HISTORY

OF

CHRISTIAN NAMES

BY

CHARLOTTE M. YONGE,

AUTHOR OF "THE HEIR OF REDCLYFFE," "UNKNOWN TO HISTORY," ETC. ETC.

NEW EDITION, REVISED

London

MACMILLAN AND CO.

1884

REPUBLISHED BY GALE RESEARCH COMPANY, BOOK TOWER, DETROIT, 1966

LONDON

R. CLAY, SONS, AND TAYLOR, PRINTERS,

BREAD STREET HILL.

PAPER USED IN THIS EDITION IS
A FINE ACID FREE PERMANENT/DURABLE PAPER
COMMONLY REFERRED TO AS "300-YEAR" PAPER

Library of Congress Catalog Card No. 66-25691

PREFACE TO FIRST EDITION.

I CANNOT put forth this attempt without a few words of apology for having undertaken it at all. The excuse is, chiefly, the attraction that the subject has had for me for at least twenty years, from the time when it was first taken up as matter of amusement. The difficulty of gaining information, and the inconsistencies of such as I did acquire, convinced me that the ground was almost untrodden; but the further I advanced on it, the more I perceived that it required a perfect acquaintance with language, philology, ethnology, hagiology, universal history, and provincial antiquities; and to me these were so many dark alleys, up which I only made brief excursions to knock my head against the wall of my own ignorance.

But the interest of the subject carried me on—often far beyond my depth, when the connection between names and words has lured me into the realms of philology, or where I have ventured upon deductions of my own. And I have ventured to lay the result of my collections before the public, in the hope that they may at least show the capabilities of the study of comparative nomenclature, and by classifying the subject, may lead to its being more fully studied, as an illustration of language, national character, religion, and taste.

Surnames and local names have been often discussed, but the Christian name has been usually considered too fortuitous to be worthy of notice. Camden did indeed review the current ones of his own day, and gave many correct explanations, chiefly from the German author Luther Dasipodius. Verstegen followed him up, but was more speculative and less correct; and since that date (as far as I am aware) no English author has given any real trustworthy information to the subject, as a subject. A

few lists of names and meanings now and then have appeared
in magazines and popular works, but they have generally been
copies of Verstegen, with childishly shallow and incorrect
additions. One paper which long ago appeared in *Chambers'
Journal*, was the only really correct information on English
names *en masse* that I have met with.

The Anglo-Saxon names had been, however, treated of by
Sharon Turner in his history, and Mr. Kemble put forth a very
interesting lecture on *Names, Surnames, and Nicknames among
the Anglo-Saxons*. Thierry, moreover, gives several explanations, both of Saxon and Frank ones, in the notes to his
Conquête d'Angleterre and *Récits des Rois Merovingiens*. These
were groundwork. Neither Turner nor Thierry is always right,
for want of having studied the matter comparatively ; but they
threw light on one another, and opened the way to the dissec-
tion of other names, neglected by them, with the aid of an
Anglo-Saxon dictionary.

The Scriptural class of names was studied with less difficulty.
Every Hebrew one has been fully discussed and examined
by the best scholars ; and the Greek, both biblical and classical,
have received the same attention, and are in fact the most easy
of all, as a class. With regard to Latin, much must be doubtful
and inexplicable, but the best information at present attained to
was easily accessible.

The numerous race of German appellations has received full
attention from many ripe German philologists, and I have made
much use of their works. The Scandinavian class has been
most ably treated by Professor Munch of Christiania, in a series
of contributions to the *Norsk Maanedskrifts*, of which I have
been kindly permitted to make free use, and which has aided
me more than any other treatise on Teutonic nomenclature.

Our Keltic class of names has presented far greater difficulties.
For the Cymric department, I have gathered from many
quarters, the safest being Lady Charlotte Guest's notes to
the *Mabinogion* and M. de Villemarqué's elucidations of King
Arthur's romances, Rees's *Welsh Saints*, Williams's *Ecclesiastical
Antiquities*, and Chalmers's *Caledonia ;* the least safe, Davies's
various speculations on British antiquities and the *Cambro-
Briton*. These verified by Dr. Owen Pugh's *Welsh Dictionary*,
and an occasional light from Diefenbach and Zeuss, together
with a list kindly extracted for me from the *Brut*, have been
my authorities in the Welsh and Breton departments. In the
Erse and Gaelic names I was assisted by a very kind letter from

the lamented Dr. O'Donovan, whose death deprived me of his promised revision of this extremely difficult class, and left me to make it out to the best of my ability from his contributions to the publications of the Archæological Society, from the notes to those of the Ossianic Society, Chalmers's *Caledonia*, and the Highland Society's *Gaelic Dictionary*.

From the first, however, I had perceived that the curiosity of the study does not lie merely in the meanings of the sounds by which men in one country are distinguished from one another. The changes through which the word passes is one great interest, and for this I had been collecting for years, from dictionaries, books of travels, histories, and popular tales, whenever people were so good as to give the genuine word, instead of translating it into English. Dr. G. Michaelis' *Vergleichendes Wörterbuch der Gebrauchlichsten Taufnamen* left in me little to desire in this respect, especially with regard to German dialects, and I have used it copiously.

The history of names, however, seemed to have been but little examined, nor why one should be popular and another forgotten —why one should flourish throughout Europe, another in one country alone, another around some petty district. Some of these questions were answered by history, some by genealogy, many more by the tracing of patron saints and their relics and legends. Here my great aid has been a French edition of Alban Butler's *Lives of the Saints*, where, in the notes, are many accounts of the locality and translations of relics ; also, Mrs. Jamieson's *Sacred and Legendary Art*, together with many a chance notice in histories or books of travels. In each case I have tried to find out whence the name came, whether it had a patron, and whether the patron took it from the myths or heroes of his own country, or from the meaning of the words. I have then tried to classify the names, having found that to treat them merely alphabetically utterly destroyed all their interest and connection. It has been a loose classification, first by language, then by meaning or spirit, but always with the endeavour to make them appear in their connection, and to bring out their interest.

In general I have only had recourse to original authorities where their modern interpreters have failed me, secure that their conclusions are more trustworthy than my own could be with my limited knowledge of the subjects, which could never *all* be sufficiently studied by any one person.

Where I have given a reference it has been at times to

the book whence I have *verified* rather than originally obtained my information, and in matters of universally known history or mythology, I have not always given an authority, thinking it superfluous. Indeed, the scriptural and classical portion is briefer and less detailed than the Teutonic and Keltic, as being already better known.

I have many warm thanks to render for questions answered and books consulted for me by able and distinguished scholars, and other thanks equally warm and sincere to kind friends and strangers who have collected materials that have been of essential service to me.

Lastly, let me again present my apologies for my presumption, when the necessity of tracing out the source and connections of a word has led me to wander beyond my proper ken ; let me hope that apparent affectations may be excused by the requirements of the subject, and express my wish for such corrections as may in time render the work far more accurate and complete. Let it be remembered, that it is the popular belief, not the fact, that spreads the use of a name, and that if there is besides matter that seems irrelevant, it has been rather in the spirit of Marmion's palmers,—

> ' To charm a weary hill
> With song, romance, or lay.
> Some ancient tale, or glee, or jest,
> Some lying legend at the least,
> They bring to cheer the way.'

March 9th, 1863.

After one-and-twenty years, I have been able to bring out the revised edition for which I have long wished, having noted corrections as they were kindly sent to me, and as I was able to make them. I am sensible that the work is entirely incomplete, and as I have not studied philology much in the interval, I fear the book has not gained by the delay as much as it ought to have done. But at any rate, many errors have been taken out, as well as much that was entirely useless and irrelevant ; and as no subsequent publication has taken quite the same ground, I hope that the present form of the History of Christian Names may occupy the niche all the better for the cutting off its excrescences. With thanks to the many who have aided in the correction,

C. M. YONGE.

July 25th, 1884.

CONTENTS.

PART II.

PART III.

CHAPTER I.

CHAPTER II.

CHAPTER III.

CHAPTER IV.

CHAPTER V.

PART IV.

CHAPTER I.

CHAPTER II.

CHAPTER III.

CHAPTER IV.

CHAPTER V.

CHAPTER VI.

CHAPTER VII.

PART V.

CHAPTER I.

CHAPTER II.

CHAPTER III.

CHAPTER IV.

PART VI.

CHAPTER I.

CHAPTER II.

CHAPTER III.

CHAPTER IV.

CHAPTER V.

GLOSSARY OF CHRISTIAN NAMES.

THE names here given are referred, as far as possible, first to the language in which the form occurs, then to their root.

The original names, in their primary form, are in capitals, the shapes they have since assumed are in Roman type, the contractions in italics. A table is here given of the main stems and branches, with the abbreviations used for them in the glossary.

HEBREW . . . { Modern Jew (Jew.)
(Heb.)   { Aramæan (Aram.)

ANCIENT PERSIAN { Persian (Pers.)
(Zend)

GREEK . . . . { Modern Greek (Mod. Gr.)
(Gr.)   { Russian (Russ.)

LATIN . . . . { Italian (It.)
(Lat.) | Venetian (Ven.)
                   | Spanish (Span.)
                   | Portuguese (Port.)
                   | Provençal (Prov.)
                   | Wallachian (Wall.)
                   | French (Fr.)

KELTIC . . . .
(Kelt.)

Cymric . . . { Ancient British
(Cym.) | (Brit.)
                   | Welsh
                   | Breton
                   | (Bret.)
                   | Cornish
                   | (Corn.)

Gadhaelic . . { Ancient Irish
(Gad.) | (Erse)
                   | Modern Irish Dialect
                   | (Ir.)
                   | Gaelic
                   | (Gael.)
                   | Scottish
                   | (Scot.)
                   | Manx

TEUTONIC
(Teu.)

- Northern (Nor.)
  - Icelandic (Ice.)
  - Norwegian (Nor.)
  - Swedish (Swed.)
  - Danish (Dan.)
  - Norman (Norm.)

- Anglo-Saxon (A.S.)
  - English (Eng.)
  - Scottish (Scot.)
  - Frisian (Fris.)
  - Dutch
  - Irish
  - American (Am.)

- Old German (O. G.)
  - German (Ger.)
  - Bavarian (Bav.)
  - Hamburgh (Ham.)
  - Dantzig (Dan.)
  - Swiss

- Frank — French

- Gothic (Goth.)
  - Spanish (Span.)
  - Portuguese (Port.)

- Lombardic (Lomb.)
  - Italian (It.)

SLAVONIC
- Russian (Russ.)
- Slovak (Slov.)
- Bohemian (Bohm.)
- Polish (Pol.)
- Hungarian (Hung.)
- Lithuanian (Lith.)
- Lettish (Lett.)
- Illyrian (Ill.)

A

Aaron, *m. Eng.* Heb. mountain, 27

AASBJORN, *m. Nor.* Teu. divine bear, 290

AASIR, *m. Nor.* Teu. the gods, 289.

AASOLFR, *m. Nor.* Teu. divine wolf, 290

AASTA, *f. Nor.* Teu. love, 401

AASVALDR, *m. Nor.* Teu. divine power, 291

Abacuck, *m. Scot.* Heb. embracing, 51

Abban, m. Fr. Lat. white, 157

Abel, *m. Eng.* Heb. breath, 11

Abelard, *m. Eng.* Teu. noble firmness.

Abellona, *f. Dan.* Gr. of Apollo, 65

Abigail, *f. Eng.* Heb. father of joy, 12

Abimelech, *m. Eng.* Heb. father of the king, 12

Abishalom, *m. Eng.* Heb. father of peace, 12

Abner, *m. Eng.* Heb. father of light.

Abiud, m. Eng. Dan. Heb. father of praise, 20

Abra, f. Cambrai, Heb. father of a multitude, 11

Abram, *m. Eng.* Heb. father of height, 11

Absalom, *m. Eng.* Dan. Heb. father of peace, 12

Aby, m. Am. Heb. father of multitudes, 12

Accepted, *m. Eng.* Accius, *m. Lat.* 140

Achaius, *m. Lat.* Kelt. horseman, 276

Achashverosh, *m. Heb.* Zend. venerable king, 57

Achill, *m. Ger.* Gr. without lips (?), 74

Achilla, *f. Lat.* Gr. without lips (?), 74

Achille, *m. Fr.* Gr. without lips (?), 74

Achillea, *f. It.* Gr. without lips (?), 74

Achilles, *m. Eng.* Gr. without lips (?), 74

ACHILLEUS, *Gr.* (?) without lips, 74

Achim, *m. Ger.* Heb. the Lord will judge, 38

Achsah, *f. Eng.* Heb. anklet, 38

Acim, m. Ill. Heb. the Lord will judge, 38

Acima, f. Ill. Heb. the Lord will judge, 38

Ada, *f. Eng.* Teu. happy.

Adah, *f. Eng.* Heb. ornament, 7

Adalard, *m. Fr.* Teu. nobly firm, 412

ADALBERT, *m. Ger.* Teu. nobly bright, 410

Adalfieri, *m. It.* Teu. noble pledge, 409

ADALGAR, *m. Lom.* Teu. noble spear, 412

ADALGISE, *f. Fr.* Teu. noble pledge, 409

ADALGISL, *m. Lom.* Teu. noble pledge, 409

ADALHARD, *m. Ger.* Teu. nobly stern, 412

ADALHEID, *f. Ger.* Teu. noble cheer, 412

ADALPOLT, *m. Ger.* Teu. nobly bold, 412

ADALRIK, *m. Goth.* Teu. noble king, 412

Adalrik, *m. Ger.* Teu. noble ruler, 412

ADALTAC, *m. Ger.* Teu. noble day, 413

Adam, *m. Eng.* Fr. Dutch, Ger. Dan. Heb. red earth, 10

Adamina, *f. Scot.* Heb. red earth, 10

Adamk, m. Lus. Heb. red earth, 10

Adamnan, m. Scot. Heb. Lat. dwarf Adam, 10

Adamnanus, m. Lat. Heb. dwarf Adam, 10

Adamo, *m. Ital.* Heb. red earth, 10

Adams, m. Lett. Heb. red earth, 10

Addala, f. Lett. Teu. noble cheer, 412

Addo, m. Fris. Teu. noble cheer, 412

Addy, f. Eng. Teu. noble threatener, 411

Ade, m. Flem. Heb. red earth, 10

Adela, *f. Eng.* Teu. noble cheer, 411

Adelaïda, *f. Rom.* Russ. Teu. noble cheer, 411

Adelaide, *f. Fr.* Eng. Ger. Teu. noble cheer, 411

Adelaïs, *f. Old. Fr.* Teu. noble cheer, 411

Adelajda, *f. Slov.* Teu. noble cheer, 411

ADELAR, *m. Ger.* Teu. noble eagle, 412

ADELBERN, *m. Ger.* Teu. noble bear, 412

Adelbert, *m. Ger.* Teu. nobly bright, 412

Adelberta, *f. Ger.* Teu. nobly bright, 412

Adelbold, *m. Ger.* Teu. nobly bold, 412

Adelbrecht, *m. Ger.* Teu. nobly bright, 412

Adelburg, *f. Ger.* Teu. noble protection, 412

Adelchis, *m. Lat.* Teu. noble pledge, 412

Adèle, *f. Fr.* Gr. Teu. noble cheer, 411

Adeleve, *f. Eng.* Teu. noble gift, 412

ADELFRID, *m. Ger.* Teu. noble peace, 412

ADELGAR, noble spear, 412

Adelgard, *m. Ger.* Teu. noble guard, 412

Adelgis, noble pledge, 412

Adelgonda, *f. Rom.* Teu. noble war, 412

Adelgonde, *f. Fr.* Teu. noble war, 412

Adelgunde, *f. Ger.* Teu. noble war, 412

ADELHART, *m. Ger.* Teu. nobly firm, 412

Adelhelm, noble helmet, 412

ADELHELM, *m. Ger.* Teu. noble helmet, 412

ADELHILD, *f. Ger.* Teu. noble battle maid, 413

Adelhold, *m. Ger.* Teu. nobly firm, 412

Adelicia, *f. Lat.* Teu. noble cheer, 412

Adelina, *f. Eng.* Teu. noble manner, 413

Adelinde, *f. Ger.* Teu. noble snake, 413

Adeliñe, *f. Eng.* Teu. noble snake, 413

Adelschalk, *m. Ger.* Teu. noble servant, 413

Adelswinde, *f. Ger.* Teu. noble strength, 413

Adeltrude, *f. Ger.* Teu. noble maid, 412

Adelulf, *m. Ger.* Teu. noble wolf, 412

Adelwin, *m. Ger.* Teu. noble friend, 412

Ademaro, *m. Ital.* Teu. fierce greatness, 304

Adeodat, *m. Ger.* Lat. by God given, 188

ADEODATUS, *m. Lat.* by God given, 188

Adhémar, *m. Fr.* Teu. fierce greatness, 304

Adilo, *m. Ger.* Teu. noble, 412

Ado, m. Fris. Teu. noble, 412

Adolf, *m. Ger.* Teu. noble wolf, 409

Adolfine, *f. Ger.* Teu. noble wolf, 409

Adolfo, *m. Ital.* Teu. noble wolf, 409

Adolphe, *m. Fr.* Teu. noble wolf, 409

Adolphus, *m. Eng.* Teu. noble wolf, 409

Adoncia, *f. Span.* Lat. sweet, 196

Adosinda, *f. Span.* Teu. fierce strength, 305

Adriaan, *m. Dutch.* Lat. from Adria, 156

Adrian, *m. Eng.* Ger. Lat. from Adria, 156

Adriana, *f. Ital.* Lat. from Adria, 156

Adriane, *f. Ger.* Lat. from Adria, 156

Adriano, *m. Ital.* Lat. from Adria, 156

ADRIANUS, *m. Lat.* N.L.D. Lat. from Adria, 157

Adrien, *f. Fr.* Lat. from Adria, 156

Adrienne, *f. Fr.* Lat. from Adria, 156

Aed, *m. Welsh.* Kelt. fire, 226

Aeddon, *m. Welsh.* Kelt. 226

AEDH, *m. Erse.* Kelt. fire, 226

Ægidius, *m. Lat.* Gr. with the Ægis, 79

ÆLF, *m. A. S.* Teu. elf, 380

ÆLFGIFU, *f. A. S.* Teu. elf gift, 380

ÆLFHÆG, *m. A. S.* Teu. high as an elf, 381

ÆLFHELM, *m. A. S.* Teu. elf helmet, 381

ÆLFRED, *m. A. S.* Teu. elf council, 381

ÆLFRIC, *m. A. S.* Teu. elf ruler, 381

ÆLFTHRYTH, *f. A. S.* Teu. threatening elf, 382

ÆLFWINE, *m. A. S.* Teu. elf darling, 382

ÆLFWOLD, *m. A. S.* Teu, elf ruler, 382

ÆLIANUS, *m. Lat.* Gr. of the sun, 191

Ælla, *m. A. S.* Teu. elf friend, 382

Ælle, *m. A. S.* Teu. elf friend, 382

ÆMILIA, *f. Lat.* work (?), 141

Æmiliana, *f. Lat.* work (?), 141

Æmilianus, *m. Lat.* work (?), 141

ÆMILIUS, *m. Lat.* work (?), 141

Æneas, *m. Lat.* praise (?), 74

AENGHAS, *m. Erse,* Kelt. excellent virtue, 242

ÆTHELBALD, *m. A. S.* Teu. noble prince, 349

ÆTHELBRYHT, *m. A. S.* Teu. nobly bright, 412

ÆTHELFLED, *f. A. S.* Teu. noble increase, 412

ÆTHELGIFU, *f. A. S.* Teu. noble gift, 409

ÆTHELHILD, *f. A. S.* Teu. noble battle maid, 412

ÆTHELRED, *m. A. S.* Teu. noble council, 410

ÆTHELRIC, *m. A. S.* Teu. noble ruler, 409

ÆTHELSTAN, *m. A. S.* Teu. noble stone, 412

ÆTHELTHRYTH, *f. A. S.* Teu. noble threatener, 411

ÆTHELWARD, *m. A. S.* Teu. noble guard, 412

ÆTHELWINE, *m. A. S.* Teu. noble friend, 412

ÆTHELWOLF, *m. A. S.* Teu. noble wolf, 409

Aëtius, m. Lat.

Afanassij, *m. Russ.* Gr. undying, 109

Affonso, *m. Port.* eagerness for war, 305

Affrica, *f. Manx,* Irish, Kelt. pleasant, 230

Afonso, *m. Port.* eagerness for war, 305

Agafia, *f. Russ.* Gr. good, 82

Agafon, *m. Russ.* Gr. good, 82

Agape, *f. Gr.* love, 113

Agapit, *m. Russ.* Gr. loved, 113

Agata, *f. It.* Span. Swed. Slov. Ger. good, 82

AGATHA, *f. Eng.* Hung. Gr. good, 82

Agathe, f. Fr. Ger. Gr. good, 82

AGATHIAS, *m. Gr.* good, 82

Agathocles, *m. Gr.* good fame, 82

Agathon, *m. Ger.* Gr. good, 82

Aggate, *f. Lett.* Gr. good, 82

Aggie, *f. Eng.* Gr. pure, 119

Agilard, *m. Fr.* Teu. formidably bright, 323

Agilbert, *m. Frank.* Teu. formidably bright, 323

Agilo, *m. Ger.* Teu. formidable, 322

Agiltrude, *f. Ger.* Teu. formidable maiden, 323

Agilulf, *m. Frank.* Teu. formidable wolf, 323

Agilward, *m. Norm.* Teu. formidable guardian, 323

AGINHAR, *m. Nor.* Teu. formidable warrior, 323

Aglaé, *f. Fr.* Gr. brightness, 72

AGLAIA, *f. Lat.* Gr. brightness, 72

Aglaja, *f. Ger.* Gr. brightness, 72

Aymund, m. Nor. awful protection, 323

Agnar, *m. Nor.* Teu. formidable warrior, 323

Agne, m. Nor. Teu. formidable warrior, 323

Agnello, *m. It.* Gr. pure, 119

AGNES, *f. Dan.* Eng. Ger. Fr. Gr. pure, 119

Agnesca, *f. It.* Gr. pure, 119

Agnese, *f. It.* Gr. pure, 119

Agnesija, *f. Russ.* Gr. pure, 119

Agnessa, *f. Russ.* Gr. pure, 119

Agneta, *f. Eng.* Swiss, Gr. pure, 119

Agnete, *f. Dan.* Gr. pure, 119

Agnies, *f. Fr.* Gr. pure, 119

Agnizka, *f. Pol.* Gr. pure, 119

Agnola, *f. It.* Gr. angel, 53

Agnolo, *m. It.* Gr. angel, 53

Agnyta, *f. Lett.* Gr. pure, 119

Agostina, *f. It.* Lat. venerable, 158

Agostinha, *f. Port.* Lat. venerable, 158

Agostinho, *f. Port.* Lat. venerable, 158

Agostino, *m. It.* Lat. venerable, 158

Agoston, *m. Hung.* Lat. venerable, 158

Agrafina, *f. Russ.* Lat. born with the feet foremost, 156

AGRICOLA, *m. Lat.* Lat. field tiller.

AGRIPPA, *m. Lat.* Lat. born with the feet foremost, 156

Agrippina, *f. Lat.* Lat. born with the feet foremost, 156

Agrippine, *f. Fr.* Lat. born with the feet foremost, 156

Agueda, *f. Port.* Gr. pure, 57

Ahasuerus, *m. Eng.* Pers. venerable king.

Ahrens, m. Ger. Teu. powerful eagle, 342

Ahrold, *m.* powerful eagle, 342

AIAS, *m. Gr.* Gr. eagle, 342

Aidan, *m. Eng.* Kelt. fire, 226

AIGIDIOS, *m. Gr.* with the Ægis, 79

Aileen, *f. Ir.* Gr. light, 67

Aileve, *f. Eng.* Teu. elf gift, 380

Ailie, f. Scot. Teu. famed war, 406

Aimable, *f. Fr.* Lat. lovable.

Aimée, *f. Fr.* Lat. loved.

Aimerich, m. Ger. Teu. work rūler, 331

Aimery, m. Eng. Teu. work ruler, 331

AINÈ, *f. Erse.* Kelt. joy, 230

Aineceallach, *m. Gael.* Kelt. joyful war, 230

AINEIAS, *m. Gr.* Gr. praise, 174

AISTULF, *m. Ger.* Gr. swift wolf, 335

Akilina, *f. Russ.* Lat. eagle, 156

Akim, m. Russ. Heb. the Lord will judge, 38

Akulnia, *f. Russ.* Lat. eagle, 156

Ala, *m. Eng.* Teu. holy (?), 402

Alaf, *m. Nor.* Teu. forefather's relic, 332

Alain, *m. Fr.* It. Lat. cheerful (?), Kelt. harmony, 279

Alan, *m. Scot.* Ger. Lat. cheerful (?), Kelt. harmony, 279

Alane, *f. Ger.* Lat. cheerful; Kelt. harmony, 279

Alard, m. Ger. Teu. nobly stern, 409

Alaric, *m. Eng.* Teu. noble ruler, 409

Alarich, *m. Ger.* Teu. noble ruler, 409

Alaster, *m. Gael.* Ger. helper of men, 85

Alatea, *f. Span.* Gr. truth, 126

ALAWN, *m. Cym.* Kelt. harmony, 279

Alban, *m. Eng.* Lat. white, 157

ALBANUS, *m. Lat.* white, 157

Albany, *m. Scot.* Kelt. white, 157

Albar, *m. Lat.* Span. white, 157

Alberia, *f. Span.* Lat. white (?), 157

Alberic, *m. Eng.* Teu. elf king, 380

Alberich, *m. Ger.* Teu. elf king, 380

Alberico, *m. It.* Teu. elf king, 380

Albert, *m. Eng.* Fr. Russ. Pol. Teu. nobly bright, 410

Alberta, *f. Eng.* Teu. nobly bright, 410

Albertine, *f. Ger.* Teu. nobly bright, 410

Albertino, *m. It.* Teu. nobly bright, 410

Alberto, *m. It.* Teu. nobly bright, 410

Albin, *f. Erse.* Kelt. white (?), 157

Albin, *m. Ger.* Lat. white, 157

Albina, *f. Ger.* Lat. white, 157

Albinia, *f. Eng.* Kelt. white (?), 157

Albino, *m. Rom.* Lat. white, 157

Alboin, *m. Fr.* Teu. elf friend, 380

Alboino, *m. Lomb.* Teu. elf friend, 380

Albrecht, *m. Ger.* Teu. nobly bright, 412

Albwin, *m. Ger.* Teu. elf friend, 380

Alcuin, m. Eng. Teu. hall friend, 382

Alcuinus, m. Lat. Teu. hall friend, 382

Alda, *f. It. Lat.* Eng. Teu. rich, 376

Aldclatha, *f. Gael.* Kelt. decaying beauty.

Aldebert, *m. Eng.* Ger. Teu. nobly bright, 410

Aldegonde, *f. Flem.* Teu. noble war, 410

Alderich, *m. Ger.* Teu. noble ruler, 412

Aldgitha, *f. Eng.* Teu. noble gift, 412

Aldhelm, *m. Eng.* Teu. noble helmet, 412

Aldobrando, *m. Ital.* Teu. battle sword, 318

Aldonça, *f. Span.* Lat. the sweet, 196

Aldrovando, *m. Ital.* Teu. battle sword, 318

Aléard, *m. Prov.* Teu. nobly stern, 412

Aléarda, *f. Prov.* Teu. nobly stern, 412

Aleardo, *m. Ital.* Teu. nobly stern, 412

Aleixo, *m. Port.* God helper, 85

Alejandro, *m. Span.* Teu. helper of men, 85

Alejo, *m. Span.* Gr. helper, 85

Aleks, *m. Lett.* Gr. helper, 85

Aleksa, *m. Serv.* Gr. helper, 85

Aleksajeder, *m. Slav.* Gr. helper of men, 85

Aleksander, *m. Russ.* Gr. helper of men, 85

Aleksije, *m. Russ.* Gr. helper of men, 85

Ales, m. Slov. Gr. helper, 85

Alessandra, *f. Ital.* Gr. helper of men, 84

Alessandro, *m. Ital.* Gr. helper of man, 85

Alessio, m. Ital. Gr. helper, 85

Aletea, *f. Span.* Gr. truth, 126

ALETHEA, *f. Eng.* Ger. Gr. truth, 126

Alexander, *m. Eng.* Gr. helper of men, 85

Alexandr, *m. Bohm.* Gr. helper of men, 84

Alexandra, *Eng.* Gr. 84

Alexandre, *m. Fr.* Gr. helper of men, 85

Alexandrina, *f. Eng.* Gr. helper of men, 84

Alexandrine, *f. Fr.* Gr. helper of men, 84

ALEXANDROS, *m. Gr.* helper of men, 85

Alexe, *m. Fr.* Gr. helper, 85

Alexia, *f. Ger.* Gr. helper, 84

Alexis, *m. Eng.* Ger. Gr. helper, 85

ALEXIOS, *m. Gr.* Gr. helper, 85

Alexius, *m. Lat.* Gr. helper, 85

ALFDIS, *f. Nor.* Teu. household spirit, 380

ALFGEJR, *m. Nor.* Teu. elf spear, 380

ALFGERDUR, *f. Nor.* Teu. elf woman, 380

ALFHEIDUR, *f. Nor.* Teu. elf cheerfulness, 380

Alfhild, f. Eng. Teu. elf battle maid, 380

Alfhiotr, f. Nor. Teu. elf terror, 380

Alfonso, *m. Span.* Teu. eager for battle, 320

Alfred, *m. Eng.* Fr. Teu. elf council, 380

Alfreda, *f. Eng.* Teu. elf council, 380

Alfredo, *m. It.* Teu. elf council, 380

Alfried, *m. Ger.* Teu. elf council, 380

ALFR, *m. Nor.* Teu. elf, 380

Algar, m. Eng. Teu. hall spear, 380

ALGERNON, *m. Eng.* Fr. with wiskers, 427

Alice, *f. Eng.* Teu. noble cheer, 409

Alicia, *f. Ir.* Teu. noble cheer, 409

Alick, m. Scot. Gr. helper of men, 85

Alienor, *f. Prov.* Gr. light, 67

Aline, f. Ger. Teu. noble, 409

Alison, *f. Scot.* Teu. famous war, 406

Alitea, *f. It.* Gr. truth, 126

Alix, *f. Fr.* Teu. noble cheer, 409

Allan, *m. Eng.* Lat. cheerful (?), 280

Allen, *m. Eng.* Lat. cheerful (?), 280

Allighiero, *m. Ital.* Teu. noble spear, 412

ALMA, *f. Lat.* fair, 224

ALMA, *f. Erse,* Kelt. all good, 224

Alma, f. Eng. Russ. (from the river), 224

Almedha, *f. Welsh,* Kelt. shapely (?), 273

Almeric, *m. Eng.* Teu. work ruler, 331

Almerigo, *m. Sp.* Teu. work ruler, 331

Almund, *m. Eng.* Teu. hall protection, 382

Aloïs, *m. Ger.* Teu. famous war, 405

Aloisia, *f. Ger.* Teu. famous war, 405

Aloïsio, *m. It.* Teu. famous war, 405

Aloizia, *f. Bohm.* Teu. famous war, 405

Alonso, *m. Span.* Teu. eager for battle, 320

Aloys, *m. Prov.* Teu. famous war, 405

Alphege, *m. Eng.* Teu. tall as an elf, 381

Alphonse, *m. Fr.* Teu. battle eager, 320

Alphonsine, *f. Fr.* Teu. battle eager, 320

Alphonso, *m. Eng.* Teu. battle eager, 320

Alpin, m. Scot. Kelt. elf, 380

Alpinolo, m. Ital. Teu. elf friend, 380

Alric, m. Eng. Teu. hall ruler, 380

Alswytha, *f. Eng.* Teu. hall strength, 380

ALTHEA, *f. Eng.* Gr. wholesome, 126

Alured, m. Eng. Teu. elf peace, 380

Alvar, *m. Span.* Port. Lat. white, 157

Alwine, *f. Ger.* Teu. elf friend, 380

Alysander, *m. Eng.* Gr. helper of man, 85

Amabel, *f. Eng.* Lat. lovable, 182

AMABILIS, *m. Lat.* lovable, 182

Amable, *m. Fr.* lovable, 181

AMADAS, *m. Eng.* Kelt. husbandman, 182

Amadé, *m. Fr.* Lat. love God, 182

Ama oe, *m. Ital.* Lat. love God, 182

AMADEUS, *m. Ger.* Lat. love God, 182

Amadigi, *m. Ital.* Lat. love God, 182

Amadis, *m. Span.* Lat. love God, 182

Amadore, *m. Flor.* Lat. lover, 182

AMAETHON, *m. Kymric.* Kelt. husbandman, 182

AMALA, *f. Lomb.* work, 330

Amalasontha, *f. Lat.* Teu. work strength, 330

AMALASWIND, *f. Lomb.* Teu. work strength, 330

AMALBERGA, *f. Ger.* Teu. work protection, 330

AMALBERT, *m. Ger.* Teu. work bright, 330

AMALBERTA, *f. Ger.* Teu. work bright, 330

AMALFRIED, *m. Ger.* Teu. work peace, 330

AMALFRIDA, *f. Ger.* Teu. fair work, 330

AMALGAID, *m. Erse,* Kelt. work, or spotless (?), 330

Amalgund, f. Ger. Teu. work war, 330

Amalia, *f. Ital.* Teu. work, 330

Amalie, *f. Ger.* Teu. work, 330

Amalija, *f. Russ.* Slov. Teu. work, 330

Amalilda, f. Ger. Teu. work battle maid, 330

AMALINA, *f. Goth.* Teu. work serpent, 330

AMALRICH, *m. Ger.* Teu. work ruler, 330

Amaltrude, f. Ger. Teu. work maiden, 330

Amand, *m. Fr.* Lat. worthy to be loved, 181

Amanda, *f. Eng.* Lat. worthy to be beloved, 181

Amandine, *f. Fr.* Lat. worthy to be beloved, 181

Amando, *m. Ital.* Lat. worthy to be beloved, 181

AMANDUS, *m. Lat.* worthy to be loved, 182

AMATA, *f. Lat.* beloved, 181

AMATUS, *m. Lat.* Lat. beloved, 182

Amaury, m. Fr. Teu. work ruler, 330

Amberkelleth, *m. Gael.* Kelt. joyful war, 231

Ambrogio, *m. Ital.* Gr. immortal, 109

Ambroise, *m. Fr.* Gr. immortal, 109

Ambrose, *m. Eng.* Gr. immortal, 109

Ambrosio, *m. Span.* Gr. immortal, 109

AMBROSIOS, *m. Gr.* immortal, 109

Ambrosius, *m. Lat.* Gr. 109

Ambroz, *m. Bohm.* Gr. immortal, 109

Ambrozij, *m. Pol.* Gr. immortal, 109

Ambrus, *m. Hung.* Gr. immortal, 109

Amé, *m. Fr.* Lat. loved, 182

Amedée, *m. Fr.* Lat. love God, 182

Amelia, *f. Eng.* Port. Teu. work, 330

Amélie, *f. Fr.* Teu. work, 330

Amelius, *m. Eng.* Teu. work, 330

Amelot, m. Fr. Teu. work, 330

AMELUNG, *m. Teu.* work, 330

Americo, *m. Port.* Teu. work ruler, 331

Amerigo, *m. Ital.* Teu. work ruler, 331

Amias, *m. Eng.* Lat. love God, 182

Amice, *f. Eng.* Lat. beloved, 182

Amicia, *f. Eng.* Lat. beloved, 182

Amicie, *f. Cambrai.* Lat. beloved, 182

Amlaidh, *m. Erse,* Teu. forefather's relic, 332

AMMA, *f. Nor.* Teu. grandmother, 332

Amone, *m. Ital.* Teu. home, 311

AMOS, *m. Eng.* Heb. burthen, 50

Amund, *m. Nor.* Teu. awful protection, 323

Amrrossij, m. Russ. Gr. immortal, 109

Amy, *f. Eng.* Lat. beloved, 182

Amyas, *m. Eng.* Lat. love God, 182

Amyot, *m. Eng.* Lat. love God, 182

Ana, *f. Span.* Bohm. Slov. Heb. grace, 42

Analo, *m. Ger.* Teu. ancestral, 332

ANANIAS, *m. Gr.* Heb. grace of the Lord, 42

Anarawd, *f. Welsh,* free of shame, 279

Anastagio, *m. Ital.* Gr. who shall rise again, 110

Anastase, *m. Fr.* Gr. who shall rise again, 110

Anastasia, *f. Eng.* Ital. Russ. Gr. who shall rise again, 110

Anastasij, *m. Russ.* Gr. who shall rise again, 110
ANASTASIOS, *m. Gr.* who shall rise again, 110
Anastasius, *m. Lat.* Gr. who shall rise again, 110
Anastasl, *m. Bav.* Gr. who shall rise again, 110
Anastazy, *m. Pol.* Gr. who shall rise again, 110
Anatola, *m. Fr.* Gr. eastern, 200
Anatolia, *f. Gr.* Gr. eastern, 200
Anatolius, *m. Gr.* Gr. eastern, 200
Anbiorn, m. Nor. Teu. eagle bear, 342
Anca, f. Bohm. Heb. grace, 42
Ancela, f. Pol. Gr. angel, 53
Ancelin, servant, 262
Ancelot, *m. Fr.* Lat. servant, 262
Ancelote, *f. Fr.* Lat. servant, 262
Ancika, f. Bohm. Gr. grace, 42
Ancilée, *f. Fr.* Lat. servant, 262
Anders, m. Dan. Gr. man, 86
ANDRAGATHIUS, *m. Gr.* good man, 86
André, m. Fr. Gr. man, 86
Andrea, *m. Ital.* Gr. man, 86
Andreana, *f. Ital.* Gr. man, 86
Andréas, *f. Ger.* Gr. man, 86
Andrée, *f. Fr.* Gr. man, 86
Andreian, *m. Russ.* Lat. from Adria, 156
Andrej, *m. Lus.* Gr. man, 86
Andrejek, *m. Slav.* Gr. man, 86
Andres, *m. Span.* Gr. man, 86
Andrew, *m. Eng.* Gr. man, 86
Andrezck, m. Pol. man, 86
Andrien, *m. Fr.* Gr. man, 86
Andries, *m. N.L.D.* Gr. man, 86
Andrija, *m. Serv.* Gr. man, 86
Andronicus, *m. Lat.* Gr. man's victory, 86
Andy, m. Ir. Gr. man, 86
Ane, f. Lith. Heb. grace, 42
Anessil, 242
Aneta, f. Serv. Heb. grace, 42
Aneurin, *m. Welsh.* Gr. man of excellence.
Anczka, f. Bohm. Gr. pure, 119
ANGANTYR, *m. Nor.* Teu. favourite of Tyr, 306
Ange, *m. Fr.* Gr. angel, 53
Angel, *f. Eng.* Gr. angel, 53
Angela, *f. Eng.* Span. It. Gr. angel, 53

Angèle, *f. Fr.* Gr. angel, 53
Angelica, *f. Ital.* Ger. Gr. angelic, 53
Angelico, *m. Ital.* Gr. angelic, 53
Angelina, *f. Eng.* Ital. Gr. angel, 53
Angeline, *f. Fr.* Gr. angel, 53
Angelino, *m. Ital.* Gr. angel, 53
Angelique, *f. Fr.* Gr. angelic, 53
ANGELOS, *m. Gr.* Gr. angel, 53
Angelot, *f. Eng.* Gr. angel, 53
Anges, *f. Fr.* Gr. angels, 53
Angharawd, *f. Welsh,* Kelt. free from shame, 279
ANGILBALD, Ing's prince, 325
ANGILRICH, Ing's king, 325
ANGILTRUD, Ing's maid, 325
Angiolo, m. It. Gr. angel, 53
Angus, *m. Scot.* Kelt. excellent virtue, 242
Anicet, *m. Fr.* Gr. unconquered, 90
Aniceto, *m. Rom.* Gr. unconquered, 90
Anicsika, f. Serv. Heb. grace, 42
Aniello, m. Neap. Gr. angel, 53
Anikita, *m. Russ.* Gr. unconquered, 90
Anikke, f. Lith. Heb. grace, 42
Anisia, f. Eng. Gr. complete, 94
Anita, f. Span. Heb. grace, 42
Anjela, *f. Bohm.* Gr. angel, 53
Anjelika, *f. Bohm.* Gr. angelic, 53
Anjelina, *f. Bohm.* Gr. angel, 53
Anjuska, f. Serv. Heb. grace, 42
Anjutoka, f. Serv. Heb. grace, 42
Ankaret, *f. Eng.* Gr. Kelt. free from shame, 279
ANLAFF, *m. Eng.* Teu. ancestor's relic, 332
ANMCHA, *m. Erse,* Kelt. courageous, 224
Ann, *f. Eng.* Heb. grace, 42
Anna, *f. Gr.* It. Swed. Serv. Heb. grace, 42
Annabel, *f. Teu.* Heb. eagle heroine (?), 41
Annabella, *f. Teu.* Heb. eagle heroine (?), 41, 343
Annali, f. Swiss, Heb. grace, 42
Annaple, f. Scot. Heb. eagle heroine (?), 41, 343
Annas, *m. Eng.* Heb. grace of the Lord, 41
Annchen, f. Ger. Heb. grace, 42
Annchel, f. Flem. Heb. grace, 42
Anne, f. Eng. Fr. Heb. grace, 42

Annerl, f. Bav. Heb. grace, 42
Annes, f. Eng. Gr. complete, 94
Annetta, f. Ital. Heb. grace, 42
Annette, f. Fr. Heb. grace, 42
Annibal, ⎫ *m.* 41
Annibale, ⎬ *f. Ital.* Phœn. grace of
⎪ Baal, 40
Annibas, ⎭ 40
Annice, f. Eng. Heb. grace, 42
Annika, f. Dan. Heb. grace, 42
Anninka, f. Russ. Heb. grace, 42
Annjuscha, f. Russ. Heb. grace, 42
Annonciada, *f. Span.* Lat. announced, 30
Annonciade, *f. Fr.* Lat. announced, 30
Annora, *f. Eng.* Heb. grace (?), 68, eagle of Thor, 343
Annot, *f. Scot.* Heb. Light, 42
Annunciata, *f. Lat.* announced, 30
Annunziata, *f. Ital.* Lat. announced, 30
Annusche, f. Lett. Heb. grace, 42
Annuschka, f. Russ. Lat. grace, 42
Annusia, *f. Russ.* Gr. complete, 94
Annys, *f. Eng.* Gr. complete (?), 94
Annze, f. Lith. Heb. grace, 42
Anquetil, *m. Fr.* Teu. divine kettle, 290
Ans, m. Lett. Heb. grace of the Lord, 45
ANSBRANDO, *m. Pol.* Teu. divine sword, 290
Anschar, *m. Ger.* Teu. divine spear, 290
Anselm, *m. Eng.* Teu. divine helmet, 290
Anselme, *m. Fr.* Teu. divine helmet, 290
Anselmo, *m. Rom.* Teu. divine helmet, 290
Anselot, *m. Fr.* Lat. servant, 263
ANSGAR, *m. Frank.* Teu. divine war, 290
Ansgard, *f. Eng.* Teu. divine guard, 290
Ansgisil, *f. Lom.* Teu. divine pledge, 290
ANSHELM, *m. Lom.* Teu. divine helmet, 290
Ansis, m. Lett. Heb. grace of the Lord, 45
ANSKETIL, *m. Frank.* Teu. divine cauldron, 291

Ansmunt, divine protection, 291
Anso, *m. Gr.* Teu. divine helmet, 291
Anstace, *f. Eng.* Gr. resurrection, 110
Anstice, *m. Eng.* resurrection, 110
Anstys, *m. Eng.* resurrection, 110
ANSVALD, *Gr. Teu. m.* divine power, 292
Anta, m. Lapp. Gr. man, 86
Antal, m. Hung. Lat. inestimable, 142
Antek, m. Pol. Lat. inestimable, 142
Antelmo, *m. It.* Teu. divine helmet, 290
Anthiball, *m. Corn.* Gr. surrounding.
ANTHONIUS, *m. Dutch.* Lat. inestimable, 142
Anthony, *m. Eng.* Lat. inestimable, 142
Antoine, *m. Fr.* Lat. inestimable, 142
Antoinette, *f. Fr.* Lat. inestimable, 142
Antolin, *m. Ger.* Lat. inestimable, 142
Anton, *m. Ger.* Russ. Lat. inestimable, 142
Antonetta, *f. Russ.* Lat. inestimable, 142
Antonetta, f. Swiss, Lat. inestimable, 142
Antoni, m. Pol. Lat. inestimable, 142
Antonia, *f. Ital.* Span. Lat. inestimable, 142
Antonie, *f. Ger.* Lat. inestimable, 142
Antonica, f. Rom. Lat. inestimable, 142
Antonietta, *f. Rom.* Lat. inestimable, 142
Antonina, *f. Ital.* Span. Eng. Lat. inestimable, 142
Antonino, *m. Ital.* Lat. inestimable, 142
Antonio, *m. Ital.* Span. Lat. inestimable, 142
ANTONIUS, *m. Lat.* inestimable, 142
Antons, m. Lett. Lat. inestimable, 142
Antony, *m. Eng.* Lat. inestimable, 142
Antoonje, m. Dutch, Lat. inestimable, 142
Antos, m. Pol. Lat. inestimable, 142
Ants, m. Esth. Heb. grace of the Lord, 45

Anty, f. Ir. Gr. resurrection, 110

Anysia, f. Gr. complete, 94

Anzioleto, m. Ven. Gr. angel, 53

Anziolina, f. Ven. Gr. angel, 53

Anziolo, Ven. Gr. angel, 53

AODH, *m. Gael.* Kelt. fire, 227

Aodhfin, m. Gael. Kelt. white fire, 227

Aogostino, *m. Pol.* Lat. venerable, 158

AOIBHIN, *f. Erse,* Kelt. pleasant, 227

AOIBHIR ALLUIN, *f. Gad.* pleasantly excellent, 227

AOIBHIR CAOMHA, *Gad.* pleasantly amiable, 227

AOIDHNE, *f. Erse,* Kelt. fire, 227

AOIFE, *f. Erse,* Heb. pleasant, 227

AONGHAS, *f. Erse,* Kelt. excellent virtue, 242

Aonio, *m. Ital.* Gr. inestimable, 142

APER, *Lat.* boar, 152

Apolline, f. Fr. Gr. of Apollo, 65

APOLLODORUS, *m. Lat.* Gr. gift of Apollo, 65

APOLLONIA, *f. Lat.* Gr. of Apollo, 65

APOLLOS, *m. Eng.* Gr. of Apollo, 65

Appo, m. Ger. Teu. wild boar, 337

AQUILA, *m. Eng.* Lat. eagle, 156

Aquilina, f. Lat. Lat. eagle, 156

Arabella, f. Eng. Teu. eagle heroine (?), 343

Arbell, f. Eng. Teu. eagle heroine (?), 343

Archambault, *m. Fr.* Teu. holy prince, 328

Archangel, *m. Eng.* Gr. archangel, 73

Archibald, *m. Scot.* Teu. holy prince, 329

Archie, m. Scot. Teu. holy prince, 329

Archimbald, *m. Ger.* Teu. holy prince, 329

Arcibaldo, *m. Ital.* Teu. holy prince, 329

ARDH, *m. Erse,* Kelt. high, 266

Ardisheer, m. Pers. Zend. fire king, 224

AREGWYDD, *Cym.* Kelt.

Areh, m. Slov. Teu. ever king, 400

Arend, m. Dutch, Teu. eagle power, 343

Areta, f. Corn. Gr. virtuous rule, 64

ARETHUSA, *f. Gr.* Gr. virtuous, 83

Aretino, *m. Ital.* Gr. virtuous, 83

ARGYRO, *f. Gr.* Gr. silver, 125

Ari, m. Nor. Teu. eagle, 342

ARIANWEN, *f. Welsh,* Kelt. silver, 125, 282

ARINBIORN, *m. Nor.* Teu. hearth bear, 342

Ariovistus, *m. Lat.* Teu. host leader, 342

Arisa, f. Russ. Arab, 449

Aristagoras, Gr. Eng. best assembly, 83

Aristarchus, *m. Lat.* Gr. best governor, 83

Aristide, *m. Fr.* Gr. son of the best, 83

ARISTIDES, *m. Eng.* Gr. son of the best, 83

Aristippus, Gr. Eng. best horse, 83

Aristobulus, *m. Lat.* Gr. best council, 83

Aristocles, Gr. Eng. best fame, 83

Arje, m. Dutch, Lat. from Adria, 156

Arkles, m. Eng. Gr. noble fame (?), 63

Armand, *m. Fr.* Teu. public, 327

Armando, *m. Span.* Teu. public, 327

Armanno, *m. It.* Teu. public, 327

Armantine, f. Fr. Teu. public, 327

Armine, *m. Eng.* Teu. public, 327

Arminius, *m. Lat.* Teu. public, 327

Armyn, *m. Eng.* Teu. public, 327

Arnaldo, *m. Span.* Prov. Teu. eagle power, 342

Arnalldr, *m. Nor.* Teu. eagle power, 342

Arnaud, *m. Fr.* Teu. eagle power, 342

Arnaut, m. Fr. Teu. eagle power, 342

ARNBIORG, *f. Nor.* Teu. eagle defence, 342

ARNBIORN, *m. Nor.* Teu. eagle bear, 342

ARNDIS, *f. Nor.* eagle spirit, 342

Arne, m. Dutch, Lat. from *Adria,* 156

Arneidur, f. Nor. Teu. eagle haste, 342

ARNFINN, *m. Nor.* Teu. white eagle, 342

ARNFRIDUR, *f. Nor.* Teu. fair eagle, 342

ARNGEIR, *m. Nor.* Teu. eagle spear, 342

ARNGRIM, *m. Nor.* Teu. eagle mask, 342

ARNGRIMER, *m. Nor.* Teu. eagle mask, 342

Arnhold, *m. Ger.* Teu. eagle power, 342

Arnkatla, *f. Nor.* Teu. eagle cauldron, 342

Arnkjell, *m. Nor.* Teu. eagle cauldron, 342

Arnlaug, f. Ger. Teu. eagle liquor, 342

Arnleif, *m. Nor.* Teu. eagle relic, 342

Arnliotor, *m. Nor.* Teu. eagle terror, 342

Arnmodr, *Nor.* Teu. eagle wrath, 342

Arnold, *m. Ger.* Eng. Teu. eagle power, 342

Arnoldine, *f. Ger.* Teu. eagle power, 342

Arnolf, *m. Ger.* Teu. eagle wolf, 342

Arnost, *m. Bohm.* Teu. eagle stone (?), 342

Arnostinrka, f. Bohm. Teu. eagle stone, 342

Arnoud, *m. Fr.* Teu. eagle power, 342

Arnoul, m. Fr. Teu. eagle wolf, 342

ARNRIDUR, *f. Nor.* Teu. eagle haste, 343

ARNSTEIN, *m. Nor.* Teu. eagle stone, 342

ARNTHONA, *f. Nor.* Teu. eagle maiden, 343

ARNTHOR, *m. Nor.* Teu. eagle of Thor, 343

Arnthora, *f. Nor.* Teu. eagle of Thor, 343

Arnulf, *m. Eng.* Teu. eagle wolf, 343

ARNULV, *m. Nor.* Teu. eagle wolf, 343

ARNVALLDR, *m. Nor.* Teu. eagle power, 343

ARNVID, *m. Nor.* Teu. eagle of the wood, 343

Arri, f. Lith. Lat. honourable, 191

Arrian, m. Dutch, Lat. of *Adria,* 156

Arrighetta, f. Ital. Teu. home ruler, 310

Arrighetto, m. Ital. Teu. home ruler, 310

Arrigo, m. Ital. Teu. home ruler, 310

Arrigozo, m. Ital. Teu. home ruler, 310

Arriguccio, m. Ital. Teu. home ruler, 310

Arsaces, *m. Gr.* Zend. venerable, 57

ARSHA, *m. Pers.* Zend. venerable, 57

ARSHK, *m. Pers.* Zend. venerable, 57

ARSINOE, *f. Fr.* Gr. venerable, 57

Artabanus, *Pers.* fire worshipper. Artabanus, fire guardian.

Artamenes, *Pers.* great minded.

ARTAKSHATRA, *m. Zend.* fire king, 56

Artaxerxes, m. Gr. Zend. fire king, 56

Artemidore, *m. Fr.* Gr. gift of Artemis, 65

Artemidorus, *m. Lat.* Gr. gift of Artemis, 65

Artemise, *f. Fr.* Gr. of Artemis, 65

Artemisia, *f. It.* Gr. of Artemis, 65

ARTH, *m. Scot.* Kelt. high, 266

Arthegal, *m. Eng.* Kelt. high courage, 266

ARTHGAL, *m. Erse,* Kelt. high courage, 266

Arthmael, *m. Erse,* Kelt. high chief, 266

ARTHUR, *m. Eng.* Kelt. high, 266

Arthurine, f. Eng. Kelt. high, 266

Arthwys, *m. Welsh,* 266

Arturo, *m. Ital.* Kelt. high, 266

Artus, *m. Fr.* Kelt. high, 266

Arve, m. Dan. Teu. eagle of the wood, 342

Arviragus, *m. Lat.* Kelt. high king, 267

Arwystli, *m. Welsh,* Gr. best council, 83

ASBERA, *f. Nor.* Teu. divine bear, 291

ASBJORG, *f. Nor.* Teu. divine protection, 291

ASBJORN, *m. Nor.* Teu. divine bear, 291

ASBRAND, *m. Ice.* Teu. divine sword, 291

Ascelin, *m. Eng.* Lat. servant, 268

ASGARD, *f. Ice.* Teu. divine guard, 291

Asgaut, m. Nor. Teu. divine good, 291

Asgjer, m. Nor. Teu. divine spear, 291

Asgrim, *m.* *Ice.* Teu. divine wrath, 291

Asher, *m.* *Eng.* Heb. blessed, 7

Askatla, divine cauldron, 290

Askel, *m.* *Ice.* Teu. divine cauldron, 290

Asketyl, *m.* *Ice.* Teu. divine cauldron, 290

Askjell, *m.* *Nor.* Teu. divine cauldron, 290

Aslak, *m.* *Nor.* Teu. divine sport, 290

Aslavg, *f.* *Nor.* Teu. divine liquor, 290

Asleif, *m.* *Nor.* Teu. divine relic, 290

Asmundr, *m.* *Nor.* Teu. divine hand, 290

Asmus, *m.* *Dutch,* Gr. beloved, 113

Aspamirtas, *m.* *Gr.* Pers. horse lover, 78

Aspasia, *f.* *Gr.* Gr. welcome, 60

Assrenta, *f.* *Ital.* Lat. taken up into heaven, 30

Assur, *m.* *Eng.* Teu. the gods, 289

Asta, f. *Ger.* Lat. venerable, 158

Astolfo, *m.* *Ital.* Teu. swift wolf, 335, 401

Astrid, *f.* *Nor.* Teu. impulse of love, 401

Asuerues, *m.* *Fr.* Zend. venerable king, 57

Asvald, *m.* *Nor.* Teu. divine power, 290

Asvard, *m.* *Nor.* Teu. divine ward, 290

Asvor, *m.* *Nor.* Teu. divine prudence, 290

Asvora, *f.* *Nor.* Teu. divine prudence, 290

Ata, *m.* *Lapp.* Gr. man, 86

Atalik, *m.* *Hung.* Tatar, father-like, 13

Atanacko, *m.* *Serv.* Gr. undying, 109

Atanagio, *m.* *Ital.* Gr. undying, 109

Atanasia, *m.* *Ital.* Gr. undying, 109

Atanasio, *m.* *It.* Gr. undying, 109

Athanase, *m.* *Fr.* Gr. undying, 109

Athanasios, *m.* *Gr.* undying, 109

Athanasius, *m.* *Eng.* Lat. Ger. Gr. undying, 109

Athelstan, *m.* *Eng.* Teu. noble stone, 349

Athelwold, *m.* *Eng.* Teu. noble power, 349

Athenagoras, *m.* *Gr.* Athene's assembly, 64

Athenaios, *m.* *Gr.* Gr. of Athene, 64

Athenais, *f.* *Fr.* Gr. of Athene, 64

Athenodorus, *m.* *Lat.* Gr. Athene's gift, 64

Atli, *m.* *Nor.* Tatar, father-like, 13

Atte, *m.* *Lett.* Teu. rich, 376

Attila, *m.* *Lat.* Tatar, father-like, 13

Attilius, *m.* *Lat.* father-like (?), 13

Attinsch, *m.* *Lett.* Teu. rich, 376

Attok, *m.* *Lapp.* Gr. man, 86

Atty, *m.* *Ir.* Kelt. high, or horseman, 266

Aubrey, *m.* *Eng.* Teu. elf ruler, 380

Aubri, *m.* *Fr.* Teu. elf ruler, 380

Aud, *f.* *Ice.* Teu. rich, 376

Auda, *f.* *Eng.* Teu. rich, 376

Audafrei, *m.* *Fr.* Teu. rich peace, 376

Audard, *m.* *Fr.* Teu. people's firmness, 375

Audgrie, *m.* *Nor.* Teu. rich helmet, 376

Audgunnr, *f.* *Nor.* Teu. rich war, 376

Audoacer, *m.* *Goth.* Teu. treasure watcher, 376

Audoenus, *m.* *Lat.* Teu. rich friend, 376

Audofled, *f.* *Frank.* Teu. rich increase, 376

Audoin, *m.* *Lomb.* rich friend, 376

Audovard, *m.* *Nor.* Teu. rich guard, 376

Audr, *m.* *Nor.* Teu. rich, 376

Audrey, *f.* *Eng.* Teu. noble threatener, 410

Audulf, *m.* *Ice.* Teu. rich wolf, 335

Audur, *m.* *Ice.* Teu. rich, 376

Audvakr, *m.* *Goth.* Teu. treasure watcher, 376

Audwine, *m.* *Frank.* Teu. rich friend, 376

Augen, rich war, 376

Augmund, *m.* *Nor.* Teu. awful protection, 323

August, *m.* *Ger.* Lat. venerable, 157

Augusta, *f.* *Eng.* Ger. Lat. venerable, 157

Auguste, *m.* *Fr.* Lat. venerable, 157

Augusteen, *f.* *Ir.* Lat. venerable, 158

Augustin, *m. Eng.* Ger. Lat. vener-
able, 158
Augustina, *f. Ger.* Lat. venerable,
158
Augustine, *f. Fr.* Lat. venerable, 158
Augustino, *m. Span.* Lat. venerable,
158
Augustinus, *m. Lat.* Lat. venerable,
158
Augusts, *m. Lett.* Lat. venerable, 157
AUGUSTUS, *m. Lat.* Eng. Lat. vener-
able, 157
Augustyn, *m. Pol.* Lat. venerable, 158
Auhy, Ir. Kelt. horseman, 276
AUJUSTS, *m. Lett.* Lat. venerable, 157
AULUS, *m. Lat.* Lat. sustaining (?),
or cockle (?), or hall, 131
Aurelia, *f. Eng.* Lat. golden, 143
Aurélie, *f. Fr.* Lat. golden, 143
AURELIUS, *m. Lat.* golden, 143
AURORA, *f. Eng.* Ger. Lat. dawn, 169
Aurore, *f. Fr.* Lat. dawn, 169
Austin, m. Eng. Lat. venerable, 158
Authaire, *m. Teu.* rich warrior, 378
Avald, m. Nor. Teu. 323
AVARDDWY, *m. Cym.* Kelt. 224
Avel, m. Russ. Heb. breath, 11
Aveline, *f. Norman,* Heb. pleasant,
232
Averil, f. Eng. Teu. wild boar battle
maid, 337
Averkie, m. Wall. Teu. noble ruler,
412
Avgust, *m. Russ.* Lat. venerable, 157
Avgusta, *f. Russ.* Lat. venerable, 157
Avgusta, *f. Russ.* Slov. Lat. venerable,
157
Avgustin, *m. Russ.* Slov. Lat. vener-
able, 157
Avice, *f. Eng.* Teu. war refuge, 305
Avicia, *f. Lat.* Teu. war refuge, 305
Avis, *f. Eng.* Teu. war refuge, 305
Avraam, m. Russ. Heb. father of
multitudes, 12
Avramij, m. Russ. Heb. father of
multitudes, 12
Awdry, *f. Eng.* Teu. noble threatener,
310
Awel, m. Russ. Heb. breath, 11
Awlay, *m. Scott.* Kelt. work, 330
Awnan, m. Ir. Heb. Lat. Adam, the
dwarf, 10
Awst, *m. Welsh,* Lat. venerable, 157

Axel, m. Dan. Teu. divine reward,
13
Ayelt, m. Fris. Teu. formidable firm-
ness, 323
Ayldo, m. Fris. Teu. formidable firm-
ness, 323
Aylmer, *m. Eng.* Teu. formidable
fame, 323
Aylward, *m. Eng.* Teu. formidable
guard, 323
Aylwin, m. Eng. Teu. formidable
friend, 323
Aylwin, m. Eng. Teu. formidable
fame, 323 ; elf friend, 266
Aymar, *m. Eng.* Teu. work ruler, 331
Aymon, *m. Fr.* Teu. home, 311
Ayoub, m. Arab. Heb. persecuted, 26
Azalaïs, *f. Prov.* Teu. noble cheer, 411
Azalbert, *m. Prov.* Teu. nobly bright,
411
Azelin, m. Norman, Tatar, father-
like, 13
Azemar, m. Prov. Teu. fierce fame,
412
Azo, *m. Ital.* Lat. from Acca, 140
Azor, *m. Norman,* Teu. the gods, 289
Azzo, *m. Ital.* Lat. from Acca, 140
Azzolino, *m. Ital.* Lat. from Acca,
140

B

Baaje, m. Nor. Teu. bow, 351
Bab, f. Eng. Gr. stranger, 117
Baba, f. Lus. Swiss, Gr. stranger, 117
Babali, f. Swiss, Gr. stranger, 117
Babbe, f. Lett. Gr. stranger, 117
Babeli, f. Swiss, Gr. stranger, 117
Babet, f. Fr. Heb. God's oath, 35
Babette, f. Fr. Heb. God's oath, 35
Babiche, f. Fr. Heb. stranger, 117
Babichon, f. Fr. Heb. God's oath, 35
Babic, f. Scot. Gr. stranger, 117
Babuscha, f. Lus. Gr. stranger, 117
Baccio, m. Ital. Lat. babbler, 159
Badezom, m. Bret. Gr. baptizer, 44
Badilo, m. Ger. Teu. messenger, 413
Bado, *m. Ger.* Teu. messenger, 413
BAEZ, *m. Welsh,* Kelt. boar, 152
Bahee, *f. Manx,* life, 243
Bal, m. Lus. Pers. war council (?), 211
Bal, m. Lus. Lat. healthy, 152
Balas, *m. Hung.* Lat. babbler, 159

Balawn, m. Welsh, Lat. strong, 153
BALBUS, *m. Lat.* stammerer, 159
BALDAG, *m. A.S.* Teu. white day, 303
Baldassare, *m. Ital.* Pers. war council, 211
Baldbrecht, *m. Ger.* princely splendour, 303
BALDEFLEDE, *f. Eng.* Teu. princely increase, 303
BALDEGISEL, *m. Frank.* Teu. prince pledge, 303
BALDEMAR, *m. Ger.* Teu. princely fame, 303
BALDEMUND, *m. Ger.* Teu. princely protection, 303
BALDERICH, *m. Ger.* Teu. prince ruler, 303
BALDERIK, *m. Swiss,* Teu. prince ruler, 303
Balderik, *m. Swed.* Teu. prince ruler, 303
Balderyk, *m. Pol.* Teu. prince ruler, 303
BALDETRUD, *m. Ger.* Teu. princely maid, 303
BALDFRIED, *m. Ger.* Teu. prince peace, 303
Baldie, m. Scot. Teu. sacred prince, 303
Baldo, m. Ger. Teu. prince, 303
Baldovino, *m. Ital.* Teu. prince friend, 303
BALDRAMM, *m. Eng.* Teu. prince raven, 303
BALDRED, *m. Eng.* Teu. prince council, 303
BALDRIC, *m. Eng.* Teu. prince ruler, 303
BALDUR, *m. Nor.* Teu. white, 303
Baldwin, *m. Eng.* Teu. prince friend, 304
BALDWINE, *m. Eng.* Teu. prince friend, 304
Balint, m. Lith. Lat. strong, 153
Balk, m. Lus. Pers. war council (?), 211
Balk, m. Lus. Lat. healthy, 153
Balsys, m. Lith. Pers. war council (?), 211
Balta, m. Ill. Pers. war council (?), 211
Baltasar, *m. Span.* Pers. war council (?), 211

Baltasard, *m. Fr.* Pers. war council (?), 211
Baltassare, *m. Ital.* Pers. war council (?) 211
Baltazar, *m. Ill.* Pers. war council(?), 211
Balthasar, *m. Ger. Eng.* Pers. war council (?), 211
Balto, m. Ill. Pers. war council (?), 211
Baltramejus, m. Lith. Heb. son of furrows, 25
Baltras, m. Lith. Heb. son of furrows, 25
Baltyn, m. Lus. Pers. war council (?), 211
Bältzel, m. Swiss, Pers. war council(?), 211
Balz, m. Swiss, Pers. war council (?), 211
BANAN, *Erse,* white, 244
Banej, m. Slov. Lat. of the city, 202
Bandi, m. Hung. Gr. man, 86
Banquo, *m. Eng.* Kelt. white, 244
BAOTHGALACH, *m. Erse,* Kelt. youthful courage, 224
Baptist, *m. Russ. Ger. Eng.* Gr. baptizer, 44
Baptista, *m. Port.* Gr. baptizer, 44
Baptiste, *m. Fr.* Gr. baptizer, 44
Baptysta, *m. Pol.* Gr. baptizer, 44
Barak, *m. Eng.* Heb. lightning.
Barba, f. Ill. Span. Eng. Slav. Gr. stranger, 117
BARBARA, *f. Ger. It. Russ.* Gr. stranger, 117
Barbary, *f. Eng.* Gr. stranger, 117
Barbe, *f. Fr. Lett. Ger.* Gr. stranger, 117
Barbeli, f. Gr. Gr. stranger, 117
Barbica, f. Slov. Gr. stranger, 117
Barbora, *f. Lus.* Gr. stranger, 117
Barbota, f. Bohm. Gr. stranger, 117
Barbraa, f. Dutch, Gr. stranger, 117
Barbule, f. Lett. Gr. stranger, 117
Barbutte, f. Lith. Gr. stranger, 117
Barca, *m. Lat.* Phœn. lightning,
Bardo, m. Dan. Heb. son of furrows, 25
Bardolf, *m. Eng.* Teu. bright wolf, 335
BARDR, *m. Nor.* Ice. beard, 427
Barend, m. Dutch, Teu. firm bear, 339

Barna, m. Ital. Heb. son of consolation, 24

Barnaba, *m. Ital. Ger.* Heb. son of consolation, 24

Barnabas, *m. Eng.* Heb. son of consolation, 24

Barnabé, *m. Fr.* Heb. son of consolation, 24

Barnaby, *m. Eng.* Heb. son of consolation, 24

Barnard, *m. Ir.* Teu. firm bear, 339

Barney, m. Ir. Teu. firm bear, 339

Barry, *m. Ir.* Kelt. looking straight at the mark, 224

Bart, m. Dutch, Heb. son of furrows, 25

Bartek, m. Pol. Heb. son of furrows, 25

Bartel, m. Heb. son of furrows, 25

Barteo, m. Ill. Heb. son of furrows, 25

Barthel, m. Ger. Heb. son of furrows, 25

Barthelemi, *m. Fr.* Heb. son of furrows, 25

Bartholomœus, *Lat.* Heb. son of furrows, 25

Bartholomao, *m. Port.* Heb. son of furrows, 25

Bartholomew, *m. Eng.* Heb. son of furrows, 25

Bartholomieu, *m. Fr.* Heb. son of furrows, 25

Barthram, *m. Scot.* Teu. bright raven, 415

Bartl, m. Bav. Heb. son of furrows, 25

Bartleme, m. Swiss, Heb. son of furrows, 25

Bartley, m. Ir. Heb. son of furrows, 25

Bartli, m. Swiss, Heb. son of furrows, 25

Bartlme, m. Bav. Heb. son of furrows, 25

Bartlomiej, m. Pol. Heb. son of furrows, 25

Barto, m. Lus. Heb. son of furrows, 25

Bartold, *m. Ger.* Teu. bright power, 415

Bartolik, m. Ill. Heb. son of furrows, 25

Bartolo, m. Span. Heb. son of furrows, 25

Bartolomée, *m. Fr.* Heb. son of furrows, 25

Bartolome, *m. Span.* Heb. son of furrows, 25

Bartolomeo, *m. Ital.* Heb. son of furrows, 25

Bartram, m. Litt. Teu. bright raven, 345, 415

Bartramusch, m. Litt. Teu. bright raven, 345

BARTULF, *m. Ger.* Teu. bright wolf, 345

Bartuo, m. Ill. Heb. son of furrows, 25

Barzillai, *m. Eng.* Heb. son of iron, 25

Bascho, m. Swiss, Gr. awful, 111

Basil, *m. Ger. Eng.* Gr. kingly, 112

Basile, *m. Fr.* Gr. kingly, 112

Basilia, *f. Eng.* Gr. kingly, 112

Basilio, *m. Ital.* Gr. kingly, 112

Basine, *f. Prov.* Gr. kingly, 112

Baste, m. Nor. Ger. awful, 111

Basti, m. Bav. Gr. awful, 111

Bastia, m. Swiss, Gr. awful, 111

Bastiali, m. Swiss, Gr. awful, 111

Bastian, m. Ger. Gr. awful, 111

Bastiano, m. Ital. Gr. awful, 111

Bastiao, m. Port. Gr. awful, 111

Bastien, m. Fr. Gr. awful, 111

Bat, m. Eng. Heb. son of furrows, 25

BATHANAT, *m.* Kelt. son of the boar, 224

BATHILDA, *f. Eng.* Teu. commanding battle maid, 338, 413

Bathilde, *f. Fr.* Teu. commanding battle maid, 413

Bathsheba, *f. Eng.* Heb. daughter of the oath.

Bathshua, *f. Eng.* Heb. daughter of the oath.

Bâtiste, *m. Fr.* Gr. baptizer, 44

Batiste, m. Fr. Gr. baptizer, 44

Batram, m. Lus. Teu. bright raven, 345, 415

Batramusch, m. Lus. Teu. bright raven, 345, 415

Battista, *f. Fr.* Gr. baptizer, 44

Baud, m. Fr. Teu. prince, 303

BAUDOUIN, *m. Fr.* Teu. princely friend, 303

Baudoin, f. Fr. Teu. princely friend, 303

Baudri, *m. Fr.* Teu. bold ruler, 303

BAUDHILDUR, *f. Nor.* Teu. commanding battle maid, 413

Baudrand, *m. Fr.* Teuton, prince raven, 303

Baudouin, *m. Fr.* Teu. prince friend, 303

BAUGE, *m. Ice.* Teu. bow, 351

BAUGISEL, *m. Ice.* Teu. bow pledge, 351

Bauista, *m. Span.* Gr. baptizer, 44

Bazyli, m. Pol. Gr. kingly, 112

BEADWEIG, *m. A.S.* Teu. battle war.

Brearck, Lat. Ill. babbler, 158

Beat, *m. Fr.* Lat. blessed, 183

Beata, *f. Eng.* Lat. blessed, 183

Beate, *f. Fr.* Lat. blessed, 183

Peatrica, *f. Slov.* Lat. blesser, 183

Beatrice, *f. Ital. Eng. Ger.* Lat. blesser, 183

Beatriks, *f. Russ.* Lat. blesser, 183

BEATRIX, *f. French, Port.* Lat. blesser, 183

BEATUS, *m. Lat.* blessed, 183

Bebba, f. Swiss, Heb. God's oath, 35

Bebbeli, f. Swiss, Heb. God's oath, 35

BEBINN, *f. Gael.* Kelt. melodious, 224

Becky, f. Eng. Heb, noosed cord, 14

BEDAWS, *m. Cym.* Kelt. life, 254

Bede, *m. Eng.* Kelt. life, Teu. prayer, 254

Bedrich, m. Bohm. Teu. peace ruler, 296

Bedriska, f. Bohm. Teu. peace ruler, 296

BEDWULF, *m. Eng.* Teu. commanding wolf, 335, 413

Bees, *f. Eng.* Teu. praying—Kelt. life, 253

Beffana, f. It. Gr. manifestation, 212

Bega, *f. Eng.* Kelt. life—Teu. prayer, 253

Begga, *f. Nor.* Kelt. life—Teu. prayer, 253

Beieli, m. Swiss, Heb. goodness of the Lord, 49

Bejmia, m. Lus. Gr. fair fame, 88

Bela, f. Span. Heb. God's oath, 35

Bela, m. Hung. Teu. nobly bright, 410

Belinda, *f. Eng.* Ital. (?) serpent, 464

Belisarius, *m. Lat.* Slav. white prince, 211

BELITZAR, *m.* Slav. white prince, 211

Belle, f. Eng. Phœn. oath of Baal, 35

BELLONA, *f. Eng.* Lat. warlike, 169

Bellovisus, *m. Lat.* beautiful to behold, 352

Belphœbe, *f. Eng.* Gr. far light, 65

Beltran, *m. Span.* Teu. bright raven, 415

Bema, f. Lus. Gr. fair speech, 88

Ben, m. Eng. Heb. son of the right hand, 7

Bendik, m. Nor. Lat. blessed, 184

Bendikkas, *m. Lett.* Lat. blessed, 184

Bendzus, m. Lett. Lat. blessed, 184

Benedek, *m. Hung.* Lat. blessed, 184

Benedetta, *f. Ital.* Lat. blessed, 184

Benedetto, *m. Ital.* Lat. blessed, 184

Benedict, *m. Eng.* Lat. blessed, 184

Benedicta, *f. Port. Eng.* Lat. blessed, 184

Benedictine, *f. Ger.* Lat. blessed, 184

Benedicto, *m. Port.* Lat. blessed, 184

BENEDICTUS, *m. Lat.* blessed, 184

Benedikt, *m. Ger.* Lat. blessed, 184

Benedickta, *f. Ger.* Lat. blessed, 184

Benedit, m. Ill. Lat. blessed, 184

Benedix, m. Ger. Lat. blessed, 184

Benedykt, m. Pol. Lat. blessed, 184

Bengt, *Swed.* Lat. blessed, 184

Benigna, *f. Ger.* Lat. kind, 183

Benigne, *m. Fr.* Lat. kind, 183

BENIGNUS, *m.* Lat. kind, 183

Beniesch, Lus. Lat. blessed, 184

Benin, m. Fr. Lat. kind, 183

Benita, *f. Span.* Lat. blessed, 184

Benito, *m. Span.* Lat. blessed, 184

BENJAMIN, *m. Eng.* Heb. son of the right hand, 7

Benjamino, *m. It.* Heb. son of the right hand, 7

Benjie, m. Scot. Heb. son of the right hand, 7

Bennéad, m. Bret. Lat. blessed, 184

Bennéged, m. Bret. Lat. blessed, 184

Bennet, *m. Eng.* Lat. blessed, 183

Benno, m. Ger. Teu. firm bear, 339

Benoit, *m. Fr.* Lat. blessed, 184

Benoite, *f. Fr.* Lat. blessed, 184

Benoni, *m. Eng.* Heb. son of sorrow, 7

Bent, m. Dan. Lat. blessed, 184

c

Benvenuto, m. It. welcome, 185

Benyna, *f. Lith.* Lat. kind, 183

Benzel, m. Swiss, Lat. blessed, 184

Benzli, m. Swiss, Lat. blessed, 184

BEORN, *m. A.S.* Teu. bear, 339

BEORNULF, *m. A.S.* Teu. bear wolf, 339

BEORNWALD, *m. A.S.* Teu. bear power, 339

BEORHTRIC, *m. A.S.* Teu. bright ruler, 415

BEOWULF, *m. A.S.* Teu. harvest wolf, 335

Beppo, m. It. Heb. addition, 23

Bera, *f. Nor.* Teu. bear, 339

BERACH, *m. Erse,* Kelt. looking straight at the mark, 224

Béranger, *m. Fr.* Teu. bear spear, 339

Bérangerè, *f. Fr.* Teu. bear spear, 339

Berault, m. Fr. Teu. bear power, 340

BERCHTA, *f. Ger.* Teu. bright, 415

BERCHTHILDA, *f. Frank.* Teu. bright battle maid, 415

BERCHTIRAMM, *m. Frank.* Teu. bright raven, 345, 415

BERCHTVOLD, *m. A.S.* Teu. bright power, 339, 415

Berdrand, m. Ger. Teu. bright raven, 345, 415

Berend, m. Ger. Teu. firm bear, 339

Berengar, *m. Ger.* Teu. bear spear, 339

Berengaria, *f. Eng.* Teu. bear spear, 339

Berenger, *m. Eng. Span.* Teu. bear spear, 339

Berenguela, *f. Span.* Teu. bear spear, 339

BERENICE, *f. Macedonian,* Gr. bringing victory, 90

Berents, Lett. Teu. bear firm, 339

Berghild, *f. Nor.* Teu. protecting battle maid, 419

BERGLIOT, *f. Swed.* Teu. mountain terror, 419

Berge, f. Lett. Kelt. 236

BERGSWAIN, *m. Nor.* Teu. protecting youth, 419

BERGTHOR, *m. Nor.* Teu. protecting Thor, 419

BERGTHORA, *f. Nor.* Teu. protecting Thor, 419

Bernal, *m. Span.* Teu. firm bear, 339

Bernaldo, m. Fr. It. Teu. bear's power, 339

Bernard, *m. Eng.* Teu. firm bear, 340

Bernardek, m. Slov. Teu. firm bear, 339

Bernardin, m. Fr. Teu. firm bear, 339

Bernardina, *f. Ital.* Teu. firm bear, 339

Bernardine, *f. Fr.* Teu. firm bear, 339

Bernardino, m. Ital. Teu. firm bear, 339

Bernardo, *m. Ital.* Teu. firm bear, 339

Bernardu, *m. Wallach.* Teu. firm bear, 339

Bernat, m. Hung. Teu. firm bear, 339

Bernclo, *m. Bav.* Teu. bear's claw, 339

Bernd, m. Fris. Teu. bear firm, 339

Berner, *m. Ger.* Teu. bear warrior, 339

Berngard, *m. Russ.* Teu. bear firm, 339

Bernhard, *m. Ger.* Teu. bear firm, 339

Berngard, *f. Dan.* Teu. bear spear, 339

Bernhardine, *f. Ger.* Teu. bear firm, 339

Bernice, Eng. Gr. bringing victory, 90

Bernold, *m. Ger.* Teu. bear power, 339

Berns, m. Lett. Teu. bear firm, 339

Bersi, *m. Nor.* Teu. bear, 339

Berta, *f. Ital. Pol.* Teu. bright (Epiphany night), 212, 415

Bertalda, *f. Ger.* Teu. bright battle maid, 415

Bertaldo, *m. It.* Teu. bright firm, 415

Bertar, *m. Ger.* Teu. bright warrior, 415

Bertel, m. Ger. Heb. son of furrows, 25

Bertel, Dan. Teu. noble brightness, 415

Bertelmes, m. Dutch, Heb. son of furrows, 25

BERTHA, *f. Eng. Ger.* Teu. bright (Epiphany night), 212, 415

Berthe, *f. Fr.* Teu. bright (Epiphany night), 212, 415

Berthilda, *f. Ger.* Teu. bright battle maid, 414

Berthold, *m. Ger.* Teu. bright firm, 415

Bertille, *f. Fr.* Teu. bright battle maid, 414

Bertin, *m. Fr.* Teu. bright friend, 415

Berto, *m. Ger.* Teu. bright.

Bertok, m. Hung. Teu. bright raven, 414

Bertold, *m. Ger.* Teu. bright power, 414

Bertoldo, *m. Ital.* Teu. bright firm, 414

Bertolf, *m. Ger.* Teu. bright wolf, 335

Bertoud, *m. Fr.* Teu. bright firm, 415

Bertrade, *f. Fr.* Teu. bright speech, 415

Bertram, *m. Ger. Eng.* Teu. bright raven, 415

Bertran, *m. Prov. Span.* Teu. bright raven, 415

Bertrand, *m. Fr. Ger.* Teu. bright raven, or shield, 415

Bertrão, *m. Span.* Teu. bright raven, 415

Bertrich, *m. Ger.* Teu. bright rule, 415

Bertrud, *f. Ger.* Teu. bright maid, 415

Bertuccio, m. Ital. Teu. bright friend, 415

Bertulf, *m. Ger.* Teu. bright wolf, 335, 415

BERTWINE, *m. Ger.* Teu. bright friend, 415

Berzske, f. Lett. Kelt. strength, 236

Bess, f. Eng. Heb. God's oath, 35

Besse, *m. Nor.* Teu. bear, 339

Bessie, f. Scot. Heb. God's oath, 35

Bessy, f. Eng. Heb. God's oath, 35

Bet, f. Eng. Heb. God's oath, 35

Beta, f. Lus. Heb. God's oath, 35

BETH, *f. Gael.* Kelt. life, 253

Betha, f. Swiss, Heb. God's oath, 35

Bethia, *f. Eng.* Kelt. life, 253

Bethlem, m. Hung. Heb. house of bread, 39

BETHOC, *f. Gael.* Kelt. life, 253

Betsey, f. Eng. Heb. God's oath, 35

Betta, f. It. Lat. blessed, 183

Bette, f. Ger. Heb. God's oath, 35

Bettina, f. It. Lat. blessed, 183

Bettine, f. Ger. Heb. God's oath, 35

Bettino, m. Ital. Lat. blessed, 183

Betto, m. Ital. Lat. blessed, 183

Bettrys, *f. Welsh,* Lat. blesser, 183

Betty, f. Eng. Heb. God's oath, 35

Bevis, *m. Eng.* Teu. bow, 351

Biagio, *m. Ital.* Lat. babbler, 159

Bianca, *f. Ital.* Teu. white, 428

Biasio, *m. Ital.* Lat. babbler, 159

Bibiana, *f.* Lat. living, 197

Bibianus, *m.* Lat. living, 197

Biddulph, *f. Eng.* Teu. commanding wolf, 413

Biddy, f. Ir. Kelt. strength, 235

Bice, f. It. Lat. blesser, 183

Bildaberta, f. Ger. 212

Bilichilde, *f. Fr.* Teu. resolute battle maid, 314

Bilippos, m. Macedonian, Gr. loving horses, 79

Bill, m. Eng. Teu. helmet of resolution, 314

Bille, f. Lith. Lat. wise old woman, 313

Bindus, m. Lett. Lat. blessed, 183

Bine, f. Serv. Lat. kind, 184

Binkentios, *m. Gr.* Lat. conquering, 197

BIORGULV, *m. Nor.* protecting wolf, 419

Birge, 419

Birger, *m. Dan.* Teu. protecting warrior, 419

Birre, f. Esth. Kelt. strength, 236

Bisch, Swiss, Gr. baptism, 44

Bischeli, Swiss, Gr. baptism, 44

Bjorgulv, m. Ice. Teu. mountain wolf, 419

BJORN, *m. Nor.* Teu. bear, 339

BJORNAR, *m. Nor.* Teu. bear warrior, 339

BJORNGJAR, *m. Nor.* Teu. bear spear, 339

Bjorngjerd, *m. Nor.* Teu. bear spear.

BJORNHARD, *m. Nor.* Teu. stern bear, 339

BJORNHEDINN, *m. Nor.* Teu. bear fury, 339

BJORNSTERN, *m. Nor.* Teu. bear star, 339

BJORNULV, *m. Nor.* Teu. bear wolf, 339

Blaas, *m. Dutch,* Teu. babbler, 159

Blagodvoj, *m. Ill.* Slav. good war, 444

BLAGOGOST, *m. Slav.* good guest, 444

Blagoje, Ill. Slav. good war, 444

BLAGOROD, *m. Ill.* Slav. good birth, 444

BLAGOSLAV, *m. Ill.* Slav. good glory, 444

Blaise, *m. Fr.* Lat. babbler, 159

Blaisot, m. Fr. Lat. babbler, 159

Blanca, *f. Ger. Span.* Teu. white, 429

Blanch, *f. Eng.* Teu. white, 428

BLANCHE, *f. Fr.* Teu. white, 429

Blanchefleur, *f. Fr.* Teu. white flower, 172, 428

Blanco, *m. Span.* Teu. white, 429

Blas, *m. Span.* Lat. babbler, 159

Blase, *m. Eng.* Lat. babbler, 159

Blasek, m. Ill. Lat. babbler, 159

Blasi, m. Ger. Lat. babbler, 159

Blasia, *f. Ger.* Lat. babbler, 159

Blasio, *m. It.* Lat. babbler, 159

BLASIUS, *m. Ger. Lat.* Lat. babbler, 159

Blasko, m. Ill. Lat. babbler, 159

Blasok, m. Bav. Lat. babbler, 159

Blaszej, *m. Pol. Bohm.* Lat. babbler, 159

Blathnaid, *f. Erse,* Kelt. white flower, 428

Blaz, *m. Ill.* Lat. babbler, 159

Blaze, *m. Eng.* Lat. babbler, 159

Blazek, *m. Ill.* Lat. babbler, 159

BLAZENA, *f. Slav.* Slav. happy, 444

Blazko, m. Ill. Lat. babbler, 159

BLENDA, *f. Swed.* Teu. dazzling, 429

Boadicea, *f. Lat.* Kelt. victory, 227

Boaventura, *m. Port.* Ital. well met, 185

Bob, m. Eng. Teu. bright fame, 392

Bobbo, m. Ger. Teu. father, 333

Bobo, m. Ger. Teu. father, 333

Bodil, f. Nor. Teu. commanding battle maid, 413

Bodild, f. Nor. Teu. commanding battle maid, 413

BODMOD, *m. Dan.* Teu. battle fury, 414

BODNAR, *m. Dan.* Teu. battle leader, 414

Bodo, m. Ger. Teu. commander, 413

Bodulf, *m. Dan.* Teu. commanding wolf, 413

BODVULF, *m. A.S.* Teu. commanding wolf, 413

BODVULF, *m. Dan.* Teu. battle wolf, 414

Boel, f. Nor. Teu. commanding battle maid, 413

Boemondo, *m. It.* Slav. God's love (?).

Boethius, *m. Lat.* Kelt. youthful courage.

Bogasav, m. Ill. Slav. God's glory, 438

BOGDAN, *m. Slav.* Slav. God's gift, 438

BOGDANA, *f. Slav.* Slav. God's gift, 438

BOGE, *m. Nor.* Teu. bow, 352

Bogislaus, *m. Eng.* Slav. God's glory, 438

BOGO, *m. Ger.* Teu. bow, 352

BOGOBOJ, *m. Slav.* Slav. God's battle, 438

BOGOHVAL, *m. Slav.* Slav. God's praise, 438

BOGOMIL, *m. Ill.* Slav. God's love, 438

BOGOSLAV, *m. Slav.* Slave, God's glory, 438

Bogue, m. Eng. Teu. bow, 352

Bohdan, *m. Bohm.* Slav. God's gift, 438

Bohdana, *m. Bohm.* Slav. God's gift, 438

Bohemond, *m. Eng.* Slav. God's love (?), 438

Bohumil, m. Bohm. Slav. God's love, 438

Bohumir, m. Bohm. Slav. God's peace, 438

BOIDH, *m. Gadhaelic,* Erse, yellow, 252

Boldisar, m. Hung. Pers. war council, 211

Boleslao, *m. Span.* Slav. stronger glory, 441

Boleslas, *m. Fr.* Slav. strong glory, 441

Boleslau, *m. Port.* Slav. strong glory, 441

BOLESLAV, *m. Slav.* Slav. strong glory, 441

Bolta, m. Ill. Pers. 211

Boltazar, *m. Slov.* Pers. 211

BONA, *f. It.* Ger. Lat. good, 185

BONAVENTURA, *m. It.* well met, 185

Bonaventure, *m. Fr.* It. well met, 185

BONDR, *m. Nor.* farmer, 332

Bonifac, *m. Bohm.* Lat. well doer, 185

Boniface, *m. Eng. Fr.* Lat. well doer, 185

Bonifacij, *m. Russ.* Lat. well doer, 185

Bonifacio, *m. It.* Lat. well doer, 185

BONIFACIUS, *m. Ger.* Lat. well doer, 185

Bonifacy, *m. Pol.* Lat. well doer, 185

Bonifaz, *m. Ger.* Lat. well doer, 185

Bonifazio, *m. It.* Lat. well doer, 185

Bonne, *f. Fr.* Lat. good, 185

Bopp, m. Swiss, Heb. supplanter, 17

Boppi, f. Swiss, Heb. addition, 23

BORIS, *m. Russ.* fight, 441

Borka, m. Russ. Slav. fight, 441

Borinka, m. Russ. Slav. fight, 441

Borivor, *m. Bohm.* Slav. fight, 441

BORGNY, protecting freshness, 419

Borny, protecting freshness, 419

Borbola, Hung. stranger, 117

Boris, Hung. stranger, 117

Bors, *m. Eng.* Kelt. boar, 152

Bortolo, m. It. Heb. son of furrows, 25

Boso, *m. Ger.* Teu. commander, 413

Bostej, m. Sl. Gr. awful, 111

Bostjan, m. Sl. Gr. awful, 111

Botheric, *m. Goth.* Teu. commanding king, 413

Bothild, *f. Dan.* Teu. commanding heroine, 413

Botho, m. Ger. Teu. commander, 413

Botolph, *m. Eng.* Teu. commanding wolf, 413

Botzhild, *f. Ger.* Teu. commanding heroine, 413

Botzo, m. Ger. Teu. commander, 413

Botzulf, *m. Ger.* Teu. commanding wolf, 413

Boyd, *m. Scot.* Kelt. yellow, 252

Bozena, *m. Slov.* Slav. Christmas child, 438

Bozicko, m. Slov. Slav. Christmas child, 438

BOZIDAR, *m. Slov.* Slav. God's gift, 438

BOZIDARA, *m. Slov.* Slave, God's gift, 438

Bozo, *m. Ger.* Teu. commander, 413

Bozo, *m. Slov.* Slav. Christmas child, 438

BRAGICAN, *m. Ill.* Slav. brother, 444

Brajan, m. Ill. Slav. brother, 444

Bram, m. Dutch. Heb. father of nations, 12

BRAN, *m. Gael.* Kelt. raven, 235

BRAN, *m. Cym.* Kelt. raven, 235

Branca, Port. Teu. white, 429

Brancaleone, *m. Ital.* arm of a lion, 77

BRAND, *m. Ger.* Teu. sword, 351

Brandolf, m. Nor. Teu. sword wolf, 351

BRATOLJUB, *m. Ill.* Slav. brother's love, 444

BRAVAC, *m. Ill.* Slav. wild boar, 441

Braz, *m. Port.* Lat. babbler, 159

Brazil, *m. Manx,* Kelt. strong, 235

BREASAL, *m. Erse,* Kelt. 235

Brenda, *f. Scot.* Teu. sword (?), 351

Brengwain, *f. Eng.* Kelt. white bosom, 230

Brenhilda, *f. Span.* Teu. breast-plate battle maid, 360

Brennus, *m. Lat.* Kelt. strong, 232

Brenzis, f. Esth. Lat. laurel, 174

BRIAN, *m. Ir.* Kelt. strong, 235

Brichteva, *f. Nor.* Teu. bright gift, 415

BRICHTFLED, *f. A.S.* Teu. bright increase, 415

BRICHTFRID, *m. A.S.* Teu. bright peace, 415

BRICHTMAR, *A.S.* Teu. bright fame, 415

BRICHTRIC, *m. A.S.* Teu. bright king, 415

BRICHTSEG, *m. A.S.* Teu. bright warrior, 415

BRICHTSTAN, *m. A.S.* Teu. bright stone, 415

Bride, *f. Scot.* Kelt. strength, 236

Bridget, *f. Eng.* Kelt. strength, 236

Brien, *m. Fr.* Kelt. strength, 236

Brietta, f. Ir. Kelt. strength, 236

Brieuc, *m. Bret.* Kelt. strength, 236

BRIGHID, *f. Erse,* Kelt. strength, (goddess of smiths,) 236

Brigida, *f. It.* Kelt. strength, 236

Brigide, *f. Fr.* Kelt. strength, 236

Brigitta, *f. Swed. Ger.* Kelt. strength, 236

Brigitte, *f. Fr.* Kelt. strength, 236

Brischia, f. Lus. Kelt. strength, 236

Brita, f. Swed. Kelt. strength, 236

Brites, f. Port. strength, 236

Brithomar, m. Kelt. great Briton, 224

BRITHRIC, *m. Eng.* Teu. bright ruler, 415

BRITOMARTIS, *f. Crete,* Gr. sweet maid, 236

Britte, f. Lett. Kelt. strength, 236

Brockwell, m. Eng. Kelt. strong champion (?), 236

Brocmael, *m. Welsh,* Kelt. strong champion (?), 236

BRONISLAV, *m. Slav.* Slav. weapon glory, 441

BRONISLAVA, *f. Slav.* Slav. weapon glory, 441

BRONWEN, *f. Welsh,* Kelt. white bosom, 229

Bros, m. Lus. Gr. immortal, 109

Brosk, m. Lus. Gr. immortal, 109

Brunehault, *f. Fr.* Teu. breast-plate battle maid, 360

Brunilla, f. Nor. Teu. breast-plate battle maid, 360

BRUNO, *m. Ger.* Teu. brown, 428

Brush, m. Eng. Gr. immortal, 109

Bryan, *m. Ir.* Kelt. strong, 235

Bryney, m. Ir. Kelt. strong, 235

BRYNHILD, *m. Ger.* Teu. breast-plate battle maid, 360

BRYNJAR, *m. Nor.* Teu. breast-plate warrior, 360

BRUNULF, *m. Nor.* Teu. breast-plate wolf, 360

BUADHACH, *m. Erse,* Kelt. victorious, 227

Budhic, m. Bret. Kelt. victorious, 227

Buddud, f. Welsh, Kelt. victory, 227

BUDDUG, *f. Welsh,* Kelt. victory, 227

Bugge, m. Dan. Teu. bow, 352

Buovo, *It. Nor.* Teu. bow, 352

BURAC, *m. Serv.* Slav. storm, 439

BURGENHILD, *A.S.* Teu. protecting battle maid, 419

Burja, m. Serv. Slav. storm, 439

BURRHED, *m. A.S.* Teu. pledge of council, 419

Byrger, *m. Dan.* Teu. protecting warrior, 419

C

CACCIAGUIDO, *m. It.* conquering war, 451

CADELL, *m. Welsh,* Kelt. war defence, 251

CADFER, *m.* stout in battle, 251

Cadffrawd, *m. Welsh,* Kelt. brother's war, 252

Cado, *m. Welsh,* Kelt. 251

Cadoc, *m. Eng.* Kelt. 251

Cadogan, *m. Eng.* Kelt. 251

Cados, *m. Fr.* Kelt. war, 251

Caduad, m. Brit. Kelt. war, 251

Caduan, *m. Bret.* Kelt. war horn, 251

CADVAN, *m. Welsh,* Kelt. war horn, 252

CADWALADYR, *m. Welsh,* Kelt. battle arranger, 252

Cadwallader, *m. Eng.* Kelt. battle arranger, 251

CADWALLON, *m. Welsh,* Kelt. war lord (?), 251

CADWGAN, *m. Welsh,* Kelt. war, 252

CÆCILIA, *f. Lat.* blind, 144

Cäcilie, f. Ger. Lat. blind, 144

CÆCILIUS, *m. Lat.* blind, 144

Caemhan, m. Erse, Kelt. handsome, 256

CÆSAR, *m. Lat.* hairy (?), 159

Cäsar, *m. Ger.* Lat. hairy (?), 159

CAETANO, *m. Span.* Lat. of Caieta, 132

Caharija, f. Slov. Heb. remembrance of the Lord, 51

Cahir, *m. Ir.* Kelt. battle slaughter, 252

CAIA, *f. Lat.* rejoiced in, 131

Caieta, *f. Lat.* rejoiced in, 131

Cailein, *m.* dove, 261

CAILLEACH, *f. Erse,* Kelt. handmaid, 261

CAILLEACH AONGHAS, *f. Erse,* Kelt. handmaid of Angus, 261

CAILLEACH COEIMGHIN, *f. Erse,* Kelt, handmaid of Kevin, 261

CAILLEACH DE, *f. Erse,* Kelt. handmaid of God, 261

Cain, *m. Eng.* Heb. possession, **7**

Cainan, *m. Eng.* Heb. gaining, **7**

CAINNEACH, *m. Gael.* Kelt. comely, 256

CAINTIGERN, *f. Erse,* Kelt. fair lady, 258

Caio, *m. Ital.* Lat. rejoiced in, 131

CAIRBRE, *m. Erse,* Kelt. strong man, 250

Caislav, m. Pol. Slav. honour glory, 442

CAIUS, *m. Lat.* rejoiced in, 131

Cajetano, *m. Span.* Lat. of Gaeta, 131

Caleb, *m. Eng.* Heb. dog, 38

Caligula, *m. Lat.* of the sandal, 131

CALIXTUS, *m. Lat.* of the chalice.

Callum, *m. Gael.* dove, 261

Calvandre, *m. Fr.* 57

CAMILLA, *f. Lat. Eng. It.* Lat. attendant at a sacrifice, 160

Camille, *m. f. Fr.* Lat. attendant at a sacrifice, 160

Camillo, *m. Ital.* Lat. attendant at a sacrifice, 160

CAMILLUS, *m. Lat.* attendant at a sacrifice, 160

Camilo, *m. Span.* Lat. attendant at a sacrifice, 160

CANDIDE, *f. Fr.* Lat. white, 270

Cane, *m. It.* Lat. dog, 247

Canute, *m. Eng.* Teu. hill, 433

Canutus, *Lat.* Teu. hill, 433

CAOIMGHIN, *m. Kelt.* comely, 256

Caoimhghin, m. Erse, Kelt. handsome, 256

CAOIN, *Erse,* Kelt. comely, 256

CAOINEACH, *Gael.* comely, Kelt. 256

CAOINNACH, *Erse,* Kelt. comely, 256

CAOMH, *Erse,* Kelt. comely, 256

Cara, f. Gr. Kelt. friend, 234

Caractacus, *m. Lat.* Kelt. beloved, 233

Caradoc, *m. Eng.* Kelt. beloved, 234

CARADWG, *m. Welsh,* Kelt. beloved, 234

Carel, m. Dutch, Teu. man, 386

Carl, *m. Ger.* Teu. man, 386

Carlina, *f.* Ital. Teu. man, 386

Carlo, *m. Ital.* Teu. man, 386

Carloman, *m. Fr.* Teu. strong man, 386

Carlos, *m. Span.* Teu. man, 386

Carlota, *f. Span.* Teu. man, 386

Carlotta, *f. Ital.* Teu. man, 386

Carmela, *f. Ital.* Heb. vineyard, 36

Carmichael, m. Scot. Kelt. friend of Michael, 260

Carmine, *f. Ital.* Heb. vineyard, 36

Carnation, *Gyp.* Lat. incarnation, 31

Carolina, *f. Ital.* Teu. man, 386

Caroline, *f. Eng. Fr. Ger.* Teu. man, 386

Carolus, *m. Lat.* Teu. man, 386

Carry, f. Eng. Teu. man, 386

Carvilius, *m. Lat.* Kelt. friend of power, 224

Casimir, *m. Fr.* Slav. show forth peace, 443

Casimiro, *m. Ital.* Slav. show forth peace, 443

Caslav, m. Slav. honour glory, 443

Casparo, *m. Ital.* Pers. treasure master, 211

Cassandra, *f. Eng.* Gr. 75

Cassivellaunus, *m. Lat.* Kelt. lord of great hate, 224

CASTIBOG, *m. Slav.* fear God, 444

CASTIMIR, *m. Slav.* honour peace, 442

CASTISLAV, *m. Slav.* honour glory, 444

Caswallon, *m. Eng.* Kelt. lord of great hate (?), 224

Catalina, *f. Span.* Gr. purer, 123

Cataut, f. Fr. Gr. pure, 123

Categern, *m. Eng.* Kelt. head chief, 258

Caterina, *f. It.* Gr. pure, 123

Caterino, *m. It.* Gr. pure, 123

Cathal, *Irish,* eye of battle, 252

CATHAOIR, *m. Erse,* Kelt. battle slaughter, 252

Catharina, *f. Eng.* Gr. pure, 123

Catharine, *f. Eng.* Gr. pure, 123

CATHBAR, *m. Erse,* Kelt. battle chief, 252

CATHBAT, *m. Gael.* Kelt. battle (?), 252

Catherine, *f. Fr.* Gr. pure, 123

Cathir, *m.* battle slaughter, 252

Cathmor, *m. Gael.* great in battle, 252

CATHUIL, *m. Gael.* Kelt. eye of battle, 252

Cathwg, f. Welsh, Gr. pure, 123

Catin, f. Fr. Gr. pure, 123

CATO, *m. Lat.* cautious, 164

Caton, *m. Fr.* Lat. cautious, 164
Caton, m. Fr. Gr. pure, 123
CATTWG, *m. Welsh*, Kelt. war, 252
Ceadda, *m. Lat.* Kelt. war, 252
Ceadwalla, *m. A.S.* Kelt. war lord, 252
CEARA, *f. Erse*, Kelt. ruddy, 256
CEARAN, *m. Erse*, Kelt. black, 256
Cecca, f. Ital. Teu. free, 299
Ceccarella, f. It. Teu. free, 299
Ceccina, f. It. Teu. free, 299
Cecco, m. Ital. Teu. free, 299
Cecil, *m. f. Eng.* Lat. blind, 144
Cecile, *f. Fr.* Lat. blind, 144
Cecilia, *f. It. Eng.* Lat. blind, 144
Cecilie, *f. Ger.* Lat. blind, 144
Cecilija, *f. Ill.* Lat. blind, 144
Cecilio, *m. Ital.* Lat. blind, 144
Cecily, *f. Eng.* Lat. blind, 144
Cedd, *m. A.S.* Kelt, war, 252
CEDOLJUB, *m. Sl.* child love, 444
CEDOMIL, *m. Sl.* child love, 444
CEILE PETAIR, *m. Erse*, Kelt. vassal of Peter, 261
CEIN, *f. Welsh*, Kelt. jewel, 260
CEINWEN, *f. Welsh*, Kelt. jewel, the virgin, 260
Ceirin, *m. Erse*, Kelt. black, 255
Celamire, f. Fr. 57
Celeste, *f. Fr.* Lat. heavenly, 193
Celestin, *m. Fr.* Lat. heavenly, 193
Celestine, *f. Fr.* Lat. heavenly, 193
Celestino, *m. Ital.* Lat. heavenly, 193
Celia, *f. Eng.* Lat. 145
Celie, *f. Fr.* Lat. 145
Celine, *f. Fr.* Lat. 145
CENBYRHT, *m. A.S.* Teu. bold brightness, 424
CENFUS, *m. A.S.* Teu. bold eagerness, 424
CENFUTH, *m. A.S.* Teu. bold peace, 424
CENHELM, *m. A.S.* Teu. bold helmet, 424
CENRED, *m. A.S.* Teu. bold council, 423
CENVULF, *m. A.S.* Teu. bold wolf, 423
CEOL, *m. A.S.* Teu. ship, 429
CEOLNOTH, *m. A.S,* Teu. ship compulsion, 429
CEOLRED, *m. A.S.* Teu. ship council, 429

CEOLWALD, *m. A.S.* Teu. ship power, 429
CEOLWULF, *m. A.S.* Teu. ship wolf, 429
CEORL, *m. A.S.* Teu. man, 386
CEPHAS, *m. Eng.* Aram. stone, 107
Cesar, *m. Fr.* Lat. hairy (?), 159
Cesare, *m. It.* Lat. hairy (?), 159
Cesarina, *f. It.* Lat. hairy (?), 159
Ceslav, m. Ill. Slav. honour glory, 443
Cestislav, m. Ill. Slav. honour glory, 443
Chad, *m. Eng.* Kelt. war, 252
CHARALMPIOS, *m. Gr.* joy lamp, 216
CHARIBERT, *m. Frank.* Teu. bright warrior, 417
Charilaus, *m. Eng.* Gr. grace of the people, 73
CHARIMUND, *m. Teu.* 417
Charinus, *m. Eng.* Gr. grace, 73
Chariovalda, *Pat.* Teu. warrior power, 417
Charissa, *f. Eng.* Gr. love, 73
CHARITON, *f. Gr.* Gr. love, 73
Charity, *f. Eng.* Gr. love, 73
CHARIWULF, warrior wolf, 417
Charlemagne, *m. Fr.* Teu. Lat. Charles the Great, 386
Charles, *m. Eng. Fr.* Teu. man, 386
Charlet, *f. Eng.* Teu. man, 386
Charley, m. Eng. Teu. man, 386
Charlie, m. Scot. Teu. man, 386
Charlot, m. Fr. Teu. man, 386
Charlotte, *f. Eng. Fr. Ger.* Teu. man, 386
Chatty, f. Eng. Teu. man, 386
Chérie, f. Fr. Lat. fair, 196
Cherry, f. Eng. Gr. love, 73
Cherubino, *m. Ital.* Heb. little cherub, 53
Chiara, *f. Ital.* Lat. famous, 185
Childebert, *m. Frank.* Teu. battle bright, 318
Childeberte, *f. Frank.* Teu. battle bright, 318
Childebrand, *m. Frank.* Teu. battle brand, 318
Childerich, *m. Frank.* Teu. battle ruler, 318
Chilperic, *m. Frank.* Teu. helping ruler, 318
Chim, m. Ger. Heb. the Lord will judge, 38

Chlaus, m. Swiss, Gr. victory of the people, 92

CHLODHILDA, *f. Lat. Frank.* Teu. famous battle maid, 404

CHLODOALD, *m. Frank.* Teu. famous power, 404

CHLODOBERT, *m. Frank.* Teu. famously bright, 404

Chlodobeu, *m. Prov.* Teu. holy fame, 404

Chlodio, *m. Frank.* fame, 404

CHLODOMIR, *Frank.* Teu. loud fame, 404

CHLODOSIND, *f. Frank.* Teu. famous strength, 404

Chlodoswintha, *f. Goth.* Teu. famous strength, 404

Chlodoweh, *m. Frank.* Teu. holy fame, 404

CHLOE, *f. Eng.* Gr. blooming, 70

CHLOTER, *m. Frank.* Teu. famous warrior, 407

Chochilaicus, *m. Lat.* Teu. sport of thought, 354

Chosroes, *m. Gr.* Zend. sun (?), 56

CHRAMNE, *m. Frank.* Teu. raven, 345

Chresta, m. Swiss, Gr. Christian, 105

Chresteli, m. Swiss, Gr. Christian, 105

Chrestien, *m. Fr.* Gr. Christian, 105

Chrestienne, *f. Fr.* Gr. Christian, 105

Chrestoffel, *m. Swiss,* Gr. Christ bearer, 106

Chrétien, *Fr.* Gr. Christian, 105

Chriemhild, *f. Ger.* Teu. helmeted battle maid, 360

Chrissanth, m. Russ. Fr. gold flower, 125

Chris, Eng. Gr. Christ bearer, 106

Chrissie, f. Scot. Gr. Christian, 105

Christabel, *f. Eng.* fair Christian, 104

Christackr, m. M.Gr. Gr. Christ bearer, 106

Christal, m. Scot. Gr. Christ bearer, 106

Christian, *f. Scot. Dan.* Gr. Christian, 105

Christiana, *f. Eng.* Gr. Christian, 105

Christiane, *f. Nor.* Gr. Christian, 105

Christiern, *m. Dan.* Gr. Christian, 105

Christina, *m. Eng.* Gr. Christian, 105

Christine, *m. Fr.* Gr. Christian, 105

Christinha, *f. Port.* Gr. Christian, 105

Christmas, *m. Eng.* 209

Christof, *m. Russ.* Gr. Christ bearer, 106

Christofer, *m. Russ.* Gr. Christ bearer, 106

Christoph, *m. Ger.* Gr. Christ bearer, 106

Christophe, *m. Fr.* Gr. Christ bearer, 106

Christopher, *m. Eng.* Gr. Christ bearer, 106

Christophera, *f. Eng.* Gr. Christ bearer, 106

CHRISTOPHOROS, *m. Gr.* Gr. Christ bearer, 106

CHRISTOPHILON, *Ger.* Gr. Christ loved, 106

Christophine, *f. Ger.* Gr. Christ bearer, 106

Christovao, *m. Port.* Gr. Christ bearer, 106

Chrodehilde, *f. Fr.* Teu. famous heroine, 404

CHRODO, *m. Fr.* Teu. fame, 404

Chrodogang, *m. Frank.* Teu. famed progress, 406

Chrodoswintha, *f. Fr.* Teu. famous strength, 407

Chrysanth, *m. Bav.* Gr. gold flower, 125

CHRYSANTHOS, *m. Gr.* Gr. gold flower, 125

Chryseis, *f. Gr.* golden, 125

Chrysostom, *m. Eng.* Gr. gold mouth, 43

Chrysostome, *m. Fr.* Gr. gold mouth, 43

CHRYSOSTOMOS, *m. Gr.* Gr. gold mouth, 43

CHRYSOUCHA, *f. M. Gr.* Gr. golden, 43

Chuedi, m. Swiss, Teu. bold council, 423

Chuedli, m. Swiss, Teu. bold council, 423

Chuercd, m. Swiss, Teu. bold council, 423

CHUONMUND, *m. Old Ger.* Teu. bold protection, 423

CHUONRATH, *m. Old Ger.* Teu. bold council, 423

CIAN, *m. Erse,* vast, 258

CICERO, *m. Lat.* vetch, 129

Cicily, *f. Eng.* Lat. blind, 144

Cila, f. Ill. Lat. blind, 144

Cile, f. Hamb. Lat. blind, 144
Cilika, f. Ill. Lat. blind, 144
Ciprian, *m. Eng.* Lat. of Cyprus, 199
Cipriano, *m. It.* Lat. of Cyprus, 199
Ciriaco, *m. Ital.* Gr. Sunday child, 217
Ciril, *m. Ill.* Gr. lordly, 217
Cirilo, *m. Span. Ital. Ill.* Gr. lordly, 217
Cirjar, *m. Ill.* Gr. Sunday child, 217
Cirko, m. Ill. Gr. Sunday child, 217
Ciro, *m. Slov. Ill.* Gr. lordly, 217
Cis, f. Eng. Lat. blind, 144
Cislav, m. Slav. pure glory, 444
Cistislav, m. Slav. pure glory, 444
Clair, *m. Fr.* Lat. famous, 185
Claire, *f. Fr.* Lat. famous, 185
CLARA, *f. Eng. Span.* Lat. famous, 185
Clare, *f. Eng.* Lat. famous, 185
Clarina, *m. Eng.* Lat. famous, 185
Claribel, *f. Eng.* Lat. brightly fair, 185
Clarice, *f. Ital.* Lat. rendering famous, 185
Clarimond, *Eng.* 185
Clarinda, *f. Eng.* Lat. brightly fair, 185
Clarissa, *f. Eng.* Lat. rendering famous, 185
Clarisse, *f. Fr.* Lat. rendering famous, 185
CLARUS, *m.* Lat. famous, 185
Clas, m. Dutch, Gr. victory of the people, 92
Claud, *m. Eng.* Lat. lame, 146
Claude, *f. m. Fr.* Lat. lame, 146
CLAUDIA, *f. Ger. It.* Lat. lame, 146
Claudie, *f. Prov.* Lat. lame, 146
Claudina, *f. It.* Lat. lame, 146
Claudine, *f. Ger. Fr.* Lat. lame, 146
Claudio, *m. It.* Lat. lame, 146
CLAUDIUS, *m. Lat.* lame, 146
Claus, m. Dutch, Gr. victory of the people, 92
Cleanthe, *Fr.* Gr. famous bloom, 95
Clem, m. Eng. Lat. merciful, 160
Clémence, *f. Fr.* Lat. merciful, 160
Clemency, *f. Eng.* Lat. merciful, 160
CLEMENS, *m. Ger.* Lat. merciful, 160
Clement, *m. Eng. Fr.* Lat. merciful, 160
Clemente, *m. It.* Lat. merciful, 160

Clementia, *f. Ger. It.* Lat. merciful, 160
Clementina, *f. Eng. It.* Lat. merciful, 160
Clementine, *f. Ger. Fr.* Lat. merciful, 160
Clemenza, *f. It.* Lat. merciful, 160
Cleomachus, *m.* Gr. famous war, 407
Cleopatra, *f. Eng.* Gr. fame of her father, 95
Clobes, m. Ger. Gr. victory of the people, 90
Clodoveo, *m. Span.* Teu. holy fame, 404
Clodius, *m.* Lat. lame, 146
Clotilda, *f. Lat.* Teu. famous battle maid, 404
Clotilde, *f. Fr.* Teu. famous battle maid, 404
Clovd, m. Fr. Teu. famous power, 404
Clovis, *m. Lat.* Teu. holy fame, 404
CNÆUS, *m. Lat.* with a birth mark, 131
Cnogher, m. Ir. Kelt. strong aid, 247
Cnud, *m. Eng.* Teu. hill, 433
CŒLIA, *f. Lat.* 145
CŒLINA, *f. Lat.* 145
Coenrad, m. Dutch, Teu. bold speech, 423
Cohat, Prov. Teu. bold speech, 423
Cort, Dan. Teu. bold speech, 423
Col, Welsh, Kelt.
Cola, m. It. Gr. victory of the people, 92
Colan, *m. Corn.* Lat. dove, 261
Colas, m. Fr. Gr. victory of the people, 92
Colbert, *m. Fr. Eng.* Teu. cool brightness, 429
Colbrand, *m. Eng.* Teu. cool sword, 429
Colborn, *m. Eng.* Teu. black bear, 429
Colin, m. Fr. Gr. victory of the people, 92
Colin, *m. Scot.* Lat. dove, 261
Colin, m. Fr. Gr. victor, 90, 388
Colinette, *f. Eng.* Lat. dove, 261
Colman, *m. Ger.* Lat. dove, 187
Colombina, *f. Ital.* Lat. dove, 187
Columb, *m. Eng.* Lat. dove, 187, 261
COLUMBA, *m. Lat.* dove, 187, 261
Columbanus, *m. Lat.* Lat. dove, 187, 261

COLUMBINE, *f. Eng.* Lat. dove, 261

Columbkill, *m. Ir.* Lat. dove of the cell, 261

Côme, *m. Fr.* Gr. order, 125

Como, *m. It.* Heb. supplanter, 17

CON, *m. Erse,* Kelt. wisdom, 247

Conachar, *m. Scot.* Kelt. strong help.

CONAN, *m. Bret.* Kelt. wisdom, 247

Concepcion, f. Span. Lat. in honour of the immaculate conception, 30

Concetta, f. It. Lat. in honour of the immaculate conception, 30

Conchita, f. Span. Lat. in honour of the immaculate conception, 30

CONCHOBHAR, *m. Erse,* Kelt. strong help, 248

CONCORDIA, *f. Ger.* Lat. concord.

CONGAL, *m. Erse,* Kelt. chief courage, 247

Coniah, *m. Eng.* Heb. appointed, 38

CONMOR, *m. Ir.* Kelt. strength great, 247

CONN, *m. Erse,* Kelt. wisdom, 247

CONNAIRE, *m. Gael.* Kelt. hound of slaughter, 250

Connal, *m. Ir.* Kelt. chief's courage, 247

Connel, *m. Ir.* Kelt. chief's courage, 247

Connor, *m. Ir.* Kelt. hound of slaughter, 250

Connull, *m. Scot.* Kelt. wise strength, 247

Conquhare, m. Scot. Kelt. strong help, 248

Conrad, *m. Eng.* Teu. able speech, 423

Conrade, *m. Fr.* Teu. able speech, 423

Conradin, m. Fr. Teu. able speech, 423

Conrado, *m. Ital.* Teu. able speech, 423

Consalvo, *m. Ital.* Teu. war wolf, 363

Constança, *f. Span.* Lat. firm, 161

Constance, *f. Eng. Fr.* Lat. firm, 161

Constancia, *f. Eng. Port.* Lat. firm, 161

Constancio, *m. Port.* Lat. firm, 161

CONSTANS, *m. Ger.* Lat. firm, 161

Constant, *m. Ir. Eng.* Lat. 161

Constantine, *m. Eng.* Lat. firm, 161

Constantino, *m. Ital.* Lat. firm, 161

CONSTANTINUS, *m.* Lat. firm, 161

CONSTANTIUS, *m.* Lat. firm, 161

Constanz, *m. Ger.* Lat. firm, 161

Constanze, *f. Ger.* Lat. firm, 161

Conwal, m. Scot. Kelt. strength and valour, 247

Cooey, m. Irish, Kelt. hound of the meadow, 250

Coppo, m. Ital. Heb. supplanter, 17

Coralie, *f. Fr.* coral,

CORA, *f. Gr.* maiden, 60

CORCRAN, *m. Erse,* Kelt. rosy.

Cordelia, *f. Eng.* Kelt. jewel of the sea, 230

Cordelie, *f. Fr.* Kelt. jewel of the sea, 230

Cordula, f. Ger. Kelt. jewel of the sea, 220

Corinna, f. Gr. maiden, 60

Corinne, f. Fr. a maiden, 60

CORMAC, *m. Erse,* Kelt. son of a chariot, 249

Cormick, Irish, Kelt. son of a chariot, 249

Corneille, m. Fr. Lat. horn (?), 146

Cornelia, *f. Eng. Ital.* Lat. horn (?), 146

Cornelie, *f. Fr.* Lat. horn (?), 146

Cornelio, *m. Ital.* Lat. horn (?), 146

CORNELIUS, *m. Eng.* Lat. horn (?), 146

Corney, m. Ir. Lat. horn (?), 146

Corradino, m. It. Teu. bold council, 423

Cosimo, *m. Ital.* Gr. order, 125

Cosmo, *m. Ital.* Gr. order, 125

Cospatrick, *m. Scot.* Gael. Lat. boy of Patrick, 260

Costanza, *f. Span.* Lat. firm, 161

Costanza, *f. Ital.* Lat. firm, 161

Cotahelm, *m. Ger.* Teu. divine helmet, 287

Cotahram, *m. Ger.* Teu. good raven, 287

Cotalint, *m. Ger.* Teu. divine serpent, 287

Court, m. Neth. Teu. bold council, 423

Cradock, m. Eng. Kelt. beloved, 233

CREIRDYDDLYDD, *f. Welsh,* Kelt. jewel of the sea, 230

CREIRWY, *f. Welsh,* Kelt. token, 229

Crepet, m. Fr. Lat. curly, 162

Crepin, *m. Fr.* Lat. curly, 162

Crescence, *f. Fr.* Lat. growing, 198

Crescencia, *f. Ital.* Lat. growing, 198

Crescencio, *f. Ital.* Lat. growing, 198

CRESCENS, *m.* Lat. growing, 198
Crescent, *m. Fr.* Lat. growing, 198
Crescentia, *f. Ger.* Lat. growing, 198
Crescenz, *f. Bav.* Lat. growing, 198
Crisostomo, *m. Span.* Gr. golden mouth, 125
Crispian, *m. Eng.* Lat. curly, 162
CRISPIANUS, *m. Lat.* curly, 162
Crispin, *m. Eng. Fr.* Lat. curly, 162
Crispino, *m. It.* Lat. curly, 162
CRISPINUS, *m. Lat.* curly, 162
Cristiano, *m. Rom.* Gr. Christian, 105
Cristina, *f. It. Span.* Gr. Christian, 105
Cristinha, *f. Port.* Gr. Christian, 105
Cristofano, m. Ital. Gr. Christ bearer, 106
Cristoforo, m. Ital. Gr. Christ bearer, 106
Cristoval, m. Span. Gr. Christ bearer, 106
Crogher, m. Irish, Kelt. strong help, 248
Crohoore, m. Irish, Kelt. strong help, 248
CUCHAISIL, *m. Erse,* Kelt. hound of Cashel, 248
Cuchullin, *m. Scot.* Kelt. hound of Ulster, 248
Cuddie, m. Scot. Teu. noted brightness, 423
CUGAN-MATHAIR, *m. Erse,* Kelt. hound without a mother, 248
Cuillean, *m. Gael.* Kelt. whelp, 248
CUMHAIGHE, *m. Erse,* Kelt. hound of the plain, 246
Cunibert, *m. Ger.* Teu. bold brightness, 423
Cunegonda, *f. Ital.* Teu. bold war, 423
Cunegundis, Port. Teu. bold war, 423
Cunegonde, *f. Fr.* Teu. bold war, 423
Cunobelinus, *m. Lat.* Kelt. lord of the sun (?), war (?), 232
Cunzo, m. Ger. Teu. bold council, 423
Currado, *m. It.* Teu. bold council, 423
CU-SIONNA, *m. Erse,* Kelt. hound of the Shannon, 248
CUSLIEBNE, *m. Erse,* Kelt. hound of the mountain, 248
Custance, *f. Eng.* Lat. firm, 162
Cutha, *m. A.S.* Teu. skilled, 422
Cuthbert, *m. Eng.* Teu. well known splendour, 422

CUTHBURH, *f. A.S.* Teu. skilled pledge, 422
CUTHBRYHT, *m. A.S.* Teu. noted splendour, 422
CUTHWALD, *m. A.S.* skilled power, 422
CUTHWINE, *m. A.S.* Teu. skilled friend, 422
CU-ULADH, *m. Gadhael.* Kelt. hound of Ulster, 248
CWENBURH, *f. A.S.* Teu. queen pledge.
Cwrig, *m. Welsh,* Gr. Sunday child, 217
Cyaxares, *m. Eng.* Zend. beautiful eyed, 56
Cymbeline, *m. Eng.* Kelt. lord of the sun, war (?), 232
Cyndeyrn, *m. Welsh,* Kelt. head chief, 258
CYNEBALD, *m. A.S.* Teu. prince lineage, 424
CYNEBRIGHT, *m. A.S.* lineage of splendour, 424
CYNEBURH, *m. A.S.* Teu. pledge of kindred, 424
CYNEFRYTH, *m. A.S.* Teu. able kindred of peace, 424
Cynegundis, *f. Port.* Teu. bold war (?), 423
CYNRIC, *m. A.S.* Teu. royal kin, 424
CYNETHRYTH, *f. A.S.* Teu. threatening kindred, 424
CYNEWALD, *m. A.S.* Teu. kin of power, 424
Cynthia, *f. Eng.* Gr. of Cynthus, 65
Cynvelin, *m. Welsh,* Kelt. lord of war (?), 258
Cyprian, m. Eng. Ger. Gr. Lat. of Cyprus, 199
CYPRIANUS, *m.* Lat. of Cyprus, 199
Cyprien, *m. Fr.* Gr. Lat. of Cyprus, 199
Cyr, *m. Fr.* Gr. Sunday child, 217
Cyran, *m. Fr.* Lat. spear man, 177
Cyrenius, *m. Gal. Eng.* Lat. spear man, 177
Cyriac, *m. Fr.* Gr. the Sunday child, 217
Cyriacus, *m. Lat.* Gr. Sunday child, 217
Cyriak, *m. Ger.* Gr. Sunday child, 217
Cyril, *m. Eng.* Gr. lordly, 217

Cyrill, *m. Ger.* Gr. lordly, 217
Cyrilla, *f. Ger.* Gr. lordly, 217
Cyrille, *m. Fr.* Gr. lordly, 217
Cyrillo, *m. Port.* Gr. lordly, 217
Cyrin, *m. Gr.* Lat. spear man, 177
Cyrus, *m. Eng.* Pers. the sun (?), 56
Cystenian, *m. Welsh,* Lat. firm, 161
Czenzi, f. Hung. Lat. increasing, 198

D

Daan, m. Dutch, Heb. the judging
God, 49
Daarte, f. Dan. Gr. gift of God, 102
Dabit, m. Lus. Heb. beloved, 46
Dabko, m. Lus. Heb. beloved, 46
Dafod, *Welsh,* 46
DAG, *m. Goth.* Teu. day, 334
DAGFINN, *m. Nor.* Teu. white as day,
46, 334
Dageid, cheerful as day, 334
DAGHEID, cheerful as day, 334
Dagmar, *f. Dan.* Teu. Dane's joy, 335
DAGNY, *f. Nor.* Teu. fresh as day, 334
Dago, *m. Span.* Teu. day, 334
Dagobert, *m. Fr.* Teu. day bright, 334
DAGOBRECHT, *m. Frank.* Teu. day
bright, 334
DAGOLF, *m. Ger.* Teu. day wolf, 334
DAGR, *m. Ice.* Teu. day, 334
DAGRAD, *m. Ger.* Teu. day council.
Dalphin, m. Fr. Gr. of Delphi, 66
DAMALIS, *f. Gr.* Gr. taming, 126
Damaris, *f. Eng.* Gr. taming, 126
DAMASPIA, *f. Pers.* Pers. horse tamer,
78
Damian, *m. Ger. Eng. Russ.* Gr. tam-
ing, 126
Damiano, m. Ital. Gr. taming, 126
DAMIANOS, *m.* Gr. taming, 126
Damianus, *m. Lat.* Gr. taming, 126
Damiao, *m. Port.* Gr. taming, 126
Damien, *m. Fr.* Gr. taming, 126
DAMHNAIT, *f. Erse,* Kelt. 271
DAN, *m. Eng.* Heb. judge, 7, 49
Dandie, m. Scot. Gr. man, 86
Dancel, m. Dutch, Heb. the judging
God, 49
DANICA, *f. Slav.* Slav. morning star,
441
DANIEL, *m. Eng.* Heb. the judging
God, 49

Danielle, *m. It.* Heb. the judging God,
49
Danihel, *m. N.L.D.* Heb. the judging
God, 49
Danil, *m. Russ.* Heb. the judging God,
49
Danila, *m. Slov.* Heb. the judging God,
49
Danjels, m. Lett. Heb. the judging
God, 49
DANKHERI, *m. Ger.* Teu. thankful
warrior, 372
DANKRAD, *m. Ger.* Teu. thankful
speech, 372
DANKMAR, *m. Ger.* Teu. thankful
fame, 372
DANKWART, *m. Ger.* Teu. thankful
ward, 372
Dannel, *m. Swiss,* Teu. the judging
God, 49
Dante, m. It. Lat. lasting, 186
DAPHNE, *f. Gr.* Gr. bay tree.
Darby, *m. Ir.* Kelt. freeman, 249
Darcy, m. Eng. Erse, dark, 225
Darija, f. Russ. Gr. gift of God, 102
Darkey, f. Eng. Erse, dark, 225
Darius, *m. Eng.* Pers. king, 57 ?
Darte, m. Lett. Gr. gift of God, 102
Dascha, f. Russ. Gr. gift of God, 102
Daschenka, f. Russ. Gr. gift of God,
102
DATHI, *m. Erse,* Kelt. far darting, 46
Datsch, m. Danzig, Heb. beloved, 46
Daulf, m. Ger. Teu. day wolf, 334
Davced, m. Russ. Heb. beloved, 46
DAVID, *m. Fr. Eng. Ger.* Heb. be-
loved, 46
Davidas, m. Lett. Heb. beloved, 46
Davidde, m. Ital. Heb. beloved, 46
Davidu, m. Wallach. Heb. beloved,
46
Davie, m. Scot. Heb. beloved, 46
DAVORIN, *m. Slav.* Slav. of the war
god, 445
DAVROSLAV, *m. Slav.* Slav. Davor's
glory, 445
DAVROSLAVA, *f. Slav.* Slav. Davor's
glory, 445
Davy, m. Eng. Heb. beloved, 46
Dawfydd, m. Welsh, Heb. beloved, 46
Dé, m. Fr. Kelt. fire, 227
DEARBHFORGAIL, *f. Erse,* Kelt. purely
fair daughter, 255

DEARG, *m. Erse*, Kelt. red, 253
Deb, f. Eng. Heb. bee, 14
Deborah, *f. Eng.* Heb. bee, 2, 14
DECIMA, *f. Eng.* Lat. tenth, 139
DECIMUS, *m. Lat.* tenth, 139
Decius, m. Lat. tenth, 139
Dedo, m. Ger. Teu. people's ruler, 374
DEGEN, Ger. Teu. warrior, 351
DEGENHARD, *m. Ger.* Teu. firm warrior, 351
DEICOLA, *m. Lat.* God's worshipper, 188
Deinhard, Ger. Teu. firm warrior, 351
Deiniol, m. Welsh, Heb. the judging God, 49
Delia, f. Eng. Gr. of Delos, 65
Delicia, *f. Eng.* Lat. delightful, 196
Delizia, *f. Ital.* Lat. delightful, 196
Delphine, *f. Fr.* Gr. of Delphi, 66
Delphinia, *f. Gr.* Gr. of Delphos, 66
Delphinus, *m. Lat.* Gr. of Delphi, 66
Demeter, *m. Slov.* Gr. of Demeter, 69
Demetre, *m. Fr.* Ger. of Demeter, 69
Demetria, *m. It.* Gr. of Demeter, 69
DEMETRIOS, *m. Gr.* Gr. of Demeter, 69
Demetrius, *m. Lat. Eng.* Gr. of Demeter, 69
Demjan, *m. Russ.* Gr. taming, 126
DEMODOKOS, *m.* Gr. people's teacher, 95
DEMOLEON, *m.* Gr. people's lion, 95
Denis, *m. Fr.* Gr. of Dionysos, 70
Denise, *f. Fr.* Gr. of Dionysos, 70
Dennet, *f. Eng.* Gr. of Dionysos, 70
Dennis, *m. Eng.* Gr. of Dionysos, 70
Denys, *m. O.Fr.* Gr. of Dionysos, 70
Deodati, *m. Ital.* Lat. God given, 188
Deodatus, *m. Eng.* Lat. God given, 188
DEOGRATIAS, *m. Lat.* thanks to God, 188
Derdre, f. Erse, Kelt. fear, 224
Derede, f. Bav. Gr. gift of God, 102
DERGO, *m. Scot.* Kelt. red, 253
Dermot, *m. Ir.* Kelt. freeman, 249
Derrick, m. Eng. Teu. people's wealth, 373
DESIDERATUS, *m. Lat.* beloved, 188
Desiderio, *m. It.* Lat. beloved, 188
Desiderius, *m. Lat.* beloved, 188
Desirata, *f. It.* Lat. beloved, 188
Desirée, *f. Fr.* Lat. beloved, 188

Desse, f. Ill. Gr. God given, 102
Detrich, Bohm. Teu. people's ruler, 374
DEUSDEDIT, *m. Lat.* God gave, 188
DEUSVULT, *m. Lat.* God wills, 188
Devnet, f. Ir. Kelt. 271
Devorgil, *f. Scot.* Kelt. purely fair daughter, 255
DEVOSLAV, *m. Slav.* maiden glory, 445
DEVOSLAVA, *f. Slav.* maiden glory, 445
DHUBODA, *Gael.* black, 255
DHUGAL, *m. Gael.* Kelt. black stranger, 255
Di, f. Eng. Lat. goddess, 170
Diago, m. Port. Heb. supplanter, 17
DIAMANTO, *f. M. Gr.* Gr. diamond, 125
DIANA, *f. Eng.* Lat. goddess, 170
Diane, *f. Fr.* Lat. goddess, 170
DIARMAID, *m. Gael.* Kelt. freeman, 46, 225, 249
Dibble, m. Eng. Teu. people's prince, 374
Diccon, m. Eng. Teu. firm ruler, 399
Dick, *m. Eng.* Teu. firm ruler, 399
Didders, m. Lett. Lat. beloved, 46
Didhrikr, *m. Nor.* Teu. people's ruler, 374
Didier, *m. Fr.* Lat. beloved, 49
Didière, beloved, 188
Diederike, *f. Ger.* Teu. people's ruler, 374
Didrik, m. Nor. Teu. people's ruler, 374
Didschis, m. Lett. Teu. people's ruler, 374
Didymus, *m. Eng.* Ger. twin, 22
Diego, m. Span. Heb. supplanter, 17
Diel, m. Fr. Lat. God's worshipper, 188
Dielle, f. Franche-comté, Lat. God's worshipper, 188
Dienes, m. Hung. Gr. of Dionysos, 70
Diephold, m. Ger. Teu. people's prince, 374
Dierk, m. Dutch, Teu. people's ruler, 374
Dietberga, *m. f. Frank.* Teu. people's protection, 375
Dietbert, *m. Frank.* Teu. people's brightness, 375

Dietbold, *m. Ger.* Teu. people's prince, 374

Dietbrand, *m. Ger.* Teu. people's sword, 375

Dietfrid, *m. Ger.* Teu. people's peace, 375

Dietger, *m. Ger.* Teu. people's spear, 375

Diethard, *m. Ger.* Teu. people's firmness, 375

Diethelm, *m. Ger.* Teu. people's helmet, 375

Dietl, m. Ger. Teu. people's ruler, 374

Dietleib, *m. Ger.* Teu. people's relic, 374

Dietlind, *m. Ger.* Teu. people's snake, 375

Dietman, *m. Ger.* Teu. people's man, 375

Dietmar, *m. Ger.* Teu. people's fame, 375

Dieto, *m. Ger.* Teu. the people, 374

Dietolf, *m. Ger.* Teu. people's wolf, 374

Dietram, *m. Ger.* Teu. people's raven, 374

Dieterico, *m. It.* Teu. people's rule, 374

Dieterich, *m. Ger.* Teu. people's rule, 374

Dietrl, m. Bav. Teu. people's rule, 374

DIEUDONNÉ, *m. Fr.* Lat. God given, 188

Diez, Ger. Teu. supplanted, 17

Diggory, *m. Eng.* French, the almost lost, 462

Dimitar, *m. Slov.* Gr. of Demeter, 70

Dimitrij, *m. Russ.* Gr. of Demeter, 70

Dimitrija, *m. Ill. Gr.* of Demeter, 70

Dimitrije, *m. Ill.* Gr. of Demeter, 70

Dinah, *f. Eng.* Heb. judgment, 26

Dinis, m. Port. Gr. of Dionysos, 70

Ditlev, m. Ger. Teu. people's relic, 375

Dinko, m. Slav. Lat. Sunday child, 218

Diodor, m. Ger. Gr. God's gift, 102

Dionetta, *f. Eng.* Gr. of Dionysos, 70

Dionigi, *m. It.* Gr. of Dionysos, 70

Dionigio, *m. It.* Gr. of Dionysos, 70

Dionis, *m. Span.* Gr. of Dionysos, 70

Dionisia, *f. Rom.* Gr. of Dionysos, 70

Dionisij, *m. Russ.* Gr. of Dionysos, 70

Dionisio, *m. Rom.* Gr. of Dionysos, 70

Dionys, *m. Ger.* Gr. of Dionysos, 70

Dionysia, *f. Eng. Ger.* Gr. of Dionysos, 70

Dionysio, *m. Port.* Gr. of Dionysos, 70

DIONYSIOS, *m. Gr.* of Dionysos, 70

Dionysius, *m. Eng. Lat.* Gr. of Dionysos, 70

DIONYSOS, *m. Gr.* god of Nysos (?), 70

DIORO, *m. Ger.* Teu. dear, 426

Diotisalvi, m. It. Lat. God save thee, 188

Diotrich, m. Ger. Teu. people's ruler, 374

Dippold, *m. Ger.* Teu. people's prince, 374

Diriks, *m. Lett.* Teu. people's ruler, 374

Dirk, *m. Dutch,* Teu. people's ruler, 374

DISA, *f. Nor.* Teu. active spirit, 307

Dith, m. Swiss, Heb. praise, 21

Ditrik, m. Hung. Teu. people's ruler, 374

Diura, m. Ger. Teu. dear, 426

Diuthilt, *f. Ger.* Teu. people's heroine, 375

Diutrat, people's council, 375

Diwis, m. Bohm. Gr. of Dionysos, 70

Dix, m. Ger. Lat. blessed, 184

Djoulija, m. Serv. Gr. well born, 87

Djuradj, m. Ill. Gr. husbandman, 116

Djurdj, m. Ill. Gr. husbandman, 116

Djurica, m. Ill. Gr. husbandman, 116

Dmitar, m. Serv. Gr. of Demeter, 70

Dmitra, f. Slav. Gr. of Demeter, 70

Dmitri, m. Russ. Gr. of Demeter, 70

Dmitrij, m. Russ. Gr. of Demeter, 70

Dobrana, *f. Slav.* Slav. good, 443

Dobrija, *f. Slav.* Slav. good, 443

DOBROGOST, *m. Pol.* Slav. good guest, 443

DOBROLJUB, *m. Slav.* Slav. good lover, 443

DOBROSLAV, *m. Slav.* Slav. good glory, 443

DOBROVOJ, *m. Ill.* Slav. good warrior, 443

DOBROVUK, *m. Ill.* Slav. good wolf, 443

DOBROTIN, *m. Slav.* Slav. good doer, 443

DOBROTINA, *f. Slav.* Slav. good doer, 443

Dodd, m. Eng. Teu. of the people, 374

Dolfine, f. Ger. Teu. noble wolf, 66

Dolfino, *m. Ven.* Gr. of Delphi, 66

Dolly, f. Eng. Gr. gift of God, 102

Dolores, *f. Span.* Lat. sorrows, 2, 30

Dolph, m. Eng. Teu. noble wolf, 400

Dolphin, *m. Fr.* Gr. of Delphi, 66

Domas, Lus. Aram. twin, 22

Domask, Lus. Aram. twin, 22

DOMHNALL, *m. Erse,* Kelt. great chief, 253

Domingo, *m. Span.* Lat. Sunday child, 218

Domingos, *m. Port.* Lat. Sunday child, 218

Dominic, *m. Ger. Eng.* Lat. Sunday child, 218

Dominica, *f. It.* Lat. Sunday child, 218

Dominichino, m. It. Lat. Sunday child, 218

Dominico, *m. It.* Lat. Sunday child, 218

Dominicus, *m. Ger.* Lat. Sunday child, 218

Dominik, *m. Slav.* Lat. Sunday child, 218

Dominique, *m. Fr.* Lat. Sunday child, 218

Domnech, *m. Ir.* Lat. Sunday child, 218

Domogoj, *m. Slav.* Lat. Sunday child, 218

Domokos, m. Hung. Lat. Sunday child, 218

DON, *m. Ir.* Kelt. brown, 253

DONACHA, *m. Gael.* Kelt. brown warrior, 50, 253

Donald, *m. Scot.* Kelt. proud chief, 253

Donath, *m. Ir.* Lat. given, 188

Donato, *m. It.* Lat. given, 188

Donatus, *m. Lat.* given, 188

DONNAN, *m. Erse,* Kelt. brown, 50

Donnet, f. Eng. Gr. of Dionysos, 70

Donnet, f. Eng. Lat. gift of God, 188

Donoghue, *m. Ir.* Kelt. brown chief, 50, 153

Donough, *m. Ir.* Kelt. brown warrior, 50, 153

DONUMDEI, *m. Lat.* gift of God, 188

Dora, f. Eng. Ger. Ill. Gr. gift of God, 102

Doralice, f. Fr. Gr. gift, 102

Dorcas, *f. Eng.* Gr. gazelle, 50

DORCHAIDE, *m. Erse,* dark, 225

Dore, m. Florentine, Lat. lover, 182

Dore, f. Ger. Gr. gift of God, 102

DORENN, *f. Erse,* Kelt. sullen, 2

Dorette, f. Fr. Gr. gift of God, 102

Dorfei, f. Russ. Gr. gift of God, 102

Dorinda, f. Eng. Gr. gift, 102

Dorka, f. Russ. Gr. gift of God, 102

Dorlisa, f. Lus. Gr. Heb. Dorothea Elizabeth, 102

Dornadilla, f. Lat. Kelt. purely fair daughter, 255

Dorofei, m. Russ. Gr. gift of God, 102

Doroltya, Hung. Gr. gift of God, 102

Dorosia, f. Pol. Bohm. Gr. gift of God, 102

Dorota, f. Pol. Bohm. Gr. gift of God, 102

Dorotea, *f. It.* Gr. gift of God, 102

Doroteja, *f. Ill.* Gr. gift of God, 102

Dorothea, *f. Span. Eng. Gr.* Gr. gift of God, 102

Dorothée, *f. Fr. Ger.* Gr. gift of God, 102

DOROTHEUS, *m. Lat.* Gr. gift of God, 102

Dorothy, *f. Eng.* Gr. gift of God, 102

Dorothya, *f. Hung.* Gr. gift of God, 102

Dort, f. Dutch, Gr. gift of God, 102

Dortchen, f. Dutch, Gr. gift of God, 102

Douce, *f. Fr.* Lat. sweet, 196

Dougal, *m. Scot.* Kelt. black stranger, 253

Douglas, *m. Scot.* Kelt. dark grey, 259

Dowsabel, *f. Eng.* Lat. sweet fair, 196

Dowsie, *f. Eng.* Lat. sweet, 196

Dragan, *m. Slav.* Slav. dear, 444

Dragana, *f. Slav.* Slav. dear, 444

Draganka, f. Slav. Slav. dear, 444

Dragija, *m. Slav.* Slav. dear, 444

Dragilika, m. Slav. Slav. dear, 444

Dragojila, *f. Slav.* Slav. dear, 444

Dragoslav, *m. Slav.* Slav. dear glory, 444

Dragotinka, m. Slav. Slav. dear, 444
Drenka, f. Ill. Lat. horn, 146
Drew, *m. Eng.* Teu. skilful (?), 451
Dries, m. Dutch, Gr. manly, 86
DROGO, *m. Ital.* Teu. skilful, 451
Drogon, *m. Fr.* Teu. skilful, 451
Drot, m. Nor. Teu. maiden, 318
Dru, *m. Fr.* Teu. skilful, 451
DRUST, *m. Pict.* Kelt. proclaimer, 464
DRUSILLA, *f. Lat.* strong, 162
DRUSUS, *m. Lat.* strong, 162
Drutje, f. Neth. Teu. spear maid, 368
Duarte, *m. Port.* Teu. rich guard, 378
DUBDAINTUATH, *m. Erse,* Kelt. black man of two lordships, 254
DUBDAINBER, *m. Erse,* Kelt. black man of two rivers, 253
DUBDALETHE, *m. Erse,* Kelt. black, 253
DUBHAN, *m. Erse,* Kelt. black, 254
DUBHCOHBLAITH, *f. Erse,* Kelt. black victory, 254
DUCHOMAR, *m. Gael.* Kelt. black well-shaped man, 253
DHUBDOTHRA, *m. Erse,* Kelt. black man of the Dodder, 253
DUBADEASA, *f. Erse,* Kelt. black beauty, 254
DUBHESSA, *f. Erse,* Kelt. black nurse, 254
DUBISLAV, *m. Slav.* Slav. oak glory, 438
Ducia, *f. Eng.* Lat. sweet, 196
Dudde, m. Fris. Teu. people's ruler, 374
Dudon, *m. Fr.* Lat. God-given, 188
Dudone, *m. It.* Lat. God-given, 188
Duessa, *f. Eng.* Kelt. black nurse, 254
Dugald, *m. Scot.* Kelt. black stranger, 253
Duff, *m. Scot.* Kelt. black, 253
Dulce, *f. Eng.* Lat. sweet, 196
Dulcia, *f. Span.* Lat. sweet, 196
Dulcibella, *f. Eng.* Lat. sweet fair, 196
Dulcinea, *f. Span.* Lat. sweet, 196
Dummas, m. Lith. Aram. twin, 22
Duncan, *m. Scot.* Kelt. brown chief, 255
Dunstan, m. A.G.S. Teu. hill stone, 350
Dunulf, m. A.G.S. Teu. hill wolf, 350

Dunko, m. Slav. Lat. Sunday child, 218
Dunwalton, Cym. Kelt. 254
Durand, *m. Fr.* Lat. lasting, 187
Durante, *m. It.* Lat. lasting, 187
Durandarte, *m. Span.* Lat. lasting, 187
Durans, *m. Lat.* lasting, 187
Duredel, f. Bav. Gr. gift of God, 102
Durl, f. Bav. Gr. gift of God, 102
Dusa, f. Ill. Slav. happy, 444
DUSCHA, *f. Russ.* Slav. happy, 444
Duschinka, f. Russ. Slav. happy, 444
Dusica, f. Russ. Slav. happy, 444
DWYNWEN, *f. Welsh,* Kelt. white wave, 270
Dye, f. Eng. Lat. goddess, 170
Dyfan, *m. Welsh,* Greek, taming, 125
Dymphna, *f. Irish,* Kelt. 271
Dynawd, *m. Welsh,* Lat. given, 188
Dynval, *m. Cym.* Kelt. of the weaned couch (?), 252
Dyonizy, m. Pol. Gr. of Dionysos, 70
DYRE, *m. Dan.* Teu. dear, 426
Dyterych, m. Pol. Teu. people's ruler, 374

E

EACH, *m. Kelt.* Norse, 276
EACHAID, *m. Gael.* Kelt. horseman, 276
EACHAN, *m. Gael.* Kelt. horseman, 276
EACHMARCHACH, *Erse,* Kelt. horse rider, 276
EACHMILIDH, *m. Erse,* Kelt. horse warrior, 276
EAD, *f. Eng.* Teu. rich, 378
EADBALD, *f. m. A.S.* Teu. rich prince, 378
EADBRYHT, *f. m. A.S.* Teu. rich splendour, 378
EADBURG, *f. A.S.* Teu. rich protection, 378
EADBURH, *f. A.S.* Teu. rich pledge, 378
EADFLED, *f. A.S.* Teu. rich increase, 378
EADFRITH, *m. A.S.* Teu. rich peace, 378
EADGAR, *m. A.S.* Teu. rich spear, 378

d

EADGIFU, *f. A.S.* Teu. rich gift, 378
EADGYTH, *f. A.S.* Teu. rich gift, 378
EADHILD, *f. A.S.* Teu. rich battle maid, 378
EADMUND, *m. A.S.* Teu. rich protection, 378
EADRED, *m. A.S.* Teu. rich council, 378
EADRIC, *m. A.S.* Teu. rich ruler, 378
EADSWITH, *f. A.S.* Teu. rich strength, 378
EADULF, *m. A.S.* Teu. rich wolf, 336
EADWALD, *m. A.S.* Teu. rich power, 378
EADWARD, *m. A.S.* Teu. rich guard, 378
EADWIG, *m. A.S.* Teu. rich war, 378
EADWINE, *m. A.S.* Teu. rich friend, 378
EAL, *f. Bret.* Kelt. angel.
EALHFLED, *f. A.S.* Teu. hall increase, 382
EALHFRITH, *m. A.S.* Teu. hall peace, 382
EALHRED, *m. A.S.* Teu. hall speech, 382
EALHSWITH, *m. A.S.* Teu. hall strength, 382
EALHWINE, *f. m. A.S.* Teu. hall friend, 382
Easter, *f. Eng.* Teu. Easter child, 215
Ebba, f. Ger. Teu. firm wild boar, 337
Ebbe, Fris. Fris. Teu. firm wild boar, 337
Ebbert, m. Fris. Teu. formidably bright, 323
Ebbo, m. Ger. Teu. firm wild boar, 337
EBERHARD, *m. Ger.* Teu. firm wild boar, 337
Eberhardine, *f. Ger.* Teu. firm wild boar, 337
EBERHILD, *f. Ger.* Teu. wild boar battle maid, 337
EBERNUND, *m. Frank.* Teu. wild boar protection, 337
EBERIK, *m. Ger.* Teu. wild boar king, 337
Ebert, m. Ger. Teu. firm wild boar, 337
EBERULF, *m. Frank.* Teu. wild boar wolf, 337

EBERWINE, *m. Goth.* Teu. wild boar friend, 337
Ebilo, m. Ger. Teu. firm wild boar, 337
Ebles, m. Prov. Teu. firm wild boar, 337
Ebo, m. Ger. Teu. firm wild boar, 337
Eborico, *m. Span.* Teu. wild boar king, 337
EBRIMUTH, *m. Ger.* Teu. wild boar protection, 337
Ebroin, *m. Frank.* Teu. wild boar friend, 337
Ebur, m. Ger. Teu. wild boar, 337
EBURBERO, *m. Ger.* Teu. wild boar bear, 337
Eccelino, m. It. Tartar, father-like, 13
ECGBERHT, *m. A.S.* Teu. formidable bright, 323
ECGFRITH, *m. A.S.* Teu. formidable peace, 323
Eckart, m. Ger. Teu. formidable firmness, 323
Eckhardt, *m. Ger.* Teu. formidable firmness, 323
Edan, m. Scot. Kelt. fire, 226
Edanus, m. Lat. Kelt. fire, 226
Edburg, f. Ger. Teu. rich protection, 378
Edde, f. Fris. Teu. war refuge, 305
Eddeve, f. Eng. Teu. rich gift, 378
Ede, f. Fris. Teu. war refuge, 305
Ede, Neth. Teu. rich guard, 378
Eddo, f. Esth. Teu. war refuge, 305
Edelberge, *f. Ger.* Teu. noble protection, 411
Edeline, *f. Ger.* Teu. noble cheer, 411
Edelmar, *m. Eng.* Teu. noble greatness, 413
Edeltrud, *f. Ger.* Teu. noble maid, 411
Edeva, f. Eng. Teu. rich gift, 378
Edgar, *m. Eng.* Teu. rich spear, 378
Edgard, *m. Fr.* Teu. rich spear, 378
Edgardo, *m. It.* Teu. wealth spear, 378
Edie, m. Scot. Heb. red earth, 10
Ediltrude, f. Eng. Teu. noble maid, 411
Edith, *f. Eng.* Teu. rich gift, 379
Edmond, *m. Fr.* Teu. rich protection, 377

Edmund, *m. Eng.* Teu. rich protection, 377

Edmondo, *m. Ital.* Teu. rich protection, 377

Edom, m. Eng. Heb. red, 10

Edouard, *m. Fr.* Teu. rich guard, 378

Eduard, *m. Ger.* Teu. rich guard, 378

Eduardo, *m. Ital.* Teu. rich guard, 378

Eduart, *m. Dutch,* Teu. rich guard, 377

Eduige, *m. f. Ital.* Teu. war refuge, 305

Eduino, *m. Ital.* Teu. rich friend, 377

Edvald, *m. Ger.* Teu. rich power, 378

Edwald, *m. Eng.* Teu. rich power, 378

Edward, *m. Eng.* Teu. rich guard, 378

Edwin, *m. Eng.* Teu. rich friend, 377

Edwy, *m. Eng.* Teu. rich war, 377

Eed, f. Eng. Teu. wealth, 377

Eegnatie, *m. Russ.* Lat. fiery, 194

Eelia, *m. Russ.* Heb. God the Lord, 36

Eereenia, *f. Russ.* Gr. peace, 113

Eernest, *m. Lett.* Teu. eagle stone (?), 344

Eernst, Lett. Teu. eagle stone (?), 344

Eesaia, *Russ.* salvation of the Lord, 48

Eers, m. Esth. Teu. eternal rule, 400

Eesidor, *m. Russ.* Gr. strong gift, 103

Effie, f. Scot. Gr. fair speech, 231

EGA, *m. Frank.* Teu. formidable, 323

Egbert, *m. Eng.* Teu. formidably bright, 323

Egbertine, *f. Ger.* Teu. formidably bright, 323

Eggerich, *m. Fries.* Teu. formidable king, 323

Eggert, m. Ger. Teu. formidable king, 323

Eggo, m. Fries. Teu. formidable king, 323

Egica, *m. Span.* Teu. formidable, 323

Egide, *m. Fr.* Gr. with an ægis, 79

Egidia, *f. Scot.* Gr. with the ægis, 79

Egidio, *m. Ital.* Gr. with the ægis, 79

Egidius, *m. Dutch,* Gr. with the ægis, 79

EGIHERI, *m. Ger.* Teu. formidable warrior, 323

Egilbert, *m. Fr.* Teu. formidable brightness, 323

Egilhart, *m. Ger.* Teu. formidable firmness, 323

Egilolf, *m. Fr.* Teu. formidable wolf, 323

Egilmar, *Ger.* Teu. formidable fame, 323

Egilona, *f. Span.* Teu. formidable, 323

Egils, *Nor.* Teu. formidable, 323

Eginhard, *m. Fr.* Teu. formidable firmness, 323

Egmond, *m. Ger.* Teu. terrible protection, 323

Egor, m. Russ. Gr. husbandman, 116, 325

Egorka, m. Russ. Gr. husbandman, 116

Ehregott, *m. Ger.* Teu. honour God, 468

Ehrenbrecht, *m. Ger.* Teu. honour bright, 468

Ehrenpries, reward of honour, 468

Ehrenfried, *m. Ger.* Teu. honour peace.

Eigils, *m. Nor.* Teu. awful, 323

Eilart, m. Ger. Teu. formidable firmness, 323

Eilbert, m. Ger. Teu. formidable brightness, 323

Eileen, f. Ir. Gr. light, 68

Eilif, *m. Nor.* Teu. ever living, 400

Eiliv, *m. Nor.* Teu. ever living, 400

Eimund, *m. Nor.* Teu. ever guarding, 400

Eilo, m. Ger. Teu. formidable firmness, 323

EINAR, *f. Nor.* Teu. chief warrior, 323

EINDRIDE, *f. Nor.* Teu. chief rider, 323

EINIAWN, *m. Welsh,* Kelt. just, 282

Eino, m. Fries. Teu. awful firmness, 323

EIRENAIOS, *m. Gr.* peaceful, 113

EIRENÈ, *f. Gr.* peace, 113

EIRIK, *m. Nor.* Teu. ever king, 400

Eisaak, *m. Russ.* Heb. laughter, 14

Eisenbart, *m. Ger.* Teu. iron bright, 348

Eisenbolt, *m. Ger.* Teu. iron prince, 348

Eisenhardt, *m. Ger.* Teu. iron firm, 348

Eivind, m. Nor. Teu. island Wend, 431

Ekard, m. Ger. Teu. formidably firm, 323

Ekatrina, f. Russ. Gr. pure, 123

Ekiel, m. Eng. Heb. strength of God, 48

Ela, *f. Eng.* Nor. holy (?), 403

Elaine, *f. Eng.* Gr. light, 68

Elayne, *f. Eng.* Gr. light, 68

Elberich, *m. Ger.* Teu. elf king, 380

Eldred, *m. Eng.* Teu. battle counsel, 382

Eldrid, *m. Nor.* Teu. battle counsel, 382

Eleanor, *f. Eng.* Gr. light, 68

Eleazar, *m. Eng.* Heb. the Lord's help, 33

Elek, m. Hung. Gr. helper of men, 85

Elena, *f. Ital.* Gr. light, 68

Elene, f. m. Gr. Gr. light, 68

Eleonora, *f. Eng.* Gr. light, 68

Eléonore, *f. Eng. Ger.* Gr. light, 68

Eleonorka, f. Slav. Gr. light, 68

Elfleda, *f. Eng.* Teu. hall increase, 382

Elfrida, *f. Eng.* Teu. elf threatener, 380

Elgiva, *f. Eng.* Teu. elf gift, 380

Elia, *m. Ital.* Heb. God the Lord, 36

Eliakim, *m. Eng.* Heb. the Lord will judge, 37

Elian, m. W. Lat. cheerful, 280

Elias, *m. Eng. Dutch*, Heb. God the Lord, 35

Elie, m. Fr. Heb. God the Lord, 36

Elidure, m. Eng. Gr. sun's gift.

Elidi, m. W. Gr. sun's gift.

Elidan, f. Welsh, Lat. downy, 151

Eliezer, m. Heb. God will help, 33

Elihu, *m. Eng.* Heb. God the Lord, 35

Elija, *m. Slov.* Heb. God the Lord, 36

ELIJAH, *m. Eng.* Heb. God the Lord, 35

ELINED, *f. Welsh*, Kelt. shapely, 273

Elinor, *f. Eng.* Gr. light, 68

Elisa, *f. Ital.* Heb. oath of God, 35

Elisabet, *f. Gr.* Heb. oath of God, 35

Elisabetta, *f. Ital.* Heb. oath of God, 35

Elisabeth, *Ger. Fr.* Heb. oath of God, 35

Elisavetta, *f. Russ. Eng.* Heb. oath of God, 35

Elischeba, *f.* Heb. oath of God, 35

Elise, *f. Fr.* Heb. oath of God, 35

Eliseo, *m. It.* Heb. God my salvation, 36

Eliseus, *m. Lat.* Heb. God my salvation, 36

Elisha, *m. Eng.* Heb. God my salvation, 36

Elisif, *f. Russ.* Heb. God's oath, 35

Eliza, *f. Eng.* Heb. God's oath, 35

Elizabeth, *f. Eng.* Heb. God's oath, 35

Ella, f. m. Eng. Teu. elf friend, 382

ELLANHERI, *m. Ger.* Teu. battle warrior, 382

ELLANPERAHT, *m. Ger.* Teu. battle splendour, 382

Elle, m. Fris. Teu. battle, 382

Ellen, *f. Eng.* Gr. light, 68

Ellend, m. Nor. Teu. stranger, 432

Ellin, f. Welsh, Gr. light, 68

Elling, m. Nor. Teu. 333

Ellinor, f. Eng. Gr. light, 68

Ellis, *m. Eng.* Heb. God the Lord, 36

Ello, m. Fris. Teu. battle, 382

Ello, f. Esth. Heb. God's oath, 35

Elmark, m. Fris. Teu. helmed king, 351

Elmo, m. It. Gr. amiable, 113

Eloi, *m. Fr.* Lat. worthy of choice.

Eloïsa, *f. Ital.* Teu. famous holiness, 405

Eloïse, *f. Fr.* Teu. famous holiness, 405

Eloy, *m. Fr.* Lat. worthy of choice.

Elsabet, f. Ger. Heb. God's oath, 35

Elsbet, f. Ger. Heb. God's oath, 35

Elsbeth, f. Swiss, Heb. God's oath, 35

Else, f. Ger. Teu. noble cheer, 411

Elscbin, f. Dan. Heb. God's oath, 35

Elshender, m. Scot. helper of men, 85

Elshie, m. Scot. helper of men, 85

Elsie, *f. Eng.* Teu. noble cheer, 411

Elspeth, f. Scot. Heb. God's oath, 35

Elspie, f. Scot. Heb. God's oath, 35

Elts, f. Esth. Heb. God's oath, 35

ELVIRA, *f. Span.* Lat. white, 382

Elzbieta, f. Pol. Heb. God's oath, 35

Elzbietka, f. Pol. Heb. God's oath, 35

Elzea, m. Fr. Heb. God will help, 33

Ema, *f. Span.* Teu. grandmother, 331

Emanuel, *m. Ger.* Heb. God with us, 36

Emerence, *f. Fr.* Lat. deserving, 190

Emerentia, *f. Ger.* Lat. deserving, 190
Emerentiana, f. Dan. Lat. deserving, 190
EMERENTIUS, *m.* Lat. deserving, 190
Emeranz, f. Ger. Lat. deserving, 190
Emerick, *m. Slov.* Teu. work ruler, 330
Emery, m. Eng. Teu. work rule, 141
Emelin, *f. Eng.* Teu. work ruler, 141
Emile, *m. Fr.* Lat. work (?), 141
EMILIA, *f. Ital.* Lat. work (?), 141
Emilie, *f. Fr.* Lat. work, 141
Emilija, *m. Slav.* Lat. work (?), 141
Emilio, *m. Ital.* Lat. work (?), 141
EMILIUS, *m. Eng.* Lat. work (?), 141
Emily, *f. Eng.* Lat. work (?), 141
Emlyn, *f. Eng.* Teu. work serpent, 333
Emm, *f. Eng.* Teu. grandmother, 333
Emma, *f. Eng.* Teu. grandmother, 333
Emme, *f. Fr.* Teu. grandmother, 333
Emmeline, *f. Eng.* Teu. work serpent, 330
Emmerich, *m. Ger.* Teu. work rule, 333
Emmery, *m. Eng.* Teu. work rule, 331
Emmon, Erse, Teu. rich protection, 378
Emmott, *f. Eng.* Teu. grandmother (?), 333
Emrys, *m. Welsh,* Gr. immortal, 109
Emund, m. Nor. Dan. island protection, 431
ENCARNACION, *f. Span.* Lat. being made flesh, 30
Endrede, f. Nor. Teu. superior rider, 323
Endres, m. Ger. Gr. manly, 86
Endrikis, m. Lett. Teu. home ruler, 310
Endruttis, m. Lett. Teu. home ruler, 310
Enea, *m. It.* Gr. praise, 74
Eneca, *f. Span.* Lat. fiery, 194
Eneco, *m. Span.* Lat. fiery, 194
Enée, *m. Fr.* Gr. praise, 74
ENGEL, *m. Ger.* Gr. angel, 325
ENGELBERGA, *f. Ger.* Teu. angel of protection, 325
Engelbert, m. Ger. Teu. bright angel, 325
Engelchen, m. Ger. Gr. angel, 325

ENGLEFRID, *m. Ger.* Gr. Teu. angel peace, 325
ENGELHARD, *m. Ger.* Teu. Ing's firmness, 325
Engelke, f. Nor. Teu. Ing's battle maid, 325
ENGELSCHALK, *m. Ger.* Gr. Teu. angel's disciple, 325
Engeltje, f. Dutch, Gr. angelic, 325
ENGELRAM, *m. Ger.* Gr. Teu. Ing's raven, 325
Engerrand, *m. Fr.* Gr. Teu. Ing's raven, 325
Enghus, m. Scot. Kelt. excellent virtue, 241
Engracia, *f. Span.* Lat. grace, 194
Ennica, m. Sp. Lat. Lat. fiery, 194
Ennicus, m. Sp. Lat. Lat. fiery, 194
Ennan, m. Fr. Heb. Lat. Adam the dwarf, 10
Enoch, *m. Eng.* Heb. dedicated, 11
Enos, *m. Eng.* Heb. mortal man, 11, 241
Enrichetta, *f. It.* Teu. home ruler, 310
Enrico, *m. It.* Teu. home ruler, 310
Enrik, *m. Slov.* Teu. home ruler, 310
Enrika, *f. Slov.* Teu. home ruler, 310
Enrique, *m. Span.* Teu. home ruler, 310
Enriqueta, *f. Span.* Teu. home rule, 310
Enselis, m. Lett. Heb. the Lord's grace, 45
Ensilo, m. Ger. Teu. divine, 291
Enskys, m. Lett. Heb. the Lord's grace, 45
Enz, m. Swiss, Lat. laurel, 174
Enzeli, m. Swiss, Lat. laurel, 174
Enzio, m. Ital. Teu. home rule, 309
Enzius, m. Lat. Teu. home rule, 309
EOCHAID, *m. Erse,* Kelt. horseman, 276
EOGHAN, *m. Gael.* Kelt. young warrior, 273
Eoghania, *f. Erse,* Kelt. young warrior, 273
Eoin, m. Erse, Heb. grace of the Lord, 45
EORCONBERHT, *m. A.S.* Teu. sacred brightness, 328
EORCONGOT, *m. A.S.* Teu. sacred goodness, 329

EORCONWALD, *m. A.S.* Teu. sacred power, 329

EORCONWINE, *m. A.S.* Teu. sacred friend, 328

EORMENBURG, *f. A.S.* Teu. public protection, 327

EORMENBURH, *f. A.S.* Teu. public pledge, 327

EORMENGILD, *f. A.S.* Teu. public pledge, 327

EORMENGYTH, *f. A.S.* Teu. public gift, 327

EORMENRIC, *m. A.S.* Teu. public rule, 327

Eostafie, *m. Slav.* Gr. healthy, 88

EPHRAIM, *m. Eng.* Heb. two-fold increase.

Ephrem, *m. Russ.* Heb. two-fold increase.

Epifania, *f. Ital.* Gr. manifestation, 212

Epifanio, *m. Rom.* Gr. of the manifestation, 212

Epilo, m. Ger. Teu. wild boar, 337

EPIMETHEUS, *m.* Gr. after-thought.

Epiphanie, *f. Fr.* Gr. manifestation, 212

EPIPHANIOS, *m.* Gr. of the manifestation, 212

Epiphanius, *m. Lat.* Gr. manifestation, 212

Eppie, f. Scot. Gr. fair fame, 88

Eppo, m. Ger. Teu. firm wild boar, 337

Epurhard, m. Ger. Teu. firm wild boar, 337

EPURHELM, *m. Ger.* wild boar helm, 337

Equitius, *m. Lat.* Kelt. horseman, 276

Eraric, m. Ger. Teu. warrior king, 400

Erasme, m. Fr. Ger. amiable, 113

Erasmo, m. It. Gr. amiable, 113

Erasmus, *m. Dutch, Lat. Eng. Ger.* Gr. amiable, 113

Erchenold, *m. Ger.* Teu. sacred prince, 329

Erchimperto, *m. It.* Teu. sacred brightness, 328

Ercole, *m. It.* Gr. noble fame, 63

ERDMUTH, *Ger.* earth courage, 328, 468

Erembert, m. Fr. Teu. public splendour, 327

Eremburga, f. Eng. Teu. public protection, 328

Eric, *m. Ir. Eng.* Teu. ever king, 400

Erich, *m. Russ. Ger.* Teu. ever king, 400

Erik, *m. Slov.* Teu. ever king, 400

Erik, *m. Swed. Esth.* Teu. ever king, 400

Erika, *f. Swed.* Teu. ever king, 400

Eriks, *m. Lett.* Lett. ever king, 400

Erivigio, m. Span. Teu. warrior battle, 400

Erkenoald, *m. Frank.* Teu. sacred power, 328

ERL, *m. Nor.* Teu. earl, 333

ERLEBALD, *Ger.* Teu. earl prince, 333

ERLEBRYHT, *Ger.* Teu. bright earl, 333

ERLHER, *Nor.* Teu. earl warrior, 333

ERLHILD, *Nor.* Teu. earl maiden, 333

ERLING, earl's son, 333

ERLEND, *f. m. Nor.* Teu. stranger, 432

Erling, m. Nor. Teu. stranger, 432

Ermas, *m. Lith.* Teu. public, 327

Erme, m. Fr. Teu. public, 327

Ermelinda, *f. Ital.* Teu. world serpent, 327

Ermengard, *f. Ger.* Teu. public guard, 327

Ermengarde, *f. Eng.* Teu. public guard, 327

ERMENIGILD, *m. Russ.* Teu. public pledge, 327

Ermentrud, *f. Eng.* Teu. maiden of the nation, 327

Ermesinda, *f. Span.* Teu. public strength, 327

Ermin, f. Burg. Teu. public, 327

Ermin, *f. Welsh,* Lat. lordly, 147

Erminia, f. Ital. Lat. lordly, 147

Ermo, m. Ital. Gr. amiable, 113

Ermo, m. Ital. Teu. public, 327

Ermolaj, m. Russ. Gr. people of Hermes, 71

Ernest, *m. Eng. Pol.* Teu. eagle stone, 344

Erneste, *m. Fr.* Teu. eagle stone (?), 344

Ernestine, *f. Ger.* Teu. eagle stone (?), 344

Ernesto, *m. Ital.* Teu. eagle stone (?), 344

Erneszt, *m. Hung.* Teu. eagle stone (?), 344

Ernijo, m. Hung. Gr. peaceful, 113

Ernst, *m. Ger.* Teu. eagle stone (?), 344

Ernstine, f. Ger. Teu. eagle stone (?), 344

Erszok, f. Hung. Heb. God's oath, 35

Erulf, m. Ger. Teu. boar wolf, 337

Ervigo, m. Span. Teu. army war, 417

Eryk, m. Pol. Teu. ever king, 400

Erzebet, f. Hung. Heb. God's oath, 35

Erzok, f. Hung. Heb. God's oath, 35

Esa, f. A.S. Teu. the gods, 289

Esaia, *m. It.* Heb. salvation of the Lord, 48

Esaias, *m. Eng. Ger.* Heb. salvation of the Lord, 48

Esaie, *m. Fr.* Heb. salvation of the Lord, 48

ESAU, *m. Eng.* Heb. hairy.

Esay, m. Eng. Heb. salvation of the Lord, 48

Esbern, *m. Dan.* Teu. divine bear, 290

Esc, *f. m. A.S.* Teu. ash tree, 324

Esclairmonde, *f. Fr.* Lat. Teu. famous protection, 186

Escwine, m. A.S. Teu. ash friend, 324

Esdras, *m. Eng.* Heb. rising of light, 51

Esmeralda, *f. Span.* Gr. emerald, 125

Esperança, *f. Span.* Lat. hope, 196

Esperance, *f. Fr.* Lat. hope, 196

Esperanza, *f. Span.* Lat. hope, 196

ESSA, *f. Ir.* Kelt. nurse, 254

Essie, f. Eng. Pers. star, 57

Estanislau, *m. Port.* Slav. camp glory, 440

Esteban, *m. Span.* Gr. crown, 96

Estella, *f. Span.* Lat. star, 57

Estelle, *f. Fr.* Lat. star, 57

Ester, *f. It. Hung.* Pers. star, 57

Esterre, *f. It.* Pers. star, 57

Estephania, *f. Port.* Gr. crown, 96

Estevan, *m. Span.* Gr. crown, 96

Estevao, *m. Port.* Gr. crown, 96

Estevennes, *m. Fr.* Gr. crown, 96

Esther, *f. Eng.* Pers. star, 57

Estienne, *m. Fr.* Gr. crown, 96

Estolfo, *m. Span.* Teu. swift wolf, 401

Estrith, *f. Dan.* Teu. impulse of love, 401

ESYLT, *f. Cym.* Kelt. fair, 269, 275

Eth, *m. Scot.* Kelt. fire, 227

Ethel, f. Eng. Teu. noble, 410

Ethelburga, *f. Eng.* Teu. noble protection, 410

Etheldred, *f. Eng.* Teu. noble threatener, 410

Ethelind, *f. Eng.* Teu. noble snake, 410

Ethelmar, *m. Eng.* Teu. work ruler, 331

Ethelred, *m. Eng.* Teu. noble council, 410

Ethered, m. Eng. Teu. noble council, 410

Ethert, m. Eng. Teu. noble council, 410

Ethfinn, m. Scot. Teu. white fire, 227

Etienne, *m. Fr.* Gr. crown, 96

Etiennette, *f. Fr.* Gr. crown, 97

Etta, f. Ger. Teu. home ruler, 310

Etto, m. Ger. Teu. firm wild boar, 337

Ettore, *m. It.* Gr. defender, 74

Etzel, *m. Ger.* Tartar, father like, 13

Eubul, *m. Ger.* Gr. happy council, 88

Eucaria, *f. m. Ital.* Gr. happy hand, 87

Euchaire, *m. Fr.* Gr. happy hand, 87

Euchar, *m. Ger.* Gr. happy hand, 87

Euchario, *m. Port.* Gr. happy hand, 87

EUCHARIS, *f.* Gr. happy grace, 88

Euchary, *m. Pol.* Gr. happy hand, 87

EUCHEIR, *m.* Gr. happy hand, 87

Eucherius, *m. Lat.* Gr. happy hand, 87

Eudbaird, *m. Erse,* Teu. rich guard, 376

EUDES, *m. Fr.* Teu. rich, 376

Eudocia, *f. Lat.* Gr. approval, 87

Eudocie, *f. Fr.* Gr. approval, 87

Eudokhia, *f. Russ.* Gr. approval, 87

Eudon, *m. Fr.* Teu. rich, 376

EUDORA, *f. Lat.* Gr. happy gift, 87

Eudore, *f. Fr.* Gr. happy gift, 87

Eudossia, *f. It.* Gr. approval, 87

EUDOXIA, *f. Russ.* Gr. happy glory, 87

Eudoxie, *f. Fr.* Gr. happy glory, 87

Eufemia, *f. It.* Gr. fair fame, 88

Eufrosina, *f. Rom.* Gr. mirth, 72

Eugen, *m. Ger.* Gr. well born, 87

Eugene, *m. Fr. Eng.* Gr. well born, 87
EUGENES, *m.* Gr. well born, 87
Eugenia, *f. It. Span. Eng.* Gr. well born, 87, 273
Eugenie, *f. Fr. Ger.* Gr. well born, 87
Eugenio, *m. Rom.* Gr. well born, 87
Eugenius, *m. Lat.* Gr. well born, 87
Eugeniusz, *m. Pol.* Gr. well born, 88
Euginia, *f. Erse,* Kelt. warrior, 273
EULALIA, *f. It. Span. Eng.* Gr. fair speech, 88
Eulalie, *f. Fr.* Gr. fair speech, 88
EUNICE, *f. Eng.* Gr. happy victory, 88
Euphame, *f. Scot.* Gr. fair fame, 88
EUPHEMIA, *f. Eng. Scot. Dutch,* Gr. fair fame, 88
Euphemie, *f. Fr.* Gr. fair fame, 88
EUPHRASIA, *f. Eng.* Gr. mirth, 72
Euphrasie, *f. Fr.* Gr. mirth, 72
Euphrosine, *f. Fr.* Gr. mirth, 72
EUPHROSYNE, *f. Eng. Ger.* Gr. mirth, 72
Eustace, *m. Eng.* Gr. happy in harvest, 88
Eustache, *m. Fr.* Gr. happy in harvest, 88
Eustachia, *f. Eng.* Gr. happy in harvest, 88
Eustachie, *f. Fr.* Gr. happy in harvest, 88
EUSTACHYS, *m.* Gr. happy in harvest, 88
Eustachius, *m. Lat.* Gr. happy in harvest, 88
EUSTATHIOS, *m.* Gr. healthy, 88
Eustazia, *f. It.* Gr. happy in harvest, 88
Eustazio, *m. It.* Gr. happy in harvest, 88
Eustathius, m. Russ. Gr. Gr. healthy, 88
Eustochium, *f. Lat.* Gr. good thought, 88
EVA, *f. Ger. Dan. Lat.* Heb life, 11
Evald, f. Fr. Teu. wild boar power, 337
Evan, *m. Scot. Welsh,* Kelt. young warrior, 273
Evangeline, *f. Am.* Gr. happy messenger, 87
Evangelista, *m. It.* Gr. happy messenger, 87

Eve, *f. Eng.* Heb. life, 11
Eveleen, *f. Ir.* Kelt. pleasant, 231
Evelina, *f. Eng.* Kelt. pleasant, 231
Eveline, *f. Eng.* Kelt. pleasant, 232
Evelyn, *m. Eng.* Lat. hazel nut, 232
Even, m. Nor. Teu. island Wend, 431
Everard, *m. Fr. Eng.* Teu. firm wild boar, 337
Everardo, *m. It.* Teu. firm wild boar, 337
Everhard, *m. Ger.* Teu. firm wild boar, 337
Everhilda, *f. Eng.* Teu. wild boar battle maid, 337
Everilda, *f. Eng.* Teu. wild boar battle maid, 337
Evers, m. L. Ger. Teu. wild boar firm, 337
Evert, m. Ger. Teu. wild boar firm, 337
Evgen, m. Slov. Gr. well born, 87
Evgenij, f. Slov. Gr. well born, 87
Evir, f. Scot. pleasant, 231
Evirallin, f. Scot. Kelt. pleasantly excellent, 231
Evircoma, *f. Scot.* Kelt. pleasantly amiable, 231
Evlalija, *f. Slov.* Gr. fair speech, 88
Evrand, *m. Fr.* Teu. firm wild boar, 337
Evre, *m. Fr.* Teu. wild boar, 337
Evremond, *m. Fr.* Teu. wild boar protection, 337
Evrols, m. Fr. Teu. wild boar wolf, 337
Evroud, m. Fr. Teu. wild boar power, 337
Evva, f. Russ. Heb. life, 11
Ewa, *f. Ger.* Heb. life, 11
Ewan, *m. Scot.* Kelt. warrior. 273
Ewart, m. Eng. Teu. firm wild boar, 337
Ewarts, m. Lett. Teu. firm wild boar, 337
Ewe, f. Lus. Heb. life, 11
Eweline, *f. Ger.* Kelt. pleasant, 231
Ewert, m. Esth. Teu. firm wild boar, 337
Ewerts, m. Lett. Teu. firm wild boar, 337
Ewusche, f. Lett. Heb. life, 11
EYAR, *m. Nor.* Teu. island warrior, 431

EYDIS, *f. Nor.* Teu. island sprite, 431

EYFREY, *f. m. Nor.* Teu. island peace, 431

EYGERD, *f. Nor.* Teu. island maid, 431

EYMUND, *m. Nor.* Teu. island protection, 431

EYSTEIN, *m. Nor.* Teu. island stone, 431

EYTHIOF, *m. Nor.* Teu. island thief, 431

EYNY, *f. Nor.* Teu. island freshness, 431

EYULF, *m. Nor.* Teu. island wolf, 335

EYVAR, *m. Nor.* Teu. island prudence, 431

EYVIND, *m. Nor.* Teu. island Wend, 431

Ezechiel, *m. Ger.* Heb. strength of God, 48

Ezekias, *m. Gr.* Heb. strength of the Lord, 48

Ezekiel, *m. Eng.* Heb. strength of God, 48

Ezra, *m. Eng.* Heb. rising of light, 51

F

FABIA, *It.* Lat. bean grower, 146

Fabian, *m. Eng.* Lat. bean grower, 146

Fabiano, *m. It.* Lat. bean grower, 146

Fabien, *f. Fr.* Lat. bean grower, 146

Fabio, *m. It.* Lat. bean grower, 146

Fabiola, *f. It.* Lat. bean grower, 146

FABIUS, *m.* Lat. bean grower, 146

Fabijan, *m. Slov.* Lat. bean grower, 146

Fabrice, *m. Fr.* Lat. mechanic, 147

FABRICIUS, *m.* Lat. mechanic, 147

Fabron, *m. Ger.* Lat. mechanic, 147

Fabronio, *m. It.* Lat. mechanic, 147

FACHTNA, *m. Erse,* 224

Facio, m. It. Lat. good worker, 185

Fadrique, *m. Span.* Teu. peace rule, 296

Faik, f. Bret. Kelt. white wave, 270

Faith, f. Eng.

Fanchette, f. Fr. Teu. free, 300

Fanchon, f. Fr. Teu. free, 300

Fanny, f. Eng. Teu. free, 300

Fantik, f. Bret. Teu. free, 330

FARABERT, *m. Frank.* Teu. travelled splendour, 432

FARAMOND, *m. Frank.* Teu. travelled protector, 432

Fardorougha, *m. Irish,* Kelt. blind man, 238

Farghy, m. Irish, Kelt. excellent valour, 238

FARGRIM, *Nor.* Teu. travelled Grim, 432

FAROLD, *m. Ger.* travelled power, 432

Farquhar, m. Scot. Kelt. manly, 238

FARTHEGN, *m. Nor.* Teu. travelled servant, 432

FARULF, *m. Nor.* Teu. travelled wolf, 432

FASTBURG, *f. Frank.* Teu. firm protection, 421

FASTMANN, *m. Frank.* Teu. firm man, 421

FASTMUND, *m. Frank.* Teu. firm guard, 421

FASTOLF, *m. Ger.* Teu. firm wolf, 421

FASTRADE, *f. Fr.* Teu. firm council, 421

FAUSTA, *f. It.* Lat. lucky, 163

Faustine, *f. m. Ger.* Lat. lucky, 163

Faustina, *f. It.* Lat. lucky, 163

Faustine, *f. Fr.* Lat. lucky, 163

Fausto, *m. It.* Lat. lucky, 163

FAUSTUS, *m.* Lat. lucky, 163

Favour, m. Eng. 177

FAXABRANDR, *m. Ice.* white hair, 427

FAXI, *m. Ice.* hair, 427

Fazio, m. It. Lat. good worker, 185

FEARACHUR, *m. Gael.* manly, 237

FEARGHAL, *m. Erse,* Kelt. man of valour, 237

FEARGHUS, *m. Erse,* Kelt. man of strength, 237

Feargus, *m. Ir.* Kelt. man of strength, 237

Febe, *f. It.* Gr. light, 65

Febo, *m. Span.* Gr. light, 65

FEBRONIA, *f. It.* Lat. 176

Federico, *m. It.* Teu. peace ruler, 296

Federiga, *f. It.* Teu. peace ruler, 296

Federigo, *m. It.* Teu. peace ruler, 296

FEDLEMI, *f. Erse,* Kelt. ever good, 256

FEDLIM, *m. Irish,* Kelt. good, 256

Fedor, *f. m. Russ.* Gr. God's gift, 101

Feeleep, *m. Russ.* Gr. lover of horses, 78

FEIDLIM, *m. Erse,* Kelt. ever good, 256

Feidrik, *Bret.* Teu. peace ruler, 296

FEITHFAILGE, *f. Erse,* Kelt. honeysuckle ringlets, 224

Felice, *m. It.* Lat. happy, 163

Felicia, *f. Eng.* happy, 163

Felicidad, *f. Span.* Lat. happiness, 163

Felicidade, *f. Port.* Lat. happiness, 163

Felicie, *f. Fr.* Lat. happy, 163

Felicità, *f. It.* Lat. happiness, 163

Felicité, *f. Fr.* Lat. happiness, 163

Feliks, *m. Russ.* Lat. happy, 163

Felim, *m. Irish,* Kelt. ever good, 163, 257

Felimy, *m. Irish,* Kelt. ever good, 163, 257

Felipa, *f. Port.* Gr. lover of horses, 79

Felipe, *f. m. Span.* Gr. lover of horses, 79

Felipinho, *m. Port.* Gr. lover of horses, 79

Felipo, *m. Span.* Gr. lover of horses, 79

Felippe, *m. Span.* Gr. lover of horses, 79

Felise, *f. Fr.* Lat. happy, 163

FELIX, *m. Fr. Eng. Span. Slov.* Lat. happy, 163, 257

Feliz, *m. Port.* Lat. happy, 163

Fenella, *f. Scot.* Kelt. white shouldered, 245

Feo, *m. It.* Heb. gift of the Lord, 15

Feodor, *m. Russ.* Gr. God's gift, 101

Feodora, *f. Russ.* Gr. God's gift, 101

Feodosia, *m. Russ.* Gr. God given, 103

Feoris, *m. Erse,* Gr. stone, 108

Ferabras, *m. Fr.* Kelt. strong arm, 234

FERAHBALD, *m. Ger.* Teu. prince of life, 433

FERAHMUND, *m. Ger.* Teu. protection of life, 433

Ferdinand, *m. Ger. Fr. Eng.* Teu. adventuring life, 433

Ferdinanda, *f. Ger.* Teu. adventuring life, 433

Ferdinandine, *f. Fr.* Teu. adventuring life, 433

Ferdinando, *m. It.* Teu. adventuring life, 433

Ferdynand, *m. Pol.* Teu. adventuring life, 433

Ferencz, *m. Hung.* Teu. free, 300

Ferghal, *m. Erse,* Kelt. man of strength, 237

FERHONANTHS, *m. Goth.* Teu. adventuring life, 433

Fergus, *m. Scot.* Kelt. man's strength, 237

Fergusiana, *f. Scot.* Kelt. man's strength, 237

Feriga, *f. It.* Teu. peace ruler, 296

Ferko, *m. Hung.* Teu. free, 300

Fernanda, *f. Span.* Teu. adventuring life, 433

Fernando, *m. It.* Teu. adventuring life, 433

Ferrand, *m. Prov.* Teu. adventuring life, 433

Ferrante, *m. It.* Teu. adventuring life, 433

Ferry, *m. Fr.* Teu. peace ruler, 296

FESTUS, *m. Lat.* 224

Ffraid, *f. Welsh,* Kelt. fiery dart, 236

FIACHRA, *m. Erse,* Kelt. eagle, 252

Fiacre, *m. Fr.* Kelt. eagle, 252

FIAMMA, *f. It.* Lat. 451

Ficko, *m. Fris.* Teu. peace rule, 296

Fiddy, *f. Ir.* Teu. peace strength, 296

Fidrik, *m. Lus.* Teu. peace rule, 296

Ficchen, *f. Ger.* Gr. wisdom, 107

Fieke, *f. Ger.* Gr. wisdom, 107

Fifine, *f. Fr.* Heb. addition, 23

Filep, *m. Hung.* Gr. horse lover, 79

Filibert, *m. Fr.* Teu. bright will, 316

Filiberto, *m. It.* Teu. bright will, 316

Filikitata, *f. Russ.* Lat. happiness, 163

Filip, *m. Swed. Slav. Wall.* Gr. lover of horses, 79

Filippa, *f. It.* Gr. lover of horses, 79

Filippino, *m. It.* Gr. lover of horses, 79

Filippo, *m. It.* Gr. lover of horses, 79

Filomena, *f. It.* daughter of light, 207

FINABHOR, *f. Erse,* Kelt. fair eyelids, 172

FINBIL, *f. Erse,* Kelt. white blossom, 172

Finan, m. Irish, Kelt. fair offspring, 244

Finbo, f. Nor. Kelt. white bow, 244

FINDATH, *f. Erse,* Kelt. fair colour, 245

FINDELVH, *f. Erse,* Kelt. fair face, 245

Fineen, m. Irish, Kelt. fair offspring, 245

Finella, f. Irish, Kelt. fair shoulders, 245

Finette, f. Fr. Heb. addition, 23

Fingal, *m. Scot.* Kelt. white stranger, 244

FINGHIN, *m. Erse,* Kelt. fair offspring, 244

Finian, m. Irish, Erse, Kelt. fair offspring, 244

FINN, *m. Nor.* Kelt. white, 244

FINNA, *f. Nor.* Kelt. white, 244

FINNBOGI, *m. Nor.* Kelt. white bow, 244

FINNGARD, *m. Nor.* Kelt. Nor. white defence, 244

FINNGEIR, *Nor.* Kelt. Nor. white spear, 244

Finni, m. Ice. Kelt. white, 245

Finnkatla, f. Nor. Teu. white kettle, 245

FINNKETIL, *m. Nor.* Teu. white kettle, 245

Finnkjell, m. Nor. Kelt. Nor. white kettle, 245

FINNLEIK, *m. Nor.* Teu. Finn's sport, 245

FINNVARDR, *m. Nor.* Kelt. Nor. Finn's guard, 245

FINNVIDR, *m. Nor.* Teu. Finn's wood, 245

FINSCOTH, *f. Erse,* Kelt. white blossom, 245

Fintan, Irish, Kelt. white, 240

Finvola, f. Irish, Kelt. white shoulders, 245

FIONN, *m. Gael.* Kelt. white, 244

Fionnagal, m. Erse, Kelt. white, 245

FIONNGHAL, *m. Gael.* Kelt. white stranger, 245

FIONNGHALA, *f. Erse,* Kelt. white shouldered, 245

Fiore, f. Ital. Lat. flower, 171

Fiorentino, *m. It.* Lat. flourishing, 171

Fithil, m. Erse, Kelt. 171

FJORLEIF, *m. Nor.* Teu. relic of life, 434

FLAVIA, *f. It.* Lat. yellow, 147

Flavian, *m. Eng.* Lat. yellow, 147

Flavianus, *m.* Lat. yellow, 147

Flavilla, *f.* Lat. yellow, 147

Flavio, *m. It.* Lat. yellow, 147

FLAVIUS, *m.* Lat. yellow, 147

Flidrik, m. Breton, Teu. peace rule, 296

Flipote, f. Fr. Gr. horse lover, 79

Flobert, m. Fr. Teu. wise splendour, 425

Floberte, f. Ir. Teu. wise splendour, 425

FLORA, *f. Eng.* Lat. flowers, 171

Flore, *f. Fr.* Lat. flowers, 171

Florence, *f. Eng.* Lat. flourishing, 171

Florence, *m. Ir.* Lat. flourishing, 171

Florentin, *m. Fr.* Lat. flourishing, 171

Florentine, *f. Fr.* Lat. flourishing, 171

FLORENTIUS, *m.* Lat. flourishing, 171

Florentz, *m. Ger.* Lat. flourishing, 171

Florette, f. Fr. Lat. flowers, 171

Florian, *m. Ger.* Lat. flowery, 171

Florie, *f. Gael.* Lat. flowery, 171

Flory, f. Scot. Lat. flowers, 171

Foka, *m. Russ.* Gr. a Phocian, 200

Fokke, *m. Nor.* Teu. people's guard, 371

Folkart, *m. Ger.* Teu. people's guard, 371

FOLKER, *m. Ger.* Prov. people's guard, 371

Folkwar, *m. Ger.* Teu. people's greatness, 371

Folko, *m. Ger.* Teu. people's guard, 371

FOLKPERAHT, *m. Ger.* Teu. people's brightness, 371

FOLKWART, *m. Ger.* Teu. people's guard, 371

FOLKWINE, *m. Ger.* Teu. people's friend, 371

FOLRAD, *m. Ger.* Teu. people's council, 371

FOLKRICH, *m. Ger.* Teu. people's ruler, 371

Foma, m. Russ. Aram, twin, 22

Fomida, f. Russ. Aram, twin, 22

FORTUNATUS, *m. Lat.* fortune, 176

Fortune, *f. Eng.* 176
Fortunio, *m. Span.* Lat. fortunate, 176
Foulques, *m. Fr.* Teu. people's guard, 371
Fouques, m. Fr. Teu. people's guard, 371
Franc, *m. Slov.* Teu. free, 299
Frances, *f. Eng.* Teu. free, 299
Francesca, *f. Ital.* Teu. free, 299
FRANCESCO, *m. Ital.* Teu. free, 299
Francie, m. Scot. Teu. free, 299
Francilo, m. Span. Teu. free, 299
Francina, f. Dutch, Teu. free, 299
Francis, *m. Eng.* Teu. free, 299
Francisca, *f. Port. Span.* Teu. free, 300
Francisco, *m. Port. Span.* Teu. free, 299
Franciscus, *m. Lat.* Teu. free, 299
Francisek, m. Slov. Teu. free, 299
Francisk, *m. Wall.* Teu. free, 299
Franciska, f. Dan. Teu. free, 300
Franciske, f. Slov. Ger. Teu. free, 300
Franciskus, m. Ger. Teu. free, 300
Francisque, f. Fr. Teu. free, 300
Francisquinho, m. Port. Teu. free, 300
Franciszek, *m. Pol.* Teu. free, 300
Franck, m. Pol. Teu. free, 300
Franciszka, f. Pol. Teu. free, 300
Franco, m. It. Teu. free, 300
François, *m. Fr.* Teu. free, 300
Françoise, *f. Fr.* Teu. free, 299
Francyhtje, f. Dutch, Teu. free, 300
Franek, m. Pol. Teu. free, 300
Franica, f. Slov. Teu. free, 300
Franja, f. Slov. Teu. free, 300
Franjo, m. Slov. Teu. free, 300
Frank, f. Eng. Teu. free, 300
Frankel, m. Ger. Teu. free, 300
Franko, m. O. Ger. Teu. free, 300
Frans, m. Swed. Teu. free, 300
Franse, m. Bret. Teu. free, 300
Franseza, f. Bret. Teu. free, 300
Franzje, f. Dutch, Teu. free, 300
Franta, *m. Span.* Teu. free lord, 300
Frantisek, f. Bohm. Teu. free, 300
Frantiska, f. Bohm. Teu. free, 300
Franulka, f. Pol. Teu. free, 300
Franusia, f. Pol. Teu. free, 300
Franz, m. Ger. Teu. free, 300
Franzisk, m. Russ. Teu. free, 300
Franziska, f. Russ. Teu. free, 300
Franziske, *f. Ger.* Teu. free, 300

FREAVINE, *m. Nor.* Teu. free friend, 295
Fred, m. Eng. Teu. peace ruler, 296
Freddy, m. Eng. Teu. peace ruler, 296
Fredegonde, *f. Fr.* Teu. peace war, 295
FREDEGUNT, *f. Frank.* Teu. peace war, 295
Frederic, *m. Fr.* Teu. peace ruler, 296
Frederica, *f. Eng. Span. Port.* Teu. peace ruler, 296
Frederick, *m. Eng.* Teu. peace ruler, 296
Frederico, *m. Port.* Teu. peace ruler, 296
Frederigo, *m. Span.* Teu. peace ruler, 296
Frederik, m. Dan. Teu. peace ruler, 296
Frederigue, *f. m. Fr.* Teu. peace ruler, 296
Fredewolt, *m. Fris.* Teu. peace power, 295
Fredi, m. Fris. Teu. peace power, 297
Frediswid, *f. Eng.* Teu. peace strength, 295
Fredli, m. Swiss, Teu. peace ruler, 296
Fredreg, m. Norm. Ger. peace ruler, 296
Fredrik, *m. Swed.* Teu. peace rule, 296
Fredrika, *f. Swed.* Teu. peace rule, 296
Freerik, m. Dutch, Ger. peace ruler, 296
Freidank, m. Ger. Ger. free thought, 295
Freimund, *m. Ger.* Teu. free protection, 295
Freimuth, *m. Ger.* Ger. free courage, 295
Frek, m. Fris. Teu. peace ruler, 296
Fremont, *m. Fr.* Teu. peace protection, 295
Frenz, *m. Dutch,* Teu. free, 296
FREODHORIC, *m. A.S.* Teu. peace ruler, 296
Frerk, m. Fris. Teu. peace rule, 296
FRETHESANTHA, *f. Eng.* Teu. strength of peace, 295
Frewen, *m. Eng.* Teu. free friend, 295

Frewissa, f. Eng. Teu. strength of peace, 295

FREYGERDUR, *Ice.* Teu. free home, 295

Fridbald, *m. Ger.* Teu. peace prince, 295

Fridbert, *m. Ger.* Teu. peace bright, 295

Fridburg,*f. Ger.* Teu. peace protection, 295

FRIDEGER, *f. m. Ger.* Teu. spear of peace.

Frider, *m. Ger.* Teu. peace warrior, 297

Friderik, *m. Slov.* Teu. peace ruler, 296

Fridgerda, *f. Ger.* Teu. peace guard, 297

Fridgund, *f. Frank.* Teu. peace war, 297

FRIDHELM, *m. Ger.* Teu. peace helmet, 297

FRIDHERI, *m. Ger.* Teu. peace warrior, 297

FRIDHREKR, *m. O. Nor.* Teu. peace ruler, 296

Fridiswid,*f. Eng.* Teu. peace strength, 295

FRIDLEIFR, *m. Nor.* Teu. peace relic, 295

Fridli, m. Swiss, Teu. peace rule, 295

Fridlib, m. Ger. Teu. peace relic, 295

FRIDLINA, *f. Ger.* Teu. peace snake, 295

Fridman, m. Ger. Teu. peace man, 295

Fridmar, m. Ger. Teu. peace fame, 295

FRIDMUND, *m. Ger.* Teu. peace protection, 295

Frido, m. Ger. Teu. peace, 295

Fridold, *m.Ger.* Teu. peace power, 295

FRIDOLF, *m. Ger.* Teu. peace wolf, 295

Fridolin, *m. Ger.* Teu. peace, 295

Fridrad, *m. Ger.* Teu. peace council, 295

Fridrada,*f. Ger.* Teu. peace councillor, 295

Fridrich, *m. Russ. Ger.* Teu. peace ruler, 295

Fridrik, *m. Hung.* Teu. peace ruler, 296

Fridrike,*f. Ger.* Teu. peace ruler, 296

FRIDRIKR, *m. Nor.* Teu. peace ruler, 295

Fridrun, *f.* peace wisdom, 295

FRIDUHERI, *m. O. Ger.* Teu. peace warrior, 295

FRIDULF, *m. Nor.* Teu. peace wolf, 295

Friedel, m. Ger. Teu. peace wolf, 295

Friedrich, *m. Ger.* Teu. peace rule, 295

Friko, m. Fris. Teu. peace ruler, 296

FRITHIOF, *m. Nor.* Teu. free thief, 295

Frithlaf, *m. A.S.* Teu. peace relic, 295

FRITHOGAR, *m. A.S.* Teu. peace spear, 295

FRITHSWITH, *f. A.S.* Teu. peace strength, 295

FRITHWALD, *m. A.S.* Teu. peace power, 295

FRITHWOLF, *m. A.S.* Teu. peace wolf.

Fritz, m. Ger. Teu. peace ruler, 296

Fritze, f. Ger. Teu. peace ruler, 296

Fritzinn, f. Ger. Teu. peace ruler, 296

FRODA, *m. Nor.* Teu. wise, 425

Frodbert, *m. Ger.* Teu. wise bright, 425

Frodberta, *f. Ger.* Teu. wise bright, 425

Frodine, f. Ger. Teu. wise friend, 425

FRODHR, *m. Nor.* Teu. wise, 425

FRODWIN, *m. Nor.* Teu. wise friend, 425

Froila, *m. Span.* Teu. Lord, 295

Fromsais, *m. Erse,* Teu. free, 296

Frowin, *m. Ger.* Teu. free friend, 295

Fruela, *m. Span.* Teu. Lord, 295

Fryc, m. Pol. Teu. peace ruler, 296

Fryderyk, *m. Pol.* Teu. peace ruler, 296

Frydryka, *f. Pol.* Teu. peace ruler, 296

Fulbert, *m. Eng.* Teu. bright resolution, 316

Fulcher, m. Fr. Teu. people's guard, 371

Fulberto, *m. Rom.* Teu. bright resolution, 316

Fülip, m. Hung. Gr. horse lover, 79

Fulk, *m. Eng.* Teu. people's guard, 371

FULKO, *m. Ger.* Teu. people's guard, 371

Fulrad, *m. Ger.* Teu. people's councillor, 371

FULVIA, *f. It.* Lat. yellow, 147

Fulvio, *m. It.* Lat. yellow, 147

FULVIUS, *m.* Lat. yellow, 147

Fynballa, f. Scot. Kelt. fair shouldered, 245

Fynvola, f. Scot. Kelt. fair shouldered, 245

Fynwald, f. Scot. Kelt. fair shouldered, 245

G

Gab, m. Eng. Heb. hero of God, 55

Gabe, m. Bav. Heb. hero of God, 55

Gabela, m. Swiss, Heb. hero of God, 55

Gaberjels, m. Lett. Heb. hero of God, 55

Gaberl, m. Bav. Heb. hero of God, 55

Gabilo, *m. Ger.* Teu. giver, 379

Gabor, m. Hung. Heb. hero of God, 55

Gabriel, *m. Span. Eng. Fr. Ger.* Heb. hero of God, 55

Gabriele, *f. Ger.* Heb. hero of God, 55

Gabriella, *f. Span. It. Eng.* Heb. hero of God, 55

Gabrielle, *f. Fr.* Heb. hero of God, 55

Gabriello, *m. It.* Heb. hero of God, 55

Gabris, Lett. hero of God, 55

Gabryell, Pol. hero of God, 55

Gad, m. Eng. Heb. troop, 7

Gaddo, m. It. Pers. treasure master, 211

Gaetan, *m. Fr.* Lat. of Gaeta, 132

Gaetano, *m. It.* Lat. of Gaeta, 132

Gaius, *m. Eng.* Lat. rejoiced, 131

Gajo, *m. Slov.* Lat. of Gaeta, 131

GAL, *m. Erse,* Kelt. valour, 246

Galahad, *Eng.* milky way (?), 263

GALATH, *Welsh,* milky way (?), 263

Galdfridus, m. Lat. Teu. good peace, 287

Galeas, *m. Eng.* Teu. helmeted, 163

Galeaz, *m. Ger.* Lat. helmeted, 163

Galeazzo, *m. It.* Lat. helmeted, 163

Galeran, *m. Fr.* Teu. or Lat. healthy or slaughter rule, 317

Galerano, *m. It.* Teu. slaughter rule, 317

Galileo, *m. It.* Kelt. a cock (?) or Galilean, 163

GALL, *m. Gadhael.* Kelt. stranger, 246

Gallo, *m. It.* Lat. cock, 163

GALLUS, *m.* Lat. cock, 163

Gandolf, *m. Ger.* Teu. progress of a wolf, 434

GANDOLF, *m. Ger.* Teu. progress of a wolf, 434

Gandolfo, *m. It.* Teu. progress of a wolf, 434

Ganivre, f. Eng. Kelt. white wave, 269

Ganore, f. Eng. Kelt. white wave (?), 269

Gappe, m. Bav. Pers. treasure master, 211

Garalt, *m. Fr.* Teu. firm spear, 369

Garcia, *m. Span.* Teu. spear, 369

Garcilasso, m. Span. Teu. spear, 369

GARD, *m. Nor.* Teu. dwelling place, 322

GARDHAR, *m. Nor.* Teu. warrior of his country, 322

GARDBRAND, *m. Nor.* Teu. sword of his country, 322

GARDMUND, *m. Nor.* Teu. protection of his country, 322

Garibaldo, *m. It.* Teu. war prince, 369

Garnier, m. Fr. Teu. protecting warrior, 369

Garratt, m. Eng. Teu. spear firm, 368

Garret, m. Teu. firm spear, 368

Garsendis, *f. Span.* Teu. spear strength, 368

Garsias, m. Span. Teu. spear, 368

Gaso, m. Ill. Pers. treasure master, 211

Gaspar, *m. Span. It. Pol.* Pers. treasure master, 211

Gaspard, *m. Fr.* Pers. treasure master, 211

Gasparde, *f. Fr.* Pers. treasure master, 211

Gaspardo, m. It. Pers. treasure master, 211

Gaspare, *m. It.* Pers. treasure master, 211

Gasparro, *m. It.* Pers. treasure master, 211

Gaspe, m. Bav. Pers. treasure master, 211

Gaspero, *m. It.* Pers. treasure master, 211

Gaston, *m. Span. Fr.* 453

Gastone, *m. Span.* 453

Gaton, f. Fr. Gr. pure, 123

Gattirsch, m. Lett. Teu. God's firmness, 288

Gatty, f. Eng. Teu. spear maid, 368

Gaubert, m. Fr. Teu. slaughter bright, 316

Gaucher, m. Fr. Teu. slaughter spear, 316

Gaud, *m. Fr.* Teu. power, 425

GAUDENTIUS, *m.* Lat. rejoicing, 191

Gaudenzio, *m. It.* Lat. rejoicing, 191

Gaugl, m. Swiss, Heb. supplanter, 17

GAUTA, *m. Swed.* Teu. Goth. 288

Gautrek, *m. Swed.* Teu. Goth's king, 288

Gautulf, *m. Swed.* Teu. Goth wolf, 288

Gavin, *m. Scot.* Kelt. hawk of battle, 272

Gavra, f. Slav. Heb. hero of God, 55

Gavre, m. Ill. Heb. hero of God, 55

Gavriil, m. Russ. Heb. hero of God, 55

Gavril, m. Ill. Heb. hero of God, 55

Gavrila, f. Slav. Heb. hero of God, 55

Gavrilo, m. Ill. Heb. hero of God, 55

Gawain, *m. Eng.* Kelt. hawk of battle, 232

Gayorgee, m. Russ. Gr. husbandman, 115

Gebert, m. O. Ger. Teu. strong giver, 378

Gebhard, m. Ger. Teu. strong giver, 378

Gebhardine, f. Ger. Teu. strong giver, 378

Gedde, f. Lett. Teu. spear maid, 368

Gedderts, m. Lett. Teu. God's firmness, 286

Gédéon, *m. Fr.* Heb. destroyer, 38

Geert, m. Dan. Lus. Teu. firm spear, 370

GEIR, *m. Nor.* Teu. spear, 332, 370

GEIRMUND, *f. Nor.* Teu. spear protection, 370

GEIRNY, *f. Nor.* Teu. spear freshness, 370

GEIRRANDUR, *f. Nor.* Teu. spear house, 370

GEIRRIDUR, *f. Nor.* Teu. spear impulse, 370

GEIRTHIOF, *m. Nor.* Teu. spear thief, 370

GEIRBJORG, *f. Nor.* Teu. spear protection, 370

GEIRFUSS, *m. Nor.* Teu. spear eagerness, 370

GEIRHILDA, *f. Nor.* Teu. spear heroine, 370

GEIRLAUG, *f. Nor.* Teu. spear drink, 370

GEIRTHRUD, *f. Nor.* Teu. spear maid, 370

GEIRULF, *m. Nor.* Teu. spear wolf, 370

Geitult, goat heroine, 341

Geitwald, goat prince, 341

GELASIUS, *m. Lat.* Gr. laugher, 113

GELGES, *f. Gr.* swan white, 246

Gellies, m. Dutch, Teu. warring, 418

GELIMIR, *m. Vandal,* Teu. pledge of fame, 366

GELTFRID, *m. Ger.* Teu. pledge of peace, 366

Geltruda, f. It. Teu. spear maid, 368

GEMLORG, *f. Er.* gem like, 125

GEMMA, *f. It.* gem, 125

Genevieve, *f. Fr.* Kelt. (?) white wave, 270

Genevion, f. Fr. Kelt. (?) white wave, 270

Gennaro, *m. It.* Lat. of Janus, 170

Genovefa, *f. Ger.* Kelt. (?) white wave, 270

Genoveffa, *f. It.* Kelt. white wave, 270

Genovefica, *f. Ill.* Kelt. white wave (?), 270

Genoveva, *f. Port.* Kelt. white wave (?), 270

Genserich, *m. Ger.* Teu. spear ruler, 369

Geoffrey, *m. Eng.* Teu. God's peace, 288

Geoffroi, *m. Fr.* Teu. God's peace, 288

Geordie, m. Scot. Gr. husbandman, 115

Georg, *m. Ger. Dan.* Gr. husbandman, 115

George, *m. Eng.* Gr. husbandman, 115

Georges, *m. Fr.* Gr. husbandman, 115

Georget, m. Fr. Gr. husbandman, 115

Georgeta, f. Port. Gr. husbandman, 115
Georgette, f. Fr. Gr. husbandman, 115
Georgey, m. Eng. Gr. husbandman, 115
Georgiana, *f. Eng.* Gr. husbandman, 115
Georgie, m. Wall. Gr. husbandman, 115
Georgij, m. Russ. Gr. husbandman, 115
Georgina, *f. Eng. Ital.* Gr. husbandman, 115
Georgine, *f. Fr. Ger.* Gr. husbandman, 115
Georgio, *m. Ital.* Gr. husbandman, 115
GEORGIOS, *m. Gr.* husbandman, 115
Georgius, *m. N.L.D.* Gr. husbandman, 115
Georgy, m. Eng. Gr. husbandman, 115
Gerald, *m. Eng.* Teu. spear power, 369
Geraldine, *f. Eng.* Teu. spear power, 369
Gerard, *m. Eng. Fr.* Teu. spear firm, 369
Gerardo, m. Rom. Teu. spear firm, 369
Gerart, m. O. Fr. Teu. spear firm, 369
Gerasimus, *m. Lat.* Gr. venerable, 113
Gerand, m. Fr. Teu. spear firm, 369
Gerberge, *f. Fr.* Teu. spear protection, 369
Gerbert, *m. Fr.* Teu. spear bright, 369
GERBOLD, *m. Ger.* Teu. war prince, 369
GERDA, *f. Nor.* Teu. enclosure, 322
Gerde, f. Lett. Teu. spear maid, 322, 368
GERDRUD, *f. Ger.* Teu. spear maid, 368
GERDUR, *f. Nor.* Teu. enclosure, 322
Gerel, m. Fris. Teu. spear power, 368
Gerelt, m. Fris. Teu. spear power, 369
Geremia, *m. Ital.* Heb. exalted of the Lord, 49
Gerga, m. Ill. Gr. watchman, 114
Gergeli, m. Hung. Gr. watchman, 114

Gergen, m. Slov. Gr. watchman, 114
GERHARD, *m. Ger.* Teu. spear firm, 369
Gerhardine, f. Ger. Teu. firm spear, 369
GERHOLD, *m. A.S.* Teu. firm spear, 369
Gerkis, m. Lett. Teu. firm spear, 369
Gerlach, *m. Ger.* Teu. spear sport, 370
Gerlib, *m. Ger.* Teu. spear relic, 370
Germain, *m. Eng. Fr.* Lat. German, 202
Germaine, *f. Fr.* Lat. German, 202
Germana, *f. Span.* Lat. German, 203
Germann, *m. Ger.* Lat. German, 203
Germano, *m. Ital.* Lat. German, 203
GERMANUS, *m.* Lat. German, 203
GERMAR, *m. Ger.* Teu. spear fame, 369
GERNOT, *m. Ger.* Teu. spear compulsion, 370
Gero, m. Hung. Gr. watchman, 114
Gero, f. Nor. Teu. divine wisdom, 286
Gerold, m. Ger. Teu. spear firm, 369
GEROLF, *m. Ger.* Teu. spear wolf, 370
Geronimo, *m. It.* Gr. holy name, 89
Gerontius, *m. Lat.* Gr. old man.
GERRAMN, *m. Ger.* Teu. spear raven, 369
Gerritt, m. Dutch, Teu. firm spear, 370
Gerte, f. Lett. Teu. spear maid, 368
Gerts, m. Lett. Teu. firm spear, 369
Gertraud, *f. Ger.* Teu. spear maid, 368
Gertrud, *f. Hung. Ger.* Teu. spear maid, 368
Gertruda, *f. It. Russ.* Teu. spear maid, 368
Gertrude, *f. Eng. Fr.* Teu. spear maid, 368
Gertrudes, *f. Port.* Teu. spear maid, 368
Gervais, *m. Fr.* Teu. war eagerness, 370
GERWALD, *m. Ger.* Teu. spear power, 370
Gervas,* *m. Eng.* Teu. war eagerness, 370
Gervasio, *m. It.* Teu. war eagerness, 370
Gervazij, *m. Slav.* Teu. war eagerness, 370
Gerwart, *m. Ger.* Teu. spear ward, 370

* Sts. Gervasius and Protasius were martyrs disinterred by St. Ambrose, at Milan. The name is therefore probably from a classical source, unless it was originally that of a Teutonic slave.

Gerwas, *m.* *Ger.* Teu. war eagerness, 370

Gerwin, *m.* *Ger.* Teu. spear friend, 370

Geta, *m.* *Lat.* Teu. Goth. 289

Gevald, m. *Ger.* Teu. power giver, 379

Gherardo, *m.* *It.* Teu. spear firm, 370

Ghita, f. *It.* Teu. pearl, 121

Giacinta, *f.* *It.* Gr. purple, 81

Giacinto, *m.* *It.* Gr. purple, 81

Giacobba, *f.* *It.* Heb. supplanter, 17

Giacobbe, *m.* *It.* Heb. supplanter, 17

Giacomma, *f.* *It.* Heb. supplanter, 17

Giacomo, *m.* *It.* Heb. supplanter, 17

Giacopo, *m.* *It.* Heb. supplanter, 17

Gian, m. *It.* Heb. the Lord's grace, 45

Gianbattista, m. *It.* Heb. John the Baptist, 108

Giankos, m. *M. Gr.* Heb. grace of the Lord, 45

Giannakes, m. *M. Gr.* Heb. grace of the Lord, 45

Giannes, m. *M. Gr.* Heb. the Lord's grace, 45

Gianina, f. *It.* Heb. the Lord's grace, 46

Giannino, m. *It.* Heb. the Lord's grace, 45

Gianozzo, m. *It.* Heb. the Lord's grace, 45

Gib, m. *Eng.* Teu. bright pledge, 366

Gibichs, m. *Ger.* Teu. giver, 344

Gibbon, m. *Eng.* Teu. bright pledge, 366

Gideon, m. *Eng.* Heb. destroyer, 38

Giertruda, *f.* *Pol.* Teu. spear maid, 368

Gil, m. *Span.* Lat. downy (?), 149

Gilavij, m. *Russ.* Lat. cheerful, 191

Gilbert, *m.* *Eng. Fr. Ger.* Teu. bright pledge, 366

Gilberto, *m.* *It.* Teu. bright pledge, 366

Gilbrid, *m.* *Scot.* Kelt. servant of Bridget, 260

Gilchrist, *m.* *Scot.* Kelt. servant of Christ, 260

Gilcolum, *m.* *Scot.* Kelt. servant of Columba, 260

Gildas, *m.* *Lat.* Kelt. servant of God, 260

Gileber, m. *Fr.* Teu. bright pledge, 366

Giles, m. *Eng.* Gr. with the ægis, 79

Gilescop, *m.* *Gael.* Kelt. servant of the bishop, 261

Gilfred, m. *Ger.* Teu. pledge of peace, 366

Gill, f. *Eng.* Lat. downy, 150

Gilleneaomh, *m.* *Gael.* Kelt. servant of the saints, 260

Gilles, *m.* *Fr.* Gr. with the ægis, 79

Gillespie, *f.* *Scot.* Kelt. bishop's servant, 260

Gillet, *f.* *Eng.* Lat. downy, 150

Gilli, Flem. Teu. bright pledge, 336

Gillian, *f.* *Eng.* Lat. downy, 149

Gillies, m. *Scot.* servant of Jesus, 261

Gilmichel, *m.* *Scot.* Kelt. servant of Michael, 261

Gilmory, f. *Scot.* Kelt. servant of Mary, 261

Gilmoir, *f.* *Gael.* Kelt. servant of Mary, 261

Gils, *m.* *Nor.* Teu. pledge, 224

Gilpatrick, m. *Scot.* Kelt. servant of Patrick, 195, 261

Giodoco, *m.* *It. Lat.* joyful, 191

Giofred, m. *It.* Teu. God's peace, 287

Ginevra, *f.* *Ital.* Kelt. white wave (?), 270

Giobbe, *m.* *It.* Heb. persecuted, 26

Gioachimo, m. *It.* Heb. the Lord will judge, 38

Gioachino, m. *It.* Heb. the Lord will judge, 38

Giolla Brighde, *m.* *Erse,* Kelt. servant of Bridget, 261

Giolla Christ, *m.* *Erse,* Kelt. servant of Christ, 261

Giolla Cheallaich, *m.* *Erse,* Kelt. servant of Ceallach, 261

Giolla Choluin, *m.* *Erse,* Kelt. servant of Columba, 261

Giolla Chomhghaill, *m.* *Erse,* Kelt. servant of Congall, 261

Giolla De, *m.* *Erse,* Kelt. servant of God, 261

Giolla Dubdh, *m.* *Erse,* Kelt. servant of the black, 261

Giolla Earch, *m.* *Erse,* Kelt. servant of Earc, 261

Giolla Josa, *m.* *Erse,* Kelt. servant of Jesus, 261

Giolla-na-naomh, *m.* *Erse,* Kelt. servant of the saints, 261

e

GIOLLA PHADRIG, *m. Erse,* Kelt. servant of Patrick, 195, 261

GIOLLA RHIOBACH, *m. Erse,* Kelt. servant of the swarthy, 260

Giordano, *m. It.* Heb. the Jordan, 39

Giorgio, *Gr. It.* husbandman, 115

Gioseffo, *m. Ital.* Heb. addition, 23

Giotto, m. Ital. Teu. God's peace, 288

Giovachino, m. Ital. Heb. the Lord will judge, 38

Giovanna, *f. Ital.* Heb. the Lord's grace, 46

Giovanni, *m. Ital.* Heb. the Lord's grace, 45

Giovannina, f. Ital. Heb. the Lord's grace, 46

Giovanino, m. Ital. Heb. the Lord's grace, 45

Giovanetto, m. Ital. Heb. grace of the Lord, 45

Giovio, *m. Ital.* Lat. of Jupiter, 169

Girairs, m. Fr. Teu. firm spear, 370

Giralda, *f. Ital.* Teu. spear power, 369

Giraldo, *m. Ital.* Teu. spear power, 369

Giraldus, *m. Lat.* Teu. spear power, 369

Girart, *m. Prov.* Teu. firm spear, 369

Girault, m. Fr. Teu. spear power, 369

Girioel, m. Welsh, Gr. lordly, 217

Girroald, *m. Fr.* Teu. spear power, 369

Girolamo, *m. It.* Lat. holy name, 89

Girzie, f. Scot. Gr. Teu. golden battle maid, 291

Gisbert, f. m. Ger. Teu. pledge bright, 366

Gisborn, m. Eng. Teu. pledge bear, 366

Gisala, *f. Ger.* Teu. pledge, 366

Gisbert, m. Dutch, Teu. bright pledge, 366

Gisebryht, m. Dutch, Teu. bright pledge, 366

GISEL, *f. Frank.* Teu. pledge, 366

Giselbert, m. Ger. Teu. bright pledge, 366

GISELBERGE, pledged protection, 366

Gisèle, *f. Fr.* Teu. pledge, 366

GISELFRID, *m. Ger.* Teu. pledge of peace, 366

GISELHART, *m. Ger.* Teu. pledge of firmness, 366

GISELHER, *m. Ger.* Teu. pledge warrior, 366

GISELHILDA, *f. Ger.* Teu. pledged heroine, 366

GISELOF, pledged relic, 366

GISELRICO, *m. Goth.* Teu. pledged ruler, 366

Gisla, *f. Nor.* Teu. pledge, 366

GISLAUG, *f. Nor.* Teu. pledge drink, 366

Gismonda, f. Ger. Teu. conquering protection, 366

Gismondo, m. Ger. Teu. conquering protection, 366

Gissur, m. Ice. Teu. pledged warrior, 366

Gith, f. Eng. Teu. happy gift, 379

Giubileo, m. It. Lat. of the jubilee, 191

Giuda, m. It. Heb. praise, 21

Giuditta, f. It. Heb. praise, 21

Giuka, m. Ill. Gr. husbandman, 116

Giuko, m. Ill. Gr. husbandman, 116

Giulia, *f. It.* Lat. downy bearded, 149

Giuliana, *f. It.* Lat. downy bearded, 149

Giuliano, *m. It.* Lat. downy bearded, 149

Giulietta, *f. It.* Lat. downy bearded, 150

Giulio, *m. It.* Lat. downy bearded, 149

Giuro, m. Ill. Gr. husbandman, 259

Giuseppe, *m. It.* Heb. addition, 23

Giuseppina, *f. It.* Heb. addition, 23

Giusta, *f. It.* Lat. just, 192

Giustina, *f. It.* Lat. just, 192

Giustino, *m. It.* Lat. just, 192

Giusto, *m. It.* Lat. just, 192

GJAFLAUG, *f. Nor.* Teu. liquor giver, 343

GJAVVALD, *m. Nor.* Teu. liquor giver, 343

GJERD, *m. Nor.* Teu. bond, 240

GJERHILD, *f. Nor.* Teu. spear battle maid, 370

GJERLEIV, *m. Nor.* Teu. spear relic, 370

GJERMUND, *m. Nor.* Teu. spear protection, 370

GJERULV, *m. Nor.* Teu. spear wolf, 370

Gjorghic, *m. Ill.* Gr. husbandman, 115

Gjosta, *m. Swed.* Teu. Goth's staff, 289

Gjuko, *m. Nor.* Teu. giver, 116, 379

Gjuraj, *m. Ill.* Gr. husbandman, 116

Gjurgjija, *f. Ill.* Gr. husbandman, 116

Gjurginka, *f. Ill.* Gr. husbandman, 116

Gjuro, *m. Ill.* Gr. husbandman, 259

Gjutha, *f. Nor.* Teu. giver, 379

Gladus, *m. Welsh*, Lat. lame, 146

Gladuse, *f. Eng.* Lat. lame, 146

Gladys, *f. Welsh*, Lat. lame, 146

GLASAN, *m. Erse*, Kelt. blue, 106

Claud, *m. Scot.* Lat. lame, 146

GLEB, *m. Russ.* Slav. 460

GLOUKERA, *f. Russ.* Gr. sweet, 80

Glycère, *f. Fr.* Gr. sweet, 80

GLYKERA, *f. Gr.* Gr. sweet, 80

Goçalak, *m. Ill.* Teu. God's servant, 286

Godafrei, *m. Prov.* Teu. God's peace, 288

Godard, *m. Fr.* Teu. divine firmness, 287

Goddard, *m. Eng.* Teu. divine firmness, 287

Godebert, *m. Ger.* Teu. divine brightness, 288

Godeberta, *f. Frank.* Teu. divine brightness, 288

GODEGISEL, *m. Ger.* Teu. divine pledge, 288

Godefroi, *m. Fr.* Teu. God's peace, 287

GODEFRIED, *m. Ger.* Teu. God's peace, 287

Gödel, *m. Ger.* Teu. divine peace, 287

Godeleva, *f. m. Lat.* Teu. divine gift, 286

GODELIND, *f. Ger.* Teu. good serpent, 288

GODEMAR, *m. Ger.* Teu. good fame, 288

Goderic, *m. Fr.* Teu. divine king, 286

Godescalco, *m. It.* Teu. God's servant, 286

GODESKALK, *m. Frank.* Teu. God's servant, 286

Godfrey, *m. Eng.* Teu. God's peace, 287

Godfried, *m. Holl.* Teu. God's peace, 287

GODGIFU, *f. A.S.* Teu. God's gift, 286

Godine, *f. m. Cambrai*, Teu. divine friend, 286

Godinette, *f. Cambrai*, Teu. divine friend, 286

Godiva, *f. Eng.* Teu. divine gift, 286

Godon, *m. Fr.* Lat. lame, 146

Godric, *m. Eng.* Teu. divine king, 286

Godwin, *m. Eng.* Teu. divine friend, 286

GODWINE, *m. A. G. S.* Teu. divine friend, 286

GODWULF, *m. A. G. S.* Teu. divine wolf, 286

Goelen, *f. Flemish*, Teu. war, 363

Goetz, *m. Ger.* Teu. God's peace, 287

Goffredo, *m. It.* Teu. God's peace, 287

Gogo, *m. Fr.* Gr. pearl, 121

Gollaa, *f. Nor.* Teu. divine sea, 286

GOLUBICA, *f. Ill.* Slav. dove, 187

Gombert, *m. Fr.* Teu. war prince, 363

Gonçalo, *m. Port.* Teu. 363

Gondaberge, *f. Ger.* Teu. war protection, 363

Gondebaldo, *m. Span.* Teu. war prince, 363

Gondebault, *m. Fr.* Teu. war bold, 363

Gondebert, *m. Fr.* Teu. war bright, 363

Gondemir, *m. Span.* Teu. war fame, 364

GONDERIC, *m. Frank.* Teu. war chief, 364

Gonderico, *m. Span.* Teu. war chief, 364

Gondesind, *f. Span.* Teu. war strength, 364

GÖNDOL, *f. m. Nor.* Teu. good, 364

Gondoline, *f. Ger.* Teu. war serpent, 364

GONDOMAR, *m. Span.* Teu. war fame, 364

Gondomire, *m.* Span. war fame, 364

Gonorij, *m. Russ.* Lat. honoured, 394

Gonsalve, *m. Fr.* Teu. war wolf, 363

Gonsalvo, *m. It.* Teu. war wolf, 363

Gonstan, *m. Bret.* Teu. hill stone, 295

Gonthery, *m. Fr.* Teu. war rule, 363

Gonthier, *m. Fr.* Teu. war army, 363

Gonthere, *m. It.* Teu. war army, 363

Gontrada, *f. Span.* Teu. war council, 364

Gontram, *m. Fr.* Teu. war raven, 364

Gönz, m. Ger. Teu. war, 363

Gonzalo, *m. Span.* Teu. war wolf, 361

Gonzalve, *m. Fr.* Teu. war wolf, 363

Goratij, m. Russ. Lat. watchman, 114, 148

Gorm, m. Nor. Teu. war serpent, 363

Gormfhlait, f. Erse, Teu. blue lady, 253

Gospatrick, *m. Scot.* Gael. Lat. boy of Patrick, 195

Gospava, f. Ill. Slav. lady.

Gosta, m. Swed. Teu. Goth's staff, 289

Gostanza, *f. Span.* Lat. firm, 162

GOSTOMIL, *m. Ill.* Slave, hospitality, 439

Gotardo, m. It. Lat. good firm, 287

Gotfryd, *m. Pol.* Teu. God's peace, 288

Goton, f. Fr. Gr. pearl, 121

GOTTFRIED, *m. Ger.* Teu. God's peace, 288

Gottgabe, *m. Ger.* Teu. God's gift, 288

Gottgetreu, *m. Ger.* Teu. faithful to God, 288

GOTTHARD, *m. Ger.* Teu. divine firmness, 286

Gotthelf, *m. Ger.* Teu. God's help, 288

Gotthold, *m. Ger.* Teu. God's power, 288

GOTTLEIP, *m. Ger.* Teu. remains of divinity, 288

Gottlieb, *m. Ger.* Teu. God's love, 288

Gottlob, *m. Ger.* Teu. God's praise, 288

GOTTSCHALK, *m. Ger.* Teu. God's servant, 286

Gottseimitdir, *m. Ger.* Teu. God be with thee, 288, 468

GOTTWALD, *m. Ger.* Teu. God's power, 288

Goule, f. Brabant, Teu. war, 363

Govert, m. Dutch, Teu. God's peace, 288

GOZSTAV, *m. Swed.* Teu. Goth's staff, 289

GRACE, *f. Eng.* Lat. grace, 195

Gracie, *f. Scot.* Lat. grace, 195

Gradlon, *m. Bret.* Kelt. love, 250

GRAIDHNE, *f. Erse,* Kelt. love, 250

GRAINE, *f. m. Irish,* Kelt. love, 195, 249

Gratianus, *m. Lat.* thanks, 195

Graziella, *f. It.* Lat. thanks, 195

Grazian, *m. It.* Lat. thanks.

Greagair, *m. Erse,* Kelt. watchman, 114

Gredel, f. Bav. Gr. pearl, 121

Greg, m. Scot. Kelt. fierce, 114

Grega, m. Slov. Gr. watchman, 114

Gregoire, *m. Fr.* Gr. watchman, 114

Gregor, *m. Ger.* Gr. watchman, 114

Gregori, *m. It.* Gr. watchman, 114

GREGORIOS, *m. Gr.* Gr. watchman, 114

Gregorius, m. Lat. Gr. watchman, 114

Gregory, *m. Eng.* Gr. watchman, 114

Gregos, m. Dan. Gr. watchman, 114

Gregur, *m. Slov.* Gr. watchman, 114

Gregus, m. Dan. Ger. Gr. watchman, 256

Greis, m. Swed. Gr. watchman, 114

GREIS, *m. Nor.* Teu. stone, 349

Grel, f. Bav. Gr. pearl, 121

Greszkus, m. Lith. Gr. watchman, 114

Greta, f. Lith. Gr. pearl, 121

Gretchen, f. Ger. Eng. pearl, 121

Grete, f. Ger. Gr. pearl, 121

Gretel, f. Bav. Gr. pearl, 121

Grethe, f. Ger. Gr. pearl, 121

Gretje, f. Dutch, Gr. pearl, 121

Gretli, f. Swiss, Gr. pearl, 121

Gries, watchman, 114

Griffith, *m. Welsh,* Lat. ruddy, 167

Grifone, *m. It.* Lat. ruddy, 167

Grigge, m. Let. Gr. watchman, 114

Grigorie, *m. Wall.* Gr. watchman, 114

Grigorij, *m. Russ.* Gr. watchman, 114

Grigory, *m. Ill.* Gr. watchman, 114

GRIM, *m. Nor.* Teu. helmeted, 293

Grimaldo, *m. It.* Teu. fierce power, 293

Grimaltos, *m. Span.* Teu. fierce power, 293

Grimaud, m. Fr. Teu. fierce power, 293

Grimar, m. Nor. Teu. helmeted warrior, 293

GRIMBALD, *m. Eng.* Teu. fierce power, 293

GRIMBERT, *m. Ger.* Teu. helmeted warrior, 293

GRIMHERI, *m. Ger.* Teu. helmeted warrior, 293

GRIMHILD, *f. m. Nor.* Teu. helmeted battle maid, 293

GRIMKETYL, *m. Nor.* Teu. hidden cauldron, 293

Grimkjell, m. Nor. Teu. hidden cauldron, 293

GRIMWALD, *m. Ger.* Teu. helmeted power, 293

GRIMULF, *m. Eng.* Teu. helmeted wolf, 293

Grischa, f. Russ. Gr. watchman, 114

GRIOTGARD, *f. Nor.* Teu. stone maid, 349

Grischha, f. Russ. Gr. watchman, 115

Griselda, *f. It. Eng.* Gr. Teu. stone heroine, 349

Grisostomo, *m. It.* Gr. golden mouth, 43

Grissel, *f. Eng.* Gr. Teu. stone heroine, 349

Gristovalo, *m. It.* Gr. Christ bearer, 106

Gritty, f. Eng. Gr. pearl, 121

Grizel, *f. Scot.* Gr. Teu. stone heroine, 349

GROZDANA, *f. Serv.* Slav. rich in grapes, 438

GRUACH, *f. Gael.* Kelt. hairy.

Gruffin, *m. Welsh,* Lat. ruddy, 167

Gruffydd, *m. Welsh,* Lat. ruddy, 167

Grunja, f. Russ. Lat. born with feet foremost, 156

Gruscha, f. Russ. Lat. born with feet foremost, 156

Grygallis, m. Lett. Gr. watchman, 113

Gryta, f. Lith. Gr. pearl, 121

Grzegorz, *m. Pol.* Gr. watchman, 114

Guadalupe, *f. m. Span.* 371

Gualberto, m. It. Teu. slaughter bright, 317

Gualter, *m. Port.* Teu. powerful army, 425

Gualthier, *m. Fr.* Teu. powerful army, 425

Gualtiero, *m. It.* Teu. powerful army, 425

Guarin, *m. Fr.* Teu. spear friend, 369

Guarino, *m. It.* Teu. spear friend, 369

Guarniero, *m. It.* Teu. protecting warrior, 369

Guérin, *m. Fr.* Teu. protecting warrior, 369

Guccio, m. It. Teu. home rule, 310

Guda, *f. Nor.* Teu. divine, 285

GUDBIORG, *f. Nor.* Teu. divine protection, 286

GUDBRAND, *m. Nor.* Teu. divine sword, 286

GUDFINN, divine whiteness, 286

GUDFINNA, divine whiteness, 286

GUDHR, *f. Nor.* Teu. divine, 286

Gudiskako, servant of God, 286

GUDLEIF, *m. Nor.* Teu. divine relic, 286

GUDLEIFR, *m. Nor.* Teu. divine relic, 286

GUDLEIK, *m. Nor.* Teu. divine praise, 286

GUDMUND, *m. Nor.* Teu. divine protection, 286

GUDNY, *m. Nor.* Teu. divine freshness, 286

GUDOLV, *m. Nor.* Teu. divine wolf, 286

GUDRID, *f. Nor.* Teu. divine impulse, 286

GUDRIDUR, *f. Nor.* Teu. divine impulse, 286

GUDRUNA, *f. Nor.* Teu. divine wisdom, 286

Gudule, *f. Ger.* Teu. war, 364

GUDVAR, *m. Nor.* Teu. divine prudence, 286

GUDVEIG, *f. Nor.* Teu. divine liquor, 286

Guelfo, m. It. Teu. wolf, 335

Guendolen, *f. Eng.* Kelt. white browed, 268

GUENNEAN, *f. Bret.* Kelt. angel, 270

Guennever, *f. Eng.* Kelt. white lady, 268

Guennolé, *f. Bret.* Kelt. white, 268

Guennolà, *f. Bret.* Kelt. white, 268

Guerin, m. Fr. Teu. war friend, 369

Guglielma, *f. It.* Teu. helmet of resolution, 315

Guglielmo, *m. It.* Teu. helmet of resolution, 315

Gui, m. Fr. Kelt. sense, 228

Guides, m. Fr. Kelt. sense, 228

Guido, m. It. Eng. Kelt. sense, 228

lxx GLOSSARY.

Guidon, m. Fr. Kelt. sense (?), 228
Guidone, m. It. Kelt. sense (?), 228
Guiette, f. Fr. Kelt. sense (?), 228
Guilbaldo, *m. Port.* Teu. bold prince, 314
Guilhermo, *m. Port.* Teu. helmet of resolution, 315
Guillarn, m. Bret. Teu. will helmet, 315
Guillerm, m. Bret. Teu. will helmet, 315
Guillym, m. Welsh, Teu. will helmet, 315
Guillaume, *m. Fr.* Teu. helmet of resolution, 315
Guillaumette, *f. Fr.* Teu. helmet of resolution, 315
Guillaumine, *f. Fr.* Teu. helmet of resolution, 315
Guillene, *m. Prov.* Teu. helmet of resolution, 315
Guillena, *f. Prov.* Teu. will helmet, 315
Guillermo, *m. Span.* Teu. helmet of resolution, 315
Guillette, f. Fr. Teu. helmet of resolution, 315
Guillibaud, *m. Fr.* Teu. resolute prince, 315
Guillot, m. Fr. Teu. helmet of resolution, 315
Guirauld, *m. Fr.* Teu. spear power, 369
Guiscard, *m. Fr.* Teu. wise war, 321
Guiscardo, *m. It.* Teu. wise war, 321
Gulla, f. Nor. Teu. divine sea, 286
Gullaug, f. Nor. Teu. divine liquor, 286
Gullbrand, m. Nor. Teu. war sword, 286
Gulleik, m. Nor. Teu. war sport, 286
Gulleiv, m. Nor. Teu. divine relic, 286
Gulmar, m. Nor. Teu. war greatness, 364
Gulmund, m. Nor. Teu. divine protection, 286
Gumpert, m. Ger. Teu. war splendour, 364
GUNBJORG, *f. Nor.* Teu. war protection, 364
GUNBJORN, *f. Nor.* Teu. war bear, 364

Gunborg, *f. Nor.* Teu. war protection, 364
GUNDAHARI, *m. O. Ger.* Teu. warrior, 364
GUNDEKAR, *m. Ger.* Teu. war spear, 364
GUNDLIN, *f. Ger.* Teu. war serpent, 364
Gundolf, *m. Ger.* Teu. war wolf, 364
Gundrada, f. Ger. Teu. war council, 364
Gundred, *f. Eng.* Teu. war council (?), 364
GUNDRIDUR, *f. Nor.* Teu. war impulse, 364
Gundula, *f. Ger.* Teu. war, 364
GUNDULF, *m. Norm.* Teu. war wolf, 364
GUNDVAR, *f. Nor.* Teu. war prudence, 364
Gunhild, f. Nor. Teu. war heroine, 364
Guni, f. Nor. Teu. divine freshness, 286
GUNLAUG, *f. Nor.* Teu. war liquor, 364
GUNLEIF, *m. Nor.* Teu. war love, 364
GUNLEIK, *m. Nor.* Teu. war sport, 364
Gunnar, *f. Nor.* Teu. war, 364
GUNNDERICH, *m. Nor.* Teu. war ruler, 364
GUNNHILDUR, *f. Nor.* Teu. war maid, 364
Gunnilda, f. Eng. Teu. war battle maid, 364
GUNNOLFR, *m. Ice.* Teu. war wolf, 364
Gunnora, *f. Eng.* Teu. war protection, 364
Gunnrod, *f. Nor.* Teu. war council, 364
GUNNSTEIN, *m. Nor.* Teu. war stone, 364
GUNNR, *f. Nor.* Teu. war, 364
GUNNULV, *m. Nor.* Teu. war wolf, 364
GUNNWALD, *m. Nor.* Teu. war power, 364
Gunthar, *m. Frank.* Teu. warrior, 362
Gunthe, f. Ger. Teu. war, 362
GUNTHRAM, *m. Fr.* Teu. war raven, 363

GUNTRUD, *f. Nor.* Teu. war maid, 364

Gunula, f. Ger. Teu. war, 364

Guossalvo, *m. Prov.* Teu. war wolf, 264

Gurn, f. Nor. Teu. divine wisdom, 286

Gurth, *m. Eng.* Teu. bond, 322

Guru, f. Nor. Teu. divine wisdom, 286

Gushtasp, *m. Pers.* Zend. possessing horses, 137

Gussie, f. Eng. Lat. venerable, 158

Gust, m. Dutch, Teu. Goth's staff, 289

Gusta, f. Lus. Ger. Lat. venerable, 158

Guste, f. Lus. Ger. Lat. venerable, 158

Gustel, f. Ger. Lat. venerable, 158

GUSTAF, *m. Swed.* Teu. Goth's staff, 289

Gustav, *m. Ger.* Teu. Goth's staff, 289

Gustave, *m. Fr.* Teu. Goth's staff, 289

Gustavo, *m. Rom.* Teu. Goth's staff, 289

Gustavus, *m. Eng.* Teu. Goth staff, 289

Gusts, m. Lett. Teu. Goth's staff, 289

Gustylka, f. Lus. Lat. venerable, 157

Gutha, *f. Ger.* Teu. war, 286

Guthlac, *m. A.S.* Teu. war sport, 286

GUTHORM, *m. Dan.* Teu. war serpent, 286

Guthrum, *m. Eng.* Teu. war serpent, 286

Gutmar, m. Ger. Teu. war strength, 286

Guttiere, *m. Span.* Teu. powerful warrior, 286

Guttorm, m. Eng. Teu. war serpent, 286

Guy, *m. Eng.* Kelt. sense (?), 228

Guyon, *m. Fr.* Kelt. sense, 228

Guzman, *m. Span.* Teu. good man, 288

GWALCHMAI, *m. Welsh,* Kelt. hawk of battle, 272

GWALLAWG, *m. Welsh,* Kelt. stammerer, or hawk, 272

Gwirydd, m. Welsh, Kelt. 281

GWEN, *f. Welsh,* Kelt. white, 268

GWENDOLEN, *f. Welsh,* Kelt. white browed, 265

Gwendoleu, *m. Welsh,* Kelt. white browed, 268

GWENEAL, *f. Bret.* Kelt. white angel, 269

GWENHWYFAR, *f. Welsh,* Kelt. white wave, 269

GWENFREWI, *f. Welsh,* Kelt. white stream, 269

GWENWYNWYN, *m. Welsh,* Kelt. thrice fair (?), 269

Gwethalyn, *m. Welsh,* Lat. of life, 197

GWIAWN, *m. Welsh,* Kelt. sense, 228

GWIAWN, *m. Cym.* Kelt. sense (?), 228

Gwric, *m. Welsh,* Gr. Sunday child, 217

Gwril, *m. Welsh,* Gr. lordly, 217

GWRTHEYRN, *m. Welsh,* excelling king, 238

GWYDYR, *m. Welsh,* Kelt. wrathful, 363

Gwynaeth, f. Eng. Kelt. bliss, 271

Gyda, f. Nor. gift, 379

Gyllys, m. Fris. Teu. warring, 363

Gyneth, f. Eng. Kelt. blessed, 271

GYRTHR, *m. Dan.* Teu. bond, 322

Gytha, f. Eng. Teu. gift, 379

Gysbert, m. Dutch, Teu. bright pledge, 366

H

Haagan, *m. Nor.* Teu. high kin, 365

HAAKATHA, *m. Nor.* Teu. 365

Haake, m. Nor. Teu. high kin, 365

HAAKEN, *m. Nor.* Teu. high kin, 365

HAAMUND, *m. Nor.* Teu. high protection, 365

HAAVARD, *m. Nor.* Teu. high protection, 365

Habbakuk, *m. Eng.* Heb. embracing, 5

Habor, m. Nor. Teu. dexterous brightness, 365

Hacco, *m. Nor.* Teu. high kin, 365

Häcke, *m. Swiss,* Teu. axe (?)

Hackel, *m. Swiss,* Teu. axe (?)

Haco, *m. Lat.* Teu. high kin, 365

Hacon, *m. Scot.* Teu. high kin, 365

Hada, f. Lus. Teu. war refuge, 304

Hadamk, m. Lus. Heb. red earth, 10

Hadassah, *Eng. Pers.* Heb. myrtle, 57

HADRIANUS, *m. Lat.* from Adrian, 157

HADUFRID, *m. Ger.* Teu. war peace, 305

HADUFUNS, *m. Ger.* Teu. war eagerness, 305

HADULINT, *f. Ger.* Teu. war spear, 305

Haduman, *m. Ger.* Teu. Hodur's man, 304

HADUMAR, *m. Ger.* Teu. fierce fame, 304

HADUPALD, *m. Ger.* Teu. fierce prince, 305

HADUPRACHT, *m. Ger.* Teu. war's brightness, 305

HADUPARC, *f. Ger.* Teu. war protection, 305

HADUSWINTH, *f. Goth.* Teu. war strength, 305

HADUWALD, *m. Ger.* Teu. war prince, 305

HADUWIG, *f. Ger.* Teu. war refuge, 305

HAFGRIM, *m. Nor.* Teu. sea obscured, 432

HAFLIDE, *m. Nor.* Teu. sea wanderer, 432

HAFLOK, *m. Nor.* Teu. sea relic, 432

HAFTHOR, *m. Nor.* Teu. sea Thor, 432

HAGBART, *Nor.* Teu. dexterous brightness, 365

HAGBRAND, *Nor.* Teu. dexterous sword, 365

Haggai, *m. Eng.* Heb. festival of the Lord, 51

HAGAN, *m. Dan.* Teu. hook, 365

Haggy, f. Eng. Gr. good, 82

HAGTHOR, *m. Nor.* Teu. dexterous Thor, 365

HAIRUWULF, *m. Goth.* sword wolf, 351

Hake, m. Nor. Teu. high kin, 365

Hakona, m. Nor. Teu. high kin, 365

Hal, m. Eng. Teu. home rule, 310

Halbe, m. Ger. Teu. half, 431

Halbert, *m. Scot.* Teu. bright stone, 349

HALBJORG, *f. Nor.* Teu. stone protection, 349

Halbdan, *m. Nor.* Teu. half Dane, 431

HALBTURING, *m. Ger.* Teu. half Thuringian, 431

HALBWALAH, *m. Ger.* Teu. stranger, half Wallachian, 431

Haldanus, *m. Lat.* Teu. half Dane, 431

HALDIS, *f. Nor.* Teu. stone spirit, 349

Halex, m. Lus. Gr. helper of men, 85

Half, m. Ice. Teu. half, 431

HALFDAN, *m. Nor.* Teu. half Dane, 431

HALFRID, *f. Nor.* Teu. hall fair, 349

Hali, m. Kaffir, Teu. home rule, 310

Halldora, *f. Nor.* Teu. stone of Thor, 349

Halgerd, f. Nor. Teu. stone fence, 319

HALGJER, *m. Nor.* Teu. stone spear, 319

HALLGRIM, *f. m. Nor.* Teu. stone helmet, 349

HALLGRIMA, *f. Nor.* Teu. stone helmet, 349

Halkatla, *f. Nor.* Teu. stone kettle, 349

Hallkjell, *m. Nor.* Teu. stone kettle, 349

HALLRID, *f. Nor.* Teu. stone vehemence, 349

HALLTHORA, *f. Nor.* Teu. stone of Thor, 349

HALLWARD, *m. Nor.* Teu. stone guardian, 349

HALVAR, *m. Nor.* Teu. stone prudence, 349

Hameline, f. Fr. Teu. home, 309

Hamish, m. Gael. Heb. supplanter, 17

Hamlyn, *m. Eng.* Teu. home, 309

Hamo, *m. Nor.* Teu. home, 309

Han, m. Esth. Swiss, Heb. grace of God, 45

Hananeel, *m. Eng.* Heb. grace of God, 46

Hanani, *m. Eng.* Heb. grace of God, 46

Ha˘ aniah, *m. Eng.* Heb. grace of the Lord, 40

Hanchen, f. Ger. Heb. grace of the Lord, 42

Hancicka, f. Lus. Heb. grace, 42

Handrej, m. Lus. Gr. man, 86

Hanka, f. Lus. Heb. grace of the Lord, 46

Hanke, m. Netherlands, Heb. grace of the Lord, 45

Hanna, f. Lus. Heb. grace, 42

Hannah, *f. Eng.* Heb. grace, 42

Hanne, f. Ger. Heb. grace of the Lord, 46

Hanneken, m. Dutch, Heb. grace of the Lord, 45

Hannes, m. Dutch, Heb. grace of the Lord, 45

Hannibal, m. Eng. Phœn. grace of Baal, 40

Hanno, m. Lat. Corn. Phœn. grace, 40

Hannyball, m. Swiss, Ger. Phœn. grace of Baal, 40

Hans, m. Ger. Dutch, Heb. grace of the Lord, 45

Hanschen, m. Ger. Heb. grace of the Lord, 45

Hansel, m. Bav. Heb. grace of the Lord, 45

Hansli, m. Swiss, Heb. grace of the Lord, 45

Hanto, m. Lus. Lat. inestimable, 142

Hanusia, f. Pol. Heb. grace of the Lord, 46

Hanza, f. Lus. Gr. pure, 119

Hanzyzka, f. Lus. Heb. grace, 42

Happen-to-be, m. Eng.

Harald, *m. Nor.* Teu. warrior power, 417

Harding, *m. Nor.* Teu. firm, 421

Hardiknut, *m. Dan.* Teu. bold and able, 421

Hardouin, *m. Fr.* Teu. firm friend, 421

Hardrada, m. Nor. Teu. hardy, 421

Hardwig, *m. Eng.* Teu. hard war, 421

Hardwin, *m. Ger.* Teu. firm friend, 421

Harenc, m. Fr. Teu. army, 416

Haribert, bright warrior, 417

Haring, m. Dan. Teu. army, 416

Harivald, *m.* warrior power, 416

Harm, m. Netherland, Gr. holy name, 89

Harold, *m. Eng.* Teu. warrior power, 417

Haroun, m. Arab. Heb. mountain, 27

Harriet, *f. Eng.* Teu. home rule, 310

Harry, *m. Eng.* Teu. home rule, 310

Harthagrepa, *f. Nor.* Teu. hard grip, 420

Harthaknut, *m. Dan.* Teu. firm hill, 420

Hartrich, *m. Ger.* Teu. firm ruler, 421

Hartmod, *m. Ger.* Teu. firm spirit, 421

Hartmund, *m. Ger.* Teu. firm protection, 421

Hartwig, *m. Ger.* Teu. firm war, 421

Harvey, *m. Eng.* Kelt. bitter, 281

Hasli, m. Swiss, Heb. grace of the Lord, 15

Hasting, *m. Dan.* Teu. swift, 402

Hati, f. Swiss, Gr. pure, 123

Hatili, f. Swiss, Gr. pure, 123

Hatto, *m. Ger.* Teu. Hessian, 432

Hatty, f. Eng. Teu. home rule, 310

Hauk, *m. Ice.* Teu. hawk, 344

Hauleik, *m. Nor.* Teu. sport of thought, 354

Havisia, *f. Lat.* Teu. war refuge, 305

Havoys, *f. Eng.* Teu. war refuge, 305

Hawoise, *f. Eng.* Teu. war refuge, 305

Haymo, m. Eng. Teu. home, 311

Haymon, m. Eng. Teu. home, 311

Hazzo, *m. Ger.* Teu. Hessian, 422

Hazzy, m. Eng. Zend. venerable king, 57

Hector, *m. Eng.* Gr. defender, 74

Heddo, m. Fris. Teu. war, 305

Hedinn, *m. Nor.* Teu. fury, 305

Hedviga, *f. Hung.* war refuge, 305

Hedviga, *f. Fr.* war refuge, 305

Hedwig, *f. Ger.* Teu. war refuge, 305

Heerdegen, *m. Ger.* Teu. warrior blade, 351, 417

Heimbert, m. Ger. Teu. home bright, 311

Heimirich, *m. Ger.* Teu. home ruler, 309

Heimrad, m. Ger. Teu. home council, 309

Heimrich, m. Ger. Teu. home rule, 310

Hein, m. Ger. Teu. home rule, 310

Heine, m. Ger. Teu. home rule, 310

Heinel, m. Ger. Teu. home rule, 310

Heinrich, *m. Ger.* Teu. home rule, 310

Heintje, m. Dutch, Teu. home rule, 310

Heintz, m. Ger. Teu. home rule, 310

Hejba, f. Lus. Heb. life, 11

HEKTOR, *m. Ger.* Gr. defender, 74

Helbing, m. Ger. Teu. half, 431

Helaine, *f. Eng.* Gr. light, 68

Helen, *f. Scot.* Gr. light, 68

HELENA, *f. Port. Eng. Span.* Gr. light, 68

Helène, *f. Fr.* Gr. light, 68

Helenka, f. Russ. Gr. light, 68

Helewise, *f. Eng.* Teu. famous holiness, 405

Helfrich, *m. Ger.* helping ruler, 420

HELGA, *f. Nor.* Teu. holy, 403

Helie, *m. Fr.* Heb. God the Lord, 36

Helier, *m. Fr.* Lat. cheerful, 280

HELGI, *m. Nor.* Teu. holy, 403

Heliodorus, *m. Lat.* Gr. sun's gift, 67

Heliogabalus, *m. Lat.* Gr. sun's gift, 67

Helier, m. Jersey, Lat. cheerful, 191, 280

HELMAR, *m. Ger.* Teu. helmeted warrior, 351

HELMBOLD, *m. Ger.* Teu. helmed prince, 351

HELMERICH, *m. Ger.* Teu. helmet king, 351

HELMICH, *m. Ger.* Teu. helmet, 351

Helmhart, *m. Ger.* Teu. firm helmet, 351

HELMTAC, *m. Ger.* Teu. helmet day, 351

Helmut, *m. Ger.* Teu. helmet rage, 351

Helmine, f. Ger. Teu. will helmet, 351

Helmold, m. Ger. Teu. helmet power, 351

HELOISE, *f. Fr.* Teu. famous holiness, 405

Helsa, f. Dan. Ger. Heb. God's oath, 35

Hendrik, *m. Dan. Dutch,* Teu. home rule, 310

Hendrika, *f. Dutch,* Teu. home rule, 310

Hendrijshka, m. Lus. Gr. man, 86

Henghist, m. A.S. Teu. horse, 340

Hennike, m. Ger. Teu. home ruler, 309

Henning, *m. Ger.* Teu. home ruler, 309

Henny, *f. Eng.* Teu. home ruler, 310

Henri, *m. Fr.* Teu. home rule, 310

HENRIETTA, *f. Eng.* Teu. home rule, 310

Henriette, *f. Fr. Ger.* Teu. home ruler, 310

Henrika, f. Swed. Teu. home ruler, 310

Henriot, m. Fr. Teu. home ruler, 310

Henrique, m. Port. Teu. home ruler, 310

Henriqueta, f. Port. Teu. home ruler, 310

Henry, *m. Eng.* Teu. home ruler, 310

Henryketa, f. Pol. Teu. home ruler, 310

Henryk, *m. Pol.* Teu. home ruler, 310

HEORUWARD, *m. A.S.* sword guardian, 351

Hephzibah, *f. Eng.* Heb. my delight is in her, 49

Hepsy, f. Am. Heb. my delight is in her, 49

Heraclius, *m. Lat.* Gr. noble fame, 63

Heraclidas, *m. Lat.* Gr. noble fame, 63

Heracleonas, *m. Lat.* Gr. noble fame, 63

HERAKLES, *m. Ger.* Gr. lordly fame, 63

Heraric, *m. Ger.* Teu. warrior king, 417

Herberge, *f. Fr.* Teu. warrior protection, 417

Herbert, *m. Eng.* Teu. bright warrior, 417

Herbjorn, *m. Nor.* Teu. warrior bear, 417

Herbrand, *m. Nor.* Teu. warrior sword, 417

Herchenhold, *m. Ger.* Teu. sacredly firm, 329

Hercule, *m. Eng.* Gr. lordly fame, 63

Hercules, *m. Eng.* Gr. lordly fame, 63

Herdegen, *m. Ger.* Teu. warrior blade, 351, 417

Hertag, m. Ger. Teu. army day, 351, 417

Heremon, *m. Erse,* Kelt. 241

Hereward, *m. Eng.* Teu. sword guardian, 351

HERUWULF, *m. Ger.* Teu. sword wolf, 351

Hergils, *m. Ger.* Teu. warrior pledge, 417

Heribert, *m. Fr.* Teu. warrior bright, 417

Heribold, *m. Ger.* Teu. warrior prince, 417

Herimar, *m. Ger.* Teu. warrior fame, 417

HERIOLD, *m. Ger.* Teu. warrior power, 417

HERJOLF, *m. Nor.* Teu. warrior wolf, 417

HERLAUG, *f. Nor.* Teu. warrior drink, 417

HERLEIF, *m. Nor.* Teu. warrior love relic, 417

HERLEIK, *m. Nor.* Teu. warrior sport, 417

Herluin, m. Fr. Teu. warrior friend (?), 417

Hermagoras, m. Gr. assembly of Hermes, 71

Herma, Swiss, Teu. public, 327

HERMAN, *m. Ger.* Teu. public army man, 327

HERMANGILD, *m. Goth.* Teu. public pledge, 327

HERMANFRIED, *m. Ger.* Teu. public peace, 327

Hermanfroy, *m. Fr.* Teu. public peace, 327

HERMANRICH, *m. Ger.* Teu. public rule, 327

HERMESIND, *f. Goth.* Teu. public strength, 328

HERMES, *f. Lat.* Gr. of the earth, 71

HERMIA, *f. Eng.* Gr. of Hermes, 71

Hermine, *f. It.* Lat. lordly, 147, 327

HERMINIUS, *m. Lat.* lordly, 147, 327

HERMIONE, *f. Lat.* Gr. of Hermes, 71

Hermolaus, *m. Lat.* Gr. Hermes' people, 71

Hermocrates, m. Lat. Gr. Hermes' judge, 71

Hermogenes, m. Lat. Gr. Hermes' descendant, 351

Hermund, m. Nor. Teu. army protection, 351

Hernan, m. Span. Teu. adventuring life, 433

Hernanda, f. Span. Teu. adventuring life, 433

Hernando, m. Span. Teu. adventuring life, 433

Hero, *f. Eng.* Gr. lady, 63

Herod, *m. Eng.* Gr. of a hero, 63

Herodias, *m. Eng.* Gr. of a hero, 63

Herodotus, *m. Eng.* Gr. noble gift, 63

Herulf, *m. Nor.* Teu. army wolf, 351

Hervé, *m. Fr.* Kelt. bitter, 281

Herwin, m. Ger. Teu. army friend, 416

Hery, m. Bret. Teu. home ruler, 310

Hesekiel, *m. Ger.* Heb. strength of God, 48

Hesje, f. Dutch, Pers. star, 57

Hester, *f. Eng.* Pers. star, 57

Hesthera, *f. Lat.* Pers. star, 57

Hezekiah, *m. Ger.* Heb. strength of the Lord, 48

Hetty, f. Eng. Pers. star, 57

Heva, f. Lat. Heb. life, 11

Hew, m. Eng. Kelt. mind, 353

HEZEKIAH, *m. Eng.* Heb. strength of the Lord, 48

HIALFREK, *m. Nor.* Teu. helping ruler, 420

HIALPERIK, *m. Frank.* Teu. helping ruler, 420

Hierom, *m. Eng.* Gr. holy name, 89

Hieronim, *m. Pol.* Gr. holy name, 89

Hieronimo, *m. It.* Gr. holy name, 89

Hieronimus, *m. Lat. Ger.* Gr. holy name, 89

Hieronôme, *m. Fr.* Gr. holy name, 89

Hieronomette, *f. Fr.* Gr. holy name, 89

Hieronymus, *Lat.* Gr. holy name, 89

Hics, m. Bav. Heb. gift of the Lord, 15

Hiesel, m. Bav. Heb. gift of the Lord, 15

Hilaire, *m. Fr.* Lat. cheerful, 191

Hilaria, *f. Eng.* Lat. cheerful, 191

Hilariao, *m. Port.* Lat. cheerful, 191

Hilario, *m. Sp. Port.* Lat. cheerful, 191

Hilarion, *m. Fr.* Lat. cheerful, 191

HILARIUS, *m. Lat.* Lat. cheerful, 191

Hilary, *m. f. Eng.* Lat. cheerful, 191

HILDA, *f. Eng.* Teu. battle maid, 317

Hildebert, *m. Frank.* Teu. battle bright, 318

Hildaberta, *f. Ger.* Teu. battle bright, 318

HILDEBJORG, *f. Nor.* Teu. battle maid protection, 318

HILDEBOLD, *m. Ger.* Teu. battle prince, 318

Hildebrand, *m. Eng.* Teu. battle sword, 318

HILDEGAR, *m. Ger.* Teu. battle spear, 318

Hildegarde, *f. Ger.* Teu. battle maid protection, 318

HILDEGUND, *f. Nor.* Teu. battle maid's war, 318

HILDEGUNNA, *f. Ice.* Teu. battle maid's war, 318

Hildelildis, *f. Lat.* Teu. battle maid, 318

Hildemand, *m. Ger.* Teu. battle man, 318

Hildemunda, *m. Ger.* Teu. battle maid's protection, 318

Hilderich, *m. Ger.* Teu. battle rule, 318

Hilderik, *m. Frank.* Teu. battle rule, 318

Hildert, f. Fries. Teu. battle council, 318

HILDEWARD, *m. Frank.* Teu. battle ward, 318

Hildewig, *f. Frank.* Teu. battle maid war, 318

Hildiridur, *f. Ice.* Teu. battle hastener, 318

Hildrad, m. Ger. Teu. battle council, 318

Hilduara, *f. Nor.* Teu. battle prudence, 318

HILDUR, *f. Nor.* Teu. battle maid, 318

Hillert, m. Fr. Teu. battle bright, 318

HILPERIK, *m. Frank.* Teu. battle rule, 318

Hilram, m. Ger. Teu. battle raven, 318

Hilza, f. Lus. Heb. God's oath, 35

Hilzbeta, Lus. Heb. God's oath, 35

Hilzizka, Lus. Heb. God's oath, 35

Hiltrude, *f. Ger.* Teu. battle maiden, 319

Hime, m. Fris. Heb. the Lord will judge, 38

Himmeltrud, f. Ger. Teu. heavenly maid.

Hinmarc, m. Fr. Teu. Ing's fame, 325

Hinko, m. Ger. Teu. Ing, 325

Hinrik, m. Fris. Swed. Teu. home rule, 310

Hiob, m. Ger. Heb. persecuted, 20

HIORDIS, *f.* sword spirit, 351

HIORGEIR, *m.* sword war, 351

HIORLEIF, *m.* sword relic, 351

HIORULF, *m.* sword wolf, 351

HIPPODAMUS, *m. Gr.* horse tamer, 78

HIPPODAMEIA, *f. Gr.* horse tamer, 78

Hippolyt, *m. Ger.* Gr. horse destruction, 78

Hippolyta, *f. Eng.* Gr. horse destruction, 78

Hippolyte, m. Fr. Gr. horse destruction, 78

HIPPOLYTOS, *m.* Gr. horse destruction, 78

Hippolytus, *m. Eng. Lat.* Gr. horse destruction, 78

Hirsch, m. Ger. Teu. stag.

Hirus, m. Pol. Gr. with a holy name, 89

HJALMAR, *m. Nor.* helmed warrior, 351

Hjarrande, *Nor.* Teu. sword horse, 351

HLOD, *m. Frank.* Teu. famous, 405

HLODIO, *m. Frank.* Teu. famous, 405

HLODHERI, *m. Frank.* Teu. famous army, 405

HLODHILD, *f. Frank.* Teu. famous battle maid, 405

HLODMAR, *m. Frank.* Teu. loud fame, 405

HLODWIG, *m. Frank.* Teu. famous war, 405

Hob, m. Eng. Teu. bright fame, 405

Hobbie, m. Scot. Teu. bright stone, 417

Hocke, m. Dutch. Teu. mind, 353

Hodaiah, *m. Eng.* Heb. praise, 21

Hodge, m. Eng. Teu. spear of fame, 390

Hoel, *m. Welsh*, Kelt. lordly, 276

Hogni, *m. Dan.* Teu. deft (?), 364

Holda, *f. Ger.* Teu. gentle, 214

Holcx, m. Lus. Gr. helper of men, 85

Holger, *m. Dan.* Teu. holy, 403

Holla, *f. Ger.* Teu. faithful, 214

Homfroi, m. Fr. Teu. support of peace, 350

Honor, *f. Eng.* Lat. honour, 190

Honora, *f. Ir.* Lat. honour, 190

Honoratus, *m. Lat.* honoured, 190

Honoré, *m. Fr.* Lat. honoured, 190

Honoria, *f. Eng.* Lat. honourable, 190

Honorine, *f. Fr.* Lat. honour, 190

Honorius, *m. Lat.* honourable, 190

Horace, *m. Fr. Eng.* Lat. 148

Horacio, *m. Span.* Lat. 148

Horatia, *f. Eng.* Lat. 148

Horatio, *m. Eng.* Lat. 148

Horatius, *m. Lat.* 148

Horatz, *m. Ger.* Lat. 148

Hordaknut, m. Dan. Teu. firm hill, 420

Horsa, *m. A.S.* Teu. horse, 340

Horta, f. Lus. Gr. gift of God, 102

Hortense, *f. Fr. Lat.* gardener, 147

Hortensia, *f. Ger. Eng.* Lat. gardener, 147

Hortensius, *m. Lat.* gardener, 147

Hortija, f. Lus. Gr. gift of God, 102

Hosch, m. Walloon, thought, 353

Hoscha, f. Lus. Lat. bear, 411

Hoshea, *m. Eng.* Heb. salvation, 36

Houerv, *m. Bret.* Kelt. bitter, 282

Hovleik, *m. Nor.* Teu. sport of thought, 354

Hrafen, *m. Icc.* Teu. raven, 344

Hrafenhildur, *f. Ice.* Teu. raven battle maid, 344

Hrafenkjell, *m. Ice.* Teu. raven kettle, 344

Hrista, m. Ill. Gr. Christian, 105

Hrodbern, *m. Nor.* Teu. famous bear, 341

Hrodhild, *f. Ger. Nor.* Teu. famous heroine, 393

Hrodfrid, *f. Ger. Nor.* Teu. famous peace, 393

Hroi, m. Teu. Nor. famous, 393

Hrodny, *f. Teu.* Nor. famous freshness, 393

Hrollaug, famous liquor, 393

Hrollaf, m. Teu. Nor. relic of fame, 393

Hrodsind, *f. Nor.* Teu. famous strength, 393

Hrodstein, *m. Nor.* Teu. famous stone, 393

Hrudo, *Nor.* Teu. fame, 393

Hroar, m. Nor. Teu. famous spear, 393

Hrolf, m. Nor. Teu. wolf of fame, 393

Hrosbert, *m. Ger.* Teu. bright horse, 341

Hroshelm, *m. Ger.* Teu. horse helmet, 341

Hrosmund, *f. m.* Teu. famed protection, 341

Hroswith, *f. Lomb.* Teu. horse strength, 341

Hrosswald, *m. Nor.* Teu. horse power, 341

Hrothulf, *m. Nor.* famous wolf, 393

Hrothgar, *A.S.* spear of fame, 393

Hrothmund, *m. Nor.* Teu. famous protection, 393

Hrothrekr, *m. Nor.* Teu. famous king, 393

Hrorekr, *m. Nor.* Teu. famous king, 393

Hrothulf, *m. Nor.* Teu. famous wolf, 393

Hruodgar, *m. Ger.* Teu. famed spear, 393

Hruodgjer, *m. Nor.* Teu. famed spear, 393

Hruodland, *m. Frank.* Teu. fame of land, 393

Hruodmar, *m. Nor.* Teu. famed renown, 393

Hruodperacht, *m. Nor.* Teu. bright fame, 393

Hruoderich, *m. Nor.* Teu. famed rule, 393

Hrudrolf, *m. Nor.* Teu. wolf of fame, 393

Hu, *m. Cym.* Kelt. mind, 226, 353

Huard, *m. Ger.* Teu. firm in mind, 353

Hubbard, m. Eng. Teu. mind bright, 354

Hubert, *m. Eng. Fr.* Teu. mind bright, 354

Huberto, *m. It.* Teu. mind bright, 354

Hucpraht, *m. Ger.* Teu. 354

Hues, *m. Fr.* Teu. mind, 226, 353

Huet, *m. Fr.* Teu. Kelt. (?) mind, 226, 353

Huette, f. Fr. Teu. Kelt. mind, 226, 353

Hugh, *m. Eng.* Teu. mind, 226, 353

Hugi, *m. Nor.* Teu. mind, 226, 353

Hugibald, *m. Fr.* Teu. mind prince, 353

Hugibert, *m. Ger.* Teu. mind bright, 353

Hugihardt, *m. Ger.* Teu. firm mind, 353

Hugleik, *m. Nor.* Teu. sport of the mind, 353

Hugo, *m. Span. Lat. Port.* Teu. mind, 226, 353

Hugoleik, *m. Frank.* Teu. sport of the mind, 353

Hugolin, *m. Fr.* Teu. mind, 352

Hugr, *m. Nor.* Teu. mind, 353

Hugues, *m. Fr.* Teu. mind, 353

Huguenin, m. Fr. Teu. mind, 353

Hugur, *m. Nor.* Teu. mind, 353

Huig, *m. Dutch,* Teu. thought, 353

Huldr, *f. Swed.* Teu. muffled, 214

Hulla, *f. Swed.* Teu. muffled, 214

Humbert, *m. Fr.* Teu. support of brightness, 350

Humfrey, *m. Eng.* Teu. support of peace, 350

Humfreid, *m. Ger.* Teu. support of peace, 350

Humphrey, *m. Eng.* Teu. support of peace, 350

Humps, m. Eng. Teu. support of peace, 350

Hunaud, m. Fr. Teu. support of power, 350

Hund, *m. Dan.* Teu. dog, 336

Hundolf, dog wolf, 336

Hungerdur, *f. Nor.* Teu. supporting maiden, 351

Hungus, m. Scot. Kelt. excellent virtue, 242

Hunibert, m. Nor. Teu. support of brightness, 350

Hunnerich, *m. Ger.* Teu. support ruler, 350

Hunold, *m. Fr.* Teu. support of power, 350

Huon, m. Fr. Teu. mind, 226, 352

Huprecht, m. Lus. Teu. bright fame, 354

Hutcheon, *m. Scot.* Teu. mind, 226, 353

Hyacinth, *m. Ir.* Gr. purple, 81

Hyacinthe, *f. Fr.* Gr. purple, 81

Hyacinthie, f. Ger. Gr. purple, 81

Hygelac, *m. A.G.S.* Teu. sport of thought, 353

Hynek, m. Bohm. Lat. fiery, 194

Hystaspes, *m. Gr.* Zend. possessing horses.

Hywel, *m. Welsh,* Kelt. lordly, 276

Hywgi, *m. Welsh,* Teu. mind, 226

I

Iachimo, m. It. Heb. supplanter, 17

Iago, m. Span. Heb. supplanter, 17

Ian, m. Scot. Heb. grace of the Lord, 45

Iarngard, *m. Nor.* iron defence, 348

Ib, f. Eng. Phœn. oath of Baal, 35

Ibald, m. Ger. Teu. bow prince, 326

Ibbot, f. Scot. Teu. oath of Baal, 35

Ibert, m. Ger. Teu. bright bow, 326

Ibraheem, *m. Arab.* Heb. father of nations, 12

Ichabod, m. Eng. Heb. the glory is departed, 2

Ida, *f. m. Ger. Eng.* Teu. happy, 411

Ida, *f. Erse,* Kelt. thirsty, 224

Ide, *m. Ger.* Teu. rich, 376

Idette, f. Flem. Teu. rich, 376

Idonea, f. Eng. Teu. she who ever works, 307

Iduberge, f. Fr. Teu. happy protection, 378

Idune, *f. Ger. Nor.* Teu. she who works, 307

Iggerich, m. Fris. Teu. awful king, 323

Ignace, *m. Russ.* Lat. fiery, 194

Ignacij, *m. Slov.* Lat. fiery, 194

Ignacio, *m. Rom.* Lat. fiery, 194

Ignacy, *m. Pol.* Lat. fiery, 194

Ignascha, m. Russ. Lat. fiery, 194

Ignatie, *m. Wallach.* Lat. fiery, 194

Ignatij, *m. Russ.* Lat. fiery, 194

Ignatius, *m. Eng.* Lat. fiery, 194

Ignaz, *m. Ger.* Lat. fiery, 194

Ignazia, *m. Bav.* Lat. fiery, 194

Ignazio, *m. It.* Lat. fiery, 194

Ignes, *f. Span.* Gr. pure, 119

Igor, m. Russ. Gr. husbandman, 115
Ike, m. Fris. Teu. awful firmness, 323
Ikey, m. Eng. Heb. laughter, 41
Ilar, *m. Welsh*, Gr. cheerful, 191
Ilaria, *m. Russ.* Lat. cheerful, 191
Ilareeij, *Russ.* Lat. cheerful, 191
Ilario, *m. It.* Lat. cheerful, 191
Ilarion, *m. Russ.* Lat. cheerful, 191
Ildefonso, *m. Span.* Teu. eager for battle, 320
Ildefonsus, *m. Span.* Teu. eager for battle, 320
Ilderico, m. It. Teu. battle rule, 320
Iliska, f. Slov. Lat. downy bearded, 149
Ilja, m. Russ. Heb. God, the Lord, 36
Ilona, Hung. Gr. light, 68
Ilse, f. Ger. Heb. God's oath, 35
Ilse, f. Ger. Teu. noble cheer, 411
Imagina, f. Ger.
IMMANUEL, *m. Eng.* Heb. God with us, 36
Imogen, f. Eng. 233
Incarnaçion, *f. Span.* Lat. incarnation, 30
Indes, Lett. home ruler, 310
Indrikis, Lett. home ruler, 310
Indus, Lett. home ruler, 310
Indride, m. Nor. chief rider, 323
Iñes, *f. Span.* Gr. pure, 119
Inesila, f. Span. Gr. pure, 119
Iñaz, *Port.* Gr. pure, 119
Ing, m. Nor. Teu. Ing, 324
Ingebera, *f. Nor.* Teu. Ing's bear, 325
Ingeberge, *f. Nor.* Teu. Ing's protection, 325
INGEBJERG, *f. Nor.* Teu. Ing's protection, 325
INGEBRAND, *m. A.S.* Teu. Ing's sword, 325
INGEGJERD, *f. Nor.* Teu. Ing's guard, 325
Ingeltram, *m. Eng.* Teu. Ing's raven, 325
INGELIEF, *m. Nor.* Teu. Ing's relic, 325
INGEMUND, *m. Nor.* Teu. Ing's protection, 325
INGERIDUR, *f. Nor.* Teu. Ing's eagerness, 325
INGHILD, *f. Nor.* Teu. Ing's battle maid, 325

Ingjard, *m. Nor.* Teu. Ing's spear, 325
Ingoberga, *f. Lat.* Teu. Ing's protection, 325
INGRIMR, *m. Nor.* Teu. helmeted Ing, 325
Ingram, m. Eng. Teu. Ing's raven, 325
INGULF, *m. Eng.* Teu. Ing's wolf, 325
Ingulphus, *m. Lat.* Teu. Ing's wolf, 325
INGUNNA, *f. Nor.* Teu. Ing's maiden, 325
INGVE, *m. Nor.* Teu. Ing's consecration, 325
Ingvaldr, *m. Nor.* Teu. Ing's power, 325
Ingvar, *m. Nor.* Teu. Ing's warrior, 325
INGVECHILD, *f. Nor.* Teu. Ing's battle maid, 325
Iñiga, *f. m. Span.* Gr. fiery, 194
Iigo, *m. Span.* Gr. fiery, 194
Innocent, *m. Eng.* Lat. harmless, 193
INNOCENTIUS, *m. Lat.* harmless, 193
Innocenz, *m. Ger.* Lat. harmless, 193
Innocenzie, *f. Ger. Lat.* harmless, 193
Innocenzio, *m. It.* Lat. harmless, 193
Innokentij, *m. Russ.* Lat. harmless, 193
Iola, m. Bret. Lat. downy bearded, 149
Iolo, m. Welsh, Lat. downy bearded, 140
Ippolita, *f. It.* Gr. horse destruction, 78
Ippolito, *m. It.* Gr. horse destruction, 78
Irene, *f. Eng. It. Fr.* Gr. peace, 113
Irenæus, *m. Lat.* Gr. peaceful, 113
IRING, *m. Thuringian*, Teu. 327
Irmanfrit, *m. Ger.* Teu. public peace, 327
Irnvrit, m. Thu. Teu. public peace, 327
IRUNG, *m.* bright, 416
Isa, f. Ger. Teu. iron, 348
Isaac, *m. Fr. Eng.* Heb. laughter, 14
Isaak, *m. Russ. Ger.* Heb. laughter, 14
Isabeau, *f. Fr.* Heb. oath of Baal, 35
Isabel, *f. Span. Eng. Port.* Heb. oath of Baal, 35

Isabelinha, f. Port. Heb. oath of Baal, 35

Isabella, *f. It.* Heb. oath of Baal, 35

Isabelle, *f. Fr.* Heb. oath of Baal, 35

Isaiah, *m. Eng.* Heb. salvation of the Lord, 48

ISAMBART, *m. Fr.* Teu. iron bright, 348

Isambaus, *m. Fr.* Teu. iron prince, 348

Isbel, f. Scot. Heb. God's oath, 35

Isbrand, m. Nor. Teu. iron sword, 348

Isebald, m. Ger. Teu. iron prince, 348

Isenbrand, m. Ger. Teu. iron sword, 348

ISENGARD, *m. Ger.* Teu. iron defence, 348

ISENGRIM, *m. Ger.* Teu. iron mask, 348

Isenhard, *m. Ger.* Teu. iron firm, 348

Isculte, f. Fr. Kelt. fair, 275

ISFUNDEAR, *m. Pers.* Zend.

Isgar, m. Ger. Teu. iron spear, 348

ISGIER, *m. Nor.* Teu. iron spear, 348

Ishmael, *m. Eng.* Heb. heard of God, 2

Isidor, *m. Span. Ger.* Gr. strong gift, 103

Isadora, *f. Span.* Gr. strong gift, 103

Isidore, *f. m. Fr.* Gr. strong gift, 103

Isidoro, *m. It.* Gr. strong gift, 103

ISIDORUS, *m. Lat.* Gr. strong gift, 103

Ising, *m. Nor.* Teu. son of iron, 348

Iskender, *m. Turk.* Gr. helper of men, 85

Isobel, *f. Scot.* Heb. oath of God, 35

Isolda, *f. It.* Kelt. fair, 275

Isolde, *f. Eng.* Kelt. fair, 275

Isolt, *f. Eng.* Kelt. fair, 275

ISRID, *f. Nor.* Teu. iron vehemence, 348

Issachar, *m. Eng.* Heb. hire, 7

Issaak, *m. Russ.* Heb. laughter, 14

Istvan, *m. Hung.* Gr. crown, 96

ISULF, *m. Nor.* Teu. iron wolf, 348

Ita, *f. Erse,* Kelt. thirsty, 224

Itzig, m. Pol. Heb. laughter, 14

Ivan, *m. Russ.* Heb. grace of God, 45

Ivancica, f. Russ. Gr. Teu. grace of the Lord, 46

Ivanjuscha, m. Russ. Heb. grace of the Lord, 45

Ivanku, f. Bulg. Heb. grace of the Lord, 46

Ivanna, f. Russ. Heb. grace of the Lord, 46

IVAR, *m. Dan.* Teu. archer, 325

IVBALD, *m. Ger.* Teu. bow prince, 325

IVBERT, *m. Ger.* Teu. bright bow, 325

Iver, *m. Dan.* Teu. archer, 325

Ives, *m. Eng.* Teu. archer, 325

Ivka, f. Ill. Heb. grace of the Lord, 45

Ivo, *m. Eng.* Teu. archer, 325

Ivon, *m. Bret.* Teu. bow bearer, 325

Ivor, *m. Scot.* Teu. bow bearer, 325

Ivory, *m. Irish,* 325

Izaak, *m. Eng.* Heb. laughter, 15

Izabela, f. Pol. Heb. oath of Baal, 35

Izabella, f. Hung. Heb. oath of Baal, 35

Izod, *f. Eng.* Kelt. fair, 275

Izoldo, *f. Eng.* Kelt. fair, 275

Izydor, m. Pol. Gr. strong gift, 103

J

Jaak, m. Esth. Heb. supplanter, 17

Jaap, m. Dutch, Heb. supplanter, 17

Jaapje, f. Dutch, Heb. supplanter, 17

Jabez, *m. Eng.* Heb. sorrow, 2

Jachym, m. Pol. Heb. the Lord's judgment, 37

Jacim, Slov. Ill. the Lord's judgment, 37

Jacinta, *f. Span.* purple, 81

Jacintha, *f. Eng.* Gr. purple, 81

Jacinthe, *m. Fr.* Gr. purple, 81

Jack, *m. Eng.* Heb. grace of God, 45

Jackel, m. Bav. Heb. supplanter, 17

Jacob, *m. Eng. Fr.* Heb. supplanter, 1, 17

Jacobéa, f. Fr. Heb. supplanter, 17

Jacobello, m. It. Heb. supplanter, 17

Jacobina, *f. Scot.* Heb. supplanter, 17

Jacobine, *f. Ger.* Heb. supplanter, 17

Jacobo, *m. It. Span.* Heb. supplanter, 17

Jacobus, *m. Lat.* Heb. supplanter, 17

Jacopo, *m. It.* Heb. supplanter, 17

Jacot, m. Fr. Heb. supplanter, 17

Jacov, m. Russ. Heb. supplanter, 17

Jacovina, f. Russ. Heb. supplanter, 17

Jacques, *m. Fr.* Heb. supplanter, 17

Jacqueline, *f. Fr.* Heb. supplanter, 17
Jacqueminot, m. Fr. Heb. supplanter, 17
Jacquetta, f. Eng. Heb. supplanter, 17
Jacquette, f. Fr. Heb. supplanter, 17
Jaddæus, *m. Lat.* Heb. known of God, 8
Jaddua, *m. Eng.* Heb. known of God, 8
Jadwiga, *f. Pol.* Teu. war refuge, 305
Jaga, m. Eng. Heb. supplanter, 17
Jaggeli, m. Bav. Heb. supplanter, 17
JAGODA, *m. Slav.* Slav. strawberry, 438
Jahus, *m. Dutch,* Heb. grace of the Lord, 45
Jaime, m. Aram. Heb. supplanter, 17
Jaka, m. Slov. Heb. supplanter, 17
Jakab, m. Hung. Heb. supplanter, 17
Jako, m. Ill. Heb. supplanter, 17
Jakob, *m. Esth. Dutch, Ger. Pol.* Heb. supplanter, 17
Jakoba, *f. Dutch, Ger.* Heb. supplanter, 17
Jakobos, *m. Gr.* Heb. supplanter, 17
Jakobine, *f. Ger.* Heb. supplanter, 17
Jakov, m. Russ. Ill. Wall. Heb. supplanter, 17
Jakova, f. Hung. Heb. supplanter, 17
Jakobika, f. m. Ill. Heb. supplanter, 17
Jaffrez, *m. Bret.* Teu, God's peace, 287
James, *m. Eng.* Heb. supplanter, 17
Jamesina, *f. Eng.* Heb. supplanter, 17
Jamie, m Scot. Heb. supplanter, 17
Jan, m. Nor. Dutch, Eng. Heb. grace of the Lord, 45
Jannik, m. Bret. Heb. grace of the Lord, 45
Janas, m. Lett. Heb. grace of the Lord, 45
Janak, Pol. Heb. grace of the Lord, 45
Janckzi, m. Hung. Heb. grace of the Lord, 45
Jane, *f. Eng.* Heb. grace of the Lord, 46
Janck, m. Scot. Heb. grace of the Lord, 45
Jancsika, f. Slov. Heb. grace of the Lord, 46
Janet, f. Scot. Heb. grace of the Lord, 46

Janez, m. Slov. Heb. grace of the Lord, 45
Janja, f. Serv. Gr. pure, 119
Janke, m. Lus. Heb. grace of the Lord, 45
Janne, m. Dan. Heb. grace of the Lord, 45
Jannedik, f. Bret. Heb. grace of the Lord, 45
Janos, m. Hung. Heb. grace of the Lord, 45
Janotje, f. Dutch, Heb. grace of the Lord, 46
Jantina, f. Dutch, Heb. grace of the Lord, 46
Jantje, f. Dutch, Heb. grace of the Lord, 46
JANUARIUS, *m. Lat.* January born, 171
Janus, m. Dutch, Lat. from Adria, 156
Jaques, *m. Fr.* Heb. supplanter, 17
Jaquette, *f. Fr.* Heb. supplanter, 17
JARLAR, *m. Swed.* Heb. earl warrior, 333
JAROMIR, *m. Bohm.* Slav. firm peace, 333
JAROPOLK, *m. Russ.* Slav. firm peace, 333
JAROSLAV, *f. Russ.* Slav. firm peace.
Jarratt, *m. Eng.* Teu. spear firm, 369
Jartrud, *m. Nor.* Teu. spear truth, 368
Jascha, m. Russ. Heb. supplanter, 17
Jaschenka, m. Russ. Heb. supplanter, 17
Jaschis, m. Lett. Heb. addition, 23
Jaseps, *m. Lett.* Heb. addition, 23
Jasper, *m. Eng.* Pers. treasure master, 211
Jatmund, *m. Dan.* Teu. rich protection, 377
Jaubert, m. Fr. Teu. good bright, 288
Jauffré, m. Prov. Teu. God's peace, 287
Jantje, m. Dutch, Heb. grace of the Lord, 45
Javotte, f. Fr. Kelt. white stream, 270
Jaward, *m. Nor.* Teu. rich guardian, 378
Jayme, *m. Sp. Port.* Heb. supplanter, 17

f

Jeames, m. Eng. Heb. supplanter, 17

Jean, *m. Fr.* Heb. grace of the Lord, 45

Jean, *f. Scot.* Heb. grace of the Lord, 46

Jeanne, *f. Fr.* Heb. grace of the Lord, 46

Jeannette, f. Fr. Heb. grace of the Lord, 46

Jeannetton, f. Fr. Heb. grace of the Lord, 46

Jeannot, m. Fr. Heb. grace of the Lord, 45

Jebbe, f. Fris. Teu. wild boar battle maid, 337

Jeconiah, m. Eng. Lat. appointed of the Lord, 38

Jedert, f. Slov. Teu. war maid, 368

Jedrzej, m. Pol. Gr. manly, 86

Jeffrey, *m. Eng.* Teu. good peace, 287

Jefronissa, f. Russ. Gr. mirth, 72

Jehan, *m. Fr.* Heb. grace of the Lord, 45

Jehanne, *f. Fr.* Heb. grace of the Lord, 46

Jehoash, given by the Lord, 37

Jehoram, *m. Eng.* Heb. the Lord is exalted, 37

Jehoiachin, *m. Eng.* Heb. appointed of the Lord, 37

Jehoiada, *m. Eng.* Heb. known of God, 37

Jehoiakim, *m. Eng.* Heb. the Lord will judge, 38

Jehu, *m. Eng.* Heb. the Lord is He, 38

Jeka, m. Lett. Heb. supplanter, 17

Jekups, m. Lett. Heb. supplanter, 17

Jela, f. Serv. Gr. light, 68

Jelena, f. Slov. Gr. light, 68

Jelica, f. Russ. Slov. Gr. light, 68

Jelisavka, f. Serv. Heb. God's oath, 35

Jelissaveta, f. Russ. Heb. God's oath, 35

Jellon, m. Scot. Lat. downy bearded, 150

Jemmy, m. Eng. Heb. supplanter, 17

Jemima, *f. Eng.* Heb. dove, 26

Jendriska, f. Bohm. Teu. home ruler, 310

Jenkin, m. Eng. Heb. grace of the Lord, 45

Jennifer, *f. Corn.* Kelt. white wave, 270

Jenny, f. Eng. Heb. grace of the Lord, 46

Jenovefa, *m. Bret.* Kelt. white stream, 270

Jens, m. Dan. Heb. grace of the Lord, 45

Jeoffroi, *m. Fr.* Teu. divine peace, 288

Jeps, m. Lett. Heb. addition, 23

Jerassim, m. Russ. Gr. beloved, 113

Jerast, m. Russ. Gr. amiable, 113

Jera, f. Slov. Teu. war maid, 368

Jeremej, *m. Russ.* Heb. exalted of the Lord, 49

Jeremiah, *m. Ger. Slov.* Heb. exalted of the Lord, 49

Jeremiah, m. Fr. Eng. Heb. exalted of the Lord, 49

Jeremias, *m. Fr. Eng.* Heb. exalted of the Lord, 49

Jeremie, *m. Fr. Wall.* Heb. exalted of the Lord, 49

Jeremija, *m. Russ. Serv.* Heb. exalted of the Lord, 49

Jeremy, *m. Eng.* Heb. exalted of the Lord, 49

Jerica, f. Slov. Teu. war maid, 368

Jerko, m. Serv. Gr. with a holy name, 89

Jermyn, *m. Eng.* Lat. German, 416

Jernej, m. Ill. Heb. son of furrows, 25

Jerolim, m. Serv. Gr. with holy name, 89

Jerom, *m. Ger.* Gr. holy name, 89

Jeromette, *f. Fr.* Gr. holy name, 89

Jerome, *m. Eng. Fr.* Gr. holy name, 89

Jeronimo, m. Port. Gr. with a holy name, 89

Jerram, *m. Eng.* Teu. war raven, 370

Jerry, *m. Eng.* Heb. exalted of the Lord, 49

Jervis, *m. Eng.* Teu. spear war, 369

Jervoise, m. Eng. Teu. spear war, 369

Jerzy, m. Pol. Gr. husbandman, 115

Jesaia, *m. Ger.* Heb. help of God, 49

Jesekijel, *m. Russ.* Heb. strength of God, 49

Jespers, *m. Lett.* Pers. treasure master, 211

Jeshua, *m. Eng.* Heb. the Lord my salvation, 37

Jessica, f. Eng. 46
Jesse, m. Eng. Heb. the Lord is, 46
Jessie, f. Scot. Heb. grace of the Lord, 46
Jettchen, f. Ger. Teu. home ruler, 310
Jette, f. Ger. Teu. home ruler, 310
Jettje, f. Dutch, Teu. home ruler, 310
Jeva, f. Serv. Gr. fair speech, 88
Jeva, f. Lett. Serv. Heb. life, 11
Jevan, Welsh, young warrior, 273
Jevva, f. Russ. Heb. life, 11
Jevchariz, m. Russ. Gr. happy hand, 87
Jevdoksia, f. Russ. Gr. happy glory, 88
Jevginnia, f. Russ. Gr. well born, 88
Jevginij, m. Russ. Gr. well born, 88
Jevfimija, f. Russ. Gr. fair fame, 88
Jevlalija, f. Russ. Gr. fair speech, 88
Jevstachij, m. Russ. Gr. fair harvest, 88
Jewa, f. Lith. Heb. life, 11
Jewele, f. Lett. Heb. life, 11
Jezia, m. Lett. Heb. supplanter, 17
Jill, f. Eng. Lat. downy beard, 150
Jillet, f. Eng. Lat. downy beard, 150
Jillian, f. Eng. Lat. downy beard, 150
Jitka, f. Pol. Heb. praise, 20
Jim, m. Eng. Heb. supplanter, 17
Jiri, m. Bohm. Gr. husbandman, 115
Jjewa, f. Lus. Heb. life, 11
Joa, m. Span. Heb. the Lord will judge, 37
Joachim, m. Eng. Heb. the Lord will judge, 37
Joachim, m. Russ. Eng. Fr. Heb. God will judge, 38
Joachime, f. Fr. Heb. God will judge, 37
Joahim, m. Slov. Heb. God will judge, 38
Joakim, m. Russ. Heb. God will judge, 38
Joan, f. Eng. Heb. the Lord's grace, 46
Joanna, f. Eng. Pol. Heb. the Lord's grace, 46
Joannes, m. Gr. Heb. the Lord's grace, 45
Joanico, m. Port. Heb. the Lord's grace, 45
Joaniniha, f. Port. Heb. the Lord's grace, 46

Joao, m. Port. Heb. the Lord's grace, 45
Joaozinho, m. Port. Heb. the Lord's grace, 45
Joaquim, *m. Span.* Heb. the Lord will judge, 37
Joaquin, *m. Span. Port.* Heb. the Lord will judge, 37
Joquina, *f. Port.* Heb. the Lord will judge, 37
Joash, *m. Eng.* Heb. given by the Lord, 38
Job, *m. Eng.* Heb. persecuted, 26
Jobs, m. Ger. Lat. sportive, 191
Jobst, m. Bav. Lat. sportive, 191
Jocelin, m. Fr. Eng. Lat. sportive, 191
Jochebed, *f. Eng.* Heb. person of merit, 27
Jocheli, m. Swiss, the Lord will judge, 37
Johann, *m. Bav.* Heb. the Lord will judge, 37
Jock, m. Scot. Heb. the Lord's grace, 45
Jock, m. Swiss, Heb. supplanter, 17
Jockel, m. Ger. Heb. supplanter, 17
Jockey, m. Eng. Heb. the Lord's grace, 45
Jocosa, f. Eng. Lat. merry, 191
Jocosus, *m. Lat.* merry, 191
Jodel, m. Bav. Lat. sportive, 191
Jodetel, m. Fr. Lat. sportive, 191
Jodoca, *f. Eng.* Lat. sportive, 191
Jodocus, *m. Lat.* sportive, 191
Jodoke, *f. Ger.* Lat. sportive, 191
Jodokus, *m. Ger.* Lat. sportive, 191
Joar, horse warrior, 341
Jodis, horse sprite, 341
Jofan, the Lord's grace, 45
Jofred, horse peace, 341
Jofrid, fair horse, 341
Jogeir, horse spear, 341
Jogrim, horse mask, 341
Jokell, horse kettle, 341
Joketyl, horse kettle, 341
Joreid, horse eagerness, 341
Jostein, horse stone, 341
Jorunna, horse lady, 341
Jornandes, Jordan, 39
Jøren, Nor. Teu. glittering man, 416
Jørund, *Nor.* Teu. glittering man, 416
Joel, *m. Eng.* Heb. strong willed, 50

Joe, m. Eng. Heb. addition, 23

Joeran, m. Dan. Gr. husbandman, 115

Jofa, m. Lapp. Heb. the Lord's grace, 45

Jofan, m. Lapp. Heb. the Lord's grace, 45

Jogg, m. Swiss, Heb. supplanter, 17

Joggeli, m. Swiss, Heb. supplanter, 17

Johan, *m. Swiss, Esth.* Heb. the Lord's grace, 45

Johanan, *Eng.* Heb. the Lord's grace, 45

Johanna, *f. Ger. Esth.* Heb. the Lord's grace, 46

Johanna, *f. Eng.* Heb. the Lord's grace, 46

Johanne, *f. Ger.* Heb. the Lord's grace, 46

JOHANNES, *m. Ger.* Heb. the Lord's grace, 45

John, *m. Eng.* Heb. the Lord's grace, 45

Johnnie, Scot. Heb. the Lord's grace, 45

Johnny, Eng. Heb. the Lord's grace, 45

Johum, Dan. Heb. the Lord will judge, 37

Joletta, *f. Eng.* Lat. violet, 206

Joliette, f. Fr. Lat. downy bearded, 150

Jompert, m. Fr. Teu. war splendour, 363

Jonah, *m. Eng.* Heb. dove, 26

Jonas, *m. Lat.* Heb. dove, 26

Jonaszus, *m. Lith.* Heb. dove, 26

Jonathan, *m. Eng.* Heb. the Lord's gift, 25

Jonelis, m. Lith. Heb. the Lord's grace, 45

Jonka, m. Lapp. Heb. dove, 26

Jonkus, m. Lith. Heb. the Lord's grace, 45

Jonkuttelis, m. Lith. Heb. the Lord's grace, 45

Jonuttis, m. Lith. Heb. the Lord's grace.

Joram, m. Eng. Heb. the Lord is exalted, 37

JORDAN, *m. Eng.* Heb. descender, 39

Jorens, m. Norse, Lat. laurel, 174

Jorge, *Port.* husbandman, 115

Joris, Dutch, Gr. husbandman, 115

Jortz, *Gr. Prov.* husbandman, 115

Jorwarth, *m. Welsh,* Teu. rich guard, 378

Jos, m. Eng. Heb. the Lord is salvation, 37

Joscelin, *m. Eng.* Lat. just, 192

Joscelind, f. Eng. Lat. just, 192

Jose, *m. Span. Port.* Heb. addition, 23

Josef, *m. Span. Swed.* Heb. addition, 23

Josefa, *f. Span.* Heb addition, 23

Josefina, *f. Swed.* Heb. addition, 23

Josep, *m. Prov. Fr.* Heb. addition, 23

Joseph, *m. Fr. Eng. Ger.* Heb. addition, 17

Josepha, *f. Port.* Heb. addition, 23

Josephe, *f. Ger. Fr.* Heb. addition, 23

Josephina, *f. Port.* Heb. addition, 23

Josephine, *f. Fr. Eng.* Heb. addition, 23

Joses, *m. Gr.* Heb. addition, 23

Joshua, *m. Eng.* Heb. the Lord is salvation, 37

Josiah, *m. Eng.* Heb. yielded to the Lord, 37

Jossif, *m. Wall.* Heb. addition, 23

Josipe, *f. Ill.* Heb. addition, 23

Josip, *m. Ill.* Heb. addition, 23

Josipa, f. Ill. Heb. addition, 23

Josipac, m. Ill. Heb. addition, 23

Josipica, f. Ill. Heb. addition, 23

Joska, f. Ill. Heb. addition, 23

Josko, m. Ill. Heb. addition, 23

Josh, m. Bav. Heb. addition, 23

Josse, m. Fr. Lat. sportive, 191

Josselin, m. Fr. Lat. sportive, 191

Jossif, m. Russ. Heb. addition, 23

Jossué, *m. Fr.* Heb. the Lord is salvation, 37

Jost, m. L. Ger. Lat. just, 192

Jost, m. Swiss, Lat. sportive, 23

Jost, m. Ger. Lat. sportive, 191

Jostli, m. Swiss, Lat. sportive, 191

Josts, m. Lett. Lat. just, 192

Jourdain, m. Fr. Heb. descender, 39

Jov, m. Russ. Heb. persecuted, 26

Jovan, m. Ill. Swiss, Heb. the Lord's grace, 45

Jovana, f. Ill. Heb. the Lord's grace, 46

Jovanna, f. Port. Heb. the Lord's grace, 46

Jovica, f. Ill. Heb. the Lord's grace, 46

Joy, f. Eng. 191
Joyce, *f. Eng.* Lat. sportive, 191
Joycelin, *m. Eng.* Lat. just, 192
Joza, m. Slov. Heb. addition, 23
Joze, *m. Port.* Heb. addition, 23
Jozef, *m. Pol. Slav.* Heb. addition, 23
Jozefa, f. Pol. Heb. addition, 23
Jozo, m. Ill. Heb. addition, 23
Jozefa, *f. Hung.* Heb. addition, 23
Jra, f. Slov. Teu. spear maid, 368
Juan, *m. Span.* Heb. the Lord's grace, 45
Juana, *f. Span.* Heb. the Lord's grace, 46
Juanito, m. Span. Heb. the Lord's grace, 45
Juczi, *f. Hung.* Heb. praise, 21
Judah, *m. Eng.* Heb. praise, 20
Judas, *m. Scot.* Heb. praise, 20
Jude, *m. Eng.* Heb. praise, 20
Judical, *m. Bret.* Lat. sportive, 191
Judit, *f. Hung.* Heb. praise, 21
JUDITH, *f. Ger. Eng.* Heb. praise, 21
Juditha, *f. Ger.* Heb. praise, 21
Judithe, *f. Fr.* Heb. praise, 21
Judy, f. Eng. Heb. praise, 21
Jugge, f. Eng. Heb. praise, 21
Jukums, m. Lith. Heb. the Lord will judge, 38
Jukkinum, m. Esth. Heb. the Lord will judge, 38
Jules, m. Lith. Lat. downy bearded, 149
Jules, *m. Fr.* Lat. downy bearded, 149
Juli, *f. Hung.* Lat. downy bearded, 149
Julia, *f. Eng.* Lat. downy bearded, 149
Juliaantje, *f. Dutch,* Lat. downy bearded, 150
Julian, *m. f. Eng. Span.* Lat. downy bearded, 150
Juliana, *f. Eng. Span. Port. Wall.* Lat. downy bearded, 150
Juliane, *f. Ger.* Lat downy bearded, 150
Juliano, *m. Span.* Lat. downy bearded, 150
Julianus, *m.* Lat. downy bearded, 150
Juanito, f. Span. Heb. the Lord's grace, 45
Juliao, *m. Port.* Lat. downy bearded, 150

Julie, *f. Ill. Fr. Wall.* Lat. downy bearded, 150
Julien, *m. Fr.* Lat. downy bearded, 150
Julienne, *f. Fr.* Lat. downy bearded, 150
Juliet, *f. Eng.* Lat. downy bearded, 151
Julietta, *f. Span.* Lat. downy bearded, 151
Juliette, *f. Fr. Ger.* Lat. downy bearded, 151
Julij, *m. Slav.* Lat. downy bearded, 149
Julija, *f. Russ.* Lat. downy bearded, 149
Julijan, *m. Slov.* Lat. downy bearded, 150
Julijana, *f. Slov.* Lat. downy bearded, 149
Julio, *m. Span.* Lat. downy bearded, 149
Julis, *f. Hung.* Lat. downy bearded, 149
Juliska, *f. Hung.* Lat. downy bearded, 149
JULIUS, *m. Lat. Eng. Ger.* Lat. downy bearded, 149
Julka, *f. Pol.* Lat. downy bearded, 149
Julyan, *f. Eng.* Lat. downy bearded, 150
JUNIUS, *m.* Lat. of Juno, 151
Jurek, m. Slav. Gr. husbandman, 115
Jurgan, m. Fris. Neth. Gr. husbandman, 115
Jurgis, m. Lett. Gr. husbandman, 115
Jurguttis, m. Lett. Gr. husbandman, 115
Jurica, m. Ill. Gr. husbandman, 115
JURISA, *m. Ill.* Slav. storm.
Jurn, m. Fris. Esth. Gr. husbandman, 115
Juro, m. Ill. Gr. husbandman, 115
Jurriaan, m. Dutch, Gr. husbandman, 115
Jurric, m. Dutch, Gr. husbandman, 115
Jurrusch, m. Lett. Gr. husbandman, 115
Just, *m. Ger.* Lat. just, 193
Justa, *f.* Lat. just, 193
Juste, *m. Fr.* Lat. just, 193

Juste, *f. Ger.* Lat. just, 193
Justin, *m. Eng. Ger.* Lat. just, 193
Justina, *f. Eng. Span.* Lat. just, 193
Justine, *f. Fr. Ger.* Lat. just, 193
Justinian, *m. Ger. Eng.* Lat. just, 193
Justinien, *m. Fr.* Lat. just, 193
Justino, *m. Span.* Lat. just, 193
JUSTINUS, *m.* Lat. just, 193
Justs, *m. Lett.* Lat. just, 193
Justyn, *m. Pol.* Lat. just, 193
Juthe, *f. Hung. Ger.* Heb. praise, 21
Jutka, *f. Hung.* Heb. praise, 21
Jutta, *f. Ger.* Heb. praise, 21
Juzeth, *f. Bret.* Heb. praise, 21
Juzzis, *m. Lett.* Heb. God will judge, 38
Jvan, *m. Bulg.* Heb. the Lord's grace, 45
Jvic, *m. Ill.* Heb. the Lord's grace, 45
Jvica, *m. Ill.* Heb. the Lord's grace, 45

K

Kaat, *f. Dutch,* Gr. pure, 123
KAARI, *m. Nor.* Teu. god of the winds, 322
Kaatje, *f. Dutch,* Gr. pure, 123
Kaddo, *f. Esth.* Gr. pure, 123
Kadl, *f. Bav.* Gr. pure, 123
KAJETAN, *m. Slov.* Lat. of Gaeta, 132
Kajsa, *f. Swed.* Gr. pure, 123
Kalle, *m. Swed.* Teu. man, 386
Kaaurentina, *f. Bret.*
Kapo, *m. Lus.* Pers. treasure master (?), 211
Kapp, *m. Bav.* Pers. treasure master (?), 211
Karel, *m. Esth. Dutch, Bohm. Dan.* Teu. strong man, 386
Karen, *f. Dan.* Gr. pure, 123
Kalle, *m. Swed.* Teu. man, 386
Kantemir, *m. Russ. Turk.* happy iron.
Karadek, *m. Bret.* Kelt. beloved, 233
Karl, *m. Swiss,* Teu. god of the winds, 386
Karin, *f. Dan.* Teu. pure, 123
Karl, *m. Swed. Ger.* Teu. man, 386
Karla, *f. Slov.* Teu. man, 386
Karlic, *m. Ill.* 386

Karlica, *m. Ill.* 386
Karlo, *m. Russ. Ill.* Teu. man, 386
Karlmann, *m. Ger.* Teu. strong man, 386
Karlko, *m. Lus.* Teu. man, 386
Karls, *m. Lett.* Teu. man, 386
Karol, *m. Pol. Slov.* Teu. man, 386
Karolek, *m. Pol.* Teu. man, 386
Karolina, *f. Slav.* Teu. man, 386
Karolinka, *f. Slov.* Teu. man, 386
Karoly, *m. Hung.* Teu. man, 386
Karsten, *m. Slav. L. Ger.* Teu. Christian, 105
Karstin, *f. Dan.* Gr. Christian, 105
Kasche, *f. Dantzig,* Gr. pure, 123
Kasch, *m. Dantzig,* Teu. man, 386
Kaschis, *m. Lett.* Slav. showing peace, 443
Kasen, *f. Dan.* Gr. pure, 123
Kashuk, *m. Lett.* Slav. show forth peace, 442
Kasia, *f. Pol.* Gr. pure, 123
Kasimir, *m. Ger.* Slav. show forth peace, 443
Kasimira, *f. Ger.* Slav. show forth peace, 443
Kasimirs, *m. Lett.* Slav. show forth peace, 443
Kaspar, *m. Ger. Russ. Bohm.* Pers. treasure master (?), 211
Kaspe, *m. Bav.* Pers. treasure master (?), 211
Kasper, *m. Swed.* Pers. treasure master (?), 211
Kasperl, *m. Bav.* Pers. treasure master (?), 211
Kaspers, *m. Lett.* Pers. treasure master (?), 211
Kaspor, *m. Lus.* Pers. treasure master (?), 211
Kass, *m. Bav.* Pers. treasure master (?), 211
Kata, *f. Ill.* Gr. pure, 123
Katalin, *f. Hung.* Gr. pure, 123
Katarina, *f. Swed. Ill. Russ.* Gr. pure, 123
Katarzina, *f. Pol.* Gr. pure, 123
Kate, *f. Eng. Ill.* Gr. pure, 123
Katel, *f. Bret.* Gr. pure, 123
Katelik, *f. Bret.* Gr. pure, 123
Katerina, *f. Bohm.* Gr. pure, 123
Katharine, *f. Eng. Ger.* Gr. pure, 123
Kätchen, *f. Ger.* Gr. pure, 123

Kathe, f. Ger. Gr. pure, 123
Katherine, f. Eng. Gr. pure, 123
Kathleen, f. Ir. Gr. pure, 123
Kathri, f. Swiss, Gr. pure, 123
Kathrili, f. Swi s, Gr. pure, 123
Kathrina, f. Dan. Gr. pure, 123
Kali, f. Hung. Gr. pure, 123
Katica, f. Ill. Gr. pure, 123
Katicza, f. Hung. Gr. pure, 123
Katie, f. Scot. Gr. pure, 123
Katinka, f. Russ. Gr. pure, 123
Katya, f. Russ. Gr. pure, 123
KATLA, *f. Nor.* Teu. cauldron, 346
Katra, f. Slov. Gr. pure, 123
Katreij, f. Slov. Gr. pure, 123
Katrin, f. Bav. Gr. pure, 123
Katrina, f. Slov. Gr. pure, 123
Katrine, f. Eng. Bav. Lett. Gr. pure, 123
Kats, f. Esth. Gr. pure, 123
Katsehe, f. Lett. Gr. pure, 123
Kattel, f. Bav. Gr. pure, 123
Katty, f. Ir. Gr. pure, 123
Kavzma, m. Russ. Gr. order, 125
Kay, *m. Eng.* Lat. rejoicing, 131
KAZIMIR, *m. Ill. Pol. Slov. Bohm.* Slav. show forth peace, 211
Kazimierz, m. Pol. Slav. show forth peace, 211
Kean, *m. Irish,* vast, 258
Kee, f. Dutch, Lat. horn (?), 146
Kees, m. Dutch, Lat. horn (?), 146
Keetje, f. Dutch, Lat. horn (?), 146
Keeldar, m. Scot. Teu. battle army.
Keereel, *m. Russ.* Gr. lordly, 217
Keira, Lapp. Teu. ever king, 56
Kenneth, *m. Scot.* Kelt. comely, 256
Kenny, *m. Ir.* Kelt. vast, 256
Kentigern, m. Welsh, Kelt. head chief, 258
Kentigerna, *f. Welsh,* Kelt. head chief, 258
Kephas, *m. Gr.* Aram. stone, 107
Kerenhappuch, f. Heb. box of paint, 26
Kerestel, m. Hung. Christian, 105
Keresteli, m. Hung. Christian, 105
Keriadek, *m. Bret.* Kelt. beloved, 233
Kerstan, m. Lus. Gr. Christian, 105
Kerste, f. Lett. Gr. Christian, 105
Kersti, m. Est. Gr. Christian, 105
Kerstiteli, m. Ill. Gr. baptizer, 106
Kersto, m. Ill. Gr. Christian, 105

Kester, m. Eng. Teu. Christ bearer, 106
Kert, Esth. Teu. spear maid, 268
KETELBIORN, *m. Nor.* Teu. cauldron bear, 347
KETELRIDIR, *f. Nor.* Teu. cauldron fury, 347
Ketterle, f. Bav. Gr. pure, 123
KETYL, *m. Nor.* Teu. cauldron, 347
Kevin, *m. Irish,* Kelt. comely, 256
Keyne, f. Eng. Kelt. jewel, 271
Kezia, *f. Eng.* Bret. cassia, 26
Khaoos, *m. Pers.* Zend. beautiful eyed.
Kharalamm, *m. Russ.* Gr. joy of Easter, 216
Kharalample, *m. Russ.* Gr. joy of Easter, 216
Kharitoun, m. Russ. Gr. love, 73
Khevronia, m. Russ. Lat. purifying, 176
Khoosroo, m. Pers. Zend. sun (?), 56
Khur, m. Pers. Zend. sun (?), 56
Khshayarsha, Zend. venerable king, 56
Kissey, f. Eng. Heb. cassia, 26
Kieren, *m. Irish,* Kelt. black, 256
Kilian, *m. Ger.* Lat. blind, 144
Kina, f. Swiss, Gr. Christian, 105
Kirin, m. Ill. Lat. spearman, 177
Kit, m. Eng. Gr. Christ bearer, 106
Kiogeir, m. Nor. Teu. people's spear, 375
Kitto, m. Lus. Gr. Christ bearer, 106
Kitty, f. Eng. Gr. pure, 123
Kiodvala, Nor. people's power, 375
Kjogjer, Nor. people's spear, 375
Kjol, Nor. people's wolf, 375
Kjold, Nor. people's wolf, 375
Kjoille, Nor. people's heroine, 375
Kjoval, Nor. people's power, 375
Kjostol, m. Nor. harsh wolf, 419
Kjartan, m. Nor. Kelt. sea warrior, 146
Kjelljorg, f. Nor. Teu. kettle protection, 346
Kjell, m. Nor. Teu. kettle, 346
Klaatje, m. Dutch, Lat. famous, 186
Klaas, m. Dutch, Lat. victory of the people, 90
Klaasji, m. Dutch, Lat. victory of the people, 90
Klaada, m. Bret. Lat. lame, 146
Klara, f. Sl. Lat. famous, 185

Klas, m. Bav. Dan. Gr. victory of the people, 90

Klasel, m. Bav. Gr. victory of the people, 90

Klassis, m. Lat. Gr. victory of the people, 90 ·

Klaudij, *m. Ill.* Lat. lame, 146

Klaus, m. Ger. Esth. Lat. victory of the people, 90

Klavde, m. Slov. Lat. lame, 146

Klavdij, *m. Russ.* Lat. lame, 146

Klavinsh, m. Lett. Gr. victory of the people, 90

Klavs, m. Lett. Gr. victory of the people, 90

KLEANTHES, *m.* Gr. famous bloom, 95

Klemen, m. Slov. Hung. Lat. merciful, 160

Klemente, *m. Ill.* Lat. merciful, 160

Klemet, *m. Esth.* Lat. merciful, 160

Klemin, m. Ger. Lat. merciful, 160

Klunans, m. Russ. Lat. merciful, 160

KLEOPATRA, *f.* Gr. fame of her father, 95

Klothilde, f. Ger. Teu. famous battle maid, 404

Knelis, m. Dutch, Lat. horn (?), 146

Knel, m. Dantzig, Lat. horn (?), 146

KNUD, *m. Dan.* Teu. hill, 433

Knut, *m. Dan.* Teu. hill, 433

Koadou, m. Bret. Kelt. wood liver.

Kodders, m. Lett. Gr. divine gift, 101, 282

Koenraed, *m. Netherlands,* Teu. bold council, 423

KOL, *m. Ice.* Teu. cool, 429

KOLBEIN, *m. Ice.* Teu. cold iron bone, 429

KOLBJORN, *m. Ice.* Teu. black bear, 429

Kolina, f. Swed. Gr. pure, 123

KOLBIORN, *m. Nor.* Teu. black bear, 429

KOLFINN, *m. Nor.* Teu. cool white, 429

KOLFINNA, *f. Nor.* Teu. cool white, 429

KOLGRIM, *m. Nor.* Teu. cool mask, 429

KOLGRIMA, *f. Nor.* Teu. cool mask, 427

Kolinka, m. Russ. Gr. victory of the people, 90

Kolja, m. Russ. Gr. victory of the people, 90

KOLOMAN, *m. Hung.* slave council man, 443

KOLSKEGG, *m. Ice.* Teu. black beard, 427

Kondratij, m. Russ. Teu. bold council, 423

Konrad, *m. Hung. Swed. Ger. Russ.* Teu. bold council, 423

Konradin, m. Ger. Teu. bold council, 423

Konradine, f. Ger. Teu. bold council, 423

Konstantia, *f. Ill. Slav.* Lat. firm, 161

Konstanij, m. Slav. Lat. firm, 161

Konstanczia, *f. Hung.* Lat. firm, 161

Konstantin, *m. Teu. Slav. Russ.* Lat. firm, 161

Konstanz, m. Ger. Lat. firm, 161

KORE, *f. Gr.* Gr. maiden, 60

Kored, bold council, 423

Koredli, bold council, 423

Kordel, f. Bav. Kelt. jewel of the sea, 230

Kordule, *f. Gr.* Kelt. jewel of the sea, 230

Kormak, *m. Ice.* Kelt. son of a chariot, 249

Koreish, m. Heb. Zend. sun (?), 56

Kornel, m. Dutch, Lat. horn (?), 146

Kornelie, f. Wall. Dutch, Lat. horn (?), 146

Kornelij, m. Slav. Lat. horn (?), 146

Korstiaan, *m. Dutch,* Gr. Christian, 105

KOSMOS, *m.* Gr. order, 125

Kostadin, m. Slov. Lat. firm, 161

Kostancia, f. Slav. Lat. firm, 161

Koste, m. Slav. Lat. firm, 161

Kostja, m. Russ. Lat. firm, 161

Kostusin, m. Pol. Lat. firm, 161

Kotka, Ill. Slov. Lat. firm, 161

Koulna, m. Bret. Lat. dove, 186

Koulum, m. Bret. Lat. dove, 186

Kowzma, m. Russ. Gr. order, 125

KRASISLAV, *m. Slav.* Slav. fair glory, 443

KRASIMIR, *m. Slav.* fair peace, 443, 445

KRASOMIL, *m. Slav.* fair love, 443

Kret, f. Esth. Gr. pearl, 121

Krikshte, m. Ill. Gr. Christian, 105

Kriemhild, f. Ger. Teu. helmet battle maid, 361
Krispin, m. Dutch, Lat. curly, 162
Krista, f. Swiss, Gr. Christian, 105
Kristal, m. Ger. Gr. Christ bearer, 106
Kristagis, m. Lett. Gr. Christ bearer, 106
Kristoppis, m. Lett. Gr. Christ bearer, 106
Kriste, f. Lett. Gr. Christian, 105
Kristel, f. Ger. Gr. Christian, 105
Kristi, f. Esth. Gr. Christian, 105
Kristian, *m. Swed. Ill.* Gr. Christian, 105
Kristiane, *f. Slav.* Gr. Christian, 105
Kristijan, f. Slav. Gr. Christian 105
Kristina, *f. Slav.* Gr. Christian, 105
Kristinsch, m. Lett. Gr. Christian, 105
Kristof, *m. Ill. Slav.* Gr. Christ bearer, 106
Kristofer, *m. Swed.* Gr. Christ bearer, 106
Kristoffel, m. Swiss, Gr. Christ bearer, 106
Kristofor, m. Slov. Ill. Gr. Christ bearer, 106
Kristscho, m. Lus. Gr. Christian, 105
Kristuppas, m. Lith. Gr. Christ bearer, 106
Kroet, f. Esth. Gr. pearl, 121
Kruschan, m. Gr. Christian, 105
Krustinn, f. Bulg. Gr. Christian, 105
Krustjo, m. Bulg. Gr. Christian, 105
Kryspyn, m. Pol. Lat. curly, 162
Kryslof, m. Pol. Gr. Christ bearer, 106
Krystyan, m. Pol. Gr. Christian, 105
Ksersas, m. Ill. Zend. venerable king, 56
Kub, m. Lus. Pol. Heb. supplanter, 17
Kuba, m. Pol. Heb. supplanter, 17
Kubischu, m. Lett. Heb. supplanter, 17
Kunel, m. Bav. Teu. bold speech, 424
Kuhnhardt, m. Ger. Teu. bold and firm, 424
Kuhnrat, m. Ger. Teu. bold speech, 423
Kunat, m. Lus. Teu. bold speech, 423
Kundel, f. Ger. Teu. bold war, 424
Kunds, m. Ger. Teu. bold speech, 423
Kunigunde, f. Ger. Teu. bold war, 423
Kunimund, m. Ger. Teu. bold protection, 423

Kuno, m. Ger. Teu. bold, 424
Kunrad, m. Bohm. Teu. bold speech 423
Kunrat, m. Russ. Teu. bold speech, 423
Kunsch, m. Slav. Teu. bold speech, 423
Kunz, m. Ger. Teu. bold speech, 423
Kupina, *f. Ill.* Slav. gooseberry, 438
KUPJENA, *f. Ill.* Slav. gooseberry, 438
Kurt, m. Ger. Teu. bold speech, 423
Kustas, m. Esth. Teu. Goth's staff, 289
Kustav, m. Esth. Teu. Goth's staff, 289
Kwedders, m. Lett. Gr. divine gift, 182
KUREISH, *m.* Zend. sun (?), 56
Kusteninn, *m. Bret.* Lat. firm, 161
Kymbelin, m. Eng. Kelt. lord of the lion, 232
Kygeir, m. Nor. Teu. people's spear, 374
Kythe.
Kyer, m. Nor. Teu. people's spear, 374
KYNAN, *m. Welsh,* Kelt. chief, 247
KYRIAKOS, *m. Gr.* Sunday child, 217
KYRILLOS, *m. Gr.* lordly, 217

L

Labrenzis, m. Lett. Lat. laurel, 174
Lachlan, *m. Scot.* Kelt. warlike, 255
LACHTNA, *m. Erse,* Kelt. green, 256
Lacko, m. Ill. Slav. ruling with fame, 442
Laco, m. Ill. Slav. ruling with fame, 442
Laczko, m. Hung. Slav. ruling with fame, 442
Ladislao, *m. Span. It.* Slav. ruling with fame, 442
Ladislas, *m. Fr.* Slav. ruling with fame, 442
Ladislao, *m. Port.* Slav. ruling with fame, 442
Ladislaus, *m. Lat.* Slav. ruling with fame, 442
LAIDRAD, *m. Ger.* Teu. fierce speech, 418

LAIDWALD, *m. Ger.* Teu. fierce power, 418

LAIDWIG, *m. Ger.* Teu. fierce war, 418

Lælia, *f. Lat.* 151

LÆLIUS, *m. Lat.* 151

LÆTITIA, *f. Eng.* Lat. gladness, 192

Lajos, m. Hung. Teu. famous war, 405

LALA, *f. Serv.* Slav. tulip, 438

LALAGE, *f. Lat.* Gr. prattler, 463

Lambert, *m. Fr. Eng. Dutch, Ger.* Teu. country's brightness, 431

Lambertine, *f. Ger.* Teu. country's brightness, 431

Lamberto, *m. It.* Teu. country's brightness, 431

Lambrecht, *m. Ger.* Teu. country's brightness, 481

Lamech, *m. Eng.* Heb. smitten.

Lammert, m. Dutch, Teu. country's brightness, 431

Lance, m. Eng. Lat. servant, 263

Lancelot, *m. Eng. Fr.* Lat. servant, 263

Lancilotto, *m. It.* Lat. servant, 263

LANDERICH, *m. Frank.* Teu. land ruler, 431

Landerico, *m. Ital.* Teu. land ruler, 431

Landfranc, *m. Eng.* Teu. land free, 431

LANDFRANG, *m. Ger.* Teu. land free, 431

LANDFRIED, *m. Ger.* Teu. land peace, 431

Landinn, *f. Ger. Fr.* Teu. country, 431

Lando, *m. Ger.* Teu. country, 431

LANDOLF, *m. Ger.* Teu. country wolf, 431

LANDRAD, *m. Ger.* Teu. country's council, 431

LANDWIN, *m. Gr.* Teu. country friend, 431

Landfranco, *m. It.* Teu. country free, 431

LANN, *f. Erse,* Kelt. sword.

LANTPERAHT, *m. O. Ger.* Teu. country's brightness, 430

Lanty, m. Ir. Lat. laurel, 174

LAODAMAS, *Gr.* people's tamer, 95

LAODAMIA, *f. It.* Gr. people's tamer, 95

LAODIKE, *f.* Gr. people's justice, 95

Lapo, m. It. Heb. supplanter, 17

Lara, f. Finn. Lat. famous, 185

Laris, m. Fris. Lat. cheerful, 191

Larkin, m. Eng. Lat. laurel, 174

Larry, m. Ir. Lat. laurel, 174

Lars, m. Dan. 174

Larse, m. Swed. Lat. laurel, 174

Lasar, m. Russ. Heb. God will help, 33

Lasche, f. Lett. Teu. famous war, 405

LASSAIR, *f. Erse,* Kelt. flame, 224

LASSARFHINA, *f. Erse,* Kelt. flame of wine, 224

Lassla, m. Hung. ruling with fame, 442

Latte, f. Lett. Teu. man, 386

Launart, m. Fr. Teu. lion strong, 77

Laur, m. Lapp. Esth. Lat. laurel, 174

Laura, *f. Eng. Ital. Ger.* Lat. laurel, 174

Laure, *f. Fr.* Lat. laurel, 174

Laurenza, *f. Eng. Port.* Lat. laurel, 174

Laurence, *m. Eng.* Lat. laurel, 174

Laurencho, *m. Port.* Lat. laurel, 174

Laurençya, *f. Port.* Lat. laurel, 174

Laurens, *m. Nor.* Lat. laurel, 174

Laurent, *m. Fr.* Lat. laurel, 174

Laurentia, *f. Lat.* laurel, 174

LAURENTIUS, *m. Lat.* laurel, 174

Laures, *m. Lap.* Lat. laurel, 174

Lauretta, f. Eng. Lat. laurel, 174

Laurette, f. Fr. Lat. laurel, 174

Laurie, m. Scot. Lat. laurel, 174

Lauris, *m. Lett.* Lat. laurel, 174

Lauritz, m. Dan. Lat. laurel, 174

Laurus, m. Esth. Lat. laurel, 174

Laus, m. Esth. Gr. people's victory, 90

Lav, *m. Slov.* Gr. lion, 77

LAVINIA, *f. Eng.* of Latium, 176

LAVOSLAV, *m. Slav.* Slav. lion glory, 77

Lavrentic, *m. Wall.* Lat. laurel, 174

Lavrentij, *m. Russ.* Lat. laurel, 174

Lavrentija, *f. Russ.* Lat. laurel, 174

Lavrenzis, *m. Lett.* Lat. laurel, 174

Lawise, f. Lett. Teu. famous war, 405

Lawrence, *m. Eng.* Lat. laurel, 174

Lazar, m. Ill. Hung. Heb. God will help, 33

Lazare, *m. Fr.* Heb. God will help, 33

Lazarillo, m. Span. Heb. God will help, 33

LAZARO, *m. Span. It.* Heb. God will help, 33

Lazarus, *m. Lat.* Heb. God will help, 33

L*a*zarro, *m. It.* Heb. God will help, 33

Lazarz, m. Pol. Heb. God will help, 33

Laze, m. Ill. Heb. God will help, 33

Lazo, m. Ill. Heb. God will help, 33

Lazzaro, *m. It.* Heb. God will help, 33

Leah, *f. Eng.* Heb. weary, 7, 15

Leander, *m. Eng.* Gr. lion man, 77

Leandre, *m. Fr.* Gr. lion man, 77

Leandro, *m. It. Span.* Gr. lion man, 77

LEANDROS, *m. Gr.* Gr. lion man, 77

Leăo, m. Port. Gr. lion, 77

Lear, *m. Eng.* Kelt. sea, 229

Lebbœus, *m. Eng.* Aram. praise, 20

LEBRECHT, *m. Ger.* live right, 468

Lebwin, *m. Ger.* Teu. beloved friend, 426

LECH, *m. Pol.* Slav. a woodland spirit.

Lechsinska, *f. Pol.* Slav. a woodland spirit.

Leger, *m. Teu.* people's spear, 430

Leen, m. Dutch, Teu. lion strong, 77

Leendert, m. Dutch, Teu. lion strong, 77

Left shoulder forward, m .Eng. 10, 463

Leentje, f. Dutch, Heb. of Magdala, 31

Leifr, *m. Nor.* relic, 332

Leila, f. Moorish.

LEIKNY, *f. Nor.* Teu. fresh sport, 354

Leiul, m. Nor. Teu. fierce wolf, 418

Leisje, f. Dutch, Heb. God's oath, 35

Leks, m. Slav. helper of men, 85

Leli, f. Swiss, Heb. of Magdala, 30

Lelia, f. It. Lat. 151

Lelie, f. It. Lat. 151

Lelio, m. It. Lat. 151

Lelika, f. Slov. Gr. fair speech, 308

Lena, f. Alb. Lett. Gr. light, 68

Lemet, m. Esth. Lat. merciful, 161

Lenardo, m. It. Teu. lion strong, 77

Lenort, m. Teu. lion strong, 77

Lenchen, f. Ger. Heb. of Magdala, 31, 68

Lencica, f. Slov. Gr. light, 68

Lendrts, m. Lett. Teu. lion strong, 77

Lene, f. Ger. Heb. of Magdala, 32

Lenhart, m. Ger. Teu. lion strong, 77

Lenia, f. Alb. Gr. light, 68

Lenka, f. Slov. Gr. light, 68

Lenny, m. Eng. Teu. lion strong, 77

Lenore, *f. Ger.* Gr. light, 68

Leno, f. Esth. Gr. light, 68

Lenz, m. Swiss, Lat. laurel, 174

LEO, *m. Ger. Span.* Gr. lion, 76

LEOBGYTHA, *f. A.S.* Teu. love gift, 426

LEOBHARD, *m. Frank.* Teu. love strength, 426

Leocadia, *f. Span.* Gr. 77

Leocadie, *f. Span.* Gr. 77

Leodegarius, *m. Lat.* Teu. people's spear, 430

Leodowald, *m. A.S.* Teu. people's power, 430

LEOFRIC, *m. Eng.* Teu. beloved rule, 426

LEOFISTAN, *m. A.S.* Teu. beloved stone, 426

LEOFWINE, *m. A.S.* Teu. beloved friend, 426

Leoline, *m. Eng.* Kelt. Lat. 280, 426

Leon, *m. It. Russ.* Gr. lion, 76

Leonard, *m. Eng. It.* Teu. lion strong, 77

Leonarda, *f. Span. Ger.* Teu. lion strong, 77

Leonarde, *f. It. Ger.* Teu. lion strong, 77

Leonardine, *f. Ger.* Teu. lion strong, 77

Leonardo, *m. Rom.* Teu. lion strong, 77

Léonce, *m. Fr.* Gr. lion like, 77

Leoncie, *f. Fr.* Gr. lion like, 77

Leoncio, *m. It.* Gr. lion like, 77

Leone, *m. It.* Gr. lion, 76

Leongard, *m. Russ.* Teu. lion strong, 77

Leonhard, m. Ger. Teu. lion strong, 77

Leanhardine, *m. Ger.* Teu. lion strong, 77

LEONIDAS, *m. Gr.* lion like, 77

Leonie, *f. Fr.* Gr. lion, 77

Leonor, *f. Span.* Gr. light, 68

Leonora, *f. It. Eng.* Gr. light, 68

Leonore, *f. Fr.* Gr. light, 68

Leontia, *f. Lat.* Gr. lion like, 77
Leontij, *m. Russ.* Gr. lion like, 77
Leontin, *m. Ger. Fr.* Gr. lion like, 77
Leontine, *f. Ger. Fr.* lion like, 77
LEONTIUS, *m.* Lat. lion like, 77
Leonz, *m. Ger.* Teu. lion strong, 77
Leopo, m. Ger. Teu. people's prince, 430
Leopold, *m. Ger. Fr.* Teu. people's prince, 430
Leopoldine, *f. Ger.* people's prince, 430
Leopoldo, *m. Slav. It.* Teu. people's prince, 430
Leovigildo, *m. Span.* Teu. love pledge, 426
Leszek, m. Pol. Gr. helper of men, 85
Letitia, *f. Eng.* Lat. gladness, 192
Lettice, *f. Eng.* Lat. gladness, 192
Lethard, *m. Ger.* Teu. fierce firmness, 418
Lethild, *f. Ger.* Teu. fierce battle maid, 418
Letizia, *f. It.* Lat. gladness, 192
Leto, 64
Let'y, *f. Ir.* Gr. truth, 126
Letty, *f. Eng.* Lat. gladness, 192
Leudomir, *m. Frank.* Teu. people's fame, 430
Leufroi, *m. Gr.* Teu. people's peace, 430
Leunairs, m. Fr. Teu. lion strong, 77
Leupold, *m. Ger.* Teu. people's prince, 430
LEUTGAR, *m. Ger.* Teu. people's spear, 429
LEUTGARDE, *f. Ger.* Teu. people's guard, 430
LEUTPOLD, *m. Ger.* Teu. people's prince, 429
Lev, m. Pol. Slov. Gr. lion, 77
Levi, *m. Eng.* Heb. joining, 7, 15
Lew, m. Slav. Gr. lion, 77
Levor, m. Nor. Teu. gate ward, 421
Lewis, *m. Eng.* Teu. famous war, 405
Lia, *f. It.* Heb. dependence, 15
Libby, f. Eng. Heb. God's oath, 35
LIBUSA, *f. Bohm.* Slav. darling, 443
Lida, f. Bohm. Slav. people's love, 432, 443
LIDVARD, *m. Nor.* Teu. gate ward, 421

LIDWINA, *f. Bohm.* Slav. people of Vina, 443
LIEBE, *f. Flem.* Ger. love, 426
Liebhard, *m. Ger.* Teu. love strength, 426
Liebtrud, *f. Ger.* Teu. love maiden, 426
Liedulf, *m. Nor.* Teu. fierce wolf, 418
Lienhardt, m. Bav. lion strength, 77
Lienl, m. Ger. Teu. lion strong, 77
Lienzel, m. Russ. Teu. lion strong, 77
Liert, m. Swiss, Teu. lion strength, 77
Lieschen, f. Ger. Teu famous, 405
Lievina, f. Flem. Teu. love, 426
Ligach, f. Gael. Kelt. pearly, 224
Ligaire, m. Fr. Teu. people's spear, 430
Likelas, m. Bav. Gr. victory of the people, 90
Lilian, *f. Eng.* Lat. lily, 145
Lilias, *f. Scot.* Lat. lily, 145
Liliola, f. It. Lat. blind, 144
Lilla, f. Eng. Heb. oath of God, 35
Lilly, *f. Eng.* lily, 145
Lina, f. Ger. Teu. man, 386
Line, f. Ger. Teu. man, 386
Linet, f. Eng. Kelt. shapely (?), 145
Linnea, *f. Nor.* Teu. lime tree, 470
LINTRUDE, *f. Ger.* Teu. serpent maid, 347
Linuscha, f. Dant. Teu. man, 386
Lionardo, *m. It.* Teu. lion strong, 77
Lionel, *m. Eng.* Lat. lion, 77
Lionello, *m. It.* Lat. little lion, 77
Liovigotona, *f. Span.* Teu. love Goth, 426
Lipo, m. Lus. Teu. remains of divinity, 288
Lipp, m. Bav. Gr. loving horses, 79
Lipp, m. Dant. Teu. relic of divinity, 288
Lippa, m. Bav. Gr. loving horses, 79
Lippo, m. It. Gr. loving horses, 79
Lipsts, m. Lett. Gr. loving horses, 79
Lisa, f. Dan. Lus. Heb. God's oath, 35
Lisbet, f. Ger. Heb. God's oath, 35
Lisbeta, f. Lett. Heb. God's oath, 35
Lise, f. Ger. Heb. God's oath, 35
Liserli, f. Swiss, Heb. God's oath, 35
Lisetle, f. Fr. Teu. famous war, 405

Lisilka, f. Russ. Heb. God's oath, 35
Lisi, f. Bav. Heb. God's oath, 35
Liska, f. Lus. Heb. God's oath, 35
Liso, f. Esth. Heb. God's oath, 35
Lisrl, f. Bav. Heb. God's oath, 35
Liuba, f. Flem. Teu. love, 426
LIUTBERGA, *f. Ger.* Teu. people's protection, 430
LIUTBERT, *m. Ger.* Teu. people's brightness, 430
LIUTFRED, *m. Ger.* Teu. people's peace, 430
LIUTHOLD, *m. Ger.* Teu. people's firmness, 430
LIUTMAR, *m. Ger.* Teu. people's fame, 430
LIUTPOLD, *m. Ger.* Teu. people's valour, 430
LIUTPRAND, *m. Frank.* Teu. people's sword, 430
Liuva, *m. Span.* Teu. love, 426
Liza, f. Russ. Heb. God's oath, 35
Lizbeta, f. Slov. Heb. God's oath, 35
Lizbetha, f. Russ. Heb. God's oath, 35
Lizika, f. Slov. Heb. God's oath, 35
Lizzie, f. Scot. Heb. God's oath, 35
Ljena, f. Albanian, Gr. light, 68
LJODOLD, *m. Nor.* Teu. people's firmness, 430
LJOT, *m. Nor.* Teu. people, 430
Ljubica, f. Serv. Slav. love, 443
Ljubima, f. Serv. Slav. love, 443
Ljubka, f. Russ. Slav. love, 443
LJUBMILA, *f. Slav.* Slave, loving, 443
LJUBOMIR, *m. Slav.* Slav. love peace, 443
LJUBOSLAV, *m. Slov.* Slav. love glory, 443
LJUBOV, *f. Russ.* Slav. love, 443
Ljudevit, m. Slov. Teu. famous war, 405
LJUDOMILA, *f. Slav.* Slav. people's love, 430
LJUDOMIR, *m. Slav.* Slav. people's peace, 430
Lles, *m. Welsh,* Lat. light, 132
Lleulu, *f. Welsh,* light, 132
LLEURWG, *m. Welsh,* Kelt. light, 281
LLEW, *m. Welsh,* Kelt. lion.
LLEW, *m. Welsh,* Kelt. light, 281
Llewellyn, *m. Eng.* Kelt. lightning, 281
Lleufer, m. Welsh, Lat. light, 281

LLEWRWG, *f. Welsh,* Lat. light, 76
LLYR, *m. Welsh,* Kelt. sea, 230
Lloyd, *m. Eng.* Kelt. grey, 230
LLWYD, *m. Welsh,* Kelt. grey, 230
LLYWELWYN, *m. Welsh,* Kelt. lightning, 281
Lobo, *m. Port.* Lat. wolf, 198
Lodewick, *m. Dutch,* Teu. famous war, 405
Lodoiska, *f. Pol.* Teu. famous war, 405
Lodovico, *m. It.* Teu. famous war, 405
Lodowick, *m. Scot.* Teu. famous war, 405
Lodowig, *m. Ger.* Teu. famous war, 405
Lodve, m. Nor. Teu. famous war, 405
Lodward, *m. Nor.* Teu. famous guard, 405
Lois, *m. Br.* Teu. famous war, 405
Loiseach, m. Erse, Kelt. 405
Loïz, *m. Bret.* Teu. famous war, 405
Lola, f. Span. Teu. man, 386
Lolotte, *f. Fr.* Teu. man, 386
Lood, *m. Dutch,* Teu. famous war, 405
Looys, *m. Fr.* Teu. famous war, 405
Lope, *m. Span.* Lat. wolf, 198
Lopko, *m. Lus.* Teu. God's praise, 288
Lopo, *m. Lus.* Teu. God's praise, 288
Lora, *f. Eng.* Lat. laurel, 174
Lorenço, *m. It.* Lat. laurel, 174
Lorenz, *m. Ger. Dan.* Lat. laurel, 174
Lorenzo, *m. It.* Lat. laurel, 174
Lori, *m. Swiss,* Lat. laurel, 174
Lorinez, *m. Hung.* Lat. laurel, 174
Loritz, m. Esth. Lat. laurel, 174
Lorl, *f. Ger.* Gr. light, 174
Lorus, *m. Lith.* Lat. laurel, 174
Lot, *m. Eng.* Heb.
Lot, *m. Eng.* Kelt. lion, 281
Lotario, *m. Span. It.* Teu. famous warrior, 407
Lothaire, *m. Fr.* Teu. famous warrior, 407
Lothar, *m. Ger.* Teu. famous warrior, 407
Lothario, *m. Eng.* Teu. famous warrior, 407
Lotta, f. Swed. Teu. man, 386
Lotte, f. Ger. Teu. man, 386
Lotty, f. Eng. Teu. man, 386

Lotze, m. Ger. Teu. famous war, 407

LOUARN, *m.* Kelt. fox, 224, 242

Louis, *m. Fr.* Teu. famous war, 405

Louisa, *f. Eng.* Teu. famous war, 405

Louise, *f. Ger. Fr.* Teu. famous war, 405

Louison, f. Fr. Teu. famous war, 405

Lova, f. Swed. Teu. famous war, 405

LOVE, *f. Eng.* Teu. love, 464

LOVEDAY, *f. Corn.* Teu. love (?), 464

Lovisa, *f. Swed.* Teu. famous war, 405

Lovisje, *f. Dutch,* Teu. famous war, 405

Lovra, f. m. Serv. Lat. laurel, 174

Lovre, m. Slov. Lat. laurel, 174

Lovrenika, f. Ill. Lat. laurel, 174

LOWENHARD, *m. Frank.* Teu. stern lion, 281

LOWENCLO, *m. Bav.* Teu. lion claw, 281

Loys, *m. Fr.* Teu. famous holiness, 405

Lozoik, *m. Prov.* Teu. famous holiness, 405

Lubin, *m. Ir. Eng.* Teu. love friend, 426

LUBOMIRSKI, *m. Pol.* Slav. loving peace, 443

Luca, *m. Fr.* Lat. light, 133

Luca, *m. It.* Lat. light, 133

LUCANUS, *m. Gr.* Lat. light, 133

Lucas, *m. Span.* Lat. light, 133

Luce, *m. Fr.* Lat. light, 133

LUCIA, *f. It.* Lat. light, 132

Lucian, *m. Eng.* Lat. light, 133

Luciana, *f. It.* Lat. light, 132

Luciano, *m. It.* Lat. light, 133

Lucianus, *m.* Lat. light, 133

Lucie, *f. Fr.* Lat. light, 132

Lucien, *m. Fr.* Lat. light, 133

Lucienne, *f. Fr.* Lat. light, 132

Lucifer, *m. Eng.* Lat. light bringer, 133

LUCIFERUS, *m. Lat.* Lat. light bringer, 133

Lucile, *f. Fr.* Lat. light, 132

Lucilla, *f. Eng.* Lat. light, 132

LUCINDA, *f. Eng.* Lat. light, 132

Lucio, *m. It.* Lat. light, 133

LUCIUS, *m. Eng.* Lat. light, 133

Lucrece, *f. Fr.* Lat. gain (?), 134

Lucretia, *f. Eng.* Lat. gain (?), 134

LUCRETIUS, *m.* Lat. gain (?), 134

Lucrezia, *f. It.* Lat. gain (?), 134

LUCY, *f. Eng.* Lat. light, 132

Lucya, *f. Pol.* Lat. light, 132

Lucza, *f. Hung.* Lat. light, 132

Ludevic, *m. Wall.* Teu. famous holiness, 405

Ludgar, m. Ger. Teu. people's spear, 430

Ludi, m. Swiss, Teu. famous holiness, 405

Ludmila, *f. Ger. Slav.* people's love, 430, 442

Ludolf, m. Ger. Teu. people's wolf, 430

LUDOMILLA, *f. Ger.* Slav. people's love, 430

LUDOMIR, *m. Ger.* Slav. people's peace, 430

Ludomir, *m. Ger.* Teu. famous greatness, 405

Ludovic, *m. Wall.* Teu. famous holiness, 405

Ludovica, *f. Swed.* Teu. famous holiness, 405

Ludovick, *m. Scot.* Teu. famous holiness, 405

Ludovico, *m. It.* Teu. famous holiness, 406

Ludovicus, *m. Lat.* Teu. famous war, 405

Ludovike, *f. Ger.* Teu. famous war, 405

Ludvig, *m. Swed.* Teu. famous war, 405

Ludvik, *m. Pol. Bohm. Slov.* Teu. famous war, 405

Ludvika, *f. Pol.* Teu. famous war, 405

Ludvis, *m. Pol.* Teu. famous war, 405

Ludvisia, *f. Pol.* Teu. famous war, 405

LUANMAISI, *f. Erse,* Kelt. fair as the moon, 224

LUGHAID, *m. Erse,* Kelt. light (?), 133

Luigi, *m. It.* Teu. famous war, 405

Luis, *m. Port. Span.* Teu. famous war, 405

Luisa, *f. Span. Port.* Teu. famous war, 405

Luise, *f. Ger.* Teu. famous war, 405

Luitbert, m. Ger. Teu. people's brightness, 430

Luitberga, *f. Ger.* Teu. people's guard, 430

Luitbrand, *m. Ger.* Teu. people's sword, 430

Luitger, *m. Ger.* Teu. people's spear, 430

Luitgarde, *f. Ger.* Teu. people's guard, 430

Luithard, *m. Ger.* Teu. people's firmness, 430

Luitmar, *m. Ger.* Teu. people's fame, 430

Luitpold, *m. Ger.* Teu. people's valour, 430

Luiza, f. Port. Teu. famous war, 405

Luizinha, f. Port. Teu. famous war, 405

Luka, m. Russ. Wall. Lat. light, 133

Lukacz, m. Hung. Lat. light, 134

LUKAS, *m. Ger. Bohm.* Lat. light, 133

Lukasch, m. Lus. Lat. light, 134

Lukaschk, m. Lus. Lat. light, 134

Lukasz, m. Slav. Pol. Lat. light, 134

Luke, *m. Eng.* Lat. light, 133

Lukez, m. Slov. Lat. light, 134

Luned, *f. Welsh,* Kelt. shapely (?), 273

Lunette, *f. Fr.* Kelt. shapely (?), 273

Lupo, *m. Ital.* Lat. wolf, 198

LUPUS, *m.* Lat. wolf, 198

Lusche, f. m. Lett. Teu. famous holiness, 405

Luther, *m. Ger.* Teu. famous warrior, 405

Lutters, m. Lett. Teu. famous warrior, 405

Luzia, f. Rom. Lat. light, 132

Luzian, m. Russ. Lat. light, 133

Luziano, m. It. Lat. light, 133

Luzija, f. Russ. Lat. light, 133

Luzio, m. It. Lat. light, 133

LYCOS, *m.* Gr. wolf.

Lycurgus, *m. Lat.* Gr. wolf driver.

LYDIA, *f. Eng.* Gr. of Lydia, 200

Lyntje, f. Dutch, Gr. light, 132

Lys, f. Dutch, Heb. God's oath, 35

Lysje, f. Dutch, Heb. God's oath, 35

Lyulf, m. Scot. Teu. fierce wolf, 418

M

Maatfred, *m. Ger.* Teu. mighty peace, 422

Maatulf, *m. Ger.* Teu. mighty wolf, 422

Mab, *f. Ir.* Kelt. mirth (?), 258

Mabel, *f. Eng.* Lat. beloved, 258

Mabelle, *f. Fr.* Lat. beloved, 258

Macaire, *m. Ir.* Gr. happy, 447

Macario, *m. It.* Gr. happy, 447

MACBEATH, *m. Gael.* Kelt. son of life, 253

Macbeth, *m. Scot.* Kelt. son of life, 253

Mace, m. Fr. Aram. gift of the Lord, 15

Machtild, f. Ger. Teu. mighty heroine, 422

MAKARIOS, blessed, Gr. 447

Macias, m. Span. Heb. gift of the Lord, 15

Maciej, m. Pol. Aram. gift of the Lord, 15

Macsen, *m. Welsh,* Lat. greatest, 167

Madawc, *m. Welsh,* Kelt. beneficent, 227

Maddalena, *f. Ital.* Heb. of Magdala, 32

Maddalene, *f. Lett.* Heb. of Magdala, 32

Madde, f. Pol. Heb. of Magdala, 32

Madeleine, *f. Fr.* Heb. of Magdala, 32

Madelena, *f. Span.* Heb. of Magdala, 32

Madeline, *f. Eng.* Heb. of Magdala, 32

Madelina, *f. Russ.* Heb. of Magdala, 32

Madelon, f. Fr. Heb. of Magdala, 32

Maddis, m. Esth. Heb. gift of the Lord, 15

Madge, f. Eng. Gr. pearl, 121

Madlen, f. Bav. Heb. of Magdala, 32

Madlena, f. Slov. Lus. Heb. of Magda'a, 32

Madlenka, f. Lus. Heb. of Magdala, 32

Madli, f. Esth. Heb. of Magdala, 32

Madlyna, f. Lith. Heb. of Magdala, 32

Madoc, *m. Eng.* Kelt. beneficent, 227

Madoc, *f. m Welsh*, Kelt. beneficent, 227

Mads, m. Dan. Heb. gift of the Lord, 15

Madsche, f. Lett. Ger. pearl, 121

MADWG, *m. Welsh, Kelt.* beneficent, 227

MAEL, *m. Ir.* Kelt. disciple, 259

MAELBRIDH, *m. Erse*, Kelt. disciple of St. Bridget, 259

MAELCLULTH, *m. Erse*, Kelt. youth of the game, 261

MAELCOLUIN, *m. Gael.* Kelt. disciple of Columba, 261

MAELDEARG, *m. Erse*, Kelt. red chief, 261

MAELDOG, *m. Erse*, Kelt. servant of the star, 261

MAELDUBH, *m. Erse*, Kelt. black chief, 261

MAELDUINE, *m. Gael.* Kelt. brown chief, 261

MAELEOIN, *m. Erse*, Kelt. servant of John, 261

MAELFHIONN, *m. Erse*, Kelt. servant of Finn, 261

MAELGWAS, *m. Cym.* Kelt. chief, 261

MAELGWN, *m. Cym.* Kelt. chief, 261

MAELIOSA, *m. Erse*, Kelt. servant of JESUS, 261

MAELMORDNA, *m. Erse*, Kelt. majestic chief, 261

MAELPATRAIC, *m. Erse*, Kelt. servant of Patrick, 261

MAELRUADH, *m. Erse*, Kelt. 261

MAELSEACHLAIN, *m. Erse*, Kelt. servant of Secundus, 261

Maffea, f. Ital. Heb. gift of the Lord, 15

Maffeo, m. Ital. Heb. gift of the Lord, 15

Mag, f. Eng. Gr. pearl, 121

Maga, f. Swiss, Heb. bitter, 29

Magan, *m. Nor.* Teu. power, 422

Magdalen, *f. Eng.* Heb. of Magdala, 32

Magdalena, *f. Russ. Span. Port.* Heb. of Magdala, 32

Magdalene, *f. Ger.* Heb. of Magdala, 32

Magdeleine, *f. Fr.* Heb. of Magdala, 32

Magdelina, *f. Russ.* Heb. of Magdala, 32

Magdolna, f. Hung. Heb. of Magdala, 32

Magdosia, f. Pol. Heb. of Magdala, 32

Magge, f. Lett. Gr. pearl, 121

Maggie, f. Scot. Gr. pearl, 121

Maginbert, *m. Ger.* Teu. mighty brightness, 422

MAGINFRIED, *m. Ger.* Teu. mighty peace, 422

MAGINHILD, *f. Nor.* Teu. mighty battle maid, 422

Magmild, *f. Nor.* Teu. mighty battle maid, 422

MAGNUS, *m. Nor.* Lat. great, 166

Magsheesh, m. Erse, Heb. drawn out, 27

Mahault, *f. Fr.* Teu. mighty battle maid, 422

Mahe, m. Bav. Heb. gift of the Lord, 15

Mahon, *m. Erse*, Kelt. bear, 257

MAHTHILD, *f. Ger.* Teu. mighty battle maid, 422

Mai, f. Esth. Gr. pearl, 121

Maida, 464

Maidoc, *m. Ir.* Kelt. beneficent, 227

Maie, f. Esth. Heb. of Magdala, 32

Maie, f. Esth. Gr. bitter, 29

Maieli, f. Swiss, Heb. bitter, 29

Maije, f. Lett. Gr. pearl, 122

Maika, f. Russ. bitter, 29

Maillard, f. Cambrai. Heb. bitter, 29

Mainfroi, m. Fr. mighty peace, 321

Mainfroy, m. Eng. mighty peace, 321

Maion, f. Fr. Heb. bitter, 29

Mair, *f. Welsh*, Heb. 29

Mairgreg, *Erse*, Gr. pearl, 121

Maisie, f. Scot. Gr. pearl, 121

Maja, f. Swiss, Heb. bitter, 29

Majken, f. Swed. Heb. bitter, 29

Maksa, f. m. Ill. Lat. greatest, 166

Maksica, f. Ill. Lat. greatest, 166

Maksimilian, *m. Russ.* Lat. greatest Æmilian, 166

Maksymilian, *m. Pol.* Lat. greatest Æmilian, 166

Mal, f. Dutch, Teu. work, 330

Mal, f. Eng. Heb. bitter, 29

Mal, f. Esth. Heb. of Magdala, 32

Malachi, *m. Eng.* Heb. angel of the Lord, 52

Malalcel, m. Eng. Heb. shining of God.

Malberg, *f. Nor.* work protection, 331
Malchen, f. Ger. Teu. work, 330
Malcolm, *m. Scot.* Kelt. servant of Columba, 261
Male, f. Ger. Teu. work, 330
Malfrid, f. Nor. Teu. fair work, 330
Malgherita, *f. It.* Gr. pearl, 121
Malgorzata, f. Pol. Gr. pearl, 121
Malgosia, f. Pol. Gr. pearl, 121
Mali, f. Kaffir, Heb. bitter, 29
Malise, *m. Scot.* Kelt. disciple of Jesus, 260
Malk, m. Esth. Pers. king, 211
Malkin, f. Eng. Heb. bitter, 29
Maltrud, f. Nor. Teu. workmaid, 330
Malvina, *f. Gael.* Kelt. handmaid (?), 250
Malvine, *f. Fr.* Kelt. handmaid (?), 250
Manasseh, *m. Eng.* Heb. forgetting, 24
Manasses, *m. Lat.* Heb. forgetting, 24
Manda, f. Lat. Heb. of Magdala, 32
Mandelina, f. Serv. Heb. of Magdala, 32
MANDURRATH, *m. Cym.* Kelt. man of black treason, 224
Manfred, *m. Eng.* Teu. mighty peace, 421
Manfredi, *m. It.* Teu. mighty peace, 421
Manna, f. Bav. Heb. bitter grace, 29
Manna, m. Lapp. Lat. great, 327
Mannas, m. Lapp. Lat. great, 327
Manoel, *m. Port.* Heb. God with us, 36
Manon, m. Fr. Heb. bitter, 29
Manovello, *m. It.* Heb. God with us, 36
Manuel, *m. Fr. Eng. Span.* Heb. God with us, 36
Manuelita, f. Span. Heb. God with us, 36
Manuelito, m. Span. Heb. God with us, 36
Manus, m. Dutch, Teu. public, 327
Manus, *m. Irish,* Lat. great, 327
MAEL EOIN, *m. Er.* Heb. disciple of John, 260
Mara, f. Lus. Heb. bitter, 29
Marc, *m. Fr.* Lat. of Mars, 135
Marca, *f. Ger.* Lat. of Mars, 135
Marcel, *m. Fr.* Lat. of Mars, 135

Marcella, *f. Ir.* Lat. of Mars, 135
Marcelli, *f. Fr.* Lat. of Mars, 135
Marcellianus, *m.* Lat. of Mars, 135
Marcellin, *m. It.* Lat. of Mars, 135
Marcellino, *m. It.* Lat. of Mars, 135
Marcello, *m. It.* Lat. of Mars, 135
MARCELLUS, *Lat.* of Mars, 135
MARCH, *m. Erse,* Kelt. horse, 275
Marchell, *Welsh,* Lat. horse, 275
Marcia, *f. Ir.* Lat. of Mars, 135
Marcian, *m. Ger.* Lat. of Mars, 135
Marciano, *m. It.* Lat. of Mars, 135
MARCIANUS, *m.* Lat. of Mars, 135
Marcie, f. Fr. Lat. of Mars, 135
Marcin, m. Pol. Lat. of Mars, 135
MARCIUS, *m.* Lat. of Mars, 135
Marco, *m. It.* Lat. of Mars, 135
Marcos, *m. Span.* Lat. of Mars, 135
MARCUS, *m. Eng.* Lat. of Mars, 135
Mare, Lith. Heb. bitter, 29
Mareiel, Bav. Heb. bitter, 29
Mareili, Swiss, Heb. bitter, 29
Marek, Pol. Lat. of Mars, 135
Maret, f. Dan. Gr. pearl, 121
Marete, f. Lett. Gr. pearl, 121
Marenze, f. Lett. Lat. deserving, 190
Marczi, m. Hung. Lat. of Mars, 135
Marfa, *f. Russ.* Heb. becoming bitter, 32
Margaret, *f. Eng.* Gr. pearl, 121
Margareta, *f. Hung. Ger. Pol.* Gr. pearl, 121
Margarete, *f. Swiss,* Gr. pearl, 121
Margarethe, *f. Ger.* Gr. pearl, 121
Margarida, *f. Port.* Gr. pearl, 121
Margarita, *f. Span. Russ.* Gr. pearl, 121
MARGARITE, *f.* Gr. pearl, 121
Margarith, *f. Dutch,* Gr. pearl, 121
Margery, *f. Eng.* Gr. pearl, 121
Marget, f. Eng. Gr. pearl, 121
Margherita, *f. It.* Gr. pearl, 121
Marghet, Ger. Gr. pearl, 121
Margit, f. Hung. Gr. pearl, 121
Margot, f. Fr. Gr. pearl, 121
Margoton, f. Fr. Gr. pearl, 121
Margrete, *f. Lett.* Gr. pearl, 121
Margryta, *f. Lith.* Gr. pearl, 121
Marguerite, *f. Fr.* Gr. pearl, 121
Mari, *f. Hung. Irish,* Heb. bitter, 29
Maria, *f. (Universal)* Heb. bitter, 29
Marialit, f. Jew. Gr. pearl, 121
Mariam, *f. Gr.* Heb. bitter, 29

9

Mariamna, *f. Russ.* Heb. bitter grace, 29

MARIAMNE, *f.* Heb. bitter, 29

Mariana, *f. Port. Span.* Heb. bitter, 29

Mariane, *f. Ger.* Heb. bitter, 29

Marica, *f. Ill.* Heb. bitter, 29

Marie, *f. Ger. Fr. Bav.* Heb. bitter, 29

Mariedel, f. Slav. Heb. bitter, 29

Marieke, f. Dutch, Heb. bitter, 29

Mariel, f. Bav. Heb. bitter, 29

Marietta, f. It. Heb. bitter, 29

Mariette, f. It. Heb. bitter, 29

Marija, *f. Russ.* Heb. bitter, 29

Marike, f. L. Ger. Heb. bitter, 29

Marina, f. It. Lat. marine, 203

Marinha, f. Span. Heb. bitter, 29

Marino, f. It. Lat. marine, 203

Mario, f. m. It. Lat. of Mars, 135

Marion, f. Fr. Scot. Heb. bitter, 29

Mariquinhas, f. Port. Heb. bitter, 29

Mariquita, f. Port. Heb. bitter, 29

Maritornes, f. Span. Heb. bitter, 29

Marius, *m. Lat.* of Mars, 135

Marl, f. Bav. Heb. bitter, 29

Marja, *f. Lapp.* Heb. bitter, 29

Marjarita, Slav. Gr. pearl, 121

Marjeta, Slav. Gr. pearl, 121

Marjeta, f. Slov. Heb. bitter, 29

Marjorie, f. Scot. Gr. pearl, 121

Mark, *m. Eng. Russ. Esth.* Lat. of Mars, 135

Marka, f. Hung. Heb. bitter, 121

Markell, m. Russ. Lat. of Mars, 135

Markellin, *m. Russ.* Lat. of Mars, 135

Marko, *m. Wall.* Lat. of Mars, 135

Markos, *m. Gr.* Lat. of Mars, 135

Markota, f. Bohm. Gr. pearl, 131

Markulf, *m. Ger.* Teu. border wolf, 426

Markus, *m. Hung.* Lat. of Mars, 135

Markusch, *m. Lus.* Lat. of Mars, 135

Markward, m. Ger. Teu. border ward, 426

Markwin, m. Ger. Teu. border friend, 426

Marl, f. Bav. Heb. bitter, 29

Marlena, f. Lus. Heb. of Magdala, 32

Marmaduke, *m. Eng.* Kelt. sea leader (?), 281

Marquard, m. Fr. Teu. border ward, 425

Marret, f. Esth. Gr. pearl, 121

Marri, f. Esth. Heb. bitter, 29

Marrije, f. Lett. Heb. bitter, 29

Marsali, f. Gael. Gr. pearl, 121

Mart, m. Esth. Lat. of Mars, 135

Marta, *f. It. Boh.* Heb. becoming bitter, 31

Marten, *m. Swed. Dutch,* Lat. of Mars, 135

MARTHA, *f. Hung. Eng. Port.* Heb. becoming bitter, 31

Marthe, *f. Fr.* Heb. becoming bitter, 31

Marthon, *f. Fr.* Heb. becoming bitter, 31

Martia, m. Swiss, Lat. of Mars, 135

Martijn, *m. Dutch,* Lat. of Mars, 135

Martili, m. Swiss, Lat. of Mars, 135

Martin, *m. Fr. Russ. Eng. Port. Slov.* Lat. of Mars, 135

Martina, *f. Eng.* Lat. of Mars, 135

Martine, *f. Fr.* Lat. of Mars, 135

Martinho, *m. Port.* Lat. of Mars, 135

Martino, *m. Span. It.* Lat. of Mars, 135

MARTINUS, *m. Ger.* Lat. of Mars, 135

Martius, *m.* Lat. of Mars, 135

Martoni, m. Hung. Lat. of Mars, 135

Martschis, m. Lett. Lat. of Mars, 135

Martyn, *m. Eng.* Lat. of Mars, 135

Maruscha, f. Lus. Heb. bitter, 29

Marusche, f. Lett. Heb. bitter, 29

Marute, f. Lett. Heb. bitter, 29

Mary, *f. Eng.* Heb. bitter, 29

Marya, *f. Pol.* Heb. bitter, 29

Maryke, f. Lith. Heb. bitter, 29

Marynia, f. Pol. Heb. bitter, 29

Marysia, f. Pol. Heb. bitter, 29

Marzellin, *m. Russ.* Lat. of Mars, 135

Marzia, f. It. Lat. of Mars, 135

Marzocco, *m. Ven.* Lat. of Mars, 135

Masaccio, *m. Ital.* Aram. twin, 22

Masaniello, *m. Ital.* Aram. Ger. twin, 22

Mascha, f. Russ. Heb. bitter, 29

Masche, f. Lett. Gr. pearl, 121

Maschinka, f. Russ. Heb. bitter, 29

Maso, m. It. Aram. twin, 22

Massimiliano, *m. It.* Lat. greatest Æmilianus, 166

Massimo, *m. It.* Lat. greatest, 166

Massuccio, m. It. Aram. twin, 22

Mat, m. Eng. Heb. gift of the Lord, 15

Mateo, *Span.* Heb. gift of the Lord, 15

Mate, Hung. Heb. gift of the Lord, 15

Mataus, m. Bohm. Heb. gift of the Lord, 15

Mateusz, m. Pol. Heb. gift of the Lord, 15

Matfei, m. Russ. Heb. gift of the Lord, 15

Matevz, m. Slov. Heb. gift of the Lord, 15

Mathe, m. Bav. Heb. gift of the Lord, 15

MATH-GHAMHAIN, *m. Erse,* Kelt. bear, 257

Mathia, m. Wall. Heb. gift of the Lord, 15

Mathias, m. Swed. Fr. Swiss, Heb. gift of the Lord, 15

Mathieu, m. Prov. Heb. gift of the Lord, 15, 257

Mathilda, *m. Hung.* Teu. mighty battle maid, 422

Mathilde, *f. Ger.* Teu. mighty battle maid, 422

Matija, m. Serv. Heb. gift of the Lord, 15

Matilda, *f. Eng. It.* Teu. mighty battle maid, 422

Matilde, *f. Fr.* Teu. mighty battle maid, 422

MATTANIAH, *m. Eng.* Heb. gift of the Lord, 15

Mats, m. Swed. Heb. gift of the Lord, 15

Mattea, *f. It.* Heb. gift of the Lord, 15

Matteo, m. It. Heb. gift of the Lord, 15

Matthäus, *m. Ger.* Heb. gift of the Lord, 15

Matthes, *m. Ger.* Heb. gift of the Lord, 15

Matthew, *m. Eng.* Heb. gift of the Lord, 15

Matthia, *m. Ger.* Heb. gift of the Lord, 15

Matthies, *m. Fr.* Bav. gift of the Lord, 15

Matthieu, *m. Port.* Heb. gift of the Lord, 15

Matthias, *m. Eng.* Heb. gift of the Lord, 15

Matthis, m. Ger. Heb. gift of the Lord, 15

Matthys, m. Dutch, Lett. Heb. gift of the Lord, 15

Mattia, *m. Ital.* Heb. gift of the Lord, 15

Mattija, *m. Slov.* Heb. gift of the Lord, 15

Matty, f. Eng. Heb. becoming bitter, 15

Matty, f. Eng. Teu. mighty battle maid, 422

Matvei, *m. Russ.* Heb. gift of the Lord, 15

Matyas, *m. Pol. Hung.* Heb. gift of the Lord, 15

Maude, f. Eng. Teu. mighty battle maid, 422

Maudlin, f. Eng. Heb. of Magdala, 32

Maun, f. Eng. Heb. of Magdala, 32

Mauna, m. Lapp. Lat. great, 166

Maunes, m. Lapp. Lat. great, 166

Maur, *m. Fr.* Lat. dark, 200

Maura, *f. It. Ger.* Lat. dark, 200

Maure, *f. Fr.* Lat. dark, 200

Maurice, *m. Fr. Eng.* Lat. Moorish, 201

Mauricio, *m. Port. Span.* Lat. Moorish, 201

Maurids, *m. Dan.* Lat. Moorish, 201

MAURITIUS, *m.* Lat. Moor, 201

Maurits, *m. Dutch,* Lat. Moor, 201

Maurizio, *m. Ital.* Lat. Moor, 201

Mauro, *m. Rom.* Lat. Moor, 201

MAURUS, *m.* Lat. Moor, 201

Maurycij, *m. Pol.* Lat. Moor, 201

Mave, *f. Irish,* Kelt. mirth (?), 258

Mavia, *f. Russ.* Lat. dark, 201

Mavritij, *m. Russ.* Lat. dark, 201

Mavruscha, f. Russ. Lat. dark, 201

Mawkin, f. Eng. Heb. bitter, 29

Max, *m. Ger.* Lat. greatest, 166

Maxa, f. Ger. Lat. greatest, 166

Maxime, *m. Fr.* Lat. greatest, 166

Maximien, *m. Fr.* Lat. greatest, 166

Maximilian, *m. Ger.* Lat. greatest Æmilianus, 166

MAXIMILIANE, *f. Ger.* Lat. greatest Æmilianus, 166

Maximiliao, *m. Port.* Lat. greatest Æmilianus, 166

Maximilien, *m. Fr.* Lat. greatest Æmilianus, 166

MAXIMUS, *m.* Lat. greatest, 166

Maxl, m. Bav. Lat. greatest Æmilianus, 166

MAWDWEN, *f. Cym.* Kelt. mannerly, 271

May, f. Eng. Heb. bitter, 29

May, f. Scot. Gr. pearl, 121

Maynard, m. Eng. Teu. mighty firmness, 421

Mayne, m. Eng. Teu. mighty, 421

Mazalein, f. Pro. Heb. of Magdala, 32

MEADHBH, *f. Erse,* Kelt. mirth, 258

MEAGHAR, *m. Erse,* Kelt. merry, 259

Meara, *m. Irish,* Kelt. merry, 259

Meave, *f. Erse,* Kelt. mirth (?), 259

Mechel, f. Bav. Teu. mighty battle maid, 422

Mechtild, *f. Bav.* Teu. mighty battle maid, 422

Medal, f. Bav. Heb. bitter, 29

Médé, f. Fr. my delight, 196

Meews, m. L.G. Heb. son of furrows, 25

Meg, f. Eng. Gr. pearl, 121

MEGINHARD, *m. Ger.* Teu. mighty firmness, 421

MEGINHERI, *m. Ger.* Teu. mighty warrior, 421

Mehaut, f. Fr. Teu. mighty battle maid, 421

Mehetabel, *f. Eng.* Heb. beneficent, 26

Meinbern, m. Ger. Teu. mighty bear, 421

Meinbert, *m. Ger.* Teu. mighty brightness, 421

Meinbot, m. Ger. Teu. mighty commander, 421

Meinfred, *m. Ger.* Teu. mighty peace, 421

Meinhard, *m. Ger.* Teu. mighty firmness, 421

Meino, *m. Ger.* Teu. mighty, 421

Meinolf, *m. Ger.* Teu. mighty wolf, 421

Meinrad, *m. Ger.* Teu. mighty council, 421

Meinward, *m. Ger.* Teu. mighty guard, 421

Meirchawn, *m. Pict.* Kelt.

MEIRIADWG, *m. Welsh,* Kelt. sea protector, 280

Mekel, m. L. Ger. Heb. who is like to God, 54

Melanell, f. m. Eng. Kelt. honey (?), 282

MELANIA, *f. Eng. It.* Gr. black, 70

Melanie, *f. Fr.* Gr. black, 70

Melany, *f. Eng.* Gr. black, 70

Melchior, *m. Span. Ger. Pers.* king, 211

Melchiore, *m. It.* Pers. king, 211

Melchiorre, *m. It.* Pers. king, 211

MELCHISEDEC, *m. Eng.* Heb. king of righteousness, 15

MELETIUS, *m.* Lat. honied, 282

Melicent, *f. Eng.* Teu. work strength, 330

Melicerte, *f. Fr.* Teu. work strength, 330

MELIOR, *f. Eng.* Lat. better, 193

Melisenda, *f. Span.* Teu. work strength, 330

MELISSA, *f. It. Eng.* Lat. bee, 80

Melisse, *f. Fr.* Lat. bee, 80

Melite, *f. Fr.* Lat. bee, 80

Melitus, *m.* Lat. honied, 80

Melony, *f. Eng.* Gr. dark, 70

Melusina, *f. Eng.* Teu. work strength, 80, 330

Melusine, *f. Fr. Ger.* Teu. work strength, 80, 330

Melva, *m. Eng.* Kelt. chief, 262

Memba, m. Fris. Teu. mighty bear, 421

Memmo, m. Fris. Teu. mighty bear, 421

Mencia, f. Span. Lat. Sunday child (?), or adviser (?), 218

Mendez, m. Span. Lat. Sunday child, 218

Menica, f. It. Lat. Sunday child, 218

Menico, m. It. Lat. Sunday child, 218

Menie, f. Scot. Heb. bitter, 29

Menno, m. Ger. Teu. mighty strength, 421

Meno, m. Ger. Teu. mighty strength, 421

Mens, m. Ger. Lat. merciful, 160

Mente, m. Ger. Lat. merciful, 160

Mentzel, m. Ger. Lat. merciful, 160

Menz, m. Dan. Lat. merciful, 160

Menz, Serv. Lat. Sunday child, 218

Menzel, Serv. Lat. Sunday child, 218

Meo, m. It. Heb. son of furrows, 25

Meraud, *f. Eng.* Gr. emerald, 125
Mercede, *f. It.* Lat. favours, 30
MERCEDES, *f. Span.* Lat. favours, 30
MERCY, *f. Eng.*
MERDDHIN, *m. Welsh,* Kelt. sea hill, 280
Meredith, *m. Eng.* Kelt. sea protector, 280
MEREWINE, *m. A.S.* Teu. famed friend, 425
Meriadoc, *m. Bret.* Kelt. sea protector, 280
Merica, f. Eng. Teu. work rule, 330
Merich, m. Ger. Teu. work ruler, 330
Merrik, m. Ger. Teu. work ruler, 330
Merlin, *m. Eng. Fr.* Kelt. sea hill, 280
Merlino, *m. It.* Kelt. sea hill, 280
MEROHELM, *m. A.S.* Teu. famed helm, 425
Merovée, *m. Fr.* Teu. famed war, 425
Meroveus, *m.* Lat. Teu. famed war, 425
MEROWALD, *m. A.S.* Teu. famed power, 425
Mertil, m. Ger. Lat. of Mars, 135
Mertin, m. Bav. Lat. of Mars, 135
Meriel, f. Eng. Gr. myrrh, 125
MEROVEH, *m. Frank.* Teu. famed holiness, 425
MEROVINE, *m. A.S.* Teu. famed, 425
Mervyn, *m. Eng.* Kelt. sea hill, 280
Mesdélices, *f. Fr.* my delight, 196
Meta, f. Ger. Ger. pearl, 121
Mete, f. Ger. Gr. pearl, 121
Metelill, f. Dan. pearl, 121
Methusalem, *m. Eng.* Heb. man of the dart.
Metje, f. Dutch, Gr. pearl, 121
Metrophanes, *m. Ger.* Slav. fire glory (?), 440
Mette, f. Dan. Gr. pearl, 121
Meurisse, m. Fr. Lat. Moor, 201
Meuriz, *m. Welsh,* Lat. Moor, 201
Mewes, m. Ger. Heb. son of furrows, 25
Meyrick, m. Eng. Teu. work ruler, 330
Micah, *m. Eng.* Heb. who is like the Lord, 54
Micha, *m. Ger.* Heb. who is like to God, 54
Michael, *m. Ger. Eng.* Heb. who is like to God, 54

Michaella, *f. It.* Heb. who is like to God, 54
Michaele, *f. m. It.* Heb. who is like to God, 54
Michaeline, *f. Ger.* Heb. who is like to God, 54
Michaelis, *m. Ger.* Heb. who is like to God, 54
Michail, *m. Russ.* Heb. who is like to God, 54
Michaila, *m. Russ.* Heb. who is like to God, 54
Michal, *m. Bohm. Pol. Lus.* Heb. who is like to God, 54
Michau, m. Fr. Heb. who is like to God, 54
Michée, m. Fr. Heb. who is like to God, 54
Michej, m. Russ. Heb. who is like to God, 54
Michel, *m. Fr.* Heb. who is like to God, 54
Michele, *m. It.* Heb. who is like to God, 54
Michelle, *m. Fr.* Heb. who is like to God, 54
Micheltje, m. Dutch, Heb. who is like to God, 54
Michiel, *m. Dutch,* Heb. who is like to God, 54
Michon, m. Fr. Heb. who is like to God, 54
Mick, m. Ir. Heb. who is like to God, 54
Mickel, m. Swed. Heb. who is like to God, 54
Miedal, f. Bav. Heb. bitter, 29
Mieke, f. Dutch, Heb. bitter, 29
Miel, f. Bav. Heb. bitter, 29
Mieli, f. Swiss, Heb. 29
Micral, f. Bav. Heb. bitter, 29
Mies, m. Swiss, Heb. exalted of the Lord, 49
Mietje, f. Dutch, Heb. bitter, 29
Miguel, *m. Span. Port.* Heb. who is like to God, 54
Miguela, *f. Port. Span.* Heb. who is like to God, 54
Miha, m. Slov. Heb. who is like to God, 54
Mihail, *m. Wall.* Heb. who is like to God, 54
Mihal, m. Slov. Hung. Heb. who is like to God, 54

Mihaly, m. Hung. Heb. who is like to God, 54

Miho, m. Serv. Heb. who is like to God, 54

Mija, f. Swiss, Heb. bitter, 29

Mijailo, m. Serv. Heb. who is like to God, 54

Mik, m. Esth. Heb. who is like to God, 54

Mikael, *m. Swed.* Heb. who is like to God, 54

Mikas, m. Swed. Heb. who is like to God, 54

Mike, f. Dutch, Heb. bitter, 29

Mikel, m. Esth. Heb. who is like to God, 54

Mikelina, f. Russ. Lett. Heb. who is like to God, 54

Mikkas, m. Lett. Heb. who is like to God, 54

Mikke, m. Lett. Heb. who is like to God, 54

Mikkeles, m. Lith. Lett. Heb. who is like to God, 54

Miklaoz, m. Slov. Gr. people's victory, 90

Miklaos, m. Lus. Gr. people's victory, 90

Mikli, m. Esth. Heb. who is like to God, 54

Miklos, m. Hung. Gr. people's victory, 90

Mikolxj, m. Pol. Gr. people's victory, 90

Mikulas, m. Bohm. Gr. people's victory, 90

Mila, f. Slav. Slav. lovely, 444

Mila, f. Lus. Lat. work (?), 141

Milan, m. Bret. Gr. crusher, 97

Milan, f. m. Slov. Lat. lovely, 97

Milari, m. Slov. Lat. cheerful, 191

Milborough, *f. Eng.* Teu. mild pledge, 427

MILBURGA, *f. Lat.* Teu. mild pledge, 427

Milcah, *f. Eng.* Heb. queen.

MILDBURH, *f. A.S.* Teu. mild pledge, 427

MILDGYTH, *f. A.S.* Teu. mild gift, 427

Mildred, *f. Eng.* Teu. mild threatener, 427

Mildreda, *f. Lat.* Teu. mild threatener, 427

Mildrid, *f. Dan.* Teu. mild threatener, 427

MILDTHRYTH, *f. A.S.* Teu. mild threatener, 427

Miles, *m. Eng.* Gr. crusher, 97

Milhan, m. Span. Lat. affable, 141

Milica, f. Slov. Slav. love, 444

Milicent, *f. Eng.* Teu. work strength.

MILIDH, *m. Erse,* Kelt. warrior, 97

Milivo, m. Slav. Slav. love war, 444

Miljo, m. Serv. Heb. who is like to God, 54

Milka, m. Lus. Lat. work or affable, 141

Millicent, *m. Eng.* Teu. work strength, 330

Millica, f. Ill. Heb. bitter, 29, 444

Milly, f. Eng. Teu. work strength, 330

Milo, *m. Lat.* Gr. crusher, 97

Milon, *m. Fr. & Gr.* Gr. crusher, 97

Milone, *m. Ital.* Gr. crusher, 97

MILOSLAV, *m. Slov.* Slav. love glory, 441

Mimi, f. Fr. Teu. helmet of resolution, 315

Mimmeli, f. Swiss, Teu. helmet of resolution, 315

Mine, *f. Ger.* Teu. helmet of resolution, 315

Minella, f. Eng. Teu. helmet of resolution, 315

MINERVINA, *f.* Lat. of Minerva, 171

Minette, f. Fr. Teu. helmet of resolution, 315

Minka, *f. Pol.* Teu. helmet of resolution, 315

Minne, f. Ger. Teu. helmet of resolution, 315

Minna, *f. Scot.* Teu. memory.

MINNE, *f. Ger.* Teu. memory.

Minnehaha, *f. Red Indian,* laughing water.

Miranda, *f. Eng.* Lat. to be admired.

Miriam, *f. Eng.* Heb. bitter, 29

Mirko, m. Slov. Teu. work rule, 331

MIROSLAV, *f.* Slav. peace glory, 442

Misa, m. Serv. Heb. who is like to God, 54

Mischa, m. Russ. Heb. who is like to God, 54

Mischenka, m. Russ. Heb. who is like God, 54

Miska, m. Serv. Hung. Heb. who is like to God, 54

Mistislaus, *m. Lat.* Slav. avenging glory, 441

Mitar, m. Serv. Ill. Gr. of Demeter, 69

Mithridates, *m. Gr.* Pers. given to the sun.

Mitra, f. Slav. Gr. of Demeter, 69

MITROFAN, *m. Russ.* fire glory (?), 440

MLADEN, *m. Serv.* Slav. young, 445

Modestine, *f. Fr.* Lat. modest, 193

MODESTUS, *m. Lat.* modest, 193

Modesty, *f. Eng.* Lat. 193

Medwenna, *f. Welsh,* Kelt. 271

MOEDOG, *m. Erse,* Kelt. servant of the star, 227

Moggy, m. Eng. Gr. pearl, 121

Mogue, *m. Erse,* Kelt. amiable, 227

Moina, *f. Scot.* Kelt. soft.

Moise, *m. Fr.* Heb. drawn out, 27

Moises, *m. Port.* Heb. drawn out, 27

Moisi, *m. Wall.* Heb. drawn out, 27

Moissej, *m. Russ.* Heb. drawn out, 27

Moissey, *f. Manx,* Heb. bitter, 29

Mojsia, *m. Serv.* Heb. drawn out, 27

Mojsilo, m. Serv. Heb. drawn out, 27

Mojzesz, *m. Pol.* Heb. drawn out, 27

Mojzisch, m. Boh. Heb. drawn out, 27

Mojzija, m. Slov. Heb. drawn out, 27

Molde, f. Eng. Teu. mighty battle maid, 422

Molly, f. Eng. Heb. bitter, 29

Monacella, *f. Lat.* little nun, 282

Moncha, *f. Erse,* Lat. adviser, 218

Monegonde, f. Flem. Heb. thoughtful war.

MONGFINN, *f. Erse,* Kelt. fair haired.

Moni, *f. Swab.* Lat. adviser, 218

MONICA, *f. It. Eng.* Lat. adviser (?), 218

Monike, *f. Ger.* Lat. adviser, 218

Monique, *f. Fr.* Lat. adviser, 218

Moore, *f. Scot.* Kelt. great, 258

MOR, *f. Erse,* Kelt. great, 258

Morag, f. Scot. Kelt. great, 258

Morets, *m. Dan.* Lat. moor, 280

Morgance, f. m. French, Kelt. sea dweller, 280

Morgan, *m. Welsh,* Kelt. sea dweller, 280

Morgana, f. Eng. Kelt. sea dweller, 280

Morguc, f. Fr. Kelt. sea dweller, 280

MORGWEN, *f. Welsh,* Kelt. sea lady, 280

MORGWN, *m. Welsh,* Kelt. sea dweller, 280

Moric, *m. Bohm. Slov.* Lat. Moor, 201

Moricz, *m. Hung.* Lat. Moor, 201

Moritz, *m. Dan.* Lat. Moor, 201

Moritz, *m. Ger.* Lat. Moor, 201

Moriz, *m. Russ.* Lat. Moor, 201

MORMAN, *m. Bret.* Kelt. sea man, 201

Morna, f. Scot. Kelt. beloved (?), 251

Morolt, m. Eng. Kelt. sea protection, 280

Morough, *m. Ir.* Kelt. sea protection, 280

Morris, *m. Ir.* Lat. Moor, 201

Mortough, *m. Ir.* Kelt. sea warrior, 280

Morty, m. Ir. Kelt. sea warrior, 280

MORVEN, *m. Bret.* Kelt. sea man, 280

MORVREN, *m. Welsh,* Kelt. sea raven, 280

MORVRYN, *m. Welsh,* Kelt. sea hill, 280

Mose, *m. It.* Heb. drawn out, 27

Moses, *m. Eng. Ger.* Heb. drawn out, 27

Mote Mahal, *f.* Arab. pearl of the harem, 2

Mousa, *m. Arab.* Heb. drawn out, 27

Mozes, *m. Dutch, Slov.* Heb. drawn out, 27

Mozses, *m. Hung.* Heb. drawn out, 27

MRENA, *f. Serv.* Slav. white in the eyes, 445

Mros, m. Lus. Gr. immortal, 109

Mrosk, m. Lus. Gr. immortal, 109

MSTISLAV, *m. Slav.* avenging glory, 441

MUIRCHEARTACH, *m. Erse,* Kelt. sea warrior, 280

MUIREADHACH, *m. Erse,* Kelt. sea protector, 280

MUIRGIS, *m. Erse,* Kelt. sea, 280

Mukkel, m. Bav. Slov. helpless, 43

Mukki, m. Bav. Slov. helpless, 43

Mun, m. Eng. Teu. rich protection, 378

Muna, *f. Span.* Basque, 460

MUNGHU, *m. Gael.* Kelt. loveable, 258

Mungo, *m. Scot.* Kelt. loveable, 258

Munila, f. Span. Basque, 460

MUNO, *m. Span.* Basque, 460

Murdoch, *m. Scot.* Kelt. sea protector, 280

Muriel, *f. Eng.* Gr. myrrh, 125

Murphy, m. Ir. Kelt. sea warrior, 280

MURRIN, *f. Erse,* Kelt. long haired, 100

Murtagh, *m. Ir.* Kelt. sea warrior, 280

Murtough, *m. Fr.* Kelt. sea warrior, 280

Musidora, f. Eng. Gr. gift of the Muses, 72

Myles, *m. Ir.* Gr. crusher, 77

Myne, Lith. Teu. helmet of resolution, 315

Mynette, Lith. Teu. helmet of resolution, 315

Myra, f. Eng.

Mysie, f. Scot. Gr. pearl, 121

MYVANWY, *f. Welsh,* Kelt. 279

N

Naatje, f. Dutch, Heb. grace, 42

Nace, m. Slov. Lat. fiery, 194

Nada, *f. Serv.* Slav. hope, 439

Nadan, f. Serv. Slav. hope, 439

NADEZNA, *f. Russ.* Slav. hope, 439

Nadine, *f. Fr.* Slav. hope, 439

Nafaniel, *m. Russ.* Heb. gift of God, 25

Nahum, *m. Eng.* Heb. comfort, 51

Nan, f. Eng. Heb. grace, 42

Nancy, f. Eng. Heb. grace, 42

Nandel, m. Ger. Teu. adventuring life, 433

Nanette, f. Fr. Heb. grace, 42

Nani, f. Hung. Heb. grace, 42

NANNA, *f. Nor.* Teu. bold, 304

Nanna, f. It. Heb. grace, 42

Nanneli, f. Swiss, Heb. grace, 42

Nannerl, f. Bav. Heb. grace, 42

Nanni, m. Ital. Heb. the Lord's grace, 45

NANNO, *m. Fris.* Teu. bold, 304

Nannon, f. Fr. Heb. grace, 42

Nannos, m. Gr. Heb. grace of the Lord, 45

Nanny, f. Eng. Heb. grace, 42

Nanon, f. Fr. Heb. grace, 42

Nanty, m. Scot. Lat. inestimable, 142

Naomi, *f. Eng.* Heb. pleasant, 28

Nap, m. Eng. Lat. of the new city, 200

Naphthali, *m. Eng.* Heb. wrestling, 7

Napo, m. Ger. Lat. of the new city, 200

Napoleon, *m. Fr.* Gr. of the new city, 200

Napoleone, *m. It.* Gr. of the new city, 200

Napolio, *m. It.* Gr. of the new city, 200

Narcisse, *m. Fr.* Gr. daffodil, 81

Narcissus, *m. Eng.* Gr. daffodil, 81

Narkiss, *m. Russ.* Gr. daffodil, 81

Nastagio, f. m. It. Gr. of the resurrection, 110

Nastassja, f. Russ. Gr. of the resurrection, 110

Naste, f. m. Lett. Lat. Christmas child, 210

Nastenka, f. Russ. Gr. of the resurrection, 110

Nat, m. Eng. Heb. gift of God, 25

Natale, *m. It.* Lat. Christmas child, 209

Natalia, *f. It. Span.* Lat. Christmas child, 209

Natalie, *f. Fr. Ger.* Lat. Christmas child, 209

Natalija, *f. Russ.* Lat. Christmas child, 209

Natalita, *f. Span.* Lat. Christmas, child, 209

Natanaelle, m. It. Heb. gift of God, 25

Natascha, *f. Russ.* Lat. Christmas child, 209

Nataschenka, f. Russ. Lat. Christmas child, 210

NATHAN, *m. Eng.* Heb. gift, 25

NATHANAEL, *m. Eng.* Heb. gift of God, 25

Nathanial, *m. Wall.* Heb. gift of God, 25

Nathaniel, *m. Fr.* Heb. gift of God, 25

Natividad, *f. Span.* Lat. birth, 209

Navarino, *m. Eng.*

Nazji, m. Bav. Lat. fiery, 194

Nazarene, m. Ger. Heb. of Nazareth, 39

Naze, m. Bav. Lat. fiery, 194
Nazel, m. Bav. Lat. fiery, 194
Neal, m. Ir. Kelt. chief, 240
Neapolio, *m. It.* Gr. of the new city, 200
Neapoleon, *m. It.* Gr. of the new city, 200
Necek, m. Slov. Gr. man, 86
Ned, m. Eng. Teu. rich guard, 378
NEDA, *f. Bulg.* Slav. Sunday, 218
Nedan, *m. Bulg.* Slav. Sunday, 218
Nedelko, *m. Bulg.* Slav. Sunday, 218
Nedeljka, *f. Bulg.* Slav. Sunday, 218
Nedelschko, m. Ill. Slav. Sunday, 218
Nedo, *m. Ill.* Slav. Sunday, 218
Neeldje, m. Dutch, Lat. horn (?), 314
Nehemiah, *m. Eng.* Heb. comfort of the Lord, 51
NEIDHARD, *m. Ger.* Teu. firm compulsion, 418
NEILL, *m. Gadhael.* Kelt. champion, 240
Nelle, f. Dutch, Lat. horn (?), 146
Nelle, f. Ger. Gr. stone, 108
Nelly, f. Eng. Gr. light, 68
NEOT, *m. A.S.* compulsion, 418
Nepomucen, *m. Pol.* Slav. helpless, 43
NEPOMUK, *m. Bohm.* Slav. helpless, 43
Nese, f. Lett. Gr. pure, 119
Nesle, *m. Fr.* Lat. black, 168
Nessie, f. Manx, Gr. pure, 119
Nest, f. Welsh, Gr. pure, 119
Neto, f. Esth. Gr. pure, 119
Neza, f. Slov. Gr. pure, 119
Nezica, f. Slov. Gr. pure, 119
Nial, *m. Nor.* Kelt. champion, 240
Nib, f. Eng. Heb. God's oath, 35
Nicholas, *m. Eng.* Gr. victory of the people, 90
Nichon, f. Fr. Heb. grace, 42
Nick, m. Eng. Gr. victory of the people, 90
Nickel, m. Bav. Gr. victory of the people, 90
Nicodème, *m. Fr.* Gr. victory of the people, 90
Nicodemus, *m. Eng.* Gr. victory of the people, 90
Nicol, m. Scot. Gr. victory of the people, 90

Nicola, *m. It.* Gr. victory of the people, 90
Nicolaas, *m. Dutch,* Gr. victory of the people, 90
Nicolas, *m. Fr.* Gr. victory of the people, 90
Nicolau, *m. Port.* Gr. victory of the people, 90
Nicole, *m. Fr.* Gr. victory of the people, 90
Nicolette, *f. Fr.* Gr. victory of the people, 90
Nicolina, *f. Gr.* Gr. victory of the people, 90
Nicolo, *m. Ital.* Gr. victory of the people, 90
Nidbert, *m. Ger.* Teu. bright compelling, 418
Nidhert, *m. Ger.* Teu. firm compelling, 418
Niels, *m. Scot.* Kelt. champion, 240
Niel, m. Dan. Gr. victory of the people, 90
Nigel, *m. Scot.* Lat. black, 168, 241
NIGELLUS, *m. Lat.* black, 168
NIGER, *m. Lat.* black, 168
NIKIAS, *m. Gr.* conquering, 90
Nikka, m. Lapp. Gr. victory of the people, 90
Nikkelis, *m. Lett.* Gr. victory of the people, 90
Nikki, m. Finn. Gr. victory of the people, 90
Nikla, m. Bav. Gr. victory of the people, 90
Niklaas, *m. Dutch,* Gr. victory of the people, 90
Niklas, m. Ger. Swed. Gr. victory of the people, 90
Niklau, m. Bav. Gr. victory of the people, 90
Nikodem, *m. Gr.* Gr. victory of the people, 90
NIKODΓMOS, *m. Gr. Slov. Bulg.* victory of the people, 90
Nikola, *m. Russ.* Gr. victory of the people, 90
Nikolaj, *m. Russ.* Gr. victory of the people, 90
Nikolas, *m. Dutch,* Gr. victory of the people, 90
Nikolascha, m. Russ. Gr. victory of the people, 90

NIKOLAUS, *m. Ger.* Gr. victory of the people, 90
NIKON, *m. Russ.* Gr. victory, 90
Niku, m. Finn. Gr. victory of the people, 90
Niles, m. Finn. Gr. victory of the people, 90
Nille, Nor. Gr. stone, 108
Nillon, f. Fr. Heb. grace, 42
Nilo, m. Finn. Gr. victory of the people, 90
Nils, m. Swed. Gr. victory of the people, 90
Ninetta, f. Ital. Heb. grace, 42
Ninette, f. Fr. Heb. grace, 42
Ninian, *m. Scot.* Kelt. 240
NINIDH, *m. Erse,* Kelt. 240
Ninon, f. Fr. Heb. grace, 42
NIORD, *m. Nor.* Teu. sea god, 306
Nithard, *m. Ger.* Teu. firm compulsion, 418
Nitz, m. Ger. Teu. firm compulsion, 418
Njal, *m. Ice.* Teu. champion, 240
Noa, *m. It.* Heb. rest, 9
Noah, *m. Dutch,* Heb. rest, 9
NOACHAS, *m. Gr.* Heb. rest, 9
Noah, *m. Eng.* Heb. rest, 9
Noe, *m. Fr. Russ.* Heb. rest, 9
Noël, *m. Fr.* Lat. Christmas, 209
Noll, m. Eng. Teu. olive, 208
Nöll, m. Dutch, Lat. horn, 314
Nona, *f. Eng.* Lat. ninth, 138
Nonna, *f.* Lat. ninth, 138
Nonne, *m. Fris.* Teu. bold, 304
Nora, f. Ir. Lat. honour, 190
Norah, f. Ir. Lat. honour, 190
NORBERT, *m. Ger.* Teu. Niord's brightness, 306
NORDHILDA, *f. Ger.* Teu. Niord's battle maid, 306
Norman, *m. Scot.* Teu. Niord's man, 306
Notberg, *f. Ger.* Teu. compelling protection, 418
Notger, *m. Ger.* Teu. compelling spear, 418
Notto, m. Nor. Teu. compelling wolf, 418
NOTTULF, *m. Nor.* Teu. compelling wolf, 418
Novak, *m. Ill.* Slov. new.
Novia, *f. Ill.* Slav. Lat. new.

Nozzo, m. It. Heb. grace of the Lord, 46
Nuala, f. Ir. Kelt. fair shoulders, 245
Numps, m. Eng. Heb. staff of peace, 350
Nuño, *f. Span.*
Nuno, *m. Span.*
Nunziata, f. It. Lat. announced, 30

O

Oado, m. Esth. Heb. red earth, 10
Obadiah, *m. Eng.* Heb. servant of the Lord, 50
Obramas, *m. Lith.* Heb. father of nations, 11
Octave, *f. Fr.* Lat. eighth, 138
Octavia, *f. Eng.* Lat. eighth, 138
Octaviano, *m. Rom.* Lat. eighth, 138
OCTAVIANUS, *m. Lat.* eighth, 138
Octavien, *m. Fr.* Lat. eighth, 138
Octavie, *f. Fr.* Lat. eighth, 138
OCTAVIUS, *m. Lat.* eighth, 138
Ocko, m. Fris. Teu. noble rich, 409
ODA, *f. Ger.* Teu. rich, 376
ODBJORG, *f. m. Ger.* Teu. rich protection, 378
ODDE, *m. Ger.* Teu. rich, 376
ODDGRIM, *m. Nor.* Teu. rich helmet, 378
ODDLAUG, *f. Nor.* Teu. rich liquor, 378
ODDLEIF, *m. Nor.* Teu. rich relic, 378
ODDMUND, *m. Nor.* Teu. rich protection, 378
ODDNY, *m. Nor.* Teu. rich freshness, 378
Oddo, *f. m. Nor.* Teu. rich, 378
ODDR, *f. m. Nor.* Teu. rich, 378
ODDVEIG, *m. Nor.* Teu. rich liquor, 378
ODDWARD, *m. Ger.* rich guard, 378
Ode, f. Nor. Teu. rich, 376
Odes, *m. It.* Teu. rich, 376
ODELBURGA, *f. Ger.* Teu. noble guard, 411
Odelbrecht, *m. Ger.* Teu. noble brightness, 411
ODELGIS, *m. Ger.* Teu. noble pledge, 411
ODELIND, *f. Ger.* Teu. noble snake, 411
Odelric, *m. Ger.* Teu. noble rule, 411

Odgisl, m. Nor. Teu. rich pledge, 411
ODGJER, *m. Nor.* Teu. rich spear, 411
ODGUND, *f. Ger.* Teu. rich war, 411
ODILA, *f. Ger. Fr.* Teu. rich, 411
ODILE, *f. Fr.* Teu. rich, 411
Odilo, *m. Ger.* Teu. rich, 378
Odilon, *m. Fr.* Teu. rich, 378
Odkatla, *f. Nor.* rich kettle, 376
Odkel, m. Nor. rich kettle, 376
Odli, m. Swiss, Heb. red earth, 10
Odmar, *Nor.* Teu. rich fame, 378
Odo, *m. Ger. Eng.* Teu. rich, 378
Odoacer, *m. Lat.* Teu. treasure watcher, 377
Odoardo, *m. It.* Teu. rich guard, 378
Odolf, m. Ger. Teu. rich wolf, 378
Odon, *m. Fr.* Teu. rich, 378
Odorico, *m. It.* Teu. rich ruler, 378
Odulf, *m. Ger.* Teu. noble wolf, 378
Odvald, *m. Ger.* Teu. rich power, 378
ODVIN, *m. Ger.* Teu. rich friend, 378
Ody, m. Fr. Kelt. lamb, 140
ODYSSEUS, *m. Gr.* hater, 75
ŒGILIV, *m. Nor.* Teu. Œgir's relic, 323
ŒGILS, *m. Nor.* Teu. awful, 323
ŒGULV, *m. Nor.* Teu. awful wolf, 323
ŒGUNN, *m. Nor.* Teu. awful maiden, 323
ŒGWIND, *m. Nor.* awful Wend, 323
Oëlrich, *m. Ger.* Teu. noble ruler, 409
Offa, *m. A.G.S.* Teu. wild boar (?), 334
Ofura, f. Lat. Teu. island prudence, 431
Offy, f. Eng. Gr. divine love, 100
Oggiero, *m. Ital.* Teu. holy, 402
OGMUND, *m. Nor.* Teu. awful protection, 323
Ogier, m. Fr. Teu. holy, 402
OGNOSLAV, *m. Ill.* Slav. fire glory.
OGVALLD, *m. Nor.* awful power, 323
Oieif, m. Nor. Teu. island wolf, 431
Oiel, m. Nor. Teu. island wolf, 431
Oighrigh, *f. Gael.* Gr. fair speech, 88
OISEAN, *m. Gadhael.* Kelt. 243
OLAF, *m. Nor.* Teu. ancestor's relic, 332
Olaüs, *m. Lat.* Teu. ancestor's relic, 332
Olav, *m. Nor.* Teu. ancestor's relic, 332
Olave, *m. Eng.* Teu. ancestor's relic, 332

Olbracht, *m. Pol.* Teu. noble brightness, 411
Oldrich, m. Bohm. Teu. nobler ruler, 409
Ole, m. Nor. Teu. ancestor's relic, 332
Oleg, *m. Russ.* Teu. holy, 68
Olery, m. Fr. Teu. noble ruler, 409
Olfert, m. Ger. Teu. noble peace, 411
Olga, *f. Russ.* Teu. holy, 68
Olger, *m. Dan.* Teu. holy, 68
Olier, *m. Bret.* Lat. olive, 203
Olimpia, *f. Ital.* Gr. Olympian, 97
Olinka, f. Russ. Teu. holy, 448
Olive, *f. Eng.* Lat. 203
Oliviëros, *m. Port. S.* Lat. olive, 203
Oliver, *m. Eng.* Lat. olive, 203
Oliverio, *m. Port.* Lat. olive, 203
Oliveros, *m. Span.* Lat. olive, 203
Olivia, *f. Eng.* Lat. olive, 203
Olivier, *m. Fr.* Lat. olive, 203
Oliviero, *m. It.* Lat. olive, 203
Olop, m. Esth. Teu. ancestor's relic, 332
Olve, *m. Nor.* Teu. ale, 432
OLVER, *m. Nor.* Teu. ale, 432
Olympe, *f. Fr.* Gr. Olympian, 97
Olympia, *f. Eng.* Gr. Olympian, 97
OLYMPIAS, *f. Eng.* Gr. Olympian, 97
Olympie, *f. Ger.* Gr. Olympian, 97
Onan, m. Ir. Heb. Lat. dwarf Adam, 10
Ondrej, m. Bohm. Gr. man, 86
Onfroi, *m. Fr.* Teu. support of peace, 350
Onofredo, *m. Ital.* Teu. support of peace, 350
Onofrio, *m. It.* Teu. support of peace, 350
Onora, *m. Erse,* Lat. honour, 190
Onoré, m. Fr. Lat. honoured, 190
Onorij, m. Slov. Lat. honoured, 190
Onuphrius, *m. Lat.* Teu. support of peace, 350
Onufrio, *m. It.* Teu. support of peace, 350
Ophelia, *f. Eng.* Gr. serpent, 346
Orac, *m. Slov.* Lat. 148
Orazia, *f. It.* Lat. 148
Orazio, *m. It.* Lat. 148
Orban, *m. Hung.* Lat. citizen, 202
Ordoño, *m. Span.* Teu. rich friend (?), 376

ORFLATH, *f. Erse*, Kelt. golden lady, 125

Orlando, *m. Ital.* Teu. fame of the land, 389

ORM, *m. Ice.* Teu. serpent, 346

ORMAR, *m. Nor.* Teu. serpent warrior, 346

ORMILDA, *f. Ice.* Teu. serpent battle maid, 346

Orsch, *f. Swiss*, Lat. bear, 199

Orscheli, f. Swiss, Lat. bear, 199

Orse, *f. Hung.* Heb. oath of God, 35

Orseline, *f. Dutch*, Lat. bear, 199

Orsike, f. Hung. Heb. oath of God, 35

Orsola, *f. Ital.* Lat. bear, 199

Orsolya, *f. Hung.* Lat. bear, 199

Orson, *m. Eng.* Lat. bear, 199

Ortensia, *f. It.* Lat. gardener, 147

Ortensio, *m. It.* Lat. gardener, 147

Ortleip, *m. Ger.* Teu. rich relic, 378

Ortgrim, *m. Ger.* Teu. rich helm, 378

ORTGAR, *m. Ger.* Teu. rich spear, 378

Orto, *m. Ger.* Teu. rich, 378

ORTWIN, *m. Ger.* Teu. rich friend, 378

Ortwulf, *Ger.* Teu. rich wolf, 378

Orzil, m. Prov. Teu. rich, 378

Osbert, *m. Ger.* Teu. divinely bright, 290

Osberta, *f. Ger.* Teu. divinely bright, 290

OSBORN, *m. Eng.* Teu. divine bear, 290

Osberga, *f. Eng.* Teu. divine pledge, 290

Oscar, *m. Fr.* Kelt. bounding warrior, 251, 291

OSCETYL, *m. A.S.* Teu. divine kettle, 291

Oseep, m. Russ. Heb. addition, 23

Osfred, m. Eng. Teu. divine peace, 290

OSGAR, *m. Gael.* Kelt. bounding warrior, 251

OSGIFU, *f. m. A.S.* Teu. Asagod's gift, 290

OSGOD, *m. Dan.* Teu. Asagod, 290

Oska, f. Lus. Lat. bear, 199, 291

Oskar, m. Ger. Teu. divine spear, 290

OSKETYL, *m. Dan.* Teu. divine cauldron, 291

OSLAC, *m. Eng.* Teu. divine sport, 291

Oslaf, *m. Eng.* Teu. divine legacy, 291

Osmod, *Ger.* Teu. divine wrath, 291

Osmond, *m. Eng.* Teu. divine protection, 291

Osmont, *m. Fr.* Teu. divine protection, 291

Osred, *m. Eng.* Teu. divine council, 291

Osric, *m. Eng.* Teu. divine rule, 291

Ossian, m. Eng. Kelt. 66

OSTHRYTH, *f. Eng.* divine threatener, 291

OSULF, *m. Eng.* Teu. divine wolf, 291

OSWALD, *m. Eng.* Teu. divine power, 291

OSWINE, *m. A.S.* Teu. divine friend, 291

Oswy, m. Eng. Teu. divine holiness, 291

Osyth, *f. Eng.* Teu. divine strength, 291

Otemar, m. Ger. Teu. rich fame, 378

Otfried, *m. Ger.* Teu. rich peace, 376

Othao, *m. Port.* Teu. rich, 376

Othello, *m. It.* Teu. rich, 376

OTHER, *m. Ger.* Teu. happy warrior, 376

Othes, *m. Fr.* Teu. rich, 376

Othilia, *f. m. Fr.* Teu. rich battle maid, 341

OTHO, *m.* Lat. Teu. happy (?), 376

Otpald, m. Ger. happy bold, 376

Otpraht, m. Ger. happy bright, 376

Ottavia, *f. m. It.* Lat. eighth, 138

Ottavio, *m. It.* Lat. eighth, 138

Otte, *m. Ger.* Teu. happy, 376

OTTHILD, *f. Ger.* Teu. happy battle maid, 376

Ottilia, *f. Lat.* Teu. happy battle maid, 376

Ottmar, m. Ger. Teu. happy fame, 376

Otto, *m. It. Ger.* Teu. rich, 376

OTTOKAR, *m. Ger.* Teu. happy spear, 376

Ottone, *m. It.* Teu. happy, 376

Ottorino, m. It. Teu. happy, 376

OTTUR, *m. Nor.* Ger. awful, 356

Ouen, m. Fr. Teu. rich friend, 376

Ougunna, *f. Nor.* Teu. rich war, 376

Oulf, Nor. Teu. rich wolf, 376

Ours, *m. Fr.* Lat. bear, 199

Ovind, m. Nor. Teu. island Wend, 431

Owain, *m. Welsh,* Kelt. lamb, or warrior, 273

Owen, *m. Eng.* Kelt. lamb, or young warrior, 273

P

Pablo, *m. Span.* Lat. little, 165

Pacifico, *m. It.* Lat. pacific, 190

Paddy, m. Ir. Lat. noble, 195

Padrig, *m. Erse,* Lat. noble, 195

Pagano, *m. It.* Lat. countryman, 202

Paganus, *m.* Lat. countryman, 202

Pain, *m. Eng.* Lat. countryman, 202

Pal, m. Hung. Lat. little, 165

Palko, m. Hung. Lat. little, 165

Palladius, *m. Lat.* Gr. of Pallas, 64

Pallig, *m. Dan.* 419

Palne, *m. Dan.* 419

Pamela, *f. Eng.* 464

Pancrace, *m. Ir.* Gr. all ruler, 90

Pancracio, *m. Rom.* Gr. all ruler, 90

Pancracy, *m. Pol.* Gr. all ruler, 90

Pancras, *m. Eng.* Gr. all ruler, 90

Pancrazio, *m. Ital.* Gr. all ruler, 90

Pankratios, *m. Gr.* all ruling, 90

Panna, f. Hung. Heb. grace, 42

Panni, f. Hung. Heb. grace, 42

Pantaleon, *m. Fr.* Gr. all a lion, 90

Pantaleone, *m. It.* Gr. all a lion, 90

Paola, f. It. Lat. little, 165

Paolina, *f. It.* Lat. little, 165

Paolino, *m. It.* Lat. little, 165

Paolo, *m. It.* Lat. little, 165

Pappo, m. Ger. Teu. father, 333

Parascha, f. Russ. Slav. Good Friday child, 216

Parysatis, *f. Gr.* Zend. fairy born (?).

Paraskeva, *f. Russ.* Slav. Good Friday child, 216

Pari, m. Fr. Lat. fatherly, 195

Parnel, f. Eng. Gr. stone, 108

Parthenois, *m. Gr.* Gr. of the virgin, 64

Parthenope, *m. Eng.* Gr. the virgin's city, 64

Pas, m. Pol. Lat. little, 165

Pascal, m. Span. Heb. passover child, 215

Pascha, f. Russ. Slav. Good Friday child, 215

Pascha, *f. Russ.* Slav. Good Friday child, 215

Paschal, *m. Fr.* Heb. Easter child, 215

Paschina, *f. It.* Heb. Easter child, 215

Paschino, *m. It.* Heb. Easter child, 215

Pascoal, *m. Port.* Heb. Easter child, 215

Pascoe, *m. Eng.* Heb. Easter child, 215

Pascual, *m. Span.* Heb. Easter child, 215

Pasinek, m. Pol. Lat. little, 165

Pasquale, *m. It.* Heb. Easter child, 215

Passion, *m. Eng.* Lat. suffering, 215

Pat, m. Ir. Lat. noble, 195

Pate, m. Scot. Lat. noble, 195

Paternus, *m. Lat.* fatherly, 195

Patie, m. Scot. Lat. noble, 195

Patience, *f. Eng.* Lat. bearing up, 193

Patiens, *m. Lat.* patient, 193

Patrice, *m. Fr.* Lat. noble, 195

Patricia, *f. Scot.* Lat. noble, 195

Patricio, *m. Rom.* Lat. noble, 195

Patricius, *m.* Lat. noble, 195

Patrick, m. Eng. Lat. noble, 195

Patrikij, *m. Russ.* Lat. noble, 195

Patriz, *m. Ger.* Lat. noble, 195

Patrizia, *f. It.* Lat. noble, 195

Patrizio, *m. It.* Lat. noble, 195

Patty, f. Eng. Heb. becoming bitter, 29

Paul, *m. Fr. Ger. Eng.* Lat. little, 165

Paula, *f. Span. Port.* Lat. little, 165

Paule, *f. Ger.* Lat. little, 165

Paulette, f. Fr. Lat. little, 165

Paulin, *m. Ger.* Lat. little, 165

Paulina, *f. Rom. Eng. Span.* Lat. little, 165

Pauline, *f. Ger. Fr.* Lat. little, 165

Paulino, *m. It.* Lat. little, 165

Paulinus, *m.* Lat. little, 165

Paulisca, f. Ger. Lat. little, 165

Paulo, *m. Rom. Port.* Lat. little, 165

Paulot, m. Fr. Lat. little, 165

Paultje, *m. Dutch,* Lat. little, 165

Paulus, *m. Ger.* Lat. little, 165

Pav, m. Lapp. Lat. little, 165

Pava, m. Ill. Lat. little, 165
Paval, m. Lapp. Lat. little, 165
Pavck, m. Esth. Lapp. Lat. little, 165
Pavel, m. Russ. Wall. Pol. Bohm. Lat. little, 165
Pavelek, m. Pol. Lat. little, 165
Pavils, m. Lett. Lap. little, 165
Pavko, m. Ill. Lat. little, 165
Pavl, *m. Ill.* Lat. little, 165
Pavla, f. Russ. Lat. little, 165
Pavli, m. Esth. Lat. little, 165
Pavlcnka, m. Russ. Lat. little, 165
Pavlika, f. m. Slav. Lat. little, 165
Pavlija, m. Ill. Lat. little, 165
Pavlin, *m. Slav.* Lat. little, 165
Pavlina, *f. Slav.* Lat. little, 165
Pavluscha, m. Russ. Lat. little, 165
Pavol, *m. Lus.* Lat. little, 165
Pawel, *m. Pol.* Lat. little, 165
Payen, *m. Fr.* Lat. countryman, 202
Payne, *m. Eng.* Lat. countryman, 202
Peace, *f. Eng.*
Peder, *m. Nor.* Gr. stone, 108
Pcdo, m. Esth. Gr. stone, 108
Pcdrinho, m. Port. Gr. stone, 108
Pedro, *m. Port. Span.* Gr. stone, 108
Peggy, f. Eng. Gr. pearl, 121
Peira, m. Prov. Gr. stone, 108
Pejo, m. Ill. Gr. stone, 108
Pelage, *m. Fr.* Gr. of the sea, 203
Pelagia, *f. m. Gr.* of the sea, 203
Pelagio, *m. Rom.* Gr. of the sea, 203
Pelagius, *m.* Lat. Gr. of the sea, 203
Pelayo, *m. Span.* Gr. of the sea, 203
PELEG, *m. Eng.* Heb. dispersion, 15
Pclci, m. Swiss. Gr. of the sea, 203
Pelgrim, *m. Du'ch*, Gr. stranger, 203
Pellegrino, *m. It.* Lat. pilgrim, 203
Pen, f. Eng. Gr. weaver, 75
PENELOPE, *f. Eng.* Gr. weaver, 75
Penny, f. Eng. Gr. weaver, 75
Pent, m. Lapp. Lat. blessed, 184
Pcnta, m. Lapp. Lat. blessed, 184
Pentecost, *m. Eng.* Gr. Whitsuntide, 216
Pentecoste, *f. Eng.* Gr. Whitsuntide, 216
Pepa, f. Span. Heb. addition, 23
Pcpe, m. Span. Heb. addition, 23
Pepin, *m. Fr.* Teu. father, 333
Pepino, *m. Rom.* Teu. father, 333
Pepita, f. Span. Heb. addition, 23

Pepito, m. Span. Heb. addition, 23
Peppo, m. It. Heb. addition, 23
Pcpsa, m. Ill. Heb. addition, 23
Per, m. Swiss. Gr. stone, 108
PERAHTHERI, *m. O. Ger.* Teu. bright army, 415
PERAHTHILD, *f. O. Ger.* Teu. bright battle maid, 415
PERAHTMAR, *m. O. Ger.* Teu. bright fame, 415
PERAHTOLF, *m. O. Ger.* Teu. bright wolf, 415
PERAHTRAM, *m. O. Ger.* Teu. bright raven, 415
Percival, *m. Eng.* Kelt. companion of the chalice, 278
PEREDUR, *m. Welsh*, Kelt. companion of the chalice, 278
Pérégrin, *m. Fr.* Lat. traveller, 203
Peregrine, *m. Eng.* Lat. traveller, 203
PEREGRINUS, *m.* Lat. traveller, 203
Peregrino, m. It. Lat. stranger, 203
Perent, m. Esth. Teu. bear firm, 340
Perctte, f. Fr. Gr. stone, 108
Pcrino, m. It. Gr. stone, 108
PERIZADA, *f. Pers.* Pers. fairy born.
Pcrnel, f. Eng. Gr. stone, 108
Pero, m. It. Gr. stone, 108
Pcro, m. Esth. Teu. bear firm, 340
PERPETUA, *f. It.* Lat. lasting, 197
Pcrrin, m. Fr. Ger. stone, 108
Pcrrine, f. Fr. Gr. stone, 108
Perronik, Bret. 108
Pert, m. Esth. Heb. son of furrows, 25
Pet, m. Esth. Gr. stone, 108
Petar, *m. Ill.* Gr. stone, 108
Peter, *m. Eng.* Ger. Gr. stone, 108
Peteris, m. Lett. Gr. stone, 108
Peters, *m. Lctt.* Gr. stone, 108
Petko, m. Lus. Bulg. Gr. stone, 108
Peto, m. Lus. Gr. stone, 108
Petr, m. Bohm. Russ. Gr. stone, 108
Petra, m. Esth. Gr. stone, 108
Petra, f. Ill. Gr. stone, 108
Pctraca, f. Ger. Gr. stone, 108
Petrarca, m. It. Gr. stone, 108
Petras, m. Lett. Gr. stone, 108
Petrica, m. Ill. Gr. stone, 108
Petrija, f. Ill. Gr. stone, 108
Petrik, m. Bret. Gr. stone, 108
Petrina, *f. Scot.* Gr. stone, 108
Petrine, *f. Fr.* Gr. stone, 108

Petrinka, *m. Russ.* Gr. stone, 108
Petrisse, *f. Ger.* Gr. stone, 108
Petronella, *f. Ger. Eng. It.* Gr. stone, 108
Petronelle, *f. Fr.* Gr. stone, 108
Petronilha, *f. Port.* Gr. stone, 108
PETROS, *m. Gr.* stone, 108
Petru, *m. Wall.* Gr. stone, 108
Petrus, *m. Lat.* Gr. stone, 108
Petrusa, *f. Ill.* Gr. stone, 108
Petruscha, *m. Russ.* Gr. stone, 108
Petsch, *m. Lus.* Gr. stone, 108
Petur, *m. Bulg.* Gr. stone, 108
Pewlin, *m. Welsh*, Lat. little, 165
Phaddei, *m. Russ.* Aram. praise, 20
Phadrig, *m. Erse*, Lat. noble, 195
Pharamond, *m. Eng.* Teu. travelled protector, 432
Phelim, *m. Ir.* Kelt. Erse, good, 257
Phemie, *f. Scot.* Gr. fair fame, 88
Pheodor, *m. Russ.* Gr. divine gift, 101
Pheodora, *f. m. Russ.* Gr. divine gift, 101
Pheodosij, *m. Russ.* Gr. divine gift, 103
Pheodosia, *f. m. Russ.* Gr. divine gift, 103
PHERENIKE, *f. Gr.* bringing victory, 90
Phil, *m. Eng.* Ger. love horses, 79
PHILADELPHIA, *f. Eng.* Gr. love of brethren, 93
PHILALETHES, *m.* Gr. love of truth, 94
PHILANDER, *m. Eng.* Gr. love man, 94
Philaret, *m. Gr.* Gr. love virtue, 94
PHILARETOS, *m.* Gr. love virtue, 94
PHILE, *f.* Gr. love, 93
PHILEMON, *m. Eng.* Gr. loving thought, 94
Philetus, *m. Am.* Gr. love, 94
Philibert, *m. Fr.* Teu. will bright, 315
Philine, *f. Ger.* Gr. love, 94
Philip, *m. Eng.* Gr. love horses, 79
Philipp, *m. Ger.* Gr. love horses, 79
Philippa, *f. Eng.* Gr. love horses, 79
Philippe, *m. Fr.* Gr. love horses, 79
Philippine, *f. Ger. Fr.* Gr. love horses, 79
PHILIPPOS, *m.* Gr. loving horses, 79

Philippot, *m. Fr.* Gr. love horses, 79
Philippole, *f. Fr.* Gr. love horses, 79
Philippus, *m. Lat.* Gr. love horses, 79
Philologus, *m. Eng.* Gr. love the word, 94
Philothée, *f. m. Fr.* Gr. love God, 94
Philotheus, *m. Eng.* Gr. love God, 94
Philumena, *f.* Lat. daughter of light, 208
Philumène, *f.* Lat. daughter of light, 208
Phillis, *f. Eng.* Gr. foliage, 81
Philon, *m. Fr.* Gr. love, 94
Philoxène, *f. Fr.* Gr. loving the stranger, 93
Phocas, *m. Lat.* Gr. Phocian, 200
Phœbe, *f. Eng.* Gr. shining, 65
Phœbus, *m. Lat.* Gr. shining, 65
PHOKAS, *m. Gr.* Phocian, 200
Photinee, *f. Gr.* light, 65
Photius, *m. Gr.* light, 65
Phrankiskos, *m. M. Gr.* Teu. free, 300
Phroso, *f. M. Gr.* Gr. mirth, 72
PHYLLIS, *f. Eng.* Gr. green bough, 81
Pia, *f. It. Lat.* pious, 193
Pico, *m. It. Lat.* woodpecker, 176
PICUS, *m. Lat.* woodpecker, 176
Pie, *m. Fr.* Lat. pious, 193
Pier, *m. It.* Gr. stone, 108
Pieran, *m. Corn.* Kelt. black, 255
Pierce, *m. Eng.* Gr. stone, 108
Piere, *m. O. Fr.* Gr. stone, 108
Piero, *m. It.* Gr. stone, 108
Pieron, *m. Fr.* Gr. stone, 108
Pierot, *m. Fr.* Gr. stone, 108
Pierre, *m. Fr.* Gr. stone, 108
Pierrot, *m. Fr.* Gr. stone, 108
Piers, *m. Eng.* Gr. stone, 108
Pies, *m. Pol.* Gr. stone, 108
Piet, *m. Dutch*, Gr. stone, 108
Pieter, *m. Dutch*, Gr. stone, 108
Picti, *m. Pol.* Gr. stone, 108
Pietro, *m. It.* Gr. stone, 108
Pietruccio, *m. It.* Gr. stone, 108
Piety, *f. Eng.* Lat. piety, 193
Pij, *m. Russ.* Lat. pious, 193
Pikka, *f. Lapp.* Kelt. strength, 236
Pikke, *f. Lapp.* Kelt. strength, 236
Pil, *m. Esth.* Lat. wise old woman, 179
PILAR, *f. Span.* Lat. pillar, 30
Pilgrim, *m. Eng.* Lat. traveller, 203

Pimme, f. Esth. Gr. fair fame, 88
Pine, f. Ger. Gr. loving horses, 79
Pinna, m. Lapp. Lat. blessed, 184
Pint, m. Lapp. Lat. blessed, 184
Pinus, m. Ger. Gr. loving horses, 79
Pio, m. It. Lat. pious, 193
Piotr, m. Pol. Gr. stone, 108
Pipin, *m. Ger.* Teu. father, 333
Pippa, f. It. Gr. loving horses, 79
Pippin, m. Dutch, Eng. Teu. father, 333
Pippo, m. It. Gr. loving horses, 79
Pirket, f. Lapp. Kelt. strength, 236
Pirimona, m. Maori, Gr. loving thought.
Pirrit, f. Esth. Kelt. strength, 236
Pius, *m. It.* Lat. pious, 193
Pjetr, *m. Lus.* Gr. stone, 108
Pjetrik, *m. Lus.* Gr. stone, 108
Plaxy, f. Corn. Gr. active.
Plectrude, *f. Fr.* Teu. lightning battle maid.
Pobjus, m. Lith. Lat. of a bean, 146
Poldo, m. Slav. Teu. people's prince, 430
Polei, m. Swiss, Lat. of the sea, 203
Polidoro, *m. It.* Gr. many gifted, 93
Polieukt, *m. Russ.* Gr. much desired, 93
Poliksenija, *f. Russ.* Gr. much hospitality, 93
Polly, f. Eng. Heb. bitter, 29
Polonia, f. Slov. Gr. of Apollo, 65
Polonija, f. Slov. Gr. of Apollo, 65
Polycarp, *m. Eng.* Gr. much fruit, 93
Polydore, *m. Eng.* Gr. much gifted, 93
POLYDORUS, *m. Lat.* Gr. much gifted, 93
POLYEUKTOS, *m. Gr.* much longed for, 93
POLYHYMNIA, *f. Eng.* Gr. of many hymns, 72
POLYKARPOS, *m.* Gr. much fruit, 93
Polyksenija, *f. Russ.* Gr. much hospitality, 93
POLYXENA, *f.* Gr. much hospitality, 93
Polyxène, *f. Fr.* Gr. much hospitality, 93
Pompée, *m. Fr.* Lat. of Pompeii, 151
Pompeio, *m. It.* Lat. of Pompeii, 151
POMPEIUS, *m.* Lat. of Pompeii, 151

Pompey, *m. Eng.* Lat. of Pompeii 151
Ponce, *m. Span.* Lat. fifth, 138
Poncio, *m. Rom.* Lat. fifth, 138
Pons, *m. Fr.* Lat. fifth, 138
PONTIUS, *m. Lat.* fifth, 138
Ponzio, *m. It.* Lat. fifth, 138
Poppo, *m. Ger.* Teu. father, 333
PORCIA, *f. Ger.* Lat. of the pigs, 151
PORCIUS, *m. Lat.* of the pigs, 151
Portia, *f. Eng.* Lat. of the pigs, 151
Porzia, *f. It.* Lat. of the pigs, 151
POSTHUMUS, *m.* Lat. the last, 136
Poto, m. Ger. Teu. commander, 414
Prancas, m. Lith. Teu. free, 209
Prascovie, *f. Fr.* Slav. Good Friday child, 215
Prassede, *f. Ital.* Gr. active, 94
PRAVDOSLAV, *m. Ill.* Slav. upright glory, 444
PRAVDOSLAVA, *f. Ill.* Slav. upright glory, 444
Pravoje, m. Ill. Slav. upright glory.
PRAXEDES, *f. Lat.* Gr. active, 94
Prechtl, m. Bav. Teu. bright fame, 213
Premislaus, *m. Eng.* Slav. thoughtful glory, 444
Preban, *m. Dan.* Slav. 444
Predbiorn, *m. Dan.* Slav. 444
Pribislav, *m. Slav.* 444
Pribislava, *f. Slav.* 439
Priczus, m. Lith. Teu. peace ruler, 296
Pridrik, m. Lett. Teu. peace rule, 296
PRIMUS, *m.* Lat. first, 137
PRISCILLA, *f. Eng.* Lat. ancient, 163
PRISCUS, *m. Lat.* ancient, 163
Priske, *f. Ger.* Lat. ancient, 163
Prissie, f. Eng. Lat. ancient, 163
Prizzis, m. Lett. Teu. peace ruler, 296
PROCHOROS, *m. Gr.* leader of the dance, 126
Prochorus, *m. Eng.* Lat. leader of the dance, 126
PROCOPIUS, *m. Lat.* Gr. progressive, 126
Prokhor, *m. Russ.* Gr. leader of the dance, 126
Prokop, *m. Bohm.* Gr. progressive, 126
Prokopij, *m. Russ. Gr.* progressive, 126

Prokupek, *m. Bohm.* Gr. progressive, 126

PROMETHEUS, *m. Gr.* love thought.

Prospero, *m. It.* Lat. prosperous, 192

Prudence, *f. Eng.* 193

PRUDENTIUS, *m. Lat.* prudent, 193

Prydas, m. Litt. Teu. peace ruler, 296

Prydikis, m. Lith. Teu. peace ruler, 296

PRZEMYSL, *m. Bohm.* Slav. thoughtful, 439

PRZEMYSLAVA, *f. Pol.* Slav. thoughtful glory, 439

PSYCHE, *f. m. Gr.* soul, 447

PULCHERIA, *f. Ger. It.* Lat. fair, 196

Pulcherie, *f. Fr.* Lat. fair, 196

PURVAN, *m. Bulg.* Slav. first, 442

PURVANCE, *m. Bulg.* Slav. first, 442

Q

QUADRATUS, *m. Lat.* fourth, 137

QUARTINUS, *m. Lat.* fourth, 137

QUARTUS, *m. Lat.* fourth, 137

Quenburga, *f. Eng.* Lat. queen pledge, 319

Quendrida, *f. Eng.* Lat. queen threatener, 319

Quencs, m. Fr. Teu. bold speech, 423

Quentin, *m. Scot.* Lat. fifth, 138

Qucran, m. Flem. Scot. Kelt. black, 255

Quintianus, *m.* Lat. fifth, 138

QUINTILIANUS, *m. Lat.* fifth, 138

QUINTUS, *m. Lat.* fifth, 138

Quiric, m. Fr. Gr. Sunday child, 217

QUIRINUS, *m. Lat.* spearman, 177

QUOD-VULT-DEUS, *m. Lat.* what God wills, 188

R

RAADGJER, *m. Nor.* Teu. spear of fame, 394

Raadgjerd, *f. Nor.* Teu. council guard, 394

Raamund, m. Nor. Teu. council protection, 394

Rab, m. Scot. Teu. bright fame, 392

Rabba, m. Fris. Teu. council commander, 394

Rabbe, m. Fris. Teu. council commander, 394

Rabbo, m. Fris. Teu. council commander, 394

Rachel, *f. Fr. Eng. Ger.* Heb. ewe, 14

Rachele, *f. It.* Heb. ewe, 14

Radagaisus, *m. Lat.* Teu. council pledge, 394

Radak, *m. Slav.* Slav. joy, 439

Radan, *m. Slav.* Slav. joy, 439

RADBERT, *m. Ger.* Teu. council bright, 394

RADBOD, *m. Ger.* Teu. council commander, 394

RADEGAR, *m. Lom.* Teu. council spear, 394

RADEGISL, *m. Lom.* Teu. council pledge, 394

RADEGONDE, *f. Fr.* Teu. council war, 394

RADEGUNDA, *f. Span.* Teu. council war, 394

Radelchis, *m. Lat.* Teu. council pledge, 394

Radfried, *m. Ger.* Teu. council peace, 394

Radgund, *f. Ger.* Teu. council war, 394

RADINKA, *m. Slav.* Slav. joyful peace, 439

Radinko, m. Slav. joy, 439

Radko, m. Slav. joy, 439

Radman, *m. Slav.* Slav. joy, 439

RADMIL, *m. Slav.* Slav. joyful love, 439

RADIVOJ, *m. Slav.* Slav. joyful war, 439

Radoje, m. Slav. joyful war, 439

Radolf, *m. Eng.* Teu. house wolf, 421

RADULFUS, *m. Lat.* Teu. house wolf, 421

RADOSLAV, *m. Slav.* Slav. joyful glory, 439

Rafael, *m. Span. Hung.* Heb. healing of God, 55

Rafe, *m. Eng.* Teu. house wolf, 421

Raffaelle, *m. It.* Heb. healing of God, 55

Raffaello, *m. It.* Heb. healing of God, 55

Rafn, *m. Nor.* Teu. raven, 345

Rafnulf, *m. Nor.* Teu. raven wolf, 345

RAGANO, *m. O. Ger.* Teu. judgment, 396

RAGINBALD, *m. Ger.* Teu. prince of judgment, 398

RAGINFRED, *m. Frank.* Teu. judgment of peace, 398

h

RAGINFRIDA, *f. Ger.* Teu. judgment of peace, 398

RAGINHARD, *m. Frank.* Teu. firm judge, 396

RAGINHEID, *f. Nor.* Teu. impulse of justice, 398

RAGINHERI, *m. A.S. Frank.* Teu. warrior of judgment, 396

RAGINHILD, *f. Frank.* Teu. battle maid of judgment, 398

RAGINHOLD, *m. Frank.* Teu. judging firmly, 396

RAGINLEIF, *m. Nor.* Teu. relic of judgment, 396

RAGINMUND, *m. Frank.* Teu. judge's protection, 396

RAGINHAR, *m. Frank.* Teu. great judgment, 396

RAGINWALD, *m. Frank.* Teu. judge ruler, 396

RAGINWARD, *m. Nor.* Teu. guardian of judgment, 396

RAGNAR, *m. Nor.* Teu. warrior of judgment, 397

RAGNFRID, *f. Nor.* Teu. wise fair one, 398

Ragnold, *m. Frank.* Teu. wise judge ruler, powerful judge, 395

Ragnrid, f. Nor. Teu. wise fair one, 398

Rahel, *f. Pol.* Heb. ewe, 15

Raimond, *m. Fr.* Teu. judge's protection, 396

Raimondo, *m. It.* Teu. judge's protection, 395

Raimons, *m. Prov.* Teu. council strengthening protection, 397

Rainiald, *m. Eng.* Teu. power of judgment, 395

Rainardo, *m. Ital.* Teu. firm judgment, 396

Rainart, *m. Prov.* Teu. firm judgment, 396

Rainhard, *m. Hung.* Teu. firm judgment, 396

Rainer, m. Eng. Teu. warrior of judgment, 396

Rainulf, m. O. Fr. Teu. wolf of judgment, 335

Rajnold, m. Pol. Teu. power of judgment, 396

Ralf, *m. Eng.* Teu. house wolf, 421

Ralph, *m. Eng.* Teu. house wolf, 421

Rambert, *Ger.* raven bright, 345

Ramiro, *m. Span.* Teu. great judge, 396

Ramon, *m. Span.* Teu. judge's protection, 397

Rampold, *m.* raven prince, 345

Ranald, *m. Scot.* Teu. power of judgment, 397

Ramusio, *m. Span.* Teu. raven, 345

Randal, *m. Eng.* Teu. house wolf, 421.

Randi, f. Nor. Teu. wise fair one, 396

Randid, m. Nor. Teu. wise fair one, 396

Randle, *m. Eng.* Teu. house wolf, 335

Randolph, *m. Eng.* Teu. house wolf, 335, 421

Randve, *m. Nor.* Teu. house consecration, 321

Randver, m. Nor. Teu. house consecration, 321

RANDVID, *m. Nor.* Teu. house consecration, 321

Rane, f. Nor. Teu. warrior of judgment, 396

Ranieri, *m. It.* Teu. warrior of judgment, 396

Ranmod, f. Nor. Teu. house courage, 421

Ranna, f. Lapp. Teu. battle maid of judgment, 396

Rannmod, m. Nor. Teu. house courage, 421

Rannog, f. Nor. Teu. house liquor, 421

Ranssu, m. Finn. Teu. free, 300

Ranulf, *m. Eng.* Teu. house wolf, 421

RANVEIG, *f. m. Nor.* Teu. house liquor, 421

Raonmill, *m. Erse,* Teu. power of judgment, 396

Raoul, *m. Fr.* Teu. wolf of fame, 335

Raphael, *m. Eng. Fr. Ger.* Heb. healing of God, 55

Rasche, f. Pol. Lat. rose, 204

Rasia, f. Pol. Lat. queen, 31

Rasine, f. Lith. Lat. rose, 204

Rasine, f. Pol. Lat. queen, 31

Rasl, m. Bav. Gr. amiable, 113

Rasmus, m. Dutch, Gr. amiable, 113

Ratulf, *m. O. Ger.* Teu. council bright, 394

Raul, m. Rom. Teu. house wolf, 421.

Raulus, m. Lith. Lat. laurel, 174

Ravelina, f. Mentone, Heb. medicine of God, 55

Ravelin, m. Eng. Teu. council wolf, 335

Ravengar, *Eng.* Teu. raven spear, 345

Ravenswar, *Eng.* Teu. raven spear, 345

Raymond, *m. Eng.* Teu. wise protection, 397

Raynard, *m. Pol.* Teu. firm judgment, 396

Rayner, *m. Eng.* Teu. warrior of judgment, 396

RAZOOMNIK, *m. Russ.* Slav. wise man, 449

Rebecca, *f. Lat.* Heb. noosed cord, 14

Rebekah, *f. Eng.* Heb. noosed cord, 14

Recaredo, *m. Span.* Teu. ruling by council, 399

Rechiarius, *m: Lat.* Teu. ruling an army, 399

Rechilda, *f. Lat.* Teu. ruling battle maid, 399

Rechimiro, *m. Span.* Teu. ruling fame, 399

Recimir, *m. Goth.* Teu. ruling fame, 399

Redmond, *m. Ir.* Teu. council protection, 31

Redwald, *m. Eng.* Teu. council power, 31

REGINA, *f. It. Ger.* Lat. queen, 31

Reginald, *m. Eng.* Teu. powerful judgment, 396

Reginard, *m. Frank.* Teu. firm judge, 396

Reginand, *m. Fr.* Teu. powerful judgment, 396

Reginbert, *m. Ger.* Teu. splendour of judgment, 396

REGINTAG, *m. Frank.* Teu. judgment day, 396

Reginwart, *m. Frank.* Teu. guardian of judgment, 396

Regl, f. Bav. Lat. queen, 398

Regnard, m. Fr. Teu. firm judge, 396

Regnault, *m. Fr.* Teu. power of judgment, 396

Regnier, *m. Fr.* Teu. warrior of judgment, 396

REGULUS, *m. Lat.* king, 355

Rehur, watchman.

Reichart, m. Ger. Teu. ruling firmness, 399

Reigl, f. Ger. Teu. queen, 398

Rein, m. Esth. Teu. power of judgment, 396

Reinaldo, *m. Span.* power of judgment, 396

Reinbold, *m. Ger.* Teu. prince of judgment, 396

Reine, f. Fr. Lat. queen, 36

Reiner, *m. Ger.* Teu. warrior of judgment, 398

Reinette, f. Fr. Lat. queen, 31

Reinfrid, *m. Ger.* Teu. peace of judgment, 396

Reingard, *m. Russ.* Teu. protection of judgment, 398

Reinger, *m. Ger.* Teu. spear of judgment, 398

Reinhard, *m. Ger.* Teu. firm judge, 398

Reinhild, *f. Ger.* Teu. battle maid of judgment, 398

Reinner, *m. Ger.* Teu. great judgment, 398

Reinhold, *m. Ger.* Teu. firmness of judgment, 398

Reinis, m. Lett. Teu. power of judgment, 398

Reino, m. Ger. Teu. power of judgment, 398

Reinolf, *m. Ger.* Teu. wolf of judgment, 398

Reinward, *m. Ger.* Teu. guard of judgment, 398

Rekkerts, m. Lett. Teu. spear of fame, 399

Remarkable, f. American.

Rembald, *m. Ger.* Teu. prince of judgment, 398

Rembert, *m. Fris.* Teu. splendour of judgment, 396

Remi, m. Fr.

Remma, m. Fris. Teu. guardian of judgment, 396

Remward, m. Fris. Teu. guardian of judgment, 396

Renard, *m. Fr.* Teu. firm judge, 396

Renart, *m. Fr.* Teu. firm judge, 396

Renata, *f. m. It.* Teu. warrior of judgment, 396

Renato, *m. It.* Teu. warrior of judgment, 396

h 2

Renaud, m. Fr. Teu. power of judgment, 396
Renauld, m. Fr. Teu. power of judgment, 396
Renbold, m. Ger. Teu. prince of judgment, 396
René, *m. Fr.* Teu. warrior of judgment, 396
Renée, *f. Fr.* Teu. warrior of judgment, 396
Renfred, m. Eng. Teu. judgment of peace, 396
Rennert, m. Fris. Teu. firm judge, 396
Rennold, m. Fris. Teu. power of judgment, 396
Renz, m. Ger. Teu. firm judge, 396
Renzo, m. It. Lat. laurel, 174
Res'l, f. Bav. Gr. carrying ears of corn, 124
RESTITUTUS, *m.* Lat. restored, 193
Restyn, *m. Welsh,* Lat. restored, 193
REUBEN, *m. Eng.* Heb. behold a son, 7
Reta, f. Finn. Gr. pearl, 121
Reynard, *m. Eng.* Teu. firm judge, 396
Reynold, *m. Eng.* Teu. power of judgment, 396
Rhesa, m. Eng. Chal. prince, 277
Rhoda, *f. Eng.* Gr. rose, 31
RHODE, *f.* Gr. rose, 31
RHODEIA, *f.* rosy cheeked, 31, 204
RHODOPIS, *f.* rosy cheeked, 31, 204
RHONWEN, *f. Welsh,* Kelt. white skirt, 239
RHYDDERCH, *m. Welsh,* Kelt. 255
RHYS, *m. Welsh,* Kelt. warrior, 277
Ricardo, *m. Port.* Teu. stern king, 399
Riccardo, *m. It.* Teu. stern king, 399
Ricbert, *m. Ger.* Teu. bright king, 399
Ricciardetto, m. It. Teu. stern king, 399
Ricciardo, *m. It.* Teu. stern king, 399
Rice, m. Eng. Welsh, warrior, 277, 399
RICEHARD, *m. A.S.* stern king, 399
Richard, *m. Fr. Eng.* Teu. stern king, 399
Richenza, f. Ger. Teu. ruling firmness, 400
Richer, *m. Ger.* Teu. ruling warrior, 399

Richila, *f. Span.* Teu. ruling battle maid, 399
Richilde, *f. Fr.* Teu. ruling battle maid, 399
Richiza, *f. Ger.* Teu. ruling firmness, 399
RICKOLF, *m. Ger.* Teu. king wolf, 400
Riciberga, *f. Span.* Teu. ruling guard, 400
Ricimir, *m. Lat.* Teu. great king, 399
Rickel, m. Bav. Teu. noble ruler, 399
Rictrude, *f. Fr.* Teu. ruling maid, 400
Ridolfo, m. It. Teu. fame ruler, 391
Rietu, m. Finn. Teu. peace ruler, 296
Rieuk, m. Bret. Kelt. warrior, 277
Right-about-face, m. Eng. 10
Rigonthe, f. O. Fr. Teu. ruling war, 400
Riik, m. Neth. Teu. ruling firmness, 400
Riikert, m. Neth. Teu. ruling firmness, 399
Rikchen, f. Ger. Teu. peace ruler, 296
Rike, f. Ger. Teu. peace ruler, 296
Rikheri, *m. O. Fr.* Teu. ruling warrior, 399
Rikomar, *m. Ger.* Teu. ruling fame, 399
Rikulf, *m. Ger.* Teu. ruling wolf, 399
Rikwald, *m. Ger.* Teu. ruling power, 400
Rinaldo, *m. It.* Teu. power of judgment, 396
Rinnert, m. Fris. Teu. firmness of judgment, 396
Riok, *m. Bret.* Kelt. warrior, 277
Riowal, *m. Bret.* Kelt. lordly, 277
Rita, f. It. Gr. pearl, 121
Ritchie, *m. Scot.* Teu. ruling firmness, 399
Roald, *m. Nor.* Teu. famous power, 392
Roar, m. Nor. Teu. spear of fame, 392
Rob, *m. Scot.* Teu. bright fame, 392
Robbie, *m. Scot.* Teu. bright fame, 392
Robers, *m. Fr.* Teu. bright fame, 392
Robert, *m. Eng. Fr.* Teu. bright fame, 392
Roberto, *m. Ital.* Teu. bright fame, 392
Robin, *m. Fr. Eng.* Teu. bright fame, 392
Robina, *f. Scot.* Teu. bright fame, 392

Robinet, *m. Fr.* Teu. fame bright, 392

Roderic, *m. Fr.* Teu. famous king, 255, 393

Roderich, *m. Ger.* Teu. famous king, 255, 393

Roderick, *m. Eng.* Teu. famous king, 255, 393

Rodolf, *m. Ger.* Teu. wolf of fame, 391

Rodolfo, *m. It.* Teu. wolf of fame, 391

Rodolph, *m. Eng.* Teu. wolf of fame, 391

Rodolphe, *m. Fr.* Teu. wolf of fame, 391

Rodri, *m. Welsh*, Teu. famous king, 255, 393

Rodrigo, *m. Span. Port.* Teu. famous king, 255, 393

Rodrigue, *m. Fr.* Teu. famous king, 255, 393

Rodulfo, *Span.* wolf of fame, 391

Roese, *f. Eng.* Teu. fame, 204

Roesia, *f. Eng.* Teu. fame, 204

Roger, *m. Eng.* Teu. spear of fame, 390

Rogero, *m. It.* Teu. spear of fame, 390

Rogier, *m. Neth.* Teu. spear of fame, 390

Rognwald, *m. Nor.* Teu. power of judgment, 396

Rohais, *f. Eng.* Teu. fame, 204

Rohlops, *m. Lett.* Teu. wolf of fame, 390

Roibin, *m. Erse*, Teu. bright fame, 392

Roeland, *m. Neth.* Teu. fame of the land, 389

Roland, *m. Ir. Eng.* Teu. fame of the land, 389

Rolando, *m. Port.* Teu. fame of the land, 389

Roldan, *m. Span.* Teu. fame of the land, 389

Roldao, *m. Port.* Teu. fame of the land, 389

Rolf, *m. Ger.* Teu. wolf of fame, 391

Rollaug, *m. Nor.* Teu. famous liquor, 393

Rolleik, *m. Nor.* Teu. famous sport, 389

Rolph, *m. Eng.* Teu. wolf of fame, 391

Rollo, *m. Lat.* Teu. wolf of fame, 391

Rolv, *m. Nor.* Teu. wolf of fame, 391

Romain, *m. Fr.* Lat. Roman, 178

Romano, *m. It.* Lat. Roman, 178

Roman, *m. Slav.* Lat. Roman, 178

ROMANUS, *m. Lat.* Roman, 178

Romao, *m. Port.* Lat. Roman, 178

Romeo, *m. Ital.* Teu. fame, 393

Romola, *f. Ital.* Lat. fame (?), 178

Romolo, *m. Ital.* Lat. fame (?), 178

ROMUALD, *m. Fr.* Teu. famed power, 390

ROMUALDO, *m. It.* Teu. famed power, 390

ROMULUS, *m. Lat.* fame (?), 178

Rona'd, *m. Scot.* judge power, 390

Ronan, *m. Scot.* Kelt. seal (?), 253

Ronat, *f. Erse*, Kelt. seal (?), 253

RONDOLFR, *m. Nor.* Teu. house wolf, 421

Ronnan, *f.* house liquor, 393

Rory, *m. Ir.* Kelt. red, 255

ROSA, *f. It. Span.* Lat. rose, 204

Rosabel, *f. Eng.* Lat. rose fair, 204

Rosaclara, *f. Eng.* Lat. rose clear, 204

Rosalba, *f. It.* Lat. rose white, 204

Rosalbe, *f. Fr.* Lat. rose white, 204

Rosalia, *f. It.* Lat. rose, 204

Rosalie, *f. Ger. Fr. Eng.* Lat. rose, 204

Rosalija, *f. Russ.* Lat. rose, 204

Rosalind, *f. Eng.* Teu. fame serpent, 204

Rosaline, *f. Eng.* Teu. famed serpent, 204

Rosamond, *f. Eng.* Teu. famed protection, 204

Rosamunda, *f. It. Span.* Teu. famed protection, 204

Rosamunde, *f. Ger.* Teu. famed protection, 204

Rosanne, *f. Eng.* Lat. rose, 204

Rosaura, *f. It.* Lat. rose, 204

Roschana, *f. Pers.* Zend. dawn of day, 58

Roschen, *f. Ger.* Lat. rose, 204

ROSCRANA, *f. Gael.* Kelt. rose bush.

Rose, *f. Eng.* Lat. rose, 204

Rosel, *f. Swiss*, Teu. rose, 204

Roseli, *f. Swiss*, Teu. rose, 204

Rosemonde, *f. Fr.* Teu. famed protection, 204

Roseta, *f. Port.* Lat. rose, 204

Rosetta, *f. It.* Lat. rose, 204

Rosette, *f. Fr.* Lat. rose, 204

ROSHILDA, *f. Ger.* Teu. famed battle maid, 206

Rosi, *f. Swiss,* Lat. rose, 204

Rosia, *f. Eng.* Teu. fame, 204, 398

Rosilde, *f. Ger.* Teu. horse battle maid, 341

Rosimonda, *f. It.* Teu. horse protection, 341

Rosina, *f. Eng. It.* Lat. rose, 204

Rosine, *f. Fr. Ger.* Lat. rose, 204

Rosita, *f. Span.* Lat. rose, 204

ROSSKETYL, horse kettle, 341

Rosskjell, horse kettle, 341

Rosmer, *m. Dan.* Teu. sea horse, 341

Rosmund, *f. Ger.* Teu. horse protection, 341

Rospert, bright horse, 341

Rostiophus, *m. Lat.* Teu. horse thief, 341

ROSTISLAV, *m. Slav.* increasing fame, 441

Roswald, *m. Scot.* Teu. horse power, 341

Roswald, *m. Dan.* Teu. horse power, 341

Roswida, *f. Ger.* Teu. horse strength, 341

ROSWITH, *f. Frank.* Teu. horse strength, 341

Rota, *m. Maori,* Heb.

Rotholf, *m. Fris.* Teu. famed wolf, 391

Rotija, *f. Ill.* Gr. gift of God, 102

Rottgers, *m. Ger.* Teu. famed spear, 392

Rotlandus, *m. Lat.* Teu. fame of the country, 389

Rou, *m. Fr.* Teu. wolf of fame, 390

Roul, *m. Fr.* Teu. wolf of fame, 390

Rowena, *f. Eng.* Kelt. white skirt, 239

Rowland, *m. Eng.* Teu. fame of the land, 389

Roxana, *f. Pers.* Fr. dawn of day, 58

Roy, *m. Scot.* Kelt. red, 255

Roza, *f. Pol.* Lat. rose, 204

Rozalia, *f. Pol.* Lat. rose, 204

Rozalija, *f. Slov.* Lat. rose, 204

Rozer, *m. Russ.* Teu. famed spear, 390

Rozia, *f. Pol.* Lat. rose, 204

Rozina, *f. Slov. Bohm.* Lat. rose, 204

Rozsi, *f. Hung.* Lat. rose, 204

Rozyna, *f. Pol.* Lat. rose, 204

Ruadh, *m. Erse,* Kelt. red, 167, 255

Ruadri, *m. Gael.* Kelt. red, 255

RUADRIGH, *m. Gadhael.* Kelt. red, 255

Ruaridh, *m. Gael.* Kelt. 255

Rudbert, *m. Ger.* Teu. bright fame, 392

Ruben, *m. Ger.* Heb. behold a son, 7

Rubert, *m. It.* Teu. bright fame, 392

Rudhard, *m. Ger.* Teu. famed firmness, 392

Rudiger, *m. Ger.* Teu. famed spear, 392

Rudland, *m. Ger.* Teu. fame of the land, 392

Rudolf, *m. Ger.* Teu. wolf of fame, 391

RUDOLPHE, *m. Fr.* Teu. wolf of fame, 391

Rudolphine, *f. Ger.* Teu. wolf of fame, 391

Ruedi, *m. Swiss,* Teu. wolf of fame, 391

Ruedli, *m. Swiss,* Teu. wolf of fame, 391

RUEDOLF, *m. Bav.* Teu. wolf of fame, 390

Ruffo, *m. It.* Lat. red, 167

Ruffin, *m. Fr.* Lat. red, 167

RUFINA, *f. It.* Lat. red, 167

Rufine, *f. Fr.* Lat. red, 167

Rufino, *m. It.* Lat. red, 167

RUFINUS, *m. Ger.* Lat. red, 167

RUFUS, *m. Am.* Lat. red, 167

Ruggero, *m. It.* Teu. famed spear, 390

Ruggiero, *m. It.* Teu. famed spear, 390

Rule, *m. Scot.* Lat. king.

Ruland, *m. Ger.* Teu. fame of the land, 389

Rulef, *m. Fris.* Teu. wolf of fame, 390

Rulf, *m. Ger.* Teu. wolf of fame, 390

Rulves, *m. Fris.* Teu. wolf of fame, 390

Rumilde, *f. Ger.* Teu. famed battle maid, 398

Rupert, *m. Ger. Eng.* Teu. bright fame, 392

Rûperto, *m. It.* Teu. bright fame, 392

Ruprat, *m. Slov.* Teu. bright fame, 392

Ruprecht, *m. Ger.* Teu. bright fame, 392

Rurik, *m. Russ.* Teu. famed rule, 392

Rutger, *m. Neth.* Teu. spear of fame, 390

Ruth, *f. Eng.* Heb. beauty, 39

Ruy, m. Span. Teu. famed rule, 398

Ruzalia, *f. Ill.* Lat. rose, 204

Rycolf, *m. Fris.* Teu. ruling wolf, 392

Rydygier, *m. Pol.* Teu. spear of fame, 390

Rykert, *m. Dutch,* Teu. stern king, 399

Ryklof, *m. Fris.* Teu. ruling wolf, 390

Ryszard, m. Pol. Teu. stern king, 399

S

SABAS, *m. Ger.* Heb. rest (?), 216

Sabea, *f.* 216

Sabee, *m. Russ.* Heb. rest (?), 216

Sabina, *f. It. Eng.* Lat. Sabine, 164

Sabine, *f. Ger. Fr.* Lat. Sabine, 164

SABINUS, *m.* Lat. Sabine, 164

Sabrina, *f. Eng.* the Severn, 164

Sabra, 216

Sacha, f. Russ. Gr. helper of men, 85

Sachar, m. Russ. Heb. remembrance of the Lord, 51

Sacharija, *m. Russ.* Heb. remembrance of the Lord, 51

Sadof, *m. Russ.* Pers. (?), 49

SADOVIT, *m. Ill.* Slav. fruitful.

Sadwrn, *m. Welsh,* Lat. of Saturn, 179

Sæbert, m. A.S. Teu. conquering brightness, 356

Sæmund, m. A.S. conquering protection, 359

Sæwald, conquering power, 359

Sæward, conquering protection, 359

Saffi, f. Dan. Gr. wisdom, 107

Saher, m. Eng. Teu. conquering army, 359

Sahlke, f. Ger. Lat. rose, 204

Sakaria, *m. Ill.* Heb. remembrance of the Lord, 51

Sakchej, *m. Russ.* Heb. remembrance of the Lord, 51

Sakerl, m. Dan. Heb. remembrance of the Lord, 51

Sakkarias, *m. Esth.* Heb. remembrance of the Lord, 51

SAKSE, *m. Nor.* Teu. rock, 51

Sal, f. Eng. Heb. princess, 13

Salamans, *m. Lett.* Heb. peaceful, 47

Salamao, *f. Port.* Heb. peaceful, 47

Salamon, *m. Fr. Hung.* Heb. peaceful, 47

Salaun, *m. Bret.* Heb. peaceful, 47

Sally, f. Eng. Heb. princess, 13

Salomao, *f. m. Fr. Port.* Heb. peaceful, 47

Salomaun, *m. Bohm.* Heb. peaceful, 47

Salome, *f. Eng. Russ. Ger.* Heb. peaceful, 47

Salomea, *f. Pol.* Heb. peaceful, 47

Salomée, *f. Fr.* Heb. peaceful, 47

Salomeli, f. m. Swiss, Heb. peaceful, 47

Salomo, *m. Ger.* Heb. peaceful, 47

Salomone, *m. Ital.* Heb. peaceful, 47

Salvador, *m. Span.* Lat. saviour, 193

Salvatore, *m. Ital.* Lat. saviour, 193

Salvestro, *m. Ital.* Lat. woody, 179

Sam, m. Eng. Heb. asked of God, 20

Samel, m. Esth. Heb. asked of God, 20

Sameli, m. Swiss, Heb. asked of God, 20

Sammel, *m. Swiss,* Heb. asked of God, 20

Sampson, *m. Eng.* Heb. splendid sun, 39

Samsao, *m. Port.* Heb. splendid sun, 39

Samson, *m. Eng. Ger.* Heb. splendid sun, 39

Samuel, *m. Ger. Eng. Fr.* Heb. asked of God, 20

Samuele, m. It. Heb. asked of God, 20

Samuil, m. Wall. Heb. asked of God, 20

Samuls, m. Lett. Heb. asked of God, 20

Sancha, *f. Span.* Lat. holy, 175

Sanchica, f. m. Span. Lat. holy, 175

Sanche, *f. Fr.* Lat. holy, 175

Sancho, *m. Span.* Lat. holy, 175

Sancia, *f. Ger.* Lat. holy, 175

Sancie, *f. Fr.* Lat. holy, 175

Sancto, *m. It.* Lat. holy, 175

SANCTUS, *m. Lat.* holy, 175

Sanders, *m. Lett.* Gr. helper of men, 85

Sandor, *m. Hung.* Gr. helper of men, 85

Sandrl, *f. Bav.* Heb. lily, 50

Sandro, *m. Ital.* Gr. helper of men, 85

Sandy, *m. Scot.* Gr. helper of men, 85

Sanerl, *f. Bav.* Heb. lily, 50

Sanne, *f. Dutch,* Heb. lily, 50

Sanson, *Fr.* Heb. splendid sun, 39

Sansone, *It.* Heb. splendid sun, 39

Santerl, *m. Bav.* Gr. gold flower, 125

Santiago, *m. Span.* Lat. Heb. holy James, 17

Santje, *f. Dutch,* Heb. lily, 50

Santo, *m. Rom.* Lat. holy, 175

Santos, *m. Span.* Lat. the saints, 175

Sanzio, *m. Ital.* Lat. holy, 175

Sapor, *m.* Gr. Zend. venerable king, 57

SAPPHERO, *f. M. Gr.* Gr. sapphire, 125

Sappi, *f. Lith.* Gr. wisdom, 107

Sara, *f. Fr. Hung. Ill. Ger. Ill.* Heb. princess, 13

Sarah, *f. Eng.* Heb. princess, 13

Sarai, *f. Eng.* Heb. quarrelsome, 13

SARAID, *f. Erse,* Kelt. excellent, 13

Sarica, *f. Hung.* Heb. princess, 13

Sarotte, *f. Fr.* Heb. princess, 13

SASAN, *m.* Zend. venerable king, 57

Sasze, *m. Fris.* Gr. Christian, 105

Sativola, *f. Lat.* Kelt. 282

SATURNINUS, *m. Lat.* of Saturn, 179

Saul, *m. Eng.* Heb. longed for.

Saunders, *m. Scot.* Gr. helper of men, 85

Sava, *m. Russ.* Heb. rest, 216

Saverij, *m. Ill.* Arabic, bright, 299

Savero, *m. It.* Arab. bright, 299

Sawney, *m. Scot.* Gr. helper of men, 85

Saxo, *m. Lat.* Teu. rock, 324

Sayer, *m. Eng.* Teu. conquering army, 359

Scczpan, Lus. Gr. crown, 96

Sczrpan, Pol. Gr. crown, 96

Schelluf, *m. Nor.* Teu. shield wolf, 35

Schmul, m. Ger. Heb. asked of God, 20

SCHOLASTICA, *f. Eng.* Lat. scholar, 184

Scholastike, *f. Ger.* Lat. scholar, 184

Scholastique, *f. Fr.* Lat. scholar, 184

Schombel, m. Lus. Heb. asked of God, 20

SCHWANHILDE, *Ger.* Teu. swan maid, 346

SCHWANBERGE, *Ger.* Teu. swan protection, 346

Schymank, m. Lus. Heb. obedient, 19

Schymanz, m. Lus. Heb. obedient, 19

Science, *f. Eng.* Lat. science, 175

SCIENTIA, *f. Eng.* Lat. science, 175

SCIPIO, *m. Eng.* Lat. staff, 164

Scipion, *m. Fr.* Lat. staff, 164

Scipione, *m. It.* Lat. staff, 164

SCROFA, *m.* Lat. pig, 152

Seachnall, *m. Ir.* Lat. second, 52

Seabert, *m. Eng.* Teu. conquering brightness, 359

Seaforth, *m. Eng.* Teu. conquering peace, 359

SEALBFLAITH, *f. Erse,* Kelt. lady of possessions, 259

SEALBHACH, *m.* rich, 359

Searlus, *m. Erse,* Teu. man.

SEAXBALD, *m. A.S.* Teu. rock bold, 324

SEAXBERT, *m. A.S.* Teu. rock bright, 324

SEAXBURH, *f. A.S.* Teu. rock pledge, 324

Seaward, *f. m. Eng.* Teu. conquering guardian, 359

Sebald, m. Ger. Fr. Teu. conquering valour, 359

Sebastian, *f. m. Ger. Eng. Span.* Gr. venerable, 111

Sebastiana, *f. It.* Gr. venerable, 111

Sebastiane, *f. Ger.* Gr. venerable, 111

Sebastiano, *m. It.* Gr. venerable, 111

SEBASTIANUS, *m. Lat.* Gr. venerable, 111

Sebastiao, *m. Port.* Gr. venerable, 111

Sebastien, *m. Fr.* Gr. venerable, 111

Sebastienne, *f. Fr.* Gr. venerable, 111

Sebastyan, *m. Pol.* Gr. venerable, 111

Sebesta, f. Bohm. Gr. venerable, 111

Sebestyen, *m. Hung.* Gr. venerable, 111

Sebila, *f. Span.* Lat. wise old woman, 178

SECUNDUS, *m. Lat.* second, 137

Sedecias, *m. Lat.* Heb. justice of the Lord, 49

Seemeon, *m. Russ.* Heb. obedient, 19

Sefa, f. Swiss, Heb. addition, 23

Seifred, *m. Ger.* Teu. conquering peace, 356

Selbflaith, *f. Erse,* Kelt. lady of possessions, 259

Selima, *f. Arab.* Heb. peace, 47

Selina, *f. Eng.* Gr. moon, 67

Selinde, *f. Ger.* Teu. conquering snake, 358

Selma, *f. Scot.* Kelt. fair (?).

Selvach, m. Scot. Kelt. rich in cattle, 259

Selvaggia, *f. Ital.* Lat. wild, 179

Selvaggio, *m. It.* Lat. wild, 179

Seoin, *m. Erse,* Heb. grace of the Lord, 46

Seorgi, m. Erse, Gr. husbandman, 116

Seph, m. Bav. Heb. addition, 23

Sepherl, m. Bav. Heb. addition, 23

Sepp, m. Swiss, Bav. Heb. addition, 23

Seppeli, f. Swiss, Heb. addition, 23

Seppi, m. Swiss, Heb. addition, 23

Seppli, m. Swiss, Heb. addition, 23

Septime, *m. Fr.* Lat. seventh, 138

Septimia, *f. Eng.* Lat. seventh, 138

SEPTIMUS, *m. Eng.* Lat. seventh, 138

Serafina, *f. Span. It.* Heb. seraph, 53

Serafino, *m. Span. It.* Heb. seraph, 53

Seraphine, *Fr.* Heb. seraph, 53

SERENA, *Dan. Eng.* Lat. serene, 164

Serene, *f. Fr. Ger.* Lat. serene, 164

Serge, *m. Fr.* 152

Sergio, *m. Lom.* 152

SERGIUS, *m.* Lat. 152

Serlo, *m. Norseman,* Teu. armour, 352

Sersa, *m. Ill.* Zend. venerable king, 57

Sessylt, *Welsh,* Lat. blind, 144

Seth, *m. Eng.* Heb. appointed, 11

Seumuis, *m. Erse,* Heb. supplanted, 17

Sevilla, *f. Span.* Lat. wise old woman, 178

SEXTUS, *m. Eng.* Lat. sixth, 138

SHAPOOR, *m. Pers.* Zend. venerable king, 57

Shawanie-Jassan, Red Indian, fierce wolf, 182

Shawn, *m. Ir.* Heb. grace of the Lord, 45

Sheelah, *f. Ir.* Lat. blind, 144

Sholto, *m. Scot.* Kelt. sower (?), 254

Siade, m. Fris. conquering firmness, 357

Siard, m. Fris. Teu. conquering firmness, 311

Sib, f. Ir. Lat. wise old woman, 178

Sibbald, m. Eng. Teu. conquering prince, 359

Sibbaldo, m. It. Teu. conquering prince, 359

Sibbe, m. Ger. Teu. conquering commander, 359

Sibbel, *m. Eng.* Lat. wise old woman, 178

Sibbern, m. Fris. Teu. conquering bear, 359

Sibbie, f. Scot. Lat. wise old woman, 178

Sibel, *m. Fris.* Teu. conquering prince, 359

Sibella, *f. Eng.* Lat. wise old woman, 178

Siber, f. Nor. Teu. conquering protection, 359

Sibert, m. Fris. Teu. conquering brightness, 359

Sibila, f. It. Lat. wise old woman, 178

Sibilla, f. It. Lat. wise old woman, 178

Sibille, f. Fr. Lat. wise old woman, 178

Sibo, m. Fris. Teu. conquering messenger, 359

Sibod, m. Fris. Teu. conquering messenger, 359

Sibold, m. Fris. Teu. conquering prince, 359

Siborg, f. Nor. Teu. conquering protection, 359

Sibrand, m. Fris. Teu. conquering sword, 359

Sibyl, *f. Eng.* Lat. wise old woman, 178

SIBYLLA, *f. Eng.* Lat. wise old woman, 178

Sibylle, *f. Ger. Fr.* Lat. wise old woman, 178

Siccard, m. Fr. Teu. conquering firmness, 359

Sicco, m. Nor. Teu. conquering peace, 357

Sichelgaita, *f. It.* Teu. Sicilian goat, 341

Sidbolt, m. Fris. Teu. conquering prince, 357

Sidde, m. Fris. Teu. conquering brightness, 357

Sidders, m. Lith. Lat. beloved, 188

Sidoine, *m. Fr.* Lat. of Sidon, 200

SIDONIA, *f. m. It.* Lat. of Sidon, 200

Sidonie, *f. Ger. Fr.* Lat. of Sidon, 200

Sidwell, *f. Eng.* Kelt. 282

SIDONIUS, *m. Lat.* of Sidon, 200

SIEGFRIED, *m. Ger.* Teu. conquering peace, 357

Siegmund, m. Ger. Teu. conquering protection, 359

Siem, m. S. Ger. Heb. obedient, 19

Siewars, m. Nor. Teu. conquering peace, 359

Siffredo, m. It. Teu. conquering peace, 359

Siffroi, m. Fr. Teu. conquering peace, 359

SIGBALD, *m. Ger.* Teu. conquering prince, 359

SIGBERT, *m. Ger.* Teu. conquering brightness, 359

SIGBOD, *m. Ger.* Teu. conquering commander, 359

SIGBIORG, *f. Nor.* Teu. conquering protection, 357

SIGBRAND, *m. Ger.* Teu. conquering sword, 357

SIGEBALD. *m. A.S.* Teu. conquering prince, 357

SIGEBERG, *m. Frank.* Teu. conquering brightness, 357

SIGEBURGE, *f. Ger.* conquering protection, 357

SIGEFRED, *m. A.S.* Teu. conquering peace, 357

Sigefredo, *m. Ital.* Teu. conquering peace, 357

Sigfreda, *f. Ger.* Teu. conquering peace, 357

Sigefroi, *m. Fr.* Teu. conquering peace, 357

SIGEHARD, *m. A.S.* Teu. conquering firmness, 357

SIGEHELM, *m. Ger.* Teu. conquering helmet, 357

SIGEHERI, *m. A.S.* Teu. conquering warrior, 357

SIGELIND, *f. Ger.* Teu. conquering snake, 357

SIGEWOLF, *m. A.S.* conquering wolf, 357

Sigfrid, *m. Ger.* Teu. conquering peace, 357

Sigfrida, *f. Ger.* Teu. conquering peace, 358

SIGFUS, *m. Nor.* Teu. conquering zeal, 358

Sighar, *m. Ger.* Teu. conquering warrior, 359

Sighard, *m. Ger.* Teu. conquering firmness, 359

SIGHELM, *m. Ger.* Teu. conquering helmet, 359

Sigher, *m. Ger.* Teu. conquering warrior, 358

Sigismond, *m. Fr.* Teu. conquering protection, 358

Sigismonda, *f. Span. It.* Teu. conquering protection, 358

Sigismondo, *m. It.* Teu. conquering protection, 358

Sigismund, *m. Eng.* Teu. conquering protection, 358

Sigismunda, *f. Eng.* Teu. conquering protection, 358

Sigismundo, *m. Port.* Teu. conquering protection, 358

Sikko, m. Ger. Teu. conquering peace, 356

Sigl, m. Bav. Teu. conquering peace, 356

Siglind, f. Ger. Teu. conquering snake, 356

Sigmar, m. Ger. Teu. conquering fame, 356

Sigmund, *m. Ger.* Teu. conquering protection, 356

Sigmunda, f. Ger. Teu. conquering protection, 359

SIGMUNDR, *m. Nor.* Teu. conquering protection, 359

Sigo, m. Ger. Teu. conquering, 359

Sigrad, m. Ger. Teu. conquering council, 359

SIGRIDUR, *f. Nor.* Teu. conquering impulse, 359

Sigrada, f. Ger. Teu. conquering council, 359

Sigri, f. Nor. Teu. conquering impulse, 359

Sigrich, *m. Ger.* Teu. conquering rule, 357

Sigrid, *f. Nor.* Teu. conquering council, 357

Sigtrud, *f. Nor.* Teu. conquering maid, 359

SIGTRYGGE, *m. Nor.* conquering security, 359

Sigufrit, *m. Ger.* Teu. conquering peace, 359

Sigulf, m. Nor. Teu. conquering wolf, 359

Sigurd, *m. Nor.* Teu. conquering guard, 359

SIGVALLDR, *m. Nor.* Teu. conquering power, 359

Sigvor, m. Nor. Teu. conquering prudence, 359

Sigwald, *m. Ger.* Teu. conquering power, 359

SIGWARD *m. Ger.* Teu. conquering guard, 359

Silas, *m. Eng.* Lat. living in a wood, 179

Sile, f. Erse, Lat. 179

Silvain, *m. Fr.* Lat. living in a wood, 179

Silvano, *m. It.* Lat. living in a wood, 179

SILVESTER, *m. Eng.* Lat. living in a wood, 179

Silvestre, *m. Fr.* Lat. living in a wood, 179

Silvia, *f. It.* Lat. living in a wood, 179

Silvie, *f. Fr.* Lat. living in a wood, 179

Silvio, *m. It.* Lat. living in a wood, 179

Sim, m. Eng. Heb. obedient, 19

SIMAITH, *m.* Kelt. peaceful, 47

Simanas, *m. Lett.* Heb. obedient, 19

Simao, *m. Port.* Heb. obedient, 19

Simej, *m. Ill.* Heb. obedient, 19

SIMEON, *m. Eng. Ger. Fr.* Heb. obedient, 7, 19

Simmas, m. Lith. Heb. obedient, 19

Simo, m. Ill. Heb. obedient, 19

Simon, *m. Fr. Eng. Ger. Span.* Heb. obedient, 19

Simonas, *m. Lett.* Heb. obedient, 19

Simone, *m. It.* Heb. obedient, 19

Simonette, f. Fr. Heb. obedient, 19

Simson, *m. Fr.* Heb. splendid sun, 39

Simo, m. Ill. Heb. obedient, 19

SINDBALD, *m. Ger.* Teu. sparkling prince (?), 379

SINDBERT, *m. Ger.* Teu. sparkling bright, 379

SINDOLF, *m. Ger.* Teu. sparkling wolf, 379

SINDRAM, *m. Ger.* Teu. sparkling raven, 379

Sinibaldo, m. It. Teu. sparkling prince, 379

Sinovij, m. Russ. Arab. father's ornament, 62

Sinovija, f. Russ. Arab. father's ornament, 62

Sintram, *m. Ger.* Teu. sparkling raven, 379

SIOLTIACH, *m. Gael.* Kelt. sower, 254

Sipp, m. Bav. Heb. addition, 23

Sired, f. Norman, Teu. conquering impulse, 359

Siri, f. Nor. Teu. conquering impulse, 359

SIROSLAV, *m. Slav.* Slav. far famed, 435

Siseberto, *m. Span.* Teu. conquering brightness, 359

Sisebuto, *m. Span.* Teu. conquering commander, 359

Sis, f. Eng. Lat. blind, 144

Sisley, f. Eng. Lat. blind, 144

Sisman, m. Ill. Teu. conquering protection, 359

Sismonde, m. It. Teu. conquering protection, 359

Sisto, *m. It.* Lat. sixth, 138

Sitto, m. Fries. Teu. conquering brightness, 359

Siurd, m. Nor. Teu. conquering guard, 359

Siulf, m. Nor. Teu. conquering wolf, 359

Siward, *m. Eng.* Teu. conquering guardian, 359

Sixte, *m. Fr.* Lat. sixth, 138

Sixtus, *m. Eng.* Lat. sixth, 138

Sizo, *m. Ger.* Teu. conquering brightness, 359

Sjovald, *m. Nor.* Teu. conquering power, 359

Sjovar, *m. Nor.* Teu. conquering prudence, 359

Sjul, *m. Nor.* Teu. conquering guard, 359

Sjurd, *m. Nor.* Teu. conquering guard, 359

Skak, *m. Nor.* Teu. servant.

Skarphedinn, *Nor.* Teu. sharp attack, 304

Skegg, *m. Nor.* Teu. beard, 427

Skend r, *m. Slav.* helper of man, 85

Skerste, *m. Lett.* Gr. Christian, 105

Skersts, *m. Lett.* Gr. Christian, 105

Skialde, *m. Nor.* Teu. shield, 352

Skiolde, *m. Nor.* Teu. shield, 352

Skioldbiorn, *m. Nor.* Teu. shield bear, 352

Skioldulf, *m. Nor.* Teu. shield wolf, 352

Skioldvar, *m. Nor.* Teu. shield caution, 352

Sklear, *m. Bret.* Lat. famous, 185

Skleara, *f. Bret.* Lat. famous, 185

Skuldr, *f. Nor.* Teu. shall, 306

Skule, *m. Nor.* Teu. shield, 352

Slavoje, *m. Slav.* Slav. glorious love, 435

Slavofjub, *m. Slav.* Slav. glorious love, 435

Slavomil, *m. Slav.* Slav. glorious friend, 435

Slavomir, *m. Slav.* Slav. glorious peace, 435

Smaragda, *f. M. Gr.* Gr. emerald, 124

Smaragdos, *m. M. Ger.* Gr. emerald, 125

Smil, *m. Slav.* Slave, beloved, 439

Smiljan, *m. Slav.* Slave, everlasting flower, 438

Smiljana, *f. Slav.* Slav. everlasting flower, 438

Smoljan, *m. Ill.* Slav. long-nosed, 446

Smoljana, *f. Ill.* Slav. long-nosed, 445

Snæbiorn, *m. Nor.* Teu. snow bear, 348, 339

Snæfrid, *f. Nor.* Teu. snow fair, 348

Snælaug, *f. m. Nor.* Teu. snow ocean, 348

Snæulf, *m. Nor.* Teu. snow wolf, 348

Snorre, *m. Nor.* Teu. striving, 418

Snorro, *m. Lat.* Teu. striving, 418

Sodomina, *f. Erse*, Kelt. good lady, 258

Sofia, *f. Hung. It.* Gr. wisdom, 107

Sol, *f. Span. Nor.* Teu. sun.

Solle, *m. Nor.* Teu. armour, 352

Soloma, *f. Eng.* Heb. peace, 48

Sölmund, *m. Dan.* Teu. healing protection, 352

Solomon, *m. Eng.* Heb. peaceful, 48

Solva, *f. Nor.* Teu. healing drink, 352

Solvar, healthy warrior, 352

Solve, *m. Dan.* Teu. healthy warrior, 352

Solveig, *f. m. Nor.* Teu. healing drink, 352

Somerled, *m. Scot.* Teu. summer wanderer, 432

Somhle, *m. Gael.* Teu. summer wanderer, 432

Sophia, *f. Eng.* Gr. wisdom, 107

Sophie, *f. Fr. Ger.* Gr. wisdom, 107

Sophocles, *m. Lat.* Gr. wise fame, 107

Sophonisba, *f. Eng.* Phœn.

Sophron, *m. Eng.* Gr. of sound mind.

Sophronia, *f. Eng.* Gr. of sound mind.

Sophy, *f. Eng.* Gr. wisdom, 107

Sorcha, *f. Erse*, Kelt. bright, 13

Sorle, *m. Nor.* Teu. armour, 352

Sosana, *f. Wall.* Heb. lily, 50

Speranza, *f. It.* Lat. hope, 196

Sperata, *f. It.* Lat. hoped for, 196

Spira, *f. Ill.* Gr. round basket, 124

Spiridion, *m. Ill.* Gr. round basket, 124

Spiridione, *m. It.* Gr. round basket, 124

Spranzis, *m. Lett.* Teu. free, 299

Sprinzchen, *f. N. Lands*, Teu. free, 299

Sprizzis, *m. Lett.* Teu. peace ruler, 296

Spyridōn, *m. M. Gr.* Gr. round basket, 124

Spyro, *m. M. Gr.* Gr. round basket, 124

Ssachka, m. Russ. Gr. helper of men, 85

Ssachnika, m. Russ. Gr. helper of men, 85

Ssava, *m. Russ.* Heb. rest (?), 216

Ssemar, m. Russ. Heb. obedient, 19

Ssenka, m. Russ. Heb. obedient, 19

Sszrezeca, Russ. Lat. 152

Ssergii, *m. Russ.* Lat. 152

Ssevastjan, *m. Russ.* Gr. awful, 111

Ssevastjana, *f. Russ.* Gr. awful, 111

Ssevilla, *f. Russ.* Lat. wise old woman, 178

Ssimeon, *m. Russ.* Heb. obedient, 19

Ssimon, *m. Russ.* Heb. obedient, 19

Ssofija, *f. Russ.* Gr. wisdom, 107

Ssonia, f. Russ. Gr. wisdom, 107

Ssoninska, f. Russ. Gr. wisdom, 107

Ssusanna, *f. Russ.* Heb. lily, 50

STAALE, *m. Nor.* Teu. steel, 349

Stach, m. Pol. Slav. camp glory, 44

Stacherl, m. Bav. Gr. happy harvest, 89

Staches, m. Bav. Gr. happy harvest, 89

Stachis, m. Lett. Slav. camp glory, 440

Stachus, m. Bav. Gr. happy harvest, 89

Stacy, f. Ir. Gr. resurrection, 110

Stanca, f. Ill. Lat. firm, 162

Stanel, m. Bav. Slav. camp glory, 440

Stanerl, m. Bav. Slav. camp glory, 440

Stanes, m. Bav. Slav. camp glory, 440

Stanisav, *m. Ill.* Slav. camp glory, 440

Stanisl, m. Bav. Slav. camp glory, 440

Stanislao, *m. Port.* Slav. camp glory, 440

Stanislaus, *m. Ger.* Slav. camp glory, 440

STANISLAV, *m. Pol.* Slav. camp glory, 440

Stanislaos, *m. Lett.* Slav. camp glory, 440

Stanko, m. Ill. Slav. camp glory, 440

Stanze, f. Ger. Lat. firm, 161

Stas, m. Bav. Gr. of the resurrection, 110

Stas, m. Pol. Slav. camp glory, 440

Stasi, m. Bav. Gr. of the resurrection, 110

Stasrl, m. Bav. Gr. of the resurrection, 110

STASTNY, *m. Bohm.* Slav. happy, 441

Statire, *f. Fr.* Zend. 58

Stefan, *m. Slov. Swiss, Pol.* Gr. crown, 96

Stefanida, f. Russ. Gr. crown, 96

Stefanie, *f. Fr.* Gr. crown, 96

Stefano, *m. It.* Gr. crown, 96

Steffano, *m. It.* Gr. crown, 96

Steffel, m. Bav. Gr. crown, 96

STEIN, *m. Nor.* Teu. stone, 349

STEINARNA, *f. m. Nor.* Teu. stone eagle, 349

STEINAR, *m. Nor.* Teu. stone warrior, 349

STEINBJORN, *m. Nor.* Teu. stone bear, 349

Steindor, m. Nor. Teu. stone of Thor, 349

STEINFINN, *m. Nor.* Teu. stone white, 349

STEINGRIM, *m. Nor.* Teu. stone helmet, 349

STEINHAR, *m. Ger.* Teu. stone warrior, 349

STEINTHOR, *m. Nor.* Teu. stone of Thor, 349

STEINULV, *m. Nor.* Teu. stone wolf, 349

STEINVOR, *m. Nor.* Teu. stone prudence, 349

Stella, *f. Eng.* Lat. star, 57

Sten, *m. Ger.* Teu. stone, 349

Stenka, m. Russ. Gr. crown, 96

Stenzel, m. Schleswig. Slav. camp glory, 440

Stepan, *m. Russ. Bohm.* Gr. crown, 96

Stepania, *f. Ill.* Gr. crown, 96

Stepanida, *f. Russ.* Gr. crown, 97

Stephan, *m. Ger.* Gr. crown, 96

Stephana, *f. Eng.* Gr. crown, 96

Stephanie, *f. Ger. Fr.* Gr. crown, 96

Stephanine, *f. Ger.* Gr. crown, 96

STEPHANOS, *m.* Gr. crown, 96

Stephen, *m. Eng.* Gr. crown, 96

Stepica, *m. Ill.* Gr. crown, 96

Stepka, m. Russ. Gr. crown, 96

Stepko, m. Ill. Gr. crown, 96

Stepo, m. Ill. Gr. crown, 96

STERKULV, *m. Nor.* Teu. strong wolf, 336

Steven, *m. Dutch,* Gr. crown, 96

STIGAND, *m. Eng.* Teu. mounting, 434

Stilicho, *m. Lat.* Teu. steel, 349

Stine, f. Ger. Gr. Christian, 105

Stoffel, m. Bav. Swiss, Gr. Christ bearer, 106

Stoppel, m. Bav. Gr. Christ bearer, 106

Strachota, m. Bohm. Slav. terror.

STRASIMIR, *m. Slav.* Slav. terrible peace, 440

STRASISLAV, *m. Slav.* Slav. terrible glory, 440

Stratonice, *f. Eng.* Gr. army victory, 212

STYGE, *m. Nor.* Teu. rising, 434

STYGGE, *m. Nor.* Teu. rising, 434

Styntje, f. Dutch, Gr. Christian, 105

Styrk, *f. Dan.* Teu. strong, 424

Styrker, *m. Nor.* Teu. strong, 424

Sue, f. Eng. Heb. lily, 50

Sueno, *m. Lat.* Teu. strong, 424

Suintila, *m. Goth.* Teu. strength, 424

Sukey, f. Eng. Heb. lily, 50

Sulia, m. Bret. Lat. downy beard, 150

Suliana, f. Bret. Lat. downy beard, 150

Suleiman, *m. Arab.* Heb. peaceful, 47

Sulpice, *m. Fr.* Lat. red spotted face, 152

SULPICIUS, *m.* Lat. red spotted face, 152

Sulpoy, *m. Ger.* Lat. red spotted face, 152

SUMALIDE, *m. Nor.* Teu. summer wanderer, 432

Susan, *f. Eng.* Heb. lily, 50

Susana, *f. Span.* Heb. lily, 50

Susanna, *f. Ger.* Heb. lily, 50

Susannah, *f. Eng.* Heb. lily, 50

Susechen, *f. Ger.* Heb. lily, 50

Suse, f. Lett. Heb. lily, 50

Susette, f. Fr. Heb. lily, 50

Susie, f. Eng. Heb. lily, 50

Suska, f. Slav. Heb. lily, 50

Suson, f. Fr. Heb. lily, 50

Suzanne, f. Fr. Heb. lily, 50

Suzette, f. Fr. Heb. lily, 50

Suzan, f. Fr. Heb. lily, 50

Suzsi, f. Hung. Heb. lily, 50

SVEIN, *m. Nor.* Teu. youth, 424

Sven, m. Nor. Teu. youth, 424

Svewke, *m. Nor.* Teu. youth, 424

Svenbjorn, *m. Nor.* Teu. young bear, 424

SVERKE, *m. Nor.* Teu. swarthy, 428

Sverkir, *m. Nor.* Teu. swarthy, 428

SVEVLAD, *m. Slov.* Slav. all ruler, 442

SVJATOPOLK, *m. Russ.* Slav. holy government, 441

SVJATOSLAV, *m. Russ.* Slav. holy glory, 441

Swain, *m. Eng.* Teu. youth, 424

SWANA, *f. Nor.* Teu. swan, 346

Swanbrecht, *m. Ger.* Teu. swan bright, 346

SWANHILD, *f. Nor.* Teu. swan battle maid, 346

SWANHOLD, *m. Ger.* Teu. swan firm, 346

SWANLAUG, *f. Nor.* Teu. swan water, 346

SWANHWITE, *f. Nor.* Teu. swan white, 346

SWEND, *m. Dan.* Teu. strong youth, 424

Swenike, m. Nor. Teu. strong, 424

SWETLANA, *f. Russ.* Teu. star, 439

Swibert, *m. Fris.* Teu. brightness, 424

SWIDBIORG, *f. Nor.* Teu. strong protection, 424

SWIDGER, *m. Nor.* Teu. strong spear, 424

SWINTFRIED, *m. Ger.* Teu. strong peace, 424

SWITHBEORHT, *m. A.S.* Teu. strong brightness, 424

SWITHELM, *m. A.S.* Teu. strong helmet, 424

SWITHUN, *m. Eng.* Teu. strong friend, 424

Sylvanus, *m. Lat.* living in a wood, 179

SYLVESTER, *m. Eng.* Lat. living in a wood, 179

Sylvia, *f. Eng.* Lat. living in a wood, 179

Sylvius, *m. Lat.* living in a wood, 179

SYGFRYD, *m. Pol.* Teu. conquering peace, 357

Syver, m. Nor. Teu. conquering guard, 357

Syvert, m. Nor. Teu. conquering guard, 357

Szymon, *m. Pol.* Heb. obedient, 18

T

Tabby, f. Eng. Aram. gazelle, 50

Tabcia, f. Ger. Aram. gazelle, 50

Tabbern, m. Fris. Teu. people's sword, 375

TABITHA, *f. Eng.* Aram. gazelle, 50

Taddeo, *m. Ill.* Aram. praise, 20

Tade, m. Ill. Aram. praise, 20

Tade, m. Fris. Teu. people's ruler, 375

Tadeiv, m. Nor. Thor's relic, 302

Tadeo, *m. Span.* Aram. praise, 20

TADGH, *m. Erse,* Kelt. poet, 257

Tadia, m. Ill. Aram. praise, 20

Taedlef, m. Fris. Teu. people's relic, 374

Tuffy, m. Welsh, Heb. beloved, 46

Tafline, f. Welsh, Heb. beloved, 46

Taganwart, *m. O. Ger.* Teu. day guard, 334

Tago, *m. Span.* Teu. day, 334

Tajo, *m. Span.* Teu. day, 344

TAKAPERAHT, *m. O. Ger.* Teu. day bright, 334

Talitha Cumi, f. Eng. Aram. damsel arise.

TALLWCH, *Cym.* Kelt. torrent, 275

Tam, m. Scot. Aram. twin, 22

Tamar, *f. Eng.* Heb. palm, 26

Tamas, m. Hung. Aram. twin, 22

Tamassa, m. Lat. Aram. twin, 22

Tamasine, *f. Eng.* Aram. twin, 22

Tamkus, m. Lett. Aram. twin, 22

Tamlane, m. Scot. Aram. twin, 22

Tammy, f. Eng. Aram. twin, 22

Tamoszus, m. Lett. Aram. twin, 22

Tamzin, f. Eng. Aram. twin, 22

Tancar, *m. Ger.* Teu. grateful warrior, 371

Tancard, *m. Eng.* Teu. grateful guard, 371

Tancred, *m. Eng.* Teu. grateful speech, 371

Tancredi, *m. It.* Teu. grateful speech, 371

Taniel, m. Esth. Heb. judgment of God, 50

Tankred, *m. Ger.* Teu. thankful speech, 371

Tanne, m. Lett. Lat. inestimable, 142

Tanneguy, *m. Bret.* Kelt. 252

Tanni, m. Esth. Heb. judgment of God, 50

TATE, *f. A.S.S.* cheerful, 429

Tavid, m. Esth. Heb. beloved, 46

Teague, *m. Ir.* Kelt. poet, 257

Tearlach, *m. Gael.* Teu. man, 386

Tebaldo, *m. It.* Teu. people's valour, 374

Tebes, m. Swiss, Heb. goodness of the Lord, 49

Tecla, *f. It.* Ger. divine fame, 100

Ted, m. Eng. Teu. rich guard.

Tedor, m. Hamburgh, Gr. divine gift, 101

Tedric, m. Norman, Teu. people's rule, 374

Tegan Euvron, *m. Welsh,* Kelt. golden beauty, 234

TEITR, *m. Nor.* Teu. cheerful, 429

Telemachus, *m. Lat.* Gr. distant battle, 75

Telemaque, *m. Fr.* Gr. distant battle, 75

Temperance, *f. Eng.* Lat.

Tennis, m. Lett. Gr. of Dionysos, 70

Tennis, m. Lett. Lat. inestimable, 142

Tents, m. Lett. Gr. of Dionysos, 70

Teobald, m. Pol. Teu. people's valour, 374

Teobaldo, *m. It.* Teu. people's valour, 374

Teodor, m. Pol. Slov. Gr. divine gift, 101

Teodora, *f. It.* Gr. divine gift, 101

Teodorico, *m. It.* Teu. people's ruler, 373

Teodoro, *f. It.* Gr. divine gift, 101

Teodosia, *f. It. Russ.* Gr. divine gift, 101

Teodosio, *m. It.* Gr. divine gift, 101

Teodorico, *m. It.* Teu. people's rule, 373

Teofil, *m. Slav.* Gr. divinely loved, 100

Teofila, *f. It.* Gr. divinely loved, 100

Teofilo, *m. It.* Gr. divinely loved, 100

Terence, *m. Ir.* Lat. tender, 152

Terentia, *f.* Lat. tender, 152

Terentilla, *f.* Lat. tender, 152

TERENTIUS, *m.* Lat. tender, 152

Terenz, *m. Ger.* Lat. tender, 152

Teresa, *f. It. Span.* Gr. carrying ears of corn, 124

Teresina, f. Pol. Gr. carrying ears of corn, 124

Teresita, f. It. Span. Gr. carrying ears of corn, 124

Terezia, *f. Ill.* Gr. carrying ears of corn, 124

Terezia, f. Hung. Gr. carrying ears of corn, 124

Terezie, *f. Bohm.* Gr. carrying ears of corn, 124

Terezyga, *f. Pol.* Gr. carrying ears of corn, 124

Terry, m. Eng. people's rule, 375

Terza, f. Ill. Gr. carrying ears of corn, 124

TERTIA, *m.* Lat. third, 137

TERTIUS, *m.* Lat. third, 137

TERTULLA, third, 137

TERTULLIANUS, 137

Tetje, m. Hamb. Gr. divine gift, 101

Teunis, m. Dutch, Lat. inestimable, 142

Teuntje, f. Dutch, Lat. inestimable, 142

Tewa, m. Esth. Gr. crown, 96

Tewdur, *m. Welsh,* Gr. divine gift, 101

Tewdews, *f. Welsh,* divinely given, 101

Tewes, m. Hamburgh, Heb. goodness of the Lord, 49

Thaddä, m. Ger. Aram. praise, 20

THADDÆUS, *m. Eng.* Aram. praise, 20, 257

Thaddej, *m. Russ.* Aram. praise, 20

Thaddea, *m. Port.* Aram. praise, 20

Thady, m. Ir. Aram. praise, 20

Thaiter, Erse, Teu. powerful warrior, 425

Thakkraad, *Nor.* Teu. thankful speech, 371

Thalia, *f. Eng.* Gr. bloom, 72

Thangbrand, *Nor.* Teu. thankful sword, 371

Thean, m. Fr. Teu. people's rule, 375

Thecla, *f. Eng.* Gr. divine fame, 100

Thecle, *f. Fr.* Gr. divine fame, 100

Thedo, m. West Fris. Gr. divine gift, 100

THEKLA, *f. Ger.* Gr. divine fame, 100

Theobald, *m. Eng.* Teu. people's prince, 374

Theobalda, *f. Ger.* Teu. people's prince, 374

Theobaldo, *m. Port.* Teu. people's valour, 374

Theobul, *m. Ger.* Gr. divine council, 100

Theobulaire, *f. Ger.* Gr. divine council, 100

THEOBOULUS, *m. Lat.* Gr. divine council, 100

THEODEBALD, *A.S.S.* 373

THEODOMAIR, 373

Theodemaro, 374

Theodisclo, Span. Teu. people's pledge, 374

Theodolf, m. Ger. Teu. people's wolf, 374

THEODHARD, *m. Fr.* Teu. people's firmness, 375

Theodofredo, *m. Span.* Teu. people's peace, 375

Theodor, *m. Ger.* Gr. divine gift, 101

THEODOKAR, *m. Frank.* Teu. people's spear, 375

THEODORA, *f. Eng. Ger.* Gr. divine gift, 101

Theodorada, *f. Ger.* Teu. people's council, 373

Theodore, *m. Eng. Fr.* Gr. divine gift, 101

Theodoric, *m. Frank.* Teu. people's rule, 373

THEODORICO, *m. Port.* Teu. people's rule, 373

Theodoro, *m. Port.* Gr. divine gift, 101

THEODOROS, *m. Gr.* divine gift, 101

Theodorus, *m. Lat.* Gr. divine gift, 103

Theodose, *m. Fr.* Gr. divine gift, 103

Theodosia, *f. Ger. Eng.* Gr. divine gift, 103

Theodosio, *m. Port.* Gr. divine gift, 103

Theodosius, *m. Lat.* Gr. divinely given, 103

Theodotos, *m. Gr.* Gr. divinely given, 103

Theodric, Eng. Teu. people's ruler, 373

Theodrekr, *m. Nor.* Teu. people's rule, 373

Theodule, *f. Fr.* Gr. God's servant, 103

Theone, *f. Ger.* Gr. godly, 103

Theophanes, *m. Lat.* Gr. divine manifestation, 212

THEOPHANIA, *f. Ger. Lat.* Gr. divine manifestation, 212

Theophanie, *f. Fr.* Gr. divine manifestation, 212

Theophano, *f. N.Ger.* Gr. divine manifestation, 212

Theophil, *m. Ger.* Gr. divinely loved, 100

Theophila, *f. Eng.* Gr. divinely loved, 100

Theophile, *m. Fr.* Gr. divinely loved, 100

Theophilo, *m. Port.* Gr. God loved, 100

THEOPHILOS, *m. Gr.* Gr. divinely loved, 100

Theophilus, *m. Eng.* Gr. God beloved, 100

Theotari, m. Finn. Gr. divine gift, 103

THERESA, *f. Eng.* Gr. carrying ears of corn, 124

Thérèse, *f. Fr.* Gr. carrying ears of corn, 124

Theresia, *f. Ger.* Gr. harvester, 124

Theresie, *f. Ger.* Gr. harvester, 124

Theudebaldo, *m. Span.* Teu. people's prince, 375

THEUDEBOLD, *m. Frank.* Teu. people's prince, 374

Theudebert, *m. Frank.* Teu. people's brightness, 374

Theudebrand, *m. Ger.* Teu. people's sword, 375

Theudefred, *m. Goth.* Teu. people's peace, 375

Theudegisle, *m. Ger.* Teu. people's pledge, 375

Theudis, *m. Span.* Teu. the people, 375

THEUDHILDA, *f. Frank.* Teu. people's heroine, 375

THEUDOLIND, *f. Ger.* Teu. people's snake, 375

THEUDOMIR, *m. Frank.* Teu. people's fame, 375

THEUDOWIN, *m. Frank.* Teu. people's friend, 375

Theunis, m. Dutch, Lat. inestimable, 142

Thiadmar, m. Fris. Teu. people's fame, 375

Thiadelef, m. Fris. Teu. people's love, 375

Thias, m. Eng. Heb. gift of God, 15

Thieu, m. Fr. Teu. people's ruler, 374

Thebald, m. Fr. Teu. people's prince, 374

Thiebault, *m. Fr.* Teu. people's prince, 374

Thibaud, *m. Fr.* Teu. people's prince, 374

Thibault, *m. Fr.* Teu. people's prince, 374

Thierry, m. Fr. Teu. people's ruler, 374

Thiesli, m. Swiss, Heb. gift of God, 15, 103

Thiess, m. L.Ger. Heb. gift of God, 15

THIEDOLF, *m. Nor.* Teu. people's wolf, 375

THIOSTAN, *m. Nor.* Teu. harsh warrior, 419

THIOSTOLF, *m. Nor.* Teu. harsh wolf, 419

THIOSTWALD, *m. Nor.* Teu. harsh power, 419

Thiou, m. Fr. Teu. people's wolf, 375

Thirza, *f. Ger.* Heb. pleasantness, 38

THJODGEIR, *m. Nor.* Teu. people's spear, 375

THJODHILDR, *f. Nor.* Teu. people's heroine, 375

THJODHJALM, *m. Nor.* Teu. people's helmet, 375

THJODLEIF, *m. Dan.* people's relic, 375

THJODULV, *m. Nor.* Teu. people's wolf, 375

THJODVALD, *m. Nor.* Teu. people's power, 375

THJODVAR, *m. Nor.* Teu. people's prudence, 375

Thoddeiv, m. Nor. Teu. Thor's relic, 302, 332

Tholliev, m. Nor. Teu. Thor's relic, 302, 332

i

Thoma, *m. Wall.* Aram. twin, 21

Thomas, *m Fr. Eng.* Aram. twin, 21

Thomasia, *f. Ger.* Aram. twin, 22

Thomasin, *f. Ger.* Aram. twin, 22

Thomasine, *f. Eng.* Aram. twin, 22

Thor, *m. Ger.* Teu. the thunder god, 301

Thora, *f. Nor.* Teu. thunder, 302

Thorald, *m. Nor.* Teu. Thor's power, 302

Thoralfr, *m. Nor.* Teu. Thor's elf, 302

Thorarin, *m. Nor.* Teu. Thor's eagle, 302

Thorarna, *f. Nor.* Teu. Thor's eagle, 302

Thorbera, *f. Nor.* Teu. Thor's she bear, 302

Thorberg, *f. Ger.* Teu. Thor's protection, 302

Thorbert, *m. Nor.* Teu. Thor's splendour, 302

Thorbjorg, *f. Nor.* Teu. Thor's protection, 302

Thorbjorn, *m. Nor.* Teu. Thor's bear, 302

Thorbrand, *m. Ice.* Teu. Thor's sword, 302

Thord, *m. Nor.* Teu. thunder, 302

Thorer, *m. Nor.* Teu. Thor's warrior, 302

Thordis, *f. Nor.* Teu. Thor's household spirit, 302, 308

Thorfinn, *m. Nor.* Teu. Thor's white man, 302

Thorfinna, *f. Nor.* Teu. Thor's white woman, 302

Thorgard, *m. Nor.* Teu. Thor's guard, 302

Thorgautr, *m. Nor.* Teu. Thor the good, 302

Thorgerda, *f. Nor.* Teu. Thor's maiden, 302

Thorgestur, *m. Nor.* Teu. Thor's guest, 302

Thorgils, *m. Nor.* Teu. Thor's pledge, 302

Thorgisla, *f. Dan.* Teu. Thor's pledge, 302

Thorgrim, *m. Ice.* Teu. Thor the helmeted, 302

Thorgunna, *f. Nor.* Teu. Thor's war, 302

Thorhall, *m. Nor.* Teu. Thor's stone, 302

Thorhalla, *f. Nor.* Teu. Thor's stone, 302

Thorhilda, *f. Nor.* Teu. Thor's battle maid, 302

Thorhilde, *f. Ger.* Teu. Thor's battle maid, 302

Thorismondo, *m. Span.* Teu. Thor's protection, 302

Thorismund, *m. Goth.* Teu. Thor's protection, 302

Thorkatla, *f. Nor.* Teu. Thor's cauldron, 302

Thorketyl, *m. Nor.* Teu. Thor's cauldron, 302

Thorkjell, m. Nor. Teu. Thor's cauldron, 302

Thorlaug, *f. Nor.* Teu. Thor's liquor, 302

Thorleif, *m. Nor.* Teu. Thor's relic, 302

Thorleik, *m. Nor.* Teu. Thor's sport, 302

Thormod, *m. Nor.* Teu. Thor's mood, 302

Thorold, *m. Eng.* Teu. Thor's power, 302

Thorolf, *m. Ger.* Teu. Thor's wolf, 302

Thorothea, f. M. Gr. Gr. gift of God, 102

Thorstein, *m. Nor.* Teu. Thor's jewel, 302

Thorulva, *f. Nor.* Teu. Thor's wolf woman, 302

Thorunna, f. Ice. Teu. Thor's free woman, 302

Thorvalldr, *m. Nor.* Teu. Thor's power, 302

Thorvid, *m. Nor.* Thor's consecration, 302

Thorwald, *m. Ger.* Teu. Thor's power, 302

Thrall, *m. Nor.* Teu. serf, 331

Thrine, f. Ger. Gr. pure, 123

Thrudr, *f. Nor.* Teu. battle maid of constancy, 319

Thumas, *m. O. Fr.* Aram. twin, 21

Thursday, m. Eng. 445

Thurstan, *m. Eng.* Teu. Thor's jewel, 302

Thyrgils, m. Swed. Teu. Thor's pledge, 302

Thyra, *f. Nor.* Teu. belonging to Tyr, 306

Thyrza, *f. Eng.* Heb. pleasantness, 38

Tiabbern, m. Fris. Teu. people's sword, 375

Tiaddo, m. Fris. Teu. people's ruler, 374

Tiadelef, m. Fris. Teu. people's ruler, 374

Tiaderik, *m. Fris.* Teu. people's ruler, 374

Tiado, m. Fris. Teu. people's ruler, 374

Tiago, m. Span. Heb. supplanter, 17

Tiallef, m. Fris. people's ruler, 374

Tiard, m. Fris. Teu. people's prince, 374

Tiarik, m. Fris. Teu. people's ruler, 375

Tiark, m. Fris. Teu. people's ruler, 374

Tiart, m. Fris. Teu. people's prince, 374

Tib, m. Eng. Teu. people's prince, 374

Tibal, *m. Eng.* Teu. people's prince, 374

Tiballa, *m. Eng.* Teu. people's prince, 374

Tibaut, *m. Fr.* Teu. people's prince, 374

Tibbie, f. Scot. Heb. God's oath, 35

Tibble, m. Eng. Teu. people's prince, 374

Tibelda, *f. Eng.* Teu. people's prince, 374

Tibotta, *f. Eng.* people's prince, 374

Tibout, m. Fr. Teu. people's prince, 374

Tide, m. Fris. Teu. people's ruler, 374

Tidmer, m. Fris. Teu. people's fame, 374

Tido, m. Fris. Teu. people's ruler, 374

Ticbold, m. Ger. Teu. people's prince, 374

Tiedmer, m. Fris. Teu. people's fame, 375

Tienette, f. Fr. Gr. crown, 97

Tiennon, m. Fr. Gr. crown, 96

Tiennot, m. Fr. Gr. crown, 96

Tiernan, *m. Ir.* Kelt. kingly, 258

Tietje, m. Neth. Teu. people's rule, 375

Tiffany, *f. Eng.* Gr. divine manifestation, 212

Tiga, f. Lett. Gr. God's gift, 101

TIGHEARNACH, *m. Erse,* Kelt. kingly, 257

Tigo, m. Lett. Gr. God's gift, 102

TIHOMIL, *m. Slav.* Slav. silent love, 445

TIHOMIR, *m. Slav.* Slav. silent peace, 445

TIHOSLAV, *m. Slav.* Slave, silent glory, 445

Tike, f. Lett. Gr. God's gift, 101

TIKLA, *f. Pol.* Slav. goddess of good luck.

Til, f. Eng. Teu. mighty battle maid, 422

Tilda, f. Eng. Teu. mighty battle maid, 422

Tile, m. Neth. Teu. people's rule, 373

Tille, f. Ger. Teu. mighty battle maid, 422

Tilo, m. Fris. Teu. people's rule, 375

Tim, m. Ir. Gr. fear God, 104

Timofei, *m. Russ.* Gr. fear God, 104

Timoscha, m. Russ. Gr. fear God, 104

Timoteo, *m. It.* Gr. fear God, 104

Timothea, *f. Eng.* Gr. fear God, 104

Timothée, *m. Fr.* Gr. fear God, 104

TIMOTHEOS, *m.* Gr. fear God, 104

Timotheus, *m. Ger.* Lat. fear God, 104

Timothy, *m. Eng.* Lat. fear God, 104

Timotij, *m. Pol.* Gr. fear God, 104

Timotij, *m. Slav.* Gr. fear God, 104

Tina, f. It. Teu. man, 359

Tine, f. Ger. Gr. Christian, 105

Tio, f. Esth. Gr. gift of God, 101

Tirzah, *f. Eng.* Heb. pleasantness, 38

Tiphaïne, *f. Fr.* Gr. divine manifestation, 212

Tit, *m. Esth.* Lat. safe (?), 136

TITA, *m. It.* Lat. safe, 136

Tite, *m. Fr.* Lat. safe, 136

TITIANUS, *m.* Lat. safe, 136

Tito, *f. It.* Lat. safe (?), 136

TITURIUS, *m.* Lat. safe, 136

TITUS, *m.* Lat. safe, 136

Tivador, m. Hung. Gr. divine gift, 101

Tiz, Lett. Teu. people's ruler, 375

Tiziano, m. It. Lat. safe, 136

Tjerri, m. Russ. Teu. people's ruler, 375

TJOD, *m. Nor.* Teu. the people, 375

TJODGJER, *m. Nor.* Teu. people's spear, 375

TJODREKR, *m. Nor.* Teu. people's ruler, 375

TJODULV, *m. Nor.* Teu. people's wolf, 375

TJODWALD, *m. Nor.* Teu. people's power, 375

TJOKLE, *f. Russ.* Gr. divine fame, 103

Tobeis, m. Swiss, Heb. goodness of the Lord, 49

Tobej, m. Russ. Heb. goodness of the Lord, 49

Tobia, m. It. Ger. Heb. goodness of the Lord, 49

Tobias, *m. Hung. Eng. Span.* Heb. goodness of the Lord, 49

Tobiasz, m. Pol. Heb. goodness of the Lord, 49

Tobies, m. Swiss, Heb. goodness of the Lord, 49

Tobija, m. Russ. Slov. Heb. goodness of the Lord, 49

Toby, m. Eng. Heb. goodness of the Lord, 49

Tobysas, *m. Lett.* Heb. goodness of the Lord, 49

Todo, m. Fris. Teu. people's ruler, 375

Todor, *m. Ill. Slov.* Gr. divine gift, 101

Todorik, *m. Slov.* Teu. people's ruler, 375

Toff, m. Neth. Gr. Christ bearer, 106

Toffel, m. Neth. Gr. Christ bearer, 106

Toger, Nor. Teu. people's spear, 375

Toinette, f. Fr. Lat. inestimable, 142

Toinon, f. Fr. Lat. inestimable, 142

TOIRDELVACH, *m. Erse,* Kelt. tall as a tower, 259

TOKE, *m. Dan.* raving, 419

Tolla, f. Rom. Lat. victor, 197

Tollo, m. Rom. Lat. victor, 197

Tolomieu, m. Fr. Heb. son of furrows, 25

Tolv, m. Dan. Teu. Thor's wolf, 302

Tom, m. Eng. Aram. twin, 21

Toma, m. Ill. Aram. twin, 21

TOMALHAID, *m. Erse,* Kelt. 21

Tomas, *m. Span. Ill.* Aram. twin, 21

Tomasa, *f. Span.* Aram. twin, 21

Tomasz, *m. Pol.* Aram. twin, 21

Tome, *m. Span.* Aram. twin, 21

Tommasso, *m. It.* Aram. twin, 21

Tonček, m. Slov. Lat. inestimable, 142

Tone, m. Slov. Lat. inestimable, 142

Tonek, m. Slov. Lat. inestimable, 142

Toni, m. Bav. Lat. inestimable, 142

Tonietto, m. It. Lat. inestimable, 142

Tonio, m. It. Lat. inestimable, 142

Tonisech, m. Lus. Lat. inestimable, 142

Tonjes, m. Fris. Lat. inestimable, 142

Tonk, m. Lus. Lat. inestimable, 142

Tonneli, m. Swiss, Lat. inestimable, 142

Tonnies, m. Fris. Lat. inestimable, 142

Tonnio, m. Esth. Lat. inestimable, 142

Tonnis, m. Esth. Lat. inestimable, 142

Tool, m. Dutch, Lat. inestimable, 142

Toole, *Ir.* Kelt. lordly, 258

Toon, m. Dutch, Lat. inestimable, 142

Toontje, m. Dutch, Lat. inestimable, 142

Torchel, m. Norman, Teu. Thor's cauldron, 301

Toribio, m. Span. Teu. Thor's bear (?), 302

Torkel, m. Dan. Teu. Thor's cauldron, 302

Torketyl, m. Nor. Teu. Thor's cauldron, 302

Torli, f. Swiss, Gr. gift of God, 101

Tormaid, *m. Gael.* Teu. Niord's man, 306

Torquato, *m. It.* Lat. wearing a neck chain, 164

TORQUATUS, *m.* Lat. wearing a neck chain, 164

Torquil, m. Eng. Teu. Thor's pledge or cauldron, 164, 302

Toso, m. Ill. Gr. divine gift, 302

Tostain, m. Nor. Teu. Thor's stone, 302

Tostig, m. Eng. Teu. harsh day, 419

Tostein, m. Fr. Teu. Thor's stone, 302

Totila, *m. Lat.* Teu. battle leader, 302

Tott, m. Ger. Teu. people, 374

Tots, m. Lett. Gr. fear God, 104

Toussaint, *m. Fr.* Lat. all saints, 219

Tovi, *m. Swiss,* Heb. beloved, 47

Toveli, *m. Swiss,* Heb. beloved, 47

Tracy, *f. Eng.* Gr. carrying ears of corn, 124

TRAHERNE, *m. Welsh,* Lat. 164

Trajano, *m. It.* Lat. 164

TRAJANUS, *Lat.* 164

Traudl, *f. Bav.* Teu. spear maid, 368

Traugott, *m. Ger.* trust God, 468

Trenel, *m. Bav.* Gr. pure, 123

Treschen, *f. Hamb.* Gr. harvester, 124

Treuhold, *m. Ger.* faithful, 456

Tri, *f. Swiss,* Gr. pure, 123

Trili, *f. Swiss,* Gr. pure, 123

Trine, *f. Swiss,* Gr. pure, 123

Trineli, *f. Swiss,* Gr. pure, 123

Trinette, *f. French,* Gr. pure, 123

Trino, *f. Esth.* Gr. pure, 123

Tristan, *m. Fr.* Kelt. herald, 274

Tristano, *m. It.* Kelt. herald, 274

Tristram, *m. Eng.* Kelt. herald, 275

Trix, *f. Eng.* Lat. blesser, 184

Trod, *f. Eng.* Nor. constant battle maid, 319

Trofeem, *m. Russ.* Gr. nourishing, 94

Trophimus, *m. Lat.* Gr. nourishing, 94

Troth, *f. Eng.* Teu. constant battle maid, 319

Trudchen, *f. Ger.* Teu. spear maid, 368

Trude, *f. Ger. Lett.* Teu. spear maid, 368

Trudel, *f. N. Lands.* Teu. spear maid, 368

Trudje, *f. Neth.* Teu. spear maid, 368

Truta, *f. Esth.* Teu. spear maid, 368

Truto, *f. Esth.* Teu. spear maid, 368

TRWST, *m. Cym.* Kelt. proclaimer, 275

Tryg, *m. Nor.* Teu. true, 319

TRYGGVE, *m. Nor.* Teu. true, 421

Tryn, *f. Dutch,* Gr. pure, 123

TRYPHENA, *f. Eng.* Gr. dainty, 94

TRYPHON, *m.* Gr. dainty, 94

TRYPHOSA, *f. Eng.* Gr. dainty, 94

TRYSTAM, *m. Eng.* Kelt. herald, 275

Tsassen, *f. Fris.* Gr. Christian, 105

TUATHAL, *m. Erse,* Kelt. lordly, 258

TUALTHFLAITH, *f. Erse,* Kelt. noble lady, 258

Tudor, *m. Welsh,* Gr. divine gift, 101

TUGENDREICH, *m. Ger.* Teu. virtue rich.

Tullia, *f. It.* Lat. spout of blood (?), 130

TULLIUS, *m.* Lat. spout of blood (?), 130

TULLUS, *m.* Lat. spout of blood (?), 130

Tunstal, *m. Eng.* Teu. Thor's wolf, 302

Tunstan, *m. Eng.* Teu. Thor's stone, 302

Tuomas, *m. Finn.* Aram. twin, 21

Turcetyl, *m. A.S.* Teu. Thor's kettle, 302

Turgar, *m. Eng.* Teu. Thor's spear, 302

Turketul, *m. Eng.* Teu. Thor's kettle, 302

Turlozgh, *m. Ir.* Kelt. tower like, 259

TVERDIMIR, *m. Slav.* firm peace, 442

TVERDISLAV, *m. Slav.* firm glory, 442

Tverdko, *m. Slav.* firm, 442

Twudor, *m. Hung.* Gr. divine gift, 101

Tybal, *f. Eng.* Teu. people's prince, 374

Tyballa, *f. Eng.* Teu. people's prince, 374

Tybalt, *m. Eng.* Teu. people's prince, 374

Tycho, *m. Lat.* Teu. raging, 419

Tyeddemar, *m. Fris.* Teu. people's fame, 374

TYKE, *m. Dan.* Teu. raging, 419

Tyge, *m. Dan.* Teu. raging, 419

Tymolensz, *m. Slav.* Gr. fear God, 104

Tyno, *m. Lus.* Lat. healthy, 153

TYRE, *m. Dan.* Teu. divine, 306

Tziasso, *m. Fris.* Gr. Christian, 105

U

UADELBRECHT, *m. O. Ger.* Teu. nobly bright, 409

UADALRICH, *m. O. Ger.* Teu. noble ruler, 410

UAILSI, *f. Erse,* Kelt. proud, 224

Ubald, *m. Ger.* Teu. mind prince, 354

Ubalde, *m. Fr.* Teu. mind prince, 354

Ubaldo, *m. It.* Teu. mind prince, 354

Uberto, *m. Span. It.* Teu. mind bright, 354

Uc, *m. Prov.* Teu. mind, 353

Uchtred, *m. Eng.* Teu. mind council, 353

Ucko, m. Fris. Teu. noble rule, 412

Uda, f. Ger. Teu. rich, 378

Udalland, *m. Ger.* Teu. noble country, 412

Udalrich, *m. Ger.* Teu. noble ruler, 409

Udalrike, *f. Ger.* Teu. noble ruler, 409

Udalrique, *f. Fr.* Teu. noble ruler, 409

Udolfo, *m. Ital.* Teu. noble wolf, 409

Udve, m. Nor. Teu. rich war, 378

Ueli, m. Swiss, Teu. noble ruler, 412

Uffo, *m. Ger.* Teu. wild boar, 337

Uggieri, *m. It.* Teu. holy, 402

Ugo, *m. It.* Teu. mind, 353

Ugolino, m. It. Teu. mind, 353

Ugon, *m. Ill.* Teu. mind, 353

Ugone, *m. It.* Teu. mind, 353

Ugotto, m. It. Teu. mind, 353

Uguccione, m. Ital. Teu. mind, 353

Ugues, *m. O. Fr.* Teu. mind, 353

Uisdean, *m. Gael.* Teu. mind, 353

Uladislaus, *m. Lat.* Slav. ruling glory, 442

Uland, m. Ger. Teu. noble country, 412

Ulbrecht, m. Ger. Teu. noble splendour, 410

Uldriks, m. Lett. Teu. noble ruler, 409

Ulerk, m. Fris. Teu. noble ruler, 409

Ulf, *m. Nor.* Teu. wolf, 336

Ulfac, m. Eng. Teu. tall wolf, 336

Ulfar, *m. Nor.* Teu. wolf warrior, 336

Ulfener, m. Eng. Teu. wolf, 336

Ulferd, m. Ger. Teu. noble peace, 410

Ulfilas, *m. Lat.* Teu. wolf, 336

Ulfried, m. Ger. Teu. noble peace, 410

Ulfric, *m. Eng.* Teu. wolf ruler, 336

Ulfhedinn, *m. Ice.* Teu. wolf fury, 336

Ulfherdur, *m. Ice.* Teu. wolf guard, 336

Ulick, *m. Fr.* Teu. mind reward, 75

Uliseo, *m. It.* Gr. hater, 75

Ulisse, *m. Fr.* Gr. hater, 75

Ulfliotr, *m. Ice.* wolf warrior, 336

Ulk, f. m. Fris. Teu. noble rule, 410

Ull, *m. Nor.* Teu. will, 314

Ulla, *f. Nor.* Teu. will, 314

Ullr, *m. Nor.* Teu. 314

Ulphilas, *m. Lat.* Teu. wolf, 336

Ulric, *m. Bohm. Fr.* Teu. noble ruler, 409

Ulrica, *f. Eng. Rom.* Teu. noble ruler, 409

Ulrick, *m. Ger.* Teu. noble ruler, 409

Ulrico, *m. Ital.* Teu. noble ruler, 409

Ulrih, *m. Slov.* Teu. noble ruler, 409

Ulrik, *m. Fris.* Teu. noble ruler, 409

Ulrika, *f. Russ.* Teu. noble rule, 409

Ulrike, *f. Ger.* Teu. noble rule, 409

Ulrique, *f. Fr.* Teu. noble rule, 409

Ulryk, *m. Pol.* Teu. noble rule, 409

Ulryka, *f. Pol.* Teu. noble rule, 409

Ulv, *m. Nor.* Teu. wolf, 336

Ulva, *f. Nor.* Teu. wolf, 336

Ulvhildur, *f. Nor.* Teu. wolf battle maid, 336

Ulysses, *m. Lat.* Gr. hater, 75

Una, *f. Erse,* Kelt. famine, 254

Unchi, *f. Erse,* Kelt. contentious, 224

Undine, *f. Ger.* Lat. of the waves.

Unna, *f. Ice.* Teu. woman, 307

Uoli, f. Swiss, Teu. noble ruler, 411

Uote, *f. Ger.* Teu. rich, 378

Uppo, *m. Ger.* Teu. wild boar, 337

Upravda, *m. Slav.* uprightness, 444

Urania, *f. Eng.* Gr. heavenly, 72

Uranie, *f. Fr.* Gr. heavenly, 72

Uranius, *m. Lat.* Gr. heavenly, 72

Urbain, *m. Fr.* Lat. of the town, 202

Urban, *m. Ger. Eng.* Lat. of the town, 202

Urbana, *f. Ger.* Lat. of the town, 202

Urbano, *m. It.* Lat. of the town, 202

Urbanus, *m. Lat.* of the town, 202

Urgel, *m. Span.* Teu. holy, 403

Urraca, *f. Span.* Teu. council of war, 394

Urien, *m. Welsh,* Gr. heavenly, 72

Uric, m. Eng. Teu. noble ruler, 409

Ursa, *f. Slov.* Lat. bear, 199

Urschel, f. Ger. Lat. bear, 199

Urschla, *f. Swiss,* Lat. bear, 199

Ursel, *f. Eng.* Lat. bear, 199

Ursello, *m. Rom.* Lat. bear, 199

Ursilo, *m. It.* Lat. bear, 199

Ursin, *m. Fr.* Lat. bear, 199
Ursino, *m. It.* Lat. bear, 199
Ursley, f. Eng. Lat. bear, 199
Ursola, *f. Span.* Lat. bear, 199
Urssula, *f. Russ.* Lat. bear, 199
Ursula, *f. Ger. Eng.* Lat. bear, 199
Ursule, *f. Fr.* Lat. bear, 199
URSUS, *m.* Lat. bear, 199
Ursyn, m. Pol. bear, 199
Urszula, *f. Pol.* Lat. bear, 199
Urte, f. Lith. Gr. gift of God, 102
Urvan, *m. Russ.* Lat. of the town, 202
Uta, *f. Ger.* Teu. rich, 378
UTHYR, *m. Welsh,* Kelt. terrible, 267
Utz, m. Ger. Teu. noble ruler, 409
Uzziah, *m. Eng.* Heb. might of the Lord, 9

V

Vaceslav, m. Bohm. Slav. crown glory, 441
Vaclav, m. Bohm. Pol. Slav. crown glory, 441
Vacslav, m. Bohm. Slav. crown glory, 441
Val, m. Eng. Lat. healthy, 153
VALBJORG, *f. Nor.* Teu. slaughter protection, 316
Valborg, *f. Swed.* Teu. slaughter protection, 316
Valburg, *f. Swed.* Teu. slaughter protection, 317
VALD, *m. Nor.* Teu. power, 424
Valdemar, *m. Fr.* Teu. powerful fame, 315
VALDIS, *f. Nor.* Teu. spirit of slaughter, 317
Valdus, m. Lat. Teu. power, 215
Valericus, m. Lat. Teu. slaughter spear, 316
Valck, m. Bohm. Lat. healthy, 153
Valente, *m. It.* Lat. healthy, 153
Valentim, *m. Port.* Lat. healthy, 153
Valentin, *m. Fr.* Lat. healthy, 153
Valentina, *f. It.* Lat. healthy, 153
Valentine, *m. Eng.* Lat. healthy, 153
Valentine, *f. Fr.* Lat. healthy, 153
Valentino, *m. It.* Lat. healthy, 153
Valentinus, *m. Lat.* healthy, 153
Valentyn, *m. Pol.* Lat. healthy, 153

Valer, *m. Ger.* Lat. healthy, 152
Valasquita, *f. Span.* Teu. slaughter, 317
Valère, *m. Fr.* Lat. healthy, 152
Valeria, *f. It. Ger.* Lat. healthy, 152
VALERIANUS, *m.* Lat. healthy, 152
Valerie, *f. Fr. Ger.* Lat. healthy, 152
Valerien, *m. Fr.* Lat. healthy, 152
Valerij, *m. Russ.* Lat. healthy, 152
Valerio, *m. It.* Lat. healthy, 152
VALERIUS, *m.* Lat. healthy, 152
Valery, *m. Fr.* Teu. slaughter ruler, 317
Valeska, f. Slav. Slav. ruling glory, 441
Valgard, m. Nor. Teu. foreign spear, 316
Valgjer, m. Ice. Teu. foreign spear, 316
Valjgerda, *m. Ice.* Teu. foreign guard, 316
Valheri, *m. Frank.* Teu. slaughter host, 316
Vallia, m. Span. Teu. slaughter, 316
Valmont, m. Fr. Teu. slaughter protection, 316
Valpurgis, f. Ger. Teu. slaughter protection, or powerful protection, 317
Valtheof, *m. Nor.* Teu. foreign thief, 316
VALTRUD, *f. Nor.* Teu. slaughter maid, 317
Vanjuscha, Dutch. grace of God, 45
Vanka, m. Russ. Heb. grace of God, 45
Vanni, m. It. Heb . grace of God, 45
Vanora, f. Scot. Kelt. white wave, 270
Vara, f. Ill. Gr. stranger, 117
Varfolomei, *m. Russ.* Aram. son of furrows, 25
Varinka, f. Russ. Gr. stranger, 117
Varnava, *m. Russ.* Aram. son of consolation, 24
Vartholomei, *m. Wall.* Aram. son of furrows, 25
Varvara, *f. Russ.* Gr. stranger, 117
Vaschka, m. Russ. Gr. kingly, 57
Vashti, f. Eng. Pers. 57
Vasilij, *m. Ill.* Gr. royal, 112
Vaso, m. Ill. Gr. royal, 112
Vassilij, *m. Russ.* Gr. royal, 112
Vassja, m. Russ. Gr. royal, 112

Vasska, *m. Russ.* Gr. royal, 112

VATROSLAV, *m. Slov.* Slav. fiery glory, 441

Vaubert, *m. Fr.* Teu. bright slaughter, 317

Vaubourg, *f. Fr.* Teu. slaughter protection, 317

Vaudru, *f. Fr.* Teu. slaughter maid, 317

Vautrude, *f. Fr.* Teu. slaughter maid, 317

Vavrinec, m. Bohm. Lat. laurel, 174

Vavrzynec, m. Pol. Lat. laurel, 174

VEBJORN, *m. Nor.* Teu. sacred bear, 320

VEBRAND, *m. Nor.* Teu. sacred sword, 320

VEDIS, *f. Nor.* Teu. sacred sprite, 320

VEDORM, *m. Nor.* Teu. sacred snake, 321

VEGJER, *m. Nor.* Teu. sacred spear, 321

VEDHELM, *m. Nor.* Teu. sacred helmet, 321

VEDHILD, *f. Nor.* Teu. sacred battle maid, 321

Vefeli, f. Ill. Kelt. white wave, 270

Vehka, Bulg. great glory, 441

Veicht, *m. Bav.* Teu. living, 198

Veidl, *m. Bav.* Teu. living, 198

VEKOSLAV, *m. Slav.* eternal glory, 441

VEKOSLAVA, *f. Slav.* eternal glory, 441

Veleda, f. Teu. wise woman, 441

VELISLAV, *f. m. Bulg.* Slav. great glory, 441

VELIKA, *f. Bulg.* Slav. great, 441

VELIMIR, *m. Bulg.* Slav. great peace, 441

VENCESLAV, *m. Slov.* Slav. crown glory, 441

Venedikt, *m. Russ.* Lat. blessed, 184

Venetia, f. Eng. Kelt. blessed, 184

Venice, f. Eng. Kelt. blessed, 184

Ventura, m. It. Lat. well met, 185

VENUS, *m.* Lat. fair (?)

Venzeslaus, *m. Ger.* Slav. crown glory, 441

VENZESLAV, *m. Russ.* Slav. crown glory, 441

Vera, *f. Serv.* Slav. faith, 449

Verban, *m. Slov.* Lat. of the city, 202

Vercingetorix, *m. Lat.* Kelt. chief of one hundred heads, 237

Verena, *Ger.* Teu. sacred wisdom, 331

Verena, f. Ger. Lat. Gr. true picture, 207

Verenchen, f. Ger. Lat. Gr. true picture, 227

Verenund, m. Nor. Teu. guardian protector, 377

Vergosillanus, *m. Lat.* Kelt. man of the banner, 236

Vermudo, *m. Span.* bear's protection, 339

Vernulfo, *m. Span.* Teu. bear wolf, 339

Verra, f. Ill. Slav. faith, 449

Veronica, *f. It. Eng.* Lat. Gr. true image, 207

Veronike, *f. Ger.* Lat. Gr. true picture, 207

Veronique, *f. Fr.* Lat. Gr. true picture, 207

VERRES, *m. Lat.* boar, 337

Vestan, *m. Nor.* sacred stone, 321

VESTESLAV, *m. Bohm.* Slav. crown glory, 441

VESTLIDE, *m. Nor.* Teu. western wanderer, 432

VETILIDE, *m. Nor.* Teu. winter wanderer, 432

Veva, f. Ill. Kelt. white wave, 270

Vevay, f. Bav. Kelt. white wave, 270

Vevina, f. Scot. Kelt. melodious woman, 224

Victoire, *f. Fr.* Lat. victorious, 197

VICTOR, *m. Ger. Fr. Eng.* Lat. conqueror, 197

Victoria, *f. Eng.* Lat. conqueror, 197

Victorie, *f. Ger.* Lat. victorious, 197

Victorine, *f. Fr.* Lat. victorious, 197

Vid, *m. Bohm.* Lat. life, 320

Vida, *m. Hung.* Lat. life, 198, 320

Vida, f. Eng. Heb. beloved, 320

VIGBRAND, *m. Ger.* Teu. war sword, 418

Vigelius, *m. Lat.* Teu. warring, 418

VIGFUS, *m. Ger.* Teu. war eagerness, 418

VIGHEARD, *m. A.S.* Teu. war firmness, 418

VIGLAF, *m. A.S.* Teu. war relic, 418

VIGLEIK, *m. Nor.* Teu. war sport, 418

Viktor, *m. Slav.* Lat. conqueror, 197

Vikentij, *m. Russ.* Lat. conqueror, 197

VIKING, *m. Nor.* Teu. bay inhabitant, 432

VILBJORG, *f. Nor.* Teu. resolute protection, 314

Vilem, *m. Bohm.* Teu. resolute helmet, 314

Vilelm, *m. Pol.* Teu. resolute helmet, 314

Vilgelm, *m. Russ.* Teu. resolute helmet, 314

VILGERD, *m. Nor.* Teu. resolute protection, 314

Vilhelm, *Slov. Hung.* Teu. resolute helmet, 314

Vilhelmine, *f. Swed.* Teu. resolute helmet, 314

Viljalm, *m. Nor.* Teu. resolute helmet, 314

Vilibaldo, *m. Port.* Teu. resolute prince, 314

Vincenc, *m. Bohm.* Lat. conquering, 197

Vincencio, *m. Span.* Lat. conquering, 197

VINCENS, *m. Ger.* Lat. conquering, 197

Vincent, *m. Eng. Fr.* Lat. conquering, 197

Vincente, *m. Port.* Lat. conquering, 197

Vincenty, *m. Pol.* Lat. conquering, 197

Vincenz, *m. Ger.* Lat. conquering, 197

Vincenzio, *m. It.* Lat. conquering, 197

VINCIGUERRA, *m. It.* Lat. Teu. conquering war, 197

Vincislao, *m. It.* Slav. crown glory, 441

Vincze, m. Hung. Lat. conquering, 197

Viola, *f. It.* Lat. violet, 206

Violante, *f. Span.* Lat. violet, 206

Violet, *f. Scot.* Lat. violet, 206

Violette, *f. Fr.* Lat. violet, 206

Virdumarus, *m. Lat.* Kelt. great dark man, 237

Virgil, *m. Eng.* Lat. flourishing, 153

Virgile, *m. Fr.* Lat. flourishing, 153

Virgilio, *m. It.* Lat. flourishing, 153

VIRGILIUS, *m.* Lat. flourishing, 153

Virginia, *f. It. Eng.* Lat. flourishing, 153

Virginie, *f. Fr.* Lat. flourishing, 153

Virginio, *m. It.* Lat. flourishing, 153

VIRGINIUS, *m.* Lat. flourishing, 153

Viriathus, *m. Lat.* Kelt. man of fire (?), 237

Viridis, *f. It.* Lat. green, 206

VISHTASPA, *m. Pers.* Zend. possessor of horses.

Vita, m. Russ. Bohm. Lat. living, 197

Vjta, m. Bohm. Lat. living, 197

Vital, *m. Fr. Ger.* Lat. of life, 197

Vitale, *m. It.* Lat. of life, 197

Vitaliana, *f. Ger.* Lat. of life, 197

Vitalianus, *m.* Lat. of life, 197

Vitalij, *m. Russ.* Lat. of life, 197

VITALIS, *m. Lat.* of life, 197

Vitgeir, m. Ice. Teu. wise man, 321

Vittore, *m. It.* Lat. conqueror, 197

Vittoria, *f. It.* Lat. conqueror, 197

VITUS, *m.* Lat. living, 197

VIVIA, *f.* Lat. lively, 197

Vivian, *m. f. Eng.* Lat. lively, 198

Viviana, *f. It.* Lat. lively, 198

Viviano, *f. It.* Lat. lively, 198

Vivien, *m. Fr.* Lat. lively, 198

Vivienne, *f. Fr.* Lat. lively, 198

VJERA, *f. Russ.* Slav. faith, 439

VLADIMIR, *m. Russ.* Slav. ruling the world, 442

VLADISAV, *m. Serv.* Slav. ruling the world, 442

VLADISLAV, *m. Russ.* Slav. ruling the world, 442

VLADIVOJ, *m. Russ.* Slav. ruling the army, 442

VLADYSLAV, *m. Pol.* Slav. ruling the world, 442

VLADISLAVKA, *f. Pol.* Slav. ruling the world, 442

Vlaho, m. Hung. Lat. babbler, 159

Vlass, m. Russ. Lat. babbler, 159

Vlassij, m. Russ. Lat. babbler, 159

VOJCIECH, *m. Pol.* Slav. warrior, 441

VOJTECH, *m. Bohm.* Slav. warrior, 441

VOJTEH, *m. Slav.* Slav. warrior, 441

Volfgango, *m. It.* Teu. wolf's progress, 336

Volker, *m. Ger.* Teu. people's guard, 371

Volkmar, *m. Ger.* Teu. people's fame, 371

Volguard, m. Ger. Teu. people's guard, 371

Volgvard, *m. Ger.* Teu. people's guard, 371

Volodia, *m. Russ.* Slav. ruling the world, 442

Volodinka, *m. Russ.* Slav. ruling the world, 442

VOLUNDR, *m. Nor.* Teu. artful (?), 313

Vortigern, *m. Eng.* Kelt. great king, 238

Vortya, *f. Lus.* Gr. gift of God, 102

VRATISLAV, *m. Slav.* Slav. brilliant fame, 441

Vrcad, *f. Erse,* Gr. pearl, 123

Vreneli, *f. Swab.* Lat. Gr. true image, 207

VSELAV, *m. Slav.* Slav. all glory, 442

VSEVOLOD, *m. Slav.* Slav. all ruler, 442

VUC, *m. Slav.* Slav. wolf, 336

VUKMIL, *m. Slav.* Slav. wolf love, 335

VUKMIR, *m. Slav.* Slav. wolf peace, 335

VUKSLAV, *m. Slav.* Slav. wolf glory, 335

VULFGAR, *m. A.S.* Teu. wolf spear, 335

VULFHERE, *m. A.S.* Teu. wolf warrior, 335

VULFHILDA, *f. m. A.S.* Teu. wolf battle maid, 335

VULFMAR, *m. A.S.* Teu. wolf fame, 335

VULFNOT, *m. A.S.* Teu. wolf violence, 335

VULFSTAN, *m. A.S.* Teu. wolf stone, 335

Vye, *f. Fris.* wisdom, 107

VYSFSLAV, *m. Slav.* Slav. highest glory, 442

Vyvyan, *f. Eng.* Lat. living, 198

W

Wabel, *m. Bav.* Aram. son of furrows, 25

Wabishaw, *m. Red Indian,* red leaf.

Wabm, *m. Bav.* Aram. son of furrows, 25

WAITKUS, *m. Lith.* Slav. warrior.

Wala, *m. Span.* Teu. slaughter, 311

Walaheri, *m. Frank.* Teu. slaughter host, 317

Walamund, *m. Frank.* Teu. slaughter protection, 317

Walarik, *m. Frank.* Teu. slaughter king, 317

Walaram, *m. Frank.* Teu. slaughter raven, 317

Walber, *f. Esth.* Teu. slaughter protection, 317, 425

Walbert, *m. Ger.* Teu. power bright, 317, 425

Waldburga, *f. Eng.* Teu. powerful protection,* 317, 425

WALDEMAR, *m. Eng. Ger.* Teu. powerful fame, 425

WALDHERI, *m. Frank.* Teu. powerful warrior, 425

Waldl, *m. Bav.* Teu. will bold, 315

Waldo, *m. Frank.* Teu. power, 425, 315

Waldobert, *m. Ger.* Teu. power bright, 425

Waldrich, *m. Ger.* Teu. powerful rule, 425

Walen, *m. Eng.* Teu. foreign thief, 316

Waleran, *m. Flem.* Teu. or Lat. healthy, 152

Walfrid, *m. Ger.* Teu. powerful peace, 316

Wallinsch, *m. Lith.* Lat. healthy, 152

Walmar, *m. Ger.* Teu. slaughter fame, 316

Walpert, *m. Ger.* Teu. slaughter bright, 311

Walpl, *f. Bav.* Teu. powerful protection, 311, 428

Walpora, *f. Lus.* Teu. slaughter protection, 316

Walpurd, *f. Flem.* Teu. slaughter protection, 311, 425

Walpurg, *f. Ger.* Teu. slaughter protection, 311

Walram, *m. Ger.* Teu. slaughter raven, 316

---

* This, one of the English missionary nun princesses in Germany, is the patroness of the celebrated Valpurgisu ,cht. She died at Heidenheim, and her right feast is on the 25th of February; but being translated to Crichstadt on the 1st of May, and minced into numerous relics, the latter day was also hers, and strangely became connected with the witches' sabbath.

Walstan, *m. Eng.* Teu. slaughter stone, 311

Walter, *m. Eng.* Teu. powerful warrior, 425

Waltfrid, *m. O. Ger.* Teu. powerful peace, 425

Waltheof, *m. Eng.* Teu. foreign thief, 316

Walther, *m. Ger.* Teu. powerful warrior, 425

Waltier, *m. O. Fr.* Teu. powerful warrior, 425

Waltinsh, *m. Lett.* Lat. healthy, 151

Waltl, *m. Bav.* Teu. powerful warrior, 425

Walwyn, *m. Eng.* Kelt. hawk of battle, 272

WAMBA, *m. Span.* Teu. belly, 427

Wanders, *f. Scot.* Kelt. white wave, 270

WARAND, *m. Ger.* Teu. protecting, 420

Warmund, *m. Ger.* Teu. protecting guard, 420

Warner, *m. Eng.* Teu. protecting warrior, 420

Warno, *m. Ger.* Teu. protecting, 420

Warnfrid, *m. Ger.* Teu. protecting peace, 420

WARNEBOLD, *m. Ger.* Teu. protecting prince, 420

Warren, *m. Eng.* Teu. protecting friend, 420

Wastel, *m. Bav.* Gr. venerable, 111

Wat, *m. Eng.* Teu. powerful warrior, 425

Watagimat, *m. Red Indian*, eagle's nest.

Water, *m. Eng.* Teu. powerful warrior, 425

Waters, *m. Lett.* Teu. powerful warrior, 425

Watier, *m. O. Fr.* Teu. powerful warrior, 425

Watlis, *m. Swiss*, Teu. powerful warrior, 425

Wattles, *m. Eng.* Teu. powerful warrior, 425

Watty, 425

Wawyn, *m. Eng.* Kelt. hawk of battle, 272

Wawel, *m. Bav.* Aram. son of furrows, 25

Wayland, *m. Eng.* Teu. artful (?), 313

Weigel, *m. Fris.* Teu. warring, 418

WEALTHEOF, *m. A.S.* Teu. foreign thief, 316

Welf, *m. Ger.* Teu. wolf, 335

Welfhard, *m. Ger.* Teu. wolf strong, 335

Wenceslaus, *m. Eng.* Slav. crown glory, 441

Wendel, *f. m. Ger.* Teu. wandering.

Wendela, *f. Ger.* Teu. wandering.

Wendelgard, *f. m. Ger.* Teu. wandering guard.

Wendelgar, *m. Ger.* Teu. wandering spear.

Wendelin, *m. Ger.* Teu. wanderer.

Wendeline, *f. Ger.* Teu. wanderer.

Wenefride, *f. Eng.* Kelt. white wave, 270

Wendis, *m. Lett.* Slav. ruling glory, 441

Wenzel, *m. Ger.* Slav. crown glory, 441

Werburgha, *f. Eng.* Teu. powerful protection, 420

Werlands, *m. Lett.* Teu. adventuring life, 433

Werner, *m. Ger.* Teu. protecting army, 420

WERNHARD, *m. Ger.* Teu. protecting firmly, 420

WERNHER, *m. Ger.* Teu. protecting army, 420

Wetu, *m. Finn.* Teu. peace ruler, 296

Wetukka, *m. Finn.* Teu. peace ruler, 296

Wiart, *m. Fris.* Teu. war firmness, 418

Wicko, *m. Fris.* Teu. war bright, 418

Wido, *m. O. Ger.* Teu. life, 321

WIG, *m. A.S.* Teu. war, 418

WIGAND, *m. Ger.* Teu. warring, 418

WIGBALD, *m. Ger.* Teu. war prince, 418

WIGBERT, *m. Ger.* Teu. war bright, 418

WIGBURGA, *f. Ger.* Teu. war protection, 418

Wige, *m. Ger.* Teu. warring, 418

WIGHARD, *m. Ger.* Teu. war firm, 418

WIGHELM, *m. Ger.* Teu. war helmet, 418

WIGHER, *m. Ger.* Teu. warrior, 418

WIGLAF, *f. Ger.* Teu. war relic, 418
WIGLIND, *f. Ger.* Teu. war snake, 418
WIGMANN, *m. Ger.* Teu. war man, 418
WIGMAR, *m. Ger.* Teu. war fame, 418
WIGRAM, *m. Ger.* Teu. war raven, 418
Wihts, m. Lett. Lat. life, 320
Wike, f. Lett. Gr. wisdom, 107
Wilbrand, *m. Ger.* Teu. willing sword, 314
Wilfred, *m. Eng.* Teu. resolute peace, 314
WILFRITH, *m. Eng.* Teu. resolute peace, 314
Wilfroy, *m. Eng.* Teu. resolute peace, 314
WILHELM, *m. Swiss, Ger.* Teu. helmet of resolution, 315
Wilhelmina, *f. Eng.* Teu. helmet of resolution, 315
Wilhelmine, *f. Ger.* Teu. helmet of resolution, 315
Wilip, m. Fris. Gr. horse lover, 79
Wilips, m. Lett. Gr. horse lover, 79
Will, m. Eng. Teu. helmet of resolution, 315
Willaume, *m. O. Fr.* Teu. helmet of resolution, 315
Wille, m. Swiss, Teu. helmet of resolution, 315
Willebald, *m. Dutch,* Teu. resolute prince, 314
WILLEHAD, *m. Ger.* Teu. resolute battle, 314
Willelme, *m. Fr.* Teu. helmet of resolution, 314
Willan, m. Lus. Netherlands, Teu. helmet of resolution, 314
Willemin, *f. Dutch,* Teu. helmet of resolution, 314
Willempje, f. Dutch, Teu. helmet of resolution, 314
William, *m. Eng.* Teu. helmet of resolution, 315
Williamina, *f. Eng.* Teu. helmet of resolution, 315
WILLIBALD, *m. Ger.* Teu. resolute prince, 314
WILLIBERT, *m. Ger.* Teu. bright will, 314
WILLIBRORD, *m. A.S.* Teu. 314
WILLIBURG, *f. Ger.* Teu. resolute protection, 314

Willie, m. Scot. Teu. helmet of resolution, 315
WILLIGIS, *m. Ger.* Teu. pledge of resolution, 314
WILLIHARD, *m. Ger.* Teu. willing firmness, 314
WILLIHERI, *m. Ger.* Teu. resolute warrior, 314
WILLIHILD, *f. Frank.* Teu. resolute battle maid, 314
WILLIHOLD, *m. A.S.* Teu. resolute power, 314
WILLIMAR, *m. Ger.* Teu. resolute fame, 314
WILLIRAM, *m. Ger.* Teu. willing raven, 314
WILLIRAT, *m. Ger.* Teu. willing resolute council, 314
WILLIRIK, *m. Ger.* Teu. willing resolute ruler, 314
Willo, m. Fris. Teu. willing helmet, 314
WILLIWOLF, *m. Ger.* Teu. willing wolf, 314
Willy, m. Eng. Teu. helmet of resolution, 315
WILMAR, *m. Ger.* Teu. willing fame, 314
Wilmett, f. Eng. Teu. helmet of resolution, 316
WILMOD, *m. Ger.* Teu. resolute mood, 315
Wilmot, *m. Eng.* Teu. resolute mood, 314
WILRICH, *m. Ger.* Teu. resolute ruler, 314
WILTRUD, *f. Ger.* Teu. resolute battle maid, 314
Winfred, *m. Eng.* Teu. friend of peace, 427
WINFRITH, *m. A.S.* Teu. friend of peace, 427
Wingallok, *m. Bret.* Kelt. white, 270
Wingar, *m. Ger.* Teu. friend of war, 427
WINIBALD, *m. A.S.* Teu. friend of valour, 427
Winifrid, *f. Eng.* Kelt. white stream, 270
WINMAR, *m. Ger.* Teu. friend of fame, 427
WINRAD, *m. Ger.* Teu. friend's council, 427

WINRICH, *m. Ger.* Teu. friend of rule, 427

Winny, f. Ir. Kelt. famine, 70

Wippert, m. Ger. Teu. war bright, 418

Wippold, m. Ger. Teu. war prince, 418

Wiremo, m. Maori, Teu. will helmet, 315

Wisdom, f. Eng. 421

Wishard, m. Ger. Teu. wise strength, 321

WITGAR, *m. Ger.* Teu. wood spear, 321

Witiza, *m. Span.* Teu. wood dweller, 321

Witold, *m. Ger.* Teu. wood power, 321

WITOLF, *m. Ger.* Teu. wood wolf, 321, 325

WITRAM, *m. Ger.* Teu. forest raven, 321

WITTOKIND, *m. Ger.* Teu. forest dweller, 321

Wittich, *m. Ger.* Teu. wood dweller, 321

Wittig, *m. Ger.* Teu. wood dweller, 321

Wladimir, *m. Pol.* Slav. ruling peace, 442

Wladis, m. Lett. Slav. ruling glory, 442

Wladislav, *m. Pol.* Slav. ruling glory, 442

Wolbrecht, *m. Ger.* Teu. wolf brightness, 335

Wolder, m. Dutch, Teu. powerful warrior, 425

WOLF, *m. Ger.* Teu. wolf, 335

Wolfer, *m. Ger.* Teu. wolf army, 335

WOLFGANG, *m. Ger.* wolf's progress, 335

WOLFHART, *m. Ger.* Teu. wolf's firmness, 335

WOLFMAR, *m. Ger.* Teu. wolf fame, 335

WOLFRAD, *m. Ger.* Teu. wolf's advice, 335

WOLFRAMM, *m. Ger.* Teu. wolf raven, 335

WOLFRICH, *m. Ger.* Teu. wolf ruler, 335

Wouter, m. Dutch, Teu. powerful warrior, 425

Worsola, f. Bohm. Lat. bear, 199

Wridriks, m. Lett. Teu. peace ruler, 296

Wrizzis, m. Lett. Teu. peace ruler, 296

WULFSTAN, *m. A.S.* Teu. wolf stone, 335

Wursla, *f. Lus.* Lat. bear, 199

Wya, m. Ger. Teu. warring, 418

Wygard, m. Fris. Teu. warring, 418

X

XANTHIPPE, *f. Gr.* yellow horse, 78

XAVER, *m. Span.* Arab. bright, 299

Xavier, *m. Fr.* Arab. bright, 299

Xaverie, *f. Span.* Arab. bright, 299

Xaveric, *m. Wall.* Arab. bright, 299

Xaverio, *m. It.* Arab. bright, 299

Xavery, *m. Pol.* Arab. bright, 299

Xenia, *f. Russ.* Gr. hospitality, 93

Xerxes, *m. Eng.* Pers. venerable king.

Ximen, *m. Span.* 330

Ximena, *f. Span.* 330

Ximon, *m. Span.* Heb. obedient, 17

Xiste, *m. Fr.* Lat. sixth, 138

Y

Yago, m. Span. Heb. supplanter, 17

Yatmund, m. Dan. Teu. happy protection, 378

Yestin, *m. Welsh,* Lat. just, 192

YNGVAR, *m. Nor.* Teu. Ing's warrior, 325

YNGVE, *m. Nor.* Teu. 325

Ynyr, *m. Welsh,* Lat. honourable, 190

Yolande, *f. Prov.* Lat. violet, 206

Yolette, *f. Fr.* Lat. violet, 206

Yorwarth, m. Welsh, Teu. happy guard, 378

Ysabel, f. Span. Heb. God's oath, 35

Ysaie, m. Fr. Heb. salvation of the Lord, 48

Yseulte, *f. Fr.* Kelt. spectacle, 275

Ysonde, *f. Fr.* Kelt. spectacle, 275

Ysolt, *f. Eng.* Kelt. spectacle, 275

Yueins, *m. Fr.* Kelt. young warrior, 273

Yvain, *m. Bret.* Kelt. young warrior, 273

Yvon, *m.* *Ir.* Teu. archer, 326

Ywain, *m.* *Welsh,* Kelt. young warrior, 273

Z

Zacarias, *m.* *Span.* Heb. remembrance of the Lord, 51

Zaccaria, *m.* *It.* Heb. remembrance of the Lord, 51

Zach, *m.* *Eng. Bav.* Heb. remembrance of the Lord, 51

Zacharia, *m.* *Ger.* Heb. remembrance of the Lord, 51

ZACHARIAH, *m.* *Eng.* Heb. remembrance of the Lord, 51

Zacharias, *m.* *Port.* Heb. remembrance of the Lord, 51

Zacharie, *m.* *Fr.* Heb. remembrance of the Lord, 51

Zachary, *m.* *Eng.* Heb. remembrance of the Lord, 51

Zacharyasz, *m.* *Pol.* Heb. remembrance of the Lord, 51

Zachée, *m.* *Fr.* Heb. remembrance of the Lord, 51

Zacheo, *m.* *It.* Heb. remembrance of the Lord, 51

Zachers, *m.* *Bav.* Heb. remembrance of the Lord, 51

Zachereis, *m.* *Bav.* Heb. remembrance of the Lord, 51

Zaches, *m.* *Bav.* Heb. remembrance of the Lord, 51

Zacheo, *m.* *Port.* Heb. remembrance of the Lord, 51

Zaccheus, *m.* *Eng. Ger.* Heb. remembrance of the Lord, 51

Zaidée, *f.* *Fr.* 458

Zakarias, *m.* *Esth.* Heb. remembrance of the Lord, 51

Zackelina, *f.* *Russ.* Heb. supplanter, 18

Zakharias, *m.* *Hung.* Heb. remembrance of the Lord, 51

Zakheus, *m.* *Hung.* remembrance of the , 1

Zako, *m.* *Ill.* Heb. remembrance of the Lord, 51

Zan, *m.* *Dantzig,* Gr. Christian, 105

Zan, *m.* *Gr.* Heb. supplanter, 17

Zaneta, *f.* *Russ.* Heb. grace of the Lord, 46

Zaqueo, *m.* *Span.* Heb. remembrance of the Lord, 51

Zara, *f.* *Arab.* Heb. princess, 13

Zasso, *m.* *Fris.* Gr. Christian, 105

Zebulon, *m.* *Eng.* Heb. dwelling.

Zechariah, *m.* *Eng.* Heb. remembrance of the Lord, 51

Zedekiah, *m.* *Eng.* Heb. justice of the Lord, 49

Zedena, *f.* *Ger.* Lat. of Sidon, 200

ZEENAB, *f.* *Arab.* father's ornament, 62

ZELIMIR, *m.* Slav. wishing peace.

Zelinde, conquering snake, 347

ZELISLAV, *m.* Slav. wishing glory.

ZENAÏDA, *f.* *Russ.* Gr. daughter of Zeus, 62

Zenaïde, *f.* *Fr.* Gr. daughter of Zeus, 62

Zenevieva, *f.* *Russ.* Kelt. white wave, 270

ZENO, *m.* Gr. from Zeus, 62

ZENOBIA, *f.* *Lat.* Aram. father's ornament, 62

Zenobie, *f.* *Fr.* Arab. father's ornament, 62

Zenobio, *m.* *Milan.* Gr. from Zeus, 62

Zenobius, *m.* Lat. 62

ZENON, *m.* *Gr.* Gr. from Zeus, 62

Zenovia, *f.* *Russ.* Arab. father's ornament, 62

ZENOVIA, *f.* *Russ.* Slav. goddess of hunting, 440

Zenz, *f.* *Bav.* Lat. increasing, 198

Zenz, *m.* *Bav.* Lat. conquering, 197

Zenzel, *m.* *Bav.* Lat. conquering, 197

Zenzl, *f.* *Bav.* Lat. increasing, 198

Zephaniah, *m.* *Eng.* Heb. protected of the Lord, 50

Zephyrine, *f.* *Fr.* Gr. like the zephyr.

Zerah, *m.* *Eng.* Heb. rising of light, 51

Zerdosht, *m.* *Pers.* Zend. gold star, 57, 437

Zerubabel, *m.* *Eng.* Heb. born at Babel.

Zesk, *Sav.* Teu. free, 300

Zezilija, *f.* *Russ.* Lat. blind, 144

Zikmund, *m.* *Bohm.* Teu. conquering protection, 358

Zilia, *f.* *Ven.* Lat. 145

Ziliola, *f.* *Ven.* Lat. 145

Zillah, *f.* *Eng.* Heb. shadow, 11

Zinevra, *f. Ven.* Kelt. white wave, 270

Ziroslav, *m.* acorn glory.

Zivan, *m. Slav.* living, 198

Zivana, *f.* living, 198

Zizi, f. Russ. Arab. father's ornament, 62

Zlata, *f. Slov.* Slav. gold, 445

Zlatana, *f. Slov.* Slav. gold, 445

Zlatibor, *m. Slov.* Slav. gold, 445

Zlatke, m. Slov. Slav. gold, 445

Zlatoje, m. Slov. Slav. gold love, 445

Zlatoljub, *m. Slov.* Slav. gold love, 445

Zlatoslav, *m. Slov.* Slav. gold love, 445

Zlatoust, *m. Russ.* Slav. gold mouth, 445

Zoe, *f. Fr.* Gr. life, 11

Zofia, *f. Pol.* Gr. wisdom, 107

Zoia, *f. Russ.* Gr. life, 11

Zomelis, m. Lett. Heb. asked of God, 20

Zon, f. Fr. Gr. carrying ears of corn, 124

Zora, *f. Ill.* Slav. dawn, 437

Zorana, *f. Ill.* Slav. dawn, 437

Zore, f. Ill. Heb. princess, 14

Zorica, *f.* Slav. dawn, 437

Zorislava, *f. Ill.* Slav. dawn of glory, 437

Zoroaster, *m. Eng.* Pers. golden star (?), 57, 437

Zosa, f. Swiss, Heb. lily, 50

Zosel, f. Swiss, Heb. lily, 50

Zosia, f. Pol. Gr. wisdom, 107

Zsiga, m. Hung. Teu. conquering protection, 356

Zsigmund, m. Hung. Teu. conquering protection, 356

Zsoflie, f. Hung. Gr. wisdom, 107

Zsofe, f. Hung. Gr. wisdom, 107

Zsusane, f. Lett. Heb. lily, 50

Zsusanna, f. Hung. Heb. lily, 50

Zwetlana, *f. Russ.* Slav. star, 437

Zygmunt, m. Pol. Heb. conquering protection, 358*

---

* Every form of every name given in the index is not to be found in the text ; but in all cases where a reference is given, the history, as far as ascertainable, of the leading portion of the original name will be found.

HISTORY OF CHRISTIAN NAMES.

INTRODUCTORY CHAPTER.

THE SPIRIT OF NOMENCLATURE.

MUCH has been written upon the Surname, a comparatively modern invention, while the individual, or, as we term it, the Christian name, has barely received, here and there, a casual notice from English authors, and has seldom been treated of collectively or comparatively. Yet there is much that is extremely curious and suggestive in the rise and signification of the appellations of men and women, their universal or partial popularity, the alterations by which they have been adapted to different languages, their familiar abbreviations, the patronymics formed from them, and the places or articles called from them. In fact, we shall find the history, the religion, and the character of a nation stamped upon the individuals in the names which they bear.

It is to Christian names, properly so called, that our attention will chiefly be directed. Other names, not acknowledged at any time as baptismal, or only given so exceptionally as not to deserve notice, are here omitted, or only treated of when their analogy is needed to illustrate the history of a true Christian name.

The original proper names of men and women arose—

First, from some circumstance connected with the birth, such as Esau, hairy ; Jacob, taking by the heel ; Agrippa, born with the feet foremost.

Secondly, from the complexion, *e. g.*, Edom, red ; Flavius and Fulvius, yellow ; Don, brown ; Ruadh, red ; Boidh, yellow ; Blanche, fair.

Thirdly, from the qualities desired for the child, such as David, meaning beloved ; the Persian Aspamitas and Greek Philippos, both lovers of horses ; the Keltic Eochaidh, a horseman ; the Teutonic Eadgifu, happy gift ; the Slavonic Przemyszl, the thoughtful.

B

Fourthly, from an animal, Deborah, the bee; Jonah, Columba, Golubica, the dove; Zeeb, Lycos, Lupus, Ulf, Vuk, all signifying that strangely popular wild beast the wolf.

Fifthly, from a weapon, as the Teuton Gar, a spear.

Sixthly, from a jewel, Mote Mahal, in Persian, pearl of the harem; the Greek, Margarite, a pearl in Greek; the Teutonic Stein, a stone or jewel in Teutonic.

Seventhly, religious names, dedicating the child to the Divinity, such as Ishmael, heard of God; Elijah, God the Lord; and among idolaters, Artemidorus, gift of Artemis; Jovianus, belonging to Jupiter; Brighid, the Irish goddess of smiths and poets; Thorgils, Thor's pledge.

To these we may add a few names of flowers, chiefly borne by women, and always indicating a poetical nation, such as Susanna, Lilias, Rhoda, Rose, and the Slavonic Smiljana, the amaranth, a description of name never found among the unimaginative Romans.

Also a few indicating a time of deep sorrow and distress, when the child was born, such as Beriah, son of evil, named when it went ill with his father Ephraim; Jabez, sorrow; Ichabod, the glory is departed. These being of ill omen, never prevailed among the joyous Greeks; but among the quick-feeling Kelts we find Una, famine, and Ita, thirsty, names recording, no doubt, times of sorrow. Also Posthumus and Tristan, though not originally bearing the meaning since attributed to them, and Dolores, a name of Spanish Roman Catholic growth, have all been applied to express the mournful circumstances of some "child of misery, baptized in tears."

Natural defects have likewise furnished names, such as Balbus, the stammerer; the Irish Dorenn, the sullen; and Unchi, the contentious. These are most common among the Romans, owing to their habit of continuing a father's name, however acquired, to the son. And the Romans likewise stand almost alone in their strange and uncomplimentary fashion of giving individual names from numbers, one in which they have not been imitated, except now and then, where the number of a family has become so remarkable as to be deemed worthy of commemoration in the names of the younger children. There is, however, said to be a family in Michigan where the sons are called One, Two, Three Stickaway, and the daughters First, Second, Third Stickaway.

The invention of original names usually takes place in the early stages of a people's history, for a preference soon arises for established names, already borne by kindred, and as the spoken tongue drifts away from the primitive form, the proper name becomes a mere appellative, with the original meaning forgotten, and often with a new one incorrectly applied to it. The names in popular use almost always belong to a more ancient language than that spoken by the owners; or else they are imported from some other nation, and adapted to the mouths of those who use them. Flexibility of speech is only acquired at a very early age, and persons who have never spoken any other than their mother tongue, have no power to catch foreign sounds, and either distort them, or assimilate them to words of their own. The ear catches the word imperfectly, the lips pronounce it after their own fashion, and the first writer who hears it, sets it down to the best of his ability, to be read, as it may chance, by others, ignorant of the sound the letters were meant to represent, and thus striking out absolute novelties. Even where it travels by the medium of writing, the letters of one language are so inadequate to express the sounds of another, that great changes take place in pronunciation, even while the spelling remains unaltered, and these become visible in the popular contractions.

Thus a foreign conquest, or the fusion of one nation into another, while introducing two orders of names to the same country, and in breaking up and intermixing their original forms of speech, yet leaves untouched the names belonging to the old language, though the spoken tongue goes on living, growing, and altering.

The Hebrew is an instance of this process. It was a living tongue up to the Babylonish captivity, and constantly formed new names from the ordinary speech of the people ; but when the Jews returned they spoke the Aramean dialect ; the old Hebrew was dead. They still called their children by mangled and contracted Hebraisms, inherited from their forefathers, but were in general not aware of their meaning, and were willing to give them Greek terminations to suit the literary taste of the East. That there was no vigour to throw out new names, is attested by the very scanty number of Aramean derivation. Yet it is these corrupted Hebrew names, marred by Aramean pronunciation, by Greek writing, and by the speech of every country, that are the most universally loved and honoured in every Christian land.

Greek may be said to have never died, and it has, from first to last, been the most vigorous of all languages in creating and spreading names, which are almost all easily explicable. Hellas, though frequently conquered, has by its glorious literature, both pagan and Christian, gained wide dominion for its language, and even the present vernacular of the peasant and sailor is not so decayed but that they can comprehend a line of Homer or a verse of St. John. Thus there is a long list of Greek names ever new, with comparatively few importations from other tongues, and for the most part conveying their meaning and augury.

On the contrary, before Latin was born, the dialects that had produced Latin names were decaying, and those who, by inheritance, bore the scanty stock that came down to them, were often at a loss for their meaning ; nor in general is it so much the names actually borne by ancient Romans, as appellations formed out of the Latin language, that have been the Latin contribution to Christian nomenclature. The universal victors chiefly spread Roman names by adopting the conquered as their clients, and conferring their own nomina when they bestowed the right of citizenship.

Keltic still lives in its corners of the world, and its old names have for the most part continued in use, but usually each with a name by the side from some more fashionable tongue, supposed to translate it to the civilized ear. For instance, Tadhg, which means, in Erse, a poet, is called in English speech, Teague or Thady; and then further transformed into the Aramean Thaddeus (praise); or the Greek Timothy (honour God); with an utter loss of the true association.

The Teutonic names are taken from the elder branches of the Teuton languages, before they became commingled in different degrees with the later progeny of Latin, and with one another. We here use the word Teutonic, because it is the most convenient term by which to express the class of languages spoken by the great Germanic family, though we are aware that it is not absolutely correct as a class-appellation including the whole. Iceland and Scandinavia use their ancient tongue, but slightly altered, and there may be found the true forms and interpretations of the greater number of the appellations in common use. Modern German continues the old High German, but it is no safe guide to the meaning of names which belong to a much earlier form than that in which we now see it, and it has only created a few modern ones of its own. Anglo-Saxon explains most of its own names, but it cannot be safely trusted without comparison with the other branches. It was a language deteriorated by the Norman conquest, just as the Norse of the invaders had been previously smothered by their conquest of Neustria, and the English which grew up among them used more of the High Dutch names adopted by the Normans in France, than of its own Anglo-Saxon ones; and only after the Reformation was there an attempt, and that not a very successful one, at the fabrication of native English names. France kept Dutch names, and clipped them, while High Dutch minced Latin. Lombardy, too, used the old heroic names of the fair-haired barbarians, even while its speech was constant to the flowing Latin; and Spain has much more of the nomenclature than of the tongue of her Goths.

The Slavonic has corrupted itself, but become Christian, and has sent a few names of great leaders into the general stock of nomenclature, which has been formed by contributions from these six original branches, with a few chance additions from other quarters.

Each nation had a stock of its own at first, but as tribes became mixed, their names were interchanged, and varied by the pronunciation of those who adopted them; and when Christianity produced real union, making the saint of one country the glory and example of the entire Church, the names of the holy and the great became a universal link, and a token of the brotherhood established from land to land.

It was not at first, however, that this fusion of names commenced. The first Christians were Jews, with Hebrew, Aramean, Greek, or Latin names of their own, and their converts already bore Greek or Latin appellations, which were seldom altered. In the case of the Romans, children almost necessarily succeeded to family names, and the Greeks alone could at first exercise any choice, forming words of Christian meaning for their children, or adopting those of their revered instructors in the faith; and afterwards, persons using the Latin tongue, but not encumbered with the numerous names of a citizen, followed their example. The Teutons, when converted, were baptized by the names they already bore, and gave the like to their children ; nor does it seem to have been till the older forms of the languages were expiring, that the introduction of old saintly names became by any means frequent. When names were mere appellations, not descriptions, a favourite character was sought for in the legends of the saints, and the child was dedicated to, or placed under the protection of, the patron whose name he bore. The theory was, that the festival in the calendar on which the birth took place, established the claim of the infant to the care of the patron, and thus fixed the name, an idea which still prevails in the Greek Church, but it was more usual to select a favourite patron, and instead of keeping the child's birth-day, to feast him upon the holy day of the saint, a custom still observed in Roman Catholic countries.

The system of patron saints was greatly established by the veneration of relics. It was the presence of a supposed fragment of the body that was imagined to secure the protection of the saint to country, to city, to village, or family ; and often the 'translation' of a relic can be traced as the cause of the nationality of a name, as the Diego of Spain, the Andreas of Flanders, the Marco of Venice, the Adrianus of Holland, the Radegonde of Poitiers, the Anne of Prague. Or the prominence of a fresh doctrine is shown in nomenclature, as by the outburst of Scripture names in all Calvinist countries ; so that in French pedigrees, Huguenotism may be traced by the Isaacs and other patriarchal apparitions in the genealogy, and Puritanism has in England produced the quaint Old Testament appellations to be found in every parish register. On the other hand, the increasing devotion to the Blessed Virgin is indicated by the exaggerated use of Mary in Roman Catholic lands, the epithets coupled with it showing the peculiar phases of the homage paid to her, and almost gauging the amount of superstition in the country.

Religion has thus been in general the primary guide to individual nomenclature, and next in order must be ranked the family feeling that renders Christian names almost hereditary. In many places where primitive customs are kept up, it was an almost compulsory token of respect to call the eldest son after his paternal grandfather. This has indeed been almost universal. The ancient Greeks always did so unless the grandfather were alive, in which case the child was thought to take his place by bearing his name, and thus to bring death upon him.

In Scotland and in the north of England, the paternal grandfather and grandmother have namesakes in the eldest son and daughter, then comes the turn of the grand-parents on the mother's side, then of the parents themselves, after which fancy may step in. In Germany the same practice prevails as regards the two eldest ; and likewise in the south of France, where the child, whatever its sex, bears the grandfather's name, thus accounting for various uncouth feminines ; but though thus christened, the two eldest children are never so called, but always by the diminutive of their surname.

However, distinguished, or wealthy, or beloved godparents interfered with these regular successions, and in this manner queens have been the great conductors of female names, bestowing them on their nobility, from whom they spread to the commonalty.

Literature requires considerable cultivation before it spreads many names. It gave some in the latter days of Greece, and more after the old hereditary customs of Rome were broken up; then, during the dark ages, its influence was lost, except at Byzantium; and only when the chivalrous romance became fashionable, did a few poetic knights and dames call their children after the heroes of the Round Table, or the paladins of Charlemagne, and then it must have been in defiance of the whole system of patron saints until the convenient plan of double names, first discovered by the Germans and French, accomplished the union of fancy and dedication, or compliment.

The revival of learning in the fifteenth century, however, filled Italy with classical names, some of which spread into France, and a few into Germany; but as a general rule in modern times, France, England, and America have been the countries whose nomenclature has been most affected by literature; France, especially so, the prevalence of different tastes and favourite novels being visible from the fifteenth century downwards, through its Arcadian, its Augustan, its Infidel, its Revolutionary periods; while England, since the Reformation, has slightly partaken of all these tastes in turn, but with her own hereditary fashions and religious influences mingling with them; and America exaggerates every variety in her mixed population.

PART I.

CHAPTER I.

HEBREW NOMENCLATURE.

HEBREW, the sacred language, and the medium of all our earliest knowledge of the world and of man, furnishes almost all of the first names known to us, which are in general, verbs, substantives, or adjectives from that tongue, suggested either by inspiration or by some of the natural motives observed in the former chapter.

The minute history of the naming of the twelve patriarchs, furnish the best illustrations of the presaging spirit of early nomenclature.

Reuben, "behold a son," cries the mother in her first pride; Simeon, "He that heareth," because He had heard her prayer; Levi, a joining, in the trust that her husband would be joined with her; Judah, praise, in praise of Him who had given these four sons, and Judah, "thou art he whom thy brethren shall *praise*," is repeated by Jacob; Dan, a judge, is so called by his adoptive mother because her cause is judged, "and Dan shall *judge* his people" is his father's blessing; Naphtali commemorates Leah's wrestling with her sister; Gad is one of the *troop* round Leah, "and a *troop* shall overcome him," saith Jacob; Asher, is *blessed*, and Moses cries, "let Asher be blessed;" Issachar, is *hire;* and Zebulon, a *dwelling*, because Leah hoped her husband would dwell with her, and his promise from his father is that he shall *dwell*. Rachel cannot name her long-desired first-born without a craving that God would add to her another son, and thus Joseph means an *addition*, and when that second child was given, and she felt that it was at the cost of her own life, she mourned over him as Benoni, son of my sorrow; but his father with more hopeful augury called him (probably at his circumcision) Benjamin, son of my right hand.

The earlier names were very simple, such as Leah, weary; Adah, ornament. But about the time of the going into Egypt compound words were employed, family names began to grow traditional, and several of Egyptian etymology were acquired.

The Aramaic became the Jewish vernacular, and so continued after the return from Babylon, nor has it ceased to prevail, under the name of Syriac, among a considerable portion of the natives of the East.

Moreover, the Greek invasion of the East, and the establishment of the Macedonian dynasties of Egypt and Syria, rendered the Grecian the language of foreign relations and of literature, and caused it to be understood by all who pretended to polite education, or meddled with politics and commerce. The Septuagint, or Alexandrian version of the Scriptures, was used in private by the Græcised Jews, and was the form in which their sacred books became known to those of foreign nations who took interest in them.

The Roman conquest in like manner brought in a certain amount of influence from the Latin language, though not to the same extent, since all cultivated Romans were by this time instructed in Greek as part of their education, and even those of inferior rank used it as the medium of communication with the people of the East.

Thus, in the time of the Gospel history, the learned alone entered into the full import of the old Hebrew names, nor were new ones invented to suit the occasion, with a very few exceptions, and these few were formed from the vernacular Aramean. The custom was to recur to the old family names belonging to ancestors or kindred, and in the account of the circumcision of St. John the Baptist we see that a deviation from this practice excited wonder. Tradition and change of language had, however, greatly marred these old Hebraisms; Jehoiadah, (*j* pronounced *y*,) (known of God,) had after the captivity lost its significance in the form of Jaddua, then was Græcized, as 'Ιωδαέ, (Hiodae,) and was Latinized as Jaddeus! These corrupted ancient appellations were the favourites, but imitation and compliment caused some Greek ones and even some Latin ones to be adopted, some persons using their national name at home, and bearing another for their external relations, such as John or Mark, Saul or Paul.

The persons most revered by Christians, and who have had the most influence on nomenclature, thus bore either corrupt Hebrew, or else Aramean, Greek, or Latin names, which all have been handed down to us through the medium of Greek authorship, afterwards translated into Latin, and thence carried by word of mouth into every Christian land, and taking shape from the prevalent pronunciation there.

Eastern Christians have gone directly to the Greek; but the Western Church used nothing but the Vulgate translated from the Septuagint and from the original New Testament. Thus the Old Testament personages, as well as those of the Gospel, were known to mediæval Europe, and are so still to the greater part of the continent in their Greco-Latin shape.

But King James I. caused his translators to go back to the fountain-head, using the original Hebrew and Greek—and only applying to the Septuagint and Vulgate as means of elucidation, not as authorities. In consequence, many of the Old Testament names assumed their original shape, as far as it could be expressed by English letters, but these were mostly those but slightly known to the world, not those of the principal characters, since the translators were instructed not to make needless alterations such as should make the objects of ancient veneration appear in a form beyond recognition. Therefore it is that some English Old Testament names are unlike those of other nations.

Those who were at work on the New Testament, however, left the ancient names, there occurring, as they found them in the Greek, and thus arose the disparity we remark in the title given to the same individual, Noah or Noe, Korah or Core, Uzziah or Ozias.

For the most part Old Testament names, as such, have had little prevalence excepting under the influence of Calvinism. The Roman Catholic Church neglected them because they did not convey patronage, and Lutherism has not greatly adopted them, but they were almost a badge of the Huguenot party in France ; and in England, about the latter part of the reign of Elizabeth, a passion for the most extraordinary and unusual Scripture names prevailed, for which the genealogist must have carefully searched. William L'Isle, in 1623, complains of some "devising new names with apeish imitation of the Hebrew," and in effect there are few of these that do not give an impression of sectarianism or Puritanism. In England and America, the more obscure and peculiar ones are chiefly adopted by the lower classes ; in Ireland several prevail for another cause, namely, their supposed resemblance to the native Erse appellations that were long proscribed by the conquerors.

Those that were borne by the remnant of faithful Jews, who were the stock on which the Christian Church was grafted, have gone out into all lands, infinitely modified by the changes they have undergone in their transit from one people to another.*

* Books consulted :—Max Müller's *Lectures on Language ; Proper Names of Scripture ;* Smith's *Dictionary of the Bible.*

CHAPTER II.

PATRIARCHAL NAMES.

SECTION I.—*Adam.*

THE oldest of all proper names comes from a word signifying red, and refers to the red earth (adama) out of which the first man was taken, reminding us that dust we are, and unto dust shall we return.

Some say that it should be translated 'likeness,' and that it comes from the same root as '*adama*,' red earth, because red earth is always alike, wherever found. In this case, the first man would have been called from his likeness to his Creator, but the other explanation is preferable, especially as the same adjective, pronounced with a change in the vowel sound, so as to make it Edom, was the surname of Esau (hairy), on account both of the ruddiness of his complexion and of the *red* lentile pottage for which he sold his birthright.

No Israelites or Jews appear to have been called after our first father, and the first time Adam comes to light again, is among the Keltic Christians of Ireland and Scotland. It is not improbable that it was first adopted according to a frequent Gaelic fashion, as the ecclesiastical name most resembling the native one of Aedh or fire; but however this may be, there was in the seventh century a distinguished abbot of Iona, called in the dog Latin of the time, Adamnanus or dwarf Adam, and best known as Adamnan. Though not recognized by the Roman calendar, he was regarded as a saint in his own country, but his name has been much corrupted. At Skreen in Ireland, where he founded a church, he is styled St. Awnan, at Raphoe he is patron, as St. Ennan, in Londonderry he is St. Onan; but in Scotland, Adam has become a national Christian name. The family who most affected it were the 'gay Gordons.' *Edie* is the Scottish contraction. The feminine *Adamina* has been a recent Scottish invention.

In Germany and the neighbouring countries there prevails an idea that Adam is always long-lived, and if the first infant of a family dies, the life of its successor is secured by calling it either Adam or Eve. In consequence it has various contractions and alterations. In Lower Lusatia it is *Hadamk* in familiar speech; the Swiss abbreviation is *Odli;* the Esthonian *Ado* or *Oado*, the Lettisu was *Adums*. With its contraction, *Ade*, it seems to have been very common at Cambrai through the middle ages.

" The mother of all living"—received from the lips of Adam a

name signifying life, sounding in the original like *Chavva*, as it began
with a rough aspirate. It was not copied by any of her daughters
for a long time, and when first the Alexandrian Jews came on it in
their translation, they rendered it by *Zoe* (life), in order to show the
connection of the name with the prophecy ; but afterwards in the
course of the narrative they merely made it Eva, or in Latin the
Heva or *Eva*, which English has changed into Eve.

The Eva of Ireland and Scotland, and the Aveline or Eveline of
the Normans, were probably only imitations of the old Keltic names
Aoibhiun and Aoiffe, and will therefore be considered among the
Keltic class.

Eve has been seldom used in England, though old parish registers
occasionally show a pair of twins christened Adam and Eve.

The same notion of securing a child's life that has spread the use
of Adam in Germany and its vicinity has had the same effect upon
his wife, so that Eva is common in both Germany and Scandinavia.
Russia has Evva or Jevva, though not often as a name in use ; the
Letts as Ewe or Ewusche ; the Lithuanians as Jewa or Jewele, the
first letter of course pronounced like *Y ;* and in Lusatia her namesakes are called Hejba or Hejbka.*

The murdered son of Adam is called by a Hebrew word meaning
breath, vapour, or transitoriness, and as some think may have been
so termed in remembrance of his short life. The sound of the
original word was more like Hebel, but through the Greek we receive
it as Abel.

It is not absolutely a modern Puritan name, for an Abel existed in
Essex in the time of Henry III., and Awel is known in Russia ; but
it is generally given direct from the Bible, as are also Seth (appointed),
and Enoch (dedicated).

Adah (ornament), the wife of Lamech, is often supposed to be the
origin of our English Ada, but this last is the hereditary Latinized
form of Eed (rich), and is the same as the German Ida. Zillah (or
shadow), the other wife of Lamech, is a Gypsy name.

SECTION II.—*Abi.*

Common to both the Semitic and Indo-European tongues, and
traceable through all their branches, is the parental title first uttered
by the infant ; Abba, Abi, Aba ; Atta among the Slavonians, and
again among the Goths ; Athair among the Irish, the pater of Greece,
fondly called at home papa, and apphys the *pater* of Rome, the
German Vater, and our own father—*il babbo* in Italy, and daddy in
English cottages.

In the East a parent is more usually called the father of his son
than by his own name. This, however, is probably a late affectation,
not applying to the time when the greatest of the patriarchs received
his original name of Abram (father of height or elevation), which was
changed by Divine appointment into Abraham (father of a multitude),

* Smith's *Dictionary ;* Michaelis, *Personen Namen.*

foretelling the numerous and enduring offspring that have descended from him, and even to the present hour revere his name.

No one, however, seems to have presumed to copy it as long as the Israelites dwelt in their own land, and the first resuscitations of it appear to have been among the Christians of the patriarch's native land, Mesopotamia, towards the end of the fourth century, when a hermit called Abraham, living near Edessa, obtained a place in the Coptic, Greek, and Roman calendars; and about the same time another Abraham was among the martyrs who were put to death by the fire worshipping zeal of the Sassanid dynasty in Persia. Two other Mesopotamian SS. Abraham lived in the next century, and died, one at Constantinople, the other in Auvergne, whither in some unaccountable manner he had been carried between foul winds and man-stealing barbarians when on a journey to visit the solitaries in Egypt.

As one of the patrons of Clermont, this Abraham must have been the means of diffusing namesakes in France, especially on the side towards the Low Countries. Abraham often occurs in the registers of Cambray; and in compliance with the fashion of adapting the name of the father to the daughter, Abra was there formed, though apparently not earlier than 1644. Indeed the Netherlands and Holland are the only countries where this patriarchal name is really national, generally shortened into Abram and Bram; and the Dutch settlers carried it into America, where it is generally called either Bram or Aby.

Many other Scripture names bear this prefix, but it would be contrary to our plan to dwell upon those that have not been in subsequent use or are devoid of peculiar interest.

Abigail (father of joy), strikes us as inappropriate to a woman, till we remember that the eastern nations use this expression for an abstract quality, and that the title would stand for joyfulness. Her ready courtesy to David seems to have recommended her to the earliest readers of the English Bible, for Abigail occurs in registers as early as 1573, and was for many years very frequent. Abigail Masham's back-stair influence over Queen Anne has been generally supposed to have rendered it a soubriquet for a lady's maid; but Mr. Bardsley, in his *Curiosities of Puritan Nomenclature*, shows it to have been the name of the waiting gentlewoman in Beaumont's Comedy, *The Scornful Ladie*, played in 1616. And in a play of Killigrew's, some thirty years later, the term 'Abigail' is used for a waiting-maid, when the back-stair influence and supposed arts of Abigail Masham in the bedchamber of Queen Anne gave it a sudden fall. Abigail turned into a cant term for a lady's maid, and thenceforth has been seldom heard even in a cottage.

Counter to his name was the course of the "Father of Peace." He is Abishalom, or Absalom in the narrative of his life, a history that one would have thought entailed eternal discredit on the name ; but it seems that in the earlier Christian times of Denmark, as well as in some other countries, a fashion prevailed, especially among the clergy, of supplementing the native name with one of Scriptural or ecclesiastical sound, and thus, about the middle of the twelfth century, Absalom was adopted by a distinguished Danish bishop as the synonym of what Professor Munch conjectures to have been his own name of Aslak (reward of the gods), though Danish tradition has contracted it into Axel. This last is a national Danish name, and it seems as if Absalom had been popularly supposed to be the Latin for Axel; since, in a Latin letter of 1443, Olaf Axelsson is turned into Olaus Absalonis.

Before quitting this prefix Ab, it seems to be the place to remark upon a name coming to us through the Tartar stock of languages, from the same source—Ab. Ata, (father, the source of Atalik, (fatherlike or paternal,) is to the present day a title among the Usbeks of Bokhara. Thence that regent of the Huns, the scourge of God, who spread terror to the gates of Rome, would have been called Attalik among his own people, and thus historians have written his name of terror Attila.

In the tales of the Nibelungen, the great Hun, whom Kriemhild marries after the death of Siegfried, and at whose court the general slaughter takes place, is called Etzel in the German poem, Atli in the Northern saga, and this has generally been regarded as identifying him with Attila and fixing the date of the poem; but the monarch of the Huns is hospitable and civilized, with few features in common with the savage of Roman history; and if Attalik were a permanent regal title among the Huns, the chieftain may have been any other of the royal dynasty. His occurrence in that favourite poem, sung alike by all the Teutonic race, has rendered Atli very common from early times in the North as well as Etzel in Germany. The Lombards took it to Italy, where it turned into Eccelino, and in the person of the fierce mountain-lord, Eccelino di Romagna, became as fearful as Attila had ever been to the Romans.

The verb to fight or to rule furnished both the names of the wife of Abraham; Sarai (quarrelsome) was thus converted into Sarah (the princess). If we may judge from the example of the bride of Tobias, the daughters of Sarah were occasionally called by her name, and Zara has been, with what correctness I know not, used as an eastern name.

Sarah now and then occurs in England, as with Sara Beauchamp, (temp. Ed. I.,) but I suspect that she as well as Sarrota de Multon, who lived in the former reign, were alterations of some of the derivatives of the Teutonic prefix Sig—victory, as the masculine Saher or Serlo certainly came from Sigcheri. Sarah was never commonly used till after the Reformation, when it began to grow very popular, with its contraction Sally; and at the same time it was adopted as the equivalent for no less than three Irish names—Sadhbh (pronounced Soyv), Sorcha (bright), and Saraid (excellent). The two first are still in use; but Highlanders make a still stranger use of Sarah, which they use to translate their native More (great), perhaps in consequence of its meaning.

Elsewhere the name is occasionally used without the h that our biblical translators gave it. It is not, however, very popular, though the French have used it enough to make it Sarotte; in Illyria its diminutive is Sarica; in Lithuania it is Zore.*

When the first glad tidings of the Child of Promise were announced, Sarah laughed for very joy and wonder, and Laughter (Yizchak) became the name of her son; known in Greek as Ἰσαάκ, in Latin and to the European world as Isaac.

It was not revived among the early Jews; but, like Abraham, it was used by the eastern Christians, and St. Isaac, bishop of Beth Seleucia, was put to death with other Christian martyrs by Sapor II. of Persia. Another eastern Isaac was a hermit at Spoleto, in the sixth century, and Isaak has always been a favourite name in the Greek Church. Several of the family of Comnenus, both at Constantinople and Trebizond, rendered Isaak a royal name; and Isaak or Eisaak, whose feast falls on the 30th of May, is the patron of the cathedral at Petersburg. The name is frequently used in Russia and the other Greco-Slavonic countries, though not much varied.

It had not much favour in the West, though it appears once in Domesday Book, and occurs in the Cambray registers. Mr. Bardsley thinks that it, with some other Patriarchal names, became familiar through Mystery plays. But its chief popularity was after the Reformation, when it is continually to be found among the Huguenots, and it seems to have passed from them to other French families, since it is sometimes found in pedigrees, and the noted de Sacy, a grandson of the Arnauld family, was thus christened long after his forefathers had conformed to the Roman Catholic Church.

With us Izaak, as our ancestors spelt it, is just so prevalent among us as to have a recognized contraction, Ike or Ikey.

Isaac's wife was called from *rabak* (to bind). The word Ribkâ meant a cord with a noose, and probably was given as conveying the firmness of the marriage bond. The Septuagint and Latin gave Rebecca; the authorized version Rebekah; and both spellings are adopted by those bearing the name, who are generally called Becky.

Here too should be mentioned the faithful nurse of Rebekah, who was so lamented that the tree beneath which she was buried was known as the oak of weeping. Her name of Deborah came from a verb meaning to hum or buzz, and signified a bee, or, in after times, eloquent.

Deborah found no favour as a name except among English Puritans, and has acquired a certain amount of absurdity from various literary associations, which prevent ' Deb.' from being used except by the peasantry.

Of Rebekah's two daughters-in-laws, Rachel signified a ewe.

Dante made *l'antica Rachele*, with her beautiful eyes, the type of heavenly contemplation, ever gazing at the mirror that reflected heavenly glory; but her name was not popular, although the Manx princess, otherwise called Affrica, assumed it upon her marriage with Somerled, Lord of the Isles, somewhere about the eleventh century.

* Books consulted:—*Proper Names of the Bible;* Le Beau's *Histoire du Bas Empire;* O'Donovan on *Irish Proper Names;* Michaelis, *Personen Namen.*

But Puritan days loved the sound of the word, and "that sweet saint who sat by Russell's side" has given it a place in many an English family. Polish Jews call it Rahel; in which form it was borne by the metaphysical lady who became the wife of Varnhagen von Ense.

Rachel's less beloved and less favoured sister had a name that came from *lawah* (hanging upon, dependence, or, as in her case it is explained, weariness)—Leah, in French Lea, in Italian Lia, under which title Dante makes her the emblem of active and fruitful, as is her sister of meditative, love. It was from the same word that she named her third son Levi, when she hoped that her husband would be more closely united or dependent on her. Levi's name was carried on into the Gospel times, and belonged to the publican who was called from the receipt of custom to become an Apostle and an Evangelist. His Aramean name was, however, that by which he calls himself in his own narrative, or more correctly speaking, by its Græcized form. The old Hebrew Mattaniah (gift of the Lord) was probably the origin of both the names that we have in the Greek Testament as Ματθαῖος and Ματθίας, Matthæus and Matthias as the

English.	German.	Bavarian.
Matthias	Matthæus	Mathies
Matthew	Matthia	Mahe
Mat	Matthes	Hies
	Matthis	Hiesel
		Mathe

Swiss.	Swedish.	Danish.
Mathias	Mathias	Mathias
Thies	Mats	Mads
Thiesli		

Friesland.	French.	Italian.
Matthies	Matthieu	Matteo
Hise	Macé	Maffeo
Hisse		Feo
		Mattia

Spanish.	Russian.	Polish.
Mateo	Matfei	Mateusz
	Matvej	Maciei
		Maciek
		Matyas

Hungarian.	Slovak.	Esthonian.
Matyas	Matevz	Maddis
Mate	Tevz	Mats
	Mattija	

Latin renders them. Some, however, make the first mean a faithful man ; but it is not possible to distinguish between the various forms that have risen out of the two among persons who, probably, had no idea that the Apostle who supplied the place of Judas was a different person from the Evangelist. The Emperor Charles V. was born on St. Matthias' day, and the text " The lot fell on Matthias " was regarded as a good augury, whence Matthias came into favour in Austria and its dependencies. The name has been more popular in Germany and its dependencies. Matteo heads the Milanese Visconti, who were mostly named after the Evangelists.

Apostolic names are particularly common in Bavaria, probably from the once frequent representations of the Mystery of the Passion. In Germany, SS. Matthew and Matthias have produced the surnames Matthies, Matys, Thiess, and Thiessen, Latinized after a queer scholarly fashion into Thysius.

Section III.—*Jacob.*

The twin sons of Isaac and Rebekah were called from the circumstances of their birth, Esau, the hairy, and Ja'akob, the latter word being derived from *âkêb*, the heel, because in the words of the Prophet " he took his brother by the heel in the womb." This, the action of tripping up, confirmed the mother's faith in the previous prediction that " the elder should serve the younger," and thus that the younger should supplant the elder. " Is he not rightly named Jacob, for he hath *supplanted* me these two times," was accordingly the cry of Esau.

By the time of the return from Babylon we find two if not three persons mentioned as bearing the name of Akkub, and that this was meant for Jacob, is shown by its etymology ; as it likewise means the supplanter, by its likeness in sound to Yacoub, the form still current among the Arabs, and by the fact that the Akkub, who in the book of Nehemiah stands up with Ezra to read the law to the people, is in the book of Esdras, written originally in Greek, called Ἰάκοβος (Jakobos).

So frequent was this Jakobos among the returned Jews that it occurs in the royal genealogy in St. Matthew's Gospel, and was borne by two of the twelve apostles, by him called the Great, who was the first to be martyred, and by him termed the Less, who ruled the Church at Jerusalem.

It is the Great Apostle, the son of Zebedee, who is the saint, in whose honour most of those bearing this name in Europe have been christened. A belief arose that he had preached the Gospel in Spain before his martyrdom at Jerusalem ; and though there was no doubt that the Holy City was the place of his death, yet it was declared that his relics were brought to Galicia in a marble ship without oar or sail, which arrived at the port of Aria Flava, since called Patron. A little farther inland arose what was at first termed in Latin the shrine of Sanctus Jacobus Apostolus. Men's tongues quickly turned this into Sancto Jacobo Apostolo, and thence, confounding the title with the place, arrived at Santo Jaco de Compostella, or Santiago de Compostella.

A further legend arose that in the battle of Clavijo with the Moors, the spirits of the Christian Spaniards were revived by the sight of Santiago mounted on a white steed, waving a white banner, and leading them on to victory. Thenceforth Santiago became their war-cry, and the saint was installed as a champion of Christendom. Subsequently no less than three Spanish orders of knighthood were instituted in his honour, and his shrine became one of the most universal places of pilgrimage in Europe, more especially as the most marvellous fables of miracles were forged thereat. His saintly title had become so incorporated with his name that his votaries were in some perplexity where to separate them, and in Castille his votaries were christened Tiago or Diego. Even as early as the tenth century the Cid's father was Don Diego de Bivar, and he himself Don Rodrigo Diaz de Bivar, Diaz being the patronymic.

In 1207, Maria, Queen of Aragon, considering her infant son and heir to have been granted at the especial intercession of the twelve apostles, resolved to baptize him after one of their number, and impartially to decide between them by naming twelve tapers after the apostles, and calling the child after him whose candle burnt longest. Southey has comically described the Queen's agitations until the victorious candle proved to be that of the great Saint of Galicia, whom Aragonese tongues called Jayme. The child thus christened became the glory of his kingdom, and was known as El Conquestador, leaving Jayme to be honourably borne by Kings of Aragon, Majorca, and Sicily as long as his family remained distinct. Giacopo Apostolo was the Italian version of the name, whence they made their various Giacopo, Jacopo, Giacomo, Como, Iachimo, and Iago according to their various dialects. Germany recurred to the original Jakob ; but the French coming home with their own variety talked of Jiac Apostol, and named their children Jacques, or fondled them as Jacquot and Jacqueminot. The great church of St. Jacques, at Liège, spread the love of the name in Flanders as is testified by Jacob von Arteveldt, the Brewer of Ghent ; and so universal throughout France was it, that Jacques Bonhomme became the nickname of the peasantry, and was fearfully commemorated in the Jacquerie, the insurrection of which English chroniclers supposed James Goodman to have been the leader. It must have been when English and French were mingled together in the camps of the Black Prince and Henry V. that Jack and Jock became confounded together. Henry V. called the wild Jacqueline of Hainault, Dame Jack. She, like his other Flemish sister-in-law, Jacquette of Luxemburg, must have been named in honour of the saint of Liège. Edward VI.'s nurse, whom Holbein drew by the soubriquet of Mother Jack, was perhaps a Jacquette ; Iacolyn and Jacomyn are also found in old registers, but this feminine never took root anywhere but in France, where Jacobée also occurs. James had found its way to Scotland ere the birth of the Black Douglas, and was already a national name before it was given to the second son of Robert III., in accordance with a vow of

C

the queen. This James was brought to the throne by the murder of
his brother David, Duke of Rothsay ; and thus was the first of the
royal Stuarts, by whom it was invariably borne till the sixth of the
line hoped to avert the destiny of his race by choosing for his sons
more auspicious names. James and Jamie thus became great favourites
in Scotland, and came to England with the Stuarts. The name had
indeed been previously used, as by the brave Lord James Audley
under Edward III., but not so frequently, and the old English form
was actually Jeames. Norden dedicates his *Survey of Cornwall* to
James I. as Jeames ; and Archbishop Laud so spells the word in his
correspondence. In fact, Jemmy and Jim are the natural offsprings
of Jeames, as the word was pronounced in the best society till the
end of the last century. Then the gentry spoke according to the
spelling ; Jeames held his ground among the lower classes, and finally
—thanks to *Jeames's Diary*—has become one of the stock terms of
conventional wit ; and in modern times Jacobina and Jamesina were
coined for female wear.

The Highlanders call the name Hamish ; the Irish, Seumuis. In
fact, its variations are almost beyond enumeration. In Italy the full
name has the three varieties, Giacomo, Jacopo, Giacobbe, so no
wonder the abbreviations are Coppo and Lapo.

Due honour is paid in the Greek and Slavonic Church to both the
veritable apostles, but not to the mythical Santiago de Compostella,
whom we have traced as the root of all the Jameses of the West.

The great Jakobos, who appeared at the Council of Nicea, and
gloriously defended the city of Nisibis, handed on the apostolic name
in the East ; and it has almost as many Greek and Slavonian variations as Latin and Teutonic ones.

English.	Scotch.	Erse.	Gaelic.	Dutch.
Jacob	James	Seumuis	Hamish	Jacob
James	Jamie			Jaap
Jem				
Jemmy				

French.	German.	Swiss.	Italian.	Spanish.
Jacob	Jakob	Jakob	Jacopo	Jacobo
Jacques	Jackel	Bopp	Iachimo	Santiago
Jacquot	Jockel ⎱ Bav.	Jock	Giakobbe	Diego
Jacqueminot	Gaugl ⎰	Jogg	Coppo	Yago
		Jagli	Lapo	Jago
			Jacobello	Jayme

Portuguese.	Russian.	Polish.	Lett.	
Jayme	Jakov	Jakob	Jekups	
	Jascha	Kuba	Jeka	
	Jaschenka	Kub	Jezis	
			Kubischu	

The Russian nameday is the 30th of April, either for the sake of St. James the Less, whose eve it is, or for that of a namesake who perished in Numidia in the time of Valerian, and whose feast falls on that day. Jakov gets called Jascha and Jaschenka, and his feminine Jacovina and Zakelina. The Illyrians twist the masculine into Jakovica, and the Lithuanians into Jeka or Kubinsch.*

SECTION IV.—*Simeon.*

Of the twelve sons of Jacob, four only have names of sufficient interest to deserve individual notice, and among these, the first requiring notice is Simeon, from *schama*, to hear.

Simeon's name passed on to numerous Jews, and was very common in the Gospel times, no less than five personages being so called, namely, the aged man in the Temple, the son of Jonas, the other apostle called the Zealot or the Canaanite, and the leper, besides the tanner of Joppa, and the magician whose attempt to purchase spiritual gifts has given the title of simony to sins of the same nature.

By this time, however, the Hebrew Simeon had been confounded with the Greek Σίμων (Simon), snub-nosed. St. James, in his discourse at Jerusalem, called St. Peter 'Simeon,' and it would thus seem likely that this was used as their true national name, and that Simon was a Græcism used in intercourse with strangers, or in writing.

The anchorite who took that strangest freak of fanaticism, the perching himself for life upon a column, is called both Simeon and Simon Stylites, but the latter form has generally been the prevalent one, and has belonged to numerous saints in both the Eastern and Western Church. The Greek Church has both St. Seemeön on the 3rd of February, and St. Ssimon on the 10th of May, and the Russian contractions are Ssemen and Ssenka. The West, too, had sundry Simons of its own, besides those common to all Christendom. We had a monastic St. Simon Stock, and though the Christian name is now uncommon, it has left us many varieties of surnames, as Simmonds, Simkins, Simpson, Simcoe, Sykes, etc., the spelling but slightly varied. It was more used among the French peasantry, and acquired the feminine Simonette. The Italian Simone was not unfrequent, and has made the surname Simoncelli; the Portuguese had Sima; the Spaniards, Ximon; and the Slavonians have the odd varieties of the Polish Szymon, the Illyrian Simej, the Lusatian Schymanz.

It is the same word Schama that named the first of the prophets of Israel. " Asked of God " is the import of Samuel, a name so endeared by the beautiful history of the call to the child in the temple, that it could not be quite forgotten. A Samuel, native of Palestine, who perished in the persecution of Maximian, obtained a martyr's place in the calendar, and his name has been a favourite in the Eastern Church, as Samuil, Samoilo, in Russia ; Schombel in Lusatia ; Zomelis

---

* Smith's *Dictionary of the Bible ;* Southey's Poems ; Jamieson's *Sacred and Legendary Art ;* Butler ; Michaelis ; Pott ; Brand's *Popular Antiquities.*

in Lithuania. The reading of the Holy Scriptures was, however, no doubt, the cause of its use here and in Switzerland, since we scarcely find it before the Reformation, though now Samuel is common in Switzerland, and Sam here.*

SECTION V.—*Judah.*

In her exultation at having borne so many promising sons, Leah called her fourth Jehudah (he will be praised) ; meaning brought forward by her husband Jacob when, in his death-bed blessing of his sons, he exclaimed, " Judah, thou art he whom thy brethren shall praise."

Thus, too, it has been with the individual name of Judah. Unused before the captivity, it was revived again after it, and carried to the highest fame and popularity by the brave Maccabee, who newly founded Judea and restored it, for a time, to freedom and honour. His surname is by some derived from a word meaning the Hammerer, by others from Makkabi, formed by initial letters of the motto on his standard, "Who among the gods is like unto Thee, O Lord ?" Judas Maccabeus, early as was his death, and imperfect as was the deliverance of his country when he was slain, was one of the chief heroes of the world, and occupied a far larger space in the imagination of our mediæval ancestors than he does in ours. Not only were the books of Maccabees considered as of equal authority with the canonical Scriptures, but, before 1240, a French metrical romance had recounted his exploits, and by Chaucer's time Judas Maccabeus was ranked among the nine worthies—the subject of many a ballad and chap-book.

But his name has never occurred ! Frequent, indeed, it was among his own countrymen after his time, but of them was that man who rendered it for ever accursed.

Another apostle bore the same name, but this did not suffice to redeem it, though altered into Jude to mark the distinction. The Saint had, however, two Aramean names, Lebbæus, supposed to mean hearty, or else from the town of Lebba, and Thaddæus, which is satisfactorily explained as an Aramean form of the same word Praise, Græcized and Latinized of course before it came to us.

It is not, however, popular. Italy has indeed used it a good deal as Taddeo, and Spain knows it as Tadeo ; but though Ireland swarms with Thadys, who write themselves Thaddeus, this is only as a supposed English version of their ancient Erse, Tadhg (a poet). The Slavonic nations use it more than the West ; it is a favourite Polish name, and the Russians call it Phaddéi ; and the Illyrians, Tadia. No name has been so altered as Judah ; it is Hodaiah after the captivity, and Abiud, or rather Ab-jud, in St. Luke's genealogy.

The feminine form of the name, Jehudith, or Judith, belonged primarily to the Hittite wife of Esau, who was a grief of heart to

* *Proper Names of the Bible ;* Butler ; Lower's *English Surnames ;* Michaelis ; P.ot.

Rebekah, but its fame is owing to the heroine of Bethulia, whose name is, however, said rather to mean a Jewess than to be exactly the feminine of Judah. Indeed some commentators, bewildered by the difficulties of chronology, have supposed the history to be a mere allegory in which she represents the Jewish nation. However, on the uncritical mind of the eighth or ninth century, her story made a deep impression, and a poem was in circulation in Europe recording her adventurous deed, and mentioning among the treasures of Holofernes' tent a mosquito net, whence the learned argue that the narrative must have been derived from some eastern source independent of the Apocryphal book.

At any rate, hers was the first name not belonging to their own language that was borne by Teutonic ladies, and long preceded that of any saint. Perhaps it was supposed to be the equivalent of the German Juthe from Ganthe, war ; at any rate Juditha, Jutha, or Jutta was in high favour at the court of the Karling Kaisers, and came to England with the step-mother, who gave the first impulse to our great Alfred's love of learning. Her subsequent marriage took it to Flanders, and we had it back again with the niece of William the Conqueror, the wicked wife of Waltheof, and afterwards of Simon de St. Lis. Her uncle cites her as a witness to a charter by the familiar abbreviation of Jugge, which was long used as the regular contraction, though Judy has since become more usual, and is exceedingly common in Ireland.

Even French families gave their daughters the name of Judith, which belonged to the gentle Comtesse de Bonneval. The Breton form is Juzeth ; and the Swiss ruthlessly turn it into Dith, but across the Alps it comes forth more gracefully as Giuditta ; and the Poles make it Jitka ; the Hungarians, Juczi or Jutka.

On the authority of Eusebius we venture to add a third to those who bore the name of Judah in the apostolic college, namely, him whom we know by the Aramaic and Greek epithets Thomas and Didymus, both meaning a twin. Tradition declares that his fellow-twin was a sister called Lysia. India is believed to have been the region of his labours and of his death ; the Christians there were called after him ; and when, in the sixteenth century, the Portuguese attained their object of reaching India by sea, they thought they discovered his tomb at Meliapore, transported the relics to Goa, and created San Tomàs or Tomè into their patron saint. Long ere this, however, in every part of Europe had Thomas been revived with other apostolic names, but its great prominence was derived from the murdered Archbishop Becket, or St. Thomas of Canterbury. His shrine at Canterbury was the English Compostella, visited by foreign as well as native pilgrims, and the greater proportion of churches so termed were under the invocation of the archbishop instead of the apostle, although it is only by charter or by wake-day that the dedication can be traced, since Henry VIII. did his utmost to de-canonize and destroy all memorials of the bold prelate whom he would most certainly have beheaded instead of assassinating. In Italy a martyr for ecclesiastical prerogatives was certain to be in high repute ;

carvings, glass, paintings, and even needlework still bear his history and figure, always denoted by the clean cutting off of his scalp above the tonsure, and Tomasso flourishes greatly as a Christian name, the Italians, as usual, abbreviating by the omission of the first syllable instead of the last, so that where we say Tom, they say Maso, and thence Masuccio, as we call one of their earliest great painters. Tomasso Agnello was the true name which, contracted into Masaniello, was the wonder of the day at Naples, and made the Spanish power there totter on its throne.

The feminine Thomassine, Tamzine, and Tammie, are comparatively recent inventions. They were frequent in the 17th century, and then went out of fashion.

English.	Scotch.	French.
Thomas	Thomas	Thomas
Tom	Tam	Thumas
Fem. { Thomassine	Tamlane	
Tamzine		
Spanish.	Italian.	Russian.
Tomas	Tomaso	Foma
Tome	Maso	*Fem.*—Fomaida
Fem.—Tomasa	Masuccio	
	Masaccio	
German.	Polish.	Lower Lusatian.
Thoma	Tomasz	Domas
Fem.—Thomasia		Domask
Lithuanian.	Hungarian.	Finland.
Tamkus	Tamas	Tuomas
Tamoszus		
Dummas		

Thomas is the accepted equivalent for the Irish Tomalhaid, Tomaltach, and Toirdelvach, tall as a tower.

Section VI.—*Joseph.*

When, after long waiting and hoping, a son was at length granted to Rachel, she called him Joseph from a word signifying an addition, because she hoped that yet another child would be added to her family.

Joseph, beloved and honoured as he was for his own beautiful character and eventful history, has perhaps at the present day the greater number of direct namesakes among the Arabs, who still are frequently called Yussuf.

Only two Josephs occur again in the Scripture before the captivity in Babylon, but afterwards they were exceedingly numerous, and in the Gospel history two remarkable characters are so named, as well as three others whom we know by the Græcized form of the name as Joses, *i. e.* a fourth brother of the royal family of James, Simon, and Jude; he who was usually called by his surname of Barnabas, and he who was also called Barsabas, whose lot was cast with that of Matthias. The Latinized form we know' as the name of the historian Flavius Josephus. Legend loved to narrate that Joseph of Arimathea brought the Gospel to England, and that his staff was the Christmas-flowering thorn of Glastonbury; nay, that he carried thither the Sancgreal and the holy lance, the mystic objects of the adventures of the Round Table.

Yet, in spite of the reputation of this holy man, and of the universal reverence for 'the just man' of Nazareth, Joseph was scarcely used as a name in Europe till in 1621 a festival day was fixed by the pope in honour of St. Joseph, the husband of the Blessed Virgin. Therewith an enthusiasm broke forth in Roman Catholic Europe for the name. All the world in Italy began to call itself Giuseppe or Gioseffo; or for short, Peppo and Beppo have swarmed ever since in every village.

Spain delighted in Josef or Jose, and the more devout in Jose Maria, with Pepe or Pepito for the contraction; Pepita for the Josefa, who, of course, arose at the same time, these becoming the most common of all Peninsular names.

Not to be behindhand in devotion, the Emperor Leopold christened his son Joseph, and thus recommended it to all his subjects; and, perhaps, the Tyrol is the greatest of all the strongholds of the Josephs, the name being there called by its last syllable in all endearing varieties, Sepp, Sepperl, &c.; while the Swiss, on the other side, have Sipp and Sippli. Maria Josepha was a daughter of Maria Theresa, and these two are seldom separated in Germany, Italy, or France; but as Maria forms part of the name of every Roman Catholic woman, and of most men, the second name is the one for use. Marie Josephe Rose was the Christian name of her whom we know and pity as the Empress Josephine, and to whom it is owing that France was once full of young ladies usually called Fifine or Finette; while the rougher damsels of Lucerne are content to be Boppi in familiar life.

The Slavonians use the varieties Josko and Joska; the Letts turn the name into Jaschis or Jeps. It is in fact broken into as many odd contractions as it can possibly undergo. It is Joseef or Oseep in Russia.

England having freed herself from Roman Catholic influence before this mighty crop of Josephs sprang up, merely regarded the name as one of the Scripture names chiefly used by Puritans, although Joseph Addison has given it distinction in literature; and there Joe is of uncertain origin, as it is as often the contraction of Josiah or Joshua as of Joseph. In some parts of England, Joseph and Mary are considered appropriate to twins. Josephine is with us a mere introduction from the French.

Joseph, or Joses, as he was called since, coming from Cyprus—he was one of the Hellenistic Jews—is best known to us under his

surname of Barnabas, which St. Luke explains from the Aramaic as
υἱὸς παρακλησέος (uios parakleseos), the son of comfort, a word which
bears different interpretations, since comfort may be either exhort-
ation or consolation ; and it is in the latter sense that St.
Chrysostom and our translators have understood the word, though there are
many who prefer the other meaning.

Barnabas has not been a very common name, though, with an
apostle for its origin, it could not fail to be everywhere known ; but
it was never royal ; and the only historical character so called,
Bernabo Visconti, was enough to give any name an evil odour. We
make it Barnaby when we do use it, the Irish call it Barney and
confuse it with Brian, and the Russians call it Varnava. One Barnabas Hutchinson, proctor of the chapter of Durham, who died in
1633, is thus commemorated in his epitaph :—

> " Under this thorne tree
> Lies honest Barnabee." *

Joseph had named his two sons Manasseh (forgetting), because he
said, "God hath made me *forget* all my toil," and Ephraim (twofold
increase). The first was early adopted by the Israelites ; we find it
belonging to the son of Hezekiah, and to the father of Judith, and, to
our amazement, to a mediæval knight, whose friends may perhaps
have brought it from the Crusades. Two early bishops of Cambrai
bore the name of Manassès, and there is one among the under-tenants
in Domesday Book. In Ireland, the name of Manus, a corruption of
Magnus, derived from the Northmen who invented it, is turned into
Manasses.

Ephraim, like other patriarchal names, lived on in Mesopotamia ;
and St. Ephrem of Edessa, who lived in the beginning of the fourth
century, is esteemed as a doctor of the Church, and is the name-saint
of numerous Russians, who keep his day on the 28th of January,
though the Roman Church marks it in July.†

SECTION VII.—*Benjamin.*

When the long-desired 'addition,' the second son, was given to
Rachel, and in the words of Jacob she " died by him when there was
but a little way to come to Ephrath," she called the infant who had
cost her life Ben-oni (son of my sorrow) ; but this was changed by
his father into Ben-Yamin (son of my right hand, *i. e.* prosperous).

In spite of Rare Ben Jonson, Benjamin is an essentially Puritan
and Jewish name ; such a feminine as Benjamina has even been
perpetrated. Oddly enough the Bretons call Benjamin Benoni.

Benoni, "the child of sorrow," and Ichabod, "the glory is departed,"
were so frequent among the Puritans of the time of James I. that Mr.
Bardsley thinks that they could not have been so much allusions
to family distress as to the afflictions of the Puritan sect. Benoni
occurs in the rate of six to one compared with Benjamin in the
registers of the period.

* Kitto's *Biblical Cyclopædia;* Trollope's *Greek Testament ;* Michaelis.
† *Proper Names of the Bible ;* Michaelis ; O'Donovan's *Irish Names.*

Afterwards the place of Ben was taken by the Syriac Bar, the earliest instance being that of old Barzillai, the Gileadite, whose name signified the son of iron.　It seems as though under the Herodean kingdom the custom was coming in that forms the first surnames, that of calling the son by his patronymic almost in preference to his own individual appellation, and thus arose some of the double titles that confuse us as to the identity of the earlier saints.　Thus, the "Israelite without guile," is first introduced as Nathanael, the same as the ancient Nethaneel, captain of the tribe of Issachar, and meaning the gift of God, being compounded of the Divine Word and nathan (a gift).　Nathan was the name of the prophet who rebuked David, and of the son whose descendants seem to have taken the place of the royal line.　Elnathan occurs as father to the wife of one of the kings, and Jonathan has exactly the same meaning, the gift of God.　In the list of apostles, Nathanael is called by his patronymic Bartholomaios, as it stands in the Greek, and Tholomaios is referred to Talmai (furrows), which occurs in the list of the sons of Anak, and also as belonging to the King of Geshur, Absalom's grandfather.

In the uncertainty whether it was really the apostle, Nathanael was left unused until those English took it up, by whom it was made into Nat.

The other form, though not popular, is of all nations, and from its unwieldy length has endless contractions, perhaps the larger number being German, since it is most common in that central Teutonic land.

English.	German.	Dutch.	Swiss.
Bartholomew	Bartholomaus	Bartelmês	Bartleme
Bart	Bertel		Bartli
Bartley	Barthol		
Bat	Mewes		
	Bartold		

Bavarian.	French.	Danish.	Spanish.
Bartlmê	Bartholomieu	Bartholomeuis	Bartolome
Bartl	Bartolomée	Bartel	Bartolo
Wawel	Tolomieu	Bardo	
Wabel			
Wabm			

Portuguese.	Italian.	Russian.	Polish.
Bartolomeu	Bartolomeo	Varfolomei	Bartlomiej
	Bortolo		Bartek
	Meo		

Illyrian.	Lusatian.	Esthonian.	Lithuanian.
Bartuo	Bartolik	Partel	Baltras
Barteo	Barto	Pert	Baltramejus
Jernij	Batram		
Vratolomije			

Section VIII.—*Job*.

We must not quit the patriarchal names without mentioning that of Job. This mysterious person is stated in the margin of the Alexandrian version to have originally borne the name of Jobab, which means shouting ; and a tradition of the Jews, adopted by some of the Christian fathers, makes him the same as the Jobab, prince of Edom, mentioned in the genealogy in the 33rd chapter of Genesis, a supposition according with his evident position as a great desert sheik, as well as with the early date of his history.

Job, however, as he is called throughout his book, is explained by some to mean persecuted ; by others a penitent ; and it is evident from a passage in the Koran that this was the way that Mahommed understood it. The tradition of his sufferings lived on among the Arabs, who have many stories about Eyub, or Ayoub, as they pronounce the name still common among them, and their nickname for the patient camel is Abi Ayub, father of Job.

Jöv, probably from their eastern connections, is a name used by the Russians, and has belonged to one of their patriarchs. Otherwise it is a very infrequent name even in England.

Job's three daughters, Jemima, Kezia, and Kerenhappuch, are explained to mean a dove, cassia, and a horn of stibium. This latter is the paint with which eastern ladies were wont to enhance the beauty of their eyelashes, and it is curious to find this little artifice so ancient and so highly esteemed as to give the very name to the fair daughter of the restored patriarch, perhaps because her eyes were too lovely to need any such adornment. Hers has never been a popular name, only being given sometimes to follow up those of her sisters ; Kezia is a good deal used in England, and belonged to a sister of Wesley, who was called Kissy ; but Jemima is by far the most general of the three.

The Hebrew interpretation of Jemima makes it a day, but the Arabic word for a dove resembles it more closely, and critics, therefore, prefer to consider it as the Arab feminine version of that which the Israelites had among them as Jonah (a dove). This belonged to the prophet of Nineveh. It is not usual in Europe, but strangely enough the Lithuanians use it as Jonsazus, and the Lapps as Jonka.

What strange fancy can have made Mehetabel, the wife of one of the princes of Edom, leave her four syllables to be popular in England ? Many village registers all over the country show it. Was it a remnant of the East in Cornwall, or did Puritans choose it for its meaning, God is beneficent ? It was at Jarrow as early as 1578.

Tamar, a palm tree, it may here be mentioned, has continued common among eastern Christians, especially since a distinguished Armenian queen was so called. Now and then very great lovers of biblical names in England give it, and likewise Dinah (judgment).*

* Smith's *Dictionary of the Bible ;* Kitto's *Biblical Cyclopædia ; Proper Names of the Bible.*

CHAPTER III.

ISRAELITE NAMES.

SECTION I.—*Moses and Aaron.*

AT the time of the Exodus, the Israelites had become a nation, and their names, though still formed from a living language, were becoming more hereditary and conventional than those of the patriarchal times. That of Moses himself, interpreted by the Scripture as meaning drawn out of the water, belongs rather to the Egyptian than to the Hebrew language. It probably came from the Coptic *mo*, water, and *usha*, saved ; though the Hebrew, *mâshâh*, also presents a ready derivation : the great Law-giver. It has never been forgotten in the East, where the Arabs in the desert point out Gebel Mousa, the rock of Moses, whence they say the water flowed, and Wady Mousa, the vale of Moses. Mousa is a frequent name among the Arabs to this day, and among the gallant Moors of Granada, none stands so prominently forward in the noble rivalry of Abencerrages and Zegris as does the champion Muza.

Moses was unused by the Jews while they continued a nation, but has been very common in their dispersion, and in Poland has come to be pronounced Mojzesz. The frequent Jewish surname Moss is taken from one of these continental corruptions of the name of the great Law-giver. In Ireland the name Magsheesh has been adopted by the inhabitants as an imitation of Moses ; but no form of Moses is used elswhere, except as a direct Scripture name.

The name of Thermuthis has been found on a tombstone, given apparently in honour of Pharaoh's daughter, whom Josephus thus denominates.

Aaron's name is in like manner considered to be Egyptian, and the meaning is very doubtful, though it is commonly explained as a high mountain.

Aaron seems to have been assumed as a name by some of our old British Christians, or else it was accepted as an equivalent for something Keltic, for Aaron and Julius were among our very few British martyrs under Diocletian's persecution, and a later Aaron was an abbot in Brittany ; but it has never been a name in use.*

The sister of Moses and Aaron, who led the songs of the Israelites when they saw their enemies dead upon the sea-shore, was the first

* *Proper Names of the Bible;* Liddell and Scott's *Greek Lexicon;* Butler's *Lives of the Saints;* Dean Stanley.

owner of that name which was to be the most highly honoured among those of women.

Yet it is a name respecting which there is great contention. Gesenius derives it from *Merî* (stubbornness), with the addition of the third person plural, so as to make it mean their rebellion. Other commentators refer it to the word *Marah* (bitterness), and thence the bitter gum, myrrh, the same term that was applied to the brackish springs in the desert, and to which the desolate widow of Bethlehem declared her right, when she cried, "Call me not Naomi (pleasant), call me Marah (bitter)." This is on the whole the most satisfactory derivation, but in the middle ages it was explained as Myrrh of the Sea, Lady of the Sea, or Star of the Sea, the likeness to the Latin, Keltic, and Teutonic *mar* being probably the guide. Star of the Sea is the favourite explanation among Roman Catholics, as the loftiest and most poetical, and it is referred to in many of their hymns and other devotional compositions.

Miriam does not seem to have been repeated until after the captivity, when it took the Greek forms of Mariam and Mariamne, and became very frequent among Jewish women, probably in the expectation of the new deliverance from the bondage that galled them like that of Egypt of old. It was the name of the Asmonean princess in whom the brave Maccabean line was extinguished by Herod the Great ; it belonged to three if not to four of the women of the Gospel ; and we find it again marking the miserable being who is cited as having fulfilled the most terrible of all the woes denounced by Moses upon the daughters of Jerusalem.

The name of Mariam continued in the East, but was very slow in creeping into the Western Church, though not only the Blessed Virgin herself had borne it, but two very popular saints, namely, the Magdalen, and the Penitent of Egypt, whose legends were both current at a very early period.

The first Maria whom I can find of undoubted western birth was a Spanish maiden, who was martyred by the Moors at Cordova in 851. Michaelis tells us that the old Spanish name of Urraca is the same as Maria, but this can hardly be true.

It seems to have been the devotion of the Crusaders that first brought Maria into Europe, for we find the first instances about the middle of the twelfth century all at once ; Maria of Antioch, a Crusader's daughter, who married the Emperor Manuel Comnenus ; her daughter, Maria Comnena, married to the Marquis of Montferrat ; Marie, the daughter of Louis VII. of France, and our Eleanor of Guienne, named probably during their Crusader's fervour ; then Marie, the translator of the Breton legends for Henry III. ; Marie, the nun daughter of Edward I., and at the same time Marie all over the western world.

Probably the addition of the German diminutive *chen*, in French *on*, formed the name of

> " A bonny fine maid of noble degree,
> Maid Marion called by name."

Very soon had her fame travelled abroad, for in 1332 the play of *Robin et Marion* was performed by the students of Angers, one of them appearing as a *fillette déguisée*. The origin of *Marionettes*, puppets disguised to play the part of Maid Marion, is thus explained. They may, however, have received their name from the habit of calling small images of the Blessed Virgin Mariettes, or Marionettes. Several streets of old Paris, in which were such images, were called Rue des Mariettes, or later, Rue des Marionettes. All puppets there came to be called Mariettes and Marmousets; and two streets of Paris were down to the last century called Rue des Marmousets. Henri Etienne says: "Never did the Egyptians take such cruel vengeance for the murder of their cats, as has been wreaked in our days on those who had mutilated some Marmouset or Marionette." Even the bauble of a licensed fool was a Marotte, from the little head at its point, and the supernatural dolls of sorcerers, in the form of toads or apes, were described as Marionettes in an account of a trial for witchcraft in 1600. The term Marmoset passed to the daintiest and most elegant of the monkey tribe, by which it is now monopolized. Marion became a common name in France, and contracted into Manon, and expanded into Marionette, as in a poem of the 13th century where Marion is thus addressed; and in Scotland, where "Maid Marion, fair as ivory bone," likewise figured in rustic pageantry, she took a stronger hold than anywhere else, is in common life yclept Menie, and has escaped her usual fate of confusion with Marianne. With us, the Blessed Virgin's name, having come through the French, was spelt in their fashion till the translation of the Bible made our national Mary familiar. Mary II. was the first of our queens who dropped the *ie*. The chief contractions and endearments are as follows :—

English.	French.	Italian.	Spanish.
Maria	Marie	Maria	Maria
Mary	Marion	Marietta	Marinha
Marion	Manon	Mariuccia	Mariquinhas
Moll	Maion		Mariquita
Molly	Mariette		Maritornes
Polly	Maillard		
Malkin	(Cambrai)		
Mawkes			
Mawkin			
May *			

Keltic.	Swedish.	Bavarian.	Swiss.
Mair (W.)	Maria	Marie	Marie
	Majken	Mariel	Mareili
Moissey		Mariedel	Maga
(Manx)		Marei	Maieli
Mari (Ir.)		Mareiel	Mija
		Marl	Mieli
		Medal	
		Miel	

* Marriott occurs in a Cornish register as a feminine in 1666.

Dutch.	Russian.	Polish.	Illyrian.
Maria	Marija	Mary	Maria
Marieke	Maika	Marysia	Marica
Mike	Mascha	Marynia	Millica
	Mashinka		

Lusatian.	Esthonian.	Lapland.	Hungarian.
Mara	Marri	Marja	Maria
Maruscha	Mai		Mari
	Maie		Marka

Our Latin Maria is a late introduction, brought in by that taste which in the last century made everything feminine end with an *a*.

It is only during the last three centuries that Maria has reigned supreme in Roman Catholic countries, marking the exaggerated devotion paid to the original. Indeed, the Italian proverb, answering to the needle in a bottle of hay, is " *Cercar Maria in Ravenna,*" so numerous are the Marias there. Even in Ireland there were few Marys till comparatively recent times ; but now the Môr that in some parts of the island was translated by Sarah, is changed into Mary.

Since Marys have been thus multiplied, the attributes of the first Mary have been adopted into the Christian name, and used to distinguish their bearer. The earliest and best of these was the Italian Maria Annunciata, or Annunziata, contracted into Nunziata ; and followed up in Spain by Maria Anonciada ; and in France, by Marie Annonciade. Soon there followed Maria Assunta, in honour of her supposed assumption bodily into glory, but this never flourished beyond Italy, Spain, and her colonies.

France has Marie des Anges, at least as a conventual appellation ; as in Spain the votaress of the merciful interceding patroness is called Maria de Mercedes ; and she whose parents were mindful of the Seven Sorrows supposed to have pierced the heart of the Holy Mother, would choose for their child Maria de Dolores. There was a legend that Santiago had seen a vision of the Blessed Virgin standing on a pillar of jasper and bidding him found at Zaragoza the church thence called Neustra Señora del Pilar, whence, in Spain at least, Pilar has become a female name, as Guadalupe has likewise in honour of a miraculous image of St. Mary, preserved in the church of the mountain once covered with hermitages. Moreover, a district in Mexico, formerly called Tlaltelolco, contained a temple to a favourite goddess of the Aztec race. After the Spanish conquest, the same site became the scene of a vision of Neustra Señora, who appeared to a Christian Indian, and intimated that a church was there to be built in her honour. As a token of the reality of the vision, roses burst forth on the bare rock of the Tepeyac, and it further appeared impressed with a miraculous painting, which has been the great subject of adoration from the Mexicans ever since.

Guadalupe, a free translation into Spanish of the native name of
Tlaltelolco, has been ever since a favourite name with the damsels of
Mexico, and is even adopted by such of the other sex as regard the
shrine with special veneration. Maria del Incarnaçion is also Spanish.
An English gipsy woman lately said ' Carnation ' was her daughter's
name, and had been her grandmother's. Was it from this source ?

As queen of heaven, Maria has votaries, called in Italy Regina or
Reina. The latter was frequent in early times at Florence. In
France we find Reine and Reinette, and Regina is a favourite in
some parts of Germany, where it has been confused with the
derivatives of the old Teutonic Ragin, Council.

Since the promulgation of the new dogma, young ladies in Spain
have been called Maria de la Concepcion ; in Italy, Concetta. Surely
the superstition of these races is recorded in their names. The custom
of adding Maria to a man's name seems to have begun in Italy about
1360, and now most individuals in Italy, and probably likewise in
Spain, as well as in the more devout French families, bear the name
of Maria ; and the old Latin Marius and Virginius, though entirely
unconnected except by the sound, have been pressed into the service,
and made to do duty as Mario and Virginio in her honour.

Perhaps the Jews had in some degree adopted the Roman fashion
of similar names in a family, since the sister of the Blessed Virgin
bears the same as her own, and there is a great similarity between
those of the sisters of Bethany, which both probably come from *mara*
(bitter), although some deduce Martha from the Aramean *mar* (a
lord), which we often hear as the title of Syrian bishops, as Mar
Elias, &c.

Even the earliest writers on the Gospels were at a loss whether to
identify the meek contemplative Mary of Bethany, by the woman
that was a sinner, who is recorded as performing the same act of
devotion, and with Mary Magdalen, once possessed by seven devils
and afterwards first witness of the Resurrection. While inquiry was
cautious, legend was bold, and threw the three into one without the
slightest doubt, going on undoubtingly to narrate the vain and sinful
career of Mary Magdalen, describing her luxury, her robes, and in
especial her embroidered gloves and flowing hair, and all the efforts
of Martha to convert her, until her final repentance. The story proceeded to relate how the whole family set out on a mission to Provence,
where Martha, by holding up the cross, demolished a terrific dragon ;
and Mary, after having aided in converting the country, retired to a
frightful desert with a skull for her only companion.

It is this legendary Magdalen, whom painters loved to portray in
all her dishevelled grief.

The word itself is believed to be a mere adjective of place, meaning
that she came from Magdala, which, in its turn, means a tower or
castle, and is represented by the little village of Mejdel, on the lake
of Tiberias, so that her proper designation would be Mary of Magdala,
i. e. of the tower, probably to distinguish her from Mary of Bethany
with whom she is confounded.

It is curious to observe how infinitely more popular her name has been than her sister's, *i. e.* accepting the mediæval belief that they *were* sisters. The Marfa of Russia is of course like the English Martha, Matty, Patty, the true housewifely Martha, independent of the legend of the dragon, and has there been a royal name occurring frequently among the daughters of the earlier Tzars; and the Martha used in Ireland is only as an equivalent for the native Erse Meabhdh, Meave, or Mab, once a great Irish princess, who has since become the queen of the fairies. Martha used also to be used for Mor. But the Marthe and Marthon of the south of France, and the rarer Marta of Italy and Spain, were all from the Provençal dragon-slayer, and as to the popularity of Magdalen, the contractions in the following table will best prove it:

English.	German.	Swiss.	Danish.
Magdalene	Magdalene	Magdalene	Magdelene
Maudlin	Madlen		Malin
Maun	Lene	Leli	Magli
Madeline	Lenchen		Mali

Italian.	French.	Polish.	Servian.
Maddalena	Magdelaine	Magdelina	Mandelina
	Mazaline—*old*	Magdusia	Manda
Spanish.	Madeleine	Magdosia	
Magdalena	Madelon	Madde	
Madelena			

Lusatian.	Esthonian.	Ung.	Lettish.
Madlena	Madli	Magdalena	Madlene
Marlena	Mai	Magdolna	Maddalene
Marlenka	Male		Madde
Madlenka			

The penitent Mary of Egypt has had her special votaresses. Maria Egyptiaca was a princess of Oettingen in 1666.*

Section II.—*Elisheba, &c.*

The names of the wife and son of Aaron bring us to a style of nomenclature that was very frequent among the Israelites at the period of the Exodus, and had begun even earlier. This was the habit of making the name contain a dedication to the Deity, by beginning or ending it with a word of Divine signification.

The Divine title known to man before the special revelation to

* Smith's *Dictionary of the Bible;* Michaelis; Jameson's *Legends of the Madonna; Sacred and Legendary Art; Romancero del Cid;* Warton's *History of Poetry;* Grimm, *Deutsche Mythologie;* O'Donovan, *On Irish Names; Festivals and their Household Words; Christian Remembrancer;* Mme. Calderon de la Borca, *Mexico.*

Moses in the burning bush, was the Hebrew word El, in the plural Elohim, which corresponds to our term Deity or God-head. It was by a derivative from this word that Jacob called the spot where he beheld the angels, Beth El (the House of God), and again the place where he built an altar, El Elohe Israel (the God of Israel), as indeed his own name of Israel meant prevailing with God.

This termination is to be found in the names of several of his grandsons; but we will only in the present section review the class of names where it serves as a prefix.

The first of all of these is Eliezer (God of help), the name of Abraham's steward who went to bring home Rebecca, and again of the second son of Moses. A very slight change, indicated in our version by the change of the vowels, made it Eleazar, or God will help, the name of Aaron's eldest surviving son, the second high priest. Both continued frequent among the Jews before the captivity, and after it the distinction between them was not observed, though Eleazar was in high repute as having belonged to the venerable martyr in the Antiochian persecution, as well as to the brave Maccabee, who perished under the weight of the elephant he had stabbed.

In the Gospels, Eleazar has become Lazarus, and in this form is bestowed upon the beggar of the parable, as well as on him who was raised from the dead. It is curious to observe the countries where it has been in use. The true old form once comes to light in the earlier middle age as St. Elzéar, the Comte de St. Sabran, who became a devotee of St. Francis, and has had a scanty supply of local namesakes. The beggar's name has been frequently adopted in Spain as Lazaro or Lazarillo; Italy has many a Lazzaro; Poland, shows Lazarz; Russia, Lasar; Illyria, Lazo and Laze.

Aaron's wife was Elischeba, meaning God hath sworn, i. e. an appeal to his covenant. It recurred again in the priestly family in the Gospel period, and had become, in its Greek form, Ελισαβετ; in Latin, Elisabeth.

The mother of the Baptist was not canonized in the West, though, I believe, she was so in the East, for there arose her first historical namesake, the Muscovite princess Elisavetta, the daughter of Jaroslav, and the object of the romantic love of that splendid poet and seaking, Harald Hardràda, of Norway, who sung nineteen songs of his own composition in her praise on his way to her from Constantinople, and won her hand by feats of prowess. Although she soon died, her name remained in the northern peninsula, and figures in many a popular tale and Danish ballad, as Elsebin, Lisbet, or Helsa. It was the Slavonic nations, however, who first brought it into use, and from them it crept into Germany, and thence to the Low Countries.

Elisabeth of Hainault, on her marriage with Philippe Auguste, seems to have been the first to suffer the transmutation into Isabelle, the French being the nation of all others who delighted to bring everything into conformity with their own pronunciation. The royal name thus introduced became popular among the crown vassals, and Isabelle of Angoulême, betrothed to Hugues de Lusignan, but married to King John, brought Isabel to England, whence her daughter, the wife of Friedrich II., conveyed Isabella to Germany and Sicily. Meantime the lovely character of Elisabeth of Hungary—or Erzsebet as she is called in her native country—earned saintly honours, and caused the genuine form to be extremely popular in all parts of Germany. Her namesake great-niece was, however, in Aragon turned into Isabel, and when married into Portugal, received the surname of De la Paz, because of her gentle, peace-making nature. She was canonized ; and Isabel, or Ysabel, as it is now the fashion to spell it in Spain, has ever since been the chief feminine royal name in the Peninsula, and was rendered especially glorious and beloved by Isabel the Catholic.

In the French royal family it was much used during the middle ages, and sent us no fewer than two specimens, namely, the 'She-Wolf of France,' and the child-queen of Richard II. ; but though used by the Plantagenets and their nobility, it took no hold of the English taste ; and it was only across the Scottish border that Isobel or Isbel, probably learned from French allies, became popular, insomuch that its contraction, Tibbie, has been from time immemorial one of the commonest of all peasant names in the Lowlands. The wicked and selfish wife of Charles VI. of France was always called Isabeau, probably from some forgotten Bavarian contraction ; but she brought her appellation into disrepute, and it has since her time become much more infrequent in France.

The fine old English ballad that makes 'pretty Bessee' the grand-daughter of Simon de Montfort is premature in its nomenclature ; for the first Bess on record is Elizabeth Woodville, whose mother, Jacquetta of Luxemburg, no doubt imported it from Flanders. Shakespeare always makes Edward IV. call her Bess ; and her daughter Elizabeth of York is the lady Bessee of the curious verses recording the political courtship of Henry of Richmond. Thence came the name of Good Queen Bess, the most popular and homely of all borne by English women, so that, while in the last century a third at least of the court damsels were addressed as 'Lady Betty,' it so abounded in villages that the old riddle arose out of the contractions.

During the anti-Spanish alliance between England and France, Edward VI. was sponsor to a child of Henri II., who received the Tudor name of Elisabeth, but could not become the wife of Philip II., without turning into Isabel ; indeed, the Italian Elisabetta Farnese—a determined personage—was the only lady who seems to have avoided this transformation.

Poetry did not improve our Queen Elizabeth by making her into Eliza, a form which, however, became so prevalent in England during the early part of the present century, that Eliza and Elizabeth are sometimes to be found in the same family. No name has so many varieties of contraction, as will be seen by the ensuing list, where, in deference to modern usage, Elizabeth is placed separately from Isabella.

English.	Scotch.	German.	Bavarian.	Swiss.
Elizabeth	Elizabeth	Elisabeth		Elsbeth
Eliza	Elspeth	Elise		Betha
Bessy	Elspie	Lise	Lisi	Bebba
Betsey	Bessie	Lischen	Liserl	Bebbeli
Betty	Lizzie	Elsabet		Liserli
Lizzy		Elsbet		
Libby		Elsabe		
Lisa		Bettine		
		Bette		
		Ilse		

Danish.	French.	Italian.	Russian.	Polish.
Elisabeth	Elisabeth	Elisabetta	Jelissaveta	Elzbieta
Elsebin	Elise	Elisa	Lisa	Elzbietka
Helsa	Babet	Betta	Lisenka	
	Babette	Bettina		
	Babichon	Lisettina		

Servian.	Slovak.	Esthonian.	Hungarian.	Lusatian.
Jelisaveta	Lizbeta	Ello	Erzebet	Hilzbeta
Jelisavka	Liza	Elts	Erzsi	Hilza
Liza	Lizika	Liso	Erszok	Hilzizka
			Orse	Lisa
			Orsike	Liska
				Beta

Lise and Lisette are sometimes taken as contractions of Elisabeth, but they properly belong to Louise.

English.	Scotch.	French.	Spanish.	Portuguese.
Isabella	Isabel	Isabeau	Ysabel	Isabel
Isabel	Isbel	Isabelle	Bela	Isabelhina
Belle	Tibbie			
Nib				
Ibbot				
Ib				

Scotland and Spain are the countries of Isabel; England and Germany of Elizabeth.

The noblest prophet of the kingdom of Israel was called by two Hebrew words, meaning God the Lord, a sound most like what is represented by the letters Eliyahu, the same in effect as that of the young man who reproved Job and his friends, though, in his case, the Hebrew points have led to his being called in our Bible Elihu, while we know the prophet as Elijah, the translators probably intending us to pronounce the *j* like an *i*. The Greek translators had long before formed ʼΗλιας, the Elias of the New Testament.

When the Empress Helena visited Palestine, she built a church on Mount Carmel, around which arose a cluster of hermitages, and thus the great prophet and his miracles became known both to East and West.

When the Crusaders visited the Mount of Carmel frowning above Acre, and beheld the church and the hermits around it, marked the spot where the great prophet had prayed, and the brook where he slew the idolaters, no wonder they became devoted to his name, and Helie became very frequent, especially among the Normans. Helie de la Flèche was the protector of Duke Robert's young son, William Clito ; and Helie and Elie were long in use in France, as Ellis must once have been in England, to judge by the surnames it has left. Elias is still very common in the Netherlands.

The order of Carmelites claimed to have been founded by the prophet himself ; but when the Latins inundated Palestine, it first came into notice, and became known all over the West. It was placed under the invocation of St. Mary, who was thus called in Italy the Madonna di Carmela or di Carmine, and, in consequence, the two names of Carmela and Carmine took root among the Italian ladies, by whom they are still used. The meaning of Carmel, as applied to the mountain, is vineyard or fruitful field.

Elisha's name meant God of Salvation. It becomes Eliseus in the New Testament, but has been very seldom repeated ; though it is possible that the frequent Ellis of the middle ages may spring from it.

Here, too, it may be best to mention the prophetic name by which the Humanity of the Messiah was revealed to Isaiah—Immanuel (God with us), *Imm* meaning with ; *an* being the pronoun.

The Greeks appear to have been the first to take up this as a Christian name, and Manuel Komnenos made it known in Europe. The Italians probably caught it from them as Manovello ; and the Spaniards and Portuguese were much addicted to giving it, especially after the reign of Dom Manoel, one of the best of the noble house of Avis. Manuelita is a feminine in use in the Peninsula. When used as a masculine, as it is occasionally in England and France, the first letter is generally changed to *E*.*

Section IV.—*Joshua, &c.*

A still more sacred personal Divine Name was revealed to Moses upon Mount Horeb—the name that proclaimed the eternal self-exist-ence of Him who gave the mission to the oppressed Israelites.

The meaning of that Name we know, in its simple and ineffable majesty ; the pronunciation we do not know, for the most learned doubt whether that the usual substitute for it may not be a mistake. The Jews themselves feared to pronounce it commonly in reading their scriptures, and substituted for it Adonai, that which is indicated by the 'LORD,' in capital letters in our Bibles, while the French try

* *Proper Names of the Bible;* Michaelis ; Grimm, *Deutscha Mythologie.*

to give something of the original import by using the word *l'Éternel*, and thus the tradition of the true sound has been hidden from man, and all that is known is that the three consonants employed in it were J, or rather Y V H.

Yet, though this holy name was only indicated in reading, it was very frequent in combination in the names of the Israelites, being the commencement of almost all those that with us begin with *je* or *jo*, the termination of all those with *iah*. Nay, the use of the name in this manner has received the highest sanction, since it was by inspiration that Moses added to Hoshea, salvation—the syllable that made it Jehoshea or Joshua, "the Lord my salvation," fitly marking out the warrior, who, by Divine assistance, should save Israel, and place them safely in the promised land.

That name of the captain of the salvation of Israel seems to have been untouched again till the return from the captivity, when probably some unconscious inspiration directed it to be given to the restorer of the Jews, that typical personage, the high priest, in whom we find it altered into Jeshua ; and the Greek soon made it into the form in which it appears as belonging to the author of the book of Ecclesiasticus, and which, when owned by the apostate high priest, under Antiochus Epiphanes, was made by him from Jesus into Jason, to suit the taste of the Greek rulers. It had become common among the Jews ; it was the current name for the ancient Joshua, when it was assumed by Him Who alone had a right to it.

A feast in honour of that Name "to which every knee shall bow," has been marked by the Western Church, and it is probably in consequence of this that the Spanish Americans actually have adopted this as one of their Christian names—a profanation whence all the rest of Christendom has shrunk. There too *a* and *ita* are added to it to make it feminine.

In the unfortunate son and grandson of the good Josiah (yielded to the Lord), we see some curious changes of name. The son was called both Eliakim and Jehoiakim, in which the verb meant "will establish or judge ;" the only difference was in the Divine Name that preceded it. This miserable prince died during the first siege of Jerusalem, and his son Jehoiachin (appointed of the Lord), reigned for three months till the city was taken, and he was carried away to Babylon. The above-mentioned seems to have been his proper name, but he was commonly called Jeconiah, and Jeremiah denounces his punishment without the prefix, as "this man Coniah."

After the death of Nebuchadnezzar, Jehoiachin was brought out of prison, and lived in some degree of ease and favour at Babylon ; and by Greek authors a sort of compromise was made between his name and his father's, and he becomes sometimes Jeconias, and sometimes Joacim.

There was an early tradition that Joachim had been the name of the father of the Blessed Virgin, but her private history did not assume any great prominence till about 1500, and in consequence the names of her parents are far less often used before than after that era. Her mother's name, as we shall see, had a history of its own ; and was earlier in general use than that of her father, which scarcely came into England at all, and was better known to us when Murat ascended the throne of Naples than at any other time. Being however found in the apocryphal Gospels, it was in use in the Greek Church, and is therefore to be found in Russia. Its forms are,

German.	Bavarian.	Frisjan.	Swiss.
Joachim	Jochum	Hime	Jocheli
Jochim	Jochem		
Achim			
Chim			

Spanish.	French.	Italian.	Danish.
Joaquim	Joachim	Gioachimo	Joachim
Joquim		Gioachino	Johum
Joa		Giovachino	

Russian.	Polish.	Lett.	Illyrian.
Joachim	Jachym	Jukkums	Jacim
Akim		Juzziz	Accim

The Germans, French, and Portuguese have the feminine Joachime, Joaquima; or, in Illyrian, Acima.*

The Book of Judges has not furnished many names to collective Europe. Caleb, the faithful spy, who alone finally accompanied Joshua into the Land of Promise out of all the 600,000 who had come out of Egypt, had a name meaning a dog, seldom copied except by the Puritan taste, and only meeting in one language a personal name of similar signification, namely, the Irish *cu* (gen.) *con.*

Caleb's daughter, Achsah, probably from the shortness and pretty sound of her name, which means a tinkling ornament for the ancle, has a good many namesakes in remote village schools, where it is apt to be spelt Axah. Tirzah (pleasantness) was one of those five daughters of Zelophehad, whose heiress-ship occupies two chapters of the Book of Numbers. She probably was the origin of Thirza, the name of Abel's wife in Gessner's idyll of the *Death of Abel,* a great favourite among the lower classes in England, whence Thyrza has become rather a favourite in English cottages.

Gideon (a feller or destroyer) seems by his martial exploits to have obtained some admirers among the Huguenots of the civil wars of France, for Gédéon was in some small use among them.

The name of the mighty Nazarene, whose strength was in his hair, is not clearly explained. Schimschon seems best to represent the Hebrew sound, but the Greek had made it Σαμψων ; and our trans-

* Dr. Pusey's *Commentary on the Prophets;* Kitto's *Biblical Dictionary;* Jameson's *Legends of the Madonna;* Michaelis.

lation, Samson. Some translate it splendid son, others as the diminutive of sun.

The Greek Church and her British daughter did not forget the mighty man of valour, and Samson was an early Welsh Bishop and saint, from whom this became a monastic appellation, as in the instance of Mr. Carlyle's favourite Abbot Samson. The French still call it Simson, which is perhaps more like the original; and our Simpson and Simkins may thus be derived from it, when they do not come from Simon, which was much more frequent.

The name of the gentle and faithful Ruth has never been satisfactorily explained. Some make it mean trembling; others derive it from a word meaning to join together; and others from Reûth (beauty), which is perhaps the best account of it. In spite of the touching sweetness of her history, Ruth's name has never been in vogue, except under the influence of our English version of the Bible.

Perhaps this may be the fittest place to mention the prevalence of names taken from the river Jordan during the period of pilgrimages. The Jordan itself is named from Jared (to descend), and perhaps no river does descend more rapidly throughout its entire course than does this most noted stream, from its rise in the range of Libanus to its fall in the Dead Sea, the lowest water in the world. To bathe in the Jordan was one of the objects of pilgrims, and flasks of its water were brought home to be used at baptisms—as was done for the present family of Royal children. It was probably this custom that led to the adoption of Jordan as a baptismal name, and it is to be supposed that it was a fashion of the Normans, since it certainly prevailed in countries that they had occupied. In Calabria, Count Giordano Lancia was the friend of the unfortunate Manfred of Sicily, and recognized his corpse. Jourdain was used in France, though in what districts I do not know, and Jordan was at one time recognized in England. Jordan de Thornhill died in 1200; Jordan de Dalden was at the battle of Lewes in 1264, and two namesakes of his are menitoned in the pedigree of his family. Jordan de Exeter was the founder of a family in Connaught, who became so thoroughly Hibernicized, that, after a few generations, they adopted the surname of, Mac Jordan. Galileo dei Gaililei probably took both his names from Galilee, which comes from *Galil*, a circle.

Bethlem Gabor will seem to the mind as an instance of Bethlehem (the place of bread), having furnished Christian names for the sake of its associations, and Nazarene has also been used in Germany.

SECTION V.—*Names from Chaanach.*

Perhaps no word has given rise to a more curious class of derivatives than this from the Hebrew Chaanach, with the aspirate at each end, signifying favour, or mercy, or grace.

To us it first becomes known in the form of Hannah, the mother of Samuel, and it was also used with the Divine syllable in the masculine, as Hananeel, Hanani, Hananiah, or Jehohanan, shortened into Johanan.

Exactly the same names were current among the Phœnicians, only we have received them through a Greek or Latin medium. Anna, the companion sister of Dido, was no doubt Hannah, and becoming known to the Romans through the worship paid to her and Elisa by the Carthaginians, was, from similarity of sound, confused by them with their Italian goddess, Anna Perenna, the presiding deity of the circling year (*Annus*). Virgil, by-and-by, wove the traditions of the foundation of Carthage, and the death of Dido, into the adventures of Æneas ; and a further fancy arose among the Romans that after the self-destruction of Dido, Anna had actually pursued the faithless Trojan to Italy, and there drowned herself in the river Numicius, where she became a presiding nymph as Anna Perenna ! A fine instance of the Romans' habit of spoiling their own mythology and that of every one else ! Oddly enough, an Anna has arisen in Ireland by somewhat the same process. The river Liffey is there said to owe its name to Lifé, the daughter of the chief of the Firbolg race being there drowned. In Erse, the word for river was Amhain, the same as our Avon ; but on English tongues Amhain Lifé became Anna Liffey, and was supposed to be the lady's name ; another version declared that it was Lifé, the horse of Heremon the Milesian, who there perished.

Hanno, so often occurring in the Punic wars, was another version of the Hebrew Hanan, and the far-famed Hannibal himself answered exactly to the Hananiah or Johanan of the Holy Land, saying that it was the grace of Baal that unhappily he besought by his very appellation. The Greeks called him Annibas, and the Romans wavered between Annibal and Hannibal as the designation of their great enemy. In the latter times of Rome, when the hereditary prænomina were discarded, Annibal and Annibalianus were given among the grand sounds that mocked their feeble wearers, and Annibale lingered on in Italy, so as to be known to us in the person of Annibale Caracci.

It is a more curious fact, however, that Hannibal has always been a favourite with the peasantry of Cornwall. From the first dawn of parish registers Hannyball is of constant occurrence, much too early, even in that intelligent county, to be a mere gleaning from books ; and the west country surname of Honeyball must surely be from the same source. A few other eastern names, though none of them as frequent or as clearly traced as the present, have remained in use in this remote county, and ought to be allowed due weight in favour of the supposed influence of the Phœnician traders over the races that supplied them with tin and lead.

The usual changes were at work upon the Jewish names Hannah and Hananiah. Greek had made the first 'Anna, the second Ananias, or Annas. Indeed Hannah is only known, as such, to the readers of the English version of the Bible, from whom the Irish have taken it to represent their native Ainè (joy). All the rest of Europe calls her, as well as the aged prophetess in the temple, Anne.

The apocryphal Gospels which gave an account of the childhood of the Blessed Virgin, called her mother Anna, though from what tradition is not known. St. Anna was a favourite with the Byzantines from very early times; the Emperor Justinian built a church to her in 550, and in 710 her relics were there enshrined. From that time forward Greek damsels, and all those of the adjoining nations who looked to Constantinople as their head, were apt to be christened Anna. In 988, a daughter of the Emperor Basil married and converted Vladimir, Grand Prince of Muscovy, whence date all the numerous Russian Annas, with their pretty changes of endearment. The grand-daughter of this lady, Anne of Muscovy, sister of Harald Hardrada's Elisif, carried her name to France, where it grew and flourished.

St. Anne became the patron saint of Prague, where a prodigious festival is yearly holden in her honour, and great are the rejoicings of all the females who bear her name, and who are not a few. It was from Prague that the Bohemian princess, Anne of Luxemburg, brought it to England, and gave it to her name-child, Anne Mortimer, by whom it was carried to the house of York, then to the Howards, from them to Anne Boleyn, and thereby became an almost party word in England.

Abroad it had a fresh access of popularity from a supposed appearance of the saint to two children at Auray, in Brittany, and not only was the Bretonne heiress, twice Queen of France, so named, but she transferred the name to her god-sons, among whom the most notable was the fierce Constable, Anne de Montmorency. Her Italian goddaughter, Anna d'Este, brought it back to the House of Guise, and shortly after a decree from Rome, in 1584, made the name more popular still by rendering the feast obligatory, and thenceforth arose the fashion of giving the names of the Blessed Virgin and her mother in combination, as Anne Marie, or Marianne. This is usually the source of the Marianne, Mariana, or Manna, so often found on the continent; in England, Marianne is generally only a corruption of Marion, and Anna Maria is in imitation of the Italian.

Hardly susceptible of abbreviation, no name has undergone more varieties of endearment, some forms almost being treated like independent names, such as the Annot of Scotland, an imitation of the French Annette, showing the old connection between France and Scotland; and in the present day, there has arisen a fashion of christening Annie, probably from some confusion as to the spelling of Ann or Anne.

All these Annes can distinctly be traced from the Byzantine devotion to the mother of the Blessed Virgin spreading westwards, and at Rome magnified by Mariolatry. There are however what seem like forms of Anne in the West before the adoption of the name from Russia and Bohemia. Welsh Angharawd (far from shame), which is treated as Anne's equivalent. The Scottish Annaple and Annabella are likewise too early to come from St. Anne, and are probably either from Ainè (joy), a favourite name in early Gaelic times, or from the Teutonic Arnhilda—Eagle heroine.

Annabella by no means is to be explained to mean fair Anna, as is generally supposed. *Bellus* did, indeed, signify handsome in Latin, and became the *beau* and *belle* of French, but the habit of putting it

English.	Scotch.	French.	Spanish.	Italian.
Hannah	Hannah	Anne	Ana	Anna
Anna		Annette	Anita	Annica
Anne	Anne	Nanette		Nanna
Nan	Nannie	Nanon		Ninetta
Nancy	Annot	Ninon		
Nanny		Ninette		
		Nichon		
		Nillon		

German.	Dutch.	Danish.	Swiss.	Bavarian.
Anne	Anna	Anna	Anne	Anne
Annchen	Antje	Annika	Annali	Annerl
	Naatje		Nann	Nannerl
	Annechet		Nanneli	

Bohemian.	Russian.	Servian.	Lusatian.	Lett.
Ana	Anna	Anna	Anna	Anne
Ancika	Anninka	Annuschka	Hanna	Annusche
Anca	Anjuska	Aneta	Hanzyzka	
	Anjutka	Anica	Hancicka	
	Annuschka	Anicsika		
		Anka		

Lithuanian.		Hungarian.		Polish.
Ane	Annze	Anna	Panni	Anna
Anikke		Nani	Panna	Anusia

at the end of a name, by way of ornament, was not invented till the late period of seven-leagued names of literature. Annys, or Anisia, is a separate name with a saint in the Greek calendar, and was used in England from the Norman Conquest down at least to 1690. Mr. Bardsley thinks, however, that this was really Agnes; and certainly the unfortunate Scotchwoman, who was supposed to have raised the tempest before the wedding of James VI., is called indifferently Agnes or Annis Simpson.

'Ιώαννα, or 'Ιαννης, for the masculine, 'Ιώαννα for the feminine, were already frequent among the natives of Judea, though they appear not to have been used in the family of Zacharias when he was commanded so to call his son.

The Evangelist who was surnamed Mark, and Joanna the wife of Herod's steward, both had received their names independently, and thus Joannes became a most universal baptismal name, given from the first in the East and at Rome. There were many noted bishops so called in the fourth century, the earliest time when men began to be baptized in memory of departed saints, rather than by the old Roman names. The first whose name is preserved is Joannes of Egypt, one of the hermits of the Thebaïd; the next is the great deacon of Antioch, and patron of Constantinople, Joannes Chrysostomos (John of the golden mouth), whose Greek surname, given him for his eloquence, has caused him to be best known as St. Chrysostom, and has perpetuated in Italy, Grisostomo; in Spain, Crisostomo; whilst the Slavonian nations translate the name and make it Zlatoust.

At Constantinople, the partiarch St. Joannes the Silent, at Rome, the martyr Pope St. Johannes I., at Alexandria, the beneficent patriarch St. Joannes the Almoner, all renewed the popularity of their name. The last mentioned was originally the patron of the order of Hospitallers, though when these Franks were living at enmity to the Greek Church, they discarded him in favour of the Baptist. Each of the two Scriptural saints had two holidays,—the Baptist on the day of his nativity, and of his decollation; the Evangelist, on the 27th of December, as well as on the 6th of May, in remembrance of his confession in the cauldron of boiling oil.

Thus the festivals were so numerous that children had an extra chance of the name, which the Italians called Giovanni, or for short, Vanni; and the French, Jehan.

It was still so infrequent at the time of the Norman Conquest, that among the under-tenants in Domesday Book, to 68 Williams, 48 Roberts, and 28 Walters, there are only 10 Johns, but it was flourishing in the Eastern Church, where one of the Komneni was called, some say from his beauty, others from the reverse, Kaloioannes, or handsome John, a form which was adopted bodily by his descendants, the Komneni of Trebizond.

It had come into Ireland at first as Maol-Eoin (shaveling, or disciple of John), the Baptist sharing with St. Patrick the patronage of the island; but Shawn or Seoln soon prevailed in Ireland, as did Ian in Scotland; but not till the Crusades did French or English adopt it to any great extent, or the English begin to Anglicize it in general by contracting the word and writing it John.

The misfortunes of the English Lackland and of the French captive of Poictiers caused a superstition that theirs was an ill-omened royal name, and when John Stuart came to the Scottish throne, he termed himself Robert III., without, however, averting the doom of his still more unhappy surname. It did not fare amiss with any Castilian Juan or Portuguese João; and in Bohemia a new saint arose called Johanko von Nepomuk, the Empress's confessor, who was thrown from the bridge of Prague by the insane Emperor Wenzel for refusing to betray her secrets.

As St. Nepomucene, he had a few local namesakes, who get called Mukki or Mukkel. The original word is said to mean helpless.

Double names, perhaps, originated in the desire to indicate the individual patron, where there were many saints of similar name, and thus the votaries of the Baptist were christened Gian Battista, or Jean Baptiste, but only called by the second Greek title—most common in Italy—least so in England.

English.	French.	Spanish.	Italian.	Swiss.	Polish.
Baptist	Baptiste Batiste	Bautista	Battista	Bisch Bischli	Baptysta

The Illyrians, using the word for christianizing instead of that for baptizing, make the namesakes of the Baptist Kerstiteli.

It was probably in honour of St. John the Evangelist's guardian-ship of the Blessed Virgin that her name became commonly joined with his. Giovanni Maria Visconti of Milan, appears in the fifth century, and Juan Maria and Jean Marie soon followed in Spain and France.

Johann was the correct German form, usually contracted into Hans; and it was the same in Sweden, where Johann I., in 1483, was known as King Hans; and in Norway, Hans and Jens, though both abbreviations of Johan, are used as distinct names, and have formed the patronymics, Hanson and Jensen, the first of which has become an English surname. Ivan the Terrible, Tzar of Muscovy, was the first prince there so called, though the name is frequent among all ranks, and the sons and daughters are called Ivanovitch and Ivanovna.

Rare as patronymic surnames are in France, this universal name has there produced Johannot, while the contraction is Jeannot, answering to the Spanish Juanito and the patronymic Juanez. Jan is very frequent in Brittany, where the diminutive is Jannik.

Jock is the recognized Scottish abbreviation, and it would seem to have been the older English one according to the warning to Jockey of Norfolk, at Bosworth. Jack sounds much as if the French Jacques had been his true parent; but "sweet Jack Falstaff, old Jack Falstaff" has made it alienable from John.

Though Joanna was a holy woman of the Gospel, her name did not come into favour so early as the male form, and it is likely that it was adopted rather in honour of one of the St. Johns than of herself, since she is not canonized; and to the thirty feasts of the St. Johns, in the Roman calendar, there are only two in honour of Joannas, and these very late ones, when the name was rather slipping out of fashion. Its use seems to have begun all at once, in the twelfth century, in the south of France and Navarre, whence ladies called Juana in Spanish, Jehanne or Jeanne in France, came forth, and married into all the royal families of the time. Our first princess so called was daughter to Henry II., and married into Sicily ; and almost every king had a daughter Joan, or Jhone, as they preferred spelling it. Joan Make-peace was the name given to the daughter of Edward II., when the long war with the Bruces was partly pacified by her marriage ; and Joan Beaufort was the maiden romantically beloved by the captive James I. The Scots, however, usually called the name Jean, and adopted Janet from the French Jeanette, like Annot from Annette.

The various forms and contractions are infinite :—

English.	Scotch.	Welsh.	Breton.	Gaelic.	Erse.	German.	Danish.	Dutch.
John	John	Jan	Jan	Ian	Shawn	Johannes	Johan	Jan
Johnny	Johnnie	Jenkin	Jannik		Eoin	Hans	Janne	Jantje
Jack	Jock					Hanschen	Jens	
Jenkin							Hans	
							Jantje	

Belgian.	Bavarian.	Swiss.	French.	Spanish.	Portuguese.	Italian.	Modern Greek.	Russian.
Jehan	Johan	Johan	Jean	Juan	Joao	Giovanni	Ιωάννης	Ivan
Jan	Hansl	Han	Jeanno	Juanito	Joaminho	Gianni	Jannes	Vanja
Hannes		Hansli	Jehan—*old*		Joanico	Gian	Giannes	Vanka
Hanneken		Hasli			Joaozinho	Giovanoli	Giankos	Ivanjuschka
Hanka						Giammino	Giannakes	Vanjuschka
						Vanni	Joannoulos	Vanjucha
						Nanni	Nannos	
						Gianozzo		

Polish.	Bohemian.	Slavonic.	Illyrian.	Lett.	Lithuanian.	Esthonian.	Hungarian.	Lapp.
Jan	Jan	Jovan	Jovan	Janis	Jonas	Johan	Janos	Jofan
Janek		Ivan	Jovica	Janke	Ancas	Hannus	Jani	Jofa
		Janez	Jvo	Ans	Jonkus	Ants		
			Jveica	Ansis	Jonkuttis			
			Jvic		Enselis			
					Enskis			

Jessie, though now a separate name, is said to be short for Janet. Queen Joans have been more uniformly unfortunate than their male counterparts. Twice did a Giovanna reign in Naples in disgrace and misery ; and the royalty of poor Juana la Loca in Castille was but one long melancholy madness. There have, however, been two heroines, so called, Jeanne of Flanders, or Jannedik la Flamm, as the Bretons call her, the heroine of Henbonne, and the much more noble Jeanne la Pucelle of Orleans. The two saints were Jeanne de Valois, daughter of Louis XI., and discarded wife of Louis XII., and foundress of the Annonciades, and Jeanne Françoise de Chantel, the disciple of St. François de Sales.

Johanna is a favourite with the German peasantry, and is contracted into Hanne. It was not till the Tudor period, as Camden states, that Jane came into use ; when Jane Seymour at once rendered it so fashionable that it became the courtly title ; and Joan had already in Shakespeare's time descended to the cottage and kitchen.

English.	Scotch.	German.	Dutch.	French.
Johanna	Joanna	Johanna	Jantina	Jehanne
Joanna	Jean	Hanne	Janotje	Jeanne
Joan	Jeanie		Jantje	Jeannette
Jane	Jenny			Jeannetton
Jone	Janet			
Jenny	Jessie			
Janet	Gael.			
Janetta	Seonaid			

Spanish.	Portuguese.	Italian.	Russian.	Polish.
Juana	Jovanna	Giovanna	Ivanna	Joanna
Juanita	Johannina	Giovannina	Zaneta	Hanusia
			Anniuscka	Anusia

Slovak.	Illyrian.	Bulgarian.	Lusatian.	
Jovana	Ivana	Ivanku	Hanka	
Janesika	Jovana			
Ivancica	Jovka			
	Ivka			

Section VI.—*David.*

" The man after God's own heart " was well named from the verb to love, David, still called Daood in the East. It was Δαυιδ in the Septuagint ; Δαβιδ and Δαυειδ in the New Testament ; and the Vulgate made it the name well known to us.

The Eastern Church, in which the ancient Scriptural names were in greater honour than in the West, seems to have adopted David among her names long before it was revived among the Jews, who never seem to have used it since the days of their dispersion. It has always been common among the Armenians and Georgians. Daveed is frequent in Russia, in honour of a saint, who has his feast on the 29th of July ; and in Slavonic it is shortened into Dako ; in Esthonia it is Taved ; in Lusatia, Dabko.

The influence of eastern Christianity is traceable in the adoption of David in the Keltic Church. Early in the 6th century, a Welshman of princely birth (like almost all Welsh saints), by name David, or Dawfydd, lived in such sanctity at his bishopric of Menevia, that it has ever since been known as St. David's, the principal Welsh see having been there transplanted from Caerleon in his time. Dewi was the vernacular alteration of his name, and the Church of Llan Dewi Brevi commemorates a synod held by him against the Pelagians. Dafod, or Devi, thus grew popular in Wales, and when ap Devi ceased to be the distinction of the sons of David—Davy, Davis, and Davies became the surname, Taffy the contraction, and Taffline or Vida the feminine. The Keltic bishop was revered likewise in Scotland, and his name was conferred upon the third son of Malcolm Ceanmohr, the best sovereign whom Scotland ever possessed, and whom she deservedly canonized, although his Protestant descendant James VI. called him "a sore saint to the crown," because of his large donations of land to the clergy—at that time the only orderly subjects in the country. Affection and honour for the royal saint filled the Lowlands with Davids, and this has continued a distinctively Scottish name.

The Anglicizing Irish took David as the synonym of Dathi (far darting) ; and Diarmaid (a freeman) ; and the Danes made it serve for Dagfinn (day white).*

SECTION VII.—*Salem*.

It is remarkable to observe how the longing for peace is expressed in the names of almost every nation. The warlike Roman may be an exception, but the Greek had his Eireneos ; the German, his Friedrich ; the Kelt, his Simaith ; the Slave, his Lubomirski ; testifying that even in the midst of war, there was a longing after peace and rest ! And, above all, would this be the case with the Hebrew, to whom sitting safely and at peace, beneath his own vine and his own fig-tree, was the summit of earthly content.

Schalem (peace) ! By the Prophet-King it was bestowed upon the two sons to whom he looked for the continuance of his throne, and the continuance of the promises of ' peace,'—Absalom (father of peace), and afterwards with a truer presage, Salomo, or Solomon, (the peaceful) !

Long before his time, however, Welsh and Breton saints had been called Solomon, as well as one early Armorican prince ; and likewise an idiot boy, who lived under a tree at Auray, only quitting it when in want of food, to wander through the villages muttering "Salaum hungry"—the only words, except *Ave Maria*, that he could pronounce.

* *Proper Names of the Bible ;* Rees, *Welsh Saints ;* Jones, *Welsh Sketches ;* O'Donovan, *Irish Names ; Seven Champions of Christendom.*

When he died, the neighbours, thinking him as soulless as a dog, buried him under his tree; but, according to the legend, their contempt was rebuked by a beauteous lily springing from his grave, and bearing on every leaf the words *Ave Maria.* Certain it is that an exquisite church was there erected, containing the shrine of Salaun the Simple, who thus became a popular saint of Brittany, ensuring tender reverence for those who, if mindless, were likewise sinless, and obtaining a few namesakes.

Salomon and Salomone are the French and Italian forms; and Solomon is so frequent among the Jews as to have become a surname.

Russia and Poland both use it, and have given it the feminines, Ssolominija and Salomea; but Schalem had already formed a true feminine name of its own, well known in Arabic literature as Suleima, Selma, or Selima.

But returning to the high associations whence the names of Christians should take their source, we find Salome honoured indeed as one of the women first at the sepulchre; and it is surprising that thus recommended, her name should not have been more frequent. It sometimes does occur in England, and Salomée is known in France; but it is nowhere really popular except in Switzerland, where, oddly enough, Salomeli is the form for the unmarried, and Salome is restricted to the wife.

In Denmark, similarity of sound led Solomon to be chosen as the ecclesiastical name, so to speak, of persons whose genuine appellation was Solmund, or sun's protection. Perhaps it was in consequence that the Lord Mayor of London, of 1216, obtained the name of Solomon de Basing. The county of Cornwall much later shows a Soloma.* It is a question whether Lemuel be another name for Solomon. It means "to God," or "dedicated to God," and was a favourite at one time with Puritan mothers. Swift made it famous; but Lemuel Gulliver was by no means an improbable north country name, and Lemuel is not wholly disused even now.

SECTION VIII.—*Later Israelite Names.*

By the time the kingdom was established most of the Israelite names were becoming repetitions of former ones, and comparatively few fresh ones come to light, though there are a few sufficiently used to be worth cursorily noting down.

Hezekiah meant strength of the Lord, and in the Greek became Ezekias. Ezekiel is like it, meaning God will strengthen. The great prophet who was the chief glory of Hezekiah's reign was Isaiah (the salvation of the Lord), made by Greek translators into Esaias, and thence called by old French and English, Esaie, or Esay. The Russians, who have all the old prophetic names, have Eesaia; but it is not easy to account for the choice of Ysaie le Triste as the name of the child of Tristram and Yseulte in the romance that carried on

* *Proper Names of the Bible;* Souvestre, *Derniers Bretons.*

their history to another generation, unless we suppose that Ysaie was supposed to be the masculine of Yseulte ! the one being Hebrew, and meaning as above, the other Keltic, and meaning a sight.

Contemporary with Hezekiah, and persecuted by the Assyrian monarch when he returned to Nineveh after the miraculous destruction of his host, was the blind Israelite of the captivity whose name is explained to have been probably Tobijah (the goodness of the Lord), a name occurring again in the prophet Zechariah, and belonging afterwards to one of the Samaritan persecutors. Probably, in Greek, came the variation of the names of the father and son ; perhaps the latter was once meant for Tobides, the son of Tobias.

The marvellous element in the book of Tobit gained for it much popularity ; scenes from it appeared in art. Thus Tobias had a diffusion in the later middle ages much greater than the names of his contemporaries of far more certain history, and in Ireland Toby has enjoyed the honour, together with Thaddeus and Timothy, of figuring as an equivalent for Tadgh, a poet.

English.	French.	Swiss.	Hamburg.	Italian.	Russian.
Tobias	Tobie	Tobies	Tewes	Tobia	Tobija
Tobit		Tebes			Tobej
Toby		Tebos			
		Beiali			

Hephzibah (my delight is in her), was the wife of Hezekiah, and it may have been in allusion to her that Isaiah spoke of the land being called Hephsibah. It has been rather a favourite name in America, where it gets turned into Hepsy.

As Judah sinned more and more and her fate drew on, Jeremiah stood forth as her leading prophet. His name meant exalted of the Lord, and became Jeremias in the Greek, Jeremy in vernacular English. As the name of some of the early eastern saints it has had a partial irregular sort of use in the West, and is adopted direct from the prophet in the Greco-Slavonic Churches. The French, struck by the mournful strain of the prophet, use Jeremiade to express a lamentation ; and the English are rather too ready to follow their example. Jeremy is considered as another variety of equivalent for the Gaelic Diarmaid, and this has led to the frequency of Jerry among families of Irish connection. In Switzerland, Jeremias is contracted into Meies or Mies ; in Russia it is Jeremija ; but nowhere has it been so illustrious in modern times as in the person of our own Jeremy Taylor. The king whom Jeremiah saw led into captivity was Zedekiah (justice of the Lord).

The prophet of the captivity, Daniel, bore in his name an amplification of that of Dan (a judge). The termination signified God the judge, and the alias Belteshazzar, imposed upon him by the Chaldean monarch, is considered to translate and heathenize the name, making Bel the judge. It is observable that Daniel never calls himself thus, though he gives these heathen titles to his three companions.

E

Daniel has always flourished as a name in the East. Daniel and Verda (a rose), were martyred by Shapoor in 344; another Daniel was crazy enough to succeed Simeon Stylites on his pillar; and thus the Armenian, Montenegrin, and Slavonian races are all much attached to Daniela, or Daniil, as they call it in Russia; or in Esthonia, Taniel or Tanni. The Welsh adopted it as Deiniol, the name of the saint who founded the monastery of Bangor, the High Choir, in the sixth century, and it was thus known to the Bretons; and in Ireland it was adopted as the equivalent to Domnall, Donacha, and other names from Don (or brown-haired), thus causing Dan to be one of the most frequent of Irish contractions.

St. Jerome "transfixed with a dagger"—with his pen—the additional chapters of the Book of Daniel relating to the story of Susanna, to show that he did not regard it as genuine, but, like the story of Judith, it was greatly more popular than the narratives in the canonical books, and was commemorated in ballad, mystery, tapestry, and painting. The name was properly Schuschannah (a lily), though we know it as Susannah. It belonged to one of the holy women at the sepulchre, and it was likewise in the calendar, for two virgin martyrs, named Susanna, had suffered in the times of persecution, and though not commemorated in the Western Church, Queen Susanna, the "Lily of Tiflis," had died for the truth in the hands of Mahometans. The name has been chiefly popular in France and Switzerland, as in England. The Swiss contraction, Züsi-Ketti, for Susanne-Catherine, is quaint.*

English.	German.	Bavarian.
Susannah	Susanne	Susanne
Susan	Suschen	Sanrl
Susie	Suse	Sandrl
Sukey		
Sue		

Swiss.	French.	Lithuanian.
Susanne	Susanne	Zuzane
Zosa	Suzette	
Zosel	Suzon	
Zösel		

This may be the best place to mention the Aramean Tabitha, explained by St. Luke as the same as Dorcas (a roe or gazelle), the Greek word being from its full dark eye. Tabitha and Dorcas both have associations unsuited to the "dear gazelle." As the charitable disciple raised by St. Peter, her names were endeared to the Puritans.

Of the minor prophets, the names have been little employed. Joel meant strong-willed; Amos, a burthen; Obadiah, servant of the

* *Proper Names of the Bible;* Jones, *Welsh Sketches;* Michaelis; O'Donovan; Butler.

Lord, has been slightly more popular, perhaps, in honour of him who hid the prophets in a cave, with whom the mediæval imagination confounded the prophet, so that loaves of bread are the emblem of Obadiah in ancient pictures of the twelve prophets. Even the Abbacuc, as the Apocrypha calls him, who, in the story of *Bel and the Dragon* is carried off by the hair to feed Daniel in the den of lions, seems to have been likewise supposed to be the same person in the strange notions of Scripture history that once floated among our forefathers. The name of Abacuck, or Habbakkuk, was conferred upon a child by one of the last persons one would have suspected of such a choice, namely, Mary, Queen of Scots. On her way to mass, she was waylaid by one of her caterers, who acquainted her that he had a child to be baptized, and desired her to give the name. " She said she would open the Bible in the chapel, and whatever name she cast up, that should be given to the child;" and for the child's misfortune it proved to be ' Abacuck!' The name comes from the verb to clasp, and means embracing.

Micah is a contraction of Micaiah, and means " Who is like unto the Lord." Nahum—to us connected with " Tate and Brady"—was consolation; Nehemiah expanded it, adding the Divine termination; Zephaniah is, protected of the Lord; Haggai (festival of the Lord), called Aggae, when brought through a Greek medium, is rather a favourite in Russia.

Zachariah (remembrance of the Lord), has been more in favour. After belonging to a king of Israel and to the priest murdered by King Jehoash, it came forth after the captivity as Zechariah with the prophet; and in the New Testament, as Zacharias, names the father of the Baptist; and the mysterious martyr who was to fill up the measure of the iniquity of the Jews; and again appears as Zaccheus, the publican of Jericho. It was rather frequent among Eastern Christians, and belonged to the pope who first invited the Franks into Italy to protect him from the Lombards; nor has it ever quite died away in the West, although nowhere popular.

English.	French.	Italian.	Danish.
Zacharias	Zacharie	Zaccaria	Sakerl
Zachary			
Zach			

Bavarian.	Russian.	Slavonic.	Illyrian.
Zachereis	Sacharija		Sakarie
Zacherl	Sachar	Charija	Zaro
Zacher			Zako
Zaches			
Zach			

Of those to whom these later prophets were sent, Ezra's name is thought to be the same as that of Zerah, son of Judah, the rising of light, from whom likewise Heman, the writer of the 88th Psalm, is

termed the Ezrahite. The name of Ezra is hardly to be recognized
in that of Esdras, as the Greek translators rendered it.* The house
of Aphrah, mentioned in the Prophet Micah, means the house of dust,
or ashes, and the Puritans, with their love of piteous names, adopted
Aphra as a name. As well it appears as ' Dust ' and ' Ashes ' in actual
English.†

SECTION IX.—*Angelic Names.*

We have thrown these together, because, though our common term
for those spiritual messengers is Greek, yet all the other words for
them, as well as the three individual angelic designations that have
come into use as baptismal names, are derived from the Hebrew.

Moreover, the first of these belonged to the last of the prophets,
Malach-jah, the angel or messenger of God. It has even been thought
by some commentators that this title of the prophet was the quota-
tion of his own words, " Behold, I send my messenger (or Malachi)
before my face."

Malachi would never have been a modern name, but for the Irish
fancy that made it the equivalent of Maelseachlain, the disciple of
St. Sechnall, or Secundus, a companion of St. Patrick ; and as the
era of him who is now called King Malachi with the collar of gold,
was particularly prosperous, the name has come into some amount of
popularity.

The Septuagint always translated Malach by Ἄγγελος, even in that
first sentence of the prophet, which in our version bears his name.
Angelos had simply meant a messenger in Greek, as it still does ; but
it acquired the especial signification of a heavenly messenger, both in
its own tongue, and in the Latin, whither Angelus was transplanted
with this and no other sense.

Angelos first became a name in the Byzantine Empire. It probably began as an epithet, since it comes to light in the person of
Konstantinos Angelos, a young man of a noble family of Philadelphia,
whose personal beauty caused him, about the year 1100, to become
the choice of the Princess Theodora Komnena. It is thus highly
probable that Angelos was first bestowed as a surname, on account
of the beauty of the family. They were on the throne in 1185, and
Angelos continued imperial till the miserable end of the unhappy
Isaac, and his son, Alexios, during the misdirected crusade of the
Venetians. Angelos thus became known among the Greeks ; and
somewhere about 1217, there came a monastic saint, so called, to
Sicily, who preached at Palermo, and was murdered by a wicked
count, whose evil doings he had rebuked. The Carmelites claimed
St. Angelo as a saint of their order, and his name, both masculine
and feminine, took hold of the fancy of Italy, varied by the Neapoli-
tan dialect into Agnolo or Aniello—*e. g.*, the wonderful fisherman,
Masaniello, was, in fact, Tomasso Angelo ; by the Venetian into
Anziolo, Anzioleto, Anzioleta ; and by the Florentine, into Angiolo,

* *Proper Names of the Bible ;* Michaelis ; Chambers, *Records of Scotland.*
† Bardsley, *Puritan Nomenclature.*

Angioletto, and thence into the ever-renowned contraction Giotto, unless indeed this be from Gotofredo. It passed to other nations, but was of more rare occurrence there, except in the feminine. The fashion of complimenting women as angels, left the masculine Ange to be scantily used in France, and Angel now and then in England ; but in Italy alone did Angiolo, and its derivative Angelico, thrive. All the other countries adopted the feminine, either in the simple form or the diminutive, or most commonly, the derivative, Angelica (angelical), noted in romance as the faithless lady, for whose sake Orlando lost his heart, and his senses. She was a gratuitous invention of Boiardo and Ariosto ; whose character for surpassing beauty made her name popular, and thus Angelica and Angelique have always been favourites.

English.	German.	French.
Angela	Engel	Angele
Angelot	Engelchen	
Angelina	Angelina	Angeline
Angelica	Angelica	Angelique

Italian.	Polish.	Bohemian.
Angiola	Ancela	Anjela
Angioletta		Anjelina
Angelica		Anjelika
Agnola		
Anzioleta		

Angel was most often a man's name in England. We find it at Hadleigh, Suffolk, in 1591, and sometimes likewise in Cornwall.

Archangel has even been used as an English name.

The mysterious creatures that are first mentioned as " keeping the way of the tree of life," then were represented in the tabernacle over-shadowing the ark, and afterwards were revealed in vision to the Prophet Ezekiel and to the Apostle St. John, combined in their forms the symbols of all that was wisest, bravest, strongest, and loftiest in creation—the man, the lion, the ox, and eagle.

In the lands where Art made the Cherub a mere head with wings, Cherubino arose as a Christian name, for it is hardly ever to be met with out of Spain and Italy.

Equally misused is Seraph—now a lady's name, as Seraphine in France ; Serafina, in Spain and Italy. The word seraph, or saraph, signifies burning, or fiery, and would apply to that intensity of glory that Ezekiel struggles to express in the cherubim by comparisons to amber and to glowing embers, or to their intense fervour of love.

Three individual angels have been revealed to us by name as of the seven that stand in the presence of God, and foremost of these is Michael (who is like unto God), he who was made known to Daniel as the protector of the Jewish people ; to Zechariah, as defending

them from Satan ; to St. Jude, as disputing with Satan for the body
of Moses ; and to St. John, as leading the hosts of Heaven to battle
with the adversary and prevailing over him.

His name would have seemed in itself fit only for an archangel,
yet before apparently he had been made known, it had been borne
by the father of one of David's captains, and by a son of Jehoshaphat,
and it was almost the same as Micaiah, the name of him who foretold
the destruction of Ahab.

Constantine the Great dedicated a church in his new city in
honour of St. Michael, the archangel, and thenceforth Mickaelion, or
Mikael, have been favourites with all branches of the Eastern Church.

An appearance of the archangel in Colosse led the way to another
legend of his descent upon Monte Galgano in Apulia, somewhere
about 493. Then came a more notable vision, seen by Gregory the
Great himself, of the angel standing with outstretched sword on the
tomb of Adrian, which has ever since been called the castle of St.
Angelo. In 706, St. Michael was again seen to take his stand upon
the isolated rock on the Norman coast, so noted as the fortress and
convent of Mont St. Michel. Moreover tradition placed him upon
the Cornish rock,—

> " When the great vision of the guarded mount
> Looked towards Namancos and Bayona's hold."

He was above all others the patron of the Christian warrior ; his
armour-clad effigy was seen in almost every church ; the young
knight was dubbed in his name, as well as that of the national saint ;
and since the prevalence of saintly names, his name has been frequently bestowed. It is, perhaps, most common in the Greek and
Slavonic countries ; but Ireland makes great use of it ; and Italy has
united it with the epithet angel, in the one distinguished instance of
Michelangelo Buonarotti.

English.	French.	Spanish.	Italian.
Michael	Michel	Miguel	Michele
Mick	Michon		
Mike	Michau		
German.	**Dutch.**	**Swedish.**	**Russian.**
Michael	Michiel	Mikael	Michail
Micha	Micheltje	Mikel	Michaila
		Mikas	Misha
			Mischenka
Slavonic.	**Servian.**	**Lett.**	**Hungarian.**
Miha	Miljo	Mikkelis	Mihaly
Mihal	Miho		Mihal
Mihaljo	Misa		Miska
	Mijailo		

There is some confusion in the German mind between it and the old *michel* (mickle, large), which, as a name, it has quite absorbed. It has the rare feminines,

French.	Russian.	Portuguese.
Michelle	Micheline	Miguella
Michée	Mikelina	

Legend has been far less busy with Gabriel, "the hero of God;" the angel who strengthened Daniel, and who brought the promise to Zacharias and to the Blessed Virgin. His name is chiefly used by the Slavonians; and in Hungary we find it in combination with Bethlehem, belonging to that noted chieftain, Bethlem Gabor.

It was known and used everywhere, however; and the Swedish house of Oxenstjerna considered it to have been the saving of their line from extinction, all their sons having died in the cradle, owing, it was thought, to Satan's strangling them; till at length one was named Gabriel; and having thus obtained the protection of the guardian angel, survived to be the ancestor of the minister of the great Gustavus. The feminine, Gabrielle, has been a favourite in France ever since la belle Gabrielle gave it a reputation for beauty.

English.	German.	Bavarian.	Swiss.	Italian.
Gabriel	Gabriel	Gabe	Gabëler	Gabriello
Gab		Gaberl		

Russian.	Polish.	Illyrian.	Lett.	Hungarian.
Gavrül	Gabryel	Gabriel	Gaberjels	Gabriel
Gavrila		Gavrilo	Gabris	Gabor
		Gavril		
		Gavro		

FEMININE.				
French.	German.	Slavonic.		
Gabrielle	Gabriele	Gavrila		
		Gavra		

Raphael (the medicine of God), is the angel who guided Tobias and healed his father. Italy and Spain are the countries where his name is most used, and well it may, in the first named, after the fame of him who has made it the highest proverb in art. It hardly varies, except by the double *ff* of Italian, and the single one of Spain, to supply its Greek *φ*. I have heard of a girl at Mentone called Ravelina, probably Raffaellina.*

* Smith, *Dictionary of the Bible; Proper Names of the Bible;* Williams, *Commentary on the Gospels;* Jameson, *Sacred and Legendary Art;* Ruskin, *Modern Painters;* Marryat, *Sweden,*

PART II.

SECTION I.—*The Persian Language.*

SCANTY as are the Christian names derived from the Persian race, they are very curious and interesting, partly on account of the changes that they have undergone, and still more because the language whence they are derived belongs to the same group as our own, and testifies in many of its words to the common origin.

To begin with the sovereign to whom all alike look up ; him who is " called by name in the book of Isaiah," as the shepherd who should restore Judah after the Captivity. Kuru is a name said to be older than the Sanscrit and of unknown signification ; although some derive it from Khur, one name for the sun. Kureish was the original form ; Koreish to the Hebrews ; Kyros to the Greeks, whence the Romans took the Cyrus by which he is known to Europe. His only namesake in his own line was he who invited the 10,000 from Greece and perished at Cunaxa, and of whom is told the story of his willing acceptance of the water of the river Kur or Cyrus, whose name sounded like his own. When the Sassanids revived the old Achæmenid names they pronounced the royal word as Khoosroo, and the Byzantines recorded it as Chosröes, when Chosröes Nushirvan, or the magnanimous, almost rivalled the glory of his ancestor—Kai Khoosroo, as the *Shahnameh* called him.

Not only had the fire-worshippers revived the name, but it had been borne by various Christians in the East, one of whom, a physician of Alexandria, suffered in one of the persecutions, having been detected in visiting a Christian prisoner. He was buried at Canope, in Egypt, and was called in the Coptic calendar Abba Cher, or Father Cyrus ; in the Greek, Abba Cyrus. His relics were afterwards transported to Rome, where the Church built over them was called, by the Italians, Saint Appassara. Like a fixed star, the original Cyrus had shone through adjacent darkness, evident by his lustre, but his lineaments lost in distance, and thus Ferdosi makes him a mere mythical hero. Herodotus copied some distorted tradition ; Xenophon pourtrayed imaginary perfection in his *Cyropœdia ;* and moderns have taken even greater liberties with him. *Artaban, ou le grand Cyrus,* the ponderous romance of Mlle. de Scudery, was a stately French tale of love and war, containing a long amorous correspondence between Cyrus and his beloved, the model and admiration of the *précieuses* in their glory, and absolutely not without effect upon nomenclature. In one village in Picardy there still exist living specimens of Oriane, Philoxène, Célamire, Arsinoe, Calvandre, all derived from vassals named by their enthusiastic seigneurs in honour of the heroines of the fashionable romances, and still inherited by their posterity long after the seigneurs and the heroines are alike forgotten.

Either from his being mentioned in the Bible, or from the *Cyropœdia,* Cyrus has had some currency as an English baptismal name.*

Section II.—*Esther.*

Khshayarsha, from *Kshaya* (a king), and *arsha* (venerable), was the word that was converted in Hebrew into Achashverosh, and in our Bible into Ahasuerus, while the Greeks called it Xerxes. In Illyria people are christened from him Kserksas, and called Sersa, and a few seekers of Scripture names, chiefly in America, have called their sons Ahasuerus, in common life Hazzy.

The reigning wife of Xerxes is known to have been Amestris, the daughter of an Achæmenian noble, and she might well have been Vashti, set aside only for a time when the address of the nobles gained a victory over her. The fair daughter of the tribe of Benjamin, whose royalty ensured her people's safety, was in her own tongue Hadassah, or the Myrtle ; some say, Atossa ; but the Persian epithet by which we know her may have been taken from *satarah*, a word showing the ancient union of the languages, since Aster is Arab and Greek ; and from thence and the Latin *stella* have sprung the modern *étoile, estrella,* star, *stern, stjorna,* which the Septuagint gave as 'Εστὴρ, the Romans as Esthera and Hestera ; whence the occasional variations in English of Esther or Essie, and Hester or Hetty.

Not till the days of Racine was Esther much in vogue. The tragedian, being requested to write a sacred drama to be acted by the young ladies of St. Cyr, chose this subject in compliment to Madame de Maintenon, as the faultless Esther preferred before the discarded Vashti, namely, Madame de Montespan ! Esther thereupon became a favourite lady's name in France, and vied in popularity with the cumbrous splendours taken from the Scudery cycle of romance. At the same time it was borne by the two ladies who had the misfortune to be the object of Dean Swift's affection, Esther Johnson and Esther Vanhomrigh, whom he called, one by the Latin name Stella ; the other, by the generic title of our finest English butterflies, Vanessa.

* Rawlinson, *Herodotus ;* Malcolm, *Persia ;* Le Beau, *Bas Empire ;* Rollin, *Ancient History ;* Butler, *Lives of the Saints ;* Dunlop, *History of Fiction.*

Estrella was the heroine of a Spanish pastoral, whence the Abbé Florian borrowed his theatrical shepherdess Estelle, which thus became a French name, though chiefly on the stage, and both Estelle and Stella are sometimes used as Epiphany names for girls.

Roschana, as it is now pronounced, is still common in Persia, and means the dawn of day. Roxane and Statire, as rival heroines of Racine, became proverbs in France for the stately or the languishing form of tragedy dame. Roxana, or Roxy, is one of the favourite American grandiloquent style of names.

PART III.

CHAPTER I.

NAMES FROM THE GREEK.

PASSING from Persian to Greek names, we feel at once that we are nearer home, and that we claim a nearer kindred in thoughts and habits, if not in blood, with the sons of Javan, than with the fire-worshippers. The national names are thus almost always explicable by the language itself, with a few exceptions, either when the name was an importation from Egypt or Phœnicia, whence many of the earlier arts had been brought.

Each Greek had but one name, which was given to him by his father either on or before the tenth day of his life, when a sacrifice and banquet was held. Genealogies were exceedingly interesting to the Greeks, as the mutual connection of city with city, race with race, was thus kept up, and community of ancestry was regarded as a bond of alliance, attaching the Athenians, for instance, to the Asiatic Ionians as both sons of Ion, or the Spartans to the Syracusans, as likewise descended from Doros. Each individual state had its deified ancestor, and each family of note a hero parent, to whom worship was offered at every feast, and who was supposed still to exert active protection over his votaries. The political rights of the citizens, and the place they occupied in the army, depended on their power of tracing their line from the forefather of a recognized tribe, after whose name the whole were termed with the patronymic termination *ides* (the son of). This was only, however, a distinction, for surnames were unknown, and each man possessed merely the individual personal appellation by which he was always called, without any title, be his station what it might. Families used, however, to mark themselves by recurring constantly to the same name. It was the correct thing to give the eldest son that of his paternal grandfather, as Kimon, Miltiades, then Kimon again, if the old man were dead, for if he were living it would have been putting another in his place, a bad omen, and therefore a father's name was hardly ever given to a son. Sometimes, however, the prefix was preserved, and the termination varied, so as to mark the family without destroying the individual identity. Thus, Leonidas, the third son of Anaxandridas, repeated with an augmentative his grandfather's name of Leo (a lion), as his father, Anaxandridas, did that of *his* own great grandfather, Anaxandras (king of man), whose son Eurycratidas was named from his grandfather Eurycrates. A like custom prevailed among the old English.

After the Romans had subdued Greece and extended the powers of becoming citizens, the name of the adopting patron would be taken by his client, and thus Latin and Greek titles became mixed together. Later, Greek second names became coined, either from patronymics, places, or events, and finally ran into the ordinary European system of surnames.

Among the names here ensuing will only be found those that concern the history of Christian names. Many a great heart-thrilling sound connected with the brightest lights of the ancient world must be passed by, because it has not pleased the capricious will of after-generations to perpetuate it, or so exceptionally as not to be worth mentioning.

Some of the female Greek names were appropriate words and epithets ; but others, perhaps the greater number, were merely men's names with the feminine termination in *a* or *e*, often irrespective of their meaning. Some of these have entirely perished from the lips of men, others have been revived by some enterprising writer in search of a fresh title for a heroine. Such is Corinna (probably from Persephone's title Κόρη (Koré), a maiden, the Bœotian poetess, who won a wreath of victory at Thebes, and was therefore the example from whom Mdme. de Staël named her brilliant Corinne, followed in her turn by numerous French damsels ; and in an Italian chronicle of the early middle ages, the lady whom we have been used to call Rowena, daughter of Henghist, has turned into Corinna ; whilst Cora, probably through Lord Byron's poem, is a favourite in America. Such too is Aspasia (welcome), from the literary fame of its first owner chosen by the taste of the seventeenth century as the title under which to praise the virtues of Lady Elizabeth Hastings. In the *Rambler* and *Spectator* days, real or fictitious characters were usually introduced under some classical or pastoral appellation, and ladies corresponded with each other under the soubriquets of nymph, goddess, or heroine, and in virtue of its sound Aspasia was adopted among these. It has even been heard as a Christian name in a cottage. "Her name's Aspasia, but us calls her Spash." *

* Bishop Thirlwall, *Greece ;* Smith, *Dictionary of Greek and Roman Antiquities ;* Lappenberg, *Anglo-Saxons.*

CHAPTER II.

Section I.

GREEK appellations may be divided into various classes; the first, those of the gods and early heroes are derived from languages inexplicable even by the classical Greeks. These were seldom or never given to human beings, though derivatives from them often were.

The second class is of those formed from epithets in the spoken language. These belonged to the Greeks of the historical age, and such as were borne by the Macedonian conquerors became spread throughout the East, thus sometimes falling to the lot of early saints of the Church, and becoming universally popular in Christendom. Of others of merely classic association a few survived among the native Greeks, while others were resuscitated at intervals; first, by the vanity of decaying Rome; next, by the revival of ancient literature in the Cinque-cento; then, by the magniloquent taste of the Scudery romances in France; again, in France, by the republican mania; and, in the present time, by the same taste in America, and by the reminiscences of the modern Greeks.

After the preaching of the Gospel, Greece had vigour enough to compose appropriate baptismal names for the converts; and it is curious to observe that no other country could have ever been so free from the trammels of hereditary nomenclature, for no other has so complete a set of names directly bearing upon Christianity. So graceful are they in sound as well as meaning, and so honoured for those who bore them, that many have spread throughout Europe.

Lastly, even modern Greek has thrown out many names of graceful sound, which are, however, chiefly confined to the Romaic.

Section II.—*Names from Zeus.*

At the head of the whole Greek system stands the mighty Zeus (Ζεύς), a word that has been erected into a proper name for the thundering father of gods and men, whilst the cognate θεὸς (theos) passed into a generic term; just as at Rome the Deus Pater (God-Father), or Jupiter, from the same source, became the single god, and *deus* the general designation.

All come from the same source as the Sanscrit Deva, and are connected with the open sky, and the idea of light that has produced our word day. We shall come upon them again and again; but for the present we will confine ourselves to the personal names produced by

Zeus, in his individual character, leaving those from Theos to the Christian era, to which most of them belong.

Their regular declension of Zeus made *Dios* the genitive case ; and thus Diodorus, Diogenes, &c., ought, perhaps, to be referred to him ; but the more poetical, and, therefore, most probably the older, form, was *Zenos* in the genitive ; and as Dios also meant heaven, the above names seem to be better explained as heaven-gift and heaven-born, leaving to Zeus only those that retain the same commencement.

Ζηνων, or, as it is commonly called, Zeno, was a good deal used in Greece throughout the classical times, and descending to Christian times, named a saint martyred under Gallienus, also a bishop of Verona, who left ninety-three sermons, at the beginning of the fourth century, and thus made it a canonical name, although the rules of the Church had forbidden christening children after heathen gods. Except for the Isaurian Emperor Zeno, and an occasional Russian Sinon, there has not, however, been much disposition to use the name.

Zenobios, life from Zeus, is by far the easiest way of explaining the name of the brilliant Queen of Palmyra ; but, on the other hand, she was of Arabian birth, the daughter of Amrou, King of Arabia, and it is highly probable that she originally bore the true Arabic name of Zeenab (ornament of the father) ; and that when she and her husband entered on intercourse with the Romans, the name Zenobia was bestowed upon her as an equivalent, together with the genuine Latin Septima as a mark of citizenship.   When her glory waned, and she was brought as a prisoner to Rome, she and her family were allowed to settle in Italy ; and her daughters left descendants there. Zenobius, the Bishop of Milan, who succeeded St. Ambrose, bore her name, and claimed her blood ; and thus Zenobio and Zenobia still linger among the inhabitants of the city.

The romance of her story caught the French fancy, and Zénobie has been rather in fashion among modern French damsels.

A Cilician brother and sister, called Zenobius and Zenobia, the former a physician and afterwards Bishop of Ægæ, were put to death together during the persecution of Diocletian, and thus became saints of the Eastern Church, making Sinovij, Sinovija, or for short, Zizi, very fashionable among the Russians.

It is much more difficult to account for the prevalence of Zenobia in Cornwall.   Yet many parish registers show it as of an early date : and dear to the West is the story of a sturdy dame called Zenobia Brengwenna, (Mrs. Piozzi makes the surname Stevens,) who, on her ninety-ninth birthday, rode seventeen miles on a young colt to restore to the landlord a 99 years' lease that had been granted to her father, in her name, at her birth.

Probably Zenaïda means daughter of Zeus.   Although not belonging to any patron saint, it is extensively popular among Russian ladies ; and either from them, or from the modern Greek, the French have recently become fond of Zenaïde.*

* Smith, *Dictionary ;* Butler, *Lives ;* Gibbon, *Rome ;* Miss Beaufort, *Egyptian Sepulchres and Syrian Shrines ;* Hayward, *Mrs. Piozzi.*

SECTION III.—Ἡρα—Hera.

The name of the white-armed, ox-eyed queen of heaven, Ἡρα or Ἡρη (Hera or Heré), is derived by philologists from the same root as the familiar German *herr* and *herrinn*, and thus signifies the lady or mistress. Indeed the masculine form ἥρως, whence we take our hero, originally meant a free or noble man, just as *herr* does in ancient German, and came gradually to mean a person distinguished on any account, principally in arms; and thence it became technically applied to the noble ancestors who occupied an intermediate place between the gods and existing men. The Latin *herus* and *hera* are cognate, and never rose out of their plain original sense of master and mistress, though the *heros* was imported in his grander sense from the Greek, and has passed on to us.

It is curious that whereas the wife of Zeus was simply the lady, it was exactly the same with Frigga, who, as we shall by-and-by see, was merely the Frau—the free woman or lady.

Hera herself does not seem to have had many persons directly named after her, though there was plenty from the root of her name. The feminine Hero was probably thus derived,—belonging first to one of the Danaïdes, then to a daughter of Priam, then to the maiden whose light led Leander to his perilous breasting of the Hellespont, and from whom Shakespeare probably took it for the lady apparently "done to death by slanderous tongues."

It is usual to explain as Ἡρα-κλῆς (fame of Hera) the name of the son of Zeus and Alcmena, whose bitterest foe Hera was, according to the current legends of Greece; but noble fame is a far more probable origin for Herakles, compound as he is of the oft-repeated Sun-myth mixed with the veritable Samson, and the horrible Phœnician Melkarth or Moloch, with whom the Tyrians themselves identified Herakles.

A few compounds, such as Heraclius, Heraclidas, Heracleonas, have been formed from Herakles, the hero ancestor of the Spartan kings, and therefore specially venerated in Lacedæmon. The Latins called the name Hercules; and it was revived in the Cinque-cento, in Italy, as Ercole. Thus Hercule was originally the baptismal name of Catherine de Medici's youngest son; but he changed it to François at his confirmation, when hoping to mount a throne. Exceptionally, Hercules occurs in England; and we have known of more than one old villager called Arkles, respecting whom there was always a doubt whether he were Hercules or Archelaus.

Hence, too, the name of the father of history, Herodotus (noble gift); hence, likewise, that of Herodes. Some derive this last from the Arab *hareth* (a farmer); but it certainly was a Greek name long before the Idumean family raised themselves to the throne of Judea, since a poet was so called who lived about the time of Cyrus. If the Herods were real Edomites, they may have Græcized Hareth into Herodes; but it is further alleged that the first Herod, grandfather of the first king, was a slave, attached to the temple of Apollo at

Ascalon, taken captive by Idumean robbers. Hateful as is the name in its associations, its feminine, Herodias, became doubly hateful as the murderess of John the Baptist.

SECTION IV.—*Athene.*

The noble goddess of wisdom, pure and thoughtful, armed against evil, and ever the protector of all that was thoughtfully brave and resolute, was called 'Αθήνη (Athene), too anciently for the etymology to be discernible, or even whether her city of Athens was called from her, or she from the city.

Many an ancient Greek was called in honour of her, but the only one of these names that has to any degree survived is Athenaïs.

There were some Cappadocian queens, so called; and so likewise was the daughter of a heathen philosopher in the fourth century, whom the able Princess Pulcheria selected as the wife of her brother Theodosius, altering her name, however, to Eudocia at her baptism.

It must have been the Scudery cycle of romance that occasioned Athenaïs to have been given to that Demoiselle de Mortémar, who was afterwards better known as Madame de Montespan.

Athenaios (Athenian), Athenagoras (assembly of Athene), Athenadgoros (gift of Athene), were all common among the Greeks.

Athene's surname of Pallas is derived by Plato from πάλλειν, to brandish, because of her brandished spear; but it is more likely to be from πάλλαξ (a virgin), which would answer to her other surname of παρθένος, likewise a virgin, familiar to us for the sake of the most beautiful of all heathen remains, the Parthenon, as well as the ancient name of Naples, Parthenope. This, however, was a female name in Greece, and numerous instances of persons called Parthenios and Palladios attest the general devotion to this goddess, perhaps the grandest of all the imaginings of the Indo-European.

There is something absolutely satisfactory in seeing how much more the loftier and purer deities, Athene, Apollo, Artemis, reigned over Greek nomenclature than the embodiments of brute force and sensual pleasure, Ares and Aphrodite, both probably introductions from the passionate Asiatics, and as we see in Homer, entirely on the Trojan side. An occasional Aretas and Arete are the chief recorded namesakes of Ares, presiding god of the Areopagus as he was; and thence may have come the Italian Aretino, and an Areta, who appears in Cornwall. Aphrodite seems to have hardly one derived from her name, which is explained as the Foam Sprung.*

SECTION V.—*Apollo and Artemis.*

The brother and sister deities, twin children of Zeus and Leto, are, with the exception of Athene, the purest and brightest creations of Greek mythology.

* Smith, *Dictionary of Greek and Roman Mythology;* Le Beau, *Bas Empire;* Gladstone, *Homer*

The sister's name, Artemis, certainly meant the sound, whole, or vigorous ; that of the brother, Apollōn, is not so certainly explained ; though Æschylus considered it to come from ἀπόλλυμι, to destroy.

They both of them had many votaries in Greece ; such names as Apollodorus (gift of Apollo), Apollonius, and the like, arising in plenty, but none of them have continued into Christian times, though Apollos was a companion of St. Paul. The sole exception is Apollonia, an Alexandrian maiden, whose martyrdom began by the extraction of all her teeth, thus establishing St. Apolline, as the French call her, as the favourite subject of invocation in the tooth-ache. Abellona, the Danish form of this name, is a great favourite in Jutland and the isles, probably from some relic of the toothless maiden. The Slovaks use it as Polonija or Polona.

The votaries of Artemis did not leave a saint to perpetuate them ; but Artemisia, the brave queen of Halicarnassus, had a name of sufficient stateliness to delight the *précieuses*. Thus Artémise was almost as useful in French romances as the still more magnificient Artémidore, the French version of Artemidorus (gift of Artemis).

It was a late fancy of mythology, when all was becoming confused, that made Apollo and Artemis into the sun and moon deities, partly in consequence of their epithets Phœbus, Phœbe, from φάω (to shine). The original Phœbe seems to have belonged to some elder myth, for she is said to have been daughter of Heaven and Earth, and to have been the original owner of the Delphic oracle. Afterwards she was said to have been the mother of Leto (the obscure), and thus grand-mother of Apollo and Artemis, who thence took their epithet. This was probably a myth of the alternation of light and darkness ; but as we have received our notions of Greek mythology through the dull Roman medium, it is almost impossible to disentangle our idea of Phœbus from the sun, or of Phœbe from the crescent moon. In like manner the exclusively modern Greek φωτεινή (bright), Photinee, comes from φώς phos (light), as does Photius, used in Russia as Fotie.

Strangely enough, we find Phœbus among the mediæval Counts of Foix, who, on the French side of their little Pyrenean county were Gaston Phœbus ; on the Spanish, Gastone Febo. Some say that Phœbus was originally a soubriquet applied to one of the family on account of his personal beauty, though it certainly was afterwards given at baptism ; others, that it was an imitation of an old Basque name.

Phœbe was a good deal in use among the women of Greek birth in the early Roman empire ; and " Phœbe, our sister," the deaconness of Cenchrea, is commended by St. Paul to the Romans ; but she has had few namesakes, except in England ; the Italian Febe only being used as a synonym for the moon.

Cynthia was a title belonging to Artemis, from Mount Cynthus, and has thence become a title of the moon, and a name of girls in America.

Delia, another title coming from Delos, the place of her nativity, has been preferred by the Arcadian taste, and flourished in shepherdess poems, so as to be occasionally used as a name in England, but more often as a contraction for Cordelia.

F

Delphinios and Delphinia were both of them epithets of Apollo and Artemis, of course from the shrine at Delphi. Some say that shrine and god were so called because the serpent Python was named Delphinè ; others, that the epithet was derived from his having metamorphosed himself into a dolphin, or else ridden upon one, when showing the Cretan colonists the way to Delphi.

The meaning of *Delphys adelphus* is the womb ; and thus the Greeks believed Delphi to be the centre of the earth, just as the mediæval Christians thought Jerusalem was. It is from this word that delphis (a brother) is derived, and from one no doubt of the same root, that was first a mass, and afterwards a dolphin, the similarity of sound accounting for the confusion of derivatives from the temple and the fish. Again, the dolphin is said to be so called as being the fish of the Dolphièm god.

It was probably as an attribute of the god that Delphinos was used as a name by the Greeks ; and it makes its first appearance in Christian times in two regions under Greek influence, namely, Venice and Southern France, which latter place was much beholden for civilization to the Greek colony of Massilia. Dolfino has always prevailed in the Republic of St. Mark ; and Delphinus was a sainted bishop of Bourdeaux, in the fourth century, from whom many, both male and female, took the name, which to them was connected with the fish of Jonah, the emblem of the Resurrection.

In 1125, Delfine, heiress of Albon, married Guiges, Count of Viennois. She was his third wife ; and to distinguish her son from the rest of the family, he was either called or christened, Guiges Delphin, and assumed the dolphin as his badge, whence badge and title passed to his descendants, the Counts Dauphins de Viennois. The last of these left his country and title to Charles, son of King Jean of France ; and thence the heir-apparent was called the Dauphin.

Dalphin appears at Cambrai before 1200 ; and Delphine de Glandèves, sharing the saintly honours of her husband, Count Elzéar de St. Sabran, became the patroness of the many young ladies in compliment to *la dauphine.*

It is startling to meet with 'Dolphin' as a daughter of the unfortunate Waltheof, Earl of Mercia ; but unless her mother, Judith, imported the French Delphine, it is probable that it is a mistake for one of the many forms of the Frank, Adel, which was displacing its congener the native Æthel. Indeed, Dolfine, which is very common among German girls now, is avowedly the contraction of Adolfine, their feminine for Adolf (noble wolf).

SECTION VI.—*Hele.*

The sun-god who drove his flaming chariot around the heavenly vault day by day, and whose eye beheld everything throughout the earth, was in Homer's time an entirely different personage from the "far darting Apollo," with whom, thanks to the Romans, we confound him. Helios was his name, a word from the root *elé* (light), the same that has furnished the Teutonic adjective *hell* (bright or clear), and that is met again in the Keltic *heol* (the sun).

This root ele (heat or light) is found again in the Greek name of the moon, Sēlēnē once a separate goddess from Artemis. One of the Cleopatras was called Selene ; but it does not appear that this was used again as a name till in the last century, when Selina was adopted in England, probably by mistake, for the French Céline, and belonged to the Wesleyan Countess of Huntingdon.

From ēlē again sprang the name most of all noted among Greeks, the fatal name of Ἐλένε, Helene, the feminine of Helenos (the light or bright), though Æschylus, playing on the word, made it ἑλένας (the ship-destroying).

> " Wherefore else this fatal name,
> That Helen and destruction are the same."

A woman may be a proverb for any amount of evil or misfortune, but as long as she is also a proverb for beauty, her name will be copied, and Helena never died away in Greece, and latterly was copied by Roman ladies when they first became capable of a little variety.

At last it was borne by the lady who was the wife of Constantius Chlorus, the mother of Constantine, and the restorer of the shrines at Jerusalem. St. Helena, holding the true cross, was thenceforth revered by East and West. Bithynia on the one hand, Britain on the other, laid claim to have been her birth-place, and though it is unfortunately most likely that the former country is right, and that she can hardly be the daughter of " Old King Cole," yet it is certain that the ancient Britons held her in high honour. Eglwys Ilan, the Church of Helen, still exists in Wales, and the insular Kelts have always made great use of her name. Ellin recurs in old Welsh pedigrees from the Empress's time. Elayne is really the old Cambrian form occurring in registers from early times, and thus explaining the gentle lady Elayne, the mother of Sir Galahad, whom Tennyson has lately identified with his own spinning Lady of Shalott. Helen, unfortunately generally pronounced Ellen, was used from the first in Scotland ; Eileen or Aileen in Ireland.

Nor are these Keltic Ellens the only offspring of the name. Elena in Italy, it assumed the form of Aliénor among the Romanesque populations of Provence, who, though speaking a Latin tongue, greatly altered and disguised the words. Indeed there are some who derive this name from ἕλεος (pity), but there is much greater reason to suppose it another variety of Helena, not more changed than many other Provençal names. Aliénor in the land of troubadours received all the homage that the Languedoc could pay, and one Aliénor at least was entirely spoilt by it, namely, she who was called Eléonore by the French king who had the misfortune to marry her, and who became in time on English lips our grim Eleanor of the dagger and the bowl, the hateful Acquitanian grandmother, who bandies words with Constance of Brittany in *King John*. Her daughter, a person of far different nature, carried her name to Castille, where, the language being always disposed to cut off a commencing *e*, she was known as Leonor, and left hosts of namesakes.   Her descendant, the daughter of San Fernando, brought the name back to England, and, as our " good Queen Eleanor," did much to redeem its honour, which the levity of her mother-in-law, the Provençal Aliénor of Henry III., had greatly prejudiced.   Eleanor continued to be a royal name as long as the Plantagenets were on the throne, and thus was widely used among the nobility, and afterwards by all ranks, when of course

Greek.	Latin.	English.	Scotch.
Ἑλένη	Helena	Helena	Helen
		Helen	Ellen
		Elaine	
		Ellen	
		Eleanor	
Ἑλενίσκη		Elinor	
		Nelly	
Ἑλεναιαι		Leonora	
		Annora	
		Annot	
		Lina	
		Linot	

Irish.	German.	Italian.	Spanish.
Helena	Helène	Elena	Helena
Eileen	Eleonore	Eleonora	
Nelly			
	Lenore	Leonora	Leon

Russian.	Polish.	Slavonic.	Servian.
Jelena	Helena	Jelena	Jelena
	Helenka	Jela	Jela
		Jelika	Jelika
		Lenka	
		Lencica	

Lett.	Esthonian.	Ung.	Albanian.
Lena	Leno	Ilona	Ljena
			Lenia

it lost its proper spelling and was turned into Ellinor and Elinor, still, however, owning its place in song and story.   Annora, frequent in Northern England, was the contraction of Eleanora, and was further contracted into Annot.   Also Ellen was Lina, or Linot.

Meantime the Arragonese conquests in Italy had brought Leonora thither as a new name independent of Elena, and it took strong root there, still preserving its poetic fame in the person of the lovely

Leonora d'Este, the object of Tasso's hopeless affection. To France again it came with the Galigai, the Maréchale d'Ancre, the author of the famous saying about the power of a strong mind over a weak one ; and unpopular as she was, Léonore has ever since been recognized in French nomenclature, and it went to Germany as Lenore.

The Greek Church was constant to the memory of the Empress, mother of the founder of Constantinople, and Helena has always been frequent there. And when the royal widow Olga came from Muscovy to seek instruction and baptism, she was called Helena, which has thus become one of the popular Russian names. It is sometimes supposed to be a translation of Olga, but this is a mistake founded on the fact that this lady, and another royal saint, were called by both names. Olga is, in fact, the feminine of Oleg (the Russian form of Helgi), which the race of Rurik had derived from their Norse ancestor, and it thus means holy.

Sweden also has a Saint Helene, who made a pilgrimage to Rome, and was put to death on her return by her cruel relations in 1160. Her relics were preserved in Zealand, near Copenhagen, making Ellin a favourite name among Danish damsels.

Helena has a perplexing double pronunciation in English, the central syllable being made long or short according to the tradition of the families where it is used. The Greek letter was certainly the short *e*, but it is believed that though the quantity of the syllable was short, the accent was upon it, and that the traditional sound of it survives in the name of the island which we learnt from the Portuguese.

SECTION VII.—*Demeter.*

Among the elder deities in whom the primitive notion of homage to the Giver of all Good was lost and dispersed, was the beneficent mother Demeter (Δημητήρ). Some derive the first syllable of this name from γῆ (the earth), others from the Cretan δῆαι (barley), making it either earth mother, or barley mother ; but the idea of motherhood is always an essential part of this bounteous goddess, the materializing of the productive power of the earth, "filling our hearts with food and gladness."

Formerly Demeter had numerous votaries, especially among the Macedonians, who were the greatest name-spreaders among the Greeks, and used it in all the "four horns" of their divided empire. It occurs in the Acts, as the silversmith of Ephesus, who stirred up the tumult against St. Paul, and another Demetrius is commended by St. John. The Latin Church has no saint so called ; but the Greek had a Cretan monk of the fourteenth century, who was a great ecclesiastical author ; and a Demetrios, who is reckoned as the second great saint of Thessalonika. Hence Demetrios is one of the most popular of names in all the Eastern Church, and the countries that have ever been influenced by it ; among whom must be reckoned the Venetian dominions which considered themselves to belong to the old Byzantine empire till they were able to stand alone. Dimitri has always

been a great name in Russia. The Slavonian nations give it the contraction Mitar, and the feminine Dimitra or Mitra. The modern
Greek contraction is Demos.

In some parts of Greece, Demeter was worshipped primarily as the
gloomy winterly earth, latterly as the humanized goddess clad in
black, in mourning for her daughter, whence she was adored as
Melaina. Whether from this title of the goddess or simply a dark
complexion, there arose the female name of Melania, which belonged
to two Roman ladies, grandmother and granddaughter, who were
among the many who were devoted to the monastic Saint Jerome,
and derived an odour of sanctity from his record of their piety.
Though not placed in the Roman calendar, they are considered as
saints, and the French Mélanie and the old Cornish Melony are
derived from them.

On the contrary, her summer epithet was Chloe, the verdant, as
protectress of green fields, and Chloe seems to have been used by the
Greeks, as a Corinthian woman so called is mentioned by St. Paul,
and has furnished a few scriptural Chloes in England. In general,
however, Chloe has been a property of pastoral poetry, and has thence
descended to negroes and spaniels.*

Section VIII.—*Dionysos.*

The god of wine and revelry appears to have been adopted into
Greek worship at a later period than the higher divinities embodying loftier ideas. So wild and discordant are the legends respecting
him, that it is probable that in the Bacchus, or Dionysos, whom the
historical Greeks adored, several myths are united; the leading ones
being, on the one hand, the naturalistic deity of the vine; on the
other, some dimly remembered conqueror.

Dionysos has never been satisfactorily explained, though the most
obvious conclusion is that it means the god of Nysa—a mountain
where he was nursed by nymphs in a cave. Others make his mother
Dione one of the original mythic ideas of a divine creature, the
daughter of Heaven and Earth, and afterwards supposed to be the
mother of Aphrodite.

Names given in honour of Dionysos were very common in Greece,
and especially in the colony of Sicily, where Dion was also in use.
Dionysios, the tyrant, seemed only to make the name more universally
known, and most of the tales of tyranny clustered round him—such
as the story of his ear, of the sword of Damocles, and the devotion of
Damon and Pythias.

In the time of the Apostles, Dionysius was very frequent, and gave
the name of the Areopagite mentioned by St. Paul, of several more
early saints, and of a bishop who, in 272, was sent to convert the Gauls,
and was martyred near Paris. The Abbey erected on the spot where
he died was placed under the special protection of the Counts of

---

* Smith, *Dictionary;* Keightley's *Mythology;* Montalembert, *Monks of the
West;* Michaelis.

Paris ; and when they dethroned the sons of Charlemagne and became kings of France, St. Denys, as they called their saint, became the patron of the country ; the banner of the convent, the Oriflamme, was unfurled in their national wars, and *Mont joie St. Denys* was their war-cry. St. Denys of France was invoked, together with St. Michael, in knighting their young men ; and St. Denys of France was received as one of the Seven Champions of Christendom.

The Sicilians, having a certain confusion in their minds between the champion and the tyrant of Syracuse, have taken San Dionigi for their patron ; he is also in high favour in Portugal as Diniz, and in Spain as Dionis. Denis is a very frequent Irish name, as a substitute for Donogh ; and, to judge by the number of the surnames, Dennis, Denison, and Tennyson or Tenison, it would seem to have been more common in England than at present. The Russians have Dionissij ; the Bohemians, Diwis ; the Slavonians, Tennis ; the Hungarians, Dienes. The feminine is the French Denise ; English, Dionisia, Donnet, Dennet or Diot, which seem to have been at one time very common in England.*

Section IX.—*Hermes.*

The origin is lost of the name of Hermes, the swift, eloquent, and cunning messenger of Zeus ; but it is supposed to come from hĕra (the earth), and was called Hermas, Hermes, or Hermeias.

A long catalogue of Greeks might be given bearing names derived from him ; and it was correctly that Shakespeare called his Athenian maiden Hermia.

Hermas is mentioned in the Epistle to the Romans, and is thought to be the same with the very early Christian author of the allegory of *The Shepherd,* but his name has not been followed.

Hermione was, in ancient legend, the wife of Cadmus, the founder of Thebes, and shared his metamorphosis into a serpent. Afterwards, another Hermione was the daughter of Helen and Menelaus, and, at first, wife of Neoptolemus, though afterwards of Orestes, the heroine of a tragedy of Euripides, where she appears in the unpleasant light of the jealous persecutor of the enslaved Andromache.

Hermione is generally supposed to be the same as the Italian Erminia and the French Hermine ; but these are both remains of the Herminian gens, and are therefore Latin.

Hermocrates, Hermagoras, Hermogenes, every compound of this god's name prevailed in Greece ; but the only one that has passed on to Christianity is Hermolaos (people of Hermes), a name that gave a saint to the Greek Church, and is perpetuated in Russia as Ermolaï.†

Descending from the greater deities of Olympus, we must touch upon the Muses, though not many instances occur of the use of their names. Μοῦσαι (Mousai), their collective title, is supposed to come

* Liddell and Scott, Keightley, Michaelis, Smith.
† Keightley's *Mythology ;* Cave's *Lives of the Fathers ;* Smith, *Dictionary ;* Potter's *Euripides.*

from μάω (mao), to invent ; it furnished the term mousikos, for songs and poetry, whence the Latin *musa, musicus,* and all the forms in modern language in which we speak of music and its professors.

Musidora (gift of the Muses) was one of the fashionable poetical soubriquets of the last century, and as such figures in Thomson's *Seasons.*

As to the individual names, they have scarcely any owners except Polymnia, she of many hymns, whose modern representative, Polyhymnia, lies buried in a churchyard on Dartmoor, and startles us by her headstone. The West Indian negresses, sporting the titles of the ships of war, however, come out occasionally as Miss Calliope, Miss Euterpe, &c.

The only Muse who has left namesakes is hardly a fair specimen ; for Urania (the heavenly), her epithet, as the presiding genius of astronomers, is itself formed from one of the pristine divinities of Greece, himself probably named from heaven itself, of which he was the personification. Οὐρανός (Ouranos), Uranus, is in Greek both the sky and the first father of all. The word is probably derived from the root *or,* which we find in ὄρος (a mountain), and ὄρνυμι (to raise), just as our heaven comes from to heave.

Uranius was not uncommon among the later Greeks, especially in Christian names ; a Gaulish author was so called, and it was left by the Romans as a legacy to the British. It makes its appearance among the Welsh as Urien, a somewhat common name at one time. "Brave Urien sleeps upon his craggy bed ;" but Camden, or some one else before him, thought proper to identify it with George, which has led to its decay and oblivion.

Urania was revived in the days of euphuistic taste, when Sir Philip Sidney called himself Sidrophel, and the object of his admiration, Urania ; it became a favourite poetic title both in England and France, and in process of time, a family name.

Θάλεια (Thaleia), though both Muse of Comedy, and one of the Three Graces, and signifying bloom, has not obtained any namesakes, though both her sister Graces have.

These nymphs were the multiplied personifications of Χάρις (Charis) grace, beauty, or charity. The Greeks were not unanimous as to the names or numbers of the Charites ; the Athenians and Spartans adored only two, and the three usually recognized were defined by Hesiod. Thalia (bloom), Aglaia (brightness), Euphrosyne (mirth, cheerfulness, or festivity).

It has been almost exclusively by Greeks that the name has been borne ; it was a great favourite among the Romaic Greeks, figuring again and again amongst the Porphyrogenitai, and to this present day it is common among the damsels of the Ionian Isles. I have seen it marked on a school-child's sampler in its own Greek letters. In common life it is called Phroso. In Russia it is Jefronissa.

The other Grace, Aglaia, comes to light in Christian legend, as the name of a rich and abandoned lady at Rome, who, hearing of the value that was set on the relics of saints, fancied them as a kind of roc's egg to complete the curiosities of her establishment, and sent

Boniface, both her steward and her lover, to the East to procure some for her. He asked in jest whether, if his bones came home to her, she would accept them as relics ; and she replied in the same spirit, little dreaming that at Tarsus he would indeed become a Christian and a martyr, and his bones be truly sent back to Rome, where Aglaia received them, became a penitent, took the veil, and earned the saintly honours that have ever since been paid to her. It is unfortunate for the credibility of this story that the date assigned to it is between 209 and 305, a wide space indeed, but one in which relic worship had not begun, and even if it had, the bones of martyrs must have been only too plentiful much nearer home. However, the French have taken up the name of Aglaë, and make great use of it.

A few ancient Greeks had names compounded of Charis, such as Charinus, and Charilaus, the nephew of Lycurgus ; but it was reserved for Christianity to give the word its higher sense. Charis, through the Latin caritas, grew to be the Christian's Charity, the highest of the three Graces : Faith, Hope, Love, that had taken the place of Bloom, Mirth, and Brightness. And thus it was that, after the Reformation, Charity, contracted into Cherry, became an English Christian name, perhaps in remembrance of the fair and goodly Charity of the House Beautiful, herself a reflex of the lovely and motherly Charissa, to whom Una conducted the Red Cross Knight. Chariton, Kharitoon, in Russian, is a name in the Greek Church, from a confessor of Sirmium, who under Aurelius was flogged with ox-hides and imprisoned, but was liberated on the Emperor's death, and made a pilgrimage to Jerusalem.

Perhaps this is the place, among these minor mythological personages, to mention that Zephyr (the West wind) has absolutely a whole family of name-children in France, where Zephirine has been greatly the fashion of late years.*

Section X.—*Heroic Names.*

Not very many of the heroic names—glorious in poetry—have passed on ; but we will select a few of those connected with the siege of Troy, and handed on upon that account. Mostly they were not easy of comprehension even to the Greeks themselves, and were not much copied among them, perhaps from a sense of reverence. It was only in the times of decay, and when the recollection of the fitness of things was lost, that men tried to cover their own littleness with the high-sounding names of their ancestors. Moreover, by that time, Greek associations were at a discount. Rome professed to descend from Troy, not from Greece ; and, after her example, modern nations have tried to trace themselves back to the Trojan fugitives—the Britons to Brut, the French to Francus, &c.—and thus Trojan names have been more in vogue than Greek. However, be it observed that the Trojan names are Greek in origin. The Trojans

* Smith, *Dictionary;* Keightley, *Mythology;* Montalembert.

were of Pelasgic blood, as well as most of their opponents ; but they
were enervated by residence in Asia, while the superior race of
Hellenes had renovated their Greek relatives ; making just the difference that the Norman Conquest did to the English Saxon in opposition to his Frisian brother.

One of these inexplicable names was borne by Ἀχιλλεύς (Achilleus),
the prime glory of Homer and of the Trojan war.   The late Greek
traditions said that his first name had been Ligyron, or the whining,
but that he was afterwards called Achilles, from A privative and
χεῖλη (cheile), lip ; because he was fed in his infancy on nothing but
lions' hearts and bears' marrow.   This legend, however, looks much
as if the true meaning of the word had been forgotten, and this was
a forgery to account for it.   However this may be, modern Greece
and France alone repeat the name, and it is much disguised by the
French pronunciation of Achille.   A martyr in Dauphiné was called
Achilles ; and an Achilla appears, as a lady, early in the Visconti
pedigree.

Gallant Hector, who, perhaps, is the most endearing of all the
Trojan heroes, from the perfection of his character in tenderness,
devotion, and courage, and the beautiful poetry of his parting with
his wife and son, bore a name that is an attribute of Zeus, Ἕκτωρ
(holding fast), i. e., defending, from Ἔχω (hecho), to have or to hold
—a word well-befitting the resolute mainstay of a falling cause.

Italy, where the descent from the Trojans was early credited and
not, perhaps, impossible, is the only country where his name has been
genuinely imitated, under the form of Ettore.   The Hector of Norway
is but an imitation of the old Norse Hagtar (hawk of Thor), and the
very frequent Hector of Scotland is the travestie of the Gaelic Eachan
(a horseman).   In like manner the Gaelic Aonghas (excellent valour)
and the Welsh Einiawn (the just), are both translated into Æneas ;
indeed it is possible that the early Welsh Saint, Einiawn, may indeed
have been an Æneas ; for, in compliment to the supposed descent of
the Julii from Æneas, this name is very common in the latter times
of the empire : it appears in the book of Acts, and belonged to several
writers.   Latterly, in the beginning of the classical taste of Italy, the
name of Enea Silvio was given to that Piccolomini who afterwards
became a pope.   This form is in honour of that son of Æneas and
Lavinia who was said to have been born in a wood after his father's
death.   A son of the Earl of Hereford was called Æneas (temp. Ed.
III.).

The pious Æneas owes his modern fame to Virgil.   In the time of
Homer, even his goddess-mother had not raised him into anything
like the first rank of the heroes who fought before Troy.   His name
in the original is Αἰνείας (Aineias), and probably comes from αἰνέο
(aineo), to praise.

The poem that no doubt suggested the *Æneid*, the Homeric story of
the Greek wanderer, contains some of those elements that so wonderfully show the kindred of far distant nations.   We are content to
call this wonderful poem by something approaching to its Greek
title, though we are pleased to term the hero by the Latin travestie

of his name—Ulysses, the consequence, it is supposed, of some transcriber having mistaken between the letters Δ and Λ. The Romans, likewise, sometimes called him Ulixes; the Greek σσ and ξ being, by some, considered as the same letter. Ὀδυσσεύς (Odysseus), his true name, is traced to the root δυς (dys), hate, the Sanscrit *dvish*, and from the same source as the Latin *odio*. Italians talked of Uliseo, and Fenelon taught the French to honour his favourite hero as *le fils du grand Ulisse;* but the only place where the name is now used is Ireland, probably as a classicalism for the Danish legacy of Ulick—Hugleik, or mind reward. The Irish Finnghuala (white shoulders) was not content with the gentle native softenings of her name into Fenella and Nuala, but must needs translate herself into Penelope; and it is to this that we owe the numerous Penelopes of England, down from the Irish Penelope Devereux, with whom is connected the one shade on Sidney's character, to the Pen and Penny so frequent in many families.

The faithful queen of Ithaca was probably named Πηνελόπη, or Πηνελόπεια, from her diligence over the loom, since πήνη (pēnē) is thread on the bobbin, πηνίζομαι is to wind it off; but a later legend declared that she had been exposed as an infant, and owed her life to being fed by a kind of duck called πηνέλοψ (penelops), after which she was therefore called. This has since been made the scientific name of the turkey, and translators of Christian names have generally set Penelope down as a turkey-hen, in oblivion that this bird, the D'Inde of France, the *Wälsche Hahn* of Germany, always in its name attesting its foreign origin, came from America 3000 years after the queen of Ithaca wove and unwove beneath her midnight lamp.

Her son Telemachus (distant battle) had one notable namesake in the devoted hermit who for ever ended the savage fights of the amphitheatre; but, though Télémaque was a triumph of genius and tender religious feeling in spite of bad pseudo-classical taste, has not been again repeated.

Cassandra appears in Essex in 1560, and named the sister of Jane Austen.

CHAPTER III.

NAMES FROM ANIMALS, ETC.

SECTION I.—*The Lion.*

MUCH of the spirit of the nation is to be traced in the animals whence their names are derived. The Jew, whose temper, except when thoroughly roused, was peaceful and gentle, had hardly any save the names of the milder and more useful creatures : the ewe, the lamb, the bee, the fawn, &c. The Indo-European races, on the other hand, have the more brave and spirited animals, many of them running through the entire family of nations thus derived, and very possibly connected with that 'beast epic,' as Mr. Dasent calls it, which crops out everywhere ; in the East, in apologues and fables; and towards the West, in '*mahrchen*,' according to the expressive German term. It is just as if in the infancy of the world, there was the same living sympathy with the animal creation that we see in a young child, and that the creatures had at one time appeared to man to have an individual character, rank, and history of their own, explained by myths, in which these beings are the actors and speakers, and assumed a meaning divine, symbolic, didactic, or simply grotesque, according to the subsequent development of the peoples by whom they were handed down.

The lion is one of these universal animals, testifying how long dim memories of the home in Asia must have clung to the distant wanderers.

Leon, or Leo, was early a favourite name among the Greeks ; and Herodotus thinks, on account of its meaning, that the captive Leo was the first victim of the Persians. It passed on in unceasing succession through Greeks of all ranks till it came to Byzantine emperors and Roman bishops. Two popes, to whom Rome owed the deepest debt of gratitude—to the one, for interceding with Attila ; to the other, for turning away the wrath of the Saracens—were both called Leo, and it thus became a favourite on the papal throne, and was considered to allude to the Lion of the Tribe of Judah, which was therefore sculptured on St. Peter's, in the time of the Medicean Leo X.

Leone, and Léon, and Léonie have continued in use in France and Italy. The word has been much compounded from the earlier Greek times, Leontius, Leontia, whence the modern French Léonce. The

name Leonidas, the glorious self-devoted Spartan, after entire desuetude, has been revived in Greece and America.

The Romanized Britons adopted the Lion name, which amongst
them became Llew, the Lot of the romances of the Round Table.
Here likewise figured the gallant Sir Lionel, from whom Edward III.,
in chivalrous mood, named his third son, the ancestor of the House
of York. An unfortunate young Dane, to whom the Dutch republic
stood sponsor, received the name of Leo Belgicus. The Slavonic
forms are Lev, Lav, and Lew, which, among the swarms of Jews in
Poland, have become a good deal confounded with their hereditary
Levi.

Leandros, Leander, as we call it, means lion-man. Besides the
unfortunate swimming lover whose exploit Byron imitated and
Turner painted, it belonged to a sainted bishop of Seville, who, in
590, effected the transition of the Spanish Visigoths from Arianism to
orthodoxy. Very likely his name was only a classicalizing of one of
the many Gothic names from *leut* (the people), which are often confused with those from the lion ; but Leandro passed on as a Christian
name in Spain and Italy.

The name Leocadia, a Spanish maiden martyred by the Moors,
had probably some connection with a lion ; but it cannot be traced
in the corrupted state of the language. Léocadie has travelled into
France.

The Slavonians have Lavoslav (lion-glory), which they make the
equivalent of the Teutonic Liutpold or Leopold, really meaning the
people's prince.

Löwenhard (the stern lion, or lion strong), was a Frank noble, who
was converted at the same time as his sovereign, Clovis, and became
a hermit near Limoges. Many miracles were imputed to him, and
St. Leonard became a peculiarly popular saint both in France and
England. Leonard is a favourite name in France ; and has some
popularity in England, chiefly, it is said, in the north, and in the
Isle of Wight. Lionardo is Italian, witness Lionardo da Vinci ; and,
according to Gil Blas, Leonarda is a Spanish feminine ; Germany has
in surnames Lenhardt, Lehnart, Leinhardt, Lowen ; Italy invented
the formidable Christian name, Brancalleone (Brachium leonis), or
arm of a lion ; and Bavaria has Lowenclo (lion-claw).

English.	French.	German.	Swiss.	Italian.
Leonard	Léonard	Leonhard	Liert	Lionardo
	Leunairs	Lienhard	Liertli	
	Launart	Lienl	Lienzel	

Section II.—*The Horse.*

The horse is as great a favourite as the lion, and is prominent in
many a myth from the Caspian to the Frozen Ocean. His name
in Sanscrit *açva*, in Zendish *esp* or *asp*, comes forth in the Greek

ἵππος or ἴκκος, showing its identity with the Latin *equus*, the Gaelic *each*, and it may be with the Teutonic *hengst*.

Among these various races it is the Persian, the Greek, and the Gael who have chiefly used the term for this noble animal in their nomenclature.

The Persian feminine Damaspia is said exactly to answer to the Greek Hippodameia, the female of Hippodamus (horse-tamer), and Hippos forms part of far too many Greek names to be here enumerated, except where they have become popular elsewhere.

One would have imagined that Hippos and λύω (to destroy) must have suggested the name of Hippolytus, the son of Theseus, who was destroyed by his own horse, terrified by a sea monster; but, on the other hand, he appears to have been named after his mother Hippolita, the beautiful queen of the Amazons, whom Shakespeare has shown us hunting in his wondrous Attic forest. However this may be, Hippolytus has many namesakes; among them an early Christian writer, and also a priest at Rome, who in the year 252 was condemned by the persecuting judge to die the death his name suggested. The Christians buried him in a catacomb, which bears his name. Sant 'Ippolito became a parish church at Rome, and of course gave a title to one of the cardinals, and Ippolito and Ippolita have always been fashionable Italian names. He was also the patron of horsemen and horses, and the latter were solemnly blessed in his name. Xanthippe's name is feminine of Xanthippus (a yellow horse!) What a pity it was not a grey one!

The Persian Aspamitras (horse-lover) exactly corresponds to the Greek Φίλιππος (loving horses). Thus were named many obscure kings of Macedon, before that sagacious prince who prepared the future glories of his son by disciplining his army, and crushing Greece in spite of those indignant orations of Demosthenes, which have made Philippics the generic term for vehement individual censure.

Macedon, by colonizing the East, spread Philippos over it, and thus was named the apostle of Bethsaida, and likewise one of the deacons, chosen for his 'Grecian' connections.

The apostle was martyred at Hierapolis; nevertheless an arm of his, according to the Bollandists, was brought to Florence from Constantinople, in 1205, and made Filippo, Filippa, Lippo, Pippo, Pippa, great favourites in Northern Italy.

Greece and her dependent churches always used the name of Philip, or Feeleep, as they call it in Russia; and it was the eldest son of the Muscovite Anne, Queen of Henri I., who was the first Philippe to wear the crown of France. He transmitted his name to five more kings, and to princes innumerable, of whom one became Duke of Burgundy. His descendant, the half Flemish, half Austrian Philippe the handsome, married Juana la Loca of Castille and Aragon, and their grandson was known as Felipe II. in Spain. During his brief and ill-omened stay in England, he was godfather to Philip Sidney, whose name commemorated the gratitude of his mother to the King Consort for having interceded for the life of his father the Duke of Northumberland.

Philip, in both genders, was, however, already common in England. Queen Philippe, as she called herself, our admirable Hainaulter, was the god-daughter of Philippe de Valois, her husband's rival; and many a young noble and maiden bore her honoured name, which one female descendant carried to Portugal, and another to Sweden, where both alike worthily sustained the honour of Plantagenet.

The name of Philippe is particularly common in the Isle of Jersey, so that it has become a joke with sailors to torment the inhabitants by calling them Philip as they would term an Irishman Paddy.

Filippo is additionally popular in Italy at present from the favourite modern Saint Filippo Neri.*

English.	Scotch.	French.	German.	Italian.
Philip	Phillipp	Philippe	Philipp	Filippo
Phil		Philipot	Lipp	Pippo
Phip			Lipperl	Lippo

Portuguese.	Spanish.	Russian.	Lett.	Hungarian.
Felippe	Felipe	Feeleep	Wilips	Fülip
Felipinho			Lipsts	

		FEMININE.		

English.	French.	Portuguese.	Dutch.	Italian.
Philippa	Philippine	Felipa	Pine	Filippa
	Flipote			Pippa

SECTION III.—*The Goat.*

The goat (αἴξ) stands out prominently in northern mythology, though there scarcely, if at all, used in nomenclature. In Greek mythology he appears, though not distinctly, and the names derived from him are manifold.

The goat was the standard of Macedon (the rough goat was the King of Grecia), as Daniel had announced while Greece was yet in her infancy, and Macedon in barbarism, not even owned as of the Hellenic confederacy. The unfortunate posthumous son of Alexander was therefore called Aigos, or Ægos, in addition to his father's name.

The aigis, ægis, or shield of Pallas Athene, though said to bear the gorgon's head, was probably at first a goat skin. From it is formed Aigidios, Ægidius. In 475, there was an Ægidius, a Roman commander in Gaul, who was for a time an independent sovereign, ruling over both Romans and Franks. About two centuries later, an Athenian, as it is said, by name Ægidius, having worked a miraculous cure by laying his cloak over the sick man, fled to France to avoid the veneration of the people, and dwelt on the

* Rawlinson's *Herodotus;* Keightley's *Mythology;* Butler; Michaelis.

banks of the Rhone, living on the milk of a hind. The creature was chased by the king of France, and, flying wounded to her master, discovered him to the hunters. Thenceforth he has been revered as St. Giles, and considered as the patron of numbers thus called. Now, is Giles a contraction of Ægidius, or is it the corruption of the Latin Julius; or, again, is it the Keltic Giolla, a servant, or the Teutonic Gils, a pledge? Every one of these sounds more like it than the Greek word, and it does seem probable that the Athenian, if Athenian he were, was seized upon as patron by aliens to his name, and then cut down to suit them. However, Ægidius continued to be treated as the Latin for Giles; Egidio became an Italian name; and as St. Giles was patron of Edinburgh, Egidia was used by Scottish ladies; one of the sisters of King Robert II. was so called, and even now it is not quite extinct.*

Section IV.—*The Bee.*

The word μεῖλα (soothing things) gave the verb μειλίσσω, or μελίσσω (melisso), to soothe or sweeten, whence the name of honey, and of the honey-bee. Melissa was sometimes said to have been the name of the nymph who first taught the use of honey, and bees, perhaps from their clustering round their queen, became the symbol of nymphs. Thence Melissa grew to be the title of a priestess as well as a lady's name in classic times.

Melissa was invented by the Italian poets as the beneficent fairy who protected Bradamante, and directed Ruggero to escape from Atlante, and afterwards from Alcina, upon the hippogriff. Thus she entered the domain of romance, and became confounded with the Melusine and Melisende, who had risen out of the Teutonic Amalaswinth; and Melisse and Melite were adopted into French nomenclature.

Akin to Melissa is Γλυκηρά (Glykera), the sweet. This was not a feminine in good repute in ancient Athens, but it has since belonged to a saint of the Greek Churches, namely, the daughter of Macarius, thrice consul, who in the time of Antoninus suffered torments for a long time at Trajanopolis; and Gloukera is prevalent in Russia; and Glykera, or Glycère, in France.†

Section V.—*Names from Flowers.*

It was not common in Greece to name persons from flowers, but two names in occasional use are connected with legends of transformation, though in each case it is evident that the name belonged originally to the flower, and then was transferred to the man.

Thus the Narcissus, named undoubtedly from ναρκάω (narkao), to

* Keightley's *Fairy Mythology;* Croker's *Fairy Legends;* Tooke's *History of Russia;* Butler.
† Liddell and Scott; Professor Munch; Junius.

put to sleep, has become the object of a graceful legend of the cold-hearted youth, for whose sake the nymph Echo pined away into a mere voice, and in retribution was made to see his own beauty in the water and waste from hopeless love for his own image, until his corpse became the drooping golden blossom, that loves to hang above still pools of water, like the "dancing daffodils" of Wordsworth.

Narcissus seems to have been a name among the Greek slaves of the Romans, for we twice find it belonging to freedmen of the Emperor. St. Narcissus was Bishop of Jerusalem in 195, and presided at the council that fixed the great festival of the Resurrection on a Sunday instead of on the day fixed by the full moon like the Jews. The Russians call it Narkiss; the Romans, Narcisso; and it has even been found belonging to an English peasant.

Hyacinthus ('Υάκινθος) was a beautiful Spartan youth, who, being accidentally killed by Apollo in a game with the discus, was caused by the sorrowing divinity to propagate from his blood a flower bearing on its petals either his initial Υ or the αἰ (alas), the cry of lamentation. A yearly feast was held at Sparta in honour of Hyacinthus, and his name was perpetuated till Christian times, when a martyr bore it at Rome, and thus brought it into favour in Italy as Giacinto; also a Polish Dominican Jacinthus in the thirteenth century, is commemorated as the Apostle of the North, because he preached Christianity in great part of Russia and Tartary; but curiously enough it is in Ireland alone that Hyacinth has ever flourished as a man's name, probably as a supposed equivalent to some native Erse name. There it is very common among the peasantry, and is in common use as Sinty, while in France, Italy, and Spain, though apparently without a saintly example of their own sex, Jacinthe, Giacinta, and Jacinta are always feminine, and rather popular peasant names.

'Ρόδος (Rhodos), the rose, is a word connected in its source with the origin of the Teuton roth, Keltic ruadh, and Latin rufus. Roses are the same in almost every tongue, and they almost always suggest female names; of which the most interesting to us is Rhoda, "the household maid, of her own joy afraid," who "opened not the gate for gladness" when she knew the voice of St. Peter as he stood without the door after his release from prison and death. Her name, as a Scripture one, has had some use in England, though, in general, the Roses of each country have grown upon their own national grafts from the one great stock, or, more strangely, are changed from horses.

Φύλλις (Phyllis), a green leaf or bough, has another story of transformation. She was a Thalian damsel who hung herself because her lover did not keep his promise of returning to marry her, and was accordingly changed into an almond tree. Phyllis was the name of Domitian's nurse, and in process of time found her way among the dramatis personæ of Arcadian poetry; and arrived at being somewhat popular as a name in England.

G

CHAPTER IV.

HISTORICAL GREEK NAMES CONSISTING OF EPITHETS.

SECTION I.—*Agathos.*

AFTER passing from the fascinating but confused tales and songs that group around the ship Argo, the doomed family of Œdipus, and the siege of Troy, the Greeks are well-nigh lost for a time, but emerge again in the full and distinct brilliancy of the narratives of Herodotus and his followers, who have rendered their small aggregate of fragmentary states and their gallant resistance to Asiatic invasion the great nucleus of interest in the ancient world.

In the days of these wise and brave men, the nomenclature was, for the most part, expressive and appropriate, consisting of compounds of words of good augury from the spoken language, and, usually, as has been before shown, with a sort of recurring resemblance, from generation to generation, so as to make the enumeration of a pedigree significant and harmonious.

Of these was ἀγαθός (the good), precisely the same word as our own *good* and the German *guth*, only with the commencing *a* and a Greek termination.

Classical times showed many an Agathon, and Agathias, and numerous compounds, such as Agathocles (good fame), to be repeated in the Teutonic Gudred, and other varieties; but the abiding use of the word as an European name was owing to a Sicilian girl, called Agatha, who in the Decian persecution was tortured to death at Rome. Sicily considered her as one of its guardian saints. Thus, the festival day of this martyred virgin is observed by both the Eastern and Western Churches, and her name is found among all the nations that ever possessed her native island. Greece has transmitted it to Russia, where the *th* not being pronounceable, it is called Agafia; and the masculine, which is there used, Agafon; and the Slavonian nations derive it from the same quarter. The Normans adopted it and sent it home to their sisters in Neustria, where it was borne by that daughter of William the Conqueror who was betrothed to the unfortunate Earl Edwin, and afterwards died on her way to a state marriage in Castille. In her probably met the Teutonic Gytha and the Greek Agatha, identical in meaning and root, and almost in sound, though they had travelled to her birth-place in Rouen by two such different routes from their Eastern starting-place. Agatha was once much more common as a name than at present in England, and seems still to prevail more in the northern than the southern counties. Haggy, or Agatha, is the maid-servant's name in Southey's *Doctor*, attesting its prevalence in that class before hereditary or peculiar names were discarded as at present.

France did not fail to take up Agatha. Spain had her Agatha like that of the Italians, both alike omitting the *h* of *θ*. Portugal makes it Agneda; and the only other change worth noting is that the Letts cut it short into Apka.

Aristos (best) was a favourite commencement with the Greeks. Aristides, most just of men, was thus called the son of the best.   He has reappeared in his proper form in modern Greece; as Aristide in republican France; as Aristides in America.

Aristobulus (best counsel) came originally from an epithet of Artemis, to whom Themistocles built a temple at Athens, as Aristoboulè, the best adviser. It was very common in the various branches of the Macedonian empire, and was thus adopted in the Asmonean family, from whom it came to the Herodian race, and thence spread among the Jews. In the Epistle to the Romans, St. Paul sends his greetings to the household of Aristobulus; and Welsh ecclesiastical antiquaries endeavour to prove that Arwystli, whom the Triads say was brought by Bran the blessed to preach the Gospel in Britain, was the same with this person.

Aristarchus (best judge) is also a Scriptural name; and besides these we have Aristocles (best fame), Aristippos (best horse), Aristagoras (best assembly), and all the other usual Greek compounds among the Greeks.

Perhaps this is the fittest place to mention that Arethusa is in use among the modern Greeks, and interpreted by them to mean the virtuous, as coming from this source. Aretino has been used in Italy.*

Section II.—*Alexander, &c.*

Conquering Macedon was the portion of Greece, if Greece it could be called, that spread its names most widely and permanently; and as was but right, no name was more universally diffused than that of the great victor, he who in history is as prominent as Achilles in poetry. Ἀλέξανδρος (Alexandros), from ἀλέξω (alexo), to help, and ἄνδρες (andres), men, was said to have been the title given to Paris by the shepherds among whom he grew up, from his courage in repelling robbers from the flocks. It was afterwards a regular family name among the kings of Macedon, he who gave it fame being the third who bore it. So much revered as well as feared was this mighty conqueror, that his name still lives in proverb and song throughout the East. The Persians absolutely adopted him into their own line, and invented a romance by which 'Secunder' was made the son of a native monarch. Among the eastern nations, Iskander became such a by-word for prowess, that even in the sixteenth century the Turks would find no greater title of fear for their

* Smith: Jameson; Rees, *Welsh Saints.*

foe, the gallant Albanian, Georgios Kastriotes, than Skander Beg, or
Lord Alexander.

Not only did the great conqueror possess many namesakes,—as
indeed, there is a story that all the children born the year of his
conquest of India were called after him,—but Alexandros was already
frequent in Greece; and among the kingdoms formed out of the
fragments of his empire, it recurred so as to become usual all over
the Græcized East.   Even the Maccabean Jews used it, and it was
common in Judea, as well as elsewhere, in the time of the Gospels, so
that a large proportion of saints and martyrs bore it and handed it
on, especially in Greece and Italy.   A pope, martyred in the second
century, rendered it a papal assumed name; and the Italians used it
frequently as Alessandro, shortened into Sandro.   Nowhere, however,
is it so thoroughly national as in Scotland, imported thither, apparently, with other Greek names, by Margaret Ætheling, who learnt
them in the Hungarian court where she was born and brought up.
Her third son was the first of the three Scottish Alexanders, under
whom the country spent her most prosperous days.

No wonder his namesakes were numerous.   In the Highlands
they came to be Alaster, and formed the surname MacAlister; in the
south, the contractions were Alick, Saunders, or Sandy, and the
feminine Alexa, Alexandrina, and Alexandra, are chiefly German
and Russian, though now and then occurring in France.

The first half of this name, Alexios, a defender, was in use in
ancient Greece, where it belonged to a noted sculptor.   Its saintly
honours did not begin till the fifth century, when a young Roman
noble, called Allexius or Alexis, is said to have been so much bent
on a monastic life, that being compelled by his parents to marry, he
fled away on his wedding day, and lived seventeen years in a convent
in Syria; but, finding his reputation for sanctity too much for his
humility, he came home in guise of a poor pilgrim, and spent another
seventeen years as a beggar maintained on the scraps of his father's
kitchen, and constantly mocked and misused by the servants, until
in his dying moments, he made himself known to his parents.   His
church at Rome, called St. Alessio, gives a title to a cardinal; and his
day, July 17th, is observed by the Greeks as well as the Romans';
and yet so strange is his history that it almost seems as if it might
have been one of those instances in which an allegory acquired the
name of a real saint, and attached itself to him as a legend.   Alessio
has in consequence always been an Italian name, and with the family
of the Komnenoi, Alexios came into use among the Byzantine Greeks,
with whom it was very frequent.   Alexia is often found as a lady's
name in old records and accounts of the middle ages; but it is apparently intended merely as the Latin equivalent for Alice, which we
shall show by-and-by to have had an entirely different origin.

English.	Scotch.	French.	Italian.	Spanish.
Alexander	Alexander	Alexandre	Alessandro	Alejandro
Alex	Alick		Sandro	
	Sanders			
	Sandy			
	Sawny			
	Elshender			
	Elshie			
	Alaster			

Russian.	Polish.	Slavonic.	Ung.	
Aleksander	Aleksander	Aleksander	Sandor	
Ssachka		Skender		
Ssaschinka	Leszek			

English.	Italian.	Portuguese.	Spanish.	French.
Alexis	Alessio	Aleixo	Alejo	Alexis
				Alexe

Russian.	Slavonic.	Servian.	Lusatian.	Hungarian.
Alexei	Ales	Aleksa	Alex	Elek
Alescha	Leks		Halex	
			Holex	

SECTION III.—*Aner, Andros.*

We come to the names derived from ἀνήρ, gen. ἀνδρός (aner, andros), a man. The word itself has connections in the Sanscrit *nara*, and Zend *ner;* but its compounds are all from its oblique cases.

The most interesting of these is formed by the corrupt Greek dialect used in Syria, namely, that which fell to Ανδρέας (Andreas), the Galilean fisherman, whom the Church Universal reveres as one of the foremost in the Glorious Company of the Apostles. The saint was martyred at Patras in Achaia, whence some of his relics were carried in the fourth century to Scotland, and were thus the occasion of St. Andrew's becoming the Metropolitan see. Shortly after, the vision of Hungus, King of the Picts, of St. Andrew's Cross, promising him victory, rendered the white saltire the national ensign, and St. Andrew became not only the patron saint, but in due time the knightly champion of Scotland, and made Andrew one of the most universal of names, and the patronymic Anderson very common. The other relics went first to Constantinople, and after the taking of that city, were dispersed through Europe. Philip the Good, of Burgundy, obtained some of them, and made St. Andrew the patron

of the order of the Golden Fleece, and Andreas became a frequent
Flemish and Dutch name.　It has a feminine in the countries where
it is most popular, and its variations are as follows :—

English.	Scotch.	Dutch.	Danish.
Andrew	Andrew	Andreas	Anders
Andy	Dandie	Andries	
		Dries	

French.	German.	Italian.	Spanish.
André	Andreas	Andrea	Andres
Andrien			

Russian.	Slavonic.	Polish.	Bohemian.
Andrej	Andrej	Andrezej	Ondrej
	Andias	Jedrzej	
	Necek		
	Andrejeek		

Lusatian.	Esthonian.	Hungarian.	Lapland.
Handrej	Andras	Andras	Anta
Rajka	Andrus	Bandi	Attok
Hendrijshka			Ats

The feminines are the French Andrée and Italian Andreana.　The
Russians use Andrean as an equivalent for Henry!

Andronicus, man's victory, was a great favourite, and occurs in
St. Paul's Epistle to the Romans, probably having belonged to
a Corinthian who had gone from the busy city of traffic on the
Isthmus to the great Capital of the world.　The name continued
among the Greeks, and belonged to numerous emperors, but has not
been subsequently in much favour.

Section IV.—*Eu.*

The word εὖ (well or happily) was the commencement of many a
name of good augury from the earliest times, and mingles as much
among Christian as among classical associations.

Thus in company with ἄγγελος, angelos (a messenger), it formed
evangelus, happy messenger, or bearer of good tidings, the first time
applied to a shepherd, who brought to Ephesus the tidings of a quarry
of beautiful marble for the building of the temple that was the glory
of the city and of all Asia.　Adored with heroic honours as he was,
the title must have seemed to the Ephesian Christians, above all, to
befit those spiritual shepherds who brought the best of tidings, and
Evangelista became the term for a preacher, as Evangelium of his
doctrine, both becoming in time restricted to the four writers of the

personal history of our Lord, and their narrative, as being the very core and centre of the Good Tidings. Evangelista was an old Italian name ; and Longfellow appears to have invented Evangeline for the heroine of his poem, whence many of the name have sprung up in America.

Εὔχειρ (Eucheir), dexterous hand, was no doubt at first a mere epithet of a sculptor, but afterwards considered as a name, and belonging to no less than four distinguished sculptors of ancient Greece.

Thence the Latinized Eucherius, which belonged to a Bishop of Lyons, a great author of ecclesiastical works, who died about A.D. 450 ; from him comes the Portuguese Euchario, the Italian Eucario, the French Euchaire, the Russian Jevcharij, the Polish Euchary.

Εὐδώρη (Eudora), happy gift, was one of the Nereids, and afterwards did duty as Eudore in French romance.

Eudocia and Eudoxia are so much alike as to be often confused, but have different significations. The first is Εὐδοκία (approval), the second Εὐδοξία (good fame of glory). Both were great favourites with the Greek empresses, and were assumed by imperial brides possessed of some appellation not supposed to befit the purple. Saints of the Greek Church handed Eudokhia on into Russia, where it has been worn upon the throne, and becomes in common parlance Jevdoksija.

Εὐγενής (Eugenes), well born, was a very old Greek author ; but Eugenios was the more usual form in classical times, and was carried on as Eugenius by the Romans. St. Eugenius was an African Confessor, and another Eugenius was Bishop of Toledo in 646. Both these gave much popularity to their name ; the first in the East, the second in Italy, where Eugênio came to that high-spirited Savoyard who, growing weary of lingering at the court of Louis XIV., and hearing himself called *le petit Abbé du Roi*, rendered the sound of Prince Eugène dear to Austria and England ; terrible to France and Turkey. Foe as he was, it is to his fame that the great popularity of Eugène in France is owing, whilst even in the country for which he fought Eugen is far less common. The Russians have it as Jevgenij ; and the Servians as Djoulija ; indeed, well may these last remember the gallant prince who turned back the wave of Turkish invasion.

Eugenius stands forth again and again in the early roll of Scottish kings, but whether these sovereigns ever lived or not, their appellation was certainly not Eugenius, nor any corruption from it ; but the Keltic Eoghan, Ewan, or Evan, still extremely common in the Highlands, and meaning a young warrior, though, after the favourite custom of the Gael, Anglicized and Latinized by names of similar sound. The Welsh Owain or Ywain appears to have had the same fate, as the first means a lamb ; but this is not equally certain, as the British had many Latin and Greek names current among them, and this *may* be a corruption of Eugenius.

Eugenia was a virgin Roman martyr, of whom very little is known ; but this convenient feminine for Eugène has been in favour in the countries where the masculine was popular, and the Empress Eugénie rendered it the reigning name in France.

The names beginning with this favourite adverb are almost beyond enumeration, and it is only possible to select those of any modern interest. Εὐνίκη (Eunike), Eunice, happy victory, was one of the fifty Nereids, from whom the name passed to Greek women, and thus to Eunice, the Jewish mother of Timothy, whence this has become a favourite with English lovers of Bible names.

John Bunyan would have been reminded of his town of *Fair Speech* by the number of Greeks called by words of this signification: Eulalius, Eulogius, Euphemius, all with their feminines, besides Euphrasia.

The feminines were more enduring than the masculines. Eulalia was a child of ten or twelve years old, who, with that peculiar exaggeration of feeling that distinguishes Spanish piety, made her escape from the place of safety where her parents had taken refuge, entered Merida, and proclaiming herself a Christian, was martyred with the utmost extremity of torture in the persecution of Diocletian, and was sung by the great Christian poet Prudentius, himself a Spaniard. His verses spread her fame into the East, where the Russians carry on her name as Jevlalija ; the Servians, as Evlalija or Lelica. Another virgin martyr of the same name, under the same persecution, died at Barcelona, whence her relics spread into Guienne and Languedoc, and thus named the villages of Ste. Olaille, Ste. Aulazie, and Ste. Aulaire, the last a familiar seignoral title ! Eulalia and Eulalie have been often used in Spain and France, and the former is found in the register of Ottery St. Mary, Devon—also frequently in Cornwall.

Euphemia originally meant at once fair speech and abstinence from the reverse, so that almost in irony it signified silence, and was applied to the stillness that prevailed during religious rites, or to the proclamation of silence. The Euphemia who was the parent of the wide-spread name, was a virgin-martyr of Bithynia, whose legend of constancy, unshaken and invulnerable, alike by lion and flame, strongly impressed both the East and the West. Jevfimija, in Russia ; Jeva, in Servia ; Bema, in Lusatia ; and Pimmie, in Lithuania. Then she is almost as much changed as by the Effie and Phemie of Scotland, which together with Euphame have prevailed since very early times. It is a question whether this Scottish Euphame were really one of the Greek names brought from Hungary by Queen Margaret, or if it be only another attempt to translate the Keltic Aoiffe. In the Highlands, however, the name is called Oighrigh ; which, to English eyes and ears, seems equally distant from either Aoiffe or Euphemia. The church of Santa Eufemia at Rome gives title to a cardinal, and has spread the name in Italy and France.

It remains somewhat doubtful whether Eustace should be referred to Εὐστάθηος (steadfast), or to Εὔσταχος (happy in harvest). The Eostafie, or Eustathius, of the Greco-Slavonic Church, certainly has the same festival-day (September 20th) as the Eustachius of the Latin ; but the Latin Church has *likewise* a St. Eustachius, a different personage with a different day. He of September 20th was a Roman soldier, who lived and suffered under the Emperor Adrian, but his wild poetical legend is altogether a work of the Western mind. It begins like that of St. Hubert, with his conversion by the apparition of a crucifix planted between the horns of a stag, and a voice telling him that he should suffer great things. A soldier saint was sure to be a great favourite in the middle ages, and the supposed transport of St. Eustace's relics to St. Denis, in very early times, filled France with Eustache, and thence Eustace, Wistace, or Huistace, as English tongues were pleased to call it, came over in plenty at the Norman Conquest. Eustace 'Comes,' who holds land in Domesday Book before the Conquest, must have been he of Boulogne who had such a desperate quarrel with the Godwin sons. There were six householders of this name after the Conquest, and they, or their descendants, sometimes called their daughters Eustachie, or Eustachia. Eustachia, a kinswoman of Henry II., married Geoffrey de Mandeville; and Eustacie was once in favour in France ; but all these have a good deal lost their popularity, though we sometimes hear of Eustace in these days. The Bavarian contraction is Staches. Eusebius and Eusebia mean gentle or holy, and have not been frequent.*

SECTION V.—*Hieros.*

The word ἵερος (hieros), sacred, gave the term for a priest, or any other person or thing set apart, and thus formed several names in the family of the kings of Syracuse, Hieron, Hieracles (holy fame), Hieronymus, *i. e.* Ἱερώνυμος (with a holy name). These continued in use among the Greeks, and came at length to that Dalmatian scholar and hermit, Eusebius Hieronymus Sophronius, who is reckoned as one of the greatest of the Latin fathers. As a saint of high reputation, his name underwent the Italian process of changing its aspirate into a *G*, and he became San Geronimo, or even Girolamo, whence the French took their frequent Jerome, and we followed their example. The Germans did indeed hold fast to Hieronymus ; and the old English reformers would quote St. Hierom ; but Jerome is the abiding name by which the saint, his namesakes, and the friars who took his rule are called.

In Ireland, Jerome, like Jeremiah and Edward, has been forced into representing the good old Keltic Diarmaid.

English.	Portuguese.	Spanish.	Italian.
Hierom	Jeromino	Jeromo	Geronimo
Jerome	Hieronimo	Jeromino	Girolamo

French.	Russian.	Polish.	Servian.
Jerôme	Jeronim	Hieronim	Jerolim
		Hirus	Jerko

* Liddell and Scott; Smith; Jameson; Sir Isumbras; Ellis, *Domesday Book;* Michaelis.

In Cambrai, Hieronome was the form, with the Hieronomette for a feminine; and among the Swinburnes of Yorkshire, in the seventeenth century, Jeronima thrice occurs.*

Section VI.—*Pan.*

A few words beginning with πᾶς (all) must here be mentioned, such as Pankratios (all ruling). A boy thus called is said to have suffered at Rome, in his 14th year, in 304, under Diocletian. Even in the time of Gregory of Tours, it was supposed that certain vengeance followed false oaths made at his shrine, and his relics were therefore very valuable. A present of some from Pope Vitalian to our King Oswy brought St. Pancras into fashion in England, and Pancrace and Pancragio have also named many churches in France and Italy. The lily called *pancratium* claims by its name to excel all others.

Πανταλέων, Pantaleon (altogether a lion), was one of the numerous Christian physicians who suffered martyrdom. He died at Nicodemia, but his relics were brought to Constantinople, and thence to France, where he is the chief saint of the largest church at Lyons, and he is the patron of doctors next after St. Luke. His name was in use in France and Italy before. As a peasant name, he fell, with Arlechino and Colombina, into comedy. His dress was on the stage made to fit tight to his body, as if all in one piece, and he was always a feeble old man, whence Shakespeare speaks of the lean and slippered pantaloon. Thence again, when the entire leg was covered by the trousers instead of by stockings and breeches meeting at the knee, the name of pantaloon was applied to the new garment.

Νίκη (victory) was an auspicious word, which, being of feminine gender, as befitted a goddess, was a favourite close for women's names; such as Stratonike (army victory), Φερενίκη, Pherenike (bringing victory). Berenike was the Macedonian pronunciation of this last, and was in constant use among princesses of the two Greek kingdoms of Syria and Egypt. From these ladies, those of the Herod family took the name, and thus it was borne by that Bernice who heard St. Paul's defence. Oddly enough, the peasants of Normandy are fond of calling their daughters Berenice. Veronica is sometimes said likewise to be a corrupt form.

In men's names Nike was the prefix, as in Nikon, Niklias, Nikodemos (conquering people), Nikolaos (Νίκολαος), a word of like meaning. This last, after belonging to one of the seven first deacons, and to the founder of a heresy doomed in the Apocalypse, came to the Bishop of Myra, from whom it acquired a curious legendary fame that made it universal. St. Nicholas is said to have supplied three destitute maidens with marriage portions by secretly leaving money at their window, and as his day occurred just before Christmas, he thus was made the purveyor of the gifts of the season to all children in Flanders and Holland, who put out their shoe or stocking in the

* Grimm; Smith; Scott.

confidence that Santa Klaus or Knecht Clobes, as they call him, will put in a prize for good conduct before the morning. The Dutch element in New England has introduced Santa Klaus to many a young American who knows nothing of St. Nicholas or of any saint's day. Another legend described the saint as having brought three murdered children to life again, and this rendered him the patron of boys, especially school-boys.

A saint of both the East and West, with a history so endearing, and legends still more homely and domestic, Nicholas was certain of many followers throughout Christendom, and his name came into use in Europe among the first of the sainted ones. To us it came with the Norman Conquest, though not in great abundance, for only one Nicolas figures in Domesday Book, but his namesakes multiplied. The only English pope was Nicolas Breakspear; and Nicole or Nicola de Camville was the brave lady who defeated the French invaders at Lincoln, and secured his troublesome crown to Henry III. She deserves to have had more ladies called after her in her own country, but the feminines are chiefly confined to France, where, in the fifteenth century, its contraction was beatified in the person of a shoemaker's daughter, Collette Boilet, who reformed the nuns of St. Clara, and died in the odour of sanctity. The southern nations almost always contract their names by the omission of the first syllables, as the northern ones do by leaving out the latter ones; and thus, while the English have Nick, the Italians speak of Cola, a contraction that became historical when the strange fortunes of "Cola di Rienzi, the tribune of the people," raised him to his giddy height of honour, and then dashed him down so suddenly and violently, that "You unfortunate Rienzi" has ever since been a proverbial expression of pity in Italy.

The French language generally has both varieties of contractions, perhaps according as it was influenced by the Provençal or the Frank pronunciation, and thus its Nicolas becomes Nicole or Colas, sometimes Colin. Thence it has been suggested that Colin Maillard, or blind-man's-buff, may be Colin seeking Maillard, the diminutive of Marie, which would drolly correspond to the conjecture that the "N or M" of our catechism and marriage service, instead of being merely the consonants of *nomen*, stand for Nicholas and Mary as the most probable names. The French Colin is probably Nicolas, and is the parent of all the Arcadian Colins who piped to their shepherdesses either in the rural theatricals of the ancient regime, in Chelsea china, or in pastoral poetry. The Scottish Colin may, perhaps, have been slightly influenced by French taste, but he bears no relation to Nicolas, being, in fact, formed from the Irish missionary, Saint Columba. The true Scottish descendant of the patron of scholars is to be found in that quaint portrait, Baillie Nicol Jarvie. The *h* with which Nicolas is usually spelt in English was probably introduced in the seventeenth century, which seemed to think good spelling consisted in the insertion of superfluous letters.

Niel, a pure Keltic word, which was adopted by the Northmen, and became naturalized in Scandinavia and Normandy, has also been translated by Nicolas, but quite incorrectly. Nils is the only *real* Nicolaus except Klaus used in the North, though Niel, and even Nigel, are sometimes confounded with it. Denmark has had a King Klaus; otherwise this popular name has only been on the throne in the instance of that great Tzar whom we had respected till the last year of his life, when his aggression forced us into war.

English.	Scotch.	French.	Danish.
Nicholas	Nicol	Nicolas	Nikolaus
Nick		Nicole	Niklaas
		Colas	Klaus
		Colin	Nils

Dutch.	German.	Bavarian.	Swiss.
Niklaas	Nikolaus	Niklau	Chlaus
	Niklas	Nickel	
Klasse	Klaus	Likelas	
		Klasl	

Italian.	Portuguese.	Russian.	Slavonic.
Nicola	Nicolaio	Nikolaj	Nikola
Nicolo		Nikolascha	Miklaoz
Cola		Kolinka	
		Kolja	

Polish.	Lett.	Finland.	Ung.
Mikolej	Klavinsh	Laus	Mikos
	Klassis	Nilo	
		Niku	Lapland.
		Niles	Nikka

The German Sieg answers exactly to the Greek Nike.

With the *a* before it, which in Greek contradicts the ensuing word, like the Latin *in*, and Teutonic *un*, we have 'Ανίκητος, Aniketos, Anicetus, unconquered, the name of a pope, a friend of St. Polycarp, and an opponent of heresy, whence he is a saint both of East and West, and is called Aniceto at Rome, Anicet in France, and Anikita in Russia.*

Section VII.—*Polys*.

Πολύς (Polys), much, very, or many, was a frequent opening for Greek names. Polydoros (Πολύδωρος), many-gifted, was the youngest and last survivor of the sons of Priam; and as mediæval Europe had a strong feeling for the fate of Troy, and the woes of 'Polydore' had an especial attraction for them, so Polidoro was revived in Italy, and has never quite died away.

* Liddell and Scott; Rollin; Jameson; Butler; Michaelis; Ellis, *Domesday Book;* Warton, *English Poetry*.

His sister Polyxena, the feminine of very hospitable, had an equally piteous fate, being slain by the Greeks at the tomb of Achilles. According to the legends of the Eastern Church, a lady named Eusebia (gentle), who had been born at Rome, fled from an enforced marriage with a king, and took refuge, first at Alexandria, and then in the Isle of Cos, where she was called Xena, or the stranger. She founded a monastery at Mylassa in Caria, and there died in the 5th century. Kseenia, as she is called in Russia, has many namesakes, and probably was made ornamental by being lengthened into Poliksenja, which is likewise in use, with the contraction Polinka ; and Polixene has also been used from an early period in Germany.

Πολύευκτος (Polyeuctos), much longed for, answering to the Desiderio of Italy, and Desirée of France, was an old classic name, and an officer who was martyred in Lesser Armenia about the middle of the third century, was placed in the martyrology of both East and West ; but only has namesakes in Russia, where he is called Polieukt.

Πολύκαρπος (Polycarpos), that glorious Bishop of Smyrna, "faithful unto death," and "receiving a crown of life when he played the man in the fire," has had still fewer imitators of his suitable Christian name, much-fruit.

SECTION VIII.— *Phile, &c.*

Φίλος (Philos) was a most obvious and natural opening for names. It stood alone as that of several Macedonian ladies, and again with numerous men called Philon.

Philemon (loving thought) was the good old Phrygian who, with his wife Baucis, entertained Zeus and Hermes, and were rewarded with safety when their churlish neighbours were destroyed. Philemon was very common among the Greeks, and the Epistle of St. Paul to the Colossian master of the runaway Onesimus, has made it one of the Scriptural names of the English. The Maories call it Pirimona.

The Ptolemys of Egypt were particularly fond of surnaming themselves after their love to their relations, though they generally contrived so to treat them as to make the epithet sound ironical : Ptolemy Philadelphos (love brother), *because* he murdered his brother ; Ptolemy Philopater, *because* he poisoned his father ; though at least Philometer does seem to have had a good mother, and to have loved her. Such surnames were imitated by the Greek kings of Pergamus, all of whom were named Attalus, and it was from Attalus Philadephus, the second of them, that the city of Philadelphia, mentioned in the Apocalypse, took its title. This perished city of brotherly love seemed to William Penn to afford a suitable precedent for the title of the capital of his Quaker colony, which has ever since been Philadelphia. Less happily, Philadelphia has even been used among English women, apparently desirous of a large mouthful of a name.

Whether Philadelphia set the fashion, or whether the length of name is the allurement, Americans have a decided turn for all these commencements with 'Phile'; and Philetus, Philander, &c., are to be found continually among the roughest inhabitants of the back-woods and far-west. With us they are at a discount, probably owing to the fashion of the last century of naming imaginary characters from the qualities they possessed.

Philaret, fond of virtue, is however popular in Russia, for the sake of some Eastern saint, who no doubt derived it from Philaretos, a Greek physician.

The verb πράσσω (prasso), to do or act, and the substantives πρᾶγμα (pragma), πρᾶξις (praxis), business, were fertile in derivatives.

The Christian interest of the words from this source is through Praxedes, who, according to the legend, was the daughter of the house in which St. Peter lodged at Rome, and devoted herself, together with her sister, to attending on Christians in prison, and burying them when they were put to death; a course of life that resulted in a glorious martyrdom. In honour of these two faithful women was built one of the first churches of Rome, consecrated, it is said, as early as 141, and still existing in all the glory of its ancient mosaics. Santa Prassede, as modern Rome terms it, gives title to a cardinal; and the admirable Carlo Borromeo was thus distinguished, deserving, perhaps, more than any other known 'hinge-priest' of Rome to be called after the saint of holy activity. Prassede has continued in vogue among Italian women, who frequently learn their names from Roman churches. I have found Plaxy in Cornwall, possibly from this source. Here, too, we should place Anysia ('Ανύσια), from ἀνύω (anuo), to accomplish or complete. She was a maiden of Thessalonica, put to death there under Maximian. Her day is the 30th of October, in the Greek calendar, and Annusia is a Russian name, but she is not in the Roman calendar; and how the Normans heard of her it is hard to guess, unless it was either from the Sicilian Greeks, or in the Crusades; nevertheless, we are often met by Annys, Anisia, Annice, or Annes, in older pedigrees. The latter form occurs down to 1597 in the registers of the county of Durham. In later times the form was absorbed by Anne.

Τροφή, Trophe (food or nourishment), formed Τρόφιμος, Trophimos (the fruitful or nourishing), the name of an old Greek sculptor, and afterwards of the Ephesian companion of St. Paul who was left sick at Miletus. The people at Arles consider that he afterwards preached the Gospel in their city, and have made him the patron of their cathedral; but it is Russia that continues the use of his name as Trofeem.*

Even nong the heathen Greeks, Τρυφή, Tryphe (daintiness, soft-ness, or licacy), had not a respectable signification. Yet Τρύφον, or Tryphon, was a favourite with persons of inferior rank—artists, architects, and physicians; and in the Decian persecution, a martyr so called was put to the extremity of torture in Bithynia, and has remained highly honoured in the calendar of the Greek Church; Trypho continuing in use as a Russian name.

* Butler; Surius; Sir Cuthbert Sharpe, *Extracts from Parish Registers.*

The feminine form, Τρυφαίνα (Tryphæna), was given to two of the daughters of the Ptolemys in Egypt, where it was far from inappropriate ; but, probably, the two women whom St. Paul greets so honourably at Rome as Tryphæna and Tryphosa, were either Alexandrian Jewesses whom he had met at Corinth on their way to Rome, or else merely so called as being the daughters of some Tryphon. They were not canonized, and the dainty Tryphæna has only been revived in England by the Puritan taste.

SECTION IX.—*Names connected with the Constitution.—Laos, &c.*

The democratic Greeks delighted in names connected with their public institutions—ἀγορά (agora), the assembly, δῆμος (dêmos), the public, λαός, also the people, gave them numerous names, with which were closely connected the formations from δίκη (dike), justice, and κλέος (kleos), fame.

Λαοδάμας (Laodamas), people-tamer, had a feminine Λαόδαμεία (Laodameia), principally noted for the beautiful legend of her bitter grief for her husband, the first to fall at Troy, having recalled him to earth for three hours under the charge of Hermes. Probably Florence must have had a local saint named Laodamia, for it has continued in vogue there.

The demos better answered to the commons ; they expressed less the general populace than the whole voting class of free citizens, and were more select. We find them often at the beginning or end of Greek names, like the Theut of the Teutons : Demodokos, people's teacher ; Demoleon, people's lion ; Nikodemos, conquering people, etc.

Κλέος (Kleos), fame, from κλείω (kleio), to call, had as many derivatives as the Frank *hlod*, or loud, for renowned, but most of them have passed out of use, though Κλεάνθης (Kleanthes), famous bloom, the name of a celebrated sculptor, so struck the fancy of the French that Cleanthe—their epicene form—was one of the favourite soubriquets for their portraits of living characters. Even Cleopatra (Κλέοπατρα), fame of her father, with all her beauty and fame, did not hand on the name which she had received in common with a long course of daughters of Egypto-Greek kings. Russia alone accepts it as a frequent Christian name, and it is occasionally to be found in England and America.

The wreath of the conqueror was an appropriate allusion to those games where the Greek youth delighted to contend, and very probably the first Stephanos (Στέφανος) was so called by an exulting family whose father had returned with the parsley, or pine-leaf, crown upon his brow, and named the infant in honour of the victory. For Stephanos was an old Greek name, which had belonged among others to a son of Thucydides, before it came to that Hellenist deacon who first of all achieved the greatest of all the victories, and won the crown.

Besides St. Stephen's own day, another on the 3rd of August for "the invention of St. Stephen's relics," which were pointed out in a dream to a priest of Caphargamala in the year 415, by no less a person than the Jewish doctor, Gamaliel, in a white robe, covered with plates of gold. The bones were carried to the church on Mount Sion, and thence dispersed into all quarters; even St. Augustin rejoiced in receiving a portion at Hippo, other fragments were taken to the Balearic Isles, while Ancona laid claim to the possession of a bone, carried off at the time of the saint's martyrdom!

No wonder the name is common. Seven saints bore it besides the proto-martyr, and among them, that admirable King of Hungary, who endeared it to his people, and left the crown so highly honoured at Prague. Our name of Stephen is probably due to the acquaintance of the Normans with Ancona, whence William the Conqueror obtained such interest in St. Stephen as to dedicate to him the Abbey built at Caen. There is no instance of the name in Domesday Book, and our king of turbulent memory derived it from his father, the Count de Blois. In the roll of Winchester householders in Stephen's reign we find, however, already Stephen de Crickeled and "Stephen the Saracen." Could this last have been a convert brought home from the East, and baptized in honour of the pious Count de Blois, father of the king— perhaps an adherent of the family? It is everywhere in use, varied according to the manner in which the tongue treated the double consonant. The feminine began at Cambrai at least as early as the thirteenth century, and it is frequent in Caen, probably in honour of St. Stephen's Abbey at Caen.

English.	German.	French.	Italian.
Stephen	Stephan Steffel	Etienne Tiennon Tiennot Estevennes	Stefano Steffano
Spanish.	**Portuguese.**	**Dutch.**	**Russian.**
Estevan Esteban	Estevao	Steven	Stefan Stepan Stenka Stepka
Polish.	**Illyrian.**	**Esthonian.**	**Hungarian.**
Sscezepan	Stepan Stepo Stepko Stepika	Tewa	Istvan
Lusatian. Scezpan			

FEMININE.			
English.	**French.**	**Portuguese.**	**Russian.**
Stephana	Estephanie	Estephania	Stefanida
	Stefanie		Stepanida
	Etiennette		**German.**
	Tiennette		Stephanine

I venture here to include the numerous names of which the leading word is Ὀλυμπ. They are generally derived from Mount Olympos, the habitation of the gods; but I cannot help thinking them more likely to be connected with the Olympian games, and to have been first invented for children born in the year of an Olympiad.

There were numerous varieties, but none have survived except the feminine Olympias, belonging to the proud but much beloved mother of Alexander, and, like all other Macedonian names, spreading through the East. A Byzantine widow, of great piety and charity, who stood faithful to St. Chrysostom during his persecution by the empress, was canonized, and sent Olympias on to be a favourite with the Greeks, so that it flourishes among all ranks in the Ionian Islands. Italy had her Olimpia, probably through the Greek connections of Venice; and the noble and learned Olimpia Morata rendered it famous. It was brought to France by the niece of Mazarin, the Comtesse de Soissons, of evil fame as a poisoner, and yet the mother of Prince Eugène. From her, apparently, Olympe spread among French ladies and long continued fashionable, and Surtee's *History of the County Palatine of Durham* mentions an Olympia Wray, married in 1660.

Here, too, must be mentioned Milone, though its connection with the subject is only through Milon, the famous Greek wrestler of Crotona, who carried a heifer through the Stadium at Olympia, and afterwards ate her up in a single meal; killed a bull with one stroke of his fist; and finally, was caught by the hands in the recoil of a riven oak, and there imprisoned till eaten by the wolves. Michaelis thinks the root of the word is the same with that of the old German verb *milan*, to beat or crush, the relation of our *mills*. Thence may likewise have come the Latin *Miles*, and the Keltic *Milidh*, both meaning a warrior.

Milo belonged to the realms of romance. In the story of the Golden Ass of Apuleius, Milon is the master of the house where the unfortunate hero undergoes his transformation; and having thus entered the world of imagination, Milon, or Milone as Italian poets call him, became a paladin of Charlemagne; Milan was a Welsh knight in one of Marie of Bretagne's lays; and in a curious old French romance, Miles is the father of two children, one of whom is brought up by a lion, and defended by an ape as his champion. These stories, or their germs, must have struck the Norman fancy, for a Milo appears among the newly installed landholders in Domesday Book, and Milo

H

Fitzwilliam stands early in the Essex pedigrees, but very soon the vernacular form became Miles. Among the Norman settlers in Ireland, Miles was a frequent name; and in the Stanton family, when it had become so thoroughly Hibernicized as to dislike the Norman appellation, one branch assumed the surname of MacAveely, son of Milo, according to the change of pronunciation undergone by Erse consonants in the genitive. Miles or Myles itself was adopted as an English equivalent for the native Erse Maelmordha, or majestic chief, and has now become almost an exclusively Irish name, though sometimes used in England by inheritance from Norman ancestors, and generally incorrectly derived from the Latin *Miles*, whereas its immediate parent is certainly the Greek Milo.*

* Liddell and Scott; Butler; Neale, *Hymns of the Greek Church;* Smith; Dunlop, *History of Fiction;* Hanmer, *Chronicle of Ireland; Publications of Irish and Ossianic Societies.*

CHAPTER V.

CHRISTIAN GREEK NAMES.

SECTION I.

THE names that we place in this class are such as arose under the Christian dispensation. Some, indeed, are older, and many more may be so, and may have been in use among slaves, peasants, and persons of whom history took no cognizance ; but the great mass, even if previously invented, were given with a religious meaning and adaptation, and many embodied ideas that no heathen could have devised. Greek, above all others the ecclesiastical tongue, has sent forth more widely diffused names of truly Christian meaning than any other language ; the formations of Latin, German, and English, in imitation of these are, in comparison, inharmonious and ungainly, carrying their meaning too openly displayed.

Among these are here mixed, when they belong evidently to the same race, the exclusively modern Greek names, which have arisen since Greece and her dependencies ceased to be the great store-house of martyrs and saints, and the dispenser of sacred thought to the Christian world. Many, indeed, of these names may be of equally ancient date, only not belonging to any individual of sufficient renown to have transmitted them to other countries.

Perhaps no land has been less beholden to others in her nomenclature than modern Greece. Hebrew names have, indeed, come in through her religion ; a very few were accepted from the Latin in the days when Constantinople was the seat of the Roman empire, and when the churches were one ; but scarcely one of the wide-spread 'Frank' names has ever been adopted by the Greeks. Even in Slavonic Russia the nomenclature remains almost exclusively Byzantine ; the native Slave names are comparatively few, and those that come in from other nations are discarded, as at Constantinople, for some supposed Greek equivalent.

SECTION II.—*Names from Theos.*

Already in speaking of Zeus it has been explained that this and Θεός (Theos) are but differing forms of the same term for Divinity, although one became restricted to the individual Deity ; the other was a generic term in heathen days, retaining, however, so much of spiritual majesty that it was employed in the Septuagint to express the true Creator, and thus Christians embraced it as the designation of the supreme object of worship.

The word Theos itself had been assumed as a surname by one of the worst of the line of the Syrian Antiochus, and Theon had never been infrequent among the Greeks. Θεόφιλος (Theophilos), God-beloved, to whom is dedicated the Gospel of St. Luke, must have been so called before his Christianity. Thenceforward Theophilus became a name in the Church; but it has been less used on the Continent than in England. There, probably from its occurrence in Holy Scripture, and also from being generally the title of the favourite speaker in religious dialogues, it has been in some use. The feminine, Theophila, was the name of the mother of Sir Joshua Reynolds.

English.	French.	Italian and Spanish.	Portuguese.
Theophilus	Théophile	Teofilo	Theophilo

Theokles (Θεοκλῆς), divine fame, was an ancient heathen name, and it is most probable that Θεκλα (Thekla) is the contraction of the feminine. St. Thekla was said to have been a disciple of St. Paul, at Inconium, and to have been exposed to lions at Antioch. Though they crouched at her feet instead of tearing her, she is considered as the first virgin martyr, and it was deemed that the highest possible praise for a woman was to compare her to St. Thekla. Another Thekla of Alexandria is believed to have been the scribe of that precious copy of the Gospels given by Cyril Lucar to Charles I., and now in the British Museum; and thus Thekla has always had high reputation in the East, though less known in the West, except that 'Tecla' is the patroness of Tarragona.

German.	French.	Italian.	Russian.
Thekla	Técla	Tecla	Tjokle

Θεόδορος (Theodoros), and Θεόδορα (Theodora), divine gift, are the most usual of these names; the first universal in the East and West, the second prevalent in the Eastern Church, but less common in the Western than the incorrect feminine Dorothea.

There were numerous saints called Theodorus; the favourite of the West being he of Heraclea, a young soldier, who burnt the temple of Cybele, and was martyred in consequence. The Venetians brought home his legend, and made him their champion and one of their patron saints, whence Teodoro has prevailed in the city of the Doge; and from a church dedicated to him at Rome the Spaniards must have taken their Teodor, the French their Théodore, and the Germans the similar Theodor, which has always been frequent there.

The ancient Britons must have known and used this name ; for among their host of obscure saints of princely birth appears Tewdwr ; and the Welsh made so much use of this form that when the handsome Owen ap Tewdwr won the heart of the widow of Harry of Monmouth, Tudor was an acknowledged surname, and in two generations more it became a royal one.

Here, however, the Theodores are a recent introduction. They seem only to have been really hereditary in Wales, Greece, and Venice. By Greece is also meant all those Greco-Slavonic countries that received their nomenclature from Constantinople, in especial Russia, where the *th* is exchanged for *ph*, so as to produce the word Feodor ; and the Germans, receiving it again, spell it Pheodor.

Welsh. Tewdwr	French. Théodore	Portuguese. Theodoro	Spanish and Italian. Teodoro
English. Theodore			
German. Theodor Pheodor	Hamburg. Tedor Tetje	Russian. Feodor Fedor	Polish. Feodor
Slavonic. Todor	Illyrian. Todor Toso	Lett. Kodders Kwedders	Hungarian. Twador
			Finland. Theotari

The feminine Theodora has two independent saints, a martyr and a Greek empress. It suffers no alterations except the Russian *F* at the commencement, and is not common except in the East. The West prefers the name reversed, and rendered incorrect. Dorotheus and Theodorus may indeed be exact equivalents ; but the invention of Theodora makes the giver feminine instead of the gift. It is the beauty of the legend of St. Dorothea that has made her name so great a favourite. Never did pious fancy form a more beautiful dream than the story of the Cappadocian maiden, who sent the roses of paradise by angelic hands as a convincing testimony of the joy that she was reaping. The tale is of western growth, and the chief centre of St. Dorothea's popularity as a patroness was in Germany ; but the name was likewise in great favour in England, where Massinger composed a drama on her story. Dorothy was once one of the most usual of English names ; and 'Dolly' was so constantly heard in every household, that it finally became the generic term for the wooden children that at least as late as the infancy of Elizabeth Stuart, were called babies or puppets. In the days of affectation, under the House of Hanover, Dorothy fell into disuse, but was regarded as of the same old Puritan character as Abigail or Tabitha. Probably from the influence of German literature, the German contraction Dora, or more properly Dore, has come in as almost an independent name, which, perhaps, ought to be translated as simply a gift, though often used as a contraction for Dorothea. The fashion has again come round, and Dorothy has become the favourite name. In the last century, Dorinda was a fashionable English fancy embellishment, Doralice a French one—perhaps from the German Dorlisa —Dorothea Elisa. The Russian Darija is reckoned as a translation ; but it does not seem probable, for the patroness of this latter was an Athenian lady, martyred with her husband, Chrysanthus, at Rome, and buried in a catacomb, which was opened in the days of Constantine the Great. The modern Greeks call the name, Thorothea.

English.	French.	German.	Bavarian.
Dorothea	Dorothée	Dorothea	Derede
Dorothy	Dorette	Dore	Duredel
Dolly	Doralice	Dorlisa	Durl
Dora			
Dorinda			

Swiss.	Dutch.	Danish.	Spanish.
Torli	Dört	Daarte	Dorotea
	Dortchen		

Portuguese.	Italian.	Russian.	Polish.
Dorothea	Dorotea	Dorofei	Dorota
		Darija	Dorosia
		Darha	
		Daschenka	
		Dorka	

Illyrian.	Lusatian.	Lett.	Esthonian.
Doroteja	Dora	Darte	Tigo
Dora	Horta	Tike	Tio
Rotija	Horteja	Tiga	
	Vortija		

Lithuanian.	Ung.		
Urte	Doroltya		

Before leaving the word *doros*, we may mention the name Isidoros, a very old and frequent one among the ancient Greeks, and explained by some to mean Gift of Isis ; but this Egyptian deity is an improbable origin for a name certainly in use before the Greek kingdom in Egypt was established, and it seems more satisfactory to refer the first syllable to *ἰς* (strength), a word which when it had its digamma was Ϝἰς, exactly answering to the Latin *vis* (force or strength). It commenced many old Greek names, but none that have passed on to Christian times except Isidorus, which was first borne by one of the grim hermits of Egypt, then by an Alexandrian author, and then by three Spanish bishops of Cordova, Seville, and Badajos. They probably received it as a resemblance of the Gothic names beginning with *eisen* (iron). In consequence, Isidoro and the feminine Isidora have continued national in Spain, and Isodoros in Greece, whence Russia has taken Eesidor.

Theodotos (God-given) was in common use among the Greeks of the early empire, and apparently in Spain was corrupted into Theodosius, since Spain was the native land of him who rendered this form illustrious. Theodosia has been in favour in many parts of Europe, copied probably from some of the Byzantine princesses. The canonized personages of the masculine and feminine forms are, however, by no means imperial; the one being a hermit, the other a virgin martyr. Theone is also a German feminine.

English. Theodosius		French. Théodose	Italian. Teodosia
English. Theodosia	Italian. Teodosia	Russian. Feodosia	Illyrian. Desse

The entire race of Greek words thus derived must be carefully distinguished from the Gothic ones, which at first sight appear to resemble them : such as Theodoric, Theudebert, &c., but are all, in fact, taken from the Teuton word *Theut* (the people).

Of Theophanos we shall speak among the names taken from sacred festivals, but we must not leave these titles of pious signification without mentioning Τιμόθεος (honour God), from τιμή (honour or worship), the noun formed from τίω (to honour or esteem), connected of course with the Latin *timor* (fear).

Timotheus had been in use even in heathen times, as in the case of Alexander's musician.

But probably it was with a full religious meaning that the good Eunice chose it for that son who was to be the disciple of St. Paul and the first bishop of Ephesus. From him, and from several subsequent Saints, the East and West both learnt it, but at the present day it flourishes chiefly in Russia as Teemofe. In Ireland, it was taken as one of the equivalents of the native Tadgh (a bard), and the absurdities of Irish Tims have cast a ridiculous air over it, mingled with the Puritan odour of the Cromwellian days, such as to lower it from the estimation its associations deserve. Mr. Timothy Davison, in 1670, named his daughter Timothea, but happily his example does not seem to have been followed.[*]

---

[*] Smith; Jameson; Butler; Liddell and Scott; Hartwell Horne, *Introduction to the Bible* ; Le Beau, *Bas Empire* ; Michaelis.

English.	French.	Italian.	Russian.
Timothy	Timothée	Timoteo	Timofei
Tim			Timoscha

Polish.	Slavonic.	Lett.	
Tymotensz	Timoty	Tots	

SECTION III.—*Names from Christos.*

The Greek verb χρίω (chrio), to touch, rub, or anoint, formed the term Χριστός, which translated the old Hebrew prophetic Messiah (the Anointed), and thence became the title of the Saviour, the very touch-stone of faith.

Therefore it was that at Antioch the disciples came to be called Χριστιανοι (Christianoi), a Greek word with a Latin termination, the title that they accepted as their highest glory, and which has ever since been the universal and precious designation of a believer. The first person who is known to have been baptized after this title, was St. Christina, a Roman virgin of patrician birth, who was martyred in 295. Her marvellous legend declares that she was thrown into lake Bolsena, with a mill-stone round her neck, but that she floated to the surface, supported by angels, and that she was at last shot to death with arrows. She is therefore, of course, patroness of Bolsena and of the Venetian States, where Cristina is frequent ; and her fame travelled to Greece, Bohemia, and Hungary, from which last place the Atheling family brought it to England and Scotland in the person of Christina, Abbess of Romsey. Christian, like the other Greek names of this importation, took deep root in Scotland, where Kirstin is its abbreviation among the peasantry ; and Christina, or Stine, and Tine, is common in Germany. John Bunyan's Christiana, as the feminine of his allegorical Christian, has made this form the most common in England. Christine, either through Germany or Scotland, found its way to Scandinavia, where the contraction is Kirste, or Kirstine. Being vigorous name-makers at the time of their conversion, the Northmen were not content to leave this as a mere lady's name inherited from the saint, but invented for themselves a masculine Christian, or Christiern as they call it in Denmark, which has belonged to many a sovereign in that kingdom, where it is especially national, and contracts into Kirsten.

Christabel was already a name before Coleridge's time. It is to be found in Cornwall, in 1727, and in the North of England. It occurs at Crayke, in Yorkshire, between 1538 and 1652.

From the same holy title was derived that of Χριστοφόρος (Christ-bearer), claimed by many an early Christian as an expression of his membership, as St. Ignatius on his trial spoke of himself as Θεοφορος. To this title was attached the beautiful allegory of the giant ever in search of the strongest master, whom he found at last in the little

English.	German.	French.	Swedish.
Christian	Christian	Chrestien Chrétien	Kristian

Danish.	Netherlands.	Dantzig.	Frisian.
Christian	Kerstan Karston Krischân Kruschan	Zan	Tsassen Tziasso Zasso Sasze
		Dutch. Korstiaan	

Swiss.	Polish.	Slavonic.	Illyrian.
Krista Chresta Chresteli	Krystyan	Kristijan	Kristian Kersto Hristo

Lusatian.	Bulgarian.	Lett.	ː Esthonian.
Khrystjan Kristo Kito	Krustjo	Kristo Skersto	Kersti
			Hungarian. Kcrestel

FEMININE.

English.	French.	German.	Bulgarian.
Christiana Christian Christina Chrissie Xina	Christine	Christiane Christine Stine Tine Kristel	Khrustina
			Lithuanian. Krikszte

Portuguese.	Spanish.	Italian.	Danish.
Christinha	Cristine	Cristina	Karstin

Slavonic.	Lusatian.	Lett.	Esthonian.
Kristina Kina	Krystla Kita Kitka	Kristine Kersti Skerste	Kirstin Kirste

child that he bore on his shoulders over the river. Simplicity soon turned the parable into credited fact, and St. Christopher became the object of the most eager veneration, especially as there had been a real martyr so called, and mentioned in the Mozarabic service-book. He was put to death in Lycia, and his relics were supposed to have been at first at Toledo and afterwards at St. Denis. The sight of St. Christopher's image was thought to be a protection from sickness, earthquake, fire, or flood, for the rest of the day, and it was therefore carved out and painted in huge proportions outside churches and houses, especially in Italy, Spain, and Germany. The cumbrous length is cut down in England into Kit, Kester, and Chris. The modern Greeks shorten Christophoros into Christachi. The two feminine are the German Christophine and English Christophera.

English.	Scotch.	French.	Swedish.
Christopher	Christopher	Christophe	Kristofer
Kester	Christal		Kristofel
Kit			
Chris			

Netherlands.	German.	Swiss.	Italian.
Toffel	Christoph	Chrestoffel	Cristoforo
Toff	Stoffel	Stoffel	Cristovano
	Stoppel		Gristovalo

Portuguese.	Spanish.	Russian.	Polish.
Christovao	Cristoval	Christofer	Kristof
		Christof	

Lusatian.	Lett.	Lithuanian.	
Kitto	Kristoppis	Kristuppas	
	Kristagis		

Christopher was once far more common in England than it is at present. In the list of voters at Durham in the year 1500, there were thirteen Christophers, and in 1813 there were as many as ten. The Germans have also Christophilon, meaning, loved by Christ.*

Section IV.—*Sophia.*

Perhaps we ought to consider Sophia (Σοφία) as one of the words most closely connected with divine attributes, since its use as a name was owing to the dedication of that most gorgeous of Christian temples by which Justinian declared that he had surpassed Solomon. It was called, and it has borne the title through its four hundred years of bondage to Islam, Sta. Sophia (the holy wisdom of God), that figurative wisdom whom Christians considered the Book of Proverbs to point out as the Word of God. Moreover, the words of the 'Preacher,' in the Book of Ecclesiasticus, "Wisdom (Σοφία) is the mother of fair Love and Hope and holy Fear," suggested an allegory of a holy woman with three daughters so called, and thus, in compliment, no doubt, to the glorious newly-built church, the niece of Justinian's empress, afterwards wife to his nephew and successor, was called Sophia, a name which thenceforward became the fashion among

* Milman, *Christianity;* Liddell and Scott; Jameson.

the purple-born daughters, and spread from them among the Slavonian nations, who regarded Constantinople as the centre of civilization.

Through these Slavonians Sophia spread to Germany. A Hungarian princess was so called in 999 ; another, the daughter of King Geysa, married Magnus of Saxony, in 1074, and Saxony scattered its Sophias in the next centuries all over the neighbouring states and into Denmark, where it has always been a royal name. Very nearly had the Electress Sophia brought it to our throne, and though the unhappy Sophia Dorothea of Zelle never took her place in the English Court, her grand-daughters made it one of the most fashionable ladies' names under the House of Hanover ; and though its reign has passed with the taste for ornamental nomenclature, yet the soft and easy sound of Sophy still makes her hold her own.

English.	French.	German.	Danish.	Frisian.
Sophia Sophy	Sophie	Sophia Fieke	Saffi	Vye

Italian.	Russian.	Polish.	Lett.	Hungarian.
Sofia	Ssofija Ssonia Ssoniuska	Zofia Zosia	Sappe Wike	Zsofia Zsofe

SECTION V.—*Petros.*

Great is the controversy that hangs on the form of Πέτρος, the surname divinely bestowed upon the faithful disciple Simon Barjona, when he made his great confession of faith in the Godhead and Messiahship of his Master.

" Thou art *Petros* (a stone), and on this *Petra* (a rock) I will build my Church," are the words.

The apostle was sometimes called in his own lifetime by the Hebrew or Syriac equivalent Κηφᾶς, or Cephas ; but Petros, or Petrus, being both Greek and Latin words, he went down to posterity thus distinguished. Many a Pietro was called after him in Italy, to be cut down into Piero or Pier, and amplified into Pietruccio, or Petruccio and Petraccio. The devout Spaniards caught up the name, and had many a Pedro, nay, three Pedros at once were reigning at a time in three Peninsular kingdoms, and the frequency of Perez as a surname shows how full Spain is of the sons of Pedro. France had many a Pierre, Pierrot, or, in Brittany, Perronnik. Perrault, a common surname, may be a derivation from it, as is St. Pierre, one of the territorial designations. Before the Revolution, La Pierre and La France were the unvarying designations of the two lackeys that every family of any pretension always kept in those days of display.

England had Peter, which Peter-pence, perhaps, hindered from being a favourite, and borrowed from the French, Piers and Pierce.

Feories is the Irish version of Pierce. Pedder or Peer are both much used in the North, and Peter in Germany; while the great Muscovite made Petr notable in his empire. The Irish, regardless of the true history of Patricius, want to make St. Patrick a namesake of St. Peter, and therefore the Paddys own not only their national apostle, but the prince of apostles, for their patrons. The feminines of Peter are Petronilla, said to have been his daughter, and whence has come Petronilla in Spanish, Petronille shortened into Nille in Norway, Pernel or Parnel, once exceeding common, though now forgotten, in England; but other female names have been made direct from that of the saint, Peronetta in Italy, Perretta in France, and even Petrina in Scotland and Sweden.

English.	French.	Swedish.	Danish.
Peter	Pierre	Per	Peder
Piers	Pierrot		
Pierce	Perrin		
	Peire		

Dutch.	Italian.	Spanish.	Portuguese.
Pieter	Pietro	Pedro	Pedro
Piet	Piero		Pedrinho
	Pier		
	Pietruccio		

Russian.	Polish.	Illyrian.	Lusatian.
Petr	Picti	Petai	Pjeti
Petruscha	Pies	Pero	Petsch
Petrinka		Petrica	Peto
		Pejo	

Bulgarian.	Lett.	Esthonian.	Kelt.
Petur	Peteris	Pedo	Pétar } *Erse*
Petko		Pet	Feoris }
			Per } *Breton*
			Petrik }

FEMININE.			
English.	French.	Italian.	Portuguese.
Petrina	Perette	Petronilla	Petronilha
Petronella	Petronelle		
Pernel	Petrine	German.	Illyrian.
		Petronille	Petra
		Nelle	Petrija
		Nillel	Petrusa

SECTION VI.—*Names of Immortality.*

Rejoicing that "life and immortality had been brought to light" quickly broke out in the very names given to Christians at their baptism, and full of import were the appellations invented in these early ages of the Church, to express the joyful hope of everlasting life.

Even in the Sanscrit, *a-mrita* expresses the elixir of life, "the amreeta cup of immortality," which terminates the woes of Kailyal in the *Curse of Kehama,* and according to Hindoo myth was produced by the celebrated churning of the ocean. The name is traced to *a* privative and *mri,* a word to be met with again in *mors, murder,* &c., and the notion of a water of life continued to pervade all the Indo-European races. Among the Greeks this life-giving elixir was ἀμβροσία (ambrosia), immediately derived from ἄμβροτος (immortal), a word from the same source. In various legends this ambrosia served to express the human craving for heavenly and immortal food, until at length, in later times, ambrosia came to be regarded as the substantial meat of the gods, as nectar was their drink.

It was reserved for Christianity to proclaim the true ambrosia, the veritable food of Paradise, and thus it was that Ambrosios became a chosen name, borne in especial by that great Archbishop of Milan, who spent one of the most illustrious lives recorded in Church history. The Church has never forgotten this great saint; and Milan, where his own liturgy has never been discontinued, is especially devoted to her Sant' Ambrogio, but his history is perhaps a little too much in the clear light of day to afford the convenient shadow requisite for name-spreading legend, and his name has but moderate popularity. Already, as we may suppose, his fame had spread to Britain when Aurelius Ambrosius, the brave champion who so long withstood the Saxon invaders, bore it and left it to the Welsh as Emrys.

English.	French.	Italian.	Spanish.	Russian.
Ambrose Brush	Ambroise	Ambrogio	Ambrosio	Amvrossij
Polish.	Bohemian.	Lusatian.	Hungarian.	Welsh.
Ambrozij	Ambroz	'Bros Mros Brosk Mrosk	Ambrus	Emrys

In the same spirit was formed 'Αθανασιος (Athanasios), from the word θάνατος (death). The Undying was in itself a name of good hope for a Christian, and it became dear to the Church at large through the great Alexandrian patriarch, the bulwark of the faith. It is in the East that his name has been kept up; the West, though of course knowing it and using it for him individually, shows few namesakes except in Italy, where it is probably a remnant of the Greek influence upon Venice and Naples. The feminine Atanasia is, I believe, solely Italian.

French.	Italian.	Russian.	Servian.
Athanase	Atanasio Atanagio	Afanassij	Atanacko

So again the new Christians took the old word ἀνάστασις (meaning an awakening or raising), from ἀνίστημι (to make to stand up), and used it to signify the Resurrection; then formed from it ᾿Αναστάσιος (Anastasios), of the Resurrection,—having the elements of the Resurrection within him or her, for the feminine Anastasia was as early and as frequent as the masculine. Indeed the strange caprices of fate have decreed that, though the masculine form is exceedingly common all over the Eastern Church, it should, in spite of three saints in the calendar, one of papal dignity, be almost unused in the West, except in Bavaria, whilst the feminine, borne by two virgin martyrs, is prevalent everywhere, and chiefly in Ireland. England once used the name more than at present, and then Anglicized it into Anstace. Anstiss, Anstish, Anstyce, all occur frequently as *female* names in the elder pages of a Devonshire parish register, where Anstice is now a surname. Anstis Squire is in the Froxfield register in 1587, and the name must once have been much more usual.

French.	Italian.	Polish.	Bavarian.
Anastase	Anastagio	Anastazij	Anastasl Stas Stasl Stasi

FEMININE.			
English.	Irish.	French.	Russian.
Anastasia Anstace	Anastasia Anty Stacy	Anastasie	Anastasia Nastassja Nastenka

Amongst these well-chosen baptismal titles may be mentioned Ζωή (Life), no doubt given as meaning that the principle of Eternal Life was then implanted. It is strange that neither the Eastern nor Western calendar shows a Zoë, though a woman thus entitled was said to have been cured of dumbness by a miracle of St. Sebastian, and afterwards to have been the first of the martyrs in the persecution in which he died, about the year 286. After this, Zoë became frequent among the women of the Greek Church, belonging to many of the royal ladies of the Blachernal, among others to her who endeavoured to shake the constancy of the sea-king, Harald Hardrada, to his Muscovite Elisif. From the lower empire it travelled to Russia, where Zoia is at present very common, and in the time of romantic interest in the new Greek kingdom, Zoé became fashionable in France, and still is much used there.*

SECTION VII.—*Royal Names.*

Σέβας (Sebas), awe or veneration, was compounded into the word Σεβαστός (Sebastos), as a translation for Augustus, the imperial title coined by Octavianus to express his own peculiar sacred majesty.

It was not, however, apparently used for the original Augustus; at least St. Luke calls him Αὔγουστος; and its technical use probably did not begin till the division of the empire by Diocletian, and his designation of two emperors as Augusti or Sebastoi, with their heirs as Cæsars.

Subsequently to this arrangement no one would have dared to assume the name so intimately connected with the jealous wearers of the purple; and, accordingly, it was a contemporary of the joint emperors, who is the martyr-saint of this name—Sebastianus, a soldier at Rome, who, when other Christians fled, remained there to encourage the flock in the first outburst of the last persecution. He endured a double martyrdom; first, by the well-known shower of arrows directed against him; and next, after his recovery under the care of a pious widow, who had carried away his supposed corpse to

English.	French.	Italian.	Spanish.
Sebastian	Sebastien	Sebastiano	Sebastian
	Bastien	Bastiano	
		Basto	

Portuguese.	German.	Norse.	Bavarian.
Sebastião	Sebastian	Sebastian	Bastian
Bastiao	Bastian	Baste	Basti
			Wastel

Swiss.	Russian.	Slavonic.	Hungarian.
Bastia	Ssevastjan	Bostjan	Sebestyen
Bastiali		Bostej	
Bascho			

FEMININE.			

German.	French.	Russian.	Bohemian.
Sebastiane	Sebastienne	Ssevastjana	Sebesta

* Liddell and Scott ; Southey, Notes to *Curse of Kehama ;* Snorre, Sturleson, *Heimskringla ;* Le Beau, *Bas Empire.*

bury it, he defied the emperor again, and was beaten to death in the arena by clubs.

Devout women buried him in the catacombs, and his name slept for at least a hundred years till Pope Damasus built a church over his catacomb, which has ever since been called after him, and subsequent popes made presents of his relics to Tuscany, France, and other countries. A notion arose, Mrs. Jameson thinks, from his arrows reminding the classical world of the darts of Apollo, that he was connected with pestilence. His name is thus found all over Europe, though less commonly in England and the Protestant parts of Germany than farther south. Indeed its especial home is Portugal, where it must have been specially cherished in memory of the rash Don Sebastião, the last of the glorious House of Avis, for whose return from the fatal African campaign his country so long looked and longed.

More ancient was the term βασιλεύς (basileus), a king or prince, properly answering to the Latin *rex*, as did Sebastos to Augustus, but usually applied in the Greek-speaking countries to the emperor. Thence came many interesting words, such as the term used in the empire for courts of royal judgment, Basilica, whence upon their conversion into places of Christian worship, the title Basilicon became synonymous with church.

So, too, that royal-looking serpent who was supposed to wear a crown on his head, and to kill with a look, was the basilisk ; and the familiar basilicon ointment was so termed as being fit for a king.

Βασίλειος (kingly) was not infrequent among the early Christians, and gained popularity through that great father of the Church, the Bishop of Neo-Cæsarea, as well as other more obscure saints. It is extremely common in the Eastern Church, and especially in Russia, where the first letter suffers the usual change into *V*. The feminine, Basilia, is still in use among the modern Greeks, and once even seems to have been known among English ladies, since the sister of Earl Strongbow is thus recorded in history, but its use has died away amongst us.

English.	French.	Italian.	Russian.	Polish.
Basil	Basile Basine	Basilio	Vassilij Vasska	Bazyli
				Illyrian.
				Vassilij Vaso

SECTION VIII.—*Irene.*

In heathen days Εἰρήνη (Eirene), peace, was personified and adored as a goddess ; in Christian times, when peace on earth was preached, it was formed into a name—that which we know as Irene. Irene was the pious widow, whose care revived St. Sebastian after his first martyrdom, and in 303, three sisters, Agape (love), Irene, and Chionia underwent martyrdom at Thessalonica, but Irene seems to have absorbed almost all the subsequent honour, although Agapè is occasionally to be found in modern Greece, and formed the masculine surname Agapetus, once the property of a pope, and still used in Russia.

Irene was extremely frequent among the Greek empresses, and belonged to the lady who would fain have added herself to the list of Charlemagne's many wives. Thence the Russians have it as Eereena, and in that ancient Greek colony at Sorrento, where the women's features so strongly recall their Hellenic descent, Irene is continued as one of their baptismal names.

Thence was derived the name of the great father of the Church, Εἰρηναῖος (Eirenaios), Irenæus; but few of the fathers had popular names, and Irenæus has been little copied, except in Eastern Europe, where the Russians call it Irinej, and the Hungarians, Ernijó.

The Teuton *fried* and Slavonic *mir* have been infinitely more fruitful in names than the Greek Irene, and as to the Roman *pax*, its contributions to nomenclature are all posthumous.

Erasmus comes from ἰράω (iráo), to love, and is related to Eros. The first Erasmus was tortured to death in Diocletian's persecution, at Formici, whence his relics were transferred to Gaeta, and he there became the patron of the Mediterranean sailors, who used to invoke him as St. Ermo or St. Elmo, at the approach of a storm, and he thus was thought to send the pale pure electric light that shimmers on the topmast, warning the sailor of the impending storm. The name of Erasmus was assumed by the learned Dutchman, under the belief that it translated his name of Gerhard (*really* spearhard), and from him Rasmus and Asmus are common in Holland, and Rasl has somehow found its way to Bavaria. Russia, too, has Jerassom, but this name lies in doubt between Erasmus and Gerasimus (the venerable), one of the early ascetics of Palestine.

Gelasius, the laugher, was the name of a pope, and for that reason was considered as appropriate and ecclesiastical. It has had the strange lot of being used in Ireland as the substitute for their native name of Giolla Iosa, or servant of JESUS, and was actually so used by the Primate reigning at the time of the English annexation of Ireland.*

SECTION IX.—*Gregorios.*

Γρηγόριος (Gregorios), came from γρηγορέω, a late and corrupt form of the verb ἐγείρω (to wake or watch). A watchman was a highly appropriate term for a shepherd of the Church, and accordingly Gregorios was frequent among early bishops. Gregorios Nazianzen the friend of St. Basil, Gregorios Thaumaturgos or the wonder-worker, and others of the same high fame, contributed to render it highly popular in the East, and in the West it was borne by the great pope,

---

* Le Beau; Smith; Michaelis.

I

for whose sake it became a favourite papal title, so that it has been borne by no less than sixteen occupants of the chair of St. Peter.

It has, however, been far less popular among those who own their sway than among the Eastern Christians who are free from it, and though we find it in Scandinavia, this is only as a modernization of the Norse Grjotgard, while the Macgregors of Scotland draw their descent not from Gregory, but from Grig or Gairig, a Keltic word meaning the fierce.*

English.	French.	Italian.	Danish.
Gregory	Gregoire	Gregorio	Gregos
			Gregus
	German.		
	Gregor		Swedish.
	Gregus		Greis
Russian.	Polish.	Bohemian.	Slavonic.
Grigorij	Grzegorz	Rehor	Gregor
Grischa			Grega
			Gorej
Illyrian.	Lett.	Lithuanian.	Hungarian.
Gregorije	Grigg	Greszkus	Gergelj
Gerga		Grygallis	Gero

SECTION X.—*Georgos.*

The Maronite Christians have a tradition that Georgos was a Christian sentinel at Damascus, who connived at the escape of St. Paul, when he was let down in the basket, and was therefore put to death ; but whether this be true or false, among what may be called the allegorical saints of the Greek Church, one of the most noted is our own patron Γῆ (Ge), earth, and ἔργω (ergo), anciently Γέργω (fergo), descended from the same source as our own verbs to work and to urge, formed Γεωργός (earthworker or husbandman). A Cappadocian saint and martyr, of whom nothing was known but that he had been a soldier and died in the last persecution, bore the name of Georgios, and was deeply reverenced in the East, where Constantine erected a church in his honour at Byzantium. As in the case of St. Christopher, and probably of St. Alexis, this honoured name became the nucleus of the allegory, of the warrior saint contending with the dragon, and delivering the oppressed Church, and of course the lovers of marvel turned the parable into substance. In 494, Pope Gelasius tried to separate the true Georgius from the legend, which he omitted from the offices of the Church, but popular fancy was too strong for the pope, and the story was carried on till the imaginations of the Crusaders before Jerusalem fixed upon St. George as the miraculous

* Michaelis ; Butler.

champion whom they beheld fighting in their cause, as Santiago had done for Galicia. Thereby Burgundy and Aquitaine adopted him as their patron saint ; and the Burgundian Henry carried him to Portugal, and put that realm under his protection ; as a hundred years later Richard I. did by England, making "St. George for merry England" the most renowned of battle-cries. From Burgundy he was taken by the Germans as a patron ; and Venice, always connected with Greece, already glorified him as her patron, so that "In the name of St. George and St. Michael I dub thee knight," was the formulary throughout half Europe, and no saint had so many chivalrous orders instituted in his honour.

Still the name was less early used in the West than might have been expected, perhaps from the difficulty of pronunciation. Georgios always prevailed in the East, and came to Scotland in the grand Hungarian importation, with the ancestor of the House of Drummond, who bear three wavy lines on their shield in memory of a great battle fought by the side of a river in Hungary, before the Atheling family were brought back to England, attended by this Hungarian noble. On the usurpation of Harold, he fled with them to Scotland, and there founded a family where the Eastern Christian name of George has always been an heir-loom. It was probably from the same Hungarian source that Germany first adopted Georg, or Jürgen, as it is differently spelt, and thence sent it to England with the House of Brunswick ; for, in spite of George of Clarence, brother of Edward IV., and a few other exceptions, it had been an unusual name previously, and scarcely a single George appears in our parish registers before 1700, although afterwards it multiplied to such an extent as to make it doubtful whether George, John, or Charles be the most common designation of Englishmen.

The feminine is quite a modernism. The first English lady on record, so called, was a godchild of Anne of Denmark, who caused her to be christened Georgia Anna. The name had, however, previously existed on the Continent.

Venice took its Giorgio direct from Greece, but the name was not popular elsewhere in Italy ; and at Cambrai, an isolated instance occurs in the year 1300, nor has it ever been common in France. The Welsh Urien (Uranius) descends from heaven to earth by considering George as his equivalent. The Irish translate the name into Keltic as Seoirgi.*

English.	Scotch.	French.	Italian.
George	George	Georges	Giorgio
Georgy	Geordie	Georget	

Spanish.	Portuguese.	Wallachian.	Provençal.
Jorge	Jorge	Georgie	Jortz
	Jorgezinho		

* Liddell and Scott ; Jameson ; Butler ; Michaelis ; O'Donovan.

German.	Frisian.	Bavarian.	Swiss.
Georg	Jurgen	Görgel	Jörg
Jurgen	Jurn	Gergel	

Swedish.	Danish.	Dutch.	Russian.
Göran	Georg	Georgius	Gayeirgee
	Jorgen	Joris	Georgij
		Jurriaan	Jurgi
		Jurria	Egor
			Egorka

Polish.	Bohemian.	Slavonic.	Illyrian.
Jerzy	Jiri	Jurg	Giuraj
		Jurck	Giuro
			Giuko
			Djuradj
			Djurica
			Juro
			Jurica

Lusatian.	Lett.	Lithuanian.	Esthonian.
Juro	Jorrgis	Jurgis	Jurn
Jurko	Jurrusch	Jurguttis	

FEMININE.			

English.	French.	German.	Portuguese.
Georgiana	Georgine	Georgine	Georgeta
Georgina	Georgette		
			Illyrian.
			Gjurjija
			Gjurgjinka

Section XI.—*Barbara.*

Of the four great virgin saints, revered with almost passionate affection in the Roman Catholic Church, each has been made the representative of an idea. Probably Agnes, Barbara, Katharine, and Margaret were veritable maidens who perished in the early persecutions, and whose lives, save for some horrible incident in their tortures, were unknown ; but around them crystallized the floating allegories of the Church, until Agnes became the representative of the triumph of innocence, Margaret of the victory through faith, Katharine of intellectual, and Barbara of artistic devotion. There was a speedy lapse from the allegory to the legend, just as of old, from the figure to the myth ; and the virgins' popularity in all countries depended, not on their shadowy names in the calendar, but on the implicitly credited tales of wonder connected with them.

Barbara was said to be a maiden of Heliopolis, whose Christianity was revealed by her insisting that a bath-chamber should be built with three windows instead of two, in honour of the chief mystery of the Creed. Her cruel father beheaded her with his own hands, and was immediately destroyed by thunder and lightning. Here, of course, was symbolized the consecration of architecture and the fine arts to express religious ideas, and St. Barbara became the patroness of architects, and thence of engineers, and the protectress from thunder and its mimic, artillery. The powder room in a French ship is still known as *la sainte Barbe*. Her name has thus been widely spread, though chiefly among the daughters of artificers and soldiers, seldom rising to princely rank. Barbara is the feminine of βάρβαρος (a stranger), the term applied by the Greeks to all who did not speak their own tongue. Horne Tooke derives it from the root *bar* (strong), and thinks it a repetition of the savage people's own reduplicated bar-bar (very strong); but it is far more probably an imitation of the incomprehensible speech of the strangers ; as, in fact, the Greeks seem rather to have applied it first to the polished Asiatic, who would have given them less the idea of strength than the Scyth or the Goth, to whose language *bar* belonged in the sense of force or opposition. It is curious to observe how, in modern languages, the progeny of the Latin *barbarus* vary between the sense of wild cruelty and mere rude ignorance, or ill-adapted splendour.

English.	Scotch.	French.	Italian.
Barbara	Babie	Barbe	Barbara
Bab			
Barbary			

Danish.	German.	Swiss.	Russian.
Barbraa	Barbara	Baba	Varvara
	Barbeli	Babali	Varinka
	Barbechen	Babeli	

Slavonic.	Illyrian.	Bohemian.	Lusatian.
Barbara	Barbara	Barbora	Baba
Barba	Varvara		Babuscha
Barbica	Bara		
	Vara		
	Barica		

Lett.	Lithuanian.	Hungarian.	
Barbule	Barbe	Borbola	
Barbe	Barbutte	Boris	
Babbe			

The true old English form is Barbary. It appears thus in all the unlatinized pedigrees and registers ; and the peasantry still call it so, though unluckily it is generally turned into Barbara in writing.*

SECTION XII.—*Agnes.*

The word ἄγος (agos), a thing to which religious awe attaches, gave the adjective ἄγνος (agnos), sacred or pure, whence was named the tree whose twigs the Greek matrons strewed on their beds during the festival of Demeter, and which the Romans called by a reduplication of its title in both languages, the Agnus Castus. Agnus, the Latin for a lamb, is said to have come from the consecration of those creatures to sacred purposes ; and thence, too, came Agnes, the name of the gentle Roman maiden, the place of whose martyrdom named the church of Sant' Agnese. It is said to have been built by Constantine the Great only a few years after her death, on the spot where she was put to the utmost proof ; and it retains an old mosaic, representing her veiled only by her long hair, and driven along by two fierce soldiers.

Another very ancient church of Sant' Agnese covers the catacomb where she was interred, and she has always been a most popular saint both in the East and West, but most especially at her native city. There a legend became current, probably from her name, that as her parents and other Christians were weeping over her grave in the catacomb, she suddenly stood before them all radiant in glory, and beside her a lamb of spotless whiteness. She assured them of her perfect bliss, encouraged them, and bade them weep no more ; and thus in all later representations of her, a lamb has always been her emblem, though it does not appear in the numerous very early figures of her that are still preserved.

A saint who was the object of so many legends could not fail of numerous votaries, and Agnes was common in England and Scotland, and was a royal name in France and Germany. The Welsh form is Nest. A Welsh Nest was the mother of Earl Robert of Gloucester. Iñes, as the Spaniards make it, indicating the liquid sound of the *gn* by the cedilla, gained a mournful fame in Portugal by the fate of Iñez de Castro, and Iñesila has been derived from it, while the former English taste for stately terminations to simple old names made the word Agneta. It is more common in Devonshire than in other counties. In Durham, there is a curious custom of calling any female of weak intellect, "a Silly Agnes." Italy has invented the masculine Agnolo and Agnello, often confounded with Angelo, and used as its contraction.†

* Jameson ; Horne Tooke ; Michaelis.
† Jameson ; Brand, *Popular Antiquities ;* Liddell and Scott ; Michaelis.

English.	Welsh.	Manx.	French.
Agnes	Nest	Nessie	Agnes
Aggie			Agnies
Agneta			
Italian.	Spanish.	Portuguese.	Swedish.
Agnese	Ines	Inez	Agnes
Agnete	Inesila		Agneta
Agnesca			
Danish.	Russian.	Polish.	Slavonic.
Agnes	Agnessa	Agnizka	Neza
Agnete	Agnessija		Nezika
		Bohemian.	
		Anezka	
Servian.	Lett.	Esthonian.	Lithuanian
Janja	Agnese	Neto	Agnyta
	Nese		
Lusatian.			
Hanza			

Section XIII.—*Margaret.*

No name has been the occasion of more pretty fancies than Μαργαρίτης (a pearl), itself taken from the Persian term for the jewel, Murvarid (child of light), in accordance with the beauteous notion that the oysters rising to the surface of the water at night and opening their shells in adoration, received into their mouths drops of dew congealed by the moon-beams into the pure and exquisite gem, resembling in its pure pale lustre nothing so much as the moon herself, "*la gran Margherita*," as Dante calls her. The thought of the pearl of great price, and of the pearl gates of the celestial city, no doubt inspired the Christian choice of Margarite for that child of light of the city of Antioch in Pisidia, whose name as virgin martyr standing in the Liturgy without any authentic history, became, before the fifth century, the recipient of the allegory of feminine innocence and faith overcoming the dragon, even as St. George embodied the victory of the Christian warrior. Greek though the legend were, as well as the name, neither flourished in the Eastern Church; but Cremona laid claim to the maiden's relics, and Hungary in its first Christianity eagerly adopted her name, and reckons two saints so called in the eleventh century, besides having sent forth the sweet Margaret Ætheling, the wife of Malcolm Ceanmohr, the gentle royal saint of the Grace Cup, who has made hers the national Scottish female name. From Scotland it went to Norway with the daughter

of Alexander III., whose bridal cost the life of Sir Patrick Spens;
and it had nearly come back again from thence with her child, the
Maid of Norway; but the Maid died on the voyage, and Margaret
remained in Scandinavia to be the dreaded name of the Semiramis
of the North, and was taken as the equivalent of Astrid and of
Grjotgard. From Cremona Germany learnt to know the child-like
Margarethe, one of the saints and names most frequently occurring
there; and Provence, then an integral part of the Holy Roman
Empire, likewise adopted her. From her was called the eldest of the
four heiresses of Provence, who married St. Louis, leaving Marguérite
to numerous French princesses. Her niece, the daughter of Henry
III., was the first English Margaret; but the name was re-imported
from France in the second wife of Edward I., and again in Margaret
of Anjou, from whom was called Margaret Beaufort, mother of Henry
VII., and founder of the Lady Margaret professorship.

In her grand-daughter, Margaret Tudor, it ceased to be royal in
England, though it had taken root among the northern part of the
population, while, strangely enough, it hardly ever occurs among
the southern peasantry. The Italian reverence for Margherita, or
Malgherita, as they called her, was increased by the penitence of
Margherita of Cortona, whose repentance became so famed that she
was canonized. Many are the contractions of this favourite name,
since it is too long for the popular mouth. The oldest is probably
the Scottish Marjorie, as Bruce's daughter was called, and which cut
down into Maisie, the "proud Maisie" of the ballad, and later into
Mysie, and was treated as a separate name. Mr. Lower tells us that
the surname of Marjoribanks is derived from the barony of Raltio,
granted to Marjorie Bruce on her marriage with the High Steward of
Scotland. Margaret turned into Meg before the time of "Muckle-
moued Meg of the Border," and this as well as Maggie was shared
with England, which likewise had Margery and Marget, as well as
the more vulgar Peggy and Gritty, and likewise Madge.

The French contraction was in the sixteenth century Margot,
according to the epitaph, self-composed, of the Austrian, Flemish, or
French damsel, who was so nearly Queen of Spain:

> "Ci gît Margot, la gentille demoiselle,
> Qui a deux maris et encore est pucelle."

But Gogo is not an improvement. Marcharit is the Breton form.

In Germany Grethel figures in various '*Mahrchen*,' but Gretchen
is now most common, and is rendered classical by Goethe. Mete
in the time of Klopstock's sway over the lovers of religious poetry
was very fashionable; and Meta almost took up her abode in
England, though the taste for simplicity has routed her of late.

Denmark, where the Semiramis of the North has domesticated the
name, calls it Mette and Maret, and places it in many a popular tale
and ballad as Metelill, or little Margaret.

Even the modern German Jews use it and call it Marialit; and

the Vernacular Gaelic contraction used in Ireland is Vread, though
Mairgreg is the proper form. *

English.	Scotch.	French.	Italian.
Margaret	Margaret	Marguérite	Margherita
Margaretta	Marjorie	Margot	Malgherita
Margery	Maisie	Margoton	Ghita
Maggy	Maidie	Goton	Rita
Meggy	Maggie	Gogo	
Madge	Meg		
Marget	May		
Peggy			
Gritty			
Meta			

Spanish.	German.	Swiss.	Danish.
Margarita	Margarethe	Margarete	Margarete
	Grete	Gretli	Mette
Portuguese.	Gretchen		Maret
Margarida	Grethe		Melletel
	Grethel		
	Grel		
	Marghet		
	Mete		

Polish.	Bohemian.	Slavonic.	Finland.
Margareta	Markota	Marjarita	Reta
Malgorzata		Marjeta	
Malgosia			

Lett.	Esthonian.	Lithuanian.	Hungarian.
Margrete	Maret	Magryta	Margarta
Greta	Kret	Gryta	Margit
Maije	Krot	Greta	
Madsche			

SECTION XIV.—*Katharine.*

The maiden martyr, whose name was chosen as the centre of the
allegory of intellectual religion, was Καθαρινή (Kathariné), Catharina
in Latin, from a virgin martyr of Alexandria, whose history being
unknown, became another recipient of a half-allegorical legend. It
is not found recorded earlier than the eighth century, and, indeed,
the complete ignorance of the state of the Roman empire, shown by

* Reeves, *Conchology ;* Liddell and Scott; Butler; Michaelis; Grimm ;
Weber, *Northern Romance,*

making her the daughter of a king of Egypt, argues its development at a very late period. Her exceeding wisdom, her heavenly espousals, her rejection of the suit of Maximus, the destruction of the wheels that were to have torn her in pieces, her martyrdom by the sword, and the translation of her body by angels to Mount Sinai, are all familiar through the numerous artistic works that have celebrated her. The legend is thought to have grown up to its full height among the monks of the convent that bears her name at the foot of Mount Sinai. And the many pilgrims thither had the zest of a new and miraculous legend, such as seems always to have been more popular than the awful truth beside which it grew up; but it never obtained credit enough in the East to make Katharina come into use as a name in the Greek Church, and it was only when the Crusaders brought home the story that it spread in ballad and mystery throughout the West. Indeed, the name did not prevail till it had been borne by the Italian devotee, Santa Caterina of Sienna, who tried to imagine the original Katharina's history renewed in herself, and whose influence is one of the marvels of the middle ages. Before this, however, the fair Katharine, Countess of Salisbury, had been the heroine of the Garter, and John of Gaunt had named the daughter, who, as Queen of Castille, made Catalina a Spanish name, whence it returned to us again with Katharine of Aragon ; but in the mean time Catherine de Valois, the Queen of Henry V., had brought it again from France.

The cause of the various ways of spelling this word would appear to be that the more ancient English made no use of the letter K, which only came in with printing and the types imported from Germany. Miss Catherine Fanshaw wrote a playful poem in defence of the commencement with C, avouching K to be no Saxon letter, and referring to the shrewish Katharina and the Russian empress as examples of the bad repute of the K ; but her argument breaks down, since the faithful Spanish Catalina, as English queen, wrote herself Katharine, while the 'Shrew' in Italy could only have been Caterina, and the Russian empress is on her coins Ekaterina. On the whole, Katherine would seem properly to be a namesake of the Alexandrian princess, Catherine, the Votaress of Sienna. No name is more universal in all countries and in all ranks, partly from its own beauty of sound, partly from association, and none has more varied contractions. Our truest old English ones are Kate and Kitty —the latter was almost universal in the last century, though now supplanted by the Scottish Katie and the graceful Irish Kathleen.

Catherine has even produced a masculine name. Perhaps Anne and Mary are the only others which have been thus honoured ; but the sole instance is Caterino or Catherin Davila, the historian, who had the misfortune to have Catherine de Medici for his godmother.

English.	Scotch.	Irish.	Welsh.
Katharine	Catharine	Kathleen	Cathwg
Catherine	Katie	Katty	
Catharina			
Ka'e	Dutch.		Bret.
Kitty	Kaat		Katel
Katrine	Kaatje		Katelik

French.	Portuguese.	Spanish.	Italian.
Cathérine	Catharine	Catalina	Caterina
Catant			
Caton			
Gaton			
Trinette			
Cataut			

Swedish.	Danish.	German.	Dantzic.
Katarina	Kathrina	Katharine	Trien
Kajsa	Karina	Kathchen	Kasche
Kolina	Karen	Kathe	
	Kasen	Thrine	

Bavarian.	Swiss.	Russian.	Polish.
Katrine	Kathri	Ekaterina	Katarnyna
Kadreinl	Kathrili	Katinka	Kasia
Treinel	Tri	Katinsha	
Kadl	Trili	Katja	
Kattel	Trine		
Ketterle	Hati		
	Hatili		

Slovak.	Illyrian.	Esthonian.	Hungarian.
Katrina	Katarina	Katri	Katalin
Katra	Katica	Kaddo	Kati
Katrej		Kats	Katicza

Section XV.—*Harvest Names.*

From θέρω (to heat) was derived θέρος (summer), which, in sunny Greece, came likewise to mean the summer crop, just as in Germany *Herbst* serves for both autumn and harvest. θερίζω (to reap or gather in the crop), and from this verb comes the pretty feminine Theresa, the reaper. "The first to bear the predestined name of Theresa," as Montalembert says, was a Spanish lady, the wife of a Roman noble called Paulinus, both devotees under the guidance of St. Jerome, whose writings most remarkably stamped the memory of his friends

upon posterity ; and this original Theresa was copied again and
again by her own countrywomen, till we find Teresa on the throne of
Leon in the tenth century. The name was confined to the Peninsula
until the sixteenth century, when that remarkable woman, Saint
Teresa, made the Roman Catholic Church resound with the fame of
her enthusiastic devotion. The Spanish connection of the House of
Austria rendered it a favourite with the princesses both of Spain and
Germany. The Queen of Louis XIV. promoted it in France as
Thérèse, and it is specially common in Provence as Térézon, for
short, Zon. The empress-queen greatly added to its fame ; and it
is known everywhere, though more in Roman Catholic countries and
families than elsewhere. That it nowhere occurs in older English
pedigrees is one of the signs that it was the property of a saint whose
claims to reverence began after the Reformation.

English.	French.	Portuguese.	Spanish.
Theresa	Thérèse	Theresa	Teresa
Terry	Térézon		Teresita
Tracy	Zon		

Italian.	German.	Hamburg.	Bavaria.
Teresa	Theresia	Tresa	Res'l
Teresina		Trescha	

Bohemian.	Slavonic.	Illyrian.	Hungarian.
Terezie	Terezija	Tereza	Terezia
		Terza	Threzsi

The real popularity of the word, witnessed by its many changes of
sound, is, be it observed, in those Eastern domains of the empress
where her noble spirit won all hearts to the well-remembered cry
"*Moriamur pro Rege nostrâ Maria Theresa.*"

Eustaches has already been explained as one of these harvest
names. And to these may be added that of the old Cypriot shepherd
hermit Σπυρίδων (Spiridōn), from σπυρίς (a round basket). He was
afterwards a bishop, and one of the fathers of Nicea, then going
home, died at a great age, asleep in his corn field; in honour of
whom Spiridione, or Spiro, as the Italianized Greeks call it, is one
of the most popular of all names in the Ionian Islands, and has the
feminine Spira.*

SECTION XVI.—*Names from Jewels.*

Margaret, which has been spoken of elsewhere, is the most noted
of jewel names, and it probably suggested the few others that have
prevailed.

Σμάραγδος (Smaragdos) is supposed to have been named from μαίρω

* Liddell and Scott; Montalembert; Surius; Anderson, *Genealogies.*

or μαρμαίρω (to twinkle or sparkle), whence the dog-star was called Μαῖρα (Maira). This beauteous precious stone, bearing the colour of hope, was further recommended to Christians because the rainbow of St. John's vision was "in sight like unto an emerald." Thus, Smaragdos was one of the early martyrs; and the same occurs occasionally in early times, once as an exarch of Ravenna; but it was never frequent enough to be a recognized name, except in two very remote quarters, namely, as the Spanish Esmeralda and the Cornish Meraud, the last nearly, if not quite, extinct.

The Sapphire was erased for ever from the nomenclature of Christians by the fate of the unhappy Sapphira, except that Σαπφήρω (Sapphèro), a name thus derived, is used among the modern Greeks of the Ionian Islands; and so also is Διαμάντω (Diamanto).

For want of a better place, the Italian name Gemma must here be mentioned, though purely Latin, and coming from a word meaning the young crimson bud of a tree, though since used for a gem or jewel. In Erse Gemlorg, gem-like, is almost exactly the same in sound and spirit.

Moreover, both precious metals are used as female names in modern Greece, 'Αργύρω (Argyro), silver, connecting itself with the Arianwen, or silver lady, of Wales; and Χρυσωῦχα (Chrysoucha) from Χρυσός (Chrysós), gold. This latter word has formed many other names, beginning from Chryses and his daughter Chryseis, whose ransom was the original cause of "Achilles' wrath of mighty woes the spring." In the soubriquet of Chrysostomos, or Golden Mouth, we have already seen it, and it is found also in Χρύσανθος (Chrysanthos), golden flower, the husband of Saint Daria, in whose honour prevails the Bavarian Chrysanth or Santerl.

Muriel, an old English name, comes from μύρον (myrrh). Both it and Meriel were once common, and have lately been revived.*

SECTION XVII.—*Kosmos and Damianos.*

The pursuit of the relics of saints had already begun even in the fourth century. No church was thought thoroughly consecrated save by the bones of some sainted Christian, and it was during the first fervour that led men to seek the bodies of the martyrs in their hiding-places, that St. Ambrose discovered the bodies of two persons at Milan, whom a dream pronounced to be Kosmos and Damianos, two martyred Christians.

They, of course, were placed among the patrons of Milan, and their names became favourites in Italy. Kosmos originally meant order; but, having been applied to the order of nature, has in our day come usually to mean the universe.

Cosimo, or Cosmo, as the Italians called it, was used at Milan and Florence, where it gained renown in the person of the great man who made the family of Medici eminent, and who prepared the way for their aspirations to the elevation that proved their bane and corruption.

* Smith, *Life of Chaucer;* Butler; Michaelis.

France calls the word Côme without using it as a name, and Russia adopts it as Kauzma.

Damianos was from the verb δαμάω, identical with our own tame, which we have already seen in composition. He had a good many chivalrous namesakes, as Damiano, Damiao, Damien, and the Russians call him Demjan. The old Welsh Dyfan is another form strangely changed by pronunciation.

Section XVIII.—*Alethea, &c.*

'Αλήθεια (Aletheia), truth, came from α and λήθω (to hide), and thus means openness and sincerity.

When it first came to be used as a name is not clear. Aletha, of Padua, appears in 1411 ; and the princess, on whose account Charles I., when Prince of Wales, made his journey to Spain, was Doña Maria Aletea. About that time Alethea made her appearance in the noble family of Saville, and either to a real or imaginary Alethea were addressed the famous lines of the captive cavalier :—

> " Stone walls do not a prison make,
> Nor iron bars a cage."

Moreover, in 1669, Alethea Brandling, at the age of nine, was married to one Henry Hitch, esq., and the name occurs several times in Durham pedigrees.

As far as the English Alethea is concerned, she is probably the alteration of an Irish name, for she chiefly belongs to the other island, and is there called Letty. What feminine it was meant to translate must be uncertain, perhaps Tuathflaith (the noble lady). Tom Moore called his Egyptian heroine Atethe, from the adjective, and this has been in consequence sometimes used as a name.

The name Althea must not be confounded with it. This last is 'Αλθεια (wholesome). It belonged of old to the unfortunate mother of Meleager, and now designates a genus of mallows, in allusion to their healing power.

We find the prefix πρό, forming part of the word προκοπή (progress), whence the name Προκόπιος (Prokopios) ; in Latin, Procopius, progressive. It was the name of a martyr under Diocletian, in Palestine, and is a favourite in the Greek Church. The short-lived successor of Jovian was so called ; also the great Byzantine historian ; and now Prokopij is very common among the Russian clergy ; and Prokop or Prokupek has found its way into Bohemia. Russia, likewise, uses in the form of Prokhor, the name of Próchorus (Πρόχορας), one of the seven deacons, and much Græcized indeed must the imaginations of his Jewish parents have been when they gave him such an appellation, signifying the leader of the choral dances in the Greek theatres.

PART IV.

CHAPTER I.

LATIN NOMENCLATURE.

HITHERTO we have had to deal with names at once explained by the language of those who originally bore them. With a very few exceptions, chiefly in the case of traditional deities, the word has only to be divided into its component parts, and its meaning is evident, and there was a constant fabrication of fresh appellations in analogy with the elder ones, and suited to the spirit of the times in which they were bestowed.

But on passing the Gulf of Adria we come upon a nation of mingled blood, and even more mingled language, constantly in a condition of change; their elder history disguised by legends, their ancient songs unintelligible to the very persons who sang them, their very deities and rites confused with those of Greece, till they were not fully understood even by their most cultivated men; and their names, which were not individual but hereditary, belonging to forgotten languages, and often conveying no signification to their owner.

The oldest inhabitants of Italy are thought to have been Pelasgi, which is argued, among other causes, from the structure of the language resembling the Greek, and from the simple homely terms common to both; but while the Pelasgi of the Eastern Peninsula became refined and brought to perfection by the Hellenes, the purest tribe of their own race, those of the Western Peninsula were subjected to the influence of various other nations. In the centre of Italy the Pelasgians appear to have been overrun by a race called Oscans, Priscans, or Cascans, who became fused with them, and called themselves Prisci Latini, and their country Latium or Lavinium. Their tongue was the elder Latin, and the Oscan is believed to have supplied the element which is not Greek, but has something in common both with Kelt and Teuton. These Latins were, there can be no doubt, the direct ancestors of the Romans, whose political constitution, manners, and language, were the same, only in an advanced condition.

Roman legend and poetry brought the fugitive Æneas from Troy to conquer Latium, and found Alba Longa; and after the long line of Alban kings, the twins, Romulus and Remus, founded the City of the Seven Hills, and filled it with Latins, *i. e.* the mixed Pelasgic and

Oscan race of Latium. The first tribe of pure Oscans who came in contact with the Romans were the Sabines, who, after the war begun by the seizure of the Sabine women, made common cause with Rome, and thus contributed a fresh Oscan element to both blood and language. The Oscan race extended to the South, divided into many tribes, and their language was spoken in a pure state by the southern peasantry far on into Roman history. The numerous Greek colonies which caused the South to be termed Magna Græcia, became in time mingled with the Oscans, and gave the whole of Apulia, Bruttium, and Calabria, a very different character from that of central Italy.

Northward of Latium was the powerful and mysterious race calling themselves the Raseni, and known to the Romans as Tusci. They are usually called Etruscans, and their name still survives in that of Tuscany. They are thought by some to have been Keltic, but their tongue is not sufficiently construed to afford proof, and their whole history is lost. Their religion and habits were unlike those of their Roman neighbours, and they were in a far more advanced state of civilization. In the time of Tarquinius Priscus they obtained considerable influence over Rome, many of whose noblest works were Etruscan; and though this power was lost in the time of Tarquinius Superbus, and long wars were waged between Rome and Etruria, the effects of their intercourse lasted, and many institutions were traceable to the Etruscan element. Of the Roman families, some considered themselves descended from different Latin tribes, others from Sabines, others from Etruscans; and their genealogy was carefully observed, as their political position depended upon it.

Their nomenclature was, in fact, the immediate parent of our own.

Every Roman citizen had necessarily two names. The second of these was the important one which marked his hereditary position in the state, and answered to our surname. It was called the *nomen*, or name, *par excellence*, and was inherited from his father, belonging also to the entire *gens*, or tribe, who considered themselves to have a common ancestor, and who, all alike, whether wealthy or otherwise, took the rank of their gens, whether patrician, equitial, or plebeian. The daughters of the gens were called by the feminine of its name, and sometimes took that of the gens of their husband, but this was not always the custom.

Besides these large tribes, there were lesser ones of families. If an ancestor had acquired an additional appellation, whether honourable or ludicrous, it passed to all his male descendants, thus distinguishing them from the rest of their gens, and was called the cognomen. For instance, after Marcus Manlius had saved the capitol, Capitolinus would be the cognomen not merely of himself but of his posterity.

Clients and freedmen took the gentile name of their patron, and when the freedom of Rome was granted to a stranger, he took the gentile name of him from whom it was received, thus infinitely spreading the more distinguished nomina of the later republic and early empire, and in the Romanized countries gradually becoming the modern hereditary surname, the convenience of the family distinction causing it to be gradually adopted by the rest of the world. When the last of a gens adopted the son of another clan to continue his line, the youth received the nomen and one or more cognomina of his new gens, but brought in that of his old one with the augmentative *anus*. As for instance, Publius Æmilius Paullus being adopted by Publius Cornelius Scipio Africanus, became Publius Cornelius Scipio Africanus Æmilianus, and his daughter was simply Cornelia. Again, Caius Octavius, as adopted into the Julian gens, became Caius Julius Cæsar Octavius; and the emperors being all adopted, arrived at such a multitude of names that the accumulation was entirely useless, and they were called by a single one.

Added to all these family names, each man had his own individual name, which was bestowed in later times, or more properly registered when, at the age of fourteen, he laid aside the childish tunic and bulla, or golden ball, which he had worn from infancy, put off the toga prætextala, and assumed the *toga virilis*, or manly gown, white edged with purple, which was the regular official Roman dress. In the latter days, the prænomen was given on the eighth day, with a lustratio or washing of the infant. There was a very small choice of Roman prænomina, not above seventeen; an initial was sufficient to indicate which might be intended, nor did ladies receive their feminines in the earlier times. By which name a man might be called was arbitrary; the gentile name was the distinction of rank, and perhaps the most commonly used by his acquaintance, unless the tribe were very large, when the cognomen would be used; and among brothers the prænomen was brought in first as the Christian name is with us. The great Marcus Tullius Cicero was called Cicero by those who only knew him politically, while to his correspondents he was Tullius; his son, of the same name, was termed Marcus Cicero; his brother, Quintus Cicero; and Caius Julius Cæsar figures in contemporary correspondence as C. Cæsar.

In Christian times, the lustratio at the giving of the prænomen became Holy Baptism, thus making our distinction between baptismal and hereditary names. The strict adherence to the old prænomina had been already broken into, especially in favour of women, who had found the universal gentile name rather confusing, and had added to it feminine prænomina or agnomina, had changed it by diminution or augmentation, or had taken varieties from the other gentes to which they were related. Christianity had given individuality to woman, and she was no longer No. 1, or No. 2, the property of the gens. Significant names, Greek names, or saintly ones were chosen as prænomina, and the true Christian name grew up from the old Roman seventeen. Besides these, the numerous slaves, who formed a large part of the Roman population, had each a single name. Some of these were in their own language, disguised by Latin pronunciation; others were called by Greek or Latin words; others bore their masters' names. Many of these slaves were among the martyrs of the Church, and their names were bestowed on many an infant Christian. Others were afterwards formed from significant Latin words, but far fewer than from Greek words, the rigid hereditary customs of Latin nomenclature long interfering with the vagaries of invention, and most of these later not being far removed from classical Latinity.

It should be observed that the original Latin word, especially if descriptive or adjectival, usually ends in *us*, representing the Greek *ος*, and in the oblique cases becoming *i* and *o*—in the vocative *e*. When it was meant to signify one of or belonging to this first, the termination was *ius*—thus from Tullus comes one belonging to Tullus —Tullius, in the vocative *i* ; and again, one of the gens adopted into another, would become Tullianus,—Tullus, Tullius, Tullianus. The diminutive would be *illus*, or *iolus*, and in time became a separate name : Marcus, Marcius, Marcianus, Marcellus. In the adoption of Latin by the barbarous nations, the language was spoken without the least attention to declension ; the Italians and Spanish used only the dative termination, making all their words end in *o* ; but the former preserving the nominative plural *i*, and the latter the accusative plural *os*, while the French stopped short at the simple elementary word, and while finishing it in writing with an *e*, discarded all pronunciation of its termination. The vocative was their favourite case in pronunciation, and has passed to us in our usual terminal *y*. The *a* of feminine names was retained by Italy and Spain ; cut off by France, Germany, and England.*

* Niebuhr, *Rome ;* Arnold, *Rome ;* Smith, *Dictionary of Greek and Roman Antiquities ;* Max Müller.

CHAPTER II.

LATIN PRÆNOMINA.

SECTION I.—*Aulus, Caius, Cnœus, Cœso.*

FOR the sake of convenient classification, it may be best to begin the Latin names with the original prænomina and their derivatives, few in number as they are, and their origin involved in the dark antiquity of the Roman pre-historic times. The chief light thrown upon them is in a work entitled *De Factis Dictisque Memorabilibus*, compiled by one Marcus Valerius Maximus, in the Augustan age, to which is appended a dissertation on Roman prænomina of doubtful authorship; but whether this be by Valerius himself, or by his abridger and imitator, it is the earliest information we possess as to these home appellations of the stern conquerors of the world.

Caius, or Caiius as the elders spelt it, was one of the most common of all Roman prænomina, and was pronounced Gaius, as it is written in St. Paul's mention of "Gaius mine host." Men indicated it by the initial C; women who bore it, used the same C reversed (ↄ) on coins or inscriptions. Valerius, or his imitator, deduces it from *gaudium parentum*, the parents' joy, but it is more probably from the root-word *gai*. When a Roman marriage took place with the full ceremonies such as rendered divorce impossible, the names Caius and Caia always stood for those of the married pair in the formulary of prayer uttered over them while they sat on two chairs with the skin of the sheep newly sacrificed spread over their heads; and when the bride was conducted to her husband's house, spindle and distaff in hand, she was demanded who she was, and replied, "Where thou art Caius, I am Caia;" and having owned herself his feminine, she was carried over his threshold, to prevent the ill omen of touching it with her foot, and set down on a sheepskin within. From this rite all brides were called Caiæ. It is said that it was in honour of Tanaquil, whose Roman name was Caia Cæcilia, and who was supposed to be the model Roman woman, fulfilling the epitome of duties expressed in the pithy saying, *Domum mansit, lanam fecit* (she staid at home and spun wool), and was therefore worshipped by Roman maids and matrons. The Romans introduced Caius into Britain, and the Sir Kay, seneschal of Arthur's court, who appears in the romances of the Round Table, was probably taken from a British Caius; but the Highland clan, Mackay, are not sons of Caius, but of Ey.

It was probably from a word of the same source, that the Italian

K 2

town and promontory of Caieta were so called, though the Romans believed the name to be taken from Caieta, the nurse of Æneas, a dame who only appears among Latin authors. The city has become Gaeta in modern pronunciation, and from it has arisen the present Italian Gaetano. Who first was thus christened does not appear, but the popularity of the name began on the canonization of Gaetano di Thienna, a Vicentine noble and monk, who, in 1524, instituted the Theatine order of monks. He himself had been called after an uncle, a canon of Padua, learned in the law ; but I cannot trace Gaetano back any further. It is in right of this saint, however, that it has become a great favourite in Italy. The Portuguese call it Caetano, the Spaniards, Cajetano ; the Slavonians (who must have it through Venice), Kajetan or Gajo. It was a family name in Dante's time, and his contemporary, Pope Boniface VIII., of whom he speaks with some scorn, had been Benedetto Gaëtano.*

Section II.—*Lucius.*

Lux (light) gave the very favourite prænomen Lucius, one born at daylight, or, as some say, with a fair complexion. Many an L at the opening of a Roman inscription attests the frequency of this name, which seems first to have come into Rome with the semi-mythical Lucius Tarquinius Priscus, and was derived from his family by the first Brutus. The feminine Lucia belonged to a virgin martyr of Syracuse, whose name of light being indicated by early painters by a lamp or by an eye, led to the legend that her beautiful eyes had been put out.

The Sicilian saints were, as has been already said, particularly popular, and Santa Lucia is not only the patroness of the Italian fishermen, and the namesake of their daughters, but she was early adopted by the Normans ; and even in the time of Edward the Confessor, the daughter of the Earl of Mercia had been thus baptized, unless indeed her husband, Ivo Taillebois, translated something English into Lucia. The house of Blois were importers of saintly names, and Lucie, a sister of Stephen, was among those lost in the White Ship. The name has ever since flourished, both in England and France, but was most popular in the former during the seventeenth century, when many noble ladies were called Lucy, but poetry chose

English.	Welsh.	French.	Italian.
Lucy	Lleulu	Lucie	Lucia
Luce		Luce	Luzia
Lucinda			

Russian.	Polish.	Hungarian.	Spanish.
Luzija	Lucya	Lucza	Lucia

* Smith ; Diefenbach, *Celtica ;* Butler ; Michaelis.

to celebrate them as Lucinda, or by some other fashionable variety of this sweet and simple word.

The lady has here had the precedence, because of her far greater popularity, but the masculine is also interesting to us. The root *luc* (light) is common to all the Indo-European languages; and ancient Britain is said to have had a king called Lleurwg ap Coel ap Cyllin, or Llewfer Mawr (the Great Light), who was the first to invite teachers of the Gospel to his country. He is Latinized into Lucius, and this word has again furnished the Welsh Lles. Nothing can be more apocryphal than the whole story, but it probably accounts for the use of Lucius amongst Englishmen just after the Reformation, when there was a strong desire among them to prove the conversion of their country to be anterior to the mission of Augustine. Named at this time, Lucius Cary, Viscount Falkland, rendered the sound honourable, though it has not become common. Lucio, or Luzio, is hereditary in Italy. The Irish Lucius is the equivalent of the native Lachtna and Loiseach.

The Lucillian gens of the plebeian order was formed from Lucius, and thence arose Lucilla, borne by several Roman empresses, and by a local saint at Florence; and in later times considered as another diminutive of Lucy.

Lucianus, on the other hand, was a derivative, and having belonged to several saints, continued in use in Italy as Luciano or Luziano, whence Lucien the Buonaparte derived the appellation, so plainly marking him, like his brother, as an Italian Frenchified.

Luciana has continued likewise in Italy, and was anciently Lucienne in France. Perhaps the English Lucy Anne may be an imitation of it.

Lucianus contracted into Lucanus as a cognomen, and thus was named the Spanish poet, Marcus Annæus Lucanus, usually called in English Lucan; but it has a far nearer interest to us. Cognomina in *anus*, contracted into the Greek *aç*, were frequently bestowed on slaves or freed-men, especially of Greek extraction. These were often highly educated, and were the librarians, secretaries, artists, and physicians of their masters, persons of Jewish birth being especially employed in the last-mentioned capacity. Thus does the third Evangelist, the beloved physician and reputed painter, bear in his name evidence of being a Greek-speaking protégé of a Roman house, Λουκας (Lukas) being the Greek contraction of Lucanus or Lucianus. "His sound hath gone out into all lands," and each pronounces his name in its own fashion; but he is less popular as a patron than his brethren, though more so in Italy than elsewhere.

English. Luke	French. Luc	Italian. Luca	Spanish and Portuguese. Lucas
German. Lukas	Russian. Luka	Wallachian. Luka	Bohemian. Lukas

Slavonic.	Lusatian.	Hungarian.	
Lukash	Lukash	Lukacz	
	Lukaschk		

Lucretius, the name of a noted old gens, is probably from the same source, though some take it from *lucrum* (gain). "Lucrece, combing the fleece under the midnight lamp," that fine characteristic Roman tale, furnished Shakespeare with an early poem; and Lucrezia was one of the first classic names revived by the Italians; and though borne by the notorious daughter of the Borgia, has continued fashionable with them and with the French, who make it Lucrèce; while we have now and then a Lucretia, learnt probably from the fanciful designations of the taste of the eighteenth century.*

SECTION III.—*Marcus.*

The origin of Marcus, represented by the *M*, so often a Roman initial, is involved in great doubt. It has been deduced from the Greek μαλακός (soft or tender), a very uncongenial epithet for one of the race of iron. Others derive it from *mas* (a male), as implying manly qualities; and others, from Mars, or more correctly, Mavers or Mamers, one of the chief of the old Latin deities. Diefenbach thinks also that it may be connected with the Keltic Marc (a horse), and with the verb to march.

It extended into all the provinces, and was that by which John, sister's son to Barnabas, was known to the Romans. Tradition identifies him with the Evangelist, who, under St. Peter's direction, wrote the Gospel especially intended for "strangers of Rome," and who afterwards founded the Church of Alexandria, and gave it a liturgy. In consequence, Markos has ever since been a favourite Greek name, especially among those connected with the Alexandrian patriarchate. In the days, however, when relic-hunting had become a passion, some adventurous Venetians stole the remains of the Evangelist from the pillar in the Alexandrian church, in which they had been built up, and transferred them to Venice.

Popular imagination does not seem to have supposed the saints to have been one whit displeased at any sacrilegious robberies, for San Marco immediately was constituted the prime patron of the city; and, having been supposed to give his almost visible protection in perils by fire and flood, the Republic itself and its territory were known as his property, and the special emblem of the state was that shape among the Cherubim which had been appropriated as the token suited to his Gospel, namely, the lion with eagle's wings, the Marzocco, as the populace termed it, and another such Marzocco figures at Florence.

Marco was the name of every fifth man at Venice, and the winged

* Smith; Butler; Kitto; Jameson.

lion being the stamp on the coinage of the great merchant city, which was banker to half the world, a marc became the universal title of the piece of money which, though long disused in England, has left traces of its value in the legal fee of six-and-eightpence.

The chief popularity of the Evangelist's name is in Italy, especially Lombardy ; though the Greek Church, as in duty bound, has many a Markos, and no country has ceased to make use of it. Some, such as Niebuhr for his Roman-born son, and a few classically inclined English, have revived the ancient Marcus ; but, in general, the word follows the national pronunciation.

English.	French.	Italian.	Spanish and Portuguese.
Mark Marcus	Marc	Marco	Marcos

Esthonian and Russian.	Polish and Bohemian.	Lusatian.	Hungarian.
Mark	Marek	Markusch	Markus

From Marcus sprang the nomen Martius, or, as it was later written, Marcius, belonging to a very noble gens of Sabine origin, which gave a king to Rome, and afterwards was famous in the high-spirited and gentle-hearted Cnæus Marcius Coriolanus.

The daughters of this gens were called Marcia, and this as Marzia, Marcie, Marcia, has since been used as the feminine of Mark. From Martius again came Martinus, the name of the Roman soldier who divided his cloak with the beggar, and afterwards became Bishop of Tours, and completed the conversion of the Gauls. He might well be one of the favourite saints of France, and St. Martin of Tours rivalled St. Denys in the allegiance of the French, when kings and counts esteemed it an honour to belong to his chapter ; and yet Martin occurs less frequently in French history than might have been expected, though it is to be found a good deal among the peasants, and is a surname. Dante speaks of Ser Martino as typical of the male gossips of Florence ; and from the great prevalence of the surname of Martin in England, it would seem to have been more often given as a baptismal name. Martin was a notable king of Aragon ; but zealous Romanist countries have perhaps disused Martin for the very reason that Germans love it, namely, that it belonged to "Dr. Martinus Luther," as the learned would call the Augustinian monk, whose preachings opened the eyes of his countrymen.

English.	French.	Italian and Spanish.	Portuguese.
Martyn	Martin Mertin	Martino	Martin Martinho

German.	Swiss.	Dutch.	Lett.
Martin	Märti	Martijn	Martschis
Mertil	Martili	Marten	
			Hungarian.
		Swedish.	Martoni
		Marten	

Martina was one of the young Roman girls who endured the fiery trial of martyrdom under the Emperor Decius. Her plant is the maidenhair fern, so great an ornament to the Roman fountains ; and her name, whether in her honour, or as the feminine of Martin, is occasionally found in Italy, France, and England.

Marcianus was an augmentative of Marcus, whence Marciano or Marcian were formed. Marcellus is the diminutive, and became the cognomen of the great Claudian gens. Marcus Claudius Marcellus was the conqueror of Syracuse, and the last of his direct descendants is that son of Octavia and nephew of Augustus, the prediction of whose untimely death is placed by Virgil in the mouth of his forefather, Anchises, in the Elysian Fields. St. Marcellus was a young Roman soldier who figures among the warrior saints of Venice, and now and then has a French namesake called Marcel.

Marcella was a pious widow, whose name becoming known through her friendship with St. Jerome, took the fancy of the French ; and Marcelle has never been uncommon among them, nor Marcella in Ireland.

Marcellianus, another derivative from Marcellus, was the name of an early pope, whence Marcellin is common in France.

From Mars again came Marius, the fierce old warrior of terrible memory ; but who, in the form of Mario, is supposed by the Italians to be the masculine of Maria, and used accordingly.*

Section IV.—*Posthumus, &c.*

Posthumus is generally explained as meaning a posthumous son, from *post* (after) and *humus* (ground) ; born after his father was underground ; but there is reason to think that it is, in fact, Postumus, a superlative adjective, formed from *post*, and merely signifying latest ; so that it originally belonged to the son of old age, the last born of the family. It became a frequent prænomen by imitation, and in several Roman families was taken as a cognomen.

The pseudo Valerius Maximus derives Titus from the Sabine Titurius ; others make it come from the Greek τίω (to honour), others from *tutus* (safe), the participle of *tueor* (to defend). It was one of the most common prænomina from the earliest times, and belonged to both father and son of the two emperors connected with the fall of

* Smith ; Diefenbach ; Roscoe, *History of Venice ;* Grimm ; *Transactions of Philological Society.*

Jerusalem. Both were Titus Flavius Sabinus Vespasianus, but the elder is known to us by his cognomen, the younger by his prænomen. Titus should have been a more usual Christian name in honour of the first Bishop of Crete, but it has hardly survived, except in an occasional Italian Tito; and here Dr. Titus Oates gave it an unenviable celebrity. Tita is also sometimes used in Italy. The historian, Titus Livius, has been famous enough to have his name much maltreated, we calling him Livy, the French Tite Live.

Section V.—*Numeral Names.*

Thus far and no farther went Latin invention for at least seven hundred years in the way of individual domestic names. Beyond these ten, the Romans had, with a very few exceptions, peculiar to certain families, nothing but numerals for their sons; some of which became names of note from various circumstances. The words, though not often the names, have descended into almost all our modern tongues.

Primus, the superlative of *præ* (before), *præ*, *prior*, *primus*, was only used as a slave's name, or to distinguish some person of an elder race.

Sequor (to follow) gave Secundus; the feminine of which fell sometimes to the share of daughter No. 2, to distinguish her from the elder sister, who was called by the family name. Men only had it as a cognomen, and that only in the later times. It has passed into our own tongue as well as into the more direct progeny of Latin, but Germany holds out against it. Rome likewise used Secundus in the sense of favourable, much as we speak of seconding in parliamentary language. St. Secundinus was a companion of St. Patrick, called by the Irish St. Seachnall. His disciples were christened Maol Seachlain, pupils of St. Secundinus, a name since turned into Malachi. King Malachi with the collar of gold, is truly the shaveling of the lesser follower.

Tertius barely occurs as a Roman name; but Tertia was rather more common than Secunda, and by way of endearment was called Tertulla. From this diminutive arose Tertullus and Tertullianus.

The next number is identical in all the tongues, though a most curious instance of varied pronunciation. The *quadra*, or four equal-sided Quartus, only occurs once in St. Paul's writings, and so far as we know, nowhere else. Quadratus and Quartinus were late nomina.

Why Quintus should have been so much more prevalent with the Romans than the earlier numerals does not appear, but it was one of the commonest prænomina, and was always indicated by the initial *Q*, while the Greeks called it Κοίντος. Thence came the Quintian, or Quinctian, gens, an Alban family removed by Tullus Hostilius to Rome, so plain and stern in manners that even their women wore no gold, and principally illustrious in the person of Cæso Quinctius Cincinnatus. An obscure family named Quintianus sprung again from this gens, and in time gave its name to one of the missionary martyrs of Gaul, who, in 287, was put to death at Augusta Veromanduorum on the Somme. His corpse being discovered in 641, the great goldsmith bishop of Noyon, St. Eloi, made for it a magnificent shrine, and built over it a church, whence the town took the name of St. Quentin, and Quentin became prevalent in the neighbourhood. It was also popular in Scotland and Ireland, but it is there intended to represent Cu-mhaighe (hound of the plain), pronounced Cooey. From the diminutive of the Quinctian gens came Quintilius, and thence again Quintilianus, the most noted Roman rhetorician. Pontius is thought to be the Samnite or Oscan word for fifth, related to the Greek *pente*, and Keltic *pump*, five. It was an old nomen among those fierce Italians, and belonged to the sage who gave the wise advice against either sparing or injuring by halves, the Romans at the Caudine Forks. Pontius Pilatus should, it would seem, have brought it into universal hatred, but it probably had previously become hereditary in Spain as Ponce, whence sprang the noble family of Ponce de Leon ; the French had Pons ; and the Italians, Ponzio, and our *Punch* is by some said to be another form. It may, perhaps, come from *pons* (a bridge).

Sextus was the prænomen of the hateful son of Tarquinius Superbus, but after him it was disused, although thence arose the Sextian, Sestian, and Sextilian gentes. In later times it came again into use, and a bishop of Rome, martyred under Valerian, was named Sixtus, whence this has grown to be one of the papal adopted names, and is called by the Italians Sisto, whence the Sistine chapel takes its name, and the Dresden Madonna of Raffaelle is called di San Sisto, from the introduction of one of the three sainted popes so termed. The French used to call these saints Xiste.

The Latin *septem* gave Septimus, a name exceptionally used among them, as it is among us, for a seventh son.

Some unknown Octavus (the eighth) probably founded the Octavian gens, which had only been of note in Rome for 200 years before Caius Octavius Rufus married Julia, the sister of Cæsar, and their son Caius, being adopted as heir of the Julian line, became C. Julius Cæsar Octavianus, though he afterwards merged this unwieldly title in that of Augustus. Octavius gained a certain renown through him, and Ottavio has passed on in Italy, while eighth sons are perhaps most usually named Octavius. The gentle Octavia, his sister, the most loveable of matrons, has made Ottavia an Italian name, and Octavie is one adopted by modern French taste. October is the eighth month in all modern tongues.

Nonnus, from *nonus*, the ninth, is not known as a name till very late, when Latin and Greek names were intermixed. Then it belonged to a poet, at first heathen, afterwards Christian. Nonna was the name to that female slave who wrought the conversion of Georgia to Christianity, and (we believe) has there been continued ; and in Rome Nonnius and Nonianus occur in later times as gentile appellations. Nona has been bestowed in England upon that rare personage a ninth daughter. November again bears traces of its having been the ninth month of the Romans, as does December of the tenth.

Decimus was a prænomen in the family of Junius Brutus, inherited mayhap from a tenth son, and it was at Decimus Brutus that Cæsar's dying reproach, *Et tu Brute*, is thought to have been levelled. Decimus and Decima are now and then to be found among us in unusually large families of one sex. Decius was the name of a great plebeian gens, one of the oldest in Rome, and illustrated by the self-devotion of Decius Mus.*

* Clark, *Handbook of Comparative Grammar ;* Liddell and Scott; Facciolati ; Junius; Smith; *Publications of the Irish Society ;* Butler.

CHAPTER III.

NOMINA.

SECTION I.—*Attius.*

THE Latin nomina were those that came by inheritance, and denoted the position of the gens in the state, its antiquity, and sometimes its origin. Their derivation is often, however, more difficult to trace than that of any other names, being lost in the darkness of the Oscan and Latin dialects ; and in the latter times they were very wide-spread, being adopted by wholesale by persons who received the franchise, as Roman citizens, from the individual who conferred it ; and after the time of Caracalla, A.D. 212, when all the free inhabitants of the empire became alike Roman citizens, any person might adopt whatever name he chose, or even change his own if he disliked it. The feminine of this gentile name, as it was called, was the inheritance of the daughters ; and on marriage, the feminine of the husband's nomen was sometimes, though not uniformly, assumed.

These names are here placed in alphabetical order, as there seems to be nothing else to determine their position, and it is in accordance with the rigid Roman fashion of regularity.

Thus we begin with the Accian, Attian, or Actian gens ; one of no great rank, but interesting as having been fixed on by tradition as the ancestry of the great mountain lords of Este, who were the parents of the house of Ferarra in Italy, and of the house of Brunswick, which has given six sovereigns to Britain. Accius is probably derived from Acca, the mother of the Lares, an old Italian goddess, afterwards turned into the nurse of Romulus. Valerius, however, deduces both it and Appius from a forgotten Sabine prænomen Attus. The Appian gens was not a creditable one ; but Appia was sometimes the name of mediæval Roman dames.

The genealogists of the house of Este say that Marcus Actius married Julia, sister of the great Cæsar, and trace their line downwards till modernized pronunciation had made the sound Azzo.

Him whom they count as Azo I. of Este was born in 450, and from him and his descendants Azzo and Azzolino were long common in Italy, though now discarded.

SECTION II.—*Æmilius.*

Almost inextricable confusion attends the development of the title of one of the oldest and most respectable of the plebeian gentes, namely the Æmilian, anciently written Aimilian. The family was Sabine, and the word is, therefore, probably Oscan; but the bearers were by no means agreed upon its origin, some declaring that it was αἵμυλος (flattering or witty), and called it a surname of their founder, Mamercus, whom some called the son of Pythagoras, others of Numa. The later Æmilii, again, claimed to descend from Aemylos, a son of Ascanius; and others of them, less aspiring, contented themselves with Amulius, the granduncle of Romulus. Can this most intangible Amulius be, after all, a remnant of the Teutonic element in the Roman race, and be the same with the mythical Amal, whence the Gothic Amaler traced their descent? It is curious that *maal* or *âmal* means *work* in Hebrew, while *aml* is work, likewise, in old Norse, as our *moil* is in English, though in Sanscrit *amala* is spotless. Altogether, it seems most probable that the word *mal* (a spot or stroke) may underlie all these forms, just as it does the German *mal* (time); that Amal was, in truth, the dimly remembered forefather; and that thus the proud Æmilii of Rome, and the wild Amaler of the forests, bore in their designations the tokens of a common stock.

Several obscure saints bore the name of Æmilius or Æmilianus; and Emilij has always been a prevailing masculine name in Russia. In Spain, a hermit, Saint Æmilianus, is always known as St. Milhan. Emilio was, of old-standing in Italy; but the great prevalence in France of Émile, of late, was owing to Rousseau's educational work, the hero of which had numerous namesakes among the children born in the years preceding the Revolution.

The feminine had been forgotten until Boccaccio wrote his *Teseide*, and called the heroine Emilia. It was at once translated or imitated in all languages, and became mixed up with the Amalie already existing in Germany. Amalie of Mansfeld lived in 1493; Amalie of Wurtemburg, in 1550; and thence the name spread throughout Germany, whence the daughter of George II. brought it to England, and though she wrote herself Amelia, was called Princess Emily. Both forms are recognized in most European countries, though often confounded together, and still worse, with Amy and Emma.

English.	French.	Italian.	Slovak.	Lusatian.
Emily	Émilie	Emilia	Emilija	Mila
Emilia			Milica	Milka

Section III.—*Antonius.*

Two gentes were called Antonius, a word that is not easy to trace. Some explain it as inestimable, but the Triumvir himself chose to deduce it from Antius, a son of Hercules. One of these clans was patrician, with the cognomen Merenda; the other plebeian, without any third name, and it was to the latter that the avenger of Cæsar and lover of Cleopatra belonged—Mark Anthony, Marc Antoine, or

Marcantonio, as modern tongues have clipped his Marcus Antonius. The clipping had, however, been already performed before the resuscitation of his evil fame in the fifteenth century, for both his names had become separately saintly, and therefore mutilated; Mark in the person of the Evangelist, Antonius in that of the great hermit of the fourth century—the first to practise the asceticism which resulted in the monastic system. Of Egyptian birth, his devotions, his privations, and his conflicts with Satan, were equally admired in the Eastern and Western Churches, and Antonios has been as common among the Greeks as Antonius among the Latin Christians.

St. Antony was already very popular when St. Antonio of Padua further increased the Italian devotion to the name, and Antonio has ever since been exceedingly common in Italy and Spain. Classical pedantry made Antonio Paleario turn it into Aonio in honour of the Aonian choir; but whatever he chose to call himself he made glorious by his life and death.

The Dutch seem to have needlessly added the silent h, and we probably learnt it from them. The popularity of Antony has much diminished since the Reformation in England, where perhaps it is less used than in any other country.

English.	French.	Provençal.	Italian.
Antony	Antoine	Antoni	Antonio
Anthony			Tonio
Tony			Tonetto
Antholin			

German.	Frisian.	Dutch.	Swiss.
Antonius	Tönnes	Anthonius	Antoni
Tenton	Tonjes	Theunis	Toni
Tony		Toontje	
		Tool	
		Antoonije	

Russian.	Polish.	Slovak.	Servian.
Antonij	Antoni	Anton	Antun
Anton	Antek	Tone	Antonija
	Antos	Tonek	

Lusatian.	Lett.	Esthonian.	Hungarian.
Anto	Antons	Tönnis	Antal
Hanto	Tennis	Tonnio	
Tonisch	Tanne		
Tonk			

The feminine form, Antonia, is very common in Italy and Spain. The Germans have it as Antonie, and this was the original name of Maria Antonia, whom we have learnt to regard with pitying reverence as Marie Antoinette, whence Toinette is a common French contraction.

French.	Italian.	Swedish.	Swiss.	Lithuanian.
Antoinette	Antonia	Antonia	Tonneli	Ande
Toinette	Antonietta	Antonetta		
Toinon	Antonica			

The Aurelian gens was an old Sabine one, and probably derived its name from *aurum* (gold), the *oro* of Italy and *or* of France, though others tried to take it from *Helios* (the sun).

The old name, Aurelia, for a chrysalis was, like it, taken from the glistening golden spots on the cases of some of the butterfly pupæ. The Aurelian gens was old and noble, and an Aurelia was the mother of Julius Cæsar.

Section IV.—*Cæcilius.*

The most obvious origin of the nomen of the great Cæcilian gens would be *cæcus* (blind) ; in fact *Cæcilia* means a slow-worm, as that reptile was supposed to be blind ; but the Cæcilii would by no means condescend to the blind or small-eyed ancestor ; and while some of them declared that they were the sons of Cæcas, a companion of Æneas, others traced their source to the founder of Præneste, the son of Vulcan, Cæculus, who was found beside a hearth, and called from *caleo* (to heat), the same with καίω (to burn).   There was a large gens of this name, famous and honourable, though plebeian ; but rather remarkably, the feminine form has always been of more note than the masculine.   As has been before said, Caia Cæcilia is said to have been the real name of Tanaquil, the model Roman matron, patroness of all other married dames ; and who has not heard of the tomb of Cæcilia Metella ?   But the love and honour of the Roman ladies has passed on to another Cæcilia, a Christian of the days of Alexander Severus, a wife, though vowed to virginity, and a martyr singing hymns to the last.   Her corpse was disinterred in a perfect state two hundred years after, when it was enshrined in a church built over her own house, which gives a title to a cardinal.   A thousand years subsequently, in 1599, her sarcophagus was again opened, and a statue made exactly imitating the lovely, easy, and graceful position in which the limbs remained.

This second visit to her remains was not, however, needed to establish her popularity.   She is as favourite a saint with the Roman matrons as is St. Agnes with their daughters ; and the fact of her having sung till her last breath, established her connection with music.   An instrument became her distinguishing mark ; and as this was generally a small organ, she got the credit of having invented it, and became the patroness of music and poetry, as St. Katharine of eloquence and literature, and St. Barbara of architecture and art.

Her day was celebrated by especial musical performances; even in the eighteenth century an ode on St. Cecilia's day was a special occasion for the laudation of music; and Dryden and Pope have fixed it in our minds, by their praises, not so much of Cecilia, as of Timotheus and Orpheus. Already, in the eleventh century, the musical saint had been given as a patroness; and the contemporaries, Philip I. of France, and William I. of England, had each a daughter Cécile.

From that time, Cécile in France was only less popular than the English Cicely was with all ranks before the Reformation. Cicely Neville, the Rose of Raby, afterwards Duchess of York, called "Proud Cis," gave it the chief note in England; but her princess grandchild, Cicely Plantagenet, was a nun, and thus did not transmit it to any noble family. After the Reformation, Cicely sank to the level of "stammel waistcoat," and was the milkmaid's generic name. And so the gentlewomen who had inherited Cicely from their grandmothers, were ashamed of it; and it became Cecilia, until the present reaction against fine names setting in, brought them back to Cecil and Cecily. In Ireland, the Norman settlers introduced it, and it became Sighile.

English.	French.	Italian.	German.
Cecilia	Cécile	Cecilia	Cacilia
Cecily			
Cicely			
Cecil			
Sisley			
Sis			
Sissot			
Cis			

Hamburg.	Russian.	Polish.	Illyrian.
Cile	Zezilija	Cecylia	Cecilia
			Cecilija
			Cila
			Cilika

Sessylt, the British form of the masculine, lasted on long in Wales; and the Italians kept up Cecilio. The English masculine Cecil is, however, the surname of the families of Salisbury and Exeter, adopted as a Christian name.

Moreover, Cæcilianus is supposed to be the origin of Kilian, one of the many Keltic missionaries who spread the light of the Gospel on the Continent, in the seventh century. St. Kilian is said to have been of Irish birth. He preached in Germany, and was martyred at Wurtzburg; and his name has never quite ceased to be used in the adjacent lands.*

* Facciolati; Smith; Valerius Maximus; Butler; Jameson; Michaelis; Pott.

Section V.—*Cœlius.*

Cœles Vivenna, an Etruscan general, named the Cœlian hill, and the Cœlian gens, whence the Italians have continued Celio and Celia. In Venice the latter becomes Zilia and Ziliola, and is often to be found belonging to noble ladies and the wives of doges. At Naples it was Liliola, and it seems to be the true origin of Lilian and Lilias. The Irish, too, have adopted it as Sile, or Sheelah, and Célie and Celia have been occasionally adopted by both French and English, under some misty notion of a connection with *cœlum* (heaven). The prevalence of Celia among the lower classes in English towns is partly owing to the Irish Sheelah, partly to some confusion with Cecilia.

Cœlina was a virgin of Meaux, converted to a holy life by St. Geneviève. She is the origin of the French Céline, who probably suggested the English Selina, though, as we spell this last, we refer it to the Greek Selene (the moon).

Section VI.—*Claudius.*

Another personal defect, namely lameness, probably was the source of the appellation of the Claudian gens, although by some the adjective *claudus* is rejected in favour of the old verb *clueo*, from the same root as the Greek *kleo*, I hear, and *kluo*, I am called, or I am famous, meaning to be called, *i. e.*, famed. The Claudii were a family of evil fame, with all the darker characteristics of the Roman, and they figure in most of the tragedies of the city. They were especially proud and stern, and never adopted any one into their family till the Emperor Claudius adopted Lucius Domitius Ahenobarbus, who did not improve the fame of the Claudian surname of Nero. But the reign of the Emperor Claudius and the number of his freedmen, and new citizens, gave his gentile name an extensive vogue, and from his conquests in Britain was there much adopted. Besides, the Claudia who sends her greeting to St. Timothy in St. Paul's Epistle, is believed to have been the daughter of a British prince and wife of Pudens, whose name is preserved in inscriptions at Colchester.

The epigrams of Martial speak of a British lady of the same name, and thus Claudia is marked by the concurrence of two very dissimilar authorities as one of the first British Christians, while the hereditary Welsh name of Gladys, the Cornish Gladuse, corroborate the Christian reverence for Claudia. The masculine form, Gladus, is likewise used, and in Scotland Glaud, recently softened into Claud, is not uncommon. Claudie is very common in Provence. Louis XII., who gave both his daughters male names, called the eldest Claude, and when she was the wife of François I., la Reine Claude plums were so termed in her honour. Her daughter carried Claude into the House of Lorraine, where it again became masculine, and was frequent in the family of Guise. The painter Gelée assumed the name

L

of Claude de Lorraine in honour of his patrons, and thus arose all
the picturesque associations conveyed by the word Claude.
Claudine is a favourite female Swiss form.*

English.	Scotch.	French.	Italian.	Russian.	Slovak.
Claud	Glaud	Claude Godon	Claudio	Klavdij	Klavdi
				Illyrian. Klaudij	

FEMININE.		
French. Claude Claudine Claudie	Welsh. Gladys	Italian. Claudia

SECTION VII.—*Cornelius, &c.*

The far more honourably distinguished clan of Cornelius has no
traceable origin, unless from *cornu belli* (a war horn), but this is a
suggestion of the least well-informed etymologists, and deserves no
attention. Scipio and Sylla were the most noted families of this
gens, both memorable for very dissimilar qualities; and Cornelia,
the mother of the Gracchi, inherited her name from her father,
Publius Cornelius Scipio Africanus I. The centurion of the *Italian*
band was probably a hereditary Roman Cornelius; but earliest
gentile Christian though he were, he was not canonized, and the
saint of the Western Church is a martyred Pope Cornelius of the
third century, whose relics were brought to Compiègne by Charles
the Bald, and placed in the Abbey of St. Corneille, whence again a
portion was carried to the Chapter of Rosnay, in Flanders. This
translation accounts for the popularity of both the masculine and
feminine forms in the Low Countries, in both kingdoms of which
they constantly are found, and where Cornelius gets shortened into
Kees, Knelis, Nöll, or Nelle, and Cornelia into Keetje, or Kee. As
an attempt to translate the native Keltic names beginning with *cu* or
con, Cornellius, or Corney, is one of the most frequent Irish designations. Nelleson is the Dutch surname, and Nelson is as likely to
be thus derived as from the northern Nielson. The Dantzic contraction is Knelz, and the Illyrians call the feminine Drenka!
The great Fabian gens was old Latin, and was said by Pliny to be
so called from their having been the first to cultivate the bean, *faba*,
while others say the true form was *fodius*, or *fovius*, from their having
invented the digging of pits, *foveæ*, for wolves, a proceeding rather

* Facciolati ; Smith ; Rees, *Welsh Saints.*

in character with the wary patient disposition displayed by the greatest man of the race, Quintus Fabius Maximus, whose agnomen of Cunctator so well describes the policy that wasted away the forces of the Carthaginian invader. Fabio has been occasionally a modern Italian name; Fabiola is the diminutive of Fabia; Fabianus the adoptive augmentation, whence the occasional French Fabien, and, more strange to record, the Lithuanian Pobjus.

Fabricius is probably from *Faber* (a workman), but there was no person of note of the family except Caius Fabricius Luscinus, whose interview with Pyrrhus and his elephant has caused him to be for ever remembered. Fabrizio Colonna, however, seems to be his only namesake.

Flavus and *Fulvus* both mean shades of yellow, and there were both a Flavian and a Fulvian gens, no doubt from the complexion of an early ancestor, Flavius being probably a yellow-haired mountaineer with northern blood; Fulvius a tawny Italian. It is in favour of this supposition that Constantius, who brought the Flavian gens to the imperial throne, had the agnomen Chlorus, also expressing a light complexion. Out of compliment to his family the derivatives of Flavius became common, as Flavianus, Flavia, and Flavilla. Flavio is now and then found in modern Italy, and Flavia figured in the poetry and essays of the last century. Fulvia, "the married woman," as her rival Cleopatra calls her, was the wife of Antony, and gave her name an evil fame by her usage of the head of the murdered Cicero.*

The Herminian gens is believed to be of Sabine origin, and its first syllable, that lordly *herr*, which we traced in the Greek Hera and Hercules, and shall find again in the German Herman. There is little doubt that the Roman Herminius and the brave Cheruscan chief, whom he called Arminius, were in the same relationship as were the Emilii and Amaler.

Herminius is the word that left to Italy the graceful legacy of Erminia, which was in vogue, by inheritance, among Italian ladies when Tasso bestowed it upon the Saracen damsel who was captured by Tancred, and fascinated by the graces of her captor. Thence the French adopted it as Hermine, and it has since been incorrectly supposed to be the Italian for Hermione; indeed, Scott indiscriminately calls the mysterious lady in George Heriot's house Erminia or Hermione. The Welsh have obtained it likewise, by inheritance, in the form of Ermin, which, however, they now murder by translating it into Emma.

Hortensius (a gardener), from *hortus*, a garden, belonged to an honourable old plebeian gens, and has been continued in Italy, both in the masculine Ortensio, and feminine Ortensia, whence the French obtained their Hortense, probably from Ortensia Mancini, the niece of Mazarin.

The Horatian gens was a very old and noble one, memorable for the battle of the Horatii, in the mythic times of early Rome. Some explain their nomen by *hora* (an hour), and make it mean the

* Smith; Butler; Facciolati; *Irish Society.*

L 3

punctual, but this is a triviality suggested by the sound, and the family themselves derived it from the hero ancestor, Horatus, to whom an oak wood was dedicated. The poet Horace bore it as an adoptive name, being of a freedman's family. Except for Orazio, in Italy, the name of Titian's son, it slept till Corneille's tragedy of *Les Horaces* brought it forward, and the influence of Orazio made it Horatio in England. Thus the brother and son of Sir Robert Walpole bore it, and the literary note of the younger Horace Walpole made it fashionable. Then came our naval hero to give it full glory, and that last mention of his daughter Horatia seems to have brought the feminine forward of late years. The name is not popular elsewhere, but is called by the Russians, Goratij, by the Slovaks, Orac.*

Section VIII.—*Julius.*

"At puer Ascanius, cui nunc cognomen Iulo,
    Additur Ilus erat dum res stetit Ilia regno."

" The boy Ascanius, now Iulus named—
    Ilus he was while Ilium's realm still stood,'

quoth Jupiter, in the first book of the *Æneid*, whence Virgil's commentators aver that Ascanius was at first called after Ilus, the river that gave Troy the additional title of Ilium ; but that during the conquest of Italy he was termed Iulus, from ιουλος (the first down on the chin), because he was still beardless when he killed Mezentius. The father of gods and men continues :

" Nascetur pulchrâ Trojanus origine Cæsar,
    (Imperium Oceano, famam qui terminet astris,)
    Julius, a magno nomen Iulo."

" A Trojan, by high lineage shall arise—
    Cæsar (whose conquering fame the sea and stars shall bound),
    Called Julius, from Iulus, mighty name."

The Julian gens certainly exceeded Rome in antiquity, and one of their distinguished families bore the cognomen of Iulus ; but in spite of Jupiter and Virgil, Livy makes Iulus, or Ascanius, not the Trojan son of Æneas and the deserted Creusa, but the Latin son of Æneas and Lavinia, and modern etymologists hazard the conjecture that Julus may be only a diminutive of dius (divine), since the derivation of Jupiter from Deus pater (father of gods) proves that such is the tendency of the language.

The family resided at Alba Longa till the destruction of the city by Tullus Hostilius, and then came to Rome, where, though of very high rank, they did not become distinguished till, once for all, their star culminated in the great Caius Julius Cæsar, after whom the Julii were only adoptive, though Julia was the favourite name of the emperors' daughters, and their freedmen and newly-made citizens multiplied Julius and Julianus throughout the empire.

* Butler; Michaelis.

Julius was hereditary throughout the empire, and lingered on long in Wales, Wallachia, and Italy. It is the most obvious source for the French Gilles; though, as has been already said, that word claims to be the Greek Aigidios, and is like both the Keltic Giolla and Teutonic Gil. The modern French Jules and English Julius were the produce of the revived classical taste. The latter belonged to a knight whose family name was Cæsar; and Clarendon tells a story of a serious alarm being excited in a statesman by finding a note in his pocket with the ominous words "Remember Julius Cæsar," which left him in dread of the ides of March, until he recollected that it was a friendly reminder of the humble petition of Sir Julius Cæsar.

English.	Welsh.	Breton.	French.
Julius	Iolo	Sulio	Jules
		Iola	Julot

Italian.	Spanish and Portuguese.	German.	Wallachian.
Giulio	Julio	Julius	Julie
			Slavonic.
			Julij

The feminine shared the same fate, being hereditary in Italy, and adopted as ornamental when classical names came into fashion in other countries. The heroine of Rousseau's *Nouvelle Heloïse* made Julie very common in France.

English, Spanish and Portuguese.	French and German.	Italian.	Russian.
Julia	Julie	Giulia	Julija

Polish.	Lett.	Hungarian.	Slovak.
Julia	Jule	Juli	Iliska
Julka		Julis	
		Juliska	Breton.
			Sulia

As every family that in turn mounted the imperial throne was supposed to be adopted into the Julian gens, all bore its appellation; and thus it was that out of the huge stock of nomina that had accumulated in the family of Constantius, the apostate bore by way of distinction the adoptive form of Julianus.

As the adoptive form this was more widely diffused than Julius itself in the Latinized provinces, and thus came to the Conde Julian, execrated by Spain as the betrayer of his country into the hands of the Moors.

To redeem the name of Julian from the unpopularity to which two apostates would seem to have condemned it, it belonged to no less than ten saints, one of whom was the nucleus of a legend afloat in the world. He was said to have been told by a hunted stag that he would be the murderer of his own parents; and though he fled into another country to avoid the possibility, he unconsciously fulfilled his destiny, by slaying them in a fit of jealousy before he had recognized them when they travelled after him. In penance, he spent the rest of his life in ferrying distressed wayfarers over a river, and lodging them in his dwelling; and he thus became the patron of travellers and a saint of extreme popularity.

English.	Scotch.	Welsh.	Breton.
Julian	Jellon	Julion	Sulien
French.	Spanish.	Portuguese.	Italian.
Julien	Julian	Juliao.	Giuliano
			Russian.
			Julian

The feminine was already abroad in the Roman empire in the days of martyrdom, when St. Juliana was beheaded at Nicomedia under Galerius; and in the days of Gregory the Great, her relics were supposed to be at Rome, but were afterwards divided between Brussels and Sablon. She is said to have been especially honoured in the Low Countries, and must likewise have been in high favour in Normandy, perhaps through the Flemish Duchess Matilda. Julienne was in vogue among the Norman families, and belonged to that illegitimate daughter of Henry I. whose children he so terribly maltreated in revenge for their father's rebellion; and it long prevailed in England as Julyan: witness the heraldic and hunting prioress, Dame Julyan Berners; and, indeed, it became so common as Gillian, that Jill was the regular companion of Jack, as still appears in nursery rhyme; though now this good old form has almost entirely disappeared, except in the occasional un-English form of Juliana. In Brittany, it has lasted on as Suliana, the proper name of the nun-sister of Du Guesclin, who assisted his brave wife to disconcert the night assault of their late prisoner.

English.	French.	Breton.	Italian.
Julyan	Julienne	Suliana	Giuliana
Juliana			
Gillian			
Gill			
Spanish, Portuguese, and Wallachian.	German.	Slavonic.	Hungarian.
Juliana	Juliana	Julijana	Julianja

Another feminine diminutive, Julitta, was current in the empire in the time of persecution, and belongs in the calendar to a martyr at Cæsarea in Cappadocia, as well as to her who has been already mentioned as the mother of the infant St. Kyriakos, or Cyr, a babe of three years old. She was undergoing torture herself when she beheld his brains dashed out on the steps of the tribunal, and till her own death, she gave thanks for his safety and constancy. Together the mother and child were commemorated throughout the Church; and the church of St. Gillet records her in Cornwall, as does that of Llanulid in Wales. Her name, however, when there borne by her namesakes was corrupted into Elidan. Jolitte was used among the French peasantry, and Giulietta in Italy, whence Giulietta Capellet appears to have been a veritable lady, whose mournful story told in Da Porta's novel, was adopted by Shakespeare, and rendered her name so much the property of poetry and romance, that subsequently Juliet, Juliette, and Giulietta, have been far more often christened in memory of the impassioned girl, than of the resolute Christian mother.*

SECTION IX.—*Lælius, &c.*

Lælius, an unexplained gentile name, left to the Italians, Lelio, which was borne by one of the heresiarchs Socini; also Lelia, in French Lélie, and sometimes confused with the names from Cœlius.

It was said that the city of Pompeii was so called from *pompa*, the splendour or pomp with which Hercules founded it. However this might be, it is likely that from it came the nomen of the Pompeian gens, which did not appear in Rome till a late period, and which its enemies declared was founded by Aulus Pompeius, a flute-player. The gallant Cnæus Pompeius won for himself the surname of Magnus, and made sufficient impression on the world to have his name adapted to modern pronunciation by the Pompée of the French, and the English Pompey. When a little negro boy was the favourite appendage of fine ladies of the early seventeenth century, the habit of calling slaves by classical titles, made Pompey the usual designation of these poor little fellows; from whom it descended to little dogs, and though now out of fashion, even for them, it has obtained a set of associations that is likely to prevent that fine old Roman Pompey, surnamed the big, from obtaining any future namesakes, except in Italy, where Pompeio has always flourished, probably from hereditary associations.

On Roman authority, the Porcii were the breeders of *porcus* (a pig), according to the homely, rural, and agricultural designations of old Latinity, which to modern ears have so dignified a sound. It was the clan of the two Catones, but the masculine has not prevailed; though that "woman well reputed, Cato's daughter" Porcia, or, as the Italians spelt it, Porzia, caused her name to be handed on in her

* Smith; Facciolati; Michaelis; Pott; Butler; Arrowsmith, *Geography;* Rees; Jameson; *Gesta Romanorum.*

native land, where Shakespeare took it, not only for her, but for his other heroine—

> "Nothing undervalued
> To Cato's daughter, Brutus' Portia;"

from whom Portia, as after his example we make it, has become an exceptional fancy name. The Romans thought no scorn of the title of the unclean beast, and three families in other clans likewise bore its name, Verres, Scrofa, and Aper ; the last, it is just possible, being the origin of the Sir Bors of the Round Table ; in Welsh, Baez.

The origin of Sulpicius is not known. It may possibly be connected with the obsolete word that named Sulla, from a red spotted visage ; but this is uncertain. There were three saints of the name : Severus Sulpicius, a friend of St. Martin ; Sulpicius (called the severe), Bishop of Bourges, in the sixth century ; and Sulpicius (called the gentle), also Bishop of Bourges, in the seventh. It is an arm of this last of the three that has led to the consecration of the celebrated church at Paris, in the name of St. Sulpice. In Germany, it is Sulpiz.

Terenus (soft or tender) was the origin given by the Romans to the Terentian gens, which produced Terentia, wife of Cicero, called in affection Terentilla, and likewise gave birth to the comic poet, Publius Terentius Afer, known to us as Terence, and to the Germans as Terenz. As a supposed rendering of Turlough, Terence is a very favourite name in Ireland, and is there called Terry, but it prevails nowhere else.

The meaning of the name of Sergius is not known, but the Sergian gens was very ancient, and believed itself to spring from the Trojans. From them Cataline descended, and from another branch the deputy Sergius Paullus, from whom some suppose St. Paul to have taken his name.

One saint called Sergius was martyred at the city of Rasapha, in Syria ; and was honoured by the change of the name of the place to Sergiopolis, in Justinian's time. His relics are at Rome and at Prague ; but a far greater favourite as a namesake is the Russian Ssergie, who founded a monastery near Moscow, and died there in 1292, in the highest esteem for sanctity, so that his monastery is a place of devotional pilgrimage, and Ssergij or Sserezka are favourite names in Russia.*

Section X.—*Valerius.*

Deep among the roots of Indo-European tongues lies the source of our adverb *well*, the German *wohl*, Saxon *wel*, Gothic *waila*, an evidently close connection of the Latin verb *valeo* (to be well) ; and which the Keltic *gwall* links again with the Greek καλός (well, or beautiful), related to the Sanscrit *kalya* (healthy, able, or well).

* Butler ; Michaelis ; Smith ; Facciolati ; Courson, *Peuples Bretons ;* Pott; Valerius Maximus,

Valeo was both to be sound and to be worth, and to the old Roman a sound man was necessarily *valiant*, worth something in the battle ; and *valor*, which to them and the Italians is still value, is to the chivalrous French and English *valour*.

This word of well-being named the old Sabine Valerian gens, one of the most noble and oldest in Rome, who had a little throne to themselves in the Circus, and were allowed to bury their dead within the walls of the city. The simple masculine form of the name had but two saints, and they were too obscure to be much followed, though Valère and Valerot as surnames have risen from it in France. The feminine of it was in honour at Rome for the sake of Valeria, the public-spirited lady who took the lead in persuading the mother of Coriolanus to intercede with her son to lay his vengeance aside and spare his mother-city ; Valérie is a favourite French name, but the compounds of this word have had far greater note. Valerianus, the adoptive name, was borne by Publius Sicinius Valerianus, that unhappy persecuting emperor who ended his career as a stepping-stone to Shahpoor. Saint Valerianus was Bishop of Auxerre, and though properly Valérien in French, Valerian in English, was probably the patron of the Waleran, or Galeran, occurring in the middle ages, chiefly among the Luxembourgs, Counts of St. Pol.

Valentinianus has been continued by the Welsh in the form of Balawn.

Valentinus was a Roman priest, who is said to have endeavoured to give a Christian signification to the old custom of drawing lots in honour of Juno Februata, and thus fixed his own name and festival to the curious fashion prevailing all over England and France, of either the choice of a " true Valentine," or of receiving as such the first person of the opposite sex encountered on that morning.

These customs increased the popularity of Valentine and Valentina, the latter being more probably used as the feminine of the former, than as the name of an obscure martyr who died under Diocletian.

Valentina Visconti was the wife of the Duke of Orleans, brother of Charles VI. of France, and as one of the bright lights in a corrupt court, merited that her name should have become more permanent than it has been.

The Slavonic contractions of the masculine are curious. Lower Lusatia makes it Batyn, Tyno, Bal, and Balk ; Lithuanian, Wallinsch ; and Hungary, Balint.*

It is not easy to separate the idea of Virginia from *virgo* (a virgin), especially since Sir Walter Raleigh gave that name to his American colony in honour of the Virgin Queen, and it was probably under this impression that Virginie was made by Bernardin de St. Pierre, the heroine of his tropical Arcadian romance, which reigned supreme over French, English, and German imaginations of a certain calibre, and rendered Virginie triumphant in France, and a name of sentiment in England. Nay, had the true Virginia lived and died a

---

* Liddell and Scott; Pott; Facciolati; Smith; Arnold; Jones, *Welsh Sketches ;* Brand, *Popular Antiquities ;* Michaelis.

couple of centuries earlier, her story would have passed for a myth
expressed in her appellation ; but the fact is, that she derived it from
a good old plebeian gens, who formerly spelt themselves Verginius,
thus connecting themselves with *ver* (the spring), Persian *behar*, Eolic
Βεαρ, the old Greek Γέαρ, and with all its kindred of *virga* (a rod, or
green bough), *vireo* (to flourish), *viridis* (green) ; and again with the
more remote descendants of these words in modern Europe—*vert*,
verdure, *il vero*, &c. Virginio was a name in the Orsini family, but
otherwise it has not been kept up.

CHAPTER IV.

Section I.

Roman cognomina were originally neither more nor less than nick-names, sometimes far from complimentary, but for the sake of convenience, or of honourable association, continued in the family.

Sometimes they were adjectives, such as Asper (the rough), Cæcus (the blind), Brutus (the stupid). Sometimes they were suggested by the appearance, such as Naso (the nose), or Scævola (the left-handed), the soubriquet earned by that Mutius who seared his right hand in the fire to prove to Porsenna what Roman constancy was. Sura (the calf of the leg), Sulla (the red-pimpled), Barbatus (the bearded), Dentatus (the toothed), Balbus (the stammerer), and even Bibulus and Bibacula (the drunkard).

Sometimes, like some of the gentle nomina previously mentioned, they came from animal or vegetable, connected in some way with the ancestor, either by augury, chase, or culture, such as Corvinus, from *corvus* (a raven), Buteo (a buzzard), Lentulus (a bean), Piso, from *pisum* (a pea), Cicero (a vetch), Cæpio, from *cæpe* (an onion). Others were from the birthplace of the forefather, such as Hadrianus, Albinus; others were the ablative case of the name of the tribe to which the gens belonged, as Romilia, or Palatina. Sometimes a *cognomen secundus*, or agnomen, was superadded in the case of distinguished personages, in memory of their services, such as Coriolanus, Capitolinus, Africanus, Asiaticus. The latest example of an agnomen of victory was Peloponnesiacus, which was conferred in 1688 by the Venetian Republic upon Francesco Morosini, the conqueror of the Morea.

Whatever the cognomen,—fortuitous, derisive, or honourable,—it remained attached for ever to the family, and served to designate that section of the gens, but did not naturally descend to females; though in the latter and more irregular periods, when the gentes were so extensive that the feminine was no distinction, they were usually assumed by the daughters of the house, and altered to suit their construction.

Ater, black, was the source of the name of Adria in Picenum, whence was called Adriatic Sea. A family of Ælii, migrating through Spain, were known by the cognomen of Adrianus, or Hadrianus, both place and name being usually spelt with the aspirate. The Emperor

Publius Ælius Hadrianus built our famous northern wall, still called after him, as is the city of Adrianople; but he failed in imposing his gentile name of Ælia upon Jerusalem. The Italian surname of Adriani is probably derived from the original city. An Adrianus was the first abbot of St. Augustin's, Canterbury, and another was first bishop of Aberdeen; but the most popular St. Adrianus was an officer in the imperial army who was converted by the sight of the martyrdoms under Galerius, and was martyred himself at Nicomedia, whence his relics were taken to Constantinople and to Rome, and thence again to Flanders, where they were transported from one abbey to another, and supposed to work such miracles that Adrianus has ever since been a universal name in the Low Countries, where it gets contracted into Arje, or Janus, while the more northerly nations call it, in common use, Arrian, or Arne. The French make it Adrien, and have given it the feminine Adrienne; and the Italians have not unfrequently Adriano and Adriana. In Russia it is Andreïän.

Aquila (an eagle) was a cognomen in several Roman families, either from augury or from the national feature. It reminds us of the Greek *Aias*, and of many of the Teuton names beginning with *ar*.

Aquila was a companion of St. Paul; and another Aquila, under Hadrian, wavered long between Judaism and Christianity, and translated the Old Testament into Greek; but Aquila has not been followed save here and there in England and America as a Scripture name.

Agrippa was not well understood by the Romans themselves, though they settled that it meant one born with his feet foremost. The explanation we quote from Professor Aufrecht: "He (Gellius) ascribes to that preposterous birth all the calamities which befell the world through Agrippa's ill-starred descendants. 'To fall on one's feet' was therefore no auspicious event in Italy. But how can we possibly reconcile that signification with the etymology? I think the legs peep out of the *pp*, and that *ppa* is probably a contraction of *peda*. In Greek 'Ακρόπους means only 'the beginning or tip of the foot;' but it might as well have signified an individual, who, on entering this shaky world of ours, philosophically chose to take a firm 'stand-point,' rather than begin by a foolish act, and plunge into it headlong." It was at first a prænomen, but became a cognomen in the clan of Menenius and of many others. Marcus Vipsanius Agrippa was the friend and son-in-law of Augustus. From him the Herods called themselves Agrippa; and his daughter was the first of those ladies named Agrippina, whose tragic stories mark the early years of the Roman empire. Cornelius Agrippa was probably assumed by the learned man of Cologne, who has connected it in the popular mind with alchemy and necromancy. St. Agrippina was martyred at Rome under Valerian, and her remains being transferred to Girgenti in Sicily, she became known to the Greeks. Her name is used in Russia in the softened form of Agrafina, and the rude contraction Gruscha or Grunja. Some suggest that Agrippa may be the Greek ἀργίπους (swift-footed).

The city of Alba Longa doubtless took its first name from that universal word that named the Alps, the Elbe, Elves, Albion, and

Albin from their whiteness, and left *albus* still the adjective in
Rome.   Legend declared that the city was called from the white sow
with fifty piglings, who directed Æneas to its site ; but, however this
might be, it was the source of the family of Albinus in the Postumian
gens, whence, slightly altered, came the name of the soldier Albanus,
the British martyr, whose death led to the change from Verulamium
to St. Albans, and from whom we take the English Christian name
of Alban.   Another St. Albanus, or Abban, was an Irish bishop,
consecrated by St. Patrick, and probably the source of the Scottish
Christian name Albany, which was often used as a rendering of the
Keltic Finn, also meaning white.   Another Albanus, or Albinus, of
a British family, established in Armorica, was a monastic saint and
bishop of Angers, naming the family of St. Aubin ; and perhaps
William de Albini, the ancestor of the Howards.   The modern
English feminine Albina, or Albinia, must have been formed as a
name of romance from some of these.

Section II.—*Augustus.*

Augustus is the agnomen conferred by the senate upon the second
Cæsar, meaning reverend or set apart, and was selected as hedging
him with majesty, though not offending the citizens with the word
king.   It is closely related to *avigur* or *augur*, which the Romans
said was " *ob avium garritus*," because the augur divined by the
chatter of birds ; while others make it come from *augeo* (to increase) ;
but it is not impossible that it may be related to the Teuton *æge*
(awe).   At Rome, after Diocletian, the Augustus was always the
reigning emperor, the Augusta was his wife ; and no one presumed
to take the name till the unfortunate Romulus Augustus, called
Augustulus in contempt, who ended both the independence of Rome
and the empire with the names of their founders.
    The Welsh formed the name of Awst from Augustus ; but it does

English.	French.	German.	Lett.
Augustus	Auguste	August	Anjusts
Gussy			Justs
		Russian.	Hungarian.
		Avgust	Agoston

FEMININE.			
English.	German.	Italian.	Lusatian.
Augusta	Auguste	Augusta	Avgusta
Gussie	Asta		Gusta
	Guste		Gustylka
	Gustel		

not seem to have been elsewhere used, except as an epithet which the flattering chroniclers bestowed upon Philippe III. of France, until about the middle of the sixteenth century, a fancy seized the small German princes of christening their children by this imperial title.   August of Anhalt Plotzgau appears in 1575—seven years earlier, August of Braunsweig Luneburg.   Then August of Wolfen-büttel names his daughter Anne Augusta ; and we all recollect the Elector Johann August of Saxony, memorable as the prisoner of Charles V.   Thenceforth these names flourished in Germany, and took up their abode in England with the Hanoverian race.

The diminutive had, however, been adopted under the Roman empire in later times, and was borne by the great Father Augustinus of Hippo, and his namesake, the missionary of the Saxons.   This was chosen by a Danish bishop as a Latinization of his proper name of Eystein (island stone) ; and it has always been somewhat popular, probably owing to the order of Augustin or Austin Friars, instituted in honour of the first St. Augustin, and once the greatest sheep owners in England.

English.	French.	German.	Spanish.
Augustin Austin	Augustin	Augustin	Augustino
Portuguese.	Italian.	Polish.	
Agostinho	Aogostino	Agostin	

		FEMININE.		

Irish.	French.	German.	Italian.
Augusteen	Augustine	Augustine Stine	Agostina
			Portuguese.
			Agostinha

Section III.—*Blasius.*

Some consider Blasius to be a mere contraction of the Greek *basilios* (royal) ; but long before that name prevailed, at least among historical personages, we hear of Blatius, Blattius, or Blasius, as a man of Salapia, in Apulia, whose name seems to have signified a babbler. Nevertheless, Blasio was a surname in the Cornelian gens, and Blasius was Bishop of Sebaste, in Nicomedia, where he was martyred in 316.   In the time of the Crusades, his relics were imported from the East, he became patron of the republic of Ragusa ; and from a tradition that he had been combed to death with iron combs, such an implement was his mark, and he was the favourite saint of the English wool-staplers.   The only vestige of this as a name in England

is, however, in Goldsmith's *Madam Blase;* but in Spanish Blas is
used, as no reader of *Gil Blas* can forget. Blasius is found in Bavaria ;
and Plase, Blase, Bleisig, and Bläsing, are surnames thence derived.

English.	French.	Spanish.	Portuguese.
Blaze	Blaise	Blas	Braz
Blase	Blaisot		
Italian.	**German.**	**Dutch.**	**Russian.**
Biagio	Blasius	Blaas	Vlassij
Biasio	Blasi		Vlass
Baccio	Blasol		
Servian.	**Illyrian.**	**Hungarian.**	
Blazej	Blasko	Balás	
	Vlaho		
	Bearck		

The Germans have even the feminine Blasia.*

SECTION IV.—*Cæsar, &c.*

No cognomen has ever been so much used as that of Cæsar, which
first began in the Julian gens, nearly two centuries before the time
of the great Dictator. Some derived it, like Cæso, from *cædo* (to cut) ;
others said that the eyes of the first owner of it were unusually blue
(*cæsius*), or that his hair (*cæsaries*) was wonderfully profuse ; and
a fourth explanation declared that it was the Moorish word for an
elephant, which one of the Julii had slain with his own hand in
Africa. However this might be, adoption into the family of Cæsar
was the means of obtaining that accumulation of magisterial offices
that placed the successor of Julius at the head of affairs, civil and
military ; and whilst habits of republican equality were still retained
by the emperors, Cæsar was merely used as their designation. After
the first twelve, adoption could no longer be strained into any fiction
of the continuance of the Julian clan, and Cæsar became more
properly a title. After the new arrangement of the empire under
Diocletian, Augustus was the title of the emperor who had become
an actual monarch, and Cæsar of the heir to the empire with
considerable delegated power. In consequence, when Charlemagne
relieved Rome from the attacks of the Lombards, the pope, as the
representative of the S.P.Q.R., created him Cæsar, and the title has
been carried on among his German representatives as Kaiser, though
no elected "King of the Romans" might assume this sacred title
until he had been crowned by the pope's own hand. As a Christian
name it has seldom occurred. Cesare Borgia was named, like many
Italians of his date, in the classical style, but no one wished to inherit

* Smith ; Brand ; Michaelis.

it from him, and it is seldom found except in France as Cesar; though
in some counties of England the peasantry give it in baptism, having
taken it, perhaps, from the surname Cæsar. The only feminine I
can find is Cesarina Grimaldi, in 1585. Kaiser occurs in the same
manner in Germany.

Camilla was a warlike Volscian nymph, dedicated to the service of
Diana, and celebrated in the *Æneid*. Her name is said to have been
Casmilla, and to have been given as meaning that she was a votaress
of Diana. It is believed to be an Etruscan word, and the youth of
both sexes were termed Camilli and Camillæ when employed in any
solemn office; and thus Camillus became a name in the gens of
Furius, and was noted in him who saved the capitol. Nymphs
always had an attraction for the French, and a Camille figures in
Florian's romance of *Numa Pompilius*, while Camilla was adopted in
the rage for classical names which actuated the English after the
Reformation, and in some few families it has been handed on to the
present day. Camillo was revived with classical names in Italy;
and at the time of the Revolution, Camille was very fashionable in
France. Camilla is still very common in the Abruzzi, its old classic
ground.

Clemens came in so late that it hardly deserves to be called a
cognomen, but we find it as the third name of Titus Flavius Clemens,
Vespasian's nephew, who was put to death by Domitian, on a charge
of atheism, like others who went over to the Jewish superstition, *i. e.*
to Christianity. A very early church at Rome is dedicated to him,
and he is thought by some to be the same as the Clemens mentioned
by St. Paul (Phil. iv. 3), author of two epistles, and first of nine
bishops of Rome so called. Another great Father, St. Clemens of
Alexandria, was likewise of the same name; besides a martyr of
Ancyra, all called from the adjective *clemens*, which has much the
same meaning as its derivative clement in all modern tongues. Its
origin is uncertain: some saying it meant of clear mind, others of in-
clining mind; but the substantive Clementia was a personified idea,
worshipped at Rome as a goddess, bearing a cup in one hand and a
lance in the other. "Your Clemency" became a title of the emperors,
and we find the orator Tertullus even addressing it to Felix. It is
possible that it was thus that Clemens first passed to the emperor's
kinsman. There is a pretty legend that St. Clement was martyred by
being beheaded, and thrown into the sea, where a shrine (I think of
coral) was formed round his head, and he thus became the patron of
sailors, above all, of Danes and Dutchmen. In Germany Clemens
has preserved its Latin form, but cuts down into Klenim, Mente,
Menz, Mentzel; as in Denmark into Klemet and Mens. The English
surname, Mence, may perhaps be from this source; and Clement and
Clementi are French and Italian surnames, as Clement and Clemente
are the Christian ones. Italy probably first modernized the abstract
goddess into Clemenza, whence France took up Clémence, while
Germany invented Clementine for the feminine, whence our Clementina, rendered popular for a time in honour of the Italian lady in
Sir C. Grandison. The Russians have Kliment, the Hungarians

Kelemen, and the Esthonians contract the name into Lemet. It must have been from the Dutch connections of eastern England, that Clement and Clemency were both at one time frequent.*

SECTION V.—*Constantius.*

Constantius arose likewise as late as any cognomen deserving to be reckoned. It comes from *constans* (constant), a word meaning holding together firmly, and compounded of *con* (together), and *stans*, the participle of the verb *sto* (I am, or I stand).

·So late, indeed, did Constantius become prominent in history in the person of Flavius Valerius Constantius, that he does not even seem to have had a prænomen, and his sons and grandsons varied the cognomen by way of distinction into Constans and Constantinus. Of these the first Christian emperor rendered the diminutive glorious, and though it has not been much copied in the West, Κονστάντινος is one of the very few Latin names that have been Latinized among the Greeks, as well it might be, in memory of the emperor who transported the seat of empire to a Greek city, and changed its appellation from Byzantium to Constantinopolis.

Constantius Chlorus was very popular in Britain, and—as has been said before—the belief that his wife Helena was of British birth, held the island firm in its allegiance till the death of the last emperor who claimed kindred with him. And then Constantius and Constantinus were names assumed by the rebels who first began to break the bonds of union with the empire, as if the sound were sure to win British hearts. Indeed, Cystenian has never entirely disappeared from the Welsh nomenclature, nor Kusteninn from Brittany.

Perhaps one charm of the name to a Kelt was its first syllable, which resembles the *con* or *cu* (wisdom or *hound*), which was one of their favourite beginnings. The Constantines of Hector Boece's line of Scottish kings are ornamental Congals and Conchobars; and, in like manner, Ireland has turned many a Connal and Connor into Constantine in more modern times, accounting for the prevalence of the trisyllabled Roman as a surname.

In Russia Konstantin has been carried on, especially since the days of Catharine II., as a witness to the continuation of the Byzantine empire in that of Muscovy; and here and in the other Slavonian countries alone does it really prevail as a popular name, frequent enough for vernacular contractions, such as Kostja, Kosto, Kostadin.

The feminine of both names was used by the daughters of the imperial family, and Constantia continued among the Provençal ladies, so as to be brought to the throne of France by the termagant Constance of Provence, wife to that meek sovereign, Robert the Pious. She is said to have insisted on his composing a Latin hymn in her honour, when he, not being in a mood for flattery, began to sing " *O constantia martyrum,*" which she took as a personal compliment. Constance has ever since been a royal and noble name in

* Smith ; Cave; Marryat, *Jutland ;* Michaelis.

M

France, but the unfortunate Breton duchess, mother of Arthur, probably received it as a supposed feminine to Conan, the name of her father. Italy made it Gostanza, and the Sicilian mother of Frederick II. transmitted it to Germany as Constanz, or Stanze. Her great granddaughter, the heiress of Manfred's wrongs, took it to Spain as Constanza, the traces of which we see in the Custance, by which Chaucer calls that excellent daughter of Pedro the Cruel, who was the wife of John of Gaunt. After her time it was common in England, and it is startling to find a real Constance de Beverley in disgrace in the reign of Henry VIII., not, however, for forging Marmion's letters, but for the much more excusable misdemeanour of attending the Marchioness of Exeter in a stolen visit to the Nun of Kent. In the times immediately after the Reformation, Constance died away, then came forth as Constantia in the Minerva press, and at present reigns among the favourite fancy names.

Kostancia, Kotka, Stanca are used in the Slavonian countries, but far less commonly than the masculine Constantine, which is almost entirely disregarded by the Teuton side of Europe.

Section VI.—*Crispus, &c.*

Crispus (curled, or wrinkled), the same word which has produced our crisp ; and the French *crépé* (applied to hair), became a cognomen, and in late times produced Crispinus and Crispinianus, two brothers who accompanied St. Quentin when he preached the Gospel in France. They settled at Soissons, and there, while pursuing their mission, supported themselves by making shoes until their martyrdom, A.D. 287. Shoemakers, of course, adopted them as their patrons, and theirs was a universal holiday.

> " Oh ! that we now had here
> But one ten thousand of those men in England
> Who do no work to-day."

That day being the 25th of October, that of the battle of Agincourt, of which King Henry augurs—

> " And Crispin, Crispian, shall ne'er go by,
> From this day to the ending of the world,
> But we in it shall be remembered."

Crispin has never been a frequent Christian name, but it has become a surname with us, and the French have Crêpin, Crêpet, and the Italians Crispino. *Crispin* is still the French for a shoemaker's last. Crêpin means a little stool which the Irish call a creepeen.

Drusus, a cognomen in the Livian gens, was only accounted for among the Romans by a story that its first owner took it from having killed a chieftain in Gaul named Drausus. This word is explained by comparative philologists as firm or rigid in Keltic, *Drud*, strong, in Welsh, *droth* in Erse. Either the Gaul was the real cause of the surname, or it is an instance of the Keltic element in old Italian. It is hardly worthy of notice, except that, in imitation of the sister and daughter of his patron Caligula, Herod Agrippa called his daughter by the feminine diminutive Drusilla, by which she appears by the side of Felix, hearing but little regarding the discourse of St. Paul.

The name of Felix himself was an agnomen frequently assumed by peculiarly fortunate individuals. It meant happy, and has given rise to all manner of words of good augury in the modern languages. No less than eleven saints so called are numbered in the Roman calendar, and yet it has never been a popular name, though sometimes occurring in Spain and France in the original form, and as Felice in Italy. The feminines, Felicia and Félise, in England and France, have been constructed from it, and Felicia was Queen of Navarre in 1067 ; but the abstract idea, Felicitas (happiness), once worshipped as a goddess at Rome, named the slave-martyr of Carthage, who suffered with St. Perpetua. There was another Felicitas who, with her seven sons, under Antoninus Pius, presented a Christian parallel to the mother in the Maccabees. Felicità in Italy, and Félicité in France, are the votaries of one or others of these. Felix is adopted in Ireland as a substitute for Feidlim or Phelim (ever good).

Faustus and Faustina are formed exactly in the same spirit of good augury, and Fausto is sometimes an Italian name.*

SECTION VII.—*Galerius, &c.*

The Teutonic *helm* (protection), turned in the Latin pronunciation into *galea* (helmet), named the persecuting Emperor Galerius, and continued in Lombardy till it formed that of Galeazzo, which became notable among the Visconti of Milan, and was called by the French Galeas. Old Camden augured that the first Galearono was so called from all the cocks in Milan crowing at the time of his birth, and certainly, unless the frequent Roman cognomen Gallus indicates a partly Gallic extraction, it would either be one of the farming names, and show that the owner was notable for his poultry, or be a differently spelt variety from Galea or helmet. Galileo, Galilei, and Galeotti are all Italian continuations of this old Latin name—that is, if the great astronomer's name be not in honour of Galilee. It is also possible that it may be connected with the Keltic *Gal* (courage, or a stranger), which occurs again as the Irish saint who founded an abbey in Switzerland ; but more of this in Keltic regions of names.

Niebuhr considers the Prisci to have been the original Latin tribe, whose name acquired its sense of age from their antiquity, just as Gothic was at one time a French and English synonym for antiquated. Priscus was the Porcian cognomen, probably denoting the descent of the gens from the Prisci ; and he whom we are accustomed to call Cato the elder, as a translation of Marcus Porcius Priscus Cato, was the first to add the second cognomen, the meaning of which is wary,

* Facciolati ; Diefenbach ; Smith ; Butler ; Anderson: *Irish Society ;* Grimm.

M 2

from Catus, probably a contraction from Cautus (cautious). Priscus and Prisca are both found in the Roman martyrology ; but to us the most interesting person thus named is Priscilla, the fellow-worker of St. Paul, in honour of whom this diminutive has had some preva- lence in England, though somewhat of a puritan kind.

Sabinus, of course indicating a Sabine family, occurs among the Flavii, and many other gentes. Sabina was the second name of that Poppæa, Nero's wife, whose extravagances have become a proverb, who bathed in asses' milk, and shod her mules with gold. As a frequent cognomen, this was the name of many other women, and specially of a widow who was converted by her maid, Seraphia, to the Christian faith, and was martyred in Hadrian's persecution. There is a church at Rome dedicated to her, which was formerly the first " Lent station," a fact which commended her to the notice of the Germans, and has made Sabine frequent among them. Sabina is often found among the peasantry about Gloucester, but it is possible that this may be a corruption of Sabrina (the Severn).

Serenus (serene, or good-tempered) was an old cognomen, and two saints were so called. Serena was the niece of Theodosius, and wife of Stilicho. Her appellation was chosen by Hayley for the heroine of his *Triumphs of Temper ;* but it is more often imaginary than real. In Norway, however, it has been revived as an ornamental form of Siri, the contraction of Sigrid.

Scipio means nothing but a staff ; but it is a highly honourable title, since it was given to one of the Cornelii, who served as the staff of his old blind father ; and the same filial piety distinguished the great Africanus when, at seventeen, he saved the life of his father in the battle of the Ticinus. Distinguished as is the cognomen it has not often been followed, though Scipione has occasionally occurred in Italy, and if Gil Blas may be trusted, in Spain.

Traherne, an old Welsh name, is formed from Trajanus, which belonged to others besides the emperor, whose noble qualities had made such an impression on the Italian mind as to have led to the remarkable tradition that St. Gregory the Great had obtained per- mission to recall him from the grave, and convert him to the true faith.

Torques (a neck-chain) gave the cognomen Torquatus to the fierce Lucius Manlius, who, having slain a gigantic Gaul in single combat, took the gold chain from about his neck, and hung it on his own ; and who afterwards put his son, Titus Manlius Torquatus, to death for the breach of discipline in accepting a like challenge from a Tusculan noble. Torquato Tasso is the sole modern instance of the recurrence of the surname of this " Roman Father," the northern Torquil being from an entirely different source, *i.e.* Thorgils (Thor's pledge).*

* Pott ; Michaelis ; Camden ; Diefenbach ; *Philological Society ;* Niebuhr ; Butler ; Dante ; Arnold.

SECTION VIII.—*Paullus and Magnus* [*small and large*].

The precedence must be given to the *less* on account of its far greater dignity.

There can be no doubt that the cognomen Paullus, or Paulus, the contraction of Pauxillus, originated with one of the Æmilian gens, who was small in stature. It was common in other gentes, though chiefly distinguished among the Æmilii, and was most probably the name by which "Saul of Tarsus" would have been enrolled as a citizen, either from its resemblance to his Jewish name, or from the person who had conferred liberty upon his parents.

Some, however, imagine that he assumed it out of compliment to

English.	French.	Italian.	Portuguese.
Pawl	Pol	Paolo	Paulo
Paul	Paul		
	Paulot		

Spanish.	Wallachian.	German.	Russian.
Pablo	Pawel	Paul	Pavel
			Pavlenka
		Dutch.	Pavluscha
		Paultje	

Illyrian.	Lett.	Hungarian.	Lapp.
Pavl	Pavils	Pal	Pava
Pavle		Palko	Pavck
Pavo			

	FEMININE.		

Italian.	Spanish.	Russian.	Illyrian.
Paola	Pala	Paola	Pava
			Pavlica

	DIMINUTIVE.		

Welsh.	Italian.	Spanish.	Slavonic.
Peulan	Paolino	Paulino	Pavlin

	FEMININE.		

English.	French.	Italian.	German.
Paulina	Pauline	Paolina	Pauline
	Paulette	Paoletta	
			Slavonic.
			Pavlina

the deputy, Sergius Paulus; others, that it was an allusion to his "weakness" of "bodily presence," or that he took it in his humility, meaning that he was "less than the least of the Apostles." Be that as it may, he has given it an honour entirely outshining that which is won from the Æmilii, and has spread Paul throughout Europe. The strong presumption that St. Paul preached the Gospel in Spain has rendered Pablo very common there; but, in fact, the name is everywhere more usual than in England, in spite of the tradition that the great Apostle likewise landed here, and the dedication of our great cathedral. Perhaps this may be owing to the fact that twelve other SS. Paul divide the allegiance of the Continent with the Apostle. Paula is not only honoured as his feminine, but as the name of the friend and correspondent of St. Jerome, the mother of Eustochium; and Paola is in consequence found in Italy. Paulinus (the lengthened form) became in Welsh, Pewlin, and also named three saints—among them our first Northumbria, bishop of York; but it has not been followed, except in Italy, by Paolina, and *there* is, perhaps, a mere diminutive of Paulus. Yet the feminine is far more fashionable; and Paulina, Pauline, Paolina, are the favourite forms everywhere occurring. Perhaps Pauline became the more popular in France for the sake of that favourite grandchild whose Christian name is almost the only one mentioned in Madame de Sévigné's letters. It was the only form commonly recognized in France; but it seems that the sister of Napoleon was commonly called Paulette in her own family. The direct Italian diminutive always seems to be a greater favourite with the southern blood than its relative from the northern *chen.*

The adjective of size is another word of universal kindred, though not always with the same meaning. The Sanscrit *mahat,* and Persian *mi* or *meah,* are close connections of the Gothic *mikils* (which survives in mickle and muckle, and has furnished our much), and of the Greek μεγαλος or μεγας, and Roman *magnus* and Slavonic *magi.* All these possibly may be remotely connected with the verb *magan* (may), which is the source of *macht* (might) in all Teutonic tongues.

Magnus was an agnomen added as a personal distinction, as in the case of Pompey. It was never a name till long after the Roman empire was over, when Karl der Grösse, as his Franks called him, had been Latinized into Carolus Magnus, and honoured by the French as Charlemagne. St. Olaf of Norway was known to be a great admirer of Charlemagne, whose example he would fain have imitated, and his followers, by way of a pleasant surprise and compliment to him, before they woke him to announce to him the birth of his first son, christened the child, as they thought, after the latter half of the great Emperor Carolus Magnus. That child became a much-beloved monarch, under the denomination of King Magnus Barefoot, from his having established his identity on his return from Ireland, by the ordeal of walking unshod over red-hot ploughshares. In honour of his many excellencies, as King of Norway, the entire North uses his name of Magnus, and transplanted it to Ireland, where it flourished under the form of Manus, until it became the fashion to 'Anglicize' it into Manasses. The Scottish islands, where the population is Norse, likewise use Magnus as a baptismal name; and the Lapps have turned it into Manna, or Mannas.

Maximus was likewise properly an individual agnomen of size, or of victory, as with Fabius Maximus; but it came to be a proper name, and was borne by Maximus the Monk, a great Greek ecclesiastic of the sixth century, as well as by many other obscure saints, from whom the Italians derive their Massimo, and the French Maxime, and the Welsh their old Macsen.

Maxentius and Maximinus, both named not only persecuting emperors, but Christian martyrs, whence Maxime and Maximien. Maximilianus was one of the Seven Sleepers, but he is not the origin of the German imperial name. According to Camden, this was a compound invented by the Emperor Frederick VII., and bestowed on his son in his great admiration of Fabius Maximus and Scipio Æmilianus. "The Last of the Knights," with his wild effrontery and spirited chamois-hunting might be despised by the Italians, as *Massimiliano Pochi Danari;* but he was beloved by the Austrians as "Our Max." His great grandson, Maximilian II., contributed to the popularity of his unwieldy name, and Max continues to be one of the favourite German appellations, from the archduke to the peasant, to the present day; and has even thrown out the feminine Maximiliane. The Poles and Illyrians use *ks* instead of *x* in spelling it.

SECTION IX.—*Rufus, &c.*

Rufus, the red or ruddy, was a cognomen of various families, and was, in fact, one of the adjectives occurring in the nomenclature of almost every nation; and chiefly of those where a touch of Keltic blood has made the hair vary between red and black. Flavius, Fulvius, Rufus, and an occasional Niger, were the Roman names of complexion; and it is curious to find the single instances of Chlorus (the yellow), occurring in the Flavian family. The Biondi of Italy claim to be the Flavii, and thence the Blound, Count de Guisnes, companion of William the Conqueror, took the name now Blount!

Rufus is, indeed, the Latin member of the large family of which we spoke in mentioning the Greek Rhoda; and the Kelts had, in plenty, their own Ruadh or Roy; nevertheless, such as fell under Roman dominion adopted the Roman Rufus or Rufinus; and it passed on by tradition in Wales, as Gruffin, Gruffydd, or as the English caught it and spelt it, correctly representing the sound of *dd*, Griffith. It was the name of many Welsh princes, and has passed into a frequent surname.

In its Gruffin stage, it passed into the commonwealth of romance. Among the British names that had worked through the lost world of minstrelsy, to reappear in the cycle with which Italian poets graced the camp and court of Charlemagne, is Grifone, a descendant of Bevis of Hampton. By this time, no doubt, his name was supposed to be connected with the Griffin, that creature with *griffes*, or claws; that.

after having served in earlier times, as with Dante, to represent the Italian idea of the vision of the cherubim, had been gradually degraded to a brilliant portion of the machinery of romance.

No doubt the Italians who bore the name of Grifone, thought more of the "right Griffin" and the true knight, than of the ruddy Roman whose Ruffino or Ruffo was still left lingering among them; together with Rufina, the name of a virgin martyr.

Rufus is, for some reason or other, rather a favourite at present with our American neighbours.

Niger (the black) was a cognomen of various Romans of no great note, and distinguished a teacher from Antioch, mentioned in the Acts. The diminutive Nigellus seems to have been adopted in France, by the Normans, as a translation of the Nial which they had brought from Norway, after having learned it of the Gael, in whose tongue it means the noble. In Domesday Book, twelve proprietors are recorded as Nigel, both before and after the Conquest, being probably Danish Nials thus reduced to the Neustrian French Latin. Of these was Nigel de Albini (*temp.* William I.), and Nigel de Mowbray (*temp.* Henry II.). The influx of Anglo-Normans into Scotland introduced this new-fashioned Nigel, and it was adopted as the English form of Niel, and has since become almost exclusively confined to Scotland, where it is a national name, partly perhaps in memory of the untimely fate of Niel or Nigel Bruce; and among the covenanters, for the sake of the fierce Nigel Leslie, Master of Rothes. It has shared the fate of Colin and of the true Nial, and has been taken for Nicolas. The French used a like name, which Froissart spells Nesle; but this is probably from the inference that a lengthened sound of *e* infers a silent *s*.

CHAPTER V.

NAMES FROM ROMAN DEITIES.

SECTION I.

A SHORT chapter must be given to the modern names that, in spite of the canon prohibiting the giving of names of heathen gods in baptism, are either those of Latin divinities, or are derived from them. These, though few in number, are more than are to be found in the Greek class, from the fact that where a Roman deity had become identified with a Greek one, the Latin name was used throughout Western Europe in all translations, and only modern criticism has attempted to distinguish between the distinct myths of the two races. Most of these are, or have been, in use either in France or England, the modern countries most under the dominion of fancy with regard to names.

Aurora (the dawn), so called, it is said, from *aurum* (gold), because of the golden light she sheds before her, assumed all the legends attached by the Greeks to their Eos, whose rosy fingers unbarred the gates of day. When the Cinque-cento made classic lore the fashion, Aurore came into favour with the fair dames of France, and has ever since there continued in vogue, occasionally passing into Germany. In Illyria, the dawn and the lady are both called Zora, and she in endearment Zorana.*

Bellona was not a goddess whose name one would have expected to find renewed in Christian times, yet instances have been found of it in England among those who probably had some idea that it was connected with beauty instead of with *bellum* (war). In effect, hers is not quite a proper name, being really an adjective, with the noun understood, *Bellona Dea* (the war goddess). An infant born in the streets of Weimar during the sack that followed the battle of Jena was named Angelina Bellona, as having been an angel of comfort to her parents in the miseries of war. She became a great musician, and won renown for her name in her own land.†

The old Latin deities were often in pairs, masculine and feminine. Divus, that part of their title that is still recognized as belonging to the supernatural, is from the same source as the Sanscrit *deva*, Persian *dev*, Greek δῖος, θεός, Zeus, and was applied to all. Divus Janus and Diva Jana were one of these pairs, who presided over day and night,

---

* Keightley; Michaelis.
† Keightley; Smith; Key, *Latin Grammar;* Madame Scopenhauer, *Memoirs.*

as the sun and moon. Divajana became Diana; and as groves were
sacred to her, and she was as pure a goddess as Vesta, there was every
reason for identifying her with the Greek Artemis, and giving her
possession of the temple of Ephesus, and the black stone image that
"fell down from Jupiter," or the sky; she had Apollo given as her
fellow instead of Janus, and thenceforth was the goddess of the silver
bow, daughter of Jupiter and Latona, as Artemis had been of Zeus
and Leto. Her name slept as a mere pagan device till the sixteenth
century, when romances of chivalry gave place to the semi-classical
pastoral, of which Greece was usually the scene. Jorge de Monte-
mayor, the Spanish gentleman who led the way in this flowery path,
named his heroine, Diana, and she was quickly copied by the sponsors
of Diane de Poitiers, the fair widow whose colours of black and white
were worn by Henry II. of France even to his last fatal tournament.
Diane thus became so fashionable in France, that when the Cavalier
court was there residing, the English caught the fashion, and thenceforth Lady Dye at times appeared among the Ladies Betty and Fanny
of the court. In the lower classes, Diana seems to be at times
confused with the Scriptural Dinah, though it may sometimes be
adopted as a Bible name, since a peasant has been known to pronounce
that he well knew who was "greatest 'Diana of the Ephesians,'—a
great lady of those parts, and very charitable to the poor." At Rome
Jewesses now alone bear it, and Italian Christians consequently
despise it, and only give it to dogs. However, in the eighteenth
century, a Monna Diana existed at Florence, who is recorded as an
example of the benefits of a heavy head wrapper, for a large stone
fell upon her head from a building, and she took it for a small
pebble!

Diana's fellow, Divus Janus, had a very different career. He was
sometimes called Dianus, but much more commonly Janus, and from
being merely the sun, he became allegorical of the entire year, and
had a statue with four faces for the seasons, and hands pointing the
one to 300, the other to 55, thus making up the amount of days then
given to the year; and before him were twelve altars, one for each
month. He thus presided over the beginning of everything, and the
first month of the year was from him called Januarius, as were all
gates *jani*, and doors *januæ;* and above all, that gate between the
Sabines and the Romans, which was open when they were friends,
shut when they were foes. When the two nations had become
thoroughly fused together, the gate grew to a temple; but the cere-
mony of shutting the doors was still followed on the rare occasions
when Rome was at peace, and of opening them when at war to let
the god go out, as it was now said, to help the Romans. This idea
of peace, however, turned Janus into a legendary peaceful monarch,
who only wore two heads that he might look both ways to see either
side of a question, and keys were put into his hand as the guardian
of each man's gate. His own special gate continued to be called
Janicula, and his name passed from the door, *janua*, to the porter,
janitor; and thence in modern times to St. Peter, who, bearing the
keys, was called by the Italians, *il Janitore di Cielo*, and thence the

fish, which was thought to bear the mark of St. Peter's thumb, was *il janitore*, or, as we call it, the John Dory, if not from its gilded scales, *dorée* or *dorado*. Its Spanish name of San Pedro would favour the janitor theory. The month of Janus, Janvier, January, Gennaro, Januar, has kept its name, like all the other months of the Roman calendar, in spite of the French attempt to displace them with Glacial, Pluvial, &c. Birth in the month of January occasioned the name of Januarius to be given to various persons in the time of the Roman empire, to one of the seven sons of St. Felicitas, to a martyr whose day is the 13th of October, and especially to St. Januarius, of Beneventum, who in the persecution of Diocletian was thrown to wild beasts at Pozzuoli, and on their refusal to hurt him, was beheaded. His blood was already a religious curiosity before the eighth century, when it was thought to have delivered Naples from an eruption of Mount Vesuvius, and it furnishes one of the most questionable and most hotly-defended miracles of the Church of Rome. After this Gennaro cannot fail to be a very frequent Neapolitan Christian name.*

SECTION II.—*Florentius.*

The goddess of flowers was called from their Latin name *flos*, the same that has passed into all European languages except the German. In late times the name of Florus was formed from that of the goddess, and is memorable as that of the procurator, whose harshness drove the Jews to their last rebellion. Flora was probably first used merely as the feminine of Florus. There is a church at Florence to SS. Fiore and Lucilla, otherwise the first occurrence of any variety of Flora is in Roman-Gothic Spain, where the unhappy daughter of Count Julian was called by the Spanish diminutive Florinda, and thus caused the name to be so much detested, that while Spanish ballads called her *la Cava*, the wicked, her Christian name was only bestowed upon dogs, and curiously enough it was the little spaniel (a Spanish breed), for which Flora was considered in England as an appropriate name. A Spanish maiden, however, who was martyred by the Moors in 851, brought Flora into better repute; and Flore became known to the French, though probably first adopted as a romantic epithet; and through the close connection between France and Scotland, it passed to the latter country, the especial land of floral names, and there became frequent as the English equivalent to the Gaelic Finghin. It was spelt as Florie by the island heroine of the '45. Florentius was the natural product of the goddess Flora, and named a female saint, Florentia, martyred with two others, both men, in Diocletian's persecution in Gaul, and commemorated by a monastery built over the spot. St. Florentius was likewise a Gaul, and was sent by St. Martin to preach in Poitou. His relics were at first at Saumur, but in the eleventh century were taken to Roye, and in the time of Louis XI., were divided between the two cities. As an Angevin saint, he

* Keightley; Smith; Bouterwek; *Istoria de Firenze;* Brand; Butler; *Spanish Literature.*

quite accounts for the prevalence of Florence in the masculine gender among the Anglo-Norman nobles of the middle ages; but it soon died away. The recent revival is chiefly owing to the name having been given to English girls born at the Italian city so called, and it has since acquired a deeper and dearer honour in the person of Florence Nightingale. From the city, or else as a diminutive of Florentius, arose Florentinus, a name borne by various distinguished persons in the latter days of the empire, and saintly in the person of a martyr of Burgundy. Florentina was one of the daughters of St. Leander, of Spain, and the relics of these saints scattered the names of Florentin and Florentine over a wide extent in France. Besides these, should be mentioned the romantic name, Blanchefleur. It is given to Sir Trystan's mother, and probably translates some Keltic name analogous to the Erse Blathnaid, Finbil, and Finscoth, all of which mean white flower.

The Irish Florence, or Flory, so common among the peasantry, is intended for Finghin, or Fineen (fair offspring); also for Flann, Fithil, and Flaithri.*

Section III.—*Laurentius.*

It appears natural to refer Laurentius direct to *laurus* (the bay or laurel); but there is reason to think that it, as well as the tree, must go farther back to the dim vestiges of early Roman mythology. From the Etruscans the Romans learnt the beautiful idea of guardian spirits around their hearths, whom they called by the Etruscan word *lar* or *lars*, meaning lord or master. The spirits of great statesmen or heroes became public *lares*, and watched over the welfare of the city; those of good men, or of innocent infants under forty days old, were the *lares* of their home and family. Their images, covered with dog-skins, and with the figure of a dog beside them, were placed beside every hearth; and, curiously enough, are the origin of the name dogs, still applied to the supports on either side of a wood fire-place. They were made to partake in every household festival; cups were set apart, in which a portion of every meal was poured out to them; the young bride, on being carried across her husband's threshold, made her first obeisance to these household spirits of his family; and on the nones, ides, and calends of each month, when the master returned from the war, or on any other occasion of joy, the lares were crowned with wreaths and garlands. Pairs of lares stood in niches at the entrance of the streets; other lares guarded districts in the country; and the lares of all Rome had a temple to themselves, where stood twin human figures with a dog between them. All these wore green crowns on festival days, especially on those of triumph; and thus there can be little doubt that the evergreen whose leaves were specially appropriated to the purpose was thence called *laurus*, as the poplar was from forming people's crowns. The special feast of the lares was on the 22nd of December, and it was

* Smith; Butler; *Irish Society;* Pott.

immediately followed by that of a female deity called Lara, Larunda, Larentia, Laurentia, or Acca Laurentia, who was termed in old Latin *genita mana* (good mother), received the sacrifice of a dog, and was entreated that no good domestic slave might depart. Thus much custom had preserved to the Romans; but when Greek mythology came in, flooding and corrupting all their own, poor Laurentia was turned into a nymph, so given to chattering (λαλιά) that Jupiter punished her by cutting out her tongue and sending her, in charge of Mercury, to the lower world; and the lares, now allowed to be only two, were made into her children and those of Mercury. Another story, wishing to account for all traditions in one, made her into the woman who nursed Romulus and Remus, and thus disposed of her and of the she-wolf at once, and made the twelve rural Lares her sons; whilst a third version degraded her, like Flora, and made her leave all her property to the state, in the time of Ancus Martius.

Laurentius does not occur in early history; but it belonged to the gentle Roman deacon who, on the 10th of August, 258, showed the "poor and the maimed, the halt and the blind," as the treasures of the Church, and was martyred, by being roasted over a fire on bars of iron. Constantine built a church on his tomb, and seven other Churches at Rome are likewise dedicated to him. Pope Adrian gave some of his relics to Charlemagne, who took them to Strasburg, and thus rendered him one of the regnant saints in Germany, where the prevalence of shooting stars on the night of his feast has occasioned those meteors to be called St. Lorenz's sparks. In fact, his gentle nature, his peculiar martyrdom, and his church at Rome, caused him to be a saint of universal popularity; and a fresh interest was conferred on him, in Spanish eyes, by Philip II.'s belief that the battle of St. Quentin, fought on his day, was won by his intercession, and the consequent dedication of the gridiron-palace convent of the Escurial to him.

Besides the original saint, England owns St. Laurentius among the band of Roman missionaries who accompanied St. Augustine, and, in succession, became archbishops of Canterbury. When England, in her turn, sent forth missionaries, another Laurence preached the Word in the North, with such effect as to compel the Trollds themselves to become church builders, much against their will, and to leave his name, cut down into Lars, its primitive form, as a favourite in all Scandinavia. In Ireland, Laurence, whose name I strongly suspect to have been Laghair, a son of Maurice O'Tuathail, of Leinster, was archbishop of Dublin at the time of the conquest by the Norman adventurers, and was thus brought into close connection with Canterbury and with Rome, knitting the first of the links that have made the Irish so abject in their devotion to the Papal See. It was probably on this account that he was canonized, but he was also memorable as one of the builders of St. Patrick's cathedral at Dublin, and for his charities during a terrible famine, when he supported as many as 300 destitute children. It is he who has rendered Lanty and Larry so common among the Irish peasantry. Besides all these, the modern Venetian saint, Lorenzo Justiniani, worthily maintained the honour of the Christian name already so illustrious in excellence, and it has continued in high esteem everywhere, though, perhaps, less common in England than on the Continent. Germany is the place of its special reign; and in the Harz mountains, to bow awkwardly is called *krummer Lorenz machen*.

English.	Scotch.	Irish.	French.
Lawrence	Lawrence	Laurence	Laurent
Laurence	Laurie	Lanty	
Larkin		Larry	

Italian.	Spanish.	Portuguese.	Swiss.
Lorenzo	Lorenzo	Laurençho	Lori
Renzo			Lenz
			Enz
			Enzali

German.	Wallachian.	Swedish.	Danish.
Lorenz	Lavrentia	Laurentius	Lorenz
		Lars	Lars
			Lauritz

Norse.	Russian.	Polish.	Bohemian.
Laurans	Lavrentij	Vavrzynec	Vavrinec
Jörens			
Larse			

Slovak.	Lithuanian.	Lapp.	Hungarian.
Lovre	Labrenzis	Laur	Lörencz
	Brenzis	Laures	
	Lauris	Laura	
	Raulus		

Some languages have the feminine, but it is not frequent anywhere. The Italian Lorenza is, perhaps, the most frequent.

The name of Laura is a great perplexity. It *may* be taken from Laurus, and ladies so called consider St. Laurence as their patron; but it may also be from the word Laura, the Greek Λαβρα, or Λαυρα, meaning an avenue, the same as labyrinth, and applied to the clusters of hermitages which were the germ of monasteries. Or again, a plausible derivation is that Lauretta might have commemorated the laurel-grove, or Loreto, whither Italian superstition declared that the angels transported the holy house of Nazareth away from the Turkish power on the conquest of Palestine. Those who call the milky-way the Santa Strada di Loretto, might well have used this as one of their varied forms of seeking the patronage of the Blessed Virgin. The chief objection that I can find to this theory is, that the first Lauretta that I have met with was a Flemish lady, in 1162; the next was a daughter of William de Braose, Lord of Bramber, in the time of King John, a period antecedent to the supposed migration of the holy house, which did not set out on its travels till 1294. Others think it the same with Eleonora, which I cannot believe ; but, at any rate, it was the Provençal Lora de Sades, so long beloved of Petrarch, who made this one of the favourite romantic and poetical names, above all, in France, where it is Laure, Lauretta, Loulou.*

SECTION IV.—*Sancus.*

Sancus, or Sanco-Sancus, was the divinity who presided over oaths, and guarded the marriage vow and treaties between nations. He was afterwards mixed up with Hercules, and so entirely forgotten that his altar was long supposed to have been an early Christian erection bearing the word sanctus.

This word is the past participle of the verb *sancire* (to decree). It was equivalent to instituted, and was gradually applied to mark the institutions of religion. That "all the congregation are holy," all under sanctification, all once at least saints, was a faith strong in the Church, and prompted the name of Sanctus among the first Christians.

One Sanctus was a deacon of the band of martyrs at Lyons, and another Sanctus was a Christian physician of Otriculum, a city of central Italy, and was put to death under the Antonines. There is some doubt whether he is the same physician of Otriculum who is also called St. Medicus.

Sanctus was the favourite patron in Provence, Biscay, and Navarre ; and Sancho and Sancha were constantly in royal use in the early kingdoms of the struggling Christians of Spain ; though as royalty and nobility became weary of what was national and peculiar, they were left to the peasantry, and would have been entirely forgotten, but for that wonderful personification of the shrewd, prosaic, selfish, yet faithful element in human nature, Sancho Panza, whom Cervantes has made one of the most typical yet individual characters of literature.

The Provençals had both the masculine and feminine forms in frequent use ; and the co-heiress of Provence, who married our Richard, Earl of Cornwall, king of the Romans, was Sancia, or Sancie ; but the name did not take root in England, and sorely puzzled some of our old genealogists, who record the lady as Cynthia, Scientia, or Science. This last name actually occurs several times in the seventeenth century, both in Latin and English, in the register of a small Hampshire parish ; but whether meant for Sancha, or chosen in love for abstract knowledge, those who named 'Science Dear' alone could tell.

Italy, as in duty bound, remembered her saintly physician as

---

* Smith ; Keightley ; Loudon, *Arboretum ;* Butler ; Jameson ; Grimm ; Pott ; Michaelis ; Dugdale ; Hanmer, *Chronicle of Ireland.*

Sancto at Rome, and Sanzio with the 'lingua Toscana,' where it came
as a family name to the greatest of painters.*

SECTION V.—*Old Italian Deities.*

Februus was the old Italian god both of the dead and of fertility,
to whom February was sacred.   The word is thought to mean purifi-
cation, but after the Etruscan deities were forgotten, Juno, who had
also a share in the month, absorbed it all, and was called Juno
Februata.   Thence, probably, arose the name of Febronia, a nun of
Sibapolis on the borders of Assyria, who suffered horrid torments
under her persecutors, and was at last beheaded.   She is venerated
by the Greek Church on the 25th of June, and suggested to Russia
the names Fevronia, or Khevronia.

Though not divine, the name of Lavinia should be mentioned here
as that of a mythical personage imitated by the moderns, though not
by the Romans themselves.   In Livy and in Virgil, she is the
daughter of King Latinus, and the last wife of Æneas, in whose
right he obtained a footing in Italy.   Niebuhr and his followers deny
her existence, and make her a mere personification of the Latin territory, and whether this be the case or not, hers is certainly a feminine
form of Latinus, the *t* changed to *v*, as happened in other instances.
The classical Italians of the Cinque-cento revived Lavinia for their
daughters ; and by way of recommending the story of the Book of
Ruth to the taste of the eighteenth century, Thomson had the
audacity to translate the Moabitess into "the lovely young Lavinia,"
whence it has happened that this has become rather a favourite with
those classes in England who have a taste for many syllables ending
in *ia*.

Picus was another old Italian deity who used to be represented
with a woodpecker on his head.   Whether he or the woodpecker first
had the name of Picus does not appear ; but in English that term
passed to the pyot or magpie, and some recurrence to old tradition
caused Pico to be revived in Italy in the person of the famous Pico
de Mirandola and his namesakes.

From *fors* (chance) came Fortuna, the goddess of prosperity and
success.   She was said on entering Rome to have thrown away her
globe, and shed her wings like a queen-ant, to denote that here she
took up her permanent abode.   She was adored at Rome as early as
the reign of Ancus Martius, and to her was ascribed the success of
the women's entreaty in turning away the wrath of Coriolanus.

Her name does not appear to have been used in the heathen times,
but in 212 SS. Felix and Fortunatus were martyred at Valence in
Dauphiné, and it was probably from the latter that Fortunio became
a name among the early Asturian and Navarrese sovereigns.

What shall we think of the augury of names when we find in the
parish register of St. John's, Newcastle, on the 20th of June, 1599,

* Butler; Keightley; Smith.

the marriage of Umphraye Hairope, husbandman, to Fortune Shafto, gentlewoman ?

A pair of twins, girls, of the Wycliffe family, born in 1710, were christened Favour and Fortune ; and Fortune is a surname in Scotland.*

SECTION VI.—*Quirinus.*

Quirinus, one of the oldest of the war-gods, was called from the Oscan *quiris* (a spear), which likewise was the source of the old Roman name of Quirites, and of that of the Quirinal Hill. Spearmen alike were the Quirites and their unconquerable foes ; the Gjermanner, the Germans, nay, probably *gher* and *quiris* are the very same word, equally related to the Keltic *coir.*

Others, however, call Quirinus the mere personified god of the town of Cures. When all had become confusion in the Roman mind as to their old objects of worship, and they had mingled them with " gods whom their fathers knew not," they took it into their heads that Quirinus was the deified Romulus who had been transported to the skies by his father, Mars, in the middle of a muster of his warriors in the Campus Martius ; and when a still later age distrusted this apotheosis, some rationalist Roman suggested that, weary of Romulus' tyranny, the senators had secretly assassinated him during the review, and to prevent detection had cut his body to pieces, each carried a portion home under his toga, and professed to have beheld the translation to the skies. Quirinus had become a cognomen at the Christian era, but first occurs as a Christian name in 304, when St. Quirinus was Bishop of Siscia on the Save, and after a good confession before the tyrant Maximus, was dragged in chains through the cities on the banks of the Danube, and then drowned at Sabaria, now Sarwar. His relics were afterwards taken to Rome, but are now said to be in Bavaria ; and in his honour Cyran has become a French name. As a saint connected with Germany, various chapters arose in commemoration of him ; and Mrs. Elizabeth Carter describes her meeting with a pretty little *chanoinesse* at Spa, who wore her medal of St. Quirinus, but was able to give so little account of him that Mrs. Carter, better read in Roman history than in hagiology, concluded him to be the " Saint who built Rome and killed his brother."

Quirinius was the name of the Roman governor whom St. Luke called in Greek Κυρήνιος, and our translators render Cyrenius.

The name of Romulus is thought by many to have been a mere myth made out of that of his city Roma, a word that probably signified strength, and was no inappropriate title for that empire of iron. Ῥώμη is the Greek word for strength ; the same root is found in the Latin *robur,* and it may be in the Teutonic *ruhm* (fame). Others say that *groma* (a cross-road) was the origin of this most famous of all local titles.

* Niebuhr ; Arnold ; Surius ; Keightley ; Sir C. Sharpe, *Extracts from Parish Registers.*

However this may be, after Romulus Augustulus had seen the twelve centuries of Rome fulfilled, Romolo still lingered on as a name in Italy ; the first bishop of Fiesole was thus named, and was so popular at Florence, that Catherine dei Medici was actually christened Romola.

When to be a Roman citizen was the highest benefit a man of a subject nation could enjoy, Romanus was treated as a cognomen. Pliny had two friends so called. There are seven saints thus named, and three Byzantine emperors. But when Teuton sway had made a Roman the meanest and most abject epithet, Romain or Romano died away in popularity, and only occurs now and then in French genealogy, though it is still used in Italy.

They must not be confounded with Romeo and Romuald, which are genuine Teutonic.*

SECTION VII.—*Sibylla.*

The Sibyls were beings peculiar to Roman mythology, prophetesses half human, half divine, living to a great age, but not immortal. Etymologists used to interpret their name as coming from the Greek Ζεύς and βουλή (Zeus' councils), but it is far more satisfactorily explained as coming from *sabius*, or *sabus*, an old Italian, but not a Latin word, which lives still in the vernacular *Sabio*, thus making Sibulla signify a wise old woman.

Old, indeed ! for the Cumean Sibyl, who guided Æneas to the infernal regions, was likewise said to be the same who brought the prophetic books for sale to Tarquinius Priscus, and on each refusal of the sum that she demanded for them, carried them off, destroyed one, and brought the rest back rated at a higher price. The single remaining roll bought by the king was said to contain all the mysterious prophecies that were afterwards verified by the course of events, and above all, that prediction of the coming rule of peace, which Virgil, following Theocritus, embodied in his eclogue as fulfilled in Augustus. That eclogue, flattery though it were, won for Virgil his semi-Christian fame, and caused the learned men of Italy to erect the Sibyls into the personifications of heathen presages of Gospel truth—

"Teste David cum Sibylla,"

as says the glorious hymn uniting the voices of Hebrew and Gentile prophecy ; and in this character do Michel Angelo's magnificent Sibyls adorn the Sistine Chapel ; though later painters, such as Guido and Domenichino, made them mere models of female intellectual beauty.

Sibilla, probably through the influence of Campania upon nomenclature, early spread as a Christian name. Possibly the word was the more acceptable to Northern ears from its resemblance to the Gothic *sibja* (peace, or friendship), the word familiar to us as the Scottish *sib* (related), forming with us the last syllable of gossip, in its old

* Diefenbach ; Arnold ; Livy ; Butler.

sense of god-parent. Thence came Sippia, Sib, or Sif, the lovely wife of Thor, whose hair was cut off by Lok, and its place supplied by golden tresses, which some consider to mean the golden harvest.

Perhaps it was this connection that recommended the Italian Sibila to the Norman chivalry. At any rate, Sibila of Conversana was the wife of Robert of Normandy, and Sibille soon travelled into France, and belonged to that Angevin Queen of Jerusalem, whose many marriages gave so much trouble to the Crusaders. It was very frequent among English ladies of Norman blood; and in Spain, Sevilla, or Sebilla, is frequent in the earlier ballads. Sibella, Sibyl, or Sibbie, is most frequent of all in Ireland and Scotland; but I believe that this is really as the equivalent for the ancient Gaelic Selbhflaith (lady of possessions).

Russia has the name as Ssivilla; the Lithuanians call it Bille; and the Esthonians, Pil. Sibilley is the form in which it appears in a Cornish register in 1692; in 1651 it is Sibella.*

SECTION VIII.—*Saturn, &c.*

Saturnus was a mythical king of ancient Italy, peaceful, and given to agriculture, indeed, his name is thought to come from *satus* (sown). It is very odd that he should have become the owner of all the fame of the Greek Kronos, infanticide, planet rings, and all; but so completely has he seized upon them that we never think of him as the god of seed-time, but only as the discarded king of heaven and father of Jupiter.

We should have little to do with him were it not that the later Romans formed from him the name of Saturninus, which belonged to sundry early saints, and furnished the old Welsh Sadwrn.

Sylvanus was a deity called from *sylva* (a wood), the protector of husbandmen and their crops, in the shape of an old man with a cypress-tree in his hand. His had become a Roman name just before the Christian era, and belonged to the companion of St. Paul, who is called Sylvanus in the Epistles, and, by the contraction, Silas in the Acts. This contracted form, Silas, has been revived in England as a Scripture name.

St. Sylvanus, or Silverius, was a pope whom his Church esteems a martyr, as he died in the hands of Belisarius; but sylvan, or salvage, was chiefly used in the middle ages to express a dweller in a forest, rude and hardly human. Silvano, Selvaggio, or Silvestro, was generally the name of monsters with shaggy locks, clubs, and girdles of ivy leaves, who appeared in romance; and Guidon Selvaggio was the rustic knight of Boiardo and Ariosto. Occasionally these words became names, and about the year 1200, Sylvestro Gozzolini, of Osimo, founded an order of monks, who, probably, are the cause that Sylvester became known in Ireland as a Christian name, and has come to us as a surname, while the French have it as Sylvestre.

* Max Müller, *Science of Language;* Keightley; Ruskin; Grimm; Michaelis.

The son of Æneas and Lavinia was said to have been born in a wood, and therefore called Æneas Silvius, and his name was given to one of the Piccolomini family, Enea Silvio, afterwards pope ; and also belonged to an historian.   Sylvain, Sylvan, Sylvius, Sylvia became favourite names for shepherds and shepherdesses in the time of the pastoral romance ; Sylvia turned into a poetical name for a country maid, and has since been used as a village Christian name, having been perhaps first chosen by some fanciful Lady Bountiful.

CHAPTER VI.

MODERN NAMES FROM THE LATIN.

THERE still remain a class of names derived from the Latin, being chiefly Latin words formed into names. Some of them answer to the class that we have called Christian Greek, being compound words assumed as befitting names by early Roman Christians, such as Deusvult.

There are fewer of these than of the like Greek designations, both from the hereditary system of nomenclature, and from the language being less suitable for such formations than the Greek, which was so well known to all educated Romans that a Greek appellation would convey as much meaning as a Latin one, and in that partially veiled form that always seems to have been preferred in nomenclature in the later ages of nations. Some, however, either from sound, sense, or association, have become permanent Christian names in one or more nations ; and with these, for the sake of convenience, have been classed those formed from Latin roots, and which, though coined when their ancestral language was not only dead but corrupt, are too universal to be classed as belonging to any single country of modern Europe, though sometimes the product of a Romance tongue rather than of genuine Latin, or appearing in cognate languages in different forms ; cousins, in fact, not brethren, and sometimes related to uncles sprung from the elder tongue.

SECTION I.—*From Amo.*

Of these are all the large class of names sprung from *amo*, which has descended into all the Southern languages of Western Europe nearly unaltered. The Gallic Christians seem to have had a particular delight in calling their children by derivatives of this word ; for in their early times there occur in the calendar, Amabilis (loveable), Amator (a lover), Amandus (about to be loved), and Amatus and Amata (loved) ; Amadeus (loving God) seems to have been still older. Out of this collection, St. Amand has survived as a territorial surname ; whilst Amanda, from its meaning, was one of the complimentary *noms de plume* of the eighteenth century ; and Amandine is sometimes found in France. Amabilis was a male saint of Riom, known to France as St. Amable ; nevertheless, his name passed to Aimable, the Norman heiress of Gloucester, who so strongly pro-

tested against accepting even a king's son without a surname. Her
name became on English lips Amabel, which has been handed down
unchanged in a few old English families, though country lips have
altered it into Mabel, in which form it is still used among the
northern peasantry. Ignorant etymologists have tried to make it
come from *ma belle* (my fair one), and lovers of false ornament turn
it into Mabella.

Nothing is known of the female saint, Amata, or Aimée, but that
the people of Northern France used to honour her, and she had
namesakes in old French pedigrees, so that there can be little doubt
that Norman families brought in the pretty simple Amy that has
never been entirely disused, and has been a frequent peasant name
in the West of England. St. Amatus, or Amé, was about the end of
the seventh century a hermit in the Valais, and afterwards became
Bishop of Sion, and was persecuted by one of the Merovingian kings.
He thus became the patron saint of Savoy, and for a long succession
the Counts were called Amé; but after a time, they altered the name
to Amadeus, Amadée, or Amadeo, as it was differently called on the
two sides of the mountain principality, and as it has continued to the
present time. Amyot and Amyas in England, and in Romance the
champion Amadis de Gaul, drew their names from this Savoyard
source. This notable knight is believed to have been invented in
Spain, and the Italians call him Amadigi. It is possible, however,
that he may come from the Kymry, for Amaethon, son of Don,
appears in the *Mabinogion*, and was a mystic personage in Welsh
mythology. His name meant the husbandman, another offshoot from
the universal Amal. He must have been the Sir Amadas of the
Round Table.

The old English Amicia, so often found in old pedigrees, is probably a Latinizing of Aimée. The most notable instance of it is
Amicia, the daughter of the Earl of Leicester, who brought her
county to the fierce old persecutor, Simon de Montfort, and left it to
the warlike earl, who imprisoned Henry III. His sister carried
Amicie into the Flemish family of De Roye, where it continued in
use, and it descended again into Amice in England. Amadore was
in use in Florence, cut into Dore.*

SECTION II.—*Names from Beo.*

The old verb *beo* (to make happy or bless) formed the participle
beatus (happy or blessed), which was applied by the Church to her
departed members, and in time was bestowed on the living. Indeed,
in France, *béate* was so often applied to persons who lived in the
profession of great sanctity, that *une vieille béate* has now come to be
used in the sense of a hypocritical pretender.

St. Beatus, or Béat, was an anchorite near Vendôme, in the fifth
century; but we do not find instances of his patronage having been
sought for men, though in England Beata is a prevailing female

* Butler; Pott; Dugdale; *Mabinogion;* Lady C. Guest; Dunlop, *Fiction.*

name in old registers and on tombstones up to the seventeenth century, when it dies away, having, I strongly suspect, been basely confounded with Betty. Beata and Bettrys are however still used in Wales. This last stands for Beatrice (a blesser), which seems to have been first brought into this island as a substitute for the Gaelic Bethoc (life), of which more in its place.

The original Beatrix, the feminine of Beator (a blesser), is said to have been first borne by a Christian maiden, who, in Diocletian's persecution, drew the bodies of her martyred brothers from the Tiber, and buried them: afterwards she shared their fate, and her relics were enshrined in a church at Rome, whence her fame spread to all adjacent countries; and her name was already frequent when Dante made the love of his youth, Beatrice Portinari, the theme of his *Vita Nuova*, and his guide through Paradise. Thus it was a truly national name at Florence; and Shakespeare used the Italian spelling for his high-spirited heroine, thus leading us to discard the old Latin *x*. It has been a queenly name in Spain, but less common here than it deserves.

English.	Welsh.	French.	Italian.	Spanish.
Beatrix Trix Beatrice	Bettrys	Béatrix	Beatrice Bice	Beatriz

Portuguese.	German.	Russian.	Slavonic.	
Beatrix	Beatrix	Beatriks	Beatrica	

This same *beo* is said to be the source of *benus*, the old form of *bonus*, which survives in the adverb *benè*. Both adjective and adverb are familiar in their many derivatives in the southern tongues, as well as in the *bonnie* and *bien* that testify to the close connection of France and Scotland when both alike were the foes of England.

The feminine Bona, or Bonne, was probably first invented as a translation of the old German Gutha; for we find a lady, in 1315, designated as Bona, or Gutha, of Göttingen. Bona was used by the daughters of the Counts of Savoy, and in the House of Luxemburg, and came to the crown of France with the daughter of the chivalrous Johann of Luxemburg, the blind King of Bohemia.

St. Benignus, whose name is from the same source, was a disciple of St. Polycarp, and is reckoned as the apostle of Burgundy, where he was martyred, and has been since commemorated by the splendid abbey of St. Benigne, at Dijon, whence it happens that Benin has been common among the peasantry in that part of France, and Benigne is to be found among the string of Christian names borne by the French gentry of the seventeenth and eighteenth centuries. Servia has the feminine form, Benyma, shortening it into Bine.

Benedico (to speak well) came to have the technical sense of to bless; and the patriarch of the Western monks rendered Benedictus (blessed) so universally known that different forms of it prevail in all countries, lesser luminaries adding to its saintly lustre.

English.	French.	Breton.	Italian.
Benedict	Benoît	Bennéad	Benedetto
Bennet		Bennéged	Betto
			Bettino

Spanish.	Portuguese.	German.	Swedish.
Benedicto	Benedicto	Benedikt	Bengt
Benito	Bento	Dix	

Norse.	Swiss.	Russian.	Polish.
Benedik	Benzel	Venedict	Benedykt
Benike	Benzli		
Bent			

Slavonic and Illyrian.	Lusatian.	Lithuanian.	Lapp.
Benedikt	Beniesch	Bendzus	Pent
Benedit		Bendikkas	Penta
Benko			Pint
	Lett.	Hungarian.	Pinna
	Bindus	Benedik	

There was a Visigothic nun in Spain canonized as Benedicta, but most of the feminines were meant in devotion to the original founder of the Benedictine rule. Indeed, in France, Benedicte must have been far more often assumed on the profession of a nun than have been given in baptism, except when the child was destined from her birth to a conventual life.

French.	Italian.	Spanish.	German.
Benoîte	Benedetta	Benita	Benedikta
	Betta		Benedictine
	Bettina		

How the localities of these feminines mark the extent of monasticism in modern times!

The sister of St. Benedict bore the strange name of Scholastica, a scholar, from *schola* (school). Monasticism spread the name, but it was never much in vogue, though England shows a Scholastica Conyers, in 1299.

Bonifacius (good-worker) was the name of a martyr; then of a pope; and next was assumed by our Saxon Wilfred, when in the sixth century he set out to convert his continental brethren. Perhaps, if he had kept his native name, it would have been more followed, both at home and in Germany; but in both, Boniface has withered away out of use, though Bonchurch, in the Isle of Wight, is a contraction of the Church of St. Boniface, that having probably been the last English ground beheld by the saint when he sailed on his mission. In Italy, however, Bonifacius was a papal name. Bonifazio prevailed among the Alpine lords of Monferrat, and thus is still found in Italy. It has become one of the stock names for the host of an inn, and has named the straits between Sardinia and Corsica.

English.	Italian.	Russian.	Polish.	Bohemian.
Boniface	Bonifacio Facio Bonifazio Fazio	Bonifacij	Bonifacij	Bonifac

Of modern Italian date and construction is Bonaventura. Its origin was the exclamation of St. Francis on meeting Giovanni de Fidenza, the son of a dear friend: *O buona ventura* (happy meeting). These words became the usual appellation of young Fidenza, and as he afterwards was distinguished for holiness and learning, and was called the seraphic doctor, he was canonized as San Bonaventura, and has had sundry namesakes in Italy and France; in the latter country being called Bonaventure. Benvenuto Cellini may perhaps be reckoned as one, unless his name be intended to mean welcome without reference to the saint.

SECTION III.—*From Clarus.*

Clarus (bright or clear) was used by the Romans in the sense of famous, and St. Clarus is revered as the first bishop of Nantes in Brittany, in A.D. 280. Another Clarus, said to have been a native of Rochester, was a hermit, near Rouen, where he was murdered at the instigation of a wicked woman who had vainly paid her addresses to him. Two villages of St. Clair, one on the Epte, the other near Coutance, are interesting as having (one or the other of them) named two of the most noted families in the history of Great Britain, besides the various De St. Clairs of France, who came either from thence or from a third St. Clair in Aquitaine.

A Norman family, called from one of these villages, became the De Clares. 'Red De Clare,' stout Glo'ster's earl, the foe of Henry III., was one of them; and his son marrying into the house of Geraldin, in Ireland, received from Edward I. a grant of lands in Thomond, now known from his lordship as County Clare. His heiress carried the county to the De Burghs, and their heiress again marrying Lionel, son of Edward III., the county becoming a dukedom and royal appanage, was amplified into C'arence, and gave title to Clarencieux—king-at-arms, when Thomas, brother of Henry V., was

Duke of Clarence—unless this be from Clare, in Suffolk. Clarence as a male Christian name did not solely arise when William IV. was Duke of Clarence, but began as early as 1595, when Clarence Babbington was christened at Hartlepool.

Spanish ballad lore gives a daughter, Clara, to Charlemagne, and a son, Don Claros de Montablan, to Rinaldo, and of course marries them; but it is to Italy that the feminine name, so much more universal, is owing. The first Chiara on record was the devoted disciple of St. Francis, who, under his direction, established the order of women following his rule, and called, poor Clares, or sisters of St. Clara. From them the name of Clara spread into the adjoining countries, little varied except that the French used to call it Claire, until recently, when they have added the terminal *a*, just as the English on the other hand are dropping it, and making the word Clare. The Bretons use both masculine and feminine as Sklear, Skleara; and the Finns have the feminine as Lara.

The old Latin feminine of words ending in *or*, meaning the doer, was *ix—nutor, nutrix*—and this became *ice* in modern Italian. Thus Clarice was probably intended to mean making famous. A lady thus named was the wife of Lorenzo de Medici, and France learnt it probably from her, but made the *c* silent; and England, picking it up by ear, obtained Clarissa, which, when Richardson had so named the heroine of his novel, was re-imported into France as Clarisse. Clarinda was another invention of the same date.

Esclairmonde, a magnificent name of romance, the heroine of *Huon de Bourdeaux*, walked into real life with a noble damsel of the house of Foix, in the year 1229, and was borne by various maidens of that family; but who would have thought of two ladies called Clarimond, in Devonshire, in 1613 and 1630?

Section IV.—*Columba.*

Columba is one of the sweetest and most gentle of all words in sound and sense, yet it has not been in such universal use as might have been expected from its reference to the dove of peace.

A virgin martyr in Gaul, and another in Spain, were both called Columba; and Columbina must at one time have prevailed in Italy, as a peasant name, since from the waiting damsel in the impromptu comedies that the poetical Italians loved to act, it passed to the light-footed maiden of modern farce, and now is seldom used save for her and the columbine, the dove-flower, so called from the resemblance of the curled spurs of its four purple petals to doves drinking.

It was from his gentle character that Crimthan, the great and admirable son of the House of Neill, was called Columba, a fitting name for him who was truly a dove of peace to the wild Hebrides. In Ireland this good man is generally called St. Columkill, St. Columb of the cell, or monastery, because of the numbers of these centres of Christian instruction founded by him, and he is thus distinguished from a second Columb, called after him. He has, indeed,

left strong traces on the nomenclature of the country that he evangel-
ized. Colin, so frequent among the Scots of all ranks, is the direct
descendant of Columba, though it is often confounded with the
French Colin, from Nicolas, who is the chief Colin of modern Arcadia,
and perhaps has the best right to the feminine invention of Colinette.
Besides this, it was the frequent custom to be called Gillie-colum and
Maol-colm, the disciple, or shaveling, of Columb, from whence arose
Malcolm, one of the most national of Scottish names. Colan, probably called after the patron saint of the place, was married at St.
Columb Magna, in Cornwall, in 1752 ; but earlier it was Columb for
men, Columba for women, both now disused.

Columbanus, another great Irish missionary saint, was probably
called, after old Latin custom, by the adoptive formed from Columba.
His influence on the Continent, newly broken and almost heathen-
ized by the Teutonic invasions, was so extensive, reaching as it did
from Brittany to Switzerland, and still marked by the relics of Irish
art in the books of the monasteries of his foundation, that we wonder
not to find more traces of his name. His day, November 1st, is called
by the Germans St. Colman's, and it is thought that the surnames
Kohl and Kohlmann are remains of his name, as well as the French
Coulon. So, too, the Genoese Colon was by historians identified with
Columbus, when they Latinized the mariner who "gave a new world
to Spain." Two spots in that new world bear his name, that in Terra
Firma, where he landed on his third voyage, and the bishopric newly
founded in Vancouver's Isle.

The Slavonian dove is Golubica, a cognate word to this and sometimes used as a name.*

Section V.—*Durans.*

Durans (enduring, or lasting) formed the name which no reader of
Don Quixote can forget as that of the enduring hero, lying on his
back on the marble tomb, in the cave of Montesinos, who uttered
that admirable sentiment, " Patience, cousin, and shuffle the cards ! "

The name of Durandus prevailed in other countries ; and Durand,
to our surprise, figures constantly in Domesday Book, probably having
belonged to French immigrants. A Durand and Marta, who jointly
owned a house at Winchester in the reign of Stephen, were almost
certainly Provençal, since St. Martha was hardly known except in
the scene of her exploit with the dragon. Durand Grimbald is a
specimen of a French Christian and English surname then prevailing.
Durandus is the Latinized surname of the great French lawyer of the
middle ages ; and Durandus again is familiar to the lover of mediæval
symbolism ; but none of these can approach in honour the great
Florentine Durante Alighieri, whose glory, *lasting* like that of
Homer and Shakespeare, has made his contracted appellation of
Dante stand alone and singly.

* Butler ; Hanmer, *Ireland ;* Chalmer, *Caledonia ;* Montalembert ; *Ossianic
Society ;* Pott ; Michaelis.

A great race of Christian names were fabricated, in Latin, after the pattern of the Greek Theophilus, Theophorus, &c., though hardly with equal felicity, and chiefly in the remoter provinces of the West, where Latin was, probably, a matter of scholarship. Thus, in the province of Africa, we find, just before the Vandal invasion, Quodvultdeus (what God wills) and Deogratias (thank God), neither of which had much chance of surviving. Deusvult (God wills), Deusdedit (God gave), and Adeodatus, lived nearer to Italy; indeed, Deusdedit was a pope. Adeodatus or Deodatus (God given) was a Gallic saint, called, commonly, St. Die, and with the other form, Donum Dei, continued in use for children whose birth was hailed with special joy. When Louis VII. of France at length had a son, after being "afflicted with a multitude of daughters," he called him Philippe Dieudonné; but this grateful name was discarded in favour of the imperial Auguste, by which he is distinguished. Deodati di Gozo, the Knight of Rhodes who slew the dragon, better kept his baptismal name, and it often occurs in Italian history, and is an Italian surname. Deodatus is an occasional name only found in England. The old French knightly name, Dudon, called in Italian romantic poetry Dudone, is, probably, a contraction of Dieudonné, as the surnames Donnedieu, Dondey, Dieudé, can hardly fail to be. Deicola (a worshipper of God) was invented for a pupil of St. Columbanus, who followed his master to France, lived as a hermit, and became the patron-saint of Franche Comté, where boys are still called, after him, Diel or Diez, and girls, Dielle. There is likewise an Italian name Diotisalvi, or God save thee, only to be paralleled by some of our Puritan devices.

To these may be added Donatus (given), which evidently was bestowed in the same spirit, though not mentioning the giver. It occurs, like most of this class, in the African province, and belonged to the bishop of Numidia, whose rigour against the penitent lapsed made him the founder of the exclusive schismatical church named after him. Another Donatus was St. Jerome's tutor; and, before his time, several martyrs had been canonized by his name, and it seems to have prevailed in Gaul and Britain. In Wales it was pronounced Dynawd; and, by the time St. Augustine came to England and disputed with the Cymric clergy, the history of the word had been so far forgotten that Dynawd, abbot of Bangor-Iscoed, was Latinized into Dionothius. Donat, or Donath, is found in Ireland, but it was probably there adopted for the sake of its resemblance to the native Gaelic Don, meaning brown-haired. Donato, likewise, at one time prevailed in Italy, and produced the frequent surname, Donati. Donnet was a feminine in Cornwall in 1755.

Desiderius, or Desideratus, was of the same date, and given, in like manner, to express the longing desire or love of the parents towards the child. In fact the word *desiderium*, in Latin, more properly means affection than wish, as we explain its derivatives in modern languages. The Desiderius of history was a brother of Magnentius, the opponent of Constantine, and the Desiderius of the calendar was a bishop of Bourges, in the seventh century ; but, in the mean time, the last Lombard king of Italy either had become so Italianized as to adopt it, or else used it as a translation of one of the many Teuton forms of Leofric, Leofwin, &c., for he was known to Italy as Desiderio, to France as Didier ; and his daughter, whom Charlemagne treated so shamefully, was Desiderata, Desirata, or Desirée. The latter has continued in use in France, as well as Didier and Didiere ; and the masculine likewise appears in the Slavonic countries as Zljeko, and among the Lithuanians as Didders or Sidders.

The most learned men were not perfect philologists in the sixteenth century, when they played the most curious tricks with their names. Erasmus began life as Gerhard Gerhardson, signifying, in fact, firm spear, a meaning little suited to his gentle, timid nature. He was better pleased to imagine *ger* to be the German all, and *ard* to be *erd* (earth or nature) ; of this all-nature he made out that affection embraced all, therefore he called himself Desiderius, and then, wanting another equally sounding epithet, he borrowed Erasmus from the Greek, where it had named an ancient bishop. It came from ἐράω (to love) ; and thus Desiderius Erasmus, the appellation by which he has come down to posterity, was an ingenious manufacture out of the simple Gerard.*

Section VII.—*Crescens, &c.*

The verb *cresco* (to increase or grow) has descended into all our modern languages. It has formed the French *croître* (to grow), our *increase* and *decrease*, and our *crescent*. Its participle was already adopted as a name in St. Paul's time, at least it is thus that his companion, Κρήσκης, is rendered, who had departed to Dalmatia ; and a later Crescens is said to have brought about the death of Justin Martyr, in the second century. The occasion, however, of the modern name was one of the many holy women of Sicily—Crescentia, a Christian nurse, who bred-up her charge, the infant Vitus, in her own faith, fled with him to Italy, and was there seized and martyred, under Diocletian. Crescenzia, and the masculine, Crescenzio, prevail in both Naples and Sicily ; and the election of the Angevin-Sicilian Carobert, to the throne of Hungary, carried the former thither as Czenzi ; whence Bavaria took it as Cresenz, Zenz, Zenzl.

Section VIII.—*Military Names.*

In the slender thread of connection with which we try to unite names given in the same spirit, we put together those that seem to have accorded with the tastes of the Roman army.

* Pott ; Butler ; Sismondi ; *Life of Erasmus.*

Thus *eligo* (to choose), which originally caused the title of Legion, was in the participle *electus*, and thus led to words most familiar to us in the state as political terms, to the theological term elect or chosen for salvation.

There is some doubt whether St. John's third epistle be indeed to a lady called Electa, or to an elect lady, as it is in our version ; but when a name from this source next appears, it is among the cultivated Gallo-Romans, when they had gradually worked their way to consideration among the rude Franks, who had nearly trodden out civilization in the conquered country. Eligius was the great goldsmith bishop who designed King Dagobert's throne, made shrines for almost all the distinguished relics in France, and doubtless enjoyed the fame of having made many more than could have come from his hand. He is popularly called St. Eloy, and some derive from him the Provençal Aloys ; but this is far more probably a southern form of Hlodweh, or Louis.

The Roman veterans were termed *emeriti* (having deserved) from *mereor* (to deserve). From these old soldiers must have come the name Emerentius, which is to be found as Emerenz in Germany, and Emérence in France.

St. Emerentiana was said to have been a catechumen, who was killed by soldiers who found her praying on the tomb of St. Agnes. Her name (probably her relics) passed to Denmark, and to Lithuania, where it is called Marenze, and Embrance is the old English feminine.

The very contrary, Pacifico (peaceful), is a modern Italian and Spanish name—as Peace is Puritan.

Here, too, we place that which the soldier most esteems—*honos*, or *honor*. Honor was a deity in later Rome, but no old classical names were made from him, and Honorius first appears as one of the appellations of the Spanish father of the great Theodosius ; then again inherited by that imbecile being, his grandson, the last genuine Roman emperor ; also by a niece, called Justa Grata Honoria, who dishonoured all her three honourable names. Yet some lingering sense of allegiance to the last great family that gave rulers to the empire perpetuated their names in the countries where they had reigned ; and the Welsh Ynyr long remained as a relic of Honorius, in Wales. Honorine was a Neustrian maiden, slain in a Danish invasion, and regarded as a martyr ; so that Honorine prevails in France and Germany, and one of the favourite modern Irish names, is Onora, Honor, or in common usage, Norah.

Russia has the masculine as Gonorij ; Lithuania, the feminine cut down into Arri. There were two Gallic bishops named Honoratus, whence the French Honoré, which has named a suburb of Paris, and we had one early archbishop of Canterbury so called, from whom we have derived no names, though Honor was revived in England in the days of names of abstract qualities, and Honoria was rather in fashion in the last century, probably as an ornamental form of the Irish Norah.*

* Butler ; Smith, *Antiquities ;* Le Beau.

Section IX.—*Names of Gladness.*

A large class of names of joy belonging to the later growth of the Latin tongue may be thrown together ; and first those connected with the word *jocus*, which seems to have arisen from the inarticulate shout of ecstasy that all know, but none can spell, *ίοναι* (in Greek), and with us joy, the French *joie*, and Italian *gioia*.

The original cry is preserved in the Swiss *jodel*, or shout of the mountaineers, and this indeed seems to be the sound naturally rising from the cries that peal from one hill to another, for here the Eastern meets the Western tongue. The sound at which the walls of Jericho fell, was called the Yobêl ; and the fifty years' festival of release, inaugurated with trumpet sounds, was the Yobêl (the jubilee). *Jubilo* (to call aloud), already a Latin word, also from the sound of the shout and exultation, had been connected with it even before the *annum jubileum* had come in from the Hebrews.

Giubilare and *Giubileo* made themselves at home in Italian, while German, either from the Latin or its own resources, took its own word *jubel*. Giubileo was probably born in the year of a jubilee.

From *jocus* came Jodocus, an Armorican prince, belonging to a family which migrated from Wales. He refused the sovereignty of Brittany, to live as a hermit in Ponthieu, where he is still remembered as St. Josse, and named at least three villages, perhaps also forming Josselin ; but in his native Brittany, Judicael, an old princely name, seems to have been the form of his commemoration. In *Domesday Book* we find Judicael *Venator* already a settler in England before the conquest, probably brought by the Confessor. Germany accepted this as a common peasant name, as Jost, or Jobs ; Bavaria, as Jobst, or Jodel ; Italy, as Giodoco ; and the feminine, Jodoca, is not yet extinct in Wales.

Neither is the very similar Jocosa, once not uncommon among English ladies, by whom it was called Joyce. The contractions of this name are, however, almost inextricably confused with those of Justus. Joy stands alone as one of our abstract virtue names.

Another word very nearly related to our own glad, is *gaudium* (joy), still preserved in the adjective gaudy, and in gaudy (the festival day) of a college. It named St. Gaudentius, whence the Italian Gaudenzio, and the old German name of Geila.

Hilaris (cheerful) formed Hilarius, whence was called the great doctor of the Gallican Church, known to us as St. Hilary, of Poitiers ; and to France, at St. Hilaire. A namesake was the Neustrian hermit who made Jersey his abode, and thus named St. Helier ; and moreover the Welsh called those who traditionally had been named Hilarius, first Ilar, then Elian ; and then thought they had found their patron in the Greek Ælianus.

English.	French.	Italian.	Russian.	Frisian.
Hilary	Hilaire	Ilario	Gilarij	Laris

Portugal likewise has Hilarião, and Russia Hilarion ; and the feminine, Hilaria, was once used in England, and is still the Russian Ilaria, and Slovak Milari.

Lœtus (glad) formed the substantive *lœtitia*, which was turned into a name by the Italians as Letizia, probably during the thirst for novelty that prevailed in the Cinque-cento ; and then, likewise, Lettice seems to have arisen in England, and must have become known in Ireland when Lettice Knollys was the wife of the Earl of Essex. Thence Letitia, or Letty, have been common among Irishwomen.

Prosperus, from the Latin *prosper*, formed of *pro* and *spero*, so as to mean favourable hope, formed the mediæval Roman Prospero, of which Shakespeare must have heard through the famous condottiere, Prospero Colonna, when he bestowed it upon his wondrous magician Duke of Milan.*

SECTION X.—*Jus.*

Jus (right), and *juro* (to swear), are intimately connected, and have derivatives in all languages, testifying to the strong impression made by the grand system of Roman law.

Justus, the adjective which we render as just, named the Gallic St. Justus, or St. Juste, of Lyons ; also the Dutch Jost ; Italian Giusto ; and Portuguese Justo.

Justa was a virgin martyr, but her fame was far exceeded by that of Justina, who suffered at Padua, and became the patron saint of that city, whose university made its peculiarities everywhere known. The purity of St. Justina caused her emblem to be the unicorn, since that creature is said to brook no rule but that of a spotless maiden ; and poison always became manifest at the touch of its horn, for which the twisted weapon of the narwhal did duty in collections. The great battle of Lepanto was fought on St. Justina's day, and the victory was by the Venetians attributed to her intercession ; so that Giustina at Venice, Justine in France, came for the time into the foremost ranks of popularity.

The noted Justinus, whom we call Justin Martyr, was one of the greatest of the early writers of the Church, meeting the heathen philosophers upon their own ground in argument, and bequeathing to us our first positive knowledge of Christian observances. From him the name was widely spread in the Church ; and Yestin was one of the many old Roman names that lingered on long among the Welsh. Justin was frequent in France and Germany, and has become confused in its contractions with Jodocus. Josse and Josselin seem to have been used for both in France ; and from the latter we obtained the Joscelin, or Joycelin, once far more common in England than at present. The Swiss Jost and Jostli are likewise doubtful between the two names.

In Ireland, the name of Justin has been adopted in the M'Carthy

* Kitto, *Bible Cyclopædia ;* Butler ; Pott ; Michaelis ; Dugdale ; Petre Chevalier.

family, as a translation of the native Saerbrethach (the noble judge).*

The infants whom Herod massacred at Bethlehem were termed in Latin *innocentes*, from *in* (not), and *noceo* (to hurt). These harmless ones were revered by the Church from the first, and honoured on the third day after Christmas as martyrs in deed. The relics of the Holy Innocents were great favourites in the middle ages, and are to be found as frequently as griffins' eggs in the list of treasures at Durham ; but names taken from them are almost exclusively Roman. A lawyer of the time of Constantine was called Innocentius, and a Pope contemporary with St. Chrysostom handed it on to his successors, many of whom have subsequently assumed this title, and are called by their subjects Innocenzio.

Pius, applied at first to faithful filial love, as in the case of Æneas, assumed a higher sense with Christianity, and from being an occasional agnomen, became the name of a martyr Pope, under Antoninus Pius, and thus passed on to be one of the papal appellations most often in use, called Pio at Rome, and generally left to the pontiffs, though the feminine Pia is occasionally used in Italy. The Puritans indulged in Piety, and it still sometimes occurs in England, as well as Patience and Prudence, though the givers are little aware that there were saints long ago thus called, St. Patiens, of Lyons, and St. Prudentius, the great Christian poet of primitive times.

In like manner we have Modesty, or Moddy, as a Puritan name in England, taken from the abstract virtue, while the peasant women of Southern France are christened Modestine, probably in honour of a Roman martyr called Modestus, who was put to death at Bézières. Indeed, Modestinus and Modestus were both in use even in the earlier Roman times, and were understood by those who first bore them not in the sense of 'shamefastness,' but of moderation or discretion, the word coming from *modus* (a measure).

To these, perhaps, should be added that which Italy and Spain have presumed to form from that title of the Blessed Saviour, Salvatore, or Salvador, the latter more common in South America than in the Old World.

Cœlum (heaven) formed, in late Latin, *Cœlestinus*, the name of one of the popes who was martyred, and afterwards canonized, and imitated by several successors, whence the French learned the two modern feminines, Celeste and Celestine.

Restitutus (restored), from *re* and *sisto*, seems as if it could be given only in a Christian sense, as to one restored to a new life ; yet its first owner known to us was a friend of Pliny, and an orator under Trajan. It came to Britain, and is found in Wales as Restyn.

Melior (better), is a Cornish female name, probably an imitation of some old Keltic one. It is found as early as 1574.

* Cave, *Lives of the Fathers ;* Jameson ; *Irish Society.*

O

SECTION XII.—*Ignatius.*

Ignatius is a difficult name to explain.   Its associations are with
the Eastern Church, but it occurs at a time when Latin names prevailed as much as Greek ones in the Asiatic portions of the Roman
empire, and thus the Latin *ignis* (fire) is, perhaps, the most satisfactory derivation, though it is not unlikely that the word may come
from the source both of this and of the Greek ἁγνός, purity and flame
being always linked together in Indo-European ideas.

The birth-place of the great St. Ignatius is unknown, but tradition
has marked him as the child whom our Lord set in the midst of His
disciples, and he is known to have been the pupil of St. John,
ordained by St. Peter, and at the end of his long episcopate at
Antioch, he was martyred at Rome by command of Trajan, writing
on his last journey the Epistles that are among the earliest treasures
of the Church.   So much is his memory revered in his own city, that
to the present day the schismatic patriarchs of Antioch of the Mono-
physite sect uniformly assume the name of Ignatius on their election
to their see.

The Greek Church has continued to make much use of this name,
called in Russia Ignatij, Eegnatie, or Ignascha ; and in the Slovak
dialect cut short into Nace.   The Spanish Church likewise adopted
it in early times, and among the Navarrese counts and lords of
Biscay, as far back as 750, we encounter both men and women called
Iñigo and Iñiga, or more commonly Eneco and Eneca, used indifferently with the other form, and then Latinized into Ennicus and
Ennica.

Navarre preserved the name, and it was a Navarrese gentleman,
Don Iñigo Loyola, who, while recovering from his wounds, after the
siege of Pampeluna, so read the lives of the saints as to become
penetrated with enthusiasm as fiery as his name.   Where the Jesuits
have had their will may be read in the frequency of this renewed
Iñigo, or Ignace, as it was in France, Ignaz in Roman Catholic
Germany.   It is Bohemia, where the once strong spirit of Protest-
antism was trodden out in blood and flame, that Ignaz is common
enough to have turned into Hynek, and in Bavaria that it becomes
Nazi and Nazrl.

Our English architect, whose name is associated with the unhappy
medley of Greek and Gothic which was the Stuart imitation of the
Cinque-cento style, was a Roman Catholic, and was no doubt christened in honour of Loyola.   The few stray specimens of Inigo to be
found occasionally in England are generally traceable to him ; one
occurs at St. Columb Major, in 1740.*

* Michaelis ; Cave ; Stanley, *Lectures on the Eastern Church ;* Mariana,
Istoria de España ; Anderson, *Royal Genealogies.*

Section XIII.—*Pater.*

The word *pater*, which, as we have already shown, is one of those that make the whole world kin, was the source of *patria* (the fatherland), and of far too many words in all tongues to recount. *Patres Conscripti* was the title of the senators, and the *patricii*, the privileged class of old Rome, were so called as descendants from the original thirty *patres*. *Patricius* (the noble) was as a title given half in jest to the young Roman-British Calpurnius, who was stolen by Irish pirates in his youth, and when ransomed, returned again to be the apostle of his captors, and left a name passionately revered in that warm-hearted land. The earlier Irish, however, were far too respectful to their apostle to call themselves by his name, but were all Mael-Patraic, the shaveling, or pupil of Patrick, or Giolla-Patraic, the servant of Patrick. This latter, passing to Scotland with the mission of St. Columba, turned into the Gospatric, or Cospatrick, the boy (gossoon or *garçon*) of Patrick, Earls of Galloway ; and in both countries the surname Gilpatrick, or Kilpatrick, has arisen from it.

Afterwards these nations left off the humble prefix, and came to calling themselves Phadrig in Ireland, Patrick in Scotland ; the former so universally as to render Pat and Paddy the national soubriquet. Latterly a bold attempt has been made in Ireland to unite Patrick and Peter as the same, so as to have both patron saints at once, but the Irish will hardly persuade any one to accept it but themselves. The Scotch Pate, or Patie, is frequent, though less national ; and the feminine, Patricia, seems to be a Scottish invention. The fame of the curious cave, called St. Patrick's Purgatory, brought pilgrims from all quarters, and Patrice, Patrizio, and Patricio, all are known in France, Italy, and Spain, the latter the most frequently. Even Russia has Patrikij.

Paternus (the fatherly) was the Latin name of two Keltic saints, one Armorican, the other of Avranches, where he is popularly called Saint Pari.*

Section XIV.—*Grace, &c.*

The history of the word *grace* is curious. We are apt to confuse it with the Latin *gracilis* (slender), with which it has no connection, and which only in later times acquired the sense of elegant, whereas it originally meant lean, or wasted, and came from a kindred word to the Greek γράω (grao), to consume.

Grates, on the contrary, were thanks, whence what was done *gratiis*, or *gratis*, was for thanks and nothing else, according to our present use of the word—whence our gratuitous. So again *gratus* applied to him who was thankful, and to what inspired thanks ; and *gratia* was favour, or bounty, and was used to render the Greek χάρις ; and thus have the Greek Charities come down to us as Graces.

* Arnold ; Hanmer ; *Irish Society ;* Lower.

Then, too, he was *gratiosus* who possessed the free spirit of bounty and friendliness, exactly expressed by our gracious; but, in Italy, it was degraded into mere lively good-nature, till *un grazioso* is little better than a buffoon; and *gracieux* in France means scarcely more than engaging.

Gratia was used by early Latin writers for divine favour, whence the theological meaning of grace. And from *grates* (thanks) comes our expression of "saying grace before meat."

The English name of Grace is intended as the abstract theological term, and was adopted with many others of like nature at the Reformation. Its continuation after the dying away of most of its congeners is owing to the Irish, who thought it resembled their native *Grainé* (love), and thereupon adopted it so plentifully that Grace or Gracie is generally to be found wherever there is an Irish connection.

Spain likewise has Engracia in honour of a maiden cruelly tortured to death at Zaragoza, in 304; and Italy, at least in Lamartine's pretty romance, knows Graziella.

Gratianus (favourable) rose among the later Romans, and belonged to the father and to the son of the Emperor Valens, and it left the Italians Graziano for the benefit of Nerissa's merry husband.

Pulcher (fair) turned into a name in late days, and came as Pulcheria to that noble lady on whom alone the spirit of her grandfather Theodosius in all his family descended. She was canonized, and Pulcheria thus was a recognized Greek name; but it has been little followed except in France, where Chérie is the favourite contraction.

Spes (hope) is the only one of the Christian graces in Latin who has formed any modern names; and these are the Italian Sperata (hoped for), and Speranza (hope). Esperanza in Spain, and Espérance in France, have been made Christian names.

Delicia (delightful) is an English name used in numerous families, and Languedoc has the corresponding Mesdelices, shortened into Médé, so that Mademoiselle Mesdélices is apt to be called Misé Médé in her own country. In Italy, Delizia is used.

Dulcis (sweet, or mild) is explained by Spanish authors to have been the origin of their names of Dulcia, Aldoncia, Aldonça, Adoncia, all frequent among the Navarrese and Catalonian princesses from 900 to 1200, so that it was most correct of Don Quixote to translate his Aldonça Lorenço into the peerless Dulcinea del Toboso. Probably the Moorish article was added by popular pronunciation in Spain, while Dulcia lingered in the South of France, became Douce, and came to England as Ducia in the time of the Conqueror, then turned into Dulce, and by-and-by embellished into Dulcibella, and then by Henry VIII.'s time fell into Dowsabel, a name borne by living women, as well as by the wife of Dromio. Dousie Moor, widow, was buried in 1658, at Newcastle.*

* Facciolati; Butler; Bowles, *Don Quixote con Annotaciones.*

SECTION XV.—*Vinco.*

The verb *vinco* (to conquer), the first syllable the same as our *win,* formed the present participle *vincens,* whence the name Vincentius (conquering), which was borne by two martyrs of the tenth persecution, one at Zaragoza, the other at Agen ; and later by one of the great ecclesiastical authors at Lerius, in Provence. Thus Vincent, Vincente, Vincenzio, were national in France, Spain, and Italy, before the more modern saints, Vincente Ferrer, and Vincent de St. Paul, had enhanced its honours.

English.	French.	Spanish.	Italian.	German.
Vincent	Vincent	Vincente	Vincenzio	Vincenz

Bavarian.	Russian.	Polish.	Bohemian.	Hungarian.
Zenz Zenzel	Vikentij	Vincentij	Vincenc	Vincze

Even the modern Greeks have it as Binkentios.

Conquest is a word found in all classes of names,—the Sieg of the Teuton, the Nikos of the Greek.

The past participle is *victus;* whence the conqueror is Victor—a name of triumph congenial to the spirit of early Christianity, and borne by an early pope as well as by more than one martyr, from whom Vittore descended as rather a favourite Italian name, though not much used elsewhere till the French Revolution, when Victor came into fashion in France. Tollo is the Roman contraction, as is Tolla of the feminine.

The original Victoria was a Roman virgin, martyred in the Decian persecution ; whence the Italian Vittoria, borne by the admirable daughter of the Colonne, from whom France and Germany seem to have learned it, since after her time Victoire and Victorine became very common in France ; and it was from Germany that we learnt the Victoria that will, probably, sound hereafter like one of our most national names.

SECTION XVI.—*Vita.*

Vita (life) was used by the Roman Christians to express their hopes of eternity ; and an Italian martyr was called Vitalis, whence the modern Italian Vitale and German Veitel.

Vitalianus, a name formed out of this, is hardly to be recognized in the Welsh form of Gwethalyn.

Vivia, from *vivus* (alive), was the first name of Vivia Perpetua, the noble young matron of Carthage, whose martyrdom, so circumstantially told, is one of the most grand and most affecting histories in the annals of the early Church. Her other name of Perpetua has, however, been chosen by her votaresses.

Vivianus and Viviana were names of later Roman days, often, in the West, pronounced with a *B*, and we find a Christian maiden, named Bibiana, put to death by a Roman governor, under Julian the Apostate, under pretence of her having destroyed one of his eyes by magic, a common excuse for persecution in the days of pretended toleration.   A 'church was built over her remains as early as 465, and, considering the accusation against her, it is curious to find Vyvyan or Viviana the enchantress of King Arthur's court.

Vivian has been a name for both sexes, and a Scottish Vivian Wemyss, bishop of Fife in 615, was canonized, and known to Rome as St. Bibianus.

Vitus was the child whom St. Crescentia bred up a Christian, and who died in Lucania with her.   His day was the 15th of June, and had the reputation of entailing thirty days of similar weather to its own.

Vitus is Vita, in Bohemia ; Vida, in Hungary ; Veicht and Veidl, in Bavaria ; and is used to Latinize Guy ; but it is probable that this last is truly Celtic, and it shall be treated of hereafter.*

SECTION XVII.—*Wolves and Bears.*

The Roman *lupus* had truly a right to stand high in Roman estimation, considering the good offices of the she-wolf to the founder, and the wolf and the twins will continue an emblem as long as Rome stands, in spite of the explanation that declared that the nurse was either named Lupa, or so called, because the Roman word applied to a woman of bad character, and in spite of the later relegation of the entire tale to the realms of mythology.   Lupus was accordingly a surname in the Rutilian gens, and was borne by many other Romans, thus descending to the three Romanized countries.   St. Lupus, or Loup of Troyes, curiously enough succeeded St. Ursus, and was notable both for his confutation of the Pelagian heresy, and for having saved his diocese by his intercession with Attila.   Another sainted Lupus, or Loup, was Bishop of Lyons.   Italy has the Christian name of Lupo ; Portugal, Lobo ; Spain, Lope.   The great poet, Lope de Vega, might be translated, the wolf of the meadow.

The bear was not in any remarkable favour at Rome ; but the semi-Romans adopted Ursus as rather a favourite among their names. Ursus and Ursinus were early Gallic bishops ; whence the Italian Orso and Orsino, the latter becoming the surname of the celebrated Roman family of Orsini.   Ours is very common in Switzerland, in compliment to the bears of Berne.

An old myth of the little bear and the stars seems to have been turned into the legend of Cologne, of Ursula, the Breton maiden who, on her way to her betrothed British husband, was shipwrecked on the German coast, and slain by Attila, King of the Huns, with 11,000 virgin companions.   Some say that the whole 11,000 rose out

* Fleury, *Histoire Ecclesiastique ;* Butler ; Villemarque, *Romans de la Table Ronde ;* Roscoe, *Boiardo ;* Brand, *Popular Antiquities ;* Grimm ; Michaelis.

of the V. M. for virgin martyr; others give her one companion, named Undecimilla, and suppose that this was translated into the 11,000. Skulls and bones, apparently from an old cemetery, are shown at Cologne, and their princess's name has been followed by various ladies.

French.	Swiss.	Italian.
Ours	Ours	Orso
	Orsvch	Ursilo
		Ursello

FEMININE.			
English.	French.	Spanish.	Portuguese.
Ursula	Ursule	Ursola	Ursula
Ursel			
Ursley	Dutch.		
Nullie	Orseline		
Italian.	German.	Swiss.	Russian.
Orsola	Ursel	Orscheli	Urssula
	Urschel	Urschel	
		Urschla	
Polish.	Slavonic.	Lusatian.	Hungarian.
Urszula	Ursa	Wursla	Orsolya
		Hoscha	
Bohemian.		Oscha	
Worsula			

DIMINUTIVE.		
Roman.	French.	Polish.
Ursino	Ursin	Ursyn

SECTION XVIII.—*Names from Places and Nations.*

The fashion of forming names from the original birthplace was essentially Roman. Many cognomina had thus risen; but a few more must be added of too late a date to fall under the usual denominations of the earlier classical names.

The island of Cyprus must at some time have named the family of Thascius Cyprianus, that great father of African birth, who was so noted as Bishop of Carthage; but though Cyprian is everywhere known, it is nowhere common, and is barely used at Rome as Cipriano. In 1811, Ciprian was baptized in Durham cathedral; but then he was the son of the divinity lecturer, which accounts for the choice.

Neapolis, from the universal Greek word for *new*, and the Greek πόλις (a city), was the term bestowed as frequently by the Greeks as Newtown is by Keltic influence, or Newby and Newburgh by Teutonic. One Neapolis was the ancient Sychar, and another was that which is still known as Napoli or Naples.

From some of these ' new cities' was called an Alexandrian martyr, whose canonized fame caused him to be adopted as patron by one of the Roman family of Orsini, in the course of the twelfth century. Neapolion, Neapolio, or Napoleone, continued to be used in that noble house, and spread from them to other parts of Italy, and thence to Corsica, where he received it who was to raise it to become a word of terror to all Europe, and of passionate enthusiasm to France, long after, in school-boy fashion, at Brienne, its owner had been discontented with its singularity.

The city of Sidon formed the name Sidonius, which was borne by Caius Sollius Apollinaris Sidonius, one of the most curious characters of the dark ages, a literary and married bishop of Clermont, in the fifth century, an honest and earnest man, but so little according to the ordinary type of ecclesiastical sanctity, that nothing is more surprising than to find him canonized, and in possession of the 23rd of August for a feast day. It is curious, too, that his namesakes should be ladies. Sidonie is not uncommon in France ; and, in 1449, Sidonia, or Zedena, is mentioned as daughter to George Podiebrand, of Silesia ; and Sidonia, of Bavaria, appears in 1488.

From the city of Lydia was named the seller of purple who hearkened to St. Paul at Thyatira, and to her is owing the prevalence of Lydia among English women delighting in Scriptural names.

To these should be added, as belonging to the same class, though the word is Greek, Anatolius, meaning a native of Anatolia, the term applied in later times by the Greeks to Asia Minor, and meaning the sunrise. St. Anatolius, of Constantinople, was one of the sacred poets of the Greek Church ; and after his death, in 458, his name and its feminine, Anatolia, became frequent in the countries where his hymns were used.

A Phocian is the most probable explanation of the name of Φοκας (Phocas), though much older in Greece than the date of most of those that have been here given. To us it is associated with the monster who usurped the imperial throne, and murdered Maurice and his sons ; but it had previously belonged to a martyred gardener, under Diocletian, whose residence in Pontus made him well known to the Byzantine Church ; and thus Phokas is still found among Greeks, and Foka in Russia.

The Romans called their enemies in North Africa Mauri, from the Greek ἀμαυρός, which at first was twilight or dim, but came afterwards to signify dark, or black.

. Maura was a Gallican maiden of the ninth century, whose name, it would seem highly probable, might have been the Keltic Mohr (great), still current in Ireland and the Highlands. She led a life of great mortification, died at twenty-three, was canonized, and becoming known to the Venetians, a church in her honour named the Ionian island of Santa Maura, which had formerly been Leucadia. There was, however, a genuine Greek St. Maura, the wife of Timothy, a priest, with whom she was crucified in the Thebaid, under Maximian. She is honoured by the Eastern Church on the 3rd of May, and is the subject of a poem of Mr. Kingsley's. From her, many Greek girls bear the name of Maura, and Russian ones of Mavra and Mavruscha.

Mauritius was naturally a term with the Romans for a man of Moorish lineage. The first saint of this name was the Tribune of the Theban legion, all Christians, who perished to a man under the blows of their fellow-soldiers, near the foot of the great St. Bernard. To this brave man is due the great frequency of Maurits, in Switzerland, passing into Maurizio on the Italian border, and Moritz on the German. The old French was Meurisse, the old English, Morris ; but both, though still extant as surnames, have as Christian names been assimilated to the Latin spelling, and become Maurice. The frequent Irish Morris, and the once common Scottish Morris, are the imitation of the Gaelic Moriertagh, or sea warrior.

Meuriz is in use in Wales, and appears to be the genuine produce of Maurice ; but it is very difficult to disentangle the derivations from the Moor, from ἀμαυρός, and from the Keltic *mohr* (large) and *mör* (the sea).

The Saxon Moritz, who played a double game between Charles V. and the Protestant League, was brother-in-law to the great William the Silent, and thus his name was transmitted to his nephew, the gallant champion of the United Provinces, Maurice of Nassau, in whose honour the Dutch bestowed the name of Mauritius upon their island settlement in the Indian Ocean, and this title has finally gained the victory over the native one of Cerine, and the French one of the Isle of Bourbon.

English.	Welsh.	Breton.	French.
Morris	Meuriz	Noris	Meurisse
Maurice			Maurice
Italian.	Spanish.	German.	Danish.
Maurizio	Mauricio	Moritz	Maurids
			Morets
Russian.	Polish.	Bohemian.	Hungarian.
Moriz	Maurycij	Moric	Moricz
Mavrizij			
Mavritij			

Germanus cannot be reckoned otherwise than as one of the varieties of names from countries given by the Romans. It does indeed come from the two Teutonic words *gher* (spear) and *mann ;* but it cannot be classed among the names compounded of *gher*, since the Romans were far from thus understanding it, when, like Mauritius, it must have been inherited by some 'young barbarian' whose father served in the Roman legions.

St. Germanus was greatly distinguished in Kelto-Roman Church history, as having refuted Pelagius, and won the Hallelujah victory, to say nothing of certain unsatisfactory miracles. We have various places named after him, but it was the French who chiefly kept up his name, and gave it the feminine Germaine, which was borne by that lady of the family of Foix, who became the second wife of Fernando the Catholic by the name of Germana. Jermyn has at times been used in England, and became a surname.*

SECTION XIX.—*Town and Country.*

Urbanus is one who dwells in *urbs* (a city), a person whose courtesy and statesmanship are assumed, as is shown by the words civil, from *civis* (a city), and polite, politic, polish, from the Greek πόλις of the same meaning; and thus Urbane conveys something of grace and affability in contrast to rustic rudeness.

Urbanus is greeted by St. Paul; and another Urbanus was an early pope, from whom it travelled into other tongues as Urbano, Urbani, and Urban.

English.	French.	Roman.	Russian.	Slovak.	Hungarian.
Urban	Urbain	Urbano	Urvan	Verban Banej	Orban

In opposition to this word comes that for the rustic, *Pagus*, signifying the country; the word that in Italian becomes *paese*, in Spanish *pais*, in French *pays*. The Gospel was first preached in the busy haunts of men, so that the earlier Christians were towns-folk, and the rustics long continued heathen; whence Paganus, once simply a countryman, became an idolater, a Pagan, and poetized into Paynim, was absolutely bestowed upon the Turks and Saracens in the middle ages. In the mean time, however, the rustic had come to be called *paesano, pays, paysan,* and *peasant,* independently of his religion; and Spain, in addition to her *puyo* (the countryman), had *paisano* (the lover of his country); and either in the sense of habitation or patriotism, Pagano was erected into a Christian name in Italy, and Payen in France; whence England took Payne or Pain, still one of the most frequent surnames.

The two Latin words, *per* (through) and *ager* (a field), were the source of *peregrinus* (a traveller or wanderer), also the inhabitant of the country as opposed to the Roman colonist. The same word in time came to mean both a stranger, and above all, one on a journey to a holy place, when such pilgrimages had become special acts of

* Cave; Butler; *Revue des deux Mondes;* Le Beau, *Bas Empire;* Liddell and Scott; Lower; *Les Vies des Saints.*

devotion, and were growing into living allegories of the Christian life. This became a Christian name in Italy, because a hermit, said to have been a prince of Irish blood, settled himself in a lonely hut on one of the Apennines, near Modena, and was known there as *il pellegrin*, as the Latin word had become softened. He died in 643, and was canonized as St. Peregrinus, or San Pellegrino; became one of the patrons of Modena and Lucca, and had all the neighbouring spur of the Apennines called after him. Pellegrino Pelligrini is a name that we find occurring in Italian history; and when a son was born at Wesel, to Sir Richard Bertie and his wife, the Duchess of Suffolk, while they were fleeing from Queen Mary's persecution, they named him Peregrine, "for that he was given by the Lord to his pious parents in a strange land for the consolation of their exile," as says his baptismal register, and Peregrine in consequence came into favour in the Bertie family; but in an old register the names Philgram, Pilgerlam, and Pilggerlam, occur about 1603.

English.	French.	Italian.	German.
Peregrine	Pérégrin	Pellegrino	Piligrim

To these may perhaps be added the Italian Marino and Marina, given perhaps casually to sea-side dwellers; and their Greek equivalents, Pelagios and Pelagia, both of which are still used by the modern Greeks. Pelagius was used by the Irish, or more properly Scottish, Morgan, as a translation of his own name, and thus became tainted with the connection of the Pelagian heresy; but it did not become extinct; and Pelayo was the Spanish prince who first began the brave resistance that rendered the mountains of the Asturias a nucleus for the new kingdom of Spain.

Some see in his name a sign that the Arian opinions of the Visigoths had some hereditary influence, at least, in nomenclature; and, indeed, Ario occurs long after as a Christian name; others consider Pelago's classical name to be a sign that the old Celto-Roman blood was coming to the surface above the Gothic.

Switzerland likewise has this name cut down to Pelei, or Poli.*

Section XX.—*Flower Names.*

Flower names seem to have been entirely unknown to the ancient Romans, but the Latin language, in the mouths of more poetical races, has given several graceful floral names, though none perhaps are quite free from the imputation of being originally something far less elegant.

Thus, *oliva* (the olive), the sign of peace and joy, is closely connected with the Italian Oliviero; but it is much to be suspected that it would never have blossomed into use, but for the Teutonic Olaf

* Butler; Michaelis.

(forefather's relic). Oliviero, or Ulivieri, the paladin of Charlemagne, may be considered as almost certainly a transmogrified Anlaf, or Olaf (ancestor's relic) ; and perhaps it is for this reason that his name is one of the most frequently in use among all those of the circle of paladins. He was a favourite hero of Pulci, and seems to have so nearly approached Orlando in fame, as at least to be worthy of figuring in the proverb of giving a Rowland for an Oliver. The middle ages made great use of his name in France and England. Olier, as it was called at home by the Breton knights, whom the French called Olivier, was the name of the favourite brother of Du Guesclin, as well as of the terrible Constable de Clisson. Oliver was frequent with English knights, and of high and chivalrous repute, until the eminence of the Protector rendered 'old Noll' a word of hate and would-be scorn to the Cavaliers—an association which it has never entirely overcome. The feminine was probably first invented in Italy, but the Italian literature that flowed in on us in the Tudor reigns brought it to us, and we were wise enough to naturalize Olivia as Olive, a form that still survives in some parts of the country.

Whether it is true that the "rose by any other name would smell as sweet," never appears to have been tried, for all countries seem to express both the flower and its blushing tint by the same sound ; and even the Syriac name for the oleander (the rose-laurel), "the blossoms red and bright" of the Lake of Tiberias, is *rodyon*.

The Greeks had their Rhoda, but the Romans never attained such a flight of poetry as a floral name, and the rose-wreath would hardly deserve to be relegated to a Latin root, were it not that the branches spread so widely, that it is more convenient to start from this common stem, to which all are bound by mutual resemblance ; besides which, both the saints of this name were of Romance nations. Still, I believe, that though *their* names were meant for roses when given to them, that the first use of *hrôs* among the Teutons was a meaning sometimes fame, sometimes a horse—not the flower.

Rohais, or Roesia, most probably the French and Latin of *hrôs* (fame), or else from *hros* (horse), is the first form in which the simple word appears in England. Rohais, wife of Gilbert de Gaunt, died in 1156 ; Roese de Lucy was wife of Fulbert de Dover, in the time of Henry II. ; Roesia was found at the same time among the De Bohuns and De Veres ; and some of these old Norman families must have carried it to Ireland, where Rose is one of the most common of the peasant names. Rosel and Rosette both occur at Cambrai between 900 and 1200.

During the twelfth century, probably among the Normans of Sicily, lived Rosalia, "the darling of each heart and eye," who, in her youth, dedicated herself to a hermit life in a mountain grotto, and won a saintly reputation for her name, which is frequent in her island, as is Rosalie in France, and at the German town of Duderstadt, where it is vilely tortured into Sahlke.

St. Dominic arranged a series of devotions, consisting of the meditations, while rehearsing the recurring *aves* and *paters* marked by the larger and smaller nuts, or berries, on a string. These, which we call beads from *beden* (to pray), formed the *rosarium*, or rose garden, meaning originally the delights of devotion. This *rosarium* has a day to itself in the Roman calendar, and possibly may have named the Transatlantic saint, Rosa di Lima, the whole of which appellation is borne by Peruvian señoras, and practically called Rosita.

Rosa is found in all kinds of ornamental forms in different countries, and the contractions, or diminutives, of one become the names of another. Thus Rosalia, herself, probably sprang from the endearment Rosel, which together with Rosi is common in Switzerland and the Tyrol ; the German diminutive Roschen is met again in the Italian Rosina, French Rosine, English Rosanne ; the Rasine, or Rasche, of Lithuania ; and Rosetta, the true Italian diminutive, is followed by the French Rosette.

These may be considered as the true and natural forms of Rose. Others were added by fancy and romance after the Teuton signification of fame had been forgotten, and the Latin one of the flower adopted. Of these, are Rosaura, Rosaclara ; in English, Roseclear, Rosalba (a white rose), Rosabella, or Rosabel, all arrant fancy names.

Rosamond has a far more ancient history, but the rose connection must be entirely renounced for her. The first Hrosmond (famous protection, or horse protection) was the fierce chieftainess of the Gepidæ, who was compelled by her Lombard husband to drink to his health in a ghastly goblet formed of the skull of her slaughtered father, and who avenged this crowning insult by a midnight murder. Even from the fifth century, the period of this tragedy, hers has remained a favourite name among the peasantry of the Jura, the land of the Gepidæ, but it does not appear how it came from them to the Norman Cliffords, by whom it was bestowed upon Fair Rosamond, whose fate has been so strangely altered by ballad lore, and still more strangely by Cervantes, who makes his Persiles and Sigismunda encounter her in the Arctic regions, undergoing a dreary penance among the wehr wolves. Her name, in its supposed interpretation, gave rise to the Latin epigram, *Rosa mundi, sed non Rosa munda* (the rose of the world, but not a pure rose). The sound of the word, and the popular interest of the ballad, have continued her name in England.

Hroswith, the poetical Frank nun, is certainly famous strength, or famous height, though when softened into Roswitha, she has been taken for a white rose, or a sweet rose.

Rosalind makes her first appearance in *As You Like It*, whether invented by Shakespeare cannot be guessed. If the word be really old, the first syllable is certainly *hrôs*, the last is our English *lithe*, the German *lind*, the Northern *lindre*, the term that has caused the Germans to call the snake the *lindwurm*, or supple worm. The Visigoths considered this litheness as beauty, and thus the word survives in Spanish as *lindo, linda*, meaning, indeed, a fair woman, but a soft effeminate man. Yet, the *linda*, meaning fair in Spanish, was reason enough in the sixteenth century for attaching it to many a name by way of ornament, and it is to be apprehended that thus it was that Rosalind came by her name, and possibly Rosaline, whom Romeo deserted for the sake of Juliet. However she began, she has ever since been one of the English roses.

Rosilde, or Roshilda, a German form, is in like manner either really the fame-battle, or else merely *ilda* tacked by way of ornament to the end of the rose.

Violante is a name occurring in the South of France and the North of Italy and Spain. Whence it originally came is almost impossible to discover. It may very probably be a corruption of some old Latin name such as Valentinus, or, which would be a prettier derivation, it may be from the golden violet, the prize of the troubadours in the courts of love.

The name of the flower is universal; it is *viola* in Latin, *vas* in Sanscrit; and in Greek anciently Γιον, but afterwards ἴον, whence later Greeks supposed it to have been named from having formed a garland round the head of Ion, the father of the Ionians.

That *V* is easily changed to *Y*, was plain in the treatment received by Violante, who was left to that dignified sound only in Spain; but in France was called Yolande, or for affection, Yolette; and in the confusion between *y* and *j*, figures in our own English histories in the queer-looking form of Joletta. The Scots, with much better taste, imported Yolette as Violet, learning it probably through the connections of the Archers of the Royal Guard, or it may be through Queen Mary's friends, as Violet Forbes appears in 1571, and I have not found an earlier instance. At any rate, the Scottish love of floral names took hold of it, and the Violets have flourished there ever since. Fialka is both the flower and a family name in Bohemia; as is Veigel in the Viennese dialect. Eva Maria Veigel was the young *danseuse*, called by Maria Theresa, la Violetta, under which designation she came to England, and finally became the excellent wife of Garrick. Whether Viola has ever been a real Italian name I cannot learn, or whether it is only part of the stage property endeared to us by Shakespeare. The masculine Yoland was common at Cambrai in the thirteenth century; Yolante was there used down to the sixteenth.

Viridis (green, or flourishing) was not uncommon among Italian ladies in the fourteenth century, probably in allusion to some romance.

It is much to be feared that the lily is as little traceable as the rose. There was a Liliola Gonzaga in Italy in 1340, but she was probably a softened Ziliola, or Cecilia. Lilias Ruthven, who occurs in Scotland, in 1557, was probably called from the old romantic poem of *Roswal and Lillian*, which for many years was a great favourite in Scotland. The Lillian of this ballad is Queen of Naples, and thus the name appears clearly traceable to the Cecilias of modern Italy, though it is now usually given in the *sense* of Lily; the English using Lillian; the Scots, Lillias. Indeed, it is quite possible that these, like Lilla, may sometimes have risen out of contractions of Elizabeth. Leila is a Moorish name, and Lelia is only the feminine of Lælius. On the whole, it may be said that only the Hebrew and

Slavonic tongues present us with names *really* taken from individual flowers.*

SECTION XXI.—*Roman Catholic Names.*

The two names that follow are as thorough evidences of the teachings of the Roman Church as are the epithets of the Blessed Virgin, before mentioned, and can, therefore, only be classed together, though it is rather hard upon good Latin to be saddled with them, compounded as they are of Latin and Greek.

The Latin *verus* (true), and the Greek εἰκών (an image), were strangely jumbled together by the popular tongue in the name of a crucifix at Lucca, which was called the *Veraiconica*, or Veronica; and was that Holy Face of Lucca by which William Rufus, having probably heard of it from the Lombard Lanfranc, his tutor, was wont to swear. Another Veronica is the same countenance upon a piece of linen, shown at St. Peter's. Superstition, forgetting the meaning of the name, called the relic St. Veronica's handkerchief, accounted for it by inventing a woman who had lent our Blessed Saviour a handkerchief to wipe His Face during the passage of the *Via dolorosa*, and had found the likeness imprinted upon it.

In an old English poem on the life of Pilate, written before 1305, it appears that the Emperor of Rome learnt that a woman at Jerusalem named 'Veronike' possessed this handkerchief, which could heal him of his sickness. He sent for her, and

> "Anon tho the ymage iseth, he was whole, anon,
> He honoured wel Veronike, heo ne moste fram him gon;
> The ymage he athuld that hit ne com nevereft out of Rome,
> In Seint Peteres Church it is."

Thence Veronica became a patron saint; and in the fifteenth century a real monastic Saint Veronica lived near Milan.

Véronique is rather a favourite name among French peasant women, and Vreneli in Suabia. Pott and Michaelis suggest that Veronica may be the Latin form of Berenice, or Pherenike (victory-bringer); but the history of the relic is too clear to admit of this idea. The flower, Veronica, appears to have won its name from its exquisite blue reflecting a true image of the heavens; and the Scots, who have a peculiar turn for floral names, thus seem to have obtained it.

In 1802 an inscription, with the first and last letters destroyed, was found in the catacombs standing thus, *lumena pax tecum fi.* A priest suggested that *Fi* should be put at the beginning of the sentence instead of the end, and by this remarkable trick, produced *Filumena*. There was a real Greek name Philomena, which had fallen into disuse, and of course was derived from Love, but to please the ears of the Italians, the barbarous Latin Filumen was invented.

* Michaelis; Munch; Pott; Roscoe, *Boiardo;* Anderson, *Genealogies;* Douglas, *Peerage of Scotland;* Ellis, *Specimens of Early English Poetry;* Butler, *Cervantes;* Sismondi.

Thereupon a devout artisan, a priest, and a nun, were all severally favoured by visions of a virgin martyr, who told them the story of Diocletian's love for her, of her refusal, and subsequent martyrdom ; and explained that, having once been called Lumena, she was baptized Filumena, which she explained as daughter of light ! Some, human remains near the stone being dignified as relics of St. Filomena, she was presented to Mugnano ; and, on the way, not only worked many miracles on her adorers, but actually repaired her own skeleton, and made her hair grow. So many wonders are said to have been worked by this phantom saint, the mere produce of a blundered inscription, that a book, printed at Paris in the year 1847, calls her "*La Thaumaturge du* 19*me Siècle*," and she is by far the most fashionable patroness in the Romish Church. Filomena abounds in Rome, encouraged by the example of a little Filomena, whose mosquito net was every night removed by the saint, who herself kept off the gnats. She is making her way in Spain ; and it will not be the fault of the author of *La Thaumaturge* if Philomene is not common in France. The likeness to Philomela farther inspired Longfellow with the fancy of writing a poem on Florence Nightingale, as St. Philomena, whence it is possible that the antiquaries of New Zealand, in the twenty-ninth century, will imagine St. Philomena, or Philomela, to be the heroine of the Crimean war.*

* Butler ; *Philological Society ;* Merriman, *Church in Spain ; La Thaumaturge du* 19*me Siècle.*

CHAPTER VII.

NAMES FROM HOLY DAYS.

Section I.

THE great festivals of religion have supplied names which are here classed together for convenience of arrangement, though they are of all languages. Most, indeed, are taken from the tongue that first proclaimed the glory of the days in question; but in several instances they have been translated into the vernacular of the country celebrating them. Perhaps the use of most of these as Christian names arose from the habit of calling children after the patron of their birthday, and when this fell upon a holiday that was not a saint's day, transferring the title of the day to the child. Indeed, among the French peasantry, Marcel and Marcelle are given to persons born in March, Jules and Julie to July children, and Auguste and Augustine to August children.

Section II.—*Christmas.*

The birthday of our Lord bears in general its Latin title of *Dies Natalis;* the latter word from *nascor* (to be born). The *g*, which old Latin places at the commencement of the verb and its participle, *gnatus*, shows its connection with the Greek γίγνομαι (to come into existence), with γίνεσις (origin), and the Anglo-Saxon *beginning.*

This word Natalis has furnished the title of the feast to all the Romance portion of Europe, and to Wales. There all call it the Natal day; *Nadolig* in Welsh. France has cut the word down into Noël, a word that at Angers was sung fifteen times at the conclusion of lauds, during the eight days before the feast, and which thus passed even into an English carol, still sung in Cornwall, where the popular tongue has turned the chorus into

"Now well! now well! now well!"

This cry of Noël became a mere burst of joy; and in Monstrelet's time was shouted quite independently of Christmas. Noel is a Christian name in France; Natale, in Italy; Natal, in the Peninsula. Indeed, the Portuguese called Port Natal by that title in honour of the time of its discovery, but the Spanish Natal must be distinguished from Natividad, which belongs to the Nativity of the Blessed Virgin, a feast established by Pope Sergius in 688, on the 8th of September. That same 8th of September was chosen by the Greek Church as

P

the festival day of St. Natalia, the devoted wife who attended her
husband, St. Adrian, in his martyrdom, with heroism like that of
Gertrude von der Wart.   He is the same Adrian whose relics filled
the Netherlands, and who named so many Dutchmen ; but while the
West was devoted to the husband and neglected the wife, the East
celebrated the wife and forgot the husband.   Natalia is one of the
favourite Greek Christian names ; Lithuania calls her Nastusche
and Naste ; Russia, Natalija, Nataschenka, and Natascha ; and France
has learned the word as Natalie from her Russian visitors.   Natalie,
however, occurs at Cambrai as early as 1212.

Our own name for the feast agrees with one German provincial
term Christfest.   Christmas now and then occurs in old registers
as a Christian name, as at Froxfield, Hants, in 1574, and is also
used as a surname ; but Noel is more usual for Christmas-born
children.

The Eastern Church did not originally observe the Nativity at all,
contenting itself with the day when the great birth was manifested
to the Gentiles, and for this reason there is no genuine Greek name
for Christmas-day, and Natalia, though now used as a Greek woman's
name, is of Latin origin.

The Slavonic nations have translated Christmas into Bozieni, and
their Christmas children, among the Slovak part of the race, are
the boys, Bozo, Bozko, Bozicko ; the girls, Bozena.*

SECTION III.—*The Epiphany.*

The twelfth day after Christmas was the great day with the
Eastern Church, by whom it was called Θεοφανεία, from Θεός and
φαίνω (to make known, *i.e.*, God's manifestation), or Ἐπιφάνεια (forth
showing).

The ancient Greek Church celebrated on the 6th of January the
birth of Christ, His manifestation to the Gentiles, and the baptism in
the Jordan.   Their titles, Theophania and Epiphania, were adopted
by the Latins, and when the Latin feast of the Nativity was accepted
by the Greek Church, *this* latter was frequently called Epiphania,
while the true manifestation-day was called by a name meaning the
lights, from the multitude of candles in the churches in honour of
the Light of the World and the Light of Baptism.

But in the West, it was the visit of the Magi that gave the strongest
impress to the festival.   Early did tradition fix their number at three,
probably in allusion to the three races of man descended from the
sons of Noah, and soon they were said to be descendants of the
Mesopotamian prophet Balaam, from whom they derived the expectation of the Star of Jacob, and they were promoted to be kings of
Tarsus, Saba, and Nubia, also to have been baptized by St. Thomas,
and afterwards martyred.   Their corpses were supposed to be at that
store-house of relics, Constantinople, whence the Empress Helena

* *Church Festivals and their Household Words* (*Christian Remembrancer*) *;*
Michaelis ; Butler ; Jameson ; Grimm.

caused them to be transported to Milan by an Italian, from whom a noble family at Florence obtained the surname of Epiphania. Frederick Barbarossa carried them to Cologne.

By the eleventh century, these three kings had received names, for they are found written over against their figures in a painting of that date, and occur in the breviary of Mersburg. Though their original donor is unknown, their Oriental sound makes it probable that he was a pilgrim-gatherer of Eastern legends. Gaspar, Melchior, and Balthasar, are not according to European fancy, and are not easy to explain. The first may either be the Persian, *genâshber* (treasure master), or else be taken from the red or green stone called *yashpah* in the East, ἴασπις in Greek, *jasper* in Latin. This was the only one of these names ever used in England, where it was once common. Gasparde is the French feminine; in English the masculine is Jasper. It is extremely common in Germany; and has suffered the penalty of popularity, for Black Kaspar is a name of the devil, and Kaspar is a Jack Pudding.

English. Jasper	French. Gaspard	Spanish. Gaspar	Italian. Gaspare Gaspardo Casparo
German. Kaspar	Bavarian. Kaspe Kasperl	Illyrian. Gaso	Lett. Kaspers Jespers
Frisian. Jaspar	Gaspe Gappe Kapp Kass	Lusatian. Kaspor Kapo	

Melchior is evidently the universal Eastern Malek, or Melchi (a king); but he is in much less favour than his companion; though sometimes found in Italy as Melchiorre, as well as in Germany and Switzerland in his proper form, and in Esthonia contracted to Malk.

Balthasar may be an imitation of Daniel's Chaldean name of Belteshazzar (Bel's prince). Some make it the old Persian Beltshazzar (war council, *or* prince of splendour). It is not unlike the Slavonic Beli-tzar, or White-prince, called at Constantinople Belisarius; but indeed it is probably a fancy name invented at a period when bad Latin and rude Teutonic were being mixed up to make modern languages, and the Lingua Franca of the East was ringing in the ears of pilgrims. However invented, Balthasar flourished much in Italy, and in the Slavonic countries, and very nearly came to the crown in Spain.

Italian. Baldassare	Spanish. Baltasar	Portuguese. Bathasar	Polish. Baltasar
Slovac. Boltazar	Bavarian. Hanser Hansel	Swiss. Balz Balzel	Illyrian. Baltazar Balta Bolta
Lusatian. Bal Balk Baltyn	Lett. Balsys	Hungarian. Boldisar	

Some of the Italians devoutly believed that Gaspardo, Melchiorre, and Baldassare, were the three sons of St. Beffana, as they had come to call Epiphania ; but, in general, Beffana had not nearly so agreeable an association.

In Italy the Epiphany was, and still is, the day for the presentation of Christmas gifts ; and it is likely that the pleasant fiction that la Beffana brought the presents, turned, as in other cases, such as that of St. Nicholas, into the notion that she was a being who went about by night, and must therefore be uncanny. Besides, when the carnival was over, there was a sudden immolation of the remaining weeks of the Epiphany ; and whether from thus personifying the season, or from whatever other cause, a figure was suspended outside the doors of houses at the beginning of Lent, and called la Beffana. It is now a frightful black doll, with an orange at her feet, and seven skewers thrust through her, one of which is pulled out at the end of each week in Lent ; at least, this is the case in Apulia, where she is considered as a token that those who exhibit her, mean to observe a rigorous fast.

Some parts of Italy account for the gibbeting of the unfortunate Beffana, by saying she was the daughter of Herod, *i.e.* Herodias ; and Berni (as quoted by Grimm) says in his rhymes :

" Il di Befania, vo porla per Befana alla finestra,
Perchè qualcun le dia d'una ballestra."

At Florence, however, the story was told in an entirely different way. There it is said that Beffana was the Christian name of a damsel of the Epifania family before-mentioned ; that she offended the fairies, and was by them tempted to eat a sausage in Lent, for which transgression she was sawn asunder in the piazza, and has ever since been hung in effigy at the end of the carnival, as a warning to all beholders.

In fact, Beffana is the Italian bugbear of naughty children ; and it is no wonder that this strange embodiment of the gift-bringing day should not be followed as a Christian name, though the masculine form, Epiphanius, once belonged to a Father, born near Mount

Olympus, in whose honour is named Capa Pifani, a headland on that coast, and from whom Epifanio sometimes is found at Rome.

The other form of the name of the day, Theophania, has been much more in favour ; indeed, in the days of Christine de Pisane, the feast-day was called la Tiphaïne.

Theophano was a name in common use among the Byzantine ladies, and we hear of many princesses so called—one of whom married the German Emperor, Otho II., in 962, and was then called Théophania. Probably she made the name known in Western Europe, but it is curious that its chief home in the form of Tiphaïne, was in Armorica, whence, as the grumbling rhyme of the Englishman, after the Conquest, declared,

> " William de Coningsby,'
> Came out of Brittany,
> With his wife Tiffany,
> And his maid Manfas,
> And his dog Hardigras."

Tiffany took up her abode in England, and left her progeny. The name occurs in an old Devon register, within the last two hundred years, but seems now extinct.

The high-spirited wife of Bertrand du Guesclin, was either Theophanie, or Epiphanie Ragueuel, but was commonly called Tiphaïne la Fée, on account of the mysterious wisdom by which she was able to predict to her husband his lucky and unlucky days—only he never studied her tablets till the disaster had happened. Could she have first acquired her curious title through some report of her namesake, the Fairy Beffana ? In a Cornish register I find Epiphany in 1672 ; Tiffany in 1682.

In an old German dictionary, the feast Theophania is translated " Giperahta naht" (the brightened night), a curious accordance with its Greek title. Indeed, before the relic-worship of the Three Kings of Cologne had stifled the recollection of the real signification of the day of the Manifestation, the festival was commonly termed Perchten tac, Perchten naht (bright day, or bright night). Then went on in Germany much what had befallen Beffana in Italy. By the analogy of saints' days, Perahta, or Bertha, was erected into an individual character, called in an Alsatian poem, the mild Berchte ; in whose honour all the young farming men in the Salzburg mountains go dancing about, ringing cattle bells, and blowing whistles all night. Sometimes she is a gentle white lady, who steals softly to neglected cradles, and rocks them in the absence of careless nurses ; but she is also the terror of naughty children, who are threatened with Frau Precht with the long nose ; and she is likewise the avenger of the idle spinners, working woe to those who have not spun off their hank on the last day of the year. Can this have anything to do with distaff day—the English name for the 7th of January, when work was resumed after the holidays ? Herrings and oat-bread are put outside the door for her on her festival—a token of its Christian origin ; but there is something of heathenism connected with her, for if the bread and fish are not duly put out for her, terrible vengeance is inflicted, with a plough-share, or an iron chain.

That Frau Bertha is an impersonation of the Epiphany there seems little doubt, but it appears that there was an original mythical Bertha, who absorbed the brightened night, or if the bright night gave a new title to the old mythical Holda, Holla, Hulla, Huldr (the faithful, or the muffled), a white spinning lady, who is making her feather-bed when it snows.   She, too, brings presents at the year's end ; rewards good spinners, punishes idle ones, has a long nose, wears a blue gown and white veil, and drives through the fields in a car with golden wheels.   Scandinavia calls her Hulla, or Huldr the propitious ; Northern Germany, Holda, probably by adaptation to *hold* (mild). Franconia and Thuringia recognized both Holda and Berchta ; in Alsatia, Swabia, Switzerland, Bavaria, and Austria, Berchta alone prevails.

Some have even tried to identify Holda with Huldah, the prophetess, in the Old Testament, but this is manifestly a blunder. And, on the other hand, Bertha is supposed to be a name of the goddess Freya, the wife of Odin ; but it appears that though Huldr may possibly have been originally a beneficent form of this goddess, yet that there is no evidence of Bertha's prevailing in heathen times, and therefore the most probable conclusion is that she is really the impersonation of the Epiphany, with the attributes of Holda.

Tradition made her into an ancestress, and she must have absorbed some of the legends of the swan maidens, for she is goose-footed in some of her legends ; and she is sometimes, as in Franconia and Swabia, called Hildaberta or Bildaberta, either from the Valkyr, or as a union of both Hilda and Bertha.   The goose-foot has been almost softened away by the time she appears as *Berthe aux grands pieds* (wife of Pepin, and mother of Charlemagne) ; and the connection with the distaff is again traceable in the story of Charlemagne's sister Bertha, mother of Orlando, who, when cast off on account of her marriage, and left a widow, maintained herself by spinning, till her son, in his parti-coloured raiment, won his uncle's notice by his bold demeanour.

Proverbs of a golden age when Bertha spun, are current both in France and Italy, and in Switzerland they are connected with the real Queen Bertha.

Be it observed that Bertha is altogether a Frank notion, not prevailing among the Saxons, either English or Continental, nor among the Northern races.   It is therefore quite a mistake to use Bertha, as is often done, as a name for an English lady, before the Conquest. One only historical person so called was Bertha, daughter of Chilperic, King of Paris, and wife of Ethelbert, of Kent, the same who smoothed the way for St. Augustine's mission.   She was probably called after the imaginary spinning ancestress, the visitor of Christmas night, but though bright was a common Saxon commencement or conclusion, we had no more Berthas till the Norman conquest brought an influx of Frank names.

The name was, indeed, very common in France and Germany ; and in Dante's time it was so frequent at Florence, that he places Monna Berta with Ser Martino, as the chief of the gossips.   Since those days

it has died away, but has been revived of late years in the taste for
old names; and perhaps, likewise, because Southey mentioned it as
one of the most euphonious of female appellations.   One of the early
German princesses, called Bertha, marrying a Greek emperor, was
translated into Eudoxia, little thinking that she ought to have been
Theophano.*

SECTION IV.—Easter Names.

The next day of the Christian year that has given a name is that
which we emphatically call Good Friday, but which the Eastern
Church knows by the title that it bears in the New Testament, the
Day of Preparation, Παρασκευή (Paraskewe), from πάρα (beyond), and
σκεύη (gear or implements).   Thence, a daughter born on that holy
day, was christened among the Russians Paraskeva; and the name
that has been corrupted by the French into Prascovie, and which is
called for short Pascha, is very frequent in the great empire, and
belonged to the brave maiden, Paraskeva Loupouloff, whose devotion
to her parents suggested Madame Cottin's tale of *Elizabeth, or the
Exiles of Siberia,* where the adventures, as well as the name, are
deprived of their national individuality in the fashion of the last
century.

The Passover was known from the first to the Israelites as Pasach,
or Pesach, a word exactly rendered by our Passover, and which has
furnished the Jews with a name not occurring in the Scripture—
Pesachiah, the Passover of God.

The Greek translators represented the word by Πάσχα. It is Pascha
likewise in Latin;   whence all modern languages have at least taken
some of their terms for the great feast of the Resurrection that finally
crowned and explained the Jewish Passover.

Italy inherits Pasqua; Spain, Pascua; Portugal, Pascoa, terms that
these two nations pass on to other festal Sundays.   Illyria has Paska;
Wales, Pasg; Denmark, Paaske; France, Pâques; and we ourselves
once used Pasque, as is shown by the name of the anemone or pasque
flower.

About 844, Radbert, Abbot of Corbie, put forth a book upon the
holy Eucharist, in honour of which he was surnamed Paschasius;
and, perhaps, this suggested the use of words thence derived for
children born at that season.

Cambrai has Pasqua, Pasquina, Pasquette, from 1400 to 1500.
Pasquale, Paschino, Paschina, Pasquier, Pascal, all flourished in Italy
and France;   and in Spain a Franciscan monk, named Pascual, was
canonized.   Pascoe was married in St. Columb Major, in 1452;
Paschal is there the feminine;   and many other instances can be
easily found to the further honour of the name.   There lived,
however, a cobbler at Rome, the butt of his friends, who gave his name
of Paschino to a statue of an ancient gladiator that had been newly

* *Church Festivals and Household Words;* Maury-Essaisin; *Les Légendes
Pieuses du Moyen Age; Die Stern du Weisen;* Routh; *Reliquia Sacra;*
Grimm; Brand; Stanhope, *Belisarius.*

disinterred, and set up in front of the Orsini palace, exciting the
waggery of the idle Romans by his likeness to the cobbler. Paschino,
the gladiator, proved a convenient block for posting of lampoons and
satires, insomuch that the generic term at Rome for such squibs
became paschinado, whence our English word pasquinade.

I have seen Easter as a Christian name upon a tombstone in Ripon
Cathedral, bearing the date 1813; but as I have also seen it in a
Prayer Book belonging to a woman who calls herself Esther, it is
possible that this may be a blunder of the same kind.

There was, however, soon after the Reformation, an inclination in
England to name children after the vernacular titles of holy days.
In 1675, Passion occurs at Bovey Tracey, in Devon ; another in 1712,
at Hemiock ; and Pentecost is far from uncommon in old registers.
At Madron, in Cornwall, in 1632, appear the masculine, Pentecost,
and feminine, Pentecoste ; and in Essex, an aunt and niece appear,
both called by this singular festal name, in honour of Whit Sunday.
In 1643, I find it again at St. Columb Major. It means, of course,
fifty, and is Greek.

Easter is called Λάμπα (the bright day) in Greek, because of the
lighting of candles that takes place at midnight in every church. Can
it be from this that the Eastern saint of the 10th of February, who
suffered at Antioch in Pisidia, was called Charalampios, Χαραλάμπιος,
a name which is still used in the Ionian Islands, and is imitated in
Russia as Kharalampia, or Kharalamm. Its component parts are καρα
(joy), and a derivative from λαμπάς (a torch) ; and we might explain
it either glad-light, or the joy of Easter.*

SECTION V.—*Sunday Names.*

Sabbath (rest), in Hebrew, distinguished the seventh day, set apart
from the service of the world in memory, first, of the cessation of the
work of creation, and next, of the repose of the Israelites after their
labours in Egypt.

While the Sabbath was still the sacred day, it does not appear to
have suggested any historical name, except that of the father of Joses
Barsabas, whose father must have been Sabas.   In 532, however, was
born in Cappadocia, Sabas, who became one of the most distinguished
patriarchs of the monks in Palestine ; and in 372, one of the first
converts to Christianity among the Goths, then stationed in Wallachia,
who had taken the name of Sabas, was martyred by being thrown
into the river Musæus, now Mussovi. The locality attached the
Slavonians to his name, and Sava is still common among them, as is
Ssava in Russia.

Whether Sabea or Sabra, the king of Egypt's daughter, whom St.
George saved from the dragon, was named with any view to St.
Sabas, cannot be guessed.   I have seen the name in an old English
register, no doubt in honour of the exploit of our patron saint.

* Kitto, *Bible Cyclopædia ; Church Festivals and their Household Words ;*
Grimm, *Acta Sanctorum ;* Pott ; Michaelis,

The day of rest gave place to the day of Resurrection, the Lord's day, as we still emphatically call it, after the example of the Apostles.

St. John called it Κυριακή ἡμέρα (the Lord's day), and in this he has been followed by the entire Greek Church, with whom Sundays are still Kyriakoi.

It seems to have been the translators of the Septuagint that first gave its highest sense to Κύριος (Kyrios), a lord or master, from the verb κυρέω (kyreo), to find, obtain, or possess.

St. Kyriakos, or, as Rome spelt him, Cyriacus, was martyred under Diocletian, had his relics dug up afterwards, and his arm given to the abbey of Altdorff, in Alsace. From him came the Roman Ciriaco and the French Cyriac, all of which may mean either "the Lord's," or "the Sunday child."

At the same time a little Kyriakos of Iconium, a child of three years old, fell, with his mother, Julitta, into the hands of the persecutors of Seleucia. The prefect tried to save the child, but he answered all the promises and threats alike with " I am a Christian," till, in a rage, the magistrate dashed his head on the steps of the tribunal, and his mother, in her tortures, thanked Heaven for her child's glorious martyrdom. Their touching story made a deep impression, perhaps the more from the wide dispersion of their supposed relics, which were said to have been brought from Antioch by St. Amator, to Auxerre, about the year 400, and thence were dispersed through many French towns, and villages, in which he was called St. Quiric or St. Cyr.

The ancient British Church became acquainted with the mother and child through the Gallic. Welsh hagiology owns them as " Gwyl Gwric ac Elidan ; " and Cwrig has been continued as a name in Wales, whilst, on the other hand, the child is equally honoured in his native East—by Russia, Armenia, Abyssinia, and even the Nestorian Christians. He is probably the source of the Illyrian names Cirjar and Cirko.

Kyrillos (Κύριλλος) fell to the lot of two great doctors of the Church —patriarchs, the one of Alexandria, the other of Jerusalem ; also to two martyrs, one a young boy, and thus it became widely known. The Welsh had it as Girioel, which really is nearer the pronunciation than our own Cyril, with a soft *C*. It is a name known everywhere,

English.	French.	Portuguese.	Spanish.
Cyril	Cyrille	Cyrillo	Cirilo
Italian.	German.	Russian.	Illyrian.
Cirillo	Cyrill	Keereel	Cirilo Ciril Ciro

but more in favour in the East than the West, and of honourable memory to us for the sake of Kyrillos Lucar, the Byzantine patriarch, the correspondent of Laud, and afterwards a martyr. Latterly fashion has somewhat revived it in England; and the feminine, Cyrilla, is known in Germany.

Probably, however, this is only the diminutive of kyrios (a master), and did not begin with a religious import.

The Latin equivalent for the Greek, Kyriake, was Dies Emera Dominica. The immediate derivation of this word is in some doubt. It certainly is from Dominus; but there is some question whether this word be from *domo* (to rule), a congener of the Greek δαμάω, and of our own *tame;* or if it be from *domus* (a house), a word apparently direct from the Greek δόμος, from δέμω (to build); another branch from that same root, meaning to rule or govern.

Dominicus, the adjective formed from this word, is found in the French term for the Lord's prayer, *l'Oraison Dominicale,* and it likewise named the Lord's Day, Dies Dominica; Domenica, in Italy; Domingo, in Spain; Dimanche, in France. The first saint, who was probably so called from being born on a Sunday, was San Dominico of the Cuirass, a recluse of the Italian Alps, whose mortification consisted in wearing an iron cuirass, which he never took off except to scourge himself. He died in 1024; and a still sterner disciplinarian afterwards bore the same name, that Dominico whom the pope beheld in a vision upbearing the Church as a pillar, and who did his utmost to extirpate the Albigenses; whose name is connected with the foundation of the Inquisition, and whose brotherhood spread wherever Rome's dominion was owned. He is saint for namesakes out of Romanist lands, but in these it occurs, and has an Italian feminine, Domenica; for short, Menica. Perhaps this likewise accounts for the Spanish Mendez and Mencia. This last may, however, be from Monica, the mother of St. Augustine, whose name has never been accounted for. It may be from some unknown language; but is sometimes supposed to be from *moneo,* to advise. Monique is rather a favourite with French peasants, and Moncha was Irish, but it has not been as common as it deserves.

Irish.	French.	Italian.	Spanish.
Domnech Dominic	Dominique	Domenico Domenichino Menico	Domingo Mendez
Portuguese.	Slavonic.	Hungarian.	Servian.
Domingos	Dominik Domogoj Dinko Dunko	Domokos	Dominic Menz Menzel

The Slavonians have, however, a name for their Sunday in their own tongue—Nedele; and have formed from it the Nedelco of the Bulgarians; the Nedeljko, Nedan, Nedo, and the feminine, Nedelijka and Neda, of the Illyrians.

I am aware of no other names from the days of the week, except the 'Thursday October Christian' of Pitcairn's Island, who was probably so called in recollection of the Man Friday.

All Saints' Day has furnished Spain with Santos; and France, or rather San Domingo, with Toussaint, unless this last be a corruption, or, perhaps, a pious adaptation, of Thorstein—Thor's stone, turned into All Saints.*

* Grimm; *Church Festivals and Household Words;* Butler; Rees, *Welsh Saints;* Facciolati; Michaelis.

PART V.

CHAPTER I.

SECTION I.—*The Keltic Race.*

WE now pass to a class of names whose associations belong almost entirely to the modern world, yet whose history is far more obscure than that of those on which we have previously dwelt.

From the Hebrew, the European family have derived their religion; from the Greek, their ideas; from the Roman, their laws; from the Teuton, their blood and their energy; but from the Kelt they have taken little but their fanciful romance. In only one country has the Kelt been dominant, and then with a Latinized speech, and a Teutonic name, testifying to the large modifications that he must have undergone.

Among the rugged moors and cliffs which fence Western Europe from the Atlantic waves, he did indeed preserve his freedom, but without amalgamation with other nations; and in lands where he fell under subjection, he was so lost among the conquerors as to be untraceable in language or feature, and with the exception of the Gaul, has bequeathed nothing of his character to the fused race upon his soil.

We trace the Hebrew nation with certainty from its majestic source; the Greek shines on us in a dazzling sunrise of brilliant myth; the Roman, in a grave, stern dawn of characteristic legend; but of the earlier progress of the wild, impulsive Kelt we have but the faintest indications.

Much as he loved his forefathers, keen as was his delight in celebrating the glories of his race, oral tradition contented him, and very strong was the pressure from the neighbouring nations before his bards recorded anything in writing, even the long genealogies hitherto preserved in each man's accumulated names. The beauty of their legends did indeed recommend them to the general store-house of European fancy, but though the spirit may be Keltic, the body through which it comes is almost always Teutonic.

SECTION II.—*The Keltic Languages.*

The Keltic nations used languages which showed that they came from the Indo-European root, and which are still spoken in the provinces where they remain. They have no really ancient literature, and were left at the mercy of wild tongues, so that their losses have been very great, and the divergence of dialects considerable.

The great and distinguishing feature of the entire class is their peculiar inflections, which, among other puzzling features, insert an aspirate after the primary consonant, so as entirely to change its sound, as for instance in an oblique case, *mor*, great, would become *mhor*, and be pronounced *vor*, to the eternal confusion of people of other nations, who, however the vowel or the end of a word might alter, always trusted to know it by the main syllable. A large number of guttural sounds distinguished these languages, and some of these were annihilated by the ensuing aspiration; but when spelling began, the corpses of the two internecine letters were still left in the middle of the word, to cumber the writer and puzzle the reader, so that the very enunciation of a written sentence requires a knowledge of grammar.

The vowels likewise sometimes change in the body of the word when it becomes plural, and the identification of plurals and of cases with their parent word is so difficult that few persons ever succeed in the study of Keltic, except those who have learnt it from their mothers or nurses, and even they are not always agreed how to write it grammatically.

The Keltic splits into two chief branches, so different that Cæsar himself remarked that the Gauls and Cimbrians did not use the same language. For the sake of convenience these two branches are called by philologists the Gaelic and the Cymric. The first is the stock which has since divided into the Gaelic of the Highlands, the Irish of Ireland, and the Manx of the little intermediate isle. In fact they are nearly one; old Gaelic and old Irish are extremely alike when they can be found written, and though they have since diverged, the general rules continue to be the same; and some of the chief differences may be owing to the fact, that while the Highlanders have adopted the Roman alphabet, the native Irish still adhere to the Anglo-Saxon.

The Cymric is still spoken in Wales and Brittany, and only died out a century ago in Cornwall. Welsh and Breton agree in so many points that the natives of either country are said to be able to understand one another, though they would be entirely unintelligible to an Irishman or Highlander. Indeed it may be doubted whether Greek and Latin are not more nearly akin than the two shoots of the Keltic tree. One great difference is that the *p* of the Kymric always becomes *k* or *c* hard in the Gadhaelic: thus *plant* or children in Wales, are the well-known Gaelic *clan*; *Paisg*, Easter, is *Cisg*; *pen*, a head, is *caen;* and the Cornish word *Pentyr*, the head of the land, or promontory, is the same as the Scottish *Cantyre.**

The Gauls had been completely Romanized in the South before they heard of Christianity. They gave up Greek and Roman idols rather than Druidism when they listened to the Gospel. It is thought that the first seeds were sown by St. Paul, and that afterwards the Eastern Church at Ephesus, under St. John, had much communication with them. Britain probably owed her first gleams of light to the imprisonment of Caractacus and his family at Rome; but however this might be, Gaul furnished hosts of martyrs in the persecution, and Britain did her part in testifying to the truth. Many districts long remained unconverted, however, in both countries. St. Martin is said to have completed the conversion of Gaul in the end of the third century, and in Wales St. Germain still found a host to baptize in the fifth century. Indeed, the predominance of heathen remains over Christian, have made antiquaries very doubtful whether Britain could have been by any means universally converted at the time of the fall of the Roman empire. It had, however, sent forth one great missionary, namely, St. Patrick, from the northern province of Valentia. He found a feeble Church in Ireland, but so enlarged its borders and won all hearts, that from his time that island was Christian in name, and filled with such clusters of hermitages and convents as to win its title of the Isle of Saints.

This Keltic Church, with its eastern traditions, was the special missionary Church of these little heeded times. From Ireland, St. Columba went forth to Iona, whence he and his disciples gradually converted the Picts; and though St. Gregory's mission laid the foundations of the polity of the Anglo-Saxon Church in Britain, there were the Scottish Aidan, the Welsh Chad, and Gallic Birinus doing the work quietly, in which the Roman monks had been less successful. From Ireland again, St. Columbanus, St. Gall, and many others set forth to complete the work of conversion in France and Switzerland, and many churches and convents regard as their founders and patrons, obscure Irish hermits forgotten in their own country. These have been the chief diffusers of Keltic names, being called after some hereditary native word, which their saintliness was to raise to high honour.†

SECTION III.—*Keltic Nomenclature.*

The Kelts were highly poetical and romantic in their nomenclature. In general their names were descriptive; many referred to complexion, and many more described either masculine courage or feminine grace

---

* Max Müller; *Encyclopædia Britannica;* Villemarqué, *Legoindec's Dictionary;* Haumer, *Chronicle;* Clark, *Student's Handbook of Comp. Grammar;* Prichard, *Celtic Nations.*

† Knight, *Pictorial History;* Mazzaroth; Knight, *Celt, Roman, and Saxon;* Grimm, *Deutsche Mythologie;* Jones, *Welsh Sketches; Irish Poems;* Montalembert.

and sweetness. But, unfortunately, the language is so uncertain, and its commentators are so much at war, that in dealing with these, after the well-criticized ancient tongues, is like passing from firm ground to a quaking bog, and in many cases there is but a choice of conjectures to deal with.

The names to be examined are of various kinds. First, the historical ones that have come through Latin writers, terribly disguised, but the owners of them certain to have existed. These are usually more Cymric than Gaelic, and Welsh and Breton writers find explanations for them. A few truly mythological ones will be considered with these, and placed according to the order—if order it can be called—assigned to their supposed owners in the pedigree of Brut, in which England used to believe on the word of Geoffrey of Monmouth, and the Welsh on that of their native chronicle of Brut. Then follow a most controverted collection, chiefly of the two Gaelic nations. They were the property of a set of heroes called the Feen, who are the great ancestry of the chiefs of the Scottish race in both islands, and who are said to have performed fabulous exploits at some distant period, which gains some sort of date from the poem representing Ossian, the last survivor of the band, as extremely miserable under the teaching of St. Patrick. The fact was probably that the floating myths of the Gael attached themselves to some real adventurous band, and the date is no more to be depended on than those of Geoffrey of Monmouth ; but it gives a point by which to arrange the names still in great part surviving both in Ireland and Scotland, though often confused with those imported from other languages.

After this follows the cycle of names made popular by the romances of King Arthur's court, which naturally find their place at the time of the fall of the Roman power in England. These, as far as they can be understood or interpreted at all, are Cymric, and some have become tolerably well known throughout Europe.

The different classes connected with one or other of these will nearly dispose of all the Keltic names worth notice. The remaining will chiefly belong to the saints, in which Wales, Brittany, and Ireland were particularly prolific. The odd thing is that all the Welsh saints were in some way or other of royal birth, so that the royalty of Wales must have been peculiarly pious. Brittany, likewise, had sundry hermits ; and Ireland deserved its title of the Isle of Saints, though, as will be seen, some of them were of a strangely Irish order, and regarded as strong cursing powers.

The Gaelic race had the remarkable custom of calling their children the servant, the disciple, or the votaress of the patron saint, and it is not till recent times that the prefixes Giolla, Maol, and Cailleach have been entirely dropped, and their traces are often remaining in appellations in Ireland and Scotland.

The name was entirely personal, not hereditary ; but the pride of ancestry caused the father's, grandfather's, forefather's names, to the remotest generation, to be heaped upon one head, connected in Welsh by *Mab*, or, as it was contracted, *Ap*.

The Welsh, about the fifteenth century, found these pedigree names unmanageable in contact with ordinary society, and contented themselves each with one ancestral surname for good. Some incorporated their Ap, as Pryce, Ap Rhys, Pugh, or Ap Hugh ; some, in English fashion, adding the possessive *s* to the end of the father's name, like the hosts of Joneses and Williamses; others took some favourite name from the roll of ancestry, or called themselves after their estates.

In Gaelic the word Mac, the son, or O, or *ua*, the grandson, connected the person with the ancestor whose name was chosen.

The Keltic taste in names was of the grand order, generally in many syllables, and lofty in sense and sound, much in the style of the Red Indian. Thus we find Brithomar, the great Briton ; Bathanat, son of the boar ; Louarn, the fox ; Carvilius, friend of power, among the Kymric nations of England and the Continent : and in less complimentary style, Mandubrath, man of black treason. This man of black treason was, in Britain, Avarddwy Bras, also called one of the three disgraceful men of Britain. It is said that Caswallon had murdered Avarddwy's father, and afterwards set out on what the *Triads* call one of the three unwise armaments, which weakened the force of the country. The cause is romantically described by the *Triads* to have been, that his lady-love, Flur, had been carried away by a Prince of Gascony to be presented to Julius Cæsar ; moreover, the *Mabinogion* says, he and his two friends went as far as Rome to recover her, disguised as shoemakers, whence they are called the three bold shoemakers of the Isle of Britain. The aid that he gave the Gauls does, in fact, seem to have attracted the notice of Cæsar, and the black treason was Avarddwy's invitation to the Romans. He was the father of Aregwydd Voeddog, whose second name, derived from victory, was certainly the same as Boadicea, though her deed identifies her with Cartismandua. Caswallon, or Cassivellaunus, as the Romans called him, is sometimes explained as Cas-gwall-lawn, chief of great hatred, sometimes as lord of the Cassi. The Gaels have many grand men's names, but, perhaps, have used the most poetry in those of their women. Feithfailge, honeysuckle ringlets ; Lassairfhina or Lassarina, flame or blush of the wine ; Lassair, or flame, the same in effect as the Italian Fiamma ; Alma, all good, a real old Erse name, before the babes of September 1854, were called Alma, after the Crimean river, which probably bore a Keltic name ; Bebhirn, or, as Macpherson writes it, Vevina, the sweet woman ; Essa, the nurse ; Gelges, white swan ; Luanmaisi, moon fairness ; Ligach, pearly. Yet thirst had her namesake, Ita ; Diédrè was fear ; Dorvenn, sullen ; Uailsi, pride ; Unchi, contention.

All of these, and many besides, have entirely fallen into desuetude, and all the Keltic countries have a practice of adopting names from their neighbours, supposed to answer to their own, but often without the slightest affinity thereto.

Thus Anmcha, courageous, is supposed to be translated by Ambrose ; Aneslis is rendered by Stanislaus ; Fachtna, is Festus ; Baothgalach, or rashly courageous, Boethius.

Corruptions must be permitted to our English tongues and throats, which break down at a guttural, so it is no wonder that Dorchaidha, or patronymic O'Dorchaidhe, should be sometimes turned into D'Arcy, sometimes D'Orsay, and sometimes into Darkey, which really translates the word ; and sometimes Darcy ; but it is rather hard when we have to read Archibald for Gillespie, and Edward for Diarmaid.*

* Villemarqué ; O'Donovan ; *Highland Society's Gaelic Dictionary.*

CHAPTER II.

SECTION I.—*Welsh Mythic Names.*

WELSH myths we say advisedly, for whether these were really Druidical myths or not, they have become so much disguised by Welsh bards, down to Christian times, that there is no knowing what was the original framework. Our concern is with the names connected with these traditions.

The primary personages of semi-divine rank in these traditions are Hu Gadarn, or the Mighty, the sun god, and his wife Ceridwen. It is believed that the two sacred islands of Iona and Mona were both originally Ynysgwaw Hu, the island of the worship of Hu. Others, however, say, that Iona was only I-thon, or isle of the waves.

The word Hu is not explained; but it has passed into a name in Wales and Brittany. Old French has the name inflected as Hue, Hues, Huon, and the feminine Huette; and the true Anglicized Welsh form is Hu or Hew, though it is now universally confounded with the Teutonic Hugh, from *hugur*, thought, with which it may be cognate, and the Welsh patronymic Ap Hu is always spelt Pugh.

The *Triads* speak of Aed Mawr, or Aedd, as father of Pridain, but he may have been either a title of Hu, or else the god himself. Aodh is, in fact, in sound and sense, closely related to the Greek $\alpha\iota\theta\omega$ (aitho), and our heat is of the same kin.

Dr. Meyer thinks this Aed Mawr of the *Triads* was the forefather from whom the Ædui mentioned by Cæsar were called, and further derives from him Cæer Aeddon, or Dun Aeddon, Dun Edin, or Edinburgh. Yet, on the other hand, it is a part of our English faith that Auld Reekie is our Northumbrian Edwin's burgh.

Aed, Aeddon, Aodh, Aedhan, were far more popular names than those derived from Hu. Aeddan is lamented by Aneurin as a British warrior slain among the victims of Henghist's treachery; and two Aoidhs reigned, the one in Connaught, the other in Scotland, in 570; and to the latter of these, called by Scottish historians Aidan, or Edan, they ascribe the foundation of their capital; but it was at that time in the possession of the Angles, and if called after any Aodh, it must have been after an earlier one. The Irish Aodh is said to have been about to expel the bards, but to have been prevented by the intercession of St. Columb.

At one time Ireland was afflicted with thirteen contemporary Aodhs; and at least two so called reigned in Scotland—Aodhfin, or the white, the Ethfine of historians, and Aoidh, or Eth, the swift-footed. So common was the name among the Irish that one hundred Aodhs and one hundred Aidans or Oédans were killed in the battle of Maghrath. The MacAodhas of Ireland were once many in number ; and became MacHugh or Magee ; in Scotland, Mackay ; or were sometimes translated into Hughson or Hewson. But the most interesting person so called is known to us as Aidan. He visited Wales and Scotland, became a monk of Iona, and then went forth as a missionary to the North of England. He was the friend of the admirable Oswald, free of hand, king of Deira, who used to interpet his Keltic speech to the Angle population ; and his gentle teaching won to the Church multitudes whom the harshness of former missionaries had repelled. He is reckoned as first bishop of Lindisfarn, and has left his name to sundry churches of St. Aidan. Aoidhne, or Eithne, was the Irish feminine once distinguished, but now disused.

Aidan is still a female name among some Welsh families.

Another Irish St. Aeddan, who was bishop of Ferns about the year 632, has a most curious variety of namesakes—some from his baptismal name, others from his pet appellation Móedóg, that is M'Óedóg, namely Ma Otdóg, my little Aodh. This strange custom of prefixing the possessive pronoun, first person singular, to the proper name of a saint was very general. Maodhóg, as it has since become, is still common in Wexford, where the Irish language has disappeared. It is pronounced and written Mogne, and is perpetuated in honour of the Saint of Ferns. Madog, or Madawc, was the usual form in Wales, where it has always been in great favour. Madawc, prince of Powysland, who died in 1158, in great favour with Henry II. The Latin translation of Aidan, Aideus, or Aidanus, has adhered to him in Basse Bretagne, but has there been cut down into Dé, St. Dé being the appellation of a village there, the church of which is dedicated to Mogne, is by Irish Protestants often Anglicized as Aidan, by the Roman Catholics as Moses.

The leek is said to have been used by the Welsh in the worship of Ceridwen, the wife of Hu. Afterwards a story rose that, in one of Cadwallawn's battles, his Welshmen marked themselves with leeks from a garden hard by, and the story was later transferred to the Welsh troops of the Black Prince in France.

Ced, or Cyridwen, shows no namesakes ; but buadh, or budd, victory, furnished for her the epithet of Buddug, or Buddud ; and, perhaps, she is the Boundonica mentioned by Dion Cassius as a Keltic goddess. Probably it was either as a victorious omen, or else in honour of her, that the name of Buddug was given to that fierce chieftainess of the Iceni, whose savage vengeance for her wrongs has won for her a very disproportionate fame, as much changed as her name, when we call it Bonduca, or, more usually, Boadicea. It has not met with much repetition, yet we have heard of a family so patriotic as to contain both Caractacus and Boadicea. Buadhach was, however, long a man's name in Ireland, and Budhic was one of the early Armorican princes.

Gwion, an unlucky dwarf, destroyed by Ceridwen, seems to have left his name behind him, whether it be as M. Pitre Chevalier explains it, *esprit*, sense, or be connected with the Welsh *gwyth*, and Cornish *gwg*, anger.

Aneurin mentions a knight named Gwiawn as having been slain in the battle of Cattraeth ; and Gwion is a knight of Arthur's court, figuring as Sir Guy among the knights of the Round Table, and furnishing Spenser with his Sir Guyon, the hero of the second 'Book of Courtesie' in his *Faerie Queen*.

Guy has since been a favourite name, but it has become so entangled with the Latin Vitus that it is almost impossible to distinguish the Keltic from the Roman name. It appears to have prevailed in France very early as Guy, Guies, Guyon, in the feminine Guiette ; and besides the Sicilian infant martyr, Vitus, obtained two patrons, St. Guy, the Poor Man of Anderlecht, a pilgrim to Jerusalem, who died in 1014 ; and the Italian, St. Guido, abbot of Pomposa, in Ferrara, who died in 1042. Both lived long after their name had become so popular, that it could not have depended upon them. Queen Matilda, in her Bayeux tapestry, labels as Wido, the Count Guy of Ponthieu, who captured Harold on his ill-starred expedition to Normandy, and thus she evidently does not consider him as Vitus.

Guy and Guido were both fairly frequent with us, until 'Gunpowder Treason' gave a sinister association to the sound of Guido Fawkes, and the perpetual celebrations of the 5th of November, with the burning of Guy Fawkes in effigy, have given a meaning to the term of Guy, that will probably continue long after the last tar-barrel has flamed and the last cracker exploded over his doom.

Guido and Guidone were the proper Italian forms, much used in the whole Peninsula, and appearing in Ariosto's poem in the person of Guidon Selvaggio, a rustic, uncivilized knight. From the sound it was long imagined that the names came either from *guide* or from *guidon*, a banner or ensign ; but there can be no doubt that either the Keltic Gwion or the Latin Vitus was their true origin.

Section II.—*Lear and his Daughters.*

Geoffrey of Monmouth made the eleventh of his kings, descended from Brute, to be called Leir, and live at Leircester, or Leicester, on the river Sore, somewhere about the time of the prophet Elisha.

He is one of the earliest authorities for the story of Lear and the ungrateful daughters, whom he calls Gonorilla and Regan. He gives the name of Cordeilla to the reserved but faithful daughter who could not pay lip service, but redeemed her father's kingdom when he was exiled and misused by her flattering sisters. It was a very remarkable conception of character, even thus barely narrated, without the lovely endowments with which we have since learnt to invest the good daughter. The sequel in Geoffrey's chronicle related, that after his kingdom was restored, old Leir died in peace at Leicester, and was buried by Cordeilla "in a certain vault which she ordered to be made for him under the river Sore, at Leicester, and which had been built originally under the ground to the honour of the god Janus; and here all the workmen of the city, upon the anniversary solemnity of that festival, used to begin their yearly labours."

He further narrates that Cordeilla was dethroned by her nephews, and committed suicide in despair. To this story adhered both the old ballad-monger and Spenser, in the history studied by Sir Guyon; but Shakespeare loved his sweet Cordelia too well to stain her with self-murder, and, though omitting all allusion to Christianity, made her in all her ways and actions a true Christian, and never perhaps showed more consummate art than in producing so perfect an effect with a person so chary of her words.

Whence did Geoffrey get the story which has produced such fruits?

Lear (*gen.*), Lir, is the sea. He is also a mythological personage, a god in the elder Irish belief, and father of Mänännán, the Erse Neptune.

Afterwards, later ballads humanized Lear, and made him the father of Mänännán, one of the Tuath De Danan, or early conquerors of Ireland, and Lord of the Isle of Man, which is said to be called after him. There is a tradition in Londonderry that his spirit lives in an enchanted castle in the waves of Magilligan, and that his magic ship appears every seventh year. Moreover, the daughters of Mänännán, granddaughters of Lear, were called Ainè and Aoiffè, and had a desperate quarrel about their husbands' excellence in hunting.

Wales, on its side, shows in the Isle of Anglesea a cromlech, called the tomb of Bronwen, daughter of King Llyr or Leirus. The tomb was opened in 1813, and an ancient urn, once probably containing ashes, was found there. It seems that a somewhat more substantial Llyr lived about the time of the Roman conquest, and was the father of Bronwen, who married the king of Ireland, was ill-treated by him, and received a box on the ear, which was one of the three fatal insults of the Isle of Britain. This lady is very probably the Bronwen of the cromlech; but the conjecture of the Rev. Edward Davies is, that in the story of King Lear, we may have the remains of an ancient myth.

It is certainly remarkable that the notion of Lyr, in connection with turbulent daughters or granddaughters, should be common to both Britain and Ireland. Mr. Davies explains Cordelia to have been originally Creirdyddlydd, the token of the overflowing, also called Creirwy, or the token of the egg. *Creir* is a token, the sacred article on which a man makes oath, whence it came to mean either a relic or a jewel. Creirdyddlydd might thus be the jewel of the sea, or the token of the flood. At any rate, Creirdyddlydd or Creirwy is a creation of ancient Welsh poetry, once mythical, the daughter of the sea, Llyr or Llud, on which Geoffrey seized for his history. Bronwen, or white bosom, is either another daughter of Lyr, or else Creirdyddlydd under another name, and is supposed to have been the British Proserpine. Both Bronwen and Creirwy are called Gwrvorwyn, man-maid, or

virago, and it does not seem impossible that here we see the origin of
Cordelia, Regan, and Goneril, as they have been adapted to English
pronunciation, the token of the overflowing, the fair bosom, and the
virago.　Surely these are the daughters of the ocean, rebellious and
peaceful.　Dynwen, too, is the white wave, the patroness of lovers;
and as we shall find by-and-by wave names are remarkably common
among the Welsh.

Lear is also called Llwyd, the grey, or the extended, a fitting title
for the sea, and which has passed on to form Lloyd, so common as a
Welsh Christian and surname, and adopted in England as Floyd.

Creirdyddlydd has due justice done her in the *Mabinogion*, where
we further learn that she remains with her father till the day of doom,
and that in the mean time two kings, Gwyn ab Nudd and Gwythir
mab Graidiawn, have a battle for her hand on every May-day.

Cordula is set down in Welsh and German calendars on the 22nd
of October as one of the 11,000 virgins, her feast following that of
St. Ursula.　It may be remembered that St. Ursula was said to be
Cornish; and that her only recorded companion should bear a Cymric
name, is in favour of some shade of foundation for her story.　Kordula
is in consequence a German name.　Kordula was a princess of Lingen
in 1473; and Michel and Kordel are two children in German household tradition so constantly falling into mishaps as to have become
a proverb for folly.

The Germans fancy Cordula is a diminutive of the Latin *cor*, a
heart; others have wildly made it the feminine of *Cordeleo*, lion
heart, and it has been confused with Delia, the epithet of Diana,
from Delos, her birthplace; but Creirdyddlydd is certainly its origin,
and remembering that in Welsh *d* is softened and aspirated by being
doubled, is not far from it in sound.　Cordelia is hereditary in some
Irish families; but is chiefly used for love of Shakespeare's heroine
of filial love.

Bronwen makes her appearance again in the romance of *Sir
Tristram*, under the name of Brengwain, the maid of Yseulte.
When the Lady Yseulte was sent from her home in Ireland, under
the escort of Tristram, to be married to King Mark, of Cornwall, her
mother entrusted a love potion to Brengwain to be given on the
wedding night.

Unfortunately, a tempest arose on the voyage, and, in the consequent exhaustion, "Swete Ysonde, the fre, asked Brengwain a drink."
And Brengwain, bringing the magic cup by mistake, caused the fatal
passion between Yseulte and the knight.

Even the "hound that was there biside, yclept Hodain," who licked
up the drops that were spilt of the philtre, became attached to the
knight and lady with the same magic love.

Bronwen or Brengwain has since been in use as a Welsh female
Christian name.

The names of the granddaughters of the Irish King Lear were
Aine and Aoidheal, a spark, and their dispute was whose husband
was the best hunter.　Aine means joy or praise, and also fasting.
Friday is Diah-Aoine, or fasting day in Irish.　Aine, the daughter of

Eogah-hal, was looked on as queen of the fairies of South Munster, and her abode was said to be Cnoc Aine or Knockany, the Hill of Aine, in county Limerick; Aoibhinn was queen of the fairies in Thomond or North Munster; Una, of those in Ormond.

Aine continued to be a favourite name in Ireland for many centuries; but in later times it has become the practice to Anglicize it as Anna and Hannah, and possibly Anastasia, though this may have come more directly from the Greek. In 705 reigned a Scottish king called Ainbhceallach the Good. He is turned by different authors into Arinchellar, Armkelleth, Amberkelletus, etc., and his right one is either joyful war, or agile war, or if with the *b*, ferocious war. He was too good for his savage people, and was dethroned at the end of a year, and is usually mentioned by the few historians, who name him, as Amberkelleth.

It is evident then that Aine had come to Scotland with other Gaelic names, and it is probable that this is the word that had come forth as Anaple or Annabell in Scotland long before the period of devotion to St. Anne. In 1158 Annabel Fitz Duncan, daughter to Duncan, Earl of Moray, carried the name into the Lucie family; Annabella of Strathern appears in 1244; Annaple Drummond was wife to King Robert III. of Scotland, about 1390; and thenceforth Anaple has been somewhat common in Scotland, while Anabla and Anabella are equally frequent in Ireland, and Annabella is occasionally used in England as Anna made a little finer.

Aoiffe was more generally used than Aine, but most likely is the origin of the Effie of Scotland, now always used as short for Euphemia, though the Highland version of this name is now Aoirig, or Oighrigh. In other places Aoiffe seems to have been turned into Affrica. In the beginning of the twelfth century 'Affrica,' daughter of Fergus of Galway, married 'Olaus' the Swarthy, King of Man, and her daughter 'Effrica' married Somerled, Thane of Argyle and Lord of the Isles, by whose genealogists she seems to have been translated into Rachel. Africa is still used as a female name in the Isle of Man and in Ireland. Aoiffe was the wife of Cuchullin in the Ossianic poetry, and Evir Allin and Evir Coma, properly Aoibhir Aluin and Aoibhir Caomha, the pleasantly excellent and pleasantly amiable, both appear there.

The recognized equivalent for Aoiffe was, however, Eva, beginning almost from the first Christian times, so that, until I found Aoiffe in such unquestionably heathen company as Lear and Mananàn, I had made up my mind that she was the Gadhaelic pronunciation of our first mother.

Eva is found in the oldest documents extant in Scotland, and high in their genealogies: Eva O'Dwhine carried the blood of Diarmaid to the Anglo-Norman Campbells; Eva of Menteith married one of the first Earls of Lennox; and Alan, the first High Steward of Scotland, married Eve of Tippermuir, and made her the ancestress of the Stuarts; about the same time that the Irish Aoiffe or Eva, for she at least is known to have borne both names, was being wedded to stout Earl Strongbow.

Aevin, or Evin, is occasionally found in the house of Kennedy, but

Eveleen is by far the most common form of both names in Ireland, and has held its ground unchanged. Eibhlin in Irish.

To our surprise, however, Aveline or Eveline make their appearance among the Normans long before the marriage of the Earl of Pembroke. Aveline was the name of the sister of Gunnar, the great-grandmother of William the Conqueror; and Aveline or Eveline was so favourite a Norman name that it well suits the Lady of the Garde Douloureuse in the *Betrothed*. Avelina de Longo-Campo, as the name is Latinized in old chronicles, married the last Earl of Lancaster, and was the mother of that heiress Avelina or Eveline, who, though short-lived and childless herself, carried to her husband, Edmund Crouchback, and the sons of his subsequent marriage, the great county of Lancaster, which made the power of the Red Rose formidable.

Eveline has never been frequent, but was never entirely forgotten in England, (for instance, an Eveline Elstove was baptized in 1539,) and was revived as an ornamental name by Miss Burney's *Evelina*. At present it is one of those most in vogue, but it ought not to be spelt with a *y*, unless it be intended to imitate the surname Evelyn, the old French form of the Latin *avellana*, a hazel. It was well that the tree-loving author of the *Sylva* should bear such a surname, and from him and his family, men have frequently been christened by it; but ladies do not follow the old Eveline of song and romance unless they use the true feminine termination.

It is curious that several Keltic names should have come to us with the Normans. They may either have been of the set interchanged with the Northmen at some pre-historical time, or old Keltic ones picked up from the Gallic inhabitants of Neustria, or from the Bretons on the border. In the present case, the latter supposition is the most likely, as the Scandinavians do not seem to have used Eveline. It may of course be after all a diminutive of Eve, but the alternate use of the initial *A* and *E* seems to contradict this, and identify it with Aoiffe, daughter of the Irish King Lear.

Section III.—*Bri.*

The root *brig*, meaning force or strength, is found in many branches of the Indo-European tongues. It is considered to be akin to the Sanscrit *virja*, strength, and is found in the Greek verb βρίθω (*britho*), to be heavy, or to outweigh, and the adjective βριαρός (*briaros*), strong. And thus it named the hundred-handed Titan, whom gods called Briareus, and men Ægeon, and who, in the Titanic revolution, was disposed of either in the Ægean Sea, or under Mount Ætna. Briennios, the surname of some of the eastern emperors, must have come from this root.

In the Keltic tongues it again appears in Irish as *bri* or *brigh*, force, or valour, and Bryn, height, answering to the Roman *virtus* (a near connection, as we shall presently see), and the old French word *brie*, peculiarly expressive of the gay, light Gallic courage, was a now forgotten legacy from the ancient population. Thence came Brenhin, Bren, or Bran, or, as the Romans made it, Brennus, a king or chief —well known for the forays on Italy, and capture of Rome.

Another Brennus was the leader of a division of the great host of Gauls, that, about B.C. 279, came out of Pannonia, and made a backward rush towards the East. One of their bands settled in Asia Minor, and were the parents of the Galatians; but Brennus was less successful. He marched upon Delphi, promising his followers the plunder of the Temple; but was totally defeated by the Delphians; and finding his army destroyed, and himself severely wounded, put an end to his own life.

Next time Bran comes to light, it is altogether in Welsh setting. The *Triads* and the prolific *Genealogy of Welsh Saints*, are the authorities for the existence of a prince of that name. Bran the Blessed, the son of Llyr Lledaith, and father of Caradwg, is, we are told, one of the three blessed princes of Britain, having brought home the faith of Christ from Rome, where he had been seven years as a hostage for his son Caradwg, whom the Romans put in prison after being betrayed through the enticement, deceit, and plotting of Cartismandua, or by her Welsh name, Avegwydo Foeddog, the daughter of Avarwy, who betrayed Caswallon. Her act is called by the *Triads* one of the three secret treasons of Britain.

Now Caradwg is, without a doubt, the Caractacus of Roman history, and the captivity of his family exactly coincides with the time of St. Paul's first journey to Rome. Moreover, as has been already shown under the head of Aristobulus, there is great reason to consider that Aristobulus, the friend of St. Paul, was the same as the Arwystli, whom the *Triads* commemorate as among their first missionaries. A farm-house in Glamorganshire, called Trevran, house of Bran, is pointed out as the place where Bran used to reside, and it is near Llanilid, which is considered as the oldest church in Britain.

Such is the British account of the father of Caradwg. The Roman account is, that Cunobelinus was king of the Silures, and husband of Cartismandua, queen of the Brigantes, and was a prosperous and powerful prince in league with the Romans.

Cunobelinus is in like manner a title, though not of man. Cûn is, as will be shown in due time, a chief or lord. Bel or Belin was the Keltic god of light and of war, in whose honour British coins were struck in the heathen days of Bran, whose own name the Romans thought they were reading on his coins. Beli also meant war, and more than one king was called from him.

Bran the Blessed may thus be our old friend Cymbeline, a name repeated in Cornwall, but from literature, not tradition. Cartismandua, or Aregwydd, is the wicked queen, and Caradwg one of the sons.

As to Imogen, the real charm of the play, no British lady either accounts for or explains her name; but in German genealogies we fall upon Imagina of Limburg, in 1400; and there are various other instances of the like, so that Shakespeare may be supposed to have heard of one of them, and adopted her as the heroine of the old story of the deserted and betrayed wife, which he so strangely placed at the court of the last independent British prince. Or Imogen may be a Shakespearian version of Ygnoge, daughter of Pandrasus, emperor of Greece, and wife of Brutus, according to Geoffrey of Monmouth. In Anne of Brittany's funeral oration, in 1514, her birth was deduced from this last.

Caradwg's own proper name comes from the same root as the Greek χάρις, grace, and the Latin carus, dear. It means beloved, and has the Breton form Keridak. Caer Caradoc, in Shropshire, retains the name of his camp. He had a worthy namesake in Caradawc Vreich-fras, or strong armed, called the pillar of the Kymry, and one of the three battle knights of Britain. Vreichfras means the strong arm, but the French trouveurs rendered it Brise-bras, the wasted arm ; and told of an enchanter who fixed a serpent on the knight's arm, from whose torture nothing could relieve him but that she whom he loved best should undergo it in his stead. His faithful wife offered herself ; the serpent was just about to seize on her, when her brother smote off its head with his sword ; but her husband thus never re-covered the strength of his arm ! Others, however, read Vreich-fras as Fer-a-bras, iron arm ; and thus, perhaps, from some Breton romance, was one of the Hauteville brothers called William Ferabras. Hence, again, did the French and Italian romancers name their fierce Moorish champion Ferraù, or Ferragus, the same who lost his helmet, and possessed the healing salve, valued by Don Quixote as the balsam of Fierabras !

Caradwg's wife, Tegan Euvron, or golden beauty, was mentioned by the Triads as one of the three fair ladies and chaste damsels of Arthur's court, possessing three precious things, of which she alone was worthy,—the mantle, the goblet, and the knife. Later romance and ballad have expanded these into the story of the three tests of the faithful wife ; and Sir Caradoc and his lady remain among the prime worthies of the Round Table.

In the twelfth century a saint named Caradwg retired from the world in disgust at the violence shown to him by his master, Rhys, prince of South Wales, on learning the loss of two greyhounds that had been in Caradwg's charge. He lived in various hermitages in Wales and left a well in the parish of Haroldstone, called by his name. Moreover, soon after his death, he was said to have suddenly closed his hand, in frustration of the designs of the historian, William of Malmsbury, who wanted to cut off his little finger for a relic. Our insular saints were decidedly of Shakespeare's opinion, and had no desire to have their 'bones moved ' or be made relics of.

Caradwg, Caradoc, and Keriadek continue to be used in Wales, Scotland, and Brittany.

Cara, friend, was sometimes prefixed to a saint's name by the Christian Gael, as Cara Michil, friend of St. Michael, as the name of his devout client, and thus arose such surnames as Carmichael.

This pursuit of Cymbeline and his family has carried us far from Bran the Blessed. Under this, his proper name, he stands forth in old Welsh romance as the original importer of the Sanc-greal. One very old and wild version says that King Bran brought from Ireland a magic vessel, given him by a great black man in Ireland, which healed wounds and raised the dead.

In the twelfth century the Sanc-greal had assumed its Christian character, and Bran the Blessed, as the first Christian prince of Britain, was said to have received it from St. Joseph of Arimathea, and guarded it to the end of his life. No wonder, therefore, that Brittany loved and honoured his name.

Bran was a Pictish prince, killed in 839, in battle with the Danes, and it is highly probable that St. Birinus, the Keltic apostle of Wessex, was another form of Bran.

Brian has been from very old times a favourite Christian name in both Brittany and Ireland, the first no doubt from the Christian honours of the blessed Bran, the second from the source whence he was named.

The great glory of Brian in Ireland was in the renowned Brian Boromhe, King of Leinster, or of the tribute, so called from the tribute, once shaken off by Ulster, but which he re-imposed. He defeated the Danes in twenty-five battles, and finally was slain in the great battle of Clontarf, on the Good Friday of 1014. Around that battle has centered a wonderful amount of fine legendary poetry on both sides.

Brian, or Bryan, is a very frequent Christian name, but according to the usual lot of its congeners, has an equivalent, *i. e.* Bernard, chiefly in Ulster, with which it has not the most distant connection.

Brien was always a favourite in Brittany, and is very common as a surname with the peasantry there. The Bretons, who joined in the Norman conquest, imported it to England. Two landholders, so called, are recorded in Domesday Book ; and during the first century of Norman rule it was far more common than at present, when it is considered as almost exclusively Irish. Some of our older etymologists have been beguiled into deriving it from the French *bruyant*, noisy.

The feminine Brennone is given in German dictionaries, but it, as well as Brennus, are there derived from old German, and explained as protection, which is clearly a mistake.

Brieuc was a Breton saint ; Breasal was once common in Ireland, and survives in a few families, but is generally turned into Basil, and sometimes to Brazil, in which shape the Manxmen frequently bore it.

Brîgh, or strength, is the most satisfactory explanation of Brighid, the daughter of the fire-god, and the goddess of wisdom and song, skill and poetry.

Cormac, king and bishop of Cashel, explains the word as a 'fiery dart ;' but this looks like one of the many late and untrustworthy interpretations of Keltic names.

Brighid was always a favourite female name in Ireland, and has become one of the very few Keltic ones of European popularity. This was owing to a maiden who was brought up by a bard, and afterwards became a pupil of St. Patrick ; and from a solitary recluse at Kildare, rose to be the head of five hundred nuns, and was consulted by the synod of bishops. She died in 510, and after her death, a copy of the Gospels was found in her cell, too beautiful to have been written by mortal hand, "with mystical pictures in the margent, whose colours and workmanship were, at first blush, dark and unpleasant, but in the view marvellously lively and artificiall."

It was long kept at Kildare, and a little hand-bell, such as was much used by the Irish missionaries, and which had belonged to her, and was, therefore, called Clogg Brighde, or Bridget's Bell, was exhibited to the devout, in both England and Ireland, until it was suppressed by a prohibition from Henry V., perhaps, because it tended to keep up a national spirit.

She was one of the patron saints of Ireland, and was regarded with such devotion, both there and in Scotland, that children were baptized as her servants, Maol Brighde, Giollabrid ; and to the present day, hers is the favourite name in Ireland.

St. Bride's churches are common, both in England and Scotland, and the village of Llanaffraid, in Wales, records her in her Welsh form of Ffraid. Bridewell was once the palace of St. Bride, and after its conversion into a prison, spread its sinister name to other like buildings. The Portuguese believe themselves to possess the head of St. Bridget at Lisbon, and have accordingly more than one Doña Brites among their historical ladies.

Sweden has also a St. Bridget, or rather Brigitta ; but her name is in her own tongue Bergljot, shortened to Berglit, and then confounded with the Irish Bridget. It unfortunately means mountain-fright, or guardian defect, though German antiquaries have twisted both Bridgets into *Beraht Gifu*, bright gift. Be that as it may, the Swedish Brigitta was a lady of very high birth, who, in her widowhood, founded an order of Brigittin nuns, somewhere about 1363, made a pilgrimage to Rome, and was greatly revered for her sanctity.

English.	Irish.	Scotch.	French.
Bridget	Brighid	Bride	Brigitta
Bride	Biddy		

Italian.	Portuguese.	Swedish.	German.
Brigida	Brites	Brigitta	Brigitta
Brigita		Brita	
		Begga	Esth.
		Bergliot	Pirrit
		Beret	

Lusatian.	Lettish.	Lith.	Lapp.
Brischia	Britte	Berge	Pirket
Brischa	Birte	Berzske	Pikka
	Pirre		Pikke

She named the very large class of Norwegian, German, and Swedish Bridgets or Berets, who are almost as numerous as the Irish.

SECTION IV.—*Fear, Gwr, Vir.*

The free days of the Kelt were fast ending. He fell before Roman discipline, though not without a worthy struggle.

In Cisalpine Gaul, Marcellus and Scipio themselves found Britomartus, or Viridomarus, king of the Boii, so worthy an antagonist that Marcellus, having slain him in single fight, dedicated his *spolia opima* in the temple of Jupiter Feretrius. In Spain, a Lusitanian hunter or shepherd, named Viriathus, carried on a guerilla warfare with the Roman legions for fourteen years. In Gaul, Cæsar mentions Virdumarus among his allies the Æduans, and says that their chief magistrate was termed *vergobretus*, and among his enemies, the Unelli and Arverni, he records Viridovix, Vergosillanus, and Vercingetorix.

The last chieftain was one of the most gallant men who struggled in vain against the eagles.

However, our concern is chiefly with his name. In fact, these *Virs* of Cæsar might have been placed in our preceding division, for they are from the same root, *bri*, or force, and still more resemble the Sanscrit *virja*, as well as the Latin *virtus* and *vir*. Exactly answering to *vir*, though coming in an independent stream from the same source, the Gaelic man is *fear*, plural *fir;* the Cymric is *gwr*, gen. *gyr*, plural *wyr*. Again, valour or virtue is in Welsh *gwyrth*, and *gwr* is the adjective for excelling.

Thus there can be no reasonable doubt, that the *ver* or *vir* of the Latin version of these Keltic heroes was a rendering of the *fear* of the Gael, or of the *gwr* of the Cymry, both not infrequent commencements ; and the double name of the hero of Cisalpine Gaul, Viridomarus, or Britomartus, brings us back to the original root. It may be that Britomartus referred to his great strength.

Vergobretus, the magistrate of the Ædui, is explained either as *Fear-co-breith*, man who judges, or *War-cy-fraith*, man placed over the laws ; or, taking *gwr* as excelling, and *brawd*, as justice, he would be excelling in justice.

Viriathus must be referred to *fear*, man, and, perhaps, to *aodh*, fire.

Vercingetorix himself may be translated into *Fear-cuin-cedo-righ*, man who is chief of a hundred heads ; and his cousin, Vergosillanus, is the man either of the banner or the spear, according as *sillanus* is referred to *saighean*, a banner, or to *saelan*, a spear.

Here, then, are the tokens of kindred between the Gauls of the continent and the Gael of our islands, for *Fear*, the frequent commencement in both Ireland and Scotland, is assuredly the word that Cæsar rendered by *Vir*, more correctly both in sense and sound than he knew.

Fearghus, man-deed, from *gus*, a deed, is the rendering of one of the most national of Gaelic names, though Macpherson makes it Fearguth, man of the word.

Bold genealogists place Feargus at the head of the line of Scottish kings, and make him contemporary with Alexander the Great. Another Fergus was son of Finn, and considered as even a greater bard than his nephew, Oisean. Poems said to be by him are still extant, in one of which he describes his rescue of his brother, Oisean, who had been beguiled into a fairy cave, and there imprisoned, till he discovered himself to his brother by cutting splinters from his spear, and letting them float down the stream that flowed out of the place of his captivity.

Fearghus, the son of Erc, a Dalriad prince, was, in 493, blessed by St. Patrick, and led the great migration of Scots to Albin, together with his brothers Loarn and Aonnghus, who each named their own district, while he reigned over the whole region of the Scots,—that around Argyle ; whither he had transported the stone of dominion, that sooner or later brought conquest to the race who possessed it. From these Fearghus or Farghy in Ireland, Fergus in Scotland, and the feminine Fergusiana still continue in use.

Fearachar is another Scottish form. Ferquard is given as prince of the Scots in Ireland, at some incalculable time ; and Fearchur or Ferchar was the king of the Scots just after St. Columbus' death. He is Latinized as Ferquardus ; and this was the name of an Earl of Ross in 1231 ; and as Farquhar has continued in favour in the Highlands. Feardorcha is the blind man. Fardorougha is an incorrect modern ism, and Ferdinand and Frederick the supposed equivalent.

Gwr, or *Wr*, is the Cymric form of the same word, and the parallel to Fergus among the Picts was Wrguist, or Urguist, a prince who lived about 800, and whose daughter was called after him, married the Scottish Eacha or Fergusiana, and thus led to the union of the two races under her descendant, Kenneth MacAlpin.

Gwrtigearn, excelling king, is a Silurian prince of doubtful fame. Through Latinism we know him as Vortigern. It would seem that when the usurpation of Maximus had involved the Roman empire in confusion, and left Britain without any legions to defend it against the robber nations round, that he made some attempt at a partial revival of national spirit ; but, failing this, entered into a treaty with the Anglo-Saxon invaders, and was thought to have betrayed the cause of his country.

What these doings were is another matter. We all know the romantic history of Vortigern's letter to Henghist and Horsa ; of his visit to the Saxon camp ; of Rowena and her cup ; of the Isle of Thanet marked out by strips of cow-hide ; and of the treachery of the Saxons at Stonehenge. There is nothing morally impossible in the story as it was dished up for modern history, and it used to satisfy our ancestors before they had found out that a small king on the Welsh border could hardly have dealt with Thanet, and, moreover, that the Teutonic immigration had been going on for many years past on the eastern coast.

As to the cow-hide and the massacre, they are said to be old Thuringian traditions ; and the Welsh seem to have either invented or preserved the story of the fascinations of Rowena.   At any rate, they named her ; for, alas for Saxon Rowena, there is nothing Teutonic in the word, and the Kymric form *Rhonwen*, white skirt, betrays its origin.   Rhonwen, or Bradwen, is the name by which she is called in the *Gododin*, a poem ascribed to the bard Aneurin, and, perhaps, containing some germs of truth, though its connection with the Stonehenge massacre is hotly disputed.

CHAPTER III.

GAELIC NAMES.

SECTION I.—*Scottish Colonists.*

THE strange and wild beliefs that prevailed regarding the original settlement of ancient Ireland, have left strong traces on the names still borne by the population, both there and in Scotland.

We need not go back quite to Adam's great-grandson, and the wicked race that sprang from him, and all perished, except one giant, who took up his abode in a cave, and there lived till he was baptized by St. Patrick ; nor to Fintan, who was changed into a salmon during the time that the flood prevailed, and afterwards gave rise to the proverb, " I could tell you many things were I as old as Fintan." A bard, so called, was said to have existed, and a poem is attributed to him, which gives a very queer account of the first settlers, though he does not there claim quite such a startling experience.

Fomorians, Fir Bolg, men dwelling in caves, or, more probably, ravaging men, and Tuath De Danan, *i.e.* chiefs, priests, and bards, are all conducted in turn to Erin by tradition and poetry ; but none equal in fame or interest the tribe called Milesian, from whom the purest Irish blood is supposed to descend.

The favourite legends start this famous colony from the East, where Phenius, the head of the family, was supposed to have taught the Phœnicians letters, and left them his name ! His son, Niul, not to be behindhand with him, named the Nile, having been sent on an embassy to Egypt, where he married Pharaoh's daughter ! Whether her name was Scota or not, authorities are not agreed ; but all declare that it was her father who was drowned in the Red Sea, and that a subsequent dispute with the Egyptians caused either Niul or his son to migrate to Spain.

It is this Niul, or Niale, to whom the whole legion of Niales are to be referred. The name, from *niadh*, means a champion, and was probably carried backwards to the ancestor from the various Neills, who thought they might as well claim the Nile as their namesake.

Neill of the Nine Hostages, was one of the greatest of the ancient heroes ; he was the last but one of the pagan kings of Ireland, and himself most unconsciously imported the seed of the Gospel, for it was his men who, in a piratical descent on the Roman colony of Valentia, carried off the boy who, in after days, was to become the Apostle of Ireland,—one of the many slaves by whom the Gospel has been extended. Neill of the Nine Hostages was killed by an assassin about the year 405 ; but his family, the Hy Neill, or children of Neill, became one of the leading septs in the North of Ireland. Of them the story is told, that on going to settle on the Ulster coast, one of them resolved to take seisin of the new country by touching the shore before any one else, and finding his boat outstripped, he tore out his dagger, cut off his right hand at the wrist, and threw it on the beach, so that his fingers were the first laid on the domain. Such, at least, is the tale that accounts for the O'Neill's war-cry, *Lamhdearg Aboo* (Red hand set on), and for the red hand on the shield of the O'Neills and of Ulster, afterwards given by James I. to the knights baronets, whom he created as 'undertakers' of the new colony of English, which he wished to found in Ulster.

Ireland thus frequently used Neill, or Niall, and Scotland Niel, as it is there spelt, but it is far more surprising to meet with it among the Scandinavian races. It is evidence that there must have been some considerable intercourse between Ireland and the North before the days of the piracies of the historical ages. The old Irish legends constantly speak of Norway as Lochlinn, or the land of lakes, and show visits taking place between the inhabitants ; and there are names to be found in both countries, borrowed from one another, too far back to be ascribed to the Norse invasions.

In the *Landnama Bok*, the Domesday Book of Iceland, no less than three Njals appear, and the Njalssaga, the history of the noble-spirited yet peaceful Icelander, who, even in the tenth century, had never shed blood, and preferred rather to die with his sons than to live to avenge them, is one of the finest histories that have come down to us from any age. Njal's likeness to the contraction Nils, has caused many to suppose that it also is a form of Nicolas, but the existence of Nial both in Ireland and Iceland before the conversion of either country contradicts this. Nielsen is a frequent Northern patronymic, and our renowned name of Nelson probably came to us through Danish settlers.

The Northmen apparently took their Njal to France with them, and it there was called Nesle or Nêle. Chroniclers Latinized it as Nigellus, supposing it to mean black ; and in Domesday book, twelve landholders called Nigellus appear, both before and after the Conquest, so that they may be supposed to be Danish Niels, left undisturbed in their possessions.

Nigel de Albini, brother to him who married the widow of Henry I., must have been a genuine Norman Niel ; and through the numerous Anglo-Norman nobles who were adopted into the Scottish peerage, this form was adopted in addition to the old Gaelic Nial, or as a translation of it, for the young brother of Robert Bruce is called by both names, Nigel and Nial. At present this Latinized Normanism of the old Keltic word is considered as peculiarly Scottish, chiefly because it has been kept up in that form in old Scotch families.

Fergus, Loarn, and Aonghus are said to have been the three brothers who led the migration from Erin to Caledonia, and trans-

R

ferred the name of Scotland from one isle to the other in 503, and
Loarn and Angus gave their names to two districts in Scotland.

Anguss was indeed a popular name both in Scotland and Ireland.
It comes from the numeral *aon,* one ; it also conveys the sense of pre-
eminence, means excellent strength, and it is generally pronounced
Haoonish in Gaelic. Irish genealogists make Aongus Turimheach
king two hundred and thirty-three years before the Christian era ;
and we are afterwards told of another Aongas, king of Munster, who
had a family of forty-eight sons and daughters, of whom he gave half
to St. Patrick to be monks and nuns. In Hanmer's *Chronicle,* King
Arthur visits Ireland and converses with King Anguish, which
painful title is precisely that which Henry VIII., in his correspondence, gives his brother-in-law, the Earl of Angus.

Angus is specially at home in Scotland, but there it has been
called Hungus and Ungus, likewise Enos, and is now generally
translated into Æneas, the christened name of many a Scot who
ought to be Angus ; and the Irish are too apt to change it in the
same way.*

Section II.—*The Feen.*

A remarkable cycle of traditions are cherished by the Gaelic race
regarding a band of heroes, whom they call the Fiann, or Fenians,
and whose exploits are to them what those of Jason, or Theseus,
were to the Greeks.

Scotland and Ireland claim them both alike, and point to places
named after them and their deeds ; but the balance of probability is
in favour of Ireland, as their chief scene of adventure, although they
may also have spent some time in Morven, as their legends call the
West of Scotland, since the Gaelic race was resident in both countries,
and kept together in comparative union by its hatred to the Cymry in
both. This supposition is confirmed by the semblance of a date that is
supplied through the conversion of the last survivor of the band by St.
Patrick, which would place their era in the end of the fourth century,
just when the migrations of the Scots were taking place, supposing
these to have lasted from about A.D. 250 to 500. Still, the Fian may
be only one of the ancient imaginations of the Gael, and either never
have had any corporeal existence at all, or else, genuine ancient
myths may have fixed themselves upon some forefathers, who under
their influence have been magnified into heroic—not to say gigantic—
proportions.

These tales, songs, and poems lived among the story-telling Highlanders and Irish, unnoticed, until the eighteenth century, when
the Scottish author, James Macpherson, perceived that they contained
a mine of wild beauty and heroic deeds, and were, in fact, the
genuine national poetry of his race.

He put his fragments together into the books of an epic, and

* Hanmer, *Chronicle; Ossianic Society's Transactions;* Taylor, *Hist. of
Ireland ;* Dasent, *Nialsaga ; Highland Society's Dictionary ;* Ellis, *Domesday
Book.*

wrought up the measured metre of the Gaelic into a sort of stilted English prose, rhythmical, and not without a certain grandeur of cadence and expression ; moreover, he left out a good deal of savagery, triviality, repetition, and absurdity ; and produced an exceedingly striking book, by expanding the really grand imagery of the ancient bards, and, perhaps, unconsciously imparting Christian heroism to his characters.

There had been some unscrupulousness from the first. Either from nationality or ignorance, Macpherson had entirely ignored the connection with St. Patrick, and made his heroes altogether Scottish, though passing into Ireland ; and when a swarm of critics arose, some questioning, some mocking, he did not make a candid statement of what were his materials, but left the world to divide itself between the beliefs that the whole was Ossian's, or the whole Macpherson's. Had he been truthful, he would have gained high credit, both as poet and antiquary ; but he brought on himself the reputation of an impostor, his literary talents have been forgotten, and the poems themselves are far less regarded than they deserve.

Be the truth what it may, the names of the Fianna were in constant use long before Macpherson was heard of.

In Ireland and West Scotland, the early poems represent Finn and his friends performing high feats of prowess.

Finally, the Feen either invaded Ireland, or became obnoxious to the natives, and were set upon at the battle of Garristown, or Gabhra, pronounced Gavra, loud shouting. The last survivor of them was the poet Oisean, or Ossian, as he is now called, who was said to have lived till the coming of St. Patrick, and to have been taken into his monastery, where old Irish poems show him in most piteous case, complaining much of fasts, and of the " drowsy sound of a bell."

SECTION III.—*Finn.*

Leader of the Fianna, and bestowing on them their very title, stands the great Fion, the grand centre of ancient Gaelic giant lore ; his full title being Fionn Mac Cumhail, pronounced Coul. Fingal, the name the Scots have known him by ever since the time of Barbour, is really a confusion of Faingall, the toilers of the Gaul.

There is no doubt of the meaning of *fion*. It is the same with the Cymric Gwynn, or Wynn, and like them signifies white, fair, or clear, as in the name of Lough Fyne.

One very remarkable feature in the history of Finn is that the same meaning of white attaches to it in ancient or poetical Scandinavian, though not in the other Teutonic languages ; nor is the name found in any Teuton nation but the northern ones, except that in the Saxon chronicle, Finn is Odin's fourth forefather, whereas he is his grandfather in the *Edda*.

In the great Anglian poem of *Beowolf*, Finn is king of the Frisians, but is conquered by the Danes, strangely enough, under Henghist ;

R 2

another poem, called the *Battle of Finnsburh*, records the strife—
Finn lost half his kingdom, but the next year he killed Henghist ; then
being set upon by the other Danes, lost his crown and life. It is
likely that, old as the poem is, it has been much altered, and that it
really existed before the Anglian colonization of our island ; indeed,
there is reason to suppose that it was in memory of the burgh of this
Frisian Finn, that Finsbury manor in the city of London acquired
its name.

Finn is a giant in Norway, compelled by the good Bishop Laurence
to erect the church at Lund, after which he was turned into stone by
way of payment, wife, child, and all, as may still be seen. Again in
Denmark as a trolld, he did the same service for Esbern Snare,
building Kallundborg church, on condition that if his name was not
guessed by the time the church was finished, his employer should
become his property. As in the German tale of *Rumpel Stitzchen*,
the danger was averted by the victim, just in time, overhearing this
amiable lullaby in the hole of a rock—

> "Be still, my babe, be still,
> To-morrow comes thy father Finn,
> Esbern's heart and eyes for a toy thou shalt win."

Next morning Esbern saluted Finn by his name, as he was bringing the last half-pillar, whereupon he flew away, pillar and all,
wherefore the church only stands to this day on three pillars and
a half !

Finn alone, and in combination, is rather a favourite in the North.
The *Landnama-bok*, which gives the Icelandic genealogies from the
settlements there in the ninth century down to the middle of the
thirteenth, has five men named Finnr, two, Finni, and three ladies
called Finna ; and in the three countries in the mainland it has been
equally common, even to comparatively recent times, when Finn
Magnusson was one of the chief authorities for Scandinavian antiquities. Among the compounds of the name, the Swedes have Finngaard,
which their pronunciation contrives to make sound like Fingal, with
what is called the "thick *l ;*" and in modern times it is so spelt in
allusion to Macpherson's hero. The name Finnketyl, or Finnkjell,
with the feminine Finnkatla, is explained as the cauldron or vessel
of some semi-divine Finn. Kettles are rather common in the North,
but almost always belong to some divinity of high rank. Finn has
his weapons, as Finnbogi, or Finbo, a white bow ; Finngeir, a white
spear ; his sport, as Finleik, white game or reward ; his forest, as
Finnvidr, or white wood ; as well as his guardianship, as Finn-vardr,
or white ward, all represented in northern nomenclature, in a manner
analogous to those of the national deities.

All this makes it highly probable that Finn was an idea borrowed
from the Gael by the Norsemen, especially as the hammer of Thor is
sometimes to be heard in Scottish legend resounding in the hand of
Finn. Fionn is still a name in Ireland, but in English is translated
into Albany; and in Scotland Fionnlaoch, white soldier, has become
Finlay.

There are many other Keltic names connected with Finn in the sense of white, such as Finghin, or the fair offspring, which became Finian or Fineen ; and as such was the name of two saints, one a friend of St. Patrick, and that teacher of St. Columb, who, when Columb had written out the Psalms from a book lent by him, claimed the copy on the plea that it was the offspring of his manuscript. Nevertheless, St. Columb took care that St. Finan should be duly revered in Scotland, where he has various churches, and one royal namesake, for probably he was the real original of the Finnan, whose reign is placed B.C. 134.   Another St. Finghin is patron of Ulster, and left his name to be a favourite in the families of M'Carthy, O'Sullivan, and O'Driscoll, until Finghin M'Carthy Anglicized himself as Florence, in which he has ever since been imitated by his countrymen, though the change did not bring him much good fortune, as his enemies represented that his alias showed sinister intentions ; and for other more definite misdeeds, he was thirty-six years imprisoned in the Tower of London.   It was a mistake in Lady Morgan to make Florence M'Carthy a woman, for Florence and Flory in Ireland were always men.   We do find a Florence mentioned as contemporary with St. Patrick ; but this is doubtless meant as a translation of Finghin.

The ladies, however, have not been behindhand in spoiling their derivative from Fionn.   Fionn-ghuala, or white shoulder, was a tough-looking name enough, though no one need complain of it as Finnuala, as it actually is spoken, still less as Fenella.   Early Keltic maidens used it frequently, and it is found in all manner of shapes in genealogies. In the clouds at the opening of Scottish history, we find Fynbella, or Finella, recorded as the cruel Lady of Fettercairn, who, in 994, killed King Kenneth III.

Another Fynbella was Lady of the Mearns in 1174 ; Finvola is found in the M'Leod pedigree twice in the fourteenth and fifteenth centuries.   The Macdonnells called her Finwald in 1497.   Finvola and Finola thickly stud the Irish pedigrees ; and it was perfectly correct in Scott to make Fenella the name of the little wild dumb sprite, whom he placed in the Isle of Man as a daughter of the house of Christian.   In almost all its original homes, however, Fenella has been discarded, having been ousted by its supposed equivalent, Penelope (a weaver), and only in a few Irish families is it still retained, and then in the form of Nuala.   In Scotland it has turned into the well-known Flora or Florie.

The other feminine forms of Finn have entirely passed away.   They were Finbil and Finscoth, white blossom and white flower, answering to the Blanche-fleur of Romance, which it is possible was really meant as a translation ; Findelvh, fair countenance ; Finnabhor, of the fair eyelids ; Finni, the fair ; and Findath, fair colour.

SECTION IV.—*Cu, Cun, Gal.*

We have treated the name of Fionn alone, because that is, comparatively, plain sailing, while the second syllable of the name by which we call him is beset with interminable perplexities.

If he was only Fingal, it would be easy enough to translate him by 'white courage;' but unluckily we know that this was a Lowland contraction, used indeed in Barbour's *Bruce*, in the fourteenth century, but not the original form. He was Finn Mac Cumhail; or, according to Hector Boece, in 1526, Finn, *filius Cœli*, Finn, the son of Heaven; thus making him—as every mythic worthy from Hercules to Arthur has been made—an astronomical parable.

In the first place, it may be observed that Cumhail is in pronunciation nothing but Coul, or Coyl. That murderous letter *h* has destroyed the *m*, and itself into the bargain, and their only use is to testify to what the etymology of the word has been.

Here we unite with the other branch of the language in a most curious manner, for Col, Coel, or Coll, was a highly mythic personage in Kymric legend, connected with the original population of Britain.

He is one of the three great swineherds of Britain, in the *Triads*, the other two being Pwll and Tristram; also, he is one of those who conferred benefits upon Britain, and appears in company with Hu Gadarn.

The title of the swineherd is accounted for in the Welsh tale of a sow called Henwen, the old lady, who was placed under his charge, and came swimming straight for Britain, with Coll holding by her bristles, wherever she swam. There were predictions that Britain would suffer harm from her progeny, and Arthur therefore collected his forces to oppose her landing; but at Aber Tarrogi she came to the shore, and at Wheatfield in Gwent she laid three grains of wheat and three bees, whence corn and honey are the great pride of the district. At Dyved she produced a barleycorn and a pig, to the subsequent benefit of Dyved beer and bacon. She favoured Lleyn with rye, but on Snowdon she bestowed the wolf and the eagle, and on Mona a kitten.

Without going back, like Mr. Davies, to make the sow either into the ark, or a Phœnician ship, it is worth observing that there are traces in Ireland of some pig myth. There is a famous poem called *The Hunting of the Pig*, resulting in its being slain at Muckamore; and *muc*, a pig, and *torc*, a boar, are constantly found in old names of places, as if the swine cult had been of a higher kind than that at present received by the species.

Not wholly substantial is the next British Coel-ap-Cyllin, who with Bran the Blessed, and his own son Lleurig, makes up a triad of promoters of Christianity in Britain.

We are scarcely sure of more than his existence; not quite that he left his name to Colchester, and far less that he is the father of the Empress Helena, the mother of Constantine.

Col or Gall was the name of a companion of St. Columbanus, and, like him, one of the great missionary saints of Ireland, who finished the imperfect work of conversion of the Kelts, scattered in the borders of France, Germany, and Switzerland. His name of St. Gall is still attached to the great monastery near the Lake of Constance.

The prefix *cu* is, in its primary meaning, a dog, and is thus declined: *cu* (nom.), *con* (gen.), *coin* (dat.); thus showing its kindred with the Sanscrit *çvan*, Greek κυων (cyon), and Latin *canis*, the *chien* of France, and *cane* of Italy ; *hund* and *hound* elsewhere.   Only the land of the magnificent wolf-hound would have made his designation (elsewhere a term of scorn) into the title of the brave warrior, and thence into that of a chieftain.   And so again it is the Kelts of Britain that transmuted the mungoose and snake of the Indian legend into the faithful dog and wild wolf of Bedgelert, the grave of the hound.   Caleb, and an occasional Danish Hund, have alone else-where endured the name of the most faithful of animals; but in Gaelic it is a most favourite prefix.   By the author of the *Annals of Ulster*, it is literally translated *Canis*, making us wonder whether, in the Scala family, Cane, so famous in Dante's time, could have been a rendering of some ancient Celtic Cu.

Conn, when standing alone, as in the case of Conn of the Hundred Battles, means wisdom.

Several of the most distinguished Fenians have this prefix, and have handed it on to a great number of successors.   Conghal would seem to have been the proper name of Finn's father ; and, in Mac-pherson's poem, a Congal reigns over Ulster, as many a Congal assuredly did both before and after his time.

Connal, or Connel, a name sometimes said to mean friendship, is given to one of the Ossianic heroes, who makes a great figure in Mac-pherson's epic, and is said to have named Tirconnel.   The name continued in great favour, and the popular tales of the Highlands describe a certain ingenious Conall, whose adventures are a most curious mixture of those of Ulysses and Sindbad the Sailor, and are related in the same way as those of the Three Calenders and other worthies in the *Arabian Nights*.   History says that Congal Claen, king of Ulster, slew Suibne, king of Ireland, but was then attacked and defeated by Domnall II., Suibne's successor; that he then fled to Donald-brec, or the Freckled, king of the Scots, and brought him to Ireland to be defeated at Magrath, in 637.   An Irish saint, called Congal, founded the Great Abbey of Ben-chor, in Ulster, answering to Ban-chor, in Wales, and thus formed the nursery of the great missions of the Irish Church in the sixth century.

Conan of small renown, as Macpherson calls him, was an unfortun-ate Fenian, who always served as the butt of the rest, and is called in other legends Conan Maol, the bald.   He is in character a good deal like the Sir Kay of Arthur's court.   The M'Connans now have borrowed the English names of Kenyon and Canning.   His name comes to light in the Cymric branch, in the person of the British Conan, or Kynan Meriadech, who is said to have led a migration of Britons to Armorica, and to be the patriarch of the Dukes of Brittany. Of him is told the pretty tale of the spotless ermine, that took refuge under his shield, and was spared by him, its skin thenceforth forming the cognizance of Brittany, with the motto, *Malò mori quàm fœdari*.

He is also said to have been the intended husband of St. Ursula ; and, at any rate, suggested the name of many a Conan among the Breton princes, until the father of the unfortunate Constance, a name very possibly given as a supposed feminine to Conan, since Constantine has devoured all manner of varieties of *cu* and *con*, and thus occasions the numerous occurrences of this imperial designation as labels to the grim portraits in the hall at Holyrood, who, after all, look more like Roman Constantines than Caledonian Congals, Conaires, or Conchobars.

Connchobhar is also translated as Cornelius and Charles. Here *conn* means strength, and *cobhair*, aid, or if the spelling ought to be Conchobhar, it would be wolf-dog aid, and it is a word as variously rendered by those who wish to retain its native form as by those who try to change it into an ordinary name. Macpherson calls it Conachar, and thence we have the assumed name of the unfortunate young chieftain whom Sir Walter Scott placed in the deadly fight between Clan Chattan and Clan Kay, to exemplify the struggle between constitutional timidity and fear of shame. Conchabhar, who reigned in Scotland in 847, and Cunechat or Conquhare, who was Maormar of Angus in the tenth century, are both forms of Connchobhar, which in the North-East of Ireland is vulgarly called Crogher and Crohoore. The last is said to be the best representation of the spoken word; but Connor is the usual version, and much the most euphonious to English ears; but then it is said also to represent Connaire, one endowed with strength, *aire* being a word added to form an adjective, and Conmor, also in use in the days of the Fenians. Indeed, Ireland had many royal Connors, one dignified as the Great; but Conchobar, Conmor, and Connaire, are all confused in them.

Constantine is used in the Maguire family as a rendering of Cú Connacht, the hound of Connaught; Munster's hound is Cú Mumhan; Cashel's, Cú Chaisil. The river Shannon has Cú Sionnan; the mountain has Cú-sleibhe; and, strangest of all, there is Cugan-mathair, hound without a mother. Cú-Mhidhe, hound of Meath, is simply pronounced Cooey; but in the O'Kane family has been turned into Quentin, and it may be concluded that a similar process in Scotland changed the hound of Meath into the Latin fifth, and accounts for the various Quentins.

Meath Cuchullin is the name of the hero with which Macpherson's epic opens : "Cuchullin sat by Tara's wall, by the tree of the rustling leaf." His name is explained in the note, to mean, the voice of Ullin or Ulster; Gath Ullin, voice of Ulster; but Ullin does not mean Ulster at all. It was not the hero's original name; but when young he killed a wolf-hound belonging to Culain, the smith of Ulster. He answered the owner's complaints by saying, "I will be your hound," and thus obtained the nickname of Cú Culain, Culain's dog. Cuchullin was a great hero, and a Gaelic proverb, "as strong as Cuchullin," is still in use. To Cuchullin belongs the Keltic version of the story of the single combat between the unknown father and son, only recognized too late by the tokens left with the mother. In Persia and Ireland the son is killed; in Greece, the father; in Germany alone the conclusion is happy !

As to the MacCuinns, they have dignified themselves as MacQueen in Scotland, while their cousins in Ireland from O'Cuinn have become Quin.

SECTION V.—*Diarmaid and Graine.*

Of all the heroes of the Feen, Diarmaid, whose name means free man, was one of the most distinguished, and though not brought in by Macpherson, his legend bears the same sort of relation to the main cycle, as does the story of Orlando to the Court of Charlemagne, or that of Lancelot to the Round Table.

Grainne was the daughter of Cormac MacArt, king of the fifth part of Ulster, who built at Tara for her the Grianan of one pillar, or royal palace. She was a lady of extremely quick wit, and gained the heart of Fionn by her answers to a series of questions, which tradition still preserves.

Fionn met with the usual fate of uncles in romance, for his nephew, Diarmaid, fell in love with her too, and was the more irresistible, as he had a beauty spot, which made every woman who saw it fall in love with him. The young pair fled away together, and there is an extremely long poem on their adventures and mutual affection, but fate at length overtook Diarmaid. A great hunting took place, at which all the Feen were present ; in the course of which they came on the track of a venomous boar, whose back was sixteen feet long, and soon after they found some shavings of wood made by Diarmaid in cutting out dishes with his knife. Having thus discovered his retreat, Fionn summoned his rival, and commanded him to join in the hunt, in hopes that he would thus meet his death ; but Diarmaid killed the animal without receiving damage. Fionn then remembered that Diarmaid, like Achilles and Siegfried, had a fatal spot in his foot, and desired him to measure the boar by pacing it against the hair. One of the bristles went into the fatal spot, and Diarmaid fell dying ; he asked for some water, and Fionn was bringing him some from the stream between his hands, when he thought on Grainne, and let it run through. Diarmaid died, and his corpse was brought home to his wife, whose lamentation is given as a separate poem. Diarmaid was also called Doun, the brown, and the clan descended from him were the O'Duine. The heiress of this line, Aoiffe or Eva, married Gillaspick Campbell, of an Anglo-Norman family, and Campbell has ever since been the Lowland surname of the great clan ; but in the North they are still the sons of Diarmid ; and their crest, the boar's head, is in memory of the fatal hunting.

Diarmaid continued in use both in Scotland and Ireland ; and in historical times it was Diarmaid, king of Leinster, who acted the part of Paris, and ruined his country by the abduction of Dervorgil of Meath ; and then, when forced by the superior king to give up the lady, revenged himself by calling in Earl Strongbow and the English.

Diarmid, or, as it is commonly called, Dermot or Darby, is still common among the Irish. Where the saying about Darby and Joan arose, I cannot discover. Darby is the form of Diarmid in Limerick and Tipperary ; Jeremiah, strange to say, is used for it in Cork and Kerry. Napoleon, in his enthusiasm for the Ossianic poems of Macpherson, named two of his heroes therefrom, but Diarmaid Murat died in childhood.

Grainne's name has been equally popular with that of her lover. Ancient Irish ladies constantly use it ; the most celebrated being Grainne O'Maille, a notable sailor chieftainess of the south-western coast, whence she once sallied forth to pay a friendly visit to Queen Elizabeth ; and when the two high-spirited women were together, the semi-barbarian was more than a match for the civilized queen.

Graine was soon after translated into Grace ; indeed, the piratess was also called Grace O'Malley ; and ever since, Grace has been a favourite national name in Scotland and Ireland, wherever Graine has been used ; it has been accepted for its English meaning and pleasant sound, and is now very frequent.

SECTION VI.—*Cormac.*

Cormac is a name that makes a great figure in the Ossianic poems, and perhaps the son of *Corb, i. e.*, a chariot, that is, a charioteer. Cormac, king of Ulster, was the young ward of Cuchullin ; and another Cormac, called Cairbar, or the strong, was the father of a lady called Morna, or more properly, Muirne, who when one lover returned from battle, announcing that he had slain his rival, demanded his sword stained with the blood, and then took revenge by plunging it into his breast, and finally killed herself with it. A still more misty Cormac figures in ancient pedigrees, as having been choked by the bone of an enchanted salmon ; and Cormac Cas is a more remote ancestor of the O'Briens than the great Brien Boromhe himself.

Another Cormac is named in Irish calendars, as an abbot of eminent sanctity in the days of St. Columba. He is further thought to have visited Iona, and at home enjoys the credit of having endowed the sept of the Hy Muireadach with "prosperity of cattle, the gift of eloquence, success in fosterage, the gift of good counsel, and the headship of peace and protection." His name has since been common in Ireland.

Cormac used to be barbarously spelt Cormick and Cormuck, and the MacCarthy family have substituted Charles for it. There is a long Icelandic poem on a hero named Kormak, who, though his parents and brothers have Norse names, evidently had Milesian blood as well as name, for he is described as having dark eyes and hair, with a fair skin. He was an admirable warrior and poet, but was the victim of hopeless love for a lady named Steingerda.

Cairbre, strong man, is likewise one of the Ossianic names, as well as a soubriquet of Cormac. Cairbre again is reckoned as the first of the Milesians to settle in Ulster ; and another Cairbre, son of Niall of the Nine Hostages, bequeathed his name to the district now called Carbury.

Cairbre appears as the Irish sovereign who was the greatest foe of the Fenians, and commanded at the battle of Gabhra, in which their force was broken ; and the son of Oisean, the grandson of Fionn, the beloved Osgar, was treacherously slain, by a thrust in the side, by Cairbre himself. The tears shed by the great Fionn were for his grandson Osgar, and for his faithful dog Bran ; and a great quantity of poetry has clustered round the death of this young hero. Oscar Bernadotte, another of Napoleon's Ossianic godsons, recently sat upon the Swedish throne, though amongst us, this, like others of the Fenian names, has descended to dogs. It is explained as the bounding warrior, and the MacOscars, in Ireland, have been turned into Cosgrove and Costello.

The like fate has befallen the object of Osgar's love, Malvina, as Macpherson calls her. The name is a mere invention of his own, formed perhaps from Maol, a handmaid. It has been adopted by French women to such an extent, that Malvine is one of the regular Parisienne's names, and it has further travelled to Germany. Thus Osgar and Malvina, though with few namesakes in their own country, are the only Fenians who have been commemorated in continental nomenclature.

Múirne means affection, and when Anglicized as Morna, is considered as a Highland name.

Section VII.—*Cath.*

Universal among the Kelts is Cath or Cad, a battle or defence, such a prefix that is sure to flourish in every war-like nation.

Cathuil, a derivative of Cath, is a great chieftain attended by three hundred followers ; and Cathal, as the name became, continued in use among the O'Connors, who translate it as Charles. The favourite hero there was Cathal Crobhdearg, red-handed, who fought hard against the English invaders ; and, therefore, was described by them as a blood-thirsty ruffian, and by native historians as pious and amiable, probably being both characters in turn. His name was probably the parent of the Scottish surname, Cadell ; but a Welsh saint, named Cadell, a battle-defence or shield, lived in the twelfth century. He had been a fierce warrior, and a great enemy to the English ; but during his recovery from some severe wounds, he repented, went to the Holy Land as a penitent, and finally became a monk, and the patron of many a Cadell besides.

Cathbarr means tumult of battle. Cathbarr was so renowned a chief, that to strike his shield with a spear was the summons to his clan to arm. The Welsh made great use of the same prefix. Cadwallon, apparently from *cadw*, to defend, has always been common among them. Cadwallon was the brother of the Madoc of Southey, and a much earlier Cadwallon was the father of Cadwaladyr, or battle-arranger, regarded by the two parties much as Cathal was ; for by the Saxons, Ceadwalla, as they call him, the slayer of the good Edwin and Oswald, is regarded with unmixed horror, while his own Cymric countrymen revere him as a glorious patriotic prince, second only to Arthur, and worthy of saintly honours ; indeed he was canonized by Pope Sergius in 688, and is surnamed the Blessed.

Cadwaldr in Breton, and Cadwalladyr in Welsh, continue to the present day. Cadwallader is also used in the Highlands, though, perhaps, this may be a blunder for some Gaelic Cath.

Saints of this name were numerous. Among them was Cedd, as his adopted people called him, the Good Bishop, whose Keltic ecclesiastical habits were so distasteful to the fiery Wilfred of York, and who finally is revered at Lichfield as "good St. Chad,"-a form in which his appellation lingered among the midland peasantry. The grandfather of Cadwalladyr was Cadvan, whose Latin epitaph calls him "Catamarus, *rex sapientissimus*," and whose name means battle-horn. Another Caduan, or Cadvan, was a hermit who migrated from Brittany to live on the coast of Caernarvonshire, on the isle called Bardsey by the English, and Ynis Eolli, Isle of the Current, by the Welsh. It was reputed a place of so much sanctity, that it was called the Rome of Britain ; and so many saints were buried there, that it was a saying of the bards—

> " Twenty thousand saints of yore,
> Came to lie on Bardsey's shore."

Cattwg, or Cadoc, was of princely blood, founded a monastery, and trained the veritable bard, Taliessin.

The Greek Adelphios was translated by the Welsh into Cadffrawd. Sir Cados is one of gentle Enid's enemies, in the French romance of her constancy ; but Cado, her son, in Welsh pedigree, swells the roll of saints. Cadfar, or stout in battle, is almost certainly one of the Armorican contributions to the Paladins of Charlemagne, in the shape of Sir Gadifer, the Don Gayferos of Spanish ballad and of *Don Quixote*.

Section VIII.—*Fiachra*.

Fiachra, or Fiaghra, is, as the Fiach is in Irish, a raven. Fiachere MacFhinn is a son of Fingal, who does his part among the traditions of the Fenians ; and another Fiachra was the father of the last pagan king of Ireland, who, as Erse lore relates, reigned over Erin, Albin, and Britain, and as far as the mountains of the Alps. He succeeded his uncle Niall of the Nine Hostages, in 405, and went to the Alps to revenge his death. Being still a pagan, he demolished a tower of sods and stones sixty feet high, in which lived a saint, eleven feet from the light, and was accordingly cursed by the saint, and killed by a flash of lightning ; but his servants put a lighted sponge in his mouth to imitate his breath, by way of concealing his death for some time.

Fiachra was the name of a hermit who left home to seek for solitude in France, and lived at Brenil, about two leagues from Meaux. He particularly applied himself to the cultivation of his little garden, and has ever since been considered as the patron of gardeners ; an l his austerity was such, that no woman was allowed to come within his precincts. He died about 670, and his relics began to obtain a miraculous reputation, which increased so much, that, though little known in his own country, France is full of churches dedicated to him.

Anne of Austria was particularly devoted to him ; she thought the recovery of her husband, and the birth of the great Louis XIV. himself, were due to his intercessions ; and she made a pilgrimage to his shrine, remembering so well his objections to womankind, that she never attempted to cross his threshold, but knelt before the door.

It does not appear, however, that the name of Fiacre was adopted by any one in deference to this devotion, except, perhaps, the Fiak of Brittany. All it did was to pass to the first hackney-coaches of Paris, which, from being used as a commodious mode of going on pilgrimage to the shrine of St. Fiacre, received the appellation they have had ever since. It is a whimsical concatenation that has named the *fiacres* of Paris after the misty raven of the race of Fingal.

Rín means a seal or sea-calf in Gaelic. Ronan is the derivative. He is a hero whose death is lamented in the Ossianic poetry, and his name was afterwards borne by a large number of Irish and Scottish saints, from whom came Ronan in Scotland, Ronayne in Ireland, once with the feminine Ronat.*

SECTION IX.—*Names of Complexion.*

Names of complexion were very frequent among the various branches of Kelts, often as mere affixed soubriquets, but growing from thence into absolute individual names. *Dhu* and *ciar*, the black ; *dorchaid*, the dark ; *dearg* and *ruadh*, red ; *don*, brown ; *boid*, yellow ; *finn*, white ; *odhar*, pale ; *flann* and *corcair*, ruddy ; *lachtna* and *uaithne*, green ; *glas*, which is blue in Wales, green in Ireland, and grey in the Highlands ; *gorm*, blue ; *liath*, grey ; *riabhach*, greyish, have all furnished their share of names and epithets.

Dougall and Dugald have been from time immemorial Highland names, and, together with Donald, serve as the national nickname of the Gael among the Lowlanders. Dowal is used in Ireland. Donald is the Anglicism of Donghal, brown stranger, an early Scottish and Irish name, and likewise of Domhnall, which is probably really the same, though the Irish glossographers translated it a proud chieftain, and now have turned it into Donat and Daniel, or Dan.

Donald is reckoned as the first Christian king of Scotland.

To Beath, life, may be referred Betha, an old hereditary English name, and the Latinism of Bega or Begga, for a saint, called otherwise Hien or Hayne. She was of Irish birth ; but about 620, was imported by some of the Keltic missionaries of the North of England, and St. Aidan consecrated her at Whitby as the first nun in Northumbria. Leaving St. Hilda to govern there in her stead, she founded the abbey, known by her English name of St. Bees, and at present serving as a university. A French St. Begga, whose mother was Northumbrian,

* O'Donovan; Macpherson; Maitland, *History of Scotland;* Cosmo Innes ; *Saturday Review;* Butler.

was wife to a man whose strange destiny was to be, first, Maire du Palais, then, Bishop of Metz, and lastly to be killed in the chace. After his death, she founded a monastery, which is considered by some to have been the germ of the admirable institution of *béguines*, who did the work of sisters of charity in the Netherlands long before the French order was established by St. Vincent de Paul. Some, however, deduce them from a priest at Liege, called Lambert le *bégue*, or the stammerer. Begga was probably imported by the Danes to Scandinavia, where it is still in use, though there it may be a contraction for either Bergljot or Brigitta. The Venerable Bede himself, the father of English history, called Beda in Latin, is referred to the Welsh Bedaws, another form of the word *life;* but it has been more usual to explain his name by reference to the Teuton verbs, meaning to bid or to pray. However, that several Keltic forms did prevail is certain, especially among the churchmen of the northern counties.

Macduff no doubt was so called from Dubhoda, Maormar of Fife. Another Duff had exchanged the Gaelic Maormar for the English Earl, in 1115, and Dubican was Maormar of Angus, in 939.

Among ladies the Irish had Dubhdeasa, dark beauty, Dubhchob-laith (pronounced Duvcovla), or black victory, and Dubhessa, or black nurse. Duvessa O'Farrell died in 1301 ; and this same appellation Spenser must afterwards have heard in Ireland, when, struck, no doubt, by the *du* at the commencement sounding like *two*, as did the other Irish name Una resemble *one*, he called his emblem of false-hood, or perhaps of the Church of Rome, the false Duessa, while he gave the title of Una to his lovely personation of the one truth, the one true undivided Church, the guide of the Red Cross Knight. Irish antiquaries assure us that Una means dearth or famine ; but it hardly suits this etymology. Una is queen of the fairies in the county of Ormond, in which character she appears in one version of the story of the soldier billeted on a miser. The man was amazed at his hospitable reception and entertainment, as he thought, by the avaricious squire in question, until morning disclosed that the fairy queen Una had raised the mansion and provided the supper, but from the prime cow in the miser's herd.

Una has continued in use among the Irish peasantry, though much corrupted, being often pronounced Oonagh, and Anglicized as Winny, the contraction of Winifred, the English version of the Welsh Gwenfrewi.

The female Christian name of Douglas, which belonged to one of the unfortunate wives of Queen Elizabeth's Earl of Leicester, was either a free version of one of those varieties of 'dark ladyes,' or else was one of the first specimens of a surname converted into a Christian name, perhaps in compliment to Lady Margaret Douglas, the niece of Henry VIII. and mother of Lord Darnley. Douglas was, without doubt, a territorial designation from the dark vale and stream of Douglas ; but the heralds and genealogists of the gallant lineage of the bleeding heart made out an ancestor, 'Sholto Dhu Glas' (see the dark grey man), and then Sholto was adopted as a name in the Douglas family, and crept from thence to others. I have found no instance of it before the seventeenth century in looking through the peerage of Scotland, and the probable derivation of the word would be *sioltaich*, a sower.

Duncan was either Donnachu, brown chief, or Donngal, brown stranger, both which names were rife among the Scots, and Duncan has so continued ever since. Duncan and Donald both occur as Keltic slaves in Iceland, in the Saga of Burnt Njal; and, perhaps, not only the Irish, but even the saintly Scottish David, may have been at first an Anglicized Domnhall.

Don stands alone as a name in Hanmer's list of Finn's warriors; Donnan was an Irish name, and Donchada became Donoghoe, sometimes even now baptismal, but best known as the O'Donoghoe, the great visionary horseman of Killarney.

The word is really the same as our *dun*, though that has now come to express a misty dark grey, while *don* evidently means brownhaired, as in the feminine Duinsech. Don, as it stands at the end of the name of 'The O'Connor,' simply shows that he is the head of the brown branch of that sept, which anciently split into brown and red—O'Connor Don and O'Connor Roe, like the black and red Douglases of Scotland.

Roe is the Anglicism for *ruadh*, the colour that goes by the same title in all our cognate tongues, from the Greek ροδος to the Gadhaelic *ruadh*, and Cymric *rud, rhud*. It plays the chief part in nomenclature in Ireland and Scotland, where the true undiluted Gaels are divided between the black and the red.

The Irish Ruadri, Ruadhan, Ruadhaic, the Scottish Ruaridh, and Welsh Rhydderch, have all alike disguised themselves as Roderick, which is in each case supposed to be the full name of those who in ordinary parlance call themselves Rory or Roy.

In Welsh myths we meet with Rhwddlwan Gawr, the red bony giant, and in Merddhyn's time we come upon Rhydderch Hoel, or the liberal, the champion of the Christian faith, who was the friend of St. Columba, restored St. Kentigern to Glasgow, and was promised by the former that he should never fall into the hands of his enemies, but should die with his head on his pillow—a promise that a Saxon long after would have scorned. He was a discourager of Druidism, and is reviled by Merlin. His name may come from *rhydez*, the exalted.

Several less shadowy kings reigned in Wales, the most distinguished of whom united all the three principalities till the year 877, and was called Rydderch Mawr, or, as it is barbarously called in our histories, Roderick Maur; much resembling what has been done with Roderick Dhu.

Dearbhforgail, or Derforgal, is translated by the Four Masters, 'purely fair daughter;' but later critics make it 'the true oath,' from *dearbh*, an oath, and *fior-glan*, true.

Dearbhforghal was a very tough name for the genealogists, and they had a good deal of it, for it was very fashionable in the twelfth century both in Scotland and Ireland, and was turned into Dervorgilla and Dornadilla by the much tormented chroniclers.

Lachtnan, from the Erse *lachtna*, green, is less easily accountable, unless it meant fresh and flourishing. It is now turned, in Ireland, into Loughnan, and more often into Lucius. The Scottish name so like in sound Lachlan or Loughlan, is however more probably from *laochail*, warlike.

Glas, grey, blue, or green, changes its meaning wherever it goes; but Glasan, in Irish, is its only Christian name, though it was a great epithet in all its countries, and has resulted in many a surname of Glass, besides the Highland Maglashan.

Cearan, or Ceirin, from *ciar*, black, was the name of one of the twelve Irish bishops whom St. Patrick consecrated. He betook himself to solitude in a place surrounded with bogs in Ireland, called from him Saiger, or Sier Kieran; but a tribe of disciples followed him, and a monastery arose; so, in search of loneliness, he fled to Cornwall, where he lived in a cell, and taught the inhabitants so much, that they ascribed to him even their knowledge of mining; and the 5th of March, his day, was considered as the tinners' holiday, in honour of their patron saint. His name, however, following the rule of the Cymric *p* for a Gaelic *k*, has turned into Pirin, or Perran, and is, in this form, not yet lost among the Cornish miners. His cell had a church built over it, called St. Pierans in Sabulo, or in the sand, and now Peranzabuloe. And in the sand it is, for it was absolutely choked by drifting sands, and abandoned in favour of a new one. In 1835 it was disinterred, and found to be a very curious specimen of ancient architecture. Another Ceiran was the patron of the Scots who first came from Ireland; and left his name to many a Kilkeran on the west coast. He is sometimes called St. Queran.

Cear is the soubriquet of Caoinnach I. of Scotland, who was killed in 621, after a reign of three months. The meaning of the epithet is questioned in his case, some calling it *ciar*, black; others, *cearr*, left-handed. The king himself rejoices in many varieties of name,— Caoinnach, in Irish, Coinadh; then, again, Conchad, Connadh, Kinat, and Cinead; till, finally, it has settled into the national Scottish Christian name of Kenneth in the Lowlands, Caioneach, in the Gaelic, denoting a fair and comely, or mild-tempered or peacable man.

Caoin and Caomh are closely related, and both mean kind or fair. Caoimghin was that Irish saint who is commonly known as Kevin, and owns one of the seven churches of Glendalough, as well as the cave, whence a very modern legend, versified by Moore, shows him rejecting Kathleen's visit by hurling her into the lake.*

Section X.—*Feidlim, &c.*

Feidlim was a very early Irish name, meaning the ever good, and Feidhlim Reachtmar, or the lawgiver, gained himself high reputation early in the second century, from which time Feidlim flourished in

* O'Donovan; Macpherson; Maitland, *History of Scotland;* Cosmo Innes; *Scottish Surnames; Saturday Review;* Butler; *Highland Society's Dictionary;* Pugh; Crofton Croker; *Irish Legends;* Chalmers; Hayes, *Irish Ballads.*

Ireland as Felimy or Felim, until a fashion arose of spelling it like a Greek word, Phelim, and then one Sir Phelim O'Neill, who was deeply implicated in the great Popish massacre of 1641, changed his name to Felix.   He was seized by the English army and condemned, but was offered his life by Cromwell if he would inculpate King Charles, and on his gallant refusal, was executed.   His new name caused the Irish poet M'Gee to exclaim—

> "Why when that hero age you deify,
>   Why do you pass *infelix Felix* by?"

A later Phelim O'Neill, in the last century, who made the same change, and called himself Felix Neele, was indignantly addressed in a Latin epigram :—

> " Poor paltry skulker from thy noble race,
>   *Infelix Felix*, blush for thy disgrace."

Felim once had a feminine Fedlimi, now either forgotten or transmuted into Felicia.

Tadhg is translated a poet, and was always a favourite in Ireland, where it has degenerated into Teague, Teige, or Thady, and then has been translated into Timothy, Thaddeus, Theodore, Theodosius, according to the fancy of the owner, though Tim is perhaps the most usual.

Mathew is in like manner the Anglicism of Mathghamhain, pronounced Mahoone, or Mahon, and meaning a bear.

Here again we meet with that universal Amal, as in the Roman Æmilii and Teutonic Amaler, and probably like them originally meaning work, though the direct meaning of *Amuil* in Gaelic is now, a hindrance, possibly as increasing labour.   Amalgaid was a good deal in use in the elder times.   The seven sons of Amalgith are said by Nennius to have been baptized by St. Patrick, and the race formed a sept called the Ui Amalghaid, who left their designation to the barony of Tir Awlay, in Ireland ; while their Scottish cousins became the memorable clan Macaulay, the sons of labour.   Awlay is the genuine Anglicism, not entirely disused in Scotland ; but in Ireland, intercourse with the Danish conquerors led to the substitution of Amlaidh, as the Erse spelt the Danish Anlaff, ancestor's relic, the same name as Olaf, and now this is likewise called Auley.*

SECTION XI.—*Names of Majesty.*

Foremost among these names of greatness must stand *tighearn*, a king, a word of most ancient lineage, recurring in the Greek *tyrannos.*

Tighearnach was an Irish saint, who flourished at the end of the fifth century, and whose dish is still preserved at Rappa Castle, in

* O'Donovan ; Macpherson ; Nennius ; Munch ; *Highland Society's Dictionary.*

Tirawley, by the name of Mior Tigearnan, or the dish of St. Tiernan. Tigearnach became common among Irish princes, and even appears in English history, when Tigearnach O'Rourke was robbed of his wife. It was long in dying out among the Erse population, and remains as a surname in the form of Tiernay.

Tigern was also used by the Cymry. Vortigern, as has already been shown, was Gwrthigern, the excelling king, and his far braver and better son was Kentigern, head chief ; whence he is sometimes called Categern, in modern Welsh, Cyndeyrn.

Kentigern in the North, Cyndeyrn in Wales, was the name of an early Pictish saint, who recalled his countrymen from Pelagianism, and is regarded as the apostle and patron of Glasgow. Persecution obliged him to take refuge in Wales, where he founded the church of Llandwy, being guided, as saith the legend, to the spot by a milk-white boar, which ran before him, and on arriving at the spot began to stamp and root up the ground with his tusks. Returning to Glasgow, the saint thence sent missionaries to Iceland, who no doubt were the teachers of the few inhabitants whose descendants were long after found there by the Norse settlers, and called by them *Papa*, from the title of their priests, a title still lingering in many a bay and islet of the Hebrides, attesting that there the Culdee clergy had been owned as the fathers of their flocks. After a custom that does not seem to have been uncommon among the Keltic saints, Kentigern used every night to sing through the whole Book of Psalms, standing up to his neck in water. He obtained for himself the epithet, Mwyngu, or Munghu, the amiable, by which he is best known in his own city, and which has named both it and a large number of the inhabitants and of his other countrymen, one of whom, namely, Mungo Park, has made it memorable.

Wales had a feminine St. Kentigern, perhaps named after him ; perhaps derived from the Irish Caintigern, or fair lady.

Cean, head, the first syllable of the saint's name, is found in all the Keltic tongues, forming many geographical terms, generally in the form of *can* or *ken*.

Either this or *cian*, vast, was the Irish name Cian or Kean, hereditary in the O'Hara family, but often supposed to be short for Cornelius. So common was it once that fifty Cians were killed in the battle of Magh Rath.

Tuathal, lordly, turned into Toole and O'Toole, are his descendants, and the feminine, Tuathflaith, is entirely lost. The ladies had several of these majestic names ; Uallach, the proud ; So-Domina, good lady, which must have had a Latin origin ; Dunflaith, lady of the fort ; besides Mor, which the Scots are pleased to translate by Sarah, and the Irish by Mary and Martha, though it really means a large woman. Morrigu had been the goddess of battle among the Tuath de Danan.

Martha, Maud, and Mabel, are employed to distinguish Meadhbh, Meave, or Mab, one of the very oldest and most famous of Irish names. It would be most satisfactory to take it from *meadhail*, joy ; but this is far from certain, and it may come from an old comparative of *mor*, great. But Mirth is analogous with the meaning of Ainè, the other fairy queen; and *mear*, or merry, has furnished another Irish name, namely, the masculine Meaghar or Meara. Meadhbh was the daughter of Eochaid Freidhleach, king of Erin, as it is said, A.M. 3922, and was so brilliant a heroine of Irish romance, that Congal Claen bids the men of Connaught, her husband's kingdom, to "Remember Meave in the battle." Afterwards, like other favourite Irish heroines, she became queen of the fairies; and some of the Irish settlers must have carried tidings of her to England, when Shakespeare, Drayton, and Ben Jonson made Queen Mab our own peculiar possession, if knowing how to make the best use of her establishes a claim. Meave, or Mab, has not entirely lost ground among the Irish peasantry, though generally it has an equivalent.

Toirdelvach, tall as a tower, or, more properly, tower-like, must have been taken from those riddles of Ireland, the mysterious towers, scattered throughout the island, and generally supposed to have been erected in the earliest period of Christian art, if art it may be called.

Toirdelvach was king of Connaught at the time that Dermot M'Morough carried off Devorgoil, and as supreme king of Ireland he punished the offender; nor was it till after his death that the invitation to Earl Strongbow was given. In English history, he is usually called Turlough, the later form of the name, which is still in some use, though more often turned into Terence, which has been oddly borrowed from the Latin dramatist to translate the tall Irishman.

Sealbh, cattle or possessions (for in Gaelic they are the same; just like *pecus* and *pecunia*, *vieh* and *fee*, cattel and chattels), is the origin of Sealbhach, pronounced Selvach, owned by two kings of the Scots, and of the feminine Sealbhflaith, lady of possessions, now become Sally.*

SECTION XII.—*Devotional Names.*

The early Gadhaelic Christians were too reverent to call themselves by the same name as the objects of their devotion, whether Divine or human. They were the servants, or at most the friends, of those to whom they thus looked up. They used in this manner the prefixes, *Ceile*, the companion or vassal; *Cear*, the friend; *Cailleach*, the handmaid; and far more frequently *Giolla* and *Maol*.

Giolla is the very same word as the Scottish vernacular *gillie*, a servant; and in Ireland, the *giolla eachaid*, or horse servant, resulted in the term gallowglass, which is so constantly used in English narratives of Irish wars.

The primary meaning of Maol, or Mael, is bald; thus it came to mean one who has received the tonsure, or a student of theology, and was given in the sense of a disciple.

Cealleach originally meant a devotee, one living in a cell, and was

* Diefenbach; O'Donovan; Davies; Jones, *Welsh Sketches;* Rees, *Welsh Saints.*

once perhaps a Druidess, but she afterwards was a female disciple, or nun, and finally in Scotland has become only an old woman.

It will be endless work to go through all the list of servants and disciples, and yet some of these present some of the most whimsical facts in the history of names.

Gilla is sometimes used alone, and not only in the two Gaelic languages, for we have it Latinized as Gildas, the doleful Welsh historian who rates all the contemporary princes so soundly. Culdee, the term for the first missionaries of Scotland, is also explained as Giolla De. This was in use, with Cealleach De, the handmaid of God, but are both now extinct; but not so either the servant or disciple of JESUS. Giolla Iosa was used in both countries, but sank in Scotland into the homely surname of Gillies, whilst in Ireland it was wildly transformed, in the person of the primate of Armagh, at the time of the conquest, into the Greek Gelasius, laughter; a curious specimen of the consequences of supposing that Greek must be better than their natural tongue. Maol Ioso grew into the Scottish Christian name of Malise, by which we know the Earl of Strathern at the battle of the Standard, and again, the bearer of the Fiery Cross in the *Lady of the Lake*. Nor has it ever become disused in the Highlands. Giolla Christ was a Christian name in many Scottish families of the old Keltic blood. In 1174, one Gilchrist was Earl of Angus, and another, Earl of Mar; it has not, even to the present day, fallen into disuse at baptism, and is a not uncommon surname. This may perhaps have been the origin of some of the Christians, and others may once have been Cealleach Christ.

The Archangel St. Michael was the subject of much devotion : Cara Michael has now become Carmichael; but Gilliemichael was more common, and turned into Gilmichal. The influence of the great Keltic mission at Lindisfarn, on the North of England, is visible as late as the Norman Conquest; for Domesday Book shows four northern proprietors, called respectively, Ghilemicel, Ghilander, Ghillepetair, and Ghilebrid.

Votaries of the Twelve Apostles are not, however, very common. Ireland shows Ceile Petair, and also, Mail Eoin ; but what is remarkable, it has no servant, male or female, to the Blessed Virgin. In Scotland only was there Gilmory and Gilmour ; both masculine, and now surnames. Maolmhuire was the daughter of King Kenneth M'Alpin of Scotland, and marrying into Ireland, was the mother of many kings.

Some persons were servants of all the saints, collectively ; as Giolla-na-naomh, very frequent in Irish genealogies. In the Highlands it becomes Gille-ne-ohm, and thence has occasioned the modern surnames Niven and Macniven. They are, probably, all connected with the Welsh *nen*, sky.

This word, in Cymric, leads us to the name of Ninius, prince of Cumberland, who there established Christianity, and of Nennius the British historian ; though these are too much disguised by the Latin to be easily recognized. St. Ninidh, the pious, was one of the Twelve Apostles of Ireland, and left a hand bell, which is still preserved in

the county of Fermanagh. Another bell, kept as a tenure of land,
is still extant in Galloway, and is said to have belonged to St.
Ninian, who is called by the Irish, Ringan, a prince of Cumbrian birth, who
became a monk, in 412 built the first stone church between the Forth
and Clyde, earned the title of Apostle of the Picts, and died in 432 ;
leaving Ninian and Ringan both to be Christian names in Scotland.
    The great object of Keltic veneration was, however, St. Patrick.
Nobody ventured to be Patrick alone, but many were Giolla Phadraig, or Mael Phadraig, and the descendants were Mag Giolla Phadraig, whence arises the surname Fitzpatrick, translating the Mac, and
omitting the Gillie.   Others, again, were Killpatrick ; but it is not
easy to tell whether this Kil is the contraction of Gillie, or territorial,
from the Cell or Church of St. Patrick.   The first syllable of Cospatric,
or Gospatrick, the Christian name of the Earls of Northumberland
in the tenth and eleventh centuries, is less easily explained ; but I
believe (on Mr. Lower's authority) it is the Gossoon, the boy of St.
Patrick.
    St. Patrick's pupil, Bridget, had her votaries in large numbers,
Giolla Brighde, Gilbrid, Maelbridh, all now lost but for the occasional surnames of Macbride and Kilbride, which last is sometimes
the Church of Bride.   Possibly, too, the Scottish Gilbert may have
been taken up as an equivalent to Gilbrid.
    The great St. Columba, who established the centre of his civilizing
and Christianizing efforts at Iona, had many a grateful disciple, as
Gillecolumb, or Maelcolum.   The latter form rose to the throne of
Scotland in 936, when the father, who had thus dedicated his son to
the missionary saint, retired into a convent.   The second Malcolm
was the persecutor of Lady Macbeth's family, the third was Duncan's
grandson, he of the Great Head, who, by the help of his sweet wife,
St. Margaret, was the first to lift Scotland out of her barbarism, and
begin that assimilation with the English which was in full progress
at the time of the death of his great grandson, Malcolm the Maiden,
and perhaps was the reason why no more kings were called by this
Keltic name, so puzzling to Latinizers, that in utter oblivion of St.
Columb, they call it Milcolumbus.   However, the people of Scotland
have kept it up, and in 1385, Sir Malcolm Drummond received 400
francs from France, and is designated in the conveyance as Matorme
Dromod !   Callum is considered in the Highlands as the form of
Malcolm, and Cailein of Colin.   Probably Kilian, one of the Keltic
missionary saints, popular in Germany, is another pronunciation of
the word.
    Secundinus was another pupil of St. Patrick, whom the Irish first
made into Seachnall, and then termed their children Mael-seachlain,
as his pupils.   The great Irish king, Malachy with the collar of gold,
was thus rendered to suit the weak Saxon capacity.
    Cailleach-Coeimlighin and Gilla Coeimghin are the votaries of St.
Kevin, a very unpromising object of hero-worship, if we were to
believe the legend with which Moore and other moderns have quite
gratuitously favoured Glendalough.   Cœimghin itself means fair
offspring.

Giolla Cheallaigh was common in honour of Ceallach, a very local
saint, of royal birth, who was educated by St. Kieran. On his
father's death, he was about to ascend the throne, when his tutor
interfered, probably considering this an infraction of his vows, and
on his persisting, laid him under a curse, after the usual fashion of
Irish saints. He lost his kingdom, and became a bishop, but resigned
his see for fear of his enemies, and retired to a hermitage on Lough
Con, where, however, he was murdered by four ecclesiastical students,
whose names all began with Maol. His corpse was hidden in a tree,
where for once it did not show the incorruptibility supposed to be
the property of sanctity. The murderers were all put to death on an
eminence, called from them Ardna-maol, or hill of the shavelings,
and his admirers have resulted in the surname O'Killy-kelly, or, for
short, Kelly.

Scotland had several instances of bishop's servant, Gillaspick in
Scotland, or in Northern Ireland, Giolla Easbuig, the Keltic form of
episcopus. Gillaspich Campbell, already Scotticized enough to have
been christened by this Gaelic term, married Aioffe O'Duinne, the
daughter of the line of Diarmid ; and thenceforth Gillaspick, or
Gillespie, was the hereditary Christian name in the family, till, in
the twelfth century, his fourth descendant called himself Archibald,
and thenceforth the heads of the house of Campbell have been Archibald to the Lowlands, to their own clan, Gillespik. It is a curious
fact that Gillespie Grumach and his son, the two Covenanting
Argyles, should thus have proclaimed themselves 'Bishop's gillies.'
Gillespie has become a frequent surname in Scotland.

Maelgwn, or Maelgwas, was his successor in Powys and Gwynned,
and is desperately abused by the indignant Gildas for all manner of
crimes ; while even Taliessin, who praises his beauty, rebukes his
licentiousness. Three centuries later, a bard alleges that he hid
himself in a wood, waylaid and carried off the wife of King Arthur.
In the twelfth century, Caradoc, abbot of Llancarven, adds that
Arthur besieged him in his castle, and had challenged him to single
combat, when the sage Gildas and the abbot of Glastonbury inter-
posed, and obtained the lady's restoration. Walter of Oxford adds
that this Maelgwn reigned after King Arthur, and finally died of
terror in a convent, having seen the Yellow Spectre, namely the
plague, through the chinks of the church door. Dr. Owen Pugh
further tells us, that Jack-in-the-Green, on May-day, was once a
pageant representing Melva, or Melvas, king of the country now
called Somersetshire, disguised in green boughs, as he lay in ambush
to steal King Arthur's wife as she went out hunting.

Maél-was, a servant boy, was translated into old Romance French
as the former, by the word Ancel, or Ancelot, otherwise L'Ancelot ;
Villemarqué quotes a mention of the '*fable Ancelot et Tristan,*' from
the romance of Ogier, to show that in earlier days Mael, or Ancelot,
was mentioned without the article, which has since become incorporated with it, so that Lancelot has grown to be the accepted name, and
so universally supposed to mean a lance, that the Welsh themselves,
re-importing his history, called him Palladr, a shivered lance.

Ancelot and Ancelin were certainly early chivalrous names, the latter perhaps confused with the Ansir or Æsir of the Teutons. Ancilée and Anselote are feminine names in the register of Cambrai, of the dates of 1169 and 1304 ; and as there most of the feminines are changed from those of men, it is evident that Ancil and Anselot must once have existed there, either named from the hero of romance, or translated from some Walloon Mael ; and thence no doubt the Asselin, Ascelin of our old Norman barons, and the Atscelina Fossard, mentioned in a curious old tract on female names, as having lived in the North of England. It is curious that even romance does not profess that Launcelot was the true name of the knight, thus formed from the Cambrian chieftain, though Galahad is there said to have been his proper name, afterwards given to his worthier son. Launcelot was bestowed on him by Vivian, the Lady of the Lake, who stole him in infancy from his father, King Ban, and brought him up under her crystal waves, till he was eighteen, when, as Sir Lancelot du Lac, he appeared at King Arthur's court, and became the principal figure there, foremost in every feat of chivalry, the flower of knighthood ; but in the noble severity of the English romance, he was withheld from counsels of perfection, by his guilty love for Gwenever, and lying spell-bound in a dull trance when the holy vision of the Sanc-greal past by. Finally, he broke with King Arthur, and opened the way to Mordred's fatal rebellion by his defection, too late repenting, and after Arthur's fall becoming a hermit and a penitent.

His story was told with deep warning in England, but in Italy it was 'Lancilotto' that Francesca di Rimini looked back to as the tale that had been the spark to awaken fatal passion.

He has ever since been regarded as the type of penitence for misdirected love and chivalrous prowess, and in consequence Lancelot, and its contraction Lance, have never been entirely out of use in England, though not universal.

CHAPTER IV.

SECTION I.—*The Round Table.*

IT is a very remarkable fact, that the grand cycle of our national romance and poetry, has been made to centre round the hero of a people whom we have subdued, and were holding in our power with difficulty, at the very time that minstrels were singing the adventures of the leader who had for the longest time kept our forces in check.

Many a patriot has fought as boldly as Arthur, many a nation has held out as bravely as the remains of the Britons; but as the "battle is not to the strong," so renown is not to the most able; and it was to a very peculiar concatenation of circumstances that the Britons owed it that their struggles in Somerset, Cornwall, and Strathclyde should have been magnified into victories over Rome and half Europe, and themselves metamorphosed from wild Cymry, with a little Roman polish and discipline, into ideal models of chivalry.

That they did fight there can be no doubt. If the dismal groans of the Britons were ever sent at all, it was but a small number who groaned. As to the Anglo-Saxons, they had been coming even before the Romans, and Carausius and his fleet held them in check for awhile; but there can be no doubt that they came in much greater numbers, and with more intent to settle, than in former times, in the decay of the empire. Moreover, the resistance evidently became more resolute and valid, as the tide flowed westward over the diagonally arranged strata of the island; the alluvial lands to the east have no traditions of battles, but at the chalk downs, the rounded hills have names and dim legends of fights and of camps, and cities begin to claim to be the scene of Arthur's court.

Westward again, with the sandstone hill and smiling valley, the tales multiply spots where the court was held in perplexing multitude; river upon river puts forth its old Keltic name of Cam, the crooked, and calls itself the place of the last decisive fight. And when the moorland and mountain are actually reached, and the heather stretches wide over the granite moor, with the igneous peak of stone crowning the lofty crag, there the Briton is still free, and points to his rocky summits as his hero's home.

To those fastnesses were the Cymry finally limited, if they would enjoy their native government; and though many remained as serfs,

and some as clergy, in the open country, the national spirit was confined to those who dwelt in the strongholds of the West. There did
their bards sing and tell tales, and compose *Triads* on the past glories
of their race, with a natural tendency to magnify the exploits of their
most able defender. At the same time, the Armoricans on the other
side of the water, some of whom had, probably, according to their
tradition, migrated from Britain, told their own legends, and sung
their songs on the chief who had maintained the cause of their
conntrymen.

When the Normans settled in Neustria, their lively fancy caught
up all that was imaginative among those around them. It is from
their arrival that the first dawn of French literature dates, and it
seems to have been they who first listened to the Breton lays, and
brought them forward in the French tongue. At the central court of
France, the Norman trouvère met the Provençal troubadour, and
their repertory of tales was exchanged, the one giving his native Norse
myths, tinctured with Keltic heroic tales, the other the Greco-Roman
and Arabic stories that had travelled to him. And there, both sets
of stories were steeped in that mysterious atmosphere of chivalry,
which could dream of no court that was not based on the model of
feudal France, no warrior without a horse and an esquire, a cone-
shaped helmet, and kite-shaped shield.

That true knights were all equal, was a maxim held, though
hardly carried out, in the eleventh century, and the floating notion
of a table, where all were on an equality, was ready to fix itself on
the golden age of chivalry. And when the Normans themselves
became the owners of Britain, and brought with them a fair sprinkling
of Bretons, no wonder they decided that the heroes, who, at least,
were not Saxon, should be their own property. Siegfried and
Brynhild had fallen into oblivion, and the British chiefs did veritably
flourish on their native soil. Geoffrey of Monmouth pretended to
hunt up their history in Wales and Brittany; Marie of France more
faithfully reproduced her native lays in Norman-French; and as
fresh tales were discovered or invented, metrical romances spread
them far and wide, and began all to place their scene at the court of
Arthur. Most noted among these, was the story of the San-grail, the
cup of healing and lance of wounding, that may have been a shadow
of a mighty truth, but which became myth in many countries, until,
in the hands of the Cymry, they assumed to be the veritable
original Cup of Blessing of the Last Supper, and the lance of the
soldier at the Cross.

A relic-adoring age willingly believed, that to find these treasures
was the great task of the knights it had invented. Thenceforth,
English imagination beheld the glorious past as a feudal court, where
all the good Knights of the Round Table, now an order of chivalry,
had bound themselves to seek the holy relics, that could only be
revealed to the perfectly pure and worthy. Mallory's beautiful book
preserves the main line of the allegory, though it is full of episodes,
and it is the veritable prose epic of the Round Table.

France and Lombardy likewise believed in the Round Table, but not with the same national faith. As was natural, their poems centered about the great Frank emperor, and what they wrote or told of the British knights rather dealt in the less creditable adventures of individuals, than in the ennobling religious drift of the main story.

However, it is these Round Table names that are the most widely known and used of all the Keltic nomenclature, with a reputation almost entirely romantic, and very seldom saintly. Among the Arthurian names there is not one that is Teutonic; all are either genuine Cymric, or else such modifications of Latin nomina as citizenship was sure to leave to the Britons.

Section II.—*Arthur.*

No Keltic name approaches in renown to that of the central figure of the Round Table ; yet, in the very dazzle of his brightness, his person has been so much lost, that, as the author of *Welsh Sketches* observes, " Whereas Peter Schlemihl lost his shadow, Arthur has lost his substance."

To begin with his name. He may have been a Romanized Briton named from Arctus, " Arthur's slow wain rolling his course round the pole," and Arcturus, the bear's-tail, far behind him in Boötes ; and Arth, perhaps from them, does indeed mean a bear in British.

Ard, the consonant softening into *th* in composition, means high or noble, in all the Keltic tongues but Welsh, and had been a name from time immemorial in Ireland, as Scott knew when he made the Bertram family tree bear fruit of Arths in fabulous ages. Art, a Milesian, is said to have lived B.C. 233 ; Art MacCormac appears in the Ossianic legends, " Art Oge MacMorne kept Dundorme ;" according to Hanmer's catalogue of Finn MacCoul's comrades, Art and Arth recur for ever in Erse Highland pedigree ; and in the end of the fourteenth century, Art MacMorough was the great hero of Ireland, who slew Roger Mortimer, and sorely puzzled Richard II., reigned in Leinster for forty years, and cost the English treasury twelve million marcs ; so that when he died,

> " Since Brien's death in Erin
> Such a mourning had not been."

Arthmael, bear's servant or worshipper, was a Welsh prince, but here, as in Ireland, all the Arths are now merged in Arthur.

Ardghal, or Ardal, of high valour, is an Erse name, and was long used, though it has now been suppressed by the supposed Anglicism Arnold, eagle-power. It explains the name of Arthgallo, who, in Geoffrey of Monmouth's legendary history, is the persecuting brother, whom Elidure's untiring love and generosity finally won from his cruel courses to justice and mercy. *Artegal and Elidure* was one of the best ante-Shakesperian dramas ; and Artegal was selected by Spenser as one of the best and noblest of his knights-errant, representing Arthur Lord Grey.

Ardrigh was an Erse term for the supreme monarch over their five lesser realms, and is still applied by the native Irish to the king of

France,—much as the Greeks were wont to style the Persian monarch the Great King. This most probably accounts for the term Arviragus, which we picked up by the Romans, and applied to that son of Cymbeline who was really the brave Caradwg. Ardheer is another form of this same title of the highest chief, and the later critics tell us to consider this as the origin of our hero.

He is not, indeed, mentioned by Gildas, unless he be the "dragon of the island ;" but his omission from that letter is only to his credit, and the individuality of Arthur stands on the testimony of Welsh bards up to his own date, and of universal tradition.

Arthur, or Arthwys, seems to have been the son of Uthyr, and Emrys, whom he succeeded, bearing the title of Pendragon in his own tongue, and of Imperator in Latin, which was the language of politics to the Britons. A Silurian like Caradwg, his spirit was the same, and his hereditary possessions would seem to have been on the Welsh border, with Caerleon on Uske for their capital ; but he was born at Tintagel in Cornwall, and he was prompt in flying to the aid of the British cause in all quarters. The West Saxons were his chief enemies, and his battles, twelve in number, are almost all in the kingdom of Wessex ; but he must also have been acknowledged by the northern Britons of the old province of Valentia, and have ruled over "fair Strathclyde and Reged wide" from his fortress at Carlisle. After a brave reign of forty years, he at length perished through the treachery of his nephew ; but whether his last fatal battle was fought in Strathclyde, Cornwall, or in Somerset, it seems impossible to determine.

The Cymry mourned passionately. The Welsh bards made *Triads*, and the Armoricans sang songs.

Nennius mentions Arthur in the sixth century.

In 720, a person called Eremita Britannus, or the British hermit, is said to have written about King Arthur ; the Welsh *Mabinogion*, or children's tales, were all centering on him ; and when, in the early part of the twelfth century, Geoffrey of Monmouth brought out his chronicle, it was translated all over Europe, even into Greek, and furnished myriads of romances, metrical and otherwise.

The outline of the Arthur of romance scarcely needs to be here traced; the prince, brought up in concealment, establishing his claim by pulling the sword out of the stone whence no one else could detach it ; the Christian warrior, conquering all around, and extending his victories to Rome ; the band of Knights ; the vow and quest of the Holy Grail that breaks the earthly league ; the fall and defection of the two most accomplished knights through unhallowed love, the death of one, and the rebellion of the other, the lover of Arthur's own faithless wife,— all opening the way to the fatal treason of the nephew ; and the last battle, when the wounded king causes his sword to be thrown into the river, as a signal to the fairies, who bear him away to their hidden isle. All this is our own peculiar insular heritage of romance, ennobled as it has been by old Mallory's prose in the fifteenth century, and in the nineteenth by Tennyson's poetry, the best of all the interpretations of the import of Arthur himself.

As to his name, it was not very common even in Wales. It only came forth as a matter of romance, and was given occasionally either from fancy or policy.

Constance of Brittany gave her little son this popular name, perhaps in the hope that in time British Arthur would be restored to England, and thenceforth Arzur, as the Bretons call it, was occasionally used in the duchy.

An old prophecy of Merlin was said to have declared that Richmond should come from Brittany to conquer England, and this prediction caused Henry V. to refuse all requests to allow Arthur, Comte de Richemont, son of the Duke of Brittany, to be ransomed when taken prisoner at Agincourt. His name of Arthur no doubt added to the danger, and Henry's keen eyesight might have likewise detected in him the military skill which made him so formidable an enemy to the English on his own soil, not theirs.

When Richmond really came out of Brittany and conquered England, he named his first son Arthur, but that son never wore the British crown, nor did the infant Arthur of Scotland, so named by James V., survive to be known in history. Arthur, however, had become an occasional name; but it was reserved for the great Arthur Wellesley, whose name had perhaps more to do with the old Art of Erse times than with the king of the Round Table, to make it, as it is at present, one of the most universally popular of English names. Even the French use it, for its sound, it may be presumed, rather than for its recent distinction, and they have ceased to spell it in the old form, Artus, and adopted our own. The Italians know, but do not use, Arturo; however, the name changes so little that Madame Schopenhauer's husband was justified in choosing it for his son as a useful name for a merchant, because it does not alter in being translated.

The English feminine Arthurine is occasionally used.

SECTION III.—*Gwenever.*

The staunchest supporters of Arthur's existence give him three wives. One of them was she who was stolen by Maelwas, the origin of Lancelot, and she it is who is the dame of romance.

Gwen, the commencement of her name, is used in Welsh, in the double sense of the colour, white, and of a woman, perhaps for the same reason that 'the fair' so often stands for a lady in poetry. The word is closely related to the *finn* and *ban*, both meaning white in the other branch of the Keltic tongue, and, save for the fulness of interest belonging to both, all might have been treated of together. Gwen, the feminine of Gwyn, white, becomes *wen* in composition, and as such we have already met it at the end of words.

Gwendolen is made by the Brut, and by Geoffrey of Monmouth, the daughter of Corineus, Duke of Cornwall, and wife of Locrine, son of the original Brutus. He deserted her for the sake of Estrild, a fair German captive, and she made war upon him, in the course of which he was killed, and Estrild and her daughter Sabrina, or Avern, made prisoners; whereupon, the jealous and revengeful queen caused both to be drowned in the river, thenceforth called Sabrina or Severn ; in Welsh, Hafreu, where we may hope that the damsel became the lovely nymph who "listened and saved" the lady from Comus and his crew. Estrild is Essylt (or Iseulte) in the Welsh which Geoffrey copied.

The Welsh saints give us St. Gwendolen or Gwen as the mother of Caradog Vreichfras, the excellent Sir Cradocke of the Round Table. In the *Triads* and the *Mabinogion*, Gwendolen is a beauty of Arthur's court, and in the bardic enumeration of the thirteen wonders of Britain appears the gold chess-board of Gwendolen, on which, when the silver men were placed, they would play of themselves. Gwendolen, Gwen, and Gwyn have never been disused in Wales. The first was the daughter of the last native prince, and her name is increasingly in favour with the lovers of archaisms.

Gwenhwyfar is the swelling white wave ; but the ocean names of the Britons are worth noting, when we remember that they also had Llyr, with Bronwen and Creirdydlydd, all certainly mythical.

Without consigning Queen Gwenhwyfar to the regions of Regan, it is likely that hers was a hereditary name descended from some part of the ancient faith. A Welsh couplet describes her as—

> "Gwenhwyfar, daughter of Gogyrfan the Great,
> Bad when little, worse when great."

And the various early tales in the *Mabinogion*, as well as the metrical romances, always give the same character of the beautiful queen of light conduct. In the *Morte d'Arthur*, guilty love for her paralyzes Lancelot's eyes when the San-grail passes before him, the same passion drives him to his rebellion, and finally the repentant queen takes refuge in the convent at Ambresbury, where Tennyson has described the parting between her and Arthur in the most noble and beautiful of all his poetry.

Guenever was her full English name, contracted into Ganivre, or Ganore, a form that occurs in old Welsh registers. Jennifer, as they have it in Cornwall, is still frequent there ; but nowhere else in our island has the name been followed. Scotland has a tradition of her crimes that calls her Queen Wanders, or Vanora, and Boece actually imprisons her in the great old fort on Barra Hill, in Perthshire ; but abroad she met with more favour, as Génièvre in France, and in Italy as Ginevra, or Zinevra.

Observing that the French call Gwenhwyfar, Génièvre, we can hardly doubt that either this, or Gwenfrewi, holy calm or fair peace, must have been the origin of their own Généviève, though the German etymologists try to construe her as *gan*, magic, *vaips*, a crown. But Généviève was a Gaul, born at Nanterre in 422, and could hardly have borne anything but either a Keltic or a Roman name ; and the whole family of Gwens were, as has been shown, dear to the Cymric race, whose religion was the same in Gaul and Britain.

A shepherd-maid, like Joan of Arc, Généviève anticipated her deeds of patriotism, though she wore no armour and carried no sword. When Paris was besieged by the Franks, she, unarmed, and strong only in her pious confidence, walked forth as the escort of the citizens in search of provisions, and when the city was taken, her heroic holiness so impressed the heathen Franks, Hlodwig and Hilderik, that her entreaties in behalf of their prisoners were always granted. When she died, in her 90th year, she was erected into the primary patron saint of Paris, and has so continued ever since, leaving Généviève in high esteem among Parisiennes of all degrees down from Anne Généviève de Bourbon, the sister of Condé. The numerous contractions testify to the popularity of the gentle patriot. Some of the German forms may, however, be ascribed to the apocryphal Saint Genovefa, of Brabant, to whom has attached the story, of suspicious universality, of the wife who was driven by malicious accusations to the woods, there to give birth to an infant, and to be nourished by a white doe until the final discovery of her innocence. From whatever cause the name is widely used on the Continent.

English.	French.	Breton.	Italian.
Winifred	Généviève	Jenovefa	Genoveffa
Jennifer	Javotte	Fa-ik	
	Genevion		
	Vevette		

German.	Russian.	Illyrian.	
Genovefa	Zenevieva	Genovefa	
Vevay		Genovefica	
Vefele		Veva	

Gwenfrewi was the Welsh nun whose head was cut off by a furious prince called Caradoc, because she refused his addresses; whereupon, in the usual fashion of Welsh saints, she caused a well to spring up on the spot of her martyrdom. But unlike other such wells, it is intermitting, and sufficiently impregnated with mineral substances to support its high character to miraculous powers, and, in addition, the stones are marked with red veins, which represent the blood of St. Wenefred, as our Anglo-Saxon tongues have long since made her. Such undoubted wonders made Winifred a most flourishing name in Wales, and it is occasionally found in England, though usually through a Welsh connection, and so spelt as to confuse it with the true Saxon masculine Winfrith, or friend of peace. The Irish take Winny as the equivalent of Una.

In Breton, Guennolé, also called Wingallok, in Cornish, Gunwallo, was a celebrated saint, and was the counsellor who saved King Gradlon in the inundation. Guennola is the feminine, and is used, very correctly, to translate the French Candide, as is Guennéan, the white spirit, for angel, both the being and the name.

Dwynwen, or the white wave, was invoked as the patroness of

lovers, and became a Welsh name. It is just possible that an echo of this, on the other side of the water, may be Damhnait, or Devnet, Latinized as Dymphna, or Dympna, though the more obvious likeness in sound is *damhna*, a reason. An Irish princess, so called, was obliged, about the year 600, to fly from the persecutions of her father, protected by a priest, a jester, and his wife, until near Antwerp her father overtook her and cut off her head. Hanmer adds, "the Irish in the county of Lowth do honour her ; belike her father dwelt there : " and Dympna, or Demmy, is not wholly extinct as a name.

This same *wen*, the poetical form of a woman, or fair one, enters into the composition of two other saintly Keltic names. The first, St. Mawdwen, or Modwen, was one of St. Patrick's Irish nuns ; and another later Modwen, also Irish, came to England in 840, educated Edith, daughter of King Ethelwolf, and founded an abbey at Polsworth. She was rather a favourite saint ; her name is traceable in various places ; and Modwenna continued in Cornwall. Perhaps it comes from *modh*, manners.

Cainwen is said to be Cain, the virgin. The first half means splendid or beautiful things or jewels, and is connected with the Latin Candalus. The Welsh declare that she was of princely birth ; but being determined to live a holy life, she travelled on foot beyond the Severn, and there found a solitary place where no one had ever lived, because it was infested with snakes and vipers, which she forthwith, by her prayers, turned to stone, and they may still be picked up in a petrified state in the fields. Keynsham, in Somersetshire, is, in fact, famous for ammonites, which thus have given rise to another legend like those of St. Cuthbert and St. Hilda. Camden himself saw one of these stones, and was somewhat perplexed thereby.

She afterwards repaired to St. Michael's Mount, in Cornwall, where she met her nephew, St. Cadoc, and there her name became attached to a well, in the parish of St. Neots, arched over by four trees—oak, ash, elm, and withy, all apparently growing from one root. The water was further supposed to endow whichever of a married pair first tasted it with the mastery for life. No one can forget that best of all Southey's humorous ballads, where the Cornishman confesses,—

> "I hastened, as soon as the wedding was done,
> And left my wife in the porch ;
> But, i' faith, she had been wiser than I,
> For she took a bottle to church."

Cornishmen, apparently, never forgave St. Keyne for the properties of her well ; for Carew, in his *Survey of Cornwall*, terms her "no over holy saint ; " and Norden thus vituperates her : "this Kayne is sayde to be a woman saynte, of whom it (the well) taketh name ; but it better resembleth Kayne, the devil, who had the shape of a man, the name of an apostle, and the qualitie of a traitor." Gwenllian, white linen, is still sometimes used.

Gwyn also signifies blessed or happy, and this *gwynnedd* is an epithet of some of the favourite kings. Gwynaeth, a state of bliss, is a female name still in use, and often written Gyneth, though it gets

translated into Venetia, and, in the latter form, named the lady whom
Sir Kenelm Digby rendered famous.

SECTION IV.—*Gwalchmai, Sir Gawain, and Sir Owen.*

No knight is more distinguished, either in the *Triads* or in romance,
than Gwalchmai, perhaps from Gwalch, a hawk, and maedd, a blow.

In Welsh pedigrees, he is Arthur's nephew, son of his sister
Ernnos and of Llew, king of Lothian and Orkney. He probably had
a real existence, for the *Triads* celebrate him as one of the three
golden-tongued knights of Britain, one of the three learned ones of
Britain, and one of the three most courteous men towards strangers.
In a Welsh poem, he is represented as using his courteous tongue in
behalf of his friend Trystan ; and in the *Mabinogion*, in the 'Lady
of the Fountain,' he takes such a prominent part, that the French
romance is called that of Sir Yvaine and Sir Gawaine. Walganus
and Walwyn had Latinized the Hawk of Battle, and have caused it to
be confounded with the Teutonic Walwine, slaughter-lover ; but the
Gwalchmai of Wales can be identified with the Gawain, or Wawyn,
of romance by his friendship with Trystan, his relationship to Arthur,
and his title in the romances of the *Flower of Courtesy.*

It was Sir Gawaine who in the ballad boldly adventured himself
to wed the "Loathly Lady," and was rewarded by breaking the spell,
and discovering her loveliness.   Gawaine was the hero of the great
battle with the giant Rhyence, and, though unsuccessful, was one of
the foremost in the quest of the San-grail, until warned by a dream
how the enterprise was to result. Finally, Sir Gawaine took his
uncle's side first in the war with Lancelot, then with Mordred, and
died of the renewal of a wound received in battle with the former,
writing on his death-bed a letter that brought Lancelot to repentance.

His name, whether as Walwyn, Gawain, or Gavin, was popular in
England and Scotland in the middle ages ; and in the last-mentioned
shape named the high-spirited bishop of Dunkeld, the one son of old
Bell the Cat, who could "pen a line," and who did so to such good
purpose when "he gave rude Scotland Virgil's page." Nor is Gavin
by any means extinct in Scotland.

Sir Gawain is coupled in English romance with his intimate friend,
Sir Ywaine, as in French with Sir Yvaine ; and in the Welsh story,
in the *Mabinogion*, he is Sir Owain. He there sets forth from court
in search of adventures, and falls in with a knight in black armour,
whom he conquers, and thereupon is conducted to a castle, where he
becomes guardian of an enchanted fountain, and husband of a lady in
yellow satin, with long yellow hair, and a hundred maids always
embroidering satin.   Of course, when Sir Gawain came in quest of
him, and he was allowed to go back to King Arthur's court, he forgot
the whole affair, until at the end of three years, he was recalled by
his lady's confidential handmaid, Luned, and proceeded to atone for
his unfaithfulness by another severe course of adventures, during

which he delivered a black lion from a serpent, thus binding the faithful beast to his service for ever, and after a due slaughter of giants, rejoined his wife, and lived happy ever after. The French of the thirteenth century knew him as Sir Yueins, le Chevalier du Lion ; and even the Scandinavians had his story in their *Ivent Saga*. In the *Morte d'Arthur*, he is Sir Gareth, and brother to Gawain ; but he must have been his cousin, as he was the son of Urien, and of Arthur's sister, Morgwen. In the *Morte d'Arthur*, Luned is Linet, and in the French romances she is Lunette. Her name seems to be derivable from *llun*, a shape or form, and if so, would mean the shapely ; but the hagiologists identify it with that Elined, the daughter of Brychan, who suffered martyrdom on the hill of Penginger, and was canonized as St. Almedha, a name still to be seen on the sign of an inn at Knaresborough.

Owain, Oen in Brittany, continued popular in Wales, though, perhaps, rather more usual at a late than an early period. The notable Owen Glendower, as Shakespeare has taught us to call him, was really Owain ap Gruffydd of Glendfrdwy, his estate in Merionethshire, where he kept a grand household.

It was he who made Owen the most common of Welsh names, in honour of the last Welshman who lived and died free of the English yoke.

Owain is so like the word *oen* that in Welsh stands for a sheep or lamb, that it is generally so translated ; but it is most likely that this is a case of an adaptation of a derivative from an obsolete word to a familiar one, and that Owen ought to be carried much further back to the same source as the Erse Eoghan, which comes from *éoghunn*, youth, from *og*, young, and is translated, young warrior. It has the feminine Eoghania, of course turned into Eugenia.

There were many Eoghans in Ireland. One of them, a king of Connaught, when dying of his wounds, commanded himself to be buried upright, with his red javelin in his hand, and his face turned towards Ulster, as though still fighting with his foes. As long as he thus remained, Connaught prevailed and Ulster lost ; but the Ultonians discovered the spell, and re-buried him in an opposite direction, thereby changing the tide of success.

Eoghan, in Scotland, is pronounced Yō-hăn, and indiscriminately translated by Evan, Ewan, and Hugh. Several of the early kings, who are all numbered together in Scotland as Eugenius, were properly Eoghan, and Evan or Ewan is certainly the right Anglicism, though Hugh is made to do duty for these as well as for Aodh.

The same Eoghan seems in another form to have supplied the Welsh Evan, or Evan *may* be intended for John. A certain Evan of Wales, claiming the blood of the Welsh princes, who became a mercenary under Charles V. of France, made a bold descent upon Guernsey, and was killed at the siege of Mortain-sur-mer, by what Froissart calls a short Spanish dagger, but his illuminator has made to look much more like a very large arrow. Welsh history takes no cognizance of him, but he is thought to be traceable in the national songs as Jevan Dovy.

T

Another translation of Owain is "apt to serve." A British prince of Strathcluyd was called Uen or Hoen.*

Section V.—*Trystan and Ysolt.*

The episode of Trystan is one of the most celebrated incidents of Arthur's court, and has not failed to be treated by Davies as a magnificent emblematic myth.

The *Triads* begin by declaring that the three mighty swineherds of the Isle of Britain were Pryderi, Coll, and Trystan.

Another adds,—

The third swineherd was Trystan, son of Tallwch, who kept the swine of March, the son of Meirchion, while the swineherd was conveying a message to Essylt, to appoint an assignation with her.

Again, he is one of the three heralds of Britain, also one of the three diademed chiefs, also one of the three knights who had the conducting of mysteries.

Besides, the three unchaste matrons of Britain are Penarwen, Bun, and Esyllt Fingwen.

And the tale told by the Cymric race in Cambria and Armorica has resounded throughout southern Europe. There the mighty swineherd is the son of Roland and Blanchefleur, sister of Mark, king of Cornwall. Almost at the moment of his birth, she hears the tidings of his father's death, and expires from the shock, calling her babe Tristan, or the sad. He grows up to be an accomplished knight, and after various adventures, is sent by his uncle, King Mark, to Ireland, to bring home the promised bride Ysolt the fair.

The mother of Ysolt gives her maid, Brengwain, a magic draught, which was to be administered to the pair on their bridal day, to secure their mutual affection. A storm rises on the voyage, and, intending to refresh her lady and the knight after his exertions and her alarm, Brengwain, in her confusion, gives them the fatal draught, and their passion for one another became the theme of the story-tellers who preferred guilty love to high aspirations. Tristrem was married to another Ysolt called of the white hands, or of Brittany; he was dangerously wounded, and lay sick in her castle in Brittany. Nothing could cure him but the presence of Ysolt of Cornwall, and to her he sent his squire, with his ring, entreating, like the father of Theseus, that if she came to him the sails of the ship might be white, if she refused, the squire should hoist a black sail.

She came, but the wife, Ysolt of the white hands, falsely told the sick man that the sails were black ; he sank back in despair and died, and Ysolt died of grief beside him.

Such is the story told by Thomas of Ercildoune, in the thirteenth century, as well as by hosts of romances.

* *Mabinogion ; Morte d'Arthur ; Tracts on Antiquities of the Northern Counties,* by R. D. D. ; Cambro-Briton ; Jones, *Welsh Sketches ;* Chalmers ; Percy, *Relics ;* Rees, *Welsh Saints ;* O'Donovan ; Hy Fiachrach ; Owen Pugh ; *Highland Society's Dictionary.*

Trust was really a Cymric name, and was called among the Picts Drust, or Drest.   There is a Trust or Drust, MacTallaghi among the Pictish kings, who possibly may be the origin of Tristan, since many of the legends are common to Strath Clyde, Wales, and Cornwall. The Pictish Pendragon, who was elected at the time the Romans quitted Britain, was called by his countrymen Drust of the Hundred Battles, and many of his successors bore the same name, which means din, tumult, or loud noise, and thus may poetically be translated as a proclaimer or herald.   Trwst ap Taran (tumult the son of thunder) was the poetical name of another of the line.   The influence of Latin upon Welsh, however, made *trist* really mean sad, so that it was there accepted as suited to the melancholy circumstance of the hero's birth ; and Tristram, or sad face, became identified with the notion of sorrow ; so that the child of St. Louis, born while his father was in captivity on the Nile, and his mother in danger at Damietta, was named Jean Tristan.   Never would the cheerful Greeks have accepted such a name as Tristrem, Tristan, Tristano ; but in Europe it regularly entered the ranks of the names of sorrow, and it was, no doubt, in allusion to it that Don Quixote accepted the soubriquet of the Knight of the Rueful Countenance.   The earliest form of the name was Adsalutta, a Keltic goddess, whose name occurs in two inscriptions, one at Laybach and the other at Ratschöck in Istria.   It is identified by the learned with Esyltt, and connected with *Suraya*, the Sungod of the Vedas.

Esyltt was the French Yseulte, or Ysoude, the Italian Isolta, and English Ysolte, Isolda, or Izolta, and in all these shapes was frequent in the families of the middle ages ; recurring again and again in registers, down to the seventeenth century : indeed, within the last fifty years a person was alive who bore this romantic name in the form of Izod.

Tallwch is the torrent, and seems to have been translated into Roland, from the sound of rolling, when the Armorican bards laid claim to the great Paladin of Charlemagne's court, on the score of his having been Warden of the Marches of Brittany, and wanted to make out that Roland was a name of their own.   They had thus caused Rowland to be considered as a regular Cymric name.

King Mark himself was most probably a compromise between the Roman *Marcus* and the native *march*, which belongs to all the Kelts —nay, Pausanias tells us, meant a horse, in the dialect of the tribe who tried to take Delphi.   Its fellow, *mar*, passed into Teutonic ; named Marshalls, as Marskalk, or horse servant ; and lives among us as our *mare*, in the feminine.   Indeed, Marcus may itself be another instance of the Keltic element in Latin.

Marchell was the daughter of Tewdrig, king of North Wales, and, in 382, married Brychan, son of Cormac Mac Cairbre, one of the kings of Ireland,   Her name was, no doubt, a mixture of the Keltic March and the Latin Marcella ; and it was she who must have rendered the name of Marcella so common in Ireland.

The more common Gadhaelic word is, however, *each*, first cousin to *equus*, *aspa*, and many another word for the gallant animal.

Each was the saint who spent his life in Boyne Water, and was said to have uttered the curse that caused the battle of Magh Rath, a libel disproved by his previous death.

Each, in combination, has formed sundry names,—Eachmarchach, a sort of reduplication ; Eachmilidh, horse-warrior ; Eachaid, horseman, the most famous of them belonging to many kings, and rendered into Latin—Eochodius, or Equitius, the last not so incorrect. Auhy, or Atty, were the usual ways of rendering it ; but these have been confounded with Arthur, and the name is lost.

Several other Eochaids were kings of Scotland, but they are grievously confused by Latinity, and, with the owners of the following name, turned into Eugenius ; Eochaidbuidhe, or the fair-haired, appearing as Eugenius Flavus ; and Eochoid Rinne Mhail as Eugenius Crooked Nose !

Another Eochaid has, by the capricious fancy of Scotland, been transmitted to us as Achaius. He is said to have been an ally of Charlemagne, and begun the custom of lending auxiliaries to the French, numerous Scotsmen coming to honour and dignity for their assistance in their conquest of Saxony. Achaius is also said to have married the sister of the king of the Picts, and formed an alliance with him against the Anglo-Saxons. While marching against the English forces, the cross of St. Andrew suddenly appeared in the sky giving assurance of victory, and, in consequence, was adopted as the ensign of the Picts, and afterwards of the Scots.

The "double tressure, flory and counterflory," that surrounds the field where "the ruddy lion ramps in gold," is also said to have been "first by Achaius worn," though he was probably innocent of all armorial bearings, as he died in 819.

Eachan is the most usual form of the Highland name, and has for many years been, by general consent, converted into Hector.

The feminine Eacha is an old Irish name.*

SECTION VI.—*Hoel and Ryence.*

The romances of Arthur give him, among his many nephews, one named Hoel, Duke of Brittany, whose niece Helena was seized upon by the horrible giant Ritho, and devoured upon the top of Tombelaine.

This Hoel does not seem to have been a real character. His name Higuel, the lordly or conspicuous, was a common one in Wales and Brittany ; and a prince so called seems really to have fled to Arthur for aid against the Franks, and to have returned with a fresh colony of Britons, by whose aid he became king of Armorica.

He reigned for thirty years, and died in 545. Other Hoels reigned after him, the third of whom is said to have been killed at Roncevalles.

In Wales, Hywel continued in favour, and Hywel-Dha, or the Good, who reigned in the tenth century, is famous for having gone to Rome

* Chalmers ; Villemarque ; *Mabinogion ;* O'Donovan ; Pugh ; Pitre ; Chevalier ; Sir W. Scott, Ed. of *Sir Trestram.*

to study law, by which he so profited as afterwards to draw up the famous code that has thrown so much light on the manners of the Cambrian mountaineers, the order of precedence in the king's household, and even the price of animals. He signs King Athelstan's charter as Hoel-Subregulus, or under king.

Hywel was a name in frequent use among the Welsh princes, and 'highborn Hoel's harp' was frequently sounded, for various bards were so called.

Another Hoel was that unfortunate relative of Owen Glendower whom he was said to have killed and hidden in the blasted tree.

The giant Ritho is evidently a relation of Rhitta Gawr, who, in the Welsh stories, interfered to put a stop to a furious battle between two kings named Nynniaw and Peibiaw, who had quarelled about the moon and stars. Rhitta Gawr defeated them both, and cut off their beards, and afterwards the beards of seventy-eight more kings who collected to avenge them. Of these eighty beards he made a mantle that reached from his head to his heels, for he was the largest man in Britain, and wore it as a warning to all to maintain law and order.

The romances of Arthur turned Rhitta Gawr into a fierce monarch called Rhyence, king of North Wales, an aggressor instead of a defender of justice, who, however, had his scarlet mantle purfled with the moderate number of eleven royal beards, and politely demanded that of King Arthur to complete the trimming, with what consequences no one acquainted with King Arthur can doubt.

Whence come the names of Ryence and Rhittar? They connect themselves closely with the universal words for ruler, the Gadhaelic *righ*, Teuton *rik*, Latin *rex*, and the *rajah* of India. *Rhys* is, in Welsh, a rushing man or warrior, and most likely comes from the same source ; and Rhesus, the chieftain, slain by Ulysses and Diomed, on the night of his arrival before Troy, probably was called from some extinct word of the same origin.

At any rate Rhys has ever since been a Welsh name, sometimes spelt in English according to its pronunciation as Reece, and sometimes as Rice. It has furnished the surnames of Rice, Rees.

In Brittany we meet a saint called by the diminutive of Rhys, Riok, or Rieuk. His legend begins with one of the allegories that arose from the prophecy, that the weaned child should put his hand on the cockatrice's den, for when he was almost an infant he was employed by the holy knight Derrien, to lead away in a scarf a terrible basilisk, whom the saint had tamed by making the sign of the cross over him. His parents were heathens, but were convinced by this miracle ; and he became, in after years, a great saint, living for forty-one years on a rock on the sea-coast, eating nothing but herbs and little fish, and wearing a plain garment which when it wore out was supplied by a certain ruddy moss growing all over his body. His name has continued in use in Brittany.*

---

* *Mabinogion* ; Pitre Chevalier, *Bretagne* ; Mallory, *Morte d'Arthur* ; Jones, *Welsh Sketches.*

SECTION VII.—*Percival.*

No name has had more derivations suggested for it than this. The Norman family so called came from Perche-val, the valley of the Perche ; but as to the knight of romance, he was at first supposed to be Perce-val, pierce the valley, on the principle on which Percy was hatched out of Pierce-eye, and the story invented of the Piercie who thrust his spear with the keys dangling on it into the eye of Malcolm Ceanômor at Alnwick Castle. The romance of Perceforest was even named on the principle that it was as suitable to pierce the forest as the valley. Mr. Keightley derives the name from the Arabic *Parse,* or *Parschfal,* poor dummling, who appears to have been the hero of an Eastern tale of a wonderful cup, whence arose the mysterious allegory of the Holy Greal. A Provençal Troubadour, named Kyot, or Guiot, professes to have found at Toledo a book written in heathen characters by a magician, Saracen on the father's side, but descended by his mother from Solomon. His book is lost, but two founded on it survive,—the German romance of Parzifal, by Wolfram von Eschenbach, and the Norman French, Sir Perceval, of Walter Mapes, Archdeacon of Oxford under Henry II.

Equally old, however, is a Welsh legend of Peredur, who is perhaps Pair-kedor, the warrior of the cauldron ; Pair-cyfaill would then be champion of the cauldron, or bowl ; Peredur was certainly a historical person, and may perhaps be the same as Perceval. Chrétien de Troyes has a long poem on the story of Perceval, and his adventures are almost identical with those of the Peredur of the *Mabinogion.*

The story of the orphan, stirred up to chivalry by the sight of the knight whom he took for an angel, the same as that of Mervyn les Breiz, here appears, and Perceval or Peredur shows some kindred with the dummling of Persia by his ignorance and dulness till he comes to the castle, where he sees the wounded king, the bleeding lance, and the Greal or bowl of pure gold, that are the great features in his history. Probably, the magic bowl was an Indo-European idea, but there seems to have been Druidic traditions about a magic bowl, which Bran the Blessed obtained from a great black man in Ireland, and which cured mortal wounds and raised the dead. It was one of the thirteen wonders of the Isle of Britain, and disappeared with Merddin in his glass vessel.

However, in the twelfth century, the ideas of this vessel had assumed a Christian form. It was the bowl used at the institution of the Holy Eucharist, and the lance was that of Longinus the centurion, brought to Bran by Joseph of Arimathea, and thenceforth its quest became the emblem of the Christian search for holiness through the world, only gratified by gleams here, but with full fruition hereafter. Perceval, once the companion and guard of the sacred Grail, gradually descended from his high estate, and became only a knight of the Round Table, high and pure of faith and spotless of life, but only on the same terms as the rest, and though not failing in the quest, still inferior to Galahad.

It is curious that his other name, Peredur, has by the sound been turned into Peter. One Robert de Barron tells, that from Bran, the Grail descended to Alan, and thence to Petrus his nephew; and a story of the Breton peasantry still gives the adventures of Perronik, like the original Peredur, an idiot at first, but sent to the Castle of Caerglas to fetch a diamond lance and golden cup, which would raise the dead by a touch.

The later French romances spoilt the nobleness and purity of Perceval's character, but he is always one of the best of the knights, and succeeds in finding the Sanc-greal. But Galahad, the pure and virgin knight, son of Lancelot, and predestined to occupy the Siége Perilous at the Round Table, resist all temptation, conquer all peril, and finally obtain full fruition of the Greal, then, at his own desire, pass out of the world of sin and care, has, in England, taken the place once the right of Peredur or Perceval, though Wagner's splendid 'Parcifal' has restored to him the chief place. I suspect him, as before said, to have been the separate produce of the story of Cattwg, first warrior, and afterwards hermit and saint, and that Galahad may have been an epithet from his starry purity.

In the *Mabinogion*, Perceval has a ladye love, whom, however, he only loves with distant chivalrous devotion, and who answers to his sister, who in Mallory's beautiful story gave the blood from her own veins to heal a lady who could only be cured with the life-blood of a pure virgin.

In the *Mabinogion* her name is Angharad Law-eurag, or with the hand of gold, and Angharad, or the free from shame, the undisgraced (from *angharz*), was continued in Wales, but it is now generally considered as the equivalent of Anne, and thus accounts for Anna being universally called in romance the sister of Arthur, and mother of the traitor nephew Medrawd.

The Welsh Angharawd, probably the source of Ankaret, which occurs in the family of Le Strange in 1344, is generally supposed to mean an anchorite; but as it has no parallel on the Continent, it is much more likely to be the Welsh Angharad. Annan was, however, a separate name—for the three sprightly ladies of Britain are Annan, Angharad, and Perwyr.

Myfanwy is one of the unaccountable feminine Welsh names, not yet extinct among families of strong national feeling, though in general Fanny has been substituted for it. It may possibly be Mabanwy, child of the water, or else it may be My-manwy, my fine (or rare one).

The three primary bards of Britain were Plenydd, Alawn, and Gwron, whom Mr. Davies explains as light, harmony, and virtue. Plenydd, it is thought, is related to Belenus; and Alawn is erected by ardent Cymrians into the mythic Greek Olen, who is said to have been the first writer of hymns in hexameter, and whom the Delphic poetess, Boeo, calls a Hyperborean; this name is said to mean the flute-player. At any rate, I have found Alwn Aulerv in Welsh

genealogies as brother of Bran the Blessed, and this must be the
real origin of the Breton Alan.   Elian and Hilarius were both used
as its Latinisms.*

It is first found in early Breton history, then it came to England
with Alan Fergéant, Count of Brittany, the companion of William
the Conqueror, and first holder of the earldom of Richmond, in
Yorkshire ; and, indeed, one Alan, partly Breton, partly Norman,
seems to have taken up his abode in our island before the Conquest,
and four besides the count came after it.   In the time of Henry I.,
one of these gentlemen, or his son, held Oswestry ; and as these were
the times when Anglo-Norman barons were fast flowing into Scotland,
his son Walter married a lady, whom Douglas's *Peerage of Scotland*
calls Eschina, the heiress of Molla and Huntlaw, in Roxburghshire ;
and their son, another Alan, secured another heiress, Eva, the
daughter of the Lord of Tippermuir ; and, becoming high steward of
Scotland, was both the progenitor of the race of Stuart, and the
original of the hosts of Alans and Allens, who have ever since filled
Scotland.   That country has taken much more kindly to this Breton
name than has England, in spite of Allen-a-dale, and of a few
families where Allen has been kept up ; but as a surname, spelt
various ways, it is still common.

Like *mare* in Latin, and *meer* in Teuton, the Gaelic *muir*, Welsh
môr, and Breton *mor*, are close kindred, and watery names derived
from them abound.

King Arthur's sister, Morgana, or Morgaine, Morgue la Fée, or La
Fata Morgana, as she is variously termed in different tongues, was
Morgan Maritime—the derivative from sea.   From her, or from
some lingering old Keltic notion in ancient Italy, the Sicilian
fisherman connects the towers and palaces painted on the surface
of the Mediterranean with La Fata Morgana, the lady of the sea.

Morgwn was the native name of the heresiarch, who called himself
by the Greek equivalent Pelagius, and thus named the Pelagian
heresy.   Some writers say that sundry heretic names lingered about
the Spanish Visigoths after their union with the Church, and instance
both Ario, a distinguished author, and Pelayo, the Asturian Robert
Bruce, as instances of names so borne.   However this may be,
Morgan has continued, even to the present day, to be very common
in Wales.

Morvryn may be sea-king.   "Morolt with the iron mace," as
romance calls him, the brother of Yseulte, who was killed by
Sir Trystan, is called Morogh by his own countrymen in Ireland.
It is the contraction of Muireadhach, or sea protector, a favourite
Irish name, though, after degenerating into Morogh, it was usually
rendered into Morgan, and so continues in modern Ireland.   It
is perhaps the same with Meriadek, or Meiriadwg, the title of
Conan, the chieftain who is said to have colonized Brittany, and
also with the Welsh Meredith, both as a Christian and a surname.
In Ireland, the sons of Morogh became O'Muireadaig, and then con-

* Villemarqué ; Cambro-Britain ; *Mabinogion ;* Mallory, *Morte d'Arthur.*

tracted into Murray. Muredach is said to have reigned over the
Scots from 733 to 736, and is transformed into Murdach, Murochat,
Muirtec, Mordacus. It must have become mixed with Muircheartach,
from *ceart* (a right), which has produced Moriertagh, Murtagh, or
Morty, as a Christian name in Ireland ; but it is now made into
Mortimer. It is Murdoch in Scotland, once very common, and not
yet extinct, and the North, adopting it with other Keltic names, calls
it Kjartan.

Muirgis, once common in Ireland, is rendered by Maurice, or
Morris, and Murchada has become Murphy.

And there is a name, still very common in the North of England,
that I cannot help connecting with some of these, namely Marmaduke,
which appeared among the chivalry of England about the thirteenth
century, and has never become extinct. It is most likely a corruption
of one or other of the *sea* names, in fact, it is not far from Muireadach ; or it may be the offspring of the Scottish title, Maormar, from
maor, a steward or officer, and *mor*, great, thus meaning the great
officer of the crown, the term which prevailed before the Saxon
Thegn or Danish Earl displaced it. *

SECTION VIII.—*Llew.*

We find Llew, lion, naming Lleurwg ab Coel ab Cyllyn, also called
Llewfer Mawr, the great light, and correctly translated by the Latin
Lucius, the king who is said to have sent messengers to Rome to bring
home Christianity, though some think Lucius a mere figment of
Roman writers accepted by the bards.

Llew is the name given in Welsh genealogies to the king of the
Orkneys, who married King Arthur's sister, and was the father of
Gwalchmai.

Llewel, lion-like, formed Llewelyn, which is not very early in
Wales, unless the Sir Lionel of romance be intended to represent it.
A Welsh Llewelyn seems to have come over to Ireland with Richard
Strongbow, and his descendants, after passing through the stage of
MacUighilins, are now the Quillinans.

The English have broken it down into Leoline. Llewelyn the
Great of Wales was a contemporary of King John, and from this
time the name has been much in use, partly from affection to the last
native prince, Llewelyn ap Gruffyd, who perished at Piercefield.
It is now usually Anglicized as Lewis for a Christian, Lewin for a
family, name.

The old records of Brittany give a most graceful story of the saint
who made Hervé a favourite in the duchy.

Hyvernion, a British bard, was warned by an angel in a dream to
come to Armorica in quest of his wife. Near the fountain of Rivannon,

* Villemarque ; Davies ; Ellis ; Cambro-Briton ; Geoffrey of Monmouth ;
O'Donovan ; Chalmers ; Munch.

he met a beautiful maiden drawing water, who, when he accosted her, sang "Though I am but a poor flower by the wayside, men call me the little queen of the fountain." Perceiving that she was the damsel of his vision, he married her, and they had one child, who was born blind, and was named by his parents in their sorrow, *Houerf*, or bitter. His worm-eaten oaken cradle is still shown in the parish of Trefla-ouenan, as a relic, for the blind child became both monk and poet, and according to his maxim, ' It is better to instruct a child than to gather wealth for him,' he composed numerous simple and religious poems, which have been sung by the Breton peasantry through the twelve hundred years that have passed since the death of the blind bard ; one of them, on the duties of a Christian child, is exceedingly beautiful. Arianwen, Silver woman, was another Welsh saint, whose name has continued in use.

Houerv, or Hervé, is not accepted in the *Roman Calendar*, but he was enthusiastically beloved in the country for which he had "made ballads," and Hervé has been the name of peer and peasant there ever since his time. Hervé came over to us among the many adventurers who "came out of Brittany." Two landowners so called are mentioned in Domesday Book, and the widely-spread surname of Harvey can hardly be taken from anything else, though some derive it from Heriwig, army war, a Teutonic word.

Here let us mention a Breton name, Tanneguy. There was a saint so called who founded an abbey at Finisterre, and who is claimed as a relation by the family of Du Chastel. It is curious to find Sir Tanneguy Du Chastel figuring among the heroes of Froissart, and making his old Christian name renowned.

But the local saints of the Kelts are far past enumeration, such as St. Monacella, or Melangell, whose Welsh name perhaps means honey-coloured or yellow. She was a little nun, who saved a hare hunted by Brocmael, prince of Powys, and is buried at Pennant Melangle. Also there was St. Sativola, or Sidwell, as she is called at Exeter, whose head was cut off by a mower with a scythe, and who had a well marking the spot, till the railway made away with it ; but at least she appears in her own church, with her head in one hand and a scythe in the other, and she has a window in the cathedral. Once she had namesakes, but they are all gone now.

Einion is said to signify an anvil, in Welsh, though the word most like it in Dr. Owen Pugh's dictionary is *einioes*, life. St. Einion was one of the early saints of the Cymry, after whom is named a spring at Llanvareth in Radnorshire. Another Einion was grandson of Howell Dha. The name is sometimes rendered by Æneas.

PART VI.

CHAPTER I.

THE TEUTON RACE.

SECTION I.—*Ground occupied by the Teutons.*

THE great mass of modern European nomenclature springs from the class of languages which it is convenient collectively to call Teutonic.

Nothing shows the identity of the entire Teutonic race more than the resemblance of the names in each of the branches. Many are found in each of the stems—Gothic, Scandinavian, and High and Low German—the same in sense, and with mere dialectic changes in sound, proving themselves to have sprung from a name, or from words, current in the original tribe before the various families parted from it. Others are found in some branches and not in others ; but there are comparatively very few belonging to a single tongue, and the analyzation of one into its component words is never safe till the same name has been sought for in the cognate languages. All the more popular of these personal names have gone on a little in the rear of the spoken language of the country, undergoing changes, though somewhat more slowly. Then, perhaps, some famous character has, as it were, crystallized his name for ever in the form in which he bore it, and it has been so continued, ever after, in his own country, as well as imitated by others, who often have adopted it in addition to their own original national form of the very same.

The Teutonic names were almost all compounds of two words. Sometimes a single word was used, but this was comparatively rare. For the most part, families were distinguished by each person bearing the same first syllable, with other words added to it to mark the individual, much in the same way as we have seen was the custom of the Greeks. Some families, like the royal line of Wessex, would alternate between Æthel and Ead ; others between Os and Sieg and the like. The original compounds forming names were expressive and well chosen ; but it seems as if when once certain words had come into use as component parts of names, they were apt to be put together without much heed to their appropriateness or signification, sometimes with rather droll results. Their names were individual, but every man was also called the son, every woman the daughter, of the father ; a custom that has not passed away from some parts of Norway, the Hebrides, or even the remoter parts of Lancashire, where, practically, the people use no surnames. A family was further collectively spoken of by the ancestor's or father's name, with the addition of *ing*, the derivative or patronymic ; as, in France, the sons of Meervig were the Meerwingen ; the sons of Karl, the Karlingen ; not Merovingians and Carlovingians, as Latinization has barbarously made them. Remarkable features, or distinguished actions, often attached soubriquets to individuals, and these passed on, marking off families in the genealogical songs of the Scallds ; and from these derivations, as well as from the fertile source of territorial terms, have most of our modern surnames arisen.

The words whence names were compounded were usually the names of deities and those of animals, together with epithets, or terms of office, generally conveying good auguries. They were usually connected with some great hero belonging to the various cycles of myth, in which the Teuton imagination revelled, and which, for the most part, under Christian influence, descended from the divine to the heroic, and then to the fairy tale.

These Teutonic centres of legend may be considered as threefold. There is the great Scandinavian mythological system, as elaborate and as poetical as that of the Greeks, and which belonged in part, at least, to the Goths, Franks, and Saxons, though their early conversion deprived it of five hundred years of development ; and Louis le Debonnaire unfortunately destroyed the poetry that would have shown us what it had been among them.

Next, there is the cycle of Romance, represented in Scandinavia by the latter part of the elder Edda and by the Volsunga Saga, in Denmark by the Vilkina Saga, and in the centre of Europe by the Nibelungenlied, where old myths have become heroic tales that have hung themselves round the names of Attila the Hun and Theodoric of Verona, who in Germany is the centre of a great number of ancient legends, once doubtless of deified ancestors.

Thirdly, we have the grand poetical world, in which Charlemagne has been adopted as the sovereign, and Roland as the hero—the world of French romance, Spanish ballad, and Italian poetry, which is to continental chivalry what the Round Table is to our own.

CHAPTER II.

NAMES FROM TEUTON MYTHOLOGY.

SECTION I.—*Guth.*

IT is hard to class this first class of names under those of mytho-logy, for they bear in them our own honoured word for the Deity; and though some arose when the race were worshippers of false divinities, yet under the same head are included many given in a Christian spirit.

Some philologists tell us, though they are not unanimous in the explanation, that this name is from the same source as the Sanscrit *Svadáta,* self-given or uncreate, and as the Zend *Quadatu,* Persian *Khuda,* and our own Teuton term for Deity—the Northern *Gud* and Gothic *Guth,* whence the High German *Cot* and low German *God.* Others explain it as the creating or all-pervading. Others, again, derive it from *od,* possession, and in early Christian times there was a distinction between *God* (mas.) and the neuter *god,* an idol. It is equally doubtful whether this divine word be the origin of the adjec-tive, *guth, gut, cuot, gode.* Whether they are only cognate, or whether they are absolutely alien, and the adjective be related to the Greek ἀγαθός—wherever they come from, the names derived from either God or good are so much alike, as to be inextricably mixed, so that they must be treated of together.

The North is the great region of these names; but they are not very easy to distinguish from the very large class beginning with *gund,* war, as in pronunciation, and latterly in spelling, the dis-tinctive letters, *n* and *u,* get confounded or dropped.

It is probable, however, that among those from *Gud* we may place Gudhr, which was owned by one of the Valkyrier, the battle maids of northern belief, and must, with her, have meant the brave, or the goddess; Guda was known in Scandinavia; and Germany used the name, till it was translated into Bona or Bonne, and thus passed away

In the northern version of the *Nibelungen,* the second heroine is Gudruna. The last syllable means wisdom, or counsel; it is the same as *rune,* the old northern writing, and alludes to the wisdom that Odin won at so dear a rate. Gudruna may then be translated divine wisdom, a name well suited to the inspired priestesses, so highly regarded by the Teutons. It was very common in the North; eighteen ladies so called appear in the Icelandic *Landnama;* and it was so universal there, that Johann and Gudruna there stand for man and woman, like our *N.* or *M.* In Norway, likewise, Gudruna is common; and, near Trondjem, is contracted into Guru; about Bergen, into Gern or Gero. High German tongues rendered it Kutrun.

The *Landnama-bok*, which gives all the pedigrees of the free inhabitants of Iceland for about four hundred years, namely, from the migration to the twelfth century, gives us Gudbrand, divine staff, now commonly called Gulbrand; Gudbiorg, divine protection; Gudiskalkr, God's servant, or scholar, which is the very same as Godeskalk, the name assumed by the first Christian prince of the Wends of Mecklenburg, who was martyred by his heathen subjects, and thus rendered Gottschalk a German Christian name; in Illyrian, Gocalak; and known even in Italy as Godiscalco, just like Gildas or Theodoulos. Gudleif is feminine, Gudleifr masculine, for a divine relic; and this last coming to England with the Danes, turned into a surname as Gulleiv, then shortened into Gulley, and lengthened into Gulliver—a veritable though quaint surname for the Lemuel Gulliver whom Swift conducts through Laputa and Brobdignag, with coolness worthy of northern forefathers.

Gudleik, divine service, is, perhaps, repeated by our St. Guthlac; but both these may come from *gund*. Gudmund contracts into Gulmund, divine protection. Five ladies called Gudny appear, which latter termination is a common feminine form, and comes from the same word as our *new*. If an adjective, it would mean young and pretty; if a noun, it stands for the new moon, a very graceful name for a woman. Guni is the contraction used in the North.

Gudfinn and Gudfinna must be reminiscences of Finn, whom we shall often meet in the North. Gudrid and Gudridur mean the divine shock or passion, from the word *hrid* or *hrith*, one that is constantly to be met with as a termination in northern names, and which has sometimes been taken for the same as *frid*, with the aspirate instead of the *f.* Guri is the contraction.

Gudveig's latter syllable would naturally connect itself with the *wig*, war, that is found in all the Gothic tongues; but Professor Munch translates it as liquid—divine liquor—the same meaning as Gudlaug and the masculine Gudlaugr; *laug*, from *la*, liquor, or the sea. Divine sea, would be a noble meaning for the Gulla or Gollaa to which Gudlaug is commonly reduced in Norway.

Gudvar is divine prudence or caution, the last part being our word *ware;* in fact, every combination of the more dignified words was used with this prefix in the North, and it was probably the Danes who introduced this commencement into England, for we do not find such in pedigrees before the great irruption in Ethelred I.'s time.

In spite of the romantic story of Earl Godwine's rise into honour from acting as a guide to a Danish chief, it is certain that he was of an honourable family, of Danish connection, and thus he probably obtained his name, which would mean God's beloved, and thus translate Theophilos. Few are recorded in history as bearing the same ; but there must have been some to transmit the frequent surname of Godwin and Goodwin, the latter connected to our minds with the Goodwin Sands, which were really once the estate of the ambitious earl. Godin is the remains of the same in French. It is found at Cambrai, in 1065, belonging to the " Echanson d'Ostrevant." The old French word *godeau* meant a cup, and, as Godin soon became a surname of a family which carried a cup in their arms, there might have been a double allusion to the office of the ancestor and to the sound of the name. Godine and Godinette were also in use there, but were considered as feminines to Goderic—a very old word, which, strange to say, was, at Cambrai, equivalent to *fainéant,* or 'ne'er do weel,' it must be supposed in allusion to some particularly discreditable Goderic, as everywhere else it signifies divine ruler. Our own St. Goderic was an Anglo-Saxon abbot, and the name, which means divine rule, grew so common among the English, that the Norman nobles called Henry I. and his Queen, Godric and Godiva, in derision of the lady's English blood. Goderic does, indeed, swarm in Domesday Book, and has left the surname Goodrich.

> " The woman of a thousand summers back,
> Godiva, wife to that grim Earl who ruled
> At Coventry,"

really existed, and was probably Godgifu, the gift of God, like Dorothea, as *ive* or *eva* was the Norman rendering of *gifu.* Her namesakes are in multitudes in Domesday, and, in 1070, one lived in Terouenne, a pious lady, tormented, and at last murdered, by her husband, on which account she was canonized as St. God leva.

The High Germans, however, made far more use of this commencement, and won for it the chief honour. The elder forms are according to the harsh old German sounds—*Cotahelm,* divine helmet, *Cotahramn,* divine raven, *Cotalint,* divine serpent ! But the more universal spelling prevailed, as Frankish or Allemannic saints came into honour. Gotthard, bishop of Hildesheim, was one of these. His name, which may be rendered divine resolution, or, perhaps, firm through God, was also borne by Godard, abbot of Rouen, and has adhered to the great mountain-pass of the Alps, as well as to families of Godard in France, Goddard in England. In Germany it is still used as a Christian name ; and in Lithuania is Gattinsch, Gedderts, or Kodders.

Gottfrid, divine peace, was abbot of St. Quentin early in the eleventh century, and named two godsons, the canonized bishop of Amiens, and the far more famous Gottfried of Lorraine, who might well, as leader of the crusading camp, bequeath his name to all the nations whose representatives fought under him, and thus we find it everywhere. In Florence it has become Giotto, to distinguish the artist who gave us Dante's face ; in Germany, cut down into Goetz, it distinguished the terrible, though simple-hearted, champion with the iron hand, then, falling into a surname, belonged to Göthe. We received our Godfrey from the conqueror of Jerusalem, but previously the Gottfried had been taken up by the French, and was much used

by the Angevin counts in the Gallicized form of Geoffroi. In alternation with Foulques, the name continued among the Angevins till
they came to the English throne ; and then Jaffrez, as the Bretons
called the young husband of their duchess Constance, was excited to
rebellion by the Provençals as Jaffré. Geoffrey spread among the
English, and the Latinizers made it into Galdfridus, which misled
Camden into translating it into Glad-peace.

English.	Breton.	French.	Italian.
Godfrey	Jaffrez	Godefroi	Goffredo
Geoffrey		Godafrey	Godofredo
Jeffrey		Geoffroi	Giotto
Jeff		Jeoffroi	

Spanish.	German.	Polish.	Lusatian.
Godofrédo	Gottfried	Godfrid	Frido
Gofredo	Götz		Fridko
	Gödel	Dutch.	
		Govert	

Besides these, Germany has Godegisel, divine pledge ; Godebert and
Godeberta, divine brightness ; and Gottwald, divine power : repeated
in Provence by Jaubert.

Germany also has a Gottleip, the same with the old Anglo-Saxon
Guthlaf, meaning the leavings of God, or remains of Divinity, but
which has been made in modern German into Gottlieb, or love, and
contracted in Lower Lusatia into Lipo ; in Dantzic, into Lipp. There
are several of these modern devotional German names, such as
Gottlob, the very same in meaning as belonged to the Speaker of the
Rump, Praise God Barebones, but has been continued as Lopo, or
Lopko, in Lusatia.   In fact, the Moravians use these appellations,
and thus we have the modern coinage of Gottgetreu, Gotthilf, and
Gotthilfe, and even of Gottsei-mit-dir, much like the Diotisalvi of
Italy, and not without parallel among the early Christians.

The Spanish Goths left behind them Guzman, once either divine
might (*magen*), or Man of God. Guzman el Bueno was an admirable
early Spaniard, who beheld his own son beheaded rather than
surrender the town committed to his keeping.   It became a surname,
and it may be remembered how Queen Elizabeth played with that of
Philip II.'s envoy, when she declared that if the king of Spain had
sent her a gooseman, she had sent him a man-goose.

Another old form taken by this word was Geata, or Gautr.   It was
used as an epithet of Odin, and has been explained by some to mean
the keeper, and be derived from *geata*, to keep ; but it is far more
likely that it is only another pronunciation of the same term for the
All-pervader or Creator.

Gautr is sometimes a forefather, sometimes a son of Odin ; and
there is a supposed name-father, Gaut, for the Goths of Sweden,
whether they are the same as the Goths of Italy and Spain or not.

In this form, Gaut had its own brood of derivatives, chiefly in Sweden, but with a few straying into Germany; such as Gosswin, divine friend, and Gossbert, in Provençal Joubert, Gossfried, which may be the right source of Geoffrey.

The most noted of all is, however, Gotzstaf, or Gozstaf, meaning either the divine staff, or the staff of the Goths. Twice has it been endeared to the Swedes; first by Gustaf Vasa, the brave man who delivered the country from the bondage of the union of Calmar, and whose adventures in Dalecarlia, like those of Bruce in Scotland, were more endearing than even his success. Him the country calls affectionately " *Gamle Kong Gosta*," and no less was its love and pride in his noble descendant, Gustaf Ádolf, " the Lion of the North, the bulwark of the Protestant faith," who casts the only gleam of brightness over the dull waste of the Thirty Years' War. Thus it is no wonder that so many bear his name, Gustav, Gosta, Gjosta, that it is considered in the North as the national nickname of a Swede; and it has the feminine Gustava.

English.	French.	Italian.	Swedish.
Gustavus	Gustave	Gustavo	Gozstav Gustav Gosta Gjosta
German.	Lett.	Esthonian.	
Gustaf	Gustavs Gusts	Kustav Kustas	

SECTION II.—*The Aasir.*

Tacitus tells us that the supreme god of the Germans was called Esus or Hesus, and though some have thought he meant the Keltic Hu, it is far more likely that he had heard the word *As* or *Æs*, the favourite Teutonic term for their divinities.

The word is known in all the Teutonic languages: it is *As, Aasir* in the North, *Os, Es* in Anglo-Saxon, and *Anseis* or *Ensi* in Gothic and High German. Jornandes tells us that the Goths called their deified ancestors *anses*, but it is only in the North that the literature of the Pantheon of the race was so developed that we can follow it out.

The Aasir are in northern myth a family like the Olympian gods of Greece; they inhabit Valhalla, and there receive the spirits of the worthy dead, to feast and hunt with them till the general battle and final ruin of all things, when a new and perfect world shall arise.

Blended with this notion there is a grand allegory of the contention between the seasons. The Aasir, or summer gods, are always struggling with the Hrimthusir, or frost powers, and winning the victory over them.

And further, the tradition of a migration from the warmer East,

U

and of the battles with the northern aborigines, is mixed up in the legends, and the Aasir are a band of heroic settlers from Asgard or Asia, who fix themselves in Europe, and become the ancestors of all the various races of Teutons.

So speak the *Edda* and the various sagas of the North ; and though the poetry and legends of the other nations have not come down to us, their use of the names formed from *as, os, ans,* testifies to their regard for the term as conveying the idea of deity.

To begin with the North, where the pronunciation is the purest, the word in the singular is *aas,* in the plural, *aasir* or *œsir,* and the older form of these names began with the *aa,* though usually spelt with a single *a* in Norsk and Icelandic, with an *e* in Danish. And let it be remembered throughout, that the Northern *aa* is pronounced like our *o.*

The Low Germans change the *aas* into *os,* and in this way most of the Anglo-Saxon and continental German names commence.

Ans, the High German and Gothic form, occurs in the Frank, Lombardic, and Gothic names. Asgaut or, as the Saxons call it, Osgod, and Asgrim, are both reduplications of divinity.

Asa appears in the *Landnama-bok,* and Aasir, the collective term for the gods, is used in Norway as a name corrupted into Asser, or Ozer. It is probably the same with Esa, the ancestor of the Bernician kings, who may have used ' Os ' in compliment to him. Aasketyl is the divine kettle or cauldron, probably connected with creation. It was usually called in the North Askjell, and has the feminine Askatla. Oscetyl, as the Anglo-Saxons spelt it, was used by them in Danish times, when a so-called marauder terribly tormented them ; but Frank pronunciation so affected the Normans, that they brought in the name as Ansketil ; and a person so called was settled at Winchester in 1148.

Aasbjorn, divine bear, is a queer compound, and so is Aasolfr, or divine wolf ; but as will be shown when we come to the beasts themselves, a certain divinity did hedge about these formidable animals in the days of name-coining in the North. The first Asolfr with whom I have met was a Christian, who, with twelve companions, was wrecked upon the shores of Iceland in the interval between its settlement and conversion. They erected buildings, resolutely refused all commerce with the heathen, and lived solely on the produce of their fishing. A church has since been built where they settled. The name has fallen into Asulf in the North, and was paralleled by Osulf in England. As to the divine bear, he had a wider fame, for Asbiorn came among the Northmen to Neustria, and was there Frenchified. An Osborn was the seneschal who was murdered in the sleeping chamber of William in the stormy days of the minority of the future conqueror ; and his son, William Fitzosborn, was the chief friend and confidant of the stern victor of Hastings. Osborn figures in Domesday, and has now become a common English surname, which used to be translated house-born, before comparison with the other tongues had shown the true relations of the word. Asbera is the northern feminine.

Esbern Snare, or the swift, the Danish noble, whose heart and eyes were to have furnished Finn's child with amusement, was really a powerful earl at the end of the twelfth century, and his still more celebrated twin brother, Bishop Absalom, was a great statesman and warrior, and prompted Saxo Grammaticus to write his chronicle of Norway. Bishop Absalom is believed to have, like his brother, received at baptism one of the derivatives from the old gods of Denmark, namely, Aslak, the divine sport or reward, a name which in Denmark and Sweden is always called Axel, in which shape it belonged to Oxenstjerna, the beloved minister of Gustavus Adolphus, and has ever since been a favourite national name. Aslak is in the North pronounced Atlak, and sometimes taken for the original Atli in the Volsunga Saga; but this is far more probably the Tartar Attalik. We had a Bernician Aslak of the like meaning. Never were there a more noted pair of twins than these brothers, of the *bear* and the *sport*. Well might their birth be first announced to their absent father, on his return to the isle of Soro, by' twin church steeples, built by the mother to greet his eyes over the sea. His name, Askar, or Ansgjerr, divine spear, was so common that sixteen appear in the Iceland roll, and the word Osgar gets confused with the Keltic Oscar, son of Ossian; nay, it may perhaps have been his proper name. A Frank Ansgar, born in Picardy about the year 800, was the apostle of Denmark, and afterwards bishop of Hamburgh and Bremen ; he was canonized as Anscharius, and is popularly called in his bishopric St. Scharies, by which title the collegiate church of Bremen is called. It is curious to find the Ansbrando of ancient Lombardy reflected by the Asbrandr, divine sword, of Iceland. Lombardy had likewise Anshelm, the divine helmet, softened down into Anselmo or Antelmo, the name of that mild-natured Lombardic Archbishop of ours, whose constancy cost him so dear in his contention with the furious Rufus and politic Beauclerc. That firmness, however, together with his deep theological writings, won him the honours of sanctity, though it is only on the Continent that his name took root : England had no national love for her Anselm ; and he chiefly appears in Italy, France, and Germany, where he has been cut short as Anso, endeared as Ensilo, has a feminine Ansa, and is called by the Jews Anschel.

Of other terms which, like *helm*, give the idea of protection, there are many ; the feminine Asbjorg or Asburg, divine fort, is reflected by the Anglo-Saxon Asburgha. Asgardr, divine guard, may be most probably an allusion to the abode of the gods, Asgard, the abode to which the rainbow-arch Bifrost was the access, trod, according to the grand death song of Eirikr Blodaxe, by the spirits of the courageous dead on their way to feast in the hall of Odin. As men's names appear the Norwegian Asgard, and Ansgard, a Winchester householder in Stephen's time ; but the Northern feminine Asgerdur is the divine maiden, in honour of the goddess Gerda. Asmundr is the northern form of a favourite name, giving the idea of protecting with the hand. It is called Ansmunt in old German, Osmund in Anglo-Saxon and Norman-French, and in this form was most popular,. at first perhaps,

from Osmond de Centeville, the brave Norman, who fled from Laon
with the young Richard Sans Peur, but afterwards for the sake of a
Norman Osmond, who was canonized as Bishop of Salisbury, whence
this form in England and Osmont in France have continued.
Aasvalldr, divine power, was in Germany Ansvalt, and has modernized as Asvald ; but the Anglo-Saxon Oswald was the glory of the
name in the Northumbrian monarch, "free of hand," as even his
Welsh foes called him, who has left Oswald to be an English name.
Asvor and Asvora express divine prudence.

"Aslaug, dottur Sigurdur Fafnisbana," is recorded in the *Landnama-bok* in sober earnest as having married Ragnar Lodbrog.

Divine legacy, or relic, appears in Asleif, the English Oslaf.
The northern Aasny, with Ashildur, has always been a favourite.
Osthryth, divine threatener, came out of the house of Bernicia into
Mercia, where she was murdered by the Danes, and revered as St.
Osyth with a priory in her honour.

Thoroughly English are likewise Osmod, divine mood or wrath ;
Osfrith, divine peace ; Osred, divine council ; Osgifu, divine gift ;
Oswine, divine friend, the third of the admirable but short-lived
kings of Bernicia ; Oswiu, who overthrew him, was probably named
from a word meaning sacred, of which more in its place. Osbeorht
we share with Germany, which calls it Osbert, and has the feminine
Osberta. In fact, most of these names were in use there, beginning
with *os* or *ans*, according to the dialect in which they were used.
Ansgisel was one of the Frankish forms, that section of the race
always making much use of *gisel*, a pledge.*

Section III.—*Odin, or Grîmr.*

The head of the Aasir was Odin, as we have learned to call him
from the North, which worshipped him long after we had forgotten
our Wuotan, except in the title of his day of the week. There are
various opinions as to the meaning of his name, some making it come
from the word for rage in the North, *odhr ;* in A. S., *wod;* and still
wuth in German ; and the adjective *wud* in Scottish. It thus may
allude to Odin being the god of storm and tempest. Others take the
name from O. G., *watan*, N., *vatha*, to pervade, the title of the
Divinity, as being *through* all things. This is, in fact, the same as God.

However this may be, Odin, in the higher myths, is the All-
father, standing at the head of Asgard, as Zeus does of Olympus. He
governs all things, and knows all things. He obtained this mighty
influence, says the *Edda*, by hanging for nine nights on the world-
tree, Yggdrasil, without food or drink, transfixed with a spear, as a
self-sacrifice. Then he looked down into the depth, and sank from
the tree into it; but in the abyss beneath he drank the costly poet-

* Grimm ; Turner; Munch; Lappenberg; Mallet; *Landnama-bok ;
Domesday; * Michaelis; Hermann Luning, *Edda ; Hist. of Scandinavia ;*
Marryat, *Jutland.*

mead, and learnt powerful songs, obtaining the Runes, the beginning of wisdom, by which he could compel to his will all nature : wind, sea, and fire, hate and love !

Coupled with this entirely divine Odin, there was the abiding notion of ancestry beginning with a god ; and no one, of any nobility, was content without having Odin for his forefather. Even when Christianity dethroned Odin from his place in Heaven, he was still retained as a heroic ancestor ; and somewhat grotesquely, the old chroniclers, after carrying up their kings to him, brought him down from Noah, and he became reduced to be the leader of the great migration from Asia, while the gods were made his human sons.

We do not find Odin itself forming part of any personal name ; it seems to have been avoided as Zeus was in Greece, and, to a greater degree, Jupiter in Rome. But he had no less than forty-nine epithets, all of which are rehearsed in the prose *Edda*, and his votaries were called by one or other of these.

Finn has been spoken of already as one of these ; also Gautr, as one of the forms of divinity. Grîmr is another, coming from the old Norse word *grîma*, a mask or helmet. Odin was called Grímr, meaning the concealed, or possibly the helmeted ; and the names beginning with Grim may generally be referred to the hidden god.

Grimhild, or in High German, Krimhild, was originally one of the Valkyrier, or choosers of the slain, who was so called, as being endowed with a helmet of terror. Hidden battle-maid, or helmeted battle-maid, would be her fittest translation. In the northern version of the *Nibelungenlied*, Grimhild is the witch-mother of Sigurd's wife, Gudrun, and performs a part like that of the Oda, or Uta, in the German and Danish versions, in which the heroine herself is called Kriemhild, or Chriemhild, and does her fatal part in wreaking revenge for the murder of her husband. Grimhhildur was somewhat used in the North, but nothing was so fashionable as Grim, who occurs twenty-nine times in the *Landnama-bok*, and with equal frequency in Domesday ; besides that one of these Danish settlers left his name to Grimsby, in Lincolnshire.

Grim has, of course, his kettle, in the North, Grimketyl, or Grimkjell ; in Domesday, Grimchel ; an allusion, probably, to creation, quaint as is the sound to our ears. Grimperaht, or helmeted splendour, first was turned into Grimbert, then into the common German surname of Grimmert. Grimar in the North was Grimheri in Germany. Grim was in greater favour as a prefix in the High German dialects than in the North, and chiefly in the Frankish regions.

Grimbald, helmeted prince, was a monk of St. Omer, transplanted by King Alfred to Oxford, in the hope of promoting learning, and he thus became a Saxon saint. Grimvald, helmeted ruler, was a *maire du palais* in the Faineant times of the Franks ; and in Spanish balled el Conde Grimaltos, a knight at the court of Charlemagne, was slandered and driven away with his wife to the mountains, where the lady gives birth to a son, who was baptized Montesinos, from the place of his birth, and educated in all chivalry till he was old enough to go to Charlemagne's court, refute the slander by the ordeal of battle, and restore his family to favour.   Grimaldo was a name borne by the Lombard kings, and left remains in the great Grimaldi family of Genoa.

Most of our English Grims were importations, and there are few of them, though we have Grimulf in Domesday, probably a Dane.

SECTION IV.—*Frey.*

Every false religion preserves in some form or other the perception of a Divine Trinity, and the Teutonic Triad consisted of Odin, Frey, and Thor, whose images always occupied the place of honour in the temples, and who owned the three midmost days of the week.

The history of the word *freyr* is very curious.   The root is found in *pri*, Skt., to love or rejoice, the Zend *frî*, the Greek φίλος.   To be glad was also to be free ; so *freon* or *frigon* means to free and to love, and thence *free* in all its forms (N. *fri* ; Goth. *frige* ; H. G. *frei* ; L. G. *freoh*).   Thus, again, the Germans came by *froh*, and we by *fresh.* *Fro* was both glad and dear ; and as in Gothic *frowida* was joy, so is *freude* in modern German ; and we exult in *frolics* and *freaks*.   He who loved was known by the present participle, *frigonds*, the *friend* of modern English, the same in all our Teutonic tongues ; and as the effect of love is peace, the term was *fred* or *fried*, our Saxon *frith*, which we have lost in the French-Latin word.   To be free was to be noble, so the free noble was *Frauja*, the name by which Ulfilas always translates Κύριος, in the New Testament, by a beautiful analogy, showing, indeed, that our Lord is our Friend and our Redeemer, loving us, and setting us free.

Frauja, or free, was the lord and master, so his wife was likewise *frea*, both the beloved and the free woman ; the northern *frue*, German *frau*, and Dutch *vrowe*, all, as *donna* had done in Italy, becoming the generic term for woman.

Out of all the derivatives of this fertile and beautiful term, there were large contributions to mythology, and a great number of names.

Freyr, lord, lover, was once a god of very high rank, lord of sun and moon, hermaphrodite, and regulating the seasons, blessing marriage, and guarding purity : and this was probably a universal idea brought from Asia.

As old notions formed into mythic tales, and the gods grew human, the wife of Odin was invented, and what could she be but the *frau*, the lady of Asgard, Frigga ?   Again, Freyr was brought down from his mysterious vagueness, and turned into a nephew of Odin, with the moon to take care of, and, moreover, was disintegrated into a brother and sister, called Freyr and Freya.

The sixth day of the week had probably originally belonged to Freyr, but Frigga got possession of it ; and, in right of her presiding over love and marriage, she was considered to be Venus ; and in France and Italy her day is still Vendredi and Venerdì, while we have it as Friday, the Germans as Freitag, the North as Fredag.

Freya is also a goddess of love, and drives over every battle-field with her car drawn by cats (once, perhaps, panthers, like those of Bacchus, whom her brother is thought to resemble), and chooses half the slain, whom she marshals to their seats at the banquet of Valhalla. Her husband, Othur or Odhr, curiously repeats Odin's name, as she does Frigga's. She weeps continually drops of gold when he is absent, and the metal is poetically called Freya's tears.

Her brother, Freyr, was always a chaste, dignified, beneficent personage, a sort of severe Bacchus, or grave Apollo. In the great final battle, he is to be destroyed by Surti. He is the tutelary god of Sweden, as was Odin of the Saxons.

There are hosts of names connected with these deities, or the words sprung from their source. *Frith* in Saxon, *frey* or *freya* in the North, *fried* in German, falling in France into *froi*, was a favourite termination generally masculine, and so probably in honour of Freyr ; and though it is safe to translate it peace, it probably also meant freedom.

Old Spanish has Froila, or Fruela, among the kings of the Asturias, and this may be translated lord, and compared with the Freavine, or Frowin, free darling, now become Frewen. Franta, too, was a king of the Spanish Suevi.

Fritigern, king of the Visigoths, who first fixed himself on the Danube, bore the name afterwards Frideger (spear of peace), in Germany, a compound much resembling that borne by that Jezebel of the Meerwings, Fredegunt, or Frédégonde, as she is called by French historians. Freygerdur öf the North, as found in the *Landnama-bok*, serving four men and two women, is there explained either as freedom-preserver, or peace-keeper.

But what is to be said of Fridthjof, or Frithjof, the renowned hero of the Frithjofsaga, being no better than peace-thief ? Northern pirates thought no scorn of being thieves, and we shall fall on plenty more of them ; but the compound is certainly startling.

Fridulf, or Fridolf, peace wolf, is nearly as bad ; but it seems to have contracted into Friedel in Germany, and expanded into Fridolin, probably in imitation of Fedlim, or some such Erse name, since the saint thus recorded in the calendar is one of the many Scottish missionaries of the fifth century, who preached to the Burgundians. He is the titular patron of the Swiss canton of Glarus, whose shield bears his figure in the Benedictine dress he never wore. Thence Schiller took the name of the youth in his ballad on the strange adventure of Isabel de la Paz of Portugal, which is best known through Retzch's illustrations. The German Friedel must be short for this, as Frider is for Fridheri, peace-warrior. In fact, Germany is the great land of this commencement, and has fostered the best known of the whole. There was indeed a Fridrikr in the *Land-nama-bok*, and a Fredreg, or Frederic, in Domesday, but these would have been forgotten but for an old Frisian bishop, Freod-horic, who, in the time of Louis le Debonnaire, had been murdered while praying in his chapel, and being canonized, was a patron saint of the Swabian house. Friedrich with the red beard, or

Barbarossa, a Ghibelline hero, caused Federigo to be popular among that party in Italy; and when his Neapolitan grandson's claims to the kingdom of the Two Sicilies had been transmitted, through Manfred's daughter, to the Aragonese monarchs, Fadrique became

English.	French.	Breton.	Spanish.
Frederick	Frédéric	Fèidrik	Fadrique
Fred	Ferry		
Portuguese.	**Italian.**	**German.**	**Dutch.**
Frederico	Federigo	Fridrich	Frederik
Federico		Fritz	Freerik
Frisian.	**Swedish.**	**Danish.**	**Swiss.**
Frerk	Fredrik	Frederik	Fredli
Frek			Fridli
Friko			
Russian.	**Polish.**	**Slovak.**	**Bohemian.**
Fridrich	Fryderyk	Friderik	Bedrich
	Fryc		
Lusatian.	**Lettish.**	**Lithuanian.**	**Finn.**
Fidrich	Sprizzis	Prydas	Rietu
Bedrich	Prizzis	Prydikis	Wettrikki
	Wrizzis	Priczus	Wetu
Hungarian.	Wridriks		Wetukka
Fridrik	Pridriks	**Greek.**	
		Φρεσδερικος	

FEMININE.			
English.	**French.**	**Portuguese.**	**Italian.**
Frederica	Frédérigue	Frederica	Federica
Freddie			Feriga
German.	**Swiss.**	**Polish.**	**Bohemian.**
Fridrike	Fredrika	Frydryka	Bedriska
Fritze			
Fritzinn	**Greek.**		
Rike	Φρεδερική		
Rikchen			

usual in Spain. Friedrich had grown national in Germany, and not a king of Prussia till the present has reigned without being so called, in compliment to their hero, who, while the soldiers called him Old Fritz, thought it graceful to write himself Frédéric, having, with his French tastes, taken a dislike to the sound of his own name, even in the softened spelling of his adopted language. It was from the father of this monarch that the son of George II. was called Frederick, a name we have twice had next in succession to the crown. The Danes obtained the name from their German connections, and make it alternate on the throne with Christiern. The feminine is a late invention in Germany, very common there but barely recognized elsewhere.

Probably this popular Frederick has devoured all the other forms with the same commencement ; for after the middle ages had fairly begun, we hardly ever hear of the German Fridrad, Fridrada, Fridhelm, Fridrun, Fridbald, Fridbert, Fridburg, Fridgard, Fridilind. Fridmund, peace protection, Fridwald, peace-power, has been preserved in Friesland as Fredewolt, Fredo, or Freddo. Fridleifr in the North has fallen into Friedlieb in Germany : it is the same as the Frithlaf whom our Saxon chroniclers bestowed on Wuotan by way of ancestor.

Our own Saxon saint, Frithswith, strong in peace, was the daughter of the Lord of Oxford, in the eighth century. She lived in a little cell at Thornbury, had various legendary adventures, which may be seen portrayed in a modern window of the cathedral at Oxford, and became the saintly patroness of the University and Cathedral, where, by the name of St. Fridiswid, she reigned over Alma Mater, till Wolsey laid hold of the church and its chapter for his own splendid foundation of Christchurch. Frethesantha Paynell was wife of Geoffrey Lutterell, about the fourteenth century ; and Fridiswid is by no means uncommon in the old genealogies of Essex and the northern counties. Alban Butler gives Frewissa as the contraction ; but in Ireland, according to Mr. Britton's capital story of *The Election,* it is Fiddy.

From *frei,* free, modern Germany has taken Freimund, by which they mean Freemouth, though it ought to be free protection, Freimuth, free courage, Freidank, free thought. But the older word for free plays a far more important part in modern nomenclature, namely, *Frang,* the High German form of free lord.

The nation called Cherusci by Tacitus denominated themselves Frangen when they warred on northern Gaul, overspread it, and termed it for themselves Frankreich. As their primary energy decayed their dominion divided ; Frankenland, under the Latinism of Franconia, became leagued with the lands of the Swabians, Allemanni, and Saxons, and thus became part of Deutschland and of the Holy Roman Empire, while Frankreich was leavened by the Gallo-Romans, who worked up through their Frank lords, and made their clipped Latin, or *Langue d'oui** (the tongue of aye), the national language, and yet called themselves *Les Français,* and the country France. And as the most enthusiastic and versatile of the European commonwealth, they so contrived to lead other nations, and impress their fashions on them, that the Eastern races regarded all Europeans as

* 'We-we' is the name now given by the South Sea Islanders to the French.

Franks, called their country Franghistan, and the patois spoken by them in the Levant became Lingua Franca.

Franc, or Franco, was the archbishop of Rouen who made terms with Rollo ; but the name of real fame arose otherwise.

Long before the emperor Charles V. had pronounced French to be the language for men, an Italian merchant of Assisi caused his son, Giovanni, to be instructed in it as a preparation for commerce. The boy's proficiency caused him to be called 'il Francesco,' the Frenchman, until the baptismal Giovanni was absolutely forgotten ; and as Francesco he lived his ascetic, enthusiastic life ; as Franciscus was canonized ; and the mendicant order, humbly termed by him *fratres minores*, lesser brethren, were known as Franciscans throughout the Western Church.

Many a little Italian of either sex was christened by his soubriquet, and though one of the first feminines on record was the unhappy lady whose fall and doom Dante made famous, yet the sweet renown of the devout housewife, Santa Francesca di Roma, assisted its popularity ; there was a Françoise at Cambrai even in 1300, and Cecarella is the peasant mother of a damsel in the Pentamerone.

San Francesco di Nola reformed the Franciscans into a new order, called the Minimi, or least, as the former ones were the Minores. It is to him that the spread of the name beyond the Alps is chiefly owing, for Louise of Savoy was so devoted to him, that she made him sponsor and name-father to her passionately loved son, and sewed his winding-sheet with her own hands.

The name was not absolutely new to France, for that of the grandson of the first Montfort, Duke of Brittany, had been Fransez, and so had been that of the father of the Duchess Anne, who carried her old Keltic inheritance to the crown of France ; but it was her daughter's husband, François I., the godson of the saint of Nola, who was the representative Frenchman, the type of showy and degenerate chivalry ; and thus spread François and Françoise universally among the French nobility, where they held sway almost exclusively till the memories of the House of Valois had become detestable ; but by that time the populace were making great use of it, and at the present time it is considered as so vulgar that a French servant in England was scandalized that a child of the family should be called Francis.

Franz von Sickingen is an instance that already Germany knew the name ; but it did not take root there at once. The grandchildren of François I., intermarrying with the house of Lorraine, rendered his namesakes plentiful, both in the blood-stained younger branch of Guise, and in the dull direct stem, the continuation of the Karlingen, who at length, by the marriage with Maria Theresa, were restored to the throne of Charlemagne, in the person of him whom the classicalizing Germans termed Franciskus I.   This cumbrous form is still official, but Franz is the real name in universal use in the German parts of the Austrian Empire, though the Slavonic portions generally use the other end of the word, as Zesk.

It was the same gay French monarch who sent us our forms of the name.   Mary Tudor, either in gratitude for his kindness, or in

memory of her brief queenship of France, christened her first child
Frances—that Lady Frances Brandon whose royal blood was so sore
a misfortune to her daughters, and who had numerous namesakes
among the maidens of the Tudor court ; but they do not seem to
have then made the distinction of letter that now marks the feminine,
and they used what is now the masculine contraction. "Frank,
Frank, how long is it since thou wast married to Prannel ?" was the
rebuke of the Duke of Richmond to his Howard lady when he was
pleased to take down her inordinate pride, by reminding her of her
youthful elopement with a vintner.

The modern Fanny is apparently of the days of Anne, coming
into notice with the beautiful Lady Fanny Shirley, who made it a
great favourite, and almost a proverb for prettiness and simplicity,
so that the wits of George II.'s time called John, Lord Hervey,
'Lord Fanny,' for his effeminacy. Fanny, like Frank, is often given
at baptism instead of the full word ; and, by an odd caprice, it has
lately been adopted in both France and Germany instead of their
national contractions.

The masculine came in at the same time, and burst into eminence
in the Elizabethan cluster of worthies—Drake, Walsingham, Bacon ;
but it did not take a thorough hold of the nation, and was much left
to the Roman Catholics. It was not till Frank had been restricted
to men that it took hold of the popular mind, so as to become
prevalent.

The original saint of Assisi made devout Spaniards use Francisco
and Francisca, before the fresh honour won for the first by two early
Jesuits—the Duke of Gandia, the friend and guide of Charles V.,
and Xavier, the self-devoted apostle of the Indies. His surname has
thrown out another stock. It is in itself Moorish, coming from the
Arabic Ga'afar, splendid, the same as that of our old friend, the
Giaffar of the *Arabian Nights*, the Jaffier of old historians. Wherever Jesuits have been, there it is; Savero in Italy, Xavier in
France, Xaverie in Wallachia, Xavery in Poland, Saverij in Illyria;
Xaveria for the feminine in Roman Catholic Germany, marking the
course of the counter-Reformation. Even Ireland deals in Saverius,
or Savy, though when English sailors meet a Spanish negro called
Xaver, they call him Shaver ! Savary de Bohnn, whom Dugdale
places under Henry I., was probably a form of Sigeheri, or Saher,
which may have been absorbed by Xaver in Roman Catholic lands.

English.	Erse.	Breton.	French.
Francis Frank	Fromsais	Franse	François
Spanish.	Portuguese.	Italian.	Wallachian.
Francisco Francilo	Francisco Francisquinho	Francesco Franco Cecco	Francisk

German.	Dutch.	Scotch.	Swedish.
Franciskus Franz Frank	Frenz	Francie	Frans

Polish.	Bohemian.	Slovak.	Lettish.
Franciszek Franck	Frantisek	Francisek Franc Franjo Zesk	Spranzis

Lithuanian.	Finn.	Hungarian.	Greek.
Prancas	Ranssu	Ferencz Ferko	Φραγκίσκος

FEMININE.

English.	Breton.	French.	Span. and Por.
Frances Fanny	Franseza Fantik	Françoise Francisque Fanchette Fanchon	Francisca

Italian.	German.	Dutch.	Polish.
Francesca Cecca Ceccina Ceccarella	Franziske Franze Sprinzchen (Lower German.)	Francyntje Francina Fransje	Franciszka Franulka Franusia

Bohemian.	Slovak.	Hungarian.	Greek.
Frantiska	Franciska Franika Franja	Francziska	Φραγκίσκη *

Section V.—*Thor*

The third in the Teutonic Triad is the mighty Thor, whose image stood on the other side of that of Odin, in the northern temples, whose day followed Odin's, and who was the special deity of the Norsemen, as Wuotan was of the Saxons, and Freyr of the Swedes.

The most awful phenomenon to which, in Northern Europe, human ears are accustomed—the great electric sound from heaven, could not fail to be connected with divinity, by nature, as well as by the lingering reminiscence of the revelations, when it accompanied the Voice of the Most High.

* Grimm ; Munch ; Munter ; Michaelis ; Alban Butler ; Mrs. Busk, *German Empire ;* Dugdale ; Ellis, *Domesday.*

If the classic nations knew the mighty roll as the bolts of Zeus or Jupiter, they called it βροντή (*brontè*) and *tonitru*, names corresponding to those divinities wherewith the other Aryans connected the sound— the Perun of the Slavonians, the Taran of the Cymry, the Thunnr, Donnar, or Thor of the Teuton. The Indra of the Hindu, came from *udra* or *eidan*, water, as god of the waters of the sky, while the Teutonic title was probably an imitation of the deep rolling sound, and the god must have been called after it.

In the northern myths Thor is the eldest son of Odin, mightiest of all the Aasir, partly in right of his belt of strength, which doubles his force, and of the iron gauntlets which he wields whenever he throws his mighty hammer—Mjolner, the crusher (from the word that named Milo, also mills and meal)—which, like a boomerang, always returns to him when he has hurled it. He has a palace called Thrudheim, or Thrudvangr, the abode of courage, resting on five hundred and forty pillars, which seems like a tradition of some many-columned Indian edifice. It was he who was foremost in the fight with the powers of evil; he bound Lok, the destroyer, and banished him to Utgard, where the famous visit was made that so curiously reflects Indian and Persian myths, and has dwindled into the tricks of our Giant-killer and the German *schneiderlein*. He has more adventures than any other single deity in northern story, and continues champion of the gods till the final consummation, when, after having destroyed many of the enemies, he is finally stifled by the flood of poison emitted by the Midgard snake.

Thord seems to have been a contraction of the old Low German Donarad, which has vanished; but in fact Thor, though regnant in the North, was not very popular elsewhere, and almost all the names he commences are Scandinavian; though the old Spanish Goths had a king Thorismundo, Thor's protection, the same as our Norman Tormund. They had also an Asturian bishop, Toribio, who long after was followed by a sainted namesake in Spanish South America.

Every possible change that could be rung on Thor seems to have been in use among the Northmen. The simplest masculine, Thordr, comes seventy times in the *Landnama-bok*, Thorer forty-seven times, after the early settler Thorer the silent, and the feminine Thora twenty-two, and she still flourishes in Iceland and Norway.

Thor had his elf, Thoralfr, his household spirit Thordis, his bear and his wolf. His bear, Thorbjorn, is fifty-one times in the Iceland roll, and was not without a she-bear, Thorbera; and the 'Torbern,' in Domesday, was doubtless the father of the family of Thorburn. Indeed, though Thor's hammer was not an artistic one, he has had other artist namesakes by inheritance, namely, the Flemish Terburg, an offshoot from the northern Thorbergr, with its feminine Thorbjorg, or Thorberga, and the great Danish Thorwaldsen, the son of Thorvalldr, Thor's power, or maybe of thunder-welder, the Thorwald of Germany, and Thorold or Turold of the Norman Conquest. Readers of Andersen may remember his story of the boy-sculptor mortified by the consequential little girl declaring that no one whose name ended in *sen* was worth speaking to. Thorwald, too, was one of the old Icelandic discoverers of America.

As to Thor's wolf, Thorolf, it is contracted into Tolv in Norway, and thus may be the origin of that curious Danish superstition that at noon-day (twelve being *tolv* in Danish) Kong Tolv, a terrific and mysterious personage, drives by in his chariot, invisible except to maidens inadvertently left in solitude, when they are borne off by him to his domains for seven years, which pass like a single day.

Forty-two Thorarinns, as well as a Thorarna for a feminine, assisted to people Iceland, and of course Thor's sword, spear, and kettle were there too ; Thorbrandr six times over. The spear and kettle figure again in the story of Croyland Abbey, as told by Ingulf. Turgar, the little child who escaped the destruction, is no doubt Thorgeir, and it may be feared thus betrays a Norman invention ; but Turcetyl, the good man who re-built it, was really Ethelstane's chancellor, and no doubt took his name from some of the invading Danes, who called the Thorketyl or Thorkjell of the North, Thurkil or Trukill, of which we have some traces remaining in the name Thurkell.   Thorkatla was the Icelandic feminine.

It is an evidence how greatly our population was leavened by the Danes, that though Thor names are very rare in Anglo-Saxon history, we have many among our surnames, such as Thurlow from Thorleik, Thor's sport, Tunstall and Tunstan from Thurstan, the Danish Thorstein, the proper form of Thor's stone, who is thus the 'stainless Tunstall,' whose 'banner white' waved in Flodden Field, just as long before Tostain the white had been the foremost knight at Hastings, and left his name to the northern peasantry to be confounded with Toussaint, the popular reading of All Saints' day, and thus to pass to the negro champion of Hayti, Toussaint L'Ouverture.

Thorgils, Thor's pledge, also runs into Thurkil or Trokil, and cuts down to Troels ; but coming to the Western Isles has there continued in the form of Torquil, and has been mixed up with the idea of the Latin *torques*, a neck chain.   The Swedes call it Thyrgils, and the feminine is Thorgisla.   It is Torchil in Domesday.

White Thors were Thorfinn and Thorfinna ; Thorvid, or Thor's wood, is in Denmark Truvid, Truid, Trudt, probably our Truefit. Besides these were used—

Thorbert, Thor's splendour (Torbertus in Domesday).
Thorgautr, Thor the good (or Goth).
Thorgerdur, Thor's protection (thirty-seven in *Landnama-bok*).
Thorgestur, Thor's guest.
Thorgrim, Thor the helmeted.
Thorgunna, Thor's war.
Thorhildr, Thor's battle-maid.
Thorleif, Thor's relic.
Thormod, Thor's mood.
Thorhalla, Thor's stone.
Thorlaug, Thor's liquor.*

* *Landnama-bok ;* Thierry, *Conquête d'Angleterre ;* Ellis, *Domesday ;* Munch; Mallet.

SECTION VI.—*Baldur and Hodur.*

Most beautiful of all the gods was Baldur, the fair white god, mild, beautiful, and eloquent,—beloved but fore-doomed to death. His story is well known. His mother, Frigga, vainly took an oath of all created things not to be the instrument of his fate,—she omitted the mistletoe ; and Lok, the destroyer, having, in the guise of a sympathetic old woman, beguiled her into betraying her omission, placed a shaft of the magic plant in the hands of the blind god, Hodr, when all the Aasir were in sport directing their harmless weapons against the breast of their favourite. Baldur was slain, and his beautiful wife, Nanna, died of grief for his loss. Even then Hela would have relented, and have given him back, provided every living thing would have wept for him ; but one stern giantess among the rocks refused her tears, and Baldur remains in the realms of death, until after all his brethren shall have perished in the last great conflict, when with them he shall be revivified in the times of the restitution of all things, so remarkably promised in these ancient myths.

As to the source of his name, authorities are not agreed. Baldr is a prince in several Teutonic languages, and the royal family of the Visigoths were the Balten. Balths, bald, bold, is also a word among them ; but Grimm deduces the god's title from *bjel*, or *baltas*, the word that is the first syllable of the Slavonic Belisarius, and thus would make the Anglian Baldœg mean bright as day. It is the word that lies at the root of *bellus*, pretty, whose derivations are now so universal in Romanized Europe. Others turn the name over to the Bel, or Beli, of the Kelts, or the Eastern Belus ; but on the whole, the derivation Baldr, a prince, is the least unsatisfactory.

The legend seems to have been unknown to the German races, or, at least, no trace of it has been found, and the names that constantly occur beginning and ending with *bald* or *pald*, are supposed merely to mean prince, and not to refer to the god. As an end it is more common than as a beginning, and it is peculiar to the Anglian races, our own Anglo-Saxons, the inhabitants of the Low Countries, and continental Saxons. The names that have become universal all emanated from one or other of these sources.

Baldric, or prince ruler, was Anglo-Saxon ; but the Swedes learned it as Balderik, the Poles as Balderyk, the French as Baudri. Baldred, an English-named saint, was bishop of Glasgow ; thence, too, the early French took Baldramn, prince raven, which they made Baudrand, and confused with Baldrand, prince of the house, also Baldemar, famous prince, unless this is a confusion with Waldemar.

The most general of these was, however, Baldwine, princely friend, who was very early a feudatory of the empire in Flanders, and the name continued in his family, so as to take strong hold of the population, and to spread into the adjoining lands. Baldwin was the father of William the Conqueror's Matilda, and the one Baldwinus before the Conquest has very considerably multiplied after it, so that to us

Baldwin has all the associations of a Norman name. Its European celebrity was owing to the two knights of Lorraine and Bourg, who reigned successively at Jerusalem after the first Crusade, and left this to be considered as the appropriate Christian name in their short-lived dynasty ; and again, it was borne by the unfortunate count who was thrust into the old Byzantine throne only to be demolished by the Bulgarians, or if indeed he ever returned, to be disowned as an impostor by his daughter.

English.	French.	German.	Dutch.	Italian.
Baldwin	Baudouin	Balduin	Boudewijn	Baldovino
	Baudoin			Balduino

The Germans have Baldo, the French Baud, both contractions from either Baldwin or Balderich, and there are a good many surnames therefrom in England, France, and Germany.

Examples of Baldegisel, prince pledge, Baldbrecht, Baldemund, Baldeflede, Baldetrude, have also been found, but nowhere are any such forms prevalent.

Baldur's wife, Nanna, probably comes from *nanthjan*, in Gothic, to be courageous. There are a few Frisians called Nanno, Nanne, Nonne ; but it is very probable that this old goddess may have contributed to furnish some of the inherited names now all absorbed in Anne.

Baldur's unfortunate murderer has, strange to say, many more namesakes. He was Nanna's brother, blind, and of amazing strength, and is supposed to typify unheeding rashness and violence, in opposition to prudent valour. His name is in Gothic Hathus, in old German Hadu, and in Anglo-Saxon Headho, and is said to come from *headho*, an attack or fight, so that the right way to translate it in the compounds would be by fierce when it begins the name— war when it forms the conclusion.

It has a great many different forms. The old northern Hedinn is believed to be one, belonging first to a semi-fabulous sea-king of the mythic ages, who tried to elope with the Valkyr Hildur. From him the sea was poetically called, in the strange affected versification of the North, the road of Hedinn's horses. There were eight Hedinns in the *Landnama-bok*, and the word sometimes occurred at the end of the name, as with Skarphedinn, the fierce but generous son of Njal, who dies singing to the last in the flame, with his faithful axe driven deep into the wall that the fire might not spoil its edge.

Tacitus mentions two chiefs whom he calls Catumer and Catualda, and who are supposed to be by interpretation Hadumar, or fierce fame, and Hadupald, or Haduwald, each of which would be fierce prince. Hadumar has lingered in southern France, where it has become Azimar, or Adhémar, the last, the well-known surname of the Grignan family. Hadubrand, fierce sword, is one of the heroes of the most ancient existing poem in Low German. Heddo is to be found as a name of some Frisians, contracted either from this, or from Hadubert, or one of the other compounds. Even ladies were named by this affix, as Haduburg, war protection ; Hadulint, war serpent ; Haduwig, which the old German name-writer, Luther, makes war refuge.

This last is the only usual form, owing to the saintly fame of a daughter of the Markgraf of Meranie. While one daughter, Agnes, was the victim of Philippe Auguste's irregular marriage, the happier Haduwig married a duke of Silesia, and shared his elevation to the throne of Poland, where she evinced such piety as to be canonized ; and the name she left was borne by a Polish lady in the next century, who converted her husband, the Duke of Lithuania. Thus doubly sainted, all eastern Germany delighted in it, and the French sent it to us ; they calling it Hedvige ; we took it as Hawoyse, and, descending into Avice, or Avis, it was at one time very common here, and is to be found in almost every old register.

English.	French.	German.	Polish.
Havoise	Hedvige	Hedwig	Jadviga
Hawoyse		Hedda	
Havoisia			
Avice	Italian.		
Avicia	Edvige		
Avis			
Lusatian.	Esth.	Lett.	Hungarian.
Hada	Eddo	Edde	Hedviga
	Edo		

The Spanish Goths, too, had their compounds of Hadu. The Lady Adosinda, whom Southey has placed collecting the corpses of her family in the ruins of the city destroyed by the Moors, is Haduswinth, or fierce strength ; and the Portuguese Affonso is from Hadufuns. This last syllable, namely *funs*, means vehemence, and is, in fact, no other than our own undignified *fuss ;* Affonso, Afonso, thus mean fierce fuss, though for more euphony, this lofty name of kings may be made into warlike impetuosity.

Section VII.—*Tyr.*

In Northern mythology Tyr is another son of Odin, and god of strength and victory. When, in the great fight with the powers of evil, the terrible Fenris, the wolf of the abyss, was to be bound with a fetter, slender, but which no power could break, he was only induced to stand still by Tyr's volunteering to put his right hand into the monster's mouth, as a pledge of the good faith of Asgard. Finding himself chained, the wolf at once closed his jaws, and bit off Tyr's hand ; nevertheless, the Runic letter Λ (*thorn*, the sound of *dh*),

x

which was left-handed, like the god, and therefore his sign, was esteemed the mark of truth and treaties.

Tyr has few namesakes. Tyre and Thyra, in the North, are the only direct ones; but it sometimes finishes a word, as in the case of Angantyr, favourite of Tyr, the warrior who obtained the terrible sword, Tyrfing, forged by the dwarfs, which did, indeed, always give victory, but which would never go back into its scabbard till it had been fed with, at least, one human life. The *dio*, or *thius*, of the old Gothic and German names thus arose, such as Alathius, the Latinized Halltyr, and the like.

Niörd was god of the sea, almost equal in rank to Odin himself. He was a very ancient deity, known to the German nations as Nairthus, and probably, like Freyr, male and female. The goddess Nerthus, mentioned by Tacitus, has been supposed by Grimm to mean Niörd; but Hermann Luning makes it Törd, a wife of Odin, and one of the three titles of the earth: at any rate, out of this mention has been made a goddess—Hertha, who has not been without namesakes.

Many derivations have been suggested for his name. Finn Magnusson thought it might be cognate with the Greek νηρὸς (neros), wet; Grimm, that it might be connected with the *North*, though he declines to speak positively; and Hermann Luning deduces it from *nairan*, to join, because the sea joins the land together.

Niörd's direct derivatives seem to be Nordhilda and Nordbert; the last fashionable in Germany, from a youth of imperial family, who was, at the end of the eleventh century, brought to serious thoughts by having his horse struck by lightning under him, when, like St. Paul, he cried out "What wouldst Thou have me to do?" He became a monk, and was afterwards archbishop of Magdeburg, and founder of the Præmonstratensian Order; and Norbert became known and used after he was canonized.

Niörd is used in the North; and thence too, perhaps, comes Norman, which was in use, both in France and England, at the time of the Conquest. It is puzzling to find in Domesday Book sixteen Normans possessing land in England before the Conquest, and only eight after it—one of whom, Norman d'Arcie, at least, was a Norman born. Afterwards, during the friendly thirteenth century, English nobles carried Norman to Scotland, where it was adopted in the Leslie family, and, like Nigel, became exclusively Scottish. The Highlanders called it Tormaid, which is considered to be really its Gaelic form, not an equivalent. The last Englishman I have found so called was Norman de Verdun, under Edward I.

The story of Niörd's marriage is one of the wildest tales of later Norse mythology. Iduna, the wife of Bragi, god of poetry, kept the apples of gold which renewed the youth of the gods. However, Loki, having fallen into the clutches of the great frost giant, Thiassi, in the form of an eagle, only effected his release by promising to bring Iduna and her apples to Jotunheim. He beguiled her into a forest, under pretence that he had found finer apples than her own, and there Thiassi flew away with her. The gods began to grow old without their apples, and insisted that Loki should bring her back. He arrayed himself as a falcon, and, flying to Jotunheim, turned Iduna into a sparrow and flew home with her, pursued by Thiassi. The Aasir, seeing her danger, lighted a fire with chips on the walls of Asgard, which flamed up and singed Thiassi's wings, so that he fell down among them and was slain. Afterwards, his daughter, Skadi, came to avenge his death, but was mollified by being allowed to choose a husband from the Aasir, however was only allowed the sight of the feet to select from; and thus, hoping she had taken Baldur, she obtained Niörd. Thiassi's eyes are said to have become stars; but, as usual, the northern astronomy has been ruined by the classical, and no one knows which they are.

Bragi was followed as an Icelandic name. Its etymology is uncertain; some make it cognate with Brahma; others with *braga*, to shine; others with *brain*. Braga was poetry, and thence, from the manner of recital, noun, has formed the uncomplimentary verb, to *brag*, and the *braggart*.

Iduna, or more properly, Idhuna, Ithuna, is a myth of spring reft away by winter, who dies of the warmth of the flame of the summer gods. Her name does not seem to have been adopted in the North; but it is almost certainly the origin of Idonea, which is very common in old English pedigrees. Idonea de Camville lived under Henry III.; Idonea de Vetriponte, Vieuxpont, or Oldbridge, is cited in the curious tracts on Northern curiosities, put forth some years back in Durham, which say the name is very common; and though it might be the feminine of the Latin *idoneus* (fit), its absence in the Romance countries may be taken as an indication that it was a mere classical-izing of the northern goddess of the apples of youth.

The word itself is translated by Luning in the most satisfactory manner as ' she who works incessantly,' and by Munch, as ' she who renovates incessantly.' *Idja* is to work, *unna*, love, so that others make her one who loves work. The word *unna*, however, though derived from the verb *an unna*, to love, has come to mean only a woman, and as such is frequently used as a termination, as well as now and then standing alone as a female name, Unna, of whom there are three in the *Landnama-bok*, and several in the Saga of *Burnt Njal*.

Una is likewise used in both Ireland and the North; but in the former it is said to mean famine; in the North it is most probably from that word *vin, win,* or *wine,* a friend, which we shall often meet with again, and which lies most likely at the root of *unna*.

The word *idja*, to work, the first syllable of Iduna's name, formed *deisi*, activity, and thence the person who ought to be active, the old German *itis*, and Anglo-Saxon *ides*, a woman, in the North, *deis* or *dis*. The idea of the active sprite was divided between woman-kind and certain household spirits, like the Roman genii, only femi-nine and possibly another name for the Nornir, as each man had his own, and they were sometimes visible as animals suiting with the character of their protégés : powerful chiefs had bears or bulls, crafty ones foxes ; and even on the introduction of Christianity, faith in the Disir was not abandoned, though there were no more sacrifices at their *Disir salen*, or temples. Sometimes a family would have various *disir* at war with one another, some for the old faith, some for the new. While Iceland was still in suspense between heathenism and Christianity, a young chieftain one night heard three knocks at his door, and despite the warnings of a seer, went forth to see the cause. He beheld nine women in black riding from the North, and nine from the South, the *disir* of his family, the black for heathendom, the white for Christianity. The black ones, knowing that they must vanish from the land, seized his life as their last tribute, and wounded him so that he returned a dying man to tell his tale. Probably these *disir* are either the cause or the effect of those strange phantoms which, whether of doves, dogs, heads, children, or women, portend death in certain families. They may likewise account for some of the family bearings in the form of animals.

Disa is a Norwegian and Icelandic name, now nearly disused : it is also a very frequent termination, such as in Thordis, Alfdis, Freydis, &c., and it may be most fitly translated as the sprite giving the idea of the guardian protecting spirit that woman should be. In the German names it appears as the termination *itis* or *idis*, as Adelidis, one that appears at first sight like a mere Latinism.*

Section VIII.—*Heimdall*.

The porter of Valhall is Heimdall, the son of nine sisters, who watches at the further end of the rainbow-bridge Bifrost to guard the Æsir from the giants. He sleeps more lightly than a bird, can see a hundred leagues by day or night, and can hear the grass growing in the fields, and the wool on the sheep's backs. He bears in one hand a sword, in the other a trumpet, the sound of which resounds throughout the universe.

When the powers of evil break loose, Heimdall will rouse the gods to their last conflict by a blast of his trumpet, and in the struggle will kill and be killed by Loki.

His name is explained by *heim*, home, and *dallr*, powerful. The latter half is in Anglo-Saxon *deall*, in old High German *tello*, and in the old Norse *dallr*, whence Dalla is found as a name in the *Landnama-bok*.

Heim is in Ulfilas both a field and a village, and the Anglo-Saxons use the word *dhäm* for an enclosure, and *häm* for a village; *ham* in a similar manner, as is still shown in the diminutive, hamlet, for a small village, as well as in the *ham* that concludes many local names. At the same time, the word, slightly altered, assumed that closer, dearer, warmer sense which is expressed by the terms, *heim*, *hiemme*, *hjem*, *hame*, and *home*, in all the faithful-hearted Teutonic race, yet which is so little comprehended by our southern relatives,

* Grimm; Luning; Munter; Munch; Blackwell, Mallet; Ellis, *Domesday;* Dugdale.

that they absolutely have no power of expressing such an idea as " It's hame, and it's hame, and it's hame."

Even in their heathenism "true to the kindred points of heaven and home," the guardian of the dwelling of the brave spirits of the dead was made by the Northmen no grim Cerberus nor gloomy Charon, but the *Home* ruler.

And though Heimdall nowhere occurs as a name, yet the old German Heimirich is almost identical with it ; though it should be observed that *heim* is a commencement peculiar to the Germans ; we never find a name with this first syllable originating either with the Northmen or the English.

Where Heimirich first began does not appear, but it sprung into fame with the Saxon emperor called the Fowler, and his descendant won the honours of a saint, whence this became a special favourite in Germany, where it was borne by six emperors, by princes innumerable, and by so many others that the contraction Heintz had already passed to cats when *Reinecke Fuchs* was written.

It is from the endearment, Heinz, that the handsome and unfortunate son of Frederick II., who, after his brief royalty in Sardinia, spent the rest of his life in a Genoese prison, was known to Italy as Enzio, and to history as Enzius.

From the Kaisers, the third Capetian king of France was christened Henri, a form always frequent there, though only four times on the throne. Its popularity culminated during the religious wars, when Henri de Valois, Henri de Bourbon, and Henri de Guise were fighting the war of the three Henris ; but in spite of the French love and pride in *le grand monarque*, the growing devotion to St. Louis, from whom the Bourbon rights to the throne were derived, set Henri aside from being the royal name, until the birth of him whom legitimists still call Henri V.

There are but three instances of ' Henricus,' even after the Conquest, in Domesday ; and it must have been from the reigning French monarch that William the Conqueror took Henry for his youngest son, from whom the first Plantagenet King received and transmitted it to his ungracious son, his feeble grandson, and through him to the elder House of Lancaster, then to the younger, who for three generations wore it on the throne, and for whose sake it was revived in the House of Tudor. Its right native shape is Harry ; the other form is only an imitation of French spelling. It was ' Harry of Winchester' who cried out for help at Evesham ; Harry of Bolingbroke who rode triumphant into London, and who died worn out in the Jerusalem chamber ; Harry Hotspur whose spur was cold at Shrewsbury ; Harry of Monmouth who was Hal in his haunts at Eastcheap, and jested with Fluellen on the eve of Agincourt ; Harry of Windsor who foretold the exaltation of Harry Tudor when " Richmond was a little peevish boy," and Harry VIII., or bluff King Hal, who lives in the popular mind as an English Blue Beard ; perhaps connected in some cases with the popular soubriquet of the devil.

An early Swedish bishop bore the name, and so did a bishop of Iceland before the twelfth century ; but these must have been foreigners, for there are no other instances in the North in early times, though the general fusion of European names brought in Hendrik, to the loss of the native Heidrick, just as Heinrich seems to have in Germany destroyed an independent Haginrich.

English.	French.	Spanish.	Italian.
Henry	Henri	Enrique	Enrico
Harry	Henriot		Arrigo
Hal			Enzio
Halkin	Breton.	Portuguese.	Arriguccio
Hawkin	Hery	Enrique	Arrigozzo
			Guccio

German.	Dutch.	Danish.	Frisian.
Heimirich	Hendrik	Hendrik	Enrik
Heinrich	Hendricus		
Hein	Heintje	Swedish.	Polish.
Heine		Henrik	Henryk
Heinz			
Heinecke			
Henke			
Henning			

Bohemian.	Lett.	Lithuanian.	
Jindrich	Indrikis	Endrikis	
	Indes	Endruttis	
	Induls		

FEMININE.			

English.	French.	Spanish.	Swedish.
Henrietta	Henriette	Enriqueta	Henrika
Harriet			
Harriot	Italian.	Portuguese.	German.
Harty	Enrichetta	Henriqueta	Henriette
Hatty			Jette
Etta			
Hetty			

Dutch.	Polish.	Bohemian.	Slovak.
Hendrike	Henryeta	Jendriska	Enrika
Jetje			Henrinka

The founder of the Portuguese kingdom was a Henri from Burgundy ; but the name did not greatly flourish in the Peninsula till Enrique of Trastamare climbed to the Castilian throne, and his namesakes, alternating with Juan, threw out the old national Alfonso and Fernando.

On the whole this is one of the most universal of Teutonic names, and one of the most English in use, although not Anglian in origin. The feminine seems to have been invented in the sixteenth century, probably in France, for Henriet Stuart appears in the House of Stuart d'Aubigné in 1588, and there were some Henriettes to match the Henris at the court of Catherine de Medicis. England received the name from the daughter of Henri IV., Henriette Marie, whom the Prayer Book called Queen Mary, though her godchildren were always Henrietta, so Latinized by their pedigrees, though in real life they went by the queen's French appellation, as well as English lips could frame it, so that Hawyot was formerly the universal pronunciation of Harriet, and is still occasionally used.

Heimo, or Hamo, is another old German form, becoming in French Hamon, Haymon, Aymon ; and Amone in Italian. *Les Quatre Filz Aymon* were notable freebooters in Karling romance, and in Italy were *i Quattro Figli d'Amone*. Early Norman times gave us Hamo, Hamelin, and Fitzaymon ; but except for an occasional Hamlyn in an old pedigree, they have disappeared.

Germany had Heimrod, Heimbert, and Heimfred ; but these are not easy to disentangle from the derivatives of the word *hun*, which are much more in use.*

Section IX.—*Will.*

This section has thus been headed because the Will was one of the ideas most strongly expressed in various forms in the religion of the high-spirited North.

The word *to will* is of all tongues ; the Greek βουλή, Latin *velle* or *volo*, Gothic *viljan*, Keltic *iouli*, all show a common origin, and every Teuton language has the derivatives of *will*, just as the Romance have of *volo*.

But it is the Teuton who brings the Will into his mythology. When the creation began, the cow Audumbla licked out of the stones a man named Bur, who was the grandfather of the three primeval gods, Odin, Wili, and Vê, the All-pervading, the Will, the Holy ; and it was these who together animated the first human pair. We hear no more of Vili or Hœmir, as he is also called after he thus infused feeling and will into the first man ; but we meet the word *will* again forming *valjan*, to choose, *velja* in the North.

Thence the home where Odin welcomed his brave descendants was Valhall, the hall of the chosen ; and the maidens who chose the happy who were there to dwell, were the Valkyrier, or Walcyrge, the last syllable from *kjöra*, or *curen*, to choose, the word whence an electoral prince is called in German, Kürfurst. But the passport to the hall of the chosen was a glorious death on the battle-field ; and thus it was that *val, vali, wali,* belonged to the carnage of the fight, since slaughter did but seal the marks of the Valkyr upon the brave, whose spirits were passing over the rainbow-arch, while the comets marked the

* Michaelis ; Pott ; *Edda.*

course of the chariot which glanced across the sky with weapons forged for their sport in battle and chase.

So the Hall of the Chosen became the Hall of Carnage, the abode of the slain ; and it is remarkable that no Christian writer transfers the term to Paradise, although the epithet Schildburg, the castle of shields, is once applied to Heaven as the home of the victors. Indeed, Valhall was not eternal ; the warrior there admitted had yet to fight his last fight by Odin's side, perish with him and his sons, and share with them the renovation of the universe. So deeply interwoven in the ideas of the North was a violent death with the hope of bliss, that crags in Norway affording scope for a desperate leap, were called the vestibule of Valhall, and the preference for a death on the battle-field lingered into Christian days, so that not only did fierce Earl Siward bemoan his fate in dying of sickness, albeit he rose upon his feet to draw his last breath, but even the Chevalier Bayard mourned angrily over the fever that had nearly caused him to pass away like a sick girl in his bed.

Well then might the Valkyrier be the favoured messengers of Odin, sent forth to select the champions who should become the guests of their mighty forefather, himself called Valfreyr, or Slaughter Lord. They hovered over the camp in armour with swan wings, marked those who were to fall, and wove the web of slaughter ere the battle began. Their number varies in different sagas, and so do their names, although Hildur is always the chief. Their last appearance was when the islander of Caithness beheld the twelve weaving their grisly web in a loom of lances, the weights of men's heads, on the eve of the Good Friday of the battle of Clontarf, between King Sigtrygg and Brian Boromhe, singing the weird song that Gray translated long before Teutonic antiquities were revived :

> " Horror covers all the heath,
>   Clouds of carnage blot the sun :
> Sisters, weave the web of death ;
>   Sisters, cease, the work is done."

The work done, the web was torn in sunder, and divided between the Valkyrier, who flew off, half to the North, half to the South, denoting the rending of the ancient faith.

In fact, in later sagas, the *Valkyrier* lose their wild mystery and divinity, and fall into mere magic maidens, sometimes with extraordinary strength, sometimes with swan wings, and, at the very last gasp of the supernatural, with goose feet, which at their next step become merely large feet. The mother of Charlemagne absolutely makes the transition from Bertha the goose-footed, to Berthe *aux grands pieds*.

To this source probably may be referred Wala or wise woman, the inspired priestess, also called in ancient German the Velleda. Cæsar tells us that the matrons among the Germans cast lots, and prophesied the issue of battle, and thus Wala may have been the wise or inspired woman. The great prophetic song of the fate of the Aasir is *Voluspa*, either the wise woman's spae, or the inspired spae or prophecy ; for *vola* or *volur* means inspired in ancient German (no doubt from the *wala* or prophetess), and by a very small transition, mad. Probably the Kelts borrowed it, for *fol* was inspired or mad ; and Folia of Ariminium is mentioned by Horace as a magician. Our fool is thus traceable to *vola*, inspired, but probably through the Keltic and French medium.

Vili, though his myths have been forgotten, still stands as a great ancestor. From him in Germany, either directly or through a renewal of him as a forefather, must have been named the great race of the Billingen, the first dynasty of the continental Sachsen, who gave emperors to Germany.

Billing is the son of Wili, or Will ; and so again is, in the North, Vilkin, the father of the famous smith Volundr, whose name is probably from this original root, will or mind, though its immediate source is thought to be *vel*, art or cunning, cognate with our own guile, and probably the participle of a lost verb, to devise. Some connect it with Vulcan, from the name and character of Volundr. He was the son of a sea maiden, and of Vidja the Vilkin ; and he and his two brothers each married a Valkyr, who, at the end of a stated period, had to be absent for nine years, giving to each husband magic gifts and precious stones that dimmed when disaster was about to befall them. Volundr was the fortunate brother of the three, and was the mighty smith to whom all good weapons are ascribed. From him the early part of the Norse poem ending with the slaying of Fafner is called the Volsunga Saga, as, from his father, the Danish version is the Wilkina Saga ; for the hero himself is his descendant, a Wælsing, or Vilking, and fights with his redoubted weapons. Weland again makes the impenetrable corslet of Beowulf, "the twisted breastnet which protected his life against point and edge ;" he is the Wiolent, Velint, or Wieland of Germany, and Galando of Italy, the Galant of France, who forged their Joyeuse, the sword of Charlemagne, and Cortana, that of Ogier. A skilful Weland is mentioned in an old Anglo-Saxon MS. found at Exeter, and in King Alfred's translation of Boëthius he renders the line,

" Ubi nunc fidelis ossa Fabricii jacent ? "

(meaning, of course, an artificer, the sense of the name,) " Where are now the bones of the wise Weland, the goldsmith who was most famed ?" A workman is still called in Iceland, *Völundrinjarn*, and a labyrinth is *Volundrhus*. This famous armourer took possession of a Druidical cromlech in the midst of the battle-grounds between the Danes and Saxons on the Berkshire downs, and there drove his shadowy trade as Wayland Smith, close to King Alfred's own birth-place, Wantage. He was spared from oblivion by being embalmed in *Kenilworth*, where the only blunder is in making Lancelot Wayland the real name of the estimable mountebank, who personated the mythical smith. Though Wieland is a German surname, the coincidence of an English Wayland was too much for probability ; and, in fact, Scott does not seem to have known how very ancient Wayland Smith had really been.

Names in Wal are chiefly Northern, those in Wil mostly Saxon. Ullr, or Ull, another Northern form, has been much used in Iceland ; and among the Northern isles of Scotland, where it may be remembered that Ulla Troil was the real name of Norna. Ullr was the stepson of Thor, son of Sif, and renowned as a great bow-bearer.

Wil is almost always a commencement. The Frank queen Bilichilde was, of course, Willihilda, resolute battle. Our earnest but turbulent Wilfrith, the Yorkshire bishop, hardly deserved to be called resolute peace ; but as patron of Ripon, his name has continued in the North, Wilfroy being very frequent in older registers in the neighbourhood of Ripon, though of late fashion has adopted it in the form of Wilfred.

In the seventh century, we sent Germany two missionaries with this prefix, Willibrord and Willihold ; also Willibald, resolute prince, went on pilgrimage with his father, St. Richard of Wessex, in 721, and finished his career as bishop of Aichstadt, leaving his name to take root in various forms.

English.	French.	Portuguese.	Dutch.	Bavarian.
Willibald	Guillibaud	Guilbaldo	Willebald	Willibald
Wibald		Vilibaldo		Waldl
				Waltl

Native to Germany is Williburg, which has a northern fac-simile Vilbjorg, and Vilgerd, the same in meaning, resolute protection ; Willrich, resolute ruler ; Willehad, resolute violence ; Willeram, resolute raven ; Willihard, reduplicating firmness ; Willigis, willing pledge, or pledge of the will ; Willimar, resolute fame, making our surname Wilmer. Williheri, resolute warrior, is the source of the German Willer, the English Weller, the French Villiers and Villars, which, with their aristocratic sound, betray little of their kindred to Sam Weller.

Where the most popular of all the Wills was invented it is not easy to discover, but Germany is its most likely region, since *helm* is a specially Germanic termination, and the Billings favoured the commencement ; besides which the pronunciation in that language leaves the words their natural meanings, Will-helm, resolute helmet, or, perhaps, helmet of resolution. The native northern name would be Vilhjalm, but this is never used, it being only imported bodily as Wilhelm into Denmark from Germany, just as our Ethelbert is superseded by Albert.

The cause of its adoption in Normandy cannot have been one of the eight saints in the Roman calendar who bear it ; for not one is anterior to the son of Rollo, the second Duke of Normandy, from whom William descended to the Conqueror, and became one of the most national of English names.

Old Camden's account of it is too quaint not to be here inserted : " William, *gerne*. For sweeter sound drawn from Wilehlm, which is interpreted by Luther much defence, or defence to many ; as Wiliwald, ruling many ; Wildred, much reverent fear, or awful ; Wilfred, much peace ; Wilibert, much brightness. So the French, that cannot pronounce *W*, have turned it into Philli, as Philibert for Wilibert, much brightnesse. Many names wherein we have Will

English.	Welsh.	Breton.	French.
William Will Willie Bill Wilkin	Guillim	Guillern Guillarn	Guillaume Guillemot

Old French.	Spanish.	Portuguese.	Italian.
Willelme Willeaulme	Guillermo Guillen	Guilhermo	Guglielmo

German.	Dutch.	Swiss.	Frisian.
Wilhelm Wilm	Willem Wim	Wilhelm Wille	Willo

Polish.	Bohemian.	Lett.	Greek.
Vilhelm	Vilem	Willums Wille	Goulielmos Bilelmos

FEMININE.

English.	French.	Spanish.	Italian.
Wilhelmina Wilmett Wilmot Mina Minella	Guillerume Guillemette Minette Mimi Guillette	Guillemma Portuguese. Guilhermma	Guglielma Swedish. Vilhelmine

German.	Swiss.	Lithuanian.	Dutch.
Wilhelmine Helmine Mine Minchen Minna	Mimmoli Mimmeli Polish. Minka	Myne Mynette	Willemyn Willempje

seem translated from the Greek names composed of πολύς ; as Polydamas, Polybius, Polyxenes, &c. Helm yet remained with us, and Villi, Willi, and Billi yet with the German for many. Others term William willing defender, and so it answereth the Roman Titus, if it come from *tuendo*, as some learned will have it. The Italians that liked the name but could not pronounce the *W*, if we may believe

Gesner, turned it into Galeazzo, retaining the sense in part for helm ; but the Italians report that Galeazzo, the first viscount of Millain, was so called for the many cocks that krew lustily at his birth. This name hath been most common in England since William the Conqueror, insomuch that on a festival day in the court of King Henry II., when Sir William St. John and Sir William Fitzhamon, especial officers, had commanded that none but the name of William should dine with them in the great chamber, they were accompanied with one hundred and twenty Williams, all knights, as Robert Montensis recordeth, anno 1173."

Camden's authority is not Martin Luther, but one Mr. Luther Dasipodius, by whom he sets great store, and whose 'German villi or billi, many,' must have been the word now called *viel.* Verstegan's history of William is still droller, namely, that any German who killed a Roman assumed the golden head-piece of the slain, and was thence called Gildhelm, which would of course be inconsistent with the old German form of Wilihelm. Be it observed that our *sur*name Wilmot descends from a name to be found in German as Wilmod, resolute mood ; but the feminine Wilmett, which is to be found continually in old Devon and Cornwall registers, is no doubt the same as the old French Guillemette, and it is a pity it has been discarded for the cumbrous German Wilhelmina, or the Williamina that is of no language at all.

Camden is probably right in taking Filiberto from Wiliberaht, or Wilibert, resolute splendour, though Germans refer it to *viel,* the same as our full, and the Greek *polys.* The founder of the name in the sixth century was a Frank Willibert, who founded the abbey of Jumièges, which the Normans first desolated and then restored, their Frenchified tongues bringing the patron's name to England as Fulbert, which is still occasionally found in old families. The ninth grand master of St. John meantime bore the French form, which historians wrote as Philibert ; and the old counts of Savoy alternated Filiberto with Amê, until they blossomed out into double names, as Vittore Amadeo or Filiberto Êmanuele.

The *Val* of choice, or slaughter, is not, Professor Munch tells us, to be confounded with another *Val,* taken from the word *waleh,* or *waalh,* a stranger, which, as has been already said, named Wales. Our own Waltheof, being spelt in his native tongue Wealtheof, thus removes himself and an Icelandic Valtheof from being slaughter-thieves to being foreign-thieves ; a change not much for the better. There were fierce Danish ancestors, however, to account for this predatory appellation lighting upon the earl, whom the Conqueror executed at Winchester, and the English revered as a saint ; then from him it descended to his grandson, Waltheof de St. Lys, the stepson of St. David of Scotland, companion of the excellent prince Henry, and, finally, abbot of Melross, where he was canonized as St. Walthenius, or Walen, and thus accounts for the surname of Wathen.

Walmer is, in old German, Walahmar, and thus shows itself to be foreign fame ; Walager is also foreign war, and became Valgeir in the North, Gaucher in France; and thence, too, by corruption, Valgard, the evil genius of the Njal Saga.

Walaraban, or Walram, seems appropriate as slaughter-raven, but is uncertain. The French made it Gauteran; and in the form of Waleran it was used in the House of Luxembourg, Counts of St. Pol; it is Galerano in Italy.

Walabert, a monk who died at Luxen, in 625, is the same as the northern Valbjart; and another Valbert, or Vaubert, as he is called in France, had a daughter Valtrud, canonized as St. Vautrude, or Vaudru. From Walamund, the French take Valmont; and Walarik, an Auvergne hermit, was Latinized as Valaricus, and Frenchified into St. Valery, a territorial surname.

The Gothic king Wallia is left in possession of the battle-field; and so are the northern Valdis and Valbiorg, both thorough Valkyr names, not yet disused. Valtrude, an early saint, must certainly be named from a slaughter-maiden. So probably was Walburh, slaughter-pledge, one of the English missionary ladies employed by St. Boniface in Mainz. She was a very popular saint, and is called Valpurgis, Vaubone, Vaubourg. Her English church is Wembury, in Devon. Part of her relics were translated from Eichstadt to Furnes, near Ostend, in 1109, on the 1st of May, when one of her festivals is kept. Then is supposed to follow the Valpurgis Nacht, the Witches' Sabbath, on the Brocken. Surely this strange connection with the saintly abbess must be due to some old observance in honour of a Valkyr Valburg. Valasquita, an old name found among the ladies of the Asturias, Navarre, and Biscay, was probably from this source.*

Section X.—*Hilda.*

Chief among the Valkyrier was Hildur, Hild, or Hiltia, who is never wanting in any enumeration of these warlike spirits. The word, in its original sense, means battle, and has thus attached itself to the principal war-maiden; nay, it has passed from her to be a poetical term for any maiden, and is one of the very commonest terminations to feminine names throughout the Teutonic world, and is likewise often found at the beginning of men's names, predominating perhaps in Germany.

Alone, it was only used in the North and in England, where the Deiran princess Hildur became the holy abbess Hilda of Whitby, succeeding St. Begga, and leaving a reputation for sanctity enhanced, by the sight of

> " The very form of Hilda fair
> Hovering upon the sunny air ; "

a vision which, though Clara de Clare could not see it, is to be beheld

---

* Junius ; Grimm ; Luning ; Blackwell, Mallet ; Lappenberg ; Dasent ; Munter ; Alban Butler ; Camden ; Verstegann ; Pott ; Köppen ; Michaelis ; Howitt, *Literature of the North.*

under certain conditions of light, in the windows of Whitby church to the present day ; as well as the ammonites, believed, as usual, to have been serpents turned to stone at the prayer of the saint. In honour of her, Hilda is still used as a name about Whitby.

The mother of Rolf Gangr, progenitress of our royalty, who vainly besought Harald Harfagre not to banish her sons from Norway, was named Hildr ; and the name still survives in Scandinavia and Iceland, where the *Landnama-bok* shows it to have been very plentiful, seventeen ladies being recorded as bearing it.   There, too, occurs Hildiridur, battle hastener, a thorough Valkyr name, but not very suitable to Fouqué's sweet Lady Minnetröst, of the moonlight brown eyes.

Hildelildis, Battle Spirit, is an Anglo-Norman lady's name.

The true Frank form of the aspirate was, however, exceedingly harsh, amounting to the Greek χ, and therefore, usually set down in its transitions through Latin and French as a *ch*. So we meet, among the Meerwings, with Childebert, who by translation is Hildebert, battle-splendour, and Childebrand, or battle-sword.

These two last names, in their Low German form of Hiltibrant and Hiltibraht, occur again in the old poem, already referred to, of *Hiltibrant and Hadubrant*, both meaning battle-swords, which goes through a dispute about Hadubrand's father, and, finally, leaves them in the middle of a single combat.

Hildebrand is, as we know from old German and Danish poems, the companion and friend of Dietrich of Bern. He had, like some hero in every cycle of story, married and deserted a young wife ; and after assisting his master in many adventures, and much dragon killing, and being the sole survivor of all Dietrich's men in the great massacre of the *Nibelung*, he encountered, without knowing him, his young son, Alebrand. In a single combat, where both do their devoir, the old knight is wounded, the younger overthrown. Then they discover each other, by the tokens that Hildebrand had left with the mother, and

> " Up rose the youthful Alebrand,
>   And into Bern they ride ;
>   What bears he on his helmet?
>   A little cross of gold.
>   And what on his right hand bears he ?
>   His dearest father old."

So, recommended by fame, Hildebrand continued a knightly name in England and Germany for many ages, and belonged to that battle-sword of the Church, who, on his election to the papacy, was called Gregory VII., though we still continue to think of him as Pope Hildebrand ; and the eccentric Dr. Wolff tells us that one of the dreams of his youth was to wear the tiara by the name of Hildebrand ! In Italy, pronunciation turned it into Aldobrando, then into Aldrovando, and then Latin made Aldrovandus.

Hildegunnr, battle-maid of war, was another northern name, and is the same as the German Hildegund, which was rather a favourite.

It is Aldegonde in the Cambrai register, and the territorial surname of St. Aldegonde is memorable in the revolt of the Low Countries. Hildegard, in honour of an abbess in the Palatinate, who died in 1004, is still a very common name among German ladies, and going to Denmark, has been corrupted into Ollegaard. It is exactly the same in meaning with the northern Hildebjorg. So again are Hildewig and Hildegar, and among the Gothic queens of Spain is found Hilduara, or battle prudence.

St. Hiltrude of Liessies, revered in Poitou and Hainault, unites two Valkyr titles—Hildur and Thrudr; for Thrûdr is generally enumerated among the Valkyr. The word once meant, in the North, fortitude, or firmness, and is possibly connected with truth; but in all the Teuton languages it signifies maiden, or virgin. Perhaps, in connection with the Valkyrer, Hildur might have been the patroness of courage, and Thrudr of fortitude; but, unfortunately, perhaps from the spells used by the women in soothsaying before a battle, Thrudr sank down from its high estate, and *drude*, or *drut*, means a witch, and in German, also, an evil spirit. Thrudvangr, or Constancy's abode, was one of the names of Valhall. *Thrud*, *trud*, *tru*, is, in Scandinavia and Germany, as favourite a feminine termination as Hilda, and, no doubt, with the same meaning, though its owners would fain translate it by truth; but it cannot be brought nearer than constancy, or fortitude. Sometimes it stands alone. Drot, as it has become by pronunciation, figures in the *Heimskringla*; and the Danes must have brought it to England, for in Bishop-Middleham, in the county of Durham, we meet, in 1683, with Troth Bradshau, who is again Trouth, or Troath, in the old spelling. Trott also several times occurs; and we are thus led to the conclusion that the dear old Dame Trot of the nursery bears the respected name of the Valkyr of fortitude. *Truth* is, perhaps, the same, originally coaxed by Puritan invention.

Cyndrida, or Quendrida, as the histories call her, the wife of Offa, is suspected by Mr. Kemble to have been mixed up with her namesake, Thrudr, the Valkyr. She was said to be a Frankish princess, who came floating over the waters, having been exposed in a boat for some unknown crime. Her beauty fascinated Offa, king of Mercia; he married her, and she was the only old English queen who caused her image to be stamped on her coins. She treacherously murdered her son-in-law, and was put to death by being thrown down a well. Some part of this is history; other parts are thought to be taken from an Anglian myth of an elder fabulous Offa, whose wife was almost certainly a Valkyr, and, on her marriage, lost her supernatural strength. Cyne, or Cwen, a woman, only appears again with Cwenburh, another Saxon queen, and may have been merely an affix.

Other German masculine forms are Hildeman, or Hilman; Hildemund, or Hilmund; Hildewart—in Friesland, Hilwert; Hildefrid, or Hilfrid; Hildebold; Hilding; Hildrad, the Hildert, or Hillert, of Friesland; Hilram, the contraction of Hilda's raven.

Gothic Spain coined, however, the most noted form of the name when Hildefuns, or battle vehemence, came on the Latin lips of her people to be Ildefonso, or Illefonso, as the great bishop of Toledo, of the seventh century, was called.   Then, shortening into Alfonso, and again into Alonzo, the same came to the second gallant king of the Asturias, husband of Pelayo's daughter, and became the most national of all the Peninsular names, belonging to eleven Castillian kings and nine Aragonese, and to the present king of Spain ; but never passing beyond the Peninsula as a royal name, save to the Aragonese dynasty in Sicily and Naples.   In England we nearly had it, for one of the sons of Edward I. and the Castillian Eleanor was so baptized ; but his early death saved our lips from the necessity of framing themselves to its southern flow.   Alphonse has been a favourite French name.   The Portuguese Affonso, though often used as its equivalent, is Hadufuns, very similar in meaning, but rather meaning war vehemence than battle vehemence.   The feminine is the Spanish Alfonsina, and the French Alphonsine.*

English.	German.	French.	Spanish.	Italian.
Alphonso Alonzo	Alfons	Alphonse	Ildefonso Alfonso Alonso	Alfonso

Section XI.—Ve.

The third deity who, with Odin and Wili, gave life to man, was Ve, who bestowed blood and colour.

Ve is thought to be connected with the Persian word *veh*, pure, and to lie at the root of *veihan*, to consecrate, in Mæso-Gothic; *weihan*, in German ; whence Christmas is Weihnacht, holy night.

Ve was the god in ancient German, *vear* the plural for gods ; but, moreover, *ve*, as a plural, meant sacred regions, and these, among the Teutons, were groves ; *wih*, a grove in old German, a temple in old Saxon.   Thence the northern *vid*, German *wald*, English *wood*, all passing from the sense of the consecrated forest to be merely the trees, and, in our language, the actual timber of which they are composed.

Ve appears no more ; but Vidar (Vithar), a son of Odin, explained by Luning to signify the inexhaustible force of nature, is, in the final conflict, to set his foot on the Fenris wolf, and rend him asunder, and with Vali, the chosen, to pass unscathed through fire and flood, and behold the renovation of all things.

Ve and Vid do their part in names.   Vadi, Wade, or Wato, is a giant ancestor in the Vilkinga Saga ; and the father of Volundr is, in

* Grimm; Luning; Munter; Blackwell, Mallet; Munch; *Landnama-bok ;* White, *Walking Tour ;* Roscoe, *Int. to Boiardo ;* Thierry, *Récits des Temps Merovingiens ;* Weber and Jamieson, *Northern Romance ;* Michaelis; Pott; Surtees ; Butler.

the North, Vidja or Vudga ; in Germany, Wittege or Wittich, a name mentioned by Jornandes as Vidigoja. The son of Volundr also bears the same name, Vedja or Wilken, and kills the giant Etgeir, called in the Danish ballad, Langbeen Riser, or long-legged giant. The grave and the oven of the giant are still shown in Zeeland.

It is the Vitiges whom the Byzantine writers mention among their Gothic foes in Italy, and the Vitiza of the latter Visigoths in Spain, and may fairly be rendered a dweller in a wood, though, in effect, it conveyed the sense of consecration.

Thence, too, the Widukind, or Witukind, of Saxony, the fierce old chieftain subdued by Charlemagne, whose name Scott gave to old ' Witikind, the waster,' but erroneously, for a Dane would have begun his name with Ved. Before comparison had cleared up the history of names, Witikind used, however, to be translated white child.

Germany has many of such grove names, the forest wolf and raven, as Witolf and Witram ; the forest prince, as Witrich, and his fame as Witmar ; also Witpald, Witperaht, and Witheri, the like of which last is found in Domesday Book before the Conquest, as Wither, in company with Witlac, Witgar, and Wit, and Witgils is high up in the Anglo-Saxon genealogy.

It is tempting to refer such names as these to *wit* and *wise*, both from *vidjan*, to know, and to think of the *vedas ;* but the wood and its spirit of consecration is the real source of all these, as of Vebiorn, Vebrandr, Vedis, Vedornn, Vegeir, Velaug, Vemundr, Vedny, Vedhelm, Vedhild, Vestan, all names of the North. Verena, the gentle mother of Sintram, may, perhaps, be meant for Vedrun, which would mean sacred wisdom, or for Vedrid, sacred eagerness ; just as Sigrid has formed Siri and Serena.

The only cases where *wise* or *vit* has produced a name, were Vitgeir of Iceland, who received that prefix for his magic powers, and Robert d'Hauteville, surnamed Guiscard, wise heart, or wizard, the Norman conqueror of Apulia, from whose soubriquet Guiscard was afterwards used as a name in France, whence Sir Guiscard d'Angle appears in Froissart.

Ve, or *verr*, is common at the end of northern names, as in Raadve or Randverr, and stood as *vih* at the end of the old Frankish names, where it is apt to get confused with *wig*, war. *Vid*, the forest or tree, is a favourite Norsk termination, apt to be taken for *hvit*, white.*

Section XII.—*Gerda.*

Freyr's beautiful wife, whose loveliness was reflected by land and sea, was Gerda, a word coming from *gerdhi* or *gerthi*, to gird round, and thus denoting the enclosed cornfield, the emblem of peace and blessing.

And, on the other hand, *gerd* was sometimes poetically used for the

* Blackwell ; Grimm ; Munch ; *Domesday Book ; Landnama-bok ;* Le Beau ; Mariane ; Weber and Jamieson, *Northern Romance.*

entire girding or harness of a warrior prepared for battle, and in both these senses, as well as of the dedication to the goddess, Gerdur was a favourite feminine in the North; and Gerda has still continued in use in Norway and Iceland, besides supplying a great many terminations, chiefly to Germany, in Ermengard, Hildegard, &c.

Its original source is exceedingly old, and conveys the idea of turning round, as in γῦρος (gyros), *curvus*, &c., and all their derivatives in the classical languages.

In the northern tongues arose gjorde (Nor.), gyrden (A. S.), whence all the varieties of girth and gird.   Thence came the Danish Gyrthr, which, when borne by the best and most faithful of the sons of Earl Godwin, was rendered into modern English as Gurth, and thus was bestowed by Scott upon the honest thrall of Cedric of Rotherwood. This name, then, properly means the warrior girt for battle.

Gard is part of a man's name in the North; *e.g.*, Gardar, who was the Swede who first sailed round Iceland, came from Gardhar, house-warrior, or perhaps patriot; Gardmund and Gardbrand, one the hand, another the sword of the country, are also found; but, in general, this is a termination, as with Finngard, Thorgard, Valgard.

Other names of men ending with *gerd* are generally corruptions of words from *geir*.*

Section XIII.—*Ægir*.

When the Aasir took up their abode in Asgard, they there found the Jotun, or giants, of whom the chief was Fornioti, a word meaning the aged.   He had three sons, Hler, Logi, and Kari, ruling sea, flame, and wind.   After a long contest they seem to have been promoted to the privileges of Aasir, and remained allies, if not friends, till the treason of Logi or Loki brought about the death of Baldur, after which the destroyer Loki and his children, the Fenris wolf (the wolf of the fen or abyss), Hel, or death, and the Midgard serpent, were bound till the last outbreak shall take place.

Kari and Hler appear to have retained their privileges as gods or demi-gods of wind and wave.   Kari is called Fasolt in Germany, but his name of Kaari or Kari has continued in use in Norway and Iceland, and belonged to the generous avenger of Burnt Njal and his sons.

Hler is evidently the Keltic Lyr, but on his promotion to rank with the Aasir, he took the northern name of Agir, Ygg, or Ægir.   He was on very friendly terms with the Aasir, gave them banquets, visited them at Asgard, and heard Bragi tell stories of their deeds; but his usual occupation was to raise his hoary head above the water when he meant evil to vessels; and when he raised storms, his wife Ran (from *rœina*, to spoil,) sat fishing for sailors, whose spirits she imprisoned like a water Hela, so that drowned men were said to be gone to Ran, before Davy Jones superseded her in nautical language.   His daughter, Unna, was the wave rising as in human shape.   All these images evidently arose from the wild, heaped, confused masses of

* Luning; Murch; Grimm; Tooke; Liddell and Scott; *Landnama-bok*.

waves in the North Sea, which, instead of forming the even sweep of
ridge and furrow of the Atlantic, are in tumbling masses, suggesting
the human form. Unna is said to come from the same root as *unda*,
the Latin wave ; but the word also means love, and thence a woman,
and there is a curious similitude in it to Aine, the granddaughter of
Lyr, in Irish legend. In Germany, Œgir was Ecke, but was reduced
to fresh water and rivers.

The root of the name of Œgir is, in fact, *og* or *uok*, the same as our
awe. Thence come many words, such as the Frank *ega*, cunning ;
the Saxon *ege*, fear ; also the verb *eggan*, to incite, still common in
the North ; while we have *to egg on*.

It has been extremely fertile in names, in many different forms,
the simplest being the Frank Ega, a *maire du palais*. Our own two
kings, Ecgfrith and Ecgberht, are probably thus derived, though some
explain their first syllable by *edge ;* but they are far more probably
the same with the *awe* of the North. Egbert continues in Friesland
as Ebbert.

Aug is the oldest form in the North, as in Augmund, which, however, was soon turned into Ogmund, Agmund, and Amund, a shape
in which it is common in the North, while in the Low Countries it
gave the title of Egmont to the victim of Alva. Ogwald has run
something the same course in the North, and become Avald ; Œgunn
and Œgulv are also there ; and in Germany Egiheri once existed,
and gave us the surnames of Agar and Eggar ; Eggerich makes the
Frisian Eggert, Iggerick, and Eggo.

The most famous German hero connected with the name is *der
treue Eckhardt*, who is well named awful firmness, warns travellers
from the tempting mountain of fatal delights, the Venusberg, once
belonging to Hela herself. Eckhard is chiefly Frisian in the present
day, and there it forms into Eggo, Ike, and Edzard.

It is identically the same name as Eginhard, the contemporary
chronicler of Charlemagne. The *n* being used in declining the leading
noun, is retained in the pronunciation of the name. Friesland, however, separates the two, and shortens Eginhard into Eino, Aynnert,
Aynt.

Thus again is formed the original northern Aginhar, awful warrior,
who fell down into Agnar and Agne. Einar, of which there were
twenty-two in the *Landnama-bok*, looks very much like another contraction of Aginhar ; but analogy is against it ; and Professor Munch
decides that the first syllable, both of Einar and Eindride, a rather
popular old Norsk feminine, is *ein*, one, in the sense of chief or
superior ; so that Einar would be chief warrior, Eindride, Endride,
or Indride, as it is also used, superior rider.

The dative form of Ag is Agli, whence Egils, or Eigils, has come
to be a favourite northern name, and in this shape it is a very
frequent prefix. Egilona was the unfortunate wife of Rodrigo, the
last of the Goths, and afterwards of the Moorish prince, his conqueror,
whom she forced to do homage to the Cross, by having the door of
her room opposite to it made so low that he could not enter without
stooping. Agilo was a Frank nobleman, and in Domesday we fall

upon an undoubted Agilward and Egelmar, and on what are probably
their contractions, Aylward and Aylmer, afterwards Aymar; but
both these are contractions of other names, and cannot always be
referred to the awful god of the sea.   Agilard, Agilulf, and Agilbert
were Frank forms, the last Eilbert in German ; Egilhart is Eilert, or
Eilo, in German ; Eilert, Ayelt, or Ayldo, in Frisian. And the
Spanish Gothic Egica is another of the progeny of the old sea giant.
Oht is a word also meaning terror.*

Section XIV.—*Ing—Seaxnot.*

Leaving the comparatively clear and consistent regions of Scandinavian mythology, we pass to the divinities and forefathers of whom
we know far less, those of our own Anglian ancestors ; some accepted
by them in common with the High Germans, others exclusively their
own, and some apparently known to the North, though not admitted
into the system of the *Edda.*

The northern cosmogony tells us of the first man, Buri, whom the
cow Audumbla licked out of the stone, and whose grandson Odin was.
It also tells us of the primeval man and woman, Ask and Embla,
whom Odin, Vili, and Ve, animated.

On the other hand, Tacitus, writing of the ancient Germans, makes
them start from an earth-born god, Tuisco, whose son was Mannus ;
and again, Mannus's three sons were Ingus, Iscus, and Hermius, Ing,
Esc, and Ed, from whom descended the Ingævones, Iscævones, and
Hermiones.

Tuisco is Tiu, or, more properly, the divine word in another form.
He represents the original stock of Teutonism, and also the human
sense of a divine origin, for Mannus, of course, is man.

Esk, or Ask, has scarcely formed any names, but Ing, or Yngve, was
looked on as the ancestor of the Swedish kings, who thence were
called the Ynglinga ; and the history which rationalizes Odin is thence
termed the Ynglinga Saga, as it makes Yngve his son, and deduces
the line from him.   Ing, the son of Tuisco, is, however, a far more
universal forefather, being almost without a doubt the name-father
of that great race that we have called Angeln, Anglo-Saxons, and
English.

Seaxnot, or Sahsnot, was probably another name for Ing.   The
word means stone comrade, and he was supposed to be the ancestor
of the Sachsen, or Saxons, but he has not numerous namesakes.   In
the East Saxon pedigree, we find Seaxbeohrt and Seaxbald, and in the
East Anglian Seaxburh or Sexburga ; and in Scandinavia Sakse remained as a name ; and the historian of the twelfth century, who
enlightened us so much on Danish history, is Latinized as Saxo
Grammaticus.

Ing was a great deal more popular, though not among the Angles,
either insular or continental.   The only trace of him in Germany

* Grimm ; Munch ; Blackwell ; Luning ; Michaelis.

is in the old name of Hinkmar, or Hinko ; and our Anglo-Saxon
kings enumerated Ingvi, Ingebrand, and Ingegeat as connecting links
between themselves and Wuotan. The Goths, Burgundians, and
Vandals also claimed descent from Ingvja, and their princes were
called Ingvineones.

Ingve, or Ingvar, was a royal name in Scandinavia, and so travelled
with the sons of Rurik to Russia ; where Igor, as he was there called,
led an army to strike terror into Constantinople, and the name has
since become confused with Egor, or George. Ingulf was the secre-
tary of William the Conqueror, and we would fain believe in the
history of Croyland that goes by his name. Ingebjorg found her
way into an old Saga as a demi-goddess directing wind and rain ;
but her historical interest is connected with the unfortunate Danish
princess, whom Philippe Auguste married only to repudiate, and
whom French historians translate into Ingeberge, English ones into
Ingoberga. Hers is the most common female name in Norway.

The North has likewise Ingegerdur, Ingeleif, Ingemundr, Ingeridur,
Ingiallur, Ingvilldur, Ingjard, and Ingrim. Ingvilhild has become
Engelke, or Engel, and is, in fact, now merged in the idea of the
Greek Angel. The same fate has befallen other names in Germany
and France, where that best of all puns, as far as results were concerned, that of St. Gregory between Angeli and Angli, has been
constantly repeated in nomenclature. The Eng, Ing, or Engel,
named from a forgotten tradition after Ing, was well pleased to be
dedicated to an angel ; Ingram, once Ing's raven, became Engelram,
and thought he was of angelic purity, in name if not in nature ; and
either he or Engelhard passed into France as Enguerraud, the chief
Christian name of the brave house whose proud saying was—

> " Je suis ni roi, ni comte aussi,
> Je suis le Sire de Coucy ; "

and the English called it Ingeltram, when Isabel, the daughter of
Edward III., made her love match with the brave Lord de Coucy,
whose loyalty was so sorely perplexed by his connection with her
family.

Engelfrid, Engelschalk, Engelberga, and Engelbert, are probably
originally German angels in connection with peace, discipleship,
protection, and splendour ; and Professor Munch thinks the northern
Ingobert an instinctive attempt to nationalize the last. On the other
hand, he leaves to Ing, Angilbald, Angiltrud, Angelrich ; as, in fact,
may be always done with every name of the kind that can be traced
to an owner prior to the time when angels were popular ideas among
our northern ancestors.

Ingvar was a terrible name to our Saxon ancestors, when the
Danish viking, so called, carried terror to our coasts ; but Ivar is
not the short for it, but is from *yr* ; German, *eibe* ; Dutch, *ibe* ;
English, *yew* ; and *har*, a warrior, so that Ivar is the Yew warrior,
the bow-bearer, or archer. He is Iver in Danish, and in Scotland
and Ireland MacIvor has been adopted as a rendering of one of the
old hereditary Keltic names. Ivbald and Ivbert have also been used

and cut down to Ibald and Ibert.   Ireland had a St. Ivor, or Ivory, who was considered to have prayed away from Fernegenall the *mures maiores qui vulgariter Rati vocantur* so completely that none survived ; but whether he was named by Dane or Kelt does not appear.   At any rate, St. Ivory was deemed good to invoke against rats.

It is probable that Ivhar is the real origin of Ives, the saint who named the town in Huntingdonshire ; but legend strangely makes him a Persian bishop, who chose that locality for a hermitage, in the seventh century, and whose body was discovered uncorrupt in the year 1001, thus providing a patron for many an Ivar of Danish or Norman extraction, who became Yvon, or Ivone, in France ; and Ivo in the chroniclers.   Ivo de Taillebois is the villain of the story of *Hereward* and his camp of refuge ; and the name is common with the Normans and Bretons, all the more for the sake of St. Ivo de Chartres, who was imprisoned for his resistance to the adultery of Philip I. and Bertrade of Anjou, and St. Ives of Brittany, the good lawyer, called the advocate of the poor.   These Breton Ivons may, however, be from Sir Ywain, or Owen, the same as Eoghan.*

Section XV.—*Eormen.*

The third son of Mannus was said to be Er, a word, perhaps, connected with Tyr on one side, and Ares on the other ; for Ertag is the Tuesday of Southern Germany, and Eresburg, now Mersburg, was the centre of the worship of the continental Saxons.   The day was, however, also called, in Bavaria and Austria, Ermintag, or Irminstag ; and the deity worshipped at Eresburg was Irman, or Ermin ; and perhaps the word should be considered as Er-man in conjunction. From him the Herminiones of Tacitus are said to be descended, being chiefly the old Germans and the Franks.

At Eresburg, even up to the eighth century, there stood a great central temple, containing a marble column on which stood an armed warrior, holding, in one hand, a banner bearing a rose, in the other a balance.   The crest on the helmet was a cock, on the breastplate was a bear, on the shield that hung from the shoulders was a lion in a field of flowers.   Around lived a college of priests, who exercised judgment and made biennial offerings.   Before going out to war, the host, in full armour, galloped round the figure, brandishing their spears and praying for victory.   Lesser images were carried with the army, and, on its return, captives and cowards were slain, as offerings to the great idol.

This temple was destroyed by Charlemagne, who buried the idol where afterwards stood the abbey of Corbye.   In his son's reign it was dug up, and carried off by the French as a trophy, when the Saxons rose to rescue it and a battle took place, after which it was thrown into the river Innen, but was fished out, exorcised, purified, and made to serve as a candelabrum in the church of Hillesheim.

* Grimm ; Munch ; Luning ; Kemble ; O'Donovan ; Butler.

The battle was called Armansula, and the image Irmansul; whence many have fancied that Irmansul was the chief German god.

Sul, or *saul*, is, however, a pillar; and it is a very curious fact that two sacred columns were the penates of every Teuton's hearth and city. When a migration was decided on by the Scandinavians, a solemn feast was held, the master of the house seated between his two *sulur*, or columns, which he uprooted and carried with him, and, on his approach to his intended home, he threw them overboard, and followed them with his ship, landing wherever they were cast up. It was thus that the situation of Reijkjavik, in Iceland, was determined. Such columns, down to a very late period, stood at the gates of the elder towns in Germany, and were called Ermensaulen, or, sometimes, one the Rolandsaul, the other the Ermensaul.

Eormon, in the Anglian of Beowulf, means universal; *eormoncyn*, the whole of mankind; in old Norse, *jormün* is the world, and *Jormungandr* is another name of the Midgard snake which encircles the world. Most likely, the Irmansul thus signified the universal column, the pillar adored by all men; just as the Anglo-Saxons called the great Roman road Eormenstreot, or Ermingstreet, the public road. *Er*, then, would be the divinity, *man* the human word, and Erman would thus express something revered by all; and thence, the name of the tribes of the Hermiones and Hermunduri, both meaning all the people. Later, the word *jormün*, or *eorman*, came to mean only very large; and, probably, the Saxons of Thuringia had forgotten the original signification of their columns when they gave the single one of Irmansul such an exclusive prominence. Some have tried to explain one pillar as Heermansaul, pillar of the army man, and the other as Raginholdsaul, pillar of firm judgment, as emblems of military and civil power; but though this meaning may have later been bestowed on them, the signification of Eormon is decidedly adverse to this explanation, and it is safest to translate it, when it occurs in names, as public, or general.

When the Cheruschi, themselves Herminiones, broke the heart of Augustus by cutting off the legions of Quinctilius Varus, their leader was Arminius, probably Irman or Eorman, though after-generations

English.	French.	Spanish.	Italian.
Armyn Armine	Armand	Armando	Arminio Armanno
German. Hermann	Swedish. Hermann	Dutch. Hermanus Herman Manus	Swiss. Herma Hermeli
Slovak. Jerman	Lettish. Ermannis	Esth. Herm	Lithuanian. Ermas Ermonas

explained it as Heerman or Armyman. So that the hosts of Hermans, named when national feeling was roused by French invasion, are in his honour ; previously, the Dutch Jacob Hermannsen had rendered himself into Latin as Arminius. From Holland the Norfolk name of Armyn must have been imported.

The Germans use, as the feminine, Hermine and Herminie, which properly belong to the Latin Herminius ; and the French have made their own form of Armand into Armantine. A Burgundian hermit, Ermin, too, gave St. Ermo to Italy, a name inextricably mixed with Elmo, the contraction of Erasmus ; it is the St. Erme of France.

Very early, so as to be almost mythical, was the Thuringian Irmanfrit, or Iruvrit, who hardly conduced to 'public peace' by calling in the Saxons ; but Hermanfred continued in use in Germany, and was known to the French as Hermanfroi.

The Burgundian version of the great world-girding snake was Ermelind, a name that came to a saintly virgin of the sixth century from whom Ermelinda flourished as an Italian name, being probably common to both Lombards and Burgundians, as both Vandals.

But these Irmins are most frequent in ancient Spain. The Suevi had Hermanrik, or Hermanarico, public ruler, and the Goths, Hermanegar and Hermangildo ; the last being the prince who is revered as having been converted from Arianism by his orthodox Frank wife, and whose death, by his father's persecution, sealed the triumph of Catholicism in Spain. Hermenburga was a princess, offered to, but refused by, a Frank king ; and Ermesinda, or, as Southey's poem calls her, Hermesind, the daughter of Pelayo, carried the blue blood of the Balten to the line of Alfonso. Her name meant public dignity.

Parallel to these the Anglo-Saxons enumerate Eormenric, Eormen-burh, Eormenburg, Eormengyth, Eormengild ; and after the Conquest there still continue the forms of Eremburga, Ermentrude, and Ermengarde ; the last by far the most frequent, and not yet disused in Germany.

Section XVI.—*Erce.*

The Anglo-Saxons were accustomed to perform an incantation to restore the fruitfulness of their fields. It began by the cry *Erce, Erce, Erce, Eordhan Môder*, as if it were not earth itself, but her mother that was called upon.

The same word *erce* is used for ark, chest, or ship, in the Anglo-Saxon New Testament. And Erce does not seem to have been entirely forgotten ; for Erche, or Herkja, is a famous lady in old German hero songs.

From thence, too, may have sprung the Old German adjective *ërchan*, meaning holy, genuine, or simple, which is thought to have named the famous Hercynian forest of ancient Germany, which would thus be the sacred wood.

The founder of the East Saxon kingdom in England is called both Escwine and Ercenwine, the darling of Ese, or of Erce. In the Kentish genealogy we find Eorconberht, sacred brightness, answering to the Lombardo-Italic Erchimperto ; and also Eorcongot, sacred divinity.

St. Eorconwald, holy power, was a bishop of London, about 678, and may almost be reckoned as the second founder of St. Paul's, where his shrine was greatly revered ; and about the same time Erkenoald was a *maire du palais* in France ; and Erchenold, or Herchenhold, was an old German name, meaning probably firm in truth.

In old knightly times, we find the German Erchanbald, meaning a sacred prince, from which the French took many a Sire Archambault, and the Italians Arcibaldo.

The Scots, by some strange fancy, adopted Archibald as the Lowland equivalent of Gillespie, the bishop's servant. So frequent was it in the houses of Campbell and Douglas, that, with its contractions of Archie and Baldie, it has become one of the most commonly used in Scotland, recalling many a fierce worthy, from old Archibald Bell-the-Cat downwards, and always translating the Gillespie of the Campbells to Lowland ears.*

SECTION XVII.—*Amal.*

Amal is a very remarkable word. We have had it in Greek, as Αἱμύλος ; in Latin, as Æmilius ; in the Keltic as Amalgaidh ; and in all it would seem as if one notion could be detected—that of work. Even in Hebrew Amal means to work ; *aml* is work in old Norse ; and we have still our verb *to moil*, taken therefrom. *Mahl*, be it remembered, is in German a time ; *mahl*, a stroke ; *mahlen*, to paint or make strokes ; and so in the North, *maal* is a measure, or an end, a goal. Probably there is a notion of repetition of marks, stroke upon stroke, in all cases, and the Sanscrit meaning of Amal, or spotless, without mark, is in favour of the meaning.

It is safest, however, to translate the Teutonic Amal by work, the thought most familiar to the sturdy northern nations who used it, and loved work for its own sake.

In the Vilkina Saga, the mighty smith Velint's first great trial of skill was with Amilias, an armourer at the court of King Nielung. Velint struck him with his sword Mimung ; he said he felt as if a drop of water had flowed down him. " Shake yourself," said Velint, and the unfortunate smith fell down cloven painlessly from head to heel, an example of labour *versus* skill.

Aumlung, the strong, is mentioned in the *Book of Heroes*, as feasting at the Nibelung court ; and it was at Duke Amelung's court that, according to the Danish ballad, old Sir Hildibrand had been staying for twenty-two years, before, going back to Bern, he met his unknown son Alebrand.

Amala was a favourite Lombardic commencement, and was likewise much in favour with German ladies ; it became first Amalie, and then, when Italy and France had taken up the Latin Æmilia, this old Teutonic form was mixed up with it ; and Amelia in

* Grimm, &c.

England, Amélie in France, are scarcely considered to differ from it ; and though historically Emily is the descendant of the Æmilii, Amelia of the Amaler, yet both alike come from the original Amal.

Amalaswinth, which would bear the translation, dignity of labour, though probably it was only given in the sense of dignity of the Amaler, was the unfortunate Lombardic queen, whom the Romans could not protect from the treachery of her favourites. Amalasontha is what historians call her ; but on Burgundian lips it came to be Melisenda, Melicerte, Melusine.

Melisenda is in Spanish ballad lore the wife of Don Gayferos, and, being taken captive by the Moors, was the occasion of the feats that were represented by the puppet show in which Don Quixote took an unfortunately lively interest. Melisende again was the princess who carried the uneasy crown of Jerusalem to the House of Anjou ; and, perhaps, from the Provençal connections of the English court, Lady Melisent Stafford bore the name in the time of Henry II., whence Melicent has become known in England, and never quite disused, though often confounded with Melissa, a bee, and sometimes spelt Millicent.

Melusine was a nymph who became the wife of the Lord de Leezignan, or Lusignan, on condition that he should never intrude upon her on a Saturday ; of course, after a long time, his curiosity was excited, and stealing a glance at his lady in her solitude, he beheld her a serpent from the waist downward ! With a terrible shriek, she was lost to him for ever ; but she left three sons, all bearing some deformity, of whom *Geoffroi au grand dent* was the most remarkable.

Melusina continued in use in the south of France, Holland, and Germany, and is occasionally used in England. We find Melicerte in old French chronicles.

The very ancient queens of Navarre and the Asturias have a wonderful set of aliases, and one, the oddest, is " Amelina, or Simena, or Ximena," the sister of Sancho I., of Navarre, who married Alfonso the Great. Could the Spaniards, by any possibility, have contracted the soft *Amal* into the harsh guttural *Xi*, which sounds as if it came from a Moorish throat. Yet, Goths as they were, they show no Amal, though their Ximen and Ximena reach up to 700, and Ximena survived long as a name among their ladies, and was the wife of the Cid, whence the French turned her into Chimène. Emmeline, as it is now generally spelt, came from France as Emeline, and is frequent in old ballad poetry, and in northern registers, as Emyln. It is probably another form of this same Amaline, or *lind*, Amal's serpent.

The northern races have the one much reduced name of Malfrid, from Amalafrida, of peace.

The ladies have certainly been the chief owners of Amal, as a commencement ; but it has had a brilliant part to play in the form of Amalrich, Almerich, or Emmerich, on the German side ; Almerigo in Spain ; Amalric, or Amaury, in France ; Almerick in England. Amaury was an Angevin king of Jerusalem ; and our own Sir

Almerick St. Lawrence was brother-in-arms to Sir John de Courcy, and founded the House of Howth in Ireland. The House of Lusignan, Melusina's descendants, called it Aymar; and in this form it came to England with Henry III.'s half-brother, whom he promoted to the see of Winchester, but who episcopally called himself Ethelmarus; though his nephew, Aymar de Valence, kept his proper name. Emmery is a surviving English surname, and Merica occurs in old Yorkshire genealogies.

But it is the Italian form, Amerigo, which was destined to the most noted use,—when the adventurer, Amerigo Vespucci, gave his name to the tract of land that Columbus saw for the first time in his company; little knowing that it was no island, but a mighty continent, which should hold fast that almost fortuitous title, whence thousands of miles, and millions of men, bear the appellation of the forgotten forefather of a tribe of the Goths—Amalrich, the work ruler; a curiously appropriate title for the new world of labour and of progress, on the other side the Atlantic.

Amalberge is an old Cambrai name; Malburg a Danish one; Amalgund, Amalbert, Amalbertine, and Amalhild, have also been known. The French Amelot must be the contraction of one of the masculine forms.*

SECTION XVIII.—*Forefathers.*

The deification of forefathers, or the claim to divine origin, which-ever it might be, led to the employment, as a prefix, of the very word that expressed them—that word which we use still at the beginning of *ancestors*, and that the Germans call *ahnen*. In old German the singular was *ano*, and it signified a remote forefather. The *Rigsmaal*, an old Icelandic poem which explains the origin of the various castes which the northern races acknowledged, represents Heimdall, the porter of heaven, as wandering to the earth, and being entertained by Ai and Edda, or great-grandfather and great-grand-mother, who lived in a lowly hut; then by Avi and Amma (Lat. Avus), or grandfather and grandmother, who had a comfortable dwelling-house; and lastly by Fadher and Modher, whose abode was a splendid mansion. The son of Edda was Thrall; the son of Amma was Karl; the son of Modher was Jarl; and from these descended the three castes of the North—the thralls, or slaves; the churls, bondr, or farmers; and the jarls, or nobles.

This is an absolute mythic allegory by way of explanation of existing circumstances; but the names therewith connected mostly survived, though they refer to these mere embodiments of abstract ideas.

Ai, or *ani*, enters into the composition of the Icelandic Anar, ancestral warrior, and thus, no doubt, contributed to form our sur-name of Anson, which, like almost all our great naval names, thus traces back to some ancient viking, who has done us at least as much

* Grimm; Kemble; *Int. to Beowulf;* Weber; Dugdale.

good as evil, by leaving us his sons to keep all other invaders from our shores.

The old Saxon histories call some of these enemies by the name of Anlaff, in particular the chief who visited King Æthelstan's tent in a minstrel's disguise, and betrayed himself by burying the guerdon that he was too proud to keep. The same persons whom England called Anlaff, and Ireland Amlaidh, were, in the North, Alafr, or Olafr, according to the custom of pronouncing the diphthong *a* like an *o*, and then so spelling it, *e.g.*, Aasbiorn, Osbiorn. The latter syllable is *laf* or *leif*, from the verb *lev*, the Anglo-Saxon *leafan*, our own *leave*. It is a word that never is used as a commencement, and but rarely stands alone, though the North sometimes has a Leifr, and it is used in the sense of what is remaining. Anlaff, or Olaf, is thus what is left of his forefathers, his ancestor's relic, and a very notable relic was the gallant king Olaf Trygveson, the prime hero of the *Heimskringla*, whose last battle is so nobly described there. Scarcely less noble is his relative, Olaf the saint, the ally of England, who fought her battles near London-bridge, and has left his name to the church of St. Olave, near the site of the battle, though, unluckily, English tongues made him St. Toly. St. Olaf was over-harsh in his endeavours to introduce Christianity to his subjects, and perished in a war with the rebels, assisted by Knut of Denmark and England ; but his name continued glorious, and another royal St. Olaf, in Sweden, assisted to make it one of the most national of Scandinavian names, even to the present day.

Its Latinism is Oläus, and its contraction Ole, or, rather, this answers to the very old Aale, which, in its turn, answers to the Analo, Anilo, Anelo, of the old Germans.

Leif, or *laf*, we shall often meet as a termination, both in the North and in Germany, where it generally becomes *leib* or *lip*, and then the modern Germans take it for *love*, and thus have changed the old Gottleip into Gottleib.   In the North it has scarcely fared better, especially in the case of Thorleif, or Thor's relic, who changed from Tholleiv to Thoddeiv, or Tadeiv, on the one hand, and on the other, to Tellev, which, thanks to some classically-disposed clergyman, has been written Teleph, and referred to the Greek Telephus.

Of the other names connected with the *Rigsmaal*, we find Edda, the great-grandmother, giving title to the ancient poem on cosmogony and mythology that may be regarded as the parent of all the northern songs.   Thrall was likewise, in spite of its meaning, used as a name.

The next generation, Avi, Amma, and the son Karl, are the prominent ones.   The equivalent of Karl, Bondr, a farmer, is now and then a northern name ; but it is the great Frank Karling line whose names so curiously answer to these.

Were they of the middle class of landholders, and were they proud of it, and anxious to trace their connection back to the grandfather, grandmother, and churl ? Whether there were a Frank version of the *Rigsmaal* we do not know, but the leading name of the family was Karl, the churl (of which more in its relation to the cycle of Romance), and it is found in constant company with Amma, or Emma, and alternates with one that almost certainly represented Avi, or grand-father.

Charles, Pepin l'Heristal, Charles Martel, Pepin le Bref, Charles the Great, is the succession till the alternation was broken by the death of Pepin, the eldest son of Charles the Great. Now this most undignified Pepin is traced by the best authorities to be one of the many forms of the primitive and universal *abba*, father, papa, and to answer to the old German names of Bobo, Bobbo, and Poppo. And it is not, therefore, probable that Pepin and Emma stood for the northern Avi and Amma, both alike with the son Karl?

Amme, or Emma, no doubt formed by the first lispings of a child, is *amme*, a nurse, in Germany, and *ama*, a housekeeper, in Spain. As a name, it was at first exclusively Frank, and used by the Karling daughters. The first Emma mentioned was the daughter of Charlemagne ; and the sister of Hugh Capet, who married Richard the Fearless, of Normandy, was likewise so called. Her grand-daughter was the wife, first of Ethelred the Unready, then of Knut, and the supposed heroine of the ordeal of the ploughshares. Emma was considered as so un-English that her name was translated into Ælfgifu. However, we find 'Emme' among the daughters of Dru de Baladon, who came over with the Conqueror, and thus 'Emm' and 'Emr' are by no means uncommon in the registers of Yorkshire and Durham, even down to the seventeenth century. Then Prior, when modernizing and sentimentalizing the beautiful ballad of the *Nut Browne Maid*, supposed to be on the history of the shepherd Lord Clifford, called it Henry and Emma, whence it became rather a favourite romantic name of literature. Clergymen were apt to use it, in Latin registers, as a translation of Amy, as well as of its own Em. It is also confounded with Emily, and at the present day recurs extremely often in England, while it is almost disused in France, its native home. The Welsh use it as a translation of Ermin, probably a legacy of the Roman Herminii. Emmott is another old name of northern England, probably amplified from Em ; but Emeline, as has been already said, is far more probably Amalina than any relation to Emma.

Jarl, as might be expected, was a very favourite eponym ; but not in the same pronunciation ; for it first became Irl, then Erl, in nomenclature. Erling, a name much used by the Norsemen, and often corrupted into Elling, is the son of the earl ; and the Swedish once had a Jarlar, or earl-warrior, who changed into Erlher, Erlo, Erlebald, Erlebrecht, Erlhild.

CHAPTER III.

SECTION I.—*Day.*

THE rich imagination of the North could not fail to preserve the Eastern myths of natural appearances and animals with their myths, and these ideas are as usual reflected in the names of the race.

In the *Edda*, Nôtt, or night, the dark, one of the Jotun, is the wife of Dellingr, the brilliant and beautiful, one of the Æsir, and their son is Dag or Day. Mother and son each have a chariot in which they career round the sky, in pursuit of one another. The horse of Day is Shinfaxi, of shining mane ; the horse of Night is Hrimfaxi, rime or frost name.

Day had many namesakes, though more often at the end than the beginning of a word.

Dago, Tago, or Tajo, was a Gothic bishop of Zaragoza, whom King Chindaswintha sent to Rome about 640, to bring home a copy of St. Gregory's *Comment on the Book of Job*, which had been dedicated to a King of Spain, one of the Suevi, but had been lost in the irruption of the Arian Goths. The Roman clergy had been equally careless. Pope Theodorus could not lay his hands upon the manuscript ; and the search became so tedious, that finally Bishop Tajo betook himself to prayer, and obtained a special vision of the holy Pope Gregory himself, who directed him to the depository of the manuscript.

This same Dagr figures in the *Landnama-bok ;* and the North has Dagfinn, perhaps once an allusion to the resplendent glory of Odin, but usually translated white as day. Dagulf, or Daulf, day-wolf, was no doubt in allusion to the wolf Sköll, who hunts the sun daily round the sky, and will eat her up at last ; whence to this day a parhelion is called in Sweden a sun-wolf, Sololf. Eclipses are caused when the wolf gains on the sun, who has no namesakes in Teuton nomenclature, the few that sound like it being from another source, namely, *Salv* or *sölv*, anointing or healing. The feminine *ny*, though meaning the new moon when standing alone, is only the adjective new, and means fresh and fair, so that the northern Dagny is, fair as day. The Norse ladies also have Dagheid or Dageid, cheerful as day.

Dagobert, or bright as day, was that long-haired king who, next to Clovis, impressed the French imagination. He was the employer of the great goldsmith St. Eloi, and the throne or chair of King

Dagobert, ascribed to that great artificer, is still in existence. A successor in the *fainéant* times was canonized, and together the two Dagoberts, making one, have become the theme first of heroic and then of burlesque in France. It was Takaperaht in Old German ; and there, too, Tagarat, or Dagrad, is to be found ; but in general, *dag* or *tac* comes at the end of words.

Dagmar—the favourite queen of the Danes, whose only fault was lacing her sleeves on a Sunday—is called only by her epithet, Danes' joy. Her true name was Margaret of Bohemia, and the Danish princess Dagmar, who was christened after her, was on her Russian marriage called Marie.*

Section II.—*The Wolf.*

It is for the place that he occupies in the Teutonic imagination, rather than for his own merits, that the wolf stands foremost among the creatures that have supplied Teutonic names.

He is also the most universal. Zeeb, Lycos, and Lupus, have been already mentioned ; and the midnight prowler, as the most terrible animal of Europe, held his place in imaginations, whence the lion and tiger faded for want of personal acquaintance. The French have no less than forty-nine proverbs about wolves, many no doubt remains of the beast epic.

Wolves called Geri and Freki sat on either side of Odin's throne, and devoured his share of the bears' flesh of Valhalla, a banquet he was too ethereal to require. Wolves chase the sun and moon round their daily courses ; and a terrible wolf called Mangarmr, or moon-gorger, is to devour the moon at the coming of the wolf-age, which, in the *Voluspa*, shadows the last days of the world. Fenris, the wolf of the abyss, is the son of Loki ; and though bound by the Æsir at the cost of Tyr's right hand, will finally break loose, destroy Odin himself, and only be rent asunder by Vidur in his resistless shoes.

Nevertheless, *ulf, vulf, wolf*, was highly popular as a name-root ; perhaps more common at the end than the beginning of a word, but often standing alone. It was the diminutive Vulfila that was the right name of that good bishop whose Mæso-Gothic version of the Gospels goes by his Latinism of Ulphilas.

Ulf was twenty-three times in the *Landnama-bok* ; and *ulf* in every possible form ravaged the coasts of Europe. *Wolf* was again the hereditary prefix in the House of Bavaria, where the dukes varied between Wolf and Wolfart, till Wolfen became the designation of the family, and a legend was invented to account for it. An ancestress had, it was said, given birth to twelve infants all at once, and in the spirit of the child who, being shown his twin brothers, asked " Which shall we keep," sent her maid to dispose of the eleven un-necessary ones in the river. The father met her, and asked what she had in her apron. " Only whelps," she answered ; but he was not

* Blackwell, Mallet; Munch ; Butler; Grimm ; Thierry ; Michaelis.

to be thus put off, made an inspection, saved the children's lives, and called them the Wolfen, or wolf-whelps ! The *Book of Heroes*, however, makes the Wolfings descend from the brave Sir Hildebrand, and be so called from a wolf on their shield granted them by the Emperor Wolfdietrich, in remembrance of an adventure of his own infancy, when he had been carried off by a she-wolf to her den, and remained there unhurt—whence his name of Wolfdietrich. The male line of the Wolfen, however, in time became extinct, and the heiress married one of the Italian House of Este, which adopted the German Wolf in the Italianized form of Guelfo, and constantly used it as a name. Thence when the popes set up Otto d'Este, one of the Wolfen of Bavaria, as anti-emperor in opposition to the House of Hohenstaufen, his partisans were called Welfen ; those of the Fredericks, Waiblingen, from the Swabian castle of Waibling. The Italian cities rang with the fierce cries of Guelfo and Zibelino, for the pope or the emperor, and Europe learnt to identify the Guelph with the cause of the Church ; the Ghibelline with that of the State, when the origin of the words had long been forgotten.

One of the Bavarian Wolfen d'Este became Duke of Brunswick Luneburg, and from him descended the Hanoverian line of English sovereigns, who in the time of Revolution thence were said to be properly surnamed Guelf, or even Whelps, with about as much correctness as when Louis XVI. was styled Louis Capet.

We had a wolf among our sovereigns in the days of the Heptarchy, in Vulfhere, king of Mercia, the same as the northern Ulfar, and German Wolfer, meaning wolf-warrior. Also Vulfhilda was a sainted abbess in England, while Ulvhildur colonized Iceland. We had also Vulfred, Vulfnoth, Vulfstein, better known as St. Wulstan, the admirable bishop of Worcester. These English wolves of ours have a great inclination to lapse into sheep's clothing and become wool, in which form we use them in the harmless surnames of Woolgar, Woolstone, Woolmer, Wolsey.

Ulfketill, or Ulfkjell, as odd a compound as can well be found, was one of the pirates who invested England, but is a peaceable inhabitant in Domesday, where Ulf swarms, as Ulfac, Ulfeg, Ulfert, Ulfener, Ulfric ; just as he does in the Iceland Domesday, as Ulfhedinn, Ulfherdur, Ufliotr.

In Germany, Wolfgang, perhaps best rendered as Wolf-progress, was a sainted bishop of Ratisbon, in the tenth century, whence this strange name flourished, and, coming to Göthe, became prized by all his admirers. There, too, is Wolfram, the wolf-raven, Wolfrad, and Wolfert.

Some have translated *ulf*, or *wolf*, at the end of a word by help ; but this is impossible, as though *hulf* is help in German, the *f* is the property of that language alone.

A few of the Danes seem to have learnt to respect the qualities of the magnificent Irish wolf-hound, whose qualities are highly praised in the *Heimskringla*. Then they took to calling themselves Hunde ; and a son of Sigurd, Earl of Orkney, is called both Hvalp and Hund. The name of Hundolf is, however, supposed to be either hardened from Hun, or else to be from a word meaning booty or plunder, so as to mean the wolf of plunder.*

SECTION III.—*Eber, the Boar.*

The boar, whom we found so popular in Roman nomenclature, is equally so among the southern Teutons, among whom the tusky boar was one of the prime beasts of chase. The Romans apparently viewed him and his titles in their domestic aspect ; but the Teutons honoured the fierce *Eber* of their forests as their highest and most dangerous prey, and gave him a place among their mythology.

Freyr had a boar with golden bristles, called Gullenbörsti, and when the corn waved in the wind, the saying was, "Freyr's boar is passing by." Epurhelm, an old German name, was thus an appeal to the protection of Freyr.

The boar Sehrimnar was likewise the future feast of the brave in Valhall, daily hunted and eaten, and as often resuscitated for the next day's sport and banquet. Scandinavia lay too far north for his porcine majesty ; and the Norsemen had no personal acquaintance with him in their daily life, whatever they might look forward to ; and thus *Eber*, the wild boar, does not figure in their nomenclature, and scarcely among our own insular Saxons, though he is said to have ranged our forests.

But turning to the Goths, we fall at once upon Ebroirus, an evident classicalism of Eberwine, not so much the boar's friend, as Freyr's friend. Ebrimuth, another early Goth, is wild boar's mood or wrath, and in Visigothic Spain we find Eborico, namely, Eberik, boar ruler.

Frankland produced the formidable compound of boarwolf, Eberulf ; but its two owners grew up monastic saints in the sixth and seventh centuries, and were honoured by the French as SS. Evrault, Evrols, Evrou, or Evraud. The second of these saints was a native of Normandy, and is patron of the abbey of Fontévraud, the burial-place of Henry II. and Richard Cœur de Lion, and the noblest nunnery in France.

It is difficult, however, to distinguish between the forms of the French Eberulf, and the German Eberhard, who was abbot of Einsiedlen in 934 ; indeed, it is highly probable that the Norman St. Evrhault, though derived from a saint Latinized as Eberulfus, and in German called Erulf, was supposed to be the same as Eberhard, and that this accounts for the English form of Everard, which sprung up from the four Evrards of the Domesday roll after the Conquest. Eberhard hardly reaches the rank of saint in the Roman calendar ; but his exertions in a great famine that ravaged Alsace, Burgundy, and Upper Germany, in 942, account for the nationality of his name in all that region.

---

* Grimm ; Turner, *Anglo-Saxons ;* Blackwell, Mallet ; *Dictionnaire des Proverbes Français ;* Sismondi, *Republiques Italianes ;* Anderson, *Genealogies ;* Lappenburn, *Anglo-Saxons ;* Alban Butler ; Marryat, *Jutland ;* Pott.

Z

English.	Italian.	Frisian.	German.
Everard	Everardo	Evart	Eberhard
Ewart	Eberardo	Evert	Ebert
	Ebbo		Ewart
			Eppo
French.	Dutch.	Lett.	Ebbo
Evraud	Everhard	Ewarts	Ebo
Ebles	Evert		Ebilo
			Ebin
			Etto
			Uffo
			Uppo
			Appo

The Germans likewise have a feminine from this 'boarfirm' word Eberbardine, contracted into Ebertine, or Ebba, and in Frisian, Ebbe or Jebbe. I am afraid these German forms do not certainly account for the Saxon Ebba, or Æbbe, sister of St. Oswald, and foundress of the famous priory of Coldingham. However, England had one St. Eberhilda, who was a pupil of St. Wilfrid, and foundress of a monastery called Everidisham, the locality of which cannot be discovered ; but the abbess must have left an impression on the ladies of the North, to judge by the frequency of the occurrence of Everilda, which, with the contractions of Averilla and Averil, is not yet extinct.

Offa, the Low German legendary hero—is very probably called by a contraction of the wild boar. His name is repeated by the king of Mercia, who seems to have borrowed somewhat of the legend in his story, and Offa was not extinct even in Domesday.

Ebermund, a Neustrian Frank of Meerwing days, was founder of Fontenoy Abbey, and was honoured as St. Evrémond, whence the territorial surname familiar to readers of French memoirs.

St. Evre, who is frankly Latinized into Sanctus Aper, was the seventh bishop of Toul, where the register of bishops presents a curious succession of wild beasts, and some of the Ebbos and Affos of Germany may be his rightful property, though they are now all turned over to the charitable Eberhard of Einsiedlen. Eburbero, or Boar-bear, seems to have been a German invention.

SECTION IV.—*The Bear.*

The bear does not enter into the legends of the *Edda*, but he enjoyed immense regard in the North, and was looked on as a sort of ancestor, to whom, when he was killed, polite apologies were always made, and who is still called by the pet name of the Wise Man, rather than by his own proper term. Even in France he was mysteriously alluded to as le *vieux* or le *grand père ;* and probably the Swiss veneration for the bears of Berne partly originated in the general devotion to the deliberate and almost human-looking plantigrade.

The Anglo-Saxons made Beorn the great-grandson of Wuotan, and the ancestor of the kings of Beornland ; in Latin Bernicia, or Beornia, afterwards the earldom that gave title to Richard, son of William I. Legend again declared that the stout old Earl Siward Biorn was actually the offspring of a bear, and that the ears of his parent might have been found concealed beneath his matted locks.

Norway and Iceland are, as in duty bound, the land of bears, but the Pyrenees had their share likewise ; and if the North has Bjornulf, the same bear-wolf reigned over Gothic Spain in the form of Vernulfo ; and in the Asturias and Navarre, the bear's mood was dreaded as Bermudo, or Vermudo, and his protecting hand sought as Veremundo.

In the Pyrenees, too, flourished the bear-spear, the same with the northern Bjorngjer, though southern tongues made Berenger and Berengario, in which forms it was owned by many a mountain king of Navarre and count of Roussillon, Barcelona, or Toulouse. There, too, it formed the feminine Berenguela, and this, as princesses' names always do, travelled farther ; for Berenguela was queen of Castille, and mother of St. Fernando ; another Berenguela, or Berangère, as French tongues called her, is familiar to us under that most incorrect historical title of Berengaria, the bride of Richard Cœur de Lion. Another Berenguela, who from Portugal married the king of Denmark, so misconducted herself that Bjorngard or Berngard, the Danish version of her name, stands for an abandoned woman.

Biorn of the fiery eyes was appropriately named by Fouqué ; for the *Landnama-bok* shows forty-two Biorns, and the name is still common in Norway and Iceland, where also are found still, as man's names, Bersi and Besse, also titles of the bear, and Bera by way of feminine. Bjornhedinn is also northern, and there are numerous varieties of compounds, one of them rather of late date being Bjorn-stern, bear-star, probably in reference to the Pole-star. One of the present authors in Norway bears the fierce name of Bjornsternja Bjornsen.

The most famous of all the bears is, however, of Frank growth. Some have tried to resolve it into Bairn-heart, child-hearted ; but though *barn* is of most ancient lineage, found even in Ulfilas's Gospels, all analogy is against the interpretation ; and there can be no doubt that when the first historical Biornhard was named, his parents would much have preferred his having the resolution of a bear rather than the heart of a child.

That first was an uncle of Charlemagne, and from him it was that the mountain, erst of Jupiter, was termed of Bernard, even before a second Bernard, surnamed De Menthon, fled from his home for love of a monastic life, and erected his noble hospice for the reception of travellers. Then came further glory to the name through the Cistercian monk, whose pure character was revered by all in the thirteenth century, until his became a universal name throughout Europe ; in Ireland absorbing the native Brian. In Spain, too, Bernardo del Carpio is a great legendary champion, nephew to king Alfonso II. of Leon, and who, in the battle of Roncevalles, was said

to have squeezed Roland the paladin to death in his arms. Bernal
Diaz is the simple-hearted chronicler of Cortes.

English.	French.	Italian.	Spanish.
Bernard	Bernard	Bernardo	Bernardo
Barnard	Bernadin	Bernadino	Bernal

Portuguese.	Wallachian.	German.	Dutch.
Bernaldo	Bernardu	Bernhard	Bernhart
Bernadim		Berend	Barend
		Benno	Barndt

Frisian.	Lusatian.	Lettish.	Esth.
Bernd	Bernat	Berents	Pero
		Berns	Perent

Slovak.	Hungarian.		
Bernardek	Bernät		

It has the German feminine Bernhardine. The Irish Bryan adopts
Bernard as his English synonym.

Other less celebrated German forms are Bernwald ; the French,
Berault ; and Italian, Bernaldo. Berwart, abbot of Hildesheim ;
Bernclo, the Bavarian bear's claw ; Berner, and many others where
bern or *pern* ends the word.

Bahrend, Berndt, Behr, Behring, all are surnames from the bear in
Germany, and the last very appropriately named Behring's Straits. It
is the same that came to England as Faring.*

SECTION V.—*The Horse.*

No sacred animal was in more request than the horse. The gods
had their wonderful horses. Sleipner (the Slider) was the eight-
footed steed of Odin ; Gullfaxi, or gold mane, belonged to the giant
Hrimgrim ; and the shining-maned and hoary-maned coursers of day
and night have been already mentioned.

The eastern origin of the Teutons was never more shown than by
their homage to horses. Beautiful and choice white steeds were
reserved for the gods, drawing the waggons that conveyed the images,
when the army went out to battle, or a colony migrated ; and omens
were derived from their neighings when alive, and from their heads
when killed in sacrifice. Great sacrifices of horses were made on
solemn occasions, and feasts were made upon their flesh as a religious
rite, so that the abstaining from horse-flesh became absolutely a test
of Christianity.

The horse was the national emblem of the Saxons ; and Henghist
and Horsa are both old Teuton names for the animal, the first surviving in the German *hengst* and northern *hest*, the last in our ordin-

* Munch; Lappenburg; Pott; Michaelis; Butler.

ary word *horse;* while the High German *hross* has fallen into the modern *ross.* White horses cut out in the chalky hill-sides of southern England from time immemorial, attest the antiquity of the symbol still claimed by the county of Kent, and by the Anglian-Continental kingdom of Hanover.

In the old poem of *Beowulf,* however, Hengist is a Dane, invading and oppressing Finn of Friesland, and afterwards slain. It is possible, then, that Hengist may after all be a mere mythic name erected into an ancestor by the Kentish monarchs. Some have tried to derive *hross* from *horen,* to hear or obey, in honour of the noble creature's obedience; but it is in fact only another form of the *ashva* of India, to which ἵππος, *equus,* and the Keltic *each* have been traced ; and it is curious to find that Brittany preserves the word *ronse,* as does Spain *ronzin,* the term that Don Quixote magnified into the magnificent designation of Rosinante.

The nation that sat round their cauldrons and feasted solemnly on horse-flesh might well call their sons Rossketyl, or Rosskjell. Three are to be found in the *Landnama-bok,* and Roskil is not extinct in Denmark. The agreeable title of Hrossbiorn, or horse-bear, is there to be found likewise, and Saxo-Grammaticus dignifies as Rostiophus, a gentleman who was properly called by the term of Hrossthiof, or horse-thief.

Hrossbert formed into Rospert, Hroshelm into Roselm, Hrosmod into Rosmund, Hrosswald, or horse-power, into Roswal, who was the hero of a Scottish poem called *Roswal and Lilian.* He is the disinherited heir of Naples ; and, after a series of troubles, fights his way back to honour and the hand of Lilian, the fair princess of Bealn.

The feminines Hrossmund, Hroswith, Hroshild, Hrosa, have by general consent been changed from horses to roses, giving up the old idea of the Valkyr on her tall shadowy horse, weaving her web of victory, and have been treated of under the head of Latin flowers.

Hengst seems to have been used for the male, horse for the female ; but *jor* in the North, *ehu* in Old German, *ehvus* in Gothic, meant both horse and mare ; and this *jor,* or sometimes only the *jo,* is not uncommon in Norsk names, as Jogeir, Jofred, Jogrim, Jostein, or flower of chivalry, Johar or Joar, horse warrior, Joketyll, or Jokell. The women were, Jora, Jodis, Jofrid, Joreid, Jorunna, all, be it remembered, being pronounced as with a *y.*

Afterwards Justin devoured Jostein, and George probably consumed some of the others ; indeed, some of the early specimens of Jordan among the Normans, probably accommodated their names to the river in their crusading fervour ; but, *en revanche,* the great Gothic historian, Jornandes, is supposed to have been so called by corruption from his state name of Jordanes.

Jorund, which looks very like one of this race, is referable to another source.

Probably in honour of Thor's he-goats we find the goat figuring in names, as Geitwald, Geithilt, and the wife of Robert Guiscard, Sichelgaita.*

* Grimm ; Munter ; Munch ; Dasent ; Cambro-Briton ; Blackwell, Mallet ;

Section VI.—*The Eagle.*

'There is an eagle sitting on the ash Yggdrasil who knows many things.'

He is, in the North, *aar*, in Germany *ar*, in Scotland *erne;* though we and the modern Germans use, in *eagle* and *adler*, mere contractions of the Latin *aquila.* Places named from the king of birds are found wherever there are mountains.

His influence on nomenclature was exercised from the Dovrefeld and from the Alps, for the eagle-names are chiefly either Scandinavian or High German ; we do not seem to have any native English ones.

The most noted of these southern ones are Arnwald, eagle power, and Arnulf, or eagle-wolf, and it is very difficult to distinguish their derivatives from one another. The saint of the Roman calendar was certainly Arnulf, a prince of the long-haired line, who in 614 retired into a convent at Metz, and became its bishop, when alive, and its patron, when dead. Another previous Arnulf, after whom he was probably christened, for their day is the same, was martyred by the heathen Franks, about the time of the conversion of Clovis ; and a subsequent one was bishop of Soissons, under Pope Hildebrand. Arnoul was common as a name among the Burgundian kings, and was known in Italy as Arnolfo ; but it has been swallowed up by Arnwald, or Arnvalldr, as he is in the North, perhaps because this latter was made famous in Provence by Arnaldo di Maraviglia, the troubadour ; in Italy by the unfortunate Arnoldo of Brescia, and later in Switzerland by the patriot Arnold von Melchthal, and thus it has become popular enough to have the feminines Arnolde and Arnoldine.

English. Arnold	French. Arnaud Arnaut	Italian. Arnoldo	Spanish. Arnoldo
German. Arnold Arno Ahrent Ahrens Arold	Dutch. Arnoldus Arnoud Arend	North. Arnvalld Arnalldr	

The Arnolds and Arnoldines keep their feast upon St. Arnulf's day, thus confessing that they have no patron of their own. Ernulf is an old form found in Domesday Book, and not yet quite extinct.

The northern eagles are much confused by *arin*, a hearth, the same which is found at the end of Thorarin. It contracts into *arn* at the

---

Weber and Jamieson, *Northern Romance ;* Sturleson, *Heimskringla ;* Kemble *Beowulf ;* Ellis, *Specimens of Early English Poetry ;* Pott, *Personen Namen.*

beginning of a word, so that, except when we meet with it in full, as in the case of the brave old sea-king, Arinbiorn, the hearth-bear, it is difficult to tell to which to send the owner, to the *eyrie* or the *fire-side*. And further, *arn* and *arin* both contract indiscriminately into *ar* and *an*, so that the list of Northern names is given rather in the dark. They are both masculine and feminine, for Arna was both used standing alone and as a termination.

Arnridur or Arneidur, eagle haste, one of these eagle ladies, had a curious history told in the *Landnama-bok*. She was the daughter of Asbiorn, a jarl in the Hebrides, and was taken captive by Holmfast Vedormson, who sold her to an Icelander named Ketell Thrymr. He was so much smitten with her as to pay for her twice the sum demanded by old Vedorm ; but before the departure for Iceland, she found a quantity of silver beneath the roots of a tree, sufficient for her ransom. Instead of claiming it, her new master generously gave her the choice of purchasing her freedom or remaining his wife ; she chose the latter alternative, and stands as honourable women do in the *Landnama-bok*, as the mother of a house in Iceland.

Arnthor, and his feminine Arnthora, contract into Arnor and Arnora, and this latter explains Annora, to be found in Norman pedigrees. Annora was wife of Bernard de St. Valery ; and was carried into the family of Braose by king John's victim, Maude de St. Valery, who called one of her daughters Annora. It is also said that Anora is only the contraction of Éleanora.

Ari was an adventurer who sailed to Greenland in fourteen days, fifteen years before the preaching of Christianity in Iceland.

The other old Icelandic and Norsk forms are :—

Arnbiorg, eagle defence ;	Arnlaug, eagle liquor ;
Arndis, eagle sprite ;	Arnleif, eagle relic ;
Arnfinn, white eagle ;	Arnliotr, eagle wanderer ;
Arnfridur, eagle fair one ;	Arnmodur, or Armodr, } eagle wrath ;
Arngeir, eagle war ;	
Arngrimm, or Angrim, Arngrimur, } eagle mask ;	Arnstein, eagle stone ;
Arnkatla, Arnkjell, } eagle cauldron ;	Arnthrudr, eagle maiden.

This Ari, be he eagle or hearth, seems to conduct us to the source of the first syllable of Arabella. The first lady so called, whom I can detect, was Arabella, the granddaughter of William the Lion, of Scotland, who married Robert de Quinci. Another Arabella, with her husband John de Montpynçon, held the manor of Magdalen Laver in the thirty-ninth of Henry III., and thus it was evidently a Norman name. The Normans made wild work with all that did not sound like French, and their Latin secretaries made the matter worse, so that I am much tempted to believe that both Arabella and that other perplexing name, Annabella, may once have been Arnhilda, cut down into Arbell, or Anable, and then amplified. "My Lady Arbell" was certainly what the lady was called, in her own time,

whose misfortunes are so well known to us, under the name of Arabella Stuart, and from whom Arabella has been adopted in various
families, and is usually contracted by Belle.   Some have made it
Arabella, or fair altar, others the diminutive of Arab, both equally
improbable.

The most common form of Arn at present used in Scandinavia is
Arnvid, the eagle of the wood, often contracted into Arve.

With much doubt I question whether the name of Ernest should
not be added to this catalogue. It is obvious to take its native German
form, Ernst, from *ernst*, earnest, grave, or serious, but this is quite
unlike the usual analogy of such names.   Arnust was the older
German form of the name, and some even think that this was the
proper name of Ariovistus, the German chief who fought with Cæsar,
though others consider this to be Cæsar's version of Heerfurst, or
general, and others think they detect the universal root *ar*, husbandry.

The more certain form of the name begins in Lombardy, where
Ernesto, lord of Este, was killed in battle by king Astolfo, in 752.
Is not Ernesto just what Italy would make of Arnstein, after fancying
that Arnstino was a diminutive ?   Then, over the mountains, comes
Arnust I., duke of Swabia, in right of his wife, in 1012, and Arnust
the Strenuous, Markgraff of Austria, from whom Ernst spread all
over Germany, especially after the Reformation, when Ernst, Duke
of Brunswick, had striven so hard to spread Lutheranism among his
subjects that Protestants called him the Confessor.

This is now one of the most national of German names, and it is
working its way into England, though not yet with a naturalized
sound. Its German feminine, Ernestine, is one of the many contracted
by Stine and Tine, or by Erna.   Bohemian has Arnostinka.

English.	French.	Italian.	German.
Ernest	Erneste	Ernesto	Ernst
Dutch.	Bohemian.	Lettish.	Hungarian.
Ernestus	Arnost	Ernests	Erneszt

One or two instances of Hauk occur.   Hauk Habrok was a noted
pirate ; and there are two Haukrs in the *Landnama-bok*.   The bird
is now called *hog* in Denmark, and most of our families named Hogg
are supposed to rejoice in Hawk as an ancestor.

As to Folco and his kin, though it is often attributed to the falcon,
it has, as we shall see, quite another source.*

SECTION VII.—*The Raven.*

Ferocious and predatory nations love and admire even the raven
that scents slaughter from afar, and is the comrade and emblem of

* Grimm ; Munch ; Pott ; Michaelis ; Butler ; *Landnama-bok ;* Chalmers ;
Essex Pedigrees ; Dugdale ; Anderson, *Genealogies.*

the battle-field. So as Oreb and Zeeb were among the Bedouin desolators of Israel, Hraben and Ulf were among the wasters of Christendom.

Two ravens, Mind and Memory, go forth throughout the world, then returning and perching on Odin's shoulders, reveal to him all that passes on the earth.

The raven seems to have been the special mark of Odin, and sometimes used for Thor; for amulets have been found in Sweden and Denmark, where a raven flies before the mounted figure of Odin, and again is seen in company with the hammer of Thor. And who does not know the raven banner of the sons of Ragnar, denoting probably their family *dis*, which flapped its wings before victory and drooped them before defeat?

No wonder, then, that the raven has left traces in the nomenclature of Teutonic Europe, though it is not always easy to distinguish its progeny from those of *ragn*, judgment, and *rand*, a house.

The raven, in his harshest croak, entitled the Frank sovereign Chramne, who is hard to recognize as the near kinsman of the sixteen Rafns of the *Landnama-bok*, and Rabanus Maurus, the Latinism of the learned archbishop of Mainz of the ninth century.

Hrafenhilldur, a suitable title for a Valkyr, and Hrafenkell also figure in the *Landnama-bok*, and in Domesday stand Ravengar and Ravenswar, showing the transition from the *gjer*, or spear, down to our word war.

Rafnulf is northern, but has been mixed up with the derivatives of Randolf. Rambert, successor of St. Ansgar, in Holstein, was a bright raven, Rampold a raven prince, and the Italian form Ramusio may be another variety; but in general the raven comes at the end of words as in Wolfram, Valdraban, Bertram, &c.

SECTION VIII.—*The Swan.*

The swan might well figure prominently in the northern mythology, familiar as she was, as the fair creature of the autumn, when huge squadrons of the whistling swan fly southwards, athwart the darkened heavens and pine forests, making the air resound with the solemn beat of their heavy wings, and their deep peculiar cry.

Two swans, parents of all those who dwell on earth, had their home in the holy spring of Urd, beneath the world-tree, Yggdrasil; and the power and fierceness of these magnificent, pure, calm-looking birds connected them with the Valkyrer, who were supposed to have swan wings, and to be able to change themselves into swans. When the Valkyrier began to pass into mere magic ladies, they preserved their power of changing into swans, and by-and-by had swan garments, which they put off when they wished to assume human shapes, and which were now and then captured by some happy mortal, who thus won the owner for his bride. Swanhvit, or Swan white, was thus the suitable name of one of the three Valkyrier who married the sons of Vidja in the Vilkina Saga.

The swan transformations appear again in the beautiful tale, common to all Teutonic countries, of the twelve princes transformed into swans, and of the faithful sister who redeemed them by the nettle shirts that she wove, ever in silence, through every vicissitude of life even to the verge of death.

Svana is an Icelandic name, also Svanlaug, a swan ocean, which has contracted to Svallaug. Svanhild was used both by Norway and Germany, being Swanahilda in the latter, and Svanaburg and Swangarde were also there ; but it is strange that so pretty a word for a white-skinned maiden should not have been more frequent. The Erse Gelges imitates the sense, but we have no English swan ladies, for Swanhals was only the epithet of the often commemorated lady, who is said to have discovered the corpse of Harold of Hastings.

For the most part, the swans were left to womankind ; but the Germans had a Swanbrecht and Swanahold.

Section IX.—*The Serpent.*

Either from terror, or from a shadowy remembrance of the original temptation, the implanted enmity between the serpent and man has often resulted in a species of worship.

The North believed in the Jörmungandr, or Midgardsorm, the serpent that encircled the world and was one of the monstrous progeny of Loki.

And even till late in the seventh century the Lombards had a golden image of an enormous viper to which they sacrificed, until St. Barbatus recovered them from the heathenism into which they had relapsed.

One species of ship among the Northmen was called serpent. It was long and low, with the gilded head of a dragon at the prow, a long tail raised and curling over the stern, while with coloured shields ranged along the sides, and thirty oars on either side propelling it, besides the winged sails, it must have been more like a water-dragon than any creature that has ploughed the waves since the Plesiosaurus, and this probably accounts for the prevalence of the name of Orm among the northern nations.

Twenty-two Ormrs appear in the *Landnama-bok* ; Orm and Ormar (*Ger.* Wurmhar) are both in Domesday. Orm was the founder of the Scottish house of Abernethy. Homer was considered, by the Danes of the middle ages, as the translation into Latin of the name of Ormr.

Ormilda is likewise a northern name, and it is not quite impossible that Ophelia may have been a translation of one of these serpent-names by the Greek ὄφις (ophis) ; at any rate the fair Ophelia shows no precedents for her name, and no other derivation for it occurs. The gentle maiden, with her most touching fate, is altogether an invention of Shakespeare, for though a woman appears in the old story of Amleth, she is of far other mould, and Ophelia may have been merely devised by himself. If so it is curious that he should have placed her in the chief land of serpentine names. A few lovers of its sound have used it in England and America.

Lind is another term for a serpent. The German dragons are always called *lindwurmer*, and the word is, in fact, the same as that which we still use as *lithe*, expressing supple grace ; the adjective *linths* becoming, on the one side *lind*, on the other *lithe*. The Spaniards use *lindo, linda*, for pretty, with about the same difference of sense, in the masculine or feminine, as we do when we speak of a pretty woman, or a pretty man. Norse poetry considered it a compliment to compare a gaily dressed lady to a glistening serpent, and thus the idea seems to have passed from the reptile to the woman, so that, though the German Lintrude is the only instance of a commencing *lind*, the word is one of the most common of all terminations among German and Italian names, and dropping its *d*, so as to become *linn*, was made to serve as a favourite feminine diminutive, its relation to the Spanish *linda*, fair, keeping up its reputation. Thus we have Rosalind, or Rosaline, Ethelind, and many more of the same kind.*

SECTION X.—*Kettle.*

Among mythological objects the kettle or cauldron can hardly be omitted ; certainly the very quaintest of human names, but perhaps referring originally to the cauldron of creation, and afterwards to the sacrificial cauldrons that boiled the flesh of the victims at the great *blots* or sacrifices.

In the North, the vessel is *ketil ;* in old German, *chezil ;* in English, *cytel ;* but the names from it seem to be almost entirely northern, though the cauldron is certainly the *olla*, so common a bearing in Spanish heraldry, and there at present regarded as the token of a large following, beneficently fed, somewhat in the same spirit as that in which the Janissaries used a camp kettle as their ensign.

Ketyl was the Norwegian conqueror of the Hebrides, and founder of the line of Jarls, of the Western Isles ; and the family of Ketyl was very famous in Iceland, holding in honour an ancestor called Ketyl Hæng, from *hæng*, a bull trout ; because when his father asked what he had been doing, he answered, "I am not going to make a long story of every fish I see leap ; but true it is, that I chopped a bull trout asunder in the middle," which trout turned out to be a great dragon.

Katla was Ketyl's feminine, and not uncommon. The Eyrbiggia Saga tells wonderful stories of a sorceress so called, who, when her son was in danger from his enemies, made him appear first like a distaff, then like a tame kid, and, lastly, like a hog, but all in vain, for her spells were disconcerted by a rival sorceress, and she herself stoned to death.

Ketel does not often stand at the beginning of a word ; but Ketel-biorn and Ketelridur are both Iceland names, and both the masculine

* Munch ; Mallet ; Grimm ; Chalmers ; Laing.

and feminine are very common terminations ; the masculine being, however, generally contracted into Kjel, and then into *kill* or *kel*.*

Section XI.—*Weapon Names.*

Weapons were so nearly divine, so full of the warlike temper of their owners, and so often endowed with powers of their own, that it seemed as if they themselves were living agents in the deeds wrought with them.

The sword forged by supernatural smiths, the terrific helmet, the heavenly shield, are dreams of every warlike nation, either endowing the Deity with the symbols of protection or wrath or of might, or carrying on the tradition of some weapon which, either its own intrinsic superiority or the prowess of its owner, had made an object of enthusiasm or of terror.

Some of these tales of magic weapons are perhaps, as Mr. Campbell suggests, remnants of the days when the iron age was coming in, and the mass of arms being of brass, one iron sword, "a sword of light," as Gaelic tales call it, would have given irresistible superiority to its wielder, and even, perhaps, earned the worship that was paid by Attila's Huns to the naked sword.

It accords with this theory that Iron appears as a component part of numerous names in Germany, and probably likewise in Scandinavia, though there the similarity of the sound to *Iis*, ice, occasions a doubt whether the word was intended for ice, or for iron. The North has, indeed, the cold but not inappropriate Snæulf and Snæbiorn, Snæfrid, snow peace, and even the uncomfortable Snælaug ; and when their language had dropped the form *eisarn* for the metal, and called it *jern*, as we do iron, they probably transferred to ice the meaning of the names that once meant iron.

Isa is an old German feminine. Isambart, or iron splendour, is the best known of all the varieties, having been used in France as Ysambar, and travelled to England as the suitable baptismal name of the two engineers, to whom so much of our ' iron splendour ' is due. Its German contractions are Isabert and Isbert.

Nor. Isgeir ; Ger. Isegar, Isgar—Iron spear
Nor. Isbrand ; Ger. Isebrand—Iron sword
Ger. Isebald ; Fr. Isambaus—Iron prince
Nor. Iarngard ; Ger. Isengard—Iron defence
Ger. Isenhard—Iron strong
Nor. Isrid—Iron vehemence
Nor. Isulf—Iron wolf
Nor. Ising—Son of iron

* Grimm ; Munch ; Dasent ; *Int. to Nial Saga* ; Weber and Jamieson ; Spanish Heraldry *(Quarterly Review)*.

Steel or Staale, likewise had one name from it in the North, and, perhaps, likewise named even the historical Stilicho of barbarous birth, but the sole hope of Rome in her final fall.

But the stone of the elder age was not forgotten ; the stone that at all times is the readiest weapon, and often the mark of the place honoured by conflict. To say nothing of the Seax, whether stone or stone knife of our ancestral Seaxnot, we find the North using the word Stein, both alone and as a prefix and suffix ; while in England, though it is not very frequent, we have it in the honoured names of Athelstan and Wulstan.

Norwegian.		Norwegian.	
Stein, Sten (*Dan.*),	} stone.	Steinhar, Steinar,	} stone warrior.
Steinarna, stone eagle.		Steinthor, Steindor,	} stone of Thor.
Steinbjorn, stone bear.			
Steinfinn, white stone.		Steinulf, stone wolf.	
Steingrimm, stone helmet.		Steinvar, stone prudence	

Another old word for stone is *hall*, much used in the North ; and in a few cases, such as that of the Scottish Halbert, or Hobbie, creeping to our island with its Danish invaders ; but except in this, and a few surnames, unknown away from the North, save for the Hallar, or stone warrior, of Germany.

The northern varieties, however, had much reputation in their own country. Hallgerda is in the Njal Saga the haughty wife of Gunnar, of Lithend, the dame whose virulence is the cause of all the vengeance and counter-vengeance of the story.

Hallbiorg, stone protection.		Hallkell, Halkatla,	} stone kettle.
Halldis, stone spirit.			
Hallfrid, stone fair.		Hallmund, stone protection.	
Hallgerd, stone fence.		Hallthor,	
Hallgeir, stone spear.		Haldor,	} stone of Thor.
Hallgrim, Hallgrima,	} stone helmet.	Haldora,	
		Hallvard, Halvor,	} stone guard.

Grjot, in German *gries*, is another word for a stone. It was not so common as the others ; but there was both a masculine and feminine Grjotgard, who in Denmark were rendered, the one into Gregorius, the other into Margarethe. The English lady, Græsia de Bruere (*temp.* Henry III.), must have been named from *gries*, a stone.

So too was Gries-hilda—Stone battle maid. Griselda was the perfectly patient wife whose tale was told by Boccaccio, and narrated by Petrarch to Chaucer, who told it in his own way. The Scots seem to have been peculiarly delighted with the lady Griselidis—and Grizell or Grisell acquired fresh honour with Lady Grisell Baillie. Grizzie or Girzie are the contractions, and there is a Grisley in the register of Madran, Cornwall, dated 1662.

Though in general Borg, or Bjorg, is used to mean protection, yet

Bergstein is most probably a mountain stone, and it curiously answers to two names of noted ecclesiastics from Somersetshire, whose first syllable Dun is a hill ; the same with our present word *down*, and the *dunes* on the other side of the Channel, where Dunkirk answers to our Dunchurch. The word is probably the Keltic *don*, dark brown, grey, or dun, used as the epithet of a hill, and lasting on like other Keltic local titles in the *dunum* of the Romans and the *dun* of the Teutons.

The two Somerset Duns are the hill-wolf, Dunulf, who is said by one of the traditions that ought to be true, to have been the swine-herd whose cakes King Alfred burnt, and to have been afterwards made by him bishop of Winchester, which a Dunulf certainly was. The other was Dunstan, the mighty ascetic Abbot of Glastonbury and Archbishop of Canterbury, whose career, between wisdom and devotion, frenzy and sternness, is one of the least explicable studies of history.

His place in the calendar has given this rugged mountain stone a few namesakes.

There is a race of names, chiefly German, beginning with *hun*, that it would seem natural to ascribe to the Huns of Attila ; but the original term for this race seems to have been in their own language Hiognu, and was retained in the pronunciation by other nations before writing and Latin had made the word Hun. In old Germanic poems, the Huns figure as giants or Titans, so that some translate, *huni*, or *hiune*, as a giant. The word *hun*, however, also means a stake, and it is most according to the ordinary analogy of nomenclature to suppose the names thus commencing were used in the sense of a stake, meaning either the weapon or that the bearer was strong and straight as a stake or a support, like the staff in Gustav.

The names of this commencement are Huno, Hunnerich, latterly lost in Heinrich, Hunold, the French Hunaud, Hunibert, which was corrupted in France into Humbert, and belonged to various counts of Savoy and dauphins of Auvergne, Hunigar, in Hungeir and Hunifred, which the French much affected in the form of Onfroi, which belonged to one of the short-lived kings of Jerusalem, and was Latinized as Onuphrius. In the form of Humfrey it was much used by the great house of Bohun ; and through his mother, their heiress, descended to the ill-fated son of Henry IV., who has left it an open question whether dining with Duke Humfrey alludes to the report that he was starved to death, or to the Elizabethan habit for poor gentility to beguile the dinner-hour by a promenade near the tomb of Duke Humfrey Stafford in old St. Paul's. From being a noble and

English.	French	Italian.	German.
Humfrey	Onfroi	Onufrio	Humfrid
Humphrey		Onofredo	
Humps			
Numps			

knightly name, Humphrey, as we barbarously spell it, came to be a peasant's appellation, and now is almost disused.

The northern Hundolf, or Hunnolf, and Hungerdur, are in some doubt between the dog and the stake.

The helmet is the most popular piece of armour in Germany. It comes from the word meaning to cover, the very same that furnished *hol*, whole, hale, and holy. To *heal* a wound is to cover it, and health is soundness. The Teutonic languages teem with derivatives from *hulyan* and *helan*, of which all that shall be here mentioned are our own; heel, the covered part of the foot, the hold of a ship, its hull, and the provincial hulls (chaff), and hillier (a slater).

The Latin *galea* was nearly related to the *helm* of the German, and may be from the same source. Indeed, it is, as has been said before, doubtful whether Galeazzo Visconti was the offspring of a classical or of a Gothic helmet. The only popular northern helmet is Hjalmar, the helmed warrior, apparently in honour of one of the heroes of the Orvarod Saga; but Germany has Helmar, Helmerich, in Friesland Elmark, the helmed king, Helmund, or helmet protection, Helmbold, Helmut, Helmich, Helmtac; besides numerous *helms* at the end of words, of which Wilhelm is the most notable.

The sword figures in northern and German nomenclature as Brand; but not from the verb *to burn*, but from *brandr*, an elastic staff, transferred to the blade of a sword. It would also mean the staff of a bow, and a short straight stripe of colour, whence a cow so marked is *brandet* in the north, branded with us. The Brands are many, with German and Frank commencements, such as Hildeprant, Liutprant, &c., but seldom common; though Brand sometimes stands alone in the North, and Brandolf, or sword wolf, is an old name. Perhaps the Zetland Brenda may be the feminine.

Degen, a blade, is another sword name of rarer use, and exclusively German. It also is compounded into Degenhard, then contracted into Deinhard; but the primary meaning is the hero, as it comes from the same word as *tugend*, virtue or valour.

Another very old term for a sword was *hjǫru*, or *hiru*, in the North; *hairu*, *heru*, in the Gothic; *heoru*, in Anglo-Saxon. Here we see that the Heruli and Cheruschi, as the Romans called them, were both sword men. Heoruvard, or Hereward the Saxon, was the sword guardian; Heorugar answered to the northern Hjǫrgeir; there was a Gothic Hairuwolf, or Heruwolf; in the North, Hiǫrulf, Hiǫrleif, and Hiǫrdis also occur; but the syllable gets contracted into Her, and the names are not easily distinguished from those beginning with *her*, a warrior. Hjaraande is another northern form.

Boge, the bow, is sparsely found alone, and as Bauggisel in Iceland, and now and then in Norway at the end of a name. Bogo was Old German, and the surnames in Denmark Bugge, in England Bogue. But its English fame rests upon a champion called Bogo, who was supposed by our ancestors to have been Earl of Southampton at the time of the Norman Conquest; to have fought a battle with the invaders at Cardiff, and to have left his sword as a relic at Arundel Castle. Whether this ever occurred or not, Boge was rendered by

Norman tongues into Bevis, or Beavois, and was the subject of an old metrical romance, where his great exploit is killing the tremendous giant Ascapart, who had carried off his wife, the converted Saracen princess Josyan. He lives to a good old age, sees his twin sons kings, and dies happily on the same day as his wife and his good horse Arundel, once doubtless Hirondelle, or the swallow.

His fame travelled to Italy, where Buovo d'Antona is accepted as one of the heroes of romance, though he stands alone, not fitting into any of the cycles. The etymologists of Elizabeth's time were led by the form Beavois, in which they spelt the word, to imagine that it was Bellovisus, beautiful to behold. But if 'Bevis of Hampton' was anybody, he was an Anglo-Danish 'Bow,' or Boge, a word which, like bay, bough, and boughsome or buxom, comes from *bygan*, to bend.

The spear and the breastplate, Geir and Brune, will be mentioned in the next chapter. The shield is now and then found in the North, as Skialde, Skioldbjorn, Skiolulf, and Skioldvar, shield bear, wolf, and, more appropriately, shield caution. The shield wolf is capable of being contracted into Schelluf.

Saro, saru, searu, is the entire equipment or suit of armour ; Sørle is a Norwegian name for it, contracted into Solle ; and among the Normans was called Serlo, and considered to be the same with Saher.

If there were plenty of weapons, there was also balsam to heal their wounds ; that is, if the northern names beginning with *Sölv* are rightly referred to salve, the same word in the North as with us. The *v* has for the most part been left out by pronunciation, but the dotted *o* remains to testify that Sölmund, or Saamund, has no connection with Sol, the sun, as little as with Solomon, by which the Danish bishops rendered it. Solveig, healing drink, is now Solva, and Sölvar is Sölvi.*

SECTION XII.—*Thought.*

Mind or thought amounts to a mythical character in northern fancy. The word is *hugr*, the same with *hu*, still the Scandinavian word for thought, as *heuge* is in Holland, all coming from old verbs represented by the Mæso-Gothic *gahugan*, and Anglo-Saxon *gehygan*.

The two ravens who sat on Odin's shoulders, and revealed to him all that passed in the world, were Huginn and Munninn, thought and memory ; and when Thor made his famous visit to Utgard, it was Hugi, or thought, alone that was swift enough to outstrip him in the race. At Tours, the Northern Lights are *le carrosse du roi Hugues*, perhaps originally from some connection with speed of thought, though latterly mixed up with Hugues Capet.

The name has been much used by all the Teutons, and it was not inappropriately chosen by Fouqué, as that of the old knight in the *Magic ring*, whose character he has sacrificed for the sake of making him the representative parent of all the chivalry of Europe, except

---

* Munch ; Michaelis ; Ellis ; Campbell ; Montalembert.

the English, which he considers as independently typified by Richard Cœur de Lion. This roving knight appears at home as Hugo ; Hugur in the North ; Hugues, in France ; Uguccione, in Italy ; and even as Hygies, in Greece, which last is, however, only a resemblance, not a translation.

English.	Scottish.	Gaelic.	French.
Hugh	Hugh	Uisdean.	Hugues
Hugo	Hughie		Hues
Hutchin	Hutcheon		Huon
			Huet
			Hugolin
			Huguenin
			Ugues

Provençal.	Italian.	German.	Norwegian.
Oc	Ugo	Hugo	Hugr
	Ugolino		Hugi
	Ugone		
	Ugotto		
	Uguccione		

Part of the popularity of the name was, no doubt, owing to the Cymric countries having adopted it as the nearest resemblance to the mighty Hu Gadarn, from whom the national Hugh of Wales almost certainly sprung. A Frank saint, Archbishop of Rouen, and one of the many canonized cousins of Pepin, first made Hugo current among his own race ; but the only person who wore it on the throne was the Gallican Count of Paris, who may have had it as a compromise between the Cymric Hu and Frank Hugr ; at any rate, it was long spelt without the *g* in France, and declined as Hues, Huon. The old Cambrai form was Huet, with the feminine Huette.

Hugo is very frequent in Domesday Book, and the name was much more common in earlier times than at present. In Scotland and Ireland it has been pressed into the service of Anglicizing the native Aodh, or fire ; but the Gaelic name Uisdean, pronounced something like ocean, is most likely intended as a rendering of Hutcheon, the form in which the Scots caught the Hugon of their Anglo-Norman neighbours, who revered the name doubly for the sake of the good bishop of Lincoln, and for another St. Hugh of Lincoln, *i. e.* the child murdered by the Jews, as in the *Prioress's Tale* in Chaucer. St. Hugh of Lincoln is revered in the north of Italy as well as at home ; and Ugo is common there in all manner of varieties, the most memorable, perhaps, being that of the terrible Genoese, Ugolino de Gherardesca, whose fearful fate has been rendered famous by Dante. In Dutch, it is Huig. Huig Groot was the home name of the author whom the world hailed as Hugo Grotius, and the Walloons use the contraction Hosch.

A A

Hyge was the Low German form, and Hygelac is the sea-king of the Geats, the friend and lord in the poem of *Beowulf*. The latter syllable *lac* is the northern *leik*, and Gothic *laiks*, signifying both reward and sport, the same word that in some parts of England has become *lake*, meaning to play or to be idle, and in slang, to *lark*. It is rather a favourite termination, but only a commencement in the Norse feminine Leikny, fresh sport.

Hygelac is thus the sport of thought, or it may be, the reward of thought. Hugoleik was thus not an inappropriate name for an old Frank chronicler, who has had the misfortune to descend to the world by the horrible Latinism of Chochilaicus. Hugleik was current in Norway, was transformed by the Danes into Hauleik and Hovleik, and in Ireland seems to have turned into Ulic, a favourite name, but latterly transmogrified into Ulysses.

Hugibert, or bright mind, belonged to the bishop of Liege, to whom attached the Teutonic story of the hunter's conversion by the cross-bearing stag, making him the patron of hunters, and his name very popular in France, Flanders, northern Italy, and probably once in England, since it has left us the two surnames of Hubbard and Hobart.

English.	French.	Italian.	Portuguese.	German.
Hubert	Hubert	Uberto	Huberto	Hucpraht Hugibert Hubert

It used to be wrongly translated bright of hue.

Hugibald became the German Hugbold and the Italian Ubaldo, the prince of thought; Hugihard, or firm in mind, is the French Huard.

CHAPTER IV.

HEROIC NAMES OF THE NIBELUNG.

SECTION I.—*The Nibelung.*

As the Greeks believed in the exploits of semi-divine heroes, a sort of borderers between Olympus and the human race, so the Teutonic race had its grand universal legends of beings rising above human nature, and often embodying beliefs that once had attached to the gods themselves.

The great Teutonic legend, holding the same place as the deeds of Hercules, Theseus, and the Argonauts did in Greece, or those of Fionn with the Gael, is the story of the *Nibelung.* How old it may be is past computation, but it was apparently common to the whole Gothic race, since names connected with it come from Spain, Lombardy, and France : fragments of the story are traceable in England and the Faroe Islands, and the whole is told at length in Germany, Norway, and Denmark. Each of these three latter countries claim vehemently to have originated the romance, but there is little doubt that it was one of the original imaginations of the entire race, and that each division moulded the framework their own way, though with a general likeness.

Names of historical personages, probably called from its heroes, have led many to suppose it exaggerated history ; but each attempt to fit it on to a real person has resulted in confusion, and led to the perception that the actors are really mythical, and the localities, which chiefly lie in Burgundian Germany, were only connected with it by that general law which always finds a home for every heroic adventure.

The tale is begun by the Norwegian Volsunga Saga, and, about half way through, it is taken up by the Danish Vilkina and Niflung Saga, and by the German Nibelungenlied, and it is finished by numerous Danish ballads and German tales, songs, and poems, with the sort of inconsistencies always to be found in popular versions of ancient myths, but with the same main incidents.

Nifelheim, the supposed abode of these heroes, is interpreted to be *nebelwelt,* the world of mist, or cloudland, and there can be little doubt that the heroes said to be descended from the mythic Vili, Vidga, and Velint, are, in fact, fallen deities. Germany, however, turned Nifelheim into the Netherlands, and placed the realm of Brynhild in Iceland, and the scene of Aldrian's and Gunter's court at Wurms, the centre of the Burgundians.

It is highly probable that the story is another form of the original myth, with the same idea, carried through, of the early death of the glorious victor, and of the revenge for his death, but only through a universal slaughter in which all perish. But the whole has become humanized, and the actors are men and not deities; and thus the allegory is far less traceable.

The story, as it begins in the Volsunga Saga, relates that there were three brothers, Fafner, Reginn, and Audvar, or Ottur, whose name is from the same source as φg, awe, so that he may be another form of Œgir. Transforming himself into the beast that bears his name, for the convenience of catching himself a fish dinner, Ottur was killed, in this shape, by Loki. The father and the other brothers insisted that, by way of compensation, in the Teutonic fashion, Loki should fill the dead otter's skin with treasure, which he accomplished, but laid the treasure under the curse, that it should do no good to its owner. Accordingly, the amount excited the avarice of Fafner, and after murdering his father, he transformed himself into a dragon, and kept watch over the treasure, to prevent Reginn from obtaining it.[*]

SECTION II.—*Sigurd.*

Sig, or *siga,* means, in all Teutonic tongues, conquest; and the Victor seems to have been a very old epithet for the Divinity. St. Augustin speaks of a Gothic exclamation *Sihora armen,* which he translates as Κύριε ἐλέησον, and the first word of which evidently answers to Ceadmon's epithets for the Almighty, *Sigorafrea, Sigora-god, Sigoracyning.*

Odin was called Sigfadir, or conquering father, and this accounts for the later notion that the adventurer was called Sigge, and assumed the divine appellation of Odin.

Thence the victorious god, conquering the serpent, yet afterwards dying, whether he were originally meant for Odin himself, or for another form of Baldur, sank into a human serpent-slayer, bearing the name of victory—Sigward, perhaps originally, but varied into Sigufrit, Siegfried, and Sigurd.

The main points in Siegfried's story are that he was the son of Siegmund the Volsung, and of Queen Sigelind; born, according to the *Book of Heroes,* under the same circumstances as Perdita, in the *Winter's Tale;* put, by way of cradle, into a drinking-glass, and accidentally thrown into the river, where he was picked up by the smith Mimir, and educated by him. In the *Book of Heroes* he is so strong that he caught the lions in the woods and hung them over his castle wall by their tails. Reginn incited him to fight with and slay the dragon, Fafner, and obtain the treasure, including the tarn-cap of invisibility. Also, on roasting and eating the heart of Fafner, he became able to understand the language of the birds. And by a bath in the blood he was made invulnerable, except

* Lettsom, *Niebelung;* Weber and Jamieson; Koepper; Howitt, *Northern Romance;* Grimm, *Deutsche Heldensagen.*

where a leaf had unfortunately adhered to his skin, between his shoulders, and given him, like Achilles and Diarmaid, a mortal spot. His first discovery from the song of a bird was that Reginn meant to murder him at once ; he therefore forestalled his intentions, and took possession of the fatal gift, thus incurring the curse. The *Book of Heroes* calls him Siegfried the horny, and introduces him at the court of the German favourite, Theodoric, and the *Nibelungenlied* separates the dragon from the treasure, and omits most of the marvellous in the obtaining it.

His next exploit was the rescue and awakening of Brynhild ; but he fell into a magic state of oblivion as to all that had passed with her, when he presented himself at the court of Wurms, and became the husband of Gudrun, or Chriemhild, as a recompense for having, by means of his tarn-cap, enabled Gunnar to overcome the resistance of Brynhilda herself, and obliged her to become his submissive bride. Revelations made by the two ladies, when in a passion, led to vengeance being treacherously wreaked upon Siegfried, who was pierced in his vulnerable spot while he was lying down on his face to drink from a fountain during a hunting party in the forest. The remainder of the history is the vengeance taken for his death ; and the North further holds that his child, Aslaug, was left the sole survivor of the race, and finally married Ragner Lodbrog, whence her descendants always trace their pedigree from Sigurdr Fafner's bane.

His namesakes are well-nigh innumerable. There are nineteen in the *Landnama-bok ;* and Sigurdr swarms in the earlier Scandinavian royal lines, being, perhaps, most remarkable in the person of King Sigurd the Crusader of Norway.

English.	French.	German.	Bavarian.
Sigefrid	Sigefroi	Sigefrid	Sigl
Siward	Siffroi	Siegfried	
Seaward		Sigfrid	Norwegian.
Seaforth	Italian.	Seifrid	Sigvard
Seyferth	Sigefredo	Sikko	Sigurdhr
	Siffredo	Sicco	Siurd
		Sigo	Sjurd
			Sjul
		Polish.	Syvert
		Sygfryd	Syver
			Siewers

At the instance of the king of Sweden, our Edred had sent a missionary named Sigefried, who is esteemed the apostle of Sweden, and gave a Christian sanction to the serpent-slayer's name, whence it has continued extremely common there. The stout old Danish Earl Siward, the conqueror of Macbeth, the same who had the bear's ears and would only die upon his feet, is an English version of the northern Sigurdr, and bore the name that is now Seaward. Indeed

Sœward is found among the kings of Essex in 616, and, in fact, that line have so many prefixes of *Sige*, that it is likely that they thought themselves connected with Fafner's bane.   There is a Sigefugel, or Sigewolf, in their descent from Odin, who may be another form of Sigurd.   Germany has made the feminine Sigfrida.

Some have considered the story to be chiefly Burgundian ; and Sigmund, conquering protection, the name of Sigurdr's father, was that of the first Catholic king of Burgundy, who was canonized both for the recovery of his kingdom from Arianism, and for the severity of his penance, after having killed his son, Sigeric, on a false step-dame's calumny.   His relics were carried to Prague in the fourteenth century, and the effect of the translation appeared at once in the name of the Bohemian-born Emperor Sigismund, from whom this became European, and formed the feminine Sigismunda.   Gismonda is thus an old Lombardic feminine.

English.	French.	Italian.	German.
Sigismund	Sigismond	Sigismondo	Sigmund
Sæmund		Sismondo	Sigismund
	Portuguese.		
	Sigismundo		

Norwegian.	Polish.	Illyrian.	Hungarian.
Sigmund	Zygmunt	Sisman	Zsigmond
Sæmund			Zsiga
	Bohemian.		
	Zikmund		

Some have imagined that the curious correspondence of names, when Sigebert, the Frank, married Brynhild, the Goth, is a sign that the *Nibelung* referred to the Austrasian court ; but the Frank Sigebert would have been a very poor serpent-slayer, and, no doubt, only bore the name as a remembrance of him, as did our East Saxon monarch Sæbert, and the Spanish bishop Siseberto.   It has lasted on in Germany and Friesland, to be called Sizo, Sitto, Sibert, and Sidde, and is the English surname Sebright.   Sigelind, conquering snake, now and then used by German ladies, has the Eastern-looking abbreviation Zelinde.

Sigridur, or conquering impulse, was a favourite among northern ladies.   Sigrid the haughty of Sweden, was wooed by King Olaf Trygvesson, and had accepted him ; but on her refusal to be baptized, he struck her on the face with his glove, and said, 'Why should I have thee, an old faded jade, and a heathen to boot.'   She remembered his discourtesy against him, and stirred up the war, which ended in his fatal battle with Earl Sigvalddr.   Sigrid is Sired in Domesday ; in the North, she is shortened into Siri, and then Latinized as Serena.

Sigvalldur, conquering power, curiously ran into Sjovald, from whence we take our surname Shovel, one of the many by which our naval commanders are traceable to the vikings.

Sigeheri, Sigehere, Sighar, conquering warrior, is what on Norman lips was Sagar, and then Saher, the hereditary name of the De Quincys, and as a surname spelt Sayers.[*]

The other forms are,

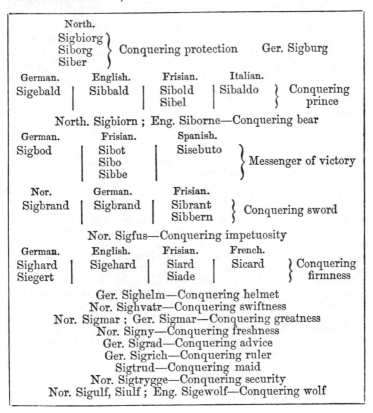

North.				
Sigbiorg ⎫ Siborg ⎬ Conquering protection　　Ger. Sigburg Siber ⎭				

German.	English.	Frisian.	Italian.	
Sigebald	Sibbald	Sibold Sibel	Sibaldo	⎰ Conquering ⎱ prince

North. Sigbiorn ; Eng. Siborne—Conquering bear

German.	Frisian.	Spanish.	
Sigbod	Sibot Sibo Sibbe	Sisebuto	⎱ Messenger of victory ⎰

Nor.	German.	Frisian.	
Sigbrand	Sigbrand	Sibrant Sibbern	⎰ Conquering sword

Nor. Sigfus—Conquering impetuosity

German.	English.	Frisian.	French.	
Sighard Siegert	Sigehard	Siard Siade	Sicard	⎰ Conquering ⎱ firmness

Ger. Sighelm—Conquering helmet
Nor. Sighvatr—Conquering swiftness
Nor. Sigmar ; Ger. Sigmar—Conquering greatness
Nor. Signy—Conquering freshness
Ger. Sigrad—Conquering advice
Ger. Sigrich—Conquering ruler
Sigtrud—Conquering maid
Nor. Sigtrygge—Conquering security
Nor. Sigulf, Siulf ; Eng. Sigewolf—Conquering wolf

SECTION III.—*Brynhild.*

A thorough Valkyr was Brynhilda, the maiden whom Odin had touched with his sleep-thorn, so that she lay in a deep slumber in the midst of a circle of flame, through which Sigurd made his way, aroused her, and won her for his own ; but became utterly and

[*] *Nibelung;* Weber and Jamieson ; Kemble, *Beowulf;* Michaelis ; Pott ; Butler ; *Heimskringla.*

magically oblivious of all that had passed as soon as he had returned
to common life.   This is the northern version, the evident origin of
our fairy tale of the *Sleeping Beauty*, pricked not by the thorn of
Odin, but by the distaff, perhaps, of one of the Nornir.   The *Book of
Heroes* reduces the circle of flame to a mere strong castle, with seven
gates ; and the *Nibelungenlied* only takes up the story at the time of
Sigfried's appearance at the court of Burgundy, and courtship of
Brynhild's rival, Chriemhild.

Brynhild had retained her matchless strength, and, like the Greek
Atalanta, was only to be won by a champion who could excel her
in games of strength, and her conquered suitors were all put to death.
Gunther, the brother of Chriemhild, being willing to obtain her on
these conditions, Siegfried, by means of his tarn-cap, invisibly van-
quished the Valkyr, while Gunther appeared to be her conqueror ;
and when she thus had been compelled to give her hand, it was
Siegfried who, again unseen, broke down her violent resistance, and
compelled her to become a submissive wife, on which she lost all
her supernatural strength.   Siegfried was rewarded by the hand of
Chriemhild, Gunther's sister.

By-and-by the two sisters-in-law had a desperate quarrel about
precedence ; in the old northern version, which should wade farthest
into the Rhine when bathing ; in the half-civilized German song,
which should first enter the cathedral of Wurms ; and in the course
of it Brynhild was roundly informed that she had not given way to
her husband, but to Siegfried.   Valkyr nature could not stand such
an affront, so Brynhild set on Hagen to assassinate Siegfried.   The
northern story makes her slay herself, and be burnt with his corpse
on a funeral pile, in Suttee fashion ; the German tames her into being
merely brought to repentance too late by the death of her husband.

No doubt Brynhild was commemorated by the name of the Gothic
princess, daughter of King Athanagild, who, for her misfortune, was
married to the Frank Sigebert, and through the whole of her long life
continued a fierce and dauntless resistance to her savage rival
Fredegund, until, when both were aged women, Brenhilda fell into
her rival's power, and was implacably sentenced to be dragged to
death by wild horses.   French historians aver that her name was at
first only Bruna, and that hilda was added to make it royal ; but
this is very unlikely, since Spanish historians call her Brenhilda.
The Latinism is Brunechildis, in French Brunehault, but the name
has not been followed, except by the northern race, whose existence
was hardly developed at the time of the misfortunes of the Austrasian
queen, and who therefore take it from her original.   Among these it
has been contracted to Brunilla and Brynil.

The meaning is the Valkyr of the Breastplate, the *byrni* of old
Scottish, *bryne* of the North, *bruniga* of the German, *broigne* in Old
French, *bronha* in Provençal.   A near connection of this name is the
northern Bryngerd, placing the gentle Gerda in this cuirass ; and the
North has likewise Brynjar, properly *hari*, the Cuirassier, and
Brynjolfr, which wolf in a breastplate was a great Icelandic ancestor,
and has been cut short into Brynjuv and Brynjo.

The Chriemhild, or Helmet Valkyr of the *Nibelung*, is the Gudrun of the northern version ; and Gudrun, as before said, would be either good wisdom, or, far more probably, war wisdom. In the *Nibelungenlied*, the action of the story begins with Chriemhild telling her mother her dream of her favourite falcon being torn to pieces by two eagles ; and when it is explained to mean her future husband, vowing that she will never marry. However, Siegfried's arrival, and his successful exertions in winning Brunhild for Gunther, overcame all the lady's scruples.

She had lived happily ten years in the Netherlands with Siegfried before, on a visit to Wurms, she was so ill-advised as to reproach Brynhild with his victory over her ; and afterwards was deluded into sewing a mark upon his garments to show where was his vulnerable spot. After his death, she found out the murderer by the ordeal of touch, and treasured up a deadly and enduring spirit of revenge ; perhaps the most terrible of all the many forms in which legend has proclaimed the old rule of blood for blood.

She was left the heiress of all Siegfried's treasure, as well as of his *Nibelungen* or Netherlandian troops, but it was taken from her by her husband's murderer, and sunk beneath the Rhine. After thirteen years of widowhood, she was induced to marry Etzel, or Atli, king of the Huns, by the promise that he would avenge all her injuries ; but still she bided her time for thirteen more years, at the end of which space she invited her brothers and all their champions to visit her in Hungary at Etzelenburg. They had not long been there before she stirred up a most tremendous battle, in which mutual destruction took place, as is minutely related in the ancient lays. Finally her brother Gunther was captured and slain at her savage command, and she herself slew the murderer Hagen with Siegfried's own sword. Immediately after, however, she was put to death as an act of justice by old Sir Hildebrand ; at least so says the *Nibelungenlied ;* but in the *Kœmpe Viser* there is a still further revenge, for the secret of the deposit of the treasure is left with the son of Hagen, who beguiles Grimhild into the cave with the hope of its restoration, and there locks her in and starves her to death.

The historical Attila is really said to have had a German wife named Kremheilch. The Gudrun of the North is a far more amiable personage. She forgives her brother, and is with difficulty persuaded to marry Atli, who is, in this version, Brynhild's brother, and lays the plot against Gunther, in order to avenge his sister's death. She does all in her power to warn them, but in vain ; and when all had been slain, her senses failed her, and in her frenzy she slew her two children by Atli, and made him drink their blood ; he died of horror, and she cast herself into the sea, but was carried alive to the land of King Jonakr, whom she married, and then underwent other misfortunes which extinguished the last remains of her family. Her name of Gudrun has already been treated of.*

* *Nibelungenlied ;* Weber and Jamieson ; Thierry ; Mariana ; Munch.

SECTION IV.—*Gunther.*

Gunth (Goth.), *guth* (A.G.S.), *gunnr* (North), *gond* or *gonz* (High German), all meant war or battle, and have an immense number of derivative names, inextricably mixed up with those from God and Gut ; and it is even thought that there may be a close connection between them, so much did the Teutons believe their deities to be gods of battle, and goodness to be courage. The word *gunth* has lived on even in Lombardy in the Gonfalon, the war banner, solemnly carried out to battle in a car as the images of the gods had formerly been, in charge of the official known as the *gonfaloniere* in the republics of northern Italy. Gundahari, warrior, was really an old name among the kings of Burgundy, who were, no doubt, called in honour of Gunther or Gunnar, the eldest brother of Kriemhild, and husband of Brynhild. He seems to have been brave but weak, led first by Sigurd, then by Hagen, but at last fighting with great spirit.

Gunthar, or Gunnar, at full length Gundahari, continued in favour with the Burgundians ; and an abbot in Brittany being canonized, left Gonthier to France, and Gontiere to Italy.

This masculine Gunnar was very common in the North, and so was likewise the feminine Gunnr, war, or Gundvar, war prudence, both confounded in Gunnar, which historians generally render as Gunnora.

Gunnhildur was in high favour in the North. One most celebrated owner was the wicked queen of Eric Blodaxe. She was said to be a native of the Orkneys, and to have filled Scandinavia with her crimes, upon the details of which, however, Norse and Danish histories are not quite agreed.

Gunhild again was the Danish princess whose murder on St. Brice's night brought her brother Sweyn down in fury upon England; and her nephew Knud likewise had a daughter so called, but who was Anglicized into Æthelthryth ; and each generation of the Godwine family records a lady Gunhild. After the Conquest, however, Gunhild died away in England ; but it has never been discarded in the North, where it is now called Gunnilda, or Gunula.

That daughter of William the Conqueror, or sister of Gherbod the Fleming, whichever she was, who was the ancestress of the Warrennes, and is buried at Lewes, has a name so much disguised as to be as doubtful as her birth. It may be Gunatrud, a Valkyr title, or Gundridur, war haste, or Gundrada, war council, the same as the Spanish Gontrado ; at any rate it has had few followers.

Gunnr and Göndol were both Valkyr titles, and the Valkyr Göndol's most noted namesake was a maiden of the Karling race, who was bred up by St. Gertrude, at Nivelle ; and on her return to her father's castle at Morzelle, used to go to her early devotions at a church half a league distant from home. On winter mornings she was lighted by a lantern, which the legend avers to have been blown out by the wind, but rekindled by her prayers. Thence comes the name of St. Gundula's lamp, applied to the *Tremella*, an orange-coloured jelly-like fungus that grows on dead branches of trees in the winter. She is the patroness of Brussels, where the church of St. Gudule is the place used for coronations ; but her common title in Flanders is Ste. Goëlan, while the convent built in her honour at Morzelle, in Brabant, is Ste. Goule.

War could not fail to have her wolf, the Gundulf of Norman England, the Gunnolfr of Iceland, the Gundolf of Germany, and, far more notable than either, the Gonsalvo or Gonzalo of Spain, always frequent among the Visigothic families, and becoming especially glorious in the person of the great captain, the brave and honourable conqueror of Naples, and the trainer of the infantry that gave the predominance to Spain for a hundred years, until they fell as one man at Rocroy.

French.	Provençal.	Spanish.	Portuguese.	Italian.
Gonsalve Gonzalve	Guossalvo	Gonzalo	Gonçalo	Consalvo

The war raven, Gunthram, figures in French history as Gontran, and the war serpent is the German Gundlin, or Gondoline, when a lady ; when a man, the terrible Guthorm, whom, as King Alfred's foe, godson, and tributary, our histories call Guthrum. In Denmark, the name was very early contracted into Gorm; but it has been so often spelt Gudthorm, that a doubt has arisen whether the latter half of the word may not be *thorm* or *thyrma*.

It is very difficult to distinguish between the derivatives of *God* and *Gund*, both being very apt to eliminate the distinctive letters. On the whole, however, it seems as if these warlike names had been some of the most universal throughout the continent, though in England they were very scarce, and do not occur in royal pedigree, nor in hagiology, except in the case of St. Guthlac, the first founder of the original Croyland Abbey, whose name in the North would be Gudleik or Gulleik, war sport.

Hosts of northern Frankish and Visigothic names thus commence, and many feminines end with this word. The other varieties thus beginning are :—

Nor. Gunbjorg ; Ger. Gondaberge ; Goth. Sp.—War protection
Nor. Gunbjorn—War bear

German.	French.	
Gondebert	Gondobert	
Gondeberta	Gombert	} War splendour
Gumpert	Jombert	

Ger. Gondebald ; Fr. Gondebaud ; Sp. Gondebaldo—War prince
Nor. Gudbrand, Guldbrand, Gulbrand—War sword
Ger. Gundekar—War spear
Nor. Gunlaug, Gullaug—War liquor
Nor. Gunleif, (Eng. Cunliffe)—War love

Nor.	German.	Spanish.	
Gudmar	Gundemar	Gondomiro	} War greatness
Gulmar	Gutmar	Gondomar	

Nor.	German.	
Gudmund	Gundemund	} War hand
Gulmund	Gunimund	

Ger. Gunderich ; Fr. Gonderic ; Sp. Gonderico—War ruler
Sp. Gondesinda—War strength
Nor. Gunnstein—War jewel

Gunthe was the old German feminine contraction for any of these warlike damsels, and being further endeared into Jutte, or Jutta, was probably the source, under the hands of chroniclers, of the Judiths, who made their appearance among the Franks so long before the days of Scripture or saintly names.[*]

Section V.—*Hagen.*

Haghen, Hagano, or Hogni, may be considered as the villain of the *Nibelungen.* In the Danish version he is the half-brother of Grimhild and Gunther, with an elf-father ; in the German, he is their wise and far-travelled uncle, who first related the adventures of the newly-arrived stranger, Siegfried, but always seems to have disliked him, and readily undertook to revenge Brynhild's injuries upon him. As Loki deceived Frigga, he persuaded his niece to mark where was the mortal spot on her husband's skin, and contrived that no wine should be taken into the forest, so that Siegfried might be reduced to lie down to drink at the stream, and thus expose the fatal place.

The body bled at his touch, and he was the chief object of Chriemhilt's vengeance, more especially after he had taken the treasure away from her, placed it in a cave beneath the Rhine, and jealously guarded the secret of the spot. When she invited the brothers to Hungary he was much averse to the journey, till he found that his disclination was imputed to fear, when he became vehemently set upon going, in spite of the omens against it. Taunts and injuries passed between him and Chriemhilt, and the next day the fierce and furious battle began, which raged till Gunther and Haghen alone were left. After Gunther had been killed, Chriemhilt offered Haghen his life,

[*] Munch ; Michaelis ; *Nibelung ;* Weber and Jamieson ; Mariana ; Thierry ; *Garland for the Year ;* Alban Butler ; Fleischner, *Onomatologie ;* Lappenberg ; Dasent, *Burnt Njal ;* Marryat, *Jutland.*

on condition that he would disclose the place where the treasure was, but he refused, and died by her hand.

There is a curious poem, called the *Duke of Aquitaine*, which is evidently another version of the same notion of Haghen. Hagano, a descendant of the Trojans, is there sent to deprecate the invasion of Attila, and afterwards assists the Burgundian king Gunther of Wurms in an attack on Duke Walther of Aquitaine, and Hildegunna, sister to Gunther, in order to recover a treasure that they had carried off from Attila's court, where they had been hostages. This version of the great central story of Europe named Hagen, Count of Aquitaine, the uncle of Charles the Bald; but the North has used it more, in the form of Hogen.

The name is either from *hagr*, deft or handy, or else from *hagi*, a hook ; most probably the latter, perhaps in connection with the other meaning, a thorn or prickle, so that here we may find a personification of the thorn destroying the victor. The word *hag* is seldom found in names, and is probably imitated from Hagen, without much regard to the meaning. It occurs only in the Danish, as Hagbrand, Hagbart, contracted as Habaar, or Habor ; Hagthor, which is incorrectly modernized as Hector ; and Hagny. The more usual form in Denmark is Hogne, probably from the German Hagano.

But there has been a confusion between this Hagan, or Hogni, and Haagan, properly Haakvin, from *haa*, high, and *kyn*, meaning of high kin, the well-known Norwegian and Danish name of many a fierce viking ; sometimes Latinized as Haquinus, Frenchified as Haquin, and called in the North Haaken, or Hakon. Domesday has it as Kaco, Hacon, Hacun, and Hakena ; and Hacon still lingers among the fishermen of the Orkneys. Other northern names, with the same opening, *haa* (pronounced *ho*), are Haamund, no doubt the parent of our Hammond, and Haavard, whence our Hayward, both alike meaning high protection.[*]

Section VI.—*Ghiseler.*

Ghiseler is one of the brothers of Gunther, an inoffensive personage, and the only one of the party of whom Chriemhild took any civil notice, when she had decoyed them to her court to their destruction. Nevertheless he did not escape, but died in combat with Wolfhart, of Bern, when the champions of Dietrich could not be withheld from the fray.

His name is tolerably clear—Giselhar, the pledged warrior. The first syllable is from *gildan, geldan, keltan*, to owe, or to pay what was due. The terms ran through all the Gothic tongues, and caused the Anglo-Saxons to call all the offerings due to the gods *gield* and *ghëlstar*.

A pledge of mutual obligation was, in Anglo-Saxon, *gisel*, and is still *gidsel* in the North ; in the German, *geissel*. Thence, far more

[*] Lettsom ; *Nibelungenlied ;* Weber and Jamieson ; Munch ; Anderson, *Royal and Noble Genealogies.*

probably than from the older word *geisli*, a beam, or nimbus, was derived the Frank Gisel, as a maiden's name. A daughter of Pepin, so called, was offered to Leo X. of Constantinople ; and afterwards the daughter of Charles the Simple, who became the pledge of amity between the Karlingen and Northmen, by her marriage with Rollo. She was called by the French Gisèle, by the Normans Gisla, in which same form it has lived on in Friesland and in Norway. The commencement is not, however, a very common one in the North, though Giselher is repeated in Gissur Isleifson, Bishop of Iceland, in the eleventh century. Gislaug, the pledge drink, is likewise northern, but though *gils* is an extremely common termination, almost all the names where it is a commencement are Frankish, or German, and thus probably Giselfrid came to the North as Gisrod.

Giselhilda, and Giselberge, were German, also Gisalhart, and Giselof ; and Gisalrico is found among the Spanish Goths. Geltfried and Giltimir are also German forms, and the latter explains Gelimer, the Vandal king in Africa, conquered by Belisarius.

Gils is a common Norwegian name, and no doubt contributed to the English Giles, French Gilles, and Spanish Gil, though all these look to the Greek hermit in France, Aigidios, as their patron. In the North, Ægidius is rendered by Ilian, Yljan, Yrjan, Orjan, but not by Giles : and it would seem as if Julius had been confounded with the name, as well as, perhaps, Giolla, a servant.

Giolla Brigde, or Bridget's disciple, is thought to have contributed the Scottish examples of Gilbert, which is incorrectly explained by some as Gelb-bert, or yellow bright ; but is clearly traceable to the old Frank Giselbert. There were four saints so called, namely, an abbot of Fontenelle, a great friend of William the Conqueror, an Auvergnat knight in the second Crusade, the English founder of the order of Gilbertine monks, and a bishop of Caithness ; and it has been a prevalent name in England, Scotland, and the Low Countries, with many contractions, especially in the latter.*

English.	French.	Italian.	German.
Gilbert	Guilbert	Gilberto	Giselbert
Gilpin	Gisebert		Gilbert
Gil	Gileber	Dutch.	Gisbert
Gibbon	Gilbert	Gysbert	Gispert
Gipp	Ghiliber		Giseprecht
		Flemish.	
		Gilli	

---

* Munter; Munch; Michaelis; Grimm; Took.

SECTION VII.—*Ghernot.*

Ghernot was Gunther's second brother, who was free from the guilt of the murder of Siegfried, and greatly displeased with Haghen for depriving Chriemhilt of the treasure ; but he shared the fate of his brothers, being killed early in the encounter by the Markgraf Rudiger

Perhaps, necessity of war, or spear compulsion, would be the best sounding translations of this remarkable name.

Ghere, the same as the northern Gejr and German Kero, is the messenger sent to invite Siegfried and Chriemhild to Wurms, when they paid the visit that had such fatal consequences; and *gher* or *gjer* is one of the most frequent of the component parts of names. Its right and original meaning is a spear, the same as that of the Latin *quiris* and Keltic *coir*. Thence the Anglo-Saxons called all other weapons *waren*, and the battle *war*, a word we still use, just as the French do *guerre*, and the Spaniards *guerra*.

Gar is *quite* in modern German, and *gher* has dropped out of the language, and thus most of the German names commencing with it have been misinterpreted to mean *all*, but it is impossible to compare them with their northern cousins without tracing the same spear in both.

The chief favourite amongst these spear titles seems to have been once a Valkyr name Gêrdrûd, or Geirthrud, the spear maid ; for, alas ! the pretty interpretation that has caused so many damsels of late to bear it, as meaning *all truth*, is utterly untenable, unless they will regard themselves as allegorically constant battle-maids, armed with the spear of Ithuriel.

The ancient popularity of this name was owing to a daughter of one of the great Pepins, in their *maire du palais* days. She founded the abbey of Nivelle, and was intensely revered by the Franks and Germans, chiefly on account of the miracles imputed to her. At old heathen feasts, the cups quaffed in honour of gods or demi-gods were prefaced by the words " *Wuotansminne, Thorsminne,*" meaning in Woden's or Thor's memory ; but the Christian teachers changed these toasts to be in the memory of the saints, such as Michelsminne for the guardian angel. *Johannisminne* was the special favourite, and was supposed to be a charm against poison, because the Evangelist was thought to have experienced the fulfilment of the promise, " If ye drink any deadly thing it shall not hurt you," as typified by the dragon in his cup. The royal nun, Gertrude, was almost as great a favourite as the Apostle with the Germans, and the regular toasts at their banquets came to be *Johannisminne* and *Gerdrutsminne,* till drinking to St. John and St. Gertrude were almost a proverb for revelry.

Let us observe, *en passant*, that *minne*, lately in honour of Minna Troil erected into a lady's name, is from the Gothic *munan*, to remember, from the Saxon form of which we take our *mind*. Minnie has lately become a favourite name, and must be referred to this source.

A second St. Gertrude, of noble blood in Saxony, was abbess of Heldelfs, had an exceedingly high reputation for sanctity, and died in 1334, leaving her name doubly popular.

English.	French.	Italian.	Portuguese.
Gertrude	Gertrude	Gertrude	Gertrudes
Gatty		Geltruda	
German.	**Bavarian.**	**Netherlands.**	**Danish.**
Gertraud	Traudl	Drutje	Gertrud
Trudchen	Traul	Trudje	Jartrud
		Trudel	
Slovak.	**Lettish.**	**Esth.**	**Polish.**
Jera	Gêrde	Kert	Giertruda
Jerica	Gerte	Truto	
Jedert	Gedde	Truta	**Lithuanian.**
Jra			Trude
			Hungarian.
			Gertrud

There is great confusion between Gerwald and Gerhard; the one meaning spear power, the other firm spear.

Though *gar* was not a common English prefix, the first Saint Gerhold was Anglo-Saxon. He migrated to Ireland, received the cowl in the monastery of Mayo, founded that of Tempul Gerald, died in 732, and became the subject of one of the Irish legends of saints. It declared that the wife of Caomhan, king of Connaught, turned him out of the fort of Cathair Mhor, with his 300 saints, who thereupon joined him in one of the peculiar prayers of Irish saints, that there never should be another king of the same race for ever. However, he afterwards relented, and only cut off from the throne the offspring of the lady herself, while to those of the king's former wife he granted the right of sitting first in the drinking house and of arraying the battle. The Irish call him Garalt, and have confused his name with the Keltic Gareth, one of the knights of the Round Table, so that Garrett and Gerald are regarded as identical.

The great prevalence of the name in Ireland is, however, chiefly owing to the Normans. There had been two Frank saints thus called in the twelfth century, Gerard of Toul, and Girroald of Fontenelle; but it was also a Lombardic name, and the old Florentine family of the Gherardi claims the parentage of one of the many Gerolds who accompanied William the Conqueror, the same whose decendant, Maurice Fitzgerald, was one of the companions of Earl Strongbow, the parent of the Fitzgeralds, or Geraldins, of Kildare, the turbulent race, who disputed with the Butlers of Ormond the supremacy of the island. Lady Elizabeth Fitzgerald, a daughter of this house, was the lady who, in imitation of Beatrice and of Laura, was erected by Surrey into the heroine of his poetry, under the title of the Fair Geraldine, thus leading to the adoption of this latter as one of the class of romantic Christian names. Gerald Barry, the Welsh chronicler who Latinizes himself as Giraldus Cambrensis, may have been rightly Gareth, and the provincial form Jarrett, still common in the North, is probably rather a remnant of the Gareth of Strathclyde, than a version of the Norman Gerald.

Another St. Gerald, bishop of Namur, left his name to be very common in the Low Countries, where we have already shown how curiously the transformation was effected of Gerhard Gerhardson into Desiderius Erasmus. Lastly, a St. Gerhard went on a mission to convert the Hungarians, and the name, or rather the two names, for there is no distinguishing between them, have become universal.

English.	French.	Provençal.	Italian.
Gerard	Gerard	Girart	Gherardo
Garrett	Giraud	Guerart	Gerardo
Jarett	Girairs		

German.	Netherlands.	Dutch.	Frisian.
Gerhard	Gerard	Gerhardus	Geerd
	Gerrit	Gerrit	
	Geert		

Danish.	Polish.	Lettish.	Hungarian.
Gerhard	Gieraud	Gerkis	Geller
Geert		Gérts	

English.	French.	Italian.	German.	Frisian.
Gerald	Giraud	Giraldo	Gerold	Gerold
	Guirauld			Gerelt
	Girault			Gerel

Gerhardine in German, and Giralda in Italian, are the feminines, besides our own Geraldine. Possibly Giralda may once have been the Valkyr name Geirhilda, which has survived in the North in the form of Jerilla, *jer* being the northern corruption of *geir*. Jerlau is thus Geirlaug, and Jeruf, or Jerul, Geirolf.

In like manner, though with different pronunciation, we make Jervis out of the old Norman Gervais, which was probably Geirfuss, or warlike eagerness. It used to be explained as *gerfast*, all firm, but this is, of course, wrong; though, as I have not found Geirfuss in the roll of northern names, and it would have been Gerfuns in Germany, where Gerwas is common, as is Gervais in France, and Gervaso in Italy, this must be doubtful.

The Gerberge of French history, the queen of Louis l'Outremer, was the same as the Geirbjorg of the North : Gerwin, or spear friend, made the Guarin of France, whence the Waryn of a few English families, and Guarino of Italy.

The old Spanish-Gothic feminine Garsendis was certainly Garswinth, or spear strength, and the equally ancient Garsias, or Garcia, so common in Galicia and Navarre, must have its commencement from the same source, though the last syllable has lost its individuality on the soft Spanish tongues. It was long a royal name, but was dropped about the thirteenth century, and makes its last public appearance in the person of the Peruvian prince and author Garcilasso de la Vega.

The spear raven, Gerramn, is the old English Jerram, that has become lost in Jerome ; and the spear prince, Gerbold, has furnished the family name of Garibaldi. *Gar* is very rare in native Anglo-Saxon names, whether as a beginning or end, but most frequent in all the other branches of the Teuton stock ; and its other form, *gais*, is the most reasonable explanation of the beginning of the name of Geisserich, the king of the Vandals, who has been made into Genserich, and then translated into the Gander king ! The remaining forms are :—

	Ger. Gerbert ; It. Gerberto—Bright spear			
	Ger. Gerfrid—Spear peace			
Nor.	German.	Neth.	Frisian.	
Gierlac	Gerlach	Garlef		Spear sport
	Gerlib	Garlaf	Garleff	Spear relic

Nor. Geirmund, Garmund—Spear hand
Nor. Geirny—Spear fresh ; Gierrandur—Spear house
Nor. Geirridur—Spear impulse ; Gierstein—Spear stone
Nor. Geirthiofr—Spear thief ; Geirvör—Spear prudence
Nor. Geirvart ; Fris. Gerber—Spear guard

Section VIII.—*Folker*.

Of all the champions of Burgundy, none is more full of gallantry and *bonhommie* than Folker, the mighty fiddler of Alsace, a true knight, always equally ready for music or for fighting. If the *Nibelungenlied* be really another form of the Eddaic myth, Folker may answer to Bragi, the god of poetry, but he has his own individual character of blithe undaunted courage. Even when the terrible battle has begun, and the heroes find themselves hemmed in by Chriemhild's warriors, Folker fiddles on, until he dies by the hand of Hildebram.

Folker's name is from our own word *folk*, the near relation of the Latin *vulgus*, whose progeny are found all over Europe in *vulgar*, *vulgo*, *foule*, &c. Most likely Folkvard is really the right version, and would mean people's guard, and Folker is rather its corruption than independently the people's warrior, and the same with Folko ; they are, therefore, all thrown together in the following table.

English.	German.	Frisian.	Nor.
Fulk	Volquard	Folkert	Folkvard
	Volkvart	Foke	Folke
French.	Folkward	Fokko	Fokke
Fulcher	Folquhard		
Feuquiers	Folkhard		
Foulques	Folker		
Fouques	Folko		
	Fulko		

In the Foulques stage, this name was borne, alternately with Geoffroi, by the counts of Anjou, and with the strange soubriquets of *Nerra* and *Réchin*. One of these counts, the grandfather of our Henry II., became king of Jerusalem ; but our English Angevins did not perpetuate the name ; and though six Fulcos are recorded in Domesday, Fulk never took root in England, and is chiefly remembered because it belonged to Fulk Greville, the friend of Sydney. It was, in fact, with all its varieties, chiefly Burgundian.

Germany shows a few other forms : Folkwin, or Volquin, which exactly answers to Demophilos, or Publicola ; Folkrad, Folkrich, and Folkmar ; also Folkbert, which some prefer to Wilibert, as the origin of the Savoyard Filiberto, and our Fulbert.*

Section IX.—*Dankwart.*

In the *Nibelungenlied* the father of Chriemhilt, who dwelt at Wurms, was 'hight Dankrat,' and the marshal at the court was Dankwart the swift, Hagen's brother. Innocent as he was of a share in his brother's crime, he was the first to be assailed while he was dining with Etzel's knights, and he had to fight his way through Chriemhild's warriors before he could return to his comrades in the hall, when he kept the door until, like all the rest, he perished in the massacre.

The first syllable of the name is the same as our word *thank*, and the name means thankful or grateful. The father of Chriemhild was thus Thank-rede, or grateful speech, and from him the Northmen seem to have taken their Thakraad, which in Normandy became Tancred, the knight of Hauteville, whose twelve gallant sons chased the Saracens from Apulia, and were the founders of the only brave dynasty that ever ruled in the enervating realms of the Two Sicilies. The son of one of these gallant knights, Tancredi di Puglia, was the foremost in the first crusade, and the favourite hero of Tasso, in whose epic he is a Christian Achilles ; and Tancredi again was the last Sicilian king of the true Norman line, the same whose bickerings with Cœur de Lion make so unpleasant an episode in the third Crusade.

* *Nibelungenlied ;* Weber and Jamieson ; Munch ; Michaelis.

Dankwart, thankful guardian, lingered in Germany ; and in 1668, a Yorkshire register records the baptism of Tankard, the son of a 'Turkey merchant,' who had probably learnt the name from some of his foreign connections. Dankheri, thankful warrior, was in Normandy Tancar. Dankker is the German surname, and has even come to Tanzen ; so that our surname Dance may have the same origin. Thangbrand was the German priest whom King Olaf Tryggvesen of Norway sent to convert Iceland, but whose severity led to his expulsion ; and Germany also mentions Dankmar ; but the prefix is almost exclusively German.*

Section X.—*Theodoric.*

Theodoric of Bern is hardly a genuine hero of the *Nibelung*, being really the main figure in a cycle of Germanic romances of his own ; but as he, under the abbreviation Dietrich, is brought in to play a considerable part in the final action of the tale, this seems the fittest place for treating of him and the names in connection with him.

He seems to have been brought into the *Nibelungenlied* because the Germanic mind could conceive of nothing considerable passing without him. He is represented as one of the four-and-twenty princes in King Etzel's train, and as anxious to prevent mischief to the visitors from Burgundy, warning them of Chriemhilt's enmity, and refusing to attack them at her request. When the great slaughter began, it was Dietrich who conveyed the king and queen safely out of the *mêlée*, and withheld his men from engaging in it, until almost at the end, when they could no longer be restrained, and rushing into the fray were all slain except old Sir Hildebrand, though on the other hand, Gunther and Haghen alone remained alive of the Burgundians. Dietrich then armed himself, and after a fierce combat, made them both prisoners, and delivered them up to Chriemhilt, fully intending that she should spare their lives ; but when her relentless fury had fallen on them, he assisted King Etzel to bury the dead, and to return the horses and armour of their fallen champions to their respective countries.

Other German romances, however, elevate this prince to a much higher rank. The *Book of Heroes*, written by Wolfram of Eschenbach and Heinrich of Ofterdingen, makes Dietrich of Bern, in Lombardy, son of King Dietmar. Hearing of Chriemhilt's rose garden, which measured seven miles round, and was guarded by twelve champions, he was seized with a desire to do battle with them, for love of battle, not of ladies, though the victor was to receive a chaplet of roses and a kiss from the young lady. The wise old Sir Hildebrand, of the Wolfing line, conducted him and his eleven companion champions to Wurms, where the single combats took place. Dietrich's knights were successful, and for the most part took the chaplets, but refused the kisses, because they disdained Chriemhild as a faithless maiden.

* *Nibelungenlied ;* Mauch ; Pott.

A Danish ballad describes 'Kong Tidrich's' tremendous battle with a Lindwurm, the progeny of one that had escaped his great-grandfather Wolfdietrich. He was led to enter on the battle by entreaties for help from a lion whom the dragon had seized; but at first he came by the worst, for his sword broke, and

> 'The Lindwurm took him on her back,
> His steed beneath her tongue,
> Bore them into the hollow hill
> To her eleven young.'

She bade them eat the horse to pass away the time while she rested, promising that on her awakening they should devour the knight. In the cave, however, Tidrich found the magic sword of Siegfried and two knives; and in spite of the threats of the young dragons, and the promises of the old one, he killed them all; but the old worm fell so as to choke the mouth of the cave, whereupon the friendly lion dug him out, and supplied the place of the slain steed by carrying him to Bern on his back.

So much for romance. History mentions a real Theodoric, son of Theudemir, and king of the Ostrogoths in Italy, from 475 to 527. He had been sent as a hostage to Constantinople, and there educated; and though he could not write his name, and had a stamp perforated with the letters Theod to enable him to sign his edicts, he was exceeding able, wise, and skilful, and Arian as he was, conciliated the love of the Catholics. Verona was his chief city, and is evidently the Bern of the romances. He lived too late for the historical Attila, who had died in 453; and though there is a report of a previous Theodoric, who meddled in a dissension between Attila's sons, and took part in a great slaughter that lasted fifteen days, it is most likely that the original Theuderik was a mythical personage, after whom these historical princes were called, and who afterwards received the credit of some of their deeds, and was localized in the places of their dominion. It is in favour of this notion that Dietrich of Berne is one of the many titles of the wild huntsman, though the Lusatians corrupt him into Dietrich Bernhard, and the Low Countries into Dirk-mit-den-Beer, or with the beard. Indeed, Dirk, the Dutch form of Theodoric, was a half-mythical king of Holland.

It was a most universal name, Anglo-Saxon and Visigothic, as well as Frank and German; and two saints made it everywhere popular in the middle ages, though the Dutch at present chiefly use it.

English.	French.	Italian.	Span. and Port.
Theodric	Theodoric	Teodorico	Theodorico
Theodoric	Thierry	Dieterico	
Derrick	Thian		
Terry	Thean		
Tedric			
(*Domesday*)			

German.	Bavarian.	Frisian.	Danish.
Diotrich	Dietl	Tiaderik	Tjodrckr
Dietrich		Tiarik	Didhrikr
Diez	**Dutch.**	Tiark	Theodrckr
Diether	Diederik	Tiado	Tidrich
	Dierk	Tiaddo	Didrik
	Dirk	Todo	
		Tade	**Slovak.**
		Tido	Todorik
		Tide	
		Dudde	

Polish.	Bohemian.	Lettish.	Hungarian.
Dytrych	Detrich	Diriks	Ditrik
		Didschis	
		Tiz	

The name of Dietmar, the father of Theodoric, is to be found in many forms; in Theudemir, a Frank, who faithfully served Constantius; in an Ostrogothic Theodomir; Spanish, Theodomiro; and the modern Frisian, Thiadmar, Tiedmer, Tyeddemer, Tidmer. It means people's greatness.

Dietleib, his friend, is rightly Ditlev; and in the North, Thjodleif, the people's relic, or what is left to them. He, too, survives in constant Friesland, as Teallef, Taedlef, Tiadelef.

The chief favourite of this class is, however, the people's prince, occurring both among the Frank and early Anglian kings, and belonging to two French hermits and one English archbishop. It took firm root in Provence, and has an aroma of crusades and courts of love surrounding it; and though it is not in Domesday, it and its contractions survive as English surnames; and in a Gloucestershire parish register of the eighteenth century, the feminine form occurs frequently in every variety of spelling; Tibelda, Tiballa, Tibotta, Tybal.

English.	French.	Spanish.	Portuguese.
Theodebald	Theudobald	Theudebaldo	Theobaldo
Theobald	Thiebault		
Tybalt	Thiebaud		
Tibble	Tibaut		
Dibble			

Italian.	German.	Dutch.	Netherlands.
Teobaldo	Dietbold	Tibout	Dippolt
Tebaldo	Diephold		

The people's wolf was canonized as a Frank hermit, who gets called St. Thiou. Our friend Theodolf, the Icelander, as Fouqué calls him, would have been in his own land Thjodolf, and the contraction is

there Kjold, or Kjol, as Kjoil, or Kjoille, is for Thjodhild, the same
as the Diuthilt of the Germans, and Theudhilda, a nun-sister of
Clovis. St. Audard has undergone a still greater change ; he was
once archbishop of Narbonne, and called Theodhard, or ward, the
Tiard of Friesland, and Thjodvar, or Kjovar, in the North.

The remaining forms are,

Ger. Dietbert ; Frank. Theudebert—People's brightness		
Ger. Dietbrand—People's sword		
Ger. Dietburg—People's protection		
Nor.	**German.**	**Frank.**
Thjodgjer ⎫		
Toger ⎪		
Kiogjeir ⎬ Dietgar	Theodokar—People's spear	
Kygeir ⎪		
Kyer ⎭		

Ger. Dietfrid ; Frank. Theodofrid—People's peace
Ger. Theodegisel ; It. Teodisclo—People's pledge
Ger. Diether—People's warrior
Nor. Thjodhjalm ; Ger. Diethelm—People's helmet
Ger. Dietlind ; Lomb. Theudelinda—People's snake
Ger. Dietman—People's man
Ger. Diutrat ; Frank. Theodorada—People's council
Ger. Dietram—People's raven
Nor. Thjodvald, Kjodvald, Kjoval—People's power.*

Section XI.—*Uta, Ortwin.*

Frau Uote was the mother of Kriemhild, who interpreted her
dream and predicted the early death of her bridegroom. Ortwin, of
Metz, was *truchsess*, or carver, and was the nephew of Hagan and
Dankwart, sharing, of course, their fate.

They are not very interesting personages, but it is curious that they
bear the only names, among all the Nibelungen, which have any
genuine Anglo-Saxon likenesses ; that is, if Uote is, indeed, from the
word in Anglo-Saxon, *ead*, in the North *aud*, in Mæso-Gothic *audr*,
in High German *od*, everywhere meaning wealth. Some ascribe it to
the same root as *good* and as *Woden*, including them with *adel*,
noble ; but its derivatives are more easy to follow than its forefathers.

In the North, *odel* is the term for property to which an entire
family retains an equal right, *all-od*, or allodial property. But when
the warriors made incursions on their neighbours, they obtained, in
addition, their share of spoil, originally cattle, *feh*, or *feo*, i. e., their
fee. So *feh-od* came to be the word for possessions gained by the
individual by personal service to his lord, and thus passed from cattle
to land itself, when held of the chief on condition of following him

* Weber and Jamieson · Munch ; Grimm ; Butler ; *Nibelung.*

in war ; and thus we have the *feudal* system, with its *feoffs* and, too often, its *feuds*.

The feminine of this word probably named Uta. It was popular everywhere. Audur-diupaudga, or Audur the deeply rich, was a female viking, one of the first Icelandic settlers, who called a promontory Kambness, because she dropped her comb upon it ; nor has her name passed from her own country, while, in Norman-England, it appears first as Auda and then as Alda, answering to Alda the wife of Orlando the Paladin, and Alda queen of Italy in 926, also to another Alda, a lady of the house of Este, in 1393. These are from the Gothic and Scandinavian *aud ;* but the High German form was also represented by Oda and the Low German by the old Saxon Ead, which was soon translated into Ide, the most common of all the early feminines in the Cambrai register, together with its diminutive Idette. Ida was the name of King Stephen's granddaughter, the Countess of Boulogne, was always used in Germany, and has of late been revived in England, from its sounding like the title of a poetical mountain of the Troad.

It is not quite clear whether Othilie, the Alsatian virgin of the seventh century, who was said to have been born blind, but to have obtained sight at her baptism, is a form of Odel, noble, or a diminutive of Oda, or whether she is Otthild, answering to our Eadhild, one of the many sisters of Æthelstane : and there is the same doubt with Odilo and Odilon, the masculines.

The masculine form of *aud* was extremely common. We had it in the person of Ida, king of Bernicia ; the North owned many an Audr ; the Germans used Odde, Orto, and Otto, and when the gallant Saxon counts won the imperial crown, they took the old Latin Otho for the rendering of their name. France, meantime, had called her Burgundian prince Eudon, but when a relay of Norman Audrs appeared, they were Odons ; and in the needlework with which Queen Matilda adorned Bayeux cathedral, her husband's doughty episcopal half-brother is always labelled 'Odo Eps.' But though we had previously had a grim Danish archbishop Odo, and though Domesday shows plenty of Eudos and Odos, neither form took root, and both are entirely continental.

French.	Provençal.	Italian.	German.	Nor.
Odon	Orzil	Otto	Odo	Audr
Eudon		Ottone	Otto	Odo
Eudes	Lettish.	Ottorino	Orto	Oddr
Othes	Atte		Otho	
	Attinsch			

Ortvin the truchsess, had his namesake in the Lombard Audoin, father to Alboin, also, in the Frank Audwine, blessed by St. Columbanus, beloved by St. Eligius, and bishop of Rouen, whose loveliest church is that of St. Audoenus, now transformed by French lips into St. Ouen. And, at home, we hail the same 'rich friend' in Eadwine, the first Christian king of Northumbria, whose conversion is the most striking portion of Bede's history. His dominion extended over the Lothians, and he disputes with Aodh and the Ædui the naming of Edinburgh. Beloved as he was, his name of Edwin never entirely died away, and became in modern times diffused by the popularity of Goldsmith's ballad, and of Beattie's *Minstrel.* It is just known upon the Continent. Ortwin, or Audoenius, is very possibly the Don Ordoño of the early Spanish kingdoms ; but Germany has chiefly dealt in the independent Odvin. Edwin, in spite of Mr. Taylor's tragedy of *Edwin the Fair,* is not the same as Edwy, namely Eadwig, rich war, a name well remembered for the unhappy fate of the owner.

Odoacer, as the Romans called him, who was put to death by Theodoric, was properly Audvakr, treasure watcher ; not quite the same as the Germanic Ottokar, or Ortgar, happy spear, which is identical with our familiar Eadgar, or Edgar. This name, after being laid to rest with the Anglo-Saxon monarchy, came to life again with the taste for antiques ; and Edgar Ravenswood, in his operatic character, has brought Edgar and Edgardo.

Eadmund, or happy protection, is one of our most English names, belonging to the king of East Anglia, who, as the first victim of the Danes, became the patron saint of Bury St. Edmund's, and the subject of various legends. The sudden deaths of Sweyn, and afterwards of Eustace de Blois, when engaged in ravaging his shrine, made him be regarded as an efficient protector ; and Henry III., when he had the good taste to make his sons Englishmen, christened the second after this national saint, so that Edmunds were always to be found in the House of Plantagenet, and thence among the nobility and the whole nation. The Irish called it Emmon, the Danes adopted it as Jatmund, in addition to their own Oddmund, the French occasionally use it as Edmond, and Italy knows it as Edmondo.

The most really noted of all our own genuine appellations is, however, Eadvard, the rich guardian. It comes to light in our royal line with the son of Alfred, and won the popular love for the sake of the young king whom St. Dunstan and the English called the martyr, in their pity for his untimely fate. And again, little as 'the Confessor had been loved in his feeble lifetime, enthusiastic affection attached to him as the last native sovereign ; while, on the one hand, it was the policy of the Norman kings to regard him as their natural predecessor, and of the barons to appeal to the laws that had prevailed in his time. All parties thus were ready to elect St. Edward to be the patron saint of England, and, in the ardour of embellishing his foundation of Westminster Abbey, it was natural to give his name to the heir of the crown, afterwards 'the greatest of the Plantage-nets.' The deaths of his three children bearing Norman or Spanish names confirmed this as the royal name, and the third king so called spread it far and wide. It was carried by his granddaughter to Portugal, and there had its honour so well sustained by her noble son, as there to find another home ; and with us it has recurred continually in every rank.

The contraction Neddy, common to all of these, is one of the titles of a donkey.

English.	Welsh.	French.	Italian.
Edward	Jorwarth	Edouard	Odoardo
Neddy	Irish.		
Teddy	Eudbaird		

Portuguese.	German.	Nor.	Netherlands.
Duarte	Eduard	Jaward	Ede
	Oddward	Audvard	

The other less celebrated parallel varieties are :—

Eng. Eadbald—Rich Prince
Eng. Eadburh—Rich pledge
Eng. Eadburge ; Nor. Oddbjorg ; Ger. Edburge—
Rich protection
Eng. Eadbryht—Rich splendour
Eng. Eadfrith ; Ger. Otfrid ; Prov. Audafrei—Rich peace
Eng. Eadfled ; Fr. Audofled—Rich increase

Nor.	German.	
Oddgrim	Ortgrim	} Rich helmet
Audgrim		

Nor. Odgisl—Rich pledge

Nor.	German.	French.	
Audgunnr	Oddgund	Augen	} Rich war
Ougunna			
Augunna			

Nor. Odkel, Odkatla—Rick kettle
Fr. Authaire—Rich warrior
Oddlaug—Rich liquor
Nor. Oddleif ; Ger. Ortleip, Ortleib—Rich relic
Eng. Eadmar ; Nor. Odmar ; Ger. Otmar—Rich greatness
Nor. Oddny—Rich freshness
Eng. Eadred—Rich council
Eng. Eadric, Edric ; Ital. Odorico—Rich king

English.	Nor.	German.	
Eadulf	Odulf	Oddulf	} Rich wolf
	Oulf	Ortwulf	

English.	German.	
Eadwald	Edvald	} Rich power.
Edwald	Odvald	

Eadswith, Eadgifu, and Eadgyth, all once separate names, together with Adelgifu and Ælfgifu, seem to have been all mixed up together by the Normans. Eadgyth was undoubtedly the name of Earl Godwin's daughter, of whom Ingulf said, ' *Sicut spina rosam, genuit Godwinus Egitham;* ' but in the roll of her lands in Domesday, she is Eddeva, Eddid, and Edeva, and for some little time Edeva seems to have been used among the Normans, though the queen of Henry I. was not allowed to retain anything so Saxon. Aline and Edith were used in a few families, but Edith survived the others.

Giav or *give* is not a very common commencement ; but in the Vilkina Saga, King Gjuko is the father of Gunnar and Gudrun, and the whole family are called Giukungr. In German, in the *Book of Heroes*, he is Gibicho, and there was really a historical Burgundian King Gibica, mentioned as a law-giver ; but in the *Nibelungen-nôt*, Gibich is only a vassal king of Etzel's. The North had Gjaflaug, liquor giver, no doubt the Hebe of the Norse banquets, Gjavvald, in German, Gevald, and perhaps Gabilo and Gavele, the Gebelius of Latinists. Germany had likewise Gebahard, a firm or perhaps a strong giver, which still survives under the unpromising sound of Gebhard.

Gyda, or Gytha, that most difficult name, sometimes sounds like Gith, the contraction of Eadgyth ; but it was evidently northern, having belonged to the proud damsel of Hordaland, who refused to marry Harald Harfagre, unless he was sole king of all Norway. Afterwards it was borne by the semi-Danish ladies of Earl Godwin's family, and melted into Gjutha, then became confounded with Jutta, which was considered as short for Juditha.

Section XII.—*Sintram.*

Sindolt was the *schenke*, or butler, at the court of Wurms, in the *Nieblungenlied ;* and in the Vilkina Saga, Sintram is one of the heroes of Thidrek's following. The derivation of the first syllable is uncertain. Michaelis takes it from the old High German *sinths*, a journey. Professor Munch refers Sindre to a word meaning sparkling or spark, and mentions a mythological dwarf who was a famous smith, and was yclept Sindre ; also a poet in Harald Harfagre's time, whose appellation was Guthorm Sindre, or the sparkling. Sundre or Sondre is, the same authority tells us, more used in the Thellmarken in Norway than elsewhere ; and another possible derivation for it is from '*sondra*,' to sunder. The forms Sunrir and Sunris are there found ; and Germany had a few others, such as Sindwald, or Sindolt, Sindbald, the Sinibaldo of Italy, Sindbert, Sindolf, and the above-mentioned Sindhram, chiefly interesting to us as chosen by Fouqué for the name of his master-piece, the wonderful allegory spun out of Albert Durer's more wonderful engraving.

SECTION XIII.—*Elberich.*

The elf king Elberich here brings in his own fairy kindred. In the *Nibelung*, he is watching over the fatal treasure when Siegfried comes to claim it, and, dwarf as he is, does such fierce battle over it that Siegfried was 'in bitter jeopardy ;' but he is at length overcome sworn to Siegfried's service, and brought by him to Wurms, where he has no more to do but to lament when Haghen makes away with the treasure.

He is called very ancient, and well he may be, for he had appeared in the *Book of Heroes* long before the time of even Hughdietrich, when King Otnit of Lombardy had set forth to win the daughter of the king of Syria, and Elberich showed himself under a linden tree in the guise of a beautiful child. Otnit was about to pick him up, but received from him a tremendous blow, and after a sharp fight came to terms, and thenceforth he assisted him in his enterprise, gave him magic armour, and assisted him to gain the lady. Much of this story is repeated in the French romance of *Huon de Bourdeaux*, where Auberon, as he is there called, gives the knight an ivory horn wherewith to summon him to his aid in an emergency, and thus arose the English Oberon, the elf-rik or king, the graceful but petulant fairy whom Drayton marries to the Irish Mab, and Shakespeare to the Greek Titania. He had his human namesakes, too ; Alberich was in fashion as a Frank name, as Ælfric was as a Saxon ; and the Domesday Book shows that while we had plenty of the latter native form, Edward the Confessor had already imported two specimens of 'Albericus comes,' and these or their sons contracted into Aubrey, which was known to fame as almost hereditary among the De Veres, earls of Oxford. France, too, had her Aubri ; and Alberico was used in Lombardy, where likewise the notable and terrible monarch Alboin, whose name as Alboino is still common among the peasantry, bore the name that Anglo-Saxons called Ælfwine, or elf-friend, perhaps likewise an allusion to the aid and friendship of 'Oberon the faëry,' whose first protégé was a Lombard. Alwine is the feminine used in Germany, and *perhaps* may be our Albinia.

The elf of England and Germany, the *alfr* of the North, was a being dear to the imagination of the people. His name means the *white*, the same word already mentioned as forming the Latin *albus*, and designating the Elbe and the Alps, as well as appearing in the Elphin of Cymric legend. The elves, or white spirits, were supposed to be beautiful shadowy gifted beings, often strangely influencing the life of mortals, so that in old Germany the Alfr were the genii of man's life, like the Disir of the North ; and Elberich probably originally attended Otnit in this capacity. Christianity did not destroy the faith in the elf-world, but the existence of these beings was accounted for by supposing them children of Eve, whom she had hidden from the face of her Maker, and He had therefore condemned to be hidden from the face of man. They were thought to mourn for their exclusion from Redemption, and to seek baptism for their infants ; but in process of time their higher attributes dropped off from them, and they were mixed up with the malicious black dwarfs. They took to stealing young maidens, as the Scottish Burd Ellen, and to exchanging infants in the cradle ; and Scotland created an Elfinland, which was a striking element of worldly vanity. In England, the traditions of the Keltic spirits, pucks and pixies, were mixed up with them, and our Elizabethan poets treated them as the males of the French fairies ; and what comes to us so recommended, surely we must accept.

These elves, in their more dignified days, played a considerable part in our native nomenclature ; nay, the most honoured of all our English sovereigns wrote himself upon his jewel Ælfred, *i.e.*, Elf in council, wise as a supernatural being. Some have tried to read the word Alfried, all peace ; but there is no doubt that the Elf is the right prefix. The English loved to continue his name, but it was Latinized as Aluredus, and thus Alured is the form in which it is borne by many persons recorded in Domesday, and is still kept up and regarded as a separate name, though Alfred has been within the last century resumed in England ; it is much used about the good king's birth-place at Wantage in Berkshire, and has of late been adopted in France and Germany.

Ælfhæg was as high as an elf ; whether given to a very small infant, or supposed to refer to a being of unearthly stature, does not appear. It was the very inappropriate name of the archbishop who, under Ethelred the Unready, was pelted to death at a Danish banquet because he would not oppress his flock to obtain a ransom. The offence given by Lanfranc in refusing to regard him as a true martyr may be judged by the large numbers called after him in Domesday. In Sussex they are set down as Ælfech ; in Hants as Ælfec ; in Nottingham as Ælfag ; and thanks to the Latinism of Alphegius, our calendar calls him Alphege.

Ælfgifu, or the elf gift, was the unfortunate Elgiva of history, a not unsuitable name for one whose beauty was like a fatal fairy gift, bringing ruin on her and on her husband ; but it was also used to translate into Saxon that of the Norman Emma, which was regarded as too foreign for the Saxons. Knut's first wife, Ælfwine (elf darling), the daughter of Ælfhelm, Earl of Southampton, is recorded by Dugdale as Ailive ; and Aileve, Ælveva, or Alveva, is very common in Domesday. Aileve indeed continued in use for many years.

In fact, it was England that made by far the most use of elf names. The North was perhaps the next in the use of them, having an immense number of instances of Alfr in the *Landnama-bok*, but there the elf at the end of a word has such an unfortunate tendency to transform himself into a wolf, that it is impossible to tell which was the original, the same person being sometimes written Thoralf, and sometimes Thorulf. There are few instances preserved from the other Teutonic branches, except as we have seen the two Lombardic names, that seem direct from Elberich.

English names in Æthel often contract into El, and when followed by an *f*, appear to be *elves ;* but they must be pursued to their original form before being so rendered.

Nor. Alfdis—Household fairy
Nor. Alfgejr ; Eng. Ælfgar—Elf spear
Nor. Alfgerdur—Elf woman
Nor. Alfheidur, Alfeidur—Elf cheerfulness
Eng. Ælfhelm—Elf helmet
Nor. Alfhild—Elf battle maid
Nor. Alfliotr—Elf terror
Eng. Ælfric—Elf king
Eng. Ælfthryth, Elfrida—Threatening elf
Eng. Ælfwold—Elf power

Alvaro and Elvira are the Spanish forms of these elf names.

A bishop of Lichfield, whose name was Ælfwine, was always called Ælla, and thus there is reason to suppose that *elves* named both the Ælle of Deira, whose name caused Gregory the Great to say that Alleluja should be sung in those regions, and also the later Ælla, who put Ragnar Lodbrog to death. Otherwise these would be referred to the word in Gothic, *aljan*, meaning battle, found in the Old German Ellanheri and Ellanperaht.

Some of our commencing *els* are no doubt from the fairy source ; but there are others very difficult to account for, beginning in Anglo-Saxon with *ealh*, which is either a hall, or without the final *h*, the adjective *all*, by which in fact they are generally translated. The most noted of them is Ealhwine, the tutor of Charlemagne's sons, generally called Alcuin, though his name has remained at home as Aylwin. Some Aylwins, are, however, certainly from Ægilwine, or awful friend ; Ealhfrith, Ealhmund, and Ealhred, are also found, and one of these must have formed the modern Eldred. Among ladies are Ealhfled, and Ealhswyth, or Alswitha. On the whole it seems to us that the *hall* is the more probable derivation ; the *h* so carefully used in the Saxon Chronicle is unlike a contraction.*

* Munch ; Weber and Jamieson ; St. Pelaye, *Huon de Bourdeaux ;* Grimm ; Keightley ; Lappenburg ; *Landnama-bok ; Domesday ;* Scott, *Minstrelsy of Scottish Border ;* Sharon Turner ; Kemble, *Names of the Anglo-Saxons.*

CHAPTER V.

THE KARLING ROMANCES.

Section I.—*The Paladins.*

Another remarkable cycle of romantic fable connected itself with a prince, not lost in the dim light of heroic legend, but described by a contemporary chronicler, and revealed in the full light of history. However, in reality, the records of Eginhard were, no doubt, as unread and unknown as if they had never existed, and with the notion that a magnificent prince had reigned over half Europe, there was ample scope for tradition to connect with him and his followers all the floating adventures that Teutonic, Keltic, or Latin invention had framed ; and, by-and-by, literature recorded them, using them as her own world of beauty and of wonder, until nothing but the names were left in common with their originals.

France, Germany, Lombardy, and Spain, all looked back to the same emperor, and hung their traditions around him, with a far more national sentiment than it was possible for them to possess for the British Arthur. In the Charles who bore the surname of the Great, all the legends centred. He was at once emperor, and, like his grandfather, champion of Europe against the Saracens, with whom in popular fancy, both his own Saxons and his grandson's Northmen were fused together ; he was besieged, like his grandson, in Paris, and lost all his best followers in the pass of Roncesvalles, by the treachery of the Navarrese.

These were the materials that fancy had to work upon. The existing feudal system supplied the machinery, and not with utter incorrectness, since it had actually then existed in its infancy, and the chiefs of the Frank court were veritably obliged to pay martial service to their head for the lands that they had received from him on the conquest of the country. *Pfalz*, the same word which we now call *palace*, the central court, furnished the title for the feudatories employed at the court ; *Pfalzen*, a word that continued in use in its proper region, Germany, naming the Pfalzgraf of the Rhine, whence we have learnt to speak of the Count Palatine and the Palatinate.

Pfalzen, then, on French tongues, became Paladins, and Paladins were supposed to have been not so much political as military, so that we regard the term as meaning a champion of high prowess. There was an idea likewise of a council of these Paladins as the twelve peers of France in the golden age of her constitution ; and the Docipairs, as the Douzepairs were sometimes run together, stood on a level in romantic imaginations with the Seven Champions of Christendom, or the Knights of the Round Table.

Spanish ballads, German lays, and Provençal songs, had been working up the stories of the Paladins, when somewhere about the year 1100, there came forth a French translation of the supposed chronicle of Turpin, who had really been archbishop of Rheims in the reign of Charlemagne. The chronicle was confirmed in 1122 by the infallible authority of the Pope, and was translated again and again, amplified and referred to by every one who wrote or sung of the Paladins, for the events they celebrated, whether it contained them or not.

The influence of the Karlingen upon our subject has been great. First, some of the genuine historical characters left hereditary Christian names ; next, several were adopted in romantic and chivalrous families, and in the poetical ages of literary Italy, they became absolutely frequent.

Paladins, however, connect themselves with hardly any genuine female names of the same period. The Ossianic Fenians have their wives and beloved maidens, the knights of the Round Table are united with ladies of Cymric title, like their own, and evidently as traditionary as themselves ; the dames of the *Nibelungenlied* are intimately connected with the whole structure of the legend ; but the knights of Charlemagne have brought with them few genuine ladye loves. Orlando once had a wife, the Alda, or Belinda, of the old traditions; but even the Clarice of Renaud in the *Quatre Fils Aymon*, betrays a late French, or rather Romanesque, influence ; and far more do the Doña Clara, Belerma, and Sebilla of the Spanish ballads, show how late they must have arisen ; whilst Angelica, Marfisa, Bradamante, Fiordespina, and Fiordiligi, and the like, are absolute Italian inventions.

The Frankish ladies seem, in fact, to have been held in little estimation. Chivalry had not blossomed into respect for womanhood, and they had probably been left behind by their lords in the march of civilization. The female names from time to time cast up in the surging tide of affairs seldom appear except for disgrace or misfortune, so that we come to the conclusion that womanhood in the Frank empire was seldom happy or honourable except in the cloister. Thus, no traditional names of woman came down with the Paladins ; and when love became an essential part of the machinery of the Italian poets, they had to invent, and entitle, the heroines for themselves.

SECTION II.—*Charles.*

Most heroes gain by becoming the subjects of romance, but this has been by no means the case with the great Karl of the Franks, for though 'il Rè Carlo' be three rolled into one, he has lost the heroism of him of the hammer, and the large-minded statesmanship of the first emperor, obtaining instead the dulness and weak credulity of him who was called the Bald.

The three Charleses are matter of history, and the Carlo Magno of romance and ballad is little more than a lay figure, always persuaded to believe traitorous stories of his best friends, and meeting with undignified adventures, as in the case of the enchanted ring that bound his affections to lady, bishop, and lake. We therefore pass on at once to this name, which a foolish old story thus accounts for. As an infant he was put out to nurse, and when brought home, much grown, his mother exclaimed, 'What great carle is this?' whence he continued to be so called, instead of by his baptismal name of David. This tale may have been suggested by the fact, that the veritable Charles the Great, when laying aside his state he became a scholar in his palace hall, under the teaching of the English Alcuin, assumed the appropriate title of David.

Karl was in fact, as we have shown in the chapter on ancestral names, the regular family name of the line, used in regular alternation from its first appearance with the grandfather of the hammering Charles, who perhaps took his soubriquet from Thor, and gradually acquiring more and more ignominious epithets till it sunk into obscurity in Lorraine, whence it only emerged again when the Karlings intermarried with Philippe Auguste, and brought the old imperial name into the French royal family, where five more kings bore it. They sent it to Naples with Charles of Anjou ; and his son, Charles Robert, or Caroberto, being elected to Hungary, had so many namesakes that Camden was led to suppose that all Hungarian kings were called Carl. It went to Germany when the son of the blind king of Bohemia received it from his father's connection with the French court, and afterwards reigned as the 4th Karl of Germany, taking up his reckoning from the old Karlingen. Again, the second ducal house of Burgundy was an off-shoot from the line of Valois, and it was from Charles the Bold that the name was transmitted to his great grandson of Ghent, soon known to Europe as Carlos I. of Spain, Karl V. of Germany, Carolus Quintus of the Holy Roman Empire. He was the real name spreader from whom this became national in Spain, Denmark, and even in Britain, for his renown impressed James I. with the idea that this must be a fortunate name ; when, in the hope of averting the unhappy doom that had pursued five James Stuarts in succession, he called his sons Henry and Charles. The destiny of the Stuart was not averted, but the fate of the 'royal martyr' made Charles the most popular of all appellations among the loyalists, and afterwards with the Jacobites, in both England and Scotland, so that rare as it formerly was, it now disputes the ground with John, George, and William, as the most common of English names.

Another namesake of Charlemagne must not be forgotten, namely, the son of St. Olaf, of Norway, whom his followers, intending an agreeable surprise to the father, baptized after the great emperor by the name of Magnus, whence the very frequent Magnus, of Scandinavia, and Manus of Ireland.

The two feminines are of late invention. The first I have been able to find was Carlota or Charlotte, of Savoy, who married Louis

English. Charles Charlie	Keltic. GAEL. Tearlach ERSE. Searlus	French. Charles Charlot	Span. and Port. Carlos German. Karl
Italian. Carlo Carolo	Swedish. Karl Kalle	Danish. Karl Karel	Dutch. Carolus Carel Karel
Polish. Karol Karolek	Bohemian. Karel Slovak. Karol	Illyrian. Karlo Karlica Karlic	Lusatian. Karlo Karlko
Lettish. Karls	Esthonian. Karl Karel	Hungarian. Karoly	Dantzig. Kasch

XI., and thus introduced this form to French royalty. Charlotte
d'Albret had the misfortune to be given in marriage to Cesare Borgia,
and had one daughter, who married into the house of La Tremouille,
whence the brave Lady Derby carried it into England, and our
registers of the seventeenth century first acknowledge Charlet. The
Huguenotism of the house of La Tremouille connected it with that
of Bouillon, where the heiress Carola, or Charlotte, was married in
1588. The house of Orange probably thence derived it, and it
became known in Germany, whence it was brought to us in full
popularity by the good queen of George III. A sentimental fame
was also bestowed on it, as the name of Göthe's heroine in *Werther*.

English. Charlotte Lotty Chatty Caroline Carry	French. Charlotte Lolotte Caroline	Spanish. Carlota Lola	Italian. Carlotta Carlota Carolina
German. Charlotte Lottchen Caroline Lina	Swedish. Lotta	Slovak. Karolina Karolinka Karla	Lettish. Latte Dantzig. Linuschca

Carolina, the other form, seems to have been at first Italian, and thence to have spread to Southern Germany, and all over that country, whence we received it with the wife of George II., by whom it was much spread among the nobility, and is now very common among the peasantry.

Ceorl was the name of an early king of Mercia, and of a thane of Alfred's, who defeated the Danes, and Carloman was almost as common as Carl in the old Karling family.*

SECTION III.—*Roland, &c.*

When the army of Charles the Great was marching back from Spain, the Gascons, Navarrese, and Goths, who were afraid of being swallowed up by his empire, if they exchanged his protection for that of the Arabs, plotted together, fell on the rear of his columns as they were passing through the defile of Roncesvalles, close to the little town of Fuente Arabia, and slaughtered the whole division that were guarding the baggage. 'There was slain Rotlandus, prefect of the Armorican border.'

So says Eginhard, the contemporary chronicler, and as he mentions only two other nobles as having been killed, it is natural to conclude that this Rotlandus was a man of mark. Who was he? Certainly Warden of the Marches of Brittany, but was he a Frank Hruodland (the country's glory), the repressor of the Kelts, or was he a Breton in the Frankish service? The Cymry have laid claim to him; they say that the rolling word is intended to render Tallwch, a rolling or overwhelming torrent, the name of the father of Tristrem; and in the later romances, this knight has actually been turned into Rowland, which thus has become a favourite national Welsh name.

It is far more likely that 'Rotlandus' was Frank, but the next question is, what were the deeds that made his birth worth contending for, and the war song of Rou be the chant of the gallant minstrel Taillefer, to cheer the Normans on to their victory at Hastings?

Eginhard is utterly silent. Turpin tells us that Rolandus was the emperor's nephew, the son of his sister Bertha, and of Milo de Anglars. With Turpin, the expedition to Spain is the prominent feature of the reign, and he gives us an account of a mingled battle and controversy between Roland and Ferragus, a giant of the race of Goliath, and only vulnerable in one point, where, however, Roland managed to pierce him. Very soon after follows the ambush of Roncesvalles, the enemy being Saracens, not Christians, but conducted by the traitor Ganelon. After a terrible battle, Roland, sorely wounded, lay down under a tree, and apostrophizing his good sword Durenda, in the most tender manner, thrice struck it upon a block of marble, and shattered it in twain, lest it should fall into the Saracen hands. Then he blew upon his horn, which had such wondrous tones that all other horns split at the sound, and this blast was with such effort that he burst all the

---

* Sismondi; Roscoe; Michaelis; Pott; Anderson, *Genealogies.*

veins in his neck, and the sound reached the king, eight miles off!
He then commended his soul to heaven, and made a most pious and
beautiful end.

That block of marble is magnified by popular fame into the mountain itself, and la Brèche de Roland is supposed to be the cleft made
by his sword! The Northern Lights, too, are said to be King Charles
riding by, and Roland bearing the banner. The Spaniards, so far as
they were Christians and Teutons, felt with the Franks; so far as
they were Celtiberians, against them, and the result was a collection
of admirable popular ballads, all prime authorities with Don Quixote,
in which *il rey Carlos* and his peers are treated as national heroes.
Nevertheless they are proud of his defeat at Roncesvalles, declare
that the emperor broke his word to Don Alfonso of Leon, and that
the attack was therefore made in which Don Alfonso's nephew,
Bernardo de Carpio, was leader, and demolished the invulnerable
Conde Roldan, by squeezing him to death in his arms.

It is the Spaniards alone who have transferred to Roldan the
invulnerability of Achilles, Siegfried, and Diarmaid; the French and
Italians bestow it only on Ferragus, who is, as already mentioned, an
evident Keltic importation through the Breton poets, being either the
Irish Fergus, or the Welsh Vreichfras, though he has since become a
Moorish giant.

The English, having their own Arthur to engage their attention,
did little more than versify Turpin, but allowed Roland's sword to
be carried away by his friend Sir Baldwin, and took vengeance for
his death.

But it was the Italians who did the most for their Orlando. Some
floating Valkyr notion had attached itself in German fancy to his
mother, who was at first Bertha the goose-footed, and then the large-
footed, and romance further related that she was the emperor's sister,
who had secretly married the knight Milone di Anglante, and therefore was driven out of the court, and forced to take refuge in a cave,
where the hero was born, and was called Rotolando, from his rolling
himself on the ground. His father went to the wars, and Berta became the diligent spinner before alluded to, but she was still so poor
that his young companions each gave her boy a square of cloth to
cover him, two white, and two red, whence he always bore those colours
quartered on his shield. Afterwards he was taken into favour, and
became the chief Paladin.

Here Luigi Pulci took him up, and made him the hero of a poem
called the *Morgante Maggiore*, from a giant whom Orlando converted,
and who followed him faithfully about through all his adventures.
Orlando is here a high-spirited Christian knight, brave, pious, and
faithfully attached to his wife Alda. When slain at Roncesvalles, he
mentions her in his last and very beautiful prayer, and his sorrow
for his comrades, and parting with his horse and sword, are very
touching.

It was Bojardo who deprived Orlando of his old traditional character of the high-minded champion, that crusading days had dwelt
upon. Led, perhaps, by the idea of the frenzy of Amadis de Gaul, he

made Orlando fall desperately in love with the fair and false Angelica, princess of Catay, and leave the court and all his duties just as the Saracen king Gradasso was invading France, to obtain possession of Durindana, Orlando's sword. The action of the poem is taken up with the adventures imposed upon Orlando by the mischievous beauty, and the pursuit of him by the other Paladins, and finally it leaves off with the whole chivalry of Charlemagne besieged in Paris by the Saracens.

Orlando was only *innamorato* according to Bojardo ; Ariosto took him up and made him *furioso*. Continuing the poem where it had dropped from Bojardo's hands, Ariosto made Angelica fall in love with an obscure youth, and marry him, whereupon Orlando, after the example of Amadis de Gaul, went into the state of frenzy that Don Quixote tried to imitate ; and the Christians suffered as much as the Greeks did without Achilles, till the champion's senses were brought back from the moon ; when he returned to his duty, restored fortune to the Christians, and saved France from becoming tributary to the infidel.

Charles VIII. of France, in his romantic youth, named one of his short-lived children, Charles Roland, by the way of union of the two heroes.

English. Roland Rowland	French. Roland	Italian. Orlando	Spanish. Roldan
Portuguese. Rolando Roldao	German. Roland Ruland Rudland	Netherlands. Roeland	

The derivation of the first syllable is the word *hruod* in Frank, *hrothr* in the North, and in modern German *ruhm*, meaning fame or glory.

Hruod is a most prolific word. As Hruodgar, famous spear, it figures in the *Nibelungenlied*, where the Markgraf Rudiger is the special friend of Dietrich, and for a long time, like him, refrains from the fray, though at last he plunges into it and is killed.

There seems to have been a veritable Hruodgar living in the time of Pepin, who married a lady whose father's name was Hector, whence it was taken for granted that she descended from Hector of Troy. Therefore the House of Este bore the white eagle in their coat of arms, because it was said he of Troy had a shield azure with a silver eagle ! Roger, Olivier, and Roland are mentioned together as subjects of minstrel songs. In the old romances there is a Ruggieri de Risa, or Reggio, who marries an Amazon, called Galaciella, but is soon after murdered, and she is carried off by sea by her enemies, whom, however, she manages to overpower and destroy on the voyage, but only to be driven to a desert island, where she dies at the birth of her twins, Ruggiero and Marfisa. This Ruggiero is the prime favourite of the Italian poets. Bojardo tells how he was bred up on lion's marrow by the enchanter Atlante, in Africa, and when his education was finished, was sent to France with the wonderful hippogriff, or winged horse. And Ariosto, probably in compliment to the House of Este, made his adventures the main plot of the *Orlando Furioso*, and completed it by converting him to Christianity, and marrying him to the brave and amiable Amazon, Bradamante.

Bojardo probably adopted Ruggiero because his country was Reggio, a country with which the name had become connected, when Roger de Hauteville had founded the kingdom of Sicily, and Ruggero, the son of his elder brother, Robert Guiscard, had been count of Apulia. These were both, of course, direct from the northern Hruodgeir, as was the turbulent Roger de Montgomery, who gave so much trouble in Normandy. It was once a famous knightly name, but is now too much discarded. Roger must once have been very frequent in England, since Hodge is still proverbial for a rustic,—whereas as a rule he is never so called, though the Registrar-General noted an extraordinary number of Roger Tichbornes in the year of the claimant's trial !

English.	French.	Italian.	Spanish.	German.
Roger Hodge	Roger	Ruggiero Rogero	Rogerio	Rüdiger Roger

Nor.	Netherlands.	Russian.	Polish.	Lettish.
Hrodgjer Raadgjer	Rogier Rutger	Rozer	Rydygier	Rekkerts

Hrothgar was also a famed name among the Angles. It appears in Beowulf, as the chief of the Scyldings, the son of Healfdane. There, too, are found Hrothmund and Hrothwulf ; and the northern names of Hroar and Hrolfr are contractions of these, though the characters they belong to are not the same as those in Beowulf. Hrolf Krake was the subject of a northern Saga ; and the father of our Norman kings, whom we are wont to call by his Latinism of Rollo, formed from the French stammer of Rou, was in fact Hrolf Gangr, or at full length, Hrothulf, Fame-Wolf. A name of fame and terror it was, when the mighty man, too weighty for steed to carry him, was expelled from his own land, and fought for a home, not for plunder, among the fertile orchards of Neustria, when his followers' rude homage overthrew the degenerate Karling, and 'the grisly old proselyte,' in his baptism, assumed, without perhaps knowing of the similarity, the French Robert. This change prevented his original name from being very prevalent among the Normans ; and the German form, Rudolf, is chiefly from a sainted Karling prince, who was bishop of Bourges, and from whom Rudolf of Hapsburg must have derived it. From him it became imperial, and other countries received it, without knowing it for their old friend.

English.	French.	Spanish.	Italian.
Rodolph	Rodolphe	Rodulfo	Rodolfo
Rolf	Raoul		Ridolfo
	Roul	Portuguese.	
	Rou	Rodolpho	

German.	Bavarian.	Frisian.	Swiss.
Rudolf	Ruedolf	Rulef	Ruedi
		Rulves	Ruedeli
		Rotholf	Rudi

Swedish.	Nor.	Lettish.	Hungarian.
Rudolf	Hruodulf	Rohlops	Rudolf
Rolf	Hrolfr		

Robert, the name assumed by Rolf Gauge at his baptism was Frank, rather than Northern, inasmuch as *bjart* is an uncommon conclusion among his native race. Hruadperaht, or bright fame, was the original form, the property of a bishop, who somewhere about the year 700 founded the first Christian church at Wurms. Honoured alike in France and Germany, he became Ruprecht in the latter, and Robert in the former. Like St. Nicolas, he is in Germany supposed to exercise a secret supervision over children ; in some places *Knecht Ruprecht* dispenses Christmas gifts, but he more often keeps watch over naughty children, and thus answers to the English Robin Good-fellow, or Hob Goblin. *Red* was long supposed to be the origin of the name, which some made Redbert, or bright speech, others Redbeard ! The German form, however, disproves both of these, and Ruprecht continued in honour in its own country, naming in especial that wise Pfalzgraf of the Rhine, who in 346 founded the university of Heidelberg ; and on the deposition of the crazy Bohemian Kaisar Wenzel, was elected Emperor of Germany, and reigned for nine years with great success and glory. It was after him that the infant, born at Prague, during the brief greatness of the Winter King, received that name of Rupert, which was so terrible to the Roundheads, but which for the most part they translated by their native Robert—native, because thoroughly Anglicized, for it was of French growth, had belonged to two or three saints, and to the hymn-writing and much persecuted king called the pious, the second of the Capet or Parisian dynasty ; but after the son of St. Louis carried it off to the House of Bourbon, it scantily appeared among the royal family. Normandy, however, cultivated it after it had been chosen at the baptism of her first duke, and sent it to Apulia with the astute Robert Guiscard, whence Roberto became national in the Neapolitan realms, and was adopted by the Angevin line, among others by the king who patronized Petrarch. The next Duke of Normandy who bore it was that wild pilgrim, whose soubriquet varies between the Devil and the Magnificent. The disinheritance of his equally wild, but more unfortunate grandson, Robert Courthose, diverted it from the English throne, but a flood of knights and nobles had poured in and established it so completely, that in a few generations more Hob was one of the established peasant names in England. Robin was its more gracious contraction—let our dearly beloved archer be who he will—either as ballad tells, the outlawed Earl of Huntingdon, or as late critics would have us believe, only another manifestation of Robin Goodfellow, or of the wild huntsman. Robin was the epithet by which Queen Elizabeth was wont to address the two earls, step-father and stepson, who so long sunned themselves in her favour; and though it has now acquired a homely sound, and the popularity of the full name has somewhat waned, it is still frequent. To Scotland it was brought by the Anglo-Norman barons, and when the English Bruces had made their distant drop of Royal Scottish blood float them to the throne, Robert the Bruce became a passionately beloved national hero, and his name one of the most favoured in the Lowlands. In Ireland it is called Roibin, a gentleman called in English Robin Lawless being in Irish, Roibin Laighleis.

English.	Scotch.	French.	Italian.
Robert	Robert	Robert	Roberto
Robin	Robin	Robers	Ruberto
Hob	Robbie	Robi	Ruperto
Bob	Rab	Robinet	
Rupert		Rupert	

German.	Bavarian.	Slovak.	Lusatian.
Hruodebert	Ruprecht	Ruprat	Huprecht
Ruprecht	Prechtl		
Rupert			
Rudbert			
Robert			

Not behindhand in glory is the northern Hrothrekr, or Germanic Hruoderich, famous ruler. In Gothic Spain, it was indeed Rodrigo,' who lost his country to the Moors, but became in his people's minds the centre for pity as much as for blame, and the subject of the beautiful legends that Southey has embodied in the finest of his poems. And it was Rodrigo Diaz de Bivar, 'Ruy mi Cid Campeador,' in whom ballad lore delighted. This became one of the most frequent of all the grand-sounding names prefaced by Don, and Rodriguez and Ruiz to be very common surnames.

The northern Hrothrekr was not long in being shortened to Hrorekr, and thence came the name of that Norseman, who, according to Russian historians, was invited by the Slaves to be their protector, and founded the Norman dynasty of Ruric, which continued on the throne during the troubled days of Tatar supremacy. Roric and Godwald were the first Northmen to obtain fiefs in France.

In Wales, Scotland, and Ireland, Roderick has a sort of false honour, being adopted as the equivalent of the native Keltic names, the Welsh Rhydderc, and the Gadhaelic Ruadh ; for Roy and Rorie, though rightly and traditionally so called by their friends, would now all make Teutons of themselves, and use the signature of Roderick.

English. Roderick	French. Rodrigue	Italian. Rodrigo	Spanish. Rodrigo Ruy
German. Roderich	Nor. Rothrekr Hrorek	Russian. Rurik	

There are numerous other forms from this prolific source. Rother, who figures in Lombardic history, is the German Hruodhari, or famous warrior, and in the North divides with Hrothgar the property of the strange abbreviation, Roar, and in the harsh old Latinisms of Frank names is Crotcharius.

There too is found Chrodovaldus, which in German was once Hrodowald, and afterwards Rudold, perhaps, too, the Danish and Scottish Ribolt, and in the North Roald, and in Italian Roaldo, the founder of an order of monks. Nay, Romeo de' Montecchi himself, the Montague of Shakespeare, bore a common Lombardic name, softened down from the Chrodomarus of Frankish Latin, as in Germany Hruotmar is Rudmar and Romar. Hromund, or Romund, must not be confused with the derivatives of Ragin, though it is most likely that the Irish Redmond is a Danish legacy from this source.

> Nor. Hrodbern—Famous bear
> Frank. Chrodogang—Famous progress
> Nor. Hrothild ; Ger. Hrodhilde ; Frank. Chrodehilda—
> Famous heroine
> Ger. Hrodfrid—Famous peace
> Ger. Hrodhard—Famous strength
> Ger. Hrudo ; Frank. Chrodo ; Nor. Hroi—Fame
> Nor. Hrodny—Famous freshness
> Nor. Hrollaug—Famous liquor
> Nor. Hrolleif—Relic of fame
> Nor. Hrodsind ; Frank. Chrodoswintha—Famous strength
> Ger. Hrodstein—Famous stone.

Ruod must have been evolved from the word meaning speech, *razda* in Gothic, *rædo* in Anglo-Saxon, whence advice became *rede* in Old English and Scottish, and *rath* in modern German.

Rad is chiefly a Frankish prefix, though we had one king Redwald. Radegond, or war council, was a Frankish queen who became a nun at Poitiers, and left a name still used by French girls in that neighbourhood. King Ordoño of Gallicia married, about the year 910, a lady recorded as Radegonda, or Arragonda, or Urraca, so that the perplexing Urraca may possibly be a contraction of this name. In the Spanish vernacular a magpie is called *urraca*, but probably from the likeness of the word to the note of the bird.

Radegist or Radelchis, and Radegar, were princes of Beneventum. Radbad, the Frisian Rabbo, and Radbert, seem to be Old German forms, but it is a word liable to be confused with *hramn*, and with *rand*, and though a common masculine termination in England, in the North it is only a corruption of *fred*, peace.

SECTION IV.—*Renaud.*

To the French, Renaud de Montauban was a far more popular and national hero than even Roland.

His name, Raginwald, was common among the Franks, and his origin is suspected to be an Aquitanian Rainaldus, who in 843 was killed in fighting with the Bretons, when in the miserable days of Charles the Bald, they invaded France under Nominoë, and were joined by the traitorous Count Lambert.

Charles the Bald, as has been said, seems to have sat for the picture of his grandfather, the Bretons turned into the Saracens, Count Lambert's treachery went to swell the account of Gano, and Rinaldus could fall at Roncevaux quite as well as at Mans!

He is just mentioned by Turpin as among the knights who accompanied Charlemagne, and were killed at Roncesvalles; and the Spanish ballads dwelt much upon the exploits of Don Reynaldos; indeed it appears that he enjoyed Don Quixote's special admiration for having carried off, in spite of forty Moors, a golden image of Mahomet, which he wanted to melt up for the payment of his men!

Such an exploit was decidedly in the line of the French hero Renaud, or Regnault, who is in romance a sort of prince of freebooters. He and his three brothers go by the title of the Quatre Fils Aymon, and he is a sort of chivalrous Robin Hood to the French mind, insomuch that country inns may still be found with the sign of the *Quatre Fils Aymon.* In the old French tale, the outlawry of Renaud is accounted for by his having been insulted by the emperor's nephew Berthelot, while playing at chess, and replying with a blow of the golden board that struck out the offender's brains. He and his brothers then lived a freebooting life, built the castle of Montalban in Gascony, the king of which country bestowed on him in marriage his daughter Clarice, and finally went on pilgrimage, made his peace with the emperor, turned his hand to the building of Cologne Cathedral, and was killed there by his jealous fellow-workmen.

In Italy Rinaldo became a wild, high-spirited Paladin, always fighting and falling in love, and retaining little in common with his French original, except the possession of his matchless horse Bayard, or Bajardo, which fought as well as his master, and on his loss ran wild in the woods. In the *Morgante*, Rinaldo mistrusts Gano, and avoids the ambush of Roncesvalles, but is afterwards carried with his brother Ricciardetto by two devils, to revenge the slaughter, which they do most effectually.

In the *Orlando Innamorato*, Rinaldo is at first ensnared by Angelica's beauty, but is cured by drinking unwittingly of the fountain of hate, while she drank of the fountain of love, and was enamoured of him. He is carried off by Malagigi to an enchanted island of delight, but returns during the great siege of Paris, takes a counter-draught of the fountain of love, fights in single combat with Ferrau, but is interrupted by Bajardo straying into a wood, whither he pursues the animal, and is there deserted by Boiardo, to be taken up by Ariosto, and after many adventures brought to relieve the Christian army in the utmost danger, and to give his sister Brada-mante in marriage to Ruggiero.

Some have thought that Tasso's one fictitious hero, Rinaldo, was partly borrowed from the Paladin, going as he does to the enchanted gardens of Armida, and being only brought back when the crusading host was in the utmost jeopardy. The chief mission of this latter Rinaldo was, however, it may be suspected, to be a compliment to the House of Este.

Some even think Roland himself only another version of Ragen-wald, but the one Paladin is undoubtedly traceable to Hruoland, as is the other to Ragenwald, though I am inclined to think that the Rolandsaulen, that accompany the Irminsaulen at the gates of old cities, may perhaps be rightly from Raginwald, judgment-power.

The Normans received this name from two sources, the French Regnault or Renaud, generally from the Paladin, and from their own northern Ragnwold or Rognwald. So Domesday has it in various forms, as Ragenald, Reynald, and Rainald, the latter fourteen times after the Conquest; and amongst them all we have derived our Christian name of Reginald, and the surname of Reynolds. The Scots took their form from the northern Rognvald, belonging to a great Jarl of the Orkneys, a noted skald, and thus obtained Ronald, which is in Gaelic Raonmill.

Ragn, or judgment, the leading word in this class of names, is connected with the Latin *rego*, to rule, and as *rectus* sprang from the one, so the Gothic *raihts* and our *right* arose from the Teutonic forms, as well as to *wreak*, and the German *rache*, vengeance, both from the old idea of justice. *Ragn*, though primarily meaning justice, is also used, as judgment is, in the sense of wisdom. Reginald Pole was in his own time known as Reynold. We get the longer name from his Latinism as Reginaldus.

Some of Renaud's freebooting fame may have come from a person whose name so closely resembles his own, that it is by no means easy to distinguish their progeny ; namely, Raginhard, or firm judge. A nobleman of this name was Count of the Palace, or Pfalzgraf, to Louis de Debonnaire, and engaged in a conspiracy against him, with

English.	Scottish.	Gaelic.	Italian.
Reginald	Ronald	Raonmill	Rinaldo
Reynold	Ranald		
Rex			

Spanish.	French.	German.	Polish.
Reynaldos	Regnauld	Reinwald	Raynold
	Renaud	Reinald	
	Regnault		

Esthonian.	Lettish.	Frisian.	
Rein	Reinis	Reinold	
Reino		Rennold	

Bernard, king of Italy. They were made prisoners, and condemned; the emperor commuted the sentence to the loss of their sight; but his wife, who wanted Bernard's inheritance, took care that so savage a person was sent to perform the operation that they both died in consequence.

Another Reginard is said by Le Grand to have been a cunning politician, who lived in Austrasia in the ninth century, and much troubled his lord by sometimes taking part with the Germans, sometimes with the French, by which means he became so much detested that he was the subject of many songs in which he was called the Little Fox. At any rate, in the great animal epic, the fox has taken the name of Reinart, or Reinecke Fuchs, and as early as 1313, when the sons of the wily Philippe le Bel were knighted, the edifying spectacle was represented before them of the life of Renard the Fox, who became successively physician, clerk, bishop, archbishop, and pope, eating however hens and chickens all the while, much after the fashion of their father's unhappy tool at Avignon. Renard has thus become the absolute name of the animal in France, to the entire exclusion of the ancient *golpe*, and in England Reynard is his universal epithet. It was not however confined to the creature, but was once prevalent among the human kind.

English.	French.	Provençal.	Italian.
Reynard	Regnard	Rainart	Rainardo
	Renart		

German.	Frisian.	Polish.	Hungarian.
Raginhart	Renert	Raynard	Reinhard
Reinhard	Rinnert		
Reineke	Rennart		
Renke	Rienit		
Renz			

Another old Frankish form is Raginmund, much in use in southern France, where there was a long line of counts of Toulouse, called Raymond, one of whom was celebrated by Tasso in the first Crusade as a gallant knight, but the last of whom, Raymond Berenger, one of the earliest examples of double names, went down before the sword of the first Simon de Montford, as a supporter of the Albigenses. The counts of Barcelona, in Spain, bore the like name, and the old Romanesque territories are still its usual home.

English.	Provençal.	Italian.	German.
Raymond	Raimons	Raimondo	Reinmund
			Reimund
French.	Spanish.		
Raimond	Ramon		

Terrible to us, but glorious to Denmark, was the name of Ragnar. Once we had it peacefully in East Anglia, as Raginhere, the warrior of judgment, but in that same East Anglia it was to have a deadly fame. The historical Ragnar seems to have been decorated with a few mythical exploits of some more ancient hero, for he is one of the dragon killers. His first wife, Thyra, had her bower encircled by a deadly poisonous serpent, the ravager of the whole country, until he won her hand by the slaughter of the serpent, having guarded himself from its venom by a suit of hairy garments covered with pitch, whence he obtained the soubriquet of Lodbrog. Afterwards he married a poor but beautiful maiden called Krake, who, after she had borne him four sons, disclosed that she was the last of the Wolsungen, the daughter of Sigurd and Brynhild. Nay, Icelandic families connect themselves through her with the heroes of Wurms ! And after this it is strange to find Jarl Ragnar sailing up the Seine, and ravaging Paris, in the days of Charles the Bald, being in fact the Agramante of the poets. Again he was the cause of bitter woe to England, falling into the hands of King Ælle of Northumbria, and being put to death by being thrown into a pit filled with vipers, where, till his last breath, he chanted the grand death song that is worthy to stand beside the dirge of King Eric Blödaxe. It was revenge for his death that brought his fierce sons with that dire armament which ravaged England—the invasion that was fatal to Edmund of East Anglia, ruined the great abbeys of the fens, and though finally mastered by Alfred, made the North of England Danish. This name of dread was brought to Normandy by his kindred, and figures in Domesday as Raynar, a frequent surname in England. In France it was cut down to René, a name that crept into the House of Anjou, and was bestowed on the prince—too much of a troubadour and knight-errant for a king—who vainly tried on so many crowns, and was hated in England because 'Suffolk gave two dukedoms for his daughter.' Why the feminine of this name, Renée, was chosen for the younger daughter of Louis XII., does not appear, but when she married into the House of Este, it was translated into Renata, and the Italians, in their revived classicalism, seem to have fancied it had some connection with regeneration. Renira is the Dutch feminine form.

English.	French.	Provençal.	German.
Rayner	Reignier	Raynier	Reiner
Rainer	Renier		
	René	Italian.	Nor.
		Renato	Ragnar
		Ranieri	

Raginmar, great judgment, still exists in Germany, as Reinmar, or Reimar, and is the most probable origin of the Ramiro, so frequent among the early kings of the small struggling Pyrenean realms.

Ragnhild, a favourite with old Norwegian dames, has become in Lapp, Ranna.

The German contraction *rein* has been often translated into pure, but this is an error, as these names can almost uniformly be traced back to *ragn*.

The remaining forms are—

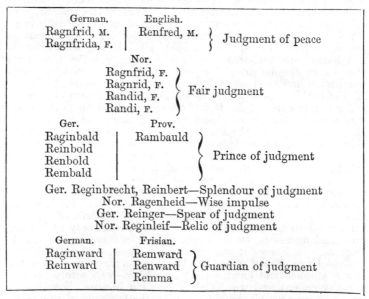

German.	English.	
Ragnfrid, M.	Renfred, M.	} Judgment of peace
Ragnfrida, F.		

Nor.
Ragnfrid, F.
Ragnrid, F. } Fair judgment
Randid, F.
Randi, F.

Ger.	Prov.	
Raginbald	Rambauld	
Reinbold		} Prince of judgment
Renbold		
Rembald		

Ger. Reginbrecht, Reinbert—Splendour of judgment
Nor. Ragenheid—Wise impulse
Ger. Reinger—Spear of judgment
Nor. Reginleif—Relic of judgment

German.	Frisian.	
Raginward	Remward	
Reinward	Renward	} Guardian of judgment
	Remma	

And lastly Regina, called in Bavaria Reigl and Regl, was originally less the Latin queen than the feminine of *ragn.* Nor in effect is the meaning far apart.*

Section V.—*Richard.*

Richard, or Richardet, was one of the Quatre Filz d'Aymon, who, according to one version, was the person who gave the fatal blow with the chess-board, instead of Renaud. He is not a very interesting personage, being rather the attendant knight than the prime hero, the rescued, not the rescuer ; but under his Italian name of Ricciardetto, he has a whole poem to himself, a mere scurrilous satire upon friars, and was the lowest depth to which romantic poetry fell.

It was not to this Paladin that his name owed its frequency, but to Ricehard, or stern king, an Anglo-Saxon monarch of Kent, who left his throne to become a monk at Lucca, and was there said to have wrought many miracles. The third Norman duke bore the name, and transmitted it to two successors, whence we obtained as many as twenty Richards at the Conquest, and have used it as a favourite national name ever since. Two more saints bore it, the excellent bishop of Chichester, and a hermit, who was made bishop of Andria, in Apulia. Three times has it been on the throne, though finally discarded by royalty after the enormities imputed to the last Plantagenet ; and latterly it has lost a little of its popularity, though it has never been entirely disused.

English.	French.	Italian.	Netherlands.
Richard	Richard	Riccardo	Rijkert
Ritchie (*Scot.*)		Ricciardo	Riikard
Diccon	Portuguese.	Ricciardetto	Riik
Dick	Ricardo		
	Polish.		
	Ryszard		

The leading syllable is from the same source as *ragn ;* it is he who executes judgment, the ruler or king, the same word as the Indian *rajah,* and the Latin *rex.* It was *reiks* in Gothic, *rich* in old German, *ryce* in Anglo-Saxon ; and its derivative *reich* was the origin of the Neustria and Austrasia, the *oster reich* and *ne oster reich,* eastern and not eastern, realms, of the Franks, and of the present Austria or eastern kingdom. *Reich* is the home term for the German empire at the present day. Our adjective *rich* is its sordid offspring, and in France a wealthy peasant is *un richart.*

Rik is more in vogue as a Gothic and Frank commencement than

* Roscoe, *Bojardo and Ariosto;* Sismondi, *Histoire de France;* Mallet; *Northern Antiquities; Spanish Ballads.*

among most of the other Teutons, though all use it as a conclusion. Richard is its only universal name ; but among the first foes of the Romans, we find among the Suevi, Rechiarius, who is the same with the German Richer, or kingly warrior, and the French saint, Riquier. Ricimar, the name of the terrible Goth who for a short time held Rome, is the great king, and was the maker and dethroner of the four last Augusti ; and his namesakes, Ricimer and Rechimiro, appear in Spain, and may, perhaps, be the right source of Ramiro. Recared, Richila, Riciburga, are also Gothic.

The Franks show Rigonthe, or royal war, a daughter of Frede-gonda ; Rictrude, a saint, as well as Richilde, also a queenly name, which continued for some time in use, and is better than the Richenza and Richarda, sometimes used in England as the feminines of Richard. Richolf endures in Friesland as Rycolf, Ryklof, or Rickel, and Germany once had Ricbert.

One great name of this derivation is the northern Eirik. The first syllable is that which we call *aye* to the present day, the word that lies at the root of the Latin *œvum*, the German *ewig*, and our own *ever*. Ei-rik is thus *Ever King*. An ancient Erik was said to have been admitted among the gods, and Earic was the second name of Æsc, the son of Henghist ; but it was the northern people who really used Eirik, which comes over and over in the line of succession of all the Northern sovereignties, figures in their ballads, and, in the person of King Eirik Blödaxe, is connected with their finest poetry. In the present day it is scarcely less popular than in old times, and has the feminine Eirika.

English. Erie	French. Eric	German. Erich	Nor. Eirik	Swedish. Erik
Polish. Eryk	Slovak. Erih Areh	Lettish. Erik	Esth. Erik Eers	Lapp. Keira

Two other names of the North have the same commencement, Eimund, ever protecting, or eternal guard, commonly called Emund, and Eilif, the ever-living, answering to the Greek Ambrosios. Eilif is also written Eiliv, Elliv, Ellef, and even Elof, and Latinized in Elavus.*

Section VI.—*Astolfo.*

Astolfo is to the Paladins what Conan is to the Feen, the butt or *grazioso*. In his full-blown perfection he is first cousin to Orlando, being the son of Milone's brother Ottone, and was also related to Rinaldo, according to the quaint genealogies of the chivalrous heroes that exact heraldry loved to draw up. He joined the four sons of

* Roscoe ; Munch ; Butler ; Michaelis.

Aymon, when they left the court after the quarrel at chess, and shared in their wild exploits; but apparently permitted no meaner interlopers in the trade, for when he caught a party of robbers, he insisted on some unfortunate hermits being their executioners, declaring such an office was quite as pleasing to Heaven, '*che dire il Pater nostro*,' and finally pummelling them into compliance.. In Bojardo, Astolfo gained possession of a magic lance, brought by Angelica from Catay, which unhorsed all its antagonists, and secure in its aid, refused when he was required to deliver up to Gradasso, Bajardo and Durindana, which had been left in his charge while their masters were wandering after Angelica, but challenged Gradasso to single combat, defeated him, and then went in search of his cousins. Ariosto conducts him into the enchanted palace, where every one was pursuing something lost; Rinaldo, his horse, Bradamante, Ruggero, Ruggero, Bradamante.

One blast of Astolfo's horn, also magical, destroyed the enchantment, and he became possessed for the time of the Hippogriff, upon whom he soared to the terrestrial paradise, and was conducted by St. John to the moon, where he obtained possession of Orlando's senses, and restored them to him. The later writers, who added to the burlesque element and diminished the chivalrous, made more and more of Astolfo's boastfulness, till he is quite the buffoon of their poems. He was finally killed at Roncesvalles; and the Spaniards call him Don Estolfo.

The person killed at the same time as Rotlandus is called, by Eginhard, Anselmus, and he, no doubt, contributed in the idea of the Astolfus, Count of Champagne, whose burial after the battle is recorded by Archbishop Turpin. But the real bearer of the name of Astolfo was one of the enemies of the Karlings, namely, Astolfo, king of the Lombards, who held his court at Pavia, and whose encroachments on the Roman territory were the first cause of the interference of the Franks in Italy. He was besieged by Pepin at Pavia in 755, and forced to come to terms; but he was evidently a very considerable sovereign; and Ernesto, Marchese d'Este, was killed in battle with him in 745. His promotion to be a Paladin is accounted for by his having been a Christian, and the character he bears, by the possibility of there having been satirical songs and poems upon him, especially at the time when Charlemagne ill-treated his granddaughter, Desirata. Astolfo is still a current name in Lombardy, though we do not find it anywhere else, and its congeners only in Scandinavia.

The meaning of the last syllable is, of course, wolf; the first is *aast* or *ast*, love or wishes, or if the sense of hot impetuosity be allowed, Astolf is the swift wolf. Aasta was rather a favourite name with the maidens of the North, and Asta is not disused, though too often treated as the short for Augusta.

Astridur is from *hridhur*, an impulse, and thus would mean swift impulse, or the impulse of love. It was greatly used by the royal ladies of the North, among whom may be specified the mother of St. Olaf, and a daughter of Knut, called by Danish pronunciation, Estridh, but transmuted into Margaret.

The diminutive of Ast, under various mispronunciations, named that most terrible of vikings, Hasting, whose ravages, though kept from England by the policy originated by Alfred, were fearful all along the French coast, and even extended to Italy. It is he who is said to have many times submitted to baptism, and then returned to his fury again ; and there is a curious report, that Rollo's Normans found him settled in France, and reproached him with the tameness of his old age, so that he dashed away again, and returned to his ships and his piracy. Hastinc occurs in Domesday, and Warren Hastings' family claimed descent from the old Sea King.*

Section VII.—*Ogier le Danois.*

One of the Paladins was, undoubtedly, the legacy of a much more ancient myth, namely, Ogier le Danois. He does not play a very prominent part in the poems of the Italians, but as Ogier the Dacian he is one of Turpin's catalogue of knights, and a ballad especially dear to Don Quixote thus commences :—

> 'De Mantua sale el Marques,
> Danes Urgel el leal.'

It proceeds to tell how he found Valdovinos, his nephew, dying under a tree, having been assassinated by the emperor's son, Carloto. The ballad further relates how the Marques proceeds to court, gets Carloto tried by his peers and doomed to death, and though el Rey Carlo banishes them all for uttering the condemnation, the sentence is carried out.

This Italian marquis is an exceedingly droll development of the old Teutonic hero, Holger Danske. In Italy he is Oggieri, Oggero, or Uggieri il Danese ; in French, Ogier le Danois ; and, at times, *le damné*, or *il dannato*, which title is further accounted for by the story that he was a Saracen who became a Christian, and that his friends wrote from home ' *tu es damné*,' whence he chose to be thus christened. In the *Reali de Francia*, Charlemagne cuts off, with his own hand, the head of an unfortunate Oldrigi, whose blood was too noble to be shed by any one else. Now this Oggier was without doubt a contribution from the stores of Norman tradition ; for Holger, or Olger, Danske is the grandest national hero of Denmark. There is a ballad, given by Weber, where he and Tidrek the Strong have a tremendous battle, and he comes off victor. Moreover, he has eaten of the fruit of the trees of the sun and moon, and has become immortal, and there he sits with his fellows in the vaults of the Castle of Kronberg, near which are two ponds, called his spectacles. A peasant, with a plough-share on his shoulders, once lost his way, and wandered in ; he found a circle of tall old men in armour, all asleep round a stone table, with their heads resting on their crossed arms. Holger Danske, who sat at the head of the table, raised his head and the stone broke asunder,

---

* Roscoe; Sismondi; Munch; Michaelis; *Histoire de Normandie.*

for his beard had grown into the stone. He asked his guest some questions about the upper world and dismissed him, offering his hand. The peasant, dreading the gigantic grip of the old champion, gave his ploughshare. 'Ha! ha!' said Holger, as he felt its firmness, 'it is well. There are still men in Denmark. Tell them that we shall come back when there are no more men left than can stand round one tun!' But the ploughshare had been twisted round by his fingers. Can this return of Holger be the Roger Bon Temps of the French peasantry?

But Holger, though I have placed him among the Paladins, might have gone even farther back than the days of Dietrich. He is a mythical king, well nigh a god, originally called Haaloge, and owing, as his sacred island, Haalogaland, or Heligoland.

His name itself is *holy*, our very word *holy*—the *halig* of the Anglo-Saxons, the *hellig* of the North, the *heilig* of Germany, and these words sprang from those denoting health; as the Latin *salve*, hail, *salvus*, safe, and *salvatio*, safety, are all related to soundness.

Leaving this, as not belonging to our main subject, we find that Helgi, the Norse form of the word for this holy old mythic king, was exceedingly popular in the North. Helgi has a poem to himself in the elder *Edda*. A son of Burnt Njal was called Helgi, and forty-two cases are found of the name in the *Landnama-bok*, and thirty-four of its feminine, Helga. In Domesday there are five called Helgi, besides fourteen Algars, very possibly meant for Holger; and it may be suspected that the Helie of the early Norman barons may have been as much due to the Helgi of their forefathers as to the prophet whom they learnt to know on Mount Carmel. Perhaps, too, Helga was the source of Ala, or Ela, by which name a good many Norman ladies are recorded, the best known of whom was Ela, heiress of Salisbury, the wife of one William Longsword and mother of the other, one of the founders of Salisbury Cathedral, and the witness of a vision of her son's death in Egypt.

Helgi's descendants towards the East are far more certain matters. Helgi, called Oleg by the Russian historians, was the son of Rurik, the first Norman grand prince of Kief, and his daughter, Olga, visited Constantinople, and was there baptized by the name of Helena, which makes the Russians suppose her two names to translate one another; but they have fortunately not discarded either Oleg or Olga, which thus remain mementoes of the northern dynasty among the very scanty number of Russian names that are neither Greek nor Slavonic.

In its own country Helgi gets contracted into Helle, and Helga into Hæge.*

Section VIII.—*Louis.*

With the throne of the Franks, the Karlingen took their favourite prefix of the old Salic line, *hlod.*

This word, the same in root as the Sanscrit *çru*, Greek κλύω (kluo), Latin *cluo*, Anglo-Saxon *hlowan*, may possibly have been originated

* Munch; Roscoe; Keightley; Marryat, *Jutland.*

by the cow, to whose voice, in our own language, the verb *to low* is now restricted. All mean to make a noise ; and the dignity of that noise increased, for κλυτός (klutos) was Greek for renowned, κλέος, fame, as we saw when dealing with Cleomenes, Cleopatra, &c. ; and in Latin, *clueo*, was to be famous, *clientes* or *callers* beset the honoured man, and *laus* was praise or fame ; and so not only have we *loud* in English, *lyde* in the North, for the ordinary adjective, but *hlod* or *hlud* was the old German term for renown, and *los* for which French knights afterwards fought and bled, and a score of other words, less relevant to our purpose, will easily suggest themselves as current in every European tongue, first cousin words from *laus* or from *hlod*.

The rough aspirate at the beginning was once an essential portion of the word, and among the Franks it must have been especially harsh, since their contemporary Latinists always render it by *ch.*

Chlodio, as they call him, is numbered as the second of the long-haired Salians, the father of ' Meroveus,' and leader of the incursions of the Franks about 428. His grandson married the Burgundian maiden, called by the Valkyr title of Hlodhild, or Chlodechilda, as the Latin civilization of her day called her, when it hailed her with delight as the converter of her husband to Christianity. Although canonized, her name was not in great use for a good many generations, and to this she probably owes it that, when it was revived as belonging to a royal saint, for the benefit of the daughter of the good dauphin, son of Louis XV., it had not been shorn of its aspirate like all the cognate ones. It has since become a favourite with French ladies.

French.	Italian.	German.
Clotilde	Clotilda	Klothilde

The husband of Clotilda was known to his own fierce Franks as Hluodowig, or famous war, or consecration ; but when his success after his prayer to the God of Hluodhild had brought him to abjure his Teuton gods, and receive baptism from St. Remi, the pope accepted the only orthodox sovereign of Europe as most Christian king and eldest son of the Church by the appellation of Chlodovisus, or Clovis, the retranslation into French.

Among his successors was found many a *fainéant* who had nothing of him but his prefix and his long hair, and one who is counted as Clovis II. When these had passed away, Charles the Great gave the name of the great founder of the former line to one of his younger sons, the only one who lived to succeed him.

What Hlodwig Haman's War was called in his own day may be seen by the curious barbaric Latin poem sung by his soldiers in honour of their exploit in setting him at liberty, when he had been treacherously made prisoner by Adelgis, Duke of Beneventum, a song that shows Latin in its first step towards the tongues of southern Europe.

> ' Audite omnes fines terre errore cum tristitia,
> Quale scelas fuit factum in civitas Beneventum
> Lluduicum comprenderunt, sancto pio Augusto.'

'Lluduicus' is now known to the French as Louis le Debonnaire, a title that some ascribe to his piety, others to his weakness. The Germans took him as Ludwig, and thenceforth these two varieties held a double course, while the softer Provençals made him Aloys, which is now regarded, owing to a saint of its own, as a separate name. Three monarchs of the Karling line bore this favourite name, and the fifth descendant of Hugh Capet brought it in again, to come to its especial honour with the saintly Crusader, ninth king so called, from whom it became so essentially connected with French royalty, that after the succession of the Bourbons, no member of the royal family was christened without it. Indeed, hardly any one of rank or birth failed to have it among their many names, till its once-beloved sound became a peril to the owners' heads in the Revolution, and it has in the present day arrived at sharing the unpopularity of François.

Elsewhere it is chiefly a French importation ; the Welsh use Lewis as an Anglicism of Llewellyn, and the Irish of Lachtna ; and the Scots make rather more use of it from their old alliances and connection through the Scottish guard. The Scottish Lodowick is probably taken from the northern form of the original word ; just as with the Italians, Luigi is the mere Italian version of Louis, Lodovico the inheritance from the Lombards or Germans, and in this shape was long current in northern Italy, belonging in particular to the unfortunate Sforza, of Milan, who perished in the first shock between France and Italy.

English.	Breton.	Scottish.	French.
Ludovick	Loiz	Lodowick	Clovis
Lewis	Loizik		Louis
Louis			Looys
			Loys

Provençal.	Italian.	Spanish.	Portuguese.
Aloys	Lodovico	Clodoveo	Luiz
Chlodobeu	Luigi	Luis	
Lozoic	Aloïsio		

German.	Swiss.	Swedish.	Dutch.
Ludwig	Ludi	Ludwig	Lodewick
Luz			Lood
Lotze	Bavarian.		
	Wickl		

Polish.	Bohemian.	Slovak.	Hungarian.
Ludvik	Ludvik	Ludvick	Lajos
Ludvis		Ljudevit	

The Provençal Aloys apparently was the first shape that threw out a feminine, the Aloyse or Heloïse, whose correspondence with Abelard was the theme of so much sentiment, and whose fame, brought by the archers to Scotland, no doubt was the origin of the numerous specimens of Alison found in that romantic nation. According to Dugdale, the wife of the Norman William Mallet was Hesilia or Helewise, no doubt the same as Heloïse. Heloïse had nearly died away in France when Rousseau's romance of *La Nouvelle Heloïse* brought it as well as Julie into fashion again.

The votaresses of St. Louis had, however, chosen to come much nearer to his name, and by the end of the fifteenth century Louise was in great vogue at the French court ; it travelled everywhere with French princesses, came to us with the House of Hanover, and has now a thorough hold of all ranks.

English.	French.	Italian.	Spanish.
Louisa	Louise	Luisa	Luisa
Louie	Lisette	Eloïsa	
	Loulou		Portuguese.
Scotch.	Heloise		Luiza
Leot	Louison		Luizinha
Alison			
Ailie			

German.	Swedish.	Polish.	Lettish.
Ludowicke	Ludovica	Ludvika	Lusche
Luise	Lovisa	Ludoisia	Lasche
	Lova	Lodoiska	Lawise

The eldest son of the great Clovis was Hlodmir, or Clodomir, great fame, made more euphonious in German as Ludomir, and furnishing such surnames as Luttmer and Lummers.

All his sons were murdered by their uncles, except one, who was shorn of his long locks to save his life, and was put into a convent, where he became a holy man, was canonized, and his harsh name of Hlodowald, or Clodvald, became the pleasant one of St. Cloud, best known for the sake of the palace near Paris. Another St. Chlodvald, of Metz, is commonly called St. Clou.

One of the uncles who killed the poor boys was Hlodhari, or Chlotachari, famous warrior, a terrible savage, but the last survivor of the brothers, and counted in the Frank history as Chlother, or Clotaire. Others of his race likewise were so baptized, and when the name passed to the Karlingen it was as Lothar. So was called the son of Louis le Debonnaire, whose portion, known at first as Lotharingen, came to be in Latin Lotharingia, and still remains Lorraine. Lothar did not pass away from Germany ; one emperor, after the separation, was so called ; and it fell into many forms of surnames, in especial into Luther ; and when Martin Luther had rendered this almost saintly to his countrymen, they over-hastily explained it by *lother*, pure ; while the Bohemians found a similar word in their own tongue, meaning a swan. Oddly enough, Huss signified a goose, and the saying arose that the Bohemian goose had let fall a quill, which had been picked up by a swan of far more distant flight.

Luther has a few namesakes in his own country on his own account, but, in general, Chloter has died out of Christian nomenclature.

English.	French.	German.	Spanish.
Lothario	Clotaire	Lothar	Clotario
Lowther	Lothaire	Luther	
			Lettish.
		Italian.	Lutters
		Lotario	

Chlodoswintha, or famous height, was a Frank princess, without namesakes beyond her own race ; in fact, the use of this prefix seems to have been exclusively Frank.*

* Sismondi, *Histoire des François, Littérature du Midi de l'Europe ;* Friedrich Pott ; Michaelis ; Thierry, *Récits des Temps Mérovingien.*

CHAPTER VI.

Section I.—*Nobility.*

THE names connected with any great cycle of interest have been nearly exhausted, and only those remain that seem to have been chosen more for sense than connection, though afterwards continued for the sake of their owners. Several of our own truly English or Anglo-Saxon names are among these, and in especial those with the prefix meaning noble, Æthel, Athel, Adel, Edel, or in High German, Adal. It is thought to come from the universal word *atta*, a father, and thus to convey that the owner has forefathers, the essence of nobility, as with the *pater* and patrician of Rome, and the *hidalgo*, the son of something, of Spain. Adel, or Æthel, is a favourite prefix in all the Teutonic branches except the Scandinavian, where it does not occur at all. It is essentially Gothic,—witness Athalaric, the formidable but gentle conqueror of Rome, who well deserved his name of Noble-King. He is generally, however, called Alaric, and his name has been deduced from *al*, all ; but the right reading seems to be that which indentifies his appellation with our own English Æthelric, and the Uadalrich of Germany.

Udalrich, archbishop of Augsburg till the year 973, is notable as the first person canonized by the pope according to the present forms, which could not, however, have included the half-century of posthumous probation, as he was placed in the calendar only twenty years after his death. Contracting his name to Ulrich, Germany made him a favourite national saint ; and we find him and his feminine spread throughout the countries influenced by the empire, and the feminine particularly prevalent in Denmark, whither it was carried by German queens. Though the ensuing table places all the forms of Athalaric together, it should be kept in mind that the forms beginning with *A* are the modern namesakes of the great Goth, those with *U* and *O* the votaries of that saint, and Adelrich is considered as a different name from Ulrich.

The successor of Alaric, who laid him in his river-grave, is known to us as Ataulfus. In his own time he was Athaulf, the Noble-Wolf, and his likeness stands in our own roll of English kings as the father of Alfred, namely, Æthelwulf ; but this good old name was dropped in England, while its German cousin, in honour of a sainted bishop of Metz, of the ninth century, became very common in the principalities of the empire, and was imported with the house of Hanover in the barbarous Latin form of Adolphus. Its feminine, coined in

English.	French.	Italian.	German.
Æthelric	Alaric	Alarico	Adelrich
Alaric	Ulric	Ulrico	Alarich
Ulrick	Olery		Uadalrich
			Ulrich
			Alerk
			Oelric

Bavarian.	Swedish.	Frisian.	Swiss.
Rickel	Alarik	Ulrik	Uoli
	Ulrik	Olrick	Ueli
		Ulerk	Uerech
		Ulk	
		Ucko	
		Ocko	

Polish.	Bohemian.	Slovak.	Lettish.
Ulryk	Ulric	Ureh	Uldriks
	Oldrich	Ulrih	

FEMININE.			

German.	French.	Roman.	Polish.
Ulrike	Ulrique	Ulrica	Ulryka

Germany, is Adolfine, usually called Dofine, and now extremely common. This may possibly be the source of the Dolphine given as the name of one of the daughters of Waltheof, Earl of Northumbria, as the habit of making barbarous feminines was just beginning in her time.

English.	French.	Italian.	German.	Finn.
Ethelwolf	Adolphe	Adolfo	Adolf	Ato
Adolphus		Udolfo	Odulf	Atu
Dolph				

Athanagild, or Athalagild, Noble Pledge, was another of these early Goths, and afterwards we meet the same meaning in Adelgis, or Adelchis, the brave son of the last Lombardic king, whose noble spirit, under his misfortunes, is the subject of a fine tragedy of Manzoni. The duke of Beneventum, who made Louis le Debonnaire prisoner, was Adelgis ; but it is curious to find the soldiers in the dog-latin poem above alluded to, terming him Adalfieri. Odelgis was old High German.

Æthel was so much used by the royal families of Kent and Wessex, that the diminutive, Ætheling, was latterly applied to designate the heir to the crown, and was thus continued even after the Conquest to the son of Henry I., who perished in the white ship.

Æthelbryht, or Noble Splendour, named our first Christian king of Kent, also a brother of King Alfred's, and a missionary of the royal blood of Northumbria, who preached in southern Germany, and died about the year 700, at Egmond, where, as St. Adelbrecht, he became patron. His name was taken at baptism by one who became archbishop of Magdeburg, who, in his turn, bestowed it on his pupil, the Bohemian Woyteich, Army-Help. This convert was afterwards bishop of Prague, and was martyred near Dantzic while preaching to the heathen Prussians in 997. Adelbrecht could not fail to become national wherever the saint had set his foot ; and when shortened to Albrecht, was adopted by Italy, and thence sent to Jerusalem with a Latin patriarch, who, being beatified, rendered Alberto freshly popular in the South. Albrecht, and the feminines Alberta and Albertine, were, however, almost entirely German, until the late Prince Consort brought the name to England, where it bids fair to become one of the most frequent of national names. Some fancy it comes from Allbright ; but the German saints, whence it was taken, are evidently direct from our English Æthelbryht, though in Germany Adelbert and Albrecht are now treated as two separate names. Bela, which belonged to an excellent blind king of Hungary, is believed to be the Magyar form of the name.

English.	French.	Provençal.	Italian.
Ethelbert	Albert	Azalbert	Alberto
Albert	Aubert		Albertino
	Albret		
	Aubertin		

German.	Wallachian.	Finn.	Danish.
Adalbert	Averkie	Alpu	Albert
Albrecht			Bertel
Ulbricht	Polish.		
	Albert		
	Olbracht		

Æthelred, Noble-speech or counsel, the brother of Alfred, was almost canonized by his subjects, and is sometimes called Ethered, whence the Scottish Ethert. The nickname of our last Ethelred was a play on his name "onreade," not meaning so much tardy as without counsel—Noble-rede the Un-reedy. Ethelred must not be confused with Etheldred, the feminine name, properly Æthelthryth, meaning in Anglo-Saxon the Noble-threatener, connected with the German Ediltrud, or noble maiden. Most likely names ending in *trut* had been brought to England, and as the Valkyr sense was forgotten, the native meaning of *threat* was attached to the word, and the spelling adapted to it. St. Æthelthryth was a queen who must have been a very uncomfortable wife, and who, finally, retired into a monastery, getting canonized as St. Etheldreda, and revered as St. Audry. From the gewgaws sold at her fairs some derive the term tawdry ; and, at any rate, Awdry has never been extinct as a name among the peasantry, and has of late been revived, though with less popularity than the other more modern contraction, Ethel, which is sometimes in modern times set to stand alone as an independent name. Addy is the common Devonian short for Audrey.

Germans do, however, seem to have used the word without another syllable, for Adilo, or Odilo, was an old name, and Ado and Addo are still current in Friesland, no doubt, the same as the Ade of the Cambrian registers. Adela and Adèle, too, occur very early ; indeed, there is reason to think that just as in England the son was the Ætheling, in Frankland the daughter was the Adalheit, or the Adelchen. This word *heit* is translated as the root of the present German *heiter*, cheerful, and thus would mean noble cheer ; but I suspect it is rather *heid*, condition, answering to the *hood* or *head* at the end of our abstract nouns, *e. g.* hardihood, and that the princess royal of each little Frankish duchy or county was thus the 'Nobleness' thereof.

All the feudal princes of the tenth and eleventh centuries seem to have had an Adelheid to offer in marriage, and to have Latinized her in all manner of ways, while practically they called her Alix (or Alisa in Lombardy), a name that was naturalized in England, when *Alix la Belle* married Henry I. Alice is our true English form, though it has been twisted into Alicia, and then referred for derivation to the Greek Alexios, so as often to appear in Latin documents of the later middle ages in the form of Alexia ; whereas in earlier times, before its origin was forgotten, it is translated by Adelicia, Adelisa, or Adelidis.

English.	French.	Provençal.	Italian.
Adelaide	Adelaide	Azalaïs	Adelaïda
Adeline	Adeline		Alisa
Adeliza	Adelais		
Adela	Adèle		
Alice	Alix		
Alicia	Aline		
Elsie			
German.	Netherlands.	Slovak.	Lettish.
Adelheid	Adelheid	Adelajda	Audule
Adeline	Adelais		Addala
Adele			
Else			
Ilse			

The French made great use of all the forms of the name ; the

Germans, in honour, perhaps, of the Italian Queen Adelaide—whose adventures before her marriage with the Emperor Otho were so curious—preferred that variety, and from them we received it again with our good Queen Adelaide, from whom it is becoming frequent amongst us. The German Alice is Else, a favourite old peasant word. This same contraction is common in northern England, but gets confused with Elizabeth, as in Scotland, with Alison ; and in Ireland, the prevalent Alicia is, perhaps, meant for Aileen, or Helen.

The Adeleve of early Norman times is probably meant for Æthelgifu, Noble-gift, a frequent Saxon lady's name, which we generally call Ethelgiva.

Æthelwold, the Saxon historian of royal blood, is Noble-power. Æthelheard, or noble resolution, answers to Adelhard, a cousin of Charlemagne, and abbot of Corbie, whom his contemporaries glorified as at once the Augustin, the Antony, and the Jeremiah of his day, and who, being canonized, left Alard and Alert to Friesland, and Aleardo, Alearda to Provence.

Æthelstan, the Noble-stone or jewel, was second only to Alfred in ability and glory, and his name lived on to the Conquest, when it is set down as Adestan and Adstan.

Adelhelm, the Noble-helmet, named the excellent and poetical Aldhelm, bishop of Sherborn, from whom the headland on the Dorset coast was once called St. Aldhelm's head, but is now corrupted into St. Alban's head.

Adelgar, or Noble-spear, was chiefly continental, first figuring in the beautiful Scottish ballad of *Sir Aldingar*, but better known in Lombardy, where Allighero sprang from it, and gave his patronymic to Dante Alighieri. Algarotti was another Italian derivative ; and in France, Augier and Augereau ; in Germany, Oehlkar, show that it once must have been much in use. It is not always easy, however, to separate between the words from Adel and from Hilda. The remaining varieties are—

Ger. Adelar—Noble eagle
Ger. Adelbar, Alpero—Noble bear
Ger. Adelbold ; Eng. Æthelbald—Noble prince
Ger. Odelburga } Noble defence
Eng. Æthelburg }
Eng. Æthelburh—Noble pledge

German.

Adelfrid ⎫
Adalfrid ⎪
Ulfrid ⎬ Noble peace
Ulfert ⎪
Olfert ⎭

Eng. Æthelfledh—Noble increase
Ger. Adelgard—Noble protection
Ger. Adelgund ; Fr. Adelgonde—Noble war

> Ger. Adelhild—Noble heroine
> Ger. Udalland, Uland—Noble land
> Ger. Adelinde, Odelind ; Eng. Ethelind (*mod.*)—Noble snake
> Ger. Adelmann, Ullman—Noble man
> Ger. Adelmund ; Eng. Edelmund (*Domes.*)—Noble protection
> Ger. Adelmar ; Eng. Ethelmar ; Fr. Ademar, Adhemar—
>   Noble greatness
> Ger. Adelschalk—Noble servant
> Ger. Adelswind—Noble strength
> Ger. Adeltac—Noble day*

Section II.—*Command.*

The Gothic *bidyan* has resulted in our verb *to bid*, the German *baten*, the Danish *byde*, besides *bote*, a messenger, and the *budstick*, bidding-stick, or summons to the muster.

All these were in the sense of command ; but from the same root grew the race of entreating words, the Scandinavian *bede*, German *bitten*, and English *beg*. When these entreaties were devotional, the Germans made the verb *beten*, and our term for prayer, *bede*, passed on to the mechanical appliance for counting beads—the *beads* of the rosary, while the pensioner bound to pray for his benefactor was his *bedesman*.

It is doubtful whether this, or the Welsh *bedaws*, life, gave his name to the Venerable Bæda, but no doubt to himself and his contemporaries it suggested the idea of prayer. There is no doubt, however, in the case of Baudhildur, or Bathilda (the commanding heroine), the daughter of king Nidudr, the lady whom Volundr carried off with him when he fled from her mother's cruelty. After her was called Bathilda, an Anglo-Saxon slave, who was elevated to be the wife of the second Hluodwig, and lived so holy a life, and exerted herself so much to obtain the redemption of slaves, that she was canonized, and, as *la reine Bathilde*, was greatly venerated in the believing days of France. Denmark also used this name, having probably taken it from England. There 'Dronning Bothild,' the wife of king Ejegod, spread the name among the maidens, so that it passed to Norway as Bodild, Bodil, and even to the contraction Boel.

Of English birth, too, was the Commanding-wolf—Bedvuolf, or Bodvulf—who, with his brother, St. Adolf, went, about the end of the sixth century, to seek religious instruction in Gallia-Belgica. Adolf became bishop of Maestricht, and eponym to the Adolphuses. Bodvulf came home, and founded the monastery of Ikano, where he died in 655, and was canonized. The monastery was destroyed by the Danes, and the situation forgotten, but the saint's relics were carried away by the fugitive monks, and dispersed into various quarters, giving title to four churches in London, besides St. Botolf's

---

* Pott; Michaelis; Lappenburg; Butler; Palgrave; Turnner.

bridge, commonly called Bottlebridge, in Huntingdonshire, and St.
Botolf's town, in Lincolnshire, usually known as Boston, whence was
called its American cousin Boston, with little relation to the saint.
The tower of the church of St. Botolf, looking forth over the Wash,
was a valued landmark, and thence the saint was apparently viewed
as a friend of travellers, and connected with the entrances to cities,
much as St. Christopher is elsewhere. Camden even supposed him
to be Boathulf, or boat helper, and his day, the 17th June, is a market
day in Christiania, under the term of Botolsok, or Botsok. In Jutland there is a church of St. Botolv ; and in the North the names of
Botol and Bottel are kept up ; while, in England, there only remain
to us the surnames of Bottle and Biddulph. The Old German forms
of the two names above-mentioned are Botzhild, Botzulf ; and Botzo,
or Boso, a Commander, was now and then used as a name with them,
as in the instance of the troublesome duke of Burgundy, whom
French historians generally call Boson, and who is apt to be translated by *böse*, wicked.

Boto, Botho, Poto, are also found in Germany, and the very earliest
specimen of this class of name is to be found in Botheric, commanding king, the name of the governor whose murder in the hippodrome
caused Theodosius to give his bitterly repented command for the
massacre of Thessalonica. Now and then *bot* occurs at the end of a
word, as in the Spanish prince Sisebuto, the messenger of victory, or
victorious commander.

These are not the same with some that look much like them,
derived from the Northern *bφd*, German *badu*, A.G.S. *beado*, war.
Beadwig, in the Wodenic ancestry, is thus battle war, and the Gothic
king of Italy, Totila, is probably made by the Romans from Bφdvhar,
battle pleader, a name still used in the North as Bφdvar. Bφdmod,
Bφdulf, and Bφdhild, or Bφdvild, have also been in use.*

Section III.—*Brightness.*

The root *brâj* furnished the Greek φλέγειν, Latin *flagrare*, and
Gothic *bairht*, the Anglo-Saxon *beohrt*, or *byrht*, the Old German
percht, and Northern *bjart*.

It is a component of Frank, German, and Anglo-Saxon nomenclature, but is rarely found in genuine Norsk ; the only instance in the
Landnama-bok is Biartmar, who is noted as of Irish birth, so may
have brought an Anglo-Saxon name.

Bertha, the most obvious of all the progeny of *biart*, has been
treated of in her character as a personification of the bright Epiphany
night, mixed up with an old epithet of Frigga and with the spinning
Holda. So, in Swabia, these legends have formed a masculine,
Berchthold, who has become the wild huntsman in that quarter.
Berchtvold was really an English prince of the Heptarchy, and

* Munch ; Michaelis ; Pott ; Sismondi ; Butler ; Camden ; Le Beau ;
Kemble.

Brichtold is in Domesday. Perahtholt is a veritable Old German name, making the modern Bartold—Niebuhr's name,—the Italian Bertaldo, and French Bertould. Bertalda is not so likely to be the feminine of this word as to come from Berchthilda, like the name of Bertille, a sainted abbess of Chelles.

It is not easy to discover whether the most popular of all thus commencing should be regarded as a single corrupted name, or the produce of two, of which one has the second syllable *hramn*, a raven, the other *rand*, a house. The patron saint of all alike is Bertich-ramnus, bishop of Mans till 623, and his Latinism leaves no doubt that he was Bright-raven. It was chiefly popular in France, whence we must have obtained it, although there is no instance of it in Domesday, and it was especially glorious in the fourteenth century, for the sake of gallant Constable du Guesclin, 'the eagle of Brittany,' whom Spanish chroniclers, by a droll perversion of his appellation, called 'Mosen Beltran Claquin,' when he came to fight their battles.

English.	Scotch.	French.	Provençal.	Italian.
Bertram	Barthram	Bertrand	Bertran	Bertrando

Spanish.	Portuguese.	German.	Lusatian.	Hungarian.
Beltran	Bertrao	Bertram Berdrand	Batram Batramusch	Bertok

The wolf was sure to accompany the raven; so Perahtolf, or Bertulf, was canonized as an abbot in Artois, and left the German Bertulf, and our own Bardolph, the flaming comrade of Falstaff.

Bertwine, or Bright friend, was the St. Bertin of France, and the Bertuccio of Italy, often found in the old Lombardic towns.

Brihtric was the English earl who so gallantly died in defending England from the Danes in the unhappy days of Ethelred the Unready, and another Brihtric was the unsuccessful suitor of Matilda of Flanders, on whom she wreaked an unworthy vengeance after the Conquest. All the Brihts in Domesday seem to be of Saxon birth, since they use the English instead of the Norman French commence-ment, which was already *Ber*, as in the instance of Bertrade de Montfort, Bright speech, the countess of Anjou, who deserted her husband for Philippe I. of France. The remaining forms are—

Ger. Bertar ; Fr. Berthier—Bright warrior

Eng. {
Brichteva—Bright gift
Bricfrid—Bright peace
Brichtmar—Bright fame
Brichsteg—Bright warrior
Britfleda—Bright increase
Brichstan—Bright stone
Bricsteg—Bright maid
}

Ger. Bertrud—Bright maid

Bert is one of the most indispensable conclusions among all the German range of names, and is far more common there than as a commencement.

Another word meaning bright, or glittering, is the Northern *jar, jor, jer*, the German *ir*. Iring, or Irinc, is a semi-mythological person. Old German tradition declared him to have been the counsellor of Irnvrit of Thuringia, and that when both had been taken by the Franks, he was deceived into slaying his sovereign, after which, in his rage, he killed the victorious Frank, laid him under his master's body, and then cut his way through the enemy, and returned home.

He appears again in the *Nibelungen-noth* as the Markgraf Irinch of Tenemarche, or Denmark, in company with Irnvrit of Düringen, *i.e.* Thuringia : he wounds Hagen, but is slain by him, and lamented over by Kriemhild. His name was sometimes subsequently used, and is, perhaps, what French histories call Harenc.

Jørund is a northern name with a similar prefix, and means a brilliant or glittering man ; but it gets called Jøren, and mixed up with Jorgen, or George.*

SECTION IV.—*War.*

In Ulfilas' Bible, 'the multitude of the heavenly host' is translated '*Haryis hunniakundis managei.*' In Anglo-Saxon, an army is *here*, in old German *heri*, in the North *her*, all perhaps coming from the ear, and *to hear*, as having been summoned, like the legion from being chosen. Thence the leader was the English Heretoga, and German Herzog, finally translated into the Latin *dux*, and becoming political and territorial. The doings of the *herr* were expressed by various old words, of which the Scottish *to harry* is the direct descendant. *Heerfurst*, or army leader, may be the Ariovistus of Cæsar.

The single warrior was *har* in the North, *hari* in Germany, and as *ar* is often found at the end of names. Many German critics translate the word by the army, instead of the warrior ; but Professor Munch considers that the warrior, *hari*, was the original meaning, and that *herjar*, his plural, afterwards came to mean the army.

The oldest and most famous of all the family is introduced to us by Tacitus as Chariovalda, a Batavian prince. It is the hardened sound of Harivald, Warrior power, or 'Army wielder,' a name that the Germans soon called Heriold, and the North Harald. This soon became one of the most renowned northern names. Harald Harfagre, or the fair-haired, was he who vowed never to trim his locks till he was sole king of Norway, and thus sent Thorer the Silent to Iceland, and Rolf-ganger to Normandy. Harald Krake, king of Sleswig, was baptized in the presence of Louis le Debonnaire, and used the already

* Grimm, *Deutcher Mythologie, Deutche Heldensage ;* Munch ; Alban Butler ; Sismondi ; *Ayale-y-z-urita.*

mentioned vow to forsake Thunner, Seaxnot, and all their works. He afterwards introduced St. Anschar to Denmark, but like all the first Christian kings of Scandinavia, was himself expelled from his realm by his subjects. Harald Hardrada, or the resolute, was the very crown of the poetic sea-kings of Norway, meeting with romantic adventures in Constantinople, singing the praises of his Russian bride all across the sea, exchanging gallant messages with his namesake Harold God-winson at Stamford Bridge, and dying as poetically as he had lived at the foot of his banner Landwaster. It was from the Danes that Harold came to England with the son of Knut, and to the son of Earl Godwin, the usurper, more than half a Dane in blood and temper, who, because he died in battle with the Normans, is regarded by the popular mind as an English patriot, and has in very modern times had a good many namesakes. Harald, or, as the Frisians call it, Herold, is only properly national in Scandinavia and the islands from Iceland to Man.

Next in note is what the Franks called Charibert, when it belonged to the king of Paris, whose daughter brought Christian doctrine to Kent, and prepared the way for St. Augustine. St. Haribert was archbishop of Cologne about the year 1000, and at that time the name became extremely common among the French nobility. A Norman settler had brought it to England even in the time of Edward the Confessor ; and one of the many Herberts founded a family in Wales, which, in the time of Henry V., was one of the first to follow the advice to use one patronymic instead of the whole pedigree of names. It is probably owing to the honours in various kinds of the branches of this family that Herbert has of late years become an exceedingly prevalent Christian name in England. Except that the Frisians call it Harber and Hero, and Italy puts an *o* at the end, it has no variations. Herman is confused with Eormen ; and the other forms are—

Ger. Herberge —Warrior protection
Ger. Herbold—Warrior prince
Nor. Herbrand ; Ger. Herbrand—Warrior sword
Nor. Herbjorn—Warrior bear
Ger. Herdegen— Warrior blade
Ger. Hertag—Warrior day
Nor. Hergils—Warrior pledge
Nor. Herlaug—Warrior drink
Nor. Herleik—Warrior sport
Nor. Herleif—Warrior relic
Ger. Herimar—Warrior greatness
Nor. Hermod ; Ger. Hermund ; Frank. Charimund—
Warrior protection
Nor. Herjolf ; Ger. Heriulf ; Frank. Chariwulf—Warrior wolf
Ger. Heraric—Warrior king

The warrior names were of the fiercest order. Leid (if it do not mean a road) was the same with the word in modern German, meaning hurt or mischief, and expressed spite or violence. The North had Liedulf, afterwards contracted into Leiul, and no doubt the Scottish Lyulf, and German Lethard, Lethild, Laidrad, Laidwald, Laidwig.

In the same spirit we have *neid* or *nöt*, meaning violence or compulsion, though it has resulted in the German *neid*, envy, and our *need*, want. We have it in the name of St. Neot, the relative and rebuker of King Alfred in his haughty days, and the hero of a legend of little fishes daily renewed for his food. Also Nidhard was a great chronicler of Frank history, and left a name surviving as Nyddert, in Friesland, and cut into Nitz, in Germany. There, too, were Notburg and Notger, Nidbert in France, and in the North, Notulf, afterwards written Notto. The terminal *nöt* is, however, more common.

Wig or Vig is war itself, and is found in the genealogy of Odin. Wægdæg, or War day, is an ancestor of the Deiran kings.

Vigleik still subsists in the North, and so does Viglaf, relic of war, the same as that of Wiglaf, the chronicler.

The other forms are—

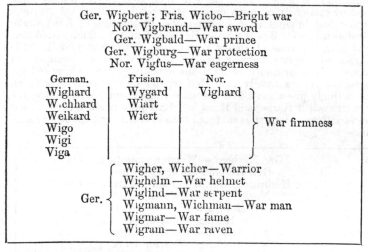

Ger. Wigbert; Fris. Wicbo—Bright war
Nor. Vigbrand—War sword
Ger. Wigbald—War prince
Ger. Wigburg—War protection
Nor. Vigfus—War eagerness

German.	Frisian.	Nor.	
Wighard	Wygard	Vighard	
Wichhard	Wiart		
Weikard	Wiert		War firmness
Wigo			
Wigi			
Viga			

Ger. { Wigher, Wicher—Warrior
Wighelm—War helmet
Wiglind—War serpent
Wigmann, Wichman—War man
Wigmar—War fame
Wigram—War raven

These are almost all German. The terminations in *wig* are often owing to German pronunciation of the word *veh*, or *vieh*, consecration, and sometimes of the northern *veig*, liquor.

The strange northern name of Snorre, famous for the sake of that Froissart of the North, Snorre Sturleson, comes from *snerra*, strife.

Styrke is the strong, the same word as that in which the old chroniclers describe William the Conqueror, as 'so very stark.' Sterkulv and a few other forms have been found in the North.

Toke is a very curious old name. It seems to mean the mad or raging, and, growing into Tyke or Tyge in Denmark, was the name that was Latinized into Tycho by the celebrated astronomer Brahe, who did not leave his madness behind him with his name. The famous Jomsburg sea-rover, a sort of northern Lycurgus of the tenth century, was Palnatoke, supposed to be properly Toke, the son of Palne. Palne is an unexplained name used by the Danes, and perhaps borrowed from the Wends ; but there are a few other instances of it, among them the Anglicized Earl Pallig, the husband of Sweyn's sister Gunhild, who was killed by Ethelred the Unready.

Thiostr means hardness or harshness, and was in use in the North as T iostulf, since contracted into Kjostol, Thiostvald, Thiostar ; and probably Tostig, the ungracious son of Godwine, who brought Harald Hardrada to invade England, took his name from thence.

SECTION V.—*Protection.*

Bar—the word for strength—has been most fertile in produce. Its progeny are far too numerous to describe ; but the most notable at present in use are the Berg, the strength of the hills, a mountain, and Burg, a fortress.

The names derived from it are, in combination, the *bjorg* of the North, in the masculine, meaning protector, and *borg*, the feminine, meaning, perhaps, protection,—the *berge* of the Germans and *burg* of the Anglo Saxons answering to the same. The Anglo-Saxon ladies also bear names ending with *burh*, also from the same root, and meaning a pledge, the strength of an engagement, and the origin of our verb, *to borrow*. Burrhed, king of Mercia, bore this name ; but instances of it are not very common.

Birger, Byrger, Birge, are the masculines much used in Scandinavia ; and the combinations were Biorgulv, Bergthor, Bergthora, the faithful wife of Njal, and Bergliot, the daughter of Thorer the Silent,—the same name that has been already mentioned as the northern one that has been mixed with the Irish Brighid, and which would mean protecting ugliness. Other forms are Bergswain, protecting youth, Berghild, answering to our Mercian princess Burgenhild, and Borgny, apt to be cut down to Borny.

This is the word to which the Burgundians owed their title, as dwellers in burghs, instead of wanderers on the open plain.

Another large race of names comes from the Gothic *warjan*, Anglo-Saxon *warian*,—the ' *ware* ' of rustic shouts in En land like the ' *gare* ' of France, the latter syllable of beware and aware, and the *wehrer* of Germany. The quality of precaution furnished the North with its favourite terminations *var* and *vara*, indicating the possession of the prudent virtue that makes a man *wary*. It does not begin names, but it often ends them, both in the North and Germany, as Geirvar, Hervar, Amalvara, Hildiwara, &c.

The inhabitant was the natural defender, and in Anglo Saxon and Norsk *ware* became synonymous with the dweller, as Cantwara, the defenders of Kent, for the Kentishmen ; Burgwara, the burghers ; and in the North, Vikvarjar, bay defender. *Ware*, a defender, is thus a commencement in the German Warimunt, Guarding protection, the Vœrmund of the Mercian genealogy, and Vermund of the North, while its surviving representatives in France are Guiremond and Vermont.

Warenheri, or Protecting-warrior, is the Guarniero of Tasso, the Garnier of France, whence this form came to England as a surname after the Edict of Nantes, whilst Warner had been the legitimate descendant of the native Vœrnhare.

Warand, the German participle name, may have assisted in forming Guérin and Warren, unless there was a Warewine to account for it. Warnfrid or Warno, Werinhold and Warnebold, are also German.

The defender was with us the *Weard*, guard-warden, and *weardian* was to ward or guard ; as in French *garde* and *garder*, in the North *vördhr*, in Germany *wart, warten*. This is the favourite termination, the *ward* of England passing the *wart* of Germany, the *vard* of the North ; but of rare appearance as a commencement, though there is an instance of a German Wartgar, or guardian-spear.

These are extremely like the words taken from *to gird*, like *gerda*, *gaard*, &c., but they are essentially different : watching is here the idea of safety, as enclosure is there.

The termination *mund*, so common among all the Teuton nations, has been a very great difficulty. Some regard it as the German *mund* or *munths*, a mouth. The fact, however, appears to be that *mund* means a hand in the elder languages, and from a hand was early transferred to him who used his hand in protection.

All the best authorities agree in translating *mund* as protection ; but as *mund*, a hand, is a feminine noun, the derivation from this source is a little doubtful, as the only lady's name thus terminated is Rosamond. It is never a prefix.

Names ending in *mund*, hand, are often confused with those finishing in *mod* or *muth*, meaning courage or wrath, the *mood* of England and *muth* of Germany. Even in very early times, Thurismund, or Thurismod, would be indifferently written ; but *mod* is not very common, and is apt to shorten into *mo*, as Thormod, Tormo.

The Germans used to imagine that all their names ending in *hulf* meant help ; but this pleasant faith was destroyed by the northern wolf, and only one real *help* name is extant, the Helfrich of modern Germany, and Hialfrek of the North, which own an ancient precedent in the old Frank Hialperik or Chilperic.

The pronunciation of *ward* runs so naturally into *hard*, that many names, which when traced to their roots, turn out to terminate with *ward*, are spelt in German and French as if they were *hard*. The word *hard* does, however, really enter into the composition of a few names, chiefly German. There is, however, a semi-mythical northern lady called by the amiable name of Harthgrepa, Firm-grip or Hard-claw ; and HartheKnad, or, as we call him, Hardicanute, seems to have had this distinguishing epithet added to his father's name. The most noted of the other forms was Hardwine, Firm friend, the Hardouin of old French chroniclers, called in Italy Ardoino.

Harding, firm	Hartmund, firm protection
Hartrich, firm king	Hartmod, firm spirit.
Hartwig, firm war	

The names in *rand* have likewise been a difficulty ; but the word is best referred to the Gothic *razn*, a house, and likewise a shield, from the protection both afford.

Rand is a northern prefix, and its derivatives are not easy to distinguish from those of Regin and Raven. Röndolfr, or House wolf, was certainly a northern name, and the same seems to have belonged to St. Radulphus, bishop of Bourges in 888, and to thirty-eight Radulfs in Domesday Book, then to the good justiciary, Ranulf de Glanville, under Henry II., to the crusading Earl Randle of Chester, and subsequently to many a Randal, Randolf, and Ralf, or, as we foolishly spell the word, Ralph.

The North had Rannveig, House-liquor, by way of a lady, and have shortened her into Rannog and Ronnau, also Rannmod, Randvid, Randve, or Randverr, house consecration.

Fast—in the sense of firm, not of quick—is found in the northern Fastolf, in the Frank queen, Fastrade, Firm council, in Fastburg, Fastmann, Fastmund. Lidvard, an old Norse name, that with us has run into Ledyard, in its own country into Levor, is the gate ward.

Tryggve, a favourite old northern name, is the true or trusty. The same word sometimes serves as a termination, as in Sigtryg or Sihtric.

Section VI.—*Power.*

Magan is the Gothic and Saxon to be able, whence our defective *may*, and a number of other words in all the various northern tongues, in especial *main* or *chief*. The names from it are chiefly of German origin. Maginfred, or Powerful-peace, was a fine Old German name, which, by the time it came to the brave but unfortunate Sicilian, son of Frederick II., had been worn down to Manfred, whence he was called by his subjects Manfredi, by his French foes Mainfroi, and by his English contemporaries Mainfroy.

Meginhard, main power, was a chronicler of the early ages, and in 1130 appears in the Cambrai registers. The Germans used it as Mainhart, and the English surname Maynard is from it. Meginrat made Meinrad, or powerful council, and Maginhild is still in use in the North as Magnild.

The *main* land is, in fact, the chief land, the *main*, the chief sheet of water, or sea, and *might* and *main* are so closely connected together, that Maginhild is the most natural step to Mahthild, Main heroine to Might heroine ; for *maht* is really the modern German *macht*, and our own *might*, and both these mighty names were in early use in Germany. Mahthild was the wife of the emperor Henry the Fowler, and afterwards became the sainted abbess of Quedlingburg. Another Swabian Mechtild was canonized after being abbess of Adilstetten ; and so fashionable did the name become, that all the French maidens, who were not Alix, seem to have been Mahthild ; and in Italy it was borne by the Countess Matilda, the friend of Gregory VII., whose bequest was one of the pope's first steps to the temporal power, and who is introduced by Dante in the flowery fields of Paradise. The Flemings call it Mahault, and thus term the lady, who, as the wife of William the Conqueror, brought it to England. Molde, as the Normans were pleased to term it, was regarded as so decidedly a Norman name, that the Scottish-Saxon Eadgyth was made to assume it, and it continued the regnant royal name until it sunk beneath the influences of the Provençal Alienor. It seems as if Matilde had been freshly introduced in Flanders when Count Philip married Matilda of Portugal ; and this, and the old traditional Mehaut, went on side by side, just as in England did the full name Matilda, and the Anglicized Norman contraction Maude. Of late years Maude has been fashionable, though not so near the original, nor so really graceful in sound as Matilda. The earlier Mall and Moll were from Matilda, not Mary, which came much later into use.

English.	French.	Italian.	Bavarian.
Matilda	Mathilde	Matilda	Mechtild
Molde	Mahaud		Mechel
Mall	Mehaut	**German.**	Melchel
Maud		Mathilde	
Tilda			
Tilly		**Hamb.**	
		Tilde	
		Tille	

Maatfred and Maatulf were old masculines.

From *may* and *might* we pass to our other defective auxiliary *can*. 'Knowledge is power,' is an idea deeply rooted in our languages, for the difference between *I ken* and *I can* is well-nigh imperceptible. The Sanscrit *gna*, forming the Greek verb γιγνώσκω (gignosco), reappears in the Latin *nosco*, and the Anglo-Saxon *cnawan*. Another Anglo-Saxon form is *cunnan*, answering to the Danish *kjende*, Iceland *kunna*, German *kennan*. Thence our word *cunning*, knowing, and *cuth*, the past participle, known, noted, or dexterous, whence came several North-Anglian names, Cutha, Cuthwealh, Noted power ; Cuthred, Noted council ; Cuthwine, Noted friend ; Cuthburh, Noted pledge ; and chief of all Cuthbryht, the great saint of Lindisfarn in his lifetime, of Durham after his death, when the wanderings of his relics rendered his fame so great that Cuthbert is still national among the peasantry of Northumbria and the Lothians.

Kann seems to have been originally a past tense of *ken*, and the Teutonic mind concluded that to have learnt is to be able, for all adopted the word *can* without an infinitive, and varied it into past tenses. To be able was likewise to dare, whence the old Teuton *kuoni*, Frank *chuon*, Saxon *cene*, German *kuhn*, bold.

Be this as it may, a large class of names has arisen from these words of knowledge and action, earliest of the bearers of which should stand Kunimund, king of the Gepidæ, and Chunimund, king of the Suevi, both meaning Able protection. Chuonrath, Able council, or Bold-speech, was also Suevic, and in the form of Konrad, afterwards a world-wide name in the Swabian house of Hohenstaufen, till the last of their generous though impetuous blood was shed on the scaffold of Corradino, as Naples fondly termed its unfortunate young heir, the Conradin of history. Pity for his untimely fate assisted to spread the name through all the German dependencies, and it has become so common that, like Vasili, Toni, and Heinz, Künz has descended to cats. It has the feminine Cunzila ; and our old Mercian King Cenred represented it in England.

English.	French.	Provençal.	Italian.
Conrad	Conrade	Cohat	Corrado
Cenred	Quenes		Currado

German.	Bavarian.	Swiss.	Swedish.
Konrad	Kadl	Chuedli	Konrad
Kunz	Kuenl	Kudli	
Kurt	Kuenz	Chuedler	Netherlands.
Kuno	Kunl	Kored	Koenraad
		Koredli	Court
		Chuered	

Danish.	Russian.	Bohemian.	Slovak.
Cort	Konrad	Kunad	Kunsch
	Kunrat		
	Kondratij	Lusatian.	
		Kunat	

Kunigund, or Bold war, was the name of a daughter of the counts of Luxemburg, who was wife to Henry of Bavaria, the sainted emperor, and shared in his canonization, rendering her name national in Bavaria. Another royal saint reigning in Hungary added to its honours, nor has it ever sunk into disuse.

French.	Italian.	Portuguese.	German.	Bavarian.
Cunigonde	Cunegonda	Cunegundis	Kunigunde	Kunl
				Kundl

The West Saxon Cenbyrht is the same with the German Kunibert ; and Wessex likewise reckoned among her kings Cenfyrth, or able peace, Cenfus, bold impetuosity ; while Mercia has Cenhelm and Cenwulf.

Alternating with these are Cynric, Cynebald, Cynewald, Cyneburh, Cynethryth, whose first syllable is *cyn*, *kin*, or *kind*, meaning, of course, kindred or lineage. Some refer Kunibert and Kunigund to this same *kin* instead of *kuhn*. This word *cyn* is one of those regarded as the root of king, *cyning*, the son of his race or kindred.

Another word seems to have had the same double meaning of ability being strength ; for *svinn*, which is wise in the northern tongues, is in those of central Europe, strong ; the English *swith*, Gothic *swinths*, German *swind ;* whence the present *geschwind*, and swift ; moreover, *swindig* is much, or many, in vulgar Dutch, and to *swindle* is probably to be too much for the victim.

Suintila was an old Gothic king of Spain, Swithbert, one of the early Anglo-Saxon missionaries, especially honoured as the converter of the kindred land of Friesland, where he was revered as St. Swibert. Swithelm was another Saxon form ; but the most noted amongst us was Swithun, the bishop of Winchester, tutor to King Alfred, and endowed with many supposed miracles, the best known of which was the forty days' rain, by which, like other honest English saints, he testified his displeasure at having his bones meddled with. The Germans have had Swidburg, Swintfried, Swidger ; but in general this has served as a feminine termination, as in Melicent, Frediswid, and in all the many *swiths* and *swinds* of the Franks and Goths.

Whether this be the root or not, Svein is in the North a strong youth, generally a servant, but in the form of Svend becoming the favourite name of the kings of Denmark, belonging to him whom Ethelred's treachery brought down on England, where it was called Swayn, and translated into Latin as Sueno, while Tasso calls the crusading Swend, Sveno. Svinbjorn occurs in Iceland, and is our Swinburn. Svenke, again, is the active or slender youth. It is amusing to see how, from a strong man, the swain became a young man, then a bachelor, then a lover, and, finally, a shepherd.

Another of the mighty words that have been formed into names is *vald*, the near relative of the Latin *valeo*. Our verb *to wield* continues the Anglo-Saxon *wealdan*, which named the wealds of Kent, nay, and the world itself.

Vald still stands alone in the North, and once was the name of a Frank abbot of Evreux ; St. Valdus, in Latin, St. Gaud, in French.

The leading name is, however, Waldheri, Powerful-Warrior appearing as the young prince of Aquitaine, who, in the curious Latin poem which seems to represent the Frankish *Nibelungenlied* in the south of France, flies from Attila's court with his fellow-hostage, the Burgundian Hildegunna, and her treasure, and repulses the pursuing Gunther and Hagano. This same Walther was said to have after-wards reigned thirty years in Aquitaine, and, no doubt, the name was already common there, when, about 990, it came to saintly glory, through a monastic saint of that dukedom, who, being followed by two others, caused it to be spread far and wide. Indeed, there are twenty-eight Walters in Domesday, and Cambrai made plentiful use of it in the same form, till, about 1300, the spelling was altered to the French Gautier. Walther von Vogelwied, the Minnesinger, who bequeathed a perpetual dole to the birds of the air at his tomb, well deserved that the memory of his name should be kept up in Germany, and it has always been very popular. Wat, as a contraction, is as old as Rufus's time, and Water was in use, at least, in Shakespeare's time, when he shows the prophecy of Suffolk's death by water fulfilled by the name of his assassin.

English.	Irish.	French.	Italian.
Walter	Thaiter	Waltier	Gualtiero
Water		Gualtier	
Wat		Wautier	Spanish.
Watty		Gatier	Guttierre
Wattles		Gautier	

Portuguese.	Netherlands.	Lettish.	Dutch.
Gualter	Gualterus	Waters	Wolder
Gualterio	Walter		
	Wouter	Swiss.	
	Wout	Watli	

Waldemar is an old German form imported by the Normans to England, and sometimes supposed to have been carried to Russia, and to have turned into Vladimir; but this has been traced to a genuine Slavonic source, though it is used by the Russians to represent Walter.

This commencement is almost exclusively German; its other varieties are Waldobert, or Walbert, the Gualberto of Italy, Waldrich, and, perhaps, Walpurg, though she is more probably from *val*, slaughter.

Frodhr, Wise or learned, is sometimes an epithet, but is also used for a name, and Latinized into Frotho. The Germans have it in combination as Frodwin, wise friend, Frodbert and Frodberta, whence the French make Flobert and Floberte.

The root *mah*, which made the Sanscrit *mahat*, Zend *maz*, Greek *megas*, Latin *magnus*, Kelt *mawr*, comes forth again in Teutonic, with *mære*, or *mara*, in Anglo-Saxon, with its comparatives *mœrre* and *mœriste*, whence our *more* and *most*. This same sense of greatness formed the word *maara*, fame, and *maren*, to celebrate, both old German, and it is the commencement of the Frank chieftain's name from whom all the princes of the earlier race were called Meerwings, Merowig, or Famed men, the Meerwig of German writers and Meroveus of Latinity, whence the Merovée of French history.

Our own Anglian Mercians had among their royal line Merowald,

Merehelm, and Merewine ; but, in general, *mer*, or *mar*, is used as a termination rather than a commencement, and then is always masculine. Merohelm is also called Merchelm, so the French saint, 'Marculphe,' *may* have been Merowulf, though he now looks more like Markulf, a border wolf *

Section VII.—*Affection.*

The Teutons had a few names denoting affection. Dyre is the same in Norse as our own word *dear*, or *dyr* in Anglo-Saxon. An inlet on the north-west corner of Iceland is still termed Dyrefiord, from one of the first settlers, and Dyre was the hero of a ballad in the *Kœmpeviser*, answering to the Scottish Katharine Janfarie, the original of young Lochinvar. The old Germans had Dioro and Diura, and the Anglo-Saxons affectionately called the young sons of their nobility Dyrling, or darling.

Leof, the German *lieb*, beloved, is much used by the Anglo-Saxons. Two bishops, one of Wells, and afterwards primate, the other of Crediton, were called Leofing, or Lyfing. The first was certainly properly Ælfstan, so it is probable that in both instances Leofing was merely an endearing name that grew up with them, and displaced the baptismal one ; but its Latin translation, Livingus, shows the origin of the surname of Livingstone.

England also had Leofwine, Beloved friend, the only native name borne by any of the sons of Earl Godwin. An earlier Leofwine was a member of St. Boniface's mission, and converted many of the heathens on the banks of the Weser ; and as St. Lebwin is patron of Deventer, probably occasioned the name of Lubin, which, from being borne by French peasants, crept into pastoral poetry.

Another of the same mission party was Leobgytha, or Dear gift, called also Liuba and Liebe, who was sent for from her convent at Wimborne to found one of the earliest nunneries in Germany. It is probably from her that Lievine became an old Cambrecis name.

Leof seems to have been the special prefix of the earls of Mercia, for we find among them, besides Leofwine, Leofstan and Leofric, the last the best known for the sake of his wife and of Coventry.

The continental instances of the prefix are among the Spanish Goths, Liuva, Leovigildo, and Liuvigotona ; and among the Franks, Leobhard, or Liebhard, a saint of Touraine.

The only present survivor of all the varieties is probably, if we exclude the occasional Puritan Love, the Cornish and Devon feminine Lovedy.

Far more universal are the names derived from the old word *vinr*, or *wine*, meaning friend or object of love, the same which has left a descendant in the German *wonne*, affection, and the Scottish adjective

* Munch; Sismondi; Butler; Junius; Kemble; Michaelis; Lappenburg; Mariana; Weber and Jamieson; Donovan.

winsome. It is a continual termination, as must have been already observed, and we had it as a commencement in our great English missionary Winfrith, or Friend of peace, the Devonian bishop who spread Christianity over Germany, but who is far better known by the Latin surname which he assumed, namely, Bonifacius. Winibald was another of our missionary saints, and Germany has also had Winrad, Winrich, and Winmar, but the Welsh Wenefred must not be confused with it.

Mild, or *mild,* is exclusively Saxon ; nay, almost exclusively Mercian, for it only occurs in one family ; that of King Merowald, who named his three daughters Mildgyth, Mildburh, and Mild-thryth. All became nuns, the two latter abbesses, one in Shropshire, the other in the isle of Thanet, and they were canonized as Milburga and Mildreda. Milborough, as the first became Anglicized, was found within the last century in Shropshire, and Mildred was never entirely disused ; it belonged to the daughter of Burleigh, and has lately been much revived, under the notion that it means mild speech ; but *red* is always masculine, and, as has been before said, *thryth* commands or threatens, so that Mildthryth is the gently strict.

Section VIII.—*Appearance.*

Miss Carolina Wilhelmina Amelia Skeggs was verily named after a beard. Skegg means neither more nor less than a beard, and strange to say, Bardr and Skegg were both fashionable names in the North ; indeed, one Icelandic gentleman rejoiced in the euphonious title of Bardr Bla-skegg, or Beard Blue-beard.

But we have an independent name of this class. William de Albini, the second husband of Henry I.'s widow, Alix of Louvaine, wore moustachios, which the Normans called *gernons,* and thus his usual title was William *als Gernons ;* and as the common ancestor of the Howards and Percys, he left this epithet to them as a baptismal name, one of the most whimsical of the entire roll. From the Percys it came to Algernon Sidney ; and partly through his admirers, partly through inheritance, and partly through the love of trisyllables, has become diffused in England.

Faxe meant the hair or tresses, as may be seen in the names of the horses of day and night, Skinfaxi and Hrinfaxi. Two instances of it are found in the *Landnama-bok,* Faxi, a colonist from the Hebrides, and Faxabrandr, most likely an epithet due to some peculiarity of hair, probably whiteness, or perhaps fieriness ; but it was not common, though it came to England to be the surname of Sir Thomas Fairfax.

The name of our excellent friend Wamba in *Ivanhoe* must probably have been taken from one of the Visigothic kings of Spain, with whom it was most likely a nickname, like that of Louis de Gros in France, for it means nothing but the belly. Epithets like this were not uncommon, and sometimes were treated as names, such as Mucel, or the big, the sobriquet of the earl of the Gevini ; or Budde, the pudding, the person who showed Knut the way over the ice. Many of those used in England were Keltic, showing that the undercurrent of Cymric population must still have been strong.

It is remarkable how very few are the Teuton names taken from the complexion—in comparison with the many used by the Kelts, and even by the Romans—either because the Teutons were all alike fair, or because they thought these casual titles unworthy to be names. Bruno was exclusively German, and may perhaps be only a nickname, but it came to honour with the monk of Cologne, who founded the Carthusian order, and has been used ever since ; and the North has Sverke, Sverkir, swarthy or dark, a famous name among the vikings.

Far more modern is the name of Blanche. The absence of colour is in all tongues of Western Europe denoted by forms of *blec*. In Anglo-Saxon, *blœc* or *blac* is the colour black, but *blœca* is a *bleak*, empty place, and *blœcan* is to bleach or whiten ; *blœco*, like the German *bleich*, stands for paleness. It is the same with German and Norse, in the latter of which *blakke hund* is not a black dog but a white one. All these, however, used their own *weiss* or *white* for the pure uncoloured snow ; while the negative *blœc*, or colourless, was adopted by the Romance languages, all abandoning the Latin *albus* in its favour. It is literally true that our *black* is the French *white; black* and *blanc* are only the absence of colour in its two opposite effects.

Blach, Blacheman, Blancus, and Blancard, all appear in Domesday ; but Blanchefleur and Blanche, seem to have been the produce of romance. The mother of Sir Tristrem was Blanchefleur, a possible translation of some of the Keltic Gwenns or Finns, and it probably crept from romance to reality among the poetical people of southern France. The first historical character so called was Blanca of Navarre, the queen of Sancho IV. of Castille, from whom it was bestowed on her granddaughter, that child of Eleanor Plantagenet, whom her uncle, King John, employed as the lure by which to detach Philippe Auguste from the support of Arthur of Brittany. The treaty only bore that the son of Philippe should wed the daughter of Alfonso of Castille ; the choice among the sisters was entrusted to ambassadors, and they were guided solely by the sound of the name borne by the younger, that of the elder sister, Urraca, being considered by them hateful to French ears, and unpronounceable to French lips. John was punished for his policy, for Blanche's royal English blood was the pretext of the pope in directing against him her husband, Louis the Lion, but no choice could have been a happier one for France, since Blanche of Castille was the first and best of her many queen-regents.

From her the name became very common in France. One of the daughters of Edward I. was so called, probably from her, in honour of his friendship for her son ; it became usual among the English nobility, and is most common in Italy, though it is somewhat forgotten in Spain.

English.	French.	Italian.	Spanish.	Portuguese.
Blanch	Blanche	Bianca	Blanca	Branca

A Swedish heroine called Blenda made this name, from *blenden*, to dazzle, common in her own country, but it is not known elsewhere.

Koll, with a double *l*, meaning head, is sometimes used in northern names, but far less commonly than *kol*, cool, or rather in the act of cooling after great heat. The great blast-bellows with which the gods charitably refreshed the horses of the sun, are called in the Eddaic poetry, *isarnkol*, or iron coolers, and there may have been some allusion to this in the names of Kol and Kale, which alternated in one of the old northern families. But as the cooling of iron involved its turning black, *kolbrünn* meant a black breastplate, and was thus used as a by-name ; and it may be in this sense of black that *kol* enters into the composition of Kolbjorn, black bear, Kolgrim, Kolgrima ; Kolskegg would thus be black-beard ; but Kolbein can hardly be black-leg, so, perhaps, it may refer to the bones being strong as wrought iron ; and Kolfinn and its feminine are either cool-white or refer to Finn's strength. Colbrand is in English romance the name of the Danish giant killed by Guy of Warwick, at Winchester ; but the Heptarchy displays a very perplexing set of Cols, as they have been modernized, though they used to be spelt Ceol. There were three Ceolwulfs in Bernicia, Mercia, and Wessex ; Ceolred in Mercia, Ceolwald in Wessex, Ceolnoth on the throne of Canterbury. Are these the relatives of the northern *kol*, cool, or are they *ceol*, keel, meaning rather a ship than merely the keel, as it does now ? Or, on the other hand, are both these, and the northern *col*, adaptations of the Keltic *col* or *gall*, like those already mentioned of Finn ? Their exclusive prevalence among the Scandinavians and Anglo-Saxons would somewhat favour the notion.

The northern feminine terminal, *frid*, belongs to this class, and means the fair, or pretty, from the old northern *fridhr*, though it is most deceitfully like *fred*, or *frey*, peace, and is probably from the same root.

Teitr is a northern man's name, meaning cheerful : *Zeiz* answers to it in old German ; and though the analogue in Anglo-Saxon does not otherwise occur in any Anglo-Saxon work, yet we find from Bede that Æthelburh, the daughter of Æthelbeorht and Bertha, of Kent, who carried her Christianity to her husband, Eadwine, was also called Tâte, by which we may gather that she was particularly lively and cheerful.

Section IX.—*Locality.*

A large and interesting class of names relate to country, and express the birthplace or the wandering habits of the original bearers.

The word *land* was one of these. Its primary meaning seems to be

the abode of the people.   Long ago we spoke of the Greek λαος, prominent in Laodamia, and many other of the like commencement.
An almost similar term runs through the Teutonic tongues ; the
Saxon *leod*, German *leute*, Frank *liade*, Northern *lydhr*.   The *leod*, or
leute, seem to have been the free inhabitants, including all ranks, and
thence we have the *laity*, for the general people, and the *lewd*, which
has sunk from the free to the ignorant, and then to the dissipated.

The great region of these names taken from the people is Germany.
Leutpold, the people's prince, was a canonized Markgraf of Austria,
in the days when that family had hardly yet begun its course of
marrying into greatness, and making Leutpold better known at every
stage, and by each new dialect differently pronounced, till it turned
into Leopold, and was confounded with the old lion names.   Indeed,
in the old Swiss ballad on the battle of Sempach, translated by Scott,
Leopold the Handsome is called the Austrian Lion.   The recurrence
of the name in the modern imperial line has made it European, and
the close connection of our own royal family with the wise king of
the Belgians has brought it to England.   Of course, it has not escaped
a modern German Leopoldine.

English.	French.	Italian.	German.	Slav.
Leopold	Léopold	Leopoldo	Luitpold Leupold Leopo	Leopoldo Poldo Poldi

Leutgar, the people's spear, was a good bishop of Antrim, who was
speared by the people, or, at least, murdered by them, in the furious
wars of the long-haired kings, and was revered as a martyr under the
Latin form of Leodigarius.   A priest of Chalons was canonized by the
same name, which is in France Leguire, and was brought as a territorial surname to England as St. Leger.

Liutgarde seems to have been a Frank saint, but there is no account
of her in Alban Butler ; but hers is one of the favourite old names at
Cambrai.   Liutprand, the people's sword, is one of the chief chroniclers
of early French history, and the other forms are Liuther, the only
one accepted by the North, and that in the form of Lyder.

Ger. Liutbert ; Fries. Liubert—People's brightness
Ger. Liutberga—People's protection
Fr. Leodefred, Leufroi—People's peace
Ger. Liutmar ; Fries. Luttmer, Lummer ; Fr. Leodemir—
People's greatness
Ger. Leuthold, Liutold ; Ags. Leodwald—People's power

The *land* itself was compounded into names chiefly among the
Franks, Germans, and Lombards, often as a conclusion, but now and
then at the beginning.   Lantperaht, or the country's brightness, is

the most noted of these, having been borne by three saints of Maestricht, Lyons, and Venice, and having thus become national in all the countries around ; but it is universally corrupted into Lambert, and has been generally derived from a lamb.

English.	French.	Italian.	German.	Dutch.
Lambert	Lambert Lanbert	Lamberto	Landbert Lambert	Lambert Lammert

Landerich, or country's ruler, was an early Frank saint, who has left Landry to be still frequent among the Flemish and French peasantry.

Landfrang, lord of the country, was the Lombardic Lanfranco, whence the Lanfranc of the archbishop of Canterbury, whom William the Conqueror imposed on the English Church, but who brought in fresh vigour and learning. Landfrid has left the surname Laffert to France ; its contraction Lando belonged to a saint, and has the feminines Landine and Landoline. There are also recorded Landolf, Landrad, Landrada, and Landinn.

If Germany and Italy talked of dwellers in the land, the North, with its seas and numerous islets, distinguished the islanders with the word Ey, or Øi, the word that we use to this very day in speaking of Guernsey Jersey, &c., of an *eyot* in a river ; and even in Sodor, that puzzling companion to the Isle of Man, which once was the Sudeyas, or South Is'es, the Hebrides.

The most famous northern island name is Eystein, or Øistein, much in use among the early kings, and especially honoured for the sake of the good brother of Sigurd the Crusader, who stayed at home and worked for his people's good, while S'gurd was killing blue m n in the land of the Saracens. The Danish Eystein was turned into Austin, or Augustin, to be more ecclesiastical, and this may be the origin of some of our Austins. Eyulf, or the island wolf, l as become, in the course of time, Øiel and Øiuf. Eyvind, who appears in the *Landnama-bok* with the unpleasant sobriquet of Skalldur Spiller, or the poet spoiler, is supposed to have been the Island Wend, a reminiscence of the Wends on the shores of the Baltic. It was a very common name, and became Øvind and Even, while Eymund, in like manner, was turned into Emund. An island thief was not wanting, as Eythiof ; nor an island warrior, as Eyar ; also Eyfrey, Eylang ; and the ladies Eygerd, Eydis, Eyny, and Eyvar, or, as Saxo calls her, Ofura.

An island is also sometimes *holm*, whence the northern Holmstein and Holmfrid, with Holmgeir, which gets mixed with Holger.

Persons of mixed birth were drolly called by the actual fractional word *half*, in Germany Halbwalah, half a foreigner, or half a Wallachian, and Halbtüring or half a Thuringian ; and in the North, generally, Halfdan, half a Dane. So early was this in use that there was a mythical king, Halfdan, from whom the name was adopted by many a true-born Dane and Northman, and has been Latinized as Haldanus.

Travellers had their epithets, which probably came to be family names. *Lide*, Wanderer, was compounded in Haflide, sea wanderer; Vestlide, west wanderer; Vetilide, winter wanderer; and Sumalide, or summer wanderer, which last was current among the lords of the Isles, and kings of Man, in the shape of Somerled, or, in Gaelic, Somhle; but 'the heirs of mighty Somerled' did not long keep up his name.

Travellers again had their name from *fara*, the modern German *fahren*, and the scarcely disused English *to fare*, meaning to journey. The most noted instance is Faramund, who, in the guise of Pharamond, is placed at the head of the long-haired Frankish dynasty, far travelled it may be, from the river Yssel whence the Salic stock took the title that was to pass to one peculiar law of succession; also Fara-bert, Farulf, and Farthegn, contracted into Farten, and Faltin, and then supposed to be a contraction of Falentin, or Valentine. *Thegn* did, in fact, originally mean a servant, so that Farthegn was either the travelled servant, or the travelled thane. Fargrim appears in Domesday; but these names are not easy to divide from those taken from *waren*, to beware.

Even the exile had his sorrows commemorated in his children's names. No doubt if we could meet with the story of the original Erland, we should find that he was born under the same circumstances as Peregrine Bertie, for the name is from the old northern *er*, out, or away from, and *land*. Erland is the Outland, the banished man, and he must have been beloved, or celebrated, for Erlendr, as the Icelanders had it, occurs plentifully, with its diminutive Erling, and perhaps the corruption Elling.

The unfortunate Bishop Hatto's name was anciently Hazzo, and is translated a Hessian.

Viking has been used as a Christian name in Norway in com-paratively modern days, in memory of the deeds of the terrible Vikingr of old; but, in spite of the resemblance in sound, it must not be suspected of any relation to sea-kings, being only the inhabitant of a vik, or bay, of course the most convenient abode for a sea-rover.

The sea, *haf*, or *hav*, as it was called in the North, named Haflide, Hafthor, and Hafgrim, as well as the mythic hero, Haflok, the Dane, whose life, according to his legend, was saved by his faithful servant Grim, the founder of Grimsby, in Lincolnshire, the native place of our own Sir Henry Havelock, who was bewailed by the Danish school-children as their own ballad hero. The two feminine termin-ations *laug* and *veig* may have been in its honour, but it is much to be feared that they only meant liquor, and at the best were allusions to the costly mead of the gods, the drink of inspiration, or the magic bowls that inflamed the Berserks. Nay, men rejoiced in the name of Ølver or Ølve, meaning neither more nor less than Ale, *øl*, which acquires a *v* in the oblique cases and plural. Ølver and Olaf have, no doubt, been confounded into the modern Oliver.

Knud, or Knut, a very common northern name, is a very puzzling one. Its origin and nationality are Danish, and it only came to Norway by intermarriages, nor does it appear at all in the *Landnama-bok*. The great Dane who brought it here is called by the chroniclers Canutus, from some notion of making it the Latin *hoary*, and thus we know him as Canute ; but even in Domesday, one landholder in Yorkshire, and another in Derbyshire, are entered as Cnud. The whole North, and the inhabitants of the Hebrides, use the name, which comes from the same root as our *knot*, and properly means a protuberance, a hill, or barrow.

Section X.—*Life.*

Life played its part among Teutonic names. One old word conveying this sense was the Gothic *ferchvus*, Saxon *feorh*, and Northern *fiorh*. The Anglo-Saxon *feorh* also meant youth, and thus passed on to mean a young man.

There are not many names from thence, but one of the few has been a great perplexity, and has been explained in many ways, *i. e.* the Gothic Ferhonanths, the last syllable being *nanth*, daring, so that its sense would be, 'adventuring his life.' It was the Spanish Goths who used this gallant name, and made it with their Romance tongues in o Fernan and Fernando. San Fernando, king of Castille, and father of our own Eleanor, made it a favourite for his royal line ; and a younger son of Castille so called, being heir of Aragon, carried it thither, and thence it passed to southern France, where the grandson of old King René was Ferrand or Ferry. Aragon again bestowed it upon Naples ; but it was there prolonged into Ferdinando, whilst Spanish elisions had at home turned it to Hernan, as the conqueror of Mexico termed himself. It was bestowed upon the second son of Juana la Loca, who was born in Spain, and long preferred there to his brother, though it was to the imperial throne that he was destined to succeed, and to render his Spanish name national through Germany, where Ferdinand has long been a sore puzzle ; sometimes explained by *fart*, a journey, and sometimes by *fried*, peace, but never satisfactorily. The contraction Nandel was the shout of the mob in the ears of Ferdinand, the obstinate, narrow-minded man who won his cause by mere force of undivided aim. It is so popular in Spain and Germany as in each to have a feminine, Fernanda and Ferdinandine.

English.	French.	Spanish.	Italian.
Ferdinand	Ferdinand	Fernando	Ferdinando
	Ferrand	Hernando	Fernando
	Ferry	Hernan	Ferrante

German.	Polish.	Lettish.	
Ferdinand	Ferdynand	Werlands	
Nandl			

Ferahbald and Ferahmund were forgotten old German forms, and Fjorleif was known in the North.

This is, probably, relic of life, as otherwise the word would be a reduplication ; but the termination *leif* or *lif* is sometimes used, being our very word life.

There are two words which may be said to form names of progress, the German *gang*, from to go, sometimes commencing as in Gangolf, but more usual at the end of a word ; and the Northern *stig*, from the universal root *stig*, found in the Greek ἐστιχον, and in our step and stile, also stairs, for the usual sense of the word implies mounting upwards ; and the name of the semi-Danish archbishop of Canterbury who crowned Harold, and was one of the Conqueror's lifelong captives, was the participle Stigand, mounting, and was long extant in the North, as well as the Danish Styge and Stygge.

PART VII.

SECTION I.—*Slavonic Races.*

THE last class of names that have had any influence upon European nomenclature are those borne by the Slavonic race dwelling to the eastward of the Teutons, and scarcely coming into notice before the period of modern history.

Nor, indeed, have they been ever very prominent. Slipping into the regions left empty by the Teutons, or depopulated by the forays of the Tatars, these nations have carried on a life for the most part obscure and industrious, though now and then drawn, either by Mongol fury on the one hand, or by Teuton ambition on the other, into gallant exertions ; but a genuine Slavonian has seldom or never extended his power far beyond his own country. Imaginative and poetical, they have nevertheless few ancestral traditions, they have no history previously to coming under the influence of other countries, and their migrations are even less known than those of the early Kelts and Teutons.

All that we do know is that by the time the ten horns of modern empire were developing themselves, there was a long strip of Slavonians, or Wends, extending from the White and Baltic seas down to the Black and Adriatic, making a division between the Teutons and the Tatars, but utterly unable to oppose a barrier when periodical fits of fury and invasion seized upon the wild hordes to the eastward of them.

Wends, or Venedi, seems to have been one universal national term ; *Slava* furnished another. The word, like the Greek κλύα and Teuton *hlod*, is from the root *çru*, and denotes fame or glory ; and it is constantly employed in the personal names, commencing Slavoljub, glorious love, Slavomir, glorious peace, Slavomil, friend of glory, and terminating Siroslav, far-famed, and many others, usually rendered as *slas* and *slaus*.

But just as Geta, the Goth, stood for a bondsman in classical literature, so when the Slav became the captive of the German, his once glorious epithet became the generic term of the thrall, bought and sold, while the derivatives of the Latin *servus* were reserved for the free hired domestic.   Glory had literally turned to slavery, perhaps the more readily because it is the Slav who, of all the Indo-European race, most readily bows beneath the yoke, so that to this day, his forms of courtesy are the most servile, his respectful address the most extravagant, used in Europe.

At our first glimpse of the Slavonic nations, the Danube flowed through the midst of a considerable settlement of them, known to classical writers as Bulgarians, and most savage foes to the Eastern empire, who lost army after army in expeditions against these barbarians.

In the North, two great merchant republics at Kief and Novgorod were conducting the trade of the North, and apparently living an honourable life of industry and self-government.

All around the east and south of the Baltic were other large territories occupied by Slavonians, from Finland to Jutland ; and, with few exceptions, most of these lands still own a Slavonian population, though only one has a native government.

The Mongols have, perhaps, chiefly influenced the changes undergone by the Slaves.   The great and terrible Tatar invasion of Attila trod them down, but by ruining the Roman empire, established homes for them, especially round the Danube.   In the kingdom now called Hungary, there is a large Slavonian population, called Slovak, from the term *slov*, a word, living mixed with the remains of the Huns, but keeping a separate language.

The mountain-girt lozenge of Bohemia was also a separate kingdom, with its own language, not the same, though nearly related, and more resembling that of the fierce elective kingdom of Poland.

The migrations of the Teutons drove most of the Wends out of Denmark into the marshy and sandy lands at the mouth of the Vistula ; and, somewhat later, home quarrels, and fears of the Tatars, impelled the republics of Russia to call in the aid of the Northmen, who quickly put an end to the freedom of the cities, and set up the principality that was the germ of the Russian empire.

The Greek Church converted the Bulgarians about the year 870; and the translations of the liturgy and Scriptures, made for their benefit, have been the authorized version of the Slavonians ever since.   The same missionaries, Cyrillus and Methodius, likewise baptized the first Christian king of Bohemia ; and in the next century, a Bohemian bishop, Adalbert of Prague, converted Hungary and Poland.   But these three realms gave their allegiance to the Western, not the Eastern Church ; and though Hungary received much of her civilization from Constantinople, her faith was with Rome.   The Norse Grand Princes of Muscovy themselves sought Christianity from Byzantium, and the Russian Church has ever since been the most earnest and conservative of the Eastern Churches.

The Baltic Slavonians held out longest against the Gospel.   Missionaries preached to them, and orders of knighthood crusaded against them on far into modern history, and the final period of their conversion and settlement into small duchies or realms, held by the conquering knights, is hardly worth tracing out.

The next step in general Slavonic history is the great Turkish outbreak, which almost crushed Muscovy, and infused a strong Tatar element into the Russian population ; and, finally, conquered the Greek empire, and with it the Bulgarian lands, which, though never Mahometanized, have ever since remained under Turkish dominion.

The kingdoms of Bohemia and Hungary, with the other western Slavonic provinces, were one by one absorbed into the German empire, or by the House of Austria—it made little difference which was the original tenure—all are ' Austrian ' now, whether willingly or not.

With the same skill, the House of Brandenburg obtained the domains of the Baltic Slaves, and formed the kingdom of Prussia, very Teutonic to the west, and very Slavonic to the east.

Meantime, after a long period of exhaustion, almost of extinction, the Muscovites came forth from the Tatar oppression stronger than ever ; and by gradual conquests from their former enemies, at length formed their huge empire of the east.

And Poland, after many a turbulent election, many a summons to German princes to hold the reins of its restless multitude, was finally and unrighteously dismembered and divided, and the cry of its wrongs has ever since rent the ears of Europe.

The existing Slavonian languages are the Russian, the literary language of the great empire ; the Livonian, or the language spoken by the persons who are not of Finnish blood in the elbow beneath the Gulf of Finland ; the Lettish and Lusatian, used by the old Prussian subjects and their neighbours in Russia ; the Polish ; the Slovak, spoken in Hungary ; the Servian, Illyrian, and Croatian, all representing the old Bulgarian.

Of all these, it is perhaps the Polish that has contributed the most names to the European stock, and they are but few ; but there were intermarriages, and friendly intercourse, besides occasional elections to the Polish throne ; and, latterly, the dispersion and exile of the Polish nobility carried their names into distant parts of Europe, and gave them a romantic interest.

Bohemia and Hungary sent a few names into the Austrian line, but they soon died out ; and Russia uses comparatively few native Slavonic names, but makes chief use of those of the saints of the Greek Church.

Slavonian languages are said to be soft in their own speech, but our letters clumsily render their sounds, and make them of cumbrous length ; and the few names that have been adopted have been severely mangled.

They are, for the most part, grand and poetical compounds, often exactly corresponding to Greek or Teutonic names, and with others more poetical than those in either of these other languages, such as Danica, the Morning star ; Zwezdana, or in Russian, Swetlana, a Star ; Zora, Zorana, Zorica, the Slovak Aurora ; and Zorislava, the

Dawn of glory ; Golubica, the Dove ; Lala, the Tulip. The Slaves
use likewise the amaranth, or everlasting flower, as a name both for
men and women, namely, Smiljan and Smiljana ; and while a man
may be called Dubislav, or Oak fame, the Servians and Illyrians call
their daughters after fruits,—Grozdana, Rich in grapes ; Jagoda, the
Strawberry ; and Kupina, or Kuviena, the Gooseberry.*

SECTION II.—*Slavonian Mythology.*

The Slavonians had a polytheistic religion, answering, in spirit, to
that of the other Indo-European nations ; but as they had no mythic
literature, like Greece and Scandinavia, we are dependent for
information upon popular ballads and superstitions, eked out by
the notices of missionaries and statements of conquerors ; and it is not
easy to perceive whether their myths were an independent branch of
the general stock, or only the Teutonic religion under another
dress.

The divine word, in all the various nations, is Bog. It was used for
God, both in the old heathen times, and afterwards in its full sense,
when Christianity became known to them. It enters into numerous
names, both before and after Christianity. The most noted is
Bogislav, or God's glory, which was borne by many a Pole and old
Prussian ; and, in 1627, it finished off the old Slavonic line of dukes
of Pomerania, from whom that state came to the acquisitive house
of Brandenburg. The historical Latinism of the name is Bogislaus ;
and it is still current in Illyria as Bogosav.

Theophilus is literally translated by Bogoljub or Bogoje in Illyria,
and Bohumil in Bohemia. This makes it probable that Robert
Guiscard thence took the name of his eldest son, Bohemond, giving
it a Norman termination. The mother is called Alvareda, and she
is said to have been divorced on the score of consanguinity ; but it is
not improbable that this was a mere excuse of the wily duke of
Calabria for ridding himself of an Illyrian wife. Bohemond is said
to have been called after a giant of romance ; but the giant has not
as yet transpired, and may have been, after all, a Slavonic divinity.
Bohemond, or Boemondo, as Tasso calls him, was the Ulysses of the
first Crusade, and left a grandson namesake.

Theodorus and Theodora are answered by Bogdan and Bogdana,
both spelt with *h* in Bohemia—Bohdan, Bohdana, and in Illyria
Bozidar, Bozidara ; and, as has been already said, the Divine birth-
night, Christmas, is commemorated by Slovak children being called
Bozo. Bogohval is Thank God, Bogoboj, God's battle, all names in
use in Poland and the kindred nations before the general names of
Europe displaced the native growth.

* Kombst, (in Johnson's) *Physical Atlas ;* Max Muller, *Lectures ;* Le Beau,
Bas Empire ; Schleicher, *Sprachen Europen ;* Zeuss, *Deutschen und die Nachbar
Stamme.*

The word does not answer to either Deus or God, but is related to the Sanscrit *bhagas*, destiny.

The word *ljube*, Love, is rather a favourite in the affectionate Slavonic nomenclature. At the outset of Bohemian history we come on the beautiful legend of Queen Libussa, or the darling. She succeeded her father in 618, governed alone for fourteen years, then, finding her people discontented, sought the wisest man in her domains for a husband, and found him, like Cincinnatus, at the plough, when he not only retained his homely cloak, iron table, and bark sandals, as marks of his origin, but bade them be produced at all future royal elections. His name, Przemysl, or the thoughtful, was continued in his line, though chroniclers cut its dreadful knot of consonants by calling it Premislaus, and the next ensuing namesake Germanized himself as Ottokar. He was afterwards elected king of Poland, where the name was used, with the feminine Przemyslava.

Russia has the feminine Ljubov, Love, fondly termed Lubuika, and, in families where French is spoken, called Aimée, though this more properly translates Ljubka and Ljubnia. The Slovaks have Ljuboslav and its feminine, and the Polish Lubomirsky is Peace-loving. The Russian Ljubov is chiefly used in allusion to the Christian grace of love; and Faith, or Vjera, and Hope, Nadezna, are both, likewise, very popular at the present day, the latter usually Frenchified into Nadine; while the Serbs have Nada, or Nadan.

The Slaves of Rugen had a terrible deity called Sviatovid, or the luminous, who was considered to answer to Mars, or Tyr, and had a temple at Acron, and an image with seven heads, which must have much resembled Indian idols. A white horse was sacred to him, and was supposed to be ridden by him during the night, and to communicate auguries by the manner in which it leaped over lances that were arranged in its path. Human sacrifices were offered to this deity both in Rugen and Bohemia; and when his image was at length overthrown, St. Vitus, from the resemblance of sound, was confounded with him by the populace, and Svantovit, as they called both alike, was still the tutelary genius of the place. Svetozor, Dawn of light, and Svetlana, a Russian lady's name still in use, are connected with light, the first syllable of his name.

Conjoined with Sviatovid, and lying on a purple bed in the temple in Rugen, was the seven-headed Rugevid, or Ranovid (whose name is explained by reference to the Sanscrit *rana*, blood-thirsty); and likewise Radegost, the god of hospitality, from *rad*, prosperous, and *gosc*, a guest, the word so often encountered. Several names began with the first syllable—Rada, Radak, Radan, Radinko, Radmir, Radivoj, Radko, Radman, Radmil, Radoje, Radoslav; and the Illyrians have the hospitable name of Gostomil, or Guest love: indeed, *gost* forms the end of many Savonic names, in accordance with the ready and courteous welcome always offered by this people.

Davor is another war god, whose name seems of very near kindred to Mavors, or Mars, and who left Davorinn, Davroslav, and Davro-slava, as names.

Tikla was the old Slavonic goddess of good luck, and, being confounded with St. Thekla, made this latter name popular in Poland, Russia, and Hungary ; and, in like manner, Zenovia, the huntress goddess, conduced to make Zenobia, and Zizi, its contraction, common in Russia.

The fire god was Znitch ; and though he does not show any direct namesakes, yet there are sundry fire-names in his honour, such as the Slovak Vatroslav and Illyrian Ognoslav, both signifying fire glory. Possibly, too, the Russian Mitrofan may be connected with the old Persian *mithras*, or sacred fire ; though in history it figures in Greek ecclesiastical guise, as the Patriarch Metrophanes.*

Section III.—*Warlike Names.*

Few more Slavonic names remain to be mentioned, and these more for their correspondence with those of other races than for much intrinsic interest.

Very few are known beyond their own limits. Stanislav, or Camp glory, is the most universal, and is one of the very few found in the Roman calendar, which has two Polish saints thus named. The first, Stanislav Sczepanowski, Bishop of Cracow, was one of the many prelates of the eleventh century who had to fight the battle of Church against king, and he was happy in that his cause was that of morality as well as discipline. Having excommunicated King Boleslav for carrying off the wife of one of the nobles, he was murdered by the king in his own cathedral ; and Gregory VII. being the reigning Pope, his martyrdom was an effectual seed of submission to the Church. The wretched king died by his own hand, and the bishop became a Slavonian Becket, was enshrined at Cracow, and thought to work miracles. His name was, of course, national, and was again canonized in the person of Stanislav Kostka, one of the early Jesuits who guided the reaction of Roman Catholicism in Poland. The name has even been used in France, chiefly for the sake of the father of the Polish queen of Louis XV., and afterwards from the influx of Poles after the partition of their kingdom.

English.	French.	Portuguese.	Italian.
Stanislaus	Stanislas	Estanislau	Stanislao

German.	Bavarian.	Polish.	Illyrian.
Stanislav	Stanes	Stanislav	Stanisav
	Stanisl	Stach	Stanko
Lettish.	Stanel	Stas	
Stanislavs	Stanerl		
Stachis			

* Tooke, *Russia ;* Eichioff, *Tableau de la Littérature du Nord au Moyen Age ;* Zeuss, *Deutschen und die Nachbar Stamme ; Universal History.*

Much in the same spirit is the Russian Boris, from the old Slavonian *borotj*, to fight. It has never been uncommon in Muscovy,
and belonged to the brother-in-law of Ivan the Terrible, Boris
Goudenoff, who was regent for his imbecile nephew Feodor ; and,
after assassinating the hopeful younger brother, Dmitri, reigned as
czar, till dethroned by a counterfeit Dmitri. Borka and Borinka are
the contractions, and Borivor was the first Christian duke of Bohemia.

Bron, a weapon, forms Bronislav and Bronislava. Voj is the
general Slavonic term for war, and is a very frequent termination.
Vojtach, the Polish Vojciech, and Lithuanian Waitkus, all mean
warrior.

It is a curious feature in nomenclature how strongly glory and
fame are the leading notion of the entire race, whose national title of
glory has had such a fall. *Slav* is an inevitable termination ; *voj*
almost as constantly used ; and even the tenderest commencements
are forced to love war, and to love fame. The old Russian Mstisslav
glories in vengeance (*mest*), but is usually recorded as Mistislaus ;
Rostislav increases glory ; Vratislav, Glowing glory, names not only
the Wratislaus of history, but the city of Breslaw. The Slovak
Vekoslav, and Vekoslava, are Eternal fame.

The two animals used in Slavonic names are warlike ; Vuk, the
wolf, and Bravac, the wild boar ; but both these are very possibly
adopted from the German Wulf and Eber.

SECTION IV.—*Names of Might.*

Boleje, strong or great, answers to the Teuton *mer*, and Boleslav is
great glory. Boleslav Chrobry, the second Christian prince of Poland,
was a devout savage and great conqueror, both in Russia and Bohemia.
He was the first Pole to assume the title of king ; and after his death,
in 1025, there are many instances of his name in both Poland and
Bohemia.

In this latter country it had, however, a far more sinister fame.
Borivor and Ludmilla, the first Christian prince and princess of that
duchy, had two grandsons, Boleslav and Vesteslav, or Venceslav, the
first a heathen, the latter a Christian.   Boleslav stirred up the pagan
population against his brother, and murdered him while praying in
church at Prague, on the 28th of September, 644, thus conferring on
him the honour of a patron saint and centre of legends. The House
of Luxemburg obtained the kingdom of Bohemia by marriage, and
Venceslav was introduced among their appellations in the form of
Wenzel ; and the crazy and furious Bohemian king of that name sat
for a few unhappy years on the imperial throne ; but in spite of the
odium of that memory, the name of good King Wenceslas, as we call
it, held its ground, and contracts into Vacslav and Vaclav.   Some
say that it is crown glory, from *vienice;* others deduce the prefix from
vest, the superlative of *veliku*, great, which furnished the Bulgarian
Velika, Veleslav, Velimir.

The familiar root that has been so often encountered in *valeo*, *wield*, &c., in the sense of power, gives the prefix *vlad* to various favourite Slavonic names. The Russian Vladimir, being of the race of Rurik, is sometimes seized upon as Wa'demar ; and, in fact, there is little difference in the sense of the first syllable. He is a great national saint, since it was his marriage with the Greek Princess Anna that obtained for the Byzantine Church her mighty Muscovite daughter ; and in honour of him, Vladimir has been perpetually used in Russia, shortened into Volodia, and expanded into Volodinka by way of endearment.

The national saint of Hungary was Vladislav, who was the restorer of the faith that had almost faded away after the death of the sainted King Stephen, and was chosen as leader of a crusade, which was pre- vented by his death in 1095. His name, and that of his many votaries, have sorely puzzled Latin and Teutonic tongues ; when not content, like the French, to term him St. Lancelot, his countrymen call themselves after him Laszlo, or Laczko, the Illyrians Lako, the Letts Wendis ; but chroniclers vary between Uladislaus and Ladislaus in Hungary and Poland ; and when the Angevin connection brought down a king from Hungary to revenge the death of his brother upon Giovanni of Naples, the Italians called him Ladislao ; and as Ladislas we recognize the last native Hungarian king, brother-in-law to Charles V. Vladislavka is a feminine, contracting into Valeska, which is still borne by Polish young ladies. Vladivoj is another of the same class, and *sve*, all, with the verb *vladati*, to rule, has formed Vsevolad and Svevlad, All ruler, and Vseslav, All fame.

Possibly there may be some connection here with the deity Volos, Weles, or Veless, invoked under these names by the Slaves, Bohemians, and Russians, as witness of their oaths, and likewise as guardian of flocks. Possibly the Roman Pales may be the same deity under another form ; but the name of Volos is still applied to shepherds, and comes, no doubt, from the Slavonic *vlas*, or Russian *volos*, the same word as wool.

The word *mir* at the end of Vladimir is somewhat doubtful. It may mean peace, or it may mean the world ; and in like manner the Slovak Miroslav stands in doubt between world-fame or peaceful- fame.

Purvan, Purvançe, is the Bulgarian *first*, whether used in the sense of chief or of first-born does not appear ; but, at any rate, bearing a most eastern sound with it.

We are familiar with the Russian *ukase*, from *ukasat*, to show forth ; and *kaze* in Polish has the same sense of command. Kazimir is thus Command of peace, a noble title for a prince, and essentially national in Poland, where it was endeared by the fame of three of the best of the earlier sovereigns. It has the feminine Kasimira, and is one of the very few Slavonic names used by Teutons. Intermarriages introduced it among the German princes ; and Johann Kasimir, a son of the Pfalzgraf of the Rhine, was a noted commander in the war of the Revolt of the Netherlands, and received the Garter from Queen Elizabeth. He was commonly called Prince Kasimir, and his name-

sakes spread in Germany ; and either for the sake of the sound, or
Polish sympathies, Casimir was somewhat fashionable in France.

French. Casimir	Polish. Kazimir Kazimierz	Bohemian. Kazimir	Lettish. Kasimirs Kasche
German. Kasimir			Kaschis Kaschuk

Kol, council, formed Koloman, somewhat noted in early Slavonic
history.

Jar, pronounced as beginning with *y*, means strength or firmness.
Jaromir, Firm peace, was prince of Bohemia in 999. Jaropolk, firm
government, was the last heathen grand prince of Muscovy ; and this
name, with Jaroslav, is very frequent in the early annals of the House
of Rurik.

From *lid*, the people, (our old friends *hleute* and λαος,) came
Ljulomir and Ludmilla, who was the first Christian duchess in
Bohemia, and was strangled by her heathen daughter-in-law,
Dragotina, the mother of Boleslav and Venceslav, leaving a sainted
name much used among all Slavonian women, and called at home
Lida and Lidiska ; in Russia, Ljudmila. Lidvina was likewise
Bohemian, from Vina, an old goddess.

SECTION V.—*Names of Virtue.*

Words signifying goodness are far from uncommon in this class of
nomenclature. *Dobry*, good, has a worthy family. Dobrija, sometimes called Dobrowka, was the Bohemian princess whose marriage,
like those of Clotilda, Bertha, and Anna, brought religion into her
new country. Her husband, Miczslav, of Poland, had been born
blind, but recovered his sight at seven years old. He had seven
wives while still a heathen, but was told that he would have no
children unless he began afresh with a Christian lady. He demanded
the Czech princess. She brought St. Adalbert, of Prague, with her ;
and Mistislaus as he is generally called in history, is counted as the
first Polish Christian king, in the year 970. So national was the
name, that the Poles altered Maria of Muscovy to Dobrija, on her
marriage with Kasimir, their king. The other names of this commencement are Illyrian—Dobrogast, Dobroljub, Dobroslav, and its
feminine Dobrovoj, Dobrvok, Dobrutin, and Dobrotina, Good guest,
Good love, Good glory, Good war, Good wolf and Beneficent.

Ssvätyj, holy, and *polk*, government, are the component parts of
the old Russian Sviatopolk, often found among the early race of
Rurik. Holy glory, Sviatoslav, was the inappropriate name of the
son of the Christian princess Olga, the same who refused baptism,

believing that all the converts were cowards, and that he should lose the support of the war gods and of his followers.

The Illyrian *blag*, good, makes Blagorod, Good birth, also, as usual, Blagovoj, Blagoslav, Blagodvor, Blagogost, and the contraction Blagoje.

Prav is upright, a connection, it may be, of *probus*, and it has formed the Slavonic Upravda, and the Illyrian Pravdoslav, Pravdoslava, Pravoje. It is, perhaps, the same with the Wend *prib*, which formed the name Pribislava. The Danes amalgamated the Wend *pred* into their own names as Predbiorn, or Preban.

Çast, or *cest*, is honour. The first letter, *ç*, should be pronounced *z;* it is rather a favourite with Poland and Bohemia. Çastibog exactly answers to the Greek Timotheus, as does Çastimir to the modern German Ehrenfried, very possibly a translation from it. Çastislav is the most popular form, like all else ending in *slav*, and has shortened into Çaslav, Çaislav, Cestislav, Ceslav.

Of the same sound is the first letter of *çist*, pure, whence Çistav and Çistislav. From *tverd*, firm, we have Tverdko, Tverdimir, Tverdislav.

Section VI.—*Names of Affection.*

The Slavonian nature has much in common with the Irish, and there is much of caressing and personal affection. *Ljub*, as has been seen, is a favourite element in names, and *dragi*, dear, does a considerable part. Dragomira, or Bear peace, was the name of the heathen mother of Boleslav and Venceslav. Dragoslav, or dear glory, is Russian, and Poland and Bohemia have used Dragan, Draganka, Dragoj, Dragojila, Dragioila, Dragnja, Dragotin, Dragotinka, Dragilika, Dragija.

Duschinka is the tender epithet which, in Russia, a serf applies to her lady in addressing her. It is properly the diminutive of Duscha, happy, which is sometimes a Christian name in Russia as well as in Illyria, where it is called Dusa and Dusica. *Stastny* is the Bohemian word for happy, and is sometimes used as a name. Blazena, meaning happy, in these tongues, is used as the South Slavonic equivalent for Beatrice.

Another word for love is *mil*. Mila and Milica are the feminines, meaning lovely, or amiable, Milan the masculine ; but all these are now confounded with the numerous progeny of the Latin Æmilius. *Mil* is a favourite termination, and is found loving war and glory— Milovoj and Miloslav.

Cedoljub and Cedomil are both most loving names, the first half of the name signifying a child, so that they signify 'child-love,' or 'filial affection.'

Brotherly love is likewise honoured as nowhere else, save in the Greek Philadelphus, which exactly renders Bratoljub, from *brata*, a word of the universal family likeness whence ἀδελφός and *hermano* are the only noted variations. Brajan and Bragican also belong to brotherhood.

Deva is a maiden, whence Devoslav and Devoslava, probably formed, or at least used, in honour of the Blessed Virgin.

SECTION VII.—*Names from the Appearance.*

A few names of extremely personal application exist, such as the Servian Mrena, white in the eyes, and Mladen, young, and the highly uncomplimentary Illyrian Smoljan and Smoljana, from *smoljo*, an overhanging nose, probably a continuation of the nickname of some favoured individual.

Krasan, beautiful, however, was used in names, as Krasimir, Krasislav, Krasomil, &c. ; and *zlata*, golden, though once used in Zlatoust, as a literal translation of Chrysostomos, in other names may, it is hoped, be employed to denote beauty ; or else Zlatoljub, with its contractions Zlatoje and Zlatko, would be a most avaricious name. Zlata, Zlatana, Zlatibor, and Zlatislav, are also used.

Tiho, silent, is a curious prefix. Tihomil, Silent love, and Tihomir, Silent peace, are clear enough ; but Tihoslav, Silent glory, is a puzzling compound, probably only arising from the habit of ending everything with *slav*.

It is remarkable, however, that there is an entire absence of the names of complexion so common among the Kelts and Romans.

CONCLUSION.

It still remains to cast a passing glance over the countries of the European commonwealth, and observe the various classes of names that have prevailed in them. It is only possible to do this, with my present information, very broadly and generally. In fact, every province has its own peculiar nomenclature; and the more remote the place the more characteristic the names, and, therefore, the most curious are the least accessible. It is the tendency of diffused civilization to diminish variations, and up to a certain point, at least, to assimilate all to one model, and this process for many years affected the educated and aristocratic community, although latterly a desire for distinctiveness and pride in the individual peculiarities of race and family, have arisen; but, on the other hand, the class below, which used to be full of individualities, has now reached the imitative stage, and is rapidly laying aside all national and provincial characteristics. The European nobility, except where some old family name has been preserved as an heirloom, thus cease, about the sixteenth century, to bear national names; but all are on one level of John, Henry, Frederick, Charles, Louisa, &c., while the native names come to light among citizens and peasants; but now, while the gentleman looks back for the most distinctive name in his remote ancestry, and proudly bestows it on his child, the mechanic or labourer shrinks from the remark and misunderstanding that have followed his old traditional baptismal name, and calls his son by the last remarkable one he can find, or by one culled from literature. These remarks apply chiefly to England, but also, in great measure, to the town population of France, and to all other places which are much affected by the universal fusion of national ideas and general intercourse of the present day.

SECTION I.—*Greece.*

Modern Greece has the most direct inheritance from the ancient, classical, and old Christian names. True, her population has undergone changes which leave but little of the proud old Ionian or Dorian blood; but her language has been victorious over the barbarous speech of her conquerors, and Latins and Bulgarians became Greek beneath her influence.

The inhabitants of her peninsulas and islands are, then, with few exceptions, called by Greek names. The exceptions are, in the first place, in favour of the Hebrew names that are in universal use, not only the never-failing Joannes and Maria, but Isaakos, David, Elias, and others, for whom the Greek Church has inculcated more constant veneration than has the Latin. Next there are the few Latin names that were accepted by the Greeks during the existence of the Byzantine empire, and either through martyrs or by favourite sovereigns, recommended themselves to the love of posterity ; but these are few in number, and Konstantinos is the only distinguished one. And, lastly, an extremely small proportion have been picked up by intercourse with the Western nations, but without taking root.

The mass of Greek names belongs to the class that I have called 'Greek Christian,' being those that were chiefly current in the years of persecution and martyrdom—some old hereditary ones from ancient time, others coined with the stamp of the Faith. These, with others expressive of favourite ideas, such as Macharios, Blessed, Sophia, Wisdom, Zoe, Life, were the staple of the Greeks until the modern revival brought forward the old heroic and historical names ; and Achilles, Alkibiades, Themistokles, &c., are again in familiar use.

In a list of names used at the present day in the Ionian Islands, I find seventeen men and four women of the old historical and heroic class ; the four ladies being Kalliope, Arethusa, Euphrosyne, and Aspasia ; and, perhaps, Psyche and Olympias ought to be added to these : twenty-three male and nineteen female of the Christian Greek class : two Hebrew, i.e. Joannes and Jakobos, of men ; three of women, Maria, Anna, and Martha. Paulos and Konstantinos, and perhaps Maura, alone represent the Latin, and Artorioos the Kelt, probably borrowed from some Englishman.

Surnames are inherited from the Latin nomina, and began earlier in Constantinople than anywhere else. They are divided between the patronymic, ending, as of old, in *ides*, the local, and the permanent nickname.

SECTION II.—*Russia.*

The European portion of the vast empire of Russia is nationally Slavonic, but much mixed with Tatar ; and the high nobility is descended, at least according to tradition, from the Norsemen. The royal line is, through intermarriages, almost Germanized. The Church continues the faith, practice, and ritual of the Greek Church, but in the old Slavonic tongue, from which the spoken language has much deviated.

The Greek element greatly predominates in the nomenclature : native saints have contributed a few Slavonic specimens, and a very few inherited from the Norsemen occur ; but the race of Rurik seem very quickly to have adopted Russian names. The Tatar population hardly contributes a Christian name to history, and the Germans almost always, on their marriage with the Russian imperial family, assumed native, *i. e.* Greek or Roman-Greek, names. The present fashions in nomenclature are, however, best explained in the following letter from an English lady residing in Russia :—

'Children (and grown-up persons in their own family) are, I may say, universally called by their diminutives. In society the Christian name and patronymic are made use of, and you seldom hear a person *addressed* by his family name, though he may be spoken of in the third person as "Romanoff," or "Romanova" (surnames take the gender and number of their bearers), except by his superiors, such as a general to his young officers, &c.

'The patronymic is formed by the addition of *vitch,* or *evitch,* to the Christian name of a person's father ; as Constantine Petrovitch, Alexander Andréevitch, in the masculine ; and of *ovna,* or *evna,* in the feminine, Olga Petrovna, Elizavetta Andréovna.

'I would call your attention to the error that is generally made in the newspapers, where these patronymics are spelt with a *W,* whereas they really are spelt and pronounced with a *V.*

'The diminutives can always be traced to the root, being derived from the first, or the accented syllable, of the full name, with the termination of a little fond syllable, *sha, ia, inka, otchka, oushka ;* for instance, Mária, Másha, Mashinka—Olga, Olinka, Olitchka : Ian, John, Vanoushka, Vanka—Alexandre, Alexandra, Sasha, Sashinka. Not in one diminutive are there such glaring differences of spelling and sound, as Dick for Richard, Polly for Mary, Patty for Martha.

'Perhaps it is not superfluous to mention, that there are diminutives of reproach as well as of affection ; if you scold Olga, she becomes Olka ; Ivan, Vanka ; and so on. This form, however, is seldom made use of by well-educated people, except in fun ; though there are some who do not hesitate to make free use of it in their kitchens and nurseries, in a private sort of a manner. Among the lower orders, and especially in the country, it is not considered reproachful, but is the general form of appellation. You observe, that this is formed by the addition of *ka* to the principal syllable.

'I find, on attentive search in the "*Monument of Faith,*" a sort of devotional book of prayer and meditations applied to every day of the year, and with the names and a short-biography of each saint, that there are 822 men's names and 204 women's in the Russian calendar. Of these, you will be surprised to hear twelve only are really Slavonic. Unfortunately I am unable to inform you of their meanings, notwithstanding every inquiry among the few educated inhabitants of this little out-of-the-way town ; but if ever I have an opportunity of seeing a real "Sclavonophile," as searchers into Russian antiquities are called, I will not fail to ask about it. The names are as follows :—

'1 Boris (*m.*), grand duke ; murdered in 1015.
'2 Gleb (*m.*), brother to Boris ; murdered in 1016.
'3 Vetcheslav (*m.*), Duke Chetsky.
'4 Vladimir (*m.*), grand duke ; baptized in 988 (1st Christian grand duke).

'5 Vsévolod (m.), duke ; he changed his name to Gabriel when baptized ; died in 1138.

'6 Igor (m.), grand duke of Tchernigoff, 1147. (Norse.)

'7 Razóomnik (m.) ; this name is taken from *rázoom*, which means sense, wisdom, and signifies a wise, sensible person.

'8 Olga (f.), grand duchess, god-mother to Vladimir. She was the first Christian duchess. (Norse.)

'9 Ludmilla (f.), god-mother to Vsevold, and martyred in the cause of Christianity.

'10 Véra (f.), means faith.

'11 Nadéjda (f.), hope.

'12 Lubov, charity, love.

'All the other names are of Greek, Latin, or Hebrew origin (with a very few exceptions, of which I will speak afterwards), and though they generally differ in termination, yet they are to be recognized instantly. I observe that in Greek names *K* is used, and not the sound of *S*, as in Kiril, Kiprian (Cyril, Cyprian). Also that *Th* takes the sound of *F*, as Féodore, Fomá (Theodore, Thomas). But the *Th* is represented by a letter distinct from that by which *Ph* or *F* are represented, the former being written Θ and the latter Ø, but both have exactly the same sound. *U* sometimes becomes *V* when used in the middle of names, as Evgenia (Eugenia), Evstafi (Eustace). *B* in many instances becomes *V*, as in Vasili (Basil), Varvara (Barbara), Varfolomey (Bartholomew).

'The names of other origin are very few, viz.:—

> 'Avenir—Indian ;
> Arisa—Arabian ;
> Daria—Persian ;
> Sadof—Persian ;
> Erminigeld—Gothic.

'German names, I may say, are not to be found in the Russo-Greek calendar.

'When I say that there are 1026 Christian names in the calendar, I must explain that the number of saints is infinitely greater ; there being from two or three to twenty or thirty every day of the year, the 29th of February included. There are sixty-one St. John's days, thirty St. Peter's, twenty-seven St. Féodor's, twenty-four St. Alexandre's, eighteen St. Gregory's, sixteen St. Vasili's, twelve St. André's, ten St. Constantine's, &c.

'Sometimes the same saint is fêted two or three times in the year, but the different saints of the same name are very many. The female saints are in less number. Maria and Anna each occur ten times in the year, Euphrosinia six times, Féodora eight, and so on. In proportion to the number of saints so are the names of the population ; so that Ivan is the most common ; next, I think, comes Vasili, André, Pëtre, Nicolas (Nikoláï), Alexandre.

'The lower orders have no idea of dates ; they always reckon by the saints' days. Ask a woman the age of her baby, she will say, "Well, I suppose it is about thirty weeks old." "What is its name?"

"Ivan." "Which Ivan?" you ask, your calculations being defeated by the sixty-one St. Johns. "Why, the Ivan that 'lives' four days after dirty Prascóvia." You then understand that the child must have been born about the 10th or 12th October, as the blessed saint is irreverently called "dirty Prascóvia" from falling on the 14th October, a very muddy time of the year in holy Russia.

'One name only can be given at baptism, and it must be taken from the orthodox calendar. German, French, and English names not to be found there cannot be bestowed, nor can a surname, as in England.'

Section III.—*Italy.*

Italy, like Greece, has her classical inheritance. Her Lucio, Marco, Tito, Giulio, bear appellations borne by their Oscan or Sabine forefathers, even before Rome was a city ; but mingled with this ancient stream there have been such an infinite number of other currents, that no land has undergone more influences, or has a more remarkable variety of personal names.

In the decay of the Roman Empire, and the growth of the Church, the old prænomina were a good deal set aside, by the heathen in his search for heroic-sounding titles, by the Christian in his veneration for the martyrs and saints of his Church. So the prosaic matter-of-fact three-storied name of the Roman was varied by importations, generally of Christian Greek, but now and then of heroic Greek ; and as the Christian element predominated, the Hebrew apostle or prophet suggested the name of the young Roman. Barbarians, acquiring rights of citizenship, ceased to adopt the nomen of their patron, retaining appellations that a Scipio or Cato would have thought only fit to be led in a triumph, but still putting on a Latin finish and regarding them as Roman. But these—disgraceful as they are now regarded—were the days that stamped the Roman impress on the world, and marked the whole South of Europe with an indelible. print of Latin civilization and language.

Goths, Vandals, Gepidæ, and Lombards came on northern Italy one after the other ; and the Lombards established a permanent kingdom that deeply influenced the north of the peninsula and Teutonized its nobility. The towns were less open to their influence ; and Venice remained the Roman and partly Byzantine city she was from her source—using a language where her *g* is still the Greek *ζ*, and christening her children by the names of later Rome in its Christian days, only with the predominance of the national saint, Marco, the guardian of the city ever since his bones were stolen from Alexandria. The recurring *ano*, or *ani*, of Venetian surnames is the adoptive *anus* of Rome—republican Rome—whose truest representative the merchant city was till her shameful degradation and final ruin.

The Italian element in the population of Cisalpine Gaul continued far too strong for the Lombardic conquerors, and ere long had taught them its own language. If they wrote, it was in their best approach to classical Latin ; when they spoke, it was in the dialectic Latin of the provinces farther broken by the inability of the victors to learn the case terminations, which were settled by making, in the first declensions, all the singular masculines end in *o*, and plurals in *i*, all the feminines in *a* and *e ;* in the others, striking a balance and calling all *ite.* But though the speech was Latin, the Lombard kept his old Teutonic name—Adelgiso, Astolfo, or the like, and handed it on to his son, softened, indeed, but with its northern form clearly traceable. Time went on, and the Lombardic kingdom was fused into the Holy Roman Empire. The towns remained self-governing, self-protecting old Roman municipalities ; the Lombardic nobles, if they had a strong mountain fastness, lived like eagles in their nests and were the terror of all ; if they had but a small home on the plains, were forced to make terms with the citizens and accept their privileges as a favour. Thus came the Teuton element into the cities, and old Lombardic names were borne by Florentine and Milanese citizens. The Roman nomina so far were preserved that a whole family would be called after its founder, whether by his name or nickname. The noted man might be originally Giacopo, but called Lapo for short. His children were, collectively, Lapi ; a single one would be either Bindo Lapo, or, latterly, *dei Lapi*, one of the Lapi. Sometimes office gave a surname, as Cancelliero, when the family became Cancellieri. One of these Cancellieri was twice married ; and one of the wives being yclept Bianca, her children were called Bianchi ; their half-brothers Neri, merely as the reverse ; and thence arose the two famous party words of the Guelfs of Florence. Latterly, when these names in *i* were recognized as surnames, it was usual to christen a boy by the singular, and thus we have Pellegrino Pellegrini, Cavaliere Cavalieri, and many other like instances, familiar to the readers of Dante and of old Italian history. Dante's own names—the first contracted from a Latin participle, the second the direct patronymic from his father—Alighiero, the Teutonic noble spear, form a fit instance of the mixed tongue, which he first reduced to the dignity of a written language. Those were its days of vigour and originality ; of fresh name-coining from its own resources,—Gemma, Fiamma, Brancaleone, Vinciguerra, Cacciaguido—words not merely of commonplace tradition, but original invention.

Meantime southern Italy had been under other influences. Long remaining a province of the Eastern empire, Calabria, Apulia, and Sicily were the marauding ground of the Saracens, till the gallant Norman race of Hauteville came to their deliverance, and imposed on them a Norman-French royalty and nobility, with their strange compound of French and Northern names—Robert and Roger, Tancred and William, Ferabras and Drogo, the latter certainly Frank, as it belonged to an illegitimate son of Charlemagne. It was brought to England by Dru de Baladon, a follower of the Conqueror ; and we find it again in Sir Drew Drury, the keeper of Mary of Scotland. It may be related to the Anglo-Saxon *dry*, a sorcerer, and *dreist*, the German skilful, but its derivation is uncertain.

When the Norman influence waned, the Swabian power gave a few German names to the Two Sicilies, but was less influential than either the French in Naples or the Aragonese in Sicily, where the one strewed Carlo, the other Fernando and Alfonso.

All this time the Christian name was the prominent one, more used and esteemed than titles throughout all ranks. Men and women would be simply spoken of as Giovanni or Beatrice, or more often, by contractions, Vanni or Bice, Massuccio, or Cecca, now and then with Ser or Monna (signor or madonna) added as titles of respect.

All the time, what may be called the Roman Catholic influence on nomenclature was growing in its great centre. The city of martyrs was filled with churches where the remains of the saint gave the title, and was thought to give the sanctity, and these suggested names to natives and pilgrims alike. Cecilia, Sebastiano, Lucia, &c., and more than can be enumerated, won their popularity from owning a church that served as a station in the pilgrimages, and thus influenced the world. Relics brought to Rome, and then bestowed as a gift upon princes, carried their saints' epithets far and wide ; and when Constantinople was in her decay, and purchased the aid of Western sovereigns by gifts of her sacred stores, the Greek and Eastern saints had their names widely diffused, as Anna, Adriano, &c. Moreover, the feasts of different events in the life of the Blessed Virgin Mary began to tell on Italian names, and Annunciata, and later, Assunta, were the produce.

Francesco is the most universal name of native Italian fabrication. It is one of what may be called the names spread by religious orders, all of which originate in Italy ; Benedetto, oldest of all and universal in Romanist lands ; Augustino, never very popular ; Domenico, not uncommon in Italy, but most used in gloomy Spain ; Francesco and Clara, both really universal in Protestant as well as Roman Catholic lands.

The revival of classical literature, produced partly by the influx of Greek scholars after the fall of Constantinople, partly by the vigour of Boccaccio and Petrarch, brought a classical influence to bear on Italy, of which her names are more redolent than those elsewhere. Emilia, Virgilio, Olimpia, Ercole, Fabrizio, all arose and flourished in Italy, and have never since been dropped, though the Romanist influence has gone on growing, and others have affected parts of the country.

Romance had some influence—Orlando, Oliviero, Rinaldo, Ruggiero —and the more remote Lancilotto, Ginevra, Isolda, Tristano, all became popular through literature ; and the great manufacture of Italian novels, no doubt, tended to keep others in vogue.

The French and German wars in Italy, the erection of the Lombardic republics into little tyrannical duchies, and the Spanish conquest of Naples, all tended to destroy much of the individuality of Italian nomenclature, and reduce that of the historical characters to the general European level. And this tendency has increased rather than diminished, as Spain devoured the North, and 'balance of power' struggled for Austrian interests, and established Bourbon kingdoms and duchies. The old national names were not utterly discarded ; there was still a Lombardic flavour in the North, a classical one in the old cities, a Norman one in Sicily ; but the favourite commonplace names predominated in the noblesse, and titles began to conceal them. Moreover, the women were all Maria, and many of the men likewise ; and the same rule at present holds good, though of late the favourites have become Filomena and Concetta—in honour, the one of the new saint, the other of the new dogma of Rome.

The House of Savoy, which is just now the hope of Italy, always had its own peculiar class of names—Humbert, Amé, Filiberto, Emanuele, Vittore, and these are likely to become the most popular in liberal Italy.

Section IV.—*Spain.*

Spain has many peculiarities of her own, to which I would fain do greater justice than is in my power. Celtiberian at first, she seems to have become entirely Latin, except in those perplexing Basque provinces, where the language remains a riddle to philologists. One Spanish name is claimed by Zamacola as Basque, *i.e.* Muño, with its feminine Muña, or Munila ; and for want of a more satisfactory history, one is inclined to suppose that Gaston, or Gastone, must be likewise Basque. It first comes to light as Gascon among the counts of Foix and Béarn, from whom the son of Henri IV. derived it, and made it French.

Rome Latinized the Spanish speech for ever, and left many an old Latin name, which, however, went on chiefly among the lower orders, while the Suevi and the Goths ruled as nobles and kings, bringing with them their Teutonic names, to be softened down to the dignified Romance tongue, which took the Latin accusative for its stately plurals in *os* and *es*. It is likely that the Latin element was working upwards at the time of the Mahometan conquest, since the traitor Julian, his daughter Florinda, the first patriot king, Pelayo, all have classically derived names ; and some of these occur in the early royal pedigrees of the Asturias and Navarre, and the lords of Biscay, as these small mountain territories proclaimed their freedom and Christianity. Here we find Sancho (Sanctus), Eneco (Ignatius), Lope, Manse, Fortunio, Adoncia, Teresa, Felicia, all undoubtedly Latin and Greek ; and curiously, too, here are the first instances of double Christian names, probably the remnant of the Latin style. Eneco Aristo, Inigo Sancho, Garcias Sancho, and the like, are frequent before the year 1000 ; and the Cid's enemy, Lain Calvo, is supposed to be Flavius Calvus. The Goths, however, left a far stronger impression on the nomenclature than on the language. Alfonso, Fernando, Rodrigo, Berengario, Fruela, Ramiro, Ermesinda, are undoubtedly theirs ; but other very early names continue extremely doubtful, such as Ximen and Ximena, Urraca, Elvira, or Gelvira,

Alvaro, Bermudo, Ordoño, Velasquita, all appearing in the earliest days of the little Christian kingdoms, though not in the palmy times of the Gothic monarchy. These names have been already mentioned, with the derivations to which they may possibly belong ; but they are far from being satisfactorily accounted for. The simple patronymic *ez* was in constant use, and formed many surnames.

As the five kingdoms expanded and came into greater intercourse with Europe, the more remarkable names gradually were discarded ; but Alfonso, Fernando, Rodrigo, Alvar, Gonzalo, were still national, and the two first constantly royal, till the House of Trastamare brought Enrique and Juan into fashion in Castille. The favourite saint was James the Great, or, more truly, Santiago de Compostella, in honour of whom Diego and his son Diaz are to be found in very early times. Maria, too, seems to have been in use in Spain sooner than elsewhere, and Pedro was in high favour in the fourteenth century, as it has continued ever since.

Aragon and Portugal had variations from the Castillian standard of language ; and Portugal now claims to have a distinct tongue, chiefly distinguished by the absence of the Moorish guttural ; and in nomenclature, by the close adherence to classic spelling, and by the terminations which would in Spanish be in *on*, or *un*, being in *aõ*, the contraction of *nho*. Aragonese has been absorbed in Castillian, and Catalan is only considered as a dialect.

After Aragon and Castille had become united, and, crushing the Moors and devouring Navarre, were a grand European power, their sovereigns lost all their nationality. French, or rather Flemish, Charles, and Greek Philip, translated as Carlo and Felipe, reigned on their throne as the House of Austria, while the native Fernando went off to be the German Ferdinand. Isabel, the Spanish version of either Jezebel, or Elizabeth, did retain her popularity, but hardly in equal measure with the universal Maria ; and as the Inquisition Romanized the national mind more and more, the attribute names of Mercedes and Dolores, and even the idolatrous Pilar, and Guadalupe, from a famous shrine, were invented. These were given in conjunction with Maria, and used for convenience' sake. Literary names seem to have been few or none, and the saint, or rather the Romanist, nomenclature, was more unmitigated in Spain and her great western colonies than anywhere else ; even in Italy, where the classics and romance always exerted their power. In the Spanish colonies, even divine names are used, without an idea of profanity.

The use of the Christian name in speech has, however, never been dropped, even under the French influence of the Bourbon monarchy ; and Don Martin, Doña Luisa, &c., would still be the proper title of every Spanish gentleman or lady.

The Spanish names that have spread most extensively have been Fernando in Germany, Iñigo and Teresa throughout all Roman Catholic countries, for the sake of the two Spanish saints who revived their old half-forgotten sound.

SECTION V.—*France.*

France, the most influential of European countries for evil or for good, can hardly be properly spoken of as *one*, in nation or language. Yet that one dialect of hers that has contrived to be the most universal tongue of Europe, that character, which by its vivacity and earnestness, and, perhaps, above all, by its hard, rigid consistency, has impressed its ideas on all other nations, and too often dragged them in its wake, though both only belonging to a fraction of the population, are still, in general estimation, *the* French, and their importance undeniable. Dislike, despise, struggle as we will, we are still influenced, through imitation and vanity, and the deference of the weaker majority, in matters of conventional taste.

Old Gaul had its brave Keltic inhabitants, and its race in Brittany, unsubdued by even Rome, were only united to the rest of the country by the marriage of their heiress, only subdued by gradual legalized tampering with their privileges. Even in the Keltic province, however, genuine Keltic names are nearly gone; though Hervé, Guennolé, Yvain, Arzur, are still found in their catalogues; and in France, Généviève, by her protection of Paris, left her ancient name for perpetual honour and imitation.

The Roman overflow came early and lasted long; it left a language and manners strongly impressed, and the names seem to have been according to Latin forms and rules. Dionysius, Pothinus, Martinus, Hilarius, are all found among the Gauls in the end of the Roman sway; and when the Franks had burst over the country and held the north of the Loire, whenever a Gaul comes to the surface, he is called by a Roman name — Gregorius, Sidonius Apollinaris, Germanus, Eligius.

Southern Gaul was, indeed, never Frank. The cities were Roman municipalities, shut their gates, and took what care of themselves they could; while the Hlodvehs and Meervehs, the Hilperics, and Hildeberts ravaged over the stony country, which still called itself Provincia. And there, though Burgundians on the east, and Goths from the Pyrenees, gradually contrived to erect little dukedoms and counties, and hold them under the empire established by Charlemagne, the country was still peopled by the Romanized Gaul, and the *Langue d'oc* was spoken and sung. This was the centre of the softened classic names, Yolande and Constance, Alienor and Delphine, while the legends of St. Marthe and of the Martyrs of Lyons supplied provincial saints. The rich literature, chiefly of amatory songs, died away, and the current remains of the language are now unwritten, falling further and further into patois, and varying more from one another. One of its curious peculiarities is to make *o* a feminine termination; Dido is there short for Marguerite, Zino for Theresine, &c.

A great number of French surnames are still Roman, such as Chauvin (Calvinus), Godon (Claudius), Marat, Salvin, and many more, showing that Latin nomenclature must long have been prevalent among the mass of the people, though as history is only concerned with the court, we hear chiefly of the Franks around the unsteady thrones of Neustria and Austrasia. The High German of these kingdoms, as used by the Meerwings, was extremely harsh ; Hlodveh and Hlodhild, Hlother and Hlodvald, were their rough legacies ; but, despised as was the name and cheap the blood of the Roman among them, his civilization was conquering his victors ; and when the Karlings, with their middle class cultivation, subdued the effete line of Meerveh, they spoke Latin as freely as Frankish, and the names they bore had softened ; Ludovicus and Lotharius, Carolus and Emma in Latin, or in German, Ludwe and Lothar, Karl and Emme. And now, among the many saints that were fostered by the religious government and missionary spirit of Frankland, arose the founders of the chief stock names of Europe—Robert, Richard, Henry, Williaume, Walther, Bernard, Bertram, Eberhard, and the like.

When, in the next generation, Germany, Lorraine, and France fell apart, the latter country was beginning to speak the *Langue d'oui*, retaining the Latin spelling, but disregarding it in speech, as though the scholar had written correctly, but the speaker had disregarded the declension, and dropped the case endings alike of Latin and Teutonic. And so Karl was Charles, and Lodwe Louis, long before the counts of Paris, with their assimilation of the Cymric Hu to the Teuton Hugur, had thrust the Karlings down into Lorraine, and commenced the true French dynasty in their small territory between the Seine and Loire.

Already had the Northmen settled themselves in Neustria, and, taking the broken Frank names and mangled Latin speech for badges of civilization and Christianity, had made them their own, and infused such vigour into the French people, that from that moment their national character and literature begin to develop.

Then it was that France exercised a genuine and honourable leadership of Europe. Her language being the briefest form of Latin, was, perhaps, the most readily understood of the broken Romance dialects ; and though Rome had the headship of the Church, and Germany the nominal empire of the West, France had the moral chieftainship.

The Pope did but sanction the Crusades ; it was France that planned them. Frenchmen were the connecting link between the Lorrainer Godfrey, the Norman Robert, the Sicilian Tancred, the Provençal Raymond, the Flemish Baldwin. The kingdom of Jerusalem, though founded by the Lorrainer, was essentially French ; the religious orders of knighthood were chiefly French ; the whole idea and language of chivalry were French ; and perhaps rightly, for France has at times shown that rare and noble spirit that can exalt a man for his personal qualities, instead of his rank, even in his own lifetime. The nation that could appreciate its St. Bernard, its Du Guesclin, its Bayard, deserved, while that temper was in it, to be a leader of the civilized world.

England was in these earlier days regarded as a foreign and semi-barbarous realm held by a French duke or count, while southern France was divided into independent fiefs of the empire. The names began to be affected by reverence for saints, and fast included more and more of the specially popular patrons, such as Jean, Jaques, Simon, Philippe. They became common to all the lands that felt the central crusading impulse, and the daughters of French princes, Alix, Matilde, the Provençal Constance, Alienor, Isabel, Marguérite, were married into all parts of Europe, and introduced their names into their new countries, often backed up by legends of their patrons.

Normandy lapsed to France through King John's crime and weakness, and the persecution of the Albigenses, and the narrower views of the popes, changed the Crusades to a mere conquest of the *Langue d'oc* by the *Langue d'oui*, completed by the marriages of the brothers of St. Louis ; and though Provence continued a fief of the empire, and the property of the Angevin kings of Naples, yet their French royal blood united it more closely to the central kingdom, and the transplanting of the papal court to Avignon, gave a French tinge to the cardinalate which it only recovered from at the expense of the Great Schism.

Philippe le Bel was the last able sovereign of France of the vigorous early middle ages ; but the brilliant character of the nobility still carried men's minds captive, and influenced the English even through the century of deadly wars that followed the accession of the House of Valois, and ended by leaving Louis XI. king of the entire French soil.

The ensuing century was that when the influence of France on other nations was at the lowest ebb. Exhausting herself first by attacks on Italy, and then by her savage civil wars, she required all the ability of Henri IV. and of Richelieu to rouse her from her depression, and make her be respected among the nations. Meantime, her nomenclature had varied little from the original set of names in use in the tenth century ; dropping a few obsolete ones, taking up a few saintly ones, recommended by fresh relics, and occasionally choosing a romantic one, but very scantily ; François was her only notable adoption. The habit of making feminines to male names seems to have spread in France about the eighteenth century, rather narrowing than widening the choice. Jeanne seems to have been the first to undergo this treatment; Philippine was not long after, then Jacqueline, and, indeed, it may have been the habit—as it is still among the peasantry of the South—always to give the father's name to the eldest child, putting a feminine to it for a girl.

With the cinque-cento came a few names of literature, of which Diane was the most permanent ; and the Huguenots made extensive use of Scripture names—Isaac, Gédéon, Benjamin, and many more ; but the Christian name was quickly falling out of fashion. People were, of course, christened, but it is often difficult to discover their names. The old habit of addressing the knight as Sire Jehan, or Sire Pierre, and speaking of him as *le Beau Sieur*, had been entirely dropped. Even his surname was often out of sight, and he was called after some estate—as le Sieur Pierre Terrail was to the whole world Chevalier

Bayard. Nay, even in the signature, the Christian name was omitted, unless from some very urgent need of distinction. Henri de Lorraine, eldest son of the duke of Guise, signs himself Le Guisard in a letter to the Dauphin Henri, son of François I. Married ladies wrote themselves by their maiden joined to their married title, and scarcely were even little children in the higher orders called by one of the many names that it had become the custom to bestow on them, in hopes of conciliating as many saints and as many sponsors as possible,—sometimes a whole city, as when the Fronde-born son of Madame de Longueville had all Paris for his godmother, and was baptized Charles Paris.

Now and then, however, literature, chiefly that of the ponderous romances of the Scudéry school, influenced a name, as Athenaïs or Sylvie ; but, in general, these magnificent appellations were more used as sobriquets under which to draw up characters of acquaintances than really given to children. Esther is, however, said to have been much promoted by the tragedy of Racine.

The Bourbons, with their many faults, have had two true kings of men among them—Henri IV. and Louis XIV.—men with greatness enough to stamp the Bourbon defects where their greatness left no likeness.

There is something very significant in the fact, that these were the days when it was fashionable to forget the simple baptismal name. There was little distinction in it, if it had been remembered ; Louis or Marie always formed part of it, with half-a-dozen others besides. As to the populace, nobody knows anything of them under Louis XIV. : they were ground down to nothing.

The lower depth, under Louis XV., brought a reaction of simplicity ; but it was the simplicity of casting off all trammels—the classicalism of the Encyclopædists. Christian names are mentioned again, and were chosen much for literary association. Emile and Julie, for the sake of Rousseau ; and, from Roman history, Jules and Camille, and many another, clipped down to that shortened form by which France always appropriated the words of other nations, and often taught us the same practice.

The Revolution stripped every one down to their genuine two names, and woe to the owners of those which bore an aristocratic sound, or even meaning. Thenceforth French nomenclature, among the educated classes and those whom they influence, has been pretty much a matter of taste. Devotion, where it exists, is satisfied by the insertion of Marie, and anything that happens to be in vogue is added to it. Josephine flourished much in the first Bonaparté days ; but Napoléon was too imperial, too peculiar, to be given without special warrant from its owner ; nor are politically-given names numerous : there are more taken from popular novels or dramas, or merely from their sound. Zephyrine, Coralie, Zaidée, Zénobie, Malvine, Séraphine, prevail not only among the ladies, but among the maid-servants of Paris ; and men have, latterly, been fancifully named by appellations brought in from other countries, never native to France—Gustave, Alfred, Ernest, Oswald, &c. Moreover, the tendency to denude words of their final syllable is being given up. The names in *us* and in *a* are let alone, in spelling, at least ; and some of our feminine English contractions, such as Fanny, have been absolutely admitted.

All this, however, very little affects the peasantry, or the provinces. Patron saints and hereditary family names, contracted to the utmost, are still used there ; and a rich harvest might be gathered by comparison of the forms in Keltic, Latin, Gascon, or German, in France.

Section VI.—*Great Britain.*

The waning space demands brevity ; otherwise, the appellations of our own countrymen and women are a study in themselves ; but they must here be treated of in general terms, rather than in detail.

The Keltic inhabitants of the two islands bore names that their descendants have, in many instances, never ceased to bear and to cherish. The Gael of Ireland and Scotland have always had their Niel and Brighd, their Fergus and Angus ; Aodh, Ardh, and Bryan, Eachan, Conan, the most ancient of all traditional names, continuing without interval on the same soil, excepting a few of the more favoured Greek and old Italian.

The Cymry, in their western mountains, have a few equally permanent. Caradoc, Bronwen, Arianwen, Llud, and the many forms of Gwen, are extremely ancient, and have never dropped into disuse. In both branches of the race there was a large mass of poetical and heroic myth to endear these appellations to the people ; and it is one of the peculiar features of our islands to be more susceptible than any other nation to these influences on nomenclature. Is it from the under-current of the imaginative Kelt that this tendency has been derived ?

Rome held England for four hundred years ; and though Welsh survived her grasp and retained its Keltic character, instead of becoming a Romance tongue, it was considerably imbued with Latin phraseology ; and the assumption of Latin names by the British princes, with the assimilation of their own, has left a peculiar class of Welsh classic names not to be paralleled elsewhere, except, perhaps, in Wallachia. Cystenian, Elin, Emrys, Iolo, Aneurin, Ermin, Gruffydd, Kay, are of these ; and there are many more, such as March, Tristrem, Einiawn, Geraint, which lie in doubt between the classic and the Cymric, and are, probably, originally the latter, but assimilated to those of their Latin models and masters. It was these Romanized Kelts who supplied the few martyrs and many saints of Britain ; whose Albanus, Aaron, and Julius left their foreign names to British love, and whose Patricius founded the glorious missionary Church of Ireland, and made his name the national one. His pupils, Brighde and Columba, made theirs almost equally venerated, though none of these saintly titles were, at first, adopted in the Gadhaelic

Churches without the reverent prefix *Gille*, or *Mael*, which are compounded with all the favourite saintly names of the Keltic calendar.

Again, the semi-Roman Kelts were the origin of the Knights of the Round Table. Arthur's own name, though thorough Keltic, is claimed by Greek. Lancelot is probably a French version of the Latin translation of Maelgwn; and the traces of Latin are here and there visible in the nomenclature of the brave men who, no doubt, aimed rather at being Roman citizens than mediæval knights.

The great Low German influx made our island English, and brought our veritable national names. An immense variety existed among the Anglo-Saxons, consisting of different combinations, generally with some favourite prefix, in each family—*Sige, Æthel, Ead, Hilde, Cuth, Ælf*, and the terminations, generally, *beorht, red, volf, veald, frith*, or, for women, *thrythe, hilde, gifu*, or *burh*. The like were in use in the Low German settlements on the Continent, especially in Holland and Friesland.

Christianity, slowly spreading through the agency of the Roman Church on the one hand and the Keltic on the other, did not set aside the old names. It set its seal of sanctity on a few which have become our genuine national and native ones. Eadward, Eadmund, Eadwine, Wilfrith, Æadgifu, Æthelthryth, Mildthryth, Osveald, and Osmund, have been the most enduring of these; and Æthelbyrht we sent out to Germany, to come back to us as Albert.

The remains of the Danish invasions are traceable rather in surnames than Christian names. The permanent ones left by them were chiefly in insular Scotland and Ireland. Torquil, Somerled, Ivor, Ronald, Halbert, are Scottish relics of the invaders; and in Ireland, Amlaidh, Redmond, Ulick.

But it was the Normans, Norsemen in a French dress, that brought us the French rather than Frank names that are most common with us. Among the thirty kings who have reigned since the Conquest, there have been ten Christian names, and of these but two are Saxon English, three are Norman Frank, two French Hebrew, one French Greek, one French, one Anglicized German Greek. Strictly speaking, Richard is Saxon, and began with a native English saint; but it was its adoption by Normans that made it popular after the Conquest; and it came in company with William, Henry, Robert, Walter, Gilbert, all in perpetual use ever since. Alberic, Bertram, Baldwin, Randolf, Roger, Herbert, Hubert, Reginald, Hugh, Norman, Nigel, and many others less universally kept up, came at the same time; and Adelheid and Mathilda were imported by the ladies; but, in general, there were more men's names than women's then planted, probably on account of William's policy of marrying Normans to English women.

Scripture names were very few. There are only two Johns in Domesday Book, and one is a Dane; but the saints were beginning to be somewhat followed; Eustace was predominant; Cecily, Lucy, Agnes, Constance, were already in use; and in the migration, Brittany contributed Tiffany, in honour of the Epiphany. At the same time she sent us her native Alan, Brian, and Aveline ; and vernacular French gave Aimée and afterwards Algernon.

It was a time of contractions. Between English and French, names were oddly twisted ; Alberic into Aubrey, Randolf into Ralph, Ethelthryth into Awdry, Eadgifu into Edith, Mathilda into Maude, Adelheid into Alice.

Saint and Scripture names seem to have been promoted by the crusading impulse, but proceeded slowly. The Angevins brought us the French Geoffrey and Fulk, and their Provençal marriages bestowed on us the Provençal version of Helena—Eleanor, as we have learnt to call their Alienor, in addition to the old Cymric form Elayne. Thence, too, came Isabel, together with Blanche, Beatrice, and other soft names current in poetical Provence. Jehan, as it was called when Lackland bore it, and its feminine Jehanne, seem to have been likewise introductions of our Aquitanian queen.

The Lowland Scots had been much influenced by the Anglo-Saxons, whose tongue prevailed throughout the Lothians ; and after the fall of Macbeth, and the marriage of Malcolm Ceanmore, English names were much adopted in Scotland. Cuthbert has been the most lasting of the old Northumbrian class. The good Queen Margaret, and her sister Christian, owed their Greek names, without a doubt, to their foreign birth and Hungarian mother, and these, with Alexander, Euphemia, and George, forthwith took root in Scotland, and became national. Probably Margaret likewise brought the habit, then more eastern than western, of using saintly names, for her son was David ; and from this time seems to have begun the fashion of using an equivalent for the Keltic name. David itself, beloved for the sake of the good king, is the equivalent of Dathi, a name borne by an Irish king before the Scottish migration. David I., nearly related to the Empress Maude, and owning the earldom of Northumbria in right of his wife, was almost an English baron ; and the intercourse with England during his reign and those of his five successors, made the Lowland nobles almost one with the Northumbrian barons, and carried sundry Norman names across the border, where they became more at home than even in England ; such as Alan, Walter, Norman, Nigel, and Robert.

Henry II. was taking advantage of the earl of Pembroke's expedition to Ireland, and the English Pale was established, bringing with it to Erin the favourite Norman names, to be worn by the newly-implanted nobles, and Iricized gradually with their owners. Cicely became Sheelah ; Margaret, Mairgreg ; Edward, Eudbaird ; and, on the other hand, the Irish dressed themselves for civilization by taking English names. Finghin turned to Florence, and Ruadh to Roderick, &c.

Henry III. had been made something like an Englishman by his father's loss of Normandy ; and in his veneration for English saints, he called his sons after the two royal saints most beloved in England, Edward and Edmund ; and the death of the elder children of Edward I. having brought the latter a second time to the throne, it was thenceforth in honour. Thomas owed its popularity to Becket, who was so christened from his birth on the feast of the Apostle, St. Thomas, and, in effect, saintly names were becoming more and more the fashion. Mary was beginning to be esteemed as the most honourable one a woman could bear ; and legends in quaint metrical English rendered Agnes, Barbara, Katharine, Margaret, and Cecily well known and in constant use.

The romances of chivalry began to have their influence. Lionel and Roland, Tristram, Ysolda, Lancelot, and Guenever, were all the produce of the revival of the tales of Arthur's court, arrayed in their feudal and chivalrous dress, and other romances contributed a few. Diggory is a highly romantic name, derived from an old metrical tale of a knight, properly called D'Egaré, the wanderer, or the almost lost, one of the many versions of the story of the father and unknown son. Esclairmonde came out of *Huon de Bourdeaux ;* Lillias, such a favourite in Scotland, came out of the tale of Sir Eger, Sir Graham, and Sir Graysteel ; Lillian out of the story of Roswal and Lillian ; and Grizel began to flourish from the time Chaucer made her patience known.

The Scots, by their alliance with France, were led to import French terminations, such as the diminutives Janet and Annot ; also the foreign Cosmo, and perhaps likewise Esmé.

Meantime we obtained fresh importations from abroad. Anne came with the Queen of Richard II. ; Elizabeth from the German connections of Elizabeth Woodville's mother, Jaquetta of Luxemburg ; Gertrude was taken from Germany ; Francis and Frances caught from France ; and Arthur was revived for his eldest son by the first Tudor ; Jane instead of Joan began, too, in the Tudor times.

But when the Reformation came, the whole system of nomenclature received a sudden shock. Patron saints were thrown to the winds ; and though many families adhered to the hereditary habits, others took entirely new fashions. Then, Camden says, began the fashion of giving surnames as Christian names ; as with Guildford Dudley, Egremont Ratcliffe, Douglas Sheffield ; and in Ireland, Sidney, as a girl's name, in honour of the lord deputy, Sir Henry, the father of Sir Philip, from whom, on the other hand, Sydney became a common English boy's name.

Then, likewise, the classical taste came forth, and bestowed all manner of fanciful varieties ; Homer, Virgil, Horatius, Lalage, Cassandra, Diana, Virginia, Julius, &c., &c., all are found from this time forward ; and here and there, owing to some ancestor of high worth, specimens have been handed on in families.

The more pious betook themselves to abstract qualities ; Faith, Hope, Charity, Prudence and Patience, Modesty, Love, Gift, Temperance, Mercy, all of which, even to the present day, sometimes are used, but chiefly by the peasantry, or in old Nonconformist families.

Between the dates 1500 and 1600 began the full employment of Scripture names, chosen often by opening the Bible at haphazard, and taking the first name that presented itself, sometimes, however, by juster admiration of the character. Thus began our use of Abraham and Sarah, Isaac and Rebecca, Rachel, Joseph, Benjamin,

Josiah, Gershom, Gamaliel, &c. ; and others more quaint and peculiar. The Puritan clergy absolutely objected to giving unedifying names. A minister was cited before Archbishop Whitgift for refusing to christen a child Richard. The Bible was ransacked for uncommon names only found in the genealogies, and parish registers show the strangest varieties, such as Hope still, Dust and Ashes, Thankful, Repent, Accepted, Hold-the-Truth, &c. These were chiefly given at the baptisms in the latter days of Elizabeth and the reign of James I. They were the real, not assumed, names of the Ironsides, but they were not perpetuated. A man called Fight-against-Sin would have too much pity for his son to transmit such a name to him. Original is, however, a family name still handed on in Lincolnshire. Probably it was at first Original Sin. The most curious varieties of names were certainly used in the 17th century. The register of the scholars admitted to Merchant Taylors' school between 1562 and 1699 shows Isebrand, Jasper, Jermyn, Polydore, Cæsar, Olyffe, Erasmus, Esme, Ursein, Innocent, Praise, Polycarpe, Tryamour, and a Sacheverell, Filgate, admitted in 1673.

Comparatively few of these Puritan names were used in Scotland ; but several were for sound's sake adopted in Ireland as equivalents ; Jeremiah for Diarmaid ; Timothy for Tadhgh ; Grace for Graine.

Charles was first made popular through loyalty to King Charles I., who had received it in the vain hope that it would be more fortunate than the hereditary James, itself brought into Scotland seven generations back by a vow of Annaple Drummond, mother of the first unfortunate James. English registers very scantily show either Charles or James before the Stuart days, but they have ever since been extremely popular. Henrietta, brought by the French queen, speedily became popular, and with Frances, Lucy, Mary, Anne, Catherine, and Elizabeth, seem to have been predominant among the ladies ; but all were contracted, as Harriet, Fanny, Molly, Nanny, Kitty, Betty. The French suppression of the Christian name considerably affected the taste of the Restoration ; noblemen dropped it out of their signature ; the knight's wife discarded it with the prefix Dame ; married daughters and sisters were mentioned by the surname only ; young spinsters foolishly adopted Miss with the surname instead of Mistress with the Christian ; but the loss was not so universal as in France, for custom still retained the old titles of knights and of the daughters and younger sons of the higher ranks of the nobility. The usual fashion was, in imitation of the French, for ladies to call themselves and be addressed in poetry by some of the Arcadian or romantic terms, a few of which have crept into nomenclature ; Amanda, Ophelia, Aspasia, Cordelia, Phyllis, Chloe, Sylvia, and the like.

The love of a finish in *a* was coming in with Queen Anne's Augustan age. The soft *e*, affectionate *ie* or *y*, that had been natural to our tongues ever since they had been smoothed by Norman-French, was twisted up into an Italian *ia :* Alice must needs be Alicia ; Lettice, Letitia ; Cecily, Cecilia ; Olive, Olivia ; Lucy, Lucinda ; and no heroine could be deemed worthy of figuring in narrative without a flourish at the end of her name. Good Queen Anne herself had an *a* tacked on to make her 'Great Anna'; Queen Bess must needs be Great Eliza; and Mary was erected into Maria; Nassau had lately been invented for William III.'s godchildren of both sexes; and Anne, after French precedent, made masculine for his successor's godsons. Belinda, originally the property of the wife of Orlando, was chosen by Pope for his heroine of *Rape of the Lock;* Clarissa was fabricated out of the Italian Clarice by Richardson; and Pamela was adopted by him out of Sir Philip Sidney's *Arcadia*, as a recommendation to the maid-servant whom he made his heroine; and these, as names of literature, all took a certain hold. Pamela is still not uncommon among the lower classes.

In the mean time the House of Brunswick had brought in the regnant names of German taste—George, of which, thanks to our national patron, we had already made an English word, Frederick, Ernest, Adolphus—a horrible English Latinism of good old German, Augustus, an adoption of German classic taste; and, among the ladies, generally clumsy feminines of essentially masculine names—Caroline, Charlotte, Wilhelmina, Frederica, Louisa, together with the less incorrectly formed Augusta, Sophia, and Amelia.

This ornamental taste flourished, among the higher classes, up to the second decade of the nineteenth century, when the affectations, of which it was one sample, were on the decline, under the growing influence of the chivalrous school of Scott, and of the simplicity upheld by Wordsworth. The fine names began to grow vulgar, and people either betook themselves to the hereditary ones of their families, or picked and chose from the literature then in fashion.

Two names, for the sake of our heroes by sea and land, came into prominence—Horatio and Arthur, the latter transcending the former in popularity in proportion to the longer career and more varied excellences of its owner. Womankind had come back to their Ellen, Mary, and Lucy; and it was not till the archaic influence had gone on much longer that the present crop sprang up, of Alice and Edith, Gertrude, Florence, and Constance, copied again and again, in fact and in fiction, and with them the Herbert and Reginald, Wilfrid and Maurice, formerly only kept up in a few old families. It is an improvement, but in most cases at the expense of nothing but imitation, the sound and the fashion being the only guides. After all, nomenclature cannot be otherwise than imitative, but the results are most curious and interesting, when it is either the continuation of old hereditary names, like the Algernon of the Howards or the Aubrey of the de Veres, or else the record of some deeply felt event, like the Giustina of Venice, in honour of the battle of Lepanto, or our own Arthur, in memory of the deeds of our great duke.

Names are often an index to family habits and temper. Unpretending households go on for generations with the same set, sometimes adopting one brought in by marriage, but soon dropping it out if it is too fine. Romantic people reflect the impressions of popular literature in their children's names; enthusiastic ones mark popular incidents,—Navarino, Maida, Alma, have all been inflicted in honour of battles. Another class always have an assortment of the fashionable type—Augusta, Amelia, and Matilda, of old; Edith and Kate at present.

Nonconformity leaves its mark in its virtue names and its Scripture names, the latter sometimes of the wildest kind. Talithacumi was the daughter of a Baptist. A clergyman has been desired to christen a boy 'Alas,' the parents supposing that 'Alas! my brother,' was a call on the name of the disobedient prophet. There is a floating tradition of 'Acts' being chosen for a fifth son, whose elder brothers had been called after the four Evangelists; and even of Beelzebub being uttered by a godfather at the font.

Among other such names may be mentioned 'Elibris,' which some people persisted belonged to their family, for it was in their grandfather's books : and so it was, being e libris (from the books), the old Latin manner of commencing an inscription in a book. Sarsaparilla was called from a scrap of newspaper. 'Valuable and serviceable' is also said to have been intended for a child, on the authority of an engraving in an old watch; and an unfortunate pair of twins were presented for the imposition of Jupiter and Orion, because their parents thought them pretty names, and 'had heard on them.'

Double names came gradually in from the Stuart days, but only grew really frequent in the present century; and the habit of calling girls by both, now so common among the lower classes in towns, is very recent.

With many families it is a convenient custom to christen the sons by the mother's maiden name in addition to their first individual name ; but the whole conversion of surnames into Christian names is exclusively English, and is impossible on the Continent, as state and church both refuse to register what is not recognized as in use. Of English surnames we need say nothing ; they have been fully treated of in other works, and as any one may be used in baptism, at any time, the mention of them would be endless.

In speaking of England we include not only our colonies but America. There our habits are exaggerated. There is much less of the hereditary ; much more of the Puritan and literary vein. Scripture names, here conspicuous, such as Hephzibah, Noah, Obadiah, Hiram, are there common-place. Virtues of all kinds flourish, and coinages are sometimes to be found, even such as 'Happen to be,' because the parents happened to be in Canada at the time of the birth.

> 'Peabody Duty perhaps keeps a store,
> With washing tubs, and wigs, and wafers stocked;
> And Dr. Quackenbox proclaims the cure
> Of such as are with any illness docked:
> Dish Alcibiades holds out a lure
> Of sundry articles, all nicely cooked;
> And Phocion Aristides Franklin Tibbs,
> Sells ribbons, laces, caps, and slobbering-bibs.'

The Roman and Greek influence has been strong, producing Cato, Scipio, Leonidas, &c. ; but the habit of calling negroes by such euphonious epithets has rather discouraged them among the other classes, and the romantic, perhaps, predominates with women, the Scriptural with men. The French origin of many in the Southern States, and the Dutch in New England, can sometimes be traced in names.

SECTION VII.—*Germany.*

What was said of Frankish applies equally to old High German, of which Frankishwas a dialect, scarcely distinguishable with our scanty sources of information.

We have seen Frankish extinguished in Latin in the West; but in the East we find it developing and triumphing. The great central lands of Europe were held by the Franks and Suevi, with the half civilized Lombards to their south, and a long slip of Burgundians on the Rhine and the Alps, all speakers of the harsh High German, all Christians by the seventh century, but using the traditional nomenclature, often that of the *Nibelungenlied.* The Low Germans, speaking what is best represented by Anglo-Saxon literature, were in the northerly flats and marshes, and were still heathens when the Franks, under Charlemagne conquered them, and the Anglo-Saxon mission of Boniface began their conversion.

The coronation of Charles by the pope was intended to establish the headship of a confederacy of sovereigns, one of them to be the Kaisar, and that one to be appointed by the choice of the superior ones among the rest. This chieftainship remained at first with the Karlingen; but after they had become feeble it remained, during four reigns, with the house of Saxony, those princes who established the strange power of the empire over Italy, and held the papal elections in their hands. It was under them that Germany became a confederation, absolutely separate from her old companion France.

There is not much to say of German nomenclature. She little varied her old traditional names. Otto, Heinrich, and Konrad, constantly appeared from the first; and the High German, as the literary tongue, has had the moulding of all the recognized forms.

The Low German continued to be spoken, and became, in time, Dutch and Frisian, as well as the popular dialect of Saxony and West Prussia. The Frisian names are, indeed, much what English ones would be now if there had been no external influences.

In spite of being the central empire, the German people long resisted improvement and amalgamation. The merchant cities were, indeed, far in advance, and the emperors were, of necessity, cultivated men, up to the ordinary mark of their contemporary sovereigns; but the nobility continued surly and boorish, little accessible to chivalrous ideas, and their unchanging names—Ulrich, Adelbert, Eberhard, marking how little they were affected by the general impressions of Europe. A few names, like Wenceslav, or Boleslav, came in by marriage with their Polish, Bohemian, and Hungarian neighbours; and Hungary, now and then, was the medium of the introduction of one used at Constantinople, such as Sophia, Anne, Elisabeth, which, for the sake of the sainted Landgraffinn of Thuringia, became a universal favourite. Friedrich came in with the Swabian dynasty ; Rudolf and Leopold, with the house of Hapsburg.

Holland and the cluster of surrounding fiefs meanwhile had a fluctuating succession, with lines of counts continually coming to an end, and others acceding who were connected with the French or English courts. The consequence was, that the gentlemen of these territories gained a strong French tinge of civilization, especially in Flanders, where the Walloons were a still remaining island of Belgæ. The Flemish chivalry became highly celebrated, and, under the French counts of Hainault and Flanders, and dukes of Burgundy, acquired a tone, which made their names and language chiefly those of France, and tinctured that of the peasantry and artisans, so as to distinguish them from the Hollanders. Andreas, Adrianus, Cornelius, saints imported by the French dukes, were both in Holland and the Netherlands, however, the leading names, together with Philip, which was derived from the French royal family. The Dutch artificers and merchants had their own sturdy, precise, business-like character— their German or saintly names, several of which are to be found among our eastern English, in consequence of the intercourse which the wool trade established, and the various settlements of Dutch and Flemish manufacturers in England.

The revival of classical scholarship in the fifteenth century was considerably felt in the great universities of the Netherlands and of Germany, and its chief influence on nomenclature is shown in the introduction of classical names ; namely, Julius and Augustus, and the Emperor Friedrich's notable compound of Maximus Æmilianus into Maximilian, but far more in finishing every other name off with the Latin *us*. Some were restorations to the original form ; Adrianus, Paulus, and the ever memorable Martinus ; but others were adaptations of very un-Latin sounds. Poppo turned to Poppius ; Wolf to Wolfius ; Ernst to Ernestus ; Jobst, instead of going back to Justinus, made himself Jobstius ; Franz, Franciscus. The surnames were even more unmanageable, being often either nicknames or local ; but they underwent the same fate ; Pott was Pottus ; Bernau, Bernavius ; while others translated them, as in the already-mentioned instance of Erasmus, from Gerhardson, and the well-known transformation of Schwarzerd into Melancthon. The Danish antiquary Broby (bridge town), figures as Pontoppidan ; Och became Bos ; Heilman, Severtus ; Goldmann, Chrysander ; Neumann, Neander ; and as to the trades, Schmidt was Faber ; Müller, Molitor ; Schneider, Sartorius ; Schuster, Sutorius ; Kellner, Cellarius.

The German Christian names did not permanently retain this affectation ; but the Netherlanders, owing probably to the great resort to their universities, retained it long and in popular speech, so that in many Dutch contractions, the *us* is still used, as in Janus for Adrianus ; Rasmus for Erasmus ; and almost always the full baptismal name includes the classical suffix. The surnames, of course, adhered, and are many of them constantly heard in Germany and Holland, while others have come to England chiefly with the fugitives from the persecution that caused the revolt of the Netherlands. The Latin left in Dacia and long spoken in Hungary must have assisted to classicalize the Germans even on their Slavonic side. The Reformation did not so much alter German as English nomenclature. The Lutherans, following their master's principle of altering only what was absolutely necessary, long retained their hereditary allegiance to their saints, and did not break out into unaccustomed names, though they modified the old Gottleip into Gottlieb. Some of their sects of Germany however, invented various religious names ; Gottseimitdir, Gottlob, Traugott, Treuhold, Lebrecht, Tugendreich, and probably such others as Erdmuth and Ehrenpreis were results of this revival of native manufacture. A few Scriptural names came up among the Calvinists, but do not seem to have taken a firm hold.

This was the land of the double Christian name. It was common among the princes of Germany, before the close of the fifteenth century, long before France and Italy showed more than an occasional specimen. It was probably necessitated, by way of distinction, by the large families all of the same rank in the little German states. They seem to have set the fashion which has gradually prevailed more and more in Europe ; indeed, there are some double names that have so grown together as to be recognized companions, such as Annstine for Anne Christine, Anngrethe for Anne Margarethe. At present it is the custom in almost all royal families to give the most preposterous number of Christian names, of which one, or at most two, is retained as serviceable, &c.

A few Slavonic names crept in ; chiefly Wenzel from Bohemia ; Kasimir from the Prussian Wends ; Stanislas from Poland ; and the house of Austria, when gaining permanent hold of the empire, spread the names derived from their various connections ; the Spanish Ferdinand, and Flemish Karl and Philipp, besides their hereditary Leopold and Rudolf, and invented Maximilian.

The counter-reformation brought the Jesuit Ignaz and Franz into the lands where the Reformation was extinguished, and canonized Stanislav. Under the horrors of the Thirty Years' War, Germany retrograded in every respect ; and when she began to emerge from her state of depression, the brilliance of the French court rendered it her model, which she followed with almost abject submission. Every one who could talked French, and was called by as French a name as might be ; the royal Fritz became Fédéric, and little Hanne, Jeannette, the French *ine* and *ette* were liberally tacked to men's names to make them feminine, and whatever polish the country possessed was French.

This lasted till the horrors of the Revolution, and the aggressions that followed it, awoke Germany to a sense of her own powers and duties as a nation. Her poets and great men were thoroughly national in spirit ; and though, after the long and destructive contest, she emerged with her grand Holy Roman Empire torn to shreds, her electoral princes turned into petty kings, her noble Hanse towns mostly crushed and absorbed in the new states, her Kaisar merely the Markgraf of Austria, enriched by the spoils of Lombardy and the Slavonic kingdoms, yet she had recovered the true loyalty to the fatherland and its institutions, cared again for her literature and her language, and had an enthusiasm for her own antiquities, a desire to develop her own powers.

German names, to a degree, reflect this. They have ceased to ape Latin or French. So far as any are literary, they come from their own national literature ; but as in most of the states only ordinary names are registered, the variety is not great. More and more German names pass to England in each generation, and become naturalized there ; but the same proportion of English do not seem to be returned.

Bavaria, having been always Roman Catholic, has more saintly names than most other parts of Germany, and, in particular, uses those of some of the less popular apostles, who probably have been kept under her notice by the great miracle plays.

Switzerland, once part of the empire, though free for five hundred years back, is a cluster of varying tongues, races, languages, and religions,—Kelt and Roman, Swabian and Burgundian, Romanist, Lutheran, Calvinist, German, French, Italian. Names and contractions must vary here ; but only those on the German side have fallen in my way, those about Berne, which are chiefly remarkable for the Ours and Ursel, in honour of the bears, and Salome among the women ; the diminutive always in *li*.

Section VIII.— *Scandinavia.*

Grand old Northmen ! They had their own character, and never lost it ; they had their own nomenclature, and kept it with the purity of an unconquered race.

The few influences that affected their nomenclature were, in the first place, in some pre-historic time, the Gaelic. Thence, when Albin and Lochlinn seem to have been on friendly terms, they derived Njal, Kormak, Kylan, Kjartan, Mælkoln, and, perhaps, Brigitte. Next, in Denmark, a few Wend names were picked up ; and, in fact, Denmark being partly peopled by Angles, and always more exposed, first to Slavonic, and then to German influences, than the North, has been less entirely national in names.

In the great piratical days the Northmen and Danes left their names and patronymics to the northern isles, from Iceland to Man, and even in part to Neustria and Italy. Oggiero and Tancredi, in the choicest Italian poems, are specimens of the wideness of their fame. Our own population, in the north-east of England, is far more Scandinavian than Anglian, and bears the impress in dialect in nanners, and in surnames, though the baptismal ones that led to them are, in general, gone out of use.

Christianity did not greatly alter the old northern names, though it introduced those of the universally honoured saints. But the clergy thought it desirable—and chiefly in Denmark—to take more ecclesiastical names to answer to their own ; so Dagfinn was David ; Sölmund, Solomon ; Sigmund, Simon ; and several ladies seem to have followed their example, so that Astrida and Griotgard both became Margarethe, and Bergliot Brigitte.

The popular nomenclature has included all the favourite saints with the individual contractions of the country. The royal lines have been influenced by the dynasties that have reigned. Gustaf grew national in Sweden after the disruption of the union of Calmar, and Denmark alternated between Christiern and Friedrich ; but the main body of the people are constant to Olaf and Eirik, Ingeborg and Gudrun ; and in the Norwegian valleys the old immediate patronymic of the father is still in use. Linnea as a feminine from Linnæus, the Latinism of their great natural historian's surname is a modern invention. Linne itself means a lime tree.

The Northmen have hitherto been the most impressing, and least impressed from without, of all the European nations ; and thus their names are the great key to those of the South.

Section IX.—*Comparative Nomenclature.*

Before entirely quitting our subject, it may be interesting to make a rapid comparison of the spirit of nomenclature, and the significative appellations that have prevailed most in each branch of the civilized family which we have been considering.

For instance—of religious names, the Hebrew race alone, and that at a comparatively late period, assumed such directly Divine appellations, as Eli, Elijah, Adonijah, Joel. The most analogous to these in spirit would be the heathen Teutonic ones, Osgod, Asthor, Aasir ; but these were, probably, rather assertions of descent than direct proclamations of glory.

The very obvious and appropriate Gift of God is in all branches save the Keltic.

Hebrew.	Greek.	Teutonic.	Persian.
Jonathan	Theodoros	Godgifu	Megabyzus
Elnathan	Dorotheus	Goftgabe	*i.e.*
Nathanael		(late)	Bagabukhsha
Mattaniah	Latin.		
Nethaniah	Adeodatus	Slavonic.	
	(late)	Bogdan	

Servant of God is everywhere but among Latins and the Slaves.

Hebrew.	Greek.	Teutonic.	Keltic.	Sanscrit.
Obadiah	Theodoulas	Gottschalk	Giolla-De	Devadasa

Greek and Gaelic likewise own the Service of Christ, by Christopheros (Christbearer), Gilchrist, and Malise ; and the Arabic has Abd-Allah, and Abd-el-Kadir, servant of the Almighty. The name of the late Sultan, Abdul Medschid, signified the servant of the All-Famed.

THE LOVE OF GOD, OR BELOVED OF GOD.				
Greek.	Latin.	Teutonic.	Slavonic.	Persian.
Theophilus Philotheus	Amadeus	Gottlieb (late)	Bogomil	Bagadaushta

HONOURING GOD.		
Greek.	Slavonic.	Persian.
Timotheus	Çastibog	Megabazus

GOD'S JUDGMENT.	
Heb.	Greek.
Daniel Jehoshaphat Jehoiachim	Theokritus

GOD'S GLORY.		HELP OF GOD.	
Greek.	Slavonic.	Hebrew.	German.
Theokles	Bogoslav	Eleazar	Gotthilf

The Greek and Slavonic have by far the most directly religious names, next to the Hebrew, from having been less pledged to hereditary names, and the time of the conversion. The Gaelic devotion was almost all expressed in the Giolla and Mael prefix.

Idol names are of course numerous, but comparison between them is not easy, as they vary with different mythologies. One point is remarkable, that the Supreme God, whether Zeus, Jupiter, Divas, or Woden, never has so many votaries as his vassal gods. Zeno, Jovius, and, perhaps, the Grim of the North, are almost exceptions. The Phœnician Baal had, indeed, many namesakes, and the Persian Ormuzd, giver of life, had several, of whom the pope, called Hormisdas, was one. In general, Ares, Mars, Thor, and Ranovit, the warlike gods, or the friendly Demeter and Gerda, the beneficent Athene, the brilliant Artemis, and Irish Brighde, the queens of heaven, Hera, Juno, Frigga, are chosen for namesakes. Mithras in Persia, and Apollo in Greece, have their share ; but, in general, the sun is not very popular, though Aurora and Zora honour the dawn ; and the North has various Dags.

Of animals the choice is much smaller than would have been

expected. The lion's home is, of course, the East, and *Sinha*, his
Sanscrit title, is represented by the Singh, so familiar in the names of
Hindu chiefs. The Arabs have Arslan in many combinations ; the
Greeks introduced Leo, which has been followed by the Romans, and
come into the rest of Europe ; but many as were the lion names of
Greece and later Rome, Leonard, and, perhaps, Lionel, alone are of
European growth.

The elephant is utterly unrepresented, unless we accept the
tradition, that the cognomen of Cæsar arose from his African name.
Persia has a few leopards, such as Chitratachna.

The bear does not show himself in favourable colours in the South,
and Ursus and Ursula are more likely to be translations of the
northern Biorn—so extremely common—than original Latin names.
The Erse, however, owns him as Mahon.

The wolf is the really popular animal. Even the Hebrews knew
Zeeb through the Midianites, the Greeks used Lycos in all sorts of
forms, the Romans had many a Lupus, the Teutons have Wolf in
every possible combination, the Slaves Vuk ; the Kelts alone avoid
the great enemy of the fold, whose frequency is almost inexplicable.
The Kelts are, however, the namesakes of the dog, the Cu and Con,
so much loathed in other lands, that only a stray Danish Hund,
Italian Cane, and the one Hebrew Caleb, unite in bearing his name
in honour of his faithful qualities.

The horse is, of course, neglected in Judea, where his use was
forbidden ; but in Sanscrit was found Vradaçva, owning great horses ;
and the horse flourished all over Persia. Aspamithras, horse's
friend, Aspachava, rich in horses, Vishtaspa, and many more, commemorate the animal ; and in Greece, Hippolytus, Hippodamos,
Hippomedon, Hipparchus, and many more, showed that riding was
the glory of the Hellenes. Rome has no representative of her *equus*,
except in Equitius, a doubtful name, more likely to be named in
honour of the equestrian order, than direct from the animal. Marcus
may, however, be from the word that formed the Keltic March,
which, with Eachan and Eochaid, and many more, represent the love
of horses among the Kelts, answering to the Eporedorix, mentioned
by Cæsar. The Slaves have apparently no horse names ; but many
of our modern Roses are properly horses, and Jostein, Rosmund, and
various other forms, keep up the horse's fame in northern Europe.

Rome dealt, to a curious degree, in the most homely domestic
names ; Mus, the surname of the devoted Decius, was, probably,
really a mouse ; for while the swine of other nations never descend
below the savage wild boar of the forest—Eber, Baezan, Bravac, the
Romans have indeed one Aper, but their others are but domestic pigs,
Verres, Porcius, Scrofa.

Goats flourished in Greece in honour of the Ægis, and of Zeus goats,
and Ægidios, with others, there arose ; but Sichelgaita, and a few
northern Geits, alone reflect them. The chamois, or mountain goat,
named Tabitha or Dorcas, and is paralleled by an occasional masculine
Hirsch, or stag, in Germany.

The sheep appears to be solely represented by Rachael, for though the lamb has laid claim to both Agnes and Lambert, it is only through a delusion of sound.

Serpents, as Orm and Lind, are peculiar to the North.

The eagle figures in Aias, Ajax, Aquila, the Russian Orlof, and many an Arn of the Teutons. It is rather surprising not to find him among the Gael; but the raven, like the wolf, is the fashionable creature, as an attendant upon slaughter—Oreb, Corvus, Morvren, Fiachra, Rafn, he croaks his name over the plunderer everywhere but among the Greeks and Slaves.

The swan has Gelges in Ireland, Svanwhit in the North; the dove named Jonah, Jemima in Palestine, Columba in Christian Latinity, Golubica in Illyria; but gentle birds are, in general, entirely neglected, unless the Greek Philomela, which properly means loving honey, were named after the nightingale. The Latin Gallus may possibly be a cock; but Genserich is not the gander king, as he was so long supposed to be.

The bee had Deborah in Hebrew, and Melissa in Greek; but, in general, insects are not popular, though Vespasian is said to come from a wasp; and among fishes, the dolphin has the only namesakes in Romance tongues, probably blunders from Delphi.

Plants were now and then commemorated; Tamar, a palm tree, Hadassah, a myrtle, are among the scanty eastern examples. Rome had a Robur, and Illyria Dobruslav, in honour of the oak; but the Slaves have almost the only genuine flower names. Rhoda is, indeed, a true Greek Rose, but the modern ones are mistakes for *hross*, a horse. Violet, probably, rose out of Valens, and Lilias from Cæcilius, Oliver from Olaf. Primrose, Ivy, Eglantine, &c., have been invented in modern books at least, and so has Amaranth.

Passing to qualities, goodness is found in many an Agathos of the Greeks, with his superlative Aristos, but early Rome chiefly dealt in Valens, leaving Bonus and Melior for her later inventors to use. The *goods* of the Teutons are rather doubtful between the names of the Deity and of war, but in passing them, the relation between Gustaf and Scipio should be observed. The Slaves have many compounds of both Dobry and Blago, and the Irish, Alma.

Love is everywhere. David represents it in Hebrew, Agape and Phile in Greek; but the grim Roman never used the compounds of his *amo*, only left them to form many a gentle modern name—Amabel, Aimée, Amy. Caradoc was the old Cymric, and Aiffe the Gadhaelic, beloved; and Wine and Leof in the German races, Ljubov, Libusa, Milica in the Slavonic, proved the warm hearts of the people. Indeed, the Slavonic names are the tenderest of all, owning Bratoljub and Çedomil, fraternal and parental love, unparalleled except by the satirical surnames of the Alexandrian kings.

Purity—a Christian idea—is found in Agnes and Katherine, both Greek; perhaps, too, Devoslava, or maiden glory, with the Slaves. Holiness is in the Hieronymus and Hagios of heathen Greece, meaning a holy name, and in the northern Ercen and Vieh, at the beginning and end of names, the Sviato of the Slavonians.

Peace, always lovely and longed-for, names both Absalom and

Solomon, and after them many an eastern Selim and Selima. Greece had Irene and Irenæus, but not till Christian days, and the Roman Pacificus was a very modern invention ; but the Friedrich, &c., of the North, and Miroslav of the Slav, were much more ancient.

The soul is to be found in Greece, as Psyche, and nowhere else but in the Welsh Enid. Life, however, figured at Rome, as Vitalis, and in the Teutonic nations as the prefix *fjor ;* and the Greek Zoë kept it up in honour of the oldest of all female names, Eve.

Grace is the Hebrew Hannah or Anna, and the *charis* in Greek compounds. Eucharis would not answer amiss to the Adelheid, or noble cheer, of Teuton damsels. Abigail, or father's joy, Zenobia, father's ornament, are in the same spirit.

Eu, meaning both happy and rich, wealthy in its best sense, is exactly followed by the Northern *ad* and Anglo-Saxon *ead.* Eulalia and Eulogios are the same as Edred, Euphrasia would answer to Odny, Eucharis and Aine likewise have the same sense of gladness. Eugenois is, perhaps, rather in the sense of Olaf, or of the host of Adels and Ethels. Patrocles and Cleopatra, both meaning the father's fame, have nothing exactly analogous to them in the Teuton and Keltic world.

Royalty is found in the Syriac Malchus, the Persian Kshahtra, or Xerxes, the Malek of the Arab, the early Archos, Ba ileus, and Tyrannos of the late Greek ; even the Roman Regulus, with Tigearnach among the Kelts, and Rik in its compounds in the Teutonic world. The loftiness and strength of the royal power is expressed in the Persian prefix *arta,* first cousin to our Keltic Art and Arthur, akin to the root that forms Ares, Arius, Arteinus, and many more familiar names from the superlative Aristos. It is the idea of strength and manhood, perhaps akin to the Latin *vir* and Keltic *fear.* Boleslav is the Wendic name, filling up the cycle of strength and manly virtue.

Majesty and greatness are commemorated by closely resembling words—the Persian Mathista or Masistes, Megas and Megalos in their Greek compounds, Latin Magnus and Maximus, Keltic Mor, Teutonic Mer ; it is only the Velika of the Slav that does not follow the same root. The crown names Stephanas and Venceslas, or crown glory.

Justice and judgment are the prevalent ideas in the Hebrew Dan and Shaphat, Greek Archos, Dike, and Krite, Latin Justinus, Northern Ragn ; perhaps, too, in the Irish Phelim and Slavonic Upravda. *Damo,* to tame, is in many Greek names ; and *ward,* or protection, answers to the Latin Titus.

Venerable is the Persian Arsaces, with Augustus and Sebastian. Power figures in Vladimir and Waldemar, and the many forms of *wald ;* and, on the other hand, the people assert themselves in the Laos and Demos of Greece, the *leutfolk* and *theod* of the Teuton, and even the *ljud* of the Slave. The lover of his people may be found under the various titles of Demophilos, Publicola, Theodwine, and the Slavonic feminine Ludmila ; their ruler, as Democritus, or Archilaus, or Theodoric ; their tamer, as Laodamos ; their justice, as Laodike.

Boulos, council, finds a parallel in the Teuton *raad ;* but Sophia, wisdom, is far too cultivated for an analogy among the name-makers of the rude North.

But fame and glory were more popular than wisdom and justice. *Slava* rings through the names of the Wends, and *klas* through the Greeks ; while *hluod* and *hruod* form half the leading names of Germanized Europe.

Clara is the late Latin name best implying fame, but answering best to Bertha, bright, like the Phlegon of Greece, and Barsines of Persia, which are all from one root. Lucius, light, translates some of these.

Conquest, that most desired of events to a warlike nation, is the Nike of the Greeks. Nikias, Victor, Sige, Cobhflaith, are all identical in meaning ; and the Greek and Teuton have again and again curiously similar compounds. Nicephorous and Sigebot, Nikoboulous and Sigfred, Stratonice would perhaps be paralleled by Sighilda. Nicolas has not an exact likeness, because the Teutons never place either *sige* or *theod* at the end of a word.

War itself has absorbed the Teuton *spear*, and is *ger* in our Teuton lands. But the Greek *mache*, and Teuton *hadu*, the Kelt *cath*, and the Slav *boj* or *voj*, all are in common use. Telemachus, or distant battle, is best represented by Siroslav, or distant glory. Stratos, meaning both army and camp, Kleostralos and Stratokles, answer to Stanislav ; and Cadwaladyr, in sound as well as sense, to Haduvald. Cathair, the Irish battle-slaughter, has likeness in the Teutonic derivatives of Val, but the North stands alone in honouring the Thiof with namesakes.

The hero, the warrior himself, the *Hero* as he really is of Greece, the *hari* of our Teutons, the *con* and *cathal* and *mal* of Ireland, the *miles* of the Roman, has namesakes in hosts. Herakles himself was not far removed from Herbert, Robert, or Lothaire, in meaning ; and Sigeher is the conquering warrior, as Nikostratos is the victorious army.

In fact, warlike names are exhausting in similarity and multitude, and our readers will discover many more for themselves. The peaceful ones are far more characteristic.

See how the ocean figures in Pelagios, in Morvan, Muircheartash, Haflide,—all the formation of maritime nations, while the Slaves have no sea names at all, and the Latin Marina is mere late coinage. It is the Welsh, however, who have the most sea names : Guenever, Bronwen, Dwynwen, &c.

The earth makes Georgos and Agricola, and its cultivators have in Greece commemorated their harvest with Eustaches and Theresa ; in Illyria, their vintage with Grozdana ; but though the old farmer citizens of Rome were called Faber, Lentulus, Cicero, and the like, produce of their fields, these were much too homely for our fierce Teuton ancestry.

Gold is not in much favour ; Chryseis, Aurelia, Orflath, and Zlata, just represent it ; and silver is to be found in Argyro, Argentine, and Arianwen ; but iron nowhere but with the Germanic races, Eisam-

bart, &c., in accordance with the weapon names in which they alone
delight. Nor are jewels many,—Esmeralda, Jasper (perhaps),
Margaret, Ligach, are almost their only representatives. Spices we
have as Kezia, Muriel, and strangest of all, Kerenhappuch, a box of
stibium for the eyes. Whether the Stein of the North is to be regarded
as a jewel does not seem clear, but it is more according to the temper
of the owners to regard it as answering to Petros, a rock. Veig,
Laug, and Øl, represent liquors, and are one of the peculiarities of
the North.

Beauty is less common than might have been expected. Kallista
is the leading owner of the word in Greece, but the Latin *bella* must
not be claimed for it, and, in spite of the *ny* and *fridhr* of the North,
it is the Kelts who deal most in names of beauty,—Findelbh, Graine,
and more than can here be specified.

Indeed, complexion names are chiefly found among the Kelts and
Romans. The white, Albanus and Finn, (which last Finn passed to
the North,) with Gwenn in Wales and Brittany ; the light-haired,
Flavius, Rufus, Ruadh, and Dearg. Fulvius, Niger, and Dubh, with
the answering Swerker, paralleled only by the late Greek Melania
have very few answering names in other lands, though the Bruno of
Germany corresponds to Don, and the Blond, now Blount, of England
is said to be meant to translate Fulvius.

On exceptional names, from the circumstances of the birth, we
have not here dwelt. They were accidental, and never became
national, except from the fame of some bearer of one. The names
derived from places are almost all Latin, at first cognomina, then
taken at baptism by converts. The number names are likewise
Latin. Those of high Christian ideas, like Anastasius, Ambrosius,
Alethea, are generally Greek ; and when Latins as Benedictus, the
blessed, and Beatrix, the blesser, are apt to be renderings of the
Greek. The early Latin names are the least explicable, and the least
resembling those of other nations ; the Keltic are the most poetical ;
the Slavonic either tender or warlike ; the Greek and the Teutonic
are the most analogous to one another in sense, and are the most in
use, except the more endeared and wide-spread of the Hebrew,—
John and Mary deservedly have the pre-eminence in the Christian
world above all others.

THE END.

LONDON: R. CLAY, SONS, AND TAYLOR, BREAD STREET HILL.

MESSRS. MACMILLAN & CO.'S PUBLICATIONS.

UNIFORM EDITION OF THE NOVELS AND TALES

OF

CHARLOTTE M. YONGE.

In Crown 8vo, Cloth extra, Illustrated, 3s. 6d. each.

1. THE HEIR OF REDCLYFFE.
2. HEARTSEASE.
3. HOPES AND FEARS.
4. DYNEVOR TERRACE.
5. THE DAISY CHAIN.
6. THE TRIAL : More Links of the Daisy Chain.
7. PILLARS OF THE HOUSE. Vol. I.
8. PILLARS OF THE HOUSE. Vol. II.
9. THE YOUNG STEPMOTHER.
10. THE CLEVER WOMAN OF THE FAMILY.
11. THE THREE BRIDES.
12. MY YOUNG ALCIDES.
13. THE CAGED LION.
14. THE DOVE IN THE EAGLE'S NEST.
15. THE CHAPLET OF PEARLS.
16. LADY HESTER, AND THE DANVERS PAPERS.
17. MAGNUM BONUM.
18. LOVE AND LIFE.
19. UNKNOWN TO HISTORY.
20. STRAY PEARLS.
21. THE ARMOURER'S 'PRENTICES.
22. THE TWO SIDES OF THE SHIELD.
23. NUTTIE'S FATHER.
24. SCENES AND CHARACTERS.
25. CHANTRY HOUSE.
26. A MODERN TELEMACHUS.
27. BYE WORDS.
28. BEECHCROFT AT ROCKSTONE.
29. A REPUTED CHANGELING.
30. MORE BYWORDS.
31. THE LITTLE DUKE.
32. THE PRINCE AND THE PAGE.
33. THE LANCES OF LYNWOOD.
34. P'S AND Q'S, AND LITTLE LUCY'S WONDERFUL GLOBE.
35. THE TWO PENNILESS PRINCESSES.
36. THAT STICK.

MACMILLAN AND CO., LONDON.

WORKS BY CHARLOTTE M. YONGE.

An Old Woman's Outlook. Crown 8vo. 3s. 6d.

A Book of Golden Deeds. 18mo. 2s. 6d. net. Globe Readings. Edition for Schools. Globe 8vo. 2s. Cheap Edition. 18mo. 1s.

The Story of the Christians and the Moors in Spain. With a Vignette by HOLMAN HUNT. 18mo. 4s. 6d.

The Lances of Lynwood. With Illustrations. New Edition. Globe 8vo. 2s. 6d.

A Storehouse of Stories. Edited by. Two Vols. Each 2s. 6d.

A Book of Worthies. Gathered from the Old Histories and written anew. 18mo. 2s. 6d. net.

The Population of an Old Pear-Tree; or, Stories of Insect Life. From the French of E. VAN BRUYSSEL. With numerous Illustrations by BECKER. New Edition. Globe 8vo. 2s. 6d.

Cameos from English History. Vol. I. From Rollo to Edward II. Extra fcap. 8vo. 5s. Vol. II. The Wars in France. 5s. Vol. III. The Wars of the Roses. 5s. Vol. IV. Reformation Times. 5s. Vol. V. England and Spain 5s. Vol. VI. Forty Years of Stuart Rule, 1603-1643. 5s. Vol. VII. The Rebellion and Restoration, 1642-1678. 5s.

Scripture Readings for Schools and Families. Genesis to Deuteronomy. Third Edition. Globe 8vo. 1s. 6d. Also with Comments. 3s. 6d.

Scripture Readings. Second Series. Joshua to Solomon. Globe 8vo. 1s. 6d. With Comments. 3s. 6d.

Scripture Readings. Third Series. Kings and Prophets. Globe 8vo. 1s. 6d. With Comments. 3s. 6d.

Scripture Readings. Fourth Series. The Gospel Times. Globe 8vo. 1s. 6d. With Comments. 3s. 6d.

Scripture Readings. Fifth Series. Apostolic Times. Globe 8vo. 1s. 6d. With Comments. 3s. 6d.

History of Christian Names. New and Revised Edition. Crown 8vo. 7s. 6d.

The Life of John Coleridge Patteson, Missionary Bishop. New Edition. Two Vols. Crown 8vo. 12s.

The Pupils of St. John. Illustrated. Crown 8vo. 6s.

Pioneers and Founders; or, Recent Workers in the Mission Field. Crown 8vo. 6s.

The Herb of the Field : Reprinted from ' Chapters on Flowers ' in *The Magazine for the Young.* A New Edition, Revised and Corrected. Crown 8vo. 5s.

The Victorian Half Century. A Jubilee Book. With a New Portrait of the Queen. Crown 8vo. Paper Covers. 1s. Cloth. 1s. 6d.

MACMILLAN AND CO., LONDON.

10.12.92.

INDEX.

INDEX.

INDEX.

MACMILLAN AND CO., LONDON.

14/50/12/94